देवाय तस्मै नमः

A HISTORY OF INDIAN PHILOSOPHY

निखिलमनुजचित्तं ज्ञानसूत्रैर्नवैर्यः
स्रजमिव कुसुमानां कालरन्ध्रैर्विधत्ते।
स लघुमपि ममैतं प्राच्यविज्ञानतन्तुं
उपहृतमतिभक्तया मोदतां मे गृहीत्वा।।

May He, who links the minds of all people, through the apertures of time, with new threads of knowledge like a garland of flowers, be pleased to accept this my thread of Eastern thought, offered, though it be small, with the greatest devotion.

A HISTORY OF INDIAN PHILOSOPHY

VOLUME 1

SURENDRANATH DASGUPTA

RUPA

Published by
Rupa Publications India Pvt. Ltd 2018
7/16, Ansari Road, Daryaganj
New Delhi 110002

Sales centres:
Bengaluru Chennai
Hyderabad Jaipur Kathmandu
Kolkata Mumbai Prayagraj

P-ISBN: 978-93-5304-108-3
E-ISBN: 978-93-5333-965-4

Fifth impression 2024

10 9 8 7 6 5

Printed in India

DEDICATION

THE work and ambition of a lifetime is herein humbly dedicated with supreme reverence to the great sages of India, who, for the first time in history, formulated the true principles of freedom and devoted themselves to the holy quest of truth and the final assessment and discovery of the ultimate spiritual essence of man through their concrete lives, critical thought, dominant will and self-denial.

NOTE ON THE PRONUNCIATION OF TRANSLITERATED SANSKRIT AND PĀLI WORDS

THE vowels are pronounced almost in the same way as in Italian, except that the sound of *a* approaches that of *o* in *bond* or *u* in *but*, and *ā* that of *a* as in *army*. The consonants are as in English, except *c*, *ch* in church; *ṭ*, *ḍ*, *ṇ* are cerebrals, to which English *t*, *d*, *n* almost correspond; *t*, *d*, *n* are pure dentals; *kh*, *gh*, *ch*, *jh*, *ṭh*, *ḍh*, *th*, *dh*, *ph*, *bh* are the simple sounds plus an aspiration; *ñ* is the French *gn*; *ṛ* is usually pronounced as *ri*, and *ś*, *ṣ* as *sh*.

PREFACE

THE old civilisation of India was a concrete unity of many-sided developments in art, architecture, literature, religion, morals, and science so far as it was understood in those days. But the most important achievement of Indian thought was philosophy. It was regarded as the goal of all the highest practical and theoretical activities, and it indicated the point of unity amidst all the apparent diversities which the complex growth of culture over a vast area inhabited by different peoples produced. It is not in the history of foreign invasions, in the rise of independent kingdoms at different times, in the empires of this or that great monarch that the unity of India is to be sought. It is essentially one of spiritual aspirations and obedience to the law of the spirit, which were regarded as superior to everything else, and it has outlived all the political changes through which India passed.

The Greeks, the Huns, the Scythians, the Pathans and the Moguls who occupied the land and controlled the political machinery never ruled the minds of the people, for these political events were like hurricanes or the changes of season, mere phenomena of a natural or physical order which never affected the spiritual integrity of Hindu culture. If after a passivity of some centuries India is again going to become creative it is mainly on account of this fundamental unity of her progress and civilisation and not for anything that she may borrow from other countries. It is therefore indispensably necessary for all those who wish to appreciate the significance and potentialities of Indian culture that they should properly understand the history of Indian philosophical thought which is the nucleus round which all that is best and highest in India has grown. Much harm has already been done by the circulation of opinions that the culture and philosophy of India was dreamy and abstract. It is therefore very necessary that Indians as well as other peoples should become more and more acquainted with the true characteristics of the past history of Indian thought and form a correct estimate of its special features.

But it is not only for the sake of the right understanding of

India that Indian philosophy should be read, or only as a record of the past thoughts of India. For most of the problems that are still debated in modern philosophical thought occurred in more or less divergent forms to the philosophers of India. Their discussions, difficulties and solutions when properly grasped in connection with the problems of our own times may throw light on the course of the process of the future reconstruction of modern thought. The discovery of the important features of Indian philosophical thought, and a due appreciation of their full significance, may turn out to be as important to modern philosophy as the discovery of Sanskrit has been to the investigation of modern philological researches. It is unfortunate that the task of re-interpretation and re-valuation of Indian thought has not yet been undertaken on a comprehensive scale. Sanskritists also with very few exceptions have neglected this important field of study, for most of these scholars have been interested more in mythology, philology, and history than in philosophy. Much work however has already been done in the way of the publication of a large number of important texts, and translations of some of them have also been attempted. But owing to the presence of many technical terms in advanced Sanskrit philosophical literature, the translations in most cases are hardly intelligible to those who are not familiar with the texts themselves.

A work containing some general account of the mutual relations of the chief systems is necessary for those who intend to pursue the study of a particular school. This is also necessary for lay readers interested in philosophy and students of Western philosophy who have no inclination or time to specialise in any Indian system, but who are at the same time interested to know what they can about Indian philosophy. In my two books *The Study of Patanjali* and *Yoga Philosophy in relation to other Indian Systems of Thought* I have attempted to interpret the Sāṃkhya and Yoga systems both from their inner point of view and from the point of view of their relation to other Indian systems. The present attempt deals with the important features of these as also of all the other systems and seeks to show some of their inner philosophical relations especially in regard to the history of their development. I have tried to be as faithful to the original texts as I could and have always given the Sanskrit or Pāli technical terms for the help of those who want to make this book a guide for further study. To understand something of these terms is indeed essential for anyone who wishes to be sure that he is following the actual course of the thoughts.

In Sanskrit treatises the style of argument and methods of treating the different topics are altogether different from what we find in any modern work of philosophy. Materials had therefore to be collected from a large number of works on each system and these have been knit together and given a shape which is likely to be more intelligible to people unacquainted with Sanskritic ways of thought. But at the same time I considered it quite undesirable to put any pressure on Indian thoughts in order to make them appear as European. This will explain much of what might appear quaint to a European reader. But while keeping all the thoughts and expressions of the Indian thinkers I have tried to arrange them in a systematic whole in a manner which appeared to me strictly faithful to their clear indications and suggestions. It is only in very few places that I have translated some of the Indian terms by terms of English philosophy, and this I did because it appeared to me that those were approximately the nearest approach to the Indian sense of the term. In all other places I have tried to choose words which have not been made dangerous by the acquirement of technical senses. This however is difficult, for the words which are used in philosophy always acquire some sort of technical sense. I would therefore request my readers to take those words in an unsophisticated sense and associate them with such meanings as are justified by the passages and contexts in which they are used. Some of what will appear as obscure in any system may I hope be removed if it is re-read with care and attention, for unfamiliarity sometimes stands in the way of right comprehension. But I may have also missed giving the proper suggestive links in many places where condensation was inevitable and the systems themselves have also sometimes insoluble difficulties, for no system of philosophy is without its dark and uncomfortable corners.

Though I have begun my work from the Vedic and Brāhmaṇic stage, my treatment of this period has been very slight. The beginnings of the evolution of philosophical thought, though they can be traced in the later Vedic hymns, are neither connected nor systematic.

More is found in the Brāhmaṇas, but I do not think it worthwhile to elaborate the broken shreds of thought of this epoch. I could have dealt with the Upaniṣad period more fully, but many works on the subject have already been published in Europe and those who wish to go into details will certainly go to them. I have therefore limited myself to the dominant current flowing through the earlier Upaniṣads. Notices of other currents of thought will be given in connection with the treatment of other systems in the second volume with which they are more intimately connected. It will be noticed that my treatment of early Buddhism is in some places of an inconclusive character. This is largely due to the inconclusive character of the texts which were put into writing long after Buddha in the form of dialogues and where the precision and directness required in philosophy were not contemplated. This has given rise to a number of theories about the interpretations of the philosophical problems of early Buddhism among modern Buddhist scholars and it is not always easy to decide one way or the other without running the risk of being dogmatic; and the scope of my work was also too limited to allow me to indulge in very elaborate discussions of textual difficulties. But still I also have in many places formed theories of my own, whether they are right or wrong it will be for scholars to judge. I had no space for entering into any polemic, but it will be found that my interpretations of the systems are different in some cases from those offered by some European scholars who have worked on them and I leave it to those who are acquainted with the literature of the subject to decide which of us may be in the right. I have not dealt elaborately with the new school of Logic (Navya-Nyāya) of Bengal, for the simple reason that most of the contributions of this school consist in the invention of technical expressions and the emphasis put on the necessity of strict exactitude and absolute preciseness of logical definitions and discussions and these are almost untranslatable in intelligible English. I have however incorporated what important differences of philosophical points of view I could find in it. Discussions of a purely technical character could not be very fruitful in a work like this. The bibliography given of the different Indian systems in the last six chapters is not exhaustive but consists mostly of books which have been actually studied or consulted in the writing of those chapters. Exact references to the pages of the texts have generally been given in footnotes in those cases where a difference of interpretation was anticipated or where it was felt that a reference to the text would make the matter clearer, or where the opinions of modern writers have been incorporated.

It gives me the greatest pleasure to acknowledge my deepest gratefulness to the Hon'ble Maharaja Sir Manindrachandra Nundy, K.C.I.E. Kashimbazar, Bengal, who has kindly promised to bear the entire expense of the publication of both volumes of the present work.

The name of this noble man is almost a household word in Bengal for the magnanimous gifts that he has made to educational and other causes. Up till now he has made a total gift of about £300,000, of which those devoted to education come to about £200,000. But the man himself is far above the gifts he has made. His sterling character, universal sympathy and friendship, his kindness and amiability make him a veritable Bodhisattva—one of the noblest of men that I have ever seen. Like many other scholars of Bengal, I am deeply indebted to him for the encouragement that he has given me in the pursuit of my studies and researches, and my feelings of attachment and gratefulness for him are too deep for utterance.

I am much indebted to my esteemed friends Dr E. J. Thomas of the Cambridge University Library and Mr Douglas Ainslie for their kindly revising the proofs of this work, in the course of which they improved my English in many places. To the former I am also indebted for his attention to the transliteration of a large number of Sanskrit words, and also for the whole-hearted sympathy and great friendliness with which he assisted me with his advice on many points of detail, in particular the exposition of the Buddhist doctrine of the cause of rebirth owes something of its treatment to repeated discussions with him.

I also wish to express my gratefulness to my friend Mr N. K. Siddhanta, M.A., late of the Scottish Churches College, and Mademoiselle Paule Povie for the kind assistance they have rendered in preparing the index. My obligations are also due to the Syndics of the Cambridge University Press for the honour they have done me in publishing this work.

To scholars of Indian philosophy who may do me the honour of reading my book and who may be impressed with its inevitable shortcomings and defects, I can only pray in the words of Hemacandra:

Pramāṇasiddhāntaviruddham atra
Yatkiñciduktam matimāndyadoṣāt
Mātsaryyam utsāryya tadāryyacittāḥ
Prasādam ādhāya viśodhayantu[1].

SURENDRANATH DASGUPTA

TRINITY COLLEGE,
CAMBRIDGE.
February, 1922.

[1] May the noble-minded scholars instead of cherishing ill feeling kindly correct whatever errors have been here committed through the dullness of my intellect in the way of wrong interpretations and misstatements.

CONTENTS

VOLUME 1

I. INTRODUCTORY 1

II. THE VEDAS, BRĀHMAṆAS AND THEIR PHILOSOPHY 10
The Vedas and their antiquity 10
The place of the Vedas in the Hindu mind 10
Classification of the Vedic literature 11
The Saṃhitās 12
The Brāhmaṇas 13
The Āraṇyakas 14
The Ṛg-Veda, its civilization 14
The Vedic Gods 16
Polytheism, Henotheism and Monotheism 17
Growth of a Monotheistic tendency; Prajāpati, Viśvakarma 19
Brahma 20
Sacrifice; the First Rudiments of the Law of Karma 21
Cosmogony—Mythological and philosophical 23
Eschatology; the Doctrine of Ātman 25
Conclusion 26

III. THE EARLIER UPANIṢADS (B.C. 700—600) 28
The place of the Upaniṣads in Vedic literature 28
The names of the Upaniṣads; Non-Brahmanic influence 30
Brāhmaṇas and the Early Upaniṣads 31
The meaning of the word Upaniṣad 38
The composition and growth of diverse Upaniṣads 38
Revival of Upaniṣad studies in modern times 39
The Upaniṣads and their interpretations 41
The quest after Brahman: the struggle and the failures 42
Unknowability of Brahman and the Negative Method 44
The Ātman doctrine 45
Place of Brahman in the Upaniṣads 48
The World 51
The World-Soul 52
The Theory of Causation 52

Doctrine of Transmigration 53
Emancipation 58

IV. GENERAL OBSERVATIONS ON THE SYSTEMS OF INDIAN PHILOSOPHY 62
In what sense is a History of Indian Philosophy possible? 62
Growth of the Philosophic Literature 65
The Indian Systems of Philosophy 67
Some Fundamental Points of Agreement 71
The Pessimistic Attitude towards the World and the Optimistic Faith in the end 75
Unity in Indian Sādhana (philosophical, religious, and ethical endeavours) 77

V. BUDDHIST PHILOSOPHY 78
The State of Philosophy in India before the Buddha 78
Buddha: his Life 81
Early Buddhist Literature 82
The Doctrine of Causal Connection of early Buddhism 84
The Khandhas 93
Avijjā and Āsava 99
Sīla and Samādhi 100
Kamma 106
Upaniṣads and Buddhism 109
The Schools of Theravāda Buddhism 112
Mahāyānism 125
The Tathatā Philosophy of Aśvaghoṣa (A.D. 80) 129
The Mādhyamika or the Sūnyavāda school—Nihilism 138
Uncompromising Idealism or the School of Vijñānavāda Buddhism 145
Sautrāntika Theory of Perception 151
Sautrāntika theory of Inference 155
The Doctrine of Momentariness 158
The Doctrine of Momentariness and the Doctrine of Causal Efficiency (Arthakriyākāritva) 163
Some Ontological Problems on which the Different Indian Systems diverged 164
Brief survey of the evolution of Buddhist Thought 166

VI. THE JAINA PHILOSOPHY 169
The Origin of Jainism 169
Two Sects of Jainism 170
The Canonical and other Literature of the Jains 171

Some General Characteristics of the Jains 172
Life of Mahāvīra 173
The Fundamental Ideas of Jaina Ontology 173
The Doctrine of Relative Pluralism (anekāntavāda) 175
The Doctrine of Nayas 176
The Doctrine of Syādvāda 179
Knowledge, its value for us 181
Theory of Perception 183
Non-Perceptual Knowledge 185
Knowledge as Revelation 186
The Jīvas 188
Karma Theory 190
Karma, Āsrava and Nirjarā 192
Pudgala 195
Dharma Adharma, Ākāśa 197
Kāla and Samaya 198
Jaina Cosmography 199
Jaina Yoga 199
Jaina Atheism 203
Mokṣa (emancipation) 207

VII. THE KAPILA AND THE PĀTAÑJALA SĀṂKHYA (YOGA) 208
A Review 208
The Germs of Sāṃkhya in the Upaniṣads 211
Sāṃkhya and Yoga Literature 212
An Early School of Sāṃkhya 213
Sāṃkhya kārikā, Sāṃkhya sūtra, Vācaspati Miśra and Vijñāna Bhikṣu 222
Yoga and Patañjali 226
The Sāṃkhya and the Yoga Doctrine of Soul or Puruṣa 238
Thought and Matter 241
Feelings, the Ultimate Substances 242
The Guṇas 243
Prakṛti and its Evolution 245
Pralaya and the disturbance of the Prakṛti Equilibrium 247
Mahat and Ahaṃkara 248
The Tanmātras and the Paramāṇus 251
Principle of Causation and Conservation of Energy 254
Change as the formation of new collocations 255
Causation as Satkāryavāda (the theory that the effect potentially exists before it is generated by the movement of the cause) 257

Sāṃkhya Atheism and Yoga Theism 258
Buddhi and Puruṣa 259
The Cognitive Process and some characteristics of Citta 261
Sorrow and its Dissolution 264
Citta 268
Yoga Purificatory Practices (Parikarma) 270
The Yoga Meditation 271

VIII. THE NYĀYA-VAIŚEṢIKA PHILOSOPHY 274
Criticism of Buddhism and Sāṃkhya from the Nyāya standpoint 274
Nyāya and Vaiśeṣika sūtras 276
Does Vaiśeṣika represent an Old School of Mīmāṃsā? 280
Philosophy in the Vaiśeṣika sūtras 285
Philosophy in the Nyāya sūtras 294
Caraka, Nyāya sūtras and Vaiśeṣika sūtras 301
The Vaiśeṣika and Nyāya Literature 305
The main doctrine of the Nyaya-Vaiśeṣika Philosophy 310
The six Padārthas: Dravya, Guṇa, Karma, Sāmānya, Viśeṣa, Samavāya 313
The Theory of Causation 319
Dissolution (Pralaya) and Creation (Sṛṣṭi) 323
Proof of the Existence of Īśvara 325
The Nyāya-Vaiśeṣika Physics 326
The Origin of Knowledge (Pramāṇa) 330
The four Pramāṇas of Nyāya 332
Perception (Pratyakṣa) 333
Inference 343
Upamāna and Śabda 354
Negation in Nyāya-Vaiśeṣika 355
The necessity of the Acquirement of debating devices for the seeker of Salvation 360
The doctrine of Soul 362
Īśvara and Salvation 363

IX. MĪMĀṂSĀ PHILOSOPHY 367
A Comparative Review 367
The Mīmāṃsā Literature 369
The Parataḥ-prāmāṇya doctrine of Nyāya and the Svatah-pramanya doctrine of Mimamsa 372
The place of sense organs in perception 375
Indeterminate and determinate perception 378
Some Ontological Problems connected with the

Doctrine of Perception 379
The nature of knowledge 382
The Psychology of Illusion 384
Inference 387
Upamāna, Arthāpatti 391
Śabda-pramāṇa 394
The Pramāṇa of Non-perception (anupalabdhi) 397
Self, Salvation, God 399
Mīmāṃsā as philosophy and Mīmāṃsā as ritualism 403

X. THE ŚAṄKARA SCHOOL OF VEDĀNTA 406
Comprehension of the philosophical issues more essential than the Dialectic of controversy 406
The philosophical situation: A Review 408
Vedānta Literature 418
Vedānta in Gauḍapāda 420
Vedānta and Śaṅkara (A.D. 788-820) 429
The main idea of the Vedānta philosophy 439
In what sense is the world-appearance false? 443
The nature of the world-appearance, phenomena 445
The Definition of Ajñāna (nescience) 452
Ajñāna established by Perception and Inference 454
Locus and Object of Ajñāna, Ahaṃkāra and Antaḥkaraṇa 457
Anirvācyavāda and the Vedānta Dialectic 461
The Theory of Causation 465
Vedānta theory of Perception and Inference 470
Ātman, Jīva, Īśvara, Ekajīvavāda and Dṛṣtisṛṣṭivāda 474
Vedānta Theory of Illusion 485
Vedānta Ethics and Vedānta Emancipation 489
Vedānta and other Indian Systems 492

XI. THE ŚAṄKARA SCHOOL OF VEDĀNTA (*continued*) 495
The World-Appearance 495
Thought and its Object in Buddhism and in Vedānta 507
Śaṅkara's Defence of Vedānta; Philosophy of Bādarāyaṇa and Bhartṛprapanca 530
Teachers and Pupils in Vedānta 540
Vedānta Doctrine of Soul and the Buddhist Doctrine of Soullessness 552
Vedāntic Cosmology 567
Śaṅkara and his School 571
Maṇḍana, Sureśvara and Viśvarūpa 576
Maṇḍana (A.D. 800) 581

Sureśvara (A.D. 800) 592
Padmapāda (A.D. 820) 596
Vācaspati Miśra (A.D. 840) 600
Sarvajñātma Muni (A.D. 900) 605
Ānandabodha Yati 610
Mahā-vidyā and the Development of Logical Formalism 612
Vedānta Dialectic of Śrīharṣa (A.D. 1150) 619
Application of the Dialectic to the Different Categories and Concepts 627
Citsukha's Interpretations of the Concepts of Śaṅkara Vedānta 641
The Dialectic of Nāgārjuna and the Vedānta Dialectic 657
Dialectical criticisms of Śāntarakṣita and Kamalaśīla (A.D. 760) as forerunners of Vedanta Dialectics 665
Dialectic of Śaṅkara and Ānandajñāna 683
Philosophy of the Prakaṭārtha-vivaraṇa (A.D. 1200) 690
Vimuktātman (A.D. 1200) 692
Rāmādvaya (A.D. 1300) 698
Vidyāraṇya (A.D. 1350) 708
Nṛsiṃhāśrama Muni (A.D. 1500) 710
Appaya Dīkṣita (A.D. 1550) 712
Prakāśānanda (A.D. 1550—1600) 714
Madhusūdana Sarasvatī (A.D. 1500) 719

XII. THE PHILOSOPHY OF THE *YOGA-VĀSIṢṬHA* 722
The Ultimate Entity 726
Origination 729
Karma, Manas and the Categories 731
The World-Appearance 734
Nature of Agency (*Kartṛtva*) and the Illusion of World Creation 736
The Stage of the Saint (*Jivan-mukta*) 739
Energy of Free-will (Pauruṣa) 746
Prāṇa and its Control 750
Stages of Progress 758
Methods of Right Conduct 761
Yoga-vāsiṣṭha, Śaṅkara Vedānta and Buddhist Vijñānavāda 762

APPENDIX TO VOLUME 1 767
INDEX 806

VOLUME 2

PREFACE ix

XIII. SPECULATIONS IN THE MEDICAL SCHOOLS 1

Āyur-veda and the Atharva-Veda 1

Bones in the Atharva-Veda and Āyur-veda 12

Organs in the Atharva-Veda and Āyur-veda 16

Practice of Medicine in the Atharva-Veda 21

The Foetus and the Subtle Body 30

Foetal Development 40

Growth and Disease 47

Vāyu, Pitta and Kapha 53

Head and Heart 68

The Circulatory and the Nervous System 72

The Nervous System of the Tantras 80

The Theory of Rasas and their Chemistry 85

The Psychological Views and other Ontological Categories 94

Logical Speculations and Terms relating to Academic Dispute 101

Did Logic Originate in the Discussions of Āyur-veda Physicians? 120

Āyur-veda Ethics 130

Springs of action in the Caraka-saṃhitā 139

Good Life in Caraka 146

Āyur-veda Literature 151

XIV. THE PHILOSOPHY OF THE *BHAGAVAD-GĪTĀ* 165

The Gītā Literature 165

Gītā and Yoga 171

Sāṃkhya and Yoga in the Gītā 183

Sāṃkhya Philosophy in the Gītā 189

Avyakta and Brahman 198

Conception of Sacrificial Duties in the Gītā 207

Sense-control in the Gītā 216

The Ethics of the Gītā and the Buddhist Ethics 221

Analysis of Action 243

Eschatology 245

God and Man 251

Viṣṇu, Vāsudeva and Kṛṣṇa 263
Bhāgavata and the Bhagavad-Gītā 273

XV. THE BHĀSKARA SCHOOL OF PHILOSOPHY 281
Date of Bhāskara 281
Bhāskara and Śaṅkara 283
The Philosophy of Bhāskara's Bhāṣya 286

XVI. THE PAÑCARĀTRA 292
Antiquity of the Pañcarātra 292
The Position of Pañcarātra Literature 294
The Pañcarātra Literature 301
Philosophy of the Jayākhya and other Saṃhitās 304
Philosophy of the Ahirbudhnya-saṃhitā 314

XVII. THE ĀṚVĀRS 343
The Chronology of the Āṛvārs 343
The Philosophy of the Āṛvārs 349
Āṛvārs and Śrī-vaisṇavas on certain points
of controversy in religious dogmas 365

XVIII. A HISTORICAL AND LITERARY SURVEY OF
THE VIŚIṢṬĀ-DVAITA SCHOOL OF THOUGHT 374
The Aṛagiyas from Nāthamuni to Rāmānuja 374
Rāmānuja 380
The Precursors of the Viśiṣṭādvaita Philosophy and the
contemporaries and pupils of Rāmānuja 385
Rāmānuja Literature 394
The Influence of the Āṛvārs on the followers
of Rāmānuja 414

XIX. THE PHILOSOPHY OF YĀMUNĀCĀRYA 419
Yāmuna's doctrine of Soul contrasted
with those of others 419
God and the World 432
God according to Rāmānuja, Veṅkaṭanātha
and Lokācārya 435
Viśiṣṭā-dvaita doctrine of Soul according to

Rāmānuja and Veṅkaṭanātha 439
Acit or Primeval Matter: the Prakṛti and its modifications 442

XX. PHILOSOPHY OF THE RĀMĀNUJA SCHOOL OF THOUGHT 445
Śaṅkara and Rāmānuja on the nature of Reality as qualified or unqualified 445
Refutation of Śaṅkara's avidyā 455
Rāmānuja's theory of Illusion—All knowledge is Real 459
Failure of theistic proofs 469
Bhāskara and Rāmānuja 472
Ontological position of Rāmānuja's Philosophy 475
Veṅkatṭnātha's treatment of Pramāṇa 481
Veṅkaṭanātha's treatment of Doubt 487
Error and Doubt according to Veṅkaṭanātha 490
Perception in the light of elucidation by the later members of the Rāmānuja School 500
Veṅkaṭanātha's treatment of Inference 505
Epistemology of the Rāmānuja School according to Meghanādāri and others 515
The Doctrine of Self-validity of Knowledge 527
Ontological categories of the Rāmānuja School according to Veṅkaṭanātha 531
God in the Rāmānuja School 576
Dialectical criticism against the Śaṅkara School 584
Meghanādāri 626
Vātsya Varada 629
Rāmānujācārya II alias Vādi-Haṃsa-Navāmvuda 632
Rāmānujadāsa alias Mahācārya 641
Prapatti Doctrine as expounded in Śrīvacana-bhūṣaṇa of Lokācārya and Saumya Jāmāts Muni's Commentary on it 654
Kastūrī Raṅgācārya 661
Śaila Śrīnivāsa 664
Raṅgācārya 675

INDEX 679

VOLUME 3

PREFACE ix

XXI. THE NIMBĀRKA SCHOOL OF PHILOSOPHY 1
Teachers and Pupils of the Nimbārka School 1
A General Idea of Nimbārka's Philosophy 6
Controversy with the Monists by Mādhava Mukunda 18
The Pramāṇas according to Mādhava Mukunda 28
Criticism of the views of Rāmānuja and Bhāskara 31
The Reality of the World 37
Vanamālī Miśra 42

XXII. THE PHILOSOPHY OF VIJÑĀNA BHIKṢU 47
A General Idea of Vijñāna Bhikṣu's Philosophy 47
The Brahman and the World according to Vijñānā-mṛta-bhāṣya 56
The Individual 62
Brahma-Experience and Experience 67
Self-Luminosity and Ignorance 70
Relation of Sāṃkhya and Vedānta according to Bhikṣu 73
Māyā and Pradhāna 78
Bhikṣu's criticism of the Sāṃkhya and Yoga 81
Īśvara-gītā, its Philosophy as expounded by Vijñāna Bhikṣu 84

XXIII. PHILOSOPHICAL SPECULATIONS OF SOME OF THE SELECTED PURĀṆAS 98

XXIV. THE BHĀGAVATA-PURĀṆA 114
Dharma 115
Brahman, Paramātman, Bhagavat and Parameśvara 124
Kapila's philosophy in the Bhāgavata-purāṇa 137
Eschatology 162

XXV. MADHVA AND HIS SCHOOL 164
Madhva's Life 164
Succession List of Madhva Gurus 169
Important Madhva Works 170
Teachers and Writers of the Madhva School 203

Rāmānuja and Madhva 207

XXVI. MADHVA'S INTERPRETATION OF THE *BRAHMA-SŪTRAS* 214
Interpretation of Brahma-sūtra I. I. 1 215
Interpretation of Brahma-sūtra I. I. 2 234
Interpretation of Brahma-sūtra I. I. 3–4 240
A general review of the other important topics of the Brahma-sūtras 242

XXVII. A GENERAL REVIEW OF THE PHILOSOPHY OF MADHVA 263
Ontology 263
Pramāṇas (ways of valid knowledge) 273
Svataḥ-prāmāṇya (self-validity of knowledge) 281
Illusion and Doubt 286
Defence of Pluralism (Bheda) 291

XXVIII. MADHVA LOGIC 294
Perception 294
Inference (Anumāna) 297
Tarka (Ratiocination) 301
Concomitance (Vyāpti) 310
Epistemological Process in Inference 313
Various Considerations regarding Inference 313
Testimony 315

XXIX. CONTROVERSY BETWEEN THE DUALISTS AND THE MONISTS 317
Vyāsa-tīrtha, Madhusūdana and Rāmācārya on the Falsity of the World 317
Nature of Knowledge 343
The World as Illusion 359

XXX. CONTROVERSY BETWEEN THE DUALISTS AND THE MONISTS (CONTINUED) 372
A Refutation of the definition of Avidyā (nescience) 372
Perception of ajñāna (ignorance) 377
Inference of ajñāna 389

	The theory of Avidyā refuted	392
	Ajñāna and Ego-hood (ahaṃkāra)	407
	Indefinability of World-appearance	414
	Nature of Brahman	418
	Refutation of Brahman as material and instrumental cause	421
	Liberation (mokṣa)	428
XXXI.	THE PHILOSOPHY OF VALLABHA	433
	Vallabha's Interpretation of the Brahma-sūtra	433
	The nature of Brahman	440
	The Categories	445
	The Pramāṇas	449
	Concept of bhakti	459
	Topics of Vallabha Vedānta as explained by Vallabha's followers	471
	Viṭṭhala's Interpretation of Vallabha's Ideas	476
	Life of Vallabha (1481–1533)	484
	Works of Vallabha and his Disciples	486
	Viṣṇusvāmin	495
XXXII.	CAITANYA AND HIS FOLLOWERS	497
	Caitanya's Biographers	497
	The Life of Caitanya	498
	Emotionalism of Caitanya	502
	Gleanings from the Caitanya-Caritāmṛta on the subject of Caitanya's Philosophical Views	503
	Some Companions of Caitanya	506
XXXIII.	THE PHILOSOPHY OF JĪVA GOSVĀMĪ AND BALADEVA VIDYĀBHŪṢAṆA, FOLLOWERS OF CAITANYA	509
	Ontology	509
	Status of the World	518
	God and His Powers	522
	God's Relation to His Devotees	523
	Nature of bhakti	528
	Ultimate Realization	541

	The Joy of bhakti	543
	The Philosophy of Baladeva Vidyābhūṣaṇa	551
XXXIV.	LITERATURE OF SOUTHERN ŚAIVISM	562
	The Literature and History of Southern Śaivism	562
	The Āgama Literature and its Philosophical Perspective	581
	Śiva-jñāna-bodha	585
	Mātaṅga-parameśvara-tantra	589
	Pauṣkarāgama	590
	Vātulāgama	599
	Vātula-tantram	599
XXXV.	VÍRA-ŚAIVISM	603
	History and Literature of Vīra-śaivism	603
	Anubhava-sutra of Māyi-deva	622
XXXVI.	PHILOSOPHY OF ŚRĪKAṆṬHA	626
	Philosophy of Śaivism as expounded by Śrīkaṇṭha in his Commentary on the Brahma-sūtra and the Sub-commentary on it by Appaya Dīkṣita	626
	The Nature of Brahman	638
	Moral Responsibility and the Grace of God	646
XXXVII.	THE ŚAIVA PHILOSOPHY IN THE PURĀṆAS	657
	The Śaiva Philosophy in the Śiva-mahāpurāṇa	657
	Śaiva Philosophy in the Vāyavīya-saṃhitā of the Śiva-mahāpurāṇa	667
XXXVIII.	ŚAIVA PHILOSOPHY IN SOME OF THE IMPORTANT TEXTS	691
	The Doctrine of the Pāśupata-sūtras	691
	The Śaiva Ideas of Māṇikka-vāchakar in the Tiru-vāchaka	710
	Mānikka-vāchakar and Śaiva Siddhanta	715
	Saiva Philosophy according to Bhoja and his commentators	720

Śrīpati Paṇḍita's Ideas on the Vedānta Philosophy, also called the *Śrikara-bhāṣya* which is accepted as the Fundamental Basis of Vīra-śaivism 734

INDEX 753

I

INTRODUCTORY

THE achievements of the ancient Indians in the field of philosophy are but very imperfectly known to the world at large, and it is unfortunate that the coalition is no better even in India. There is a small body of Hindu scholars and ascetics living a retired life in solitude, who are well acquainted with the subject, but they do not know English and are not used to modern ways of thinking, and the idea that they ought to write books in vernaculars in order to popularize the subject does not appeal to them. Through the activity of various learned bodies and private individuals both in Europe and in India large numbers of philosophical works in Sanskrit and Pāli have been published, as well as translations of a few of them, but there has been as yet little systematic attempt on the part of scholars to study them and judge their value. There are hundreds of Sanskrit works on most of the systems of Indian thought and scarcely a hundredth part of them has been translated. Indian modes of expression, entailing difficult technical philosophical terms are so different from those of European thought, that they can hardly ever be accurately translated. It is therefore very difficult for a person unacquainted with Sanskrit to understand Indian philosophical thought in its true bearing from translations. Pāli is a much easier language than Sanskrit, but a knowledge of Pāli is helpful in understanding only the earliest school of Buddhism, when it was in its semi-philosophical stage. Sanskrit is generally regarded as a difficult language. But no one from an acquaintance with Vedic or ordinary literary Sanskrit can have any idea of the difficulty of the logical and abstruse parts of Sanskrit philosophical literature. A man who can easily understand the Vedas, the Upaniṣads, the Purāṇas, the Law Books and the literary works, and is also well acquainted with European philosophical thought, may find it literally impossible to understand even small portions of a work of advanced Indian logic, or the dialectical Vedānta. This is due to two reasons, the use of technical terms and of great condensation in expression, and the hidden allusions to doctrines of other systems. The tendency to conceiving philosophical problems in a clear and unambiguous manner is an important feature of Sanskrit thought, but from the ninth century onwards, the habit of using clear, definite, and precise expressions, began to develop in a very striking manner, and as a result of that a large number of technical terms began to be invented. These terms are seldom properly explained, and it is presupposed that the reader who wants to read the works should have a knowledge of them. Anyone in olden times who took to the study of any system of philosophy, had to do so with a teacher, who explained those terms to him. The teacher himself had got it from his teacher, and he from his. There was no tendency to popularize philosophy, for the idea then prevalent was that only the chosen few who had otherwise shown their fitness, deserved to become fit students (*adhikārī*) of philosophy, under the direction of a teacher. Only those who had the grit and high moral strength to devote their whole life to the true understanding of philosophy and the rebuilding of life in accordance with the high truths of philosophy were allowed to study it.

Another difficulty which a beginner will meet is this, that sometimes the same technical terms are used in extremely different senses in different systems. The student must know the meaning of each technical term with reference to the system in which it occurs, and no dictionary will enlighten him much about the matter[1]. He will have to pick them up as he advances and finds them used. Allusions to the doctrines of other systems and their refutations during the discussions of similar doctrines in any particular system of thought are often very puzzling even to a well-equipped reader; for he cannot be expected to know all the doctrines of other systems without going through them, and so it often becomes difficult to follow the series of answers and refutations which are poured forth in the course of these discussions. There are two important compendiums in Sanskrit giving a summary of some of the principal systems of Indian thought, viz. the *Sarvadarśanasaṃgraha*, and the *Ṣaḍdarśanasamuccaya* of Haribhadra with the commentary of Guṇaratna; but the former is very sketchy and can throw very little light on the understanding of the ontological or epistemological doctrines of any of the systems. It has been translated by Cowell and Gough, but I

[1] Recently a very able Sanskrit dictionary of technical philosophical terms called Nyāyakośa has been prepared by M. M. Bhīmācārya Jhalkikar, Bombay, Govt. Press.

am afraid the translation may not be found very intelligible. Guṇaratna's commentary is excellent so far as Jainism is concerned, and it sometimes gives interesting information about other systems, and also supplies us with some short bibliographical notices, but it seldom goes on to explain the epistemological or ontological doctrines or discussions which are so necessary for the right understanding of any of the advanced systems of Indian thought. Thus in the absence of a book which could give us in brief the main epistemological, ontological, and psychological positions of the Indian thinkers, it is difficult even for a good Sanskrit scholar to follow the advanced philosophical literature, even though he may be acquainted with many of the technical philosophical terms. I have spoken enough about the difficulties of studying Indian philosophy, but if once a person can get himself used to the technical terms and the general positions of the different Indian thinkers and their modes of expression, he can master the whole by patient toil. The technical terms, which are a source of difficulty at the beginning, are of inestimable value in helping us to understand the precise and definite meaning of the writers who used them, and the chances of misinterpreting or misunderstanding them are reduced to a minimum. It is I think well-known that avoidance of technical terms has often rendered philosophical works unduly verbose, and liable to misinterpretation. The art of clear writing is indeed a rare virtue and every philosopher cannot expect to have it. But when technical expressions are properly formed, even a bad writer can make himself understood. In the early days of Buddhist philosophy in the Pāli literature, this difficulty is greatly felt. There are some technical terms here which are still very elastic and their repetition in different places in more or less different senses heighten the difficulty of understanding the real meaning intended to be conveyed.

But is it necessary that a history of Indian philosophy should be written? There are some people who think that the Indians never rose beyond the stage of simple faith and that therefore they cannot have any philosophy at all in the proper sense of the term. Thus Professor Frank Thilly of the Cornell University says in his *History of Philosophy*[1], "A universal history of philosophy would include the philosophies of all peoples. Not all peoples, however

[1] New York, 1914, p. 3.

have produced real systems of thought, and the speculations of only a few can be said to have had a history. Many do not rise beyond the mythological stage. Even the theories of Oriental peoples, the Hindus, Egyptians, Chinese, consist, in the main, of mythological and ethical doctrines, and are not thoroughgoing systems of thought: they are shot through with poetry and faith. We shall, therefore, limit ourselves to the study of the Western countries, and begin with the philosophy of the ancient Greeks, on whose culture our own civilization in part, rests. There are doubtless many other people who hold such uninformed and untrue beliefs, which only show their ignorance of Indian matters. It is not necessary to say anything in order to refute these views, for what follows will I hope show the falsity of their beliefs. If they are not satisfied, and want to know more definitely and elaborately about the contents of the different systems, I am afraid they will have to go to the originals referred to in the bibliographical notices of the chapters.

There is another opinion, that the time has not yet come for an attempt to write a history of Indian philosophy. Two different reasons are given from two different points of view. It is said that the field of Indian philosophy is so vast, and such a vast literature exists on each of the systems, that it is not possible for anyone to collect his materials directly from the original sources, before separate accounts are prepared by specialists working in each of the particular systems. There is some truth in this objection, but although in some of the important systems the literature that exists is exceedingly vast, yet many of them are more or less repetitions of the same subjects, and a judicious selection of twenty or thirty important works on each of the systems could certainly be made, which would give a fairly correct exposition. In my own undertaking in this direction I have always drawn directly from the original texts, and have always tried to collect my materials from those sources in which they appear at their best. My space has been very limited and I have chosen the features which appeared to me to be the most important. I had to leave out many discussions of difficult problems and diverse important bearings of each of the systems to many interesting aspects of philosophy. This I hope may be excused in a history of philosophy which does not aim at completeness. There are indeed many defects and shortcomings, and these would have been much less in the case of a writer abler than the present one. At any rate it may be hoped that the imperfections of the present attempt will be a stimulus to those whose better and more competent efforts will supersede it. No attempt ought to be called impossible on account of its imperfections.

In the second place it is said that the Indians had no proper and accurate historical records and biographies and it is therefore impossible to write a history of Indian philosophy. This objection is also partially valid. But this defect does not affect us so much as one would at first sight suppose; for, though the dates of the earlier beginnings are very obscure, yet, in later times, we are in a position to affirm some dates and to point out priority and posteriority in the case of other thinkers. As most of the systems developed side by side through many centuries their mutual relations also developed, and these could be well observed. The special nature of this development has been touched on in the fourth chapter. Most of the systems had very early beginnings and a continuous course of development through the succeeding centuries, and it is not possible to take the state of the philosophy of a particular system at a particular time and contrast it with the state of that system at a later time; for the later state did not supersede the previous state, but only showed a more coherent form of it, which was generally true to the original system but was more determinate. Evolution through history has in Western countries often brought forth the development of more coherent types of philosophic thought, but in India, though the types remained the same, their development through history made them more and more coherent and determinate. Most of the parts were probably existent in the earlier stages, but they were in an undifferentiated state; through the criticism and conflict of the different schools existing side by side the parts of each of the systems of thought became more and more differentiated, determinate, and coherent. In some cases this development has been almost imperceptible, and in many cases the earlier forms have been lost, or so inadequately expressed that nothing definite could be made out of them. Wherever such a differentiation could be made in the interests of philosophy, I have tried to do it. But I have never considered it desirable that the philosophical interest should be subordinated to the chronological. It is no doubt true that more definite chronological information would be a very desirable thing, yet I am of opinion that the little chronological data we have give us a fair amount of help in forming a general notion about the growth and development of the different systems by mutual association and conflict. If the condition of the development of philosophy in India had been the same as in Europe, definite chronological knowledge would be considered much more indispensable. For, when one system supersedes another, it is indispensably necessary that we should know which preceded and which succeeded. But when the systems are developing side by side, and when we are getting them in their richer and better forms, the interest with regard to the conditions, nature and environment of their early origin has rather a historical than a philosophical interest. I have tried as best I could to form certain general notions as regards the earlier stages of some of the systems, but though the various features of these systems at these stages in detail may not be ascertainable, yet this, I think, could never be considered as invalidating the whole programme. Moreover, even if we knew definitely the correct dates of the thinkers of the same system we could not treat them separately, as is done in European philosophy, without unnecessarily repeating the same thing twenty times over; for they all dealt with the same system, and tried to bring out the same type of thought in more and more determinate forms.

The earliest literature of India is the Vedas. These consist mostly of hymns in praise of nature gods, such as fire, wind, etc. Excepting in some of the hymns of the later parts of the work (probably about B.C. 1000), there is not much philosophy in them in our sense of the term. It is here that we first find intensely interesting philosophical questions of a more or less cosmological character expressed in terms of poetry and imagination. In the later Vedic works called the Brāhmaṇas and the Āraṇyakas written mostly in prose, which followed the Vedic hymns, there are two tendencies, viz. one that sought to establish the magical forms of ritualistic worship, and the other which indulged in speculative thinking through crude generalizations. This latter tendency was indeed much feebler than the former, and it might appear that the ritualistic tendency had actually swallowed up what little of philosophy the later parts of the Vedic hymns were trying to express, but there are unmistakable marks that this tendency existed and worked. Next to this come certain treatises written in prose and verse called the Upaniṣads, which contain various sorts of philosophical thoughts mostly monistic or singularistic but also some pluralistic and dualistic ones. These are not reasoned statements, but utterances of truths intuitively perceived or felt as unquestionably real and indubitable, and carrying great force, vigour, and persuasiveness with them. It is very probable that many of the earliest parts of this literature are as old as B.C. 500 to B.C. 700 Buddhist philosophy began with the Buddha from some time about B.C. 500. There is reason to believe that Buddhist philosophy continued to develop in India in one or other of its vigorous forms till some time about the tenth or eleventh century A.D. The earliest beginnings of the other Indian systems of thought are also to be sought chiefly between the age of the Buddha to about B.C. 200. Jaina philosophy was probably prior to the Buddha. But except in its earlier days, when it came in conflict with the doctrines of the Buddha, it does not seem to me that the Jaina thought came much in contact with other systems of Hindu thought. Excepting in some forms of Vaiṣṇava thought in later times, Jaina thought is seldom alluded to by the Hindu writers or later Buddhists, though some Jains like Haribhadra and Guṇaratna tried to refute the Hindu and Buddhist systems. The non-aggressive nature of their religion and ideal may to a certain extent explain it, but there may be other reasons too which it is difficult for us to guess. It is interesting to note that, though there have been some dissensions amongst the Jains about dogmas and creeds, Jaina philosophy has not split into many schools of thought more or less differing from one another as Buddhist thought did.

The first volume of this work will contain Buddhist and Jaina philosophy and the six systems of Hindu thought. These six systems of orthodox Hindu thought are the Sāṃkhya, the Yoga, the Nyāya, the Vaiśeṇika, the Mīmāṃsā (generally known as Pūrva Mīmāṃsā), and the Vedānta (known also as Uttara Mīmāṃsā). Of these what is differently known as Sāṃkhya and Yoga are but different schools of one system. The Vaiśesika and the Nyāya in later times became so mixed up that, though in early times the similarity of the former with Mīmāṃsā was greater than that with Nyāya, they came to be regarded as fundamentally almost the same systems. Nyāya and Vaiśesika have therefore been treated together. In addition to these systems some theistic systems began to grow prominent from the ninth century A.D. They also probably had their early beginnings at the time of the Upaniṣads. But at that time their interest was probably concentrated on problems of morality and religion. It is not improbable that these were associated with certain metaphysical theories also, but no works treating them in a systematic way are now available. One of their most important early works is the *Bhagavad-gītā*. This book is rightly regarded as one of the greatest masterpieces of Hindu thought. It is written in verse, and deals with moral, religious, and metaphysical problems, in a loose form. It is its lack of system and method which gives it its peculiar charm more akin to the poetry of the Upaniṣads than to the dialectical and systematic Hindu thought. From the ninth century onwards attempts were made to supplement these loose theistic ideas which were floating about and forming integral parts of religious creeds, by metaphysical theories. Theism is often dualistic and pluralistic, and so are all these systems, which are known as different schools of Vaiṣṇava philosophy. Most of the Vaiṣṇava thinkers wished to show that their systems were taught in the Upaniṣads, and thus wrote commentaries thereon to prove their interpretations, and also wrote commentaries on the *Brahma-sutra* the classical exposition of the philosophy of the Upaniṣads. In addition to the works of these Vaiṣṇava thinkers there sprang up another class of theistic works which were of a more eclectic nature. These also had their beginnings in periods as old as the Upaniṣads. They are known as the Śaiva and Tantra thought, and are dealt with in the second volume of this work.

We thus see that the earliest beginnings of most systems of Hindu thought can be traced to some time between B.C. 600 to B.C. 100 or 200. It is extremely difficult to say anything about the relative priority of the systems with any degree of certainty. Some conjectural attempts have been made in this work with regard to some of the systems, but how far they are correct, it will be for our readers to judge. Moreover during the earliest manifestation of a system some crude outlines only are traceable. As time went on the systems of thought began to develop side by side. Most of them were taught from the time in which they were first conceived to about the seventeenth century A.D. in an unbroken chain of teachers and pupils. Even now each system of Hindu thought has its own adherents, though few people now care to write any new works upon them. In the history of the growth of any system of Hindu thought we find that as time went on, and as new problems were suggested, each system tried to answer them consistently with its own doctrines. The order in which we have taken the philosophical systems could not be strictly a chronological one. Thus though it is possible that the earliest speculations of some form of Sāṃkhya, Yoga, and Mīmāṃsā were prior to Buddhism yet they have been treated after Buddhism and Jainism, because the elaborate works of these systems which we now possess are later than Buddhism. In my opinion the Vaiśesika system is also probably pre-Buddhistic, but it has been treated later, partly on account of its association with Nyāya, and partly on account of the fact that all its commentaries are of a much later date. It seems to me almost certain that enormous quantities of old philosophical literature have been lost, which if found could have been of use to us in showing the stages of the early growth of the systems and their mutual relations. But as they are not available we have to be satisfied with what remains. The original sources from which I have drawn my materials have all been indicated in the brief accounts of the literature of each system which I have put in before beginning the study of any particular system of thought.

In my interpretations I have always tried to follow the original sources as accurately as I could. This has sometimes led to old and unfamiliar modes of expression, but this course seemed to me to be preferable to the adoption of European modes of thought for the expression of Indian ideas. But even in spite of this striking similarities to many of the modern philosophical doctrines and ideas will doubtless be noticed. This only proves that the human mind follows more or less the same modes of rational thought. I have never tried to compare any phase of Indian thought with European, for this is beyond the scope of my present attempt, but if I may be allowed to express my own conviction, I might say that many of the philosophical doctrines of European philosophy are essentially the same as those found in Indian philosophy. The main difference is often the difference of the point of view from which the same problems appeared in such a variety of forms in the two countries. My own view with regard to the net value of Indian philosophical development will be expressed in the concluding chapter of the second volume of the present work.

II

THE VEDAS, BRĀHMAṆAS AND THEIR PHILOSOPHY

The Vedas and their antiquity.

THE sacred books of India, the Vedas, are generally believed to be the earliest literary record of the Indo-European race. It is indeed difficult to say when the earliest portions of these compositions came into existence. Many shrewd guesses have been offered, but none of them can be proved to be incontestably true. Max Müller supposed the date to be B.C. 1200, Haug B.C. 2400 and Bāl Gaṅgādhar Tilak B.C. 4000. The ancient Hindus seldom kept any historical record of their literary, religious or political achievements. The Vedas were handed down from mouth to mouth from a period of unknown antiquity; and the Hindus generally believed that they were never composed by men. It was therefore generally supposed that either they were taught by God to the sages, or that they were of themselves revealed to the sages who were the "seers" (*mantradraṣṭā*) of the hymns. Thus we find that when some time had elapsed after the composition of the Vedas, people had come to look upon them not only as very old, but so old that they had, theoretically at least, no beginning in time, though they were believed to have been revealed at some unknown remote period at the beginning of each creation.

The place of the Vedas in the Hindu mind.

When the Vedas were composed, there was probably no system of writing prevalent in India. But such was the scrupulous zeal of the Brahmins, who got the whole Vedic literature by heart by hearing it from their preceptors, that it has been transmitted most faithfully to us through the course of the last 3000 years or more with little or no interpolations at all. The religious history of India had suffered considerable changes in the latter periods, since the time of the Vedic civilization, but such was the reverence paid to the Vedas that they had ever remained as the highest religious authority for all sections of the Hindus at all times. Even at this day all the obligatory duties of the Hindus at birth, marriage, death, etc., are performed according to the old

Vedic ritual. The prayers that a Brahmin now says three times a day are the same selections of Vedic verses as were used as prayer verses two or three thousand years ago. A little insight into the life of an ordinary Hindu of the present day will show that the system of image-worship is one that has been grafted upon his life, the regular obligatory duties of which are ordered according to the old Vedic rites. Thus an orthodox Brahmin can dispense with image-worship if he likes, but not so with his daily Vedic prayers or other obligatory ceremonies. Even at this day there are persons who bestow immense sums of money for the performance and teaching of Vedic sacrifices and rituals. Most of the Sanskrit literatures that flourished after the Vedas base upon them their own validity, and appeal to them as authority. Systems of Hindu philosophy not only own their allegiance to the Vedas, but the adherents of each one of them would often quarrel with others and maintain its superiority by trying to prove that it and it alone was the faithful follower of the Vedas and represented correctly their views. The laws which regulate the social, legal, domestic and religious customs and rites of the Hindus even to the present day are said to be but mere systematized memories of old Vedic teachings, and are held to be obligatory on their authority. Even under British administration, in the inheritance of property, adoption, and in such other legal transactions, Hindu Law is followed, and this claims to draw its authority from the Vedas. To enter into details is unnecessary. But suffice it to say that the Vedas, far from being regarded as a dead literature of the past, are still looked upon as the origin and source of almost all literatures except purely secular poetry and drama. Thus in short we may say that in spite of the many changes that time has wrought, the orthodox Hindu life may still be regarded in the main as an adumbration of the Vedic life, which had never ceased to shed its light all through the past.

Classification of the Vedic literature.

A beginner who is introduced for the first time to the study of later Sanskrit literature is likely to appear somewhat confused when he meets with authoritative texts of diverse purport and subjects having the same generic name "Veda" or "Śruti" (from *śru* to hear); for Veda in its wider sense is not the name of any particular book, but of the literature of a particular epoch extending over a long period, say two thousand years or so. As this literature represents the total achievements of the Indian people in different directions for such a long period, it must of necessity be of a diversified character. If we roughly classify this huge literature from the points of view of age, language, and subject matter, we can point out four different types, namely the Saṃhitā or collection of verses (*sam* together, *hita* put), Brāhmaṇas, Āraṇyakas ("forest treatises") and the Upaniṣads. All these literatures, both prose and verse, were looked upon as so holy that in early times it was thought almost a sacrilege to write them; they were therefore learnt by heart by the Brahmins from the mouth of their preceptors and were hence called *śruti* (literally anything heard)[1].

The Saṃhitās.

There are four collections or Saṃhitās, namely Ṛg-Veda, Sāma-Veda, Yajur-Veda and Atharva-Veda. Of these the Ṛg-Veda is probably the earliest. The Sāma-Veda has practically no independent value, for it consists of stanzas taken (excepting only 75) entirely from the Ṛg-Veda, which were meant to be sung to certain fixed melodies, and may thus be called the book of chants. The Yajur-Veda however contains in addition to the verses taken from the Ṛg-Veda many original prose formulas. The arrangement of the verses of the Sāma-Veda is solely with reference to their place and use in the Soma sacrifice; the contents of the Yajur-Veda are arranged in the order in which the verses were actually employed in the various religious sacrifices. It is therefore called the Veda of Yajus—sacrificial prayers. These may be contrasted with the arrangement in the Ṛg-Veda in this, that there the verses are generally arranged in accordance with the gods who are adored in them. Thus, for example, first we get all the poems addressed to Agni or the Fire-god, then all those to the god Indra and so on. The fourth collection, the Atharva-Veda, probably attained its present form considerably later than the Ṛg-Veda. In spirit, however, as Professor Macdonell says, "it is not only entirely different from the *Rigveda* but represents a much more primitive stage of thought. While the *Rigveda* deals almost exclusively with the higher gods as conceived by a com-

[1] Pāṇini, III. iii. 94.

paratively advanced and refined sacerdotal class, the *Atharva-Veda* is, in the main a book of spells and incantations appealing to the demon world, and teems with notions about witchcraft current among the lower grades of the population, and derived from an immemorial antiquity. These two, thus complementary to each other in contents are obviously the most important of the four Vedas[1]."

The Brāhmaṇas[2].

After the Saṃhitās there grew up the theological treatises called the Brāhmaṇas, which were of a distinctly different literary type. They are written in prose, and explain the sacred significance of the different rituals to those who are not already familiar with them. "They reflect," says Professor Macdonell, "the spirit of an age in which all intellectual activity is concentrated on the sacrifice, describing its ceremonies, discussing its value, speculating on its origin and significance." These works are full of dogmatic assertions, fanciful symbolism and speculations of an unbounded imagination in the field of sacrificial details. The sacrificial ceremonials were probably never so elaborate at the time when the early hymns were composed. But when the collections of hymns were being handed down from generation to generation the ceremonials became more and more complicated. Thus there came about the necessity of the distribution of the different sacrificial functions among several distinct classes of priests. We may assume that this was a period when the caste system was becoming established, and when the only thing which could engage wise and religious minds was sacrifice and its elaborate rituals. Free speculative thinking was thus subordinated to the service of the sacrifice, and the result was the production of the most fanciful sacramental and symbolic

[1] A. A. Macdonell's *History of Sanskrit Literature*, p. 31.

[2] Weber (*Hist. Ind. Lit*., p. II, note) says that the word Brāhmaṇa signifies "that which relates to prayer *brahman*." Max Müller (*S. B. E.* I. p. IXVI) says that Brāhmaṇa meant "originally the sayings of Brahmans, whether in the general sense of priests, or in the more special sense of Brahman-priests." Eggeling (*S. B E.* XII. Introd. p. XXII) says that the Brāhmaṇas were so called "probably either because they were intended for the instruction and guidance of priests (brahman) generally; or because they were, for the most part, the authoritative utterances of such as were thoroughly versed in Vedic and sacrificial lore and competent to act as Brahmans or superintending priests." But in view of the fact that the Brāhmaṇas were also supposed to be as much revealed as the Vedas, the present writer thinks that Weber's view is the correct one.

system, unparalleled anywhere but among the Gnostics. It is now generally believed that the close of the Brāhmaṇa period was not later than B.C. 500.

The Āraṇyakas.

As a further development of the Brāhmaṇas however we get the Āraṇyakas or forest treatises. These works were probably composed for old men who had retired into the forest and were thus unable to perform elaborate sacrifices requiring a multitude of accessories and articles which could not be procured in forests. In these, meditations on certain symbols were supposed to be of great merit, and they gradually began to supplant the sacrifices as being of a superior order. It is here that we find that amongst a certain section of intelligent people the ritualistic ideas began to give way, and philosophic speculations about the nature of truth became gradually substituted in their place. To take an illustration from the beginning of the Bṛhadāraṇyaka we find that instead of the actual performance of the horse sacrifice (*aśvamedha*) there are directions for meditating upon the dawn (*Uṣas*) as the head of the horse, the sun as the eye of the horse, the air as its life, and so on. This is indeed a distinct advancement of the claims of speculation or meditation over the actual performance of the complicated ceremonials of sacrifice. The growth of the subjective speculation, as being capable of bringing the highest good, gradually resulted in the supersession of Vedic ritualism and the establishment of the claims of philosophic meditation and self-knowledge as the highest goal of life. Thus we find that the Āraṇyaka age was a period during which free thinking tried gradually to shake off the shackles of ritualism which had fettered it for a long time. It was thus that the Āraṇyakas could pave the way for the Upaniṣads, revive the germs of philosophic speculation in the Vedas, and develop them in a manner which made the Upaniṣads the source of all philosophy that arose in the world of Hindu thought.

The Ṛg-Veda, its civilization.

The hymns of the Ṛg-Veda are neither the productions of a single hand nor do they probably belong to any single age. They were composed probably at different periods by different sages, and it is not improbable that some of them were composed before the Aryan people entered the plains of India. They were handed down from mouth to mouth and gradually swelled through the new additions that were made by the poets of succeeding generations. It was when the collection had increased to a very considerable extent that it was probably arranged in the present form, or in some other previous forms to which the present arrangement owes its origin. They therefore reflect the civilization of the Aryan people at different periods of antiquity before and after they had come to India. This unique monument of a long vanished age is of great aesthetic value, and contains much that is genuine poetry. It enables us to get an estimate of the primitive society which produced it—the oldest book of the Aryan race. The principal means of sustenance were cattle-keeping and the cultivation of the soil with plough and harrow, mattock and hoe, and watering the ground when necessary with artificial canals. "The chief food consists," as Kaegi says, "together with bread, of various preparations of milk, cakes of flour and butter, many sorts of vegetables and fruits; meat cooked on the spits or in pots, is little used, and was probably eaten only at the great feasts and family gatherings. Drinking plays throughout a much more important part than eating[1]." The wood-worker built war-chariots and wagons, as also more delicate carved works and artistic cups. Metal-workers, smiths and potters continued their trade. The women understood the plaiting of mats, weaving and sewing; they manufactured the wool of the sheep into clothing for men and covering for animals. The group of individuals forming a tribe was the highest political unit; each of the different families forming a tribe was under the sway of the father or the head of the family. Kingship was probably hereditary and in some cases electoral. Kingship was nowhere absolute, but limited by the will of the people. Most developed ideas of justice, right and law, were present in the country. Thus Kaegi says, "the hymns strongly prove how deeply the prominent minds in the people were persuaded that the eternal ordinances of the rulers of the world were as inviolable in mental and moral matters as in the realm of nature, and that every wrong act, even the unconscious, was punished and the sin expiated[2]." Thus it is only right and proper to think that the Aryans had attained a pretty high degree

[1] *The Rigveda*, by Kaegi, 1886 edition, p. 13.

[2] *Ibid.* p. 18.

of civilization, but nowhere was the sincere spirit of the Aryans more manifested than in religion, which was the most essential and dominant feature of almost all the hymns, except a few secular ones. Thus Kaegi says, "The whole significance of the Rigveda in reference to the general history of religion, as has repeatedly been pointed out in modern times, rests upon this, that it presents to us the development of religious conceptions from the earliest beginnings to the deepest apprehension of the godhead and its relation to man[1]."

The Vedic Gods.

The hymns of the Ṛg-Veda were almost all composed in praise of the gods. The social and other materials are of secondary importance, as these references had only to be mentioned incidentally in giving vent to their feelings of devotion to the god. The gods here are however personalities presiding over the diverse powers of nature or forming their very essence. They have therefore no definite, systematic and separate characters like the Greek gods or the gods of the later Indian mythical works, the Purāṇas. The powers of nature such as the storm, the rain, the thunder, are closely associated with one another, and the gods associated with them are also similar in character. The same epithets are attributed to different gods and it is only in a few specific qualities that they differ from one another. In the later mythological compositions of the Purāṇas the gods lost their character as hypostatic powers of nature, and thus became actual personalities and characters having their tales of joy and sorrow like the mortal here below. The Vedic gods may be contrasted with them in this, that they are of an impersonal nature, as the characters they display are mostly but expressions of the powers of nature. To take an example, the fire or Agni is described, as Kaegi has it, as one that "lies concealed in the softer wood, as in a chamber, until, called forth by the rubbing in the early morning hour, he suddenly springs forth in gleaming brightness. The sacrificer takes and lays him on the wood. When the priests pour melted butter upon him, he leaps up crackling and neighing like a horse—he whom men love to see increasing like their own prosperity. They wonder at him, when, decking himself with

[1] *The Rigveda*, by Kaegi, p. 26.

changing colors like a suitor, equally beautiful on all sides, he presents to all sides his front.

> All-searching is his beam, the gleaming of his light,
> His, the all-beautiful, of beauteous face and glance,
> The changing shimmer like that floats upon the stream,
> So Agni's rays gleam over bright and never cease[1].
> R. V. I. 143. 3.

They would describe the wind (Vāta) and adore him and say

> "In what place was he born, and from whence comes he?
> The vital breath of gods, the world's great offspring,
> The God where'er he will moves at his pleasure:
> His rushing sound we hear—what his appearance, no one[2]."
> R. V. X. 168. 3, 4.

It was the forces of nature and her manifestations, on earth here, the atmosphere around and above us, or in the Heaven beyond the vault of the sky that excited the devotion and imagination of the Vedic poets. Thus with the exception of a few abstract gods of whom we shall presently speak and some dual divinities, the gods may be roughly classified as the terrestrial, atmospheric, and celestial.

Polytheism, Henotheism and Monotheism.

The plurality of the Vedic gods may lead a superficial enquirer to think the faith of the Vedic people polytheistic. But an intelligent reader will find here neither polytheism nor monotheism but a simple primitive stage of belief to which both of these may be said to owe their origin. The gods here do not preserve their proper places as in a polytheistic faith, but each one of them shrinks into insignificance or shines as supreme according as it is the object of adoration or not. The Vedic poets were the children of nature. Every natural phenomenon excited their wonder, admiration or veneration. The poet is struck with wonder that "the rough red cow gives soft white milk." The appearance or the setting of the sun sends a thrill into the minds of the Vedic sage and with wonder-gazing eyes he exclaims:

> "Undropped beneath, not fastened firm, how comes it
> That downward turned he falls not downward?
> The guide of his ascending path,—who saw it?" R. V. IV. 13. 5.

The sages wonder how "the sparkling waters of all rivers flow into one ocean without ever filling it." The minds of the Vedic

[1] *The Rigveda*, by Kaegi, p. 35.
[2] *Ibid.* p. 38.

people as we find in the hymns were highly impressionable and fresh. At this stage the time was not ripe enough for them to accord a consistent and well-defined existence to the multitude of gods nor to universalize them in a monotheistic creed. They hypostatized unconsciously any force of nature that overawed them or filled them with gratefulness and joy by its beneficent or aesthetic character, and adored it. The deity which moved the devotion or admiration of their mind was the most supreme for the time. This peculiar trait of the Vedic hymns Max Müller has called Henotheismor Kathenotheism: "a belief in singlegods, each in turn standing out as the highest. And since the gods are thought of as specially ruling in their own spheres, the singers, in their special concerns and desires, call most of all on that god to whom they ascribe the most power in the matter,—to whose department if I may say so, their wish belongs. This god alone is present to the mind of the suppliant; with him for the time being is associated everything that can be said of a divine being;—he is the highest, the only god, before whom all others disappear, there being in this, however, no offence or depreciation of any other god[1]." "Against this theory it has been urged," as Macdonell rightly says in his *Vedic Mythology*[2], "that Vedic deities are not represented 'as independent of all the rest,' since no religion brings its gods into more frequent and varied juxtaposition and combination, and that even the mightiest gods of the Veda are made dependent on others. Thus Varuṇa and Sūrya are subordinate to Indra (1. 101), Varuṇa and the Aśvins submit to the power of Viṣṇu (1.156)....Even when a god is spoken of as unique or chief (*eka*), as is natural enough in laudations, such statements lose their temporarily monotheistic force, through the modifications or corrections supplied by the context or even by the same verse[3]." "Henotheism is therefore an appearance," says Macdonell, "rather than a reality, an appearance produced by the indefiniteness due to undeveloped anthropomorphism, by the lack of any Vedic god occupying the position of a Zeus as the constant head of the pantheon, by the natural tendency of the priest or singer in extolling a particular god to exaggerate his greatness and to ignore other gods, and by the

[1] *The Rigveda*, by Kaegi, p. 27.
[2] See *Ibid.* p. 33. See also Arrowsmith's note on it for other references to Henotheism.
[3] Macdonell's *Vedic Mythology*, pp. 16, 17.

growing belief in the unity of the gods (cf. the refrain of 3, 35) each of whom might be regarded as a type of the divine[1]." But whether we call it Henotheism or the mere temporary exaggeration of the powers of the deity in question, it is evident that this stage can neither be properly called polytheistic nor monotheistic, but one which had a tendency towards them both, although it was not sufficiently developed to be identified with either of them. The tendency towards extreme exaggeration could be called a monotheistic bias in germ, whereas the correlation of different deities as independent of one another and yet existing side by side was a tendency towards polytheism.

Growth of a Monotheistic tendency; Prajāpati, Viśvakarma.

This tendency towards extolling a god as the greatest and highest gradually brought forth the conception of a supreme Lord of all beings (Prajāpati), not by a process of conscious generalization but as a necessary stage of development of the mind, able to imagine a deity as the repository of the highest moral and physical power, though its direct manifestation cannot be perceived. Thus the epithet Prajāpati or the Lord of beings, which was originally an epithet for other deities, came to be recognized as a separate deity, the highest and the greatest. Thus it is said in R. V. X. 121[2]:

In the beginning rose Hiraṇyagarbha,
Born as the only lord of all existence.
This earth he settled firm and heaven established:
What god shall we adore with our oblations?
Who gives us breath, who gives us strength, whose bidding
All creatures must obey, the bright gods even;
Whose shade is death, whose shadow life immortal:
What god shall we adore with our oblations ?
Who by his might alone became the monarch
Of all that breathes, of all that wakes or slumbers,
Of all, both man and beast, the lord eternal:
What god shall we adore with our oblations?
Whose might and majesty these snowy mountains,
The ocean and the distant stream exhibit;
Whose arms extended are these spreading regions:
What god shall we adore with our oblations?
Who made the heavens bright, the earth enduring,
Who fixed the firmament, the heaven of heavens;
Who measured out the air's extended spaces:
What god shall we adore with our oblations?

[1] Macdonell's *Vedic Mythology*, p. 17.
[2] *The Rigveda, by* Kaegi, pp. 88, 89.

Similar attributes are also ascribed to the deity Viśvakarma (All-creator)[1]. He is said to be father and procreator of all beings, though himself uncreated. He generated the primitive waters. It is to him that the sage says,

> Who is our father, our creator, maker,
> Who every place doth know and every creature,
> By whom alone to gods their names were given,
> To him all other creatures go to ask him[2]. R. V. X. 82. 3.

Brahma.

The conception of Brahman which has been the highest glory for the Vedānta philosophy of later days had hardly emerged in the Ṛg-Veda from the associations of the sacrificial mind. The meanings that Sāyaṇa the celebrated commentator of the Vedas gives of the word as collected by Haug are: (*a*) food, food offering, (*b*) the chant of the sāma-singer, (*c*) magical formula or text, (*d*) duly completed ceremonies, (*e*) the chant and sacrificial gift together, (*f*) the recitation of the hotṛ priest, (*g*) great. Roth says that it also means "the devotion which manifests itself as longing and satisfaction of the soul and reaches forth to the gods." But it is only in the Śatapatha Brāhmaṇa that the conception of Brahman has acquired a great significance as the supreme principle which is the moving force behind the gods. Thus the Śatapatha says, "Verily in the beginning this (universe) was the Brahman (neut.). It created the gods; and, having created the gods, it made them ascend these worlds: Agni this (terrestrial) world, Vāyu the air, and Sūrya the sky....Then the Brahman itself went up to the sphere beyond. Having gone up to the sphere beyond, it considered, 'How can I descend again into these worlds?' It then descended again by means of these two, Form and Name. Whatever has a name, that is name; and that again which has no name and which one knows by its form, 'this is (of a certain) form,' that is form: as far as there are Form and Name so far, indeed, extends this (universe). These indeed are the two great forces of Brahman; and, verily, he who knows these two great forces of Brahman becomes himself a great force[3]. In another place Brahman is said to be the ultimate thing in the Universe and is identified with Prajāpati, Puruṣa and Prāṇa

[1] See *The Rigveda*, by Kaegi, p. 89, and also Muir's *Sanskrit Texts*, vol. IV. pp. 5-11.

[2] Kaegi's translation.

[3] See Eggeling's translation of Śatapatha Brāhmaṇa *S.B.E.* vol. XIIV. pp. 27, 28.

(the vital air[1]). In another place Brahman is described as being the Svayambhū (self-born) performing austerities, who offered his own self in the creatures and the creatures in his own self, and thus compassed supremacy, sovereignty and lordship over all creatures[2]. The conception of the supreme man (Puruṣa) in the Ṛg-Veda also supposes that the supreme man pervades the world with only a fourth part of Himself, whereas the remaining three parts transcend to a region beyond. He is at once the present, past and future[3].

Sacrifice; the First Rudiments of the Law of Karma.

It will however be wrong to suppose that these monotheistic tendencies were gradually supplanting the polytheistic sacrifices. On the other hand, the complications of ritualism were gradually growing in their elaborate details. The direct result of this growth contributed however to relegate the gods to a relatively unimportant position, and to raise the dignity of the magical characteristics of the sacrifice as an institution which could give the desired fruits of themselves. The offerings at a sacrifice were not dictated by a devotion with which we are familiar under Christian or Vaiṣṇava influence. The sacrifice taken as a whole is conceived as Haug notes "to be a kind of machinery in which every piece must tally with the other," the slightest discrepancy in the performance of even a minute ritualistic detail, say in the pouring of the melted butter on the fire, or the proper placing of utensils employed in the sacrifice, or even the misplacing of a mere straw contrary to the injunctions was sufficient to spoil the whole sacrifice with whatsoever earnestness it might be performed. Even if a word was mispronounced the most dreadful results might follow. Thus when Tvaṣṭṛ performed a sacrifice for the production of a demon who would be able to kill his enemy Indra, owing to the mistaken accent of a single word the object was reversed and the demon produced was killed by Indra. But if the sacrifice could be duly performed down to the minutest detail, there was no power which could arrest or delay the fruition of the object. Thus the objects of a sacrifice were fulfilled not by the grace of the gods, but as a natural result of the sacrifice. The performance of the rituals invariably produced certain mystic or magical results by virtue of which the object desired

[1] See *S. B. E.* XLIII. pp. 59, 60, 400 and XLIV. p. 409.
[2] See *Ibid.* XLIV. p. 418.
[3] R. V. X. 90, Puruṣa Sūkta.

by the sacrificer was fulfilled in due course like the fulfilment of a natural law in the physical world. The sacrifice was believed to have existed from eternity like the Vedas. The creation of the world itself was even regarded as the fruit of a sacrifice performed by the supreme Being. It exists as Haug says "as an invisible thing at all times and is like the latent power of electricity in an electrifying machine, requiring only the operation of a suitable apparatus in order to be elicited." The sacrifice is not offered to a god with a view to propitiate him or to obtain from him welfare on earth or bliss in Heaven; these rewards are directly produced by the sacrifice itself through the correct performance of complicated and interconnected ceremonies which constitute the sacrifice. Though in each sacrifice certain gods were invoked and received the offerings, the gods themselves were but instruments in bringing about the sacrifice or in completing the course of mystical ceremonies composing it. Sacrifice is thus regarded as possessing a mystical potency superior even to the gods, who it is sometimes stated attained to their divine rank by means of sacrifice. Sacrifice was regarded as almost the only kind of duty, and it was also called *karma* or *kriyā* (action) and the unalterable law was, that these mystical ceremonies for good or for bad, moral or immoral (for there were many kinds of sacrifices which were performed for injuring one's enemies or gaining worldly prosperity or supremacy at the cost of others) were destined to produce their effects. It is well to note here that the first recognition of a cosmic order or law prevailing in nature under the guardianship of the highest gods is to be found in the use of the word Ṛta (literally the course of things). This word was also used, as Macdonell observes, to denote the " 'order' in the moral world as truth and 'right' and in the religious world as sacrifice or 'rite'[1] " and its unalterable law of producing effects. It is interesting to note in this connection that it is here that we find the first germs of the law of karma, which exercises such a dominating control over Indian thought up to the present day. Thus we find the simple faith and devotion of the Vedic hymns on one hand being supplanted by the growth of a complex system of sacrificial rites, and on the other bending their course towards a monotheistic or philosophic knowledge of the ultimate reality of the universe.

[1] Macdonell's *Vedic Mythology*, p. 11.

Cosmogony—Mythological and philosophical.

The cosmogony of the Ṛg-Veda may be looked at from two aspects, the mythological and the philosophical. The mythological aspect has in general two currents, as Professor Macdonell says, "The one regards the universe as the result of mechanical production, the work of carpenter's and joiner's skill; the other represents it as the result of natural generation[1]." Thus in the Ṛg-Veda we find that the poet in one place says, "what was the wood and what was the tree out of which they built heaven and earth[2] ?" The answer given to this question in Taittirīya-Brāhmaṇa is "Brahman the wood and Brahman the tree from which the heaven and earth were made[3]." Heaven and Earth are sometimes described as having been supported with posts[4]. They are also sometimes spoken of as universal parents, and parentage is sometimes attributed to Aditi and Dakṣa.

Under this philosophical aspect the semi-pantheistic Manhymn[5] attracts our notice. The supreme man as we have already noticed above is there said to be the whole universe, whatever has been and shall be; he is the lord of immortality who has become diffused everywhere among things animate and inanimate, and all beings came out of him; from his navel came the atmosphere; from his head arose the sky; from his feet came the earth; from his ear the four quarters. Again there are other hymns in which the Sun is called the soul (*ātman*) of all that is movable and all that is immovable[6]. There are also statements to the effect that the Being is one, though it is called by many names by the sages[7]. The supreme being is sometimes extolled as the supreme Lord of the world called the golden egg (Hiraṇyagarbha[8]). In some passages it is said "Brahmaṇaspati blew forth these births like a blacksmith. In the earliest age of the gods, the existent sprang from the non-existent. In the first age of the gods, the existent sprang from the non-existent: thereafter the regions sprang, thereafter, from Uttānapada[9]." The most remarkable and

[1] Macdonell's *Vedic Mythology*, p. 11.
[2] R. V. X. 81. 4.
[3] Taitt. Br. II. 8. 9. 6.
[4] Macdonell's *Vedic Mythology*, p. 11; also R. V. II. 15 and IV. 56.
[5] R. V. X. 90.
[6] R. V. I. 115.
[7] R. V. I. 164. 46.
[8] R. V. X. 121.
[9] Muir's translation of R. V. X. 72; Muir's *Sanskrit Texts*, vol. V. p. 48.

sublime hymn in which the first germs of philosophic speculation with regard to the wonderful mystery of the origin of the world are found is the 129th hymn of R. V. X.

1. Then there was neither being nor not-being.
The atmosphere was not, nor sky above it.
What covered all? and where? by what protected?
Was there the fathomless abyss of waters?

2. Then neither death nor deathless existed;
Of day and night there was yet no distinction.
Alone that one breathed calmly, self-supported,
Other than It was none, nor aught above It.

3. Darkness there was at first in darkness hidden;
The universe was undistinguished water.
That which in void and emptiness lay hidden
Alone by power of fervor was developed.

4. Then for the first time there arose desire,
Which was the primal germ of mind, within it.
And sages, searching in their heart, discovered
In Nothing the connecting bond of Being.

. . . . .

6. Who is it knows? Who here can tell us surely
From what and how this universe has risen?
And whether not till after it the gods lived?
Who then can know from what it has arisen?

7. The source from which this universe has risen,
And whether it was made, or uncreated,
He only knows, who from the highest heaven
Rules, the all-seeing lord—or does not He know[1]?

The earliest commentary on this is probably a passage in the Śatapatha Brāhmaṇa (X. 5. 3. 1) which says that "in the beginning this (universe) was as it were neither non-existent nor existent; in the beginning this (universe) was as it were, existed and did not exist: there was then only that Mind. Wherefore it has been declared by the Rishi (Rg-Veda X. 129. 1), 'There was then neither the non-existent nor the existent' for Mind was, as it were, neither existent nor non-existent. This Mind when created, wished to become manifest,—more defined, more substantial: it sought after a self (a body); it practised austerity: it acquired consistency[2]." In the Atharva-Veda also we find it stated that all forms of the universe were comprehended within the god Skambha[3].

Thus we find that even in the period of the Vedas there sprang

[1] *The Rigveda*, by Kaegi, p. 90. R. V. X. 129.

[2] See Eggeling's translation of *Ś. B.*, *S. B. E.* vol. XLIII. pp. 374, 375.

[3] *A. V.* X. 7. 10.

forth such a philosophic yearning, at least among some who could question whether this universe was at all a creation or not, which could think of the origin of the world as being enveloped in the mystery of a primal non-differentiation of being and non-being; and which could think that it was the primal One which by its inherent fervour gave rise to the desire of a creation as the first manifestation of the germ of mind, from which the universe sprang forth through a series of mysterious gradual processes. In the Brāhmaṇas, however, we find that the cosmogonic view generally requires the agency of a creator, who is not however always the starting point, and we find that the theory of evolution is combined with the theory of creation, so that Prajāpati is sometimes spoken of as the creator while at other times the creator is said to have floated in the primeval water as a cosmic golden egg.

Eschatology; the Doctrine of Ātman.

There seems to be a belief in the Vedas that the soul could be separated from the body in states of swoon, and that it could exist after death, though we do not find there any trace of the doctrine of transmigration in a developed form. In the Śatapatha Brāhmaṇa it is said that those who do not perform rites with correct knowledge are born again after death and suffer death again. In a hymn of the Ṛg-Veda (X. 58) the soul (*manas*) of a man apparently unconscious is invited to come back to him from the trees, herbs, the sky, the sun, etc. In many of the hymns there is also the belief in the existence of another world, where the highest material joys are attained as a result of the performance of the sacrifices and also in a hell of darkness underneath where the evil-doers are punished. In the Śatapatha Brāhmaṇa we find that the dead pass between two fires which burn the evildoers, but let the good go by[1]; it is also said there that everyone is born again after death, is weighed in a balance, and receives reward or punishment according as his works are good or bad. It is easy to see that scattered ideas like these with regard to the destiny of the soul of man according to the sacrifice that he performs or other good or bad deeds form the first rudiments of the later doctrine of metempsychosis. The idea that man enjoys or suffers, either in another world or by being born in this world according to his good or bad deeds, is the first beginning of the

[1] See *S. B.* 1. 9. 3, and also Macdonell's *Vedic Mythology*, pp. 166, 167.

moral idea, though in the Brahmanic days the good deeds were more often of the nature of sacrificial duties than ordinary good works. These ideas of the possibilities of a necessary connection of the enjoyments and sorrows of a man with his good and bad works when combined with the notion of an inviolable law or order, which we have already seen was gradually growing with the conception of ṛta, and the unalterable law which produces the effects of sacrificial works, led to the Law of Karma and the doctrine of transmigration. The words which denote soul in the Ṛg-Veda are *manas*, *ātman* and *asu*. The word *ātman* however which became famous in later Indian thought is generally used to mean vital breath. Manas is regarded as the seat of thought and emotion, and it seems to be regarded, as Macdonell says, as dwelling in the heart[1]. It is however difficult to understand how ātman as vital breath, or as a separable part of man going out of the dead man came to be regarded as the ultimate essence or reality in man and the universe. There is however at least one passage in the Ṛg-Veda where the poet penetrating deeper and deeper passes from the vital breath (*asu*) to the blood, and thence to ātman as the inmost self of the world; "Who has seen how the first-born, being the Bone-possessing (the shaped world), was born from the Boneless (the shapeless)? where was the vital breath, the blood, the Self (*ātman*) of the world? Who went to ask him that knows it[2]?" In Taittirīya Āraṇyaka 1. 23, however, it is said that Prajāpati after having created his self (as the world) with his own self entered into it. In Taittirīya Brāhmaṇa the ātman is called omnipresent, and it is said that he who knows him is no more stained by evil deeds. Thus we find that in the pre-Upaniṣad Vedic literature ātman probably was first used to denote "vital breath" in man, then the self of the world, and then the self in man. It is from this last stage that we find the traces of a growing tendency to looking at the self of man as the omnipresent supreme principle of the universe, the knowledge of which makes a man sinless and pure.

Conclusion.

Looking at the advancement of thought in the Ṛg-Veda we find first that a fabric of thought was gradually growing which not

[1] Macdonell's *Vedic Mythology*, p. 166 and R. V. VIII. 89.

[2] R. V. I. 164. 4 and Deussen's article on Ātman in *Encyclopaedia of Religion and Ethics*.

only looked upon the universe as a correlation of parts or a construction made of them, but sought to explain it as having emanated from one great being who is sometimes described as one with the universe and surpassing it, and at other times as being separate from it; the agnostic spirit which is the mother of philosophic thought is seen at times to be so bold as to express doubts even on the most fundamental questions of creation—"Who knows whether this world was ever created or not?" Secondly, the growth of sacrifices has helped to establish the unalterable nature of the law by which the (sacrificial) actions produced their effects of themselves. It also lessened the importance of deities as being the supreme masters of the world and our fate, and the tendency of henotheism gradually diminished their multiple character and advanced the monotheistic tendency in some quarters. Thirdly, the soul of man is described as being separable from his body and subject to suffering and enjoyment in another world according to his good or bad deeds; the doctrine that the soul of man could go to plants, etc., or that it could again be reborn on earth, is also hinted at in certain passages, and this may be regarded as sowing the first seeds of the later doctrine of transmigration. The self (*ātman*) is spoken of in one place as the essence of the world, and when we trace the idea in the Brāhmaṇas and the Āraṇyakas we see that ạtman has begun to mean the supreme essence in man as well as in the universe, and has thus approached the great Ātman doctrine of the Upaniṣads.

III

THE EARLIER UPANIṢADS[1]. (B.C. 700—600)

The place of the Upaniṣads in Vedic literature.

THOUGH it is generally held that the Upaniṣads are usually attached as appendices to the Āraṇyakas which are again attached to the Brāhmaṇas, yet it cannot be said that their distinction as separate treatises is always observed. Thus we find in some cases that subjects which we should expect to be discussed in a Brāhmaṇa are introduced into the Āraṇyakas and the Āraṇyakas materials are sometimes fused into the great bulk of Upaniṣad teaching. This shows that these three literatures gradually grew up in one

[1] There are about 112 Upaniṣads which have been published by the "Nirṇaya-Sāgara" Press, Bombay, 1917. These are 1 Īśā, 2 Kena, 3 Kaṭha, 4 Praśna, 5 Muṇḍaka, 6 Māṇḍūkya, 7 Taittirīya, 8 Aitareya, 9 Chāndogya, 10 Bṛhadāraṇyaka, 11 Śvetāśvatara, 12 Kauṣītaki, 13 Maitreyī, 14 Kaivalya, 15 Jābāla, 16 Brahma-bindu, 17 Haṃsa, 18 Āruṇika, 19 Garbha, 20 Nārāyaṇa, 21 Nārāyaṇa, 22 Paramahaṃsa, 23 Brahma, 24 Amṛtanāda, 25 Atharvaśiras, 26 Atharvaśikhā, 27 Maitrāyaṇī, 28 Bṛhajjābāla, 29 Nṛsiṃhapūrvatāpinī, 30 Nṛsiṃhottaratāpinī, 31 Kālāgnirudra, 32 Subāla, 33 Kṣurikā, 34 Yantrikā, 35 Sarvasāra, 36 Nirālamba, 37 Śukarahasya, 38 Vajrasūcikā, 39 Tejobindu, 40 Nādabindu, 41 Dhyānabindu, 42 Brahmavidyā, 43 Yogatattva, 44 Ātmabodha, 45 Nāradaparivrājaka, 46 Triśikhibrāhmaṇa, 47 Sītā, 48 Yogacūḍāmaṇi, 49 Nirvāṇa, 50 Maṇḍalabrāhmaṇa, 51 Dakṣiṇāmūrtti, 52 Śarabha, 53 Skanda, 54 Tripādvibhūtimahānārāyaṇa, 55 Advayatāraka, 56 Rāmarahasya, 57 Rāmapūrvatāpinī, 58 Rāmottaratāpinī, 59 Vāsudeva, 60 Mudgala, 61 Sāṇḍilya, 62 Paingala, 63 Bhikṣuka, 64 Mahā, 65 Śārīraka, 66 Yogaśikhā, 67 Turiyātīta, 68 Saṃnyāsa, 69 Paramahaṃsaparivrājaka, 70 Akṣamālā, 71 Avyakta, 72 Ekākṣara, 73 Annapūrnā, 74 Sūrya, 75 Akṣi, 76 Adhyātma, 77 Kuṇḍika, 78 Sāvitrī, 79 Ātman, 80 Pāśupatabrahma, 81 Parabrahma, 82 Avadhūta, 83 Tripurātāpinī, 84 Devī, 85 Tripurā, 86 Kaṭharudra, 87 Bhāvanā, 88 Rudrahṛdaya, 89 Yogakuṇḍalī, 90 Bhasmajābāla, 91 Rudrākṣajābāla, 92 Gaṇapati, 93 Jābāladarśana, 94 Tārasāra, 95 Mahāvākya, 96 Pañcabrahma, 97 Prāṇāgnihotra, 98 Gopālapūrvatāpinī, 99 Gopālottaratāpinī, 100 Kṛṣṇa, 101 Yājñavalkya, 102 Varāha, 103 Śāṭhyāyanīya, 104 Hayagrīva, 105 Dattātreya, 106 Garuḍa, 107 Kalisantaraṇa, 108 Jābāli, 109 Saubhāgyalakṣmī, 110 Sarasvatīrahasya, 111 Bahvṛca, 112 Muktika.

The collection of Upaniṣads translated by Dara Shiko, Aurangzeb's brother, contained 50 Upaniṣads. The Muktika Upaniṣad gives a list of 108 Upaniṣads. With the exception of the first 13 Upaniṣads most of them are of more or less later date. The Upaniṣads dealt with in this chapter are the earlier ones. Amongst the later ones there are some which repeat the purport of these, there are others which deal with the Śaiva, Śākta, the Yoga and the Vaiṣṇava doctrines. These will be referred to in connection with the consideration of those systems in Volume II. The later Upaniṣads which only repeat the purport of those dealt with in this chapter do not require further mention. Some of the later Upaniṣads were composed even as late as the fourteenth or the fifteenth century.

process of development and they were probably regarded as parts of one literature, in spite of the differences in their subject-matter. Deussen supposes that the principle of this division was to be found in this, that the Brāhmaṇas were intended for the householders, the Āraṇyakas for those who in their old age withdrew into the solitude of the forests and the Upaniṣads for those who renounced the world to attain ultimate salvation by meditation. Whatever might be said about these literary classifications the ancient philosophers of India looked upon the Upaniṣads as being of an entirely different type from the rest of the Vedic literature as dictating the path of knowledge (*jñāna-mārga*) as opposed to the path of works (*karma-mārga*) which forms the content of the latter. It is not out of place here to mention that the orthodox Hindu view holds that whatever may be written in the Veda is to be interpreted as commandments to perform certain actions (*vidhi*) or prohibitions against committing certain others (*niṣedha*). Even the stories or episodes are to be so interpreted that the real objects of their insertion might appear as only to praise the performance of the commandments and to blame the commission of the prohibitions. No person has any right to argue why any particular Vedic commandment is to be followed, for no reason can ever discover that, and it is only because reason fails to find out why a certain Vedic act leads to a certain effect that the Vedas have been revealed as commandments and prohibitions to show the true path of happiness. The Vedic teaching belongs therefore to that of the Karma-mārga or the performance of Vedic duties of sacrifice, etc. The Upaniṣads however do not require the performance of any action, but only reveal the ultimate truth and reality, a knowledge of which at once emancipates a man. Readers of Hindu philosophy are aware that there is a very strong controversy on this point between the adherents of the Vedānta (*Upaniṣads*) and those of the Veda. For the latter seek in analogy to the other parts of the Vedic literature to establish the principle that the Upaniṣads should not be regarded as an exception, but that they should also be so interpreted that they might also be held out as commending the performance of duties; but the former dissociate the Upaniṣads from the rest of the Vedic literature and assert that they do not make the slightest reference to any Vedic duties, but only delineate the ultimate reality which reveals the highest knowledge in the minds of the deserving.

Śaṅkara the most eminent exponent of the Upaniṣads holds that they are meant for such superior men who are already above worldly or heavenly prosperities, and for whom the Vedic duties have ceased to have any attraction. Wheresoever there may be such a deserving person, be he a student, a householder or an ascetic, for him the Upaniṣads have been revealed for his ultimate emancipation and the true knowledge. Those who perform the Vedic duties belong to a stage inferior to those who no longer care for the fruits of the Vedic duties but are eager for final emancipation, and it is the latter who alone are fit to hear the Upaniṣads[1].

The names of the Upaniṣads; Non-Brahmanic influence.

The Upaniṣads are also known by another name Vedānta, as they are believed to be the last portions of the Vedas (*veda-anta*, end); it is by this name that the philosophy of the Upaniṣads, the Vedānta philosophy, is so familiar to us. A modern student knows that in language the Upaniṣads approach the classical Sanskrit; the ideas preached also show that they are the culmination of the intellectual achievement of a great epoch. As they thus formed the concluding parts of the Vedas they retained their Vedic names which they took from the name of the different schools or branches (*śākhā*) among which the Vedas were studied[2]. Thus the Upaniṣads attached to the Brāhmaṇas of the Aitareya and Kauṣītaki schools are called respectively Aitareya and Kauṣītaki Upaniṣads. Those of the Tāṇḍins and Talavakāras of the Sāma-veda are called the Chāndogya and Talavakāra (or Kena) Upaniṣads. Those of the Taittirīya school of the Yajurveda

[1] This is what is called the difference of fitness (*adhikāribheda*). Those who perform the sacrifices are not fit to hear the Upaniṣads and those who are fit to hear the Upaniṣads have no longer any necessity to perform the sacrificial duties.

[2] When the Saṃhitā texts had become substantially fixed, they were committed to memory in different parts of the country and transmitted from teacher to pupil along with directions for the practical performance of sacrificial duties. The latter formed the matter of prose compositions, the Brāhmaṇas. These however were gradually liable to diverse kinds of modifications according to the special tendencies and needs of the people among which they were recited. Thus after a time there occurred a great divergence in the readings of the texts of the Brāhmaṇas even of the same Veda among different people. These different schools were known by the name of particular Śākhās (e.g. Aitareya, Kauṣītaki) with which the Brāhmaṇas were associated or named. According to the divergence of the Brāhmaṇas of the different Śākhās there occurred the divergences of content and the length of the Upaniṣads associated with them.

form the Taittirīya and Mahānārayaṇa, of the Kaṭha school the Kāṭhaka, of the Maitrāyaṇī school the Maitrāyaṇī. The Bṛhadāraṇyaka Upaniṣad forms part of the Śatapatha Brāhmaṇa of the Vājasaneyi schools. The Īśā Upaniṣad also belongs to the latter school. But the school to which the Śvetāśvatara belongs cannot be traced, and has probably been lost. The presumption with regard to these Upaniṣads is that they represent the enlightened views of the particular schools among which they flourished, and under whose names they passed. A large number of Upaniṣads of a comparatively later age were attached to the Atharva-Veda, most of which were named not according to the Vedic schools but according to the subject-matter with which they dealt[1].

It may not be out of place here to mention that from the frequent episodes in the Upaniṣads in which the Brahmins are described as having gone to the Kṣattriyas for the highest knowledge of philosophy, as well as from the disparateness of the Upaniṣad teachings from that of the general doctrines of the Brāhmaṇas and from the allusions to the existence of philosophical speculations amongst the people in Pāli works, it may be inferred that among the Kṣattriyas in general there existed earnest philosophic enquiries which must be regarded as having exerted an important influence in the formation of the Upaniṣad doctrines. There is thus some probability in the supposition that though the Upaniṣads are found directly incorporated with the Brāhmaṇas it was not the production of the growth of Brahmanic dogmas alone, but that non-Brahmanic thought as well must have either set the Upaniṣad doctrines afoot, or have rendered fruitful assistance to their formulation and cultivation, though they achieved their culmination in the hands of the Brahmins.

Brāhmaṇas and the Early Upaniṣads.

The passage of the Indian mind from the Brāhmanic to the Upaniṣad thought is probably the most remarkable event in the history of philosophic thought. We know that in the later Vedic hymns some monotheistic conceptions of great excellence were developed, but these differ in their nature from the absolutism of the Upaniṣads as much as the Ptolemaic and the Copernican

[1] Garbha Upaniṣad, Ātman Upaniṣad, Praśna Upaniṣad, etc. There were however some exceptions such as the Māṇḍūkya, Jābāla, Paiṅgala, Śaunaka, etc.

systems in astronomy. The direct translation of Viśvakarman or Hiraṇyagarbha into the ātman and the Brahman of the Upaniṣads seems to me to be very improbable, though I am quite willing to admit that these conceptions were swallowed up by the ātman doctrine when it had developed to a proper extent. Throughout the earlier Upaniṣads no mention is to be found of Viśvakarman, Hiraṇyagarbha or Brahmaṇaspati and no reference of such a nature is to be found as can justify us in connecting the Upaniṣad ideas with those conceptions[1]. The word puruṣa no doubt occurs frequently in the Upaniṣads, but the sense and the association that come along with it are widely different from that of the puruṣa of the Puruṣasūkta of the Ṛg-Veda.

When the Ṛg-Veda describes Viśvakarman it describes him as a creator from outside, a controller of mundane events, to whom they pray for worldly benefits. "What was the position, which and whence was the principle, from which the all-seeing Viśvakarman produced the earth, and disclosed the sky by his might? The one god, who has on every side eyes, on every side a face, on every side arms, on every side feet, when producing the sky and earth, shapes them with his arms and with his wings.....Do thou, Viśvakarman, grant to thy friends those thy abodes which are the highest, and the lowest, and the middle...may a generous son remain here to us[2]"; again in R.V.X.82 we find "Viśvakarman is wise, energetic, the creator, the disposer, and the highest object of intuition.....He who is our father, our creator, disposer, who knows all spheres and creatures, who alone assigns to the gods their names, to him the other creatures resort for instruction[3]." Again about Hiraṇyagarbha we find in R.V. 1. 121, "Hiraṇyagarbha arose in the beginning; born, he was the one lord of things existing. He established the earth and this sky; to what god shall we offer our oblation? ... May he not injure us, he who is the generator of the earth, who ruling by fixed ordinances, produced the heavens, who produced the great and brilliant waters!—to what god, etc.? Prajāpati, no other than thou is lord over all these created things: may we obtain that, through desire of which we have invoked thee; may we become masters of riches[4]." Speaking of the puruṣa the Ṛg-Veda

[1] The name Viśvakarma appears in Śvet. IV. 17. Hiraṇyagarbha appears in Śvet. III. 4 and IV. 12, but only as the first created being. The phrase Sarvāhammānī Hīraṇyagarbha which Deussen refers to occurs only in the later Nṛsiṃḥ. 9. The word Brahmaṇaspati does not occur at all in the Upaniṣads.

[2] Muir's *Sanskrit Texts*, vol. IV. pp. 6, 7.

[3] *Ibid*. p. 7.

[4] *Ibid*. pp. 16, 17.

says "Purusha has a thousand heads... a thousand eyes, and a thousand feet. On every side enveloping the earth he transcended [it] by a space of ten fingers....He formed those aerial creatures, and the animals, both wild and tame[1]," etc. Even that famous hymn (R.V. X. 129) which begins with "There was then neither being nor non-being, there was no air nor sky above" ends with saying "From whence this creation came into being, whether it was created or not—he who is in the highest sky, its ruler, probably knows or does not know."

In the Upaniṣads however, the position is entirely changed, and the centre of interest there is not in a creator from outside but in the self: the natural development of the monotheistic position of the Vedas could have grown into some form of developed theism, but not into the doctrine that the self was the only reality and that everything else was far below it. There is no relation here of the worshipper and the worshipped and no prayers are offered to it, but the whole quest is of the highest truth, and the true self of man is discovered as the greatest reality. This change of philosophical position seems to me to be a matter of great interest. This change of the mind from the objective to the subjective does not carry with it in the Upaniṣads any elaborate philosophical discussions, or subtle analysis of mind. It comes there as a matter of direct perception, and the conviction with which the truth has been grasped cannot fail to impress the readers. That out of the apparently meaningless speculations of the Brāhmaṇas this doctrine could have developed, might indeed appear to be too improbable to be believed.

On the strength of the stories of Bālāki Gārgya and Ajātaśatru (Bṛh. II. 1), Śvetaketu and Pravāhaṇa Jaibali (Chā. V. 3 and Bṛh. VI. 2) and Āruṇi and Aśvapati Kaikeya (Chā. V. II) Garbe thinks "that it can be proven that the Brahman's profoundest wisdom, the doctrine of All-one, which has exercised an unmistakable influence on the intellectual life even of our time, did not have its origin in the circle of Brahmans at all[2]" and that "it took its rise in the ranks of the warrior caste[3]." This if true would of course lead the development of the Upaniṣads away from the influence of the Veda, Brāhmaṇas and the Āraṇyakas. But do the facts prove this? Let us briefly examine the evidences that Garbe him-

[1] Muir's *Sanskrit Texts*, vol. V. pp. 368, 371.

[2] Garbe's article, "*Hindu Monism*," p. 68.

[3] *Ibid*. p. 78.

self has produced. In the story of Bālāki Gārgya and Ajātaśatru (Bṛh. II. 1) referred to by him, Bālāki Gārgya is a boastful man who wants to teach the Kṣattriya Ajātaśatru the true Brahman, but fails and then wants it to be taught by him. To this Ajātaśatru replies (following Garbe's own translation) "it is contrary to the natural order that a Brahman receive instruction from a warrior and expect the latter to declare the Brahman to him[1]." Does this not imply that in the natural order of things a Brahmin always taught the knowledge of Brahman to the Kṣattriyas, and that it was unusual to find a Brahmin asking a Kṣattriya about the true knowledge of Brahman? At the beginning of the conversation, Ajātaśatru had promised to pay Bālāki one thousand coins if he could tell him about Brahman, since all people used to run to Janaka to speak about Brahman[2]. The second story of Śvetaketu and Pravāhaṇa Jaibali seems to be fairly conclusive with regard to the fact that the transmigration doctrines, the way of the gods (*devayāna*) and the way of the fathers (*pitṛyāna*) had originated among the Kṣattriyas, but it is without any relevancy with regard to the origin of the superior knowledge of Brahman as the true self.

The third story of Āruṇi and Aśvapati Kaikeya (Chā. V. II) is hardly more convincing, for here five Brahmins wishing to know what the Brahman and the self were, went to Uddālaka Aruṇi; but as he did not know sufficiently about it he accompanied them to the Kṣattriya king Aśvapati Kaikeya who was studying the subject. But Aśvapati ends the conversation by giving them certain instructions about the fire doctrine (*vaiśvānara agni*) and the import of its sacrifices. He does not say anything about the true self as Brahman. We ought also to consider that there are only the few exceptional cases where Kṣaṭṭriya kings were instructing the Brahmins. But in all other cases the Brahmins were discussing and instructing the ātman knowledge. I am thus led to think that Garbe owing to his bitterness of feeling against the Brahmins as expressed in the earlier part of the essay had been too hasty in his judgment. The opinion of Garbe seems to have been shared to some extent by Winternitz also, and the references given by him to the Upaniṣad passages are also the same as we

[1] Garbe's article, "*Hindu Monism*," p. 74.

[2] Bṛh. II., compare also Bṛh. IV. 3, how Yājñavalkya speaks to Janaka about the *brahmavidyā*.

just examined[1]. The truth seems to me to be this, that the Kṣattriyas and even some women took interest in the religio-philosophical quest manifested in the Upaniṣads. The enquirers were so eager that either in receiving the instruction of Brahman or in imparting it to others, they had no considerations of sex and birth[2]; and there seems to be no definite evidence for thinking that the Upaniṣad philosophy originated among the Kṣattriyas or that the germs of its growth could not be traced in the Brāhmaṇas and the Āraṇyakas which were the productions of the Brahmins.

The change of the Brāhmaṇa into the Āraṇyaka thought is signified by a transference of values from the actual sacrifices to their symbolic representations and meditations which were regarded as being productive of various earthly benefits. Thus we find in the Bṛhadāraṇyaka (I. 1) that instead of a horse sacrifice the visible universe is to be conceived as a horse and meditated upon as such. The dawn is the head of the horse, the sun is the eye, wind is its life, fire is its mouth and the year is its soul, and so on. What is the horse that grazes in the field and to what good can its sacrifice lead? This moving universe is the horse which is most significant to the mind, and the meditation of it as such is the most suitable substitute of the sacrifice of the horse, the mere animal. Thought-activity as meditation, is here taking the place of an external worship in the form of sacrifices. The material substances and the most elaborate and accurate sacrificial rituals lost their value and bare meditations took their place. Side by side with the ritualistic sacrifices of the generality of the Brahmins, was springing up a system where thinking and symbolic meditations were taking the place of gross matter and action involved in sacrifices. These symbols were not only chosen from the external world as the sun, the wind, etc., from the body of man, his various vital functions and the senses, but even arbitrary alphabets were taken up and it was believed that the meditation of these as the highest and the greatest was productive of great beneficial results. Sacrifice in itself was losing value in the eyes of these men and diverse mystical significances and imports were beginning to be considered as their real truth[3].

[1] Winternitz's *Geschichte der indischen Litteratur*, I. pp. 197 ff.

[2] The story of Maitreyī and Yājñavalkya (Bṛh. II. 4) and that of Satyakāma son of Jabālā and his teacher (Chā. IV. 4).

[3] Chā. V. II.

The Uktha (verse) of Ṛg-Veda was identified in the Aitareya Āraṇyaka under several allegorical forms with the Prāna[1], the Udgītha of the Sāmaveda was identified with Om, Prāṇa, sun and eye; in Chāndogya II. the Sāman was identified with Om, rain, water, seasons, Prāṇa, etc., in Chāndogya III. 16-17 man was identified with sacrifice; his hunger, thirst, sorrow, with initiation; laughing, eating, etc., with the utterance of the Mantras; and asceticism, gift, sincerity, restraint from injury, truth, with sacrificial fees (*dakṣiṇā*). The gifted mind of these cultured Vedic Indians was anxious to come to some unity, but logical precision of thought had not developed, and as a result of that we find in the Āraṇyakas the most grotesque and fanciful unifications of things which to our eyes have little or no connection. Any kind of instrumentality in producing an effect was often considered as pure identity. Thus in Ait. Araṇ. II. 1. 3 we find "Then comes the origin of food. The seed of Prajāpati are the gods. The seed of the gods is rain. The seed of rain is herbs. The seed of herbs is food. The seed of food is seed. The seed of seed is creatures. The seed of creatures is the heart. The seed of the heart is the mind. The seed of the mind is speech. The seed of speech is action. The act done is this man the abode of Brahman[2]."

The word Brahman according to Sāyaṇa meant mantras (magical verses), the ceremonies, the hotṛ priest, the great. Hillebrandt points out that it is spoken of in R.V. as being new, "as not having hitherto existed," and as "coming into being from the fathers." It originates from the seat of the Ṛta, springs forth at the sound of the sacrifice, begins really to exist when the soma juice is pressed and the hymns are recited at the savana rite, endures with the help of the gods even in battle, and soma is its guardian (R.V. VIII. 37. 1, VIII. 69. 9, VI. 23. 5, 1. 47. 2, VII. 22. 9, VI. 52. 3, etc.). On the strength of these Hillebrandt justifies the conjecture of Haug that it signifies a mysterious power which can be called forth by various ceremonies, and his definition of it, as the magical force which is derived from the orderly cooperation of the hymns, the chants and the sacrificial gifts[3]. I am disposed to think that this meaning is closely connected with the meaning as we find it in many passages in the Āraṇyakas and the Upaniṣads. The meaning in many of these seems to be midway between

[1] Ait. Āraṇ. II. 1-3.

[2] Keith's *Translation of Aitareya Āraṇyaka.*

[3] Hillebrandt's article on Brahman, *E. R. E.*

"magical force" and "great," transition between which is rather easy. Even when the sacrifices began to be replaced by meditations, the old belief in the power of the sacrifices still remained, and as a result of that we find that in many passages of the Upaniṣads people are thinking of meditating upon this great force "Brahman" as being identified with diverse symbols, natural objects, parts and functions of the body.

When the main interest of sacrifice was transferred from its actual performance in the external world to certain forms of meditation, we find that the understanding of particular allegories of sacrifice having a relation to particular kinds of bodily functions was regarded as Brahman, without a knowledge of which nothing could be obtained. The fact that these allegorical interpretations of the Pañcāgnividyā are so much referred to in the Upaniṣads as a secret doctrine, shows that some people came to think that the real efficacy of sacrifices depended upon such meditations. When the sages rose to the culminating conception, that he is really ignorant who thinks the gods to be different from him, they thought that as each man was nourished by many beasts, so the gods were nourished by each man, and as it is unpleasant for a man if any of his beasts are taken away, so it is unpleasant for the gods that men should know this great truth[1].

In the Kena we find it indicated that all the powers of the gods such as that of Agni (fire) to burn, Vāyu (wind) to blow, depended upon Brahman, and that it is through Brahman that all the gods and all the senses of man could work. The whole process of Upaniṣad thought shows that the magic power of sacrifices as associated with Ṛta (unalterable law) was being abstracted from the sacrifices and conceived as the supreme power. There are many stories in the Upaniṣads of the search after the nature of this great power the Brahman, which was at first only imperfectly realized. They identified it with the dominating power of the natural objects of wonder, the sun, the moon, etc. with bodily and mental functions and with various symbolical representations, and deluded themselves for a time with the idea that these were satisfactory. But as these were gradually found inadequate, they came to the final solution, and the doctrine of the inner self of man as being the highest truth the Brahman originated.

[1] Bṛh. I. 4. 10.

The meaning of the word Upaniṣad.

The word Upaniṣad is derived from the root *sad* with the prefix *ni* (to sit), and Max Müller says that the word originally meant the act of sitting down near a teacher and of submissively listening to him. In his introduction to the Upaniṣads he says, "The history and the genius of the Sanskrit language leave little doubt that Upaniṣad meant originally session, particularly a session consisting of pupils, assembled at a respectful distance round their teacher[1]." Deussen points out that the word means "secret" or "secret instruction," and this is borne out by many of the passages of the Upaniṣads themselves. Max Müller also agrees that the word was used in this sense in the Upaniṣads[2]. There we find that great injunctions of secrecy are to be observed for the communication of the doctrines, and it is said that it should only be given to a student or pupil who by his supreme moral restraint and noble desires proves himself deserving to hear them. Śaṅkara however, the great Indian exponent of the Upaniṣads derives the word from the root *sad* to destroy and supposes that it is so called because it destroys inborn ignorance and leads to salvation by revealing the right knowledge. But if we compare the many texts in which the word Upaniṣad occurs in the Upaniṣads themselves it seems that Deussen's meaning is fully justified[3].

The composition and growth of diverse Upaniṣads.

The oldest Upaniṣads are written in prose. Next to these we have some in verses very similar to those that are to be found in classical Sanskrit. As is easy to see, the older the Upaniṣad the more archaic is it in its language. The earliest Upaniṣads have an almost mysterious forcefulness in their expressions at least to Indian ears. They are simple, pithy and penetrate to the heart. We can read and read them over again without getting tired. The lines are always as fresh as ever. As such they have a charm apart from the value of the ideas they intend to convey. The word Upaniṣad was used, as we have seen, in the sense of "secret doctrine or instruction"; the Upaniṣad teachings were also intended to be conveyed in strictest secrecy to earnest enquirers of high morals and superior self-restraint for the purpose of achieving

[1] Max Müller's *Translation of the Upanishads*, *S. B. E.* vol. I. p. lxxxi.

[2] *S. B. E.* vol. I. p. lxxxiii.

[3] Deussen's *Philosophy of the Upanishads*, pp. 10-15.

emancipation. It was thus that the Upaniṣad style of expression, when it once came into use, came to possess the greatest charm and attraction for earnest religious people; and as a result of that we find that even when other forms of prose and verse had been adapted for the Sanskrit language, the Upaniṣad form of composition had not stopped. Thus though the earliest Upaniṣads were compiled by B.C. 500, they continued to be written even so late as the spread of Mahommedan influence in India. The earliest and most important are probably those that have been commented upon by Śaṅkara namely Bṛhadāraṇyaka, Chāndogya, Aitareya, Taittirīya, Īśā, Kena, Kaṭha, Praśna, Muṇḍaka and Māṇḍūkya[1]. It is important to note in this connection that the separate Upaniṣads differ much from one another with regard to their content and methods of exposition. Thus while some of them are busy laying great stress upon the monistic doctrine of the self as the only reality, there are others which lay stress upon the practice of Yoga, asceticism, the cult of Śiva, of Viṣṇu and the philosophy or anatomy of the body, and may thus be respectively called the Yoga, Śaiva, Viṣṇu and Śārīra Upaniṣads. These in all make up the number to one hundred and eight.

Revival of Upaniṣad studies in modern times.

How the Upaniṣads came to be introduced into Europe is an interesting story. Dārā Shiko the eldest son of the Emperor Shāh Jahān heard of the Upaniṣads during his stay in Kashmir in 1640. He invited several Pandits from Benares to Delhi, who undertook the work of translating them into Persian. In 1775 Anquetil Duperron, the discoverer of the Zend-Avesta, received a manuscript of it presented to him by his friend Le Gentil, the French resident in Faizabad at the court of Shujā-uddaulah. Anquetil translated it into Latin which was published in 1801-1802. This translation though largely unintelligible was read by Schopenhauer with great enthusiasm. It had, as Schopenhauer himself admits, profoundly influenced his philosophy. Thus he

[1] Deussen supposes that Kauṣītaki is also one of the earliest. Max Müller and Schroeder think that Maitrāyaṇī also belongs to the earliest group, whereas Deussen counts it as a comparatively later production. Winternitz divides the Upaniṣads into four periods. In the first period he includes Bṛhadarāṇyaka, Chāndogya, Taittirīya, Aitareya, Kauṣītaki and Kena. In the second he includes Kāṭhaka, Īśā, Śvetāśvatara, Muṇḍaka, Mahānārāyaṇa, and in the third period he includes Praśna, Maitrāyaṇī and Māṇḍūkya. The rest of the Upaniṣads he includes in the fourth period.

writes in the preface to his *Welt als Wille und Vorstellung*[1], "And if, indeed, in addition to this he is a partaker of the benefit conferred by the Vedas, the access to which, opened to us through the Upanishads, is in my eyes the greatest advantage which this still young century enjoys over previous ones, because I believe that the influence of the Sanskrit literature will penetrate not less deeply than did the revival of Greek literature in the fifteenth century: if, I say, the reader has also already received and assimilated the sacred, primitive Indian wisdom, then is he best of all prepared to hear what I have to say to him.....I might express the opinion that each one of the individual and disconnected aphorisms which make up the Upanishads may be deduced as a consequence from the thought I am going to impart, though the converse, that my thought is to be found in the Upanishads is by no means the case." Again, "How does every line display its firm, definite, and throughout harmonious meaning! From every sentence deep, original, and sublime thoughts arise, and the whole is pervaded by a high and holy and earnest spirit.... In the whole world there is no study, except that of the originals, so beneficial and so elevating as that of the Oupanikhat. It has been the solace of my life, it will be the solace of my death![2]" Through Schopenhauer the study of the Upaniṣads attracted much attention in Germany and with the growth of a general interest in the study of Sanskrit, they found their way into other parts of Europe as well.

The study of the Upaniṣads has however gained a great impetus by the earnest attempts of our Ram Mohan Roy who not only translated them into Bengali, Hindi and English and published them at his own expense, but founded the Brahma Samaj in Bengal, the main religious doctrines of which were derived directly from the Upaniṣads.

[1] Translation by Haldane and Kemp, vol. I. pp. xii and xiii.

[2] Max Müller says in his introduction to the Upanishads (*S. B. E.* I. p. lxii; see also pp. lx, lxi) "that Schopenhauer should have spoken of the Upanishads as 'products of the highest wisdom' ... that he should have placed the pantheism there taught high above the pantheism of Bruno, Malebranche, Spinoza and Scotus Erigena, as brought to light again at Oxford in 1681, may perhaps secure a more considerate reception for those relics of ancient wisdom than anything that I could say in their favour."

The Upaniṣads and their interpretations.

Before entering into the philosophy of the Upaniṣads it may be worth while to say a few words as to the reason why diverse and even contradictory explanations as to the real import of the Upaniṣads had been offered by the great Indian scholars of past times. The Upaniṣads, as we have seen, formed the concluding portion of the revealed Vedic literature, and were thus called the Vedānta. It was almost universally believed by the Hindus that the highest truths could only be found in the revelation of the Vedas. Reason was regarded generally as occupying a comparatively subservient place, and its proper use was to be found in its judicious employment in getting out the real meaning of the apparently conflicting ideas of the Vedas. The highest knowledge of ultimate truth and reality was thus regarded as having been once for all declared in the Upaniṣads. Reason had only to unravel it in the light of experience. It is important that readers of Hindu philosophy should bear in mind the contrast that it presents to the ruling idea of the modern world that new truths are discovered by reason and experience every day, and even in those cases where the old truths remain, they change their hue and character every day, and that in matters of ultimate truths no finality can ever be achieved; we are to be content only with as much as comes before the purview of our reason and experience at the time. It was therefore thought to be extremely audacious that any person howsoever learned and brilliant he might be should have any right to say anything regarding the highest truths simply on the authority of his own opinion or the reasons that he might offer. In order to make himself heard it was necessary for him to show from the texts of the Upaniṣads that they supported him, and that their purport was also the same. Thus it was that most schools of Hindu philosophy found it one of their principal duties to interpret the Upaniṣads in order to show that they alone represented the true Vedānta doctrines. Any one who should feel himself persuaded by the interpretations of any particular school might say that in following that school he was following the Vedānta.

The difficulty of assuring oneself that any interpretation is absolutely the right one is enhanced by the fact that germs of diverse kinds of thoughts are found scattered over the Upaniṣads which are not worked out in a systematic manner. Thus each interpreter in his turn made the texts favourable to his own doctrines prominent and brought them to the forefront, and tried to repress others or explain them away. But comparing the various systems of Upaniṣad interpretation we find that the interpretation offered by Śaṅkara very largely represents the view of the general body of the earlier Upaniṣad doctrines, though there are some which distinctly foreshadow the doctrines of other systems, but in a crude and germinal form. It is thus that Vedānta is generally associated with the interpretation of Śaṅkara and Śaṅkara's system of thought is called the Vedānta system, though there are many other systems which put forth their claim as representing the true Vedānta doctrines.

Under these circumstances it is necessary that a modern interpreter of the Upaniṣads should turn a deaf ear to the absolute claims of these exponents, and look upon the Upaniṣads not as a systematic treatise but as a repository of diverse currents of thought—the melting pot in which all later philosophic ideas were still in a state of fusion, though the monistic doctrine of Śaṅkara, or rather an approach thereto, may be regarded as the purport of by far the largest majority of the texts. It will be better that a modern interpreter should not agree to the claims of the ancients that all the Upaniṣads represent a connected system, but take the texts independently and separately and determine their meanings, though keeping an attentive eye on the context in which they appear. It is in this way alone that we can detect the germs of the thoughts of other Indian systems in the Upaniṣads, and thus find in them the earliest records of those tendencies of thoughts.

The quest after Brahman: the struggle and the failures.

The fundamental idea which runs through the early Upaniṣads is that underlying the exterior world of change there is an unchangeable reality which is identical with that which underlies the essence in man[1]. If we look at Greek philosophy in Parmenides or Plato or at modern philosophy in Kant, we find the same tendency towards glorifying one unspeakable entity as the reality or the essence. I have said above that the Upaniṣads are

[1] Bṛh. IV. 4. 5. 22.

no systematic treatises of a single hand, but are rather collations or compilations of floating monologues, dialogues or anecdotes. There are no doubt here and there simple discussions but there is no pedantry or gymnastics of logic. Even the most casual reader cannot but be struck with the earnestness and enthusiasm of the sages. They run from place to place with great eagerness in search of a teacher competent to instruct them about the nature of Brahman. Where is Brahman? What is his nature?

We have noticed that during the closing period of the Saṃhitā there were people who had risen to the conception of a single creator and controller of the universe, variously called Prajāpati, Viśvakarman, Puruṣa, Brahmaṇaspati and Brahman. But this divine controller was yet only a deity. The search as to the nature of this deity began in the Upaniṣads. Many visible objects of nature such as the sun or the wind on one hand and the various psychological functions in man were tried, but none could render satisfaction to the great ideal that had been aroused. The sages in the Upaniṣads had already started with the idea that there was a supreme controller or essence presiding over man and the universe. But what was its nature? Could it be identified with any of the deities of Nature, was it a new deity or was it no deity at all? The Upaniṣads present to us the history of this quest and the results that were achieved.

When we look merely to this quest we find that we have not yet gone out of the Āraṇyaka ideas and of symbolic (*pratīka*) forms of worship. *Prāṇa* (vital breath) was regarded as the most essential function for the life of man, and many anecdotes are related to show that it is superior to the other organs, such as the eye or ear, and that on it all other functions depend. This recognition of the superiority of prāṇa brings us to the meditations on prāṇa as Brahman as leading to the most beneficial results. So also we find that owing to the presence of the exalting characters of omnipresence and eternality *ākāśa* (space) is meditated upon as Brahman. So also manas and Āditya (sun) are meditated upon as Brahman. Again side by side with the visible material representation of Brahman as the pervading Vāyu, or the sun and the immaterial representation as ākāśa, manas or prāṇa, we find also the various kinds of meditations as substitutes for actual sacrifice. Thus it is that there was an earnest quest after the discovery of Brahman. We find a stratum of thought which shows that the sages were still blinded by the old ritualistic associations, and though meditation had taken the place of sacrifice yet this was hardly adequate for the highest attainment of Brahman.

Next to the failure of the meditations we have to notice the history of the search after Brahman in which the sages sought to identify Brahman with the presiding deity of the sun, moon, lightning, ether, wind, fire, water, etc., and failed; for none of these could satisfy the ideal they cherished of Brahman. It is indeed needless here to multiply these examples, for they are tiresome not only in this summary treatment but in the original as well. They are of value only in this that they indicate how toilsome was the process by which the old ritualistic associations could be got rid of; what struggles and failures the sages had to undergo before they reached a knowledge of the true nature of Brahman.

Unknowability of Brahman and the Negative Method.

It is indeed true that the magical element involved in the discharge of sacrificial duties lingered for a while in the symbolic worship of Brahman in which He was conceived almost as a deity. The minds of the Vedic poets so long accustomed to worship deities of visible manifestation could not easily dispense with the idea of seeking after a positive and definite content of Brahman. They tried some of the sublime powers of nature and also many symbols, but these could not render ultimate satisfaction. They did not know what the Brahman was like, for they had only a dim and dreamy vision of it in the deep craving of their souls which could not be translated into permanent terms. But this was enough to lead them on to the goal, for they could not be satisfied with anything short of the highest.

They found that by whatever means they tried to give a positive and definite content of the ultimate reality, the Brahman, they failed. Positive definitions were impossible. They could not point out what the Brahman was like in order to give an utterance to that which was unutterable, they could only say that it was not like aught that we find in experience. Yājñavalkya said "He the ātman is not this, nor this (*neti neti*). He is inconceivable, for he cannot be conceived, unchangeable, for he is not changed, untouched, for nothing touches him; he cannot suffer by a stroke of the sword, he cannot suffer any injury[1]." He is *asat*, non-being, for the being which Brahman is, is not to be understood as such being as is known to us by experience; yet he is being, for he alone is supremely real, for the universe subsists by him. We ourselves are but he, and yet we know not what he is. Whatever we can experience, whatever we can express, is limited, but he is the unlimited, the basis of all. "That which is inaudible, intangible, invisible, indestructible, which cannot be tasted, nor smelt, eternal, without beginning or end, greater than the great (*mahat*), the fixed. He who knows it is released from the jaws of death[2]." Space, time and causality do not appertain to him, for he at once forms their essence and transcends them. He is the infinite and the vast, yet the smallest of the small, at once here as there, there as here; no characterisation of him is possible, otherwise than by the denial to him of all empirical attributes, relations and definitions. He is independent of all limitations of space, time, and cause which rules all that is objectively presented, and therefore the empirical universe. When Bāhva was questioned by Vaṣkali, he expounded the nature of Brahman to him by maintaining silence—"Teach me," said Vaṣkali, "most reverent sir, the nature of Brahman." Bāhva however remained silent. But when the question was put forth a second or third time he answered, "I teach you indeed but you do not understand; the Ātman is silence[3]." The way to indicate it is thus by *neti neti*, it is not this, it is not this. We cannot describe it by any positive content which is always limited by conceptual thought.

The Ātman doctrine.

The sum and substance of the Upaniṣad teaching is involved in the equation Ātman = Brahman. We have already seen that the word Ātman was used in the Ṛg-Veda to denote on the one hand the ultimate essence of the universe, and on the other the vital breath in man. Later on in the Upaniṣads we see that the word Brahman is generally used in the former sense, while the word Ātman is reserved to denote the inmost essence in man, and the

[1] Bṛh. IV. 5. 15. Deussen, Max Müller and Röer have all misinterpreted this passage; *asito* has been interpreted as an adjective or participle, though no evidence has ever been adduced; it is evidently the ablative of *asi*, a sword.

[2] Kaṭha III. 15.

[3] Śaṅkara on *Brahma-sutra* III. 2. 17, and also Deussen, *Philosophy of the Upanishads*, p. 156.

Upaniṣads are emphatic in their declaration that the two are one and the same. But what is the inmost essence of man? The self of man involves an ambiguity, as it is used in a variety of senses. Thus so far as man consists of the essence of food (i.e. the physical parts of man) he is called *annamaya*. But behind the sheath of this body there is the other self consisting of the vital breath which is called the self as vital breath (*prāṇamaya ātman*). Behind this again there is the other self "consisting of will" called the *manomaya ātman*. This again contains within it the self "consisting of consciousness" called the *vijñānamaya ātman*. But behind it we come to the final essence the self as pure bliss (the *ānandamaya ātman*). The texts say: "Truly he is the rapture; for whoever gets this rapture becomes blissful. For who could live, who could breathe if this space (*ākāśa*) was not bliss? For it is he who behaves as bliss. For whoever in that Invisible, Self-surpassing, Unspeakable, Supportless finds fearless support, he really becomes fearless. But whoever finds even a slight difference, between himself and this Ātman there is fear for him[1]."

Again in another place we find that Prajāpati said: "The self (*ātman*) which is free from sin, free from old age, from death and grief, from hunger and thirst, whose desires are true, whose cogitations are true, that is to be searched for, that is to be enquired; he gets all his desires and all worlds who knows that self[2]." The gods and the demons on hearing of this sent Indra and Virocana respectively as their representatives to enquire of this self from Prajāpati. He agreed to teach them, and asked them to look into a vessel of water and tell him how much of self they could find. They answered: "We see, this our whole self, even to the hair, and to the nails." And he said, "Well, that is the self, that is the deathless and the fearless, that is the Brahman." They went away pleased, but Prajāpati thought, "There they go away, without having discovered, without having realized the self." Virocana came away with the conviction that the body was the self; but Indra did not return back to the gods, he was afraid and pestered with doubts and came back to Prajapāti and said, "just as the self becomes decorated when the body is decorated, well-dressed when the body is well-dressed, well-cleaned when the body is well-cleaned, even so that image self will be blind when the body is blind, injured in one eye when the body is injured in one eye, and mutilated when the body is mutilated, and it perishes

[1] Taitt. II. 7.
[2] Chā. VIII 7-12

when the body perishes, therefore I can see no good in this theory." Prajāpati then gave him a higher instruction about the self, and said, "He who goes about enjoying dreams, he is the self, this is the deathless, the fearless, this is Brahman." Indra departed but was again disturbed with doubts, and was afraid and came back and said "that though the dream self does not become blind when the body is blind, or injured in one eye when the body is so injured and is not affected by its defects, and is not killed by its destruction, but yet it is as if it was overwhelmed, as if it suffered and as if it wept—in this I see no good." Prajāpati gave a still higher instruction: "When a man, fast asleep, in total contentment, does not know any dreams, this is the self, this is the deathless, the fearless, this is Brahman." Indra departed but was again filled with doubts on the way, and returned again and said "the self in deep sleep does not know himself, that I am this, nor does he know any other existing objects. He is destroyed and lost. I see no good in this." And now Prajāpati after having given a course of successively higher instructions as self as the body, as the self in dreams and as the self in deep dreamless sleep, and having found that the enquirer in each case could find out that this was not the ultimate truth about the self that he was seeking, ultimately gave him the ultimate and final instruction about the full truth about the self, and said "this body is the support of the deathless and the bodiless self. The self as embodied is affected by pleasure and pain, the self when associated with the body cannot get rid of pleasure and pain, but pleasure and pain do not touch the bodiless self[1]."

As the anecdote shows, they sought such a constant and unchangeable essence in man as was beyond the limits of any change. This inmost essence has sometimes been described as pure subject-object-less consciousness, the reality, and the bliss. He is the seer of all seeing, the hearer of all hearing and the knower of all knowledge. He sees but is not seen, hears but is not heard, knows but is not known. He is the light of all lights. He is like a lump of salt, with no inner or outer, which consists through and through entirely of savour; as in truth this Ātman has no inner or outer, but consists through and through entirely of knowledge. Bliss is not an attribute of it but it is bliss itself. The state of Brahman is thus likened unto the state of dreamless sleep. And he who has reached this bliss is beyond any fear. It is dearer to us than

[1] Chā. VIII. 7-12.

son, brother, wife, or husband, wealth or prosperity. It is for it and by it that things appear dear to us. It is the dearest *par excellence*, our inmost Ātman. All limitation is fraught with pain; it is the infinite alone that is the highest bliss. When a man receives this rapture, then is he full of bliss; for who could breathe, who live, if that bliss had not filled this void (*ākāśa*)? It is he who behaves as bliss. For when a man finds his peace, his fearless support in that invisible, supportless, inexpressible, unspeakable one, then has he attained peace.

Place of Brahman in the Upaniṣads.

There is the ātman not in man alone but in all objects of the universe, the sun, the moon, the world; and Brahman is this ātman. There is nothing outside the ātman, and therefore there is no plurality at all. As from a lump of clay all that is made of clay is known, as from an ingot of black iron all that is made of black iron is known, so when this ātman the Brahman is known everything else is known. The essence in man and the essence of the universe are one and the same, and it is Brahman.

Now a question may arise as to what may be called the nature of the phenomenal world of colour, sound, taste, and smell. But we must also remember that the Upaniṣads do not represent so much a conceptional system of philosophy as visions of the seers who are possessed by the spirit of this Brahman. They do not notice even the contradiction between the Brahman as unity and nature in its diversity. When the empirical aspect of diversity attracts their notice, they affirm it and yet declare that it is all Brahman. From Brahman it has come forth and to it will it return. He has himself created it out of himself and then entered into it as its inner controller (*antaryāmin*). Here is thus a glaring dualistic trait of the world of matter and Brahman as its controller, though in other places we find it asserted most emphatically that these are but names and forms, and when Brahman is known everything else is known. No attempts at reconciliation are made for the sake of the consistency of conceptual utterance, as Śaṅkara the great professor of Vedānta does by explaining away the dualistic texts. The universe is said to be a reality, but the real in it is Brahman alone. It is on account of Brahman that the fire burns and the wind blows. He is the active principle in the entire universe, and yet the most passive and unmoved. The world is his body, yet he is the soul within. "He creates all, wills all, smells all, tastes all, he has pervaded all, silent and unaffected[1]." He is below, above, in the back, in front, in the south and in the north. he is all this[2]. "These rivers in the east and in the west originating from the ocean, return back into it and become the ocean themselves. though they do not know that they are so. So also all these people coming into being from the Being do not know that they have come from the Being....That which is the subtlest that is the self, that is all this, the truth, that self thou art O Śvetaketu[3]." "Brahman," as Deussen points out, "was regarded as the cause antecedent in time, and the universe as the effect proceeding from it; the inner dependence of the universe on Brahman and its essential identity with him was represented as a creation of the universe by and out of Brahman." Thus it is said in Muṇḍ. I. I. 7:

> As a spider ejects and retracts (the threads),
> As the plants shoot forth on the earth.
> As the hairs on the head and body of the living man.
> So from the imperishable all that is here.
> As the sparks from the well-kindled fire,
> In nature akin to it, spring forth in their thousands.
> So, my dear sir, from the imperishable
> Living beings of many kinds go forth,
> And again return into him[4].

Yet this world principle is the dearest to us and the highest teaching of the Upaniṣads is "That art thou."

Again the growth of the doctrine that Brahman is the "inner controller" in all the parts and forces of nature and of mankind as the ātman thereof, and that all the effects of the universe are the result of his commands which no one can outstep, gave rise to a theistic current of thought in which Brahman is held as standing aloof as God and controlling the world. It is by his ordaining, it is said, that the sun and moon are held together, and the sky and earth stand held together[5]. God and soul are distinguished again in the famous verse of Śvetāśvatara[6]:

> Two bright-feathered bosom friends
> Flit around one and the same tree;
> One of them tastes the sweet berries,
> The other without eating merely gazes down.

[1] Chā. III. 14. 4.

[2] *Ibid.* VII. 25. I; also Muṇḍaka II. 2. 11.

[3] Chā. VI. 10.

[4] Deussen's translation in *Philosophy of the Upanishads*, p. 164.

[5] Bṛh. III. 8. 1.

[6] Śvetāśvatara IV. 6, and Muṇḍaka III. 1. 1, also Deussen's translation in *Philosophy of the Upanishads*, p. 177.

But in spite of this apparent theistic tendency and the occasional use of the word *Īśā* or *Īśāna*, there seems to be no doubt that theism in its true sense was never prominent, and this acknowledgement of a supreme Lord was also an offshoot of the exalted position of the ātman as the supreme principle. Thus we read in Kauṣītaki Upaniṣad 3. 9, "He is not great by good deeds nor low by evil deeds, but it is he makes one do good deeds whom he wants to raise, and makes him commit bad deeds whom he wants to lower down. He is the protector of the universe, he is the master of the world and the lord of all; he is my soul (*ātman*)." Thus the lord in spite of his greatness is still my soul. There are again other passages which regard Brahman as being at once immanent and transcendent. Thus it is said that there is that eternally existing tree whose roots grow upward and whose branches grow downward. All the universes are supported in it and no one can transcend it. This is that, "...from its fear the fire burns, the sun shines, and from its fear Indra, Vāyu and Death the fifth (with the other two) run on[1]."

If we overlook the different shades in the development of the conception of Brahman in the Upaniṣads and look to the main currents, we find that the strongest current of thought which has found expression in the majority of the texts is this that the Ātman or the Brahman is the only reality and that besides this everything else is unreal. The other current of thought which is to be found in many of the texts is the pantheistic creed that identifies the universe with the Ātman or Brahman. The third current is that of theism which looks upon Brahman as the Lord controlling the world. It is because these ideas were still in the melting pot, in which none of them were systematically worked out, that the later exponents of Vedānta, Śaṅkara, Rāmānuja, and others quarrelled over the meanings of texts in order to develop a consistent systematic philosophy out of them. Thus it is that the doctrine of Māyā which is slightly hinted at once in Bṛhadāraṇyaka and thrice in Śvetāśvatara, becomes the foundation of Śaṅkara's philosophy of the Vedānta in which Brahman alone is real and all else beside him is unreal[2].

[1] Kaṭha II. 6. 1 and 3.
[2] Bṛh. II. 5. 19, Śvet. I. 10, IV. 9, 10.

The World.

We have already seen that the universe has come out of Brahman, has its essence in Brahman, and will also return back to it. But in spite of its existence as Brahman its character as represented to experience could not be denied. Śaṅkara held that the Upaniṣads referred to the external world and accorded a reality to it consciously with the purpose of treating it as merely relatively real, which will eventually appear as unreal as soon as the ultimate truth, the Brahman, is known. This however remains to be modified to this extent that the sages had not probably any conscious purpose of according a relative reality to the phenomenal world, but in spite of regarding Brahman as the highest reality they could not ignore the claims of the exterior world, and had to accord a reality to it. The inconsistency of this reality of the phenomenal world with the ultimate and only reality of Brahman was attempted to be reconciled by holding that this world is not beside him but it has come out of him, it is maintained in him and it will return back to him.

The world is sometimes spoken of in its twofold aspect, the organic and the inorganic. All organic things, whether plants, animals or men, have souls[1]. Brahman desiring to be many created fire (*tejas*), water (*ap*) and earth (*kṣiti*). Then the self-existent Brahman entered into these three, and it is by their combination that all other bodies are formed[2]. So all other things are produced as a result of an alloying or compounding of the parts of these three together. In this theory of the threefold division of the primitive elements lies the earliest germ of the later distinction (especially in the Sāṃkhya school) of pure infinitesimal substances (*tanmātra*) and gross elements, and the theory that each gross substance is composed of the atoms of the primary elements. And in Praśna IV. 8 we find the gross elements distinguished from their subtler natures, e.g. earth (*pṛthivī*), and the subtler state of earth (*pṛthivīmātra*). In the Taittirīya, II. I, however, ether (*ākāśa*) is also described as proceeding from Brahman, and the other elements, air, fire, water, and earth, are described as each proceeding directly from the one which directly preceded it.

[1] Chā. VI. 11.

[2] *Ibid.* VI. 2, 3, 4.

The World-Soul.

The conception of a world-soul related to the universe as the soul of man to his body is found for the first time in R.V. X. I 21. I, where he is said to have sprung forth as the firstborn of creation from the primeval waters. This being has twice been referred to in the Śvetāśvatara, in III. 4 and IV. I2. It is indeed very strange that this being is not referred to in any of the earlier Upaniṣads. In the two passages in which he has been spoken of, his mythical character is apparent. He is regarded as one of the earlier products in the process of cosmic creation, but his importance from the point of view of the development of the theory of Brahman or Ātman is almost nothing. The fact that neither the Puruṣa, nor the Viśvakarma, nor the Hiraṇyagarbha played an important part in the earlier development of the Upaniṣads leads me to think that the Upaniṣad doctrines were not directly developed from the monotheistic tendencies of the later Ṛg-Veda speculations. The passages in Śvetāśvatara clearly show how from the supreme eminence that he had in R.V. X. 121, Hiraṇyagarbha had been brought to the level of one of the created beings. Deussen in explaining the philosophical significance of the Hiraṇyagarbha doctrine of the Upaniṣads says that the "entire objective universe is possible only in so far as it is sustained by a knowing subject. This subject as a sustainer of the objective universe is manifested in all individual objects but is by no means identical with them. For the individual objects pass away but the objective universe continues to exist without them; there exists therefore the eternal knowing subject also (*hiraṇyagarbha*) by whom it is sustained. Space and time are derived from this subject. It is itself accordingly not in space and does not belong to time, and therefore from an empirical point of view it is in general non-existent; it has no empirical but only a metaphysical reality[1]." This however seems to me to be wholly irrelevant, since the Hiraṇyagarbha doctrine cannot be supposed to have any philosophical importance in the Upaniṣads.

The Theory of Causation.

There was practically no systematic theory of causation in the Upaniṣads. Śaṅkara, the later exponent of Vedānta philosophy, always tried to show that the Upaniṣads looked upon the cause

[1] Deussen's *Philosophy of the Upanishads*, p. 201.

as mere ground of change which though unchanged in itself in reality had only an appearance of suffering change. This he did on the strength of a series of examples in the Chāndogya Upaniṣad (VI. 1) in which the material cause, e.g. the clay, is spoken of as the only reality in all its transformations as the pot, the jug or the plate. It is said that though there are so many diversities of appearance that one is called the plate, the other the pot, and the other the jug, yet these are only empty distinctions of name and form, for the only thing real in them is the earth which in its essence remains ever the same whether you call it the pot, plate, or jug. So it is that the ultimate cause, the unchangeable Brahman, remains ever constant, though it may appear to suffer change as the manifold world outside. This world is thus only an unsubstantial appearance, a mirage imposed upon Brahman, the real *par excellence*.

It seems however that though such a view may be regarded as having been expounded in the Upaniṣads in an imperfect manner, there is also side by side the other view which looks upon the effect as the product of a real change wrought in the cause itself through the action and combination of the elements of diversity in it. Thus when the different objects of nature have been spoken of in one place as the product of the combination of the three elements fire, water and earth, the effect signifies a real change produced by their compounding. This is in germ (as we shall see hereafter) the Pariṇāma theory of causation advocated by the Sāṃkhya school[1].

Doctrine of Transmigration.

When the Vedic people witnessed the burning of a dead body they supposed that the eye of the man went to the sun, his breath to the wind, his speech to the fire, his limbs to the different parts of the universe. They also believed as we have already seen in the recompense of good and bad actions in worlds other than our own, and though we hear of such things as the passage of the human soul into trees, etc., the tendency towards transmigration had but little developed at the time.

In the Upaniṣads however we find a clear development in the direction of transmigration in two distinct stages. In the one the Vedic idea of a recompense in the other world is combined with

[1] Chā. VI 2-4.

the doctrine of transmigration, whereas in the other the doctrine of transmigration comes to the forefront in supersession of the idea of a recompense in the other world. Thus it is said that those who performed charitable deeds or such public works as the digging of wells, etc., follow after death the way of the fathers (*pitṛyāna*), in which the soul after death enters first into smoke, then into night, the dark half of the month, etc., and at last reaches the moon; after a residence there as long as the remnant of his good deeds remains he descends again through ether, wind, smoke, mist, cloud, rain, herbage, food and seed, and through the assimilation of food by man he enters the womb of the mother and is born again. Here we see that the soul had not only a recompense in the world of the moon, but was re-born again in this world[1].

The other way is the way of gods (*devayāna*), meant for those who cultivate faith and asceticism (*tapas*). These souls at death enter successively into flame, day, bright half of the month, bright half of the year, sun, moon, lightning, and then finally into Brahman never to return. Deussen says that "the meaning of the whole is that the soul on the way of the gods reaches regions of ever-increasing light, in which is concentrated all that is bright and radiant as stations on the way to Brahman the 'light of lights' " (*jyotiṣām jyotiḥ*)[2].

The other line of thought is a direct reference to the doctrine of transmigration unmixed with the idea of reaping the fruits of his deeds (*karma*) by passing through the other worlds and without reference to the doctrine of the ways of the fathers and gods, the *Yānas*. Thus Yājñavalkya says, "when the soul becomes weak (apparent weakness owing to the weakness of the body with which it is associated) and falls into a swoon as it were, these senses go towards it. It (Soul) takes these light particles within itself and centres itself only in the heart. Thus when the person in the eye turns back, then the soul cannot know colour; (the senses) become one (with him); (people about him) say he does not see; (the senses) become one (with him), he does not smell, (the senses) become one (with him), he does not taste, (the senses) become one (with him), he does not speak, (the senses) become one (with him), he does not hear, (the senses) become one (with him), he does not think, (the senses) become one with him, he does not touch, (the senses) become one with him, he does not know, they say. The

[1] Chā. V. 10.

[2] Deussen's *Philosophy of the Upanishads*, p. 335.

tip of his heart shines and by that shining this soul goes out. When he goes out either through the eye, the head, or by any other part of the body, the vital function (*prāṇa*) follows and all the senses follow the vital function (*prāṇa*) in coming out. He is then with determinate consciousness and as such he comes out. Knowledge, the deeds as well as previous experience (*prajñā*) accompany him. Just as a caterpillar going to the end of a blade of grass, by undertaking a separate movement collects itself, so this self after destroying this body, removing ignorance, by a separate movement collects itself. Just as a goldsmith taking a small bit of gold, gives to it a newer and fairer form, so the soul after destroying this body and removing ignorance fashions a newer and fairer form as of the Pitṛs, the Gandharvas, the gods, of Prajāpati or Brahma or of any other being....As he acts and behaves so he becomes, good by good deeds, bad by bad deeds, virtuous by virtuous deeds and vicious by vice. The man is full of desires. As he desires so he wills, as he wills so he works, as the work is done so it happens. There is also a verse, being attached to that he wants to gain by karma that to which he was attached. Having reaped the full fruit (lit. gone to the end) of the karma that he does here, he returns back to this world for doing karma[1]. So it is the case with those who have desires. He who has no desires, who had no desires, who has freed himself from all desires, is satisfied in his desires and in himself, his senses do not go out. He being Brahma attains Brahmahood. Thus the verse says, when all the desires that are in his heart are got rid of, the mortal becomes immortal and attains Brahma here" (Bṛh. IV. iv. 1-7).

A close consideration of the above passage shows that the self itself destroyed the body and built up a newer and fairer frame by its own activity when it reached the end of the present life. At the time of death, the self collected within itself all senses and faculties and after death all its previous knowledge, work and experience accompanied him. The falling off of the body at the time of death is only for the building of a newer body either in this world or in the other worlds. The self which thus takes rebirth is regarded as an aggregation of diverse categories. Thus it is said that "he is of the essence of understanding,

[1] It is possible that there is a vague and obscure reference here to the doctrine that the fruits of our deeds are reaped in other worlds.

of the vital function, of the visual sense, of the auditory sense, of the essence of the five elements (which would make up the physical body in accordance with its needs) or the essence of desires, of the essence of restraint of desires, of the essence of anger, of the essence of turning off from all anger, of the essence of dharma, of the essence of adharma, of the essence of all that is this (manifest) and that is that (unmanifest or latent)" (Bṛh. IV. iv. 5). The self that undergoes rebirth is thus a unity not only of moral and psychological tendencies, but also of all the elements which compose the physical world. The whole process of his changes follows from this nature of his; for whatever he desires, he wills and whatever he wills he acts, and in accordance with his acts the fruit happens. The whole logic of the genesis of karma and its fruits is held up within him, for he is a unity of the moral and psychological tendencies on the one hand and elements of the physical world on the other.

The self that undergoes rebirth being a combination of diverse psychological and moral tendencies and the physical elements holds within itself the principle of all its transformations. The root of all this is the desire of the self and the consequent fruition of it through will and act. When the self continues to desire and act, it reaps the fruit and comes again to this world for performing acts. This world is generally regarded as the field for performing karma, whereas other worlds are regarded as places where the fruits of karma are reaped by those born as celestial beings. But there is no emphasis in the Upaniṣads on this point. The Pitṛyāna theory is not indeed given up, but it seems only to form a part in the larger scheme of rebirth in other worlds and sometimes in this world too. All the course of these rebirths is effected by the self itself by its own desires, and if it ceases to desire, it suffers no rebirth and becomes immortal. The most distinctive feature of this doctrine is this, that it refers to desires as the cause of rebirth and not karma. Karma only comes as the connecting link between desires and rebirth—for it is said that whatever a man desires he wills, and whatever he wills he acts.

Thus it is said in another place "he who knowingly desires is born by his desires in those places (accordingly), but for him whose desires have been fulfilled and who has realized himself, all his desires vanish here" (Muṇḍ III. 2. 2). This destruction of desires is effected by the right knowledge of the self. "He who knows his self as 'I am the person' for what wish and for what desire will he trouble the body,...even being here if we know it, well if we do not, what a great destruction" (Bṛh. IV. iv. 12 and 14). "In former times the wise men did not desire sons, thinking what shall we do with sons since this our self is the universe" (Bṛh. IV. iv. 22). None of the complexities of the karma doctrine which we find later on in more recent developments of Hindu thought can be found in the Upaniṣads. The whole scheme is worked out on the principle of desire (*kāma*) and karma only serves as the link between it and the actual effects desired and willed by the person.

It is interesting to note in this connection that consistently with the idea that desires (*kāma*) led to rebirth, we find that in some Upaniṣads the discharge of the semen in the womb of a woman as a result of desires is considered as the first birth of man, and the birth of the son as the second birth and the birth elsewhere after death is regarded as the third birth. Thus it is said, "It is in man that there comes first the embryo, which is but the semen which is produced as the essence of all parts of his body and which holds itself within itself, and when it is put in a woman, that is his first birth. That embryo then becomes part of the woman's self like any part of her body; it therefore does not hurt her; she protects and develops the embryo within herself. As she protects (the embryo) so she also should be protected. It is the woman who bears the embryo (before birth) but when after birth the father takes care of the son always, he is taking care only of himself, for it is through sons alone that the continuity of the existence of people can be maintained. This is his second birth. He makes this self of his a representative for performing all the virtuous deeds. The other self of his after realizing himself and attaining age goes away and when going away he is born again that is his third birth" (Aitareya, II. 1-4)[1]. No special emphasis is given in the Upaniṣads to the sex-desire or the desire for a son; for, being called kāma, whatever was the desire for a son was the same as the desire for money and the desire for money was the same as any other worldly desire (Bṛh. IV. iv. 22), and hence sex-desires stand on the same plane as any other desire.

[1] See also Kauṣītaki, 11. 15.

Emancipation.

The doctrine which next attracts our attention in this connection is that of emancipation (*mukti*). Already we know that the doctrine of Devayāna held that those who were faithful and performed asceticism (*tapas*) went by the way of the gods through successive stages never to return to the world and suffer rebirth. This could be contrasted with the way of the fathers (*pitṛyāna*) where the dead were for a time recompensed in another world and then had to suffer rebirth. Thus we find that those who are faithful and perform *śraddhā* had a distinctly different type of goal from those who performed ordinary virtues, such as those of a general altruistic nature. This distinction attains its fullest development in the doctrine of emancipation. Emancipation or Mukti means in the Upaniṣads the state of infiniteness that a man attains when he knows his own self and thus becomes Brahman. The ceaseless course of transmigration is only for those who are ignorant. The wise man however who has divested himself of all passions and knows himself to be Brahman, at once becomes Brahman and no bondage of any kind can ever affect him.

> He who beholds that loftiest and deepest,
> For him the fetters of the heart break asunder,
> For him all doubts are solved,
> And his works become nothingness[1].

The knowledge of the self reveals the fact that all our passions and antipathies, all our limitations of experience, all that is ignoble and small in us, all that is transient and finite in us is false. We "do not know" but are "pure knowledge" ourselves. We are not limited by anything, for we are the infinite; we do not suffer death, for we are immortal. Emancipation thus is not a new acquisition, product, an effect, or result of any action, but it always exists as the Truth of our nature. We are always emancipated and always free. We do not seem to be so and seem to suffer rebirth and thousands of other troubles only because we do not know the true nature of our self. Thus it is that the true knowledge of self does not lead to emancipation but is emancipation itself. All sufferings and limitations are true only so long as we do not know our self. Emancipation is the natural and only goal of man simply because it represents the true nature and essence of man. It is the realization of our own nature that

[1] Deussen's *Philosophy of the Upanishads*, p. 352.

is called emancipation. Since we are all already and always in our own true nature and as such emancipated, the only thing necessary for us is to know that we are so. Self-knowledge is therefore the only desideratum which can wipe off all false knowledge, all illusions of death and rebirth. The story is told in the Kaṭha Upaniṣad that Yama, the lord of death, promised Naciketas, the son of Gautama, to grant him three boons at his choice. Naciketas, knowing that his father Gautama was offended with him, said, "O death let Gautama be pleased in mind and forget his anger against me." This being granted Naciketas asked the second boon that the fire by which heaven is gained should be made known to him. This also being granted Naciketas said, "There is this enquiry, some say the soul exists after the death of man; others say it does not exist. This I should like to know instructed by thee. This is my third boon." Yama said, "It was inquired of old, even by the gods; for it is not easy to understand it. Subtle is its nature, choose another boon. Do not compel me to this." Naciketas said, "Even by the gods was it inquired before, and even thou O Death sayest that it is not easy to understand it, but there is no other speaker to be found like thee. There is no other boon like this." Yama said, "Choose sons and grandsons who may live a hundred years, choose herds of cattle; choose elephants and gold and horses; choose the wide expanded earth, and live thyself as many years as thou wishest. Or if thou knowest a boon like this choose it together with wealth and far-extending life. Be a king on the wide earth. I will make thee the enjoyer of all desires. All those desires that are difficult to gain in the world of mortals, all those ask thou at thy pleasure; those fair nymphs with their chariots, with their musical instruments; the like of them are not to be gained by men. I will give them to thee, but do not ask the question regarding death." Naciketas replied, "All those enjoyments are of tomorrow and they only weaken the senses. All life is short, with thee the dance and song. Man cannot be satisfied with wealth, we could obtain wealth, as long as we did not reach you we live only as long as thou pleasest. The boon which I choose I have said." Yama said, "One thing is good, another is pleasant. Blessed is he who takes the good, but he who chooses the pleasant loses the object of man. But thou considering the objects of desire, hast abandoned them. These two, ignorance (whose object is what is pleasant) and knowledge (whose object is what is good), are known to be far asunder, and to lead to different goals. Believing that this world exists and not the other, the careless youth is subject to my sway. That knowledge which thou hast asked is not to be obtained by argument. I know worldly happiness is transient for that firm one is not to be obtained by what is not firm. The wise by concentrating on the soul, knowing him whom it is hard to behold, leaves both grief and joy. Thee O Naciketas, I believe to be like a house whose door is open to Brahman. Brahman is deathless, whoever knows him obtains whatever he wishes. The wise man is not born; he does not die; he is not produced from anywhere. Unborn, eternal, the soul is not slain, though the body is slain; subtler than what is subtle, greater than what is great, sitting it goes far, lying it goes everywhere. Thinking the soul as unbodily among bodies, firm among fleeting things, the wise man casts off all grief. The soul cannot be gained by eloquence, by understanding, or by learning. It can be obtained by him alone whom it chooses. To him it reveals its own nature[1]." So long as the Self identifies itself with its desires, he wills and acts according to them and reaps the fruits in the present and in future lives. But when he comes to know the highest truth about himself, that he is the highest essence and principle of the universe, the immortal and the infinite, he ceases to have desires, and receding from all desires realizes the ultimate truth of himself in his own infinitude. Man is as it were the epitome of the universe and he holds within himself the fine constituents of the gross body (*annamaya koṣa*), the vital functions (*prāṇa-maya koṣa*) of life, the will and desire (*manomaya*) and the thoughts and ideas (*vijñānamaya*), and so long as he keeps himself in these spheres and passes through a series of experiences in the present life and in other lives to come, these experiences are willed by him and in that sense created by him. He suffers pleasures and pains, disease and death. But if he retires from these into his true unchangeable being, he is in a state where he is one with his experience and there is no change and no movement. What this state is cannot be explained by the use of concepts. One could only indicate it by pointing out that it is not any of those concepts found in ordinary knowledge; it is not

[1] Kaṭha II. The translation is not continuous. There are some parts in the extract which may be differently interpreted.

whatever one knows as this and this (*neti neti*). In this infinite and true self there is no difference, no diversity, no *meum* and *tuum*. It is like an ocean in which all our phenomenal existence will dissolve like salt in water. "Just as a lump of salt when put in water will disappear in it and it cannot be taken out separately but in whatever portion of water we taste we find the salt, so, Maitreyī, does this great reality infinite and limitless consisting only of pure intelligence manifesting itself in all these (phenomenal existences) vanish in them and there is then no phenomenal knowledge" (Bṛh. II. 4. 12). The true self manifests itself in all the processes of our phenomenal existences, but ultimately when it retires back to itself, it can no longer be found in them. It is a state of absolute infinitude of pure intelligence, pure being, and pure blessedness.

IV

GENERAL OBSERVATIONS ON THE SYSTEMS OF INDIAN PHILOSOPHY

In what sense is a History of Indian Philosophy possible?

IT is hardly possible to attempt a history of Indian philosophy in the manner in which the histories of European philosophy have been written. In Europe from the earliest times, thinkers came one after another and offered their independent speculations on philosophy. The work of a modern historian consists in chronologically arranging these views and in commenting upon the influence of one school upon another or upon the general change from time to time in the tides and currents of philosophy. Here in India, however, the principal systems of philosophy had their beginning in times of which we have but scanty record, and it is hardly possible to say correctly at what time they began, or to compute the influence that led to the foundation of so many divergent systems at so early a period, for in all probability these were formulated just after the earliest Upaniṣads had been composed or arranged.

The systematic treatises were written in short and pregnant half-sentences (*sūtras*) which did not elaborate the subject in detail, but served only to hold before the reader the lost threads of memory of elaborate disquisitions with which he was already thoroughly acquainted. It seems, therefore, that these pithy half-sentences were like lecture hints, intended for those who had had direct elaborate oral instructions on the subject. It is indeed difficult to guess from the sūtras the extent of their significance, or how far the discussions which they gave rise to in later days were originally intended by them. The sūtras of the Vedānta system, known as the Śārīraka-sūtras or Brahma-sūtras of Bādarāyaṇa for example were of so ambiguous a nature that they gave rise to more than half a dozen divergent interpretations, each one of which claimed to be the only faithful one. Such was the high esteem and respect in which these writers of the sūtras were held by later writers that whenever they had any new speculations to offer, these were reconciled with the doctrines of one or other of the existing systems, and put down as faithful interpretations of the system in the form of commentaries. Such was the hold of these systems upon scholars that all the orthodox teachers since the foundation of the systems of philosophy belonged to one or other of these schools. Their pupils were thus naturally brought up in accordance with the views of their teachers. All the independence of their thinking was limited and enchained by the faith of the school to which they were attached. Instead of producing a succession of freelance thinkers having their own systems to propound and establish, India had brought forth schools of pupils who carried the traditionary views of particular systems from generation to generation, who explained and expounded them, and defended them against the attacks of other rival schools which they constantly attacked in order to establish the superiority of the system to which they adhered. To take an example, the Nyāya system of philosophy consisting of a number of half-sentences or sūtras is attributed to Gautama, also called Akṣapāda. The earliest commentary on these sūtras, called the *Vātsyāyana bhāṣya*, was written by Vātsyāyana. This work was sharply criticized by the Buddhist Diṅnāga, and to answer these criticisms Udyotakara wrote a commentary on this commentary called the *Bhāṣyavāttika*[1]. As time went on the original force of this work was lost, and it failed to maintain the old dignity of the school. At this Vācaspati Miśra wrote a commentary called *Vārttika-tātparyaṭīkā* on this second commentary, where he tried to refute all objections against the Nyāya system made by other rival schools and particularly by the Buddhists. This commentary, called *Nyāya-tātparyaṭīkā*, had another commentary called *Nyāya-tātparyaṭīkā-pariśuddhi* written by the great Udayana. This commentary had another commentary called *Nyāya-nibandha-prakāśa* written by Varddhamāna the son of the illustrious Gaṅgeśa. This again had another commentary called *Varddha-mānendu* upon it by Padmanābha Miśra, and this again had another named *Nyāya-tātparyamaṇḍana* by Śaṅkara Miśra. The names of *Vātsyāyana*, Vācaspati, and Udayana are indeed very great, but even they contented themselves by writing commentaries on commentaries, and did not try to formulate any

[1] I have preferred to spell Diṅnāga after Vācaspati's *Tātparyatīka* (p. I) and not Dignāga as it is generally spelt.

original system. Even Śaṅkara, probably the greatest man of India after Buddha, spent his life in writing commentaries on the *Brahma-sūtras*, the Upaniṣads, and the *Bhagavad-gītā*.

As a system passed on it had to meet unexpected opponents and troublesome criticisms for which it was not in the least prepared. Its adherents had therefore to use all their ingenuity and subtlety in support of their own positions, and to discover the defects of the rival schools that attacked them. A system as it was originally formulated in the sūtras had probably but few problems to solve, but as it fought its way in the teeth of opposition of other schools, it had to offer consistent opinions on other problems in which the original views were more or less involved but to which no attention had been given before.

The contributions of the successive commentators served to make each system more and more complete in all its parts, and stronger and stronger to enable it to hold its own successfully against the opposition and attacks of the rival schools. A system in the sūtras is weak and shapeless as a newborn babe, but if we take it along with its developments down to the beginning of the seventeenth century it appears as a fully developed man strong and harmonious in all its limbs. It is therefore not possible to write any history of successive philosophies of India, but it is necessary that each system should be studied and interpreted in all the growth it has acquired through the successive ages of history from its conflicts with the rival systems as one whole[1]. In the history of Indian philosophy we have no place for systems which had their importance only so long as they lived and were then forgotten or remembered only as targets of criticism. Each system grew and developed by the untiring energy of its adherents through all the successive ages of history, and a history of this growth is a history of its conflicts. No study of any Indian system is therefore adequate unless it is taken throughout all the growth it attained by the work of its champions, the commentators whose selfless toil for it had kept it living through the ages of history.

[1] In the case of some systems it is indeed possible to suggest one or two earlier phases of the system, but this principle cannot be carried all through, for the supplementary information and arguments given by the later commentators often appear as harmonious elaborations of the earlier writings and are very seldom in conflict with them.

Growth of the Philosophic Literature.

It is difficult to say how the systems were originally formulated, and what were the influences that led to it. We know that a spirit of philosophic enquiry had already begun in the days of the earliest Upaniṣads. The spirit of that enquiry was that the final essence or truth was the ātman, that a search after it was our highest duty, and that until we are ultimately merged in it we can only feel this truth and remain uncontented with everything else and say that it is not the truth we want, it is not the truth we want (*neti neti*). Philosophical enquires were however continuing in circles other than those of the Upaniṣads. Thus the Buddha who closely followed the early Upaniṣad period, spoke of and enumerated sixty-two kinds of heresies[1], and these can hardly be traced in the Upaniṣads. The Jaina activities were also probably going on contemporaneously but in the Upaniṣads no reference to these can be found. We may thus reasonably suppose that there were different forms of philosophic enquiry in spheres other than those of the Upaniṣad sages, of which we have but scanty records. It seems probable that the Hindu systems of thought originated among the sages who though attached chiefly to the Upaniṣad circles used to take note of the discussions and views of the antagonistic and heretical philosophic circles. In the assemblies of these sages and their pupils, the views of the heretical circles were probably discussed and refuted. So it continued probably for some time when some illustrious member of the assembly such as Gautama or Kaṇāda collected the purport of these discussions on various topics and problems, filled up many of the missing links, classified and arranged these in the form of a system of philosophy and recorded it in sūtras. These sūtras were intended probably for people who had attended the elaborate oral discussions and thus could easily follow the meaning of the suggestive phrases contained in the aphorisms. The sūtras thus contain sometimes allusions to the views of the rival schools and indicate the way in which they could be refuted. The commentators were possessed of the general drift of the different discussions alluded to and conveyed from generation to generation through an unbroken chain of succession of teachers and pupils. Thcy wcrc however free to supplement these traditionary explanations with their own

[1] *Brahmajāla-sutla*, *Dīgha*, I. p. 12 tr.

views or to modify and even suppress such of the traditionary views with which they did not agree or which they found it difficult to maintain. Brilliant oppositions from the opposing schools often made it necessary for them to offer solutions to new problems unthought of before, but put forward by some illustrious adherent of a rival school. In order to reconcile these new solutions with the other parts of the system, the commentators never hesitated to offer such slight modifications of the doctrines as could harmonize them into a complete whole. These elaborations or modifications generally developed the traditionary system, but did not effect any serious change in the system as expounded by the older teachers, for the new exponents always bound themselves to the explanations of the older teachers and never contradicted them. They would only interpret them to suit their own ideas, or say new things only in those cases where the older teachers had remained silent. It is not therefore possible to describe the growth of any system by treating the contributions of the individual commentators separately. This would only mean unnecessary repetition. Except when there is a specially new development, the system is to be interpreted on the basis of the joint work of the commentators treating their contributions as forming one whole.

The fact that each system had to contend with other rival systems in order to hold its own has left its permanent mark upon all the philosophic literatures of India which are always written in the form of disputes, where the writer is supposed to be always faced with objections from rival schools to whatever he has got to say. At each step he supposes certain objections put forth against him which he answers, and points out the defects of the objector or shows that the objection itself is ill founded. It is thus through interminable byways of objections, counter-objections and their answers that the writer can wend his way to his destination. Most often the objections of the rival schools are referred to in so brief a manner that those only who know the views can catch them. To add to these difficulties the Sanskrit style of most of the commentaries is so condensed and different from literary Sanskrit, and aims so much at precision and brevity, leading to the use of technical words current in the diverse systems, that a study of these becomes often impossible without the aid of an expert preceptor; it is difficult therefore for all who are not widely read in all the different systems to follow any advanced work of any particular system, as the deliberations of that particular system are expressed in such close interconnection with the views of other systems that these can hardly be understood without them. Each system of India has grown (at least in particular epochs) in relation to and in opposition to the growth of other systems of thought, and to be a thorough student of Indian philosophy one should study all the systems in their mutual opposition and relation from the earliest times to a period at which they ceased to grow and came to a stop—a purpose for which a work like the present one may only be regarded as forming a preliminary introduction.

Besides the sūtras and their commentaries there are also independent treatises on the systems in verse called *kārikās*, which try to summarize the important topics of any system in a succinct manner; the *Sāṃkhya kārikā* may be mentioned as a work of this kind. In addition to these there were also long dissertations, commentaries, or general observations on any system written in verses called the vārttikas; the *Ślokavārttika*, of Kumārila or the *Vārttika* of Sureśvara may be mentioned as examples. All these of course had their commentaries to explain them. In addition to these there were also advanced treatises on the systems in prose in which the writers either nominally followed some selected sūtras or proceeded independently of them. Of the former class the *Nyāyamañjarī* of Jayanta may be mentioned as an example and of the latter the *Praśastapāda bhāṣya*, the *Advaitasiddhi* of Madhusūdana Sarasvatī or the *Vedānta-paribhāṣā* of Dharmarājādhvarīndra. The more remarkable of these treatises were of a masterly nature in which the writers represented the systems they adhered to in a highly forcible and logical manner by dint of their own great mental powers and genius. These also had their commentaries to explain and elaborate them. The period of the growth of the philosophic literatures of India begins from about B.C. 500 (about the time of the Buddha) and practically ends in the later half of the seventeenth century, though even now some minor publications are seen to come out.

The Indian Systems of Philosophy.

The Hindus classify the systems of philosophy into two classes, namely, the *nāstika* and the *āstika*. The nāstika (*na asti* "it is not") views are those which neither regard the Vedas as infallible nor try to establish their own validity on their authority. These are principally three in number, the Buddhist, Jaina and the Cārvāka. The āstika-mata or orthodox schools are six in number, Sāṃkhya, Yoga, Vedānta, Mīmāṃsā, Nyāya and Vaiśeṣika, generally known as the six systems (*ṣaḍdarśana*[1]).

The Sāṃkhya is ascribed to a mythical Kapila, but the earliest works on the subject are probably now lost. The Yoga system is attributed to Patañjali and the original sūtras are called the *Pātañjala Yoga sūtras*. The general metaphysical position of these two systems with regard to soul, nature, cosmology and the final goal is almost the same, and the difference lies in this that the Yoga system acknowledges a god *(Īśvara)* as distinct from Ātman and lays much importance on certain mystical practices (commonly known as Yoga practices) for the achievement of liberation, whereas the Sāṃkhya denies the existence of Īśvara and thinks that sincere philosophic thought and culture are sufficient to produce the true conviction of the truth and thereby bring about liberation. It is probable that the system of Sāṃkhya associated with Kapila and the Yoga system associated with Patañjali are but two divergent modifications of an original Sāṃkhya school, of which we now get only references here and there. These systems therefore though generally counted as two should more properly be looked upon as two different schools of the same Sāṃkhya system—one may be called the Kāpila Sāṃkhya and the other Pātañjala Sāṃkhya.

The Pūrva Mīmāṃsā (from the root *man* to think—rational conclusions) cannot properly be spoken of as a system of philosophy. It is a systematized code of principles in accordance with which the Vedic texts are to be interpreted for purposes of sacrifices.

[1] The word "*darśana*" in the sense of *true* philosophic knowledge has its earliest use in the *Vaiśeṣika sūtras* of Kaṇāda (IX. ii. 13) which I consider as pre-Buddhistic. The Buddhist piṭakas (B.C. 400) called the heretical opinions "*diṭṭhi*" (Sanskrit—*dṛṣṭi* from the same root *dṛś* from which darśana is formed). Haribhadra (fifth century A.D.) uses the word Darśana in the sense of systems of philosophy (*sarvadarśanavācyo ' rthaḥ—Saḍdarśanasamuccaya* 1.). Ratnakīrtti (end of the tenth century A.D.) uses the word also in the same sense ("*Yadi nāma darśane darśane nānāprakāram sattvalak-ṣaṇam uktamasti*." *Kṣaṇabhaṅgasiddhi* in *Six Buddhist Nyāya tracts*, p. 20). Mādhava (A. D. 1331) calls his Compendium of all systems of philosophy, *Sarvadarśanasaṃgraha*. The word "*mata*" (opinion or view) was also freely used in quoting the views of other systems. But there is no word to denote 'philosophers' in the technical sense. The Buddhists used to call those who held heretical views "*tairthika*." The words "siddha," "*jñānin*," etc. do not denote philosophers in the modern sense, they are used rather in the sense of "seers" or "perfects."

The Vedic texts were used as mantras (incantations) for sacrifices, and people often disputed as to the relation of words in a sentence or their mutual relative importance with reference to the general drift of the sentence. There were also differences of view with regard to the meaning of a sentence, the use to which it may be applied as a mantra, its relative importance or the exact nature of its connection with other similar sentences in a complex Vedic context. The Mīmāṃsā formulated some principles according to which one could arrive at rational and uniform solutions for all these difficulties. Preliminary to these its main objects, it indulges in speculations with regard to the external world, soul, perception, inference, the validity of the Vedas, or the like, for in order that a man might perform sacrifices with mantras, a definite order of the universe and its relation to man or the position and nature of the mantras of the Veda must be demonstrated and established. Though its interest in such abstract speculations is but secondary yet it briefly discusses these in order to prepare a rational ground for its doctrine of the mantras and their practical utility for man. It is only so far as there are these preliminary discussions in the Mīmāṃsā that it may be called a system of philosophy. Its principles and maxims for the interpretation of the import of words and sentences have a legal value even to this day. The sūtras of Mīmāṃsā are attributed to Jaimini, and Śabara wrote a bhāṣya upon it. The two great names in the history of Mīmāṃsā literature after Jaimini and Śabara are Kumārila Bhaṭṭa and his pupil Prabhākara, who criticized the opinions of his master so much, that the master used to call him guru (master) in sarcasm, and to this day his opinions pass as *guru-mata*, whereas the views of Kumārila Bhaṭṭa pass as *bhaṭṭa-mata*[1]. It may not be out of place to mention here that Hindu Law (*smṛti*) accepts without any reservation the maxims and principles settled and formulated by the Mīmāṃsā.

[1] There is a story that Kumārila could not understand the meaning of a Sanskrit sentence "*Atra tunoktam tatrāpinoktam* iti paunaruktam" (hence spoken twice). *Tunoktam* phonetically admits of two combinations, *tu noktam* (but not said) and *tunā uktam* (said by the particle *tu*) and *tatrāpi noktam* as *tatra api na uktam* (not said also there) and *tatra apinā uktam* (said there by the particle *api*). Under the first interpretation the sentence would mean, "Not spoken here, not spoken there, it is thus spoken twice." This puzzled Kumārila, when Prabhākara taking the second meaning pointed out to him that the meaning was "here it is indicated by *tu* and there by *api*, and so it is indicated twice." Kumārila was so pleased that he called his pupil "Guru" (master) at this.

The *Vedānta sūtras*, also called Uttara Mīmāṃsā, written by Bādarāyaṇa, otherwise known as the *Brahma-sūtras*, form the original authoritative work of Vedānta. The word Vedānta means "end of the Veda," i.e. the Upaniṣads, and the *Vedānta sūtras* are so called as they are but a summarized statement of the general views of the Upaniṣads. This work is divided into four books or adhyāyas and each adhyāya is divided into four pādas or chapters. The first four sūtras of the work commonly known as *Catuḥsūtrī* are (1) How to ask about Brahman, (2) From whom proceed birth and decay, (3) This is because from him the Vedas have come forth, (4) This is shown by the harmonious testimony of the Upaniṣads. The whole of the first chapter of the second book is devoted to justifying the position of the Vedānta against the attacks of the rival schools. The second chapter of the second book is busy in dealing blows at rival systems. All the other parts of the book are devoted to settling the disputed interpretations of a number of individual Upaniṣad texts. The really philosophical portion of the work is thus limited to the first four sūtras and the first and second chapters of the second book. The other portions are like commentaries to the Upaniṣads, which however contain many theological views of the system. The first commentary of the *Brahma-sūtra* was probably written by Baudhāyana, which however is not available now. The earliest commentary that is now found is that of the great Śaṅkara. His interpretations of the *Brahma-sūtras* together with all the commentaries and other works that follow his views are popularly known as Vedānta philosophy, though this philosophy ought more properly to be called Viśuddhādvaita-vāda school of Vedānta philosophy (i.e. the Vedānta philosophy of the school of absolute monism). Variant forms of dualistic philosophy as represented by the Vaiṣṇavas, Śaivas, Rāmāyatas, etc., also claim to express the original purport of the Brahma sūtras. We thus find that apostles of dualistic creeds such as Rāmānuja, Vallabha, Madhva, Śrikaṇṭha, Baladeva, etc., have written independent commentaries on the *Brahma-sūtra* to show that the philosophy as elaborated by themselves is the view of the Upaniṣads and as summarized in the *Brahma-sūtras*. These differed largely and often vehemently attacked Śaṇkara's interpretations of the same sūtras. These systems as expounded by them also pass by the name of Vedānta as these are also claimed to be the real interpretations intended by the Vedānta (Upaniṣads) and the *Vedānta sūtras*. Of these the system of Rāmānuja has great philosophical importance.

The *Nyāya sūtras* attributed to Gautama, called also Akṣapāda, and the *Vaiśeṣika sūtras* attributed to Kaṇāda, called also Ulūka, represent the same system for all practical purposes. They are in later times considered to differ only in a few points of minor importance. So far as the sūtras are concerned the *Nyāya sūtras* lay particular stress on the cultivation of logic as an art, while the *Vaiśeṣika sūtras* deal mostly with metaphysics and physics. In addition to these six systems, the Tantras had also philosophies of their own, which however may generally be looked upon largely as modifications of the Sāṃkhya and Vedānta systems, though their own contributions are also noteworthy.

Some Fundamental Points of Agreement.

I. The Karma Theory.

It is, however, remarkable that with the exception of the Cārvāka materialists all the other systems agree on some fundamental points of importance. The systems of philosophy in India were not stirred up merely by the speculative demands of the human mind which has a natural inclination for indulging in abstract thought, but by a deep craving after the realization of the religious purpose of life. It is surprising to note that the postulates, aims and conditions for such a realization were found to be identical in all the conflicting systems. Whatever may be their differences of opinion in other matters, so far as the general postulates for the realization of the transcendent state, the *summum bonum* of life, were concerned, all the systems were practically in thorough agreement. It may be worth while to note some of them at this stage.

First, the theory of Karma and rebirth. All the Indian systems agree in believing that whatever action is done by an individual leaves behind it some sort of potency which has the power to ordain for him joy or sorrow in the future according as it is good or bad. When the fruits of the actions are such that they cannot be enjoyed in the present life or in a human life, the individual has to take another birth as a man or any other being in order to suffer them.

The Vedic belief that the mantras uttered in the correct accent at the sacrifices with the proper observance of all ritualistic details, exactly according to the directions without the slightest error even in the smallest trifle, had something like a magical virtue automatically to produce the desired object immediately or after a lapse of time, was probably the earliest form of the Karma doctrine. It postulates a semi-conscious belief that certain mystical actions can produce at a distant time certain effects without the ordinary process of the instrumentality of visible agents of ordinary cause and effect. When the sacrifice is performed, the action leaves such an unseen magical virtue, called the *adṛṣṭa* (the unseen) or the *apūrva* (new), that by it the desired object will be achieved in a mysterious manner, for the *modus operandi* of the *apūrva* is unknown. There is also the notion prevalent in the Saṃhitās, as we have already noticed, that he who commits wicked deeds suffers in another world, whereas he who performs good deeds enjoys the highest material pleasures. These were probably associated with the conception of *ṛta*, the inviolable order of things. Thus these are probably the elements which built up the Karma theory which we find pretty well established but not emphasized in the Upaniṣads, where it is said that according to good or bad actions men will have good or bad births.

To notice other relevant points in connection with the Karma doctrine as established in the āstika systems we find that it was believed that the unseen (*adṛṣṭa*) potency of the action generally required some time before it could be fit for giving the doer the merited punishment or enjoyment. These would often accumulate and prepare the items of suffering and enjoyment for the doer in his next life. Only the fruits of those actions which are extremely wicked or particularly good could be reaped in this life. The nature of the next birth of a man is determined by the nature of pleasurable or painful experiences that have been made ready for him by his maturing actions of this life. If the experiences determined for him by his action are such that they are possible to be realized in the life of a goat, the man will die and be born as a goat. As there is no ultimate beginning in time of this world process, so there is no time at which any person first began his actions or experiences. Man has had an infinite number of past lives of the most varied nature, and the instincts of each kind of life exist dormant in the life of every individual, and thus whenever he has any particular birth as this or that animal or man, the special instincts of that life (technically called *vāsanā*) come forth. In accordance with these vāsanās the person passes through the painful or pleasurable experiences as determined for him by his action. The length of life is also determined by the number and duration of experiences as preordained by the fructifying actions of his past life. When once certain actions become fit for giving certain experiences, these cannot be avoided, but those actions which have not matured are uprooted once for all if the person attains true knowledge as advocated by philosophy. But even such an emancipated (*mukta*) person has to pass through the pleasurable or painful experiences ordained for him by the actions just ripened for giving their fruits. There are four kinds of actions, white or virtuous (*śukla*), black or wicked (*kṛṣṇa*), white-black or partly virtuous and partly vicious (*śukla-kṛṣṇa*) as most of our actions are, neither black nor white (*aśuklākṛṣṇa*), i.e. those acts of self-renunciation or meditation which are not associated with any desires for the fruit. It is only when a person can so restrain himself as to perform only the last kind of action that he ceases to accumulate any new karma for giving fresh fruits. He has thus only to enjoy the fruits of his previous karmas which have ripened for giving fruits. If in the meantime he attains true knowledge, all his past accumulated actions become destroyed, and as his acts are only of the aśuklākṛṣṇa type no fresh karma for ripening is accumulated, and thus he becomes divested of all karma after enjoying the fruits of the ripened karmas alone.

The Jains think that through the actions of body, speech and mind a kind of subtle matter technically called karma is produced. The passions of a man act like a viscous substance that attracts this karma matter, which thus pours into the soul and sticks to it. The karma matter thus accumulated round the soul during the infinite number of past lives is technically called *kār-maśarīra*, which encircles the soul as it passes on from birth to birth. This karma matter sticking to the soul gradually ripens and exhausts itself in ordaining the sufferance of pains or the enjoyment of pleasures for the individual. While some karma matter is being expended in this way, other karma matters are accumulating by his activities, and thus keep him in a continuous process of suffering and enjoyment. The karma matter thus accumulated in the soul produces a kind of coloration called *leśyā*, such as white, black, etc., which marks the character of the soul. The idea of the śukla and kṛṣṇa karmas of the Yoga system was probably suggested by the Jaina view. But when a man is free from passions, and acts in strict compliance with the rules of conduct, his actions produce karma which lasts but for a moment and is then annihilated. Every karma that the sage has previously earned has its predestined limits within which it must take effect and be purged away. But when by contemplation and the strict adherence to the five great vows, no new karma is generated, and when all the karmas are exhausted the worldly existence of the person rapidly draws towards its end. Thus in the last stage of contemplation, all karma being annihilated, and all activities having ceased, the soul leaves the body and goes up to the top of the universe, where the liberated souls stay for ever.

Buddhism also contributes some new traits to the karma theory which however being intimately connected with their metaphysics will be treated later on.

2. The Doctrine of Mukti.

Not only do the Indian systems agree as to the cause of the inequalities in the share of sufferings and enjoyments in the case of different persons, and the manner in which the cycle of births and rebirths has been kept going from beginningless time, on the basis of the mysterious connection of one's actions with the happenings of the world, but they also agree in believing that this beginningless chain of karma and its fruits, of births and rebirths, this running on from beginningless time has somewhere its end. This end was not to be attained at some distant time or in some distant kingdom, but was to be sought within us. Karma leads us to this endless cycle, and if we could divest ourselves of all such emotions, ideas or desires as lead us to action we should find within us the actionless self which neither suffers nor enjoys, neither works nor undergoes rebirth. When the Indians, wearied by the endless bustle and turmoil of worldly events, sought for and believed that somewhere a peaceful goal could be found, they generally hit upon the self of man. The belief that the soul could be realized in some stage as being permanently divested of all action, feelings or ideas, led logically to the conclusion that the connection of the soul with these worldly elements was extraneous, artificial or even illusory. In its true nature the soul is untouched by the impurities of our ordinary life, and it is through ignorance and passion as inherited from the cycle of karma from beginningless time that we connect it with these. The realization of this transcendent state is the goal and final achievement of this endless cycle of births and rebirths through karma. The Buddhists did not admit the existence of soul, but recognized that the final realization of the process of karma is to be found in the ultimate dissolution called Nirvāṇa, the nature of which we shall discuss later on.

3. The Doctrine of Soul.

All the Indian systems except Buddhism admit the existence of a permanent entity variously called ātman, puruṣa or jīva. As to the exact nature of this soul there are indeed divergences of view. Thus while the Nyāya calls it absolutely qualityless and characterless, indeterminate unconscious entity, Sāṃkhya describes it as being of the nature of pure consciousness, the Vedānta says that it is that fundamental point of unity implied in pure consciousness (*cit*), pure bliss (*ānanda*), and pure being (*sat*). But all agree in holding that it is pure and unsullied in its nature and that all impurities of action or passion do not form a real part of it. The *summum bonum* of life is attained when all impurities are removed and the pure nature of the self is thoroughly and permanently apprehended and all other extraneous connections with it are absolutely dissociated.

The Pessimistic Attitude towards the World and the Optimistic Faith in the end.

Though the belief that the world is full of sorrow has not been equally prominently emphasized in all systems, yet it may be considered as being shared by all of them. It finds its strongest utterance in Sāṃkhya, Yoga, and Buddhism. This interminable chain of pleasurable and painful experiences was looked upon as nearing no peaceful end but embroiling and entangling us in the meshes of karma, rebirth, and sorrow. What appear as pleasures are but a mere appearance for the attempt to keep them steady is painful, there is pain when we lose the pleasures or when we are anxious to have them. When the pleasures are so much associated with pains they are but pains themselves. We are but duped when we seek pleasures, for they are sure to lead us to pain. All our experiences are essentially sorrowful and ultimately sorrow-begetting. Sorrow is the ultimate truth of this process of the world. That which to an ordinary person seems pleasurable appears to a wise person or to a yogin who has a clearer vision as painful. The greater the knowledge the higher is the sensitiveness to sorrow and dissatisfaction with world experiences. The yogin is like the pupil of the eye to which even the smallest grain of disturbance is unbearable. This sorrow of worldly experiences cannot be removed by bringing in remedies for each sorrow as it comes, for the moment it is remedied another sorrow comes in. It cannot also be avoided by mere inaction or suicide, for we are continually being forced to action by our nature, and suicide will but lead to another life of sorrow and rebirth. The only way to get rid of it is by the culmination of moral greatness and true knowledge which uproot sorrow once for all. It is our ignorance that the self is intimately connected with the experiences of life or its pleasures, that leads us to action and arouses passion in us for the enjoyment of pleasures and other emotions and activities. Through the highest moral elevation a man may attain absolute dispassion towards world-experiences and retire in body, mind, and speech from all worldly concerns. When the mind is so purified, the self shines in its true light, and its true nature is rightly conceived. When this is once done the self can never again be associated with passion or ignorance. It becomes at this stage ultimately dissociated from *citta* which contains within it the root of all emotions, ideas, and actions. Thus emancipated the self forever conquers all sorrow. It is important, however, to note in this connection that emancipation is not based on a general aversion to intercourse with the world or on such feelings as a disappointed person may have, but on the appreciation of the state of mukti as the supremely blessed one. The details of the pessimistic creed of each system have developed from the logical necessity peculiar to each system. There was never the slightest tendency to shirk the duties of this life, but to rise above them through right performance and right understanding. It is only when a man rises to the highest pinnacle of moral glory that he is fit for aspiring to that realization of selfhood in comparison with which all worldly things or even the joys of Heaven would not only shrink into insignificance, but appear in their true character as sorrowful and loathsome. It is when his mind has thus turned from all ordinary joys that he can strive towards his ideal of salvation. In fact it seems to me that a sincere religious craving after some ideal blessedness and quiet of self-realization is indeed the fundamental fact from which not only her philosophy but many of the complex phenomena of the civilization of India can be logically deduced. The sorrow around us has no fear for us if we remember that we are naturally sorrowless and blessed in ourselves. The pessimistic view loses all terror as it closes in absolute optimistic confidence in one's own self and the ultimate destiny and goal of emancipation.

Unity in Indian Sādhana
(philosophical, religious and ethical endeavours).

As might be expected the Indian systems are all agreed upon the general principles of ethical conduct which must be followed for the attainment of salvation. That all passions are to be controlled, no injury to life in any form should be done, and that all desire for pleasures should be checked, are principles which are almost universally acknowledged. When a man attains a very high degree of moral greatness he has to strengthen and prepare his mind for further purifying and steadying it for the attainment of his ideal; and most of the Indian systems are unanimous with regard to the means to be employed for the purpose. There are indeed divergences in certain details or technical names, but the means to be adopted for purification are almost everywhere essentially the same as those advocated by the Yoga system. It is only in later times that devotion (*bhakti*) is seen to occupy a more prominent place specially in Vaiṣṇava schools of thought. Thus it was that though there were many differences among the various systems, yet their goal of life, their attitude towards the world and the means for the attainment of the goal (*sādhana*) being fundamentally the same, there was a unique unity in the practical sādhana of almost all the Indian systems. The religious craving has been universal in India and this uniformity of sādhana has therefore secured for India a unity in all her aspirations and strivings.

V

BUDDHIST PHILOSOPHY

Many scholars are of opinion that the Sāṃkhya and the Yoga represent the earliest systematic speculations of India. It is also suggested that Buddhism drew much of its inspiration from them. It may be that there is some truth in such a view, but the systematic Sāṃkhya and Yoga treatises as we have them had decidedly been written after Buddhism. Moreover it is well-known to every student of Hindu philosophy that a conflict with the Buddhists has largely stimulated philosophic enquiry in most of the systems of Hindu thought. A knowledge of Buddhism is therefore indispensable for a right understanding of the different systems in their mutual relation and opposition to Buddhism. It seems desirable therefore that I should begin with Buddhism first.

The State of Philosophy in India before the Buddha.

It is indeed difficult to give a short sketch of the different philosophical speculations that were prevalent in India before Buddhism. The doctrines of the Upaniṣads are well known, and these have already been briefly described. But these were not the only ones. Even in the Upaniṣads we find references to diverse atheistical creeds[1]. We find there that the origin of the world and its processes were sometimes discussed, and some thought that "time" was the ultimate cause of all, others that all these had sprung forth by their own nature (*svabhāva*), others that everything had come forth in accordance with an inexorable destiny or a fortuitous concourse of accidental happenings, or through matter combinations in general. References to diverse kinds of heresies are found in Buddhist literature also, but no detailed accounts of these views are known. Of the Upaniṣad type of materialists the two schools of Cārvākas (Dhūrtta and Suśikṣita) are referred to in later literature, though the time in which these flourished cannot rightly be discovered[2]. But it seems

[1] Śvetāśvatara, I. 2, *kālaḥ svabhābo niyatiryadṛcchā bhūtāni yoniḥ puruṣa iti cintyam.*

[2] Lokāyata (literally, that which is found among people in general) seems to have been the name by which all Cārvāka doctrines were generally known. See Guṇaratna on the Lokāyatas.

probable however that the allusion to the materialists contained in the Upaniṣads refers to these or to similar schools. The Cārvākas did not believe in the authority of the Vedas or any other holy scripture. According to them there was no soul. Life and consciousness were the products of the combination of matter, just as red colour was the result of mixing up white with yellow or as the power of intoxication was generated in molasses (*madaśakti*). There is no afterlife, and no reward of actions, as there is neither virtue nor vice. Life is only for enjoyment. So long as it lasts it is needless to think of anything else, as everything will end with death, for when at death the body is burnt to ashes there cannot be any rebirth. They do not believe in the validity of inference. Nothing is trustworthy but what can be directly perceived, for it is impossible to determine that the distribution of the middle term (*hetu*) has not depended upon some extraneous condition, the absence of which might destroy the validity of any particular piece of inference. If in any case any inference comes to be true, it is only an accidental fact and there is no certitude about it. They were called Cārvāka because they would only eat but would not accept any other religious or moral responsibility. The word comes from *carv* to eat. The Dhūrtta Cārvākas held that there was nothing but the four elements of earth, water, air and fire, and that the body was but the result of atomic combination. There was no self or soul, no virtue or vice. The Suśikṣita Cārvākas held that there was a soul apart from the body but that it also was destroyed with the destruction of the body. The original work of the Cārvākas was written in sūtras probably by Bṛhaspati. Jayanta and Guṇaratna quote two sūtras from it. Short accounts of this school may be found in Jayanta's *Nyāyamañjarī*, Mādhava's *Sarvadarśanasaṃ-graha* and Guṇaratna's *Tarkarahasyadīpikā*. *Mahābhārata* gives an account of a man called Cārvāka meeting Yudhiṣṭhira.

Side by side with the doctrine of the Cārvāka materialists we are reminded of the Ājīvakas of which Makkhali Gosāla, probably a renegade disciple of the Jain saint Mahāvīra and a contemporary of Buddha and Mahāvīra, was the leader. This was a thorough-going determinism denying the free will of man and his moral responsibility for any so-called good or evil. The essence of Makkhali's system is this, that "there is no cause, either proximate or remote, for the depravity of beings or for their purity. They become so without any cause. Nothing depends either on one's own efforts or on the efforts of others, in short nothing depends on any human effort, for there is no such thing as power or energy, or human exertion. The varying conditions at any time are due to fate, to their environment and their own nature[1]."

Another sophistical school led by Ajita Kesakambali taught that there was no fruit or result of good or evil deeds; there is no other world, nor was this one real; nor had parents nor any former lives any efficacy with respect to this life. Nothing that we can do prevents any of us alike from being wholly brought to an end at death[2].

There were thus at least three currents of thought: firstly the sacrificial Karma by the force of the magical rites of which any person could attain anything he desired; secondly the Upaniṣad teaching that the Brahman, the self, is the ultimate reality and being, and all else but name and form which pass away but do not abide. That which permanently abides without change is the real and true, and this is self. Thirdly the nihilistic conceptions that there is no law, no abiding reality, that everything comes into being by a fortuitous concourse of circumstances or by some unknown fate. In each of these schools, philosophy had probably come to a deadlock. There were the Yoga practices prevalent in the country and these were accepted partly on the strength of traditional custom among certain sections, and partly by virtue of the great spiritual, intellectual and physical power which they gave to those who performed them. But these had no rational basis behind them on which they could lean for support. These were probably then just tending towards being affiliated to the nebulous Sāṃkhya doctrines which had grown up among certain sections. It was at this juncture that we find Buddha erecting a new superstructure of thought on altogether original lines which thenceforth opened up a new avenue of philosophy for all posterity to come. If the Being of the Upaniṣads, the superlatively motionless, was the only real, how could it offer scope for further new speculations, as it had already discarded all other matters of interest? If everything was due to a reasonless fortuitous concourse of circumstances, reason could not proceed further in the direction to create any philosophy of the unreason. The magical

[1] *Sūmaññaphala-sutta, Dīgha*, II. 20. Hoernlé's article on the Ājīvakas, E. R. E.

[2] *Sūmaññaphala-sutta*, II. 23.

force of the hocus-pocus of sorcery or sacrifice had but little that was inviting for philosophy to proceed on. If we thus take into account the state of Indian philosophic culture before Buddha, we shall be better able to understand the value of the Buddhistic contribution to philosophy.

Buddha: his Life.

Gautama the Buddha was born in or about the year B.C. 560 in the Lumbini Grove near the ancient town of Kapilavastu in the now dense terai region of Nepal. His father was Suddhodana, a prince of the Sākya clan, and his mother Queen Mahāmāyā. According to the legends it was foretold of him that he would enter upon the ascetic life when he should see "A decrepit old man, a diseased man, a dead man, and a monk." His father tried his best to keep him away from these by marrying him and surrounding him with luxuries. But on successive occasions, issuing from the palace, he was confronted by those four things, which filled him with amazement and distress, and realizing the impermanence of all earthly things determined to forsake his home and try if he could to discover some means to immortality to remove the sufferings of men. He made his "Great Renunciation" when he was twenty-nine years old. He travelled on foot to Rājagṛha (Rajgir) and thence to Uruvelā, where in company with other five ascetics he entered upon a course of extreme self-discipline, carrying his austerities to such a length that his body became utterly emaciated and he fell down senseless and was believed to be dead. After six years of this great struggle he was convinced that the truth was not to be won by the way of extreme asceticism, and resuming an ordinary course of life at last attained absolute and supreme enlightenment. There-after the Buddha spent a life prolonged over forty-five years in travelling from place to place and preaching the doctrine to all who would listen. At the age of over eighty years Buddha realized that the time drew near for him to die. He then entered into Dhyāna and passing through its successive stages attained nirvāṇa[1]. The vast developments which the system of this great teacher underwent in the succeeding centuries in India and in other countries have not been thoroughly studied, and it will probably take yet many years more before even the materials for

[1] *Mahāparinibbānasuttanta*, *Dīgha*, XVI. 6, 8, 9.

such a study can be collected. But from what we now possess it is proved incontestably that it is one of the most wonderful and subtle productions of human wisdom. It is impossible to overestimate the debt that the philosophy, culture and civilization of India owe to it in all her developments for many succeeding centuries.

Early Buddhist Literature.

The Buddhist Pāli Scriptures contain three different collections: the Sutta (relating to the doctrines), the Vinaya (relating to the discipline of the monks) and the Abhidhamma (relating generally to the same subjects as the suttas but dealing with them in a scholastic and technical manner). Scholars of Buddhistic religious history of modern times have failed as yet to fix any definite dates for the collection or composition of the different parts of the aforesaid canonical literature of the Buddhists. The suttas were however composed before the Abhidhamma and it is very probable that almost the whole of the canonical works were completed before B.C. 241, the date of the third council during the reign of King Asoka. The suttas mainly deal with the doctrine (Dhamma) of the Buddhistic faith whereas the Vinaya deals only with the regulations concerning the discipline of the monks. The subject of the Abhidhamma is mostly the same as that of the suttas, namely, the interpretation of the Dhamma. Buddhaghoṣa in his introduction to *Atthasālinī*, the commentary on the *Dhammasaṅgaṇi*, says that the Abhidhamma is so called (*abhi* and *dhamma*) because it describes the same Dhammas as are related in the suttas in a more intensified (*dhammātireka*) and specialized (*dhammavisesatthena*) manner. The Abhidhammas do not give any new doctrines that are not in the suttas, but they deal somewhat elaborately with those that are already found in the suttas. Buddhaghoṣa in distinguishing the special features of the suttas from the Abhidhammas says that the acquirement of the former leads one to attain meditation (*samādhi*) whereas the latter leads one to attain wisdom (*paññāsampadam*). The force of this statement probably lies in this, that the dialogues of the suttas leave a chastening effect on the mind, the like of which is not to be found in the Abhidhammas, which busy themselves in enumerating the Buddhistic doctrines and defining them in a technical manner, which is more fitted to produce a reasoned insight into the doctrines than directly to generate a craving for following the path of meditation for the extinction of sorrow. The Abhidhamma known as the *Kathāvatthu* differs from the other Abhidhammas in this, that it attempts to reduce the views of the heterodox schools to absurdity. The discussions proceed in the form of questions and answers, and the answers of the opponents are often shown to be based on contradictory assumptions.

The suttas contain five groups of collections called the Nikāyas. These are (1) *Dīgha Nikāya*, called so on account of the length of the suttas contained in it; (2) *Majjhima Nikāya* (middling Nikāya), called so on account of the middling extent of the suttas contained in it; (3) *Saṃyutta Nikāya* (Nikāyas relating to special meetings), called saṃyutta on account of their being delivered owing to the meetings (*saṃyoga*) of special persons which were the occasions for them; (4) *Aṅguttara Nikāya*, so called because in each succeeding book of this work the topics of discussion increase by one[1]; (5) *Khuddaka Nikāya* containing *Khuddaka pāṭha*, *Dhammapada*, *Udāna*, *Itivuttaka*, *Sutta Nipāta*, *Vimāna-vattku*, *Petavatthu*, *Theragathā*, *Therīgāthā*, *Jātaka*, *Niddesa*, *Paṭisambhidāmagga*, *Apadāna*, *Buddhavaṃsa*, *Caryāpiṭaka*.

The Abhidhammas are *Paṭṭhāna*, *Dhammasaṅgaṇi*, *Dhātu-kathā*, *Puggalapaññatti*, *Vibhaṅga*, *Yamaka* and *Kathāvatthu*. There exists also a large commentary literature on diverse parts of the above works known as atthakathā. The work known as *Milinda Pañha* (questions of King Milinda), of uncertain date, is of considerable philosophical value.

The doctrines and views incorporated in the above literature is generally now known as Sthaviravāda or Theravāda. On the origin of the name Theravāda (the doctrine of the elders) *Dīpavaṃsa* says that since the Theras (elders) met (at the first council) and collected the doctrines it was known as the Thera Vāda[2]. It does not appear that Buddhism as it appears in this Pāli literature developed much since the time of Buddhaghoṣa (A.D. 400), the writer of *Visuddhimagga* (a compendium of theravāda doctrines) and the commentator of *Dīghanikāya*, *Dhammasaṅgaṇi*, etc.

Hindu philosophy in later times seems to have been influenced by the later offshoots of the different schools of Buddhism, but it does not appear that Pāli Buddhism had any share in it. I

[1] See Buddhaghoṣa's *Atthasālinī*, p. 25.
[2] Oldenberg's *Dīpavaṃsa*, p. 31.

have not been able to discover any old Hindu writer who could be considered as being acquainted with Pāli.

The Doctrine of Causal Connection of early Buddhism[1].

The word Dhamma in the Buddhist scriptures is used generally in four senses: (1) Scriptural texts, (2) quality (*guṇa*), (3) cause (*hetu*) and (4) unsubstantial and soulless (*nissatta nijjīva*[2]). Of these it is the last meaning which is particularly important from the point of view of Buddhist philosophy. The early Buddhist philosophy did not accept any fixed entity as determining all reality; the only things with it were the unsubstantial phenomena and these were called dhammas. The question arises that if there is no substance or reality how are we to account for the phenomena? But the phenomena are happening and passing away and the main point of interest with the Buddha was to find out "What being what else is," "What happening what else happens" and "What not being what else is not." The phenomena are happening in a series and we see that there being certain phenomena there become some others; by the happening of some events others also are produced. This is called (*paṭicca-samuppāda*) dependent origination. But it is difficult to understand what is the exact nature of this dependence. The question as *Saṃyutta Nikāya* (II. 5) has it with which the Buddha started before attaining Buddhahood was this: in what miserable condition are the people! they are born, they decay, they die, pass away and are born again; and they do not know the path of escape from this decay death and misery.

How to know the way to escape from this misery of decay and death. Then it occurred to him what being there, are decay and death, depending on what do they come? As he thought deeply into the root of the matter, it occurred to him that decay and death can only occur when there is birth (*jāti*), so they depend

[1] There are some differences of opinion as to whether one could take the doctrine of the twelve links of causes as we find it in the *Saṃyutta Nikāya* as the earliest Buddhist view, as Saṃyutta does not represent the oldest part of the suttas. But as this doctrine of the twelve causes became regarded as a fundamental Buddhist doctrine and as it gives us a start in philosophy I have not thought it fit to enter into conjectural discussions as to the earliest form. Dr E. J. Thomas drew my attention to this fact.

[2] *Atthasātinī*, p. 38. There are also other senses in which the word is used, as *dhamma desanā* where it means religious teaching. The *Laṅkāvatāra* described Dharmma as *guṇadravyapūrvakā dharmmā*, i.e. Dharmmas are those which are associated as attributes and substances.

on birth. What being there, is there birth, on what does birth depend? Then it occurred to him that birth could only be if there were previous existence (*bhava*)[1]. But on what does this existence depend, or what being there is there *bhava*. Then it occurred to him that there could not be existence unless there were holding fast (*upādāna*)[2]. But on what did upādāna depend? It occurred to him that it was desire (*taṇhā*) on which upādāna depended. There can be upādāna if there is desire (*taṇhā*)[3]. But what being there, can there be desire? To this question it occurred to him that there must be feeling (*vedanā*) in order that there may be desire. But on what does vedanā depend, or rather what must be there, that there may be feeling (*vedanā*)? To this it occurred to him that there must be a sense-contact (*phassa*) in order that there may be feeling[4]. If there should be no sense-contact there would be no feeling. But on what does sense-contact depend? It occurred to him that as there are six sense-contacts, there are the six fields of contact (*āyatana*)[5]. But on what do the six āyatanas depend? It occurred to him that there must be the mind and body (*nāmarūpa*) in order that there may be the six fields of contact[5]; but on what does nāmarūpa depend? It occurred to him that without consciousness (*viññāna*) there could be no nāmarūpa[6]. But what being there would there

[1] This word bhava is interpreted by Candrakīrti in his *Mādhyamīka vṛtti*, p. 565 (La Vallée Poussin's edition) as the deed which brought about rebirth (*punarbhava-janakaṃ karma samutthāpayati kāyena vācā manasā ca*).

[2] *Atthasālinī*, p. 385, upādānantidaḷhagahaṇaṃ Candrakīrti in explaining upādāna says that whatever thing a man desires he holds fast to the materials necessary for attaining it (*yatra vastuni satṛṣṇastasya vastuno 'rjanāya viḍhapanāya upādānamupā-datte tatra tatra prārthayate*). *Mādhyamīka vṛtti*, p. 565.

[3] Candrakīrti describes tṛṣṇā as *āsvādanābhinandanādhyavasānasthānādātmapri-yarūpairviyogo mā bhūt, nityamaparityāgo bhavediti, yeyam prārthanā*—the desire that there may not ever be any separation from those pleasures, etc., which are dear to us. *Ibid.* 565.

[4] We read also of phassāyatana and phassakāya. *M. N.* II. 261, III. 280, etc. Candrakīrti says that *ṣaḍbhirāyatanadvāraiḥ kṛtyaprakṛiyāḥ pravarttante prajñāyante. tannāmarūpapratyayaṃ ṣaḍāyatanamucyate. saḍbhyaścāyatanebhyaḥ; ṣatsparśakāyāḥ pravarttante. M. V.* 565.

[5] Āyatana means the six senses together with their objects. Āyatana literally is "Field of operation." Saḷāyatana means six senses as six fields of operation. Candrakīrti has *āyatanadvāraiḥ*.

[6] I have followed the translation of Aung in rendering nāmarūpa as mind and body, *Compendium*, p. 271. This seems to me to be fairly correct. The four skandhas are called nāma in each birth. These together with rūpa (matter) give us nāmarūpa (mind and body) which being developed render the activities through *the* six sense-gates possible so that there may be knowledge. Cf. *M. V.* 564. Govindānanda, the commentator on Śaṅkara's bhāṣya on the *Brahma-sūtras* (II. ii. 19), gives a different interpretation of Nāmarūpa which may probably refer to the Vijñānavāda view though we have no means at hand

be viññāna. Here it occurred to him that in order that there might be viññāna there must be the conformations (*saṅkhāra*)[1]. But what being there are there the saṅkhāras? Here it occurred to him that the saṅkhāras can only be if there is ignorance (*avijjā*). If avijjā could be stopped then the saṅkhāras will be stopped, and if the saṇkhāras could be stopped viññāna could be stopped and so on[2].

It is indeed difficult to be definite as to what the Buddha actually wished to mean by this cycle of dependence of existence sometimes called Bhavacakra (wheel of existence). Decay and death (*jarāmaraṇa*) could not have happened if there was no birth[3]. This seems to be clear. But at this point the difficulty begins. We must remember that the theory of rebirth

to verify it. He says—To think the momentary as the permanent is Avidyā; from there come the saṃskāras of attachment, antipathy or anger, and infatuation; from there the first vijñāna or thought of the foetus is produced; from that ālayavijñāna, and the four elements (which are objects of name and are hence called nāma) are produced, and from those are produced the white and black, semen and blood called rūpa. Both Vācaspati and Amalānanda agree with Govindānanda in holding that nāma signifies the semen and the ovum while rūpa means the visible physical body built out of them. Vijñāna entered the womb and on account of it nāmarūpa were produced through the association of previous karma. See *Vedāntakalpataru*, pp. 274, 275. On the doctrine of the entrance of vijñāna into the womb compare *D. N.* II. 63.

[1] It is difficult to say what is the exact sense of the word here. The Buddha was one of the first few earliest thinkers to introduce proper philosophical terms and phraseology with a distinct philosophical method and he had often to use the same word in more or less different senses. Some of the philosophical terms at least are therefore rather elastic when compared with the terms of precise and definite meaning which we find in later Sanskrit thought. Thus in S. *N.* III. p. 87, "*Saṇkhataṃ abhisaṇkharonti*," saṅkhāra means that which synthesises the complexes. In the *Compendium* it is translated as will, action. Mr Aung thinks that it means the same as karma; it is here used in a different sense from what we find in the word saṅkhāra khandha (viz. mental states). We get a list of 51 mental states forming saṅkhāra khandha in *Dhamma Saṅgaṇi*, p. 18, and another different set of 40 mental states in *Dharmasaṃgraha*, p. 6. In addition to these forty *cittasamprayuktasaṃskāra*, it also counts thirteen *cittavi-prayuktasaṃskāra*. Candrakīrti interprets it as meaning attachment, antipathy and infatuation, p. 563. Govindānanda, the commentator on Śaṇkara's *Brahma-sūtra* (II. ii. 19), also interprets the word in connection with the doctrine of *Pratītyasamutpāda* as attachment, antipathy and infatuation.

[2] *Saṃyutta Nikāya*, II, 7-8.

[3] Jarā and maraṇa bring in śoka (grief), paridevanā (lamentation), duḥkha (suffering), daurmanasya (feeling of wretchedness and miserableness) and upāyāsa (feeling of extreme destitution) at the prospect of one's death or the death of other dear ones. All these make up suffering and are the results of jāti (birth). *M. V.* (B. T. S. p. 208). Śaṅkara in his bhāṣya counted all the terms from jarā, separately. The whole series is to be taken as representing the entirety of duḥkhaskandha.

was enunciated in the Upaniṣads. The Bṛhadāraṇyaka says that just as an insect going to the end of a leaf of grass by a new effort collects itself in another so does the soul coming to the end of this life collect itself in another. This life thus presupposes another existence. So far as I remember there has seldom been before or after Buddha any serious attempt to prove or disprove the doctrine of rebirth[1]. All schools of philosophy except the Cārvākas believed in it and so little is known to us of the Cārvāka sūtras that it is difficult to say what they did to refute this doctrine. The Buddha also accepts it as a fact and does not criticize it. This life therefore comes only as one which had an infinite number of lives before, and which except in the case of a few emancipated ones would have an infinite number of them in the future. It was strongly believed by all people, and the Buddha also, when he came to think to what our present birth might be due, had to fall back upon another existence (*bhava*). If bhava means karma which brings rebirth as Candrakīrti takes it to mean, then it would mean that the present birth could only take place on account of the works of a previous existence which determined it. Here also we are reminded of the Upaniṣad note "as a man does so will he be born" (*Yat karma kurute tadabhi-sampadyate*, Bṛh. IV. iv. 5). Candrakīrti's interpretation of "bhava" as Karma (*punarbhavajanakam karma*) seems to me to suit better than "existence." The word was probably used rather loosely for *kammabhava*. The word bhava is not found in the earlier Upaniṣads and was used in the Pāli scriptures for the first time as a philosophical term. But on what does this bhava depend? There could not have been a previous existence if people had not betaken themselves to things or works they desired. This betaking oneself to actions or things in accordance with desire is called upādāna. In the Upaniṣads we read, "whatever one betakes himself to, so does he work" (*Yatkratur-bhavati tatkarmma kurute*, Bṛh. IV. iv. 5). As this betaking to the thing depends upon desire (*tṛṣṇā*), it is said that in order that there may be upādāna there must be taṇhā. In the Upaniṣads also we read "Whatever one desires so does he betake himself to" (*sa yathākāmo bhavati tatkraturbhavati*). Neither the word upādāna nor tṛṣṇā (the Sanskrit word corresponding

[1] The attempts to prove the doctrine of rebirth in the Hindu philosophical works such as the Nyāya, etc., are slight and inadequate.

to taṇhā) is found in the earlier Upaniṣads, but the ideas contained in them are similar to the words "*kratu*" and "*kāma*." Desire (*taṇhā*) is then said to depend on feeling or sense-contact. Sense-contact presupposes the six senses as fields of operation[1]. These six senses or operating fields would again presuppose the whole psychosis of the man (the body and the mind together) called nāmarūpa. We are familiar with this word in the Upaniṣads but there it is used in the sense of determinate forms and names as distinguished from the indeterminate indefinable reality[2]. Buddhaghoṣa in the *Visuddhimagga* says that by "Name" are meant the three groups beginning with sensation (i.e. sensation, perception and the predisposition); by "Form" the four elements and form derivative from the four elements[3]. He further says that name by itself can produce physical changes, such as eating, drinking, making movements or the like. So form also cannot produce any of those changes by itself. But like the cripple and the blind they mutually help one another and effectuate the changes[4]. But there exists no heap or collection of material for the production of Name and Form; "but just as when a lute is played upon, there is no previous store of sound; and when the sound comes into existence it does not come from any such store; and when it ceases, it does not go to any of the cardinal or intermediate points of the compass;... in exactly the same way all the elements of being both those with form and those without, come into existence after having previously been non-existent and having come into existence pass away[5]." Nāmarūpa taken in this sense will not mean the whole of mind and body, but only the sense functions and the body which are found to operate in the six doors of sense (*saḷāyatana*). If we take nāmarūpa in this sense, we can see that it may be said to depend upon the viññāna (consciousness). Consciousness has been compared in the *Milinda Pañha* with a watchman at the middle of

[1] The word āyatana is found in many places in the earlier Upaniṣads in the sense of "field or place," Chā. ɪ. 5, Bṛh. III. 9. 10, but ṣaḍāyatana does not occur.

[2] Candrakīrti interprets nāma as *Vedanādayo' rūpiṇaścatvāraḥ skandhāstatra tatra bhave nāmayantīti nāma. saha rūpaskandhena ca nāma rūpam ceti nāmarūpamucyate.* The four skandhas in each specific birth act as name. These together with rūpa make nāmarūpa. *M. V.* 564.

[3] Warren's *Buddhism in Translations*, p. 184.

[4] *Ibid.* p. 185, *Visuddhimagga*, Ch. XVII.

[5] *Ibid.* pp. 185-186, *Visuddhimagga*, Ch. XVII.

the crossroads beholding all that come from any direction[1]. Buddhaghoṣa in the *Atthasālinī* also says that consciousness means that which thinks its object. If we are to define its characteristics we must say that it knows (*vijānana*), goes in advance (*pubbaṇgama*), connects (*sandhāna*), and stands on nāmarūpa (*nāmarūpa-padaṭṭhānam*). When the consciousness gets a door, at a place the objects of sense are discerned (*ārammana-vibhāvanaṭṭhāne*) and it goes first as the precursor. When a visual object is seen by the eye it is known only by the consciousness, and when the dhammas are made the objects of (mind) mano, it is known only by the consciousness[2]. Buddhaghoṣa also refers here to the passage in the *Milinda Pañha* we have just referred to. He further goes on to say that when states of consciousness rise one after another, they leave no gap between the previous state and the later and consciousness therefore appears as connected. When there are the aggregates of the five khandhas it is lost; but there are the four aggregates as nāmarūpa, it stands on nāma and therefore it is said that it stands on nāmarūpa. He further asks, Is this consciousness the same as the previous consciousness or different from it? He answers that it is the same. Just so, the sun shows itself with all its colours, etc., but he is not different from those in truth; and it is said that just when the sun rises, its collected heat and yellow colour also rise then, but it does not mean that the sun is different from these. So the citta or consciousness takes the phenomena of contact, etc., and cognizes them. So though it is the same as they are yet in a sense it is different from them[3].

To go back to the chain of twelve causes, we find that jāti (birth) is the cause of decay and death, *jarāmaraṇa*, etc. Jāti is the appearance of the body or the totality of the five skandhas[4]. Coming to bhava which determines jāti, I cannot think of any better rational explanation of bhava, than that I have already

[1] Warren's *Buddhism in Translations*, p. 182. *Milinda Pañha* (628).

[2] *Atthasālinī*, p. 112.

[3] *Ibid.* p. 113, *Yathā hi rūpādīni upādāya paññattā suriyādayo na atthato rūpā-dīhi aññe honti ten' eva yasmin samaye suriyo udeti tasmin samaye tassa tejā-saṅ-khātam rupaṃ pīti evaṃ; vuccamāne pi na rūpādihi añño suriyo nāma atthi. Tathā cittam phassādayo dhamme upādāya paññapiyati. Atthato pan' ettha tehi aññam eva. Tena yasmin samaye cittam uppannaṃ hoti ekaṃsen eva tasmin samaye phassādihi atthato aññad eva hotī ti.*

[4] "*Jātirdehajanma pañcaskandhasamudāyaḥ,*" Govindānanda's *Ratnaprabhā* on Śaṅkara's bhāṣya, II. ii. 19.

suggested, namely, the works (*karma*) which produce the birth[1]. Upādāna is an advanced tṛṣṇā leading to positive clinging[2]. It is produced by tṛṣṇā (desire) which again is the result of vedanā (pleasure and pain). But this vedanā is of course vedanā with ignorance (*avidyā*), for an Arhat may have also vedanā but as he has no avidyā, the vedanā cannot produce tṛṣṇā in turn. On its development it immediately passes into upādāna. Vedanā means pleasurable, painful or indifferent feeling. On the one side it leads to tṛṣṇā (desire) and on the other it is produced by sense-contact (*sparśa*). Prof. De la Vallée Poussin says that Śrīlābha distinguishes three processes in the production of vedanā. Thus first there is the contact between the sense and the object; then there is the knowledge of the object, and then there is the vedanā. Depending on *Majjhima Nikāya*, iii. 242, Poussin gives the other opinion that just as in the case of two sticks heat takes place simultaneously with rubbing, so here also vedanā takes place simultaneously with sparśa for they are "produits par un même complexe de causes (*sāmagrī*)[3]."

Sparśa is produced by ṣaḍāyatana, ṣaḍāyatana by nāmarūpa, and nāmarūpa by vijñāna, and is said to descend in the womb of the mother and produce the five skandhas as nāmarūpa, out of which the six senses are specialized.

Vijñāna in this connection probably means the principle or germ of consciousness in the womb of the mother upholding the five elements of the new body there. It is the product of the past karmas (*saṅkhāra*) of the dying man and of his past consciousness too.

We sometimes find that the Buddhists believed that the last thoughts of the dying man determined the nature of his next

[1] Govindānanda in his *Ratnaprabhā* on Śaṅkara's bhāṣya, II. ii. 19, explains "bhava" as that from which anything becomes, as merit and demerit (*dharmādi*). See also *Vibhaṅga*, p. 137 and Warren's *Buddhism in Translations*, p. 201. Mr Aung says in *Abhidhammatthasaṅgaha*, p. 189, that bhavo includes kammabhavo (the active side of an existence) and upapattibhavo (the passive side). And the commentators say that bhava is a contraction of "*kammabhava*" or Karma—becoming i.e. karmic activity.

[2] Prof. De la Vallée Poussin in his *Théorie des Douze Çauses*, p. 26, says that *Śālistambhasūtra* explains the word "upādāna" as "tṛṣṇāvaipulya" or hyper-tṛṣṇā and Candrakūtti also gives the same meaning, *M. V.* (B. T. S. p. 210). Govindānanda explains" upādāna" as pravṛtti (movement) generated by tṛṣṇā (desire), i.e. the active tendency in pursuance of desire. But if upādāna means "support" it would denote all the five skandhas. Thus *Madhyamaka vṛtti* says *upādānam pañcaskandhalakṣaṇam... pañcopādānaskandhākhyam upādānam. M. V.* XXVII. 6.

[3] Poussin's *Théorie des Douze Causes*. p. 23.

birth[1]. The manner in which the vijñāna produced in the womb is determined by the past vijñāna of the previous existence is according to some authorities of the nature of a reflected image, like the transmission of learning from the teacher to the disciple, like the lighting of a lamp from another lamp or like the impress of a stamp on wax. As all the skandhas are changing in life, so death also is but a similar change; there is no great break, but the same uniform sort of destruction and coming into being. New skandhas are produced as simultaneously as the two scale pans of a balance rise up and fall, in the same manner as a lamp is lighted or an image is reflected. At the death of the man the vijñāna resulting from his previous karmas and vijñānas enters into the womb of that mother (animal, man or the gods) in which the next skandhas are to be matured. This vijñāna thus forms the principle of the new life. It is in this vijñāna that name (*nāma*) and form (*rūpa*) become associated.

The vijñāna is indeed a direct product of the saṃskāras and the sort of birth in which vijñāna should bring down (*nāmayati*) the new existence (*upapatti*) is determined by the saṃskāras[2], for in reality the happening of death (*maraṇabkava*) and the instillation of the vijñāna as the beginning of the new life (*upapatti-bhava*) cannot be simultaneous, but the latter succeeds just at the next moment, and it is to signify this close succession that they are said to be simultaneous. If the vijñāna had not entered the womb then no nāmarūpa could have appeared[3].

This chain of twelve causes extends over three lives. Thus avidyā and saṃskāra of the past life produce the vijñāna, nāma-

[1] The deities of the gardens, the woods, the trees and the plants, finding the master of the house, Citta, ill said "make your resolution, 'May I be a cakravarttī king in a next existence,' " *Saṃyutta*, IV. 303.

[2] "*sa cedānandavijñānaṃ mātuḥkukṣim nāvakrāmeta, na tat kalalam kalalatvāya sannivartteta*," *M.* V. 552. Compare *Caraka*, *Śārīra*, III. 5—8, where he speaks of a "upapāduka sattva '' which connects the soul with body and by the absence of which the character is changed, the senses become affected and life ceases, when it is in a pure condition one can remember even the previous births; character, purity, antipathy, memory, fear, energy, all mental qualities are produced out of it. Just as a chariot is made by the combination of many elements, so is the foetus.

[3] *Madhyamaka vṛtti* (B. T. S. 202-203). Poussin quotes from *Dīgha*, II. 63, "si le vijñāna ne descendait pas dans le sein maternel la namarupa s'y constituerait-il?" Govindānanda on Śaṅkara's commentary on the *Brahma-sūtras* (II. ii. 19) says that the first consciousness (vijñāna) of the foetus is produced by the saṃskāras of the previous birth, and from that the four elements (which he calls nāma) and from that the white and red, semen and ovum, and the first stage of the foetus (*kalala-budbudhāvastā*) is produced.

rūpa, ṣaḍāyatana, sparśa, vedanā, tṛṣṇā, upādāna and the bhava (leading to another life) of the present actual life. This bhava produces the jāti and jarāmaraṇa of the next life[1].

It is interesting to note that these twelve links in the chain extending in three sections over three lives are all but the manifestations of sorrow to the bringing in of which they naturally determine one another. Thus *Abhidhammatthasaṅgaha* says "each of these twelve terms is a factor. For the composite term 'sorrow' etc. is only meant to show incidental consequences of birth. Again when 'ignorance' and 'the actions of the mind' have been taken into account, craving (*tṛṣṇā*), grasping (*upādāna*) and (*karma*) becoming (*bhava*) are implicitly accounted for also. In the same manner when craving, grasping and (*karma*) becoming have been taken into account, ignorance and the actions of the mind are (implicitly) accounted for, also; and when birth, decay, and death are taken into account, even the fivefold fruit, to wit (rebirth), consciousness, and the rest are accounted for. And thus:

Five causes in the Past and Now a fivefold 'fruit.'

Five causes Now and yet to come a fivefold 'fruit' make up the Twenty Modes, the Three Connections (I. saṅkhāra and viññāna, 2. vedanā and taṇhā, 3. bhava and jāti) and the four groups (one causal group in the Past, one resultant group in the Present, one causal group in the Present and one resultant group in the Future, each group consisting of five modes)[2]."

These twelve interdependent links (*dvādaśānga*) represent the paṭiccasamuppāda (*pratītyasamutpāda*) doctrines (dependent origination)[3] which are themselves but sorrow and lead to cycles of sorrow. The term paṭiccasamuppāda or pratītyasamutpāda has been differently interpreted in later Buddhist literature[4].

[1] This explanation probably cannot be found in the early Pāli texts; but Buddhaghoṇa mentions it in *Sumaṅgalavilāsinī* on *Mahānidāna suttanta.* We find it also in *Abhidhammatthasaṅgaha,* VIII. 3. Ignorance and the actions of the mind belong to the past; "birth," "decay and death" to the future; the intermediate eight to the present. It is styled as trikāṇḍaka (having three branches) in *Abhidharmakośa,* III. 20-24. Two in the past branch, two in the future and eight in the middle "*sa pratītyasamutpādo dvādaśāngastrikāṇḍakaḥ pūrvāparāntayordve dve madhyeṣṭau.*"

[2] Aung and Mrs Rhys Davids' translation of *Abhidhammatthasaṅgaha,* pp. 189-190.

[3] The twelve links are not always constant. Thus in the list given in the *Dialogues of the Buddha,* II. 23 f., avijjā and saṅkhāra have been omitted and the start has been made with consciousness, and it has been said that "Cognition turns back from name and form; it goes not beyond."

[4] *M. V.* p. 5 f.

Samutpāda means appearance or arising (*prādurbhāva*) and pratītya means after getting (*prati+i+ya*); combining the two we find, arising after getting (something). The elements, depending on which there is some kind of arising, are called hetu (cause) and paccaya (ground). These two words however are often used in the same sense and are interchangeable. But paccaya is also used in a specific sense. Thus when it is said that avijjā is the paccaya of saṅkhāra it is meant that avijjā is the ground (*ṭhiti*) of the origin of the saṅkhāra, is the ground of their movement, of the instrument through which they stand (*nimittaṭṭhiti*), of their āyuhana (conglomeration), of their interconnection, of their intelligibility, of their conjoint arising, of their function as cause and of their function as the ground with reference to those which are determined by them. Avijjā in all these nine ways is the ground of saṅkhāra both in the past and also in the future, though avijjā itself is determined in its turn by other grounds[1]. When we take the hetu aspect of the causal chain, we cannot think of anything else but succession, but when we take the paccaya aspect we can have a better vision into the nature of the cause as ground. Thus when avijjā is said to be the ground of the saṅkhāras in the nine ways mentioned above, it seems reasonable to think that the saṅkhāras were in some sense regarded as special manifestations of avijjā[2]. But as this point was not further developed in the early Buddhist texts it would be unwise to proceed further with it.

The Khandhas.

The word khandha (Skr. skandha) means the trunk of a tree and is generally used to mean group or aggregate[3]. We have seen that Buddha said that there was no ātman (soul). He said that when people held that they found the much spoken of soul, they really only found the five khandhas together or any one of them. The khandhas are aggregates of bodily and psychical states which are immediate with us and are divided into five

[1] See *Paṭisambhidāmagga*, vol. I. p. 50; see also *Majjhima Nikāya*, I. 67, *saṅkhārā .... avijjānidānā avijjāsamudayā avijjājātikā avijjāpabhavā*.

[2] In the Yoga derivation of asmitā (egoism), rāga (attachment), dveṣa (antipathy) and abhiniveśa (self love) from avidyā we find also that all the five are regarded as the five special stages of the growth of avidyā (*pañcaparvā avidyā*).

[3] The word skandha is used in Chāndogya, II. 23 (*trayo dharmaskandhāh yajñaḥ adhyayanam dānam*) in the sense of branches and in almost the same sense in Maitrī, VII. II.

classes: (1) rūpa (four elements, the body, the senses), sense data, etc., (2) vedanā (feeling—pleasurable, painful and indifferent), (3) saññā (conceptual knowledge), (4) saṅkhāra (synthetic mental states and the synthetic functioning of compound sense-affections, compound feelings and compound concepts), (5) viññāna (consciousness)[1].

All these states rise depending one upon the other (*paṭicca-samuppanna*) and when a man says that he perceives the self he only deludes himself, for he only perceives one or more of these. The word rūpa in rūpakhandha stands for matter and material qualities, the senses, and the sense data[2]. But "rūpa" is also used in the sense of pure organic affections or states of mind as we find in the *Khandha Yamaka*, I. p. 16, and also in *saṃyutta Nikāya*, III. 86. Rūpaskandha according to *Dharma-saṃgraha* means the aggregate of five senses, the five sensations, and the implicatory communications associated in sense perceptions (*vijñapti*).

The elaborate discussion of *Dhammasaṅgaṇi* begins by defining rūpa as "*cattāro ca mahābhūtā catunnañca mahābhūtānam upādāya rūpam*" (the four mahābhūtas or elements and that proceeding from the grasping of that is called rūpa)[3]. Buddhaghoṣa explains it by saying that rūpa means the four mahābhūtas and those which arise depending (*nissāya*) on them as a modification of them. In the rūpa the six senses including their affections are also included. In explaining why the four elements are called mahābhūtas, Buddhaghoṣa says: "Just as a magician (*māyākāra*) makes the water which is not hard appear as hard, makes the stone which is not gold appear as gold; just as he himself though not a ghost nor a bird makes himself appear as a ghost or a bird, so these elements though not themselves blue make themselves appear as blue (*nīlam upādā rūpam*), not yellow, red, or white make themselves appear as yellow, red or white (*odātam upādārūpam*), so on account of their similarity to the appearances created by the magician they are called mahābhūta[4]."

In the *Saṃyutta Nikāya* we find that the Buddha says, "O Bhikkhus it is called rūpam because it manifests (*rūpyati*); how

[1] *Saṃyutta Nikāya*, III. 86, etc.

[2] *Abhidhammatthasaṅgaha*, J.P. T. S. 1884, p. 27 ff.

[3] *Dhammasaṅgaṇi*, pp. 124-179.

[4] *Atthasālinī*, p. 299.

does it manifest? It manifests as cold, and as heat, as hunger and as thirst, it manifests as the touch of gnats, mosquitos, wind, the sun and the snake; it manifests, therefore it is called rūpa[1]."

If we take the somewhat conflicting passages referred to above for our consideration and try to combine them so as to understand what is meant by rūpa, I think we find that that which manifested itself to the senses and organs was called rūpa. No distinction seems to have been made between the sense-data as colours, smells, etc., as existing in the physical world and their appearance as sensations. They were only numerically different and the appearance of the sensations was dependent upon the sense-data and the senses but the sense-data and the sensations were "rūpa." Under certain conditions the sense-data were followed by the sensations. Buddhism did not probably start with the same kind of division of matter and mind as we now do. And it may not be out of place to mention that such an opposition and duality were found neither in the Upaniṣads nor in the Sāṃkhya system which is regarded by some as pre-Buddhistic. The four elements manifested themselves in certain forms and were therefore called rūpa; the forms of affection that appeared were also called rūpa; many other mental states or features which appeared with them were also called rūpa[2]. The āyatanas or the senses were also called rūpa[3]. The mahābhūtas or four elements were themselves but changing manifestations, and they together with all that appeared in association with them were called rūpa and formed the rūpa khandha (the classes of sense-materials, sense-data, senses and sensations).

In *Saṃyutta Nikāya* (III. 101) it is said that "the four mahābhūtas were the hetu and the paccaya for the communication of the rūpakkhandha (*rūpakkhandhassa paññāpanāya*). Contact (sense-contact, phassa) is the cause of the communication of feelings (*vedanā*); sense-contact was also the hetu and paccaya for the communication of the saññākkhandha; sense-contact is also the hetu and paccaya for the communication of the saṅkhāra-kkhandha. But nāmarūpa is the hetu and the paccaya for the communication of the viññānakkhandha." Thus not only feelings arise on account of the sense-contact but saññā and saṅkhāra also arise therefrom. Saññā is that where specific knowing or

[1] *Saṃyutta Nikāya*, III. 86.
[2] *Khandhayamaka*.
[3] *Dhammasaṅgaṇi*, p. 124 ff.

conceiving takes place. This is the stage where the specific distinctive knowledge as the yellow or the red takes place.

Mrs Rhys Davids writing on saññā says: "In editing the second book of the Abhidhamma piṭaka I found a classification distinguishing between saññā as cognitive assimilation on occasion of sense, and saññā as cognitive assimilation of ideas by way of naming. The former is called perception of resistance, or opposition (*patigha-saññā*). This, writes Buddhaghoṣa, is perception on occasion of sight, hearing, etc., when consciousness is aware of the impact of impressions; of external things as different, we might say. The latter is called perception of the equivalent word or name (*adhivachānā-saññā*) and is exercised by the *sensus communis* (mano), when e.g. 'one is seated...and asks another who is thoughtful: "What are you thinking of?" one perceives through his speech.' Thus there are two stages of saññā-consciousness, 1. contemplating sense-impressions, 2. ability to know what they are by naming[1]."

About saṅkhāra we read in *Saṃyutta Nikāya* (III. 87) that it is called saṅkhāra because it synthesises (*abhisaṅkharonti*), it is that which conglomerated rūpa as rūpa, conglomerated saññā as saññā, saṅkhāra as saṅkhāra and consciousness (*viññāna*) as consciousness. It is called saṅkhāra because it synthesises the conglomerated (*saṅkhatam abhisaṅkharonti*). It is thus a synthetic function which synthesises the passive rūpa, saññā, saṅkhāra and viññāna elements. The fact that we hear of 52 saṅkhāra states and also, that the saṅkhāra exercises its synthetic activity on the conglomerated elements in it, goes to show that probably the word saṅkhāra is used in two senses, as mental states and as synthetic activity.

Viññāna or consciousness meant according to Buddhaghoṣa, as we have already seen in the previous section, both the stage at which the intellectual process started and also the final resulting consciousness.

Buddhaghoṣa in explaining the process of Buddhist psychology says that "consciousness (*citta*) first comes into touch (*phassa*) with its object (*ārammaṇa*) and thereafter feeling, conception (*saññā*) and volition (*cetanā*) come in. This contact is like the pillars of a palace, and the rest are but the superstructure built upon it (*dabbasambhārasadisā*). But it should not be thought that contact

[1] *Buddhist Psychology*, pp. 49, 50.

is the beginning of the psychological processes, for in one whole consciousness (*ekacittasmiṃ*) it cannot be said that this comes first and that comes after, so we can take contact in association with feeling (*vedanā*), conceiving (*saññā*) or volition (*cetanā*); it is itself an immaterial state but yet since it comprehends objects it is called contact." "There is no impinging on one side of the object (as in physical contact), nevertheless contact causes consciousness and object to be in collision, as visible object and visual organs, sound and hearing; thus impact is its *function*; or it has impact as its *essential property* in the sense of attainment, owing to the impact of the physical basis with the mental object. For it is said in the Commentary:— "contact in the four planes of existence is never without the characteristic of touch with the object; but the function of impact takes place in the five doors. For to sense, or five-door contact, is given the name 'having the characteristic of touch' as well as 'having the function of impact.' But to contact in the mind-door there is only the characteristic of touch, but not the function of impact. And then this Sutta is quoted 'As if, sire, two rams were to fight, one ram to represent the eye, the second the visible object and their collision contact. And as if, sire, two cymbals were to strike against each other, or two hands were to clap against each other; one hand would represent the eye, the second the visible object and their collision contact. Thus contact has the characteristic of touch and the function of impact[1]'. Contact is the manifestation of the union of the three (the object, the consciousness and the sense) and its effect is feeling (*vedanā*); though it is generated by the objects it is felt in the consciousness and its chief feature is experiencing (*anubhava*) the taste of the object. As regards enjoying the taste of an object, the remaining associated states enjoy it only partially. Of contact there is (the function of) the mere touching, of perception the mere noting or perceiving, of volition the mere coordinating, of consciousness the mere cognizing. But feeling alone, through governance, proficiency, mastery, enjoys the taste of an object. For feeling is like the king, the remaining states are like the cook. As the cook, when he has prepared food of diverse tastes, puts it in a basket, seals it, takes it to the king, breaks the seal, opens the basket, takes the best of all the soup and curries, puts them in a dish, swallows (a portion) to find out

[1] *Atthasālinī*, p. 108; translation, pp. 143-144.

whether they are faulty or not and afterwards offers the food of various excellent tastes to the king, and the king, being lord, expert, and master, eats whatever he likes, even so the mere tasting of the food by the cook is like the partial enjoyment of the object by the remaining states, and as the cook tastes a portion of the food, so the remaining states enjoy a portion of the object, and as the king, being lord, expert and master, eats the meal according to his pleasure so feeling being lord expert, and master, enjoys the taste of the object and therefore it is said that enjoyment or experience is its function[1]."

The special feature of saññā is said to be the recognizing (*paccabhiññā*) by means of a sign (*abhiññānena*). According to another explanation, a recognition takes place by the inclusion of the totality (of aspects)—*sabbasaṇgahikavasena*. The work of volition (*cetanā*) is said to be coordination or binding together (*abhisandahana*). "Volition is exceedingly energetic and makes a double effort, a double exertion. Hence the Ancients said 'Volition is like the nature of a landowner, a cultivator who taking fifty-five strong men, went down to the fields to reap. He was exceedingly energetic and exceedingly strenuous; he doubled his strength and said "Take your sickles" and so forth, pointed out the portion to be reaped, offered them drink, food, scent, flowers, etc., and took an equal share of the work.' The simile should be thus applied: volition is like the cultivator, the fifty-five moral states which arise as factors of consciousness are like the fifty-five strong men; like the time of doubling strength, doubling effort by the cultivator is the doubled strength, doubled effort of volition as regards activity in moral and immoral acts[2]." It seems that probably the active side operating in saṅkhāra was separately designated as cetanā (volition).

"When one says 'I,' what he does is that he refers either to all the khandhas combined or any one of them and deludes himself that that was 'I.' Just as one could not say that the fragrance of the lotus belonged to the petals, the colour or the pollen, so one could not say that the rūpa was 'I' or that the vedanā was 'I' or any of the other khandhas was 'I.' There is nowhere to be found in the khandhas 'I am[3]'."

[1] *Atthasālinī*, pp. 109–110; translation, pp. 145–146.

[2] *Ibid*. p. 111; translation, pp. 147–148.

[3] *Saṃyutta Nikāya*, III. 130.

Avijjā and Āsava.

As to the question how the avijjā (ignorance) first started there can be no answer, for we could never say that either ignorance or desire for existence ever has any beginning[1]. Its fruition is seen in the cycle of existence and the sorrow that comes in its train, and it comes and goes with them all. Thus as we can never say that it has any beginning, it determines the elements which bring about cycles of existence and is itself determined by certain others. This mutual determination can only take place in and through the changing series of dependent phenomena, for there is nothing which can be said to have any absolute priority in time or stability. It is said that it is through the coming into being of the āsavas or depravities that the avijjā came into being, and that through the destruction of the depravities (*āsava*) the avijjā was destroyed[2]. These āsavas are classified in the *Dhammasaṅgaṇi* as kāmāsava, bhavāsava, diṭṭthāsava and avijjāsava. Kāmāsava means desire, attachment, pleasure, and thirst after the qualities associated with the senses; bhavāsava means desire, attachment and will for existence or birth; diṭṭthāsava means the holding of heretical views, such as, the world is eternal or non-eternal, or that the world will come to an end or will not come to an end, or that the body and the soul are one or are different; avijjāsava means the ignorance of sorrow, its cause, its extinction and its means of extinction. *Dhammasaṅgaṇi* adds four more supplementary ones, viz. ignorance about the nature of anterior mental khandhas, posterior mental khandhas, anterior and posterior together, and their mutual dependence[3]. Kāmāsava and bhavāsava can as Buddhaghoṣa says be counted as one, for they are both but depravities due to attachment[4].

[1] Warren's *Buddhism in Translations* (*Visuddhimagga*, chap. XVII.), p. 17[5].

2 *M.* N. 1. p. 54. Childers translates "āsava" as "depravities" and Mrs Rhys Davids as "intoxicants." The word "āsava" in Skr. means "old wine." It is derived from "su" to produce by Buddhaghoṣa and the meaning that he gives to it is "*cira pārivāsikaṭṭhena*" (on account of its being stored up for a long time like wine). They work through the eye and the mind and continue to produce all beings up to Indra. As those wines which are kept long are called "āsavas" so these are also called āsavas for remaining a long time. The other alternative that Buddhaghoṣa gives is that they are called āsava on account of their producing saṃsāradukkha (sorrows of the world), *Atthasālinī*, p. 48. Contrast it with Jaina āsrava (flowing in of karma matter). Finding it difficult to translate it in one word after Buddhaghoṣa, I have translated it as "depravities," after Childers.

[3] See *Dhammasaṅgaṇi* p. 195.

[4] Buddhaghoṣa's *Atthasālinī*, p. 371.

The diṭṭhāsavas by clouding the mind with false metaphysical views stand in the way of one's adopting the true Buddhistic doctrines. The kāmāsavas stand in the way of one's entering into the way of Nirvāṇa (*anāgāmimagga*) and the bhavāsavas and avijjāsavas stand in the way of one's attaining arhattva or final emancipation. When the *Majjhima Nikāya* says that from the rise of the āsavas avijjā rises, it evidently counts avijjā there as in some sense separate from the other āsavas, such as those of attachment and desire of existence which veil the true knowledge about sorrow.

The afflictions (*kilesas*) do not differ much from the āsavas for they are but the specific passions in forms ordinarily familiar to us, such as covetousness (*lobha*), anger or hatred (*dosa*), infatuation (*moha*), arrogance, pride or vanity (*māna*), heresy (*diṭṭhi*), doubt or uncertainty (*vicikicchā*), idleness (*thīna*), boastfulness (*udkacca*), shamelessness (*ahirika*) and hardness of heart (*anottapa*); these kilesas proceed directly as a result of the āsavas. In spite of these varieties they are often counted as three (lobha, dosa, moha) and these together are called kilesa. They are associated with the vedanākkhandha, saññākkhandha, saṅkhārakkhandha and viññānakkhandha. From these arise the three kinds of actions, of speech, of body, and of mind[1].

Sīla and Samādhi.

We are intertwined all through outside and inside by the tangles of desire (*taṇhā jaṭā*), and the only way by which these may be loosened is by the practice of right discipline (*sīla*), concentration (*samādhi*) and wisdom (*paññā*). Sīla briefly means the desisting from committing all sinful deeds (*sabbapāpassa akaraṇam*). With sīla therefore the first start has to be made, for by it one ceases to do all actions prompted by bad desires and thereby removes the inrush of dangers and disturbances. This serves to remove the kilesas, and therefore the proper performance of the sīla would lead one to the first two successive stages of sainthood, viz. the sotāpannabhāva (the stage in which one is put in the right current) and the sakadāgāmibhāva (the stage when one has only one more birth to undergo). Samādhi is a more advanced effort, for by it all the old roots of the old kilesas are destroyed and the taṇhā or desire is removed and

[1] *Dhammasaṅgaṇi*, p. 180.

by it one is led to the more advanced states of a saint. It directly brings in paññā (true wisdom) and by paññā the saint achieves final emancipation and becomes what is called an arhat[1]. Wisdom (*paññā*) is right knowledge about the four āriya saccas, viz. sorrow, its cause, its destruction and its cause of destruction.

Sīla means those particular volitions and mental states, etc. by which a man who desists from committing sinful actions maintains himself on the right path. Sīla thus means 1. right volition (*cetanā*), 2. the associated mental states (*cetasika*), 3. mental control (*saṃvara*) and 4. the actual non-transgression (in body and speech) of the course of conduct already in the mind by the preceding three sīlas called avītikkama. Saṃvara is spoken of as being of five kinds. 1. Pāṭimokkhasaṃvara (the control which saves him who abides by it), 2. Satisaṃvara (the control of mindfulness), 3. Ñānasaṃvara (the control of knowledge), 4. Khantisaṃvara (the control of patience), 5. Viriyasaṃvara (the control of active self-restraint). Pāṭimokkhasaṃvara means all self-control in general. Satisaṃvara means the mindfulness by which one can bring in the right and good associations when using one's cognitive senses. Even when looking at any tempting object he will by virtue of his mindfulness (*sati*) control himself from being tempted by avoiding to think of its tempting side and by thinking on such aspects of it as may lead in the right direction. Khantisaṃvara is that by which one can remain unperturbed in heat and cold. By the proper adherence to sīla all our bodily, mental and vocal activities (*kamma*) are duly systematized, organized, stabilized (*samādhānam, upadhāraṇaṃ, patiṭṭhā*)[2].

The sage who adopts the full course should also follow a number of healthy monastic rules with reference to dress, sitting, dining, etc., which are called the dhūtaṅgas or pure disciplinary parts[3]. The practice of sīla and the dhūtaṅgas help the sage to adopt the course of samādhi. Samādhi as we have seen means the concentration of the mind bent on right endeavours (*kusalacittekaggatā samādhiḥ*) together with its states upon one particular object (*ekārammaṇa*) so that they may completely cease to shift and change (*sammā ca avikkhipamānā*)[4].

[1] *Visuddhimagga Nidānādikathā.*

[2] *Visuddhimagga-sīlaniddeso*, pp. 7 and 8.

[3] *Visuddhimagga*, 11.

[4] *Visuddhimagga*, pp. 84–85.

The man who has practised sīla must train his mind first in particular ways, so that it may be possible for him to acquire the chief concentration of meditation called jhāna (fixed and steady meditation). These preliminary endeavours of the mind for the acquirement of jhānasamādhi eventually lead to it and are called upacāra samādhi (preliminary samādhi) as distinguished from the jhānasamādhi called the appanāsamādhi (achieved samādhi)[1]. Thus as a preparatory measure, firstly he has to train his mind continually to view with disgust the appetitive desires for eating and drinking (*āhāre paṭikkūlasaññā*) by emphasizing in the mind the various troubles that are associated in seeking food and drink and their ultimate loathsome transformations as various nauseating bodily elements. When a man continually habituates himself to emphasize the disgusting associations of food and drink, he ceases to have any attachment to them and simply takes them as an unavoidable evil, only awaiting the day when the final dissolution of all sorrows will come[2]. Secondly he has to habituate his mind to the idea that all the parts of our body are made up of the four elements, kṣiti (earth), ap (water), tejas (fire) and wind (air), like the carcase of a cow at the butcher's shop. This is technically called catudhātuvavatthānabhāvanā (the meditation of the body as being made up of the four elements)[3]. Thirdly he has to habituate his mind to think again and again (*anussati*) about the virtues or greatness of the Buddha, the saṅgha (the monks following the Buddha), the gods and the law (*dhamma*) of the Buddha, about the good effects of sīla, and the making of gifts (*cāgānussati*), about the nature of death (*maraṇānussati*) and about the deep nature and qualities of the final extinction of all phenomena (*upasamānussati*)[4].

[1] As it is not possible for me to enter into details, I follow what appears to me to be the main line of division showing the interconnection of jhāna (Skr. *dhyāna*) with its accessory stages called parikammas (*Visuddhimagga*, pp. 85 f.).

[2] *Visuddhimagga*, pp. 341–347; mark the intense pessimistic attitude, "*Imañ ca pana āhāre paṭikulasaññāṃ anuyuttassa bhikkhuṇo rasataṇhāya cittam paṭilīyati, paṭikuṭṭati, pativaṭṭati; so, kantāranittharaṇatthiko viya puttamaṃsaṃ vigatamado āhāraṃ āhāreti yāvad eva dukkhassa niṭṭharaṇatthāya*,"p. 347. The mind of him who inspires himself with this supreme disgust to all food, becomes free from all desires for palatable tastes, and turns its back to them and flies off from them. As a means of getting rid of all sorrow he takes his food without any attachment as one would eat the flesh of his own son to sustain himself in crossing a forest.

[3] *Visuddhimagga*, pp. 347–370.

[4] *Visuddhimagga*, pp. 197–294.

Advancing further from the preliminary meditations or preparations called the upacāra samādhi we come to those other sources of concentration and meditation called the appanāsamādhi which directly lead to the achievement of the highest samādhi. The processes of purification and strengthening of the mind continue in this stage also, but these represent the last attempts which lead the mind to its final goal Nibbāna. In the first part of this stage the sage has to go to the cremation grounds and notice the diverse horrifying changes of the human carcases and think how nauseating, loathsome, unsightly and impure they are, and from this he will turn his mind to the living human bodies and convince himself that they being in essence the same as the dead carcases are as loathsome as they[1]. This is called asubhakammaṭṭhāna or the endeavour to perceive the impurity of our bodies. He should think of the anatomical parts and constituents of the body as well as their processes, and this will help him to enter into the first jhāna by leading his mind away from his body. This is called the kāyagatāsati or the continual mindfulness about the nature of the body[2]. As an aid to concentration the sage should sit in a quiet place and fix his mind on the inhaling (*passāsa*) and the exhaling (*āssāsa*) of his breath, so that instead of breathing in a more or less unconscious manner he may be aware whether he is breathing quickly or slowly; he ought to mark it definitely by counting numbers, so that by fixing his mind on the numbers counted he may fix his mind on the whole process of inhalation and exhalation in all stages of its course. This is called the ānapānasati or the mindfulness of inhalation and exhalation[3].

Next to this we come to Brahmavihāra, the fourfold meditation of mettā (universal friendship), karuṇā (universal pity), muditā (happiness in the prosperity and happiness of all) and upekkhā (indifference to any kind of preferment of oneself, his friend, enemy or a third party). In order to habituate oneself to the meditation on universal friendship, one should start with thinking how he should himself like to root out all misery and become happy, how he should himself like to avoid death and live cheerfully, and then pass over to the idea that other beings would also have the same desires. He should thus habituate himself to think that his friends, his enemies, and all those with whom he is not

[1] *Visuddhimagga*, VI.
[2] *Ibid*, pp. 239–266.
[3] *Ibid*, pp. 266–292.

connected might all live and become happy. He should fix himself to such an extent in this meditation that he would not find any difference between the happiness or safety of himself and of others. He should never become angry with any person. Should he at any time feel himself offended on account of the injuries inflicted on him by his enemies, he should think of the futility of doubling his sadness by becoming sorry or vexed on that account. He should think that if he should allow himself to be affected by anger, he would spoil all his sīla which he was so carefully practising. If anyone has done a vile action by inflicting injury, should he himself also do the same by being angry at it? If he were finding fault with others for being angry, could he himself indulge in anger? Moreover he should think that all the dhammas are momentary (*khaṇikattā*); that there no longer existed the khandhas which had inflicted the injury, and moreover the infliction of any injury being only a joint product, the man who was injured was himself an indispensable element in the production of the infliction as much as the man who inflicted the injury, and there could not thus be any special reason for making him responsible and of being angry with him. If even after thinking in this way the anger does not subside, he should think that by indulging in anger he could only bring mischief on himself through his bad deeds, and he should further think that the other man by being angry was only producing mischief to himself but not to him. By thinking in these ways the sage would be able to free his mind from anger against his enemies and establish himself in an attitude of universal friendship[1]. This is called the mettā-bhāvanā. In the meditation of universal pity (*karuṇā*) also one should sympathize with the sorrows of his friends and foes alike. The sage being more keen-sighted will feel pity for those who are apparently leading a happy life, but are neither acquiring merits nor endeavouring to proceed on the way to Nibbāna, for they are to suffer innumerable lives of sorrow[2].

We next come to the jhānas with the help of material things as objects of concentration called the Kasiṇam. These objects of concentration may either be earth, water, fire, wind, blue colour, yellow colour, red colour, white colour, light or limited space (*paricchinnākāsa*). Thus the sage may take a brown ball of earth and concentrate his mind upon it as an earth ball, sometimes

[1] *Visuddhimagga*, pp. 295–314.
[2] *Ibid*, pp. 314–315.

with eyes open and sometimes with eyes shut. When he finds that even in shutting his eyes he can visualize the object in his mind, he may leave off the object and retire to another place to concentrate upon the image of the earth ball in his mind.

In the first stages of the first meditation (*pathamam jhānam*) the mind is concentrated on the object in the way of understanding it with its form and name and of comprehending it with its diverse relations. This state of concentration is called vitakka (discursive meditation). The next stage of the first meditation is that in which the mind does not move in the object in relational terms but becomes fixed and settled in it and penetrates into it without any quivering. This state is called vicāra (steadily moving). The first stage vitakka has been compared in Buddhaghoṣa's *Visuddhimagga* to the flying of a kite with its wings flapping, whereas the second stage is compared to its flying in a sweep without the least quive of its wings. These two stages are associated with a buoyant exaltation (*pīti*) and a steady inward bliss called sukha[1] instilling the mind. The formation of this first jhāna roots out five ties of avijjā, kāmacchando (dallying with desires), vyāpādo (hatred), thīnamiddham (sloth and torpor), uddhaccakukkuccam (pride and restlessness), and vicikicchā (doubt). The five elements of which this jhāna is constituted are vitakka, vicāra, pīti, sukham and ekaggatā (one pointedness).

When the sage masters the first jhāna he finds it defective and wants to enter into the second meditation (*dutiyam jhānam*), where there is neither any vitakka nor vicāra of the first jhāna, but the mind is in one unruffled state (*ekodibhāvam*). It is a much steadier state and does not possess the movement which characterized the vitakka and the vicāra stages of the first jhāna and is therefore a very placid state (*vitakka-vicārakkhobhavirahena ativiya acalatā suppasannatā ca*). It is however associated with pīti, sukha and ekaggatā as the first jhāna was.

When the second jhāna is mastered the sage becomes disinclined towards the enjoyment of the pīti of that stage and becomes indifferent to them (*upekkhako*). A sage in this stage sees the objects but is neither pleased nor displeased. At this stage all the āsavas of the sage become loosened (*khīṇāsava*). The enjoyment of sukha however still remains in the stage and the

[1] Where there is pīti there is sukha, but where there is sukha there may not necessarily be pīti. *Visuddhimagga*, p. 145.

mind if not properly and carefully watched would like sometimes to turn back to the enjoyment of pīti again. The two characteristics of this jhāna are sukha and ekaggatā. It should however be noted that though there is the feeling of highest sukha here, the mind is not only not attached to it but is indifferent to it (*atimadhurasukhe sukhapāramippatte pi tatiyajjhāne upekkhako, na tattha sukhābhisangena ākaḍḍhiyati*)[1]. The earth ball (*paṭhavī*) is however still the object of the jhāna.

In the fourth or the last jhāna both the sukha (happiness) and the dukkha (misery) vanish away and all the roots of attachment and antipathies are destroyed. This state is characterized by supreme and absolute indifference (*upekkhā*) which was slowly growing in all the various stages of the jhānas. The characteristics of this jhāna are therefore upekkhā and ekaggatā. With the mastery of this jhāna comes final perfection and total extinction of the citta called cetovimutti, and the sage becomes thereby an arhat[2]. There is no further production of the khandhas, no rebirth, and there is the absolute cessation of all sorrows and sufferings—Nibbāna.

Kamma.

In the Katha (II. 6) Yama says that "a fool who is blinded with the infatuation of riches does not believe in a future life; he thinks that only this life exists and not any other, and thus he comes again and again within my grasp." In the Dīgha Nikāya also we read how Pāyāsi was trying to give his reasons in support of his belief that "Neither is there any other world, nor are there beings, reborn otherwise than from parents, nor is there fruit or result of deeds well done or ill done[3]." Some of his arguments were that neither the vicious nor the virtuous return to tell us that they suffered or enjoyed happiness in the other world, that if the virtuous had a better life in store, and if they believed in it, they would certainly commit suicide in order to get it at the earliest opportunity, that in spite of taking the best precautions we do not find at the time of the death of any person that his soul goes out, or that his body weighs less on account of the departure of his soul, and so on. Kassapa refutes his arguments with apt illustrations. But in spite of a few agnostics of

[1] *Visuddhimagga*, p. 163.
[2] *Majjhima Nikāya*, I. p. 296, and *Visuddhimagga*, pp. 167–168.
[3] *Dialogues of the Buddha*, II. p. 349; *D.N.* II. pp. 317 ff.

Pāyāsi's type, we have every reason to believe that the doctrine of rebirth in other worlds and in this was often spoken of in the Upaniṣads and taken as an accepted fact by the Buddha. In the *Milinda Pañha*, we find Nāgasena saying "it is through a difference in their karma that men are not all alike, but some long lived, some short lived, some healthy and some sickly, some handsome and some ugly, some powerful and some weak, some rich and some poor, some of high degree and some of low degree, some wise and some foolish[1]." We have seen in the third chapter that the same sort of views was enunciated by the Upaniṣads sages.

But karma could produce its effect in this life or any other life only when there were covetousness, antipathy and infatuation. But "when a man's deeds are performed without covetousness, arise without covetousness and are occasioned without covetousness, then inasmuch as covetousness is gone these deeds are abandoned, uprooted, pulled out of the ground like a palmyra tree and become non-existent and not liable to spring up again in the future[2]." Karma by itself without craving (*taṭhā*) is incapable of bearing good or bad fruits. Thus we read in the *Mahāsatipaṭṭhāna sutta*, "even this craving, potent for rebirth, that is accompanied by lust and self-indulgence, seeking satisfaction now here, now there, to wit, the craving for the life of sense, the craving for becoming (renewed life) and the craving for not becoming (for no new rebirth)[3]." "Craving for things visible, craving for things audible, craving for things that may be smelt, tasted, touched, for things in memory recalled. These are the things in this world that are dear, that are pleasant. There does craving take its rise, there does it dwell[4]." Pre-occupation and deliberation of sensual gratification giving rise to craving is the reason why sorrow comes. And this is the first ārya satya (noble truth).

The cessation of sorrow can only happen with "the utter cessation of and disenchantment about that very craving, giving it up, renouncing it and emancipation from it[5]."

When the desire or craving (*taṭhā*) has once ceased the sage becomes an arhat, and the deeds that he may do after that will bear no fruit. An arhat cannot have any good or bad

[1] Warren's *Buddhism in Translations*, p. 215.

[2] *Ibid*, pp. 216–217.

[3] *Dialogues of the Buddha*, II. p. 340.

[4] *Ibid*, p. 341.

[5] *Ibid*, p. 341.

fruits of whatever he does. For it is through desire that karma finds its scope of giving fruit. With the cessation of desire all ignorance, antipathy and grasping cease and consequently there is nothing which can determine rebirth. An arhat may suffer the effects of the deeds done by him in some previous birth just as Moggallāna did, but in spite of the remnants of his past karma an arhat was an emancipated man on account of the cessation of his desire[1].

Kammas are said to be of three kinds, of body, speech and mind (*kāyika*, *vācika* and *mānasika*). The root of this kamma is however volition (*cetanā*) and the states associated with it[2]. If a man wishing to kill animals goes out into the forest in search of them, but cannot get any of them there even after a long search, his misconduct is not a bodily one, for he could not actually commit the deed with his body. So if he gives an order for committing a similar misdeed, and if it is not actually carried out with the body, it would be a misdeed by speech (*vācika*) and not by the body. But the merest bad thought or ill will alone whether carried into effect or not would be a kamma of the mind (*mānasika*)[3]. But the mental kamma must be present as the root of all bodily and vocal kammas, for if this is absent, as in the case of an arhat, there cannot be any kammas at all for him.

Kammas are divided from the point of view of effects into four classes, viz. (1) those which are bad and produce impurity, (2) those which are good and productive of purity, (3) those which are partly good and partly bad and thus productive of both purity and impurity, (4) those which are neither good nor bad and productive neither of purity nor of impurity, but which contribute to the destruction of kammas[4].

Final extinction of sorrow (*nibbāna*) takes place as the natural result of the destruction of desires. Scholars of Buddhism have tried to discover the meaning of this ultimate happening, and various interpretations have been offered. Professor De la Vallée Poussin has pointed out that in the Pāli texts Nibbāna has sometimes been represented as a happy state, as pure annihilation, as an inconceivable existence or as a changeless state[5].

[1] See *Kathāvatthu* and Warren's *Buddhism in Translations*, pp. 221 ff.

[2] *Atthasālinī*, p. 88.

[3] See *Atthasālinī*, p. 90.

[4] See *Atthasālinī*, p. 89.

[5] Prof. De la Vallée Poussin's article in the *E. R. E.* on Nirvāṇa. See also *Cullavagga*, IX. i. 4; Mrs Rhys Davids's *Psalms of the early Buddhists*, I. and II., Introduction, p. XXXVII; *Dīgha*, II. 15; *Udāna*, VIII.; *Saṃyutta*, III. 109.

Mr Schrader, in discussing Nibbāna in *Pali Text Society Journal*, 1905, says that the Buddha held that those who sought to become identified after death with the soul of the world as infinite space (*ākāsa*) or consciousness (*viññāna*) attained to a state in which they had a corresponding feeling of infiniteness without having really lost their individuality. This latter interpretation of Nibbāna seems to me to be very new and quite against the spirit of the Buddhistic texts. It seems to me to be a hopeless task to explain Nibbāna in terms of worldly experience, and there is no way in which we can better indicate it than by saying that it is a cessation of all sorrow; the stage at which all worldly experiences have ceased can hardly be described either as positive or negative. Whether we exist in some form eternally or do not exist is not a proper Buddhistic question, for it is a heresy to think of a Tathāgata as existing eternally (*śāśvata*) or not-existing (*aśāśvata*) or whether he is existing as well as not existing or whether he is neither existing nor non-existing. Any one who seeks to discuss whether Nibbāna is either a positive and eternal state or a mere state of non-existence or annihilation, takes a view which has been discarded in Buddhism as heretical. It is true that we in modern times are not satisfied with it, for we want to know what it all means. But it is not possible to give any answer since Buddhism regarded all these questions as illegitimate.

Later Buddhistic writers like Nāgārjuna and Candrakīrti took advantage of this attitude of early Buddhism and interpreted it as meaning the non-essential character of all existence. Nothing existed, and therefore any question regarding the existence or non-existence of anything would be meaningless. There is no difference between the wordly stage (*saṃsāra*) and Nibbāna, for as all appearances are non-essential, they never existed during the saṃsāra so that they could not be annihilated in Nibbāna.

Upaniṣads and Buddhism.

The Upaniṣads had discovered that the true self was ānanda (bliss)[1]. We could suppose that early Buddhism tacitly pre-supposes some such idea. It was probably thought that if there was the self (*attā*) it must be bliss. The Upaniṣads had asserted that the self (*ātman*) was indestructible and eternal[2]. If we are allowed

[1] Tait. II. 5.
[2] Bṛh. IV. 5. 14. Kaṭha. V. 13.

to make explicit what was implicit in early Buddhism we could conceive it as holding that if there was the self it must be bliss, because it was eternal. This causal connection has not indeed been anywhere definitely pronounced in the Upaniṣads, but he who carefully reads the Upaniṣads cannot but think that the reason why the Upaniṣads speak of the self as bliss is that it is eternal. But the converse statement that what was not eternal was sorrow does not appear to be emphasized clearly in the Upaniṣads. The important postulate of the Buddha is that that which is changing is sorrow, and whatever is sorrow is not self[1]. The point at which Buddhism parted from the Upaniṣads lies in the experiences of the self. The Upaniṣads doubtless considered that there were many experiences which we often identify with self, but which are impermanent. But the belief is found in the Upaniṣads that there was associated with these a permanent part as well, and that it was this permanent essence which was the true and unchangeable self, the blissful. They considered that this permanent self as pure bliss could not be defined as this, but could only be indicated as not this, not this (*neti neti*)[2]. But the early Pāli scriptures hold that we could nowhere find out such a permanent essence, any constant self, in our changing experiences. All were but changing phenomena and therefore sorrow and therefore non-self, and what was non-self was not mine, neither I belonged to it, nor did it belong to me as my self[3].

The true self was with the Upaniṣads a matter of transcendental experience as it were, for they said that it could not be described in terms of anything, but could only be pointed out as "there," behind all the changing mental categories. The Buddha looked into the mind and saw that it did not exist. But how was it that the existence of this self was so widely spoken of as demonstrated in experience? To this the reply of the Buddha was that what people perceived there when they said that they perceived the self was but the mental experiences either individually or together. The ignorant ordinary man did not know the noble truths and was not trained in the way of wise men, and considered himself to be endowed with form (*rūpa*) or found the forms in his self or the self in the forms. He

[1] *Saṃyutta Nikāya*, III. pp. 44–45 ff.

[2] See Bṛh. IV. iv. Chāndogya, VIII. 7–12.

[3] *Saṃyutta Nikāya*, III. 45.

experienced the thought (of the moment) as it were the self or experienced himself as being endowed with thought, or the thought in the self or the self in the thought. It is these kinds of experiences that he considered as the perception of the self[1].

The Upaniṣads did not try to establish any school of discipline or systematic thought. They revealed throughout the dawn of an experience of an immutable Reality as the self of man, as the only abiding truth behind all changes. But Buddhism holds that this immutable self of man is a delusion and a false knowledge. The first postulate of the system is that impermanence is sorrow. Ignorance about sorrow, ignorance about the way it originates, ignorance about the nature of the extinction of sorrow, and ignorance about the means of bringing about this extinction represent the fourfold ignorance (*avijjā*)[2]. The avidyā, which is equivalent to the Pāli word avijjā, occurs in the Upaniṣads also, but there it means ignorance about the ātman doctrine, and it is sometimes contrasted with vidyā or true knowledge about the self (*ātman*)[3]. With the Upaniṣads the highest truth was the permanent self, the bliss, but with the Buddha there was nothing permanent; and all was change; and all change and impermanence was sorrow[4]. This is, then, the cardinal truth of Buddhism, and ignorance concerning it in the above fourfold ways represented the fourfold ignorance which stood in the way of the right comprehension of the fourfold cardinal truths (*āriya sacca*)—sorrow, cause of the origination of sorrow, extinction of sorrow, and the means thereto.

There is no Brahman or supreme permanent reality and no self, and this ignorance does not belong to any ego or self as we may ordinarily be led to suppose.

Thus it is said in the *Visuddhimagga* "inasmuch however as ignorance is empty of stability from being subject to a coming into existence and a disappearing from existence...and is empty of a self-determining Ego from being subject to dependence,—...or in other words inasmuch as ignorance is not an Ego, and similarly with reference to Karma and the rest—therefore is it to be understood of the wheel of existence that it is empty with a twelvefold emptiness[5]."

[1] *Saṃyutta Nikāya*, III. 46.

[2] *Majjhima Nikāya*, I. p. 54.

[3] Chā. I. I. 10. Bṛh. IV. 3. 20. There are some passages where vidyā and avidyā have been used in a different and rather obscure sense, Íśā 9–11.

[4] *Aṅg. Nikāya*, III. 85.

[5] Warren's *Budahism in Translations* (*Visuddhimagga*, chap. XVII.), p.175.

The Schools of Theravāda Buddhism.

There is reason to believe that the oral instructions of the Buddha were not collected until a few centuries after his death. Serious quarrels arose amongst his disciples or rather amongst the successive generations of the disciples of his disciples about his doctrines and other monastic rules which he had enjoined upon his followers. Thus we find that when the council of Vesāli decided against the Vṛjin monks, called also the Vajjiputtakas, they in their turn held another great meeting (Mahāsaṅgha) and came to their own decisions about certain monastic rules and thus came to be called as the Mahāsaṅghikas[1]. According to Vasumitra as translated by Vassilief, the Mahāsaṅghikas seceded in B.C. 400 and during the next one hundred years they gave rise first to the three schools Ekavyavahārikas, Lokottaravādins, and Kukkulikas and after that the Bahuśrutīyas. In the course of the next one hundred years, other schools rose out of it namely the Prajñaptivādins, Caittikas, Aparaśailas and Uttaraśailas. The Theravāda or the Sthaviravāda school which had convened the council of Vesāli developed during the second and first century B.C. into a number of schools, viz. the Haimavatas, Dharmaguptikas, Mahīśāsakas, Kāśyapīyas, Saṅkrāntikas (more well known as Sautrāntikas) and the Vātsiputtrīyas which latter was again split up into the Dharmottarīyas, Bhadrayānīyas, Sammitīyas and Channāgarikas. The main branch of the Theravāda school was from the second century downwards known as the Hetuvādins or Sarvāstivādins[2]. The *Mahābodhivaṃsa* identifies the Theravāda school with the Vibhajjavādins. The commentator of the *Kathāvatthu* who probably lived according to Mrs Rhys Davids sometime in the fifth century A.D. mentions a few other schools of Buddhists. But of all these Buddhist schools we know very little. Vasumitra (A.D. 100) gives us some very meagre accounts of

[1] The *Mahāvaṃsa* differs from *Dīpavaṃsa* in holding that the Vajjiputtakas did not develop into the Mahāsaṅghikas, but it was the Mahāsaṅghikas who first seceded while the Vajjiputtakas seceded independently of them. The *Mahābodhivaṃsa*, which according to Professor Geiger was composed A.D. 975— 1000, follows the Mahāvaṃsa in holding the Mahāsaṅghikas to be the first seceders and Vajjiputtakas to have seceded independently.

Vasumitra confuses the council of Vesāli with the third council of Pāṭaliputra. See introduction to translation of *Kathāvatthu* by Mrs Rhys Davids.

[2] For other accounts of the schism see Mr Aung and Mrs Rhys Davids's translation of *Kathāvatthu*, pp. xxxvi–xlv.

certain schools, of the Mahāsaṅghikas, Lokottaravādins, Ekavyavahārikas, Kukkulikas, Prajñaptivādins and Sarvāstivādins, but these accounts deal more with subsidiary matters of little philosophical importance. Some of the points of interest are (1) that the Mahāsaṅghikas were said to believe that the body was filled with mind (*citta*) which was represented as sitting, (2) that the Prajñaptivādins held that there was no agent in man, that there was no untimely death, for it was caused by the previous deeds of man, (3) that the Sarvāstivādins believed that everything existed. From the discussions found in the *Kathāvatthu* also we may know the views of some of the schools on some points which are not always devoid of philosophical interest. But there is nothing to be found by which we can properly know the philosophy of these schools. It is quite possible however that these so-called schools of Buddhism were not so many different systems but only differed from one another on some points of dogma or practice which were considered as being of sufficient interest to them, but which to us now appear to be quite trifling. But as we do not know any of their literatures, it is better not to make any unwarrantable surmises. These schools are however not very important for a history of later Indian Philosophy, for none of them are even referred to in any of the systems of Hindu thought. The only schools of Buddhism with which other schools of philosophical thought came in direct contact, are the Sarvāstivādins including the Sautrāntikas and the Vaibhāṣikas, the Yogācāra or the Vijñānavādins and the Mādhyamikas or the Śūnyavādins. We do not know which of the diverse smaller schools were taken up into these four great schools, the Sautrāntika, Vaibhāṣika, Yogācāra and the Mādhyamika schools. But as these schools were most important in relation to the development of the different systems in Hindu thought, it is best that we should set ourselves to gather what we can about these systems of Buddhistic thought.

When the Hindu writers refer to the Buddhist doctrine in general terms such as "the Buddhists say" without calling them the Vijñānavādins or the Yogācāras and the Śūnyavādins, they often refer to the Sarvāstivādins by which they mean both the Sautrāntikas and the Vaibhāṣikas, ignoring the difference that exists between these two schools. It is well to mention that there is hardly any evidence to prove that the Hindu writers were acquainted with the Theravāda doctrines as expressed in the Pāli works. The Vaibhāṣikas and the Sautrāntikas have been more or less associated with each other. Thus the *Abhidharmakośaśāstra* of Vasubandhu who was a Vaibhāṣika was commented upon by Yaśomitra who was a Sautrāntika. The difference between the Vaibhāṣikas and the Sautrāntikas that attracted the notice of the Hindu writers was this, that the former believed that external objects were directly perceived, whereas the latter believed that the existence of the external objects could only be inferred from our diversified knowledge[1]. Guṇaratna (fourteenth century A.D.) in his commentary *Tarkarahasyadīpikā* on *Ṣaḍdarśanasamuccaya* says that the Vaibhāṣika was but another name of the Āryasammitīya school. According to Guṇaratna the Vaibhāṣikas held that things existed for four moments, the moment of production, the moment of existence, the moment of decay and the moment of annihilation. It has been pointed out in Vasubandhu's *Abhidharmakośa* that the Vaibhāṣikas believed these to be four kinds of forces which by coming in combination with the permanent essence of an entity produced its impermanent manifestations in life (see Prof. Stcherbatsky's translation of Yaśomitra on *Abhidharmakośa kārikā*, v. 25). The self called pudgala also possessed those characteristics. Knowledge was formless and was produced along with its object by the very same conditions (*arthasahabhāsī ekasamāgryadhīnaḥ*). The Sautrāntikas according to Guṇaratna held that there was no soul but only the five skandhas. These skandhas transmigrated. The past, the future, annihilation, dependence on cause, ākāśa and pudgala are but names (*saṃjñāmātram*), mere assertions (*pratijñāmātraṃ*), mere limitations (*samvṛtamātram*) and mere phenomena (*vyavahāramātram*). By pudgala they meant that which other people called eternal and all pervasive soul. External objects are never directly perceived but are only inferred as existing for explaining the diversity of knowledge. Definite cognitions are valid; all compounded things are momentary (*kṣaṇikāḥ sarvasaṃskārāḥ*).

[1] Mādhavācārya's *Sarvadarśanasaṃgraha*, chapter II. *Śāstradīpikā*, the discussions on Pratyakṣa, Amalānanda's commentary (on *Bhāmatī*) *Vedāntakalpataru*, p. 286, "*vaibhāṣikasya bāhyo'rthaḥ pratyakṣaḥ, sautrāntikasya jñānagatākāravaicitryeṇ anumeyaḥ.*" The nature of the inference of the Sautrāntikas is shown thus by Amalānanda (A.D. 1247–1260) "*ye yasmin satyapi kādācitkāḥ te tadatiriktāpekṣāḥ*" (those (i.e. cognitions) which in spite of certain unvaried conditions are of unaccounted diversity must depend on other things in addition to these, i.e. the external objects) *Vedāntakalpataru*, p. 289.

The atoms of colour, taste, smell and touch, and cognition are being destroyed every moment. The meanings of words always imply the negations of all other things, excepting that which is intended to be signified by that word (*anyāpohaḥ śabdārtkaḥ*). Salvation (*mokṣa*) comes as the result of the destruction of the process of knowledge through continual meditation that there is no soul[1].

One of the main differences between the Vibhajjavādins, Sautrāntikas and the Vaibhāṣikas or the Sarvāstivādins appears to refer to the notion of time which is a subject of great interest with Buddhist philosophy. Thus *Abhidharmakośa* (v. 24...) describes the Sarvāstivādins as those who maintain the universal existence of everything past, present and future. The Vibhajjavādins are those "who maintain that the present elements and those among the past that have not yet produced their fruition, are existent, but they deny the existence of the future ones and of those among the past that have already produced fruition." There were four branches of this school represented by Dharmatrāta, Ghoṣa, Vasumitra and Buddhadeva. Dharmatrāta maintained that when an element enters different times, its existence changes but not its essence, just as when milk is changed into curd or a golden vessel is broken, the form of the existence changes though the essence remains the same. Ghoṣa held that "when an element appears at different times, the past one retains its past aspects without being severed from its future and present aspects, the present likewise retains its present aspect without completely losing its past and future aspects," just as a man in passionate love with a woman does not lose his capacity to love other women though he is not actually in love with them. Vasumitra held that an entity is called present, past and future according as it produces its efficiency, ceases to produce after having once produced it or has not yet begun to produce it. Buddhadeva maintained the view that just as the same woman may be called mother, daughter, wife, so the same entity may be called present, past or future in accordance with its relation to the preceding or the succeeding moment.

All these schools are in some sense Sarvāstivādins, for they maintain universal existence. But the Vaibhāṣika finds them all defective excepting the view of Vasumitra. For Dharmatrāta's

[1] Guṇaratna's *Tarkarahasyadīpikā*, pp. 46–47.

view is only a veiled Sāṃkhya doctrine; that of Ghoṣa is a confusion of the notion of time, since it presupposes the coexistence of all the aspects of an entity at the same time, and that of Buddhadeva is also an impossible situation, since it would suppose that all the three times were found together and included in one of them. The Vaibhāṣika finds himself in agreement with Vasumitra's view and holds that the difference in time depends upon the difference of the function of an entity; at the time when an entity does not actually produce its function it is future; when it produces it, it becomes present; when after having produced it, it stops, it becomes past; there is a real existence of the past and the future as much as of the present. He thinks that if the past did not exist and assert some efficiency it could not have been the object of my knowledge, and deeds done in past times could not have produced its effects in the present time. The Sautrāntika however thought that the Vaibhāṣika's doctrine would imply the heretical doctrine of eternal existence, for according to them the stuff remained the same and the time-difference appeared in it. The true view according to him was, that there was no difference between the efficiency of an entity, the entity and the time of its appearance. Entities appeared from non-existence, existed for a moment and again ceased to exist. He objected to the Vaibhāṣika view that the past is to be regarded as existent because it exerts efficiency in bringing about the present on the ground that in that case there should be no difference between the past and the present, since both exerted efficiency. If a distinction is made between past, present and future efficiency by a second grade of efficiencies, then we should have to continue it and thus have a vicious infinite. We can know non-existent entities as much as we can know existent ones, and hence our knowledge of the past does not imply that the past is exerting any efficiency. If a distinction is made between an efficiency and an entity, then the reason why efficiency started at any particular time and ceased at another would be inexplicable. Once you admit that there is no difference between efficiency and the entity, you at once find that there is no time at all and the efficiency, the entity and the moment are all one and the same. When we remember a thing of the past we do not know it as existing in the past, but in the same way in which we knew it when it was present. We are never attracted to past passions as the Vaibhāṣika suggests, but past passions leave residues which become the causes of new passions of the present moment[1].

Again we can have a glimpse of the respective positions of the Vātsīputtrīyas and the Sarvāstivādins as represented by Vasubandhu if we attend to the discussion on the subject of the existence of soul in *Abhidharmakośa.* The argument of Vasubandhu against the existence of soul is this, that though it is true that the sense organs may be regarded as a determining cause of perception, no such cause can be found which may render the inference of the existence of soul necessary. If soul actually exists, it must have an essence of its own and must be something different from the elements or entities of a personal life. Moreover, such an eternal, uncaused and unchanging being would be without any practical efficiency (*arthakriyākāritva*) which alone determines or proves existence. The soul can thus be said to have a mere nominal existence as a mere object of current usage. There is no soul, but there are only the elements of a personal life. But the Vātsīputtrīya school held that just as fire could not be said to be either the same as the burning wood or as different from it, and yet it is separate from it, so the soul is an individual (*pudgala*) which has a separate existence, though we could not say that it was altogether different from the elements of a personal life or the same as these. It exists as being conditioned by the elements of personal life, but it cannot further be defined. But its existence cannot be denied, for wherever there is an activity, there must be an agent (e.g. Devadatta walks). To be conscious is likewise an action, hence the agent who is conscious must also exist. To this Vasubandhu replies that Devadatta (the name of a person) does not represent an unity. "It is only an unbroken continuity of momentary forces (flashing into existence), which simple people believe to be a unity and to which they give the name Devadatta. Their belief that Devadatta moves is conditioned, and is based on an analogy with their own experience, but their own continuity of life consists in constantly moving from one place to another. This movement, though regarded as

[1] I am indebted for the above account to the unpublished translation from Tibetan of a small portion of *Abhidharmakośa* by my esteemed friend Prof. Th. Stcherbatsky of Petrograd. I am grateful to him that he allowed me to utilize it.

belonging to a permanent entity, is but a series of new productions in different places, just as the expressions 'fire moves,' 'sound spreads' have the meaning of continuities (of new productions in new places). They likewise use the words 'Devadatta cognises' in order to express the fact that a cognition (takes place in the present moment) which has a cause (in the former moments, these former moments coming in close succession being called Devadatta)."

The problem of memory also does not bring any difficulty, for the stream of consciousness being one throughout, it produces its recollections when connected with a previous knowledge of the remembered object under certain conditions of attention, etc., and absence of distractive factors, such as bodily pains or violent emotions. No agent is required in the phenomena of memory. The cause of recollection is a suitable state of mind and nothing else. When the Buddha told his birth stories saying that he was such and such in such and such a life, he only meant that his past and his present belonged to one and the same lineage of momentary existences. Just as when we say "this same fire which had been consuming that has reached this object," we know that the fire is not identical at any two moments, but yet we overlook the difference and say that it is the same fire. Again, what we call an individual can only be known by descriptions such as "this venerable man, having this name, of such a caste, of such a family, of such an age, eating such food, finding pleasure or displeasure in such things, of such an age, the man who after a life of such length, will pass away having reached an age." Only so much description can be understood, but we have never a direct acquaintance with the individual; all that is perceived are the momentary elements of sensations, images, feelings, etc., and these happening at the former moments exert a pressure on the later ones. The individual is thus only a fiction, a mere nominal existence, a mere thing of description and not of acquaintance; it cannot be grasped either by the senses or by the action of pure intellect. This becomes evident when we judge it by analogies from other fields. Thus whenever we use any common noun, e.g. milk, we sometimes falsely think that there is such an entity as milk, but what really exists is only certain momentary colours, tastes, etc., fictitiously unified as milk; and "just as milk and water are conventional names (for a set of independent elements) for some colour, smell (taste and touch) taken together, so is the designation 'individual' but a common name for the different elements of which it is composed."

The reason why the Buddha declined to decide the question whether the "living being is identical with the body or not" is just because there did not exist any living being as "individual," as is generally supposed. He did not declare that the living being did not exist, because in that case the questioner would have thought that the continuity of the elements of a life was also denied. In truth the "living being" is only a conventional name for a set of constantly changing elements[1].

The only book of the Sammitīyas known to us and that by name only is the *Sammitīyaśāstra* translated into Chinese between A.D. 350 to 431; the original Sanskrit works are however probably lost[2].

The Vaibhāṣikas are identified with the Sarvāstivādins who according to *Dīpavaṃsa* V. 47, as pointed out by Takakusu, branched off from the Mahīśāsakas, who in their turn had separated from the Theravāda school.

From the *Kathāvatthu* we know (1) that the Sabbatthivādins believed that everything existed, (2) that the dawn of right attainment was not a momentary flash of insight but by a gradual process, (3) that consciousness or even samādhi was nothing but

[1] This account is based on the translation of *Aṣṭamakośasthānanibaddhaḥ pudgalaviniścayaḥ*, a special appendix to the eighth chapter of *Abhidharmakośa*, by Prof. Th. Stcherbatsky, *Bulletin de l'Académie des Sciences de Russie*, 1919.

[2] Professor De la Vallée Poussin has collected some of the points of this doctrine in an article on the Sammitīyas in the *E. R. E.* He there says that in the *Abhidharmakośavyākhyā* the Sammitīyas have been identified with the Vātsīputtrīyas and that many of its texts were admitted by the Vaibhāṣikas of a later age. Some of their views are as follows: (1) An arhat in possession of nirvāṇa can fall away; (2) there is an intermediate state between death and rebirth called *antarābhava*; (3) merit accrues not only by gift (*tyagānvaya*) but also by the fact of the actual use and advantage reaped by the man to whom the thing was given (*paribhogānvaya puṇya*); (4) not only abstention from evil deeds but a declaration of intention to that end produces merit by itself alone; (5) they believe in a pudgala (soul) as distinct from the skandhas from which it can be said to be either different or non-different. "The pudgala cannot be said to be transitory (*anitye*) like the skandhas since it transmigrates laying down the burden (*skandhas*) shouldering a new burden; it cannot be said to be permanent, since it is made of transitory constituents." This pudgala doctrine of the Sammitīyas as sketched by Professor De la Vallée Poussin is not in full agreement with the pudgala doctrine of the Sammitīyas as sketched by Guṇaratna which we have noticed above.

a flux and (4) that an arhat (saint) may fall away[1]. The Sabbatthivādins or Sarvāstivādins have a vast Abhidharma literature still existing in Chinese translations which is different from the Abhidharma of the Theravāda school which we have already mentioned[2]. These are 1. *Jñānaprasthāna Śāstra* of Kātyāyanīputtra which passed by the name of *Mahā Vibhāṣā* from which the Sabbatthivādins who followed it are called Vaibhāṣikas[3]. This work is said to have been given a literary form by Aśvaghoṣa. 2. *Dharmaskandha* by Śāriputtra. 3. *Dhātukāya* by Pūrṇa. 4. *Prajñaptiśāstra* by Maudgalyāyana. 5. *Vijñānakāya* by Devakṣema. 6. *Saṅgītiparyyāya* by śāriputtra and *Prakaraṇapāda* by Vasumitra. Vasubandhu (A.D. 420–500) wrote a work on the Vaibhāṣika[4] system in verses (*kārikā*) known as the *Abhidharmakośa*, to which he appended a commentary of his own which passes by the name *Abhidharma Kośabhāṣya* in which he pointed out some of the defects of the Vaibhāṣika school from the Sautrāntika point of view[5]. This work was commented upon by Vasumitra and Guṇamati and later on by Yaśomitra who was himself a Sautrāntika and called his work *Abhidharmakośa vyākhyā*; Saṅghabhadra a contemporary of Vasubandhu wrote *Samayapradīpa* and *Nyāyānusāra* (Chinese translations of which are available) on strict Vaibhāṣika lines. We hear also of other Vaibhāṣika writers such as Dharmatrāta, Ghoṣaka, Vasumitra and Bhadanta, the writer of *Saṃyuktābhidharmaśāstra* and *Mahāvibhāṣā*. Diṅnāga (A.D. 480), the celebrated logician, a Vaibhāṣika or a Sautrāntika and reputed to be a pupil of Vasubandhu, wrote his famous work *Pramāṇasamuccaya* in which he established Buddhist logic and refuted many of the views of Vātsyāyana the celebrated commentator of the *Nyāya sūtras*; but we regret

[1] See Mrs Rhys Davids's translation *Kathāvatthu*, p. xix, and Sections I. 6, 7; II. 9 and XI. 6.

[2] *Mahāvyutpatti* gives two names for Sarvāstivāda, viz. Mūlasarvāstivāda and Āryyasarvāstivāda. Itsing (A.D. 671–695) speaks of Āryyamūlasarvāstivāda and Mūlasarvāstivāda. In his time he found it prevailing in Magadha, Guzrat, Sind, S. India, E. India. Takakusu says (*P. T. S.* 1904–1905) that Paramārtha, in his life of Vasubandhu, says that it was propagated from Kashmere to Middle India by Vasubhadra, who studied it there.

[3] Takakusu says (*P. T. S.* 1904–1905) that Kātyāyanīputtra's work was probably a compilation from other Vibhāṣās which existed before the Chinese translations and Vibhāṣā texts dated A.D. 383.

[4] See Takakusu's article *J. R. A. S.* 1905.

[5] The Sautrāntikas did not regard the Abhidharmas of the Vaibhāṣikas as authentic and laid stress on the suttanta doctrines as given in the Suttapiṭaka.

to say that none of the above works are available in Sanskrit, nor have they been retranslated from Chinese or Tibetan into any of the modern European or Indian languages.

The Japanese scholar Mr Yamakami Sogen, late lecturer at Calcutta University, describes the doctrine of the Sabbatthivādins from the Chinese versions of the *Abhidharmakośa*, *Mahāvibhāṣāśāstra*, etc., rather elaborately[1]. The following is a short sketch, which is borrowed mainly from the accounts given by Mr Sogen.

The Sabbatthivādins admitted the five skandhas, twelve āyatanas, eighteen dhātus, the three asaṃskṛta dharmas of pratisaṃkhyānirodha apratisaṃkhyānirodha and ākāśa, and the samṣkṛta dharmas (things composite and interdependent) of rūpa (matter), citta (mind), caitta (mental) and cittaviprayukta (non-mental)[2]. All effects are produced by the coming together (saṃskṛta) of a number of causes. The five skandhas, and the rūpa, citta, etc., are thus called saṃskṛta dharmas (composite things or collocations—*sambhūyakāri*). The rūpa dharmas are eleven in number, one citta dharma, 46 caitta dharmas and 14 cittaviprayukta saṃskāra dharmas (non-mental compoṣite things); adding to these the three asaṃskṛta dharmas we have the seventy-five dharmas. Rūpa is that which has the capacity to obstruct the sense organs. Matter is regarded as the collective organism or collocation, consisting of the fourfold substratum of colour, smell, taste and contact. The unit possessing this fourfold substratum is known as paramāṇu, which is the minutest form of rūpa. It cannot be pierced through or picked up or thrown away. It is indivisible, unanalysable, invisible, inaudible, untastable and intangible. But yet it is not permanent, but is like a momentary flash into being. The simple atoms are called *dravyaparamāṇu* and the compound ones *saṃghātaparamāṇu.* In the words of Prof. Stcherbatsky "the universal elements of matter are manifested in their actions or functions. They are consequently more energies than substances." The organs of sense are also regarded as modifications of atomic matter. Seven such paramāṇus combine together to form an aṇu, and it is in this combined form only that they become perceptible. The combination takes place in the form of a cluster having one atom at the centre and

[1] *Systems of Buddhistic Thought*, published by the Calcutta University.

[2] Śaṅkara in his meagre sketch of the doctrine of the Sarvāstivādins in his bhāṣya on the *Brahma-sūtras* ii. 2 notices some of the categories mentioned by Sogen.

others around it. The point which must be remembered in connection with the conception of matter is this, that the qualities of all the mahābhūtas are inherent in the paramāṇus. The special characteristics of roughness (which naturally belongs to earth), viscousness (which naturally belongs to water), heat (belonging to fire), movableness (belonging to wind), combine together to form each of the elements; the difference between the different elements consists only in this, that in each of them its own special characteristics were predominant and active, and other characteristics though present remained only in a potential form. The mutual resistance of material things is due to the quality of earth or the solidness inherent in them; the mutual attraction of things is due to moisture or the quality of water, and so forth. The four elements are to be observed from three aspects, namely, (1) as things, (2) from the point of view of their natures (such as activity, moisture, etc.), and (3) function (such as *dhṛti* or attraction, *saṃgraha* or cohesion, *pakti* or chemical heat, and *vyūhana* or clustering and collecting). These combine together naturally by other conditions or causes. The main point of distinction between the Vaibhāṣika Sarvāstivādins and other forms of Buddhism is this, that here the five skandhas and matter are regarded as permanent and eternal; they are said to be momentary only in the sense that they are changing their phases constantly, owing to their constant change of combination. Avidyā is not regarded here as a link in the chain of the causal series of pratītyasamutpāda; nor is it ignorance of any particular individual, but is rather identical with "moha" or delusion and represents the ultimate state of immaterial dharmas. Avidyā, which through saṃskāra, etc., produces nāmarūpa in the case of a particular individual, is not his avidyā in the present existence but the avidyā of his past existence bearing fruit in the present life.

"The cause never perishes but only changes its name, when it becomes an effect, having changed its state." For example, clay becomes jar, having changed its state; and in this case the name clay is lost and the name jar arises[1]. The Sarvāstivādins allowed simultaneousness between cause and effect only in the case of composite things (*saṃprayukta hetu*) and in the case of

[1] Sogen's quotation from Kumārajīva's Chinese version of Āryadeva's commentary on the *Mādhyamika śāstra* (chapter XX. Kārikā 9).

the interaction of mental and material things. The substratum of "vijñāna" or "consciousness" is regarded as permanent and the aggregate of the five senses (*indriyas*) is called the perceiver. It must be remembered that the indriyas being material had a permanent substratum, and their aggregate had therefore also a substratum formed of them.

The sense of sight grasps the four main colours of blue, yellow, red, white, and their combinations, as also the visual forms of appearance (*saṃsthāna*) of long, short, round, square, high, low, straight, and crooked. The sense of touch (*kāyendriya*) has for its object the four elements and the qualities of smoothness, roughness, lightness, heaviness, cold, hunger and thirst. These qualities represent the feelings generated in sentient beings by the objects of touch, hunger, thirst, etc., and are also counted under it, as they are the organic effects produced by a touch which excites the physical frame at a time when the energy of wind becomes active in our body and predominates over other energies; so also the feeling of thirst is caused by a touch which excites the physical frame when the energy of the element of fire becomes active and predominates over the other energies. The indriyas (senses) can after grasping the external objects arouse thought (*vijñāna*); each of the five senses is an agent without which none of the five vijñānas would become capable of perceiving an external object. The essence of the senses is entirely material. Each sense has two subdivisions, namely, the principal sense and the auxiliary sense. The substratum of the principal senses consists of a combination of paramāṇus, which are extremely pure and minute, while the substratum of the latter is the flesh, made of grosser materials. The five senses differ from one another with respect to the manner and form of their respective atomic combinations. In all sense-acts, whenever an act is performed and an idea is impressed, a latent energy is impressed on our person which is designated as avijñapti rūpa. It is called rūpa because it is a result or effect of rūpa-contact; it is called avijñapti because it is latent and unconscious; this latent energy is bound sooner or later to express itself in karma effects and is the only bridge which connects the cause and the effect of karma done by body or speech. Karma in this school is considered as twofold, namely, that as thought (*cetana karma*) and that as activity (*caitasika karma*). This last, again, is of two kinds, viz.

that due to body-motion (*kāyika karma*) and speech (*vācika karma*). Both these may again be latent (*avijñapti*) and patent (*vijñapti*), giving us the kāyika-vijñapti karma, kāyikāvijñapti karma, vācika-vijñapti karma and vācikāvijñapti karma. Avijñapti rūpa and avijñapti karma are what we should call in modern phraseology subconscious ideas, feelings and activity. Corresponding to each conscious sensation, feeling, thought or activity there is another similar subconscious state which expresses itself in future thoughts and actions; as these are not directly known but are similar to those which are known, they are called avijñapti.

The mind, says Vasubandhu, is called cittam, because it wills (*cetati*), manas because it thinks (*manvate*) and vijñāna because it discriminates (*nirdiśati*). The discrimination may be of three kinds: (1) svabhāva nirdeśa (natural perceptual discrimination), (2) prayoga nirdeśa (actual discrimination as present, past and future), and (3) anusmṛti nirdeśa (reminiscent discrimination referring only to the past). The senses only possess the *svabhāva nirdeśa*, the other two belong exclusively to manovijñāna. Each of the vijñānas as associated with its specific sense discriminates its particular object and perceives its general characteristics; the six vijñānas combine to form what is known as the Vijñānaskandha, which is presided over by mind (*mano*). There are forty-six caitta saṃskṛta dharmas. Of the three asaṃskṛta dharmas ākāśa (ether) is in essence the freedom from obstruction, establishing it as a permanent omnipresent immaterial substance (*nīrūpākkya*, non-rūpa). The second asaṃskṛta dharma, apratisaṃkhyā nirodha, means the non-perception of dharmas caused by the absence of pratyayas or conditions. Thus when I fix my attention on one thing, other things are not seen then, not because they are non-existent but because the conditions which would have made them visible were absent. The third asaṃskṛta dharma, pratisaṃkhyā nirodha, is the final deliverance from bondage. Its essential characteristic is everlastingness. These are called asaṃskṛta because being of the nature of negation they are non-collocative and hence have no production or dissolution. The eightfold noble path which leads to this state consists of right views, right aspirations, right speech, right conduct, right livelihood, right effort, right mindfulness, right rapture[1].

[1] Mr Sogen mentions the name of another Buddhist Hīnayāna thinker (about A.D. 250), Harivarman, who founded a school known as Satyasiddhi school, which propounded the same sort of doctrines as those preached by Nāgārjuna. None of his works are available in

Mahāyānism.

It is difficult to say precisely at what time Mahāyānism took its rise. But there is reason to think that as the Mahāsaṅghikas separated themselves from the Theravādins probably some time in B.C. 400 and split themselves up into eight different schools, those elements of thoughts and ideas which in later days came to be labelled as Mahāyāna were gradually on the way to taking their first inception. We hear in about A.D. 100 of a number of works which are regarded as various Mahāyāna sūtras, some of which are probably as old as at least B.C. 100 (if not earlier) and others as late as A.D. 300 or 400[1]. These Mahāyānasūtras, also called the Vaipulyasūtras, are generally all in the form of instructions given by the Buddha. Nothing is known about their authors or compilers, but they are all written in some form of Sanskrit and were probably written by those who seceded from the Theravāda school.

The word Hīnayāna refers to the schools of Theravāda, and as such it is contrasted with Mahāyāna. The words are generally translated as small vehicle (*hīna* = small, *yāna* = vehicle) and great vehicle (*makā* = great, *yāna* = vehicle). But this translation by no means expresses what is meant by Mahāyāna and Hīnayāna[2]. Asaṅga (A.D. 480) in his *Mahāyānasūtrālaṃkāra* gives

Sanskrit and I have never come across any allusion to his name by Sanskrit writers.

[1] Quotations and references to many of these sūtras are found in Candrakīrti's commentary on the *Mādhyamīka kārikās* of Nāgārjuna; some of these are the following: *Aṣṭasāhasrikāprajñāpāramitā* (translated into Chinese A.D. 164–167), *Śatasāhasrikāprajñāpāramitā*, *Gaganagañja*, *Samādhisūtra*, *Tathāgataguhyasūtra*, *Dṛḍhādhyāśayasañcodanāsūtra*, *Dhyāyitamuṣṭisūtra*, *Pitāputrasantāgamasūtra*, *Mahāyānasūtra*, *Māradamanasūtra*, *Ratnakūṭasūtra*, *Ratnacūḍāparipṛcchāsūtra*, *Ratnameghasūtra*, *Ratnarāśisūtra*, *Ratnākarasūtra*, *Rāṣṭrapālaparipṛcchāsūtra*, *Laṅkāvatārasūtra*, *Lalitavistarasūtra*, *Vajracchedikāsūtra*, *Vimalakīrttinirdeśasūtra*, *Śālīstambhasūtra*, *Samādhtrajasūtra*, *Sukhāvatīvyūha*, *Suvarṇaprabhāsasūtra*, *Saddharmapuṇḍarīka* (translated into Chinese A.D. 255), *Amitāyurdhyānasūtra*, *Hastikākhyasūtra*, etc.

[2] The word Yāna is generally translated as vehicle, but a consideration of numerous contexts in which the word occurs seems to suggest that it means career or course or way, rather than vehicle (*Lalitavistara*, pp. 25, 38; *Prajñāpāramitā*, pp. 24, 319; *Samādhtrājasūtra*, p. 1; *Karuṇāpuṇḍarīka*, p. 67; *Laṅkāvatārasūtra*, pp. 68, 108, 132). The word Yāna is as old as the Upaniṣads where we read of Devayāna and Pitṛyāna. There is no reason why this word should be taken in a different sense. We hear in *Laṅkāvatāra* of Śrāvakayāna (career of the Śrāvakas or the Theravādin Buddhists), Pratyekabuddhayāna (the career of saints before the coming of the Buddha), Buddha yāna (career of the Buddhas), Ekayāna (one career), Devayāna (career of the gods), Brahmayāna (career of becoming a Brahmā), Tathāgatayāna (career of a Tathāgata). In one place *Laṅkāvatāra* says

us the reason why one school was called Hīnayāna whereas the other, which he professed, was called Mahāyāna. He says that, considered from the point of view of the ultimate goal of religion, the instructions, attempts, realization, and time, the Hīnayāna occupies a lower and smaller place than the other called Mahā (great) Yāna, and hence it is branded as Hīna (small, or low). This brings us to one of the fundamental points of distinction between Hīnayāna and Mahāyāna. The ultimate good of an adherent of the Hīnayāna is to attain his own nirvāṇa or salvation, whereas the ultimate goal of those who professed the Mahāyāna creed was not to seek their own salvation but to seek the salvation of all beings. So the Hīnayāna goal was lower, and in consequence of that the instructions that its followers received, the attempts they undertook, and the results they achieved were narrower than that of the Mahāyāna adherents. A Hīnayāna man had only a short business in attaining his own salvation, and this could be done in three lives, whereas a Mahāyāna adherent was prepared to work for infinite time in helping all beings to attain salvation. So the Hīnayāna adherents required only a short period of work and may from that point of view also be called *hīna*, or lower.

This point, though important from the point of view of the difference in the creed of the two schools, is not so from the point of view of philosophy. But there is another trait of the Mahāyānists which distinguishes them from the Hīnayānists from the philosophical point of view. The Mahāyānists believed that all things were of a non-essential and indefinable character and void at bottom, whereas the Hīnayānists only believed in the impermanence of all things, but did not proceed further than that.

It is sometimes erroneously thought that Nāgārjuna first preached the doctrine of Śūnyavāda (essencelessness or voidness of all appearance), but in reality almost all the Mahāyāna sūtras either definitely preach this doctrine or allude to it. Thus if we take some of those sūtras which were in all probability earlier than Nāgārjuna, we find that the doctrine which Nāgārjuna expounded

that ordinarily distinction is made between the three careers and one career and no career, but these distinctions are only for the ignorant (*Laṅkāvatāra*, p. 68).

with all the rigour of his powerful dialectic was quietly accepted as an indisputable truth. Thus we find Subhūti saying to the Buddha that vedanā (feeling), saṃjñā (concepts) and the saṃskāras (conformations) are all māyā (illusion)[1]. All the skandhas, dhātus (elements) and āyatanas are void and absolute cessation. The highest knowledge of everything as pure void is not different from the skandhas, dhātus and āyatanas, and this absolute cessation of dharmas is regarded as the highest knowledge (*prajñāpāramitā*)[2]. Everything being void there is in reality no process and no cessation. The truth is neither eternal (*śāśvata*) nor non-eternal (*aśāśvata*) but pure void. It should be the object of a saint's endeavour to put himself in the "thatness" (*tathatā*) and consider all things as void. The saint (*bodhisattva*) has to establish himself in all the virtues (*pāramitā*), benevolence (*dānapāramitā*), the virtue of character (*śīlapāramitā*), the virtue of forbearance (*kṣāntipāramitā*), the virtue of tenacity and strength (*vīryyapāramitā*) and the virtue of meditation (*dhyānapāramitā*). The saint (*bodhisattva*) is firmly determined that he will help an infinite number of souls to attain nirvāṇa. In reality, however, there are no beings, there is no bondage, no salvation; and the saint knows it but too well, yet he is not afraid of this high truth, but proceeds on his career of attaining for all illusory beings illusory emancipation from illusory bondage. The saint is actuated with that feeling and proceeds in his work on the strength of his pāramitās, though in reality there is no one who is to attain salvation in reality and no one who is to help him to attain it[3]. The true prajñāpāramitā is the absolute cessation of all appearance (*yaḥ anupalambhaḥ sarvadharmāṇām sa prajñāpāramitā ityucyate*)[4].

The Mahāyāna doctrine has developed on two lines, viz. that of śūnyavāda or the Mādhyamika doctrine and Vijñānavāda. The difference between Śūnyavāda and Vijñānavāda (the theory that there is only the appearance of phenomena of consciousness) is not fundamental, but is rather one of method. Both of them agree in holding that there is no truth in anything, everything is only passing appearance akin to dream or magic. But while the Śūnyavādins were more busy in showing this indefinableness of all phenomena, the Vijñānavādins, tacitly accepting

[1] *Aṣṭasāhasrikāprajñāpāramitā*, p. 16.
[2] *Ibid*, p. 177.
[3] *Ibid*, p. 21.
[4] *Ibid*, p. 177.

the truth preached by the Śūnyavādins, interested themselves in explaining the phenomena of consciousness by their theory of beginningless illusory root-ideas or instincts of the mind (*vāsanā*).

Aśvaghoṣa (A.D. 100) seems to have been the greatest teacher of a new type of idealism (*vijñānavāda*) known as the Tathatā philosophy. Trusting in Suzuki's identification of a quotation in Aśvaghoṣa's *Śraddhotpādaśāstra* as being made from *Laṅkāvatārasūtra,* we should think of the *Laṅkāvatārasūtra* as being one of the early works of the Vijñānavādins[1]. The greatest later writer of the Vijñānavāda school was Asaṅga (A.D. 400), to whom are attributed the *Saptadaśabhūmi sūtra*, *Mahāyāna sūtra*, *Upadeśa*, *Mahāyānasamparigraha śāstra*, *Yogācārabhūmi śāstra* and *Mahāyānasūtrālaṃkāra*. None of these works excepting the last one is available to readers who have no access to the Chinese and Tibetan manuscripts, as the Sanskrit originals are in all probability lost. The Vijñānavāda school is known to Hindu writers by another name also, viz. Yogācāra, and it does not seem an improbable supposition that Asaṅga's *Yogācārabhūmi śāstra* was responsible for the new name. Vasubandhu, a younger brother of Asaṅga, was, as Paramārtha (499–569) tells us, at first a liberal Sarvāstivādin, but was converted to Vijñānavāda, late in his life, by Asaṅga. Thus Vasubandhu, who wrote in his early life the great standard work of the Sarvāstivādins, *Abhidharmakośa*, devoted himself in his later life to Vijñānavāda[2]. He is said to have commented upon a number of Mahāyāna sūtras, such as *Avataṃsaka*, *Nirvāṇa*, *Saddharmapuṇḍarīka*, *Prajñāpāramitā*, *Vimalakīrtti* and *Śrīmālāsiṃhanāda*, and compiled some Mahāyāna sūtras, such as *Vijñānamātrasiddhi*, *Ratnatraya*, etc. The school of Vijñānavāda continued for at least a century or two after Vasubandhu, but we are not in possession of any work of great fame of this school after him.

We have already noticed that the Śūnyavāda formed the fundamental principle of all schools of Mahāyāna. The most powerful exponent of this doctrine was Nāgārjuna (A.D. 100), a brief account of whose system will be given in its proper place. Nāgārjuna's kārikās (verses) were commented upon by Āryadeva, a disciple of his, Kumārajīva (A.D. 383), Buddhapālita and Candrakīrti (A.D. 550). Āryadeva in addition to this commentary wrote at

[1] Dr S. C. Vidyābhūshana thinks that *Laṅkāvatāra* belongs to about A.D. 300.

[2] Takakusu's "A study of the Paramārtha's life of Vasubandhu," *J. R. A. S.* 1905.

least three other books, viz. *Catuḥśataka*, *Hastabālaprakaraṇavṛtti* and *Cittaviśuddhiprakaraṇa*[1]. In the small work called *Hastabālaprakaraṇavṛtti* Āryadeva says that whatever depends for its existence on anything else may be proved to be illusory; all our notions of external objects depend on space perceptions and notions of part and whole and should therefore be regarded as mere appearance. Knowing therefore that all that is dependent on others for establishing itself is illusory, no wise man should feel attachment or antipathy towards these mere phenomenal appearances. In his *Cittaviśuddhiprakaraṇa* he says that just as a crystal appears to be coloured, catching the reflection of a coloured object, even so the mind though in itself colourless appears to show diverse colours by coloration of imagination (*vikalpa*). In reality the mind (*citta*) without a touch of imagination (*kalpanā*) in it is the pure reality.

It does not seem however that the Śūnyavādins could produce any great writers after Candrakīrti. References to Śūnyavāda show that it was a living philosophy amongst the Hindu writers until the time of the great Mīmaṃsā authority Kumārila who flourished in the eighth century; but in later times the Śūnyavādins were no longer occupying the position of strong and active disputants.

The Tathatā Philosophy of Aśvaghoṣa (A.D. 80) [2].

Aśvaghoṣa was the son of a Brahmin named Saiṃhaguhya who spent his early days in travelling over the different parts of India and defeating the Buddhists in open debates. He was probably converted to Buddhism by Pārśva who was an important person in the third Buddhist Council promoted, according to some authorities, by the King of Kashmere and according to other authorities by Puṇyayaśas[3].

[1] Āryadeva's *Hastabālaprakaraṇavṛtti* has been reclaimed by Dr F. W. Thomas. Fragmentary portions of his *Cittaviśuddhiprakaraṇa* were published by Mahāmahopādhyāya Haraprasāda śāstrī in the Bengal Asiatic Society's journal, 1898.

[2] The above section is based on the *Awakening of Faith*, an English translation by Suzuki of the Chinese version of *Śraddhotpādaśāstra* by Aśvaghoṣa, the Sanskrit original of which appears to have been lost. Suzuki has brought forward a mass of evidence to show that Aśvaghoṣa was a contemporary of Kaniṣka.

[3] Tāranātha says that he was converted by Āryadeva, a disciple of Nāgārjuna, *Geschichte des Buddhismus*, German translation by Schiefner, pp. 84–85. See Suzuki's *Awakening of Faith*, pp. 24–32. Aśvaghoṣa wrote the *Buddhacaritakāvya*, of great poetical excellence,

He held that in the soul two aspects may be distinguished—the aspect as thatness (*bhūtatathatā*) and the aspect as the cycle of birth and death (*saṃsāra*). The soul as bhūtatathatā means the oneness of the totality of all things (*dharmadhātu*). Its essential nature is uncreate and external. All things simply on account of the beginningless traces of the incipient and unconscious memory of our past experiences of many previous lives (*smṛti*) appear under the forms of individuation[1]. If we could overcome this smṛti "the signs of individuation would disappear and there would be no trace of a world of objects." "All things in their fundamental nature are not nameable or explicable. They cannot be adequately expressed in any form of language. They possess absolute sameness (*samatā*). They are subject neither to transformation nor to destruction. They are nothing but one soul"—thatness (*bhūtatathatā*). This "thatness" has no attribute and it can only be somehow pointed out in speech as "thatness." As soon as you understand that when the totality of existence is spoken of or thought of, there is neither that which speaks nor that which is spoken of, there is neither that which thinks nor that which is thought of, "this is the stage of thatness." This bhūtatathatā is neither that which is existence, nor that which is non-existence, nor that which is at once existence and non-existence, nor that which is not at once existence and non-existence; it is neither that which is plurality, nor that which is at once unity and plurality, nor that which is not at once unity and plurality. It is a negative concept in the sense that it is beyond all that is conditional and yet it is a positive concept in the sense that it holds all within it. It cannot be comprehended by any kind of particularization or distinction. It is only by transcending the range of our intellectual categories of the comprehension of the limited range of finite phenomena that we can get a glimpse of it. It cannot be comprehended by the particularizing consciousness of all beings, and we thus may call it negation, "śūnyatā," in this sense. The truth is that which

and the *Mahātaṃkāraśāṣtra*. He was also a musician and had invented a musical instrument called Rāstavara that he might by that means convert the people of the city. "Its melody was classical, mournful, and melodious, inducing the audience to ponder on the misery, emptiness, and non-ātmanness of life." Suzuki, p. 35.

[1] I have ventured to translate "*smṛti*" in the sense of vāsanā in preference to Suzuki's "confused subjectivity" because smṛti in the sense of vāsanā is not unlamiliar to the readers of such Buddhist works as *Laṅkāvatāra*. The word "subjectivity" seems to be too European a term to be used as a word to represent the Buddhist sense.

subjectively does not exist by itself, that the negation (*śūnyatā*) is also void (*śūnya*) in its nature, that neither that which is negated nor that which negates is an independent entity. It is the pure soul that manifests itself as eternal, permanent, immutable, and completely holds all things within it. On that account it may be called affirmation. But yet there is no trace of affirmation in it, because it is not the product of the creative instinctive memory (*smṛti*) of conceptual thought and the only way of grasping the truth—the thatness, is by transcending all conceptual creations.

"The soul as birth and death (*saṃsāra*) comes forth from the Tathāgata womb (*tathāgatagarbha*), the ultimate reality. But the immortal and the mortal coincide with each other. Though they are not identical they are not duality either. Thus when the absolute soul assumes a relative aspect by its self-affirmation it is called the all-conserving mind (*ālayavijñāna*). It embraces two principles, (1) enlightenment, (2) non-enlightenment. Enlightenment is the perfection of the mind when it is free from the corruptions of the creative instinctive incipient memory (*smṛti*). It penetrates all and is the unity of all (*dharmadhātu*). That is to say, it is the universal dharmakāya of all Tathāgatas constituting the ultimate foundation of existence.

"When it is said that all consciousness starts from this fundamental truth, it should not be thought that consciousness had any real origin, for it was merely phenomenal existence—a mere imaginary creation of the perceivers under the influence of the delusive smṛti. The multitude of people (*bahujana*) are said to be lacking in enlightenment, because ignorance (*avidyā*) prevails there from all eternity, because there is a constant succession of smṛti (past confused memory working as instinct) from which they have never been emancipated. But when they are divested of this smṛti they can then recognize that no states of mentation, viz. their appearance, presence, change and disappearance, have any reality. They are neither in a temporal nor in a spatial relation with the one soul, for they are not self-existent.

"This high enlightenment shows itself imperfectly in our corrupted phenomenal experience as prajñā (wisdom) and karma (incomprehensible activity of life). By pure wisdom we understand that when one, by virtue of the perfuming power of dharma, disciplines himself truthfully (i.e. according to the dharma) and accomplishes meritorious deeds, the mind (i.e. the *ālayavijñāna*) which implicates itself with birth and death will be broken down and the modes of the evolving consciousness will be annulled, and the pure and the genuine wisdom of the Dharmakāya will manifest itself. Though all modes of consciousness and mentation are mere products of ignorance, ignorance in its ultimate nature is identical and non-identical with enlightenment; and therefore ignorance is in one sense destructible, though in another sense it is indestructible. This may be illustrated by the simile of the water and the waves which are stirred up in the ocean. Here the water can be said to be both identical and non-identical with the waves. The waves are stirred up by the wind, but the water remains the same. When the wind ceases the motion of the waves subsides, but the water remains the same. Likewise when the mind of all creatures, which in its own nature is pure and clean, is stirred up by the wind of ignorance (*avidyā*), the waves of mentality (*vijñāna*) make their appearance. These three (i.e. the mind, ignorance, and mentality) however have no existence, and they are neither unity nor plurality. When the ignorance is annihilated, the awakened mentality is tranquillized, whilst the essence of the wisdom remains unmolested." The truth or the enlightenment "is absolutely unobtainable by any modes of relativity or by any outward signs of enlightenment. All events in the phenomenal world are reflected in enlightenment, so that they neither pass out of it, nor enter into it, and they neither disappear nor are destroyed." It is for ever cut off from the hindrances both affectional (*kleśāvaraṇa*) and intellectual (*jñeyāvaraṇa*), as well as from the mind (i.e. *ālayavijñāna*) which implicates itself with birth and death, since it is in its true nature clean, pure, eternal, calm, and immutable. The truth again is such that it transforms and unfolds itself wherever conditions are favourable in the form of a tathāgata or in some other forms, in order that all beings may be induced thereby to bring their virtue to maturity.

"Non-elightenment has no existence of its own aside from its relation with enlightenment *a priori*." But enlightenment *a priori* is spoken of only in contrast to non-enlightenment, and as non-enlightenment is a non-entity, true enlightenment in turn loses its significance too. They are distinguished only in mutual relation as enlightenment or non-enlightenment. The manifestations of nonenlightenment are made in three ways: (1) as a disturbance of the mind (*ālayavijñāna*), by the avidyākarma (ignorant action), producing misery (*duḥkha*); (2) by the appearance of an ego or of a perceiver; and (3) by the creation of an external world which does not exist in itself, independent of the perceiver. Conditioned by the unreal external world six kinds of phenomena arise in succession. The first phenomenon is intelligence (sensation); being affected by the external world the mind becomes conscious of the difference between the agreeable and the disagreeable. The second phenomenon is succession. Following upon intelligence, memory retains the sensations, agreeable as well as disagreeable, in a continuous succession of subjective states. The third phenomenon is clinging. Through the retention and succession of sensations, agreeable as well as disagreeable, there arises the desire of clinging. The fourth phenomenon is an attachment to names or ideas (*saṃjñā*), etc. By clinging the mind hypostatizes all names whereby to give definitions to all things. The fifth phenomenon is the performance of deeds (*karma*). On account of attachment to names, etc., there arise all the variations of deeds, productive of individuality. "The sixth phenomenon is the suffering due to the fetter of deeds. Through deeds suffering arises in which the mind finds itself entangled and curtailed of its freedom." All these phenomena have thus sprung forth through avidyā.

The relation between this truth and avidyā is in one sense a mere identity and may be illustrated by the simile of all kinds of pottery which though different are all made of the same clay[1]. Likewise the undefiled (*anāsrava*) and ignorance (*avidyā*) and their various transient forms all come from one and the same entity. Therefore Buddha teaches that all beings are from all eternity abiding in Nirvāṇa.

It is by the touch of ignorance (*avidyā*) that this truth assumes all the phenomenal forms of existence.

In the all-conserving mind (*ālayavijñāna*) ignorance manifests itself; and from non-enlightenment starts that which sees, that which represents, that which apprehends an objective world, and that which constantly particularizes. This is called ego (*manas*). Five different names are given to the ego (according to its different modes of operation). The first name is activity-consciousness (*karmavijñāna*) in the sense that through the agency of ignorance an unenlightened mind begins to be disturbed (or

[1] Compare Chāndogya, VI. I. 4.

awakened). The second name is evolving-consciousness (*pravṛttivijñāna*) in the sense that when the mind is disturbed, there evolves that which sees an external world. The third name is representation-consciousness in the sense that the ego (*manas*) represents (or reflects) an external world. As a clean mirror reflects the images of all description, it is even so with the representation-consciousness. When it is confronted, for instance, with the objects of the five senses, it represents them instantaneously and without effort. The fourth is particularization-consciousness, in the sense that it discriminates between different things defiled as well as pure. The fifth name is succession-consciousness, in the sense that continuously directed by the awakening consciousness of attention (*manaskāra*) it (*manas*) retains all experiences and never loses or suffers the destruction of any karma, good as well as evil, which had been sown in the past, and whose retribution, painful or agreeable, it never fails to mature, be it in the present or in the future, and also in the sense that it unconsciously recollects things gone by and in imagination anticipates things to come. Therefore the three domains (*kāmaloka*, domain of feeling—*rūpaloka*, domain of bodily existence—*arūpaloka*, domain of incorporeality) are nothing but the self manifestation of the mind (i.e. *ālayavijñāna* which is practically identical with *bhūtatathatā*). Since all things, owing the principle of their existence to the mind (*ālayavijñāna*), are produced by smṛti, all the modes of particularization are the self-particularizations of the mind. The mind in itself (or the soul) being however free from all attributes is not differentiated. Therefore we come to the conclusion that all things and conditions in the phenomenal world, hypostatized and established only through ignorance (*avidyā*) and memory (*smṛti*), have no more reality than the images in a mirror. They arise simply from the ideality of a particularizing mind. When the mind is disturbed, the multiplicity of things is produced; but when the mind is quieted, the multiplicity of things disappears. By ego-consciousness (*manovijñāna*) we mean the ignorant mind which by its succession-consciousness clings to the conception of I and Not-I and misapprehends the nature of the six objects of sense. The ego-consciousness is also called separation-consciousness, because it is nourished by the perfuming influence of the prejudices (*āsrava*), intellectual as well as affectional. Thus believing in the external world produced by memory, the mind becomes oblivious of the principle of sameness (*samatā*) that underlies all things which are one and perfectly calm and tranquil and show no sign of becoming.

Non-enlightenment is the *raison d'être* of saṃsāra. When this is annihilated the conditions—the external world—are also annihilated and with them the state of an interrelated mind is also annihilated. But this annihilation does not mean the annihilation of the mind but of its modes only. It becomes calm like an unruffled sea when all winds which were disturbing it and producing the waves have been annihilated.

In describing the relation of the interaction of avidyā (ignorance), karmavijñāna (activity-consciousness—the subjective mind), viṣaya (external world—represented by the senses) and the tathatā (suchness), Aśvaghoṣa says that there is an interperfuming of these elements. Thus Aśvaghoṣa says, "By perfuming we mean that while our worldly clothes (viz. those which we wear) have no odour of their own, neither offensive nor agreeable, they can yet acquire one or the other odour according to the nature of the substance with which they are perfumed. Suchness (*tathatā*) is likewise a pure dharma free from all defilements caused by the perfuming power of ignorance. On the other hand ignorance has nothing to do with purity. Nevertheless we speak of its being able to do the work of purity because it in its turn is perfumed by suchness. Determined by suchness ignorance becomes the *raison d'être* of all forms of defilement. And this ignorance perfumes suchness and produces smṛti. This smṛti in its turn perfumes ignorance. On account of this (reciprocal) perfuming, the truth is misunderstood. On account of its being misunderstood an external world of subjectivity appears. Further, on account of the perfuming power of memory, various modes of individuation are produced. And by clinging to them various deeds are done, and we suffer as the result miseries mentally as well as bodily." Again "suchness perfumes ignorance, and in consequence of this perfuming the individual in subjectivity is caused to loathe the misery of birth and death and to seek after the blessing of Nirvāṇa. This longing and loathing on the part of the subjective mind in turn perfumes suchness. On account of this perfuming influence we are enabled to believe that we are in possession within ourselves of suchness whose essential nature is pure and immaculate; and we also recognize that all phenomena in the world are nothing but the illusory manifestations of the mind (*ālayavijñāna*) and have no reality of their own. Since we thus rightly understand the truth, we can practise the means of liberation, can perform those actions which are in accordance with the dharma. We should neither particularize, nor cling to objects of desire. By virtue of this discipline and habituation during the lapse of innumerable āsaṅkhyeyakalpas[1] we get ignorance annihilated. As ignorance is thus annihilated, the mind (*ālayavijñāna*) is no longer disturbed, so as to be subject to individuation. As the mind is no longer disturbed, the particularization of the surrounding world is annihilated. When in this wise the principle and the condition of defilement, their products, and the mental disturbances are all annihilated, it is said that we attain Nirvāṇa and that various spontaneous displays of activity are accomplished." The Nirvāṇa of the tathatā philosophy is not nothingness, but tathatā (suchness or thatness) in its purity unassociated with any kind of disturbance which produces all the diversity of experience.

To the question that if all beings are uniformly in possession of suchness and are therefore equally perfumed by it, how is it that there are some who do not believe in it, while others do, Aśvaghoṣa's reply is that though all beings are uniformly in possession of suchness, the intensity of ignorance and the principle of individuation, that work from all eternity, vary in such manifold grades as to outnumber the sands of the Ganges, and hence the difference. There is an inherent perfuming principle in one's own being which, embraced and protected by the love (*maitrī*) and compassion (*karuṇā*) of all Buddhas and Bodhisattvas, is caused to loathe the misery of birth and death, to believe in nirvāṇa, to cultivate the root of merit (*kuśalamūla*), to habituate oneself to it and to bring it to maturity. In consequence of this, one is enabled to see all Buddhas and Bodhisattvas and, receiving instructions from them, is benefited, gladdened and induced to practise good deeds, etc., till one can attain to Buddhahood and enter into Nirvāṇa. This implies that all beings have such perfuming power in them that they may be affected by the good wishes of the Buddhas and Bodhisattvas for leading them to the path of virtue, and thus it is that sometimes hearing the Bodhisattvas and sometimes seeing them, "all beings thereby acquire (spiritual) benefits (*hitatā*)" and "entering into the samādhi of purity, they

[1] Technical name for a very vast period of time.

destroy hindrances wherever they are met with and obtain all-penetrating insight that enables them to become conscious of the absolute oneness (*samatā*) of the universe (*sarvaloka*) and to see innumerable Buddhas and Bodhisattvas."

There is a difference between the perfuming which is not in unison with suchness, as in the case of śrāvakas (theravādin monks), pratyekabuddhas and the novice bodhisattvas, who only continue their religious discipline but do not attain to the state of non-particularization in unison with the essence of suchness. But those bodhisattvas whose perfuming is already in unison with suchness attain to the state of non-particularization and allow themselves to be influenced only by the power of the dharma. The incessant perfuming of the defiled dharma (ignorance from all eternity) works on, but when one attains to Buddhahood one at once puts an end to it. The perfuming of the pure dharma (i.e. suchness) however works on to eternity without any interruption. For this suchness or thatness is the effulgence of great wisdom, the universal illumination of the dharmadhātu (universe), the true and adequate knowledge, the mind pure and clean in its own nature, the eternal, the blessed, the self-regulating and the pure, the tranquil, the inimitable and the free, and this is called the tathāgatagarbha or the dharmakāya. It may be objected that since thatness or suchness has been described as being without characteristics, it is now a contradiction to speak of it as embracing all merits, but it is held, that in spite of its embracing all merits, it is free in its nature from all forms of distinction, because all objects in the world are of one and the same taste; and being of one reality they have nothing to do with the modes of particularization or of dualistic character. "Though all things in their (metaphysical) origin come from the soul alone and in truth are free from particularization, yet on account of non-enlightenment there originates a subjective mind (*ālayavijñāna*) that becomes conscious of an external world." This is called ignorance or avidyā. Nevertheless the pure essence of the mind is perfectly pure and there is no awakening of ignorance in it. Hence we assign to suchness this quality, the effulgence of great wisdom. It is called universal illumination, because there is nothing for it to illumine. This perfuming of suchness therefore continues for ever, though the stage of the perfuming of avidyā comes to an end with the Buddhas when they attain to nirvāṇa. All Buddhas while at the stage of discipline feel a deep compassion (*mahākaruṇā*) for all beings, practise all virtues (*pāramitās*) and many other meritorious deeds, treat others as their own selves, and wish to work out a universal salvation of mankind in ages to come, through limitless numbers of *kalpas*, recognize truthfully and adequately the principle of equality (*samatā*) among people; and do not cling to the individual existence of a sentient being. This is what is meant by the activity of tathatā. The main idea of this tathatā philosophy seems to be this, that this transcendent "thatness" is at once the quintessence of all thought and activity; as avidyā veils it or perfumes it, the world-appearance springs forth, but as the pure thatness also perfumes the avidyā there is a striving for the good as well. As the stage of avidyā is passed its luminous character shines forth, for it is the ultimate truth which only illusorily appeared as the many of the world.

This doctrine seems to be more in agreement with the view of an absolute unchangeable reality as the ultimate truth than that of the nihilistic idealism of *Laṅkāvatāra*. Considering the fact that Aśvaghoṣa was a learned Brahmin scholar in his early life, it is easy to guess that there was much Upaniṣad influence in this interpretation of Buddhism, which compares so favourably with the Vedānta as interpreted by Śaṅkara. The *Laṅkāvatāra* admitted a reality only as a make-believe to attract the Tairthikas (heretics) who had a prejudice in favour of an unchangeable self (*ātman*). But Aśvaghoṣa plainly admitted an unspeakable reality as the ultimate truth. Nāgārjuna's Mādhyamika doctrines which eclipsed the profound philosophy of Aśvaghoṣa seem to be more faithful to the traditional Buddhist creed and to the Vijñānavāda creed of Buddhism as explained in the *Laṅkāvatāra*[1].

The Mādhyamika or the Śūnyavāda school—Nihilism.

Candrakīrti, the commentator of Nāgārjuna's verses known as "*Mādhyamika kārikā*," in explaining the doctrine of dependent origination (*pratītyasamutpāda*) as described by Nāgārjuna starts with two interpretations of the word. According to one the word pratītyasamutpāda means the origination (*utpāda*) of the nonexistent (*abhāva*) depending on (*pratītya*) reasons and causes

[1] As I have no access to the Chinese translation of Aśvaghoṣa's *Śraddhotpāda Śāstra*, I had to depend entirely on Suzuki's expressions as they appear in his translation.

(hetupratyaya). According to the other interpretation pratītya means each and every destructible individual and pratītyasamutpāda means the origination of each and every destructible individual. But he disapproves of both these meanings. The second meaning does not suit the context in which the Pāli Scriptures generally speak of pratītyasamutpāda (e.g. *cakṣuḥ pratītya rūpāni ca utpadyante cakṣurvijñānam*) for it does not mean the origination of each and every destructible individual, but the originating of specific individual phenomena (e.g. perception of form by the operation in connection with the eye) depending upon certain specific conditions.

The first meaning also is equally unsuitable. Thus for example if we take the case of any origination, e.g. that of the visual percept, we see that there cannot be any contact between visual knowledge and physical sense, the eye, and so it would not be intelligible that the former should depend upon the latter. If we interpret the maxim of pratītyasamutpāda as this happening that happens, that would not explain any specific origination. All origination is false, for a thing can neither originate by itself nor by others, nor by a co-operation of both nor without any reason. For if a thing exists already it cannot originate again by itself. To suppose that it is originated by others would also mean that the origination was of a thing already existing. If again without any further qualification it is said that depending on one the other comes into being, then depending on anything any other thing could come into being—from light we could have darkness! Since a thing could not originate from itself or by others, it could not also be originated by a combination of both of them together. A thing also could not originate without any cause, for then all things could come into being at all times. It is therefore to be acknowledged that wherever the Buddha spoke of this so-called dependent origination (*pratītyasamutpāda*) it was referred to as illusory manifestations appearing to intellects and senses stricken with ignorance. This dependent origination is not thus a real law, but only an appearance due to ignorance (*avidyā*). The only thing which is not lost (*amoṣadharma*) is nirvāṇa; but all other forms of knowledge and phenomena (*saṃskāras*) are false and are lost with their appearances (*sarvasaṃskārāśca mṛṣāmoṣadharmāṇaḥ*).

It is sometimes objected to this doctrine that if all

appearances are false, then they do not exist at all. There are then no good or bad works and no cycle of existence, and if such is the case, then it may be argued that no philosophical discussion should be attempted. But the reply to such an objection is that the nihilistic doctrine is engaged in destroying the misplaced confidence of the people that things are true. Those who are really wise do not find anything either false or true, for to them clearly they do not exist at all and they do not trouble themselves with the question of their truth or falsehood. For him who knows thus there are neither works nor cycles of births (*saṃsāra*) and also he does not trouble himself about the existence or non-existence of any of the appearances. Thus it is said in the Ratnakūṭasūtra that howsoever carefully one may search one cannot discover consciousness (*citta*); what cannot be perceived cannot be said to exist, and what does not exist is neither past, nor future, nor present, and as such it cannot be said to have any nature at all; and that which has no nature is subject neither to origination nor to extinction. He who through his false knowledge (*viparyyāsa*) does not comprehend the falsehood of all appearances, but thinks them to be real, works and suffers the cycles of rebirth (*saṃsāra*). Like all illusions, though false these appearances can produce all the harm of rebirth and sorrow.

It may again be objected that if there is nothing true according to the nihilists (*śūnyavādins*), then their statement that there is no origination or extinction is also not true. Candrakīrti in replying to this says that with śūnyavādins the truth is absolute silence. When the śūnyavādin sages argue, they only accept for the moment what other people regard as reasons, and deal with them in their own manner to help them to come to a right comprehension of all appearances. It is of no use to say, in spite of all arguments tending to show the falsehood of all appearances, that they are testified by our experience, for the whole thing that we call "our experience" is but false illusion inasmuch as these phenomena have no true essence.

When the doctrine of pratītyasamutpāda is described as "this being that is," what is really meant is that things can only be indicated as mere appearances one after another, for they have no essence or true nature. Nihilism (*śūnyavāda*) also means just this. The true meaning of pratītyasamutpāda or śūnyavāda is this, that there is no truth, no essence in all phenomena that appear[1]. As the phenomena have no essence they are neither produced nor destroyed; they really neither come nor go. They are merely the appearance of māyā or illusion. The void (*śūnya*) does not mean pure negation, for that is relative to some kind of position. It simply means that none of the appearances have any intrinsic nature of their own (*niḥsvabhāvatvam*).

The Madhyamaka or Śūnya system does not hold that anything has any essence or nature (*svabhāva*) of its own; even heat cannot be said to be the essence of fire; for both the heat and the fire are the result of the combination of many conditions, and what depends on many conditions cannot be said to be the nature or essence of the thing. That alone maybe said to be the true essence or nature of anything which does not depend on anything else, and since no such essence or nature can be pointed out which stands independently by itself we cannot say that it exists. If a thing has no essence or existence of its own, we cannot affirm the essence of other things to it (*parabhāva*). If we cannot affirm anything of anything as positive, we cannot consequently assert anything of anything as negative. If anyone first believes in things positive and afterwards discovers that they are not so, he no doubt thus takes his stand on a negation (*abhāva*), but in reality since we cannot speak of anything positive, we cannot speak of anything negative either[2].

It is again objected that we nevertheless perceive a process going on. To this the Madhyamaka reply is that a process of change could not be affirmed of things that are permanent. But we can hardly speak of a process with reference to momentary things; for those which are momentary are destroyed the next moment after they appear, and so there is nothing which can continue to justify a process. That which appears as being neither comes from anywhere nor goes anywhere, and that which appears as destroyed also does not come from anywhere nor go anywhere, and so a process (*saṃsāra*) cannot be affirmed of them. It cannot be that when the second moment arose, the first moment had suffered a change in the process, for it was not the same as the second, as there is no so-called cause-effect connection. In fact there being no relation between the two, the temporal determination as prior and later is wrong. The supposition that there is a self which suffers changes is also not valid, for howsoever we

[1] See *Mādhyamikavṛtti* (B.T.S.), p. 50.
[2] *Ibid*, pp. 93–100.

may search we find the five skandhas but no self. Moreover if the soul is a unity it cannot undergo any process or progression, for that would presuppose that the soul abandons one character and takes up another at the same identical moment which is inconceivable[1].

But then again the question arises that if there is no process, and no cycle of worldly existence of thousands of afflictions, what is then the nirvāṇa which is described as the final extinction of all afflictions (*kleśa*)? To this the Madhyamaka reply is that it does not agree to such a definition of nirvāṇa. Nirvāṇa on the Madhyamaka theory is the absence of the essence of all phenomena, that which cannot be conceived either as anything which has ceased or as anything which is produced (*aniruddham anutpannam*). In nirvāṇa all phenomena are lost; we say that the phenomena cease to exist in nirvāṇa, but like the illusory snake in the rope they never existed[2]. Nirvāṇa cannot be any positive thing or any sort of state of being (*bhāva*), for all positive states or things are joint products of combined causes (*saṃskṛta*) and are liable to decay and destruction. Neither can it be a negative existence, for since we cannot speak of any positive existence, we cannot speak of a negative existence either. The appearances or the phenomena are communicated as being in a state of change and process coming one after another, but beyond that no essence, existence, or truth can be affirmed of them. Phenomena sometimes appear to be produced and sometimes to be destroyed, but they cannot be determined as existent or non-existent. Nirvāṇa is merely the cessation of the seeming phenomenal flow (*prapañcapravṛtti*). It cannot therefore be designated either as positive or as negative for these conceptions belong to phenomena (*na cāpravṛttimātram bhāvābhāvcti parikalpitum pāryyate evam na bhāvābhāvanirvāṇam*, M.V. 197). In this state there is nothing which is known, and even the knowledge that the phenomena have ceased to appear is not found. Even the Buddha himself is a phenomenon, a mirage or a dream, and so are all his teachings[3].

It is easy to see that in this system there cannot exist any bondage or emancipation; all phenomena are like shadows, like the mirage, the dream, the māyā, and the magic without any real nature (*niḥsvabhāva*). It is mere false knowledge to suppose that

[1]See *Mādhyamikavṛtti* (B.T.S.), pp. 101–102.
[2]*Ibid*, p. 194.
[3]*Ibid*, pp. 162 and 201.

one is trying to win a real nirvāṇa[1]. It is this false egoism that is to be considered as avidyā. When considered deeply it is found that there is not even the slightest trace of any positive existence. Thus it is seen that if there were no ignorance (*avidyā*), there would have been no conformations (*saṃskāras*), and if there were no conformations there would have been no consciousness, and so on; but it cannot be said of the ignorance "I am generating the saṃskāras," and it can be said of the saṃskāras "we are being produced by the avidyā." But there being avidyā, there come the saṃskāras and so on with other categories too. This character of the pratītyasamutpāda is known as the coming of the consequent depending on an antecedent reason (*hetūpanibandha*).

It can be viewed from another aspect, namely that of dependence on conglomeration or combination (*pratyayopanibandha*). It is by the combination (*samavāya*) of the four elements, space (*ākāśa*) and consciousness (*vijñāna*) that a man is made. It is due to earth (*pṛthivī*) that the body becomes solid, it is due to water that there is fat in the body, it is due to fire that there is digestion, it is due to wind that there is respiration; it is due to ākāśa that there is porosity, and it is due to vijñāna that there is mind-consciousness. It is by their mutual combination that we find a man as he is. But none of these elements think that they have done any of the functions that are considered to be allotted to them. None of these are real substances or beings or souls. It is by ignorance that these are thought of as existents and attachment is generated for them. Through ignorance thus come the saṃskāras, consisting of attachment, antipathy and thoughtlessness (*rāga*, *dveṣa*, *moha*); from these proceed the vijñāna and the four skandhas. These with the four elements bring about name and form (*nāmarūpa*), from these proceed the senses (*ṣaḍāyatana*), from the coming together of those three comes contact (*sparśa*); from that feelings, from that comes desire (*tṛṣṇā*) and so on. These flow on like the stream of a river, but there is no essence or truth behind them all or as the ground of them all[2]. The phenomena therefore cannot be said to be either existent or non-existent, and no truth can be affirmed of either eternalism (*śāśvatavāda*) or nihilism (*ucchedavāda*), and it is for this reason

[1] See *Mādhyamikavṛtti* (B.T.S.), pp. 101–108.

[2] *Ibid*, pp. 209–211, quoted from *Śālistambhasūtra*. Vācaspatimiśra also quotes this passage in his *Bhāmatī* on Śaṅkara's *Brahma-sūtra*.

that this doctrine is called the middle doctrine (*madhyamaka*)[1]. Existence and non-existence have only a relative truth (*samvṛtisatya*) in them, as in all phenomena, but there is no true reality (*paramārthasatya*) in them or anything else. Morality plays as high a part in this nihilistic system as it does in any other Indian system. I quote below some stanzas from Nāgārjuna's *Suhṛllekha* as translated by Wenzel (P.T.S. 1886) from the Tibetan translation.

6. Knowing that riches are unstable and void (*asāra*) give according to the moral precepts, to Bhikshus, Brahmins, the poor and friends for there is no better friend than giving.
7. Exhibit morality (*śīla*) faultless and sublime, unmixed and spotless, for morality is the supporting ground of all eminence, as the earth is of the moving and immovable.
8. Exercise the imponderable, transcendental virtues of charity, morality, patience, energy, meditation, and likewise wisdom, in order that, having reached the farther shore of the sea of existence, you may become a Jina prince.
9. View as enemies, avarice (*mātsaryya*), deceit (*śāṭhya*), duplicity (*māyā*), lust, indolence (*kausīdya*), pride (*māna*), greed (*rāga*), hatred (*dveṣa*) and pride (*mada*) concerning family, figure, glory, youth, or power.
15. Since nothing is so difficult of attainment as patience, open no door for anger; the Buddha has pronounced that he who renounces anger shall attain the degree of an anāgāmin (a saint who never suffers rebirth).
21. Do not look after another's wife; but if you see her, regard her, according to age, like your mother, daughter or sister.
24. Of him who has conquered the unstable, ever moving objects of the six senses and him who has overcome the mass of his enemies in battle, the wise praise the first as the greater hero.
29. Thou who knowest the world, be equanimous against the eight worldly conditions, gain and loss, happiness and suffering, fame and dishonour, blame and praise, for they are not objects for your thoughts.
37. But one (a woman) that is gentle as a sister, winning as a friend, careful of your well being as a mother, obedient as a servant her (you must) honour as the guardian god(dess) of the family.
40. Always perfectly meditate on (turn your thoughts to) kindness, pity, joy and indifference; then if you do not obtain a higher degree you (certainly) will obtain the happiness of Brahman's world (*brahmavihāra*).
41. By the four dhyānas completely abandoning desire (kāma), reflection (vicāra), joy (prīti), and happiness and pain (sukha, duḥkha) you will obtain as fruit the lot of a Brahman.
49. If you say "I am not the form, you thereby will understand I am not endowed with form, I do not dwell in form, the form does not dwell in me; and in like manner you will understand the voidness of the other four aggregates."
50. The aggregates do not arise from desire, nor from time, nor from

[1] See *Mādhyamikavṛtti* (B.T.S.), p. 160.

nature (*prakṛti*), not from themselves (*svabhāvāt*), nor from the Lord (*īśvara*), nor yet are they without cause; know that they arise from ignorance (*avidyā*) and desire (*tṛṣṇā*).

51. Know that attachment to religious ceremonies (*śīlabrataparāmarśa*), wrong views (*mithyādṛṣṭi*) and doubt (*vicikitsā*) are the three fetters.
53. Steadily instruct yourself (more and more) in the highest morality, the highest wisdom and the highest thought, for the hundred and fifty one rules (of the *prātimokṣa*) are combined perfectly in these three.
58. Because thus (as demonstrated) all this is unstable (*anitya*) without substance (*anātma*) without help (*aśaraṇa*) without protector (*anātha*) and without abode (*asthāna*) thou O Lord of men must become discontented with this worthless (*asāra*) kadali-tree of the orb.
104. If a fire were to seize your head or your dress you would extinguish and subdue it, even then endeavour to annihilate desire, for there is no other higher necessity than this.
105. By morality, knowledge and contemplation, attain the spotless dignity of the quieting and the subduing nirvāṇa not subject to age, death or decay, devoid of earth, water, fire, wind, sun and moon.
107. Where there is no wisdom (*prajñā*) there is also no contemplation (*dhyāna*), where there is no contemplation there is also no wisdom; but know that for him who possesses these two the sea of existence is like a grove.

Uncompromising Idealism or the School of Vijñānavāda Buddhism.

The school of Buddhist philosophy known as the Vijñānavāda or Yogācāra has often been referred to by such prominent teachers of Hindu thought as Kumārila and Śaṅkara. It agrees to a great extent with the Śūnyavādins whom we have already described. All the dharmas (qualities and substances) are but imaginary constructions of ignorant minds. There is no movement in the so-called external world as we suppose, for it does not exist. We construct it ourselves and then are ourselves deluded that it exists by itself (*nirmmitapratimohi*)[1]. There are two functions involved in our consciousness, viz. that which holds the perceptions (*khyāti vijñāna*), and that which orders them by imaginary constructions (*vastuprativikalpavijñāna*). The two functions however mutually determine each other and cannot be separately distinguished (*abhinnalakṣaṇe anyonyahetuke*). These functions are set to work on account of the beginningless instinctive tendencies inherent in them in relation to the world of appearance (*anādikāla-prapañca-vāsanāhetukañca*)[2].

All sense knowledge can be stopped only when the diverse

[1] *Laṅkāvatārasūtra*, pp. 21–22.
[2] *Ibid*, p. 44.

unmanifested instincts of imagination are stopped (*abhūtaparikalpa-vāsanā-vaicitra-nirodha*)[1]. All our phenomenal knowledge is without any essence or truth (*nihsvabhāva*) and is but a creation of māyā, a mirage or a dream. There is nothing which may be called external, but all is the imaginary creation of the mind (*svacitta*), which has been accustomed to create imaginary appearances from beginningless time. This mind by whose movement these creations take place as subject and object has no appearance in itself and is thus without any origination, existence and extinction (*utpādasthitibhaṅgavarjjam*) and is called the ālayavijñāna. The reason why this ālayavijñāna itself is said to be without origination, existence, and extinction is probably this, that it is always a hypothetical state which merely explains all the phenomenal states that appear, and therefore it has no existence in the sense in which the term is used and we could not affirm any special essence of it.

We do not realize that all visible phenomena are of nothing external but of our own mind (*svacitta*), and there is also the beginningless tendency for believing and creating a phenomenal world of appearance. There is also the nature of knowledge (which takes things as the perceiver and the perceived) and there is also the instinct in the mind to experience diverse forms. On account of these four reasons there are produced in the ālayavijñāna (mind) the ripples of our sense experiences (*pravṛttivijñāna*) as in a lake, and these are manifested as sense experiences. All the five skandhas called *pañcavijñānakāya* thus appear in a proper synthetic form. None of the phenomenal knowledge that appears is either identical or different from the ālayavijñāna just as the waves cannot be said to be either identical or different from the ocean. As the ocean dances on in waves so the citta or the ālayavijñāna is also dancing as it were in its diverse operations (*vṛtti*). As citta it collects all movements (*karma*) within it, as manas it synthesizes (*vidhīyate*) and as vijñāna it constructs the fivefold perceptions (*vijñānen vijānāti dṛśyam kalpate pañcabhiḥ*)[2].

It is only due to māyā (illusion) that the phenomena appear in their twofold aspect as subject and object. This must always be regarded as an appearance (*samvṛtisatyatā*) whereas in the real aspect we could never say whether they existed (*bhāva*) or did not exist[3].

[1] *Laṅkāvatārasūtra*, p. 44.
[2] *Ibid*. pp. 50–55.
[3] Asaṅga's *Mahāyānasūtrālaṃkāra*, pp. 58–59.

All phenomena both being and non-being are illusory (*sadasantaḥ māyopamāḥ*). When we look deeply into them we find that there is an absolute negation of all appearances, including even all negations, for they are also appearances. This would make the ultimate truth positive. But this is not so, for it is that in which the positive and negative are one and the same (*bhāvābhāvasamānatā*)[1]. Such a state which is complete in itself and has no name and no substance had been described in the Laṅkāvatārasūtra as thatness (*tathatā*)[2]. This state is also described in another place in the *Laṅkāvatāra* as voidness (*śūnyatā*) which is one and has no origination and no essence[3]. In another place it is also designated as tathāgatagarbha[4].

It may be supposed that this doctrine of an unqualified ultimate truth comes near to the Vedantic ātman or Brahman like the tathatā doctrine of Aśvaghoṣa; and we find in Laṅkāvatāra that Rāvaṇa asks the Buddha "How can you say that your doctrine of tathāgatagarbha was not the same as the ātman doctrine of the other schools of philosophers, for those heretics also consider the ātman as eternal, agent, unqualified, all-pervading and unchanged?" To this the Buddha is found to reply thus—"Our doctrine is not the same as the doctrine of those heretics; it is in consideration of the fact that the instruction of a philosophy which considered that there was no soul or substance in anything (*nairātmya*) would frighten the disciples, that I say that all things are in reality the tathāgatagarbha. This should not be regarded as ātman. Just as a lump of clay is made into various shapes, so it is the non-essential nature of all phenomena and their freedom from all characteristics (*sarvavikalpalakṣaṇavinivrttam*) that is variously described as the garbha or the nairātmya (essencelessness). This explanation of tathāgatagarbha as the ultimate truth and reality is given in order to attract to our creed those heretics who are superstitiously inclined to believe in the ātman doctrine[5]."

So far as the appearance of the phenomena was concerned the idealistic Buddhists (*vijñānavādins*) agreed to the doctrine of pratītyasamutpāda with certain modifications. There was with them an external pratītyasamutpāda just as it appeared in the

[1] Asaṅga's *Mahāyānasūtrālaṃkāra*, p. 65.

[2] *Laṅkāvatārasūtra*, p. 70.

[3] *Ibid*, p. 78.

[4] *Ibid*, p. 80.

[5] *Ibid*, pp. 80–81.

objective aspect and an internal pratītyasamutpāda. The external pratītyasamutpāda (dependent origination) is represented in the way in which material things (e.g. a jug) came into being by the co-operation of diverse elements—the lump of clay, the potter, the wheel, etc. The internal (*ādhyātmika*) pratītyasamutpāda was represented by avidyā, tṛṣṇā, karma, the skandhas, and the āyatanas produced out of them[1].

Our understanding is composed of two categories called the *pravicayabuddhi* and the *vikalpalakṣaṇagrahābhiniveśapratiṣṭhāpikābuddhi*. The pravicayabuddhi is that which always seeks to take things in either of the following four ways, that they are either this or the other (*ekatvānyatva*); either both or not both (*ubhayānubhaya*), either are or are not (*astināsti*), either eternal or non-eternal (*nityānitya*). But in reality none of these can be affirmed of the phenomena. The second category consists of that habit of the mind by virtue of which it constructs diversities and arranges them (created in their turn by its own constructive activity—*parikalpa*) in a logical order of diverse relations of subject and predicate, causal and other relations. He who knows the nature of these two categories of the mind knows that there is no external world of matter and that they are all experienced only in the mind. There is no water, but it is the sense construction of smoothness (*sneha*) that constructs the water as an external substance; it is the sense construction of activity or energy that constructs the external substance of fire; it is the sense construction of movement that constructs the external substance of air. In this way through the false habit of taking the unreal as the real (*mithyāsatyābhiniveśa*) five skandhas appear. If these were to appear all together, we could not speak of any kind of causal relations, and if they appeared in succession there could be no connection between them, as there is nothing to bind them together. In reality there is nothing which is produced or destroyed, it is only our constructive imagination that builds up things as perceived with all their relations, and ourselves as perceivers. It is simply a convention (*vyavahāra*) to speak of things as known[2]. Whatever we designate by speech is mere speech-construction (*vāgvikalpa*) and unreal. In speech one could not speak of anything without relating things in some kind of causal

[1] *Laṅkāvatārasūtra*, p. 85.

[2] *Laṅkāvatārasūtra*, p. 87, compare the term "vyavahārika" as used of the phenomenal and the conventional world in almost the same sense by Śaṅkara.

relation, but none of these characters may be said to be true; the real truth (*paramārtha*) can never be referred to by such speech-construction.

The nothingness (*śūnyatā*) of things may be viewed from seven aspects—(1) that they are always interdependent, and hence have no special characteristics by themselves, and as they cannot be determined in themselves they cannot be determined in terms of others, for, their own nature being undetermined, a reference to an "other" is also undetermined, and hence they are all indefinable (*lakṣaṇaśūnyatā*); (2) that they have no positive essence (*bhāvasvabhāvaśūnyatā*), since they spring up from a natural non-existence (*svabhāvābhāvotpatii*); (3) that they are of an unknown type of non-existence (*apracaritaśūnyatā*), since all the skandhas vanish in the nirvāṇa; (4) that they appear phenomenally as connected though non-existent (*pracaritaśūnyatā*), for their skandhas have no reality in themselves nor are they related to others, but yet they appear to be somehow causally connected; (5) that none of the things can be described as having any definite nature, they are all undemonstrable by language (*nirabhilapyaśūnyatā*); (6) that there cannot be any knowledge about them except that which is brought about by the long-standing defects of desires which pollute all our vision; (7) that things are also non-existent in the sense that we affirm them to be in a particular place and time in which they are not (*itaretaraśūnyatā*).

There is thus only non-existence, which again is neither eternal nor destructible, and the world is but a dream and a māyā; the two kinds of negation (*nirodha*) are ākāśa (space) and nirvāṇa; things which are neither existent nor non-existent are only imagined to be existent by fools.

This view apparently comes into conflict with the doctrine of this school, that the reality is called the tathāgatagarbha (the womb of all that is merged in thatness) and all the phenomenal appearances of the clusters (*skandhas*), elements (*dhātus*), and fields of sense operation (*āyatanas*) only serve to veil it with impurities, and this would bring it nearer to the assumption of a universal soul as the reality. But the *Laṅkāvatāra* attempts to explain away this conflict by suggesting that the reference to the tathāgatagarbha as the reality is only a sort of false bait to attract those who are afraid of listening to the nairātmya (non-soul) doctrine[1].

[1] *Laṅkāvatārasūtra*, p. 80.

The Bodhisattvas may attain their highest by the fourfold knowledge of (1) *svacittadṛśyabhāvaṇā*, (2) *utpādasthitibhaṅga-vivarjjanatā*, (3) *bāhyabhāvābhāvopalakṣaṇatā* and (4) *svapratyāryyajñānādhigamābhinnalakṣaṇatā*. The first means that all things are but creations of the imagination of one's mind. The second means that as things have no essence there is no origination, existence or destruction. The third means that one should know the distinctive sense in which all external things are said either to be existent or non-existent, for their existence is merely like the mirage which is produced by the beginningless desire (*vāsanā*) of creating and perceiving the manifold. This brings us to the fourth one, which means the right comprehension of the nature of all things.

The four dhyānas spoken of in the *Laṅkāvatāra* seem to be different from those which have been described in connection with the Theravāda Buddhism. These dhyānas are called (1) *bālopacārika*, (2) *arthapravicaya*, (3) *tathatālambana* and (4) *tathāgata*. The first one is said to be that practised by the śrāvakas and the pratyekabuddhas. It consists in concentrating upon the doctrine that there is no soul (*pudgalanairātmya*), and that everything is transitory, miserable and impure. When considering all things in this way from beginning to end the sage advances on till all conceptual knowing ceases (*āsaṃjñānirodhāt*); we have what is called the vālopacārika dhyāna (the meditation for beginners).

The second is the advanced state where not only there is full consciousness that there is no self, but there is also the comprehension that neither these nor the doctrines of other heretics may be said to exist, and that there is none of the dharmas that appears. This is called the *arthapravicayadhyāna*, for the sage concentrates here on the subject of thoroughly seeking out (*pravicaya*) the nature of all things (*artha*).

The third dhyāna, that in which the mind realizes that the thought that there is no self nor that there are the appearances, is itself the result of imagination and thus lapses into the thatness (*tathatā*). This dhyāna is called *tathatālambana*, because it has for its object tathatā or thatness.

The last or the fourth dhyāna is that in which the lapse of the mind into the state of thatness is such that the nothingness and incomprehensibility of all phenomena is perfectly realized;

and nirvāṅa is that in which all root desires (*vāsanā*) manifesting themselves in knowledge are destroyed and the mind with knowledge and perceptions, making false creations, ceases to work. This cannot be called death, for it will not have any rebirth and it cannot be called destruction, for only compounded things (*saṃskṛta*) suffer destruction, so that it is different from either death or destruction. This nirvāṇa is different from that of the śrāvakas and the pratyekabuddhas for they are satisfied to call that state nirvāṇa, in which by the knowledge of the general characteristics of all things (transitoriness and misery) they are not attached to things and cease to make erroneous judgments[1].

Thus we see that there is no cause (in the sense of ground) of all these phenomena as other heretics maintain. When it is said that the world is māyā or illusion, what is meant to be emphasized is this, that there is no cause, no ground. The phenomena that seem to originate, stay, and be destroyed are mere constructions of tainted imagination, and the tathatā or thatness is nothing but the turning away of this constructive activity or nature of the imagination (*vikalpa*) tainted with the associations of beginningless root desires (*vāsanā*)[2]. The tathatā has no separate reality from illusion, but it is illusion itself when the course of the construction of illusion has ceased. It is therefore also spoken of as that which is cut off or detached from the mind (*cittavimukta*), for here there is no construction of imagination (*sarvakalpanāvirahitam*)[3].

Sautrāntika Theory of Perception.

Dharmottara (A.D. 847), a commentator of Dharmakīrtti's[4] (about A.D. 635) *Nyāyabindu*, a Sautrāntika logical and epistemological work, describes right knowledge (*samyagjñāna*) as an invariable antecedent to the accomplishment of all that a man

[1] *Laṅkāvatārasūtra*, p. 100.

[2] *Ibid*, p. 109.

[3] This account of the Vijñānavāda school is collected mainly from *Laṅkāvatārasūtra*, as no other authentic work of the Vijñānavāda school is available. Hindu accounts and criticisms of this school may be had in such books as Kumarila's *Śloka vārttika* or Śaṅkara's bhāṣya, II. ii, etc. Asaṅga's *Mahāyānasūtrālaṃkāra* deals more with the duties concerning the career of a saint (*Bodhisattva*) than with the metaphysics of the system.

[4] Dharmakīrtti calls himself an adherent of Vijñānavāda in his *Santānāntarasiddhi*, a treatise on solipsism, but his *Nyāyabindu* seems rightly to have been considered by the author of *Nyāyabinduṭīkāṭippanī* (p. 19) as being written from the Sautrāntika point of view.

desires to have (*samyagjñānapūrvikā sarvapuruṣārthasiddhi*)[1]. When on proceeding, in accordance with the presentation of any knowledge, we get a thing as presented by it we call it right knowledge. Right knowledge is thus the knowledge by which one can practically acquire the thing he wants to acquire (*arthādhigati*). The process of knowledge, therefore, starts with the perceptual presentation and ends with the attainment of the thing represented by it and the fulfilment of the practical need by it (*arthādhigamāt samāptaḥ pramāṇavyāpāraḥ*). Thus there are three moments in the perceptual acquirement of knowledge: (1) the presentation, (2) our prompting in accordance with it, and (3) the final realization of the object in accordance with our endeavour following the direction of knowledge. Inference is also to be called right knowledge, as it also serves our practical need by representing the presence of objects in certain connections and helping us to realize them. In perception this presentation is direct, while in inference this is brought about indirectly through the liṅga (reason). Knowledge is sought by men for the realization of their ends, and the subject of knowledge is discussed in philosophical works only because knowledge is sought by men. Any knowledge, therefore, which will not lead us to the realization of the object represented by it could not be called right knowledge. All illusory perceptions, therefore, such as the perception of a white conch-shell as yellow or dream perceptions, are not right knowledge, since they do not lead to the realization of such objects as are presented by them. It is true no doubt that since all objects are momentary, the object which was perceived at the moment of perception was not the same as that which was realized at a later moment. But the series of existents which started with the first perception of a blue object finds itself realized by the realization of other existents of the same series (*nīlādau ya eva santānaḥ paricchinno nīlajñānena sa eva tena prāpitaḥ tena nīlajñānam pramāṇam*)[2].

When it is said that right knowledge is an invariable antecedent of the realization of any desirable thing or the retarding of any undesirable thing, it must be noted that it is not meant

[1] Brief extracts from the opinions of two other commentators of *Nyāyabindu*, Vinītadeva and Śāntabbadra (seventh century), are found in *Nyāyabinduṭikāṭippanī*, a commentary of *Nyāyabinduṭīkā* of Dharmmottara, but their texts are not available to us.

[2] *Nyāyabinduṭikāṭippanī*, p. 11.

that right knowledge is directly the cause of it; for, with the rise of any right perception, there is a memory of past experiences, desire is aroused, through desire an endeavour in accordance with it is launched, and as a result of that there is realization of the object of desire. Thus, looked at from this point of view, right knowledge is not directly the cause of the realization of the object. Right knowledge of course directly indicates the presentation, the object of desire, but so far as the object is a mere presentation it is not a subject of enquiry. It becomes a subject of enquiry only in connection with our achieving the object presented by perception.

Perception (*pratyakṣa*) has been defined by Dharmakīrtti as a presentation, which is generated by the objects alone, unassociated by any names or relations (*kalpanā*) and which is not erroneous (*kalpanāpoḍhamabhrāntam*)[1]. This definition does not indeed represent the actual nature (*svarūpa*) of perception, but only shows the condition which must be fulfilled in order that anything may be valid perception. What is meant by saying that a perception is not erroneous is simply this, that it will be such that if one engages himself in an endeavour in accordance with it, he will not be baffled in the object which was presented to him by his perception (*tasmādgrāhye arthe vasiurūpe yadaviparyastam tadabhrāntamiha veditavyam*). It is said that a right perception could not be associated with names (*kalpanā* or *abhilāpa*). This qualification is added only with a view of leaving out all that is not directly generated by the object. A name is given to a thing only when it is associated in the mind, through memory, as being the same as perceived before. This cannot, therefore, be regarded as being produced by the object of perception. The senses present the objects by coming in contact with them, and the objects also must of necessity allow themselves to be presented as they are when they are in contact with the proper senses. But the work of recognition or giving names is not what is directly produced by the objects themselves, for this involves the unification of previous experiences, and this is certainly not what is presented

[1] The definition first given in the *Pramāṇasamuccaya* (not available in Sanskrit) of Diṅnāga (A.D. 500) was "*Kalpanāpoḍham*." According to Dharmakīrtti it is the indeterminate knowledge (*nirvikalpa jñāna*) consisting only of the copy of the object presented to the senses that constitutes the valid element presented to perception. The determinate knowledge (*savikalpa jñāna*), as formed by the conceptual activity of the mind identifying the object with what has been experienced before, cannot be regarded as truly representing what is really presented to the senses.

to the sense (*pūrvadṛṣṭāparadṛṣṭañcārthamekīkurvadvijñānam-asannihitaviṣayam pūrvadṛṣṭasyāsannihitatvāt*). In all illusory perceptions it is the sense which is affected either by extraneous or by inherent physiological causes. If the senses are not perverted they are bound to present the object correctly. Perception thus means the correct presentation through the senses of an object in its own uniqueness as containing only those features which are its and its alone (*svalakṣaṇam*). The validity of knowledge consists in the sameness that it has with the objects presented by it (*arthena saha yatsārūpyam sādṛśyamasya jñānasya tatpramāṇamiha*). But the objection here is that if our percept is only similar to the external object then this similarity is a thing which is different from the presentation, and thus perception becomes invalid. But the similarity is not different from the percept which appears as being similar to the object. It is by virtue of their sameness that we refer to the object by the percept (*taditi sārūpyam tasya vaśāt*) and our perception of the object becomes possible. It is because we have an awareness of blueness that we speak of having perceived a blue object. The relation, however, between the notion of similarity of the perception with the blue object and the indefinite awareness of blue in perception is not one of causation but of a determinant and a determinate (*vyavastkāpyavyavasthāpakabhāvena*). Thus it is the same cognition which in one form stands as signifying the similarity with the object of perception and is in another indefinite form the awareness as the percept (*tata ekasya vastunaḥ kiñcidrūpam pramāṇam kiñcitpramānaphalam na virudhyate*). It is on account of this similarity with the object that a cognition can be a determinant of the definite awareness (*vyavasthāpanaheturhi sārūpyam*), so that by the determinate we know the determinant and thus by the similarity of the sense-datum with the object (*pramāṇa*) we come to think that our awareness has this particular form as "blue" (*pramāṇaphala*). If this sameness between the knowledge and its object was not felt we could not have spoken of the object from the awareness (*sārūpyamanubhūtam vyavasthāpanahetuh*). The object generates an awareness similar to itself, and it is this correspondence that can lead us to the realization of the object so presented by right knowledge[1].

[1] See also pp. 340 and 409. It is unfortunate that, excepting the *Nyāyabindu*, *Nyāyabinduṭīkā*, *Nyāyabinduṭikāṭippanī* (St Petersburg, 1909), no other works dealing with

Sautrāntika theory of Inference[1].

According to the Sautrāntika doctrine of Buddhism as described by Dharmakīrtti and Dharmmottara which is probably the only account of systematic Buddhist logic that is now available to us in Sanskrit, inference (*anumāna*) is divided into two classes, called svārthānumāna (inferential knowledge attained by a person arguing in his own mind or judgments), and parārthānumāna (inference through the help of articulated propositions for convincing others in a debate). The validity of inference depended, like the validity of perception, on copying the actually existing facts of the external world. Inference copied external realities as much as perception did; just as the validity of the immediate perception of blue depends upon its similarity to the external blue thing perceived, so the validity of the inference of a blue thing also, so far as it is knowledge, depends upon its resemblance to the external fact thus inferred (*sārūpyavaśāddhi tannīlapratītirūpam sidhyati*).

The reason by which an inference is made should be such that it may be present only in those cases where the thing to be inferred exists, and absent in every case where it does not exist. It is only when the reason is tested by both these joint conditions that an unfailing connection (*pratibandha*) between the reason and the thing to be inferred can be established. It is not enough that the reason should be present in all cases where the thing to be inferred exists and absent where it does not exist, but it is necessary that it should be present only in the above case. This law (*niyama*) is essential for establishing the unfailing condition necessary for inference[2]. This unfailing natural connection (*svabhāvapratibandha*) is found in two types

this interesting doctrine of perception are available to us. *Nyāyabindu* is probably one of the earliest works in which we hear of the doctrine of *arthakriyākāritva* (practical fulfilment of our desire as a criterion of right knowledge). Later on it was regarded as a criterion of existence, as Ratnakirtti's works and the profuse references by Hindu writers to the Buddhistic doctrines prove. The word *arthakriyā* is found in Candrakīrti's commentary on Nāgārjuna and also in such early works as *Lalitavistara* (pointed out to me by Dr E. J. Thomas of the Cambridge University Library) but the word has no philosophical significance there.

[1] As the *Pramāṇasamuccaya* of Diṅnāga is not available in Sanskrit, we can hardly know anything of developed Buddhist logic except what can be got from the *Nyāyabinduṭīkā* of Dharmmottara.

[2] *tasmāt niyamavatorevānvayavyatirekayoḥ prayogaḥ karttavyaḥ yena pratibandho gamyeta sādhanyasa sādhyena. Nyāyabinduṭīkā*, p. 24.

of cases. The first is that where the nature of the reason is contained in the thing to be inferred as a part of its nature, i.e. where the reason stands for a species of which the thing to be inferred is a genus; thus a stupid person living in a place full of tall pines may come to think that pines are called trees because they are tall and it may be useful to point out to him that even a small pine plant is a tree because it is pine; the quality of pineness forms a part of the essence of treeness, for the former being a species is contained in the latter as a genus; the nature of the species being identical with the nature of the genus, one could infer the latter from the former but not vice versa; this is called the unfailing natural connection of identity of nature (*tādātmya*). The second is that where the cause is inferred from the effect which stands as the reason of the former. Thus from the smoke the fire which has produced it may be inferred. The ground of these inferences is that reason is naturally indissolubly connected with the thing to be inferred, and unless this is the case, no inference is warrantable.

This natural indissoluble connection (*svabhāvapratibandhā*), be it of the nature of identity of essence of the species in the genus or inseparable connection of the effect with the cause, is the ground of all inference[1]. The svabhāvapratibandha determines the inseparability of connection (*avinābhāvaniyama*) and the inference is made not through a series of premisses but directly by the liṅga (reason) which has the inseparable connection[2].

The second type of inference known as parārthānumāna agrees with svārthānumāna in all essential characteristics; the main difference between the two is this, that in the case of parārthānumāna, the inferential process has to be put verbally in premisses.

Pandit Ratnākaraśānti, probably of the ninth or the tenth century A.D., wrote a paper named *Antarvyāptisamarthana* in which

[1] *na hi yo yatra svabhāvena na pratibaddhaḥ sa tam apratibaddhaviṣayamavaśyameva na vyabhicaratīti nāsti tayoravyabhicāraniyamah. Nyāyabinduṭīkā*, p. 29.

[2] The inseparable connection determining inference is only possible when the liṅga satisfies the three following conditions, viz. (1) pakṣasattva (existence of the liṅga in the pakṣa—the thing about which something is inferred); (2) sapakṣasattva (existence of the liṅga in those cases where the sādhya or probandum existed), and (3) vipakṣāsattva (its non-existence in all those places where the sādhya did not exist). The Buddhists admitted three propositions in a syllogism, e.g. The hill has fire, because it has smoke, like a kitchen but unlike a lake.

he tried to show that the concomitance is not between those cases which possess the liṅga or reason with the cases which possess the sādhya (probandum) but between that which has the characteristics of the liṅga with that which has the characteristics of the sādhya (probandum); or in other words the concomitance is not between the places containing the smoke such as kitchen, etc., and the places containing fire but between that which has the characteristic of the liṅga, viz. the smoke, and that which has the characteristic of the sādhya, viz. the fire. This view of the nature of concomitance is known as inner concomitance (*antarvyāpti*), whereas the former, viz. the concomitance between the thing possessing liṅga and that possessing sādhya, is known as outer concomitance (*bahirvyāpti*) and generally accepted by the Nyāya school of thought. This antarvyāpti doctrine of concomitance is indeed a later Buddhist doctrine.

It may not be out of place here to remark that evidences of some form of Buddhist logic probably go back at least as early as the *Kathāvatthu* (B.C. 200). Thus Aung on the evidence of the *Yamaka* points out that Buddhist logic at the time of Aśoka "was conversant with the distribution of terms" and the process of conversion. He further points out that the logical premisses such as the udāharaṇa (*Yo yo aggimā so so dhūmavā*—whatever is fiery is smoky), the upanayana (*ayaṁ pabbato dhūmavā*—this hill is smoky) and the niggama (*tasmādayam aggimā*—therefore that is fiery) were also known. (Aung further sums up the method of the arguments which are found in the *Kathāvatthu* as follows:

"Adherent. Is *A B*? (*ṭhāpanā*).
Opponent. Yes.
Adherent. Is *C D*? (*pāpanā*).
Opponent. No.
Adherent. But if *A* be *B* then (you should have said) *C* is *D*. That *B* can be affirmed of *A* but *D* of *C* is false. Hence your first answer is refuted.")

The antecedent of the hypothetical major premiss is termed ṭhāpanā, because the opponent's position, *A* is *B*, is conditionally established for the purpose of refutation.

The consequent of the hypothetical major premiss is termed pāpanā because it is got from the antecedent. And the conclusion is termed ropaṇa because the regulation is placed on the opponent. Next:

"If *D* be derived of *C*.
Then *B* should have been derived of *A*.
But you affirmed *B* of *A*.

(therefore) That *B* can be affirmed of *A* but not of *D* or *C* is wrong."

This is the paṭiloma, inverse or indirect method, as contrasted with the former or direct method, anuloma. In both methods the consequent is derived. But if we reverse the hypothetical major in the latter method we get

If *A* is *B C* is *D*.
But *A* is *B*.
Therefore *C* is *D*.

By this indirect method the opponent's second answer is re-established[1]."

The Doctrine of Momentariness.

Ratnakīrtti (A.D. 950) sought to prove the momentariness of all existence (*sattva*), first, by the concomitance discovered by the method of agreement in presence (*anvayavyāpti*), and then by the method of difference by proving that the production of effects could not be justified on the assumption of things being permanent and hence accepting the doctrine of momentariness as the only alternative. Existence is defined as the capacity of producing anything (*arthakriyākāritva*). The form of the first type of argument by anvayavyāpti may be given thus: "Whatever exists is momentary, by virtue of its existence, as for example the jug; all things about the momentariness of which we are discussing are existents and are therefore momentary." It cannot be said that the jug which has been chosen as an example of an existent is not momentary; for the jug is producing certain effects at the present moment; and it cannot be held that these are all identical in the past and the future or that it is producing no effect at all in the past and future, for the first is impossible, for those which are done now could not be done again in the future; the second is impossible, for if it has any capacity to

[1] See introduction to the translation of *Kathāvatthu* (*Points of Controversy*) by Mrs Rhys Davids.

produce effects it must not cease doing so, as in that case one might as well expect that there should not be any effect even at the present moment. Whatever has the capacity of producing anything at any time must of necessity do it. So if it does produce at one moment and does not produce at another, this contradiction will prove the supposition that the things were different at the different moments. If it is held that the nature of production varies at different moments, then also the thing at those two moments must be different, for a thing could not have in it two contradictory capacities.

Since the jug does not produce at the present moment the work of the past and the future moments, it cannot evidently do so, and hence is not identical with the jug in the past and in the future, for the fact that the jug has the capacity and has not the capacity as well, proves that it is not the same jug at the two moments (*śaktāśaktasvabhāvatayā pratikṣaṇam bhedaḥ*). The capacity of producing effects (*arthakriyāśakti*), which is but the other name of existence, is universally concomitant with momentariness (*kṣaṇikatvavyāpta*).

The Nyāya school of philosophy objects to this view and says that the capacity of anything cannot be known until the effect produced is known, and if capacity to produce effects be regarded as existence or being, then the being or existence of the effect cannot be known, until that has produced another effect and that another *ad infinitum*. Since there can be no being that has not capacity of producing effects, and as this capacity can demonstrate itself only in an infinite chain, it will be impossible to know any being or to affirm the capacity of producing effects as the definition of existence. Moreover if all things were momentary there would be no permanent perceiver to observe the change, and there being nothing fixed there could hardly be any means even of taking to any kind of inference. To this Ratnakīrtti replies that capacity (*sāmarthya*) cannot be denied, for it is demonstrated even in making the denial. The observation of any concomitance in agreement in presence, or agreement in absence, does not require any permanent observer, for under certain conditions of agreement there is the knowledge of the concomitance of agreement in presence, and in other conditions there is the knowledge of the concomitance in absence. This knowledge of concomitance at the succeeding moment holds within itself the experience of the conditions of the preceding moment, and this alone is what we find and not any permanent observer.

The Buddhist definition of being or existence (*sattva*) is indeed capacity, and we arrived at this when it was observed that in all proved cases capacity was all that could be defined of being;—seed was but the capacity of producing shoots, and even if this capacity should require further capacity to produce effects, the fact which has been perceived still remains, viz. that the existence of seeds is nothing but the capacity of producing the shoots and thus there is no vicious infinite[1]. Though things are momentary, yet we could have concomitance between things only so long as their apparent forms are not different (*atadrūpaparāvṛttayoreva sādhyasādhanayoḥ pratyakṣeṇa vyāptigrahaṇāt*). The vyāpti or concomitance of any two things (e.g. the fire and the smoke) is based on extreme similarity and not on identity.

Another objection raised against the doctrine of momentariness is this, that a cause (e.g. seed) must wait for a number of other collocations of earth, water, etc., before it can produce the effect (e.g. the shoots) and hence the doctrine must fail. To this Ratnakīrtti replies that the seed does not exist before and produce the effect when joined by other collocations, but such is the special effectiveness of a particular seed-moment, that it produces both the collocations or conditions as well as the effect, the shoot. How a special seed-moment became endowed with such special effectiveness is to be sought in other causal moments which preceded it, and on which it was dependent. Ratnakīrtti wishes to draw attention to the fact that as one perceptual moment reveals a number of objects, so one causal moment may produce a number of effects. Thus he says that the inference that whatever has being is momentary is valid and free from any fallacy.

It is not important to enlarge upon the second part of Ratnakīrtti's arguments in which he tries to show that the production of effects could not be explained if we did not suppose

[1] The distinction between vicious and harmless infinites was known to the Indians at least as early as the sixth or the seventh century. Jayanta quotes a passage which differentiates the two clearly (*Nyāyamañjarī*, p. 22):

"*mūlakṣatikarīmāhuranavasthāṃ hi dūṣaṇam.*
mūlasiddhau tvarucyāpi nānavasthā nivāryate."

The infinite regress that has to be gone through in order to arrive at the root matter awaiting to be solved destroys the root and is hence vicious, whereas if the root is saved there is no harm in a regress though one may not be willing to have it.

all things to be momentary, for this is more an attempt to refute the doctrines of Nyāya than an elaboration of the Buddhist principles.

The doctrine of momentariness ought to be a direct corollary of the Buddhist metaphysics. But it is curious that though all dharmas were regarded as changing, the fact that they were all strictly momentary (*kṣaṇika*—i.e. existing only for one moment) was not emphasized in early Pāli literature. Aśvaghoṣa in his *Śraddhotpādaśāstra* speaks of all skandhas as kṣaṇika (Suzuki's translation, p. 105). Buddhaghoṣa also speaks of the meditation of the khandhas as khaṇika in his *Visuddhimagga*. But from the seventh century A.D. till the tenth century this doctrine together with the doctrine of arthakriyākāritva received great attention at the hands of the Sautrāntikas and the Vaibhāṣikas. All the Nyāya and Vedānta literature of this period is full of refutations and criticisms of these doctrines. The only Buddhist account available of the doctrine of momentariness is from the pen of Ratnakīrtti. Some of the general features of his argument in favour of the view have been given above. Elaborate accounts of it may be found in any of the important Nyāya works of this period such as *Nyāyamañjari*, *Tātparyyaṭīkā* of Vācaspati Miśra, etc.

Buddhism did not at any time believe anything to be permanent. With the development of this doctrine they gave great emphasis to this point. Things came to view at one moment and the next moment they were destroyed. Whatever is existent is momentary. It is said that our notion of permanence is derived from the notion of permanence of ourselves, but Buddhism denied the existence of any such permanent selves. What appears as self is but the bundle of ideas, emotions, and active tendencies manifesting at any particular moment. The next moment these dissolve, and new bundles determined by the preceding ones appear and so on. The present thought is thus the only thinker. Apart from the emotions, ideas, and active tendencies, we cannot discover any separate self or soul. It is the combined product of these ideas, emotions, etc., that yield the illusory appearance of self at any moment. The consciousness of self is the resultant product as it were of the combination of ideas, emotions, etc., at any particular moment. As these ideas, emotions, etc., change every moment there is no such thing as a permanent self.

The fact that I remember that I have been existing for

a long time past does not prove that a permanent self has been existing for such a long period. When I say this is that book, I perceive the book with my eye at the present moment, but that "this book" is the same as "that book" (i.e. the book arising in memory), cannot be perceived by the senses. It is evident that the "that book" of memory refers to a book seen in the past, whereas "this book" refers to the book which is before my eyes. The feeling of identity which is adduced to prove permanence is thus due to a confusion between an object of memory referring to a past and different object with the object as perceived at the present moment by the senses[1]. This is true not only of all recognition of identity and permanence of external objects but also of the perception of the identity of self, for the perception of self-identity results from the confusion of certain ideas or emotions arising in memory with similar ideas of the present moment. But since memory points to an object of past perception, and the perception to another object of the present moment, identity cannot be proved by a confusion of the two. Every moment all objects of the world are suffering dissolution and destruction, but yet things appear to persist, and destruction cannot often be noticed. Our hair and nails grow and are cut, but yet we think that we have the same hair and nail that we had before, in place of old hairs new ones similar to them have sprung forth, and they leave the impression as if the old ones were persisting. So it is that though things are destroyed every moment, others similar to these often rise into being and are destroyed the next moment and so on, and these similar things succeeding in a series produce the impression that it is one and the same thing which has been persisting through all the passing moments[2]. Just as the flame of a candle is changing every moment and yet it seems to us as if we have been perceiving the same flame all the while, so all our bodies, our ideas, emotions, etc., all external objects around us are being destroyed every moment, and new ones are being generated at every succeeding moment, but so long as the objects of the succeeding moments are similar to those of the preceding moments, it appears to us that things have remained the same and no destruction has taken place.

[1] See pratyabhijñānirāsa of the Buddhists, *Nyāyamañjarī*, V.S. Series, pp. 449, etc.

[2] See *Tarkarahasyadīpikā* of Guṇaratna, p. 30, and also *Nyāyamañjarī*, V.S. edition, p. 450.

The Doctrine of Momentariness and the Doctrine of Causal Efficiency (Arthakriyākāritva).

It appears that a thing or a phenomenon may be defined from the Buddhist point of view as being the combination of diverse characteristics[1]. What we call a thing is but a conglomeration of diverse characteristics which are found to affect, determine or influence other conglomerations appearing as sentient or as inanimate bodies. So long as the characteristics forming the elements of any conglomeration remain perfectly the same, the conglomeration may be said to be the same. As soon as any of these characteristics is supplanted by any other new characteristic, the conglomeration is to be called a new one[2]. Existence or being of things means the work that any conglomeration does or the influence that it exerts on other conglomerations. This in Sanskrit is called *arthakriyākāritva* which literally translated means—the power of performing actions and purposes of some kind[3]. The criterion of existence or being is the performance of certain specific actions, or rather existence means that a certain effect has been produced in some way (causal efficiency). That which has produced such an effect is then called existent or *sat*. Any change in the effect thus produced means a corresponding

[1] Compare *Milindapañha*, II. I. I.—The Chariot Simile.

[2] Compare *Tarkarahasyadīpikā* of Guṇaratna, A. S.'s edition, pp. 24, 28 and *Nyāyamañjarī*, V.S. edition, pp. 445, etc., and also the paper on *Kṣaṇabhaṅgasiddhi* by Ratnakīrtti in *Six Buddhist Nyāya tracts*.

[3] This meaning of the word "arthakriyākāritva" is different from the meaning of the word as we found in the section "sautrāntika theory of perception." But we find the development of this meaning both in Ratnakīrtti as well as in Nyāya writers who referred to this doctrine. With Vinītadeva (seventh century A.D.) the word "*arthakriyāsiddhi*" meant the fulfilment of any need such as the cooking of rice by fire (*arthaśabdena prayojanamucyate puruṣasya prayojanaṃ dārupākādi tasya siddhiḥ niṣpattiḥ*—the word *artha* means need; the need of man such as cooking by logs, etc.; *siddhi* of that, means accomplishment). With Dharmottara who flourished about a century and a half later *arthasiddhi* means action (*anuṣṭhiti*) with reference to undesirable and desirable objects (*heyopādeyārthaviṣayā*). But with Ratnakīrtti (A.D. 950) the word *arthakriyākāritva* has an entirely different sense. It means with him efficiency of producing any action or event, and as such it is regarded as the characteristic definition of existence (*sattva*). Thus he says in his *Kṣaṇabhaṅgasiddhi*, pp. 20, 21, that though in different philosophies there are different definitions of existence or being, he will open his argument with the universally accepted definition of existence as *arthakriyākāritva* (efficiency of causing any action or event). Whenever Hindu writers after Ratnakīrtti refer to the Buddhist doctrine of *arthakriyākāritva* they usually refer to this doctrine in Ratnakīrtti's sense.

change of existence. Now, that selfsame definite specific effect which is produced now was never produced before, and cannot be repeated in the future, for that identical effect which is once produced cannot be produced again. So the effects produced in us by objects at different moments of time may be similar but cannot be identical. Each moment is associated with a new effect and each new effect thus produced means in each case the coming into being of a correspondingly new existence of things. If things were permanent there would be no reason why they should be performing different effects at different points of time. Any difference in the effect produced, whether due to the thing itself or its combination with other accessories, justifies us in asserting that the thing has changed and a new one has come in its place. The existence of a jug for example is known by the power it has of forcing itself upon our minds; if it had no such power then we could not have said that it existed. We can have no notion of the meaning of existence other than the impression produced on us; this impression is nothing else but the power exerted by things on us, for there is no reason why one should hold that beyond such powers as are associated with the production of impressions or effects there should be some other permanent entity to which the power adhered, and which existed even when the power was not exerted. We perceive the power of producing effects and define each unit of such power as amounting to a unit of existence. And as there would be different units of power at different moments, there should also be as many new existences, i.e. existents must be regarded as momentary, existing at each moment that exerts a new power. This definition of existence naturally brings in the doctrine of momentariness shown by Ratnakīrtti.

Some Ontological Problems on which the Different Indian Systems Diverged.

We cannot close our examination of Buddhist philosophy without briefly referring to its views on some ontological problems which were favourite subjects of discussion in almost all philosophical circles of India. These are in brief: (1) the relation of cause and effect, (2) the relation of the whole (*avayavī*) and the part (*avayava*), (3) the relation of generality (*sāmānya*) to the specific individuals, (4) the relation of attributes or qualities and the substance and the problem of the relation of inherence, (5) the relation of power (*śakti*) to the power-possessor (*śaktimān*). Thus on the relation of cause and effect, Śaṅkara held that cause alone was permanent, real, and all effects as such were but impermanent illusions due to ignorance, Sāṃkhya held that there was no difference between cause and effect, except that the former was only the earlier stage which when transformed through certain changes became the effect. The history of any causal activity is the history of the transformation of the cause into the effects. Buddhism holds everything to be momentary, so neither cause nor effect can abide. One is called the effect because its momentary existence has been determined by the destruction of its momentary antecedent called the cause. There is no permanent reality which undergoes the change, but one change is determined by another and this determination is nothing more than "that happening, this happened." On the relation of parts to whole, Buddhism does not believe in the existence of wholes. According to it, it is the parts which illusorily appear as the whole, the individual atoms rise into being and die the next moment and thus there is no such thing as "whole[1]." The Buddhists hold again that there are no universals, for it is the individuals alone which come and go. There are my five fingers as individuals but there is no such thing as fingerness (*aṅgulitva*) as the abstract universal of the fingers. On the relation of attributes and substance we know that the Sautrāntika Buddhists did not believe in the existence of any substance apart from its attributes; what we call a substance is but a unit capable of producing a unit of sensation. In the external world there are as many individual simple units (atoms) as there are points of sensations. Corresponding to each unit of sensation there is a separate simple unit in the objective world. Our perception of a thing is thus the perception of the assemblage of these sensations. In the objective world also there are no substances but atoms or reals, each representing a unit of sensation, force or attribute, rising into being and dying the next moment. Buddhism thus denies the existence of any such relation as that of inherence (*samavāya*) in which relation the attributes are said to exist in the substance, for since there are no separate substances there is no necessity for admitting the relation of inherence. Following the same logic Buddhism also does not

[1] See *Avavavinirākaraṇa, Six Buddhist Nyāya tracts, Bibliotheca Indica*, Calcutta, 1910.

believ in the existence of a power-possessor separate from the power.

Brief survey of the evolution of Buddhist Thought.

In the earliest period of Buddhism more attention was paid to the four noble truths than to systematic metaphysics. What was sorrow, what was the cause of sorrow, what was the cessation of sorrow and what could lead to it? The doctrine of *paṭiccasamuppāda* was offered only to explain how sorrow came in and not with a view to the solving of a metaphysical problem. The discussion of ultimate metaphysical problems, such as whether the world was eternal or non-eternal, or whether a Tathāgata existed after death or not, were considered as heresies in early Buddhism. Great emphasis was laid on sīla, samādhi and paññā and the doctrine that there was no soul. The Abhidhammas hardly give us any new philosophy which was not contained in the Suttas. They only elaborated the materials of the suttas with enumerations and definitions. With the evolution of Mahāyāna scriptures from some time about B.C. 200 the doctrine of the non-essentialness and voidness of all *dhammas* began to be preached. This doctrine, which was taken up and elaborated by Nāgārjuna, Āryadeva, Kumārajīva and Candrakīrti, is more or less a corollary from the older doctrine of Buddhism. If one could not say whether the world was eternal or non-eternal, or whether a Tathāgata existed or did not exist after death, and if there was no permanent soul and all the dhammas were changing, the only legitimate way of thinking about all things appeared to be to think of them as mere void and non-essential appearances. These appearances appear as being mutually related but apart from their appearance they have no other essence, no being or reality. The Tathatā doctrine which was preached by Aśvaghoṣa oscillated between the position of this absolute non-essentialness of all dhammas and the Brahminic idea that something existed as the background of all these non-essential dhammas. This he called tathatā, but he could not consistently say that any such permanent entity could exist. The Vijñānavāda doctrine which also took its rise at this time appears to me to be a mixture of the Śūnyavāda doctrine and the Tathatā doctrine; but when carefully examined it seems to be nothing but Śūnyavāda, with an attempt at explaining all the observed phenomena. If everything was non-essential how did it originate? Vijñānavāda proposes to give an answer, and says that these phenomena are all but ideas of the mind generated by the beginningless vāsanā (desire) of the mind. The difficulty which is felt with regard to the Tathatā doctrine that there must be some reality which is generating all these ideas appearing as phenomena, is the same as that in the Vijñānavāda doctrine. The Vijñānavādins could not admit the existence of such a reality, but yet their doctrines led them to it. They could not properly solve the difficulty, and admitted that their doctrine was some sort of a compromise with the Brahminical doctrines of heresy, but they said that this was a compromise to make the doctrine intelligible to the heretics; in truth however the reality assumed in the doctrine was also non-essential. The Vijñānavāda literature that is available to us is very scanty and from that we are not in a position to judge what answers Vijñānavāda could give on the point. These three doctrines developed almost about the same time and the difficulty of conceiving śūnya (void), tathatā, (thatness) and the ālayavijñāna of Vijñānavāda is more or less the same.

The Tathatā doctrine of Aśvaghoṣa practically ceased with him. But the Śūnyavāda and the Vijñānavāda doctrines which originated probably about B.C. 200 continued to develop probably till the eighth century A.D. Vigorous disputes with Śūnyavāda doctrines are rarely made in any independent work of Hindu philosophy, after Kumārila and Śaṅkara. From the third or the fourth century A.D. some Buddhists took to the study of systematic logic and began to criticize the doctrine of the Hindu logicians. Diṅnāga the Buddhist logician (A.D. 500) probably started these hostile criticisms by trying to refute the doctrines of the great Hindu logician Vātsyāyana, in his Pramāṇasamuccaya. In association with this logical activity we find the activity of two other schools of Buddhism, viz. the Sarvāstivādins (known also as Vaibhāṣikas) and the Sautrāntikas. Both the Vaibhāṣikas and the Sautrāntikas accepted the existence of the external world, and they were generally in conflict with the Hindu schools of thought Nyāya-Vaiśeṣika and Sāṃkhya which also admitted the existence of the external world. Vasubandhu (A.D. 420–500) was one of the most illustrious names of this school. We have from this time forth a number of great Buddhist thinkers such as Yaśomitra (commentator of Vasubandhu's work),

Dharmmakīrtti (writer of Nyāyabindu A.D. 635), Vinītadeva and Śāntabhadra (commentators of Nyāyabindu), Dharmmottara (commentator of Nyāyabindu A.D. 847), Ratnakīrtti (A.D. 950), Paṇḍita Aśoka, and Ratnākara Śānti, some of whose contributious have been published in the *Six Buddhist Nyāya Tracts*, published in Calcutta in the *Bibliotheca Indica* series. These Buddhist writers were mainly interested in discussions regarding the nature of perception, inference, the doctrine of momentariness, and the doctrine of causal efficiency (*arthakriyākāritva*) as demonstrating the nature of existence. On the negative side they were interested in denying the ontological theories of Nyāya and Sāṃkhya with regard to the nature of class-concepts, negation, relation of whole and part, connotation of terms, etc. These problems hardly attracted any notice in the non-Sautrāntika and non-Vaibhāṣika schools of Buddhism of earlier times. They of course agreed with the earlier Buddhists in denying the existence of a permanent soul, but this they did with the help of their doctrine of causal efficiency. The points of disagreement between Hindu thought up to Śaṅkara (A.D. 800) and Buddhist thought till the time of Śaṅkara consisted mainly in the denial by the Buddhists of a permanent soul and the permanent external world. For Hindu thought was more or less realistic, and even the Vedānta of Śaṅkara admitted the existence of the permanent external world in some sense. With Śaṅkara the forms of the external world were no doubt illusory, but they all had a permanent background in the Brahman, which was the only reality behind all mental and the physical phenomena. The Sautrāntikas admitted the existence of the external world and so their quarrel with Nyāya and Sāṃkhya was with regard to their doctrine of momentariness; their denial of soul and their views on the different ontological problems were in accordance with their doctrine of momentariness. After the twelfth century we do not hear much of any new disputes with the Buddhists. From this time the disputes were mainly between the different systems of Hindu philosophers, viz. Nyāya, the Vedānta of the school of Śaṅkara and the Theistic Vedānta of Rāmānuja, Madhva, etc.

VI

THE JAINA PHILOSOPHY

The Origin of Jainism.

NOTWITHSTANDING the radical differences in their philosophical notions Jainism and Buddhism, which were originally both orders of monks outside the pale of Brahmanism, present some resemblance in outward appearance, and some European scholars who became acquainted with Jainism through inadequate samples of Jaina literature easily persuaded themselves that it was an offshoot of Buddhism, and even Indians unacquainted with Jaina literature are often found to commit the same mistake. But it has now been proved beyond doubt that this idea is wrong and Jainism is at least as old as Buddhism. The oldest Buddhist works frequently mention the Jains as a rival sect, under their old name Nigantha and their leader Nātaputta Varddhamāna Mahāvīra, the last prophet of the Jains. The canonical books of the Jains mention as contemporaries of Mahāvīra the same kings as reigned during Buddha's career.

Thus Mahāvīra was a contemporary of Buddha, but unlike Buddha he was neither the author of the religion nor the founder of the sect, but a monk who having espoused the Jaina creed afterwards became the seer and the last prophet (Tīrthankara) of Jainism[1]. His predecessor Pārśva, the last Tīrthaṅkara but one, is said to have died 250 years before Mahāvīra, while Pārśva's predecessor Ariṣṭanemi is said to have died 84,000 years before Mahāvīra's Nirvāṇa. The story in *Uttarādhyayanasūtra* that a disciple of Pārśva met a disciple of Mahāvīra and brought about the union of the old Jainism and that propounded by Mahāvīra seems to suggest that this Pārśva was probably a historical person.

According to the belief of the orthodox Jains, the Jaina religion is eternal, and it has been revealed again and again in every one of the endless succeeding periods of the world by innumerable Tīrthaṅkaras. In the present period the first Tīrthaṅkara was Ṛṣabha and the last, the 24th, was Vardhamāna Mahāvīra. All

[1] See Jacobi's article on Jainism, *E. R. E.*

Tīrthaṅkaras have reached mokṣa at their death, and they neither care for nor have any influence on worldly affairs, but yet they are regarded as "Gods" by the Jains and are worshipped[1].

Two Sects of Jainism[2].

There are two main sects of Jains, Śvetāmbaras (wearers of white cloths) and Digambaras (the naked). They are generally agreed on all the fundamental principles of Jainism. The tenets peculiar to the Digambaras are firstly that perfect saints such as the Tīrthaṅkaras live without food, secondly that the embryo of Mahāvīra was not removed from the womb of Devanandā to that of Triśalā as the Śvetāmbaras contend, thirdly that a monk who owns any property and wears clothes cannot reach Mokṣa, fourthly that no woman can reach Mokṣa[3]. The Digambaras deny the canonical works of the Śvetāmbaras and assert that these had been lost immediately after Mahāvīra. The origin of the Digambaras is attributed to Śivabhūti (A.D. 83) by the Śvetāmbaras as due to a schism in the old Śvetāmbara church, of which there had already been previous to that seven other schisms. The Digambaras in their turn deny this, and say that they themselves alone have preserved the original practices, and that under Bhadrabāhu, the eighth sage after Mahāvīra, the last Tīrthaṅkara, there rose the sect of Ardhaphālakas with laxer principles, from which developed the present sect of Śvetāmbaras (A.D. 80). The Digambaras having separated in early times from the Śvetāmbaras developed peculiar religious ceremonies of their own, and have a different ecclesiastical and literary history, though there is practically no difference about the main creed. It may not be out of place here to mention that the Sanskrit works of the Digambaras go back to a greater antiquity than those of the Śvetāmbaras, if we except the canonical books of the latter. It may be noted in this connection that there developed in later times about 84 different schools of Jainism differing from one another only in minute details of conduct. These were called *gacchas*, and the most important of these is the Kharatara Gaccha, which had split into many minor gacchas. Both sects of Jains have

[1] See "*Digumbara Jain Iconography* (I.a, xxxii [1903] p. 459" of J.Burgess, and Bühler's "Specimens of Jina sculptures from Mathurā," in *Epigraphica Indica*, II. pp. 311 etc. See also Jacobi's article on Jainism, *E. R. E.*

[2] See Jacobi's article on Jainism, *E. R. E.*

[3] See Guṇaratna's commentary on Jainism in *Ṣaḍdarśanasamuccaya*.

preserved a list of the succession of their teachers from Mahāvīra (*sthavirāvali*, *paṭṭāvali*, *gurvāvali*) and also many legends about them such as those in the *Kalpasūtra*, the *Pariśiṣṭa-parvan* of Hemacandra, etc.

The Canonical and other Literature of the Jains.

According to the Jains there were originally two kinds of sacred books, the fourteen Pūrvas and the eleven Aṅgas. The Pūrvas continued to be transmitted for some time but were gradually lost. The works known as the eleven Aṅgas are now the oldest parts of the existing Jain canon. The names of these are *Ācāra*, *Sūtrakṛta*, *Sthāna*, *Samavāya Bhagavatī*, *Jñātadharmakathās*, *Upāsakadaśās*, *Antakṛtadaśās Anuttaraupapātikadaśās*, *Praśnavyākaraṇa*, *Vipāka*. In addition to these there are the twelve *Upāṅgas*[1], the ten *Prakīrṇas*[2], six *Chedasūtras*[3], *Nāndī* and *Anuyogadvāra* and four *Mūlasūtras* (*Uttarādhyayana*, *Āvaśyaka*, *Daśavaikālika*, and *Piṇḍaniryukti*). The Digambaras however assert that these original works have all been lost, and that the present works which pass by the old names are spurious. The original language of these according to the Jains was Ardhamāgadhī, but these suffered attempts at modernization and it is best to call the language of the sacred texts Jaina Prākrit and that of the later works Jaina Mahārāṣṭrī. A large literature of glosses and commentaries has grown up round the sacred texts. And besides these, the Jains possess separate works, which contain systematic expositions of their faith in Prākrit and Sanskrit. Many commentaries have also been written upon these independent treatises. One of the oldest of these treatises is Umāsvāti's *Tattvārthādhigamasūtra* (A.D. 1–85). Some of the most important later Jaina works on which this chapter is based are *Viśeṣāvaśyakabhāṣya*, Jaina *Tarkavāritika*, with the commentary of Śāntyācāryya, *Dravyasaṃgraha* of Nemicandra (A.D. 1150), *Syādvādamañjarī* of Malliṣena (A.D. 1292), *Nyāyāvatāra* of Siddhasena Divākara (A.D. 533), *Parīkṣāmukkasūtralaghuvṛtti* of Anantavīryya (A.D. 1039), *Prameyakamalamārtaṇḍa* of Prabhā-

[1] *Aupapātika, Rājapraśnīya, Jīvābhigama, Prajñāpanā, Jambudvīpaprajñapti, Candraprajñapti, Sūryaprajñapti, Nirayāvali, Kalpāvataṃsikā, Puṣpikā, Puṣpacūlikā, Vṛṣṇidaśās.*

[2] *Catuḥśaraṇa, Saṃstāra, Āturapratyākhyāna, Bhaktāparijñā, Taṇḍulavaiyālī, Caṇḍāvīja, Devendrastava, Gaṇivīja, Mahāpratyākhyāna, Vīrastava.*

[3] *Niśītha, Mahāniśītha, Vyavahāra, Daśaśrutaskandha, Bṛhatkalpa, Pañcakalpa.*

candra (A.D. 825), *Yogaśāstra* of Hemacandra (A.D. 1088–1172), and *Pramāṇanayatattvālokālaṃkāra* of Deva Sūri (A.D. 1086–1169). I am indebted for these dates to Vidyābhūṣaṇa's *Indian Logic*.

It may here be mentioned that the Jains also possess a secular literature of their own in poetry and prose, both Sanskrit and Prākrit. There are also many moral tales (e.g. *Samarāicca-kahā*, *Upamitabhavaprapañca-kathā* in Prākrit, and the *Yaśastilaka* of Somadeva and Dhanapāla's *Tilakamañjarī*); Jaina Sanskrit poems both in the Purāṇa and Kāvya style and hymns in Prākrit and Sanskrit are also very numerous. There are also many Jaina dramas. The Jaina authors have also contributed many works, original treatises as well as commentaries, to the scientific literature of India in its various branches: grammar, biography, metrics, poetics, philosophy, etc. The contributions of the Jains to logic deserve special notice[1].

Some General Characteristics of the Jains.

The Jains exist only in India and their number is a little less than a million and a half. The Digambaras are found chiefly in Southern India but also in the North, in the North-western provinces, Eastern Rājputāna and the Punjab. The head-quarters of the Śvetāmbaras are in Gujarat and Western Rājputāna, but they are to be found also all over Northern and Central India.

The outfit of a monk, as Jacobi describes it, is restricted to bare necessaries, and these he must beg—clothes, a blanket, an alms-bowl, a stick, a broom to sweep the ground, a piece of cloth to cover his mouth when speaking lest insects should enter it[2]. The outfit of nuns is the same except that they have additional clothes. The Digambaras have a similar outfit, but keep no clothes, use brooms of peacock's feathers or hairs of the tail of a cow (*cāmara*)[3]. The monks shave the head or remove the hair by plucking it out. The latter method of getting rid of the hair is to be preferred, and is regarded sometimes as an essential rite. The duties of monks are very hard. They should sleep only three hours and spend the rest of the time in repenting of and expiating sins, meditating, studying, begging alms (in the afternoon), and careful inspection of their clothes and other things for the removal of insects. The laymen should try to approach the ideal of conduct of the monks

[1] See Jacobi's article on Jainism, *E. R. E.*
[2] See Jacobi, *loc. cit.*
[3] See *Ṣaḍdarśanasamuccaya*, chapter IV.

by taking upon themselves particular vows, and the monks are required to deliver sermons and explain the sacred texts in the upāśrayas (separate buildings for monks like the Buddhist vihāras). The principle of extreme carefulness not to destroy any living being has been in monastic life carried out to its very last consequences, and has shaped the conduct of the laity in a great measure. No layman will intentionally kill any living being, not even an insect, however troublesome. He will remove it carefully without hurting it. The principle of not hurting any living being thus bars them from many professions such as agriculture, etc., and has thrust them into commerce[1].

Life of Mahāvīra.

Mahāvīra, the last prophet of the Jains, was a Kṣattriya of the Jñāta clan and a native of Vaiśāli (modern Besarh, 27 miles north of Patna). He was the second son of Siddhārtha and Triśalā. The Śvetāmbaras maintain that the embryo of the Tīrthaṅkara which first entered the womb of the Brahmin lady Devanandā was then transferred to the womb of Triśalā. This story the Digambaras do not believe as we have already seen. His parents were the worshippers of Pārśva and gave him the name Varddhamāna (Vīra or Mahāvīra). He married Yaśodā and had a daughter by her. In his thirtieth year his parents died and with the permission of his brother Nandivardhana he became a monk. After twelve years of self-mortification and meditation he attained omniscience (*kevala*, cf. *bodhi* of the Buddhists). He lived to preach for forty-two years more, and attained mokṣa (emancipation) some years before Buddha in about B.C. 480[2].

The Fundamental Ideas of Jaina Ontology.

A thing (such as clay) is seen to assume various shapes and to undergo diverse changes (such as the form of a jug, or pan, etc.), and we have seen that the Chāndogya Upaniṣad held that since in all changes the clay-matter remained permanent, that alone was true, whereas the changes of form and state were but appearances, the nature of which cannot be rationally

[1] See Jacobi's article on Jainism, *E. R. E.*

[2] See Hoernlé's translation of *Uvāsagadasāo*, Jacobi, *loc. cit.*, and Hoernlé's artici on the Ājīvakas, *E. R. E.* The Śvetāmbaras, however, say that this date was B.C. 527 and the Digambaras place it eighteen years later.

demonstrated or explained. The unchangeable substance (e.g. the clay-matter) alone is true, and the changing forms are mere illusions of the senses, mere objects of name (*nāma-rūpa*)[1]. What we call tangibility, visibility, or other sense-qualities, have no real existence, for they are always changing, and are like mere phantoms of which no conception can be made by the light of reason.

The Buddhists hold that changing qualities can alone be perceived and that there is no unchanging substance behind them. What we perceive as clay is but some specific quality, what we perceive as jug is also some quality. Apart from these qualities we do not perceive any qualitiless substance, which the Upaniṣads regard as permanent and unchangeable. The permanent and unchangeable substance is thus a mere fiction of ignorance, as there are only the passing collocations of qualities. Qualities do not imply that there are substances to which they adhere, for the so-called pure substance does not exist, as it can neither be perceived by the senses nor inferred. There are only the momentary passing qualities. We should regard each change of quality as a new existence.

The Jains we know were the contemporaries of Buddha and possibly of some of the Upaniṣads too, and they had also a solution to offer. They held that it was not true that substance alone was true and qualities were mere false and illusory appearances. Further it was not true as the Buddhists said that there was no permanent substance but merely the change of passing qualities, for both these represent two extreme views and are contrary to experience. Both of them, however, contain some elements of truth but not the whole truth as given in experience. Experience shows that in all changes there are three elements: (1) that some collocations of qualities appear to remain unchanged; (2) that some new qualities are generated; (3) that some old qualities are destroyed. It is true that qualities of things are changing every minute, but all qualities are not changing. Thus when a jug is made, it means that the clay-lump has been destroyed, a jug has been generated and the clay is permanent, i.e. all production means that some old qualities have been lost, some new ones brought in, and there is some part in it which is permanent. The clay has become lost in some form, has generated itself in another, and remained permanent in still

[1] See Chāndogya, VI. 1.

another form. It is by virtue of these unchanged qualities that a thing is said to be permanent though undergoing change. Thus when a lump of gold is turned into a rod or a ring, all the specific qualities which come under the connotation of the word "gold" are seen to continue, though the forms are successively changed, and with each such change some of its qualities are lost and some new ones are acquired. Such being the case, the truth comes to this, that there is always a permanent entity as represented by the permanence of such qualities as lead us to call it a substance in spite of all its diverse changes. The nature of being (*sat*) then is neither the absolutely unchangeable, nor the momentary changing qualities or existences, but involves them both. Being then, as is testified by experience, is that which involves a permanent unit, which is incessantly every moment losing some qualities and gaining new ones. The notion of being involves a permanent (*dhruva*) accession of some new qualities (*utpāda*) and loss of some old qualities (*vyaya*)[1]. The solution of Jainism is thus a reconciliation of the two extremes of Vedāntism and Buddhism on grounds of common-sense experience.

The Doctrine of Relative Pluralism (anekāntavāda).

This conception of being as the union of the permanent and change brings us naturally to the doctrine of Anekāntavāda or what we may call relative pluralism as against the extreme absolutism of the Upaniṣads and the pluralism of the Buddhists. The Jains regarded all things as *anekānta* (*na-ekānta*), or in other words they held that nothing could be affirmed absolutely, as all affirmations were true only under certain conditions and limitations. Thus speaking of a gold jug, we see that its existence as a substance (*dravya*) is of the nature of a collocation of atoms and not as any other substance such as space (*ākāśa*), i.e. a gold jug is a *dravya* only in one sense of the term and not in every sense; so it is a *dravya* in the sense that it is a collocation of atoms and not a *dravya* in the sense of space or time (*kāla*). It is thus both a dravya and not a dravya at one and the same time. Again it is atomic in the sense that it is a composite of earth-atoms and not atomic in the sense that it is

[1] See *Tattvārthādhigamasūtra*, and Guṇaratna's treatment of Jainism in *Ṣaḍdarśanasamuccaya*.

not a composite of water-atoms. Again it is a composite of earth-atoms only in the sense that gold is a metallic modification of earth, and not any other modification of earth as clay or stone. Its being constituted of metal-atoms is again true in the sense that it is made up of gold-atoms and not of iron-atoms. It is made up again of gold-atoms in the sense of melted and unsullied gold and not as gold in the natural condition. It is again made up of such unsullied and melted gold as has been hammered and shaped by the goldsmith Devadatta and not by Yajñadatta. Its being made up of atoms conditioned as above is again only true in the sense that the collocation has been shaped as a jug and not as a pot and so on. Thus proceeding in a similar manner the Jains say that all affirmations are true of a thing only in a certain limited sense. All things (*vastu*) thus possess an infinite number of qualities (*anantadharmātmakaṃ vastu*), each of which can only be affirmed in a particular sense. Such an ordinary thing as a jug will be found to be the object of an infinite number of affirmations and the possessor of an infinite number of qualities from infinite points of view, which are all true in certain restricted senses and not absolutely[1]. Thus in the positive relation riches cannot be affirmed of poverty but in the negative relation such an affirmation is possible as when we say "the poor man has no riches." The poor man possesses riches not in a positive but in a negative way. Thus in some relation or other anything may be affirmed of any other thing, and again in other relations the very same thing cannot be affirmed of it. The different standpoints from which things (though possessed of infinite determinations) can be spoken of as possessing this or that quality or as appearing in relation to this or that, are technically called *naya*[2].

The Doctrine of Nayas.

In framing judgments about things there are two ways open to us, firstly we may notice the manifold qualities and characteristics of anything but view them as unified in the thing; thus when we say "this is a book" we do not look at its characteristic qualities as being different from it, but rather the qualities or characteristics are perceived as having no separate existence from

1 See Guṇaratna on Jainamata in *Ṣaḍdarśanasamuccaya*, pp. 211, etc., and also *Tattvārthādhigamasūtra*.

2 See *Tattvārthādhigamasūtra*, and *Viśeṣāvaśyaka dhāṣya*, pp. 895–923.

the thing. Secondly we may notice the qualities separately and regard the thing as a mere non-existent fiction (cf. the Buddhist view); thus I may speak of the different qualities of the book separately and hold that the qualities of things are alone perceptible and the book apart from these cannot be found. These two points of view are respectively called *dravyanaya* and *paryāyanaya*[1]. The dravyanaya again shows itself in three forms, and paryāyanaya in four forms, of which the first form only is important for our purposes, the other three being important rather from the point of view of grammar and language had better be omitted here. The three nayas under dravyanaya are called naigama-naya, saṃgraha-naya and vyavahāra-naya.

When we speak of a thing from a purely common sense point of view, we do not make our ideas clear or precise. Thus I may hold a book in my hand and when asked whether my hands are empty, I may say, no, I have something in my hand, or I may say, I have a book in my hand. It is evident that in the first answer I looked at the book from the widest and most general point of view as a "thing," whereas in the second I looked at it in its special existence as a book. Again I may be reading a page of a book, and I may say I am reading a book, but in reality I was reading only one of the pages of the book. I may be scribbling on loose sheets, and may say this is my book on Jaina philosophy, whereas in reality there were no books but merely some loose sheets. This looking at things from the loose common sense view, in which we do not consider them from the point of view of their most general characteristic as "being" or as any of their special characteristics, but simply as they appear at first sight, is technically called the naigama standpoint. This empirical view probably proceeds on the assumption that a thing possesses the most general as well as the most special qualities, and hence we may lay stress on any one of these at any time and ignore the other ones. This is the point of view from which according to the Jains the Nyāya and Vaiśeṣika schools interpret experience.

Saṃgraha-naya is the looking at things merely from the most general point of view. Thus we may speak of all individual things from their most general and fundamental aspect as "being." This according to the Jains is the Vedānta way of looking at things.

1 *Syādvādamañjarī*, pp. 171–173.

The vyavahāra-naya standpoint holds that the real essence of things is to be regarded from the point of view of actual practical experience of the thing, which unifies within it some general as well as some special traits, which has been existing from past times and remain in the future, but yet suffer trifling changes all the while, changes which are serviceable to us in a thousand ways. Thus a "book" has no doubt some general traits, shared by all books, but it has some special traits as well. Its atoms are continually suffering some displacement and rearrangement, but yet it has been existing as a book for some time past and will exist for some time in the future as well. All these characteristics, go to make up the essence of the "book" of our everyday experience, and none of these can be separated and held up as being the concept of a "book." This according to the Jains is the Sāṃkhya way of looking at things.

The first view of paryāya-naya called *ṛjusūtra* is the Buddhist view which does not believe in the existence of the thing in the past or in the future, but holds that a thing is a mere conglomeration of characteristics which may be said to produce effects at any given moment. At each new moment there are new collocations of new qualities and it is these which may be regarded as the true essence of our notion of things[1].

The nayas as we have already said are but points of view, or aspects of looking at things, and as such are infinite in number. The above four represent only a broad classification of these. The Jains hold that the Nyāya-Vaiśeṣika, the Vēdanta, the Sāṃkhya, and the Buddhist, have each tried to interpret and systematize experience from one of the above four points of view, and each regards the interpretation from his point of view as being absolutely true to the exclusion of all other points of view. This is their error (*nayābhāsa*), for each standpoint represents only one of the many points of view from which a thing can be looked at. The affirmations from any point of view are thus true in a limited sense and under limited conditions. Infinite numbers of affirmations may be made of things from infinite points of view. Affirmations or judgments according to any naya or standpoint cannot therefore be absolute, for even contrary affirmations of the very selfsame

[1] The other standpoints of paryāya-naya, which represent grammatical and linguistic points of view, are *śabda-naya*, *samabhirūḍha-naya*, and *evambhūta-naya*. See *Viśeṣāvaśyaka bhāṣya*, pp. 895–923.

things may be held to be true from other points of view. The truth of each affirmation is thus only conditional, and inconceivable from the absolute point of view. To guarantee correctness therefore each affirmation should be preceded by the phrase *syāt* (may be). This will indicate that the affirmation is only relative, made somehow, from some point of view and under some reservations and not in any sense absolute. There is no judgment which is absolutely true, and no judgment which is absolutely false. All judgments are true in some sense and false in another. This brings us to the famous Jaina doctrine of Syādvāda[1].

The Doctrine of Syādvāda.

The doctrine of Syādvāda holds that since the most contrary characteristics of infinite variety may be associated with a thing, affirmation made from whatever standpoint (*naya*) cannot be regarded as absolute. All affirmations are true (in some *syādasti* or "may be it is" sense); all affirmations are false in some sense; all affirmations are indefinite or inconceivable in some sense (*syādavaktavya*); all affirmations are true as well as false in some sense (*syādasti syānnāsti*); all affirmations are true as well as indefinite (*syādasti cāvaktavyaśca*); all affirmations are false as well as indefinite; all affirmations are true and false and indefinite in some sense (*syādasti syānnāsti syādavaktavyaśca*). Thus we may say "the jug is" or the jug has being, but it is more correct to say explicitly that "may be (*syāt*) that the jug is," otherwise if "being" here is taken absolutely of any and every kind of being, it might also mean that there is a lump of clay or a pillar, or a cloth or any other thing. The existence here is limited and defined by the form of the jug. "The jug is" does not mean absolute existence but a limited kind of existence as determined by the form of the jug, "The jug is" thus means that a limited kind of existence, namely the jug-existence is affirmed and not existence in general in the absolute or unlimited sense, for then the sentence "the jug is" might as well mean "the clay is," "the tree is," "the cloth is," etc. Again the existence of the jug is determined by the negation of all other things in the world; each quality or characteristic (such as red colour) of the jug is apprehended and defined by the negation of all the infinite varieties (such as black, blue, golden), etc., of its class, and it is by the combined negation of all

[1] See *Viśeṣāvaśyaka bhāṣya*, pp. 895, etc., and *Syādvādamañjarī*, pp. 170, etc.

the infinite number of characteristics or qualities other than those constituting the jug that a jug may be apprehended or defined. What we call the being of the jug is thus the non-being of all the rest except itself. Thus though looked at from one point of view the judgment "the jug is" may mean affirmation of being, looked at from another point of view it means an affirmation of non-being (of all other objects). Thus of the judgment "the jug is" one may say, may be it is an affirmation of being (*syādasti*), may be it is a negation of being (*syānnāsti*); or I may proceed in quite another way and say that "the jug is" means "this jug is here," which naturally indicates that "this jug is not there" and thus the judgment "the jug is" (i.e. is here) also means that "the jug is not there," and so we see that the affirmation of the being of the jug is true only of this place and false of another, and this justifies us in saying that "may be that in some sense the jug is," and "may be in some sense that the jug is not." Combining these two aspects we may say that in some sense "may be that the jug is," and in some sense "may be that the jug is not." We understood here that if we put emphasis on the side of the characteristics constituting being, we may say "the jug is," but if we put emphasis on the other side, we may as well say "the jug is not." Both the affirmations hold good of the jug according as the emphasis is put on either side. But if without emphasis on either side we try to comprehend the two opposite and contradictory judgments regarding the jug, we see that the nature of the jug or of the existence of the jug is indefinite, unspeakable and inconceivable—*avaktavya*, for how can we affirm both being and non-being of the same thing, and yet such is the nature of things that we cannot but do it. Thus all affirmations are true, are not true, are both true and untrue, and are thus unspeakable, inconceivable, and indefinite. Combining these four again we derive another three, (1) that in some sense it may be that the jug is, and (2) is yet unspeakable, or (3) that the jug is not and is unspeakable, or finally that the jug is, is not, and is unspeakable. Thus the Jains hold that no affirmation, or judgment, is absolute in its nature, each is true in its own limited sense only, and for each one of them any of the above seven alternatives (technically called *saptabkaṅgī*) holds good[1]. The Jains say that other Indian systems each from its own point of view asserts itself to be the absolute and the only

[1] See *Syādvādamañjarī*, with Hemacandra's commentary, pp. 166, etc.

point of view. They do not perceive that the nature of reality is such that the truth of any assertion is merely conditional, and holds good only in certain conditions, circumstances, or senses (*upādhi*). It is thus impossible to make any affirmation which is universally and absolutely valid. For a contrary or contradictory affirmation will always be found to hold good of any judgment in some sense or other. As all reality is partly permanent and partly exposed to change of the form of losing and gaining old and new qualities, and is thus relatively permanent and changeful, so all our affirmations regarding truth are also only relatively valid and invalid. Being, non-being and indefinite, the three categories of logic, are all equally available in some sense or other in all their permutations for any and every kind of judgment. There is no universal and absolute position or negation, and all judgments are valid only conditionally. The relation of the naya doctrine with the syādvāda doctrine is therefore this, that for any judgment according to any and every naya there are as many alternatives as are indicated by syādvāda. The validity of such a judgment is therefore only conditional. If this is borne in mind when making any judgment according to any naya, the naya is rightly used. If, however, the judgments are made absolutely according to any particular naya without any reference to other nayas as required by the syādvāda doctrine the nayas are wrongly used as in the case of other systems, and then such judgments are false and should therefore be called false nayas (*nayābhāsa*)[1].

Knowledge, its value for us.

The Buddhist Dharmottara in his commentary on *Nyāyabindu* says that people who are anxious to fulfil some purpose or end in which they are interested, value the knowledge which helps them to attain that purpose. It is because knowledge is thus found to be useful and sought by men that philosophy takes upon it the task of examining the nature of true knowledge (*samyagjñāna* or *pramāṇa*). The main test of true knowledge is that it helps us to attain our purpose. The Jains also are in general agreement with the above view of knowledge of the Buddhists[2]. They also

[1] The earliest mention of the doctrine of syādvāda and saptabhaṅgī probably occurs in Bhadrabāhu's (B.C. 433–357) commentary *Sūtrakṛtāṅganiryukti*.

[2] See *Pramāṇa-naya-tattvālokālaṃkāra* (Benares), p. 26; also *Parīkṣā-mukhasūtra-vṛtti* (Asiatic Society), ch. 1.

say that knowledge is not to be valued for its own sake. The validity (*prāmāṇya*) of anything consists in this, that it directly helps us to get what is good for us and to avoid what is bad for us. Knowledge alone has this capacity, for by it we can adapt ourselves to our environments and try to acquire what is good for us and avoid what is bad[1]. The conditions that lead to the production of such knowledge (such as the presence of full light and proximity to the eye in the case of seeing an object by visual perception) have but little relevancy in this connection. For we are not concerned with how a cognition is produced, as it can be of no help to us in serving our purposes. It is enough for us to know that external objects under certain conditions assume such a special fitness (*yogyatā*) that we can have knowledge of them. We have no guarantee that they generate knowledge in us, for we are only aware that under certain conditions we know a thing, whereas under other conditions we do not know it[2]. The enquiry as to the nature of the special fitness of things which makes knowledge of them possible does not concern us. Those conditions which confer such a special fitness on things as to render them perceivable have but little to do with us; for our purposes which consist only in the acquirement of good and avoidance of evil, can only be served by knowledge and not by those conditions of external objects.

Knowledge reveals our own self as a knowing subject as well as the objects that are known by us. We have no reason to suppose (like the Buddhists) that all knowledge by perception of external objects is in the first instance indefinite and indeterminate, and that all our determinate notions of form, colour, size and other characteristics of the thing are not directly given in our perceptual experience, but are derived only by imagination (*utprekṣā*), and that therefore true perceptual knowledge only certifies the validity of the indefinite and indeterminate crude sense data (*nirvikalpa jñāna*). Experience shows that true knowledge on the one hand reveals us as subjects or knowers, and on the other hand gives a correct sketch of the external objects in all the diversity of their characteristics. It is for this reason that knowledge is our immediate and most prominent means of serving our purposes.

[1] *Pramāṇa-naya-tattvālokālaṃkāra*, p. 26.

[2] See *Parīkṣā-mukha-sūtra*, II. 9, and its vṛtti, and also the concluding vṛtti of ch. II.

Of course knowledge cannot directly and immediately bring to us the good we want, but since it faithfully communicates to us the nature of the objects around us, it renders our actions for the attainment of good and the avoidance of evil, possible; for if knowledge did not possess these functions, this would have been impossible. The validity of knowledge thus consists in this, that it is the most direct, immediate, and indispensable means for serving our purposes. So long as any knowledge is uncontradicted it should be held as true. False knowledge is that which represents things in relations in which they do not exist. When a rope in a badly lighted place gives rise to the illusion of a snake, the illusion consists in taking the rope to be a snake, i.e. perceiving a snake where it does not exist. Snakes exist and ropes also exist, there is no untruth in that[1]. The error thus consists in this, that the snake is perceived where the rope exists. The perception of a snake under relations and environments in which it was not then existing is what is meant by error here. What was at first perceived as a snake was later on contradicted and thus found false. Falsehood therefore consists in the misrepresentation of objective facts in experience. True knowledge therefore is that which gives such a correct and faithful representation of its object as is never afterwards found to be contradicted. Thus knowledge when imparted directly in association with the organs in sense-perception is very clear, vivid, and distinct, and is called perceptional (*pratyakṣa*); when attained otherwise the knowledge is not so clear and vivid and is then called non-perceptional (*parokṣa*[2]).

Theory of Perception.

The main difference of the Jains from the Buddhists in the theory of perception lies, as we have already seen, in this, that the Jains think that perception (*pratyakṣa*) reveals to us the external objects just as they are with most of their diverse characteristics of colour, form, etc., and also in this, that knowledge arises in the soul

[1] Illusion consists in attributing such spatial, temporal or other kinds of relations to the objects of our judgment as do not actually exist, but the objects themselves actually exist in other relations. When I mistake the rope for the snake, the snake actually exists though its relationing with the "this" as "this is a snake" does not exist, for the snake is not the rope. This illusion is thus called *satkhyāti* or misrelationing of existents (*sat*)

[2] See *Jaina-tarka-vārttika* of Siddhasena, ch. I., and vṛtti by Śantyācārya, Pramāṇanayatattvālokālaṃkāra, ch. I., *Parīksā-mukha-sūtra-vṛtti*, ch. I.

from within it as if by removing a veil which had been covering it before. Objects are also not mere forms of knowledge (as the Vijñānavādin Buddhist thinks) but are actually existing. Knowledge of external objects by perception is gained through the senses. The exterior physical sense such as the eye must be distinguished from the invisible faculty or power of vision of the soul, which alone deserves the name of sense. We have five such cognitive senses. But the Jains think that since by our experience we are only aware of five kinds of sense knowledge corresponding to the five senses, it is better to say that it is the "self" which gains of itself those different kinds of sense-knowledge in association with those exterior senses as if by removal of a covering, on account of the existence of which the knowledge could not reveal itself before. The process of external perception does not thus involve the exercise of any separate and distinct sense, though the rise of the sense-knowledge in the soul takes place in association with the particular sense-organ such as eye, etc. The soul is in touch with all parts of the body, and visual knowledge is that knowledge which is generated in the soul through that part of it which is associated with, or is in touch with the eye. To take an example, I look before me and see a rose. Before looking at it the knowledge of rose was in me, but only in a covered condition, and hence could not get itself manifested. The act of looking at the rose means that such a fitness has come into the rose and into myself that the rose is made visible, and the veil over my knowledge of rose is removed. When visual knowledge arises, this happens in association with the eye; I say that I see through the visual sense, whereas in reality experience shows that I have only a knowledge of the visual type (associated with eye). As experience does not reveal the separate senses, it is unwarrantable to assert that they have an existence apart from the self. Proceeding in a similar way the Jains discard the separate existence of manas (mind-organ) also, for manas also is not given in experience, and the hypothesis of its existence is unnecessary, as self alone can serve its purpose[1]. Perception of an object means

[1] *Tanna indriyam bhautikam kim tu ātmā ca indriyam...anupahatacakṣurādideśeṣu eva ātmanaḥ karmakṣayopaśamastenāsthagitagavākṣatulyāni cakṣurādīni upakaraṇāni. Jaina-Vāttika-Vṛtti*, II. p. 98. In many places, however, the five senses, such as eye, ear, etc., are mentioned as senses, and living beings are often classified according to the number of senses they possess. (See *Pramāṇam īmāṃsā*. See also *Tattvārthādhigamasūtra*, ch. II. etc.) But this is with reference to the sense organs. The denial of separate senses is with

that the veil of ignorance upon the "self" regarding the object has been removed. Inwardly this removal is determined by the karma of the individual, outwardly it is determined by the presence of the object of perception, light, the capacity of the sense organs, and such other conditions. Contrary to the Buddhists and many other Indian systems, the Jains denied the existence of any nirvikalpa (indeterminate) stage preceding the final savikalpa (determinate) stage of perception. There was a direct revelation of objects from within and no indeterminate sense-materials were necessary for the development of determinate perceptions. We must contrast this with the Buddhists who regarded that the first stage consisting of the presentation of indeterminate sense materials was the only valid part of perception. The determinate stage with them is the result of the application of mental categories, such as imagination, memory, etc., and hence does not truly represent the presentative part[1].

Non-Perceptual Knowledge.

Non-perceptual knowledge (*parokṣa*) differs from pratyakṣa in this, that it does not give us so vivid a picture of objects as the latter. Since the Jains do not admit that the senses had any function in determining the cognitions of the soul, the only distinction they could draw between perception and other forms of knowledge was that the knowledge of the former kind (perception) gave us clearer features and characteristics of objects than the latter. Parokṣa thus includes inference, recognition, implication, memory, etc.; and this knowledge is decidedly less vivid than perception.

Regarding inference, the Jains hold that it is unnecessary to have five propositions, such as: (1) "the hill is fiery," (2) "because of smoke," (3) "wherever there is smoke there is fire, such as the kitchen," (4) "this hill is smoky," (5) "therefore it is fiery," called respectively *pratijñā*, *ketu*, *dṛṣṭānta*, *upanaya* and *nigamana*, except for the purpose of explicitness. It is only the first two propositions which actually enter into the inferential process (*Prameyakamalamārtaṇḍa*, pp. 108, 109). When we make an

reference to admitting them as entities or capacities having a distinct and separate category of existence from the soul. The sense organs are like windows for the soul to look out. They cannot thus modify the sense-knowledge which rises in the soul by inward determination; for it is already existent in it; the perceptual process only means that the veil which was observing it is removed.

[1] *Prameyakamalamārtaṇḍa*, pp. 8–11.

inference we do not proceed through the five propositions as above. They who know that the reason is inseparably connected with the probandum either as coexistence (*sahabhāva*) or as invariable antecedence (*kramabhāva*) will from the mere statement of the existence of the reason (e.g. smoke) in the hill jump to the conclusion that the hill has got fire. A syllogism consisting of five propositions is rather for explaining the matter to a child than for representing the actual state of the mind in making an inference[1].

As regards proof by testimony the Jains do not admit the authority of the Vedas, but believe that the Jaina scriptures give us right knowledge, for these are the utterances of persons who have lived a worldly life but afterwards by right actions and right knowledge have conquered all passions and removed all ignorance[2].

Knowledge as Revelation.

The Buddhists had affirmed that the proof of the existence of anything depended upon the effect that it could produce on us. That

[1] As regards concomitance (*vyāpti*) some of the Jaina logicians like the Buddhists prefer *antarvyāpti* (between smoke and fire) to bahirvyāpti (the place containing smoke with the place containing fire). They also divide inference into two classes, *svārthānumāna* for one's own self and *parārthānumāna* for convincing others. It may not be out of place to note that the earliest Jaina view as maintained by Bhadrabāhu in his Daśavaikālikaniryukti was in favour of ten propositions for making an inference; (1) *Pratijñā* (e.g. non-injury to life is the greatest virtue), (2) *Pratijñāvibhakti* (non-injury to life is the greatest virtue according to Jaina scriptures), (3) *Hetu* (because those who adhere to non-injury are loved by gods and it is meritorious to do them honour), (4) *Hetu vibhakti* (those who do so are the only persons who can live in the highest places of virtue), (5) *Vipakṣa* (but even by doing injury one may prosper and even by reviling Jaina scriptures one may attain merit as is the case with Brahmins), (6) *Vipakṣa pratiṣedha* (it is not so, it is impossible that those who despise Jaina scriptures should be loved by gods or should deserve honour), (7) *Dṛṣṭānta* (the Arhats take food from householders as they do not like to cook themselves for fear of killing insects), (8) *Āśaṅkā* (but the sins of the householders should touch the arhats, for they cook for them), (9) *Āśaṅkāpraliṣedha* (this cannot be, for the arhats go to certain houses unexpectedly, so it could not be said that the cooking was undertaken for them), (10) *Naigamana* (non-injury is therefore the greatest virtue) (Vidyābhūṣaṇa's *Indian Logic*). These are persuasive statements which are often actually adopted in a discussion, but from a formal point of view many of these are irrelevant. When Vātsyāyana in his *Nyāyasūtrabhāṣya*, I. 1. 32, says that Gautama introduced the doctrine of five propositions as against the doctrine of ten propositions as held by other logicians, he probably had this Jaina view in his mind.

[2] See *Jainatarkavārttika*, and *Parīkṣāmukhasūtravṛtti*, and *Ṣaḍdarśanasamuccaya* with Guṇaratna on Jainism.

which could produce any effect on us was existent, and that which could not non-existent. In fact production of effect was with them the only definition of existence (being). Theoretically each unit of effect being different from any other unit of effect, they supposed that there was a succession of different units of effect or, what is the same thing, acknowledged a succession of new substances every moment. All things were thus momentary. The Jains urged that the reason why the production of effect may be regarded as the only proof of being is that we can assert only that thing the existence of which is indicated by a corresponding experience. When we have a unit of experience we suppose the existence of the object as its ground. This being so, the theoretical analysis of the Buddhists that each unit of effect produced in us is not exactly the same at each new point of time, and that therefore all things are momentary, is fallacious; for experience shows that not all of an object is found to be changing every moment; some part of it (e.g. gold in a gold ornament) is found to remain permanent while other parts (e.g. its form as earrings or bangles) are seen to undergo change. How in the face of such an experience can we assert that the whole thing vanishes every moment and that new things are being renewed at each succeeding moment? Hence leaving aside mere abstract and unfounded speculations, if we look to experience we find that the conception of being or existence involves a notion of permanence associated with change—*paryāya* (acquirement of new qualities and the loss of old ones). The Jains hold that the defects of other systems lie in this, that they interpret experience only from one particular standpoint (*naya*) whereas they alone carefully weigh experience from all points of view and acquiesce in the truths indicated by it, not absolutely but under proper reservations and limitations. The Jains hold' that in formulating the doctrine of *arthakriyākāritva* the Buddhists at first showed signs of starting on their enquiry on the evidence of experience, but soon they became one-sided in their analysis and indulged in unwarrantable abstract speculations which went directly against experience. Thus if we go by experience we can neither reject the self nor the external world as some Buddhists did. Knowledge which reveals to us the clear-cut features of the external world certifies at the same time that such knowledge is part and parcel of myself as the subject. Knowledge is thus felt to be an expression of my own self. We do not perceive in experience that knowledge in us is generated by the external world, but there is in us the rise of knowledge and of certain objects made known to us by it. The rise of knowledge is thus only parallel to certain objective collocations of things which somehow have the special fitness that they and they alone are perceived at that particular moment. Looked at from this point of view all our experiences are centred in ourselves, for determined somehow, our experiences come to us as modifications of our own self. Knowledge being a character of the self, it shows itself as manifestations of the self independent of the senses. No distinction should be made between a conscious and an unconscious element in knowledge as Sāṃkhya does. Nor should knowledge be regarded as a copy of the objects which it reveals, as the Sautrāntikas think, for then by copying the materiality of the object, knowledge would itself become material. Knowledge should thus be regarded as a formless quality of the self revealing all objects by itself. But the Mīmāṃsā view that the validity (*prāmāṇya*) of all knowledge is proved by knowledge itself (*svataḥprāmāṇya*) is wrong. Both logically and psychologically the validity of knowledge depends upon outward correspondence (*saṃvāda*) with facts. But in those cases where by previous knowledge of correspondence a right belief has been produced there may be a psychological ascertainment of validity without reference to objective facts (*prāmāṇyamutpattau parata eva jñaptau svakārye ca svataḥ parataśca abhyāsānabhyāsāpekṣayā*)[1]. The objective world exists as it is certified by experience. But that it generates knowledge in us is an unwarrantable hypothesis, for knowledge appears as a revelation of our own self. This brings us to a consideration of Jaina metaphysics.

The Jīvas.

The Jains say that experience shows that all things may be divided into the living (*jīva*) and the non-living (*ajīva*). The principle of life is entirely distinct from the body, and it is most erroneous to think that life is either the product or the property of the body[2]. It is on account of this life-principle that the body appears to be living This principle is the soul. The soul is directly perceived (by introspection) just as the external things are. It is not a mere symbolical object indicated by a phrase or

[1] *Prameyakamalamārtaṇḍa*, pp. 38–43.
[2] See *Jaina Vārttika*, p. 60.

a description. This is directly against the view of the great Mīmāṃsā authority Prabhākara[1]. The soul in its pure state is possessed of infinite perception (*ananta-darśana*), infinite knowledge (*ananta-jñāna*), infinite bliss (*ananta-sukha*) and infinite power (*ananta-vīrya*)[2]. It is all perfect. Ordinarily however, with the exception of a few released pure souls (*mukta-jīva*), all the other jīvas (*saṃsārin*) have all their purity and power covered with a thin veil of karma matter which has been accumulating in them from beginningless time. These souls are infinite in number. They are substances and are eternal. They in reality occupy innumerable space-points in our mundane world (*lokākāśa*), have a limited size (*madhyama-parimāṇa*) and are neither all-pervasive (*vibhu*) nor atomic (*aṇu*); it is on account of this that *jīva* is called *Jivāstikāya*. The word *astikāya* means anything that occupies space or has some pervasiveness; but these souls expand and contract themselves according to the dimensions of the body which they occupy at any time (bigger in the elephant and smaller in the ant life). It is well to remember that according to the Jains the soul occupies the whole of the body in which it lives, so that from the tip of the hair to the nail of the foot, wherever there may be any cause of sensation, it can at once feel it. The manner in which the soul occupies the body is often explained as being similar to the manner in which a lamp illumines the whole room though remaining in one corner of the room. The Jains divide the jīvas according to the number of sense-organs they possess. The lowest class consists of plants, which possess only the sense-organ of touch. The next higher class is that of worms, which possess two sense-organs of touch and taste. Next come the ants, etc., which possess touch, taste, and smell. The next higher one that of bees, etc., possessing vision in addition to touch, taste, and smell. The vertebrates possess all the five sense-organs. The higher animals among these, namely men, denizens of hell, and the gods possess in addition to these an inner sense-organ namely *manas* by virtue of which they are

[1] See *Prameyakamalamārtaṇda*, p. 33.

[2] The Jains distinguish between *darśana* and *jñāna*. Darśana is the knowledge of things without their details, e.g. I see a cloth. Jñāna means the knowledge of details, e.g. I not only see the cloth, but know to whom it belongs, of what quality it is, where it was prepared, etc. In all cognition we have first darśana and then jñāna. The pure souls possess infinite general perception of all things as well as infinite knowledge of all things in all their details.

called rational (*saṃjñin*) while the lower animals have no reason and are called *asaṃjñin.*

Proceeding towards the lowest animal we find that the Jains regard all the four elements (earth, water, air, fire) as being animated by souls. Thus particles of earth, etc., are the bodies of souls, called earth-lives, etc. These we may call elementary lives; they live and die and are born again in another elementary body. These elementary lives are either gross or subtle; in the latter case they are invisible. The last class of one-organ lives are plants. Of some plants each is the body of one soul only; but of other plants, each is an aggregation of embodied souls, which have all the functions of life such as respiration and nutrition in common. Plants in which only one soul is embodied are always gross; they exist in the habitable part of the world only. But those plants of which each is a colony of plant lives may also be subtle and invisible, and in that case they are distributed all over the world. The whole universe is full of minute beings called *nigodas*; they are groups of infinite number of souls forming very small clusters, having respiration and nutrition in common and experiencing extreme pains. The whole space of the world is closely packed with them like a box filled with powder. The nigodas furnish the supply of souls in place of those that have reached Mokṣa. But an infinitesimally small fraction of one single nigoda has sufficed to replace the vacancy caused in the world by the Nirvāṇa of all the souls that have been liberated from beginningless past down to the present. Thus it is evident the saṃsāra will never be empty of living beings. Those of the *nigodas* who long for development come out and contiune their course of progress through successive stages[1].

Karma Theory.

It is on account of their merits or demerits that the jīvas are born as gods, men, animals, or denizens of hell. We have already noticed in Chapter III that the cause of the embodiment of soul is the presence in it of karma matter. The natural perfections of the pure soul are sullied by the different kinds of karma matter. Those which obscure right knowledge of details (*jñāna*) are called *jñānāvaraṇīya*, those which obscure right perception (*darśana*) as in sleep are called *darśanāvaraṇīya*, those which

[1] See Jacobi's article on Jainism, *E.R.E.*, and *Lokaprakāśa*, VI. pp. 31 ff.

obscure the bliss-nature of the soul and thus produce pleasure and pain are *vedanīya*, and those which obscure the right attitude of the soul towards faith and right conduct *mohanīya*[1]. In addition to these four kinds of karma there are other four kinds of karma which determine (1) the length of life in any birth, (2) the peculiar body with its general and special qualities and faculties, (3) the nationality, caste, family, social standing, etc., (4) the inborn energy of the soul by the obstruction of which it prevents the doing of a good action when there is a desire to do it. These are respectively called (1) *āyuṣka karma*, (2) *nāma karma*, (3) *gotra karma*, (4) *antarāya karma*. By our actions of mind, speech and body, we are continually producing certain subtle karma matter which in the first instance is called *bhāva karma*, which transforms itself into *dravya karma* and pours itself into the soul and sticks there by coming into contact with the passions (*kaṣāya*) of the soul. These act like viscous substances in retaining the inpouring karma matter. This matter acts in eight different ways and it is accordingly divided into eight classes, as we have already noticed. This karma is the cause of bondage and sorrow. According as good or bad karma matter sticks to the soul it gets itself coloured respectively as golden, lotus-pink, white and black, blue and grey and they are called the *leśyās*. The feelings generated by the accumulation of the karma-matter are called *bhāva-leśyā* and the actual coloration of the soul by it is called *dravya-leśyā*. According as any karma matter has been generated by good, bad, or indifferent actions, it gives us pleasure, pain, or feeling of indifference. Even the knowledge that we are constantly getting by perception, inference, etc., is but the result of the effect of karmas in accordance with which the particular kind of veil which was obscuring any particular kind of knowledge is removed at any time and we have a knowledge of a corresponding nature. By our own karmas the veils over our knowledge, feeling, etc., are so removed that we have just that kind of knowledge and feeling that we deserved to have. All knowledge, feeling, etc., are thus in one sense generated from within, the external objects which are ordinarily said to be generating them all being but mere coexistent external conditions.

[1] The Jains acknowledge five kinds of knowledge: (1) *matijñāna* (ordinary cognition), (2) *śruti* (testimony), (3) *avadhi* (supernatural cognition), (4) *manaḥparyāya* (thought-reading), (5) *kevala-jñāna* (omniscience).

After the effect of a particular karma matter (*karma-vargaṇā*) is once produced, it is discharged and purged from off the soul. This process of purging off the karmas is called *nirjarā*. If no new karma matter should accumulate then, the gradual purging off of the karmas might make the soul free of karma matter, but as it is, while some karma matter is being purged off, other karma matter is continually pouring in, and thus the purging and binding processes continuing simultaneously force the soul to continue its mundane cycle of existence, transmigration, and rebirth. After the death of each individual his soul, together with its karmic body (*kārmaṇaśarīra*), goes in a few moments to the place of its new birth and there assumes a new body, expanding or contracting in accordance with the dimensions of the latter.

In the ordinary course karma takes effect and produces its proper results, and at such a stage the soul is said to be in the *audayika* state. By proper efforts karma may however be prevented from taking effect, though it still continues to exist, and this is said to be the *aupaśamika* state of the soul. When karma is not only prevented from operating but is annihilated, the soul is said to be in the *kṣāyika* state, and it is from this state that Mokṣa is attained. There is, however, a fourth state of ordinary good men with whom some karma is annihilated, some neutralized, and some active (*kṣāyopaśamika*)[1].

Karma, Āsrava and Nirjarā.

It is on account of karma that the souls have to suffer all the experiences of this world process, including births and rebirths in diverse spheres of life as gods, men or animals, or insects. The karmas are certain sorts of infra-atomic particles of matter (*karma-vargaṇā*). The influx of these karma particles into the soul is called āsrava in Jainism. These karmas are produced by body, mind, and speech. The āsravas represent the channels or modes through which the karmas enter the soul, just like the channels through which water enters into a pond. But the Jains distinguish between the channels and the karmas which actually

[1] The stages through which a developing soul passes are technically called *guṇasthānas* which are fourteen in number. The first three stages represent the growth of faith in Jainism, the next five stages are those in which all the passions are controlled, in the next four stages the ascetic practises yoga and destroys all his karmas, at the thirteenth stage he is divested of all karmas but he still practises yoga and at the fourteenth stage he attains liberation (see Dravyasaṃgrahavṛtti, 13th verse).

enter through those channels. Thus they distinguish two kinds of āsravas, bhāvāsrava and karmāsrava. Bhāvāsrava means the thought activities of the soul through which or on account of which the karma particles enter the soul[1]. Thus Nemicandra says that bhāvāsrava is that kind of change in the soul (which is the contrary to what can destroy the karmāsrava), by which the karmas enter the soul[2]. Karmāsrava, however, means the actual entrance of the karma matter into the soul. These bhāvāsravas are in general of five kinds, namely delusion (*mithyātva*), want of control (*avirati*), inadvertence (*pramāda*), the activities of body, mind and speech (*yoga*) and the passions (*kaṣāyas*). Delusion again is of five kinds, namely *ekānta* (a false belief unknowingly accepted and uncritically followed), *viparīta* (uncertainty as to the exact nature of truth), *vinaya* (retention of a belief knowing it to be false, due to old habit), *saṃśaya* (doubt as to right or wrong) and *ajñāna* (want of any belief due to the want of application of reasoning powers). Avirati is again of five kinds, injury (*hiṃsā*), falsehood (*anṛta*), stealing (*cauryya*), incontinence (*abrahma*), and desire to have things which one does not already possess (*parigrahākānkṣā*). Pramāda or inadvertence is again of five kinds, namely bad conversation (*vikathā*), passions (*kaṣāya*), bad use of the five senses (*indriya*), sleep (*nidrā*), attachment (*rāga*)[3].

Coming to dravyāsrava we find that it means that actual influx of karma which affects the soul in eight different manners in accordance with which these karmas are classed into eight different kinds, namely jñānāvaraṇīya, darśanāvaraṇīya, vedanīya, mohanīya, āyu, nāma, gotra and antarāya. These actual influxes take place only as a result of the bhāvāsrava or the reprehensible thought activities, or changes (*pariṇāma*) of the soul. The states of thought which condition the coming in of the karmas is called bhāvabandha and the actual bondage of the soul by the actual impure connections of the karmas is technically called dravyabandha. It is on account of bhāvabandha that the actual connection between the karmas and the soul can take place[4]. The actual connections of the karmas with the soul are like the sticking

[1] *Dravyasaṃgraha*, Śl. 29.

[2] Nemicandra's commentary on *Dravyasaṃgraha*, Śl. 29, edited by S. C. Ghoshal, Arrah, 1917.

[3] See Nemicandra's commentary on Śl. 30.

[4] Nemicandra on 31, and *Vardhaniānapurāṇa* XVI. 44, quoted by Ghoshal.

of dust on the body of a person who is besmeared all over with oil. Thus Guṇaratna says: "The influx of karma means the contact of the particles of karma matter, in accordance with the particular kind of karma, with the soul, just like the sticking of dust on the body of a person besmeared with oil. In all parts of the soul there being infinite number of karma atoms it becomes so completely covered with them that in some sense when looked at from that point of view the soul is sometimes regarded as a material body during its saṃsāra stage[1]." From one point of view the bondage of karma is only of *puṇya* and *pāpa* (good and bad karmas)[2]. From another this bondage is of four kinds, according to the nature of karma (*prakṛti*), duration of bondage (*sthiti*), intensity (*anubhāga*) and extension (*pradeśa*). The nature of karma refers to the eight classes of karma already mentioned, namely the jñānāvaraṇīya karma which obscures the infinite knowledge of the soul of all things in detail, darśanāvaraṇīya karma which obscures the infinite general knowledge of the soul, vedanīya karma which produces the feelings of pleasure and pain in the soul, mohanīya karma, which so infatuates souls that they fail to distinguish what is right from what is wrong, āyu karma, which determines the tenure of any particular life, nāma karma which gives them personalities, gotra karma which brings about a particular kind of social surrounding for the soul and antarāya karma which tends to oppose the performance of right actions by the soul. The duration of the stay of any karma in the soul is called sthiti. Again a karma may be intense, middling or mild, and this indicates the third principle of division, anubhāga. Pradeśa refers to the different parts of the soul to which the karma particles attach themselves. The duration of stay of any karma and its varying intensity are due to the nature of the kaṣāyas or passions of the soul, whereas the different classification of karmas as jñānāvaraṇīya, etc., are due to the nature of specific contact of the soul with karma matter[3].

Corresponding to the two modes of inrush of karmas (bhāvāsrava and dravyāsrava) are two kinds of control opposing this inrush, by actual thought modification of a contrary nature and by the actual stoppage of the inrush of karma particles, and these are respectively called bhāvasaṃvara and dravyasaṃvara[4].

[1] See Guṇaratna, p. 181.
[2] *Ibid.*
[3] Nemicandra, 33.
[4] *Varddhamānapurāṇa*, XVI. 67–68, and *Dravyasaṃgrahavṛtti*, Śl. 35.

The bhāvasaṃvaras are (1) the vows of non-injury, truthfulness, abstinence from stealing, sex-control, and non-acceptance of objects of desire, (2) samitis consisting of the use of trodden tracks in order to avoid injury to insects (*īryā*), gentle and holy talk (*bhāṣā*), receiving proper alms (*eṣaṇā*), etc., (3) *guptis* or restraints of body, speech and mind, (4) *dharmas* consisting of habits of forgiveness, humility, straightforwardness, truth, cleanliness, restraint, penance, abandonment, indifference to any kind of gain or loss, and supreme sex-control[1], (5) *anuprekṣā* consisting of meditation about the transient character of the world, about our helplessness without the truth, about the cycles of world-existence, about our own responsibilities for our good and bad actions, about the difference between the soul and the non-soul, about the uncleanliness of our body and all that is associated with it, about the influx of karma and its stoppage and the destruction of those karmas which have already entered the soul, about soul, matter and the substance of the universe, about the difficulty of attaining true knowledge, faith, and conduct, and about the essential principles of the world[2], (6) the *parīṣahajaya* consisting of the conquering of all kinds of physical troubles of heat, cold, etc., and of feelings of discomforts of various kinds, (7) *cāritra* or right conduct.

Next to this we come to nirjarā or the purging off of the karmas or rather their destruction. This nirjarā also is of two kinds, bhāvanirjarā and dravyanirjarā. Bhāvanirjarā means that change in the soul by virtue of which the karma particles are destroyed. Dravyanirjarā means the actual destruction of these karma particles either by the reaping of their effects or by penances before their time of fruition, called savipāka and avipāka nirjarās respectively. When all the karmas are destroyed mokṣa or liberation is effected.

Pudgala.

The *ajīva* (non-living) is divided into *pudgalāstikāya*, *dharma stikāya*, *adharmāstikāya*, *ākāśāstikāya*, *kāla*, *puṇya*, *pāpa*. The word *pudgala* means matter[3], and it is called *astikāya* in the sense that it occupies space. Pudgala is made up of atoms

[1] *Tattvārthādhigamasūtra.*

[2] *Ibid.*

[3] This is entirely different from the Buddhist sense. With the Buddhists *pudgala* means an individual or a person.

which are without size and eternal. Matter may exist in two states, gross (such as things we see around us), and subtle (such as the karma matter which sullies the soul). All material things are ultimately produced by the combination of atoms. The smallest indivisible particle of matter is called an atom (*aṇu*). The atoms are all eternal and they all have touch, taste, smell, and colour. The formation of different substances is due to the different geometrical, spherical or cubical modes of the combination of the atoms, to the diverse modes of their inner arrangement and to the existence of different degrees of inter-atomic space (*ghanapratarabhedena*). Some combinations take place by simple mutual contact at two points (*yugmapradeśa*) whereas in others the atoms are only held together by the points of attractive force (*ojaḥpradeśa*) (*Prajñāpanopāṅgasūtra*, pp. 10–12). Two atoms form a compound (*skandha*), when the one is viscous and the other dry or both are of different degrees of viscosity or dryness. It must be noted that while the Buddhists thought that there was no actual contact between the atoms the Jains regarded the contact as essential and as testified by experience. These compounds combine with other compounds and thus produce the gross things of the world. They are, however, liable to constant change (*pariṇāma*) by which they lose some of their old qualities (*guṇas*) and acquire new ones. There are four elements, earth, water, air, and fire, and the atoms of all these are alike in character. The perception of grossness however is not an error which is imposed upon the perception of the atoms by our mind (as the Buddhists think) nor is it due to the perception of atoms scattered spatially lengthwise and breadthwise (as the Sāṃkhya-Yoga supposes), but it is due to the accession of a similar property of grossness, blueness or hardness in the combined atoms, so that such knowledge is generated in us as is given in the perception of a gross, blue, or a hard thing. When a thing appears as blue, what happens is this, that the atoms there have all acquired the property of blueness and on the removal of the darśanavaraṇīya and jñānavaraṇīya veil, there arises in the soul the perception and knowledge of that blue thing. This sameness (*samāna-rūpatā*) of the accession of a quality in an aggregate of atoms by virtue of which it appears as one object (e.g. a cow) is technically called *tiryaksāmānya*. This sȧmānya or generality is thus neither an imposition of the mind nor an abstract entity (as maintained by the Naiyāyikas) but represents only the accession of similar qualities by a similar development of qualities of atoms forming an aggregate. So long as this similarity of qualities continues we perceive the thing to be the same and to continue for some length of time. When we think of a thing to be permanent, we do so by referring to this sameness in the developing tendencies of an aggregate of atoms resulting in the relative permanence of similar qualities in them. According to the Jains things are not momentary and in spite of the loss of some old qualities and the accession of other ones, the thing as a whole may remain more or less the same for some time. This sameness of qualities in time is technically called *ūrdhvasāmānya*[1]. If the atoms are looked at from the point of view of the change and accession of new qualities, they may be regarded as liable to destruction, but if they are looked at from the point of view of substance (*dravya*) they are eternal.

Dharma, Adharma, Ākāśa.

The conception of dharma and adharma in Jainism is absolutely different from what they mean in other systems of Indian philosophy. Dharma is devoid of taste, touch, smell, sound and colour; it is conterminous with the mundane universe (*lokākāśa*) and pervades every part of it. The term *astikāya* is therefore applied to it. It is the principle of motion, the accompanying circumstance or cause which makes motion possible, like water to a moving fish. The water is a passive condition or circumstance of the movement of a fish, i.e. it is indifferent or passive (*udāsīna*) and not an active or solicitous (*preraka*) cause. The water cannot compel a fish at rest to move; but if the fish wants to move, water is then the necessary help to its motion. Dharma cannot make the soul or matter move; but if they are to move, they cannot do so without the presence of dharma. Hence at the extremity of the mundane world (*loka*) in the region of the liberated souls, there being no dharma, the liberated souls attain perfect rest. They cannot move there because there is not the necessary motion-element, dharma[2]. Adharma is also regarded as a similar pervasive entity which

[1] See *Prameyakamalamārtaṇḍa*, pp. 136–143; *Jainatarkavārttika*, p. 106.

[2] *Dravyasaṃgrahavṛtti*, 17–20.

helps jīvas and pudgalas to keep themselves at rest. No substance could move if there were no dharma, or could remain at rest if there were no adharma. The necessity of admitting these two categories seems probably to have been felt by the Jains on account of their notion that the inner activity of the jīva or the atoms required for its exterior realization the help of some other extraneous entity, without which this could not have been transformed into actual exterior motion. Moreover since the jīvas were regarded as having activity inherent in them they would be found to be moving even at the time of liberation (mokṣa), which was undesirable; thus it was conceived that actual motion required for its fulfilment the help of an extraneous entity which was absent in the region of the liberated souls.

The category of ākāśa is that subtle entity which pervades the mundane universe (*loka*) and the transcendent region of liberated souls (*aloka*) which allows the subsistence of all other substances such as dharma, adharma, jīva, pudgala. It is not a mere negation and absence of veil or obstruction, or mere emptiness, but a positive entity which helps other things to interpenetrate it. On account of its pervasive character it is called *ākāśāstikāya*[1].

Kāla and Samaya.

Time (*kāla*) in reality consists of those innumerable particles which never mix with one another, but which help the happening of the modification or accession of new qualities and the change of qualities of the atoms. Kāla does not bring about the changes of qualities, in things, but just as ākāśa helps interpenetration and dharma motion, so also kāla helps the action of the transformation of new qualities in things. Time perceived as moments, hours, days, etc., is called *samaya*. This is the appearance of the unchangeable kāla in so many forms. Kāla thus not only aids the modifications of other things, but also allows its own modifications as moments, hours, etc. It is thus a dravya (substance), and the moments, hours, etc., are its paryāyas. The unit of samaya is the time required by an atom to traverse a unit of space by a slow movement.

[1] *Dravyasaṃgrahavṛtti*, 19.

Jaina Cosmography.

According to the Jains, the world is eternal, without beginning or end. Loka is that place in which happiness and misery are experienced as results of virtue and vice. It is composed of three parts, *ūrdhva* (where the gods reside), *madhya* (this world of ours), and *adho* (where the denizens of hell reside). The mundane universe (*lokākāśa*) is pervaded with dharma which makes all movement possible. Beyond the lokākāśa there is no dharma and therefore no movement, but only space (*ākāśa*). Surrounding this lokākāśa are three layers of air. The perfected soul rising straight over the ūrdhvaloka goes to the top of this lokākāśa and (there being no dharma) remains motionless there.

Jaina Yoga.

Yoga according to Jainism is the cause of mokṣa (salvation). This yoga consists of jñāna (knowledge of reality as it is), śraddhā (faith in the teachings of the Jinas), and cāritra (cessation from doing all that is evil). This cāritra consists of *ahiṃsā* (not taking any life even by mistake or unmindfulness), *sūnṛta* (speaking in such a way as is true, good and pleasing), *asteya* (not taking anything which has not been given), *brahmacaryya* (abandoning lust for all kinds of objects, in mind, speech and body), and *aparigraha* (abandoning attachment for all things)[1]. These strict rules of conduct only apply to ascetics who are bent on attaining perfection. The standard proposed for the ordinary householders is fairly workable. Thus it is said by Hemacandra, that ordinary householders should earn money honestly, should follow the customs of good people, should marry a good girl from a good family, should follow the customs of the country and so forth. These are just what we should expect from any good and

[1] Certain external rules of conduct are also called cāritra. These are: *Īryyā* (to go by the path already trodden by others and illuminated by the sun's rays, so that proper precaution may be taken while walking to prevent oneself from treading on insects, etc., which may be lying on the way), *bhāṣā* (to speak well and pleasantly to all beings), *iṣaṇa* (to beg alms in the proper monastic manner), *dānasamiti* (to inspect carefully the seats avoiding all transgressions when taking or giving anything), *utsargasamiti* (to take care that bodily refuse may not be thrown in such a way as to injure any being), *manogupti* (to remove all false thoughts, to remain satisfied within oneself, and hold all people to be the same in mind), *vāggupti* (absolute silence), and *kāyagupti* (absolute steadiness and fixity of the body). Five other kinds of cāritra are counted in *Dravyasaṃgrahavṛtti* 35.

honest householder of the present day. Great stress is laid upon the virtues of ahiṃsā, sūnṛta, asteya and brahmacaryya, but the root of all these is ahiṃsā. The virtues of sūnṛta, asteya and brahmacaryya are made to follow directly as secondary corrollaries of ahiṃsā. Ahiṃsā may thus be generalized as the fundamental ethical virtue of Jainism; judgment on all actions may be passed in accordance with the standard of ahiṃsā; sūnṛta, asteya and brahmacaryya are regarded as virtues as their transgression leads to hiṃsā (injury to beings). A milder form of the practice of these virtues is expected from ordinary householders and this is called anubrata (small vows). But those who are struggling for the attainment of emancipation must practise these virtues according to the highest and strictest standard, and this is called mahābrata (great vows). Thus for example brahmacaryya for a householder according to the anubrata standard would be mere cessation from adultery, whereas according to mahābrata it would be absolute abstention from sex-thoughts, sex-words and sex-acts. Ahiṃsā according to a householder, according to anubrata, would require abstinence from killing any animals, but according to mahāvrata it would entail all the rigour and carefulness to prevent oneself from being the cause of any kind of injury to any living being in any way.

Many other minor duties are imposed upon householders, all of which are based upon the cardinal virtue of ahiṃsā. These are (1) *digvirati* (to carry out activities within a restricted area and thereby desist from injuring living beings in different places), (2) *bhogopabhogamāna* (to desist from drinking liquors, taking flesh, butter, honey, figs, certain other kinds of plants, fruits, and vegetables, to observe certain other kinds of restrictions regarding time and place of taking meals), (3) *anarthadaṇḍa* consisting of (*a*) *apadhyāna* (cessation from inflicting any bodily injuries, killing of one's enemies, etc.), (*b*) *pāpopadeśa* (desisting from advising people to take to agriculture which leads to the killing of so many insects), (*c*) *hiṃsopakāridāna* (desisting from giving implements of agriculture to people which will lead to the injury of insects), (*d*) *pramādācaraṇa* (to desist from attending musical parties, theatres, or reading sex-literature, gambling, etc.), (4) *śikṣāpadabrata* consisting of (*a*) *sāmayikabrata* (to try to treat all beings equally), (*b*) *deśāvakāśikabrata* (gradually to practise the *digviratibrata* more and more extensively), (*c*) *poṣadhabrata* (certain other kinds of restriction), (*d*) *atithisaṃvibhāgabrata* (to make gifts to guests). All transgressions of these virtues, called *aticāra*, should be carefully avoided.

All perception, wisdom, and morals belong to the soul, and to know the soul as possessing these is the right knowledge of the soul. All sorrows proceeding out of want of self-knowledge can be removed only by true self-knowledge. The soul in itself is pure intelligence, and it becomes endowed with the body only on account of its karma. When by meditation, all the karmas are burnt (*dhyānāgnidagdhakarma*) the self becomes purified. The soul is itself the saṃsāra (the cycle of rebirths) when it is overpowered by the four kaṣāyas (passions) and the senses. The four kaṣāyas are *krodha* (anger), *māna* (vanity and pride), *māyā* (insincerity and the tendency to dupe others), and *lobha* (greed). These kaṣāyas cannot be removed except by a control of the senses; and self-control alone leads to the purity of the mind (*manaḥśuddhi*). Without the control of the mind no one can proceed in the path of yoga. All our acts become controlled when the mind is controlled, so those who seek emancipation should make every effort to control the mind. No kind of asceticism (*tapas*) can be of any good until the mind is purified. All attachment and antipathy (*rāgadveṣa*) can be removed only by the purification of the mind. It is by attachment and antipathy that man loses his independence. It is thus necessary for the yogin (sage) that he should be free from them and become independent in the real sense of the term. When a man learns to look upon all beings with equality (*samatva*) he can effect such a conquest over rāga and dveṣa as one could never do even by the strictest asceticism through millions of years. In order to effect this samatva towards all, we should take to the following kinds of meditation (*bhāvanā*):

We should think of the transitoriness (*anityatā*) of all things, that what a thing was in the morning, it is not at mid-day, what it was at mid-day it is not at night; for all things are transitory and changing. Our body, all our objects of pleasure, wealth and youth all are fleeting like dreams, or cotton particles in a whirlwind.

All, even the gods, are subject to death. All our relatives will by their works fall a prey to death. This world is thus full of misery and there is nothing which can support us in it. Thus in whatever way we look for anything, on which we can depend, we find that it fails us. This is called aśaraṇabhāvanā (the meditation of helplessness).

Some are born in this world, some suffer, some reap the fruits of the karma done in another life. We are all different from one another by our surroundings, karma, by our separate bodies and by all other gifts which each of us severally enjoy. To meditate on these aspects is called ekatvabhāvanā and anyatvabhāvanā.

To think that the body is made up of defiled things, the flesh, blood, and bones, and is therefore impure is called aśucibhāvanā (meditation of the impurity of the body).

To think that if the mind is purified by the thoughts of universal friendship and compassion and the passions are removed, then only will good (*śubha*) accrue to me, but if on the contrary I commit sinful deeds and transgress the virtues, then all evil will befall me, is called āsravabhāvanā (meditation of the befalling of evil). By the control of the āsrava (inrush of karma) comes the saṃvara (cessation of the influx of karma) and the destruction of the karmas already accumulated leads to nirjarā (decay and destruction of karma matter).

Again one should think that the practice of the ten dharmas (virtues) of self control (*saṃyama*), truthfulness (*sūnṛta*), purity (*śauca*), chastity (*brahma*), absolute want of greed (*akiñcanatā*), asceticism (*tapas*), forbearance, patience (*kṣānti*), mildness (*mārdava*), sincerity (*ṛjutā*), and freedom or emancipation from all sins (*mukti*) can alone help us in the achievement of the highest goal. These are the only supports to which we can look. It is these which uphold the world-order. This is called dharmasvākhyātatābhāvanā.

Again one should think of the Jaina cosmology and also of the nature of the influence of karma in producing all the diverse conditions of men. These two are called *lokabhāvanā* and *bodhibhāvanā*.

When by the continual practice of the above thoughts man becomes unattached to all things and adopts equality to all beings, and becomes disinclined to all worldly enjoyments, then with a mind full of peace he gets rid of all passions, and then he should take to the performance of dhyāna or meditation by deep concentration. The samatva or perfect equality of the mind and dhyāna are interdependent, so that without dhyanā there is no samatva and without samatva there is no dhyāna. In order to make the mind steady by dhyāna one should think of *maitrī* (universal friendship), *pramoda* (the habit of emphasizing the good sides of men), *karuṇā* (universal compassion) and *mādhyastha* (indifference to the wickedness of people, i.e. the habit of not taking any note of sinners). The Jaina dhyāna consists in concentrating the mind on the syllables of the Jaina prayer phrases. The dhyāna however as we have seen is only practised as an aid to making the mind steady and perfectly equal and undisturbed towards all things. Emancipation comes only as the result of the final extinction of the karma materials. Jaina yoga is thus a complete course of moral discipline which leads to the purification of the mind and is hence different from the traditional Hindu yoga of Patañjali or even of the Buddhists[1].

Jaina Atheism[2].

The Naiyāyikas assert that as the world is of the nature of an effect, it must have been created by an intelligent agent and this agent is Īśvara (God). To this the Jain replies, "What does the Naiyāyika mean when he says that the world is of the nature of an effect"? Does he mean by "effect," (1) that which is made up of parts (*sāvayava*), or, (2) the coinherence of the causes of a non-existent thing, or, (3) that which is regarded by anyone as having been made, or, (4) that which is liable to change (*vikāritvam*). Again, what is meant by being "made up of parts"? If it means existence in parts, then the class-concepts (*sāmānya*) existing in the parts should also be regarded as effects, and hence destructible, but these the Naiyāyikas regard as being partless and eternal. If it means "that which has parts," then even "space" (*ākāśa*) has to be regarded as "effect," but the Naiyāyika regards it as eternal.

Again "effect" cannot mean "coinherence of the causes of a thing which were previously non-existent," for in that case one could not speak of the world as an effect, for the atoms of the elements of earth, etc., are regarded as eternal.

Again if "effect" means "that which is regarded by anyone as

[1] *Yogaśāstra*, by Hemacandra, edited by Windisch, in *Zeitschrift der Deutschen Morg. Gesellschaft*, Leipsig, 1874, and *Dravyasaṃgraha*, edited by Ghoshal, 1917.

[2] See Guṇaratna's *Tarkarahasyadīpikā*.

having been made," then it would apply even to space, for when a man digs the ground he thinks that he has made new space in the hollow which he dug.

If it means "that which is liable to change," then one could suppose that God was also liable to change and he would require another creator to create him and he another, and so on *ad infinitum*. Moreover, if God creates he cannot but be liable to change with reference to his creative activity.

Moreover, we know that those things which happen at some time and do not happen at other times are regarded as "effects." But the world as a whole exists always. If it is argued that things contained within it such as trees, plants, etc., are "effects," then that would apply even to this hypothetical God, for, his will and thought must be diversely operating at diverse times and these are contained in him. He also becomes a created being by virtue of that. And even atoms would be "effects," for they also undergo changes of colour by heat.

Let us grant for the sake of argument that the world as a whole is an "effect." And every effect has a cause, and so the world as a whole has a cause. But this does not mean that the cause is an intelligent one, as God is supposed to be. If it is argued that he is regarded as intelligent on the analogy of human causation then he might also be regarded as imperfect as human beings. If it is held that the world as a whole is not exactly an effect of the type of effects produced by human beings but is similar to those, this will lead to no inference. Because water-vapour is similar to smoke, nobody will be justified in inferring fire from water-vapour, as he would do from smoke. If it is said that this is so different an effect that from it the inference is possible, though nobody has ever been seen to produce such an effect, well then, one could also infer on seeing old houses ruined in course of time that these ruins were produced by intelligent agents. For these are also effects of which we do not know of any intelligent agent, for both are effects, and the invisibility of the agent is present in both cases. If it is said that the world is such that we have a sense that it has been made by some one, then the question will be, whether you infer the agency of God from this sense or infer the sense of its having been made from the fact of its being made by God, and you have a vicious circle (*anyonyāśraya*).

Again, even if we should grant that the world was created by an agent, then such an agent should have a body, for we have never seen any intelligent creator without a body. If it is held that we should consider the general condition of agency only, namely, that the agent is intelligent, the objection will be that this is impossible, for agency is always associated with some kind of body. If you take the instances of other kinds of effects such as the shoots of corn growing in the fields, it will be found that these had no intelligent agents behind them to create them. If it is said that these are also made by God, then you have an argument in a circle (*cakraka*), for this was the very matter which you sought to prove.

Let it be granted for the sake of argument that God exists. Does his mere abstract existence produce the world? Well, in that case, the abstract existence of a potter may also create the world, for the abstract existence is the same in both cases. Does he produce the world by knowledge and will? Well, that is impossible, for there cannot be any knowledge and will without a body. Does he produce the world by physical movement or any other kind of movement? In any case that is impossible, for there cannot be any movement without a body. If you suppose that he is omniscient, you may do so, but that does not prove that he can be all-creator.

Let us again grant for the sake of argument that a bodiless God can create the world by his will and activity. Did he take to creation through a personal whim? In that case there would be no natural laws and order in the world. Did he take to it in accordance with the moral and immoral actions of men? Then he is guided by a moral order and is not independent. Is it through mercy that he took to creation? Well then, we suppose there should have been only happiness in the world and nothing else. If it is said that it is by the past actions of men that they suffer pains and enjoy pleasure, and if men are led to do vicious actions by past deeds which work like blind destiny, then such a blind destiny (*adṛṣṭa*) might take the place of God. If He took to creation as mere play, then he must be a child who did things without a purpose. If it was due to his desire of punishing certain people and favouring others, then he must harbour favouritism on behalf of some and hatred against others. If the creation took place simply through his own nature, then, what is the good of admitting him at all? You may rather say that the world came into being out of its own nature.

It is preposterous to suppose that one God without the help of any instruments or other accessories of any kind, could create this world. This is against all experience.

Admitting for the sake of argument that such a God exists, you could never justify the adjectives with which you wish to qualify him. Thus you say that he is eternal. But since he has no body, he must be of the nature of intelligence and will. But this nature must have changed in diverse forms for the production of diverse kinds of worldly things, which are of so varied a nature. If there were no change in his knowledge and will, then there could not have been diverse kinds of creation and destruction. Destruction and creation cannot be the result of one unchangeable will and knowledge. Moreover it is the character of knowledge to change, if the word is used in the sense in which knowledge is applied to human beings, and surely we are not aware of any other kind of knowledge. You say that God is omniscient, but it is difficult to suppose how he can have any knowledge at all, for as he has no organs he cannot have any perception, and since he cannot have any perception he cannot have any inference either. If it is said that without the supposition of a God the variety of the world would be inexplicable, this also is not true, for this implication would only be justified if there were no other hypothesis left. But there are other suppositions also. Even without an omniscient God you could explain all things merely by the doctrine of moral order or the law of karma. If there were one God, there could be a society of Gods too. You say that if there were many Gods, then there would be quarrels and differences of opinion. This is like the story of a miser who for fear of incurring expenses left all his sons and wife and retired into the forest. When even ants and bees can co-operate together and act harmoniously, the supposition that if there were many Gods they would have fallen out, would indicate that in spite of all the virtues that you ascribe to God you think his nature to be quite unreliable, if not vicious. Thus in whichever way one tries to justify the existence of God he finds that it is absolutely a hopeless task. The best way then is to dispense with the supposition altogether[1].

[1] See *Ṣaḍdarśanasamuccaya,* Guṇaratna on Jainism, pp. 115 – 124.

Mokṣa (emancipation).

The motive which leads a man to strive for release (*mokṣa*) is the avoidance of pain and the attainment of happiness, for the state of mukti is the state of the soul in pure happiness. It is also a state of pure and infinite knowledge (*anantajñāna*) and infinite perception (*anantadarśana*). In the saṃsāra state on account of the karma veils this purity is sullied, and the veils are only worn out imperfectly and thus reveal this and that object at this and that time as ordinary knowledge (*mati*), testimony (*śruta*), supernatural cognition, as in trance or hypnotism (*avadhi*), and direct knowledge of the thoughts of others or thought reading (*manaḥparyāya*). In the state of release however there is omniscience (*kevala-jñāna*) and all things are simultaneously known to the perfect (*kevalin*) as they are. In the saṃsāra stage the soul always acquires new qualities, and thus suffers a continual change though remaining the same in substance. But in the emancipated stage the changes that a soul suffers are all exactly the same, and thus it is that at this stage the soul appears to be the same in substance as well as in its qualities of infinite knowledge, etc., the change meaning in this state only the repetition of the same qualities.

It may not be out of place to mention here that though the karmas of man are constantly determining him in various ways yet there is in him infinite capacity or power for right action (*anantavīrya*), so that karma can never subdue this freedom and infinite capacity, though this may be suppressed from time to time by the influence of karma. It is thus that by an exercise of this power man can overcome all karma and become finally liberated. If man had not this anantavīrya in him he might have been eternally under the sway of the accumulated karma which secured his bondage (*bandha*). But since man is the repository of this indomitable power the karmas can only throw obstacles and produce sufferings, but can never prevent him from attaining his highest good.

VII

THE KAPILA AND THE PĀTAÑJALA SĀṂKHYA (YOGA)[1].

A Review.

THE examination of the two ancient Nāstika schools of Buddhism and Jainism of two different types ought to convince us that serious philosophical speculations were indulged in, in circles other than those of the Upaniṣad sages. That certain practices known as Yoga were generally prevalent amongst the wise seems very probable, for these are not only alluded to in some of the Upaniṣads but were accepted by two nāstika schools of Buddhism and Jainism. Whether we look at them from the point of view of ethics or metaphysics, the two Nāstika schools appear to have arisen out of a reaction against the sacrificial disciplines of the Brāhmaṇas. Both these systems originated with the Kṣattriyas and were marked by a strong aversion against the taking of animal life, and against the doctrine of offering animals at the sacrifices.

The doctrine of the sacrifices supposed that a suitable combination of rites, rituals, and articles of sacrifice had the magical power of producing the desired effect—a shower of rain, the birth of a son, the routing of a huge army, etc. The sacrifices were enjoined generally not so much for any moral elevation, as for the achievement of objects of practical welfare. The Vedas were the eternal revelations which were competent so to dictate a detailed procedure, that we could by following it proceed on a certain course of action and refrain from other injurious courses in such a manner that we might obtain the objects we desired by the accurate performance of any sacrifice. If we are to define truth in accordance with the philosophy of such a ritualistic culture we might say that, that alone is true, in accordance with which we may realize our objects in the world about us; the truth of Vedic injunctions is shown by the practical attainment of our

[1] This chapter is based on my *Study of Patanjali*, published by the Calcutta University, and my *Yoga philosophy in relation to other Indian Systems of thought*, awaiting publication with the same authority. The system has been treated in detail in those two works.

objects. Truth cannot be determined *a priori* but depends upon the test of experience[1].

It is interesting to notice that Buddhism and Jainism though probably born out of a reactionary movement against this artificial creed, yet could not but be influenced by some of its fundamental principles which, whether distinctly formulated or not, were at least tacitly implied in all sacrificial performances. Thus we see that Buddhism regarded all production and destruction as being due to the assemblage of conditions, and defined truth as that which could produce any effect. But to such a logical extreme did the Buddhists carry these doctrines that they ended in formulating the doctrine of absolute momentariness[2]. Turning to the Jains we find that they also regarded the value of knowledge as consisting in the help that it offers in securing what is good for us and avoiding what is evil; truth gives us such an account of things that on proceeding according to its directions we may verify it by actual experience. Proceeding on a correct estimate of things we may easily avail ourselves of what is good and avoid what is bad. The Jains also believed that changes were produced by the assemblage of conditions, but they did not carry this doctrine to its logical extreme. There was change in the world as well as permanence. The Buddhists had gone so far that they had even denied the existence of any permanent soul. The Jains said that no ultimate, one-sided and absolute view of things could be taken, and held that not only the happening of events was conditional, but even all our judgments, are true only in a limited sense. This is indeed true for common sense, which we acknowledge as superior to mere *a priori* abstractions, which lead to absolute and one-sided conclusions. By the assemblage of conditions, old qualities in things disappeared, new qualities came in, and a part remained permanent. But this common-sense view, though in agreement with our ordinary experience, could not satisfy our inner *a priori* demands for finding out ultimate truth, which was true not relatively but absolutely. When asked whether anything was true, Jainism

[1] The philosophy of the Vedas as formulated by the Mīmāṃsā of Kumārila and Prabhākara holds the opposite view. Truth according to them is determined *a priori* while error is determined by experience.

[2] Historically the doctrine of momentariness is probably prior to the doctrine of *arthakriyākāritva*. But the later Buddhists sought to prove that momentariness was the logical result of the doctrine of *arthakriyākāritva*.

would answer, "yes, this is true from this point of view, but untrue from that point of view, while that is also true from such a point of view and untrue from another." But such an answer cannot satisfy the mind which seeks to reach a definite pronouncement, an absolute judgment.

The main departure of the systems of Jainism and Buddhism from the sacrificial creed consisted in this, that they tried to formulate a theory of the universe, the reality and the position of sentient beings and more particularly of man. The sacrificial creed was busy with individual rituals and sacrifices, and cared for principles or maxims only so far as they were of use for the actual performances of sacrifices. Again action with the new systems did not mean sacrifice but any general action that we always perform. Actions were here considered bad or good according as they brought about our moral elevation or not. The followers of the sacrificial creed refrained from untruth, not so much from a sense of personal degradation, but because the Vedas had dictated that untruth should not be spoken, and the Vedas must be obeyed. The sacrificial creed wanted more and more happiness here or in the other world. The systems of Buddhist and Jain philosophy turned their backs upon ordinary happiness and wanted an ultimate and unchangeable state where all pains and sorrows were for ever dissolved (Buddhism) or where infinite happiness, ever unshaken, was realized. A course of right conduct to be followed merely for the moral elevation of the person had no place in the sacrificial creed, for with it a course of right conduct could be followed only if it was so dictated in the Vedas. Karma and the fruit of karma (*karmaphala*) only meant the karma of sacrifice and its fruits-temporary happiness, such as was produced as the fruit of sacrifices; knowledge with them meant only the knowledge of sacrifice and of the dictates of the Vedas. In the systems however, karma, karmaphala, happiness, knowledge, all these were taken in their widest and most universal sense. Happiness or absolute extinction of sorrow was still the goal, but this was no narrow sacrificial happiness but infinite and unchangeable happiness or destruction of sorrow; karma was still the way, but not sacrificial karma, for it meant all moral and immoral actions performed by us; knowledge here meant the knowledge of truth or reality and not the knowledge of sacrifice.

Such an advance had however already begun in the

Upaniṣads which had anticipated the new systems in all these directions. The pioneers of these new systems probably drew their suggestions both from the sacrificial creed and from the Upaniṣads, and built their systems independently by their own rational thinking. But if the suggestions of the Upaniṣads were thus utilized by heretics who denied the authority of the Vedas, it was natural to expect that we should find in the Hindu camp such germs of rational thinking as might indicate an attempt to harmonize the suggestions of the Upaniṣads and of the sacrificial creed in such a manner as might lead to the construction of a consistent and well-worked system of thought. Our expectations are indeed fulfilled in the Sāṃkhya philosophy, germs of which may be discovered in the Upaniṣads.

The Germs of Sāṃkhya in the Upaniṣads.

It is indeed true that in the Upaniṣads there is a large number of texts that describe the ultimate reality as the Brahman, the infinite, knowledge, bliss, and speak of all else as mere changing forms and names. The word Brahman originally meant in the earliest Vedic literature, *mantra*, duly performed sacrifice, and also the power of sacrifice which could bring about the desired result[1]. In many passages of the Upaniṣads this Brahman appears as the universal and supreme principle from which all others derived their powers. Such a Brahman is sought for in many passages for personal gain or welfare. But through a gradual process of development the conception of Brahman reached a superior level in which the reality and truth of the world are tacitly ignored, and the One, the infinite, knowledge, the real is regarded as the only Truth. This type of thought gradually developed into the monistic Vedānta as explained by Śaṅkara. But there was another line of thought which was developing alongside of it, which regarded the world as having a reality and as being made up of water, fire, and earth. There are also passages in Śvetāśvatara and particularly in Maitrāyanī from which it appears that the Sāṃkhya line of thought had considerably developed, and many of its technical terms were already in use[2]. But the date of Maitrāyaṇī has not yet been definitely settled, and the details

[1] See Hille brandt's article, "Brahman" (*E. R. E.*).

[2] Kaṭha III. 10, v. 7. Śveta. v. 7, 8, 12, IV. 5, 1. 3. This has been dealt with in detail in my *Yoga Philosophy in relation to other Indian Systems of Thought*, in the first chapter.

found there are also not such that we can form a distinct notion of the Sāṃkhya thought as it developed in the Upaniṣads. It is not improbable that at this stage of development it also gave some suggestions to Buddhism or Jainism, but the Sāṃkhya-Yoga philosophy as we now get it is a system in which are found all the results of Buddhism and Jainism in such a manner that it unites the doctrine of permanence of the Upaniṣads with the doctrine of momentariness of the Buddhists and the doctrine of relativism of the Jains.

Sāṃkhya and Yoga Literature.

The main exposition of the system of Sāṃkhya and Yoga in this section has been based on the *Sāṃkhya kārikā*, the *Sāṃkhya sūtras*, and the *Yoga sūtras* of Patañjali with their commentaries and sub-commentaries. The *Sāṃkhya kārikā* (about A.D. 200) was written by Īśvarakṛṣṇa. The account of Sāṃkhya given by Caraka (A.D. 78) represents probably an earlier school and this has been treated separately. Vācaspati Miśra (ninth century A.D.) wrote a commentary on it known as *Tattvakaumudī*. But before him Gauḍapāda and Rājā wrote commentaries on the *Sāṃkhya kārikā*[1]. Nārāyaṇatīrtha wrote his *Candrikā* on Gauḍapāda's commentary. The *Sāṃkhya sūtras* which have been commented on by Vijñāna Bhikṣu (called *Pravacanabhāṣya*) of the sixteenth century seems to be a work of some unknown author after the ninth century. Aniruddha of the latter half of the fifteenth century was the first man to write a commentary on the *Sāṃkhya sūtras*. Vijñāna Bhikṣu wrote also another elementary work on Sāṃkhya known as *Sāṃkhyasāra*. Another short work of late origin is *Tattvasamāsa* (probably fourteenth century). Two other works on Sāṃkhya, viz. Sīmānanda's *Sāṃkhyatattvavivecana* and Bhāvāgaṇeśa's *Sāṃkhyatattvayāthārthyadīpana* (both later than Vijñānabhikṣu) of real philosophical value have also been freely consulted. Patañjali's *Yoga sūtra* (not earlier than B.C. 147) was commented on by Vyāsa (A.D. 40) and Vyāsa's bhāṣya commented on by Vācaspati Miśra is called *Tattvavaiśāradī*, by Vijñāna Bhikṣu *Yogavārttika*, by Bhoja in the tenth century *Bhojavṛtti*, and by Nāgeśa (seventeenth century) *Chāyāvyākhyā*.

[1] I suppose that Rājā's commentary on the *Kārikā* was the same as *Rājavārttika* quoted by Vācaspati. Rājā's commentary on the *Kārikā* has been referred to by Jayanta in his *Nyāyamañjarī*, p. 109. This book is probably now lost.

Amongst the modern works to which I owe an obligation I may mention the two treatises *Mechanical, physical and chemical theories of the Ancient Hindus* and the *Positive Sciences of the Ancient Hindus* by Dr B. N. Seal and my two works on Yoga *Study of Patanjali* published by the Calcutta University, and *Yoga Philosophy in relation to other Indian Systems of Thought* which is shortly to be published, and my *Natural Philosophy of the Ancient Hindus*, awaiting publication with the Calcutta University.

Guṇaratna mentions two other authoritative Sāṃtkhya works, viz. *Māṭharabhāṣya and Ātreyatantra*. Of these the second is probably the same as Caraka s treatment of Sāṃkhya, for we know that the sage Atri is the speaker in Caraka's work and for that it was called *Ātreyasaṃthitā* or *Ātreyatantra*. Nothing is known of the *Māṭharabhāṣya*[1].

An Early School of Sāṃkhya.

It is important for the history of Sāṃkhya philosophy that Caraka's treatment of it, which so far as I know has never been dealt with in any of the modern studies of Sāṃkhya, should be brought before the notice of the students of this philosophy. According to Caraka there are six elements (*dhātus*), viz. the five elements such as ākāśa, vāyu etc. and cetanā, called also puruṣa. From other points of view, the categories may be said to be twenty-four only, viz. the ten senses (five cognitive and five conative), manas, the five objects of senses and the eightfold prakṛti (prakṛti, mahat, ahaṃkāra and the five elements)[2]. The manas works through the senses. It is atomic and its existence is proved by the fact that in spite of the existence of the senses there cannot be any knowledge unless manas is in touch with them. There are two movements of manas as indeterminate sensing (*ūha*) and conceiving (*vicāra*) before definite understanding (*buddhi*) arises. Each of the five senses is the product of the combination of five elements but the auditory sense is made with a preponderance of ākāśa, the sense of touch with a preponderance

[1] Readers unacquainted with Sāṃkhya-Yoga may omit the following three sections at the time of first reading.

[2] Puruṣa is here excluded from the list. Cakrapāṇi, the commentator, says that the prakṛti and puruṣa both being unmanifested, the two together have been counted as one. *Prakṛtivyatiriktañcodāsīnaṃ puruṣamavyaktatvasādharmyāt avyaktāyām prakṛtāveva prakṣipya avyaktśabdenaiva gṛhṇāti.* Harinātha Viśārada's edition *of Caraka, Sārīra*, p. 4.

of air, the visual sense with a preponderance of light, the taste with a preponderance of water and the sense of smell with a preponderance of earth. Caraka does not mention the tanmātras at all[1]. The conglomeration of the sense-objects (*indriyārtha*) or gross matter, the ten senses, manas, the five subtle bhūtas and prakṛti, mahat and ahaṃkāra taking place through rajas make up what we call man. When the sattva is at its height this conglomeration ceases. All karma, the fruit of karma, cognition, pleasure, pain, ignorance, life and death belongs to this conglomeration. But there is also the puruṣa, for had it not been so there would be no birth, death, bondage, or salvation. If the ātman were not regarded as cause, all illuminations of cognition would be without any reason. If a permanent self were not recognized, then for the work of one others would be responsible. This puruṣa, called also *paramātman*, is beginningless and it has no cause beyond itself. The self is in itself without consciousness. Consciousness can only come to it through its connection with the sense organs and manas. By ignorance, will, antipathy, and work, this conglomeration of puruṣa and the other elements takes place. Knowledge, feeling, or action, cannot be produced without this combination. All positive effects are due to conglomerations of causes and not by a single cause, but all destruction comes naturally and without cause. That which is eternal is never the product of anything. Caraka identifies the avyakta part of prakṛti with puruṣa as forming one category. The vikāra or evolutionary products of prakṛti are called kṣetra, whereas the avyakta part of prakṛti is regarded as the kṣetrajña (*avyaktamasya kṣetrasya kṣetrajñamṛṣayo viduh*). This avyakta and cetanā are one and the same entity. From this unmanifested prakṛti or cetana is derived the buddhi, and from the buddhi is derived the ego (*ahaṃkāra*) and from the ahaṃkāra the five elements and the senses are produced, and when this production is complete, we say that creation has taken place. At the time of pralaya (periodical cosmic dissolution) all the evolutes return back to prakṛti, and thus become unmanifest with it, whereas at the time of a new creation from the puruṣa the unmanifest (*avyakta*), all the manifested forms—the evolutes of buddhi, ahaṃkāra, etc.—

[1] But some sort of subtle matter, different from gross matter, is referred to as forming part of *prakṛti* which is regarded as having eight elements in it (*prakṛtiścā ṣṭadhātuki*), viz. avyakta, mahat, ahaṃkāra, and five other elements. In addition to these elements forming part of the prakṛti we hear of indriyārthā, the five sense objects which have evolved out of the prakṛti.

appear[1]. This cycle of births or rebirths or of dissolution and new creation acts through the influence of rajas and tamas, and so those who can get rid of these two will never again suffer this revolution in a cycle. The manas can only become active in association with the self, which is the real agent. This self of itself takes rebirth in all kinds of lives according to its own wish, undetermined by anyone else. It works according to its own free will and reaps the fruits of its karma. Though all the souls are pervasive, yet they can only perceive in particular bodies where they are associated with their own specific senses. All pleasures and pains are felt by the conglomeration (*rāśi*), and not by the ātman presiding over it. From the enjoyment and suffering of pleasure and pain comes desire (*tṛṣṇā*) consisting of wish and antipathy, and from desire again comes pleasure and pain. Mokṣa means complete cessation of pleasure and pain, arising through the association of the self with the manas, the sense, and sense-objects. If the manas is settled steadily in the self, it is the state of yoga when there is neither pleasure nor pain. When true knowledge dawns that "all are produced by causes, are transitory, rise of themselves, but are not produced by the self and are sorrow, and do not belong to me the self," the self transcends all. This is the last renunciation when all affections and knowledge become finally extinct. There remains no indication of any positive existence of the self at this time, and the self can no longer be perceived[2]. It is the state of Brahman. Those who know Brahman call this state the Brahman, which is eternal and absolutely devoid of any characteristic. This state is spoken of by the Sāṃkhyas as their goal, and also that of the Yogins. When rajas and tamas are rooted out and the karma of the past whose fruits have to be enjoyed are exhausted, and there is no new karma and new birth,

[1] This passage has been differently explained in a commentary previous to Cakrapāṇi as meaning that at the time of death these resolve back into the prakṛti—the puruṣa—and at the time of rebirth they become manifest again. See Cakrapāṇi on śārīra, I. 46.

[2] Though this state is called brahmabhūta, it is not in any sense like the Brahman of Vedāntą which is of the nature of pure being, pure intelligence and pure bliss. This indescribable state is more like absolute annihilation without any sign of existence *(alakṣaṇam)*, resembling Nāgārjuna's Nirvāṇa. Thus Caraka writes:—*tasmimṃśarama-sannyāse samūlāḥsarvavedanāḥ asaṃjñājñānavijñānā nivṛttiṃ yāntyaśeṣataḥ, ataḥ-paraṃ brahmabhūto bhūtātmā nopalabhyate niḥsṛtaḥ sarvabhāvebhyaḥ cihnaṃ yasya na. vidyate. gatirbrahmavidāṃ brahma taccākṣaramalakṣaṇam. Caraka, Sārīra* 1. 98-100.

the state of mokṣa comes about. Various kinds of moral endeavours in the shape of association with good people, abandoning of desires, determined attempts at discovering the truth with fixed attention, are spoken of as indispensable means. Truth (tattva) thus discovered should be recalled again and again[1] and this will ultimately effect the disunion of the body with the self. As the self is avyakta (unmanifested) and has no specific nature or character, this state can only be described as absolute cessation (*mokṣe nivṛttirniḥśeṣā*).

The main features of the Sāṃkhya doctrine as given by Caraka are thus: 1. Puruṣa is the state of avyakta. 2. By a conglomeration of this avyakta with its later products a conglomeration is formed which generates the so-called living being. 3. The tanmātras are not mentioned. 4. Rajas and tamas represent the bad states of the mind and sattva the good ones. 5. The ultimate state of emancipation is either absolute annihilation or characterless absolute existence and it is spoken of as the Brahman state; there is no consciousness in this state, for consciousness is due to the conglomeration of the self with its evolutes, buddhi, ahaṃkāra etc. 6. The senses are formed of matter (*bhautika*).

This account of Sāṃkhya agrees with the system of Sāṃkhya propounded by Pañcaśikha (who is said to be the direct pupil of Āsuri the pupil of Kapila, the founder of the system) in the Mahābhārata XII. 219. Pañcaśikha of course does not describe the system as elaborately as Caraka does. But even from what little he says it may be supposed that the system of Sāṃkhya he sketches is the same as that of Caraka[2]. Pañcaśikha speaks of the ultimate truth as being avyakta (a term applied in all Sāṃkhya literature to prakṛti) in the state of puruṣa (*puruṣāvasthamavyaktam*). If man is the product of a mere combination of the different elements, then one may assume that all ceases with death. Caraka in answer to such an objection introduces a discussion, in which he tries to establish the existence of a self as the postulate of all our duties and sense of moral responsibility. The same discussion occurs in Pañcaśikha also, and the proofs

[1] Four causes are spoken of here as being causes of memory: (1) Thinking of the cause leads to the remembering of the effect, (2) by similarity, (3) by opposite things, and (4) by acute attempt to remember.

[2] Some European scholars have experienced great difficulty in accepting Pañcaśikha's doctrine as a genuine Sāṃkhya doctrine. This may probably be due to the fact that the Sāṃkhya doctrines sketched in *Caraka* did not attract their notice.

for the existence of the self are also the same. Like Caraka again Pañcaśikha also says that all consciousness is due to the conditions of the conglomeration of our physical body mind,—and the element of "cetas." They are mutually independent, and by such independence carry on the process of life and work. None of the phenomena produced by such a conglomeration are self. All our suffering comes in because we think these to be the self. Mokṣa is realized when we can practise absolute renunciation of these phenomena. The guṇas described by Pañcaśikha are the different kinds of good and bad qualities of the mind as Caraka has it. The state of the conglomeration is spoken of as the kṣetra, as Caraka says, and there is no annihilation or eternality; and the last state is described as being like that when all rivers lose themselves in the ocean and it is called aliṅga (without any characteristic)—a term reserved for prakṛti in later Sāṃkhya. This state is attainable by the doctrine of ultimate renunciation which is also called the doctrine of complete destruction (*samyagbadha*).

Guṇaratna (fourteenth century A.D.), a commentator of *Ṣaḍdarśanasamuccaya,* mentions two schools of Sāṃkhya, the Maulikya (original) and the Uttara or (later)[1]. Of these the doctrine of the Maulikya Sāṃkhya is said to be that which believed that there was a separate pradhāna for each ātman (*maulikyasāṃkhyā hyātmānamātmānam prati pṛthak pradhānam vadanti*). This seems to be a reference to the Sāṃkhya doctrine I have just sketched. I am therefore disposed to think that this represents the earliest systematic doctrine of Sāṃkhya.

In *Mahābhārata* XII. 318 three schools of Sāṃkhya are mentioned, viz. those who admitted twenty-four categories (the school I have sketched above), those who admitted twenty-five (the well-known orthodox Sāṃkhya system) and those who admitted twenty-six categories. This last school admitted a supreme being in addition to puruṣa and this was the twenty-sixth principle. This agrees with the orthodox Yoga system and the form of Sāṃkhya advocated in the *Mahābhārata*. The schools of Sāṃkhya of twenty-four and twenty-five categories are here denounced as unsatisfactory. Doctrines similar to the school of Sāṃkhya we have sketched above are referred to in some of the

[1] Guṇaratna's *Tarkarahasyadīpikā*, p. 99.

other chapters of the *Mahābhārata* (XII. 203, 204). The self apart from the body is described as the moon of the new moon day; it is said that as Rāhu (the shadow on the sun during an eclipse) cannot be seen apart from the sun, so the self cannot be seen apart from the body. The selfs (*śarīriṇaḥ*) are spoken of as manifesting from prakṛti.

We do not know anything about Āsuri the direct disciple of Kapila[1]. But it seems probable that the system of Sāṃkhya we have sketched here which appears in fundamentally the same form in the *Mahābhārata* and has been attributed there to Pañcaśikha is probably the earliest form of Sāṃkhya available to us in a systematic form. Not only does Guṇaratna's reference to the school of Maulikya Sāṃkhya justify it, but the fact that Caraka (A.D. 78) does not refer to the Sāṃkhya as described by Īśvarakṛṣṇa and referred to in other parts of *Mahābhārata* is a definite proof that Īśvarakṛṣṇa's Sāṃkhya is a later modification, which was either non-existent in Caraka's time or was not regarded as an authoritative old Sāṃkhya view.

Wassilief says quoting Tibetan sources that Vindhyavāsin altered the Sāṃkhya according to his own views[2]. Takakusu thinks that Vindhyavāsin was a title of Īśvarakṛṣṇa[3] and Garbe holds that the date of Īśvarakṛṣṇa was about A.D. 100 It seems to be a very plausible view that Īśvarakṛṣṇa was indebted for his kārikās to another work, which was probably written in a style different from what he employs. The seventh verse of his *Kārikā* seems to be in purport the same as a passage which is found quoted in the

[1] A verse attributed to Āsuri is quoted by Guṇaratna (*Tarkarahasyadīpikā*, p. 104). The purport of this verse is that when buddhi is transformed in a particular manner, it (puruṣa) has experience. It is like the reflection of the moon in transparent water.

[2] Vassilief's *Buddhismus*, p. 240.

[3] Takakusu's "A study of Paramārtha's life of Vasubandhu,"*J.R.A.S.*, 1905. This identification by Takakusu, however, appears to be extremely doubtful, for Guṇaratna mentions Īśvarakṛṣṇa and Vindhyavāsin as two different authorities (*Tarka-rahasyadīpikā*, pp. 102 and 104). The verse quoted from Vindhyavāsin (p. 104) in anuṣṭubh metre cannot be traced as belonging to Īśvarakṛṣṇa. It appears that Īśvarakṛṣṇa wrote two books; one is the *Sāṃkhya kārikā* and another an independent work on Sāṃkhya, a line from which, quoted by Guṇaratna, stands as follows:

"*Pratiniyatādhyavasāyaḥ śrotrādisamuttha adhyakṣam*" (p. 108).

If Vācaspati's interpretation of the classification of anumāna in his *Tattvakaumudī* be considered to be a correct explanation of *Sāṃkhya kārikā* then Īśvarakṛṣṇa must be a different person from Vindhyavāsin whose views on anumāna as referred to in *Ślokavārttika*, p. 393, are altogether different. But Vācaspati's own statement in the *Tātparyyaṭīkā* (pp. 109 and 131) shows that his treatment there was not faithful.

Mahābhāṣya of Patañjali the grammarian (B.C. 147)[1]. The subject of the two passages are the enumeration of reasons which frustrate visual perception. This however is not a doctrine concerned with the strictly technical part of Sāṃkhya, and it is just possible that the book from which Patañjali quoted the passage, and which was probably paraphrased in the Āryā metre by Īśvarakṛṣṇa was not a Sāṃkhya book at all. But though the subject of the verse is not one of the strictly technical parts of Sāṃkhya, yet since such an enumeration is not seen in any other system of Indian philosophy, and as it has some special bearing as a safeguard against certain objections against the Sāṃkhya doctrine of prakṛti, the natural and plausible supposition is that it was the verse of a Sāṃkhya book which was paraphrased by Īśvarakṛṣṇa.

The earliest descriptions of a Sāṃkhya which agrees with Īśvarakṛṣṇa's Sāṃkhya (but with an addition of Iśvara) are to be found in Patañjali's *Yoga sūtras* and in the *Mahābhārata*; but we are pretty certain that the Sāṃkhya of *Caraka* we have sketched here was known to Patañjali, for in *Yoga sūtra* I. 19 a reference is made to a view of Sāṃkhya similar to this.

From the point of view of history of philosophy the Sāṃkhya of Caraka and Pañcaśikha is very important; for it shows a transitional stage of thought between the Upaniṣad ideas and the orthodox Sāṃkhya doctrine as represented by Īśvarakṛṣṇa. On the one hand its doctrine that the senses are material, and that effects are produced only as a result of collocations, and that the puruṣa is unconscious, brings it in close relation with Nyāya, and on the other its connections with Buddhism seem to be nearer than the orthodox Sāṃkhya.

We hear of a *Ṣaṣṭitantraśāstra* as being one of the oldest Sāṃkhya works. This is described in the *Ahirbudhnya Sāṃhitā* as containing two books of thirty-two and twenty-eight chapters[2]. A quotation from *Rājavārttika* (a work about which there is no definite information) in Vācaspati Miśra's commentary on the *Sāṃkhya kārika* (72) says that it was called the *Ṣaṣṭitantra* because it dealt with the existence of prakṛti, its oneness, its difference from puruṣas, its purposefulness for puruṣas, the multiplicity of puruṣas, connection and separation from puruṣas, the evolution of

[1] Patañjali's Mahābhāṣya, IV. 1. 3. *Atisannikarṣādativiprakarṣāt mūrttyantara-vyavadhānāt tamasāvṛtatvāt indriyadaurvalyādatipramādāt*, etc. (Benares edition.)

[2] *Ahirbudhnya Saṃhitā*, pp. 108, 110.

the categories, the inactivity of the puruṣas and the five *viparyyayas*, nine *tuṣṭis*, the defects of organs of twenty-eight kinds, and the eight siddhis[1].

But the content of the *Ṣaṣṭitantra* as given in *Ahirbudhnya Saṃhitā* is different from it, and it appears from it that the Sāṃkhya of the *Ṣaṣṭitantra* referred to in the *Ahirbudhnya Saṃhitā* was of a theistic character resembling the doctrine of the Pañcarātra Vaiṣṇavas and the *Ahirbudhnya Saṃhitā* says that Kapila's theory of Sāṃkhya was a Vaiṣṇava one. Vijñan Bhikṣu, the greatest expounder of Sāṃkhya, says in many places of his work *Vijñānāmṛta Bhāṣya* that Sāṃkhya was originally theistic, and that the atheistic Sāṃkhya is only a *prauḍhivāda* (an exaggerated attempt to show that no supposition of Iśvara is necessary to explain the world process) though the *Mahābhārata* points out that the difference between Sāṃkhya and Yoga is this, that the former is atheistic, while the latter is theistic. The discrepancy between the two accounts of *Ṣaṣṭitantra* suggests that the original *Ṣaṣṭitantra* as referred to in the *Ahirbudhnya Saṃhitā* was subsequently revised and considerably changed. This supposition is corroborated by the fact that Guṇaratna does not mention among the important Sāṃkhya works *Ṣaṣṭitantra* but *Ṣaṣṭitantroddhāra*

[1] The doctrine of the *viparyyaya, tuṣṭi*, defects of organs, and the *siddhi* are mentioned in the *Kārikā* of Īśvarakṛṣṇa, but I have omitted them in my account of Sāṃkhya as these have little philosophical importance. The viparyyaya (false knowledge) are five, viz. avidyā (ignorance), asmitā (egoism), rāga (attachment), dveṣa (antipathy), abhiniveśa (self-love), which are also called *tamo, moka, mahāmoha, tamisrā*, and *andhatāmisra*. These are of nine kinds of tuṣṭi, such as the idea that no exertion is necessary, since prakṛti will herself bring our salvation (*ambhas*), that it is not necessary to meditate, for it is enough if we renounce the householder's life (*salila*), that there is no hurry, salvation will come in time (*megha*), that salvation will be worked out by fate (*bhāgya*), and the contentment leading to renunciation proceeding from five kinds of causes, e.g. the troubles of earning (*para*), the troubles of protecting the earned money (*supara*), the natural waste of things earned by enjoyment (*parā-para*), increase of desires leading to greater disappointments (*anuttamāmbhas*), all gain leads to the injury of others (*uttamāmbhas*). This renunciation proceeds from external considerations with those who consider prakṛti and its evolutes as the self. The siddhis or ways of success are eight in number, viz. (1) reading of scriptures (*tāra*), (2) enquiry into their meaning (*sutāra*), (3) proper reasoning (*tāratāra*), (4) corroborating one's own ideas with the ideas of the teachers and other workers of the same field (*ramyaka*), (5) clearance of the mind by long-continued practice (*sadāmudita*). The three other siddhis called pramoda, mudita, and modamāna lead directly to the separation of the prakṛti from the puruṣa. The twenty-eight sense defects are the eleven defects of the eleven senses and seventeen kinds of defects of the understanding corresponding to the absence of siddhis and the presence of tuṣṭis. The viparyyayas, tuṣṭis and the defects of the organs are hindrances in the way of the achievement of the Sāṃkhya goal.

(revised edition of *Ṣaṣṭitantra*)[1]. Probably the earlier Ṣaṣṭitantra was lost even before Vācaspati's time.

If we believe the *Ṣaṣṭitantra* referred to in the *Ahirbudhnya Saṃhitā* to be in all essential parts the same work which was composed by Kapila and based faithfully on his teachings, then it has to be assumed that Kapila's Sāṃkhya was theistic[2]. It seems probable that his disciple Āsuri tried to popularise it. But it seems that a great change occurred when Pañcaśikha the disciple of Āsuri came to deal with it. For we know that his doctrine differed from the traditional one in many important respects. It is said in *Sāṃkhya kārikā* (70) that the literature was divided by him into many parts (*tena bahudhākṛtam tantram*). The exact meaning of this reference is difficult to guess. It might mean that the original *Ṣaṣṭitantra* was rewritten by him in various treatises. It is a well-known fact that most of the schools of Vaiṣṇavas accepted the form of cosmology which is the same in most essential parts as the Sāṃkhya cosmology. This justifies the assumption that Kapila's doctrine was probably theistic. But there are a few other points of difference between the Kapila and the Pātañjala Sāṃkhya (Yoga). The only supposition that may be ventured is that Pañcaśikha probably modified Kapila's work in an atheistic way and passed it as Kapila's work. If this supposition is held reasonable, then we have three strata of Sāṃkhya, first a theistic one, the details of which are lost, but which is kept in a modified form by the Pātañjala school of Sāṃkhya, second an atheistic one as represented by Pañcaśikha, and a third atheistic modification as the orthodox Sāṃkhya system. An important change in the Sāṃkhya doctrine seems to have been introduced by Vijñāna Bhikṣu (sixteenth century A.D.) by his treatment of guṇas as types of reals. I have myself accepted this interpretation of Sāṃkhya as the most rational and philosophical one, and have there fore followed it in giving a connected system of the accepted Kapila and the Pātañjala school of Sāṃkhya. But it must be pointed out that originally the notion of guṇas was applied to different types of good and bad mental states, and then they were supposed in some mysterious way by mutual increase and decrease to form the objective world on the one hand and the

[1] *Tarkarahasyadīpikā*, p. 109.

[2] *evaṃ ṣaḍviṃśakaṃ; prāhuḥ; śarīramih mānavāḥ sāṃkhyam sāṃkhyātmakatvācca kapilādibhirucyate*. *Matsyapurāṇa*, IV. 28.

totality of human psychosis on the other. A systematic explanation of the guṇas was attempted in two different lines by Vijñāna Bhikṣu and the Vaiṣṇava writer Veṅkaṭa[1]. As the Yoga philosophy compiled by Patañjali and commented on by Vyāsa, Vācaspati and Vijñāna Bhikṣu, agree with the Sāṃkhya doctrine as explained by Vācaspati and Vijñāna Bhikṣu in most points I have preferred to call them the Kapila and the Pātañjala schools of Sāṃkhya and have treated them together—a principle which was followed by Haribhadra in his *Ṣaḍdarśanasamuccaya*.

The other important Sāṃkhya teachers mentioned by Gauḍapāda are Sanaka, Sananda, Sanātana and Voḍhu. Nothing is known about their historicity or doctrines.

Sāṃkhya kārikā, Sāṃkhya sūtra, Vācaspati Miśra and Vijñāna Bhikṣu.

A word of explanation is necessary as regards my interpretation of the Sāṃkhya-Yoga system. The *Sāṃkhya kārikā* is the oldest Sāṃkhya text on which we have commentaries by later writers. The *Sāṃkhya sūtra* was not referred to by any writer until it was commented upon by Aniruddha (fifteenth century A.D.). Even Guṇaratna of the fourteenth century A.D. who made allusions to a number of Sāṃkhya works, did not make any reference to the *Sāṃkhya sūtra*, and no other writer who is known to have flourished before Guṇaratna seems to have made any reference to the *Sāṃkhya sūtra*. The natural conclusion therefore is that these sūtras were probably written some time after the fourteenth century. But there is no positive evidence to prove that it was so late a work as the fifteenth century. It is said at the end of the *Sāṃkhya kārikā* of Īśvarakṛṣṇa that the kārikās give an exposition of the Sāṃkhya doctrine excluding the refutations of the doctrines of other people and excluding the parables attached to the original Sāṃkhya works—the *Ṣaṣṭitantraśāstra*. The *Sāṃkhya sūtras* contain refutations of other doctrines and also a number of parables. It is not improbable that these were collected from some earlier Sāṃkhya work which is now lost to us. It may be that it was done from some later edition of the *Ṣaṣṭitantraśāstra* (*Saṣṭitantroddhāra* as mentioned by

[1] Veṅkaṭa's philosophy will be dealt with in the second volume of the present work.

Guṇaratna), but this is a mere conjecture. There is no reason to suppose that the Sāṃkhya doctrine found in the sūtras differs in any important way from the Sāṃkhya doctrine as found in the *Sāṃkhya kārikā*. The only point of importance is this, that the *Sāṃkhya sūtras* hold that when the Upaniṣads spoke of one absolute pure intelligence they meant to speak of unity as involved in the class of intelligent puruṣas as distinct from the class of the guṇas. As all puruṣas were of the nature of pure intelligence, they were spoken of in the Upaniṣads as one, for they all form the category or class of pure intelligence, and hence may in some sense be regarded as one. This compromise cannot be found in the *Sāṃkhya kārikā*. This is, however, a case of omission and not of difference. Vijñāna Bhikṣu, the commentator of the *Sāṃkhya sūtras*, was more inclined to theistic Sāṃkhya or Yoga than to atheistic Sāṃkhya. This is proved by his own remarks in his *Sāṃkhyapravacanabhāṣya*, *Yogavārttika*, and *Vijñānāmṛta-bhāsya* (an independent commentary on the Brahmasūtras of Bādarāyaṇa on theistic Sāṃkhya lines). Vijñāna Bhikṣu's own view could not properly be called a thorough Yoga view, for he agreed more with the views of the Sāṃkhya doctrine of the Purāṇas, where both the diverse puruṣas and the prakṛti are said to be merged in the end in Īśvara, by whose will the creative process again began in the prakṛti at the end of each pralaya. He could not avoid the distinctively atheistic arguments of the *Sāṃkhya sūtras*, but he remarked that these were used only with a view to showing that the Sāṃkhya system gave such a rational explanation that even without the intervention of an Īśvara it could explain all facts. Vijñāna Bhikṣu in his interpretation of Sāṃkhya differed on many points from those of Vācaspati, and it is difficult to say who is right. Vijñāna Bhiksu has this advantage that he has boldly tried to give interpretations on some difficult points on which Vācaspati remained silent. I refer principally to the nature of the conception of the guṇas, which I believe is the most important thing in Sāṃkhya. Vijñāna Bhikṣu described the guṇas as reals or super-subtle substances, but Vācaspati and Gauḍapāda (the other commentator of the *Sāṃkhya kārikā*) remained silent on the point. There is nothing, however, in their interpretations which would militate against the interpretation of Vijñāna Bhikṣu, but yet while they were silent as to any definite explanations regarding the nature of the guṇas, Bhikṣu definitely came forward with a very satisfactory and rational interpretation of their nature.

Since no definite explanation of the guṇas is found in any other work before Bhikṣu, it is quite probable that this matter may not have been definitely worked out before. Neither Caraka nor the *Mahābhārata* explains the nature of the guṇas. But Bhikṣu's interpretation suits exceedingly well all that is known of the manifestations and the workings of the guṇas in all early documents. I have therefore accepted the interpretation of Bhikṣu in giving my account of the nature of the guṇas. The *Kārikā* speaks of the guṇas as being of the nature of pleasure, pain, and dullness (*sattva*, *rajas* and *tamas*). It also describes sattva as being light and illuminating, rajas as of the nature of energy and causing motion, and tamas as heavy and obstructing. Vācaspati merely paraphrases this statement of the *Kārikā* but does not enter into any further explanations. Bhikṣu's interpretation fits in well with all that is known of the guṇas, though it is quite possible that this view might not have been known before, and when the original Sāṃkhya doctrine was formulated there was a real vagueness as to the conception of the guṇas.

There are some other points in which Bhikṣu's interpretation differs from that of Vācaspati. The most important of these may be mentioned here. The first is the nature of the connection of the buddhi states with the puruṣa. Vācaspati holds that there is no contact (*saṃyoga*) of any buddhi state with the puruṣa but that a reflection of the puruṣa is caught in the state of buddhi by virtue of which the buddhi state becomes intelligized and transformed into consciousness. But this view is open to the objection that it does not explain how the puruṣa can be said to be the experiencer of the conscious states of the buddhi, for its reflection in the buddhi is merely an image, and there cannot be an experience (*bhoga*) on the basis of that image alone without any actual connection of the puruṣa with the buddhi. The answer of Vācaspati Miśra is that there is no contact of the two in space and time, but that their proximity (*sannidhi*) means only a specific kind of fitness (*yogyatā*) by virtue of which the puruṣa, though it remains aloof, is yet felt to be united and identified in the buddhi, and as a result of that the states of the buddhi appear as ascribed to a person. Vijñāna Bhikṣu differs from Vācaspati and says that if such a special kind of fitness be admitted, then there is no reason why puruṣa should be deprived of such a fitness at the time of emancipation, and thus there would be no emancipation at all, for the fitness being in the puruṣa, he could not be divested of it, and he would continue to enjoy the experiences represented in the buddhi for ever. Vijñāna Bhikṣu thus holds that there is a real contact of the puruṣa with the buddhi state in any cognitive state. Such a contact of the puruṣa and the buddhi does not necessarily mean that the former will be liable to change on account of it, for contact and change are not synonymous. Change means the rise of new qualities. It is the buddhi which suffers changes, and when these changes are reflected in the puruṣa, there is the notion of a person or experiencer in the puruṣa, and when the puruṣa is reflected back in the buddhi the buddhi state appears as a conscious state. The second, is the difference between Vācaspati and Bhikṣu as regards the nature of the perceptual process. Bhikṣu thinks that the senses can directly perceive the determinate qualities of things without any intervention of manas, whereas Vācaspati ascribes to manas the power of arranging the sense-data in a definite order and of making the indeterminate sense-data determinate. With him the first stage of cognition is the stage when indeterminate sense materials are first presented, at the next stage there is assimilation, differentiation, and association by which the indeterminate materials are ordered and classified by the activity of manas called saṃkalpa which coordinates the indeterminate sense materials into determinate perceptual and conceptual forms as class notions with particular characteristics. Bhikṣu who supposes that the determinate character of things is directly perceived by the senses has necessarily to assign a subordinate position to manas as being only the faculty of desire, doubt, and imagination.

It may not be out of place to mention here that there are one or two passages in Vācaspati's commentary on the *Sāṃkhya kārikā* which seem to suggest that he considered the ego (*ahaṃkāra*) as producing the subjective series of the senses and the objective series of the external world by a sort of desire or will, but he did not work out this doctrine, and it is therefore not necessary to enlarge upon it. There is also a difference of view with regard to the evolution of the tanmātras from the mahat; for contrary to the view of *Vyāsabhāṣya* and Vijñāna Bhikṣu etc. Vācaspati holds that from the mahat there was ahaṃkāra and from ahaṃkāra the tanmātras[1]. Vijñāna Bhikṣu however holds that both the separation of ahaṃkāra and the evolution of the tanmātras take place in the mahat, and as this appeared to me to be more reasonable, I have followed this interpretation. There are some other minor points of difference about the Yoga doctrines between Vācaspati and Bhikṣu which are not of much philosophical importance.

Yoga and Patañjali.

The word yoga occurs in the Ṛg-Veda in various senses such as yoking or harnessing, achieving the unachieved, connection, and the like. The sense of yoking is not so frequent as the other senses; but it is nevertheless true that the word was used in this sense in Ṛg-Veda and in such later Vedic works as the Śatapatha Brāhmaṇa and the Bṛhadāraṇyaka Upaniṣad[2]. The word has another derivative "yugya" in later Sanskrit literature[3].

With the growth of religious and philosophical ideas in the Rg-Veda, we find that the religious austerities were generally very much valued. Tapas (asceticism) and brahmacarya (the holy vow of celibacy and life-long study) were regarded as greatest virtues and considered as being productive of the highest power[4].

As these ideas of asceticism and self-control grew the force of the flying passions was felt to be as uncontrollable as that of a spirited steed, and thus the word yoga which was originally applied to the control of steeds began to be applied to the control of the senses[5].

In Pāṇini's time the word yoga had attained its technical meaning, and he distinguished this root "*yuj samādhau*" (*yuj* in the sense of concentration) from "*yujir yoge*" (root *yujir* in the sense of connecting). *Yuj* in the first sense is seldom used as a verb. It is more or less an imaginary root for the etymological derivation of the word yoga[6].

[1] See my *Study of Patanjali*, p. 60 ff.

[2] Compare R.V. I. 34. 9/VII. 67. 8/111. 27. 11/X. 30. 11/X. 114. 9/IV. 24. 4/1. 5. 3/1. 30. 7; Śatapatha Brāhmaṇa 14. 7. 1. 11.

[3] It is probably an old word of the Aryan stock; compare German Joch, A.S. geoc, Latin jugum.

[4] Sec Chāndogya III. 17. 4; Bṛh. 1. 2. 6; Bṛh. III. 8. 10; Taitt. I. 9. I/III. 2. I/III. 3. 1; Taitt. Brāh. II. 2. 3. 3; R.V. x. 129; Śatap. Brāh. XI. 5. 8. 1.

[5] Kaṭha III. 4, *indriyāṇi hayānahuḥ viṣayatesugocarān*. The senses are the horses and whatever they grasp are their objects. Maitr. 2. 6. *Karmendriyāṇyasya hayāḥ* the conative senses are its horses.

[6] *Yutgyaḥ* is usd from the root of *yujir yoga* and not from *yuja samādhau*. A consideration

In the *Bhagavad-gītā*, we find that the word yoga has been used not only in conformity with the root "*yuj-samādhau*" but also with "*yujir yoge*." This has been the source of some confusion to the readers of the *Bhagavad-gītā*. "Yogin" in the sense of a person who has lost himself in meditation is there regarded with extreme veneration. One of the main features of the use of this word lies in this that the *Bhagavad-gītā* tried to mark out a middle path between the austere discipline of meditative abstraction on the one hand and the course of duties of sacrificial action of a Vedic worshipper in the life of a new type of Yogin (evidently from *yujir yoge*) on the other, who should combine in himself the best parts of the two paths, devote himself to his duties, and yet abstract himself from all selfish motives associated with desires.

Kauṭilya in his *Arthaśāstra* when enumerating the philosophic sciences of study names Sāṃkhya, Yoga, and Lokāyata. The oldest Buddhist sūtras (e.g. the *Satipaṭṭhāna sutta*) are fully familiar with the stages of Yoga concentration. We may thus infer that self-concentration and Yoga had developed as a technical method of mystic absorption some time before the Buddha.

As regards the connection of Yoga with Sāṃkhya, as we find it in the *Yoga sūtras* of Patañjali, it is indeed difficult to come to any definite conclusion. The science of breath had attracted notice in many of the earlier Upaniṣads, though there had not probably developed any systematic form of prāṇāyāma (a system of breath control) of the Yoga system. It is only when we come to Maitrāyaṇī that we find that the Yoga method had attained a systematic development. The other two Upaniṣads in which the Yoga ideas can be traced are the Śvetāśvatara and the Katha. It is indeed curious to notice that these three Upaniṣads of Kṛṣṇa Yajurveda, where we find reference to Yoga methods, are the only ones where we find clear references also to the Sāṃkhya tenets, though the Sāṃkhya and Yoga ideas do not appear there as related to each other or associated as parts of the same system. But there is a remarkable passage in the Maitrāyaṇī in the conversation between Sākyāyana and Bṛhad ratha where we find that the Sāṃkhya metaphysics was offered

of Pāṇini's rule "*Tadasya brahmacaryam*," v. i. 94 shows that not only different kinds of asceticism and rigour which passed by the name of brahmacarya were prevalent in the country at the time (Pāṇini as Goldstücker has proved is pre-buddhistic), but associated with these had grown up a definite system of mental discipline which passed by the name of Yoga.

in some quarters to explain the validity of the Yoga processes, and it seems therefore that the association and grafting of the Sāṃkhya metaphysics on the Yoga system as its basis, was the work of the followers of this school of ideas which was subsequently systematized by Patañjali. Thus Śākyāyana says: "Here some say it is the guṇa which through the differences of nature goes into bondage to the will, and that deliverance takes place when the fault of the will has been removed, because he sees by the mind; and all that we call desire, imagination, doubt, belief, unbelief, certainty, uncertainty, shame, thought, fear, all that is but mind. Carried along by the waves of the qualities darkened in his imagination, unstable, fickle, crippled, full of desires, vacillating he enters into belief, believing I am he, this is mine, and he binds his self by his self as a bird with a net. Therefore, a man being possessed of will, imagination and belief is a slave, but he who is the opposite is free. For this reason let a man stand free from will, imagination and belief—this is the sign of liberty, this is the path that leads to Brahman, this is the opening of the door, and through it he will go to the other shore of darkness. All desires are there fulfilled. And for this, they quote a verse: 'When the five instruments of knowledge stand still together with the mind, and when the intellect does not move, that is called the highest state[1].' "

An examination of such Yoga Upaniṣads as Śāṇḍilya, Yoga-tattva, Dhyānabindu, Haṃsa, Amṛtanāda, Varāha, Maṇḍala Brāhmaṇa, Nādabindu, and Yogakuṇḍalī, shows that the Yoga practices had undergone diverse changes in diverse schools, but none of these show any predilection for the Sāṃkhya. Thus the Yoga practices grew in accordance with the doctrines of the

[1] Vātsyāyana, however, in his bhaṣya on *Nyāya sūtra*, I. i. 29, distinguishes Sāṃkhya from Yoga in the following way: The Sāṃkhya holds that nothing can come into being nor be destroyed, there cannot be any change in the pure intelligence (*niratiśayāḥ cetanāḥ*). All changes are due to changes in the body, the senses, the manas and the objects. Yoga holds that all creation is due to the karma of the puruṣa. Doṣas (passions) and the pravṛtti (action) are the cause of karma. The intelligences or souls (cetana) are associated with qualities. Non-being can come into being and what is produced may be destroyed. The last view is indeed quite different from the Yoga of *Vyāsabhāṣya*. It is closer to Nyāya in its doctrines. If Vātsyāyana's statement is correct, it would appear that the doctrine of there being a moral purpose in creation was borrowed by Sāṃkhya from Yoga. Udyotakara's remarks on the same sūtra do not indicate a difference but an agreement between Sāṃkhya and Yoga on the doctrine of the *indriyas* being "*abhautika*." Curiously enough Vātsyāyana quotes a passage from *Vyāsabhāṣya*, III. 13, in his bhāṣya, 1. ii. 6, and criticizes it as self-contradictory (*viruddha*).

Śaivas and Śāktas and assumed a peculiar form as the Mantra-yoga; they grew in another direction as the Haṭhayoga which was supposed to produce mystic and magical feats through constant practices of elaborate nervous exercises, which were also associated with healing and other supernatural powers. The Yogatattva Upaniṣad says that there are four kinds of yoga, the Mantra Yoga, Laya Yoga, Haṭhayoga and Rājayoga[1]. In some cases we find that there was a great attempt even to associate Vedāntism with these mystic practices. The influence of these practices in the development of Tantra and other modes of worship was also very great, but we have to leave out these from our present consideration as they have little philosophic importance and as they are not connected with our present endeavour.

Of the Pātañjala school of Sāṃkhya, which forms the subject of the Yoga with which we are now dealing, Patañjali was probably the most notable person for he not only collected the different forms of Yoga practices, and gleaned the diverse ideas which were or could be associated with the Yoga, but grafted them all on the Sāṃkhya metaphysics, and gave them the form in which they have been handed down to us. Vācaspati and Vijñāna Bhikṣu, the two great commentators on the *Vyāsabkāṣya*, agree with us in holding that Patañjali was not the founder of the Yoga, but an editor. Analytic study of the sūtras also brings the conviction that the sūtras do not show any original attempt, but a masterly and systematic compilation which was also supplemented by fitting contributions. The systematic manner also in which the first three chapters are written by way of definition and classification shows that the materials were already in existence and that Patañjali only systematized them. There was no missionizing zeal, no attempt to overthrow the doctrines of other systems, except as far as they might come in, by way of explaining the system. Patañjali is not even anxious to establish the system, but he is only engaged in systematizing the facts as he had them. Most of the criticisms against the Buddhists occur in the last chapter. The doctrines of the Yoga are described in the first three chapters, and this part is separated from the last chapter where the views of the Buddhists are

[1] The Yoga writer Jaigīṣavya wrote "*Dhāranāśāstra*" which dealt with Yoga more in the fashion of Tantra than that given by Patañjali. He mentions different places in the body (e.g. heart, throat, tip of the nose, palate, forehead, centre of the brain) which are centres of memory where concentration is to be made. See Vācaspati's *Tātparyaṭīkā* or Vātsyāyana's bhāṣya on *Nyāya sūtra*, III. ii. 43.

criticized; the putting of an "*iti*" (the word to denote the conclusion of any work) at the end of the third chapter is evidently to denote the conclusion of his Yoga compilation. There is of course another "*iti*" at the end of the fourth chapter to denote the conclusion of the whole work. The most legitimate hypothesis seems to be that the last chapter is a subsequent addition by a hand other than that of Patañjali who was anxious to supply some new links of argument which were felt to be necessary for the strengthening of the Yoga position from an internal point of view, as well as for securing the strength of the Yoga from the supposed attacks of Buddhist metaphysics. There is also a marked change (due either to its supplementary character or to the manipulation of a foreign hand) in the style of the last chapter as compared with the style of the other three.

The sūtras, 30-34, of the last chapter seem to repeat what has already been said in the second chapter and some of the topics introduced are such that they could well have been dealt with in a more relevant manner in connection with similar discussions in the preceding chapters. The extent of this chapter is also disproportionately small, as it contains only 34 sūtras, whereas the average number of sūtras in other chapters is between 51 to 55.

We have now to meet the vexed question of the probable date of this famous Yoga author Patañjali. Weber had tried to connect him with Kāpya Pataṃchala of Śatapatha Brāhmaṇa[1]; in Kātyāyana's *Vārttika* we get the name Patañjali which is explained by later commentators as *patantaḥ añjalayaḥ yasmai* (for whom the hands are folded as a mark of reverence), but it is indeed difficult to come to any conclusion merely from the similarity of names. There is however another theory which identifies the writer of the great commentary on Pāṇini called the *Mahābhāṣya* with the Patañjali of the *Yoga sūtra*. This theory has been accepted by many western scholars probably on the strength of some Indian commentators who identified the two Patañjalis. Of these one is the writer of the *Patañjalicarita* (Rāmabhadra Dīkṣita) who could not have flourished earlier than the eighteenth century. The other is that cited in Śivarāma's commentary on *Vāsavadattā* which Aufrecht assigns to the eighteenth century. The other two are king Bhoja of Dhār and Cakrapāṇidatta,

[1] Weber's *History of Indian Literature*, p. 223 N.

the commentator of *Caraka*, who belonged to the eleventh century A.D. Thus Cakrapāṇi says that he adores the Ahipati (mythical serpent chief) who removed the defects of mind, speech and body by his *Pātañjala mahābhāṣya* and the revision of *Caraka*. Bhoja says: "Victory be to the luminous words of that illustrious sovereign Raṇaraṅgamalla who by composing his grammar, by writing his commentary on the Pātañjala and by producing a treatise on medicine called *Rājamṛgāṅka* has like the lord of the holder of serpents removed defilement from speech, mind and body." The adoration hymn of Vyāsa (which is considered to be an interpolation even by orthodox scholars) is also based upon the same tradition. It is not impossible therefore that the later Indian commentators might have made some confusion between the three Patañjalis, the grammarian, the Yoga editor, and the medical writer to whom is ascribed the book known as *Pātañjalatantra*, and who has been quoted by Śivadāsa in his commentary on *Cakradatta* in connection with the heating of metals.

Professor J. H. Woods of Harvard University is therefore in a way justified in his unwillingness to identify the grammarian and the Yoga editor on the slender evidence of these commentators. It is indeed curious to notice that the great commentators of the grammar school such as Bhartṛhari, Kaiyyaṭa, Vāmana, Jayāditya, Nāgeśa, etc. are silent on this point. This is indeed a point against the identification of the two Patañjalis by some Yoga and medical commentators of a later age. And if other proofs are available which go against such an identification, we could not think the grammarian and the Yoga writer to be the same person.

Let us now see if Patañjali's grammatical work contains anything which may lead us to think that he was not the same person as the writer on Yoga. Professor Woods supposes that the philosophic concept of substance (*dravya*) of the two Patañjalis differs and therefore they cannot be identified. He holds that dravya is described in *Vyāsabhāṣya* in one place as being the unity of species and qualities (*sāmānyaviśeṣātmaka*), whereas the *Mahābhāṣya* holds that a dravya denotes a genus and also specific qualities according as the emphasis or stress is laid on either side. I fail to see how these ideas are totally antagonistic. Moreover, we know that these two views were held by

Vyāḍi and Vājapyāyana (Vyāḍi holding that words denoted qualities or dravya and Vājapyāyana holding that words denoted species[1]). Even Pāṇini had these two different ideas in "*jātyākhyā-yāmekasmin bahuvacanamanyatarasyām*," and "*sarūpānamekaśeṣamekavibhaktau*," and Patañjali the writer of the *Mahābhāṣya* only combined these two views. This does not show that he opposes the view of *Vyāsabhāṣya*, though we must remember that even if he did, that would not prove anything with regard to the writer of the sūtras. Moreover, when we read that dravya is spoken of in the *Mahābhāṣya* as that object which is the specific kind of the conglomeration of its parts, just as a cow is of its tail, hoofs, horns, etc.—"*yat sāsnālāṅgulakakudakhura-viṣāṇyartharūpam*," we are reminded of its similarity with "*ayutasiddhāvāyavabhedānugataḥ samūhaḥ dravyam*" (a conglomeration of interrelated parts is called dravya) in the *Vyāsabhāṣya*. So far as I have examined the *Mahābhāṣya* I have not been able to discover anything there which can warrant us in holding that the two Patañjalis cannot be identified. There are no doubt many apparent divergences of view, but even in these it is only the traditional views of the old grammarians that are exposed and reconciled, and it would be very unwarrantable for us to judge anything about the personal views of the grammarian from them. I am also convinced that the writer of the *Mahābhāṣya* knew most of the important points of the Sāṃkhya-Yoga metaphysics; as a few examples I may refer to the guṇa theory (1. 2. 64, 4. 1. 3), the Sāṃkhya dictum of ex nihilo nihil fit (1. 1. 56), the ideas of time (2. 2. 5, 3. 2. 123), the idea of the return of similars into similars (1. 1. 50), the idea of change *vikāra* as production of new qualities *guṇāntarādhāna* (5. 1. 2, 5. 1. 3) and the distinction of indriya and Buddhi (3. 3. 133). We may add to it that the *Mahābhāṣya* agrees with the Yoga view as regards the Sphoṭavāda, which is not held in common by any other school of Indian philosophy. There is also this external similarity, that unlike any other work they both begin their works in a similar manner (*atha yogānuśāsanam and atha śābdānuśāsanam*)—"now begins the compilation of the instructions on Yoga" (*Yoga sūtra*)—and "now begins the compilation of the instructions of words" (*Mahābhāṣya*).

It may further be noticed in this connection that the arguments

[1] Patañjali's *Mahābhāṣya*, 1. 2. 64.

which Professor Woods has adduced to assign the date of the *Yoga sūtra* between A.D. 300 and 500 are not at all conclusive, as they stand on a weak basis; for firstly if the two Patañjalis cannot be identified, it does not follow that the editor of the Yoga should necessarily be made later; secondly, the supposed Buddhist[1] reference is found in the fourth chapter which, as I have shown above, is a later interpolation; thirdly, even if they were written by Patañjali it cannot be inferred that because Vācaspati describes the opposite school as being of the Vijñāna-vādi type, we are to infer that the sūtras refer to Vasubandhu or even to Nāgārjuna, for such ideas as have been refuted in the sūtras had been developing long before the time of Nāgārjuna,

Thus we see that though the tradition of later commentators may not be accepted as a sufficient ground to identify the two Patañjalis, we cannot discover anything from a comparative critical study of the *Yoga sūtras* and the text of the *Mahā-bhāṣya*, which can lead us to say that the writer of the *Yoga sūtras* flourished at a later date than the other Patañjali.

Postponing our views about the time of Patañjali the Yoga editor, I regret I have to increase the confusion by introducing the other work *Kitāb Pātanjal*, of which Alberuni speaks, for our consideration. Alberuni considers this work as a very famous one and he translates it along with another book called *Sānka* (Sāṃkhya) ascribed to Kapila. This book was written in the form of dialogue between master and pupil, and it is certain that this book was not the present *Yoga sūtra* of Patañjali, though it had the same aim as the latter, namely the search for liberation and for the union of the soul with the object of its meditation. The book was called by Alberuni *Kitāb Pātanjal*, which is to be translated as the book of Pātañjala, because in another place, speaking of its author, he puts in a Persian phrase which when translated stands as "the author of the book of Pātanjal." It had also an elaborate commentary from which Alberuni quotes many extracts, though he does not tell us the author's name. It treats of God, soul, bondage, karma, salvation, etc., as we find in the *Yoga sūtra*, but the manner in which these are described (so

[1] It is important to notice that the most important Buddhist reference *nacaika-cittatantram vastu tadapramāṇakam tadā kim syāt* (iv. 16) was probably a line of the *Vyāsabhāṣya*, as Bhoja, who had consulted many commentaries as he says in the preface, does not count it as a sūtra.

far as can be judged from the copious extracts supplied by Alberuni) shows that these ideas had undergone some change from what we find in the *Yoga sūtra*. Following the idea of God in Alberuni we find that he retains his character as a timeless emancipated being, but he speaks, hands over the Vedas and shows the way to Yoga and inspires men in such a way that they could obtain by cogitation what he bestowed on them. The name of God proves his existence, for there cannot exist anything of which the name existed, but not the thing. The soul perceives him and thought comprehends his qualities. Meditation is identical with worshipping him exclusively, and by practising it uninterruptedly the individual comes into supreme absorption with him and beatitude is obtained[1].

The idea of soul is the same as we find in the *Yoga sūtra*. The idea of metempsychosis is also the same. He speaks of the eight siddhis (miraculous powers) at the first stage of meditation on the unity of God. Then follow the other four stages of meditation corresponding to the four stages we have as in the *Yoga sūtra*. He gives four kinds of ways for the achievement of salvation, of which the first is the *abhyāsa* (habit) of Patañjali, and the object of this abhyāsa is unity with God[2]. The second stands for vairāgya; the third is the worship of God with a view to seek his favour in the attainment of salvation (cf. *Yoga sūtra*, 1. 23 and 1. 29). The fourth is a new introduction, namely that of rasāyana or alchemy. As regards liberation the view is almost the same as in the *Yoga sūtra*, II. 25 and IV. 34, but the liberated state is spoken of in one place as absorption in God or being one with him. The Brahman is conceived as an *ūrddhvamūla avākśākha aśvattha* (a tree with roots upwards and branches below), after the Upaniṣad fashion, the upper root is pure Brahman, the trunk is Veda, the branches are the different doctrines and schools, its leaves are the different modes of interpretation. Its nourishment comes from the three forces; the

[1] Cf. *Yoga sūtra* I. 23–29 and II. 1, 45. The *Yoga sūtras* speak of Īśvara (God) as an eternally emancipated puruṣa, omniscient, and the teacher of all past teachers. By meditating on him many of the obstacles such as 'llness, etc., which stand in the way of Yoga practice are removed. He is regarded as one of the alternative objects of concentration. The commentator Vyāsa notes that he is the best object, for being drawn towards the Yogin by his concentration He so wills that he can easily attain concentration and through it salvation. No argument is given in the *Yoga sūtras* of the existence of God.

[2] Cf. Yoga II. 1.

object of the worshipper is to leave the tree and go back to the roots.

The difference of this system from that of the *Yoga sūtra* is: (1) the conception of God has risen here to such an importance that he has become the only object of meditation, and absorption in him is the goal; (2) the importance of the yama[1] and the niyama has been reduced to the minimum; (3) the value of the Yoga discipline as a separate means of salvation apart from any connection with God as we find in the *Yoga sūtra* has been lost sight of; (4) liberation and Yoga are defined as absorption in God; (5) the introduction of Brahman; (6) the very significance of Yoga as control of mental states (*cittavṛttinirodha*) is lost sight of, and (7) rasāyana (alchemy) is introduced as one of the means of salvation.

From this we can fairly assume that this was a new modification of the Yoga doctrine on the basis of Patañjali's *Yoga sūtra* in the direction of Vedānta and Tantra, and as such it probably stands as the transition link through which the Yoga doctrine of the sūtras entered into a new channel in such a way that it could be easily assimilated from there by later developments of Vedānta, Tantra and Śaiva doctrines[2]. As the author mentions rasāyana as a means of salvation, it is very probable that he flourished after Nāgārjuna and was probably the same person who wrote *Pātañjala tantra*, who has been quoted by Śivadāsa in connection with alchemical matters and spoken of by Nāgeśa as "*Carake* Patañjaliḥ." We can also assume with some degree of probability that it is with reference to this man that Cakrapāṇi and Bhoja made the confusion of identifying him with the writer of the *Mahābhāṣya*. It is also very probable that Cakrapāṇi by his line "*pātañjalamahābhāṣyacarakapratisaṃskṛtaiḥ*" refers to this work which was called "Pātañjala." The commentator of this work gives some description of the lokas, dvīpas and the sāgaras, which runs counter to the descriptions given in the *Vyāsabhāṣya*, III. 26, and from this we can infer that it was probably written at a time when the *Vyāsabhāṣya* was not written or had not attained any great sanctity or authority. Alberuni

[1] Alberuni, in his account of the book of Sāṃkhya, gives a list of commandments which practically is the same as yama and niyama, but it is said that through them one cannot attain salvation.

[2] Cf. the account of *Pāśupatadarśana* in *Sarvadarśanasaṃgraha*.

also described the book as being very famous at the time, and Bhoja and Cakrapāṇi also probably confused him with Patañjali the grammarian; from this we can fairly assume that this book of Patañjali was probably written by some other Patañjali within the first 300 or 400 years of the Christian era; and it may not be improbable that when *Vyāsabhāṣya* quotes in III. 44 as "*iti* Patañjaliḥ," he refers to this Patañjali.

The conception of Yoga as we meet it in the Maitrāyaṇa Upaniṣad consisted of six aṅgas or accessories, namely prāṇāyāma, pratyāhāra, dhyāna, dhāraṇā, tarka and samādhi[1]. Comparing this list with that of the list in the *Yoga sūtras* we find that two new elements have been added, and tarka has been replaced by āsana. Now from the account of the sixty-two heresies given in the *Brahmajāla sutta* we know that there were people who either from meditation of three degrees or through logic and reasoning had come to believe that both the external world as a whole and individual souls were eternal. From the association of this last mentioned logical school with the Samādhi or Dhyāna school as belonging to one class of thinkers called śāśvatavāda, and from the inclusion of tarka as an aṅga in samādhi, we can fairly assume that the last of the aṅgas given in Maitrāyaṇī Upaniṣad represents the oldest list of the Yoga doctrine, when the Sāṃkhya and the Yoga were in a process of being grafted on each other, and when the Sāṃkhya method of discussion did not stand as a method independent of the Yoga. The substitution of āsana for tarka in the list of Patañjali shows that the Yoga had developed a method separate from the Sāṃkhya. The introduction of ahiṃsā (non-injury), satya (truthfulness), asteya (want of stealing), brahmacaryya (sex-control), aparigraha (want of greed) as yama and śauca (purity), santoṣa (contentment) as niyama, as a system of morality without which Yoga is deemed impossible (for the first time in the sūtras), probably marks the period when the disputes between the Hindus and the Buddhists had not become so keen. The introduction of maitrī, karuṇā, muditā, upekṣā is also equally significant, as we do not find them mentioned in such a prominent form in any other literature of the Hindus dealing with the subject of emancipation. Beginning from the *Ācārāṅgasūtra*, *Uttarādhyayanasūtra*,

[1] *prāṇāyāmaḥ pratyāhāraḥ dhyānam dhāraṇā. tarkaḥ samādhiḥ ṣaḍaṅga ityucyate yogaḥ* (Maitr. 6. 8).

the *Sūtrakṛtāṅgasūtra*, etc., and passing through Umāsvāti's *Tattvārthādhigamasūtra* to Hemacandra's *Yogaśāstra* we find that the Jains had been founding their Yoga discipline mainly on the basis of a system of morality indicated by the yamas, and the opinion expressed in Alberuni's *Pātanjal* that these cannot give salvation marks the divergence of the Hindus in later days from the Jains. Another important characteristic of Yoga is its thoroughly pessimistic tone. Its treatment of sorrow in connection with the statement of the scope and ideal of Yoga is the same as that of the four sacred truths of the Buddhists, namely suffering, origin of suffering, the removal of suffering; and of the path to the removal of suffering[1]. Again, the metaphysics of the saṃsāra (rebirth) cycle in connection with sorrow, origination, decease, rebirth, etc. is described with a remarkable degree of similarity with the cycle of causes as described in early Buddhism. Avidyā is placed at the head of the group; yet this avidyā should not be confused with the Vedānta avidyā of Śaṅkara, as it is an avidyā of the Buddhist type; it is not a cosmic power of illusion nor anything like a mysterious original sin, but it is within the range of earthly tangible reality. Yoga avidyā is the ignorance of the four sacred truths, as we have in the sūtra "*anityāśuciduḥkhānātmasu nityaśuciduḥkhātmakhyātiravidyā*" (II. 5).

The ground of our existing is our will to live (*abhiniveśa*). "This is our besetting sin that we will to be, that we will to be ourselves, that we fondly will our being to blend with other kinds of existence and extend. The negation of the will to be, cuts off being for us at least[2]." This is true as much of Buddhism as of the Yoga abhiniveśa, which is a term coined and used in the Yoga for the first time to suit the Buddhist idea, and which has never been accepted, so far as I know, in any other Hindu literature in this sense. My sole aim in pointing out these things in this section is to show that the *Yoga sūtras* proper (first three chapters) were composed at a time when the later forms of Buddhism had not developed, and when the quarrels between the Hindus and the Buddhists and Jains had not reached such

[1] *Yoga sūtra*, II. 15, 16, 17. *Yathācikitsāśāstraṃ caturvyūhaṃ rogo rogahetuḥ ārogyaṃ bhaiṣajyamiti evamidamapi śāstram caturvyūhameva; tadyathā saṃsāraḥ, saṃsārahetuḥ mokṣaḥ mokṣopāyaḥ; duḥkhabahulaḥ saṃsāro heyaḥ, pradhānapuruṣayoḥ saṃyogo heyahetuḥ, saṃyogasyātyantikī nivṛttirhānaṃ hanopāyaḥ samyagdarśanam, Vyāsabhāṣya*, II. 15

[2] Oldenberg's *Buddhism*[1].

a stage that they would not like to borrow from one another. As this can only be held true of earlier Buddhism I am disposed to think that the date of the first three chapters of the *Yoga sūtras* must be placed about the second century B.C. Since there is no evidence which can stand in the way of identifying the grammarian Patañjali with the Yoga writer, I believe we may take them as being identical[1].

The Sāṃkhya and the Yoga Doctrine of Soul or Puruṣa.

The Sāṃkhya philosophy as we have it now admits two principles, souls and *prakṛti*, the root principle of matter. Souls are many, like the Jaina souls, but they are without parts and qualities. They do not contract or expand according as they occupy a smaller or a larger body, but are always all-pervasive, and are not contained in the bodies in which they are manifested. But the relation between body or rather the mind associated with it and soul is such that whatever mental phenomena happen in the mind are interpreted as the experience of its soul. The souls are many, and had it not been so (the Sāṃkhya argues) with the birth of one all would have been born and with the death of one all would have died[2].

The exact nature of soul is however very difficult of comprehension, and yet it is exactly this which one must thoroughly grasp in order to understand the Sāṃkhya philosophy. Unlike the Jaina soul possessing *anantajñāna*, *anantadarśana*, *anantasukha*, and *anantavīryya*, the Sāṃkhya soul is described as being devoid of any and every characteristic; but its nature is absolute pure consciousness (*cit*). The Sāṃkhya view differs from the Vedānta, firstly in this that it does not consider the soul to be of the nature of pure intelligence and bliss (*ānanda*)[3]. Bliss with Sāṃkhya is but another name for pleasure and as such it belongs to prakṛti and does not constitute the nature of soul; secondly, according to Vedānta the individual souls (*jīva*) are

[1] See S. N. Das Gupta, *Yoga Philosophy in relation to other Indian systems of thought*, ch. II. The most important point in favour of this identification seems to be that both the Patañjalis as against the other Indian systems admitted the doctrine of *sphoṭa* which was denied even by Sāṃkhya. On the doctrine of Sphoṭa see my *Study of Patanjali*, Appendix I.

[2] *Kārikā*, 18.

[3] See Citsukha's *Tattvapradīpikā*, IV.

but illusory manifestations of one soul or pure consciousness the Brahman, but according to Sāṃkhya they are all real and many.

The most interesting feature of Sāṃkhya as of Vedānta is the analysis of knowledge. Sāṃkhya holds that our knowledge of things are mere ideational pictures or images. External things are indeed material, but the sense data and images of the mind, the coming and going of which is called knowledge, are also in some sense matter-stuff, since they are limited in their nature like the external things. The sense-data and images come and go, they are often the prototypes, or photographs of external things, and as such ought to be considered as in some sense material, but the matter of which these are composed is the subtlest. These images of the mind could not have appeared as conscious, if there were no separate principles of consciousness in connection with which the whole conscious plane could be interpreted' as the experience of a person[1]. We know that the Upaniṣads consider the soul or ātman as pure and infinite consciousness, distinct from the forms of knowledge, the ideas, and the images. In our ordinary ways of mental analysis we do not detect that beneath the forms of knowledge there is some other principle which has no change, no form, but which is like a light which illumines the mute, pictorial forms which the mind assumes. The self is nothing but this light. We all speak of our "self" but we have no mental picture of the self as we have of other things, yet in all our knowledge we seem to know our self. The Jains had said that the soul was veiled by karma matter, and every act of knowledge meant only the partial removal of the veil. Sāṃkhya says that the self cannot be found as an image of knowledge, but that is because it is a distinct, transcendent principle, whose real nature as such is behind or beyond the subtle matter of knowledge. Our cognitions, so far as they are mere forms or images, are merely compositions or complexes of subtle mind-substance, and thus are like a sheet of painted canvas immersed in darkness; as the canvas gets prints from outside and moves, the pictures appear one by one before the light and are illuminated. So it is with our knowledge. The special characteristic of self is that it is like a light, without which all knowledge would be blind. Form and motion are the characteristics of matter, and

[1] *Tattakaumudī*, 5; *Yogavārttika*, IV. 22; *Vijñānāmṛtabhaṣya*, *p*. 74; *Yogavārttika* and *Tattvavaiśāradī*, I. 4, II. 6, 18, 20; *Vyāsabhāṣya*, I. 6, 7.

so far as knowledge is mere limited form and movement it is the same as matter; but there is some other principle which enlivens these knowledge-forms, by virtue of which they become conscious. This principle of consciousness (*cit*) cannot indeed be separately perceived *per se*, but the presence of this principle in all our forms of knowledge is distinctly indicated by inference. This principle of consciousness has no motion, no form, no quality, no impurity[1]. The movement of the knowledge-stuff takes place in relation to it, so that it is illuminated as consciousness by it, and produces the appearance of itself as undergoing all changes of knowledge and experiences of pleasure and pain. Each item of knowledge so far as it is an image or a picture of some sort is but a subtle knowledge-stuff which has been illumined by the principle of consciousness, but so far as each item of knowledge carries with it the awakening or the enlivening of consciousness, it is the manifestation of the principle of consciousness. Knowledge-revelation is not the unveiling or revelation of a particular part of the self, as the Jains supposed, but it is a revelation of the self only so far as knowledge is pure awakening, pure enlivening, pure consciousness. So far as the content of knowledge or the image is concerned, it is not the revelation of self but is the blind knowledge-stuff.

The Buddhists had analysed knowledge into its diverse constituent parts, and had held that the coming together of these brought about the conscious states. This coming together was to them the point of the illusory notion of self, since this unity or coming together was not a permanent thing but a momentary collocation. With Sāṃkhya however the self, the pure *cit*, is neither illusory nor an abstraction; it is concrete but transcendent. Coming into touch with it gives unity to all the movements of the knowledge-composites of subtle stuff, which would otherwise have remained aimless and unintelligent. It is by coming into connection with this principle of intelligence that they are interpreted as the systematic and coherent experience of a person, and may thus be said to be intelligized. Intelligizing means the expression and interpretation of the events or the happenings of

[1] It is important to note that Sāṃkhya has two terms to denote the two aspects involved in knowledge, viz. the relating element of awareness as such (*cit*), and the content (*buddhi*) which is the form of the mind-stuff representing the sense-data and the image. Cognition takes place by the reflection of the former in the latter.

knowledge in connection with a person, so as to make them a system of experience. This principle of intelligence is called puruṣa. There is a separate puruṣa in Sāṃkhya for each individual, and it is of the nature of pure intelligence. The Vedānta ātman however is different from the Sāṃkhya puruṣa in this that it is one and is of the nature of pure intelligence, pure being, and pure bliss. It alone is the reality and by illusory māyā it appears as many.

Thought and Matter.

A question naturally arises, that if the knowledge forms are made up of some sort of stuff as the objective forms of matter are, why then should the puruṣa illuminate it and not external material objects. The answer that Sāṃkhya gives is that the knowledge-complexes are certainly different from external objects in this, that they are far subtler and have a preponderance of a special quality of plasticity and translucence (*sattva*), which resembles the light of puruṣa, and is thus fit for reflecting and absorbing the light of the puruṣa. The two principal characteristics of external gross matter are mass and energy. But it has also the other characteristic of allowing itself to be photographed by our mind; this thought-photograph of matter has again the special privilege of being so translucent as to be able to catch the reflection of the *cit*—the super-translucent transcendent principle of intelligence. The fundamental characteristic of external gross matter is its mass; energy is common to both gross matter and the subtle thought-stuff. But mass is at its lowest minimum in thought-stuff, whereas the capacity of translucence, or what may be otherwise designated as the intelligence-stuff, is at its highest in thought-stuff. But if the gross matter had none of the characteristics of translucence that thought possesses, it could not have made itself an object of thought; for thought transforms itself into the shape, colour, and other characteristics of the thing which has been made its object. Thought could not have copied the matter, if the matter did not possess some of the essential substances of which the copy was made up. But this plastic entity (*sattva*) which is so predominant in thought is at its lowest limit of subordination in matter. Similarly mass is not noticed in thought, but some such notions as are associated with mass may be discernible in thought, thus the images of thought are limited, separate, have movement, and have more or less clear cut forms. The images do not extend in space, but they can represent space. The translucent and plastic element of thought (*sattva*) in association with movement (*rajas*) would have resulted in a simultaneous revelation of all objects; it is on account of mass or tendency of obstruction (*tamas*) that knowledge proceeds from image to image and discloses things in a successive manner. The buddhi (thought-stuff) holds within it all knowledge immersed as it were in utter darkness, and actual knowledge comes before our view as though by the removal of the darkness or veil, by the reflection of the light of the puruṣa. This characteristic of knowledge, that all its stores are hidden as if lost at any moment, and only one picture or idea comes at a time to the arena of revelation, demonstrates that in knowledge there is a factor of obstruction which manifests itself in its full actuality in gross matter as mass. Thus both thought and gross matter are made up of three elements, a plasticity of intelligence-stuff (*sattva*), energy-stuff (*rajas*), and mass-stuff (*tamas*), or the factor of obstruction. Of these the last two are predominant in gross matter and the first two in thought.

Feelings, the Ultimate Substances[1].

Another question that arises in this connection is the position of feeling in such an analysis of thought and matter. Sāṃkhya holds that the three characteristic constituents that we have analyzed just now are feeling substances. Feeling is the most interesting side of our consciousness. It is in our feelings that we think of our thoughts as being parts of ourselves. If we should analyze any percept into the crude and undeveloped sensations of which it is composed at the first moment of its appearance, it comes more as a shock than as an image, and we find that it is felt more as a feeling mass than as an image. Even in our ordinary life the elements which precede an act of knowledge are probably mere feelings. As we go lower down the scale of evolution the automatic actions and relations of matter are concomitant with crude manifestations of feeling which never rise to the level of knowledge. The lower the scale of evolution the less is the keenness of feeling, till at last there comes a stage where matter-complexes do not give rise to feeling

[1] *Kārikā*, 12, with Gauḍpāda and Nārāyaṇatīrtha.

reactions but to mere physical reactions. Feelings thus mark the earliest track of consciousness, whether we look at it from the point of view of evolution or of the genesis of consciousness in ordinary life. What we call matter-complexes become at a certain stage feeling-complexes and what we call feeling-complexes at a certain stage of descent sink into mere matter-complexes with matter reaction. The feelings are therefore the things-in-themselves, the ultimate substances of which consciousness and gross matter are made up. Ordinarily a difficulty might be felt in taking feelings to be the ultimate substances of which gross matter and thought are made up; for we are more accustomed to take feelings as being merely subjective, but if we remember the Sāṃkhya analysis, we find that it holds that thought and matter are but two different modifications of certain subtle substances which are in essence but three types of feeling entities. The three principal characteristics of thought and matter that we have noticed in the preceding section are but the manifestations of three types of feeling substances. There is the class of feelings that we call the sorrowful, there is another class of feelings that we call pleasurable, and there is still another class which is neither sorrowful nor pleasurable, but is one of ignorance, depression (*viṣāda*) or dullness. Thus corresponding to these three types of manifestations as pleasure, pain, and dullness, and materially as shining (prakāśa), energy (*pravṛtti*), obstruction (*niyama*), there are three types of feeling-substances which must be regarded as the ultimate things which make up all the diverse kinds of gross matter and thought by their varying modifications.

The Guṇas[1].

These three types of ultimate subtle entities are technically called *guṇa* in Sāṃkhya philosophy. Guṇa in Sanskrit has three meanings, namely (1) quality, (2) rope, (3) not primary. These entities, however, are substances and not mere qualities. But it may be mentioned in this connection that in Sāṃkhya philosophy there is no separate existence of qualities; it holds that each and every unit of quality is but a unit of substance. What we call quality is but a particular manifestation or appearance of a subtle entity. Things do not possess quality, but quality

[1] *Yogavārttika*, II. 18; Bhāvāgaṇeśa's *Tattvayāthārthyadīpana*, pp. 1–3; *Vijñānāmṛtabhāṣya*, p. 100; *Tattvakaumudī*, 13; also Gauḍapāda and Nārāyaṇatīrtha, 13.

signifies merely the manner in which a substance reacts; any object we see seems to possess many qualities, but the Sāṃkhya holds that corresponding to each and every new unit of quality, however fine and subtle it may be, there is a corresponding subtle entity, the reaction of which is interpreted by us as a quality. This is true not only of qualities of external objects but also of mental qualities as well. These ultimate entities were thus called guṇas probably to suggest that they are the entities which by their various modifications manifest themselves as guṇas or qualities. These subtle entities may also be called guṇas in the sense of ropes because they are like ropes by which the soul is chained down as if it were to thought and matter. These may also be called guṇas as things of secondary importance, because though permanent and indestructible, they continually suffer modifications and changes by their mutual groupings and re-groupings, and thus not primarily and unalterably constant like the souls (*puruṣa*). Moreover the object of the world process being the enjoyment and salvation of the puruṣas, the matter-principle could not naturally be regarded as being of primary importance. But in whatever senses we may be inclined to justify the name guṇa as applied to these subtle entities, it should be borne in mind that they are substantive entities or subtle substances and not abstract qualities. These guṇas are infinite in number, but in accordance with their three main characteristics as described above they have been arranged in three classes or types called *sattva* (intelligence-stuff), *rajas* (energy-stuff) and *tamas* (mass-stuff). An infinite number of subtle substances which agree in certain characteristics of self-shining or plasticity are called the *sattva-guṇas* and those which behave as units of activity are called the *rajo-guṇas* and those which behave as factors of obstruction, mass or materiality are called *tamo-guṇas*. These subtle guṇa substances are united in different proportions (e.g. a larger number of sattva substances with a lesser number of rajas or tamas, or a larger number of tamas substances with a smaller number of rajas and sattva substances and so on in varying proportions), and as a result of this, different substances with different qualities come into being. Though attached to one another when united in different proportions, they mutually act and react upon one another, and thus by their combined resultant produce new characters, qualities and substances. There is however one and only one stage in which the guṇas are not compounded in varying proportions. In this state each of the guṇa substances is opposed by each of the other guṇa substances, and thus by their equal mutual opposition create an equilibrium, in which none of the characters of the guṇas manifest themselves. This is a state which is so absolutely devoid of all characteristics that it is absolutely incoherent, indeterminate, and indefinite. It is a qualitiless simple homogeneity. It is a state of being which is as it were non-being. This state of the mutual equilibrium of the guṇas is called prakṛti[1]. This is a state which cannot be said either to exist or to non-exist for it serves no purpose, but it is hypothetically the mother of all things. This is however the earliest stage, by the breaking of which, later on, all modifications take place.

Prakṛti and its Evolution.

Sāṃkhya believes that before this world came into being there was such a state of dissolution—a state in which the guṇa compounds had disintegrated into a state of disunion and had by their mutual opposition produced an equilibrium the prakṛti. Then later on disturbance arose in the prakṛti, and as a result of that a process of unequal aggregation of the guṇas in varying proportions took place, which brought forth the creation of the manifold. Prakṛti, the state of perfect homogeneity and incoherence of the guṇas, thus gradually evolved and became more and more determinate, differentiated, heterogeneous, and coherent. The guṇas are always uniting, separating, and uniting again[2]. Varying qualities of essence, energy, and mass in varied groupings act on one another and through their mutual interaction and interdependence evolve from the indefinite or qualitatively indeterminate the definite or qualitatively determinate. And though co-operating to produce the world of effects, these diverse moments with diverse tendencies never coalesce. Thus in the phenomenal product whatever energy there is is due to the element of rajas and rajas alone; all matter, resistance, stability, is due to tamas, and all conscious manifestation to sattva. The particular guṇa which happens to be predominant in any phenomenon becomes manifest in that phenomenon and others become latent, though their presence is inferred by their

[1] *Yogavārttika*, II. 19, and *Pravacanabhāṣya*, I. 61.

[2] *Kaumudī*, 13-16; *Tattvavaiśāradī*, II. 20, IV. 13, 14; also *Yogavārttika*, IV. 13, 14.

effect. Thus, for example, in a body at rest mass is patent, energy latent and potentiality of conscious manifestation sublatent. In a moving body, the rajas is predominant (kinetic) and the mass is partially overcome. All these transformations of the groupings of the guṇas in different proportions presuppose the state of prakṛti as the starting point. It is at this stage that the tendencies to conscious manifestation, as well as the powers of doing work, are exactly counterbalanced by the resistance of inertia or mass, and the process of cosmic evolution is at rest. When this equilibrium is once destroyed, it is supposed that out of a natural affinity of all the sattva reals for themselves, of rajas reals for other reals of their type, of tamas reals for others of their type, there arises an unequal aggregation of sattva, rajas, or tamas at different moments. When one guṇa is preponderant in any particular collocation, the others are co-operant. This evolutionary series beginning from the first disturbance of the prakṛti to the final transformation as the world-order, is subject to "a definite law which it cannot overstep." In the words of Dr B. N.Seal[1], "the process of evolution consists in the development of the differentiated (*vaiṣamya*) within the undifferentiated (*sāmyāvasthā*) of the determinate (*viśeṣa*) within the indeterminate (*ayiśeṣa*) of the coherent (*yutasiddha*) within the incoherent (*ayutasiddha*). The order of succession is neither from parts to whole nor from whole to the parts, but ever from a relatively less differentiated, less determinate, less coherent whole to a relatively more differentiated, more determinate, more coherent whole." The meaning of such an evolution is this, that all the changes and modifications in the shape of the evolving collocations of guṇa reals take place within the body of the prakṛti. Prakṛti consisting of the infinite reals is infinite, and that it has been disturbed does not mean that the whole of it has been disturbed and upset, or that the totality of the guṇas in the prakṛti has been unhinged from a state of equilibrium. It means rather that a very vast number of guṇas constituting the worlds of thought and matter has been upset. These guṇas once thrown out of balance begin to group themselves together first in one form, then in another, then in another, and so on. But such a change in the formation of aggregates should not be thought to take place in such a way that the later aggregates appear in supersession of the former ones, so that when the former comes into being the latter ceases to exist.

[1] Dr B. N. Seal's *Positive Sciences of the Ancient Hindus*, 1915, p. 7.

For the truth is that one stage is produced after another; this second stage is the result of a new aggregation of some of the reals of the first stage. This deficiency of the reals of the first stage which had gone forth to form the new aggregate as the second stage is made good by a refilling from the prakṛti. So also, as the third stage of aggregation takes place from out of the reals of the second stage, the deficiency of the reals of the second stage is made good by a refilling from the first stage and that of the first stage from the prakṛti. Thus by a succession of refillings the process of evolution proceeds, till we come to its last limit, where there is no real evolution of new substance, but mere chemical and physical changes of qualities in things which had already evolved. Evolution (*tattvāntarapariṇāma*) in Sāṃkhya means the development of categories of existence and not mere changes of qualities of substances (physical, chemical, biological or mental). Thus each of the stages of evolution remains as a permanent category of being, and offers scope to the more and more differentiated and coherent groupings of the succeeding stages. Thus it is said that the evolutionary process is regarded as a differentiation of new stages as integrated in previous stages (*saṃsṛṣṭa-viveka*).

Pralaya and the disturbance of the Prakṛti Equilibrium.

But how or rather why prakṛti should be disturbed is the most knotty point in Sāṃkhya. It is postulated that the prakṛti or the sum-total of the guṇas is so connected with the puruṣas, and there is such an inherent teleology or blind purpose in the lifeless prakṛti, that all its evolution and transformations take place for the sake of the diverse puruṣas, to serve the enjoyment of pleasures and sufferance of pain through experiences, and finally leading them to absolute freedom or mukti. A return of this manifold world into the quiescent state (*pralaya*) of prakṛti takes place when the karmas of all puruṣas collectively require that there should be such a temporary cessation of all experience. At such a moment the guṇa compounds are gradually broken, and there is a backward movement (*pratisañcara*) till everything is reduced to the guṇas in their elementary disintegrated state when their mutual opposition brings about their equilibrium. This equilibrium however is not a mere passive state, but one of utmost tension; there is intense activity, but the activity here does not lead to the generation of new things and qualities (*visadṛśa-pariṇāma*); this course of new production being suspended, the activity here repeats the same state (*sadṛśa-pariṇāma*) of equilibrium, so that there is no change or new production. The state of pralaya thus is not a suspension of the teleology or purpose of the guṇas, or an absolute break of the course of guṇa evolution; for the state of pralaya, since it has been generated to fulfil the demands of the accumulated karmas of puruṣas, and since there is still the activity of the guṇas in keeping themselves in a state of suspended production, is also a stage of the saṃsāra cycle. The state of mukti (liberation) is of course quite different, for in that stage the movement of the guṇas ceases for ever with reference to the liberated soul. But still the question remains, what breaks the state of equilibrium? The Sāṃkhya answer is that it is due to the transcendental (non-mechanical) influence of the puruṣa[1]. This influence of the puruṣa again, if it means anything, means that there is inherent in the guṇas a teleology that all their movements or modifications should take place in such a way that these may serve the purposes of the puruṣas. Thus when the karmas of the puruṣas had demanded that there should be a suspension of all experience, for a period there was a pralaya. At the end of it, it is the same inherent purpose of the prakṛti that wakes it up for the formation of a suitable world for the experiences of the puruṣas by which its quiescent state is disturbed. This is but another way of looking at the inherent teleology of the prakṛti, which demands that a state of pralaya should cease and a state of world-framing activity should begin. Since there is a purpose in the guṇas which brought them to a state of equilibrium, the state of equilibrium also presupposes that it also may be broken up again when the purpose so demands. Thus the inherent purpose of the prakṛti brought about the state of pralaya and then broke it up for the creative work again, and it is this natural change in the prakṛti that may be regarded from another point of view as the transcendental influence of the puruṣas.

Mahat and Ahaṃkāra.

The first evolute of the prakṛti is generated by a preponderance of the sattva (intelligence-stuff). This is indeed the earliest state from which all the rest of the world has sprung forth; and it is a state in which the stuff of sattva predominates. It thus holds

[1] The Yoga answer is of course different. It believes that the disturbance of the equilibrium of the prakṛti for new creation takes place by the will of Īśvara (God).

within it the minds (*buddhi*) of all puruṣas which were lost in the prakṛti during the pralaya. The very first work of the evolution of prakṛti to serve the puruṣas is thus manifested by the separating out of the old buddhis or minds (of the puruṣas) which hold within themselves the old specific ignorance (*avidyā*) inherent in them with reference to each puruṣa with which any particular buddhi is associated from beginningless time before the pralaya. This state of evolution consisting of all the collected minds (buddhi) of all the puruṣas is therefore called *buddhitattva*. It is a state which holds or comprehends within it the buddhis of all individuals. The individual buddhis of individual puruṣas are on one hand integrated with the buddhitattva and on the other associated with their specific puruṣas. When some buddhis once begin to be separated from the prakṛti, other buddhi evolutions take place. In other words, we are to understand that once the transformation of buddhis is effected for the service of the puruṣas, all the other direct transformations that take place from the prakṛti take the same line, i.e. a preponderance of sattva being once created by the bringing out of some buddhis, other transformations of prakṛti that follow them have also the sattva preponderance, which thus have exactly the same composition as the first buddhis. Thus the first transformation from prakṛti becomes buddhi-transformation. This stage of buddhis may thus be regarded as the most universal stage, which comprehends within it all the buddhis of individuals and potentially all the matter of which the gross world is formed. Looked at from this point of view it has the widest and most universal existence comprising all creation, and is thus called *mahat* (the great one). It is called *liṅga* (sign), as the other later existences or evolutes give us the ground of inferring its existence, and as such must be distinguished from the prakṛti which is called *aliṅga*, i.e. of which no liṅga or characteristic may be affirmed.

This mahat-tattva being once produced, further modifications begin to take place in three lines by three different kinds of undulations representing the sattva preponderance, rajas preponderance and tamas preponderance. This state when the mahat is disturbed by the three parallel tendencies of a preponderance of tamas, rajas and sattva is called *ahaṃkāra*, and the above three tendencies are respectively called *tāmasika ahaṃkāra* or *bhūtādi*, *rājasika* or *taijasa ahaṃkāra*, and *vaikārika ahaṃkāra*. The rāja-sika ahaṃkāra cannot mark a new preponderance by itself; it only helps (*sahakāri*) the transformations of the sattva preponderance and the tamas preponderance. The development of the former preponderance, as is easy to see, is only the assumption of a more and more determinate character of the buddhi, for we remember that buddhi itself has been the resulting transformation of a sattva preponderance. Further development with the help of rajas on the line of sattva development could only take place when the buddhi as mind determined itself in specific ways. The first development of the buddhi on this line is called *sāttvika* or *vaikārika ahaṃkāra*. This ahaṃkāra represents the development in buddhi to produce a consciousness-stuff as I or rather "mine," and must thus be distinguished from the first stage as buddhi, the function of which is a mere understanding and general datum as thisness.

The ego or ahaṃkāra (*abhimāna-dravyd*) is the specific expression of the general consciousness which takes experience as mine. The function of the ego is therefore called *abhimāna* (self-assertion). From this again come the five cognitive senses of vision, touch, smell, taste, and hearing, the five conative senses of speech, handling, foot-movement, the ejective sense and the generative sense; the *prāṇas* (bio-motor force) which help both conation and cognition are but aspects of buddhi-movement as life. The individual ahaṃkāras and senses are related to the individual buddhis by the developing sattva determinations from which they had come into being. Each buddhi with its own group of ahaṃkāra (ego) and sense-evolutes thus forms a microcosm separate from similar other buddhis with their associated groups. So far therefore as knowledge is subject to sense-influence and the ego, it is different for each individual, but so far as a general mind (*kāraṇa buddhi*) apart from sense knowledge is concerned, there is a community of all buddhis in the buddhitattva. Even there however each buddhi is separated from other buddhis by its own peculiarly associated ignorance (*avidyā*). The buddhi and its sattva evolutes of ahaṃkāra and the senses are so related that though they are different from buddhi in their functions, they are all comprehended in the buddhi, and mark only its gradual differentiations and modes. We must again remember in this connection the doctrine of refilling, for as buddhi exhausts its part in giving rise to ahaṃkāra, the deficiency of buddhi is made good by prakṛti; again as ahaṃkāra partially exhausts itself in generating sense-faculties, the deficiency is made good by a refilling from the buddhi. Thus the change and wastage of each of the stadia are always made good and kept constant by a constant refilling from each higher state and finally from prakṛti.

The Tanmātras and the Paramāṇus[1].

The other tendency, namely that of tamas, has to be helped by the liberated rajas of ahaṃkāra, in order to make itself preponderant, and this state in which the tamas succeeds in overcoming the sattva side which was so preponderant in the buddhi, is called *bhūtādi*. From this bhūtādi with the help of rajas are generated the *tanmātras*, the immediately preceding causes of the gross elements. The bhūtādi thus represents only the intermediate stage through which the differentiations and regroupings of tamas reals in the mahat proceed for the generation of the tanmātras. There has been some controversy between Sāṃkhya and Yoga as to whether the tanmātras are generated from the mahat or from ahaṃkāra. The situation becomes intelligible if we remember that evolution here does not mean coming out or emanation, but increasing differentiation in integration within the evolving whole. Thus the regroupings of tamas reals marks the differentiation which takes place within the mahat but through its stage as bhūtādi. Bhūtādi is absolutely homogeneous and inert, devoid of all physical and chemical characters except quantum or mass. The second stadium tanmātra represents subtle matter, vibratory, impingent, radiant, instinct with potential energy. These "potentials" arise from the unequal aggregation of the original mass-units in different proportions and collocations with an unequal distribution of the original energy (*rajas*). The tanmātras possess something more than quantum of mass and energy; they possess physical characters, some of them penetrability, others powers of impact or pressure, others radiant heat, others again capability of viscous and cohesive attraction[2].

In intimate relation with those physical characters they also possess the potentials of the energies represented by sound, touch, colour, taste, and smell; but, being subtle matter, they are devoid

[1] I have accepted in this section and in the next many of the translations of Sanskrit terms and expressions of Dr Seal and am largely indebted to him for his illuminating exposition of this subject as given in Ray's *Hindu Chemistry*. The credit of explaining Sāṃkhya physics in the light of the text belongs entirely to him.

[2] Dr Seal's *Positive Sciences of the Ancient Hindus*.

of the peculiar forms which these "potentials" assume in particles of gross matter like the atoms and their aggregates. In other words, the potentials lodged in subtle matter must undergo peculiar transformations by new groupings or collocations before they can act as sensory stimuli as gross matter, though in the minutest particles thereof the sensory stimuli may be infra-sensible (*atīndriya* but not *anudbhūta*)[1].

Of the tanmātras the *śabda* or *ākāśa tanmātra* (the sound-potential) is first generated directly from the bhūtādi. Next comes the *sparśa* or the *vāyu tanmātra* (touch-potential) which is generated by the union of a unit of tamas from bhūtādi with the ākāśa tanmātra. The *rūpa tanmātra* (colour-potential) is generated similarly by the accretion of a unit of tamas from bhūtādi; the *rasa tanmātra* (taste-potential) or the *ap tanmātra* is also similarly formed. This ap tanmātra again by its union with a unit of tamas from bhūtādi produces the *gāndha tanmātra* (smell-potential) or the *kṣiti tanmātra*[2]. The difference of tanmātras or infra-atomic units and atoms (*paramāṇu*) is this, that the tanmātras have only the potential power of affecting our senses, which must be grouped and regrouped in a particular form to constitute a new existence as atoms before they can have the power of affecting our senses. It is important in this connection to point out that the classification of all gross objects as kṣiti, ap, tejas, marut and vyoman is not based upon a chemical analysis, but from the points of view of the five senses through which knowledge of them could be brought home to us. Each of our senses can only apprehend a particular quality and thus five different ultimate substances are said to exist corresponding to the five qualities which may be grasped by the five senses. In accordance with the existence of these five elements, the existence of the five potential states or tanmātras was also conceived to exist as the ground of the five gross forms.

The five classes of atoms are generated from the tanmātras as follows: the sound-potential, with accretion of rudiment matter from *bhūtādi* generates the ākāśa-atom. The touch-potentials combine with the vibratory particles (sound-potential) to generate the

[1] Dr Seal's *Positive Sciences of the Ancient Hindus*.

[2] There were various ways in which the genesis of tanmātras and atoms were explained in literatures other than Sāṃkhya; for some account of it see Dr Seal's *Positive Sciences of the Ancient Hindus*.

vāyu-atom. The light-and-heat potentials combine with touch-potentials and sound-potentials to produce the tejas-atom. The taste-potentials combine with light-and-heat potentials, touch-potentials and sound-potentials to generate the ap-atom and the smell-potentials combine with the preceding potentials to generate the earth-atom. The ākāśa-atom possesses penetrability, the vāyu-atom impact or mechanical pressure, the tejas-atom radiant heat and light, the ap-atom viscous attraction and the earth-atom cohesive attraction. The ākāśa we have seen forms the transition link from the bhūtādi to the tanmātra and from the tanmātra to the atomic production; it therefore deserves a special notice at this stage. Sāṃkhya distinguishes between a kāraṇa-ākāśa and kāryākāśa. The kāraṇa-ākāśa (non-atomic and all-pervasive) is the formless tamas—the mass in prakṛti or bhūtādi; it is indeed all-pervasive, and is not a mere negation, a mere unoccupiedness (*āvarṇābhāva*) or vacuum[1]. When energy is first associated with this tamas element it gives rise to the sound-potential; the atomic ākāśa is the result of the integration of the original mass-units from bhūtādi with this sound-potential (*śabda tanmātra*). Such an ākāśa-atom is called the kāryākāśa; it is formed everywhere and held up in the original kāraṇa ākāśa as the medium for the development of vāyu atoms. Being atomic it occupies limited space.

The ahaṃkāra and the five tanmātras are technically called *aviśeṣa* or indeterminate, for further determinations or differentiations of them for the formation of newer categories of existence are possible. The eleven senses and the five atoms are called *viśeṣa*, i.e. determinate, for they cannot further be so determined as to form a new category of existence. It is thus that the course of evolution which started in the prakṛti reaches its furthest limit in the production of the senses on the one side and the atoms on the other. Changes no doubt take place in bodies having atomic constitution, but these changes are changes of quality due to spatial changes in the position of the atoms or to the introduction of new atoms and their re-arrangement. But these are not such that a newer category of existence could be formed by them which was substantially different from the combined atoms.

[1] Dr B. N. Seal in describing this ākāśa says "Ākāśa corresponds in some respects to the ether of the physicists and in others to what may be called proto-atom (protyle)." Ray's *History of Hindu Chermistry*, p. 88.

The changes that take place in the atomic constitution of things certainly deserve to be noticed. But before we go on to this, it will be better to enquire about the principle of causation according to which the Sāṃkhya-Yoga evolution should be comprehended or interpreted.

Principle of Causation and Conservation of Energy[1].

The question is raised, how can the prakṛti supply the deficiences made in its evolutes by the formation of other evolutes from them? When from mahat some tanmātras have evolved, or when from the tanmātras some atoms have evolved, how can the deficiency in mahat and the tanmātras be made good by the prakṛti?

Or again, what is the principle that guides the transformations that take place in the atomic stage when one gross body, say milk, changes into curd, and so on? Sāṃkhya says that "as the total energy remains the same while the world is constantly evolving, cause and effect are only more or less evolved forms of the same ultimate Energy. The sum of effects exists in the sum of causes in a potential form. The grouping or collocation alone changes, and this brings on the manifestation of the latent powers of the guṇas, but without creation of anything new. What is called the (material) cause is only the power which is efficient in the production or rather the vehicle of the power. This power is the unmanifested (or potential) form of the Energy set free (*udbhūta-vṛtti*) in the effect. But the concomitant conditions are necessary to call forth the so-called material cause into activity[2]." The appearance of an effect (such as the manifestation of the figure of the statue in the marble block by the causal efficiency of the sculptor's art) is only its passage from potentiality to actuality and the concomitant conditions (*sahakāri-śakti*) or efficient cause (*nimitta-kāraṇa*, such as the sculptor's art) is a sort of mechanical help or instrumental help to this passage or the transition[3]. The refilling from prakṛti thus means nothing more than this, that by the inherent teleology of the prakṛti, the reals there are so collocated as to be transformed into mahat as those of the mahat have been collocated to form the bhūtādi or the tanmātras.

[1] *Vyāsabhāṣya* and *Yogavārttika*, IV. 3; *Tattvavaiśāradī*, IV. 3.
[2] Ray, *History of Hindu Chemistry*, p. 72.
[3] *Ibid*, p. 73.

Yoga however explains this more vividly on the basis of transformation of the liberated potential energy. The sum of material causes potentially contains the energy manifested in the sum of effects. When the effectuating condition is added to the sum of material conditions in a given collocation, all that happens is that a stimulus is imparted which removes the arrest, disturbs the relatively stable equilibrium, and brings on a liberation of energy together with a fresh collocation (*guṇasanniveśaviśeṣa*). As the owner of an adjacent field in transferring water from one field to another of the same or lower level has only to remove the obstructing mud barriers, whereupon the water flows of itself to the other field, so when the efficient or instrumental causes (such as the sculptor's art) remove the barrier inherent in any collocation against its transformation into any other collocation, the energy from that collocation flows out in a corresponding manner and determines the collocation. Thus for example the energy which collocated the milk-atoms to form milk was in a state of arrest in the milk state. If by heat or other causes this barrier is removed, the energy naturally changes direction in a corresponding manner and collocates the atoms accordingly for the formation of curd. So also as soon as the barriers are removed from the prakṛti, guided by the constant will of Īśvara, the reals in equilibrium in the state of prakṛti leave their state of arrest and evolve themselves into mahat, etc.

Change as the formation of new collocations.

It is easy to see from what we have already said that any collocation of atoms forming a thing could not change its form, unless the barrier inherent or caused by the formation of the present collocation could be removed by some other extraneous instrumental cause. All gross things are formed by the collocation of the five atoms of kṣiti, ap, tejas, marut, and vyoman. The difference between one thing and another is simply this, that its collocation of atoms or the arrangement or grouping of atoms is different from that in another. The formation of a collocation has an inherent barrier against any change, which keeps that collocation in a state of equilibrium and it is easy to see that these barriers exist in infinite directions in which all the other infinite objects of the world exist. From whichever side the barrier is removed, the energy flows in that direction and helps the formation of a corresponding object. Provided the suitable barriers could be removed, anything could be changed into any other thing. And it is believed that the Yogins can acquire the powers by which they can remove any barriers, and thus make anything out of any other thing. But generally in the normal course of events the line of evolution follows "a definite law which cannot be overstepped" (*pariṇāmakramaniyama*) or in other words there are some natural barriers which cannot be removed, and thus the evolutionary course has to take a path to the exclusion of those lines where the barriers could not be removed. Thus saffron grows in countries like Kashmere and not in Bengal, this is limitation of countries (*deśāpabandha*); certain kinds of paddy grow in the rainy season only, this is limitation of season or time (*kālāpabandha*); deer cannot beget men, this is limitation by form (*ākārāpabandha*); curd can come out of milk, this is the limitation of causes (*nimit-tāpabandha*). The evolutionary course can thus follow only that path which is not barricaded by any of these limitations or natural obstructions[1].

Change is taking place everywhere, from the smallest and least to the highest. Atoms and reals are continually vibrating and changing places in any and every object. At each moment the whole universe is undergoing change, and the collocation of atoms at any moment is different from what it was at the previous moment. When these changes are perceivable, they are perceived as *dharmapariṇāma* or changes of *dharma* or quality; but perceived or unperceived the changes are continually going on. This change of appearance may be viewed from another aspect by virtue of which we may call it present or past, and old or new, and these are respectively called the *lakṣaṇapariṇāma* and *avasthā-pariṇāma*. At every moment every object of the world is undergoing evolution or change, change as past, present and future, as new, old or unborn. When any change is in a potential state we call it future, when manifested present, when it becomes sub-latent again it is said to be past. Thus it is that the potential, manifest, and sub-latent changes of a thing are called future, present and past[2].

[1] *Vyāsabhāṣya*, *Tattvavaiśāradī* and *Yogavārttika*, III. 14.

[2] It is well to note in this connection that Sāṃkhya-yoga does not admit the existence of time as an independent entity like the Nyāya-Vaiśeṣika. Time represents the order of moments in which the mind grasps the phenomenal changes. It is hence a construction of the mind (*buddhi-nirmāṇa*). The time required by an atom to move its own measure of space is called a moment (*kṣaṇa*) or one unit of time. Vijñāna Bhikṣu regards one unit movement

Causation as Satkāryavāda (the theory that the effect potentially exists before it is generated by the movement of the cause).

The above consideration brings us to an important aspect of the Sāṃkhya view of causation as *satkāryavāda*. Sāṃkhya holds that there can be no production of a thing previously non-existent; causation means the appearance or manifestation of a quality due to certain changes of collocations in the causes which were already held in them in a potential form. Production of effect only means an internal change of the arrangement of atoms in the cause, and this exists in it in a potential form, and just a little loosening of the barrier which was standing in the way of the happening of such a change of arrangement will produce the desired new collocation—the effect. This doctrine is called *satkāryavāda*, i.e. that the kārya or effect is *sat* or existent even before the causal operation to produce the effect was launched. The oil exists in the sesamum, the statue in the stone, the curd in the milk. The causal operation (*kārakavyāpāra*) only renders that manifest (*āvirbhūta*) which was formerly in an unmanifested condition (*tirohita*)[1].

The Buddhists also believed in change, as much as Sāṃkhya did, but with them there was no background to the change; every change was thus absolutely a new one, and when it was past, the next moment the change was lost absolutely. There were only the passing dharmas or manifestations of forms and qualities, but there was no permanent underlying dharma or substance. Sāṃkhya also holds in the continual change of dharmas, but it also holds that these dharmas represent only the conditions of the permanent reals. The conditions and collocations of the reals change constantly, but the reals themselves are unchangeable. The effect according to the Buddhists was non-existent, it came into being for a moment and was lost. On account of this theory of causation and also on account of their doctrine of śūnya, they were called *vaināśikas* (nihilists) by the Vedāntins. This doctrine is therefore contrasted to Sāṃkhya doctrine as *asatkāryavāda*.

of the guṇas or reals as a moment. When by true wisdom the guṇas are perceived as they are both the illusory notions of time and space vanish. *Vyāsabhāṣya*, *Tattvavaiśāradī*, and *Yogavārttika*, III. 52 and III. 13.

[1] *Tattvakaumudī*, 9.

The Jain view holds that both these views are relatively true and that from one point of view satkāryavāda is true and from another asatkāryavāda. The Sāṃkhya view that the cause is continually transforming itself into its effects is technically called *pariṇāma-vāda* as against the Vedānta view called the *vivarttavāda:* that cause remains ever the same, and what we call effects are but illusory impositions of mere unreal appearance of name and form—mere Māyā[1].

Sāṃkhya Atheism and Yoga Theism.

Granted that the interchange of the positions of the infinite number of reals produce all the world and its transformations; whence comes this fixed order of the universe, the fixed order of cause and effect, the fixed order of the so-called barriers which prevent the transformation of any cause into any effect or the first disturbance of the equilibrium of the prakṛti? Sāṃkhya denies the existence of Īśvara (God) or any other exterior influence, and holds that there is an inherent tendency in these reals which guides all their movements. This tendency or teleology demands that the movements of the reals should be in such a manner that they may render some service to the souls either in the direction of enjoyment or salvation. It is by the natural course of such a tendency that prakṛti is disturbed, and the guṇas develop on two lines—on the mental plane, *citta* or mind comprising the sense faculties, and on the objective plane as material objects; and it is in fulfilment of the demands of this tendency that on the one hand take place subjective experiences as the changes of the buddhi and on the other the infinite modes of the changes of objective things. It is this tendency to be of service to the puruṣas (*puruṣārthatā*) that guides all the movements of the reals, restrains all disorder, renders the world a fit object of experience, and finally rouses them to turn back from the world and seek to attain liberation from the association of prakṛti and its gratuitous service, which causes us all this trouble of saṃsāra.

Yoga here asks, how the blind tendency of the non-intelligent

[1] Both the Vedānta and the Sāṃkhya theories of causation are sometimes loosely called *satkāryyavāda*. But correctly speaking as some discerning commentators have pointed out, the Vedānta theory of causation should be called satkāraṇavāda for according to it the *kāraṇa* (cause) alone exists (*sat*) and all *kāryyas* (effects) are illusory appearances of the kāraṇa; but according to Sāṃkhya the kāryya exists in a potential state in the kāraṇa and is hence always existing and real.

prakṛti can bring forth this order and harmony of the universe, how can it determine what course of evolution will be of the best service to the puruṣas, how can it remove its own barriers and lend itself to the evolutionary process from the state of prakṛti equilibrium? How too can this blind tendency so regulate the evolutionary order that all men must suffer pains according to their bad karmas, and happiness according to their good ones? There must be some intelligent Being who should help the course of evolution in such a way that this system of order and harmony may be attained. This Being is Īśvara. Īśvara is a puruṣa who had never been subject to ignorance, afflictions, or passions. His body is of pure sattva quality which can never be touched by ignorance. He is all knowledge and all powerful. He has a permanent wish that those barriers in the course of the evolution of the reals by which the evolution of the guṇas may best serve the double interest of the puruṣa's experience (*bhoga*) and liberation (*apavarga*) should be removed. It is according to this permanent will of Īśvara that the proper barriers are removed and the guṇas follow naturally an intelligent course of evolution for the service of the best interests of the puruṣas. Īśvara has not created the prakṛti; he only disturbs the equilibrium of the prakṛti in its quiescent state, and later on helps it to follow an intelligent order by which the fruits of karma are properly distributed and the order of the world is brought about. This acknowledgement of Īśvara in Yoga and its denial by Sāṃkhya marks the main theoretic difference between the two according to which the Yoga and Sāṃkhya are distinguished as Seśvara Sāṃkhya (Sāṃkhya with Īśvara) and Nirīśvara Sāṃkhya (Atheistic Sāṃkhya)[1].

Buddhi and Puruṣa.

The question again arises that though puruṣa is pure intelligence, the guṇas are non-intelligent subtle substances, how can the latter come into touch with the former? Moreover, the puruṣa is pure inactive intelligence without any touch of impurity and what service or need can such a puruṣa have of the guṇas? This difficulty is anticipated by Sāṃkhya, which has already made room for its answer by assuming that one class of the guṇas called sattva is such that it resembles the purity and the intelligence of the puruṣa to a very high degree, so much so

[1] *Tattvavaiśāradi*, IV. 3; *Yogavārttika*, I. 24; and *Pravacanabhāṣya*, V. 1–12.

that it can reflect the intelligence of the puruṣa, and thus render its non-intelligent transformations to appear as if they were intelligent. Thus all our thoughts and other emotional or volitional operations are really the non-intelligent transformations of the buddhi or citta having a large sattva preponderance; but by virtue of the reflection of the puruṣa in the buddhi, these appear as if they are intelligent. The self (puruṣa) according to Sāṃkhya-Yoga is not directly demonstrated by self-consciousness. Its existence is a matter of inference on teleological grounds and grounds of moral responsibility. The self cannot be directly noticed as being separate from the buddhi modifications. Through beginningless ignorance there is a confusion and the changing states of buddhi are regarded as conscious. These buddhi changes are further so associated with the reflection of the puruṣa in the buddhi that they are interpreted as the experiences of the puruṣa. This association of the buddhi with the reflection of the puruṣa in the buddhi has such a special fitness (*yogyatā*) that it is interpreted as the experience of the puruṣa. This explanation of Vācaspati of the situation is objected to by Vijñāna Bhikṣu. Vijñāna Bhikṣu says that the association of the buddhi with the image of the puruṣa cannot give us the notion of a real person who undergoes the experiences. It is to be supposed therefore that when the buddhi is intelligized by the reflection of the puruṣa, it is then superimposed upon the puruṣa, and we have the notion of an abiding person who experiences[1]. Whatever may be the explanation, it seems that the union of the buddhi with the puruṣa is somewhat mystical. As a result of this reflection of *cit* on buddhi and the superimposition of the buddhi the puruṣa cannot realize that the transformations of the buddhi are not its own. Buddhi resembles puruṣa in transparency, and the puruṣa fails to differentiate itself from the modifications of the buddhi, and as a result of this non-distinction the puruṣa becomes bound down to the buddhi, always failing to recognize the truth that the buddhi and its transformations are wholly alien to it. This non-distinction of puruṣa from buddhi which is itself a mode of buddhi is what is meant by *avidyā* (non-knowledge) in Sāṃkhya, and is the root of all experience and all misery[2].

[1] *Tattvavaiśāradī* and *Yogavārttika*, I. 4.

[2] This indicates the nature of the analysis of illusion with Sāṃkhya. It is the non-apprehension of the distinction of two things (e.g. the snake and the rope) that is the cause

Yoga holds a slightly different view and supposes that the puruṣa not only fails to distinguish the difference between itself and the buddhi but positively takes the transformations of buddhi as its own. It is no non-perception of the difference but positively false knowledge, that we take the puruṣa to be that which it is not (*anyathākhyāti*). It takes the changing, impure, sorrowful, and objective prakṛti or buddhi to be the changeless, pure, happiness-begetting subject. It wrongly thinks buddhi to be the self and regards it as pure, permanent and capable of giving us happiness. This is the avidyā of Yoga. A buddhi associated with a puruṣa is dominated by such an avidyā, and when birth after birth the same buddhi is associated with the same puruṣa, it cannot easily get rid of this avidyā. If in the meantime pralaya takes place, the buddhi is submerged in the prakṛti, and the avidyā also sleeps with it. When at the beginning of the next creation the individual buddhis associated with the puruṣas emerge, the old avidyās also become manifest by virtue of it and the buddhis associate themselves with the puruṣas to which they were attached before the pralaya. Thus proceeds the course of saṃsāra. When the avidyā of a person is rooted out by the rise of true knowledge, the buddhi fails to attach itself to the puruṣa and is forever dissociated from it, and this is the state of mukti.

The Cognitive Process and some characteristics of Citta.

It has been said that buddhi and the internal objects have evolved in order to giving scope to the experience of the puruṣa. What is the process of this experience? Sāṃkhya (as explained by Vācaspati) holds that through the senses the buddhi comes into touch with external objects. At the first moment of this touch there is an indeterminate consciousness in which the particulars of the thing cannot be noticed. This is called *nirvikalpa pratyakṣa* (indeterminate perception). At the next moment by the function of the *saṃkalpa* (synthesis) and *vikalpa* (abstraction or imagination) of manas (mind-organ) the thing is perceived in all its determinate character; the manas differentiates, integrates, and associates the sense-data received through the senses, and

of illusion; it is therefore called the *akhyāti* (non-apprehension) theory of illusion which must be distinguished from the *anyathākhyāti* (misapprehension) theory of illusion of Yoga which consists in positively misapprehending one (e.g. the rope) for the other (e.g. snake). *Yogavārttika*, I. 8.

thus generates the determinate perception, which when intelligized by the puruṣa and associated with it becomes interpreted as the experience of the person. The action of the senses, ahaṃkāra, and buddhi, may take place sometimes successively and at other times as in cases of sudden fear simultaneously. Vijñāna Bhikṣu differs from this view of Vācaspati, and denies the synthetic activity of the mind-organ (manas), and says that the buddhi directly comes into touch with the objects through the senses. At the first moment of touch the perception is indeterminate, but at the second moment it becomes clear and determinate[1]. It is evident that on this view the importance of manas is reduced to a minimum and it is regarded as being only the faculty of desire, doubt and imagination.

Buddhi, including ahaṃkāra and the senses, often called *citta* in Yoga, is always incessantly suffering changes like the flame of a lamp; it is made up of a large preponderance of the pure sattva substances, and is constantly moulding itself from one content to another. These images by the dual reflection of buddhi and puruṣa are constantly becoming conscious, and are being interpreted as the experiences of a person. The existence of the puruṣa is to be postulated for explaining the illumination of consciousness and for explaining experience and moral endeavour. The buddhi is spread all over the body, as it were, for it is by its functions that the life of the body is kept up; for the Sāṃkhya does not admit any separate prāṇa vāyu (vital breath) to keep the body living. What are called *vāyus* (bio-motor force) in Vedānta are but the different modes of operation of this category of buddhi, which acts all through the body and by its diverse movements performs the life-functions and sense-functions of the body.

[1] As the contact of the buddhi with the external objects takes place through the senses, the sense-data of colours, etc., are modified by the senses if they are defective. The spatial qualities of things are however perceived by the senses directly, but the time-order is a scheme of the citta or the buddhi. Generally speaking Yoga holds that the external objects are faithfully copied by the buddhi in which they are reflected, like trees in a lake:

"*tasmiṃśca darpaṇe sphāre samastā vastudṛṣṭayaḥ*
imāstāḥ pratibimbanti sarasīva taṭadrumāḥ" *Yogavārttika*, I. 4.

The buddhi assumes the form of the object which is reflected on it by the senses, or rather the mind flows out through the senses to the external objects and assumes their forms: "*indriyāṇyeva praṇālikā cittasañcaraṇamārgaḥ taiḥ saṃyujya tadgolakadvārā bāhyavastuṣūparaktasya cittasyendriyasāhityenaivārthākāraḥ pariṇāmo bhavati.*" *Yogavārttika*, I. vi. 7. Contrast *Tattvakaumudī*, 27 and 30.

Apart from the perceptions and the life-functions, buddhi, or rather citta as Yoga describes it, contains within it the root impressions (*saṃskāras*) and the tastes and instincts or tendencies of all past lives (*vāsanā*)[1]. These saṃskāras are revived under suitable associations. Every man had had infinite numbers of births in their past lives as man and as some animal. In all these lives the same citta was always following him. The citta has thus collected within itself the instincts and tendencies of all those different animal lives. It is knotted with these vāsanās like a net. If a man passes into a dog life by rebirth, the vāsanās of a dog life, which the man must have had in some of his previous infinite number of births, are revived, and the man's tendencies become like those of a dog. He forgets the experiences of his previous life and becomes attached to enjoyment in the manner of a dog. It is by the revival of the vāsanā suitable to each particular birth that there cannot be any collision such as might have occurred if the instincts and tendencies of a previous dog-life were active when any one was born as man.

The saṃskāras represent the root impressions by which any habit of life that man has lived through, or any pleasure in which he took delight for some time, or any passions which were

[1] The word saṃskāra is used by Pāṇini who probably preceded Buddha in three different senses: (1) improving a thing as distinguished from generating a new quality (*Sata utkarṣādhānaṃ saṃskāraḥ*, Kāśikā on Paṇini, VI. ii. 16), (2) conglomeration or aggregation, and (3) adornment (Pāṇini, VI. I. 137, 138). In the Piṭakas the word saṅkhāra is used in various senses such as constructing, preparing, perfecting, embellishing, aggregation, matter, karma, the skandhas (collected by Childers). In fact saṅkhāra stands for almost anything of which impermanence could be predicated. But in spite of so many diversities of meaning I venture to suggest that the meaning of aggregation (*samavāya* of Pāṇini) is prominent. The word *saṃskaroti* is used in Kauṣītaki, II. 6, Chāndogya, IV. xvi. 2, 3, 4, viii. 8, 5, and Bṛhadāraṇyaka, VI. iii. 1, in the sense of improving. I have not yet come across any literary use of the second meaning in Sanskrit. The meaning of saṃskāra in Hindu philosophy is altogether different. It means the impressions (which exist subconsciously in the mind) of the objects experienced. All our experiences whether cognitive, emotional or conative exist in subconscious states and may under suitable conditions be reproduced as memory (smṛti). The word vāsanā (*Yoga sūtra*, IV. 24) seems to be a later word. The earlier Upaniṣads do not mention it and so far as I know it is not mentioned in the Pāli; piṭakas. *Abhidhānappadīpikā* of Moggallāna mentions it, and it occurs in the Muktika Upaniṣad. It comes from the root "*vas*" to stay. It is often loosely used in the sense of saṃskāra, and in *Vyāsabhāṣya* they are identified in IV. 9. But vāsanā generally refers to the tendencies of past lives most of which lie dormant in tne mind. Only those appear which can find scope in this life. But saṃskāras are the subconscious states which are being constantly generated by experience. Vāsanās are innate saṃskāras not acquired in this life. See *Vyāsabhāṣya*, *Tattvāvaiśāradī* and *Yogavārttika*, II. 13.

engrossing to him, tend to be revived, for though these might not now be experienced, yet the fact that they were experienced before has so moulded and given shape to the citta that the citta will try to reproduce them by its own nature even without any such effort on our part. To safeguard against the revival of any undesirable idea or tendency it is therefore necessary that its roots as already left in the citta in the form of saṃskāras should be eradicated completely by the formation of the habit of a contrary tendency, which if made sufficiently strong will by its own saṃskāra naturally stop the revival of the previous undesirable saṃskāras.

Apart from these the citta possesses volitional activity (*ceṣṭā*) by which the conative senses are brought into relation to their objects. There is also the reserved potent power (*śakti*) of citta, by which it can restrain itself and change its courses or continue to persist in any one direction. These characteristics are involved in the very essence of citta, and form the groundwork of the Yoga method of practice, which consists in steadying a particular state of mind to the exclusion of others.

Merit or demerit (*puṇya, pāpa*) also is imbedded in the citta as its tendencies, regulating the mode of its movements, and giving pleasures and pains in accordance with it.

Sorrow and its Dissolution[1].

Sāṃkhya and the Yoga, like the Buddhists, hold that all experience is sorrowful. Tamas, we know, represents the pain substance. As tamas must be present in some degree in all combinations, all intellectual operations are fraught with some degree of painful feeling. Moreover even in states of temporary pleasure, we had sorrow at the previous moment when we had solicited it, and we have sorrow even when we enjoy it, for we have the fear that we may lose it. The sum total of sorrows is thus much greater than the pleasures, and the pleasures only strengthen the keenness of the sorrow. The wiser the man the greater is his capacity of realizing that the world and our experiences are all full of sorrow. For unless a man is convinced of this great truth that all is sorrow, and that temporary pleasures, whether generated by ordinary worldly experience or by enjoying heavenly experiences through the performance of Vedic sacrifices, are quite unable to

[1] *Tattvavaiśāradī* and *Yogavārttika*, II. 15, and *Tattvakaumudī*, I.

eradicate the roots of sorrow, he will not be anxious for mukti or the final uprooting of pains. A man must feel that all pleasures lead to sorrow, and that the ordinary ways of removing sorrows by seeking enjoyment cannot remove them ultimately; he must turn his back on the pleasures of the world and on the pleasures of paradise. The performances of sacrifices according to the Vedic rites may indeed give happiness, but as these involve the sacrifice of animals they must involve some sins and hence also some pains. Thus the performance of these cannot be regarded as desirable. It is when a man ceases from seeking pleasures that he thinks how best he can eradicate the roots of sorrow. Philosophy shows how extensive is sorrow, why sorrow comes, what is the way to uproot it, and what is the state when it is uprooted. The man who has resolved to uproot sorrow turns to philosophy to find out the means of doing it.

The way of eradicating the root of sorrow is thus the practical enquiry of the Sāṃkhya philosophy[1]. All experiences are sorrow. Therefore some means must be discovered by which all experiences may be shut out for ever. Death cannot bring it, for after death we shall have rebirth. So long as citta (mind) and puruṣa are associated with each other, the sufferings will continue. Citta must be dissociated from puruṣa. Citta or buddhi, Sāṃkhya says, is associated with puruṣa because of the non-distinction of itself from buddhi[2]. It is necessary therefore that in buddhi we should be able to generate the true conception of the nature of puruṣa; when this true conception of puruṣa arises in the buddhi it feels itself to be different, and distinct, from and quite unrelated to puruṣa, and thus ignorance is destroyed. As a result of that, buddhi turns its back on puruṣa and can no longer bind it to its experiences, which are all irrevocably connected with sorrow, and thus the puruṣa remains in its true' form. This according to Sāṃkhya philosophy is alone adequate to bring about the liberation of the puruṣa. Prakṛti which was leading us through cycles of experiences from birth to birth, fulfils its final purpose when this true knowledge arises differentiating

[1] Yoga puts it in a slightly modified form. Its object is the cessation of the rebirth-process which is so much associated with sorrow (*duḥkhabahulaḥ saṃsāraḥ heyaḥ*).

[2] The word *citta* is a Yoga term. It is so called because it is the repository of all subconscious states. Sāṃkhya generally uses the word buddhi. Both the words mean the same substance, the mind, but they emphasize its two different functions. Buddhi means intellection.

puruṣa from prakṛti. This final purpose being attained the prakṛti can never again bind the puruṣa with reference to whom this right knowledge was generated; for other puruṣas however the bondage remains as before, and they continue their experiences from one birth to another in an endless cycle.

Yoga, however, thinks that mere philosophy is not sufficient. In order to bring about liberation it is not enough that a true knowledge differentiating puruṣa and buddhi should arise, but it is necessary that all the old habits of experience of buddhi, all its saṃskāras should be once for all destroyed never to be revived again. At this stage the buddhi is transformed into its purest state, reflecting steadily the true nature of the puruṣa. This is the *kevala* (oneness) state of existence after which (all saṃskāras, all avidyā being altogether uprooted) the citta is impotent any longer to hold on to the puruṣa, and like a stone hurled from a mountain top, gravitates back into the prakṛti[1]. To destroy the old saṃskāras, knowledge alone not being sufficient, a graduated course of practice is necessary. This graduated practice should be so arranged that by generating the practice of living higher and better modes of life, and steadying the mind on its subtler states, the habits of ordinary life may be removed. As the yogin advances he has to give up what he had adopted as good and try for that which is still better. Continuing thus he reaches the state when the buddhi is in its ultimate perfection and purity. At this stage the buddhi assumes the form of the puruṣa, and final liberation takes place.

Karmas in Yoga are divided into four classes: (1) *śukla* or white (*puṇya*, those that produce happiness), (2) *kṛṣṇa* or black (*pāpa*, those that produce sorrow), (3) *śukla-kṛṣṇa* (*puṇya-pāpa*, most of our ordinary actions are partly virtuous and partly vicious as they involve, if not anything else, at least the death of many insects), (4) *aśuklākṛṣṇa* (those inner acts of self-abnegation, and meditation which are devoid of any fruits as pleasures or pains). All external actions involve some sins, for it is difficult to work in the world and avoid taking the lives of insects[2]. All karmas

[1] Both Sāṃkhya and Yoga speak of this emancipated state as *Kaivalya* (alone-ness), the former because all sorrows have been absolutely uprooted, never to grow up again and the latter because at this state puruṣa remains for ever alone without any association with buddhi, see *Sāṃkhya kārikā*, 68 and *Yoga sūtras*, IV. 34.

[2] *Vyāsabhāṣya* and *Tattvavaiśāradī*, IV. 7.

proceed from the five-fold afflictions (*kleśas*), namely *avidyā*, *asmitā*, *rāga*, *dveṣa* and *abhiniveśa*.

We have already noticed what was meant by avidyā. It consists generally in ascribing intelligence to buddhi, in thinking it as permanent and leading to happiness. This false knowledge while remaining in this form further manifests itself in the other four forms of asmitā, etc. Asmitā means the thinking of worldly objects and our experiences as really belonging to us—the sense of "mine" or "I" to things that really are the qualities or transformations of the guṇas. Rāga means the consequent attachment to pleasures and things. Dveṣa means aversion or antipathy to unpleasant things. Abhiniveśa is the desire for life or love of life—the will to be. We proceed to work because we think our experiences to be our own, our body to be our own, our family to be our own, our possessions to be our own; because we are attached to these; because we feel great antipathy against any mischief that might befall them, and also because we love our life and always try to preserve it against any mischief. These all proceed, as is easy to see, from their root avidyā, which consists in the false identification of buddhi with puruṣa. These five, avidyā, asmitā, rāga, dveṣa and abhiniveśa, permeate our buddhi, and lead us to perform karma and to suffer. These together with the performed karmas which lie inherent in the buddhi as a particular mode of it transmigrate with the buddhi from birth to birth, and it is hard to get rid of them[1]. The karma in the aspect in which it lies in the buddhi as a mode or modification of it is called *karmāśaya* (the bed of karma for the puruṣa to lie in). We perform a karma actuated by the vicious tendencies (*kleśa*) of the buddhi. The karma when thus performed leaves its stain or modification on the buddhi, and it is so ordained according to the teleology of the prakṛti and the removal of obstacles in the course of its evolution in accordance with it by the permanent will of Īśvara that each vicious action brings sufferance and a virtuous one pleasure.

The karmas performed in the present life will generally accumulate, and when the time for giving their fruits comes, such a life is ordained for the person, such a body is made ready for him according to the evolution of prakṛti as shall make it possible for him to suffer or enjoy the fruits thereof. The karma of the

[1] *Vyāsabhāṣya* and *Tattvavaiśāradī*, II. 3-9.

present life thus determines the particular kind of future birth (as this or that animal or man), the period of life (*āyuṣ*) and the painful or pleasurable experiences (*bhoga*) destined for that life. Exceedingly good actions and extremely bad actions often produce their effects in this life. It may also happen that a man has done certain bad actions, for the realization of the fruits of which he requires a dog-life and good actions for the fruits of which he requires a man-life. In such cases the good action may remain in abeyance and the man may suffer the pains of a dog-life first and then be born again as a man to enjoy the fruits of his good actions. But if we can remove ignorance and the other afflictions, all his previous unfulfilled karmas are for ever lost and cannot again be revived. He has of course to suffer the fruits of those karmas which have already ripened. This is the *jīvanmukti* stage, when the sage has attained true knowledge and is yet suffering mundane life in order to experience the karmas that have already ripened (*tiṣṭhati saṃskāravaśāt cakrabhramivaddhṛtaśarīraḥ*).

Citta.

The word Yoga which was formerly used in Vedic literature in the sense of the restraint of the senses is used by Patañjali in his *Yoga sūtra* in the sense of the partial or full restraint or steadying of the states of citta. Some sort of concentration may be brought about by violent passions, as when fighting against a mortal enemy, or even by an ignorant attachment or instinct. The citta which has the concentration of the former type is called *kṣipta* (wild) and of the latter type *pramūḍha* (ignorant). There is another kind of citta, as with all ordinary people, in which concentration is only possible for a time, the mind remaining steady on one thing for a short time leaves that off and clings to another thing and so on. This is called the *vikṣipta* (unsteady) stage of mind (*cittabhūmi*). As distinguished from these there is an advanced stage of citta in which it can concentrate steadily on an object for a long time. This is the *ekāgra* (one-pointed) stage. There is a still further advanced stage in which the citta processes are absolutely stopped. This happens immediately before mukti, and is called the *nirodha* (cessation) state of citta. The purpose of Yoga is to achieve the conditions of the last two stages of citta.

The cittas have five processes (*vṛtti*) (1) *pramāṇa*[1] (valid

[1] Sāṃkhya holds that both validity and invalidity of any cognition depend upon the cognitive state itself and not on correspondence with external facts or objects (*svataḥ prāmāṇyaṃ svataḥ aprāmāṇyaṃ*). The contribution of Sāṃkhya to the doctrine of

cognitive states such as are generated by perception, inference and scriptural testimony), (2) *viparyaya* (false knowledge, illusion, etc.), (3) *vikalpa* (abstraction, construction and different kinds of imagination), (4) *nidrā* (sleep, is a vacant state of mind, in which tamas tends to predominate), (5) *smṛti* (memory).

These states of mind (*vṛtti*) comprise our inner experience. When they lead us towards saṃsāra into the course of passions and their satisfactions, they are said to be *kliṣṭa* (afflicted or leading to affliction); when they lead us towards liberation, they are called *akliṣṭa* (unafflicted). To whichever side we go, towards saṃsāra or towards mukti, we have to make use of our states of mind; the states which are bad often alternate with good states, and whichever state should tend towards our final good (liberation) must be regarded as good.

This draws attention to that important characteristic of citta, that it sometimes tends towards good (i.e. liberation) and sometimes towards bad (saṃsāra). It is like a river, as the *Vyāsabhāṣya* says, which flows both ways, towards sin and towards the good. The teleology of prakṛti requires that it should produce in man the saṃsāra as well as the liberation tendency.

Thus in accordance with it in the midst of many bad thoughts and bad habits there come good moral will and good thoughts, and in the midst of good thoughts and habits come also bad thoughts and vicious tendencies. The will to be good is therefore never lost in man, as it is an innate tendency in him which is as strong as his desire to enjoy pleasures. This point is rather remarkable, for it gives us the key of Yoga ethics and shows that our desire of liberation is not actuated by any hedonistic attraction for happiness or even removal of pain, but by an innate tendency of the mind to follow the path of liberation[1]. Removal of pains

inference is not definitely known. What little Vācaspati says on the subject has been borrowed from Vātsyāyana such as the *pūtvavat*, *śeṣavat* and *sāmānyatodṛṣṭa* types of inference, and these may better be consulted in our chapter on Nyāya or in the *Tātparyaṭikā* of Vācaspati. Sāṃkhya inference was probably from particular to particular on the ground of seven kinds of relations according to which they had seven kinds of inference "*mātrānimittasaṃyogivirodhisahacāribhiḥ. Svasvāmibadhyaghātādyaiḥ sāṃ-khyānāṃ saptadhānumā*" (*Tātparyaṭīkā*, p. 109). Sāṃkhya definition of inference as given by Udyotakara (1. I. v) is "*sambandhādekasmāt pratyakṣāccheṣasiddhiranumānam.*"

[1] Sāṃkhya however makes the absolute and complete destruction of three kinds of sorrows, *ādhyātmika* (generated internally by the illness of the body or the unsatisfied passions of the mind), *ādhibhautika* (generated externally by the injuries inflicted by other men, beasts, etc.) and *ādhidaivika* (generated by the injuries inflicted by demons and ghosts) the object of all our endeavours (*puruṣārtha*).

is of course the concomitant effect of following such a course, but still the motive to follow this path is a natural and irresistible tendency of the mind. Man has power (*śakti*) stored up in his citta, and he has to use it in such a way that this tendency may gradually grow stronger and stronger and ultimately uproot the other. He must succeed in this, since prakṛti wants liberation for her final realization[1].

Yoga Purificatory Practices (Parikarma).

The purpose of Yoga meditation is to steady the mind on the gradually advancing stages of thoughts towards liberation, so that vicious tendencies may gradually be more and more weakened and at last disappear altogether. But before the mind can be fit for this lofty meditation, it is necessary that it should be purged of ordinary impurities. Thus the intending yogin should practise absolute non-injury to all living beings (*ahiṃsā*), absolute and strict truthfulness (*satya*), non-stealing (*asteya*), absolute sexual restraint (*brahmacarya*) and the acceptance of nothing but that which is absolutely necessary (*aparigraha*). These are collectively called *yama*. Again side by side with these abstinences one must also practise external cleanliness by ablutions and inner cleanliness of the mind, contentment of mind, the habit of bearing all privations of heat and cold, or keeping the body unmoved and remaining silent in speech (*tapas*), the study of philosophy (*svādhyāya*) and meditation on Īśvara (*Īśvara-praṇidhāna*). These are collectively called *niyamas*. To these are also to be added certain other moral disciplines such as *pratipakṣa-bhāvanā*, *maitrī*, *karuṇā*, *muditā* and *upekṣā*. Pratipakṣa-bhāvanā means that whenever a bad thought (e.g. selfish motive) may come one should practise the opposite good thought (self-sacrifice); so that the bad thoughts may not find any scope. Most of our vices are originated by our unfriendly relations with our fellow-beings. To remove these the practice of mere abstinence may not be sufficient, and therefore one should habituate the mind to keep itself in positive good relations with our fellow-beings. The practice of maitrī means to think of all beings as friends. If we continually habituate ourselves to think this, we can never be displeased with them. So too one should practise karuṇā or kindly feeling for sufferers, muditā

[1] See my "*Yoga Psychology*," *Quest*, October, 1921.

or a feeling of happiness for the good of all beings, and upekṣā or a feeling of equanimity and indifference for the vices of others. The last one indicates that the yogin should not take any note of the vices of vicious men.

When the mind becomes disinclined to all worldly pleasures (*vairāgya*) and to all such as are promised in heaven by the performances of Vedic sacrifices, and the mind purged of its dross and made fit for the practice of Yoga meditation, the yogin may attain liberation by a constant practice (*abhyāsa*) attended with faith, confidence (*śraddhā*), strength of purpose and execution (*vīrya*) and wisdom (*prajñā*) attained at each advance.

The Yoga Meditation.

When the mind has become pure the chances of its being ruffled by external disturbances are greatly reduced. At such a stage the yogin takes a firm posture (*āsana*) and fixes his mind on any object he chooses. It is, however, preferable that he should fix it on Īśvara, for in that case Īśvara being pleased removes many of the obstacles in his path, and it becomes easier for him to attain success. But of course he makes his own choice, and can choose anything he likes for the unifying concentration (*samādhi*) of his mind. There are four states of this unifying concentration namely *vitarka*, *vicāra*, *ānanda* and *asmitā*. Of these vitarka and vicāra have each two varieties, *savitarka*, *nirvi-tarka*, *savicāra*, *nirvicāra*[1]. When the mind concentrates on objects, remembering their names and qualities, it is called the savitarka stage; when on the five tanmātras with a remembrance of their qualities it is called savicāra, and when it is one with the tanmātras without any notion of their qualities it is called nirvicāra. Higher than these are the ānanda and the asmitā states. In the ānanda state the mind concentrates on the buddhi with its functions of the senses causing pleasure. In the asmitā stage buddhi concentrates on pure substance as divested of all modifications. In all these stages there are objects on which the mind consciously concentrates, these are therefore called the *samprajñāta* (with knowledge of objects) types of samādhi. Next to this comes the last stage of samādhi called the *asamprajñāta* or nirodha samādhi, in which the mind is without any object. By remaining

[1] Vācaspati, however, thinks that ānanda and asmitā have also two other varieties, which is denied by Bhikṣu.

long in this stage the old potencies (saṃskāras) or impressions due to the continued experience of worldly events tending towards the objective world or towards any process of experiencing inner thinking are destroyed by the production of a strong habit of the nirodha state. At this stage dawns the true knowledge, when the buddhi becomes as pure as the puruṣa, and after that the citta not being able to bind the puruṣa any longer returns back to prakṛti.

In order to practise this concentration one has to see that there may be no disturbance, and the yogin should select a quiet place on a hill or in a forest. One of the main obstacles is, however, to be found in our constant respiratory action. This has to be stopped by the practice of *prāṇāyāma*. Prāṇāyāma consists in taking in breath, keeping it for a while and then giving it up. With practice one may retain breath steadily for hours, days, months and even years. When there is no need of taking in breath or giving it out, and it can be retained steady for a long time, one of the main obstacles is removed.

The process of practising concentration is begun by sitting in a steady posture, holding the breath by prāṇāyāma, excluding all other thoughts, and fixing the mind on any object (*dhāraṇā*). At first it is difficult to fix steadily on any object, and the same thought has to be repeated constantly in the mind, this is called *dhyāna*. After sufficient practice in dhyāna the mind attains the power of making itself steady; at this stage it becomes one with its object and there is no change or repetition. There is no consciousness of subject, object or thinking, but the mind becomes steady and one with the object of thought. This is called *samādhi*[1]. We have already described the six stages of samādhi. As the yogin acquires strength in one stage of sa*m*ādhi, he passes on to a still higher stage and so on. As he progresses onwards he attains miraculous powers (*vibhūti*) and his faith and hope in the practice increase. Miraculous powers bring with them many temptations, but the yogin is firm of purpose and even though the position of Indra is offered to him he does not relax. His wisdom (*prajñā*) also increases at each step. Prajñā knowledge is as clear as perception, but while perception is limited to

[1] It should be noted that the word *samādhi* cannot properly be translated either by "concentration" or by "meditation." It means that peculiar kind of concentration in the Yoga sense by which the mind becomes one with its object and there is no movement of the mind into its passing states.

certain gross things and certain gross qualities[1] prajñā has no such limitations, penetrating into the subtlest things, the tanmātras, the guṇas, and perceiving clearly and vividly all their subtle conditions and qualities[2]. As the potencies (*saṃskāra*) of the prajñā wisdom grow in strength the potencies of ordinary knowledge are rooted out, and the yogin continues to remain always in his prajñā wisdom. It is a peculiarity of this prajñā that it leads a man towards liberation and cannot bind him to samṣāra. The final prajñās which lead to liberation are of seven kinds, namely, (1) I have known the world, the object of suffering and misery, I have nothing more to know of it. (2) The grounds and roots of samṣāra have been thoroughly uprooted, nothing more of it remains to be uprooted. (3) Removal has become a fact of direct cognition by inhibitive trance. (4) The means of knowledge in the shape of a discrimination of puruṣa from prakṛti has been understood. The other three are not psychological but are rather metaphysical processes associated with the situation. They are as follows: (5) The double purpose of buddhi experience and emancipation (*bhoga* and *apavarga*) has been realized. (6) The strong gravitating tendency of the disintegrated guṇas drives them into prakṛti like heavy stones dropped from high hill tops. (7) The buddhi disintegrated into its constituents the guṇas become merged in the prakṛti and remain there for ever. The puruṣa having passed beyond the bondage of the guṇas shines forth in its pure intelligence. There is no bliss or happiness in this Sāṃkhya-Yoga mukti, for all feeling belongs to prakṛti. It is thus a state of pure intelligence. What the Sāṃkhya tries to achieve through knowledge, Yoga achieves through the perfected discipline of the will and psychological control of the mental states.

[1] The limitations which baffle perception are counted in the *Kārikā* as follows: Extreme remoteness (e.g. a lark high up in the sky), extreme proximity (e.g. collyrium inside the eye), loss of sense-organ (e.g. a blind man), want of attention, extreme smallness of the object (e.g. atoms), obstruction by other intervening objects (e.g. by walls), presence of superior lights (the star cannot be seen in daylight), being mixed up with other things of its own kind (e.g. water thrown into a lake).

[2] Though all things are but the modifications of guṇas yet the real nature of the guṇas is never revealed by the sense-knowledge. What appears to the senses are but illusory characteristics like those of magic (māyā):

"*Guṇānāṃ paramaṃ rūpam na dṛṣṭipathamṛcchati*
Yattu dṛṣṭipatham prāptam tanmāyeva sutucchakam."

Vyāsabhāṣya, IV. 13.

The real nature of the guṇas is thus revealed only by *prajñā.*

VIII

THE NYĀYA-VAIŚEṢIKA PHILOSOPHY

Criticism of Buddhism and Sāṃkhya from the Nyāya standpoint.

THE Buddhists had upset all common sense convictions of substance and attribute, cause and effect, and permanence of things, on the ground that all collocations are momentary; each group of collocations exhausts itself in giving rise to another group and that to another and so on. But if a collocation representing milk generates the collocation of curd it is said to be due to a joint action of the elements forming the cause-collocation and the *modus operandi* is unintelligible; the elements composing the cause-collocation cannot separately generate the elements composing the effect-collocation, for on such a supposition it becomes hard to maintain the doctrine of momentariness as the individual and separate exercise of influence on the part of the cause-elements and their coordination and manifestation as effect cannot but take more than one moment. The supposition that the whole of the effect-collocation is the result of the joint action of the elements of cause-collocation is against our universal uncontradicted experience that specific elements constituting the cause (e.g. the whiteness of milk) are the cause of other corresponding elements of the effect (e.g. the whiteness of the curd); and we could not say that the hardness, blackness, and other properties of the atoms of iron in a lump state should not be regarded as the cause of similar qualities in the iron ball, for this is against the testimony of experience. Moreover there would be no difference between material (*upādāna*, e.g. clay of the jug), instrumental and concomitant causes (*nimitta* and *sahakāri*, such as the potter, and the wheel, the stick etc. in forming the jug), for the causes jointly produce the effect, and there was no room for distinguishing the material and the instrumental causes, as such.

Again at the very moment in which a cause-collocation is brought into being, it cannot exert its influence to produce its effect-collocation. Thus after coming into being it would take the cause-collocation at least another moment to exercise its influence to produce the effect. How can the thing which is destroyed the moment after it is born produce any effect? The truth is that causal elements remain and when they are properly collocated the effect is produced. Ordinary experience also shows that we perceive things as existing from a past time. The past time is perceived by us as past, the present as present and the future as future and things are perceived as existing from a past time onwards.

The Sāṃkhya assumption that effects are but the actualized states of the potential cause, and that the causal entity holds within it all the future series of effects, and that thus the effect is already existent even before the causal movement for the production of the effect, is also baseless. Sāṃkhya says that the oil was already existent in the sesamum and not in the stone, and that it is thus that oil can be got from sesamum and not from the stone. The action of the instrumental cause with them consists only in actualizing or manifesting what was already existent in a potential form in the cause. This is all nonsense. A lump of clay is called the cause and the jug the effect; of what good is it to say that the jug exists in the clay since with clay we can never carry water? A jug is made out of clay, but clay is not a jug. What is meant by saying that the jug was unmanifested or was in a potential state before, and that it has now become manifest or actual? What does potential state mean? The potential state of the jug is not the same as its actual state; thus the actual state of the jug must be admitted as non-existent before. If it is meant that the jug is made up of the same parts (the atoms) of which the clay is made up, of course we admit it, but this does not mean that the jug was existent in the atoms of the lump of clay. The potency inherent in the clay by virtue of which it can expose itself to the influence of other agents, such as the potter, for being transformed into a jug is not the same as the effect, the jug. Had it been so, then we should rather have said that the jug came out of the jug. The assumption of Sāṃkhya that the substance and attribute have the same reality is also against all experience, for we all perceive that movement and attribute belong to substance and not to attribute. Again Sāṃkhya holds a preposterous doctrine that buddhi is different from intelligence. It is absolutely unmeaning to call buddhi non-intelligent. Again what is the good of all this fictitious fuss that the qualities of buddhi are reflected on puruṣa and then again on buddhi. Evidently in all our experience we find that the soul (*ātman*) knows, feels and wills, and it is difficult to understand why Sāṃkhya does not accept this patent fact and declare that knowledge, feeling, and willing, all belonged to buddhi. Then again in order to explain experience it brought forth a theory of double reflection. Again Sāṃkhya prakṛti is non-intelligent, and where is the guarantee that she (prakṛti) will not bind the wise again and will emancipate him once for all? Why did the puruṣa become bound down? Prakṛti is being utilized for enjoyment by the infinite number of puruṣas, and she is no delicate girl (as Sāṃkhya supposes) who will leave the presence of the puruṣa ashamed as soon as her real nature is discovered. Again pleasure (*sukha*), sorrow (*duḥkha*) and a blinding feeling through ignorance (*moha*) are but the feeling-experiences of the soul, and with what impudence could Sāṃkhya think of these as material substances? Again their cosmology of a mahat, ahaṃkāra, the tanmātras, is all a series of assumptions never testified by experience nor by reason. They are all a series of hopeless and foolish blunders. The phenomena of experience thus call for a new careful reconstruction in the light of reason and experience such as cannot be found in other systems. (See *Nyāyamañjarī*, pp. 452–466 and 490–496.)

Nyāya and Vaiśeṣika sūtras.

It is very probable that the earliest beginnings of Nyāya are to be found in the disputations and debates amongst scholars trying to find out the right meanings of the Vedic texts for use in sacrifices and also in those disputations which took place between the adherents of different schools of thought trying to defeat one another. I suppose that such disputations occurred in the days of the Upaniṣads, and the art of disputation was regarded even then as a subject of study, and it probably passed then by the name of *vākovākya*. Mr Bodas has pointed out that Āpastamba who according to Bühler lived before the third century B.C. used the word Nyāya in the sense of Mīmāṃsā[1]. The word Nyāya derived

[1] *Āpastamba*, trans, by Bühler, Introduction, p. XXVII., and Bodas's article on the *Historical Survey of Indian Logic* in the Bombay Branch of J.R.A.S., vol. XIX.

from the root *nī* is sometimes explained as that by which sentences and words could be interpreted as having one particular meaning and not another, and on the strength of this even Vedic accents of words (which indicate the meaning of compound words by pointing out the particular kind of compound in which the words entered into combination) were called Nyaya[1]. Prof. Jacobi on the strength of Kauṯilya's enumeration of the *vidyā* (sciences) as Ānvīkṣikī (the science of testing the perceptual and scriptural knowledge by further scrutiny), *trayī* (the three Vedas), *vārttā* (the sciences of agriculture, cattle keeping etc.), and *daṇḍanīti* (polity), and the enumeration of the philosophies as Sāṃkhya, Yoga, Lokāyata and Ānvīkṣikī, supposes that the *Nyāya sūtra* was not in existence in Kauṯilya's time B.C. 300)[2]. Kauṭilya's reference to Nyāya as Ānvīkṣikī only suggests that the word Nyāya was not a familiar name for Ānvīkṣikī in Kauṭilya's time. He seems to misunderstand Vātsyāyana in thinking that Vātsyāyana distinguishes Nyāya from the Ānvīkṣikī in holding that while the latter only means the science of logic the former means logic as well as metaphysics. What appears from Vātsyāyana's statement in *Nyāya sūtra* I. i. 1 is this that he points out that the science which was known in his time as Nyāya was the same as was referred to as Ānvīkṣikī by Kauṭilya. He distinctly identifies Nyāyavidyā with Ānvīkṣikī, but justifies the separate enumeration of certain logical categories such as *saṃśaya* (doubt) etc., though these were already contained within the first two terms *pramāṇa* (means of cognition) and *prameya* (objects of cognition), by holding that unless these its special and separate branches (*pṛthakprasthāna*) were treated, Nyāyavidyā would simply become metaphysics (*adhyātmavidyā*) like the Upaniṣads. The old meaning of Nyāya as the means of determining the right meaning or the right thing is also agreed upon by Vātsyāyana and is sanctioned by Vācaspati in his *Nyāyavārt-tikatātparyaṭīkā* I. i. I). He compares the meaning of the word Nyāya (*pramāṇairarthaparīkṣaṇam*—to scrutinize an object by means of logical proof) with the etymological meaning of the word ānvīkṣikī (to scrutinize anything after it has been known by perception and scriptures). Vātsyāyana of course points out that so far as this logical side of Nyāya is concerned it has the widest scope for

[1] Kālidāsa's *Kumārasambhava* "*Udghāto praṇavo yāsām nyāyaistribhirudīraṇam,*" also Mallinātha's gloss on it.

[2] Prof. Jacobi's "*The early history of Indian Philosophy*" *Indian Antiquary*, 1918.

itself as it includes all beings, all their actions, and all the sciences[1]. He quotes Kauṭilya to show that in this capacity Nyāya is like light illumining all sciences and is the means of all works. In its capacity as dealing with the truths of metaphysics it may show the way to salvation. I do not dispute Prof. Jacobi's main point that the metaphysical portion of the work was a later addition, for this seems to me to be a very probable view. In fact Vātsyāyana himself designates the logical portion as a pṛthakprasthāna (separate branch). But I do not find that any statement of Vātsyāyana or Kauṭilya can justify us in concluding that this addition was made after Kauṭilya. Vātsyāyana has no doubt put more stress on the importance of the logical side of the work, but the reason of that seems to be quite obvious, for the importance of metaphysics or *adhyātmavidyā* was acknowledged by all. But the importance of the mere logical side would not appeal to most people. None of the dharmaśāstras (religious scriptures) or the Vedas would lend any support to it, and Vātsyāyana had to seek the support of Kauṭilya in the matter as the last resource. The fact that Kauṭilya was not satisfied by counting Ānvīkṣikī as one of the four vidyās but also named it as one of the philosophies side by side with Sāṃkhya seems to lead to the presumption that probably even in Kauṭilya's time Nyāya was composed of two branches, one as adhyātmavidyā and another as a science of logic or rather of debate. This combination is on the face of it loose and external, and it is not improbable that the metaphysical portion was added to increase the popularity of the logical part, which by itself might not attract sufficient attention. Mahāmahopādhyāya Haraprasāda Śāstrī in an article in the *Journal of the Bengal Asiatic Society* 1905 says that as Vācaspati made two attempts to collect the *Nyāya sūtras*, one as *Nyāyasūci* and the other as *Nyāyasūtroddhāra*, it seems that even in Vācaspati's time he was not certain as to the authenticity of many of the *Nyāya sūtras*. He further points out that there are unmistakable signs that many of the sūtras were interpolated, and relates the Buddhist tradition from China and Japan that Mirok mingled Nyāya and Yoga. He also

[1] *Yena prayuktaḥ pravarttate tat prayojanam* (that by which one is led to act is called *prayojanam*); *yamartham abhīpsan jihāsan vā karma ārabhate tenānena sarve prāṇinaḥ sarvāṇi karmāṇi sarvāśca vidyāḥ vyāptaḥ tadāśrayāśca nyāyaḥ pravarttate* (all those which one tries to have or to fly from are called prayojana, therefore all beings, all their actions, and all sciences, are included within prayojana, and all these depend on Nyāya). *Vātsyāyana bhāṣya*, I. i. 1.

thinks that the sūtras underwent two additions, one at the hands of some Buddhists and another at the hands of some Hindu who put in Hindu arguments against the Buddhist ones. These suggestions of this learned scholar seem to be very probable, but we have no clue by which we can ascertain the time when such additions were made. The fact that there are unmistakable proofs of the interpolation of many of the sūtras makes the fixing of the date of the original part of the *Nyāya sūtras* still more difficult, for the Buddhist references can hardly be of any help, and Prof. Jacobi's attempt to fix the date of the *Nyāya sūtras* on the basis of references to Śūnyavāda naturally loses its value, except on the supposition that all references to Śūnyavāda must be later than Nāgārjuna, which is not correct, since the *Mahāyāna sūtras* written before Nāgārjuna also held the Sūnyavāda doctrine.

The late Dr S. C. Vidyābhūṣaṇa in *J.R.A.S.* 1918 thinks that the earlier part of Nyāya was written by Gautama about B.C. 550 whereas the *Nyāya sūtras* of Akṣapāda were written about A.D. 150 and says that the use of the word Nyāya in the sense of logic in *Mahābhārata* I. I. 67, I. 70. 42–51, must be regarded as interpolations. He, however, does not give any reasons in support of his assumption. It appears from his treatment of the subject that the fixing of the date of Akṣapāda was made to fit in somehow with his idea that Akṣapāda wrote his *Nyāya sūtras* under the influence of Aristotle—ā supposition which does not require serious refutation, at least so far as Dr Vidyabhūṣaṇa has proved it. Thus after all this discussion we have not advanced a step towards the ascertainment of the date of the original part of the Nyāya. Goldstücker says that both Patañjali (B.C. 140) and Kātyāyana (fourth century B.C.) knew the *Nyāya sūtras*[1]. We know that Kauṭilya knew the Nyāya in some form as Ānvīkṣikī in B.C. 300, and on the strength of this we may venture to say that the Nyāya existed in some form as early as the fourth century B.C. But there are other reasons which lead me to think that at least some of the present sūtras were written some time in the second century A.D. Bodas points out that Bādarāyaṇa's sūtras make allusions to the Vaiśeṣika doctrines and not to Nyāya. On this ground he thinks that *Vaiśeṣika sūtras* were written before Bādarāyaṇa's *Brahma-sūtras*, whereas the *Nyāya sūtras* were written later. Candrakānta Tarkālaṃkāra also contends in his

[1] Goldstücker's *Pāṇini*, p. 157.

edition of Vaiśeṣika that the *Vaiśeṣika sūtras* were earlier than the Nyāya. It seems to me to be perfectly certain that the *Vaiśeṣika sūtras* were written before Caraka (A.D. 80); for he not only quotes one of the *Vaiśeṣika sūtras*, but the whole foundation of his medical physics is based on the Vaiśeṣika physics[1]. The *Laṅkāvatāra sūtra* (which as it was quoted by Aśvaghoṣa is earlier than A.D. 80) also makes allusions to the atomic doctrine. There are other weightier grounds, as we shall see later on, for supposing that the *Vaiśeṣika sūtras* are probably pre-Buddhistic[2].

It is certain that even the logical part of the present *Nyāya sūtras* was preceded by previous speculations on the subject by thinkers of other schools. Thus in commenting on I. i. 32 in which the sūtra states that a syllogism consists of five premisses (*avayava*) Vātsyāyana says that this sūtra was written to refute the views of those who held that there should be ten premisses[3]. The *Vaiśeṣika sūtras* also give us some of the earliest types of inference, which do not show any acquaintance with the technic of the Nyāya doctrine of inference[4].

Does Vaiśeṣika represent an Old School of Mīmāṃsā?

The Vaiśeṣika is so much associated with Nyāya by tradition that it seems at first sight quite unlikely that it could be supposed to represent an old school of Mīmāṃsā, older than that represented in the *Mīmāṃsā sūtras*. But a closer inspection of the *Vaiśeṣika sūtras* seems to confirm such a supposition in a very remarkable way. We have seen in the previous section that Caraka quotes a *Vaiśeṣika sūtra*. An examination of Caraka's *Sūtrasthāna* (I. 35–38) leaves us convinced that the writer of the verses had some compendium of Vaiśeṣika such as that of the *Bhāṣāpariccheda* before him. *Caraka sūtra* or *kārikā* (I. i. 36) says that the guṇas are those which have been enumerated such as heaviness, etc., cognition, and those which begin with the guṇa "*para*" (universality) and end with "*prayatna*" (effort) together with the sense-qualities (*sārthā*). It seems that this is a reference to some well-known enumeration. But this enumeration is not to be found in the *Vaiśeṣika sūtra* (I. i. 6) which leaves out the six guṇas,

[1] *Caraka, Śārīra*, 39.

[2] See the next section.

[3] Vātsyāyana's Bhāṣya on the *Nyāya sūtras*, I. i. 32. This is undoubtedly a reference to the Jaina view as found in *Daśavaikālikaniryukti* as noted before.

[4] *Nyāya sūtra* I. i. 5, and *Vaiśeṣika sūtras* IX. ii. 1–2, 4–5, and III. i. 8–17.

heaviness (*gurutva*), liquidity (*dravatva*), oiliness (*sneha*), elasticity (*saṃskāra*), merit (*dharma*) and demerit (*adharma*); in one part of the sūtra the enumeration begins with "para" (universality) and ends in "prayatna," but buddhi (cognition) comes within the enumeration beginning from para and ending in prayatna, whereas in Caraka buddhi does not form part of the list and is separately enumerated. This leads me to suppose that Caraka's sūtra was written at a time when the six guṇas left out in the Vaiśeṣika enumeration had come to be counted as guṇas, and compendiums had been made in which these were enumerated. *Bhāṣāpariccheda* (a later Vaiśeṣika compendium), is a compilation from some very old kārikās which are referred to by Viśvanātha as being collected from "*atisaṃkṣiptacirantanoktibhiḥ*"—(from very ancient aphorisms[1]); Caraka's definition of sāmānya and viśeṣa shows that they had not then been counted as separate categories as in later Nyāya-Vaiśeṣika doctrines; but though slightly different it is quite in keeping with the sort of definition one finds in the *Vaiśeṣika sūtra* that sāmānya (generality) and viśeṣa are relative to each other[2]. Caraka's sūtras were therefore probably written at a time when the Vaiśeṣika doctrines were undergoing changes, and well-known compendiums were beginning to be written on them.

The *Vaiśeṣika sūtras* seem to be ignorant of the Buddhist doctrines. In their discussions on the existence of soul, there is no reference to any view as to non-existence of soul, but the argument turned on the point as to whether the self is to be an object of inference or revealed to us by our notion of "I." There is also no other reference to any other systems except to some Mīmāṃsā doctrines and occasionally to Sāṃkhya. There is no reason to suppose that the Mīmāṃsā doctrines referred to allude to the *Mīmāṃsā sūtras* of Jaimini. The manner in which the nature of inference has been treated shows that the Nyāya phraseology of "*pūrvavat*" and "*śeṣavat*" was not known. *Vaiśeṣika sūtras* in more than one place refer to time as the ultimate cause[3]. We know that the Śvetāśvatara Upaniṣad refers to those who regard time as the cause of all things, but in none of the

[1] Professor Vanamālī Vedāntatīrtha's article in *J. A. S. B.*, 1908.

[2] Caraka (I. 1. 33) says that sāmānya is that which produces unity and viśeṣa is that which separates. V. S. II. ii. 7. Sāmānya and viśeṣa depend upon our mode of thinking (as united or as separate).

[3] *Vaiśeṣika sūtra* (II. ii. 9 and v. ii. 26).

systems that we have can we trace any upholding of this ancient view[1]. These considerations as well as the general style of the work and the methods of discussion lead me to think that these sūtras are probably the oldest that we have and in all probability are pre-Buddhistic.

The *Vaiśeṣika sūtra* begins with the statement that its object is to explain virtue, "dharma." This is we know the manifest duty of Mīmāṃsā and we know that unlike any other system Jaimini begins his *Mīmāṃsā sūtras* by defining "dharma." This at first seems irrelevant to the main purpose of Vaiśeṣika, viz., the description of the nature of padārtha[2]. He then defines dharma as that which gives prosperity and ultimate good (*niḥśreyasa*) and says that the Veda must be regarded as valid, since it can dictate this. He ends his book with the remarks that those injunctions (of Vedic deeds) which are performed for ordinary human motives bestow prosperity even though their efficacy is not known to us through our ordinary experience, and in this matter the Veda must be regarded as the authority which dictates those acts[3]. The fact that the Vaiśeṣika begins with a promise to describe dharma and after describing the nature of substances, qualities and actions and also the *adṛṣṭa* (unknown virtue) due to dharma (merit accruing from the performance of Vedic deeds) by which many of our unexplained experiences may be explained, ends his book by saying that those Vedic works which are not seen to produce any direct effect, will produce prosperity through adṛṣṭa, shows that Kaṇāda's method of explaining dharma has been by showing that physical phenomena involving substances, qualities, and actions can only be explained up to a certain extent while a good number cannot be explained at all except on the assumption of adṛṣṭa (unseen virtue) produced by dharma. The

[1] Śvetāśvatara 1. i. 2.

[2] I remember a verse quoted in an old commentary of the *Kalāpa Vyākaraṇa*, in which it is said that the description of the six categories by Kaṇāda in his *Vaiśeṣika sūtras*, after having proposed to describe the nature of dharma, is as irrelevant as to proceed towards the sea while intending to go to the mountain Himavat (Himālaya). "*Dharmaṃ vyākhyātukāmasya ṣaṭpadārthopavarṇanaṃ Himavadgantukāmasya sāgaragamanopamam.*"

[3] The sūtra "*Tadvacanād āmnāyasya prāmāṇyam* (1. i. 3 and X. ii. 9) has been explained by *Upaskāra* as meaning "The Veda being the word of Īśvara (God) must be regarded as valid," but since there is no mention of "Īśvara" anywhere in the text this is simply reading the later Nyāya ideas into the Vaiśeṣika. Sūtra X. ii. 8 is only a repetition of VI. ii. 1.

description of the categories of substance is not irrelevant, but is the means of proving that our ordinary experience of these cannot explain many facts which are only to be explained on the supposition of adṛṣṭa proceeding out of the performance of Vedic deeds. In V. i. 15 the movement of needles towards magnets, in V. ii. 7 the circulation of water in plant bodies, V. ii. 13 and IV. ii. 7 the upward motion of fire, the side motion of air, the combining movement of atoms (by which all combinations have taken place), and the original movement of the mind are said to be due to adṛṣṭa. In V. ii. 17 the movement of the soul after death, its taking hold of other bodies, the assimilation of food and drink and other kinds of contact (the movement and development of the foetus as enumerated in *Upaskāra*) are said to be due to adṛṣṭa. Salvation (mokṣa) is said to be produced by the annihilation of adṛṣṭa leading to the annihilation of all contacts and non-production of rebirths. Vaiśeṣika marks the distinction between the dṛṣṭa (experienced) and the adṛṣṭa. All the categories that he describes are founded on dṛṣṭa (experience) and those unexplained by known experience are due to adṛṣṭa. These are the acts on which depend all life-process of animals and plants, the continuation of atoms or the construction of the worlds, natural motion of fire and air, death and rebirth (VI. ii. 15) and even the physical phenomena by which our fortunes are affected in some way or other (V. ii. 2), in fact all with which we are vitally interested in philosophy. Kaṇāda's philosophy gives only some facts of experience regarding substances, qualities and actions, leaving all the graver issues of metaphysics to adṛṣṭa. But what leads to adṛṣṭa? In answer to this, Kaṇāda does not speak of good or bad or virtuous or sinful deeds, but of Vedic works, such as holy ablutions (*snāna*), fasting, holy student life (*brahmacarya*), remaining at the house of the teacher (*gurukulavāsa*), retired forest life (*vānaprastha*), sacrifice (*yajña*), gifts (*dāna*), certain kinds of sacrificial sprinkling and rules of performing sacrificial works according to the prescribed time of the stars, the prescribed hymns (mantras) (VI. ii. 2).

He described what is pure and what is impure food, pure food being that which is sacrificially purified (VI. ii. 5) the contrary being impure; and he says that the taking of pure food leads to prosperity through adṛṣṭa. He also described how feelings of attachment to things are also generated by adṛṣṭa. Throughout almost the whole of VI. i Kaṇāda is busy in showing the special conditions of making gifts and receiving them. A reference to our chapter on Mīmāṃsā will show that the later Mīmāṃsā writers agreed with the Nyāya-Vaiśeṣika doctrines in most of their views regarding substance, qualities, etc. Some of the main points in which Mīmāṃsā differs from Nyāya-Vaiśeṣika are (1) self-validity of the Vedas, (2) the eternality of the Vedas, (3) disbelief in any creator or god, (4) eternality of sound (śabda), (5) (according to Kumārila) direct perception of self in the notion of the ego. Of these the first and the second points do not form any subject of discussion in the Vaiśeṣika. But as no Īśvara is mentioned, and as all adṛṣṭa depends upon the authority of the Vedas, we may assume that Vaiśeṣika had no dispute with Mīmāṃsā. The fact that there is no reference to any dissension is probably due to the fact that really none had taken place at the time of the *Vaiśeṣika sūtras*. It is probable that Kaṇāda believed that the Vedas were written by some persons superior to us (II. i. 18, VI. i. 1–2). But the fact that there is no reference to any conflict with Mīmāṃsā suggests that the doctrine that the Vedas were never written by anyone was formulated at a later period, whereas in the days of the *Vaiśeṣika sūtras*, the view was probably what is represented in the *Vaiśeṣika sūtras*. As there is no reference to Īśvara and as adṛṣṭa proceeding out of the performance of actions in accordance with Vedic injunctions is made the cause of all atomic movements, we can very well assume that Vaiśeṣika was as atheistic or non-theistic as the later Mīmāṃsā philosophers. As regards the eternality of sound, which in later days was one of the main points of quarrel between the Nyāya-Vaiśeṣika and the Mīmāṃsā, we find that in II. ii. 25–32, Kaṇadā gives reasons in favour of the non-eternality of sound, but after that from II. ii. 33 till the end of the chapter he closes the argument in favour of the eternality of sound, which is the distinctive Mīmāṃsā view as we know from the later Mīmāṃsā writers[1]. Next comes the question of the proof of the existence of self. The traditional Nyāya view is

[1] The last two concluding sūtras II. ii. 36 and 37 are in my opinion wrongly interpreted by Śaṅkara Miśra in his *Upaskāra* (II. ii. 36 by adding an "*api*" to the sūtra and thereby changing the issue, and II. ii. 37 by misreading the phonetic combination "saṃkhyābhāva" as saṃkhyā and bhāva instead of saṃkhyā and abhāva, which in my opinion is the right combination here) in favour of the non-eternality of sound as we find in the later Nyāya-Vaiśeṣika view.

that the self is supposed to exist because it must be inferred as the seat of the qualities of pleasure, pain, cognition, etc. Traditionally this is regarded as the Vaiśeṣika view as well. But in Vaiśeṣika III. ii. 4 the existence of soul is first inferred by reason of its activity and the existence of pleasure, pain, etc., in III. ii. 6–7 this inference is challenged by saying that we do not perceive that the activity, etc. belongs to the soul and not to the body and so no certainty can be arrived at by inference, and in III. ii. 8 it is suggested that therefore the existence of soul is to be accepted on the authority of the scriptures (*āgama*). To this the final Vaiśeṣika conclusion is given that we can directly perceive the self in our feeling as "I" (*aham*), and we have therefore not to depend on the scriptures for the proof of the existence of the self, and thus the inference of the existence of the self is only an additional proof of what we already find in perception as "I" (*aham*) (III. ii. 10–18, also IX. i. 11).

These considerations lead me to think that the Vaiśeṣika represented a school of Mīmāṃsā thought which supplemented a metaphysics to strengthen the grounds of the Vedas.

Philosophy in the Vaiśeṣika sūtras.

The *Vaiśeṣika sūtras* begin with the ostensible purpose of explaining virtue (*dharma*) (I. i. 1) and dharma according to it is that by which prosperity (*abhyudaya*) and salvation (*niḥśreyasa*) are attained. Then it goes on to say that the validity of the Vedas depends on the fact that it leads us to prosperity and salvation. Then it turns back to the second sūtra and says that salvation comes as the result of real knowledge, produced by special excellence of dharma, of the characteristic features of the categories of substance (*dravya*), quality (*guṇa*), class concept (*sāmānya*), particularity (*viśeṣa*), and inherence (*samavāya*)[1]. The dravyas are earth, water, fire, air, ether, time, space, soul, and mind. The guṇas are colour, taste, odour, touch, number, measure, separations, contact, disjoining, quality of belonging to high genus or to species[2]. Action (*karma*) means upward move-

[1] *Upaskāra* notes that viśeṣa here refers to the ultimate differences of things and not to species. A special doctrine of this system is this, that each of the indivisible atoms of even the same element has specific features of difference.

[2] Here the well known qualities of heaviness (*gurutva*), liquidity (*dravatva*), oiliness (*sneha*), elasticity (*saṃskāra*), merit (*dharma*), and demerit (*adharma*) have been altogether omitted. These are all counted in later Vaiśeṣika commentaries and compendiums. It must

ment, downward movement, contraction, expansion and horizontal movement. The three common qualities of dravya, guṇa and karma are that they are existent, non-eternal, substantive, effect, cause, and possess generality and particularity. Dravya produces other dravyas and the guṇas other guṇas. But karma is not necessarily produced by karma. Dravya does not destroy either its cause or its effect, but the guṇas are destroyed both by the cause and by the effect. Karma is destroyed by karma. Dravya possesses karma and guṇa and is regarded as the material (*samavāyi*) cause. Guṇas inhere in dravya, cannot possess further guṇas, and are not by themselves the cause of contact or disjoining. Karma is devoid of guṇa, cannot remain at one time in more than one object, inheres in dravya alone, and is an independent cause of contact or disjoining. Dravya is the material cause (samavāyi) of (derivative) dravyas, guṇa, and karma; guṇa is also the non-material cause (*asamāvāyi*) of dravya, guṇa and karma. Karma is the general cause of contact, disjoining, and inertia in motion (*vega*). Karma is not the cause of dravya. For dravya may be produced even without karma[1]. Dravya is the general effect of dravya. Karma is dissimilar to guṇa in this that it does not produce karma. The numbers two, three, etc., separateness, contact and disjoining are effected by more than one dravya. Each karma not being connected with more than one thing is not produced by more than one thing[2]. A dravya is the result of many contacts (of the atoms). One colour may be the result of many colours. Upward movement is the result of heaviness, effort and contact. Contact and disjoining are also the result of karma. In denying the causality of karma it is meant that karma is not the cause of dravya and karma[3].

In the second chapter of the first book Kaṇāda first says that if there is no cause, there is no effect, but there may be the cause even though there may not be the effect. He next says that genus (*sāmānya*) and species (*viśeṣa*) are relative to the under-

be noted that "*guṇa*" in Vaiśeṣika means qualities and not subtle reals or substances as in Sāṃkhya-Yoga. Guṇa in Vaiśeṣika would be akin to what Yoga would call *dharma*.

[1] It is only when the kārya ceases that dravya is produced. See *Upaskāra* I. i. 22.

[2] If karma is related to more than one thing, then with the movement of one we should have felt that two or more things were moving.

[3] It must be noted that "karma" in this sense is quite different from the more extensive use of karma as meritorious or vicious action which is the cause of rebirth.

standing; being (*bhāva*) indicates continuity only and is hence only a genus. The universals of substance, quality and action may be both genus and species, but viśeṣa as constituting the ultimate differences (of atoms) exists (independent of any percipient). In connection with this he says that the ultimate genus is being (*sattā*) in virtue of which things appear as existent; all other genera may only relatively be regarded as relative genera or species. Being must be regarded as a separate category, since it is different from dravya, guṇa and karma, and yet exists in them, and has no genus or species. It gives us the notion that something is and must be regarded as a category existing as one identical entity in all dravya, guṇa, and karma, for in its universal nature as being it has no special characteristics in the different objects in which it inheres. The specific universals of thingness (*dravyatva*), qualitiness (*guṇatva*) or actionness (*kar-matva*) are also categories which are separate from universal being (*bhāva* or *sattā*) for they also have no separate genus or species and yet may be distinguished from one another, but bhāva or being was the same in all.

In the first chapter of the second book Kaṇāda deals with substances. Earth possesses colour, taste, smell, and touch; water, colour, taste, touch, liquidity, and smoothness (*snigdha*); fire, colour and touch; air, touch; but none of these qualities can be found in ether (*ākāśa*). Liquidity is a special quality of water because butter, lac, wax, lead, iron, silver, gold, become liquids only when they are heated, while water is naturally liquid itself[1]. Though air cannot be seen, yet its existence can be inferred by touch, just as the existence of the genus of cows may be inferred from the characteristics of horns, tails, etc. Since this thing inferred from touch possesses motion and quality, and does not itself inhere in any other substance, it is a substance (dravya) and is eternal[2]. The inference of air is of the type of inference of imperceptible things from certain known characteristics called *sāmānyato dṛṣṭa*. The name of air "*vāyu*" is derived from the scriptures. The existence of others different from us has (*asmadviśiṣṭānāṃ*) to be admitted for accounting for the

[1] It should be noted that mercury is not mentioned. This is important for mercury was known at a time later than Caraka.

[2] Substance is that which possesses quality and action. It should be noted that the word "*adravyatvena*" in II. i. 13 has been interpreted by me as "*adravyavattvena*."

giving of names to things (*saṃjñākarma*). Because we find that the giving of names is already in usage (and not invented by us)[1]. On account of the fact that movements rest only in one thing, the phenomenon that a thing can enter into any unoccupied space, would not lead us to infer the existence of ākāśa (ether). Ākāśa has to be admitted as the hypothetical substance in which the quality of sound inheres, because, since sound (a quality) is not the characteristic of things which can be touched, there must be some substance of which it is a quality. And this substance is ākāśa. It is a substance and eternal like air. As being is one so ākāśa is one[2].

In the second chapter of the second book Kaṇāda tries to prove that smell is a special characteristic of earth, heat of fire, and coldness of water. Time is defined as that which gives the notion of youth in the young, simultaneity, and quickness. It is one like being. Time is the cause of all non-eternal things, because the notion of time is absent in eternal things. Space supplies the notion that this is so far away from this or so much nearer to this. Like being it is one. One space appears to have diverse inter-space relations in connection with the motion of the sun. As a preliminary to discussing the problem whether sound is eternal or not, he discusses the notion of doubt, which arises when a thing is seen in a general way, but the particular features coming under it are not seen, either when these are only remembered, or when some such attribute is seen which resembles some other attribute seen before, or when a thing is seen in one way but appears in another, or when what is seen is not definitely grasped, whether rightly seen or not. He then discusses the question whether sound is eternal or non-eternal and gives his reasons to show that it is non-eternal, but concludes the discussion with a number of other reasons proving that it is eternal.

The first chapter of the third book is entirely devoted to the inference of the existence of soul from the fact that there must be some substance in which knowledge produced by the contact of the senses and their object inheres.

The knowledge of sense-objects (*indriyārtha*) is the reason by

[1] I have differed from *Upaskāra* in interpreting "*saṃjñākarma*" in II. i. 18, 19 as a genitive compound while *Upaskāra* makes it a *dvandva* compound. Upaskāra's interpretation seems to be far-fetched. He wants to twist it into an argument for the existence of God.

[2] This interpretation is according to Śaṅkara Miśra's *Upaskāra*.

which we can infer the existence of something different from the senses and the objects which appear in connection with them. The types of inferences referred to are (1) inference of non-existence of some things from the existence of some things, (2) of the existence of some things from the non-existence of some things, (3) of the existence of some things from the existence of others. In all these cases inference is possible only when the two are known to be connected with each other (*prasiddhipūrvakatvāt apadeśasya*)[1]. When such a connection does not exist or is doubtful, we have *anapadeśa* (fallacious middle) and *sandigdha* (doubtful middle); thus, it is a horse because it has a horn, or it is a cow because it has a horn are examples of fallacious reason. The inference of soul from the cognition produced by the contact of soul, senses and objects is not fallacious in the above way. The inference of the existence of the soul in others may be made in a similar way in which the existence of one's own soul is inferred[2], i.e. by virtue of the existence of movement and cessation of movement. In the second chapter it is said that the fact that there is cognition only when there is contact between the self, the senses and the objects proves that there is manas (mind), and this manas is a substance and eternal, and this can be proved because there is no simultaneity of production of efforts and various kinds of cognition; it may also be inferred that this manas is one (with each person).

The soul may be inferred from inhalation, exhalation, twinkling of the eye, life, the movement of the mind, the sense-affections pleasure, pain, will, antipathy, and effort. That it is a substance and eternal can be proved after the manner of vāyu. An objector is supposed to say that since when I see a man I do not see his soul, the inference of the soul is of the type of *sāmānyatodṛṣṭa* inference, i.e., from the perceived signs of pleasure, pain, cognition to infer an unknown entity to which they belong, but that this was the self could not be affirmed. So the existence of soul has to be admitted on the strength of the scriptures. But the Vaiśeṣika reply is that since there is nothing else but self to which the expression "I" may be applied, there is no need of falling back on the scriptures for the existence of the soul. But

[1] In connection with this there is a short reference to the methods of fallacy in which Gautama's terminology does not appear. There is no generalised statement, but specific types of inference are only pointed out as the basis.

[2] The forms of inference used show that Kaṇāda was probably not aware of Gautama's terminology.

then it is said that if the self is directly perceived in such experiences as "I am Yajñadatta" or "I am Devadatta," what is the good of turning to inference? The reply to this is that inference lending its aid to the same existence only strengthens the conviction. When we say that Devadatta goes or Yajñadatta goes, there comes the doubt whether by Devadatta or Yajñadatta the body alone is meant; but the doubt is removed when we think that the notion of "I" refers to the self and not to anything else. As there is no difference regarding the production of pleasure, pain, and cognition, the soul is one in all. But yet it is many by special limitations as individuals and this is also proved on the strength of the scriptures[1].

In the first chapter of the fourth book it is said that that which is existent, but yet has no cause, should be considered eternal (*nitya*). It can be inferred by its effect, for the effect can only take place because of the cause. When we speak of anything as non-eternal, it is only a negation of the eternal, so that also proves that there is something eternal. The non-eternal is ignorance (*avidyā*)[2]. Colour is visible in a thing which is great (*mahat*) and compounded. Air (*vāyu*) is not perceived to have colour, though it is great and made up of parts, because it has not the actuality of colour (*rūpasaṃskāra*—i.e. in air there is only colour in its unmanifested form) in it Colour is thus visible only when there is colour with special qualifications and conditions[3]. In this way the cognition of taste, smell, and touch is also explained. Number, measure, separateness, contact, and disjoining, the quality of belonging to a higher or lower class, action, all these as they abide in things possessing colour are visible to the eye. The number etc. of those which have no colour are not perceived by the eye. But the notion of being and also of genus of quality (guṇatva)

[1] I have differed here from the meaning given in *Upaskāra*. I think the three sūtras "*Sukhaduḥkhajñānaniṣpattyaviśeṣādekatmyam*," "*vyavasthāto nānā*," and "*śastrasāmarthyāt ca*" originally meant that the self was one, though for the sake of many limitations, and also because of the need of the performance of acts enjoined by the scriptures, they are regarded as many.

[2] I have differed here also in my meaning from the *Upaskāra*, which regards this sūtra "*avidyā*" to mean that we do not know of any reasons which lead to the non-eternality of the atoms.

[3] This is what is meant in the later distinctions of *udbhūtarūpavattva* and *anudbhūtarūpavattva*. The word *sāṃskāra* in Vaiśeṣika has many senses. It means inertia, elasticity, collection (*samavāya*), production (*udbhava*) and not being overcome (*anabhibhava*). For the last three senses see *Upaskāra* IV. i. 7.

are perceived by all the senses (just as colour, taste, smell, touch, and sound are perceived by one sense, cognition, pleasure, pain, etc. by the manas and number etc. by the visual and the tactile sense)[1].

In the second chapter of the fourth book it is said that the earth, etc. exist in three forms, body, sense, and objects. There cannot be any compounding of the five elements or even of the three, but the atoms of different elements may combine when one of them acts as the central radicle (*upaṣṭambhaka*). Bodies are of two kinds, those produced from ovaries and those which are otherwise produced by the combination of the atoms in accordance with special kinds of dharma. All combinations of atoms are due to special kinds of dharmas. Such super-mundane bodies are to be admitted for explaining the fact that things must have been given names by beings having such super-mundane bodies, and also on account of the authority of the Vedas.

In the first chapter of the fifth book action (*karma*) is discussed. Taking the example of threshing the corn, it is said that the movement of the hand is due to its contact with the soul in a state of effort, and the movement of the flail is due to its contact with the hand. But in the case of the uprising of the flail in the threshing pot due to impact the movement is not due to contact with the hands, and so the uplifting of the hand in touch with the flail is not due to its contact with the soul; for it is due to the impact of the flail. On account of heaviness (*gurutva*) the flail will fall when not held by the hand. Things may have an upward or side motion by specially directed motions (*nodanaviśeṣa*) which are generated by special kinds of efforts. Even without effort the body may move during sleep. The movement of needles towards magnets is due to an unknown cause (*adṛṣṭakāraṇaka*). The arrow first acquires motion by specially directed movement, and then on account of its inertia (*vegasaṃskāra*) keeps on moving and when that ceases it falls down through heaviness.

The second chapter abounds with extremely crude explana-

[1] This portion has been taken from the *Upaskāra* of Śaṅkara Miśra on the *Vaiśeṣika sūtras* of Kaṇāda. It must be noted here that the notion of number according to Vaiśeṣika is due to mental relativity or oscillation (*apekṣābuddhijanya*). But this mental relativity can only start when the thing having number is either seen or touched; and it is in this sense that notion of number is said to depend on the visual or the tactual sense.

tions of certain physical phenomena which have no philosophical importance. All the special phenomena of nature are explained as being due to unknown cause (*adṛṣṭakāritam*) and no explanation is given as to the nature of this unknown (*adṛṣṭa*). It is however said that with the absence of *adṛṣṭa* there is no contact of body with soul, and thus there is no rebirth, and therefore mokṣa (salvation); pleasure and pain are due to contact of the self, manas, senses and objects. Yoga is that in which the mind is in contact with the self alone, by which the former becomes steady and there is no pain in the body. Time, space, ākāśa are regarded as inactive.

The whole of the sixth book is devoted to showing that gifts are made to proper persons not through sympathy but on account of the injunction of the scriptures, the enumeration of certain Vedic performances, which brings in adṛṣṭa, purification and impurities of things, how passions are often generated by adṛṣṭa, how dharma and adharma lead to birth and death and how mokṣa takes place as a result of the work of the soul.

In the seventh book it is said that the qualities in eternal things are eternal and in non-eternal things non-eternal. The change of qualities produced by heat in earth has its beginning in the cause (the atoms). Atomic size is invisible while great size is visible. Visibility is due to a thing's being made up of many causes[1], but the atom is therefore different from those that have great size. The same thing may be called great and small relatively at the same time. In accordance with aṇutva (atomic) and mahattva (great) there are also the notions of small and big. The eternal size of *parimaṇḍala* (round) belongs to the atoms. Ākāśa and ātman are called *mahān* or *paramamahān* (the supremely great or all-pervasive); since manas is not of the great measure it is of atomic size. Space and time are also considered as being of the measure "supremely great" (paramamahat). Atomic size (parimaṇḍala) belonging to the atoms and the mind (manas) and the supremely great size belonging to space, time, soul and ether (ākāśa) are regarded as eternal.

In the second chapter of the seventh book it is said that unity and separateness are to be admitted as entities distinct from other qualities. There is no number in movement and quality; the appearance of number in them is false. Cause and effect are

[1] I have differed from the *Upaskāra* in the interpretation of this sūtra.

neither one, nor have they distinctive separateness (*ekapṛthaktva*). The notion of unity is the cause of the notion of duality, etc. Contact may be due to the action of one or two things, or the effect of another contact and so is disjoining. There is neither contact nor disjoining in cause and effect since they do not exist independently (*yutasiddhyabhāvāt*). In the eighth book it is said that soul and manas are not perceptible, and that in the apprehension of qualities, action, generality, and particularity perception is due to their contact with the thing. Earth is the cause of perception of smell, and water, fire, and air are the cause of taste, colour and touch[1]. In the ninth book negation is described; non-existence (*asat*) is defined as that to which neither action nor quality can be attributed. Even existent things may become non-existent and that which is existent in one way may be non-existent in another; but there is another kind of non-existence which is different from the above kinds of existence and non-existence[2]. All negation can be directly perceived through the help of the memory which keeps before the mind the thing to which the negation applies. Allusion is also made in this connection to the special perceptual powers of the yogins (sages attaining mystical powers through Yoga practices).

In the second chapter the nature of hetu (reason) or the middle term is described. It is said that anything connected with any other thing, as effect, cause, as in contact, or as contrary or as inseparably connected, will serve as liṅga (reason). The main point is the notion "this is associated with this," or "these two are related as cause and effect," and since this may also be produced through premisses, there may be a formal syllogism from propositions fulfilling the above condition. Verbal cognition comes without inference. False knowledge (*avidyā*) is due to the defect of the senses or non-observation and mal-observation due to wrong expectant impressions. The opposite of this is true knowledge (*vidyā*). In the tenth it is said that pleasure and pain are not cognitions, since they are not related to doubt and certainty.

[1] *Upaskāra* here explains that it is intended that the senses are produced by those specific elements, but this cannot be found in the sūtras.

[2] In the previous three kinds of non-existence, *prāgabhāva* (negation before production), *dhvaṃsābhāva* (negation after destruction), and *anyonyābhāva* (mutual negation of each other in each other), have been described. The fourth one is *sāmānyābhāva* (general negation).

A dravya may be caused by the inhering of the effect in it, for because of its contact with another thing the effect is produced. Karma (motion) is also a cause since it inheres in the cause. Contact is also a cause since it inheres in the cause. A contact which inheres in the cause of the cause and thereby helps the production of the effect is also a cause. The special quality of the heat of fire is also a cause.

Works according to the injunctions of the scriptures since they have no visible effect are the cause of prosperity, and because the Vedas direct them, they have validity.

Philosophy in the Nyāya sūtras[1].

The *Nyāya sūtras* begin with an enumeration of the sixteen subjects, viz. means of right knowledge (*pramāṇa*), object of right knowledge (*prameya*), doubt (*saṃśaya*), purpose (*prayojana*), illustrative instances (*dṛṣṭānta*), accepted conclusions (*siddhānta*), premisses (*avayava*), argumentation (*tarka*), ascertainment (*nirṇaya*), debates (*vāda*), disputations (*jalpa*), destructive criticisms (*vitaṇḍā*), fallacy (*hetvābhāsa*), quibble (*chala*), refutations (*jāti*), points of opponent's defeat (*nigrahasthāna*), and hold that by a thorough knowledge of these the highest good (*niḥśreyasa*), is attained. In the second sūtra it is said that salvation (*apavarga*) is attained by the successive disappearance of false knowledge (*mithyājñāna*), defects (*doṣa*), endeavours (*pravṛtti*), birth (*janma*), and ultimately of sorrow. Then the means of proof are said to be of four kinds, perception (*pratyakṣa*), inference (*anumāna*), analogy (*upamāna*), and testimony (*śabda*). Perception is defined as uncontradicted determinate knowledge unassociated with names proceeding out of sense contact with objects. Inference is of three kinds, from cause to effect (*pūrvavat*), effect to cause (*śeṣavat*), and inference from common characteristics (*sāmānyato dṛṣṭa*). Upamāna is the knowing of anything by similarity with any well-known thing.

Śabda is defined as the testimony of reliable authority (āpta)[2].

[1] This is a brief summary of the doctrines found in *Nyāya sūtras*, supplemented here and there with the views of Vātsyāyana, the commentator. This follows the order of the sūtras, and tries to present their ideas with as little additions from those of later day Nyāya as possible. The general treatment of Nyāya-Vaiśeṣika expounds the two systems in the light of later writers and commentators.

[2] It is curious to notice that Vātsyāyana says that an ārya, a ṛṣi or a mleccha (foreigner),

Such a testimony may tell us about things which may be experienced and which are beyond experience. Objects of knowledge are said to be self (*ātman*), body, senses, sense-objects, understanding (*buddhi*), mind (*manas*), endeavour (*pravṛtti*), rebirths, enjoyment of pleasure and suffering of pain, sorrow and salvation. Desire, antipathy, effort (*prayatna*), pleasure, pain, and knowledge indicate the existence of the self. Body is that which upholds movement, the senses and the rise of pleasure and pain as arising out of the contact of sense with sense-objects[1]; the five senses are derived from the five elements, such as pṛthivī, ap, tejas, vāyu and ākāśa; smell, taste, colour, touch, and sound are the qualities of the above five elements, and these are also the objects of the senses. The fact that many cognitions cannot occur at any one moment indicates the existence of mind (*manas*). Endeavour means what is done by speech, understanding, and body. Doṣas (attachment, antipathy, etc.) are those which lead men to virtue and vice. Pain is that which causes suffering[2]. Ultimate cessation from pain is called *apavarga*[3]. Doubt arises when through confusion of similar qualities or conflicting opinions etc., one wants to settle one of the two alternatives. That for attaining which, or for giving up which one sets himself to work is called *prayojana*.

Illustrative example (*dṛṣṭānta*) is that on which both the common man and the expert (*parīkṣaka*) hold the same opinion. Established texts or conclusions (*siddhānta*) are of four kinds, viz. (1) those which are accepted by all schools of thought called the *sarvatantrasiddhānta*; (2) those which are held by one school or similar schools but opposed by others called the *pratitantra-siddhānta*; (3) those which being accepted other conclusions will also naturally follow called *adhikaraṇasiddhānta*; (4) those of the opponent's views which are uncritically granted by a debater, who proceeds then to refute the consequences that follow and thereby show his own special skill and bring the opponent's intellect to disrepute (*abhyupagamasiddhānta*)[4]. The premisses are five:

may be an āpta (reliable authority).

[1] Here I have followed Vātsyāyana's meaning.

[2] Vātsyāyana comments here that when one finds all things full of misery, he wishes to avoid misery, and finding birth to be associated with pain becomes unattached and thus is emancipated.

[3] Vātsyāyana wants to emphasize that there is no bliss in salvation, but only cessation from pain.

[4] I have followed Vātsyāyana's interpretation here.

(1) *pratijñā* (the first enunciation of the thing to be proved); (2) *hetu* (the reason which establishes the conclusion on the strength of the similarity of the case in hand with known examples or negative instances); (3) *udāharaṇa* (positive or negative illustrative instances); (4) *upanaya* (corroboration by the instance); (5) *nigamana* (to reach the conclusion which has been proved). Then come the definitions of tarka, nirṇaya, vāda, jalpa, vitaṇḍā, the fallacies (hetvābhāsa), chala, jāti, and nigrahasthāna, which have been enumerated in the first sūtra.

The second book deals with the refutations of objections against the means of right knowledge (pramāṇa). In refutation of certain objections against the possibility of the happening of doubt, which held that doubt could not happen, since there was always a difference between the two things regarding which doubt arose, it is held that doubt arises when the special differentiating characteristics between the two things are not noted. Certain objectors, probably the Buddhists, are supposed to object to the validity of the pramāṇa in general and particularly of perceptions on the ground that if they were generated before the sense-object contact, they could not be due to the latter, and if they are produced after the sense-object contact, they could not establish the nature of the objects, and if the two happened together then there would be no notion of succession in our cognitions. To this the Nyāya reply is that if there were no means of right knowledge, then there would be no means of knowledge by means of which the objector would refute all means of right knowledge; if the objector presumes to have any means of valid knowledge then he cannot say that there are no means of valid knowledge at all. Just as from the diverse kinds of sounds of different musical instruments, one can infer the previous existence of those different kinds of musical instruments, so from our knowledge of objects we can infer the previous existence of those objects of knowledge[1].

The same things (e.g. the senses, etc.) which are regarded as instruments of right knowledge with reference to the right cognition of other things may themselves be the objects of right

[1] *Yathāpaścātsiddhena śabdena pūrvasiddham ātodyamanumīyate sādhyam ca ātodyam sādhanam ca śabdaḥ antarhite hyātodye svanataḥ anumānam bhavatīti, vīṇā vādyate veṇuḥ pūryyate iti svanaviśeṣeṇa ātodyaviśeṣam pratipadyate tathā pūrvasiddham upalabdhiviṣayam paścātsiddhena upalabdhihetunā pratipadyate. Vātsyāyana bhāṣya*, II. i. 15.

knowledge. There are no hard and fast limits that those which are instruments of knowledge should always be treated as mere instruments, for they themselves may be objects of right knowledge. The means of right knowledge (pramāṇa) do not require other sets of means for revealing them, for they like the light of a lamp in revealing the objects of right knowledge reveal themselves as well.

Coming to the question of the correctness of the definition of perception, it is held that the definition includes the contact of the soul with the mind[1]. Then it is said that though we perceive only parts of things, yet since there is a whole, the perception of the part will naturally refer to the whole. Since we can pull and draw things wholes exist, and the whole is not merely the parts collected together, for were it so one could say that we perceived the ultimate parts or the atoms[2]. Some objectors hold that since there may be a plurality of causes it is wrong to infer particular causes from particular effects. To this the Nyāya answer is that there is always such a difference in the specific nature of each effect that if properly observed each particular effect will lead us to a correct inference of its own particular cause[3]. In refuting those who object to the existence of time on the ground of relativity, it is said that if the present time did not exist, then no perception of it would have been possible. The past and future also exist, for otherwise we should not have perceived things as being done in the past or as going to be done in the future. The validity of analogy (*upamāna*) as a means of knowledge and the validity of the Vedas is then proved. The four pramāṇas of perception, inference, analogy, and scripture

[1] Here the sūtras, II. i. 20-28, are probably later interpolations to answer criticisms, not against the Nyāya doctrine of perception, but against the wording of the definition of perception as given in the *Nyāya sūtra*, II. i. 4.

[2] This is a refutation of the doctrines of the Buddhists, who rejected the existence of wholes (avayavī). On this subject a later Buddhist monograph by Paṇḍita Aśoka (ninth century A.D.), *Avayavinirākaraṇa* in *Six Buddhist Nyāya Tracts*, may be referred to.

[3] *Pūrvodakaviśiṣṭam khalu varṣodakan śīghrataram srotasā bahutaraphenaphala-pa rṇakāsṭhādivahanañcopalabhamānaḥ pūrṇatvena, nadyā upari vṛṣto deva ityanuminoti nodakabṛddhimātreṇa. Vātsyāyana bhāṣya*, II. 1. 38. The inference that there has been rain up the river is not made merely from seeing the rise of water, but from the rainwater augmenting the previous water of the river and carrying with its current large quantities of foam, fruits, leaves, wood, etc. These characteristics, associated with the rise of water, mark it as a special kind of rise of water, which can only be due to the happening of rain up the river.

are quite sufficient and it is needless to accept arthāpatti (implication), aitihya (tradition), sambhava (when a thing is understood in terms of higher measure the lower measure contained in it is also understood—if we know that there is a bushel of corn anywhere we understand that the same contains eight gallons of corn as well) and abhāva (non-existence) as separate pramāṇas for the tradition is included in verbal testimony and arthāpatti, sambhava and abhāva are included within inference.

The validity of these as pramāṇas is recognized, but they are said to be included in the four pramāṇas mentioned before. The theory of the eternity of sound is then refuted and the non-eternity proved in great detail. The meaning of words is said to refer to class-notions (*jāti*), individuals (*vyakti*), and the specific position of the limbs (*ākṛti*), by which the class notion is manifested. Class (*jāti*) is defined as that which produces the notion of sameness (*samānaprasavātmikā jātiḥ*).

The third book begins with the proofs for the existence of the self or ātman. It is said that each of the senses is associated with its own specific object, but there must exist some other entity in us which gathered together the different sense-cognitions and produced the perception of the total object as distinguished from the separate sense-perceptions. If there were no self then there would be no sin in injuring the bodies of men; again if there were no permanent self, no one would be able to recognize things as having seen them before; the two images produced by the eyes in visual perception could not also have been united together as one visual perception of the things[1]; moreover if there were no permanent cognizer then by the sight of a sour fruit one could not be reminded of its sour taste. If consciousness belonged to the senses only, then there would be no recognition, for the experience of one could not be recognized by another. If it is said that the unity of sensations could as well be effected by manas (mind), then the manas would serve the same purpose as self and it would only be a quarrel over a name, for this entity the knower would require some instrument by which it would co-ordinate the sensations and cognize; unless manas is admitted as a separate instrument of the soul, then though the sense perceptions could be explained as being the work of the

[1] According to Vātsyāyana, in the two eyes we have two different senses. Udyotakara, however, thinks that there is one visual sense which works in both eyes.

senses, yet imagining, thinking, etc., could not be explained. Another argument for the admission of soul is this, that infants show signs of pleasure and pain in quite early stages of infancy and this could not be due to anything but similar experiences in previous lives. Moreover every creature is born with some desires, and no one is seen to be born without desires. All attachments and desires are due to previous experiences, and therefore it is argued that desires in infants are due to their experience in previous existences.

The body is made up of the kṣiti element. The visual sense is material and so also are all other senses[1]. Incidentally the view held by some that the skin is the only organ of sensation is also refuted. The earth possesses four qualities, water three, fire two, air one, and ether one, but the sense of smell, taste, eye, and touch which are made respectively by the four elements of earth, etc., can only grasp the distinctive features of the elements of which they are made. Thus though the organ of smell is made by earth which contains four qualities, it can only grasp the distinctive quality of earth, viz. smell.

Against the Sāṃkhya distinction of *buddhi* (cognition) and *cit* (pure intelligence) it is said that there is no difference between the *buddhi* and *cit*. We do not find in our consciousness two elements of a phenomenal and a non-phenomenal consciousness, but only one, by whichever name it may be called. The Sāṃkhya epistemology that the antaḥkaraṇa assumes diverse forms in cognitive acts is also denied, and these are explained on the supposition of contacts of manas with the senses, ātman and external objects. The Buddhist objection against the Sāṃkhya explanation that the antaḥkaraṇas catch reflection from the external world just as a crystal does from the coloured objects that may lie near it, that there were really momentary productions of crystals and no permanent crystal catching different reflections at different times is refuted by Nyāya; for it says that it cannot be said that all creations are momentary, but it can only be agreed to in those cases where momentariness was actually experienced. In the case of the transformation of milk into curd there is no coming in of new qualities and disappearance of old ones, but

[1] It is well to remember that Sāṃkhya did not believe that the senses were constituted of the gross elements. But the Sāṃkhya-Yoga view represented in *Ātreya-saṃhitā* (*Caraka*) regarded the senses as bhautika or constituted of the gross elements.

the old milk is destroyed and the curd originates anew. The contact of manas with soul (*ātman*) takes place within the body and not in that part of ātman which is outside the body; knowledge belongs to the self and not to the senses or the object for even when they are destroyed knowledge remains. New cognitions destroy the old ones. No two recollections can be simultaneous. Desire and antipathy also belong to the soul. None of these can belong either to the body or to the mind (manas). Manas cannot be conscious for it is dependent upon self. Again if it was conscious then the actions done by it would have to be borne by the self and one cannot reap the fruits of the actions of another. The causes of recollection on the part of self are given as follows: (1) attention, (2) context, (3) repetition, (4) sign, (5) association, (6) likeness, (7) association of the possessor and the possessed or master and servant, or things which are generally seen to follow each other, (8) separation (as of husband and wife), (9) simpler employment, (10) opposition, (11) excess, (12) that from which anything can be got, (13) cover and covered, (14) pleasure and pain causing memory of that which caused them, (15) fear, (16) entreaty, (17) action such as that of the chariot reminding the charioteer, (18) affection, (19) merit and demerit[1]. It is said that knowledge does not belong to body, and then the question of the production of the body as due to adṛṣṭa is described. Salvation (*apavarga*) is effected by the manas being permanently separated from the soul (ātman) through the destruction of karma.

In the fourth book in course of the examination of doṣa (defects), it is said that moha (ignorance), is at the root of all other defects such as rāga (attachment) and dveṣa (antipathy). As against the Buddhist view that a thing could be produced by destruction, it is said that destruction is only a stage in the process of origination. Īśvara is regarded as the cause of the production of effects of deeds performed by men's efforts, for man is not always found to attain success according to his efforts. A reference is made to the doctrine of those who say that all things have come into being by no-cause (*animitta*), for then no-cause would be the cause, which is impossible.

The doctrine of some that all things are eternal is next refuted on the ground that we always see things produced and destroyed.

[1] *Nyāya sūtra* III. ii. 44.

The doctrine of the nihilistic Buddhists (śūnyavādin Bauddhas) that all things are what they are by virtue of their relations to other things, and that of other Buddhists who hold that there are merely the qualities and parts but no substances or wholes, are then refuted. The fruits of karmas are regarded as being like the fruits of trees which take some time before they can ripen. Even though there may be pleasures here and there, birth means sorrow for men, for even the man who enjoys pleasure is tormented by many sorrows, and sometimes one mistakes pains for pleasures. As there is no sorrow in the man who is in deep dreamless sleep, so there is no affliction (*kleśa*) in the man who attains apavarga (salvation)[1]. When once this state is attained all efforts (*pravṛtti*) cease for ever, for though efforts were beginningless with us they were all due to attachment, antipathy, etc. Then there are short discussions regarding the way in which egoism (*ahaṃkāra*) ceases with the knowledge of the true causes of defects (*doṣa*); about the nature of whole and parts and about the nature of atoms (*aṇus*) which cannot further be divided. A discussion is then introduced against the doctrine of the Vijñāna-vādins that nothing can be regarded as having any reality when separated from thoughts. Incidentally Yoga is mentioned as leading to right knowledge.

The whole of the fifth book which seems to be a later addition is devoted to the enumeration of different kinds of refutations (*nigrahasthāna*) and futilities (*jāti*).

Caraka, Nyāya sūtras and Vaiśeṣika sūtras.

When we compare the *Nyāya sūtras* with the *Vaiśeṣika sūtras* we find that in the former two or three different streams of purposes have met, whereas the latter is much more homogeneous. The large amount of materials relating to debates treated as a practical art for defeating an opponent would lead one to suppose that it was probably originally compiled from some other existing treatises which were used by Hindus and Buddhists alike for rendering themselves fit to hold their own in debates with their opponents[2]. This assumption is justified when

[1] Vātsyāyana notes that this is the salvation of him who has known Brahman, IV. i. 63.

[2] A reference to the *Suvarṇaprabhāsa sūtra* shows that the Buddhist missionaries used to get certain preparations for improving their voice in order to be able to argue with force, and they took to the worship of Sarasvatī (goddess of learning), who they supposed would help them in bringing readily before their mind all the information and ideas of which they stood so much in need at the time of debates.

we compare the futilities (jāti) quibbles (chala), etc., relating to disputations as found in the *Nyāya sūtra* with those that are found in the medical work of Caraka (A.D. 78), III. viii. There are no other works in early Sanskrit literature, excepting the *Nyāya sūtra* and *Caraka-saṃhitā* which have treated of these matters. Caraka's description of some of the categories (e.g. dṛṣṭānta, prayojana, pratijñā and vitaṇḍā) follows very closely the definitions given of those in the *Nyāya sūtras*. There are others such as the definitions of jalpa, chala, nigrahasthāna, etc., where the definitions of two authorities differ more. There are some other logical categories mentioned in Caraka (e.g. *pratiṣṭhāpanā*, *jijñāsā*, *vyavasāya*, *vākyadoṣa*, *vākyapraśaṃsā*, *upalambha*, *parihāra*, *abhyanujñā*, etc.) which are not found in the *Nyāya sūtra*[1]. Again, the various types of futilities (jāti) and points of opponent's refutation (*nigrahasthāna*) mentioned in the *Nyāya sūtra* are not found in *Caraka*. There are some terms which are found in slightly variant forms in the two works, e.g. *aupamya* in *Caraka*, *upamāna* in *Nyāya sūtra*, *arthāpatti* in *Nyāya sūtra* and *arthaprāpti* in *Caraka*. Caraka does not seem to know anything about the Nyāya work on this subject, and it is plain that the treatment of these terms of disputations in the *Caraka* is much simpler and less technical than what we find in the *Nyāya sūtras*. If we leave out the varieties of jāti and nigrahasthāna of the fifth book, there is on the whole a great agreement between the treatment of Caraka and that of the *Nyāya sūtras*. It seems therefore in a high degree probable that both Caraka and the *Nyāya sūtras* were indebted for their treatment of these terms of disputation to some other earlier work. Of these, Caraka's compilation was earlier, whereas the compilation of the *Nyāya sūtras* represents a later work when a hotter atmosphere of disputations had necessitated the use of more technical terms which are embodied in this work, but which were not contained in the earlier work. It does not seem therefore that this part of the work could have been earlier than the second century A.D. Another stream flowing through the *Nyāya sūtras* is that of a polemic against the doctrines which could be attributed to the Sautrāntika Buddhists, the Vijñānavāda Buddhists, the nihilists, the Sāṃkhya, the Cārvāka, and some other unknown schools of thought to which we find no

[1] Like Vaiśeṣika, Caraka does not know the threefold division of inference (*anumāna*) as *pūrvavat*, *śeṣavat* and *sāmānyatodṛṣṭa*.

further allusion elsewhere. The *Vaiśeṣika sūtras* as we have already seen had argued only against the Mīmāṃsā, and ultimately agreed with them on most points. The dispute with Mīmāṃsā in the *Nyāya sūtras* is the same as in the Vaiśeṣika over the question of the doctrine of the eternality of sound. The question of the self-validity of knowledge (*svataḥ prāmāṇyavāda*) and the akhyāti doctrine of illusion of the Mīmāṃsists, which form the two chief points of discussion between later Mīmāṃsā and later Nyāya, are never alluded to in the *Nyāya sūtras*. The advocacy of Yoga methods (*Nyāya sūtras*, IV. ii. 38–42 and 46) seems also to be an alien element; these are not found in Vaiśeṣika and are not in keeping with the general tendency of the *Nyāya sūtras*, and the Japanese tradition that Mirok added them later on as Mahāmahopādhyāya Haraprasāda Śāstrī has pointed out[1] is not improbable.

The *Vaiśeṣika sūtras*, III. i. 18 and III. ii. 1, describe perceptional knowledge as produced by the close proximity of the self (ātman), the senses and the objects of sense, and they also adhere to the doctrine, that colour can only be perceived under special conditions of *saṃskāra* (conglomeration etc.). The reason for inferring the existence of manas from the non-simultaneity (*ayaugapadya*) of knowledge and efforts is almost the same with Vaiśeṣika as with Nyāya. The *Nyāya sūtras* give a more technical definition of perception, but do not bring in the questions of saṃskāra or udbhūtarūpavattva which Vaiśeṣika does. On the question of inference Nyāya gives three classifications as pūrvavat, śeṣavat and sāmānyatodṛṣṭa, but no definition. The *Vaiśeṣika sūtras* do not know of these classifications, and give only particular types or instances of inference (V. S. III. i. 7–17, IX. ii. 1–2, 4–5). Inference is said to be made when a thing is in contact with another, or when it is in a relation of inherence in it, or when it inheres in a third thing; one kind of effect may lead to the inference of another kind of effect, and so on. These are but mere collections of specific instances of inference without reaching a general theory. The doctrine of vyāpti (concomitance of *hetu* (reason) and *sādhya* (probandum)) which became so important in later Nyāya has never been properly formulated either in the *Nyāya sūtras* or in the Vaiśeṣika. *Vaiśeṣika sūtra*, III. i. 24, no doubt assumes the knowledge of concomitance between hetu and sādhya (*prasiddhipūrvakatvāt apadeśasya*),

[1] *J.A.S.B.* 1905.

but the technical vyāpti is not known, and the connotation of the term *prasiddhipūrvakatva* of Vaiśeṣika seems to be more loose than the term *vyāpti* as we know it in the later Nyāya. The *Vaiśeṣika sūtras* do not count scriptures (*śabda*) as a separate pramāṇa, but they tacitly admit the great validity of the Vedas. With *Nyāya sūtras* śabda as a pramāṇa applies not only to the Vedas, but to the testimony of any trustworthy person, and Vātsyāyana says that trustworthy persons may be of three kinds *ṛṣi, ārya* and *mleccha* (foreigners). Upamāna which is regarded as a means of right cognition in Nyāya is not even referred to in the *Vaiśeṣika sūtras*. The *Nyāya sūtras* know of other pramāṇas, such as *arthāpatti, sambhava* and *aitihya*, but include them within the pramāṇas admitted by them, but the *Vaiśeṣika sūtras* do not seem to know them at all[1]. The *Vaiśeṣika sūtras* believe in the perception of negation (abhāva) through the perception of the locus to which such negation refers (IX. i. 1–10). *The Nyāya sūtras* (II. ii. 1, 2, 7–12) consider that abhāva as non-existence or negation can be perceived; when one asks another to "bring the clothes which are not marked," he finds that marks are absent in some clothes and brings them; so it is argued that absence or non-existence can be directly perceived[2]. Though there is thus an agreement between the Nyāya and the *Vaiśeṣika sūtras* about the acceptance of abhāva as being due to perception, yet their method of handling the matter is different. The *Nyāya sūtras* say nothing about the categories of *dravya, guṇa, karma, viśeṣa* and *samavāya* which form the main subjects of Vaiśeṣka discussions[3]. The *Nyāya sūtras* take much pains to prove the materiality of the senses. But this question does not seem to have been important with Vaiśeṣika. The slight reference to this question in VIII. ii. 5-6 can hardly be regarded as sufficient. The *Vaiśeṣika sūtras* do not mention the name of "Īśvara," whereas the *Nyāya sūtras* try to prove his existence on eschatological grounds. The reasons given in support of the existence of self in the *Nyāya sūtras* are mainly on the ground of the unity of sense-cognitions and the phenomenon of recognition, whereas the

[1] The only old authority which knows these pramāṇas is Caraka. But he also gives an interpretation of sambhava which is different from Nyāya and calls *arthāpatti arthaprāpti* (*Caraka* III. viii.).

[2] The details of this example are taken from Vātsyāyana's commentary.

[3] The *Nyāya sūtra* no doubt incidentally gives a definition of jāti as "*samānaprasavātmikā jātiḥ*" (II. ii. 71).

Vaiśeṣika lays its main emphasis on self-consciousness as a fact of knowledge. Both the Nyāya and the *Vaiśeṣika sūtras* admit the existence of atoms, but all the details of the doctrine of atomic structure in later Nyāya-Vaiśeṣika are absent there. The Vaiśeṣika calls salvation *niḥśreyasa* or *mokṣa* and the Nyāya *apavarga.* Mokṣa with Vaiśeṣika is the permanent cessation of connection with body; the apavarga with Nyāya is cessation of pain[1]. In later times the main points of difference between the Vaiśeṣika and Nyāya are said to lie with regard to theory of the notion of number, changes of colour in the molecules by heat, etc. Thus the former admitted a special procedure of the mind by which cognitions of number arose in the mind (e.g. at the first moment there is the sense contact with an object, then the notion of oneness, then from a sense of relativeness—apeksābuddhi—notion of two, then a notion of two-ness, and then the notion of two things); again, the doctrine of pilupāka (changes of qualities by heat are produced in atoms and not in molecules as Nyāya held) was held by Vaiśeṣika, which the Naiyāyikas did not admit[2]. But as the *Nyāya sūtras* are silent on these points, it is not possible to say that such were really the differences between early Nyāya and early Vaiśeṣika. These differences may be said to hold between the later interpreters of Vaiśeṣika and the later interpreters of Nyāya. The Vaiśeṣika as we find it in the commentary of Praśastapāda (probably sixth century A.D.), and the Nyāya from the time of Udyotakara have come to be treated as almost the same system with slight variations only. I have therefore preferred to treat them together. The main presentation of the Nyāya-Vaiśeṣika philosophy in this chapter is that which is found from the sixth century onwards.

The Vaiśeṣika and Nyāya Literature.

It is difficult to ascertain definitely the date of the *Vaiśeṣika sūtras* by Kaṇāda, also called Aulūkya the son of Ulūka, though there is every reason to suppose it to be pre-Buddhistic. It

[1] Professor Vanamālī Vedāntatīrtha quotes a passage from *Saṃkṣepaśaṅkarajaya*, XVI. 68-69 in *J.A.S.B.*, 1905, and another passage from a Nyāya writer Bhāsarvajña, pp. 39-41, in *J.A.S.B.*, 1914, to show that the old Naiyāyikas considered that there was an element of happiness (*sukha*) in the state of mukti (salvation) which the Vaiśeṣikas denied. No evidence in support of this opinion is found in the Nyāya or the *Vaiśeṣika sūtras*, unless the cessation of pain with Nyāya is interpreted as meaning the presence of some sort of bliss or happiness.

[2] See Mādhava's *Sarvadarśanasaṃgraha-Aulūkyadarśana.*

appears from the *Vāyu purāna* that he was born in Prabhāsa near Dvārakā, and was the disciple of Somaśarmā. The time of Praśastapāda who wrote a bhāṣya (commentary) of the *Vaiśeṣika sūtras* cannot also unfortunately be ascertained. The peculiarity of Praśastapāda's bhāṣya is this that unlike other bhāṣyas (which first give brief explanations of the text of the sūtras and then continue to elaborate independent explanations by explaining the first brief comments), it does not follow the sūtras but is an independent dissertation based on their main contents[1]. There were two other bhāṣyas on the *Vaiśeṣika sūtras*, namely *Rāvaṇa-bhāṣya* and *Bharādvāja-vṛtti*, but these are now probably lost. References to the former are found in *Kiraṇāvalībhāskara* of Padmanābha Miśra and also in *Ratnaprabhā* 2. 2. 11. Four commentaries were written on this bhāṣya, namely *Vyomavatī* by Vyomaśekharācārya, *Nyāyakandalī* by Śrīdhara, *Kiraṇāvalī* by Udayana (A.D. 984) and *Līlávatī* by Śrīvatsācārya. In addition to these Jagadīśa Bhaṭṭacārya of Navadvīpa and Śaṅkara Miśra wrote two other commentaries on the *Praśastapāda-bhāsya*, namely *Bhāṣyasūkti* and *Kaṇāda-rahasya*. Śaṅkara Miśra (A.D. 1425) also wrote a commentary on the *Vaiśeṣika sūtras* called the *Upaskāra*. Of these *Nyāya-kandalī* of Śrīdhara on account of its simplicity of style and elaborate nature of exposition is probably the best for a modern student of Vaiśeṣika. Its author was a native of the village of Bhūrisṛṣṭ in Bengal (Rāḍha). His father's name was Baladeva and mother's name was Acchokā and he wrote his work in 913 Śaka era (A.D. 990) as he himself writes at the end of his work.

The *Nyāya sūtra* was written by Akṣapāda or Gautama, and the earliest commentary on it written by Vātsyāyana is known as the *Vātsyāyana-bhāṣya*. The date of Vātsyāyana has not

[1] The bhāṣya of Praśastapāda can hardly be called a bhāṣya (elaborate commentary). He himself makes no such claim and calls his work a compendium of the properties of the categories (*Padārthadharmasaṃgraha*). He takes the categories of *dravya*, *guṇa*, *karma*, *sāmānya*, *viśeṣa* and *samavāya* in order and without raising any discussions plainly narrates what he has got to say on them. Some of the doctrines which are important in later Nyāya-Vaiśeṣika discussions, such as the doctrine of creation and dissolution, doctrine of number, the theory that the number of atoms contributes to the atomic measure of the molecules, the doctrine of pilupāka in connection with the transformation of colours by heat occur in his narration for the first time as the *Vaiśeṣika sūtras* are silent on these points. It is difficult to ascertain his date definitely; he is the earliest writer on Vaiśeṣika available to us after Kaṇāda and it is not improbable that he lived in the fifth or sixth century A.D.

been definitely settled, but there is reason to believe that he lived some time in the beginning of the fourth century A.D. Jacobi places him in A.D. 300. Udyotakara (about A.D. 635) wrote a *Vārttika* on Vātsyāyana's bhāṣya to establish the Nyāya views and to refute the criticisms of the Buddhist logician Diṅnāga (about A.D. 500) in his *Pramāṇasamuccaya.* Vācaspatimiśra (A.D. 840) wrote a sub-commentary on the *Nyāyavārttika* of Udyotakara called *Nyāyavārttikatātparyaṭīkā* in order to make clear the right meanings of Udyotakara's *Vārttika* which was sinking in the mud as it were through numerous other bad writings (*dustarakunibandhapaṅkamagnānām*). Udayana (A.D. 984) wrote a sub-commentary on the *Tātparyaṭīkā* called *Tātparyaṭīkā-pariśuddhi*. Varddhamāna (A.D. 1225) wrote a sub-commentary on that called the *Nyāyanibandhaprakāśa*. Padmanābha wrote a sub-commentary on that called *Varddhamānendu* and Śaṅkara Miśra (A.D. 1425) wrote a sub-commentary on that called the *Nyāyatātparyamaṇḍana*. In the seventeenth century Viśvanātha wrote an independent short commentary known as *Viśvanāthavṛtti*, on the *Nyāya sūtra*, and Rādhāmohana wrote a separate commentary on the *Nyāya sūtras* known as *Nyāyasūtravivaraṇa*. In addition to these works on the *Nyāya sūtras* many other independent works of great philosophical value have been written on the Nyāya system. The most important of these in medieval times is the *Nyāyamañjarī* of Jayanta (A.D. 880), who flourished shortly after Vācaspatimiśra. Jayanta chooses some of *the Nyāya sūtras* for interpretation, but he discusses the Nyāya views quite independently, and criticizes the views of other systems of Indian thought of his time. It is far more comprehensive than Vācaspati's *Tātparyaṭīkā*, and its style is most delightfully lucid. Another important work is Udayana's *Kusumāñjali* in which he tries to prove the existence of Īśvara (God). This work ought to be read with its commentary *Prakāśa* by Varddhamāna (A.D. 1225) and its sub-commentary *Makaranda* by Rucidatta (A.D. 1275). Udayana's *Ātmatattvaviveka* is a polemical work against the Buddhists, in which he tries to establish the Nyāya doctrine of soul. In addition to these we have a number of useful works on Nyāya in later times. Of these the following deserve special mention in connection with the present work. *Bhāṣāpariccheda* by Viśvanātha with its commentaries *Muktāvalī*, *Dinakarī* and *Rāmarudrī*, *Tarka-samgraha* with *Nyāyanirṇaya*, *Tarkabhāṣā* of Keśava Miśra with the commentary *Nyāyapradīpa*, *Saptapadārthī* of Śivāditya, *Tārkikarakṣā* of Varadarāja with the commentary *Niṣkaṇṭaka* of Mallinātha, *Nyāyasāra* of Mādhava Deva of the city of Dhāra and *Nyāyasiddhāntamañjarī* of Jānakīnātha Bhaṭṭācarya with the *Nyāyamañjarīsāra* by Yādavācārya, and *Nyāyasiddhāntadīpa* of Śaśadhara with *Prabhā* by Śeṣānantācārya.

The new school of Nyāya philosophy known as Navya-Nyāya began with Gaṅgeśa Upādhyāya of Mithilā, about A.D. 1200. Gaṅgeśa wrote only on the four pramāṇas admitted by the Nyāya, viz. pratyakṣa, anumāna, upamāna, and śabda, and not on any of the topics of Nyāya metaphysics. But it so happened that his discussions on anumāna (inference) attracted unusually great attention in Navadvīpa (Bengal), and large numbers of commentaries and commentaries of commentaries were written on the anumāna portion of his work *Tattvacintāmaṇi*, and many independent treatises on śabda and anumāna were also written by the scholars of Bengal, which became thenceforth for some centuries the home of Nyāya studies. The commentaries of Raghunātha Śiromaṇi (A.D. 1500), Mathurā Bhaṭṭācārya (A.D. 1580), Gadādhara Bhaṭṭācārya (A.D. 1650) and Jagadīśa Bhaṭṭācārya (A.D. 1590), commentaries on Śiromaṇi's commentary on *Tattvacintāmani*, had been very widely read in Bengal. The new school of Nyāya became the most important study in Navadvīpa and there appeared a series of thinkers who produced an extensive literature on the subject[1]. The contribution was not in the direction of metaphysics, theology, ethics, or religion, but consisted mainly in developing a system of linguistic notations to specify accurately and precisely any concept or its relation with other concepts[2].

Thus for example when they wished to define precisely the nature of the concomitance of one concept with another (e.g. smoke and fire), they would so specify the relation that the exact nature of the concomitance should be clearly expressed, and that there should be no confusion or ambiguity. Close subtle analytic thinking and the development of a system of highly technical

[1] From the latter half of the twelfth century to the third quarter of the sixteenth century the new school of Nyāya was started in Mithilā (Behar); but from the fifteenth to the seventeenth century Bengal became pre-eminently the home of Nyāya studies. See Mr Cakravarttī's paper, *J. A. S. B.* 1915. I am indebted to it for some of the dates mentioned in this section.

[2] *Iśvarānumāna* of Raghunātha as well as his *Padārthatattvanirūpaṇa* are, however, notable exceptions.

expressions mark the development of this literature. The technical expressions invented by this school were thus generally accepted even by other systems of thought, wherever the need of accurate and subtle thinking was felt. But from the time that Sanskrit ceased to be the vehicle of philosophical thinking in India the importance of this literature has gradually lost ground, and it can hardly be hoped that it will ever regain its old position by attracting enthusiastic students in large numbers.

I cannot close this chapter without mentioning the fact that so far as the logical portion of the Nyāya system is concerned, though Akṣapāda was the first to write a comprehensive account of it, the Jains and Buddhists in medieval times had independently worked at this subject and had criticized the Nyāya account of logic and made valuable contributions. In Jaina logic *Daśavaikālikaniryukti* of Bhadrabāhu (B.C. 357), Umāsvāti's *Tattvārthādhigama sūtra*, *Nyāyāvatāra* of Siddhasena Divākara (A.D. 533), Māṇikya Nandī's (A.D.800) *Parīkṣāmukha sūtra*, and *Pramāṇanayatattvālokālaṃkāra* of Deva Sūri (A.D. 1159) and *Prameyakamalamārtaṇḍa* of Prabhācandra deserve special notice. *Pramāṇasamuccaya* and *Nyāyapraveśa* of Diṅnāga (A.D. 500), *Pramāṇavārttika kārikā* and *Nyāyabindu* of Dharmakīrtti (A.D. 650) with the commentary of Dharmottara are the most interesting of the Buddhist works on systematic logic[1]. The diverse points of difference between the Hindu, Jain and Buddhist logic require to be dealt with in a separate work on Indian logic and can hardly be treated within the compass of the present volume.

It is interesting to notice that between the *Vātsyāyana bhāṣya* and the Udyotakara's *Vārttika* no Hindu work on logic of importance seems to have been written: it appears that the science of logic in this period was in the hands of the Jains and the Buddhists; and it was Diṅnāga's criticism of Hindu Nyāya that roused Udyotakara to write the *Vārttika*. The Buddhist and the Jain method of treating logic separately from metaphysics as an independent study was not accepted by the Hindus till we come to Gaṅgeśa, and there is probably only one Hindu work of importance on Nyāya in the Buddhist style namely *Nyāyasāra* of Bhāsarvajña. Other older Hindu works generally treated of

[1] See *Indian Logic Medieval School*, by Dr S. C. Vidyābhūṣaṇa, for a bibliography of Jain and Buddhist Logic.

inference only along with metaphysical and other points of Nyāya interest[1].

The main doctrine of the Nyaya-Vaiśeṣika Philosophy[2].

The Nyāya-Vaiśeṣika having dismissed the doctrine of momentariness took a common-sense view of things, and held that things remain permanent until suitable collocations so arrange themselves that the thing can be destroyed. Thus the jug continues to remain a jug unless or until it is broken to pieces by the stroke of a stick. Things exist not because they can produce an impression on us, or serve my purposes either directly or through knowledge, as the Buddhists suppose, but because existence is one of their characteristics. If I or you or any other perceiver did not exist, the things would continue to exist all the same. Whether they produce any effect on us or on their surrounding environments is immaterial. Existence is the most general characteristic of things, and it is on account of this that things are testified by experience to be existing.

As the Nyāya-Vaiśeṣikas depended solely on experience and on valid reasons, they dismissed the Sāṃkhya cosmology, but accepted the atomic doctrine of the four elements (*bhūtas*), earth (*kṣiti*), water (*ap*), fire (*tejas*), and air (*marut*). These atoms are eternal; the fifth substance (*ākāsa*) is all pervasive and eternal. It is regarded as the cause of propagating sound; though all-pervading and thus in touch with the ears of all persons, it manifests sound only in the ear-drum, as it is only there that it shows itself as a sense-organ and manifests such sounds as the man deserves to hear by reason of his merit and demerit. Thus a deaf man though he has the ākāśa as his sense of hearing, cannot hear on account of his demerit which impedes the faculty of that sense organ[3]. In addition to these they admitted the existence of time (*kāla*) as extending from the past through the present to the

[1] Almost all the books on Nyāya and Vaiśeṣika referred to have been consulted in the writing of this chapter. Those who want to be acquainted with a fuller bibliography of the new school of logic should refer to the paper called "The History of Navya Nyāya in Bengal," by Mr Cakravarttī in *J. A. S. B.* 1915.

[2] I have treated Nyāya and Vaiśeṣika as the same system. Whatever may have been their original differences, they are regarded since about A.D. 600 as being in complete agreement except in some minor points. The views of one system are often supplemented by those of the other. The original character of the two systems has already been treated.

[3] See *Nyāyakandalī*, pp. 59–64.

endless futurity before us. Had there been no time we could have no knowledge of it and there would be nothing to account for our time-notions associated with all changes. The Sāṃkhya did not admit the existence of any real time; to them the unit of kāla is regarded as the time taken by an atom to traverse its own unit of space. It has no existence separate from the atoms and their movements. The appearance of kāla as a separate entity is a creation of our buddhi (*buddhinirmāṇa*) as it represents the order or mode in which the buddhi records its perceptions. But kāla in Nyaya-Vaiśeṣika is regarded as a substance existing by itself. In accordance with the changes of things it reveals itself as past, present, and future. Sāṃkhya regarded it as past, present, and future, as being the modes of the constitution of the things in its different manifesting stages of evolution (*adhvan*). The astronomers regarded it as being due to the motion of the planets. These must all be contrasted with the Nyāya-Vaiśeṣika conception of kāla which is regarded as an all-pervading, partless substance which appears as many in association with the changes related to it[1].

The seventh substance is relative space (*dik*). It is that substance by virtue of which things are perceived as being on the right, left, east, west, upwards and downwards; kāla like dik is also one. But yet tradition has given us varieties of it in the eight directions and in the upper and lower[2]. The eighth substance is the soul (*ātman*) which is all-pervading. There are separate ātmans for each person; the qualities of knowledge, feelings of pleasure and pain, desire, etc. belong to *ātman*. Manas (mind) is the ninth substance. It is atomic in size and the vehicle of memory; all affections of the soul such as knowing, feeling, and willing, are generated by the connection of manas with soul, the senses and the objects. It is the intermediate link which connects the soul with the senses, and thereby produces the affections of knowledge, feeling, or willing. With each single connection of soul with manas we have a separate affection of the soul, and thus our intellectual experience is conducted in a series, one coming after another and not simultaneously. Over and above all these we have Īśvara. The definition

[1] See *Nyāyakandalī*, pp. 64–66, and *Nyāyamañjarī*, pp. 136–139. The *Vaiśeṣika sūtras* regarded time as the cause of things which suffer change but denied it of things which are eternal.

[2] See *Nyāyakandalī*, pp. 66–69, and *Nyāyamañjarī*, p. 140 .

of substance consists in this, that it is independent by itself, whereas the other things such as quality (*guṇa*), action (*karma*), sameness or generality (*sāmānya*), speciality or specific individuality (*viśeṣa*) and the relation of inherence (*samavāya*) cannot show themselves without the help of substance (*dravya*). Dravya is thus the place of rest (*āśraya*) on which all the others depend (*āśṛta*). Dravya, guṇa, karma, sāmānya, viśeṣa, and samavāya are the six original entities of which all things in the world are made up[1]. When a man through some special merit, by the cultivation of reason and a thorough knowledge of the fallacies and pitfalls in the way of right thinking, comes to know the respective characteristics and differences of the above entities, he ceases to have any passions and to work in accordance with their promptings and attains a conviction of the nature of self, and is liberated[2]. The Nyāya-Vaiśeṣika is a pluralistic system which neither tries to reduce the diversity of experience to any universal principle, nor dismisses patent facts of experience on the strength of the demands of the logical coherence of mere abstract thought. The entities it admits are taken directly from experience. The underlying principle is that at the root of each kind of perception there must be something to which the perception is due. It classified the percepts and concepts of experience into several ultimate types or categories (*padārtha*), and held that the notion of each type was due to the presence of that entity. These types are six in number—dravya, guṇa, etc. If we take a percept "I see a red book," the book appears to be an independent entity on which rests the concept of "redness" and "oneness," and we thus call the book a substance (*dravya*); dravya is thus defined as that which has the characteristic of a dravya (*dravyatva*). So also guṇa and karma. In the subdivision of different kinds of dravya also the same principle of classification is followed. In contrasting it with Sāṃkhya or Buddhism we see that for each unit of sensation (say

[1] *Abhāva* (negation) as dependent on bhāva (position) is mentioned in the *Vaiśeṣika sūtras*. Later Nyāya writers such as Udayana include *abhāva* as a separate category, but Śridhara a contemporary of Udayana rightly remarks that abhāva was not counted by Praśastapāda as it was dependent on bhāva—"*abhāvasya pṛthaganupadeśaḥ bhāvapāratantryāt na tvabhāvāt.*" *Nyāyakandalī*, p. 6, and *Lakṣaṇāvalī*, p. 2.

[2] "*Tattvato jñāteṣu bāhyādhyātmikeṣu viṣayeṣu doṣadarśanāt viraktasya samīhānivṛttau ātmajñasya tadarthāni karmāṇyakurvataḥ tatparityāgasādhanāni śrutismṛtyuditāni asaṅkalpitaphalāni upādadānasya ātmajñānamabhyàsyataḥ prakṛṣṭanivarttakadharmopacaye sati paripakvātmajñānasyātyantikaśarīraviyogasya bhāvāt.*" *Ibid*. p. 7.

whiteness) the latter would admit a corresponding real, but Nyāya-Vaiśeṣika would collect "all whiteness" under the name of "the quality of white colour" which the atom possessed.[1] They only regarded as a separate entity what represented an ultimate mode of thought. They did not enquire whether such notions could be regarded as the modification of some other notion or not; but whenever they found that there were some experiences which were similar and universal, they classed them as separate entities or categories.

The six Padārthas: Dravya, Guṇa, Karma, Sāmānya, Viśeṣa, Samavāya.

Of the six classes of entities or categories (*padārtha*) we have already given some account of dravya[2]. Let us now turn to the others. Of the qualities (*guṇa*) the first one called *rūpa* (colour) is that which can be apprehended by the eye alone and not by any other sense. The colours are white, blue, yellow, red, green, brown and variegated (*citra*). Colours are found only in kṣiti, ap and tejas. The colours of ap and tejas are permanent (*nitya*), but the colour of kṣiti changes when heat is applied, and this, Śrīdhara holds, is due to the fact that heat changes the atomic structure of kṣiti (earth) and thus the old constitution of the substance being destroyed, its old colour is also destroyed, and a new one is generated. Rūpa is the general name for the specific individual colours. There is the genus *rū-patva* (colourness), and the rūpa guṇa (quality) is that on which rests this genus; rūpa is not itself a genus and can be apprehended by the eye.

The second is *rasa* (taste), that quality of things which can be apprehended only by the tongue; these are sweet, sour, pungent (*kaṭu*), astringent (*kaṣāya*) and bitter (*tikta*). Only kṣiti and ap have taste. The natural taste of ap is sweetness. Rasa like rūpa also denotes the genus rasatva, and rasa as quality must be distinguished from rasa as genus, though both of them are apprehended by the tongue.

The third is *gandha* (odour), that quality which can be apprehended by the nose alone. It belongs to kṣiti alone. Water

[1] The reference is to Sautrāntika Buddhism, "*yo yo viruddhādhyāsavān nāsāve-kaḥ.*" See Paṇḍitāśoka's *Avayavinirākaraṇa, Six Buddhist Nyāya tracts*.

[2] The word "*padārtha*" literally means denotations of words.

or air is apprehended as having odour on account of the presence of earth materials.

The fourth is *sparśa* (touch), that quality which can be apprehended only by the skin. There are three kinds of touch, cold, hot, neither hot nor cold. Sparśa belongs to kṣiti; ap, tejas, and vāyu. The fifth *śabda* (sound) is an attribute of ākāśa. Had there been no ākāśa there would have been no sound.

The sixth is saṃkhyā (number), that entity of quality belonging to things by virtue of which we can count them as one, two, three, etc. The conception of numbers two, three, etc. is due to a relative oscillatory state of the mind (*apekṣābuddhi*); thus when there are two jugs before my eyes, I have the notion—This is one jug and that is another jug. This is called apekṣābuddhi; then in the two jugs there arises the quality of twoness (*dvitva*) and then an indeterminate perception (*nirvikalpa-dvitva-guṇa*) of dvitva in us and then the determinate perceptions that there are the two jugs. The conceptions of other numbers as well as of many arise in a similar manner[1].

The seventh is *parimiti* (measure), that entity of quality in things by virtue of which we perceive them as great or small and speak of them as such. The measure of the partless atoms is called *parimaṇḍala parimāṇa*; it is eternal, and it cannot generate the measure of any other thing. Its measure is its own absolutely; when two atoms generate a dyad (*dvyaṇuka*) it is not the measure of the atom that generates the aṇu (atomic) and the *hrasva* (small) measure of the dyad molecule (*dvyaṇuka*), for then the size (*parimāṇa*) of it would have been still smaller than the measure of the atom (*parimaṇḍala*), whereas the measure of the dyaṇuka is of a different kind, namely the small (*hrasva*)[2]. Of course two atoms generate a dyad, but then the number (saṃkhyā) of the atom should be regarded as bringing forth a new kind of measure, namely the small (*hrasva*) measure in the dyads. So again when three dyads (dyaṇuka) compose a tryaṇuka the number and not the measure "small"

[1] This is distinctively a Vaiśeṣika view introduced by Praśastapāda. Nyāya seems to be silent on this matter. See Śaṅkara Miśra's *Upaskāra*, VII. ii. 8.

[2] It should be noted that the atomic measure appears in two forms as eternal as in "paramāṇus" and non-eternal as in the dvyaṇuka. The parimaṇḍala parimāṇa is thus a variety of aṇuparimāṇa. The aṇuparimāṇa and the hrasvaparimāṇa represent the two dimensions of the measure of dvyaṇukas as mahat and dīrgha are with reference to tryaṇukas. See *Nyāyakandalī*, p. 133.

(*hrasva*) of the dyad is the cause of the measure "great" (*mahat*) of the tryaṇuka. But when we come to the region of these gross tryaṇukas we find that the "great" measure of the tryaṇukas is the cause of the measure of other grosser bodies composed by them. For as many tryaṇukas constitute a gross body, so much bigger does the thing become. Thus the cumulation of the tryaṇukas of mahat parimāṇa makes things of still more mahat parimāṇa. The measure of tryaṇukas is not only regarded as mahat but also as dīrgha (long) and this dīrgha parimāṇa has to be admitted as coexisting with mahat parimāṇa but not identical, for things not only appear as great but also as long (*dīrgha*). Here we find that the accumulation of tryaṇukas means the accumulation of "great" (*mahat*) and "long" (*dīrgha*) parimāṇa, and hence the thing generated happens to possess a measure which is greater and longer than the individual atoms which composed them. Now the hrasva parimāṇa of the dyads is not regarded as having a lower degree of greatness or length but as a separate and distinct type of measure which is called small (*hrasva*). As accumulation of grossness, greatness or length, generates still more greatness, grossness and length in its effect, so an accumulation of the hrasva (small) parimāṇa ought to generate still more hrasva parimāṇa, and we should expect that if the hrasva measure of the dyads was the cause of the measure of the tryaṇukas, the tryaṇukas should be even smaller than the dyaṇukas. So also if the atomic and circular (*parimaṇḍala*) size of the atoms is regarded as generating by their measure the measure of the dyaṇukas, then the measure of the dyaṇukas ought to be more atomic than the atoms. The atomic, small, and great measures should not be regarded as representing successively bigger measures produced by the mere cumulation of measures, but each should be regarded as a measure absolutely distinct, different from or foreign to the other measure. It is therefore held that if grossness in the cause generates still more greatness in the effect, the smallness and the parimaṇḍala measure of the dyads and atoms ought to generate still more smallness and subtleness in their effect. But since the dyads and the tryaṇuka molecules are seen to be constituted of atoms and dyads respectively, and yet are not found to share the measure of their causes, it is to be argued that the measures of the atoms and dyads do not generate the measure of their effects, but it is their *number* which is the cause of the measure of the latter. This explains aṇuparimāṇa, hrasva parimāṇa, mahat parimāṇa, and dīrgha parimāṇa. The parimāṇa of ākāśa, kāla, dik and ātman which are regarded as all-pervasive, is said to be paramamahat (absolutely large). The parimāṇas of the atoms, ākāśa, kāla, dik, manas, and ātman are regarded as eternal (*nitya*). All other kinds of parimāṇas as belonging to non-eternal things are regarded as non-eternal.

The eighth is *pṛthaktva* (mutual difference or separateness of things), that entity or quality in things by virtue of which things appear as different (e.g. this is different from that). Difference is perceived by us as a positive notion and not as a mere negation such as this jug is not this pot.

The ninth is *saṃyoga* (connection), that entity of guṇa by virtue of which things appear to us as connected.

The tenth is *vibhāga* (separation), that entity of guṇa which destroys the connection or contact of things.

The eleventh and twelfth *guṇas*, *paratva* and *aparatva*, give rise in us to the perceptions of long time and short time, remote and near.

The other guṇas such as *buddhi* (knowledge), *sukha* (happiness), *duḥkha* (sorrow), *icchā* (will), *dveṣa* (antipathy or hatred) and *yatna* (effort) can occur only with reference to soul.

The characteristic of *gurutva* (heaviness) is that by virtue of which things fall to the ground. The guṇa of *sneha* (oiliness) belongs to water. The guṇa of *saṃskāra* is of three kinds, (1) *vega* (velocity) which keeps a thing moving in different directions, (2) *sthiti-sthāpaka* (elasticity) on account of which a gross thing tries to get back its old state even though disturbed, (3) *bhāvanā* is that quality of ātman by which things are constantly practised or by which things experienced are remembered and recognized[1]. *Dharma* is the quality the presence of which enables the soul to enjoy happiness or to attain salvation[2]. *Adharma* is

[1] Praśastapāda says that bhāvanā is a special characteristic of the soul, contrary to intoxication, sorrow and knowledge, by which things seen, heard and felt are remembered and recognized. Through unexpectedness (as the sight of a camel for a man of South India), repetition (as in studies, art etc.) and intensity of interest, the saṃskāra becomes particularly strong. See *Nyāyakandalī*, p. 267. Kaṇāda however is silent on these points. He only says that by a special kind of contact of the mind with soul and also by the saṃskāra, memory (smṛti) is produced (IX. 2. 6).

[2] Praśastapāda speaks of *dharma* (merit) as being a quality of the soul. Thereupon Śrīdhara points out that this view does not admit that dharma is a power of karma (*na karmasāmarthyam*). Sacrifice etc. cannot be dharma for these actions being momentary

the opposite quality, the presence of which in the soul leads a man to suffer. *Adṛṣṭa* or destiny is that unknown quality of things and of the soul which brings about the cosmic order, and arranges it for the experience of the souls in accordance with their merits or demerits.

Karma means movement; it is the third thing which must be held to be as irreducible a reality as dravya or guṇa. There are five kinds of movement, (1) upward, (2) downward, (3) contraction, (4) expansion, (5) movement in general. All kinds of karmas rest on substances just as the guṇas do, and cause the things to which they belong to move.

Sāmānya is the fourth category. It means the genus, or aspect of generality or sameness that we notice in things. Thus in spite of the difference of colour between one cow and another, both of them are found to have such a sameness that we call them cows. In spite of all diversity in all objects around us, they are all perceived as *sat* or existing. This *sat* or existence is thus a sameness, which is found to exist in all the three things, dravya, guṇa, and karma. This sameness is called *sāmānya* or *jāti*, and it is regarded as a separate thing which rests on dravya, guṇa, or karma. This highest genus *sattā* (being) is called *parajāti* (highest universal), the other intermediate jātis are called *aparajāti* (lower universals), such as the genus of dravya, of karma, or of guṇa, or still more intermediate jātis such as *gotvajāti* (the genus cow), *nīlatvajāti* (the genus blue). The intermediate jātis or genera sometimes appear to have a special aspect as a species, such as *paśutva* (animal jāti) and *gotva* (the cow jāti); here however gotva appears as a species, yet it is in reality nothing but a jāti. The aspect as species has no separate existence. It is jāti which from one aspect appears as genus and from another as species.

they cannot generate the effects which are only to be reaped at a future time. If the action is destroyed its power (*sāmarthya*) cannot last. So dharma is to be admitted as a quality generated in the self by certain courses of conduct which produce happiness for him when helped by certain other conditions of time, place, etc. Faith (*śraddhā*), non-injury, doing good to all beings, truthfulness, non-stealing, sex-control, sincerity, control of anger, ablutions, taking of pure food, devotion to particular gods, fasting, strict adherence to scriptural duties, and the performance of duties assigned to each caste and stage of life, are enumerated by Praśastapāda as producing dharma. The person who strictly adheres to these duties and the *yamas* and *niyamas* (cf. Patañjali's Yoga) and attains Yoga by a meditation on the six padārthas attains a dharma which brings liberation (*mokṣa*). Śrīdhara refers to the Sāṃkhya-Yoga account of the method of attaining salvation (*Nyāyakandalī*, pp. 272–280). See also Vallabha's *Nyāyalīlāvatī*, pp. 74–75. (Bombay, 1915.)

This jāti or *sāmānya* thus must be regarded as having a separate independent reality though it is existent in dravya, guṇa and karma. The Buddhists denied the existence of any independent reality of sāmānya, but said that the sameness as cow was really but the negation of all non-cows (*apoha*). The perception of cow realizes the negation of all non-cows and this is represented in consciousness as the sameness as cow. He who should regard this sameness to be a separate and independent reality perceived in experience might also discover two horns on his own head[1]. The Nyāya-Vaiśeṣika said that negation of non-cows is a negative perception, whereas the sameness perceived as cow is a positive perception, which cannot be explained by the aforesaid negation theory of the Buddhists. Sāmānya has thus to be admitted to have a separate reality. All perception as sameness of a thing is due to the presence of this thing in that object[1]. This jāti is eternal or non-destructible; for even with the destruction of individuals comprehended within the jāti, the latter is not destroyed[2].

Through *viśeṣa* things are perceived as diverse. No single sensation that we receive from the external world probably agrees with any other sensation, and this difference must be due to the existence of some specific differences amongst the atoms themselves. The specific difference existing in the atoms, emancipated souls and minds must be regarded as eternally existing, and it

[1] The Buddhist Paṇḍitāśoka says that there is no single thing running through different individuals (e.g. cooks) by virtue of which the sāmānya could be established. For if it did exist then we could have known it simply by seeing any cook without any reference to his action of cooking by virtue of which the notion of generality is formed. If there is a similarity between the action of cooks that cannot establish jāti in the cooks, for the similarity applies to other things, viz. the action of the cooks. If the specific individualities of a cow should require one common factor to hold them together, then these should require another and that another, and we have a regressus ad infinitum. Whatever being perceptible is not perceived is non-existent (*yadyadupalabdhilakṣaṇaprāptam sannopalabhyate tattadasat*). Sāmānya is such, therefore sāmānya is non-existent. No sāmānya can be admitted to exist as an entity. But it is only as a result of the impressions of past experiences of existence and non-existence that this notion is formed and transferred erroneously to external objects. Apart from this no sāmānya can be pointed out as being externally perceptible—*Sāmānyadūṣaṇadikprasāritā*—in *Six Buddhist Nyāya Tracts*. The Vedānta also does not think that either by perception or by inference we can know jāti as a separate substance. So it discards jāti. See *Vedāntaparibhāṣā*, *Śikhāmaṇi* and *Maṇiprabhā*, pp. 69-71. See also Śrīharṣa's *Khaṇḍanakhaṇḍakhādya*, pp. 1079-1086.

[2] Similarity (*sādṛśya*) is not regarded as a separate category, for it is defined as identity in difference (*tadbhinnatve sati tadgatabhūyodharmavattvam*).

is on account of its presence that atoms appear as different to the yogins who can perceive them.

Samavāya, the inseparable relation of inherence, is a relation by virtue of which two different things such as substance and attribute, substance and karma, substance and sāmānya, kāraṇa (cause) and kārya (effect), atoms and viśeṣa, appear so unified that they represent one whole, or one identical inseparable reality. This peculiar relation of inseparable inherence is the cause why substance, action, and attribute, cause and effect, and jāti in substance and attribute appear as indissolubly connected as if they are one and the same thing. Saṃyoga or contact may take place between two things of the same nature which exist as disconnected and may later on be connected (*yutasiddha*), such as when I put my pen on the table. The pen and the table are both substances and were disconnected; the saṃyoga relation is the guṇa by virtue of which they appear to be connected for a while. Samavāya however makes absolutely different things such as dravya and guṇa and karma or kāraṇa and kārya (clay and jug) appear as one inseparable whole (*ayutasiddha*). This relation is thus a separate and independent category. This is not regarded as many like saṃyogas (contact) but as one and eternal because it has no cause. This or that object (e.g. jug) may be destroyed but the samavāya relation which was never brought into being by anybody always remains[1].

These six things are called the six padārthas or independent realities experienced in perception and expressed in language.

The Theory of Causation.

The Nyāya-Vaiśeṣika in most of its speculations took that view of things which finds expression in our language, and which we tacitly assume as true in all our ordinary experience. Thus

[1] The Vedānta does not admit the existence of the relation of samavāya as subsisting between two different entities (e.g. substance and qualities). Thus Śaṅkara says (*Brahmasūtrabhāṣya* II. ii. 13) that if a samavāya relation is to be admitted to connect two different things, then another samavāya would be necessary to connect it with either of the two entities that it intended to connect, and that another, and so there will the a vicious infinite (*anavasthā*). Nyāya, however, would not regard it as vicious at all. It is well to remember that the Indian systems acknowledge two kinds of anavasthā—*prāmāṇikī* (valid infinite, as in case of the question of the seed and the tree, or of the avidyā and the passions), and another *aprāmāṇikī anavasthā* (vicious infinite) as when the admission of anything involves an infinite chain before it can be completed.

they admitted dravya, guṇa, karma and sāmānya. Viśeṣa they had to admit as the ultimate peculiarities of atoms, for they did not admit that things were continually changing their qualities, and that everything could be produced out of everything by a change of the collocation or arrangement of the constituting atoms. In the production of the effect too they did not admit that the effect was potentially pre-existent in the cause. They held that the material cause (e.g. clay) had some power within it, and the accessory and other instrumental causes (such as the stick, the wheel etc.) had other powers; the collocation of these two destroyed the cause, and produced the effect which was not existent before but was newly produced. This is what is called the doctrine of *asatkāryavāda*. This is just the opposite of the Sāṃkhya axiom, that what is existent cannot be destroyed (*nā-bhāvo vidyate sataḥ*) and that the non-existent could never be produced (*nāsato vidyate bhāvaḥ*). The objection to this view is that if what is non-existent is produced, then even such impossible things as the hare's horn could also be produced. The Nyāya-Vaiśeṣika answer is that the view is not that anything that is non-existent can be produced, but that which is produced was non-existent[1].

It is held by Mīmāṃsā that an unseen power resides in the cause which produces the effect. To this Nyāya objects that this is neither a matter of observation nor of legitimate hypothesis, for there is no reason to suppose that there is any transcendental operation in causal movement as this can be satisfactorily explained by molecular movement (*parispanda*). There is nothing except the invariable time relation (antecedence and sequence) between the cause and the effect, but the mere invariableness of an antecedent does not suffice to make it the cause of what succeeds; it must be an unconditional antecedent as well (*anyathāsiddhiśūnyasya niyatāpūrvavarttitā*). Unconditionality and invariability are indispensable for *kāryakāraṇa-bhāva* or cause and effect relation. For example, the non-essential or adventitious accompaniments of an invariable antecedent may also be invariable antecedents; but they are not unconditional, only collateral or indirect. In other words their antecedence is conditional upon something else (*na svātantryeṇa*). The potter's stick is an unconditional invariable antecedent of the jar; but the colour

[1] *Nyāyamañjari*, p. 494.

of a stick or its texture or size, or any other accompaniment or accident which does not contribute to the work done, is not an unconditional antecedent, and must not therefore be regarded as a cause. Similarly the co-effects of the invariable antecedents or what enters into the production of their co-effects may themselves be invariable antecedents; but they are not unconditional, being themselves conditioned by those of the antecedents of which they are effects. For example, the sound produced by the stick or by the potter's wheel invariably precedes the jar but it is a co-effect; and ākāśa (ether) as the substrate and vāyu (air) as the vehicle of the sound enter into the production of this co-effect, but these are no unconditional antecedents, and must therefore be rejected in an enumeration of conditions or causes of the jar. The conditions of the conditions should also be rejected; the invariable antecedent of the potter (who is an invariable antecedent of the jar), the potter's father, does not stand in a causal relation to the potter's handiwork. In fact the antecedence must not only be unconditionally invariable, but must also be immediate. Finally all seemingly invariable antecedents which may be dispensed with or left out are not unconditional and cannot therefore be regarded as causal conditions. Thus Dr Seal in describing it rightly remarks, "In the end, the discrimination of what is necessary to complete the sum of causes from what is dependent, collateral, secondary, superfluous, or inert (i.e. of the relevant from the irrelevant factors), must depend on the test of expenditure of energy. This test the Nyāya would accept only in the sense of an operation analysable into molar or molecular motion (*paris-panda eva bhautiko vyāpāraḥ karotyarthaḥ atīndriyastu vyā-paro nāsti*. Jayanta's Mañjarī Āhnika I), but would emphatically reject, if it is advanced in support of the notion of a mysterious causal power or efficiency (*śakti*)[1]." With Nyāya all energy is necessarily kinetic. This is a peculiarity of Nyāya—its insisting that the effect is only the sum or resultant of the operations of the different causal conditions—that these operations are of the nature of motion or kinetic, in other words it firmly holds to the view that causation is a case of expenditure of energy, i.e. a redistribution of motion, but at the same time absolutely repudiates the Sāṃkhya conception of power or productive

[1] Dr P. C. Ray's *Hindu Chemistry*, 1909, pp. 249–250.

efficiency as metaphysical or transcendental (*atīndriya*) and finds nothing in the cause other than unconditional invariable complements of operative conditions (*kāraṇa-sāmagrī*), and nothing in the effect other than the consequent phenomenon which results from the joint operations of the antecedent conditions[1]. Certain general conditions such as relative space (*dik*), time (*kāla*), the will of Īśvara, destiny (*adṛṣṭa*) are regarded as the common cause of all effects (*kāryatva-prayojaka*). Those are called *sādhāraṇa-kāraṇa* (common cause) as distinguished from the specific causes which determine the specific effects which are called *asādhāraṇa kāraṇa.* It may not be out of place here to notice that Nyāya while repudiating transcendental power (*śakti*) in the mechanism of nature and natural causation, does not deny the existence of metaphysical conditions like merit (*dharma*), which constitutes a system of moral ends that fulfil themselves through the mechanical systems and order of nature.

The causal relation then like the relation of genus to species, is a natural relation of concomitance, which can be ascertained only by the uniform and uninterrupted experience of agreement in presence and agreement in absence, and not by a deduction from a certain *a priori* principle like that of causality or identity of essence[2].

The material cause such as the clay is technically called the *samavāyi-kāraṇa* of the jug. *Samavāya* means as we have seen an intimate, inseparable relation of inherence. A kāraṇa is called *samavāyi* when its materials are found inseparably connected with the materials of the effect. Asamavāyi-kāraṇa is that which produces its characteristics in the effect through the medium of the samavāyi or material cause, e.g. the clay is not the cause of the colour of the jug but the colour of the clay is the cause of the colour of the jug. The colour of the clay which exists in the clay in inseparable relation is the cause of the colour of the jug. This colour of the clay is thus called the asamavāyi cause of the jug. Any quality (*guṇa*) or movement which existing in the samavāya cause in the samavāya relation determines the characteristics of the effect is called the asamavāyi-kāraṇa. The instrumental

[1] Dr P. C. Ray's *Hindu Chemistry*, 1909, pp. 249-250.

[2] See for this portion Dr B. N. Seal's *Positive Sciences of the Ancient Hindus*, pp. 263-266. *Sarvadarśanasaṃgraha* on Buddhism. *Nyāyamañjarī, Bhāṣā-pariccheda*, with *Muktāvalī* and *Dinakarī*, and *Tarkasaṃgraha*. The doctrine of Anyathāsiddhi was systematically developed from the time of Gaṅgeśa.

nimitta and accessory (*sahakāri*) causes are those which help the material cause to produce the effect. Thus the potter, the wheel and the stick may be regarded as the nimitta and the sahakāri causes of the effect.

We know that the Nyāya-Vaiśeṣika regards the effect as non-existent, before the operation of the cause in producing it, but it holds that the guṇas in the cause are the causes of the guṇas in the effect, e.g. the black colour of the clay is the cause of the black colour of the effect, except in cases where heat comes as an extraneous cause to generate other qualities; thus when a clay jug is burnt, on account of the heat we get red colour, though the colour of the original clay and the jug was black. Another important exception is to be found in the case of the production of the parimāṇas of dvyaṇukas and trasareṇus which are not produced by the parimāṇas of an aṇu or a dyaṇuka, but by their number as we have already seen.

Dissolution (Pralaya) and Creation (Sṛṣṭi).

The docrine of pralaya is accepted by all the Hindu systems except the Mīmāṃsā[1]. According to the Nyāya-Vaiśeṣika view Īśvara wishing to give some respite or rest to all living beings desires to bring about dissolution (*saṃhārecchо bhavati*). Simultaneously with it the adṛṣṭa force residing in all the souls and forming bodies, senses, and the gross elements, ceases to act (*śakti-pratibandha*). As a result of this no further bodies, senses, or other products come into being. Then for the bringing about of the dissolution of all produced things (by the desire of Īśvara) the separation of the atoms commences and thus all combinations as bodies or senses are disintegrated; so all earth is reduced to the disintegrated atomic state, then all ap, then all tejas and then all vāyu. These disintegrated atoms and the souls associated with dharma, adharma and past impressions (*saṃskāra*) remain suspended in their own inanimate condition. For we know that souls in their natural condition are lifeless and knowledgeless, non-intelligent entities. It is only when these are connected with bodies that they possess knowledge through the activity of manas. In the state of pralaya owing to the adṛṣṭa of souls the

[1] The doctrine of pralaya and sṛṣṭi is found only in later Nyāya-Vaiśeṣika works, but the sūtras of both the systems seem to be silent on the matter.

atoms do not conglomerate. It is not an act of cruelty on the part of Īśvara that he brings about dissolution, for he does it to give some rest to the sufferings of the living beings.

At the time of creation, Īśvara wishes to create and this desire of Īśvara works in all the souls as adṛṣṭa. This one eternal desire of Īśvara under certain conditions of time (e.g. of pralaya) as accessory causes (*sahakāri*) helps the disintegration of atoms and at other times (e.g. that of creation) the constructive process of integration and unification of atoms for the world-creation. When it acts in a specific capacity in the diverse souls it is called adṛṣṭa. At the time of dissolution the creative function of this adṛṣṭa is suspended and at the time of creation it finds full play. At the time of creation action first begins in the vāyu atoms by the kinetic function of this adṛṣṭa, by the contact of the souls with the atoms. By such action the air atoms come in contact with one another and the dvyaṇukas are formed and then in a similar way the tryaṇukas are formed, and thus vāyu originates. After vāyu, the ap is formed by the conglomeration of water atoms, and then the tejas atoms conglomerate and then the earth atoms. When the four elements are thus conglomerated in the gross form, the god Brahmā and all the worlds are created by Īśvara and Brahmā is directed by Īśvara to do the rest of the work. Brahmā thus arranges for the enjoyment and suffering of the fruits of diverse kinds of karma, good or bad. Īśvara brings about this creation not for any selfish purpose but for the good of all beings. Even here sorrows have their place that they may lead men to turn from worldly attachment and try for the attainment of the highest good, mukti. Moreover Īśvara arranges for the enjoyment of pleasures and the suffering of pains according to the merits and demerits of men, just as in our ordinary experience we find that a master awards prizes or punishments according to good or bad deeds[1]. Many Nyāya books do not speak of the appointment of a Brahmā as deputy for supervision of the due disposal of the fruits of karma according to merit or demerit. It is also held that pralaya and creation were brought about in accordance with the karma of men, or that it may be due to a mere play (*līlā*) of Īśvara. Īśvara is one, for if there were many Īśvaras they might quarrel. The will of Īśvara not only brings about dissolution and creation,

[1] See *Nyāyakandalī*, pp. 48-54.

but also acts always among us in a general way, for without it our karmas could not ripen, and the consequent disposal of pleasures and sorrows to us and a corresponding change in the exterior world in the form of order or harmony could not happen. The exterior world is in perfect harmony with men's actions. Their merits and demerits and all its changes and modifications take place in accordance with merits and demerits. This desire (*icchā*) of Īśvara may thus be compared with the *icchā* of Īśvara as we find it in the Yoga system.

Proof of the Existence of Īśvara.

Sāṃkhya asserts that the teleology of the prakṛti is sufficient to explain all order and arrangement of the cosmos. The Mīmāṃsakas, the Cārvākas, the Buddhists and the Jains all deny the existence of Īśvara (God). Nyāya believes that Īśvara has fashioned this universe by his will out of the ever-existing atoms. For every effect (e.g. a jug) must have its cause. If this be so, then this world with all its order and arrangement must also be due to the agency of some cause, and this cause is Īśvara. This world is not momentary as the Buddhists suppose, but is permanent as atoms, is also an effect so far as it is a collocation of atoms and is made up of parts like all other individual objects (e.g. jug, etc.), which we call effects. The world being an effect like any other effect must have a cause like any other effect. The objection made against this view is that such effects as we ordinarily perceive may be said to have agents as their causes but this manifest world with mountains, rivers, oceans etc. is so utterly different in form from ordinary effects that we notice every day, that the law that every effect must have a cause cannot be said to hold good in the present case. The answer that Nyāya gives is that the concomitance between two things must be taken in its general aspect neglecting the specific peculiarities of each case of observed concomitance. Thus I had seen many cases of the concomitance of smoke with fire, and had thence formed the notion that "wherever there is smoke there is fire"; but if I had only observed small puffs of smoke and small fires, could I say that only small quantities of smoke could lead us to the inference of fire, and could I hold that therefore large volumes of smoke from the burning of a forest should not be sufficient reason for us to infer the existence of fire in the forest?

Thus our conclusion should not be that only smaller effects are preceded by their causes, but that all effects are invariably and unconditionally preceded by causes. This world therefore being an effect must be preceded by a cause, and this cause is Īśvara. This cause we cannot see, because Īśvara has no visible body, not because he does not exist. It is sometimes said that we see every day that shoots come out of seeds and they are not produced by any agent. To such an objection the Nyāya answer is that even they are created by God, for they are also effects. That we do not see any one to fashion them is not because there is no maker of them, but because the creator cannot be seen. If the objector could distinctly prove that there was no invisible maker shaping these shoots, then only could he point to it as a case of contradiction. But so long as this is not done it is still only a doubtful case of enquiry and it is therefore legitimate for us to infer that since all effects have a cause, the shoots as well as the manifest world being effects must have a cause. This cause is Īśvara. He has infinite knowledge and is all merciful. At the beginning of creation He created the Vedas. He is like our father who is always engaged in doing us good[1].

The Nyāya-Vaiśeṣika Physics.

The four kinds of atoms are earth, water, fire, and air atoms. These have mass, number, weight, fluidity (or hardness), viscosity (or its opposite), velocity, characteristic potential colour, taste, smell, or touch, not produced by the chemical operation of heat. Ākāśa (space) is absolutely inert and structure-less being only as the substratum of sound, which is supposed to travel wave-like in the manifesting medium of air. Atomic combination is only possible with the four elements. Atoms cannot exist in an uncombined condition in the creation stage; atmospheric air however consists of atoms in an uncombined state.

Two atoms combine to form a binary molecule (*dvyaṇuka*). Two, three, four, or five dvyaṇukas form themselves into grosser molecules of tryaṇuka, caturaṇuka, etc.[2] Though this was the generally current view, there was also another view as has been pointed out by Dr B. N. Seal in his *Positive Sciences of the Ancient Hindus*, that the "atoms have also an inherent tendency to unite," and that

[1] See Jayanta's *Nyāyamañjari*, pp. 190–204, and Udayana's *Kusumāñjali* with *Prakāśa* and *Īśvarānumāna* of Raghunātha.

[2] *Kadācit tribhirārabhyate iti tryaṇukamityucyate, kadācit caturbhirārabhyate kadācit pañcabhiriti yatheṣṭaṃ kalpanā. Nyāyakandalī*, p. 32.

they do so in twos, threes, or fours, "either by the atoms falling into groups of threes, fours, etc. directly, or by the successive addition of one atom to each preceding aggregate[1]." Of course the atoms are regarded as possessed of an incessant vibratory motion. It must however be noted in this connection that behind this physical explanation of the union of atoms there is the adṛṣṭa, the will of Īśvara, which gives the direction of all such unions in harmony with the principle of a "moral government of the universe," so that only such things are produced as can be arranged for the due disposal of the effects of karma. "An elementary substance thus produced by primary atomic combination may however suffer qualitative changes under the influence of heat (*pākajotpatti*)." The impact of heat corpuscles decomposes a dvyaṇuka into the atoms and transforms the characters of the atoms determining them all in the same way. The heat particles continuing to impinge reunite the atoms so transformed to form binary or other molecules in different orders or arrangements, which account for the specific characters or qualities finally produced. The Vaiśeṣika holds that there is first a disintegration into simple atoms, then change of atomic qualities, and then the final re-combination, under the influence of heat. This doctrine is called the doctrine of *pīlupāka* (heating of atoms). Nyāya on the other hand thinks that no disintegration into atoms is necessary for change of qualities, but it is the molecules which assume new characters under the influence of heat. Heat thus according to Nyāya directly affects the characters of the molecules and changes their qualities without effecting a change in the atoms. Nyāya holds that the heat-corpuscles penetrate into the porous body of the object and thereby produce the change of colour. The object as a whole is not disintegrated into atoms and then reconstituted again, for such a procedure is never experienced by observation. This is called the doctrine of *piṭharapāka* (heating of molecules). This is one of the few points of difference between the later Nyāya and Vaiśeṣika systems[2].

Chemical compounds of atoms may take place between the

[1] Utpala's commentary on *Bṛhatsamhitā* I. 7.

[2] See Dr B. N. Seal in P. C. Ray's *Hindu Chemistry*, pp. 190–191, *Nyāyamañjarī*, p. 438, and Udyotakara's *Vārttika*. There is very little indication in the Nyāya and *Vaiśeṣika sūtras* that they had any of those differences indicated here. Though there are slight indications of these matters in the *Vaiśeṣika sūtras* (VII. 1), the *Nyāya sūtras* are almost silent upon the matter. A systematic development of the theory of creation and atomic combinations appear to have taken place after Vātsyāyana.

atoms of the same bhūta or of many bhūtas. According to the Nyāya view there are no differences in the atoms of the same bhūta, and all differences of quality and characteristics of the compound of the same bhūta are due only to diverse collocations of those atoms. Thus Udyotakara says (III. i. 4) that there is no difference between the atom of a barley seed and paddy seed, since these are all but atoms of earth. Under the continued impact of heat particles the atoms take new characters. It is heat and heat alone that can cause the transformations of colours, tastes etc. in the original bhūta atoms. The change of these physical characters depends on the colours etc. of the constituent substances in contact, on the intensity or degree of heat and also on the species of tejas corpuscles that impinge on the atoms. Heat breaks bodies in contact into atoms, transforms their qualities, and forms separate bodies with them.

Praśastapāda (the commentator of Vaiśeṣika) holds that in the higher compounds of the same bhūta the transformation takes place (under internal heat) in the constituent atoms of the compound molecules, atoms specially determined as the compound and not in the original atoms of the bhūta entering into the composition of the compound. Thus when milk is turned into curd, the transformation as curd takes place in the atoms determined as milk in the milk molecule, and it is not necessary that the milk molecule should be disintegrated into the atoms of the original bhūta of which the milk is a modification. The change as curd thus takes place in the milk atom, and the milk molecule has not to be disintegrated into kṣiti or ap atoms. So again in the fertilized ovum, the germ and the ovum substances, which in the Vaiśeṣika view are both isomeric modes of earth (with accompaniments of other bhūtas) are broken up into homogeneous earth atoms, and it is these that chemically combine under the animal heat and biomotor force vāyu to form the germ (*kalala*). But when the germ plasm develops, deriving its nutrition from the blood of the mother, the animal heat breaks up the molecules of the germ plasm into its constituent atoms, i.e. atoms specifically determined which by their grouping formed the germ plasm. These germ-plasm atoms chemically combine with the atoms of the food constituents and thus produce cells and tissues[1]. This atomic contact is called *ārambhaka-saṃyoga*.

[1] See Dr B. N. Seal's *Positive Sciences*, pp. 104-108, and *Nyāyakandalī*, pp. 33-34, "*Śarīrārambhe paramānava eva kāraṇam na śukra-śonitasannipātaḥ kriyāvibhāgādinyāyena tayorvināśe sati utpannapākajaih paramāṇubhirārambhāt, na ca śukraśonita-*

In the case of poly-bhautik or bi-bhautik compounds there is another kind of contact called *upaṣṭambha*. Thus in the case of such compounds as oils, fats, and fruit juices, the earth atoms cannot combine with one another unless they are surrounded by the water atoms which congregate round the former, and by the infra-atomic forces thus set up the earth atoms take peculiar qualities under the impact of heat corpuscles. Other compounds are also possible where the ap, tejas, or the vāyu atoms form the inner radicle and earth atoms dynamically surround them (e.g. gold, which is the tejas atom with the earth atoms as the surrounding upaṣṭambhaka). Solutions (of earth substances in ap) are regarded as physical mixtures.

Udayana points out that the solar heat is the source of all the stores of heat required for chemical change. But there are differences in the modes of the action of heat; and the kind of contact with heat-corpuscles, or the kind of heat with chemical action which transforms colours, is supposed to differ from what transforms flavour or taste.

Heat and light rays are supposed to consist of indefinitely small particles which dart forth or radiate in all directions rectilineally with inconceivable velocity. Heat may penetrate through the interatomic space as in the case of the conduction of heat, as when water boils in a pot put on the fire; in cases of transparency light rays penetrate through the inter-atomic spaces with *pari-spanda* of the nature of deflection or refraction (*tiryag-gamana*). In other cases heat rays may impinge on the atoms and rebound back—which explains reflection. Lastly heat may strike the atoms in a peculiar way, so as to break up their grouping, transform the physico-chemical characters of the atoms, and again recombine them, all by means of continual impact with inconceivable velocity, an operation which explains all cases of chemical combination[1]. Govardhana a later Nyāya writer says that pāka means the combination of different kinds of heat. The heat that

paramāṇūnāṃ kaścidviśeṣaḥ pārthivatvāviśeṣāt....Pituḥ śukraṃ mātuḥ śonitaṃ tayos sannipātānantaraṃ jaṭharānalasambandhāt śukra-śonitārambhakeṣu paramāṇuṣu pūrvarūpādivināśe samāṇaguṇāntarotpattau dvyaṇukādikrameṇa kalalaśarīrotpattiḥ tatrāntaḥkaraṇapraveśo...tatra māturāhāraraso mātrayā saṃkrāmate, adṛṣṭavaṣāttatra punarjaṭharānalasambandhāt kalalārambhakaparamāṇuṣu kriyāvibhāgādinyāyena kalalaśarīre naṣṭe samutpannapākajaiḥ kalalārambhakaparamāṇubhiradṛṣṭavaśād upajātakriyairāhāraparamāṇubhiḥ saha sambhūya śarīrāntaramārabhyate."

[1] See Dr Seal's *Positive Sciences of the Hindus*.

changes the colour of a fruit is different from that which generates or changes the taste. Even when the colour and taste remain the same a particular kind of heat may change the smell. When grass eaten by cows is broken up into atoms special kinds of heat-light rays change its old taste, colour, touch and smell into such forms as those that belong to milk[1].

In the Nyāya-Vaiśeṣika system all action of matter on matter is thus resolved into motion. Conscious activity (*prayatna*) is distinguished from all forms of motion as against the Sāṃkhya doctrine which considered everything other than puruṣa (intelligence) to arise in the course of cosmic evolution and therefore to be subject to vibratory motion.

The Origin of Knowledge (Pramāṇa).

The manner in which knowledge originates is one of the most favourite topics of discussion in Indian philosophy. We have already seen that Sāṃkhya-Yoga explained it by supposing that the buddhi (place of consciousness) assumed the form of the object of perception, and that the buddhi so transformed was then intelligized by the reflection of the pure intelligence or puruṣa. The Jains regarded the origin of any knowledge as being due to a withdrawal of a veil of karma which was covering the all-intelligence of the self.

Nyāya-Vaiśeṣika regarded all effects as being due to the assemblage of certain collocations which unconditionally, invariably, and immediately preceded these effects. That collocation (*sāmagrī*) which produced knowlege involved certain non-intelligent as well as intelligent elements and through their conjoint action uncontradicted and determinate knowledge was produced, and this collocation is thus called pramāṇa or the determining cause of the origin of knowledge[2]. None of the separate elements composing

[1] Govardhana's *Nyāyabodhinī* on *Tarkasaṃgraha*, pp. 9, 10.

[2] "*Avyabhicāriṇīmasandigdhārthopalabdhiṃ vidadhatī bodhābodhasvabhāvā sāmagrī pramāṇam*" *Nyāyamañjarī* p. 12. Udyotakara however defined "pramāṇa" as upalabdhihetu (cause of knowledge). This view does not go against Jayanta's view which I have followed, but it emphasizes the side of vyāpāra or movement of the senses, etc. by virtue of which the objects come in contact with them and knowledge is produced. Thus Vācaspati says: "*siddhamindriyādi, asiddhañca tatsannikarṣādi vyāpārayannutpādayan karaṇa eva caritārthaḥ karṇaṃ tvindriyādi tatsannikarṣādi vā nānyatra caritarthamiti sākṣādupalabdhāveva phale vyāprīyate.*" *Tātparyaṭīkā*, p. 15. Thus it is the action of the senses as pramāṇa which is the direct cause of the production of knowledge,

the causal collocation can be called the primary cause; it is only their joint collocation that can be said to determine the effect, for sometimes the absence of a single element composing the causal collocation is sufficient to stop the production of the effect. Of course the collocation or combination is not an entity separated from the collocated or combined things. But in any case it is the preceding collocations that combine to produce the effect jointly. These involve not only intellectual elements (e.g. indeterminate cognition as qualification (viśeṣaṇa) in determinate perceptions, the knowledge of liṅga in inference, the seeing of similar things in upamāna, the hearing of sound in śabda) but also the assemblage of such physical things (e.g. proximity of the object of perception, capacity of the sense, light, etc.), which are all indispensable for the origin of knowledge. The cognitive and physical elements all co-operate in the same plane, combine together and produce further determinate knowledge. It is this capacity of the collocations that is called pramāṇa.

Nyāya argues that in the Sāṃkhya view knowledge originates by the transcendent influence of puruṣa on a particular state of buddhi; this is quite unintelligible, for knowledge does not belong to buddhi as it is non-intelligent, though it contains within it the content and the form of the concept or the percept (knowledge). The puruṣa to whom the knowledge belongs, however, neither knows, nor feels, neither conceives nor perceives, as it always remains in its own transcendental purity. If the transcendental contact of the puruṣa with buddhi is but a mere semblance or appearance or illusion, then the Sāṃkhya has to admit that there is no real knowledge according to them. All knowledge is false. And since all knowledge is false, the Sāṃkhyists have precious little wherewith to explain the origin of right knowledge.

There are again some Buddhists who advocate the doctrine that simultaneously with the generation of an object there is the knowledge corresponding to it, and that corresponding to the rise of any knowledge there is the rise of the object of it. Neither is the knowledge generated by the object nor the object by the knowledge; but there is a sort of simultaneous parallelism. It is evident that this view does not explain why knowledge should

but as this production could not have taken place without the subject and the object, they also are to be regarded as causes in some sense. "*Pramātṛ-prameyayoḥ pramāṇe caritārthatvamacaritārthatvaṃ pramāṇasya tasmāt tadeva phalahetuḥ. Pramātṛprameye tu phaloddeśena pravṛtte iti taddhetū kathañcit.*" *Ibid*, p. 16.

express or manifest its object. If knowledge and the object are both but corresponding points in a parallel series, whence comes this correspondence? Why should knowledge illuminate the object. The doctrine of the Vijñāna vādins, that it is knowledge alone that shows itself both as knowledge and as its object, is also irrational, for how can knowledge divide itself as subject and object in such a manner that knowledge as object should require the knowledge as subject to illuminate it? If this be the case we might again expect that knowledge as knowledge should also require another knowledge to manifest it and this another, and so on *ad infinitum*. Again if pramāṇa be defined as *prāpaṇa* (capacity of being realized) then also it would not hold, for all things being momentary according to the Buddhists, the thing known cannot be realized, so there would be nothing which could be called pramāna. These views moreover do not explain the origin of knowledge. Knowledge is thus to be regarded as an effect like any other effect, and its origin or production occurs in the same way as any other effect, namely by the joint collocation of causes intellectual and physical[1]. There is no transcendent element involved in the production of knowledge, but it is a production on the same plane as that in which many physical phenomena are produced[2].

The four Pramāṇas of Nyāya.

We know that the Cārvākas admitted perception (*pratyakṣa*) alone as the valid source of knowledge. The Buddhists and the Vaiśeṣika admitted two sources, pratyakṣa and inference (*anumāna*)[3]. Sāṃkhya added *śabda* (testimony) as the third source;

[1] See *Nyāyamañjarī*, pp. 12–26.

[2] Discussing the question of the validity of knowledge Gaṅgeśa, a later naiyāyika of great fame, says that it is derived as a result of our inference from the correspondence of the perception of a thing with the activity which prompted us to realize it. That which leads us to successful activity is valid and the opposite invalid. When I am sure that if I work in accordance with the perception of an object I shall be successful, I call it valid knowledge. *Tattvacintāmaṇi*, K. Tarkavāgīśa's edition, *Prāmāṇyavāda*.

[3] The *Vaiśeṣika sūtras* tacitly admit the Vedas as a pramāṇa. The view that Vaiśeṣika only admitted two pramāṇas, perception and inference, is traditionally accepted, "*pratyakṣamekaṃcārvākāḥ kaṇādasugatau punaḥ anumānañca taccāpi*, etc." Praśastapāda divides all cognition (*buddhi*) as *vidyā* (right knowledge) and *avidyā* (ignorance). Under *avidyā* he counts *saṃśaya* (doubt or uncertainty), *viparyaya* (illusion or error), *anadhyavasāya* (want of definite knowledge, thus when a man who had never seen a mango, sees it for the first time, he wonders what it may be) and *svapna* (dream). Right knowledge (*vidyā*) is of four kinds, perception, inference, memory and the supernatural

Nyāya adds a fourth, *upamāna* (analogy). The principle on which the four-fold division of pramāṇas depends is that the causal collocation which generates the knowledge as well as the nature or characteristic kind of knowledge in each of the four cases is different. The same thing which appears to us as the object of our perception, may become the object of inference or śabda (testimony), but the manner or mode of manifestation of knowledge being different in each case, and the manner or conditions producing knowledge being different in each case, it is to be admitted that inference and śabda are different pramāṇas, though they point to the same object indicated by the perception. Nyāya thus objects to the incorporation of śabda (testimony) or upamāna within inference, on the ground that since the mode of production of knowledge is different, these are to be held as different pramāṇas[1].

Perception (Pratyakṣa).

The naiyāyikas admitted only the five cognitive senses which they believed to be composed of one or other of the five elements. These senses could each come in contact with the special characteristic of that element of which they were composed. Thus the ear could perceive sound, because sound was the attribute of ākāśa, of which the auditory sense, the ear, was made up. The eye could send forth rays to receive the colour, etc., of things. Thus the cognitive senses can only manifest their specific objects by going over to them and thereby coming in contact with them. The conative senses (*vāk*, *pāṇi*, *pāda*, *pāyu*, and *upastha*) recognized in Sāṃkhya as separate senses are not recognized here as such for the functions of these so-called senses are discharged by the general motor functions of the body.

Perception is defined as that right knowledge generated by the contact of the senses with the object, devoid of doubt and error not associated with any other simultaneous sound cognition (such

knowledge of the sages (*ārṣa*). Interpreting the *Vaiśeṣika sūtras* I. i. 3, VI. i. I, and VI. i. 3, to mean that the validity of the Vedas depends upon the trustworthy character of their author, he does not consider scriptures as valid in themselves. Their validity is only derived by inference from the trustworthy character of their author. *Arthāpatti* (implication) and *anupalabdhi* (non-perception) are also classed as inference and *upamāna* (analogy) and *aitihya* (tradition) are regarded as being the same as faith in trustworthy persons and hence cases of inference.

[1] *Sāmagrībhedāt phalabhedācca pramāṇabhedaḥ*
Anye eva hi sāmagrīphale pratyakṣaliṅgayoḥ
Anye eva ca sāmagrīphale śabdopamānayoḥ. *Nyāyamañjarī*, p. 33.

as the name of the object as heard from a person uttering it, just at the time when the object is seen) or name association, and determinate[1]. If when we see a cow, a man says here is a cow, the knowledge of the sound as associated with the percept cannot be counted as perception but as sound-knowledge (*śabda-pramāṇa*). That right knowledge which is generated directly by the contact of the senses with the object is said to be the product of the perceptual process. Perception may be divided as indeterminate (*nirvikalpa*) and (*savikalpa*) determinate. Indeterminate perception is that in which the thing is taken at the very first moment of perception in which it appears without any association with name. Determinate perception takes place after the indeterminate stage is just passed; it reveals things as being endowed with all characteristics and qualities and names just as we find in all our concrete experience. Indeterminate perception reveals the things with their characteristics and universals, but at this stage there being no association of name it is more or less indistinct. When once the names are connected with the percept it forms the determinate perception of a thing called savikalpa-pratyakṣa. If at the time of having the perception of a thing of which the name is not known to me anybody utters its name then the hearing of that should be regarded as a separate auditory name perception. Only that product is said to constitute nirvikalpa perception which results from the perceiving process of the contact of the senses with the object. Of this nirvikalpa (indeterminate) perception it is held by the later naiyāyikas that we are not conscious of it directly, but yet it has to be admitted as a necessary first stage without which the determinate consciousness could not arise. The indeterminate perception is regarded as the first stage in the process of perception. At the second stage it joins the other conditions of perception in producing the determinate perception. The contact of the sense with the object is regarded as being of six kinds: (1) contact with the dravya (thing) called saṃyoga, (2) contact with the guṇas (qualities) through the thing (*saṃyukta-samavāya*) in which they inhere in samavāya (inseparable) relation, (3) contact with the guṇas (such as colour etc.) in the generic character as universals of those qualities, e.g.colourness (rūpatva), which inhere in the guṇas in the samavāya relation.

[1] Gaṅgeśa, a later naiyāyika of great reputation, describes perception as immediate awareness (*pratyakṣasya sākṣātkāritvam lakṣaṇam*).

This species of contact is called saṃyukta-samaveta-samavāya, for the eye is in contact with the thing, in the thing the colour is in samavāya relation, and in the specific colour there is the colour universal or the generic character of colour in samavāya relation. (4) There is another kind of contact called samavāya by which sounds are said to be perceived by the ear. The auditory sense is ākāśa and the sound exists in ākāśa in the samavāya relation, and thus the auditory sense can perceive sound in a peculiar kind of contact called samaveta-samavāya. (5) The generic character of sound as the universal of sound (śabdatva) is perceived by the kind of contact known as samaveta-samavāya. (6) There is another kind of contact by which negation (*abhāva*) is perceived, namely saṃyukta viśeṣaṇa (as qualifying contact). This is so called because the eye perceives only the empty space which is qualified by the absence of an object and through it the negation. Thus I see that there is no jug here on the ground. My eye in this case is in touch with the ground and the absence of the jug is only a kind of quality of the ground which is perceived along with the perception of the empty ground. It will thus be seen that Nyāya admits not only the substances and qualities but all kinds of relations as real and existing and as being directly apprehended by perception (so far as they are directly presented).

The most important thing about the Nyāya-Vaiśeṣika theory of perception is this that the whole process beginning from the contact of the sense with the object to the distinct and clear perception of the thing, sometimes involving the appreciation of its usefulness or harmfulness, is regarded as the process of perception and its result perception. The self, the mind, the senses and the objects are the main factors by the particular kinds of contact between which perceptual knowledge is produced. All knowledge is indeed *arthaprakāśa*, revelation of objects, and it is called perception when the sense factors are the instruments of its production and the knowledge produced is of the objects with which the senses are in contact. The contact of the senses with the objects is not in any sense metaphorical but actual. Not only in the case of touch and taste are the senses in contact with the objects, but in the cases of sight, hearing and smell as well. The senses according to Nyāya-Vaiśeṣika are material and we have seen that the system does not admit of any other kind of transcendental (*atīndriya*) power (*śakti*) than that of actual vibratory movement which is within the purview of sense-cognition[1]. The production of knowledge is thus no transcendental occurrence, but is one which is similar to the effects produced by the conglomeration and movements of physical causes. When I perceive an orange, my visual or the tactual sense is in touch not only with its specific colour, or hardness, but also with the universals associated with them in a relation of inherence and also with the object itself of which the colour etc. are predicated. The result of this sense-contact at the first stage is called *ālocana-jñāna* (sense-cognition) and as a result of that there is roused the memory of its previous taste and a sense of pleasurable character (*sukhasādhanatvasmṛti*) and as a result of that I perceive the orange before me to have a certain pleasure-giving character[2]. It is urged that this appreciation of the orange as a pleasurable object should also be regarded as a direct result of perception through the action of the memory operating as a concomitant cause (sahakāri). I perceive the orange with the eye and understand the pleasure it will give, by the mind, and thereupon understand by the mind that it is a pleasurable object. So though this perception results immediately by the operation of the mind, yet since it could only happen in association with sense-contact, it must be considered as a subsidiary effect of sense-contact and hence regarded as visual perception. Whatever may be the successive intermediary processes, if the knowledge is a result of sense-contact and if it appertains to the object with which the sense is in contact, we should regard it as a result of the perceptual process. Sense-contact with the object is thus the primary and indispensable condition of all perceptions and not only can the senses be in contact with the objects, their qualities, and the universals associated with them but also with negation. A perception is erroneous when it resents an object in a character which it does not possess (*atasmiṃstaditi*) and right knowledge (*pramā*) is that which presents an object with a character which it really has

[1] *Na khalvatīndriyā śaktirasmābhirupagamyate*
yayā saha na kāryyasya sambandhajñānasambhavaḥ.
Nyāyamañjarī, p. 69.

[2] *Sukhādi manasā buddhvā kapitthādi ca cakṣuṣā*
tasya karaṇatā tatra manasaivāvagamyate...
... Sambandhagrahaṇakāle yattatkapitthādiviṣayamakṣajam
jñānam tadupādeyādijñānaphalamiti bhāṣyakṛtaścetasi sthitam
sukhasādhanatvajñānamupādeyajñānam.
Nyāyamañjarī, pp. 69–70; see also pp. 66–71.

(*tadvati tatprakārakānubhava*)[1]. In all cases of perceptual illusion the sense is in real contact with the right object, but it is only on account of the presence of certain other conditions that it is associated with wrong characteristics or misapprehended as a different object. Thus when the sun's rays are perceived in a desert and misapprehended as a stream, at the first indeterminate stage the visual sense is in real contact with the rays and thus far there is no illusion so far as the contact with a real object is concerned, but at the second determinate stage it is owing to the similarity of certain of its characteristics with those of a stream that it is misapprehended as a stream[2]. Jayanta observes that on account of the presence of the defect of the organs or the rousing of the memory of similar objects, the object with which the sense is in contact hides its own characteristics and appears with the characteristics of other objects and this is what is meant by illusion[3]. In the case of mental delusions however there is no sense-contact with any object and the rousing of irrelevant memories is sufficient to produce illusory notions[4]. This doctrine of illusion is known as *viparītakhyāti* or *anyathākhyāti*. What existed in the mind appeared as the object before us (*hṛdaye parisphurato' rthasya bahiravabhāsanam*)[5]. Later Vaiśeṣika as interpreted by Praśastapāda and Śridhara is in full agreement with Nyāya in this doctrine of illusion (*bhrama* or as Vaiśeṣika calls it *viparyaya*) that the object of illusion is always the right thing with which the sense is in contact and that the illusion consists in the imposition of wrong characteristics[6].

I have pointed out above that Nyāya divided perception into two classes as nirvikalpa (indeterminate) and savikalpa (determinate) according as it is an earlier or a later stage. Vācaspati says, that at the first stage perception reveals an object as a particular; the perception of an orange at this *avikalpika* or *nir-vikalpika* stage gives us indeed all its colour, form, and also the universal of orangeness associated with it, but it does not reveal

[1] See Udyotakara's *Nyāyavārttika*, p. 37, and Gaṅgeśa's *Tattvacintāmaṇi*, p. 401, *Bibliotheca Indica*.

[2] "*Indriyeṇālocya marīcīn uccāvacamuccalato nirvikalpena gṛhītvā paścāttatropaghātadoṣāt viparyyeti, savikalpako'sya pratyayo bhrānto jāyate tasmādvijñānasya vyabhicāro nārthasya*, Vācaspati's *Tātparyatīkā*," p. 87.

[3] *Nyāyamañjarī*, p. 88.

[4] *Ibid*, pp. 89 and 184.

[5] *Ibid*, p. 184.

[6] *Nyāyakandalī*, pp. 177–181, "*Śuktisaṃyuktenendriyeṇa doṣasahakāriṇā rajatasaṃskārasacivena sādṛśyamanurundhatā śuktikāviṣayo rajatādhyavasāyaḥ kṛtaḥ.*"

it in a subject-predicate relation as when I say "this is an orange." The avikalpika stage thus reveals the universal associated with the particular, but as there is no association of name at this stage, the universal and the particular are taken in one sweep and not as terms of relation as subject and predicate or substance and attribute (*jātyādisvarūpāvagāhi na tu jātyādīnāṃ mitho viśeṣaṇa-viśeṣyabhāvāvagāhīti yāvat*)[1]. He thinks that such a stage, when the object is only seen but not associated with name or a subject-predicate relation, can be distinguished in perception not only in the case of infants or dumb persons that do not know the names of things, but also in the case of all ordinary persons, for the association of the names and relations could be distinguished as occurring at a succeeding stage[2]. Śrīdhara, in explaining the Vaiśeṣika view, seems to be largely in agreement with the above view of Vācaspati. Thus Śrīdhara says that in the nirvikalpa stage not only the universals were perceived but the differences as well. But as at this stage there is no memory of other things, there is no manifest differentiation and unification such as can only result by comparison. But the differences and the universals as they are in the thing are perceived, only they are not consciously ordered as "different from this" or "similar to this," which can only take place at the savikalpa stage[3]. Vācaspati did not bring in the question of comparison with others, but had only spoken of the determinate notion of the thing in definite subject-predicate relation in association with names. The later Nyāya writers however, following Gaṅgeśa, hold an altogether different opinion on the subject. With them nirvikalpa knowledge means the knowledge of mere predication without any association with the subject or the thing to which the predicate refers. But such a knowledge is never testified by experience. The nirvikalpa stage is thus a logical stage in the development of perceptual cognition and not a psychological stage. They would

[1] *Tātparyaṭīkā*, p. 82, also *ibid.* p. 91, "*prathamamālocito'rthaḥ sāmānyaviśeṣavān.*"

[2] *Ibid*, p. 84, "*tasmādvyutpannasyāpi nāmadheyasmaraṇāya pūrvameṣitavyo vinaiva nāmadheyamarthapratyayaḥ.*"

[3] *Nyāyakandalī*, p. 189 ff., "*ataḥ savikalpakamicchatā nirvikalpakamapyeṣitavyam, tacca na sāmānyamātram gṛhṇāti bhedasyāpi pratibhāsanāt nāpi svalakṣaṇamātram sāmānyākārasyāpi saṃvedanāt vyaktyantaradarśane pratisandhānācca, kintu sāmān-yam viśeṣañcobhayamapi gṛhṇāti yadi paramidaṃ sāmānyamayam viśeṣaḥ ityevaṃ vivicya na pratyeti vastvantarānusandhānavirahāt, piṇḍāntarānuvṛttigrahaṇāddhi sāmānyaṃ vivicyate, vyāvṛttigrahaṇādviśeṣoyamiti vivekaḥ.*"

not like to dispense with it for they think that it is impossible to have the knowledge of a thing as qualified by a predicate or a quality, without previously knowing the quality or the predicate (*viśiṣṭavaiśiṣṭyajñānam prati hi viśeṣaṇatāvacchedakaprakāraṃ jñānaṃ kāraṇaṃ*)[1]. So, before any determinate knowledge such as "I see a cow," "this is a cow" or "a cow" can arise it must be preceded by an indeterminate stage presenting only the indeterminate, unrelated, predicative quality as nirvikalpa, unconnected with universality or any other relations (*jātyādiyojanārahitaṃ vaiśiṣṭyānavagāhi niṣprakārakam nirvikalpakaṃ*)[2]. But this stage is never psychologically experienced (*atīndriya*) and it is only a logical necessity arising out of their synthetic conception of a proposition as being the relationing of a predicate with a subject. Thus Viśvanātha says in his Siddhānta-muktāvalī, "the cognition which does not involve relationing cannot be perceptual for the perception is of the form 'I know the jug'; here the knowledge is related to the self, the knower, the jug again is related to knowledge and the definite content of jugness is related to the jug. It is this content which forms the predicative quality (*viśeṣaṇatāvacchedaka*) of the predicate 'jug' which is related to knowledge. We cannot therefore have the knowledge of the jug without having the knowledge of the predicative quality, the content[3]." But in order that the knowledge of the jug could be rendered possible, there must be a stage at which the universal or the pure predication should be known and this is the nirvikalpa stage, the admission of which though not testified by experience is after all logically indispensably necessary. In the proposition "It is a cow," the cow is an universal, and this must be intuited directly before it could be related to the particular with which it is associated.

But both the old and the new schools of Nyāya and Vaiśeṣika admitted the validity of the savikalpa perception which the Buddhists denied. Things are not of the nature of momentary particulars, but they are endowed with class-characters or universals and thus our knowledge of universals as revealed by the perception of objects is not erroneous and is directly produced by objects. The Buddhists hold that the error of savikalpa perception consists in the attribution of jāti (universal), guṇa (quality),

[1] *Tattvacintāmaṇi*, p. 812.

[2] *Ibid.* p. 809.

[3] *Siddhāntamuktāvalī* on *Bhāṣāpariccheda kārikā*, 58.

kriyā (action), nāma (name), and dravya (substance) to things[1]. The universal and that of which the universal is predicated are not different but are the same identical entity. Thus the predication of an universal in the savikalpa perception involves the false creation of a difference where there was none. So also the quality is not different from the substance and to speak of a thing as qualified is thus an error similar to the former. The same remark applies to action, for motion is not something different from that which moves. But name is completely different from the thing and yet the name and the thing are identified, and again the percept "man with a stick" is regarded as if it was a single thing or substance, though "man" and "stick" are altogether different and there is no unity between them. Now as regards the first three objections it is a question of the difference of the Nyāya ontological position with that of the Buddhists, for we know that Nyāya and Vaiśeṣika believe jāti, guṇa and kriyā to be different from substance and therefore the predicating of them of substance as different categories related to it at the determinate stage of perception cannot be regarded as erroneous. As to the fourth objection Vācaspati replies that the memory of the name of the thing roused by its sight cannot make the perception erroneous. The fact that memory operates cannot in any way vitiate perception. The fact that name is not associated until the second stage through the joint action of memory is easily explained, for the operation of memory was necessary in order to bring about the association. But so long as it is borne in mind that the name is not identical with the thing but is only associated with it as being the same as was previously acquired, there cannot be any objection to the association of the name. But the Buddhists further object that there is no reason why one should identify a thing seen at the present moment as being that which was seen before, for this identity is never the object of visual perception. To this Vācaspati says that through the help of memory or past impressions (*saṃskāra*) this can be considered as being directly the object of perception, for whatever may be the concomitant causes when the main cause of sense-contact is

[1] *Nyāyamañjarī*, pp. 93–100, "*Pañca caite kalpanā bhavanti jātikalpanā, guṇakalpanā, kriyākalpanā, nāmakalpanā dravyakalpanā ceti, tāśca kvacidabhede' pi bhedakalpanāt kvacicca bhede' pyabhedakalpanāt kalpanā ucyante*." See Dharmakīrtti's theory of Perception, pp. 151–4. See also pp. 409–410 of this book.

present, this perception of identity should be regarded as an effect of it. But the Buddhists still emphasize the point that an object of past experience refers to a past time and place and is not experienced now and cannot therefore be identified with an object which is experienced at the present moment. It has to be admitted that Vācaspati's answer is not very satisfactory for it leads ultimately to the testimony of direct perception which was challenged by the Buddhists[1]. It is easy to see that early Nyāya-Vaiśeṣika could not dismiss the savikalpa perception as invalid for it was the same as the nirvikalpa and differed from it only in this, that a name was associated with the thing of perception at this stage. As it admits a gradual development of perception as the progressive effects of causal operations continued through the contacts of the mind with the self and the object under the influence of various intellectual (e.g. memory) and physical (e.g. light rays) concomitant causes, it does not, like Vedānta, require that right perception should only give knowledge which was not previously acquired. The variation as well as production of knowledge in the soul depends upon the variety of causal collocations.

Mind according to Nyāya is regarded as a separate sense and can come in contact with pleasure, pain, desire, antipathy and will. The later Nyāya writers speak of three other kinds of contact of a transcendental nature called *sāmānyalakṣaṇa*, *jñānalakṣaṇa* and *yogaja* (miraculous). The contact sāmānyalakṣaṇa is that by virtue of which by coming in contact with a particular we are transcendentally (*alaukika*) in contact with all the particulars (in a general way) of which the corresponding universal may be predicated. Thus when I see smoke and through it my sense is in contact with the universal associated with smoke my visual sense is in transcendental contact with all smoke in general. Jñānalakṣaṇa contact is that by virtue of which we can associate the perceptions of other senses when perceiving by any one sense. Thus when we are looking at a piece of sandal wood our visual sense is in touch with its colour only, but still we perceive it to be fragrant without any direct contact of the object with the organ of smell. The sort of transcendental contact (*alaukika sannikarṣa*) by virtue of which this is rendered

[1] *Tātparyaṭīkā*, pp. 88–95.

possible is called jñānalakṣaṇa. But the knowledge acquired by these two contacts is not counted as perception[1].

Pleasures and pains (*sukha* and *duḥkha*) are held by Nyāya to be different from knowledge (jñāna). For knowledge interprets, conceives or illumines things, but sukha etc. are never found to appear as behaving in that character. On the other hand we feel that we grasp them after having some knowledge. They cannot be self-revealing, for even knowledge is not so; if it were so, then that experience which generates sukha in one should have generated the same kind of feeling in others, or in other words it should have manifested its nature as sukha to all; and this does not happen, for the same thing which generates sukha in one might not do so in others. Moreover even admitting for argument's sake that it is knowledge itself that appears as pleasure and pain, it is evident that there must be some differences between the pleasurable and painful experiences that make them so different, and this difference is due to the fact that knowledge in one case was associated with sukha and in another case with duḥkha. This shows that sukha and duḥkha are not themselves knowledge. Such is the course of things that sukha and duḥkha are generated by the collocation of certain conditions, and are manifested through or in association with other objects either in direct perception or in memory. They are thus the qualities which are generated in the self as a result of causal operation. It should however be remembered that merit and demerit act as concomitant causes in their production.

The yogins are believed to have the pratyakṣa of the most distant things beyond our senses; they can acquire this power by gradually increasing their powers of concentration and perceive the subtlest and most distant objects directly by their mind. Even we ourselves may at some time have the notions of future events which come to be true, e.g. sometimes I may have the intuition that "Tomorrow my brother will come,"

[1] *Siddhāntamuktāvalī* on *Kārikā* 63 and 64. We must remember that Gaṅgeśa discarded the definition of perception as given in the *Nyāya sūtra* which we have discussed above, and held that perception should be defined as that cognition which has the special class-character of direct apprehension. He thinks that the old definition of perception as the cognition generated by sense-contact involves a vicious circle (*Tattvacintāmaṇi*, pp. 538–546). Sense-contact is still regarded by him as the cause of perception, but it should not be included in the definition. He agrees to the six kinds of contact described first by Udyotakara as mentioned above.

and this may happen to be true. This is called pratibhāna-jñāna, which is also to be regarded as a pratyakṣa directly by the mind. This is of course different from the other form of perception called mānasa-pratyakṣa, by which memories of past perceptions by other senses are associated with a percept visualized at the present moment; thus we see a rose and perceive that it is fragrant; the fragrance is not perceived by the eye, but the manas perceives it directly and associates the visual percept with it. According to Vedānta this acquired perception is only a case of inference. The prātibha-pratyakṣa however is that which is with reference to the happening of a future event. When a cognition is produced, it is produced only as an objective cognition, e.g. This is a pot, but after this it is again related to the self by the mind as "I know this pot." This is effected by the mind again coming in contact for reperception of the cognition which had already been generated in the soul. This second reperception is called anuvyavasāya, and all practical work can proceed as a result of this anuvyavasāya[1].

Inference.

Inference (*anumāna*) is the second means of proof (pramāṇa) and the most valuable contribution that Nyāya has made has been on this subject. It consists in making an assertion about a thing on the strength of the mark or liṅga which is associated with it, as when finding smoke rising from a hill we remember that since smoke cannot be without fire, there must also be fire in yonder hill. In an example like this smoke is technically called liṅga, or hetu. That about which the assertion has been made (the hill in this example) is called pakṣa, and the term " fire" is called sādhya. To make a correct inference it is necessary that the hetu or liṅga must be present in the pakṣa,

[1] This later Nyāya doctrine that the cognition of self in association with cognition is produced at a later moment must be contrasted with the *triputīpratyakṣa* doctrine of Prabhākara, which holds that the object, knower and knowledge are all given simultaneously in knowledge. Vyavasāya (determinate cognition), according to Gaṅgeśa, gives us only the cognition of the object, but the cognition that I am aware of this object or cognition is a different functioning succeeding the former one and is called anu (after) vyavasāya (cognition), "*idamahaṃ jānāmīti vyavasāye na bhāsate tad-bodhakendriyasannikarṣābhāvāt kintvidaṃviṣayakajñānatvaviśtṣṭasya jñānasya vaiśiṣtyamātmani bhāsate*; *na ca svaprakāśe vyavasāye tādṛśaṃ svasya vaiśiṣṭyaṃ bhāsitumarhati*, *pūrvaṃ viśeṣaṇasya tasyājñānāt*, *tasmādidamahaṃ jānāmīti na vyavasāyaḥ kintu anuvyavasāyah*." *Tattvacintāmaṇi*, p. 795.

and in all other known objects similar to the pakṣa in having the sādhya in it (sapakṣa-sattā), i.e., which are known to possess the sādhya (possessing fire in the present example). The liṅga must not be present in any such object as does not possess the sādhya (*vipakṣa-vyāvṛtti* absent from vipakṣa or that which does not possess the sādhya). The inferred assertion should not be such that it is invalidated by direct perception (*pratyakṣa*) or the testimony of the śāstra (*abādhita-viṣayatva*). The liṅga should not be such that by it an inference in the opposite way could also be possible (*asat-pratipakṣa*). The violation of any one of these conditions would spoil the certitude of the hetu as determining the inference, and thus would only make the hetu fallacious, or what is technically called hetvābhāsa or seeming hetu by which no correct inference could be made. Thus the inference that sound is eternal because it is visible is fallacious, for visibility is a quality which sound (here the pakṣa) does not possess[1]. This hetvābhāsa is technically called *asiddha-hetu*. Again, hetvābhāsa of the second type, technically called *viruddha-hetu*, may be exemplified in the case that sound is eternal, since it is created; the hetu " being created" is present in the opposite of sādhya (*vipakṣa*), namely non-eternality, for we know that non-eternality is a quality which belongs to all created things. A fallacy of the third type, technically called *anaikāntika-hetu*, is found in the case that sound is eternal, since it is an object of knowledge. Now "being an object of knowledge" (*prameyatva*) is here the hetu, but it is present in things eternal (i.e. things possessing sādhya), as well as in things that are not eternal (i.e. which do not possess the sādhya), and therefore the concomitance of the hetu with the sādhya is not absolute (*anaikāntika*). A fallacy of the fourth type, technically called *kālātyayāpadiṣṭa*, may be found in the example—fire is not hot, since it is created like a jug, etc. Here pratyakṣa shows that fire is hot, and hence the hetu is fallacious. The fifth fallacy, called *prakaraṇasama*, is to be found in cases where opposite hetus are available at the same time for opposite conclusions, e.g. sound like a jug is non-

[1] It should be borne in mind that Nyāya did not believe in the doctrine of the eternality of sound, which the Mīmāṃsā did. Eternality of sound meant with Mīmāṃsā the theory that sounds existed as eternal indestructible entities, and they were only manifested in our ears under certain conditions, e.g. the stroke of a drum or a particular kind of movement of the vocal muscles.

eternal, since no eternal qualities are found in it, and sound like ākāśa is eternal, since no non-eternal qualities are found in it.

The Buddhists held in answer to the objections raised against inference by the Cārvākas, that inferential arguments are valid, because they are arguments on the principle of the uniformity of nature in two relations, viz. *tādātmya* (essential identity) and *tadutpatti* (succession in a relation of cause and effect). Tādātmya is a relation of genus and species and not of causation; thus we know that all pines are trees, and infer that this is a tree since it is a pine; tree and pine are related to each other as genus and species, and the co-inherence of the generic qualities of a tree with the specific characters of a pine tree may be viewed as a relation of essential identity (*tādātmya*). The relation of tadutpatti is that of uniformity of succession of cause and effect, e.g. of smoke to fire.

Nyāya holds that inference is made because of the invariable association (*niyama*) of the liṅga or hetu (the concomitance of which with the sādhya has been safeguarded by the five conditions noted above) with the sādhya, and not because of such specific relations as tādātmya or tadutpatti. If it is held that the inference that it is a tree because it is a pine is due to the essential identity of tree and pine, then the opposite argument that it is a pine because it is a tree ought to be valid as well; for if it were a case of identity it ought to be the same both ways. If in answer to this it is said that the characteristics of a pine are associated with those of a tree and not those of a tree with those of a pine, then certainly the argument is not due to essential identity, but to the invariable association of the liṅga (mark) with the liṅgin (the possessor of liṅga), otherwise called niyama. The argument from tadutpatti (association as cause and effect) is also really due to invariable association, for it explains the case of the inference of the type of cause and effect as well as of other types of inference, where the association as cause and effect is not available (e.g. from sunset the rise of stars is inferred). Thus it is that the invariable concomitance of the liṅga with the liṅgin, as safeguarded by the conditions noted above, is what leads us to make a valid inference[1].

We perceived in many cases that a liṅga (e.g. smoke) was associated with a liṅgin (fire), and had thence formed the notion

[1] See *Nyāyamañjarī* on anumāna.

that wherever there was smoke there was fire. Now when we perceived that there was smoke in yonder hill, we remembered the concomitance (*vyāpti*) of smoke and fire which we had observed before, and then since there was smoke in the hill, which was known to us to be inseparably connected with fire, we concluded that there was fire in the hill. The discovery of the liṅga (smoke) in the hill as associated with the memory of its concomitance with fire (*tṛtīya-liṅga-parāmarśa*) is thus the cause (*anumitikaraṇa* or *anumāna*) of the inference (*anumiti*). The concomitance of smoke with fire is technically called *vyāpti*. When this refers to the concomitance of cases containing smoke with those having fire, it is called *bahirvyāpti*; and when it refers to the conviction of the concomitance of smoke with fire, without any relation to the circumstances under which the concomitance was observed, it is called *antarvyāpti*. The Buddhists since they did not admit the notions of generality, etc. preferred antarvyāpti view of concomitance to bahirvyāpti as a means of inference[1].

Now the question arises that since the validity of an inference will depend mainly on the validity of the concomitance of sign (*hetu*) with the signate (*sādhya*), how are we to assure ourselves in each case that the process of ascertaining the concomitance (*vyāptigraha*) had been correct, and the observation of concomitance had been valid. The Mīmāṃsā school held, as we shall see in the next chapter, that if we had no knowledge of any such case in which there was smoke but no fire, and if in all the cases I knew I had perceived that wherever there was smoke there was fire, I could enunciate the concomitance of smoke with fire. But Nyāya holds that it is not enough that in all cases where there is smoke there should be fire, but it is necessary that in all those cases where there is no fire there should not be any smoke, i.e. not only every case of the existence of smoke should be a case of the existence of fire, but every case of absence of fire should be a case of absence of smoke. The former is technically called *anvayavyāpti* and the latter *vyatirekavyāpti*. But even this is not enough. Thus there may have been an ass sitting, in a hundred cases where I had seen smoke, and there might have been a hundred cases where there was neither ass nor smoke, but it cannot be asserted from it that there is any relation of concomi-

[1] See *Antarvyāptisamarthana*, by Ratnākaraśānti in the *Six Buddhist Nyāya Tracts*, *Bibliotheca Indica*, 1910.

tance, or of cause and effect between the ass and the smoke. It may be that one might never have observed smoke without an antecedent ass, or an ass without the smoke following it, but even that is not enough. If it were such that we had so experienced in a very large number of cases that the introduction of the ass produced the smoke, and that even when all the antecedents remained the same, the disappearance of the ass was immediately followed by the disappearance of smoke (*yasmin sati bhavanam yato vinā na bhavanam iti bhūyodarśanaṃ*, *Nyāyamañjarī*, p. 122), then only could we say that there was any relation of concomitance (*vyāpti*) between the ass and the smoke[1]. But of course it might be that what we concluded to be the hetu by the above observations of anvaya-vyatireka might not be a real hetu, and there might be some other condition (*upādhi*) associated with the hetu which was the real hetu. Thus we know that fire in green wood (*ārdrendhana*) produced smoke, but one might doubt that it was not the fire in the green wood that produced smoke, but there was some hidden demon who did it. But there would be no end of such doubts, and if we indulged in them, all our work endeavour and practical activities would have to be dispensed with (*vyāghāta*). Thus such doubts as lead us to the suspension of all work should not disturb or unsettle the notion of vyāpti or concomitance at which we had arrived by careful observation and consideration[2]. The Buddhists and the naiyāyikas generally agreed as to the method of forming the notion of concomitance or vyāpti (*vyāptigraha*), but the former tried to assert that the validity of such a concomitance always depended on a relation of cause and effect or of identity of essence, whereas Nyāya held that neither the relations of cause and effect, nor that of essential identity of genus and species, exhausted the field of inference, and there was quite a number of other types of inference which could not be brought under either of them (e.g. the rise of the moon and the tide of the ocean). A natural fixed order that certain things happening other things would happen could certainly exist, even without the supposition of an identity of essence.

But sometimes it happens that different kinds of causes often have the same kind of effect, and in such cases it is difficult to

[1] See *Tātparyaṭikā* on anumāna and vyāptigraha.

[2] *Tātparyaṭikā* on vyāptigraha, and *Tattvacintāmaṇi* of Gaṅgeśa on vyāptigraha.

infer the particular cause from the effect. Nyāya holds however that though different causes are often found to produce the same effect, yet there must be some difference between one effect and another. If each effect is taken by itself with its other attendant circumstances and peculiarities, it will be found that it may then be possible to distinguish it from similar other effects. Thus a flood in the street may be due either to a heavy downpour of rain immediately before, or to the rise in the water of the river close by, but if observed carefully the flooding of the street due to rain will be found to have such special traits that it could be distinguished from a similar flooding due to the rise of water in the river. Thus from the flooding of the street of a special type, as demonstrated by its other attendant circumstances, the special manner in which the water flows by small rivulets or in sheets, will enable us to infer that the flood was due to rains and not to the rise of water in the river. Thus we see that Nyāya relied on empirical induction based on uniform and uninterrupted agreement in nature, whereas the Buddhists assumed *a priori* principles of causality or identity of essence. It may not be out of place here to mention that in later Nyāya works great emphasis is laid on the necessity of getting ourselves assured that there was no such upādhi (condition) associated with the hetu on account of which the concomitance happened, but that the hetu was unconditionally associated with the sādhya in a relation of inseparable concomitance. Thus all fire does not produce smoke; fire must be associated with green wood in order to produce smoke. Green wood is thus the necessary condition (*upādhi*) without which no smoke could be produced. It is on account of this condition that fire is associated with smoke; and so we cannot say that there is smoke because there is fire. But in the concomitance of smoke with fire there is no condition, and so in every case of smoke there is fire. In order to be assured of the validity of vyāpti, it is necessary that we must be assured that there should be nothing associated with the hetu which conditioned the concomitance, and this must be settled by wide experience (*bhūyodarśana*).

Praśastapāda in defining inference as the "knowledge of that (e.g. fire) associated with the reason (e.g. smoke) by the sight of the reason" described a valid reason (*liṅga*) as that which is connected with the object of inference (*anumeya*) and which exists wherever the object of inference exists and is absent in all cases where it does not exist. This is indeed the same as the Nyāya qualifications of *pakṣasattva*, *sapakṣasattva* and *vipakṣāsattva* of a valid reason (hetu). Praśastapāda further quotes a verse to say that this is the same as what Kāśyapa (believed to be the family name of Kaṇāda) said. Kaṇāda says that we can infer a cause from the effect, the effect from the cause, or we can infer one thing by another when they are mutually connected, or in opposition or in a relation of inherence (IX. ii. 1 and III. i. 9). We can infer by a reason because it is duly associated (*prasiddhipūr-vakatva*) with the object of inference. What this association was according to Kaṇāda can also be understood for he tells us (III. i. 15) that where there is no proper association, the reason (hetu) is either non-existent in the object to be inferred or it has no concomitance with it (*aprasiddha*) or it has a doubtful existence (*sandigdha*). Thus if I say this ass is a horse because it has horns it is fallacious, for neither the horse nor the ass has horns. Again if I say it is a cow because it has horns, it is fallacious, for there is no concomitance between horns and a cow, and though a cow may have a horn, all that have horns are not cows. The first fallacy is a combination of pakṣāsattva and sapakṣāsattva, for not only the present pakṣa (the ass) had no horns, but no horses had any horns, and the second is a case of vīpakṣasattva, for those which are not cows (e.g. buffaloes) have also horns. Thus, it seems that when Praśastapāda says that he is giving us the view of Kaṇāda he is faithful to it. Praśastapāda says that wherever there is smoke there is fire, if there is no fire there is no smoke. When one knows this concomitance and unerringly perceives the smoke, he remembers the concomitance and feels certain that there is fire. But with regard to Kaṇāda's enumeration of types of inference such as "a cause is inferred from its effect, or an effect from the cause," etc., Praśastapāda holds that these are not the only types of inference, but are only some examples for showing the general nature of inference. Inference merely shows a connection such that from this that can be inferred. He then divides inference into two classes, dṛṣṭa (from the experienced characteristics of one member of a class to another member of the same class), and sāmānyato dṛṣṭa. Dṛṣṭa (perceived resemblance) is that where the previously known case and the inferred case is exactly of the same class. Thus as an example of it we can point out that by perceiving that only a cow has a hanging mass of flesh on its neck (sāsnā), I can whenever I see the same hanging mass of flesh at the neck of an animal infer that it is a cow. But when on the strength of a common quality the inference is extended to a different class of objects, it is called sāmānyato dṛṣṭa. Thus on perceiving that the work of the peasants is rewarded with a good harvest I may infer that the work of the priests, namely the performance of sacrifices, will also be rewarded with the objects for which they are performed (i.e. the attainment of heaven). When the conclusion, to which one has arrived (*svani-ścitārtha*) is expressed in five premisses for convincing others who are either in doubt, or in error or are simply ignorant, then the inference is called parārthānumāna. We know that the distinction of svārthānumāna (inference for oneself) and parārthānumāna (inference for others) was made by the Jains and Buddhists. Praśastapāda does not make a sharp distinction of two classes of inference, but he seems to mean that what one infers, it can be conveyed to others by means of five premisses in which case it is called parārthānumāna. But this need not be considered as an entirely new innovation of Praśastapāda, for in IX. 2, Kaṇāda himself definitely alludes to this distinction (*asyedaṃ kāryyakāra-ṇasambandhaścāvayavādbhavati*). The five premisses which are called in Nyāya *pratijñā*, *hetu dṛṣṭānta*, *upanaya*, and *nigamana* are called in Vaiśeṣika *pratijñā*, *apadeśa*, *nidarśana*, *anusandhāna*, and *pratyāmnāya*. Kaṇāda however does not mention the name of any of these premisses excepting the second "apadeśa." Pratijñā is of course the same as we have in Nyāya, and the term nidarśana is very similar to Nyāya dṛṣṭānta, but the last two are entirely different. Nidarśana may be of two kinds, (1) agreement in presence (e.g. that which has motion is a substance as is seen in the case of an arrow), (2) agreement in absence (e.g. what is not a substance has no motion as is seen in the case of the universal being[1]). He also points out cases of the fallacy of the example

[1] Dr Vidyābhūṣaṇa says that "An example before the time of Dignāga served as a mere familiar case which was cited to help the understanding of the listener, e.g. The hill is fiery; because it has smoke; like a kitchen (example). Asaṅga made the example more serviceable to reasoning, but Dignāga converted it into a universal proposition, that is a proposition expressive of the universal or inseparable connection between the middle term and the major term, e.g. The hill is fiery; because it has smoke; all that has smoke is fiery as a kitchen" (*Indian Logic*, pp. 95, 96). It is of course true that Vatsyāyana had an imperfect example as "like a kitchen" (*śabdaḥ utpattidharmakatvādanityaḥ sthālyādivat*, I. i. 36), but Praśastapāda has it in the proper form. Whether Praśastapāda borrowed it from Diṅnāga or Diṅnāga from Praśastapāda cannot be easily settled.

(*nidarśanābhāsa*). Praśastapāda's contribution thus seems to consist of the enumeration of the five premisses and the fallacy of the nidarśana, but the names of the last two premisses are so different from what are current in other systems that it is reasonable to suppose that he collected them from some other traditional Vaiśeṣika work which is now lost to us. It however definitely indicates that the study of the problem of inference was being pursued in Vaiśeṣika circles independently of Nyāya. There is no reason however to suppose that Praśastapāda borrowed anything from Diṅnāga as Professor Stcherbatsky or Keith supposes, for, as I have shown above, most of Praśastapāda's apparent innovations are all definitely alluded to by Kaṇāda himself, and Professor Keith has not discussed this alternative. On the question of the fallacies of nidarśana, unless it is definitely proved that Diṅnāga preceded Praśastapāda, there is no reason whatever to suppose that the latter borrowed it from the former[1].

The nature and ascertainment of concomitance is the most important part of inference. Vātsyāyana says that an inference can be made by the sight of the liṅga (reason or middle) through the memory of the connection between the middle and the major previously perceived. Udyotakara raises the question whether it is the present perception of the middle or the memory of the connection of the middle with the major that should be regarded as leading to inference. His answer is that both these lead to inference, but that which immediately leads to inference is *liṅga-parāmarśa*, i.e. the present perception of the middle in the minor associated with the memory of its connection with the major, for inference does not immediately follow the memory of the connection, but the present perception of the middle associated with the memory of the connection (*smṛtyanugṛhīto liṅgaparāmarśo*). But he is silent with regard to the nature of concomitance. Udyotakara's criticisms of Diṅnāga as shown by Vācaspati have no reference to this point. The doctrine of *tādātmya* and *tadutpatti* was therefore in all probability a new contribution to Buddhist logic by Dharmakīrtti. Dharmakīrtti's contention was that the root principle of the connection between the middle and the major was that the former was either identical in essence with the latter or its effect and that unless this was grasped a mere collection of positive or negative instances will not give us

[1] Praśastapāda's bhāṣya with *Nyāyakandalī*, pp. 200—255.

the desired connection[1]. Vācaspati in his refutation of this view says that the cause-effect relation cannot be determined as a separate relation. If causality means invariable immediate antecedence such that there being fire there is smoke and there being no fire there is no smoke, then it cannot be ascertained with perfect satisfaction, for there is no proof that in each case the smoke was caused by fire and not by an invisible demon. Unless it can be ascertained that there was no invisible element associated, it cannot be said that the smoke was immediately preceded by fire and fire alone. Again accepting for the sake of argument that causality can be determined, then also cause is known to precede the effect and therefore the perception of smoke can only lead us to infer the presence of fire at a preceding time and not contemporaneously with it. Moreover there are many cases where inference is possible, but there is no relation of cause and effect or of identity of essence (e.g. the sunrise of this morning by the sunrise of yesterday morning). In the case of identity of essence (*tādātmya* as in the case of the pine and the tree) also there cannot be any inference, for one thing has to be inferred by another, but if they are identical there cannot be any inference. The nature of concomitance therefore cannot be described in either of these ways. Some things (e.g. smoke) are naturally connected with some other things (e.g. fire) and when such is the case, though we may not know any further about the nature of this connection, we may infer the latter from the former and not vice versa, for fire is connected with smoke only under certain conditions (e.g. green wood). It may be argued that there may always be certain unknown conditions which may vitiate the validity of inference. To this Vācaspati's answer is that if even after observing a large number of cases and careful search such conditions (*upādhi*) cannot be discovered, we have to take it for granted that they do not exist and that there is a natural connection between the middle and the major. The later Buddhists introduced the method of *Pañcakāraṇī* in order to determine effectively the causal relation. These five conditions determining the causal relation are (1) neither the cause nor the effect is perceived, (2) the cause is perceived, (3) in immediate succession the effect is perceived, (4) the cause disappears, (5) in

[1] *Kāryyakāraṇabhāvādvā svabhāvādva niyāmakāt avinābhāvaniyamo' darśanānna na darśanāt. Tātparyaṭīkā*, p. 105.

immediate succession the effect disappears. But this method cannot guarantee the infallibility of the determination of cause and effect relation; and if by the assumption of a cause-effect relation no higher degree of certainty is available, it is better to accept a natural relation without limiting it to a cause-effect relation[1].

In early Nyāya books three kinds of inference are described, namely pūrvavat, śeṣavat, and sāmānyato-dṛṣṭa. Pūrvavat is the inference of effects from causes, e.g. that of impending rain from heavy dark clouds; śeṣavat is the inference of causes from effects, e.g. that of rain from the rise of water in the river; sāmānyato-dṛṣṭa refers to the inference in all cases other than those of cause and effect, e.g. the inference of the sour taste of the tamarind from its form and colour. *Nyāyamañjarī* mentions another form of anumāna, namely pariśeṣamāna (*reductio ad absurdum*), which consists in asserting anything (e.g. consciousness) of any other thing (e.g. ātman), because it was already definitely found out that consciousness was not produced in any other part of man. Since consciousness could not belong to anything else, it must belong to soul of necessity. In spite of these variant forms they are all however of one kind, namely that of the inference of the probandum (*sādhya*) by virtue of the unconditional and invariable concomitance of the hetu, called the vyāpti-niyama. In the new school of Nyāya (Navya-Nyāya) a formal distinction of three kinds of inference occupies an important place, namely anvayavyatireki, kevalānvayi, and kevalavyatireki. Anvayavyatireki is that inference where the vyāpti has been observed by a combination of a large number of instances of agreement in presence and agreement in absence, as in the case of the concomitance of smoke and fire (wherever there is smoke there is fire (*anvaya*), and where there is no fire, there is no smoke (*vyatireka*)). An inference could be for one's own self (*svārthānumāna*) or for the sake of convincing others (*parārthānumāna*). In the latter case, when it was necessary that an inference should be put explicitly in an unambiguous manner, five propositions (*avayavas*) were regarded as necessary, namely pratijña (e.g. the hill is fiery), hetu (since it has smoke), udāharaṇa (where there is smoke there is fire, as in the kitchen), upanaya (this hill has smoke), nigamana (therefore it has got

[1] Vātsyāyaṇa's bhāṣya, Udyotakara's *Vārttika* and *Tātparyyaṭikā*, I. i. 5.

fire). Kevalānvayi is that type of inference, the vyāpti of which could not be based on any negative instance, as in the case "this object has a name, since it is an object of knowledge (*idaṃ, vācyam prameyatvāt*)." Now no such case is known which is not an object of knowledge; we cannot therefore know of any case where there was no object of knowledge (*prameyatva*) and no name (*vācyatva*); the vyāpti here has therefore to be based necessarily on cases of agreement—wherever there is prameyatva or an object of knowledge, there is vācyatva or name. The third form of kevalavyatireki is that where positive instances in agreement cannot be found, such as in the case of the inference that earth differs from other elements in possessing the specific quality of smell, since all that does not differ from other elements is not earth, such as water; here it is evident that there cannot be any positive instance of agreement and the concomitance has to be taken from negative instances. There is only one instance, which is exactly the proposition of our inference—earth differs from other elements, since it has the special qualities of earth. This inference could be of use only in those cases where we had to infer anything by reason of such special traits of it as was possessed by it and it alone.

Upamāna and Śabda.

The third pramāṇa, which is admitted by Nyāya and not by Vaiśeṣika, is *upamāna*, and consists in associating a thing unknown before with its name by virtue of its similarity with some other known thing. Thus a man of the city who has never seen a wild ox (*gavaya*) goes to the forest, asks a forester—"what is gavaya?" and the forester replies—"oh, you do not know it, it is just like a cow"; after hearing this from the forester he travels on, and on seeing a gavaya and finding it to be similar to a cow he forms the opinion that this is a gavaya. This knowing an hitherto unknown thing by virtue of its similarity to a known thing is called *upamāna*. If some forester had pointed out a gavaya to a man of the city and had told him that it was called a gavaya, then also the man would have known the animal by the name gavaya, but then this would have been due to testimony (*śabda-pramāṇa*). The knowledge is said to be generated by the upamāna process when the association of the unknown animal with its name is made by the observer on the strength of the experience of the similarity of the unknown animal to a known one. The naiyāyikas are thorough realists, and as such they do not regard the observation of similarity as being due to any subjective process of the mind. Similarity is indeed perceived by the visual sense but yet the association of the name in accordance with the perception of similarity and the instruction received is a separate act and is called *upamāna*[1].

Śabda-pramāṇa or testimony is the right knowledge which we derive from the utterances of infallible and absolutely truthful persons. All knowledge derived from the Vedas is valid, for the Vedas were uttered by Īśvara himself. The Vedas give us right knowledge not of itself, but because they came out as the utterances of the infallible Īśvara. The Vaiśeṣikas did not admit śabda as a separate pramāṇa, but they sought to establish the validity of testimony (*śabda*) on the strength of inference (*anumiti*) on the ground of its being the utterance of an infallible person. But as I have said before, this explanation is hardly corroborated by the Vaiśeṣika sūtras, which tacitly admit the validity of the scriptures on its own authority. But anyhow this was how Vaiśeṣika was interpreted in later times.

Negation in Nyāya-Vaiśeṣika.

The problem of negation or non-existence (*abhāva*) is of great interest in Indian philosophy. In this section we can describe its nature only from the point of view of perceptibility. Kumārila[2]

[1] See *Nyāyamañjarī* on upamāna. The oldest Nyāya view was that the instruction given by the forester by virtue of which the association of the name "wild ox" to the strange animal was possible was itself "upamāna." When Praśastapāda held that upamāna should be treated as a case of testimony (*āptavacana*), he had probably this interpretation in view. But Udyotakara and Vācaspati hold that it was not by the instruction alone of the forester that the association of the name "wild ox" was made, but there was the perception of similarity, and the memory of the instruction of the forester too. So it is the perception of similarity with the other two factors as accessories that lead us to this association called upamāna. What Vātsyāyana meant is not very clear, but Diṅnāga supposes that according to him the result of upamāna was the knowledge of similarity or the knowledge of a thing having similarity. Vācaspati of course holds that he has correctly interpreted Vātsyāyaṇa's intention. It is however definite that upamāna means the associating of a name to a new object (*samākhyāsambandhapratipattirupamānārthaḥ*, Vātsyāyaṇa). Jayanta points out that it is the preception of similarity which directly leads to the association of the name and hence the instruction of the forester cannot be regarded as the direct cause and consequently it cannot be classed under testimony (*śabda*). See Praśastapāda and *Nyāyakandalī*, pp. 220–22, Vātsyāyaṇa, Udyotakara, Vācaspati and Jayanta on *Upamāna*.

[2] See Kumārila's treatment of abhāva in the *Ślokavdrttika*, pp. 473–492.

and his followers, whose philosophy we shall deal with in the next chapter, hold that negation (*abhāva*) appears as an intuition (*mānam*) with reference to the object negated where there are no means of ordinary cognition (*pramāṇa*) leading to prove the existence (*satparicchedakam*) of that thing. They held that the notion "it is not existent" cannot be due to perception, for there is no contact here with sense and object. It is true indeed that when we turn our eyes (e.g. in the case of the perception of the non-existence of a jug) to the ground, we see both the ground and the non-existence of a jug, and when we shut them we can see neither the jug nor the ground, and therefore it could be urged that if we called the ground visually perceptible, we could say the same with regard to the non-existence of the jug. But even then since in the case of the perception of the jug there is sense-contact, which is absent in the other case, we could never say that both are grasped by perception. We see the ground and remember the jug (which is absent) and thus in the mind rises the notion of non-existence which has no reference at all to visual perception. A man may be sitting in a place where there were no tigers, but he might not then be aware of their non-existence at the time, since he did not think of them, but when later on he is asked in the evening if there were any tigers at the place where he was sitting in the morning, he then thinks and becomes aware of the non-existence of tigers there in the morning, even without perceiving the place and without any operation of the memory of the non-existence of tigers. There is no question of there being any inference in the rise of our notion of non-existence, for it is not preceded by any notion of concomitance of any kind, and neither the ground nor the non-perception of the jug could be regarded as a reason (*liṅga*), for the non-perception of the jug is related to the jug and not to the negation of the jug, and no concomitance is known between the non-perception of the jug and its non-existence, and when the question of the concomitance of non-perception with non-existence is brought in, the same difficulty about the notion of non-existence (*abhāva*) which was sought to be explained will recur again. Negation is therefore to be admitted as cognized by a separate and independent process of knowledge. Nyāya however says that the perception of non-existence (e.g. there is no jug here) is a unitary perception of one whole, just as any perception of positive existence (e.g.

there is a jug on the ground) is. Both the knowledge of the ground as well as the knowledge of the non-existence of the jug arise there by the same kind of action of the visual organ, and there is therefore no reason why the knowledge of the ground should be said to be due to perception, whereas the knowledge of the negation of the jug on the ground should be said to be due to a separate process of knowledge. The non-existence of the jug is taken in the same act as the ground is perceived. The principle that in order to perceive a thing one should have sense-contact with it, applies only to positive existents and not to negation or non-existence. Negation or non-existence can be cognized even without any sense-contact. Non-existence is not a positive substance, and hence there cannot be any question here of sense-contact. It may be urged that if no sense-contact is required in apprehending negation, one could as well apprehend negation or non-existence of other places which are far away from him. To this the reply is that to apprehend negation it is necessary that the place where it exists must be perceived. We know a thing and its quality to be different, and yet the quality can only be taken in association with the thing and it is so in this case as well. We can apprehend non-existence only through the apprehension of its locus. In the case when non-existence is said to be apprehended later on it is really no later apprehension of non-existence but a memory of non-existence (e.g. of jug) perceived before along with the perception of the locus of non-existence (e.g. ground). Negation or non-existence (*abhāva*) can thus, according to Nyāya, generate its cognition just as any positive existence can do. Negation is not mere negativity or mere vacuous absence, but is what generates the cognition "is not," as position (*bhāva*) is what generates the cognition "it is."

The Buddhists deny the existence of negation. They hold that when a negation is apprehended, it is apprehended with specific time and space conditions (e.g. this is not here now); but in spite of such an apprehension, we could never think that negation could thus be associated with them in any relation. There is also no relation between the negation and its *pratiyogi* (thing negated—e.g. jug in the negation of jug), for when there is the pratiyogi there is no negation, and when there is the negation there is no pratiyogi. There is not even the relation of opposition (*virodha*), for we could have admitted it, if the negation of the jug existed before and opposed the jug, for how can the negation of the jug oppose the jug, without effecting anything at all? Again, it may be asked whether negation is to be regarded as a positive being or becoming or of the nature of not becoming or non-being. In the first alternative it will be like any other positive existents, and in the second case it will be permanent and eternal, and it cannot be related to this or that particular negation. There are however many kinds of non-perception, e.g. (1) svabhāvānupalabdhi (natural non-perception—there is no jug because none is perceived); (2) kāraṇānupalabdhi (non-perception of cause—there is no smoke here, since there is no fire); (3) vyāpakānupalabdhi (non-perception of the species—there is no pine here, since there is no tree); (4) kāryānupalabdhi (non-perception of effects—there are not the causes of smoke here, since there is no smoke); (5) svabhāvaviruddhopalabdhi (perception of contradictory natures—there is no cold touch here because of fire); (6) viruddhakāryopalabdhi (perception of contradictory effects—there is no cold touch here because of smoke); (7) viruddhavyāptopalabdhi (opposite concomitance—past is not of necessity destructible, since it depends on other causes); (8) kāryyaviruddhopalabdhi (opposition of effects—there is not here the causes which can give cold since there is fire); (9) vyāpakaviruddhopalabdhi (opposite concomitants—there is no touch of snow here, because of fire); (10) kāraṇaviruddhopalabdhi (opposite causes—there is no shivering through cold here, since he is near the fire); (11) kāraṇaviruddhakāryyopalabdhi (effects of opposite causes—this place is not occupied by men of shivering sensations for it is full of smoke[1]).

There is no doubt that in the above ways we speak of negation, but that does not prove that there is any reason for the cognition of negation (*keturnābhāvasamvidaḥ*). All that we can say is this that there are certain situations which justify the use (*yogyatā*) of negative appellations. But this situation or yogyatā is positive in character. What we all speak of in ordinary usage as non-perception is of the nature of perception of some sort. Perception of negation thus does not prove the existence of negation, but only shows that there are certain positive perceptions which are only interpreted in that way. It is the positive perception of the ground where the visible jug is absent that

[1] See *Nyāyabindu*, p. 11, and *Nyāyamañjarī*, pp. 53–7.

leads us to speak of having perceived the negation of the jug (*anupalambhaḥ abhāvaṃ vyavahārayati*)[1].

The Nyāya reply against this is that the perception of positive existents is as much a fact as the perception of negation, and we have no right to say that the former alone is valid. It is said that the non-perception of jug on the ground is but the perception of the ground without the jug. But is this being without the jug identical with the ground or different? If identical then it is the same as the ground, and we shall expect to have it even when the jug is there. If different then the quarrel is only over the name, for whatever you may call it, it is admitted to be a distinct category. If some difference is noted between the ground with the jug, and the ground without it, then call it "ground, without the jugness" or "the negation of jug," it does not matter much, for a distinct category has anyhow been admitted. Negation is apprehended by perception as much as any positive existent is; the nature of the objects of perception only are different; just as even in the perception of positive sense-objects there are such diversities as colour, taste, etc. The relation of negation with space and time with which it appears associated is the relation that subsists between the qualified and the quality (*viśeṣya viśeṣaṇa*). The relation between the negation and its pratiyogi is one of opposition, in the sense that where the one is the other is not. The *Vaiśeṣika sūtra* (IX. i. 6) seems to take abhāva in a similar way as Kumārila the Mīmaṃsist does, though the commentators have tried to explain it away[2]. In Vaiśeṣika the four kinds of negation are enumerated as (1) *prāgabhāva* (the negation preceding the production of an object—e.g. of the jug before it is made by the potter); (2) *dhvaṃsābhāva* (the negation following the destruction of an object—as of the jug after it is destroyed by the stroke of a stick); (3) *anyonyābhāva* (mutual negation—e.g. in the cow there is the negation of the horse and

[1] See *Nyāyabinduṭīkā*, pp. 34 ff., and also *Nyāyamañjarī*, pp. 48-63.

[2] Praśastapāda says that as the production of an effect is the sign of the existence of the cause, so the non-production of it is the sign of its non-existence. Śrīdhara in commenting upon it says that the non-preception of a sensible object is the sign (*liṅga*) of its non-existence. But evidently he is not satisfied with the view for he says that non-existence is also directly perceived by the senses (*bhāvavad abhāvo' pīndriyagra-haṇayogyaḥ*) and that there is an actual sense-contact with non-existence which is the collocating cause of the preception of non-existence (*abhāvendriyasannikarṣa'pi abhāvagrahaṇasāmagrī*), *Nyāyakandalī*, pp. 225-30.

in the horse that of the cow); (4) *atyantābhāva* (a negation which always exists—e.g. even when there is a jug here, its negation in other places is not destroyed)[1].

The necessity of the Acquirement of debating devices for the seeker of Salvation.

It is probable that the Nyāya philosophy arose in an atmosphere of continued disputes and debates; as a consequence of this we find here many terms related to debates which we do not notice in any other system of Indian philosophy. These are *tarka*, *nirṇaya*, *vāda*, *jalpa*, *vitaṇḍā*, *hetvābhāsa*, *chala*, *jāti* and *nigrahasthāna*.

Tarka means deliberation on an unknown thing to discern its real nature; it thus consists of seeking reasons in favour of some supposition to the exclusion of other suppositions; it is not inference, but merely an oscillation of the mind to come to a right conclusion. When there is doubt (*saṃśaya*) about the specific nature of anything we have to take to tarka. Nirṇaya means the conclusion to which we arrive as a result of tarka. When two opposite parties dispute over their respective theses, such as the doctrines that there is or is not an ātman, in which each of them tries to prove his own thesis with reasons, each of the theses is called a *vāda*. Jalpa means a dispute in which the disputants give wrangling rejoinders in order to defeat their respective opponents. A jalpa is called a *vitaṇḍā* when it is only a destructive criticism which seeks to refute the opponent's doctrine without seeking to establish or formulate any new doctrine. Hetvābhāsas are those which appear as hetus but are really not so. *Nyāya sūtras* enumerate five fallacies (*hetvābhāsas*) of the middle (hetu): *savyabhicāra* (erratic), *viruddha* (contradictory), *prakaraṇasama* (tautology), *sādhyasama* (unproved reason) and *kālātīta* (inopportune). Savyabhicāra is that where the same reason may prove opposite conclusions (e.g. sound is eternal because it is intangible like the atoms which are eternal, and sound is non-eternal because it is intangible like cognitions which are non-eternal); viruddha is that where the reason opposes the premiss to be proved (e.g. a jug is eternal, because it is produced); prakaraṇasama is that

[1] The doctrine of negation, its function and value with reference to diverse logical problems, have many diverse aspects, and it is impossible to do them justice in a small section like this.

where the reason repeats the thesis to be proved in another form (e.g. sound is non-eternal because it has not the quality of eternality); sādhyasama is that where the reason itself requires to be proved (e.g. shadow is a substance because it has motion, but it remains to be proved whether shadows have motion or not); kālātīta is a false analogy where the reason fails because it does not tally with the example in point of time. Thus one may argue that sound is eternal because it is the result of contact (stick and the drum) like colour which is also a result of contact of light and the object and is eternal. Here the fallacy lies in this, that colour is simultaneous with the contact of light which shows what was already there and only manifested by the light, whereas in the case of sound it is produced immediately after the contact of the stick and drum and is hence a product and hence non-eternal. The later Nyāya works divide savyabhicāra into three classes, (1) sādhāraṇa or common (e.g. the mountain is fiery because it is an object of knowledge, but even a lake which is opposed to fire is also an object of knowledge), (2) asādhāraṇa or too restricted (e.g. sound is eternal because it has the nature of sound; this cannot be a reason for the nature of sound exists only in the sound and nowhere else), and (3) anupasaṃhārin or unsubsuming (e.g. everything is non-eternal, because they are all objects of knowledge; here the fallacy lies in this, that no instance can be found which is not an object of knowledge and an opposite conclusion may also be drawn). The fallacy *satpratipakṣa* is that in which there is a contrary reason which may prove the opposite conclusion (e.g. sound is eternal because it is audible, sound is non-eternal because it is an effect). The fallacy *asiddha* (unreal) is of three kinds (1) *āśrayāsiddha* (the lotus of the sky is fragrant because it is like other lotuses; now there cannot be any lotus in the sky), (2) *svarūpāsiddha* (sound is a quality because it is visible; but sound has no visibility), (3) *vyāpyatvāsiddha* is that where the concomitance between the middle and the consequence is not invariable and inevitable; there is smoke in the hill because there is fire; but there may be fire without the smoke as in a red hot iron ball, it is only green-wood fire that is invariably associated with smoke. The fallacy *bādhita* is that which pretends to prove a thesis which is against direct experience, e.g. fire is not hot because it is a substance. We have already enumerated the fallacies counted by Vaiśeṣika. Contrary to Nyāya practice

Praśastapāda counts the fallacies of the example. Diṅnāga also counted fallacies of example (e.g. sound is eternal, because it is incorporeal, that which is incorporeal is eternal as the atoms; but atoms are not incorporeal) and Dharmakīrtti counted also the fallacies of the pakṣa (minor); but Nyāya rightly considers that the fallacies of the middle if avoided will completely safeguard inference and that these are mere repetitions. Chala means the intentional misinterpretation of the opponent's arguments for the purpose of defeating him. Jāti consists in the drawing of contradictory conclusions, the raising of false issues or the like with the deliberate intention of defeating an opponent. Nigrahasthāna means the exposure of the opponent's argument as involving self-contradiction, inconsistency or the like, by which his defeat is conclusively proved before the people to the glory of the victorious opponent. As to the utility of the description of so many debating tricks by which an opponent might be defeated in a metaphysical work, the aim of which ought to be to direct the ways that lead to emancipation, it is said by Jayanta in his *Nyāyamañjarī* that these had to be resorted to as a protective measure against arrogant disputants who often tried to humiliate a teacher before his pupils. If the teacher could not silence the opponent, the faith of the pupils in him would be shaken and great disorder would follow, and it was therefore deemed necessary that he who was plodding onward for the attainment of mokṣa should acquire these devices for the protection of his own faith and that of his pupils. A knowledge of these has therefore been enjoined in the *Nyāya sūtra* as being necessary for the attainment of salvation[1].

The doctrine of Soul.

Dhūrtta Cārvākas denied the existence of soul and regarded consciousness and life as products of bodily changes; there were other Cārvākas called Suśikṣita Cārvākas who admitted the existence of soul but thought that it was destroyed at death. The Buddhists also denied the existence of any permanent self. The naiyāyikas ascertained all the categories of metaphysics mainly by such inference as was corroborated by experience. They argued that since consciousness, pleasures, pains, willing, etc. could not belong to our body or the senses, there must be

[1] See *Nyāyamañjarī*, pp. 586–659, and *Tārkikarakṣā* of Varadarāja and *Niṣkaṇṭaka* of Mallinātha, pp. 185 ff.

some entity to which they belonged; the existence of the self is not proved according to Nyāya merely by the notion of our self-consciousness, as in the case of Mīmāṃsā, for Nyāya holds that we cannot depend upon such a perception, for it may be erroneous. It often happens that I say that I am white or I am black, but it is evident that such a perception cannot be relied upon, for the self cannot have any colour. So we cannot safely depend on our self-consciousness as upon the inference that the self has to be admitted as that entity to which consciousness, emotion, etc. adhere when they are produced as a result of collocations. Never has the production of ātman been experienced, nor has it been found to suffer any destruction like the body, so the soul must be eternal. It is not located in any part of the body, but is all-pervading, i.e. exists at the same time in all places (*vibhu*), and does not travel with the body but exists everywhere at the same time. But though ātman is thus disconnected from the body, yet its actions are seen in the body because it is with the help of the collocation of bodily limbs, etc. that action in the self can be manifested or produced. It is unconscious in itself and acquires consciousness as a result of suitable collocations[1].

Even at birth children show signs of pleasure by their different facial features, and this could not be due to anything else than the memory of the past experiences in past lives of pleasures and pains. Moreover the inequalities in the distribution of pleasures and pains and of successes and failures prove that these must be due to the different kinds of good and bad action that men performed in their past lives. Since the inequality of the world must have some reasons behind it, it is better to admit karma as the determining factor than to leave it to irresponsible chance.

Īśvara and Salvation.

Nyāya seeks to establish the existence of Īśvara on the basis of inference. We know that the Jains, the Sāṃkhya and the Buddhists did not believe in the existence of Īśvara and offered many antitheistic arguments. Nyāya wanted to refute these and prove the existence of Īśvara by an inference of the sāmānyato-dṛṣṭa type.

[1] *Jñānasamavāyanibandhanamevātmanaścetayitṛtvam*, &c. See *Nyāyamañjarī*, pp. 432 ff.

The Jains and other atheists held that though things in the world have production and decay, the world as a whole was never produced, and it was never therefore an effect. In contrast to this view the Nyāya holds that the world as a whole is also an effect like any other effect. Many geological changes and landslips occur, and from these destructive operations proceeding in nature it may be assumed that this world is not eternal but a result of production. But even if this is not admitted by the atheists they can in no way deny the arrangement and order of the universe. But they would argue that there was certainly a difference between the order and arrangement of human productions (e.g. a jug) and the order and arrangement of the universe; and therefore from the order and arrangement (*sanniveśa-viśiṣṭatā*) of the universe it could not be argued that the universe was produced by a creator; for, it is from the sort of order and arrangement that is found in human productions that a creator or producer could be inferred. To this, Nyāya answers that the concomitance is to be taken between the "order and arrangement" in a general sense and "the existence of a creator" and not with specific cases of "order and arrangement," for each specific case may have some such peculiarity in which it differs from similar other specific cases; thus the fire in the kitchen is not the same kind of fire as we find in a forest fire, but yet we are to disregard the specific individual peculiarities of fire in each case and consider the concomitance of fire in general with smoke in general. So here, we have to consider the concomitance of "order and arrangement" in general with "the existence of a creator," and thus though the order and arrangement of the world may be different from the order and arrangement of things produced by man, yet an inference from it for the existence of a creator would not be inadmissible. The objection that even now we see many effects (e.g. trees) which are daily shooting forth from the ground without any creator being found to produce them, does not hold, for it can never be proved that the plants are not actually created by a creator. The inference therefore stands that the world has a creator, since it is an effect and has order and arrangement in its construction. Everything that is an effect and has an order and arrangement has a creator, like the jug. The world is an effect and has order and arrangement and has therefore a creator. Just as the potter knows all the purposes of the jug that he makes, so Īśvara knows all the purposes of this wide universe and is thus omniscient. He knows all things always and therefore does not require memory; all things are perceived by him directly without any intervention of any internal sense such as manas, etc. He is always happy. His will is eternal, and in accordance with the karma of men the same will produces dissolution, creates, or protects the world, in the order by which each man reaps the results of his own deeds. As our self which is in itself bodiless can by its will produce changes in our body and through it in the external world, so Īśvara also can by his will create the universe though he has no body. Some, however, say that if any association of body with Īśvara is indispensable for our conception of him, the atoms may as well be regarded as his body, so that just as by the will of our self changes and movement of our body take place, so also by his will changes and movements are produced in the atoms[1].

The naiyāyikas in common with most other systems of Indian philosophy believed that the world was full of sorrow and that the small bits of pleasure only served to intensify the force of sorrow. To a wise person therefore everything is sorrow (*sarvaṃ duḥkhaṃ vivekinaḥ*); the wise therefore is never attached to the so-called pleasures of life which only lead us to further sorrows.

The bondage of the world is due to false knowledge (*mithyā-jñāna*) which consists in thinking as my own self that which is not my self, namely body, senses, manas, feelings and knowledge; when once the true knowledge of the six padārthas and as Nyāya says, of the proofs (*pramāṇa*), the objects of knowledge (*prameya*), and of the other logical categories of inference is attained, false knowledge is destroyed. False knowledge can be removed by constant thinking of its opposite (*pratipakṣa-bhāvanā*), namely the true estimates of things. Thus when any pleasure attracts us, we are to think that this is in reality but pain, and thus the right knowledge about it will dawn and it will never attract us again. Thus it is that with the destruction of false knowledge our attachment or antipathy to things and ignorance about them (collectively called *doṣa*, cf. the *kleśa* of Patañjali) are also destroyed.

With the destruction of attachment actions (*pravṛtti*) for the

[1] See *Nyāyamañjarī*, pp. 190–204, *Īśvarānumāna* of Raghunātha Śiromaṇi and Udayana's *Kusumāñjalī*.

fulfilment of desires cease and with it rebirth ceases and with it sorrow ceases. Without false knowledge and attachment, actions cannot produce the bondage of karma that leads to the production of body and its experiences. With the cessation of sorrow there is emancipation in which the self is divested of all its qualities (consciousness, feeling, willing, etc.) and remains it its own inert state. The state of mukti according to Nyāya-Vaiśeṣika is neither a state of pure knowledge nor of bliss but a state of perfect qualitilessness, in which the self remains in itself in its own purity. It is the negative state of absolute painlessness in mukti that is sometimes spoken of as being a state of absolute happiness (*ānanda*), though really speaking the state of mukti can never be a state of happiness. It is a passive state of self in its original and natural purity unassociated with pleasure, pain, knowledge, willing etc.[1]

[1] *Nyāyamañjarī*, pp. 499–533.

IX

MĪMĀṂSĀ PHILOSOPHY[1]

A Comparative Review.

THE Nyāya-Vaiśeṣika philosophy looked at experience from a purely common sense point of view and did not work with any such monistic tendency that the ultimate conceptions of our common sense experience should be considered as coming out of an original universal (e.g. prakṛti of the Sāṃkhya). Space, time, the four elements, soul, etc. convey the impression that they are substantive entities or substances. What is perceived of the material things as qualities such as colour, taste, etc. is regarded as so many entities which have distinct and separate existence but which manifest themselves in connection with the substances. So also karma or action is supposed to be a separate entity, and even the class notions are perceived as separate entities inhering in substances. Knowledge (*Jñānu*) which illuminates all things is regarded only as a quality belonging to soul, just as there are other qualities of material objects. Causation is viewed merely as the collocation of conditions. The genesis of knowledge is also viewed as similar in nature to the production of any other physical event. Thus just as by the collocation of certain physical circumstances a jug and its qualities are produced, so by the combination and respective contacts of the soul, mind, sense, and the objects of sense, knowledge (*Jñāna*) is produced. Soul with Nyāya is an inert unconscious entity in which knowledge, etc. inhere. The relation between a substance and its quality, action, class notion, etc. has also to be admitted as a separate entity, as without it the different entities being without any principle of relation would naturally fail to give us a philosophic construction.

Sāṃkhya had conceived of a principle which consisted of an infinite number of reals of three different types, which by their combination were conceived to be able to produce all substances, qualities, actions, etc. No difference was acknowledged to exist between substances, qualities and actions, and it was conceived

[1] On the meaning of the word Mīmāṃsā see Chapter IV.

that these were but so many aspects of a combination of the three types of reals in different proportions. The reals contained within them the rudiments of all developments of matter, knowledge, willing, feelings, etc. As combinations of reals changed incessantly and new phenomena of matter and mind were manifested, collocations did not bring about any new thing but brought about a phenomenon which was already there in its causes in another form. What we call knowledge or thought ordinarily, is with them merely a form of subtle illuminating matter-stuff. Sāṃkhya holds however that there is a transcendent entity as pure consciousness and that by some kind of transcendent reflection or contact this pure consciousness transforms the bare translucent thought-matter into conscious thought or experience of a person.

But this hypothesis of a pure self, as essentially distinct and separate from knowledge as ordinarily understood, can hardly be demonstrated in our common sense experience; and this has been pointed out by the Nyāya school in a very strong and emphatic manner. Even Sāṃkhya did not try to prove that the existence of its transcendent puruṣa could be demonstrated in experience, and it had to attempt to support its hypothesis of the existence of a transcendent self on the ground of the need of a permanent entity as a fixed object, to which the passing states of knowledge could cling, and on grounds of moral struggle towards virtue and emancipation. Sāṃkhya had first supposed knowledge to be merely a combination of changing reals, and then had as a matter of necessity to admit a fixed principle as puruṣa (pure transcendent consciousness). The self is thus here in some sense an object of inference to fill up the gap left by the inadequate analysis of consciousness (*buddhi*) as being non-intelligent and incessantly changing.

Nyāya fared no better, for it also had to demonstrate self on the ground that since knowledge existed it was a quality, and therefore must inhere in some substance. This hypothesis is again based upon another uncritical assumption that substances and attributes were entirely separate, and that it was the nature of the latter to inhere in the former, and also that knowledge was a quality requiring (similarly with other attributes) a substance in which to inhere. None of them could take their stand upon the self-conscious nature of our ordinary thought and draw their conclusions on the strength of the direct evidence of this self-conscious thought. Of course it is true that Sāṃkhya had approached nearer to this view than Nyāya, but it had separated the content of knowledge and its essence so irrevocably that it threatened to break the integrity of thought in a manner quite unwarranted by common sense experience, which does not seem to reveal this dual element in thought. Anyhow the unification of the content of thought and its essence had to be made, and this could not be done except by what may be regarded as a make-shift—a transcendent illusion running on from beginningless time. These difficulties occurred because Sāṃkhya soared to a region which was not directly illuminated by the light of common sense experience. The Nyāya position is of course much worse as a metaphysical solution, for it did not indeed try to solve anything, but only gave us a schedule of inferential results which could not be tested by experience, and which were based ultimately on a one-sided and uncritical assumption. It is an uncritical common sense experience that substances are different from qualities and actions, and that the latter inhere in the former. To base the whole of metaphysics on such a tender and fragile experience is, to say the least, building on a weak foundation. It was necessary that the importance of the self-revealing thought must be brought to the forefront, its evidence should be collected and trusted, and an account of experience should be given according to its verdict. No construction of metaphysics can ever satisfy us which ignores the direct immediate convictions of self-conscious thought. It is a relief to find that a movement of philosophy in this direction is ushered in by the Mīmāṃsā system. The *Mīmāṃsā sūtras* were written by Jaimini and the commentary (*bhāṣya*) on it was written by Śabara. But the systematic elaboration of it was made by Kumārila, who preceded the great Śaṅkarācārya, and a disciple of Kumārila, Prabhākara.

The Mīmāṃsā Literature.

It is difficult to say how the sacrificial system of worship grew in India in the Brāhmaṇas. This system once set up gradually began to develop into a net-work of elaborate rituals, the details of which were probably taken note of by the priests. As some generations passed and the sacrifices spread over larger tracts of India and grew up into more and more elaborate details, the old rules and regulations began to be collected probably as tradition had it, and this it seems gave rise to the smṛti literature. Discussions and doubts became more common about the many intricacies of the sacrificial rituals, and regular rational enquiries into them were begun in different circles by different scholars and priests. These represent the beginnings of Mīmāṃsā (lit. attempts at rational enquiry), and it is probable that there were different schools of this thought. That Jaimini's *Mīmāṃsā sūtras* (which are with us the foundations of Mīmāṃsā) are only a comprehensive and systematic compilation of one school is evident from the references he gives to the views in different matters of other preceding writers who dealt with the subject. These works are not available now, and we cannot say how much of what Jaimini has written is his original work and how much of it borrowed. But it may be said with some degree of confidence that it was deemed so masterly a work at least of one school that it has survived all other attempts that were made before him. Jaimini's *Mīmāṃsā sūtras* were probably written about B.C. 200 and are now the ground work of the Mīmāṃsā system. Commentaries were written on it by various persons such as Bhartṛmitra (alluded to in *Nyāyaratnākara* verse 10 of *Ślokavārttika*), Bhavadāsa (*Pratijñasūtra* 63), Hari and Upavarṣa (mentioned in *Śāstradīpikā*). It is probable that at least some of these preceded Śabara, the writer of the famous commentary known as the *Śabara-bhāṣya*. It is difficult to say anything about the time in which he flourished. Dr Gaṅgānātha Jhā would have him about B.C. 57 on the evidence of a current verse which speaks of King Vikramāditya as being the son of Śabarasvāmin by a Kṣattriya wife. This bhāṣya of Śabara is the basis of the later Mīmāṃsā works. It was commented upon by an unknown person alluded to as Vārttikakāra by Prabhākara and merely referred to as "yathāhuḥ" (as they say) by Kumārila. Dr Gaṅgānātha Jhā says that Prabhākara's commentary *Bṛhatī* on the *Śabara-bhāṣya* was based upon the work of this Vārttikakāra. This *Bṛhatī* of Prabhākara had another commentary on it—*Ṛjuvimālā* by Śālikanātha Miśra, who also wrote a compendium on the Prabhākara interpretation of Mīmāṃsā called *Prakaraṇapañcikā*. Tradition says that Prabhākara (often referred to as Nibandhakāra), whose views are often alluded to as "gurumata," was a pupil of Kumārila. Kumārila Bhaṭṭa, who is traditionally believed to be the senior contemporary of Śaṅkara (A.D. 788), wrote his celebrated independent exposition of Śabara's bhāṣya in three parts known as *Śloka- vārttika* (dealing only with the philosophical portion of Śabara's work as contained in the first chapter of the first book known as Tarkapāda), *Tantravārttika* (dealing with the remaining three chapters of the first book, the second and the third book) and *Ṭupṭīkā* (containing brief notes on the remaining nine books)[1]. Kumārila is referred to by his later followers as Bhaṭṭa, Bhaṭṭapāda, and Vārttikakāra. The next great Mīmāṃsā scholar and follower of Kumārila was Maṇḍana Miśra, the author of *Vidhiviveka*, *Mīmāṃsānukramaṇī* and the commentator of *Tantravārttika*, who became later on converted by Śaṅkara to Vedantism. Pārthasārathi Miśra (about ninth century A.D.) wrote his *Śāstradīpikā*, *Tantraratna*, and *Nyāyaratnamālā* following the footprints of Kumārila. Amongst the numerous other followers of Kumārila, the names of Sucarita Miśra the author of *Kāśikā* and Someśvara the author of *Nyāyasudhā* deserve special notice. Rāmakṛṣṇa Bhaṭṭa wrote an excellent commentary on the *Tarkapāda* of *Śāstradīpikā* called the *Yuktisnehapūraṇī-siddhānta-candrikā* and Somanātha wrote his *Mayūkhamālikā* on the remaining chapters of *Śāstradīpikā*. Other important current Mīmāṃsā works which deserve notice are such as *Nyāyamālāvistara* of Mādhava, *Subodhinī*, *Mīmāṃsābālaprakāśa* of Śaṅkara Bhaṭṭa, *Nyāyakaṇikā* of Vācaspati Miśra, *Mīmāṃsāparibhāṣa* by Kṛṣṇayajvan, *Mīmāṃsānyāyaprakāśa* by Anantadeva, Gāgā Bhaṭṭa's *Bhaṭṭacintāmaṇi*, etc. Most of the books mentioned here have been consulted in the writing of this chapter. The importance of the Mīmāṃsā literature for a Hindu is indeed great. For not only are all Vedic duties to be performed according to its maxims, but even the smṛti literatures which regulate the daily duties, ceremonials and rituals of Hindus even at the present day are all guided and explained by them. The legal side of the smṛtis consisting of inheritance, proprietory rights, adoption, etc. which guide Hindu civil life even under the British administration is explained according to the Mīmāṃsā maxims. Its relations to the Vedānta philosophy will be briefly indicated in the next chapter. Its relations with Nyāya-Vaiśeṣika have also been pointed out in various places of this chapter. The views of the two schools of Mīmāṃsā as propounded by Prabhākara and Kumārila on all the important topics have

[1] Mahāmahopādhyāya Haraprasāda Śāstrī says, in his introduction to *Six Buddhist Nyāya Tracts*, that "Kumārila preceded Saṅkara by two generations."

also been pointed out. Prabhākara's views however could not win many followers in later times, but while living it is said that he was regarded by Kumārila as a very strong rival[1]. Hardly any new contribution has been made to the Mīmāṃsā philosophy after Kumārila and Prabhākara. The *Mīmāṃsā sūtras* deal mostly with the principles of the interpretation of the Vedic texts in connection with sacrifices, and very little of philosophy can be gleaned out of them. Śabara's contributions are also slight and vague. Vārttikakāra's views also can only be gathered from the references to them by Kumārila and Prabhākara. What we know of Mīmāṃsā philosophy consists of their views and theirs alone. It did not develop any further after them. Works written on the subject in later times were but of a purely expository nature. I do not know of any work on Mīmāṃsā written in English except the excellent one by Dr Gaṅgānātha Jhā on the Prabhākara Mīmāṃsā to which I have frequently referred.

The Parataḥ-prāmāṇya doctrine of Nyāya and the Svataḥ-prāmāṇya doctrine of Mīmāṃsā.

The doctrine of the self-validity of knowledge (*svataḥprāmāṇya*) forms the cornerstone on which the whole structure of the Mīmāṃsā philosophy is based. Validity means the certitude of truth. The Mīmāṃsā philosophy asserts that all knowledge excepting the action of remembering (*smṛti*) or memory is valid in itself, for it itself certifies its own truth, and neither depends on any other extraneous condition nor on any other knowledge for its validity. But Nyāya holds that this self-validity of knowledge is a question which requires an explanation. It is true that under certain conditions a piece of knowledge is produced in us, but what is meant by saying that this knowledge is a proof of its own truth? When we perceive anything as blue, it is the direct result of visual contact, and this visual contact cannot certify that the knowledge generated is true, as the visual contact is not in any touch with the knowledge

[1] There is a story that Kumārila, not being able to convert Prabhākara, his own pupil, to his views, attempted a trick and pretended that he was dead. His disciples then asked Prabhākara whether his burial rites should be performed according to Kumārila's views or Prabhākara's. Prabhākara said that his own views were erroneous, but these were held by him only to rouse up Kumārila's pointed attacks, whereas Kumārila's views were the right ones. Kumārila then rose up and said that Prabhākara was defeated, but the latter said he was not defeated so long as he was alive. But this has of course no historic value.

it has conditioned. Moreover, knowledge is a mental affair and how can it certify the objective truth of its representation? In other words, how can my perception "a blue thing" guarantee that what is subjectively perceived as blue is really so objectively as well? After my perception of anything as blue we do not have any such perception that what I have perceived as blue is really so. So this so-called self-validity of knowledge cannot be testified or justified by any perception. We can only be certain that knowledge has been produced by the perceptual act, but there is nothing in this knowledge or its revelation of its object from which we can infer that the perception is also objectively valid or true. If the production of any knowledge should certify its validity then there would be no invalidity, no illusory knowledge, and following our perception of even a mirage we should never come to grief. But we are disappointed often in our perceptions, and this proves that when we practically follow the directions of our perception we are undecided as to its validity, which can only be ascertained by the correspondence of the perception with what we find later on in practical experience. Again, every piece of knowledge is the result of certain causal collocations, and as such depends upon them for its production, and hence cannot be said to rise without depending on anything else. It is meaningless to speak of the validity of knowledge, for validity always refers to objective realization of our desires and attempts proceeding in accordance with our knowledge. People only declare their knowledge invalid when proceeding practically in accordance with it they are disappointed. The perception of a mirage is called invalid when proceeding in accordance with our perception we do not find anything that can serve the purposes of water (e.g. drinking, bathing). The validity or truth of knowledge is thus the attainment by practical experience of the object and the fulfilment of all our purposes from it (*arthakriyājñāna* or *phalajñāna*) just as perception or knowledge represented them to the perceiver. There is thus no self-validity of knowledge (*svataḥ-prāmāṇya*), but validity is ascertained by *saṃvāda* or agreement with the objective facts of experience[1].

It is easy to see that this Nyāya objection is based on the supposition that knowledge is generated by certain objective collocations of conditions, and that knowledge so produced can

[1] See *Nyāyamañjarī*, pp. 160–173.

only be tested by its agreement with objective facts. But this theory of knowledge is merely an hypothesis; for it can never be experienced that knowledge is the product of any collocations; we have a perception and immediately we become aware of certain objective things; knowledge reveals to us the facts of the objective world and this is experienced by us always. But that the objective world generates knowledge in us is only an hypothesis which can hardly be demonstrated by experience. It is the supreme prerogative of knowledge that it reveals all other things. It is not a phenomenon like any other phenomenon of the world. When we say that knowledge has been produced in us by the external collocations, we just take a perverse point of view which is unwarranted by experience; knowledge only photographs the objective phenomena for us; but there is nothing to show that knowledge has been generated by these phenomena. This is only a theory which applies the ordinary conceptions of causation to knowledge and this is evidently unwarrantable. Knowledge is not like any other phenomena for it stands above them and interprets or illumines them all. There can be no validity in things, for truth applies to knowledge and knowledge alone. What we call agreement with facts by practical experience is but the agreement of previous knowledge with later knowledge; for objective facts never come to us directly, they are always taken on the evidence of knowledge, and they have no other certainty than what is bestowed on them by knowledge. There arise indeed different kinds of knowledge revealing different things, but these latter do not on that account generate the former, for this is never experienced; we are never aware of any objective fact before it is revealed by knowledge. Why knowledge makes different kinds of revelations is indeed more than we can say, for experience only shows that knowledge reveals objective facts and not why it does so. The rise of knowledge is never perceived by us to be dependent on any objective fact, for all objective facts are dependent on it for its revelation or illumination. This is what is said to be the self-validity (*svataḥ-prāmāṇya*) of knowledge in its production (*utpatti*). As soon as knowledge is produced, objects are revealed to us; there is no intermediate link between the rise of knowledge and the revelation of objects on which knowledge depends for producing its action of revealing or illuminating them. Thus knowledge is not only independent of anything else in its own rise but in its own action as well (*svakāryakaraṇe svataḥ prāmāṇyaṃ jñānasya*). Whenever there is any knowledge it carries with it the impression that it is certain and valid, and we are naturally thus prompted to work (*pravṛtti*) according to its direction. There is no indecision in our mind at the time of the rise of knowledge as to the correctness of knowledge; but just as knowledge rises, it carries with it the certainty of its revelation, presence, or action. But in cases of illusory perception other perceptions or cognitions dawn which carry with them the notion that our original knowledge was not valid. Thus though the invalidity of any knowledge may appear to us by later experience, and in accordance with which we reject our former knowledge, yet when the knowledge first revealed itself to us it carried with it the conviction of certainty which goaded us on to work according to its indication. Whenever a man works according to his knowledge, he does so with the conviction that his knowledge is valid, and not in a passive or uncertain temper of mind. This is what Mīmāṃsā means when it says that the validity of knowledge appears immediately with its rise, though its invalidity may be derived from later experience or some other data (*jñānasya prāmāṇyam svataḥ aprāmāṇyaṃ parataḥ*). Knowledge attained is proved invalid when later on a contradictory experience (*bādhakajñāna*) comes in or when our organs etc. are known to be faulty and defective (*karaṇadoṣajñāna*). It is from these that knowledge appearing as valid is invalidated; when we take all necessary care to look for these and yet find them not, we must think that they do not exist. Thus the validity of knowledge certified at the moment of its production need not be doubted unnecessarily when even after enquiry we do not find any defect in sense or any contradiction in later experience. All knowledge except memory is thus regarded as valid independently by itself as a general rule, unless it is invalidated later on. Memory is excluded because the phenomenon of memory depends upon a previous experience, and its existing latent impressions, and cannot thus be regarded as arising independently by itself.

The place of sense organs in perception.

We have just said that knowledge arises by itself and that it could not have been generated by sense-contact. If this be so, the diversity of perceptions is however left unexplained. But in face of the Nyāya philosophy explaining all perceptions on the ground of diverse sense-contact the Mīmāṃsā probably could not afford to remain silent on such an important point. It therefore accepted the Nyāya view of sense-contact as a condition of knowledge with slight modifications, and yet held their doctrine of svataḥ-prāmāṇya. It does not appear to have been conscious of a conflict between these two different principles of the production of knowledge. Evidently the point of view from which it looked at it was that the fact that there were the senses and contacts of them with the objects, or such special capacities in them by virtue of which the things could be perceived, was with us a matter of inference. Their actions in producing the knowledge are never experienced at the time of the rise of knowledge, but when the knowledge arises we argue that such and such senses must have acted. The only case where knowledge is found to be dependent on anything else seems to be the case where one knowledge is found to depend on a previous experience or knowledge as in the case of memory. In other cases the dependence of the rise of knowledge on anything else cannot be felt, for the physical collocations conditioning knowledge are not felt to be operating before the rise of knowledge, and these are only inferred later on in accordance with the nature and characteristic of knowledge. We always have our first start in knowledge which is directly experienced from which we may proceed later on to the operation and nature of objective facts in relation to it. Thus it is that though contact of the senses with the objects may later on be imagined to be the conditioning factor, yet the rise of knowledge as well as our notion of its validity strikes us as original, underived, immediate, and first-hand.

Prabhākara gives us a sketch as to how the existence of the senses may be inferred. Thus our cognitions of objects are phenomena which are not all the same, and do not happen always in the same manner, for these vary differently at different moments; the cognitions of course take place in the soul which may thus be regarded as the material cause (*samavāyikāraṇa*); but there must be some such movements or other specific associations (*asamavāyikāraṇa*) which render the production of this or that specific cognition possible. The immaterial causes subsist either in the cause of the material cause (e.g. in the case of the colouring of a white piece of cloth, the colour of the yarns which is the cause of the colour in the cloth subsists in the yarns which form the material cause of the cloth) or in the material cause itself (e.g. in the case of a new form of smell being produced in a substance by fire-contact, this contact, which is the immaterial cause of the smell, subsists in that substance itself which is put in the fire and in which the smell is produced). The soul is eternal and has no other cause, and it has to be assumed that the immaterial cause required for the rise of a cognition must inhere in the soul, and hence must be a quality. Then again accepting the Nyāya conclusions we know that the rise of qualities in an eternal thing can only take place by contact with some other substances. Now cognition being a quality which the soul acquires would naturally require the contact of such substances. Since there is nothing to show that such substances inhere in other substances they are also to be taken as eternal. There are three eternal substances, time, space, and atoms. But time and space being all-pervasive the soul is always in contact with them. Contact with these therefore cannot explain the occasional rise of different cognitions. This contact must then be of some kind of atom which resides in the body ensouled by the cognizing soul. This atom may be called *manas* (mind). This manas alone by itself brings about cognitions, pleasure, pain, desire, aversion, effort, etc. The manas however by itself is found to be devoid of any such qualities as colour, smell, etc., and as such cannot lead the soul to experience or cognize these qualities; hence it stands in need of such other organs as may be characterized by these qualities; for the cognition of colour, the mind will need the aid of an organ of which colour is the characteristic quality; for the cognition of smell, an organ having the odorous characteristic and so on with touch, taste, vision. Now we know that the organ which has colour for its distinctive feature must be one composed of tejas or light, as colour is a feature of light, and this proves the existence of the organ, the eye—for the cognition of colour; in a similar manner the existence of the earthly organ (organ of smell), the aqueous organ (organ of taste), the ākāśic organ (organ of sound) and the airy organ (organ of touch) may be demonstrated. But without manas none of these organs is found to be effective. Four necessary contacts have to be admitted, (1) of the sense organs with the object, (2) of the sense organs with the qualities of the object, (3) of the manas with the sense organs, and (4) of the manas with the soul. The objects of perception are of three kinds, (1) substances, (2) qualities, (3) jāti or class. The material substances are tangible objects of earth, fire, water, air in large dimensions (for in their fine atomic states they cannot be perceived). The qualities are colour, taste, smell, touch, number, dimension, separateness, conjunction, disjunction, priority, posteriority, pleasure, pain, desire, aversion, and effort[1].

It may not be out of place here to mention in conclusion that Kumārila Bhaṭṭa was rather undecided as to the nature of the senses or of their contact with the objects. Thus he says that the senses may be conceived either as certain functions or activities, or as entities having the capacity of revealing things without coming into actual contact with them, or that they might be entities which actually come in contact with their objects[2], and he prefers this last view as being more satisfactory.

Indeterminate and determinate perception.

There are two kinds of perception in two stages, the first stage is called *nirvikalpa* (indeterminate) and the second *savikalpa* (determinate). The nirvikalpa perception of a thing is its perception at the first moment of the association of the senses and their objects. Thus Kumārila says that the cognition that appears first is a mere *ālocana* or simple perception, called non-determinate pertaining to the object itself pure and simple, and resembling the cognitions that the new-born infant has of things around himself. In this cognition neither the genus nor the differentia is presented to consciousness; all that is present there is the individual wherein these two subsist. This view of indeterminate perception may seem in some sense to resemble the Buddhist view which defines it as being merely the specific individuality (*svalakṣaṇa*) and regards it as being the only valid element in perception, whereas all the rest are conceived as being imaginary

[1] See *Prakaraṇapañcikā*, pp. 52 etc., and Dr Gaṅgānātha Jhā's *Prabhākaramīmāṃsā*, pp. 35 etc.

[2] *Ślokavārttika*, see *Pratyakṣasūtra*, 40 etc., and *Nyāyaratnākara* on it. It may be noted in this connection that Sāṃkhya-Yoga did not think like Nyāya that the senses actually went out to meet the objects (*prāpyakāritva*) but held that there was a special kind of functioning (*vṛtti*) by virtue of which the senses could grasp even such distant objects as the sun and the stars. It is the functioning of the sense that reached the objects. The nature of this *vṛtti* is not further clearly explained and Pārthasārathi objects to it as being almost a different category (*tattvāntara*).

impositions. But both Kumārila and Prabhākara think that both the genus and the differentia are perceived in the indeterminate stage, but these do not manifest themselves to us only because we do not remember the other things in relation to which, or in contrast to which, the percept has to show its character as genus or differentia; a thing can be cognized as an "individual" only in comparison with other things from which it differs in certain well-defined characters; and it can be apprehended as belonging to a class only when it is found to possess certain characteristic features in common with some other things; so we see that as other things are not presented to consciousness through memory, the percept at the indeterminate stage cannot be fully apprehended as an individual belonging to a class, though the data constituting the characteristic of the thing as a genus and its differentia are perceived at the indeterminate stage[1]. So long as other things are not remembered these data cannot manifest themselves properly, and hence the perception of the thing remains indeterminate at the first stage of perception. At the second stage the self by its past impressions brings the present perception in relation to past ones and realizes its character as involving universal and particular. It is thus apparent that the difference between the indeterminate and the determinate perception is this, that in the latter case memory of other things creeps in, but this association of memory in the determinate perception refers to those other objects of memory and not to the percept. It is also held that though the determinate perception is based upon the indeterminate one, yet since the former also apprehends certain such factors as did not enter into the indeterminate perception, it is to be regarded as a valid cognition. Kumārila also agrees with Prabhākara in holding both the indeterminate and the determinate perception valid[2].

Some Ontological Problems connected with the Doctrine of Perception.

The perception of the class (*jāti*) of a percept in relation to other things may thus be regarded in the main as a difference between determinate and indeterminate perceptions. The problems of jāti and avayavāvayavī (part and whole notion) were

[1] Compare this with the Vaiśeṣika view as interpreted by Śrīdhara.

[2] See *Prakaraṇapañcikā* and *Śāstradīpikā*.

the subjects of hot dispute in Indian philosophy. Before entering into discussion about jāti, Prabhākara first introduced the problem of *avayava* (part) and *avayavī* (whole). He argues as an exponent of svataḥ-prāmāṇyavāda that the proof of the true existence of anything must ultimately rest on our own consciousness, and what is distinctly recognized in consciousness must be admitted to have its existence established. Following this canon Prabhākara says that gross objects as a whole exist, since they are so perceived. The subtle atoms are the material cause and their connection (*saṃyoga*) is the immaterial cause (*asamavāyikāraṇa*), and it is the latter which renders the whole altogether different from the parts of which it is composed; and it is not necessary that all the parts should be perceived before the whole is perceived. Kumārila holds that it is due to the point of view from which we look at a thing that we call it a separate whole or only a conglomeration of parts. In reality they are identical, but when we lay stress on the notion of parts, the thing appears to be a conglomeration of them, and when we look at it from the point of view of the unity appearing as a whole, the thing appears to be a whole of which there are parts (see *Ślokavārttika*, *Vanavāda*)[1].

Jāti, though incorporating the idea of having many units within one, is different from the conception of whole in this, that it resides in its entirety in each individual constituting that jāti (*vyāśajya-*

[1] According to Sāṃkhya-Yoga a thing is regarded as the unity of the universal and the particular (*sāmānyaviśeṣasamudāyo dravyam*, *Vyāsabhāṣya*, III. 44); for there is no other separate entity which is different from them both in which they would inhere as Nyāya holds. Conglomerations can be of two kinds, namely those in which the parts exist at a distance from one another (e.g. a forest), and those in which they exist close together (*nirantarā hi tadavayavāḥ*), and it is this latter combination (*ayutasiddhāvayava*) which is called a dravya, but here also there is no separate whole distinct from the parts; it is the parts connected in a particular way and having no perceptible space between them that is called a thing or a whole. The Buddhists as Paṇḍitāśoka has shown did not believe in any whole (*avayavī*); it is the atoms which in connection with one another appeared as a whole occupying space (*paramāṇava eva hi pararūpadeśaparihāreṇotpannāḥ parasparasahitā avabhāsamānā deśavitānavanto bhavanti*). The whole is thus a mere appearance and not a reality (see *Avayavinirākaraṇa*, *Six Buddhist Nyāya Tracts*). Nyāya however held that the atoms were partless (*niravayava*) and hence it would be wrong to say that when we see an object we see the atoms. The existence of a whole as different from the parts which belong to it is directly experienced and there is no valid reason against it:

"*aduṣṭakaraṇodbhūtamanāvirbhūtabādhakam*
asandigdañca vijñānam katham mithyeti kathyate."

Nyāyamañjarī, pp. 550 ff.

vṛtti), but the establishment of the existence of wholes refutes the argument that jāti should be denied, because it involves the conception of a whole (class) consisting of many parts (individuals). The class character or jāti exists because it is distinctly perceived by us in the individuals included in any particular class. It is eternal in the sense that it continues to exist in other individuals, even when one of the individuals ceases to exist. When a new individual of that class (e.g. cow class) comes into being, a new relation of inherence is generated by which the individual is brought into relation with the class-character existing in other individuals; for inherence (*samavāya*) according to Prabhākara is not an eternal entity but an entity which is both produced and not produced according as the thing in which it exists is non-eternal or eternal, and it is not regarded as one as Nyāya holds, but as many, according as there is the infinite number of things in which it exists. When any individual is destroyed, the class-character does not go elsewhere, nor subsist in that individual, nor is itself destroyed, but it is only the inherence of class-character with that individual that ceases to exist. With the destruction of an individual or its production it is a new relation of inherence that is destroyed or produced. But the classcharacter or jāti has no separate existence apart from the individuals as Nyāya supposes. Apprehension of jāti is essentially the apprehension of the class-character of a thing in relation to other similar things of that class by the perception of the common characteristics. But Prabhākara would not admit the existence of a highest genus sattā (being) as acknowledged by Nyāya. He argues that the existence of class-character is apprehended because we find that the individuals of a class possess some common characteristic possessed by all the heterogeneous and disparate things of the world as can give rise to the conception of a separate jāti as sattā, as demanded by the naiyāyikas. That all things are said to be *sat* (existing) is more or less a word or a name without the corresponding apprehension of a common quality. Our experience always gives us concrete existing individuals, but we can never experience such a highest genus as pure existence or being, as it has no concrete form which may be perceived. When we speak of a thing as *sat*, we do not mean that it is possessed of any such class-characters as sattā (being); what we mean is simply that the individual has its specific existence or *svarū-*

pasattā. Thus the Nyāya view of perception as taking only the thing in its pure being apart from qualities, etc. (*sanmātra-viṣayam pratyakṣaṃ*) is made untenable by Prabhākara, as according to him the thing is perceived direct with all its qualities. According to Kumārila however jāti is not something different from the individuals comprehended by it and it is directly perceived. Kumārila's view of jāti is thus similar to that held by Sāṃkhya, namely that when we look at an individual from one point of view (jāti as identical with the individual), it is the individual that lays its stress upon our consciousness and the notion of jāti becomes latent, but when we look at it from another point of view (the individual as identical with jāti) it is the jāti which presents itself to consciousness, and the aspect as individual becomes latent. The apprehension as jāti or as individual is thus only a matter of different points of view or angles of vision from which we look at a thing. Quite in harmony with the conception of jāti, Kumārila holds that the relation of inherence is not anything which is distinct from the things themselves in which it is supposed to exist, but only a particular aspect or phase of the things themselves (*Ślokavārttika*, *Pratyakṣasūtra*, 149, 150, *abhedāt samavāyo' stu svarūpam dharmadharmiṇoḥ*), Kumārila agrees with Prabhākara that jāti is perceived by the senses (*tatraikabuddhinirgrāhyā jātirindriyagocarā*).

It is not out of place to mention that on the evidence of Prabhākara we find that the category of viśeṣa admitted by the Kaṇāda school is not accepted as a separate category by the Mīmāṃsā on the ground that the differentiation of eternal things from one another, for which the category of viśeṣa is admitted, may very well be effected on the basis of the ordinary qualities of these things. The quality of pṛthaktva or specific differences in atoms, as inferred by the difference of things they constitute, can very well serve the purposes of viśeṣa.

The nature of knowledge.

All knowledge involves the knower, the known object, and the knowledge at the same identical moment. All knowledge whether perceptual, inferential or of any other kind must necessarily reveal the self or the knower directly. Thus as in all knowledge the self is directly and immediately perceived, all knowledge may be regarded as perception from the point of view of self. The division of the pramāṇas as pratyakṣa (perception), anumāna (inference), etc. is from the point of view of the objects of knowledge with reference to the varying modes in which they are brought within the purview of knowledge. The self itself however has no illumining or revealing powers, for then even in deep sleep we could have knowledge, for the self is present even then, as is proved by the remembrance of dreams. It is knowledge (*saṃvid*) that reveals by its very appearance both the self, the knower, and the objects. It is generally argued against the self-illuminative character of knowledge that all cognitions are of the forms of the objects they are said to reveal; and if they have the same form we may rather say that they have the same identical reality too. The Mīmāṃsā answer to these objections is this, that if the cognition and the cognized were not different from one another, they could not have been felt as such, and we could not have felt that it is by cognition that we apprehend the cognized objects. The cognition (*saṃvedana*) of a person simply means that such a special kind of quality (*dharma*) has been manifested in the self by virtue of which his active operation with reference to a certain object is favoured or determined, and the object of cognition is that with reference to which the active operation of the self has been induced. Cognitions are not indeed absolutely formless, for they have the cognitional character by which things are illumined and manifested. Cognition has no other character than this, that it illumines and reveals objects. The things only are believed to have forms and only such forms as knowledge reveal to us about them. Even the dream cognition is with reference to objects that were perceived previously, and of which the impressions were left in the mind and were aroused by the unseen agency (*adṛṣṭa*). Dream cognition is thus only a kind of remembrance of that which was previously experienced. Only such of the impressions of cognized objects are roused in dreams as can beget just that amount of pleasurable or painful experience, in accordance with the operation of adṛṣṭa, as the person deserves to have in accordance with his previous merit or demerit.

The Prabhākara Mīmāṃsā, in refuting the arguments of those who hold that our cognitions of objects are themselves cognized by some other cognition, says that this is not possible, since we do not experience any such double cognition and also because it would lead us to a *regressus ad infinitum*, for if a second cognition is necessary to interpret the first, then that would require a third and so on. If a cognition could be the object of another cognition, then it could not be self-valid. The cognition is not of course unknown to us, but that is of course because it is self-cognized, and reveals itself to us the moment it reveals its objects. From the illumination of objects also we can infer the presence of this self-cognizing knowledge. But it is only its presence that is inferred and not the cognition itself, for inference can only indicate the presence of an object and not in the form in which it can be apprehended by perception (*pratyakṣa*). Prabhākara draws a subtle distinction between perceptuality (*saṃvedyatva*) and being object of knowledge (*prameyatva*). A thing can only be apprehended (*saṃvedyate*) by perception, whereas inference can only indicate the presence of an object without apprehending the object itself. Our cognition cannot be apprehended by any other cognition. Inference can only indicate the presence or existence of knowledge but cannot apprehend the cognition itself[1].

Kumārila also agrees with Prabhākara in holding that perception is never the object of another perception and that it ends in the direct apprehensibility of the object of perception. But he says that every perception involves a relationship between the perceiver and the perceived, wherein the perceiver behaves as the agent whose activity in grasping the object is known as cognition. This is indeed different from the Prabhākara view, that in one manifestation of knowledge the knower, the known, and the knowledge, are simultaneously illuminated (the doctrine of *tripuṭīpratyakṣa*)[2].

The Psychology of Illusion.

The question however arises that if all apprehensions are valid, how are we to account for illusory perceptions which cannot be regarded as valid? The problem of illusory perception and its psychology is a very favourite topic of discussion in Indian philosophy. Omitting the theory of illusion of the Jains called *satkhyāti* which we have described before, and of the Vedāntists, which we shall describe in the next chapter, there are three different theories of illusion, viz. (1) *ātmakhyāti*, (2) *viparītakhyāti* or *anyathākhyāti*, and (3) *akhyāti* of the Mīmāṃsā school. The

[1] See *Prabhākaramīmāṃsā*, by Dr Gaṅgānātha Jhā.
[2] *loc. cit.* pp. 26–28.

viparītākhyāti or anyathākhyāti theory of illusion is accepted by the Nyāya, Vaiśeṣika and the Yoga, the ākhyāti theory by Mīmāṃsā and Sāṃkhya and the ātmakhyāti by the Buddhists.

The commonest example of illusion in Indian philosophy is the illusory appearance of a piece of broken conch-shell as a piece of silver. That such an illusion occurs is a fact which is experienced by all and agreed to by all. The differences of view are with regard to its cause or its psychology. The idealistic Buddhists who deny the existence of the external world and think that there are only the forms of knowledge, generated by the accumulated karma of past lives, hold that just as in the case of a correct perception, so also in the case of illusory perception it is the flow of knowledge which must be held responsible. The flow of knowledge on account of the peculiarities of its own collocating conditions generates sometimes what we call right perception and sometimes wrong perception or illusion. On this view nothing depends upon the so-called external data. For they do not exist, and even if they did exist, why should the same data sometimes bring about the right perception and sometimes the illusion? The flow of knowledge creates both the percept and the perceiver and unites them. This is true both in the case of correct perception and illusory perception. Nyāya objects to the above view, and says that if knowledge irrespective of any external condition imposes upon itself the knower and the illusory percept, then the perception ought to be of the form "I am silver" and not "this is silver." Moreover this theory stands refuted, as it is based upon a false hypothesis that it is the inner knowledge which appears as coming from outside and that the external as such does not exist.

The viparītakhyāti or the anyathākhyāti theory supposes that the illusion takes place because on account of malobservation we do not note the peculiar traits of the conch-shell as distinguished from the silver, and at the same time by the glow etc. of the conch-shell unconsciously the silver which I had seen elsewhere is remembered and the object before me is taken as silver. In illusion the object before us with which our eye is associated is not conch-shell, for the traits peculiar to it not being grasped, it is merely an object. The silver is not utterly non-existent, for it exists elsewhere and it is the memory of it as experienced before that creates confusion and leads us to think of the conch-shell as silver. This school agrees with the ākhyāti school that the fact that I remember silver is not taken note of at the time of illusion. But it holds that the mere non-distinction is not enough to account for the phenomenon of illusion, for there is a definite positive aspect associated with it, viz. the false identification of silver (seen elsewhere) with the conch-shell before us.

The akhyāti theory of Mīmāṃsā holds that since the special peculiarities of the conch-shell are not noticed, it is erroneous to say that we identify or cognize positively the conch-shell as the silver (perceived elsewhere), for the conch-shell is not cognized at all. What happens here is simply this, that only the features common to conch-shell and silver being noticed, the perceiver fails to apprehend the difference between these two things, and this gives rise to the cognition of silver. Owing to a certain weakness of the mind the remembrance of silver roused by the common features of the conch-shell and silver is not apprehended, and the fact that it is only a memory of silver seen in some past time that has appeared before him is not perceived; and it is as a result of this non-apprehension of the difference between the silver remembered and the present conch-shell that the illusion takes place. Thus, though the illusory perception partakes of a dual character of remembrance and apprehension, and as such is different from the ordinary valid perception (which is wholly a matter of direct apprehension) of real silver before us, yet as the difference between the remembrance of silver and the sight of the present object is not apprehended, the illusory perception appears at the moment of its production to be as valid as a real valid perception. Both give rise to the same kind of activity on the part of the agent, for in illusory perception the perceiver would be as eager to stoop and pick up the thing as in the case of a real perception. Kumārila agrees with this view as expounded by Prabhākara, and further says that the illusory judgment is as valid to the cognizor at the time that he has the cognition as any real judgment could be. If subsequent experience rejects it, that does not matter, for it is admitted in Mīmāṃsā that when later experience finds out the defects of any perception it can invalidate the original perception which was self-valid at the time of its production[1]. It is easy to see that the Mīmāṃsā had to adopt this view of illusion to maintain the doctrine that all cognition at the moment of its production is valid. The ākhyāti theory

[1] See *Prakaraṇapañcikā*, *Śāstradīpikā*, and *Ślokavārttika*, sūtra 2.

tries to establish the view that the illusion is not due to any positive wrong knowledge, but to a mere negative factor of non-apprehension due to certain weakness of mind. So it is that though illusion is the result, yet the cognition so far as it is cognition, is made up of two elements, the present perception and memory, both of which are true so far as they are individually present to us, and the cognition itself has all the characteristics of any other valid knowledge, for the mark of the validity of a cognition is its power to prompt us to action. In doubtful cognitions also, as in the case "Is this a post or a man?" what is actually perceived is some tall object and thus far it is valid too. But when this perception gives rise to two different kinds of remembrance (of the pillar and the man), doubt comes in. So the element of apprehension involved in doubtful cognitions should be regarded as self-valid as any other cognition.

Inference.

Śabara says that when a certain fixed or permanent relation has been known to exist between two things, we can have the idea of one thing when the other one is perceived, and this kind of knowledge is called inference. Kumārila on the basis of this tries to show that inference is only possible when we notice that in a large number of cases two things (e.g. smoke and fire) subsist together in a third thing (e.g. kitchen, etc.) in some independent relation, i.e. when their coexistence does not depend upon any other eliminable condition or factor. It is also necessary that the two things (smoke and fire) coexisting in a third thing should be so experienced that all cases of the existence of one thing should also be cases involving the existence of the other, but the cases of the existence of one thing (e.g. fire), though including all the cases of the existence of the other (smoke), may have yet a more extensive sphere where the latter (smoke) may not exist. When once a permanent relation, whether it be a case of coexistence (as in the case of the contiguity of the constellation of Kṛttikā with Rohiṇī, where, by the rise of the former the early rise of the latter may be inferred), or a case of identity (as in the relation between a genus and its species), or a case of cause and effect or otherwise between two things and a third thing which had been apprehended in a large number of cases, is perceived, they fuse together in the mind as forming one whole, and as a result of that when the existence of the one (e.g. smoke) in a thing (hill) is noticed, we can infer the existence of the thing (hill) with its counterpart (fire). In all such cases the thing (e.g. fire) which has a sphere extending beyond that in which the other (e.g. smoke) can exist is called *gamya* or *vyāpaka* and the other (e.g. smoke) *vyāpya* or *gamaka* and it is only by the presence of gamaka in a thing (e.g. hill, the pakṣa) that the other counterpart the gamya (fire) may be inferred. The general proposition, universal coexistence of the gamaka with the gamya (e.g. wherever there is smoke there is fire) cannot be the cause of inference, for it is itself a case of inference. Inference involves the memory of a permanent relation subsisting between two things (e.g. smoke and fire) in a third thing (e.g. kitchen); but the third thing is remembered only in a general way that the coexisting things must have a place where they are found associated. It is by virtue of such a memory that the direct perception of a basis (e.g. hill) with the gamaka thing (e.g. smoke) in it would naturally bring to my mind that the same basis (hill) must contain the gamya (i.e. fire) also. Every case of inference thus proceeds directly from a perception and not from any universal general proposition. Kumārila holds that the inference gives us the minor as associated with the major and not of the major alone, i.e. of the fiery mountain and not of fire. Thus inference gives us a new knowledge, for though it was known in a general way that the possessor of smoke is the possessor of fire, yet the case of the mountain was not anticipated and the inference of the fiery mountain is thus a distinctly new knowledge (*deśakālādhikyādyuktamagṛhītagrāhitvam anumānasya*, *Nyāyaratnākara*, p. 363)[1]. It should also be noted that in forming the notion of the permanent relation between two things, a third thing in which these two subsist is always remembered and for the conception of this permanent relation it is enough that in the large number of cases where the concomitance was noted there was no knowledge of any case where the concomitance failed, and it is not indispensable that the negative instances in which the absence of the gamya or vyāpaka was marked by an

[1] It is important to note that it is not unlikely that Kumārila was indebted to Diṅnāga for this; for Diṅnāga's main contention is that "it is not fire, nor the connection between it and the hill, but it is the fiery hill that is inferred" for otherwise inference would give us no new knowledge (see Vidyābhūṣaṇa's *Indian Logic*, p. 87 and *Tātparyaṭikā*, p. 120.

absence of the gamaka or vyāpya, should also be noted, for a knowledge of such a negative relation is not indispensable for the forming of the notion of the permanent relation[1]. The experience of a large number of particular cases in which any two things were found to coexist together in another thing in some relation associated with the non-perception of any case of failure creates an expectancy in us of inferring the presence of the gamya in that thing in which the gamaka is perceived to exist in exactly the same relation[2]. In those cases where the circle of the existence of the gamya coincides with the circle of the existence of the gamaka, each of them becomes a gamaka for the other. It is clear that this form of inference not only includes all cases of cause and effect, of genus and species but also all cases of coexistence as well.

The question arises that if no inference is possible without a memory of the permanent relation, is not the self-validity of inference destroyed on that account, for memory is not regarded as self-valid. To this Kumārila's answer is that memory is not invalid, but it has not the status of pramāṇa, as it does not bring to us a new knowledge. But inference involves the acquirement of a new knowledge in this, that though the coexistence of two things in another was known in a number of cases, yet in the present case a new case of the existence of the gamya in a thing is known from the perception of the existence of the gamaka and this knowledge is gained by a means which is not perception, for it is only the gamaka that is seen and not the gamya. If the gamya is also seen it is no inference at all.

As regards the number of propositions necessary for the explicit statement of the process of inference for convincing others (*parārthānumāna*) both Kumārila and Prabhākara hold that three premisses are quite sufficient for inference. Thus the first three premisses pratijñā, hetu and dṛṣṭānta may quite serve the purpose of an anumāna.

There are two kinds of anumāna according to Kumārila viz. pratyakṣatodṛṣṭasambandha and sāmānyatodṛṣṭasambandha. The former is that kind of inference where the permanent

[1] Kumārila strongly opposes a Buddhist view that concomitance (*vyāpti*) is ascertained only by the negative instances and not by the positive ones.

[2] "*tasmādanavagate'pi sarvatrānvaye sarvataśca vyatireke bahuśaḥ sākityāvagamamātrādeva vyabhicārādarśanasanāthādanumānotpattiraṅgīkartavyaḥ.*" *Nyāyaratnākara*, p. 288.

relation between two concrete things, as in the case of smoke and fire, has been noticed. The latter is that kind of inference where the permanent relation is observed not between two concrete things but between two general notions, as in the case of movement and change of place, e.g. the perceived cases where there is change of place there is also motion involved with it; so from the change of place of the sun its motion is inferred and it is held that this general notion is directly perceived like all universals[1].

Prabhākara recognizes the need of forming the notion of the permanent relation, but he does not lay any stress on the fact that this permanent relation between two things (fire and smoke) is taken in connection with a third thing in which they both subsist. He says that the notion of the permanent relation between two things is the main point, whereas in all other associations of time and place the things in which these two subsist together are taken only as adjuncts to qualify the two things (e.g. fire and smoke). It is also necessary to recognize the fact that though the concomitance of smoke in fire is only conditional, the concomitance of the fire in smoke is unconditional and absolute[2]. When such a conviction is firmly rooted in the mind that the concept of the presence of smoke involves the concept of the presence of fire, the inference of fire is made as soon as any smoke is seen. Prabhākara counts separately the fallacies of the minor (*pakṣābhāsa*), of the enunciation (*pratijñābhāsa*) and of the example (*dṛṣṭāntābhāsa*) along with the fallacies of the middle and this seems to indicate that the Mīmāṃsā logic was not altogether free from Buddhist influence. The cognition of smoke includes within itself the cognition of fire also, and thus there would be nothing left unknown to be cognized by the inferential cognition. But this objection has little force with Prabhākara, for he does not admit that a pramāṇa should necessarily bring us any new knowledge, for pramāṇa is simply defined as "apprehension." So though the inferential cognition always pertains to things already known it is yet regarded by him as a pramāṇa, since it is in any case no doubt an apprehension.

[1] See *Ślokavārttika*, *Nyāyaratnākara*, *Śāstradīpikā*, *Yuktisnehapūraṇī*, *Siddhāntacandrikā* on anumāna.

[2] On the subject of the means of assuring oneself that there is no condition (*upādhi*) which may vitiate the inference, Prabhākara has nothing new to tell us. He says that where even after careful enquiry in a large number of cases the condition cannot be discovered we must say that it does not exist (*prayatnenānviṣyamāṇe aupādhikatvānavagamāt*, see *Prakaraṇapañcikā*, p. 71).

Upamāna, Arthāpatti.

Analogy (*upamāna*) is accepted by Mīmāṃsā in a sense which is different from that in which Nyāya took it. The man who has seen a cow (*go*) goes to the forest and sees a wild ox (*gavaya*), and apprehends the similarity of the gavaya with the *go*, and then cognizes the similarity of the *go* (which is not within the limits of his perception then) with the *gavaya*. The cognition of this similarity of the *gavaya* in the *go*, as it follows directly from the perception of the similarity of the *go* in the *gavaya*, is called upamāna (analogy). It is regarded as a separate pramāṇa, because by it we can apprehend the similarity existing in a thing which is not perceived at the moment. It is not mere remembrance, for at the time the *go* was seen the *gavaya* was not seen, and hence the similarity also was not seen, and what was not seen could not be remembered. The difference of Prabhākara and Kumārila on this point is that while the latter regards similarity as only a quality consisting in the fact of more than one object having the same set of qualities, the former regards it as a distinct category.

Arthāpatti (implication) is a new pramāṇa which is admitted by the Mīmāṃsā. Thus when we know that a person Devadatta is alive and perceive that he is not in the house, we cannot reconcile these two facts, viz. his remaining alive and his not being in the house without presuming his existence somewhere outside the house, and this method of cognizing the existence of Devadatta outside the house is called *arthāpatti* (presumption or implication).

The exact psychological analysis of the mind in this arthāpatti cognition is a matter on which Prabhākara and Kumārila disagree. Prabhākara holds that when a man knows that Devadatta habitually resides in his house but yet does not find him there, his knowledge that Devadatta is living (though acquired previously by some other means of proof) is made doubtful, and the cause of this doubt is that he does not find Devadatta at his house. The absence of Devadatta from the house is not the cause of implication, but it throws into doubt the very existence of Devadatta, and thus forces us to imagine that Devadatta must remain somewhere outside. That can only be found by implication, without the hypothesis of which the doubt cannot be removed. The mere absence of Devadatta from the house is not enough for making the presumption that he is outside the house, for he might also be dead. But I know that Devadatta was living and also that he was not at home; this perception of his absence from home creates a doubt as regards my first knowledge that he is living, and it is for the removal of this doubt that there creeps in the presumption that he must be living somewhere else. The perception of the absence of Devadatta through the intermediate link of a doubt passes into the notion of a presumption that he must then remain somewhere else. In inference there is no element of doubt, for it is only when the smoke is perceived to exist beyond the least element of doubt that the inference of the fire is possible, but in presumption the perceived non-existence in the house leads to the presumption of an external existence only when it has thrown the fact of the man's being alive into doubt and uncertainty[1].

Kumārila however objects to this explanation of Prabhākara, and says that if the fact that Devadatta is living is made doubtful by the absence of Devadatta at his house, then the doubt may as well be removed by the supposition that Devadatta is dead, for it does not follow that the doubt with regard to the life of Devadatta should necessarily be resolved by the supposition of his being outside the house. Doubt can only be removed when the cause or the root of doubt is removed, and it does not follow that because Devadatta is not in the house therefore he is living. If it was already known that Devadatta was living and his absence from the house creates the doubt, how then can the very fact which created the doubt remove the doubt? The cause of doubt cannot be the cause of its removal too. The real procedure of the presumption is quite the other way. The doubt about the life of Devadatta being removed by previous knowledge or by some other means, we may presume that he must be outside the house when he is found absent from the house. So there cannot be any doubt about the life of Devadatta. It is the certainty of his life associated with the perception of his absence from the house that leads us to the presumption of his external existence. There is an opposition between the life of Devadatta and his absence from the house, and the mind cannot come to rest without the presumption of his external existence. The mind oscillates between two contradictory poles both of which it accepts but

[1] See *Prakaraṇapañcikā*, pp. 113–115.

cannot reconcile, and as a result of that finds an outlet and a reconciliation in the presumption that the existence of Devadatta must be found outside the house.

Well then, if that be so, inference may as well be interpreted as presumption. For if we say that we know that wherever there is smoke there is fire, and then perceive that there is smoke in the hill, but no fire, then the existence of the smoke becomes irreconcilable, or the universal proposition of the concomitance of smoke with fire becomes false, and hence the presumption that there is fire in the hill. This would have been all right if the universal concomitance of smoke with fire could be known otherwise than by inference. But this is not so, for the concomitance was seen only in individual cases, and from that came the inference that wherever there is smoke there is fire. It cannot be said that the concomitance perceived in individual cases suffered any contradiction without the presumption of the universal proposition (wherever there is smoke there is fire); thus arthāpatti is of no avail here and inference has to be accepted. Now when it is proved that there are cases where the purpose of inference cannot be served by arthāpatti, the validity of inference as a means of proof becomes established. That being done we admit that the knowledge of the fire in the hill may come to us either by inference or by arthāpatti.

So inference also cannot serve the purpose of arthāpatti, for in inference also it is the hetu (reason) which is known first, and later on from that the sādhya (what is to be proved); both of them however cannot be apprehended at the same moment, and it is exactly this that distinguishes arthāpatti from anumāna. For arthāpatti takes place where, without the presumption of Devadatta's external existence, the absence from the house of Devadatta who is living cannot be comprehended. If Devadatta is living he must exist inside or outside the house. The mind cannot swallow a contradiction, and hence without presuming the external existence of Devadatta even the perceived non-existence cannot be comprehended. It is thus that the contradiction is resolved by presuming his existence outside the house. Arthāpatti is thus the result of arthānupapatti or the contradiction of the present perception with a previously acquired certain knowledge.

It is by this arthāpattipramāṇa that we have to admit that there is a special potency in seeds by which they produce the shoots, and that a special potency is believed to exist in sacrifices by which these can lead the sacrificer to Heaven or some such beneficent state of existence.

Śabda-pramāṇa.

Śabda or word is regarded as a separate means of proof by most of the recognized Indian systems of thought excepting the Jaina, Buddhist, Cārvāka and Vaiśeṣika. A discussion on this topic however has but little philosophical value and I have therefore omitted to give any attention to it in connection with the Nyāya, and the Sāṃkhya-Yoga systems. The validity and authority of the Vedas were acknowledged by all Hindu writers and they had wordy battles over it with the Buddhists who denied it. Some sought to establish this authority on the supposition that they were the word of God, while others, particularly the Mīmāṃsists strove to prove that they were not written by anyone, and had no beginning in time nor end and were eternal. Their authority was not derived from the authority of any trustworthy person or God. Their words are valid in themselves. Evidently a discussion on these matters has but little value with us, though it was a very favourite theme of debate in the old days of India. It was in fact the most important subject for Mīmāṃsā, for the *Mīmāṃsā sūtras* were written for the purpose of laying down canons for a right interpretation of the Vedas. The slight extent to which it has dealt with its own epistemological doctrines has been due solely to their laying the foundation of its structure of interpretative maxims, and not to writing philosophy for its own sake. It does not dwell so much upon salvation as other systems do, but seeks to serve as a rational compendium of maxims with the help of which the Vedas may be rightly understood and the sacrifices rightly performed. But a brief examination of the doctrine of word (*śabda*) as a means of proof cannot be dispensed with in connection with Mīmāṃsā as it is its very soul.

Śabda (word) as a pramāṇa means the knowledge that we get about things (not within the purview of our perception) from relevant sentences by understanding the meaning of the words of which they are made up. These sentences may be of two kinds, viz. those uttered by men and those which belong to the Vedas. The first becomes a valid means of knowledge when it is not uttered by untrustworthy persons and the second is valid in itself. The meanings of words are of course known to us before, and cannot therefore be counted as a means of proof; but the meanings of sentences involving a knowledge of the relations of words cannot be known by any other acknowledged means of proof, and it is for this that we have to accept śabda as a separate means of proof. Even if it is admitted that the validity of any sentence may be inferred on the ground of its being uttered by a trustworthy person, yet that would not explain how we understand the meanings of sentences, for when even the name or person of a writer or speaker is not known, we have no difficulty in understanding the meaning of any sentence.

Prabhākara thinks that all sounds are in the form of letters, or are understandable as combinations of letters. The constituent letters of a word however cannot yield any meaning, and are thus to be regarded as elements of auditory perception which serve as a means for understanding the meaning of a word. The reason of our apprehension of the meaning of any word is to be found in a separate potency existing in the letters by which the denotation of the word may be comprehended. The perception of each letter-sound vanishes the moment it is uttered, but leaves behind an impression which combines with the impressions of the successively dying perceptions of letters, and this brings about the whole word which contains the potency of bringing about the comprehension of a certain meaning. If even on hearing a word the meaning cannot be comprehended, it has to be admitted that the hearer lacks certain auxiliaries necessary for the purpose. As the potency of the word originates from the separate potencies of the letters, it has to be admitted that the latter is the direct cause of verbal cognition. Both Prabhākara and Kumārila agree on this point.

Another peculiar doctrine expounded here is that all words have natural denotative powers by which they themselves out of their own nature refer to certain objects irrespective of their comprehension or non-comprehension by the hearer. The hearer will not understand the meaning unless it is known to him that the word in question is expressive of such and such a meaning, but the word was all along competent to denote that meaning and it is the hearer's knowledge of that fact that helps him to understand the meaning of a word. Mīmāṃsā does not think that the association of a particular meaning with a word is due to conventions among people who introduce and give meanings to the words[1]. Words are thus acknowledged to be denotative of themselves. It is only about proper names that convention is admitted to be the cause of denotation. It is easy to see the bearing of this doctrine on the self-validity of the Vedic commandments, by the performance of which such results would arise as could not have been predicted by any other person. Again all words are believed to be eternally existent; but though they are ever present some manifestive agency is required by which they are manifested to us. This manifestive agency consists of the effort put forth by the man who pronounces the word. Nyāya thinks that this effort of pronouncing is the cause that produces the word while Mīmāṃsā thinks that it only manifests to the hearer the ever-existing word.

The process by which according to Prabhākara the meanings of words are acquired may be exemplified thus: a senior commands a junior to bring a cow and to bind a horse, and the child on noticing the action of the junior in obedience to the senior's commands comes to understand the meaning of "cow" and "horse." Thus according to him the meanings of words can only be known from words occuring in injunctive sentences; he deduces from this the conclusion that words must denote things only as related to the other factors of the injunction (*anvitābhidhāna vāda*), and no word can be comprehended as having any denotation when taken apart from such a sentence. This doctrine holds that each word yields its meaning only as being generally related to other factors or only as a part of an injunctive sentence, thus the word *gām* accusative case of *go* (cow) means that it is intended that something is to be done with the cow or the bovine genus, and it appears only as connected with a specific kind of action, viz. bringing in the sentence *gām ānaya*—bring the cow. Kumārila however thinks that words independently express separate meanings which are subsequently combined into a sentence expressing one connected idea (*abhihitānvayavāda*). Thus in *gām ānaya*, according to Kumārila, *gām* means the bovine class in the accusative character and *ānaya* independently means

[1] According to Nyāya God created all words and associated them with their meanings.

bring; these two are then combined into the meaning "bring the cow." But on the former theory the word *gām* means that it is connected with some kind of action, and the particular sentence only shows what the special kind of action is, as in the above sentence it appears as associated with bringing, but it cannot have any meaning separately by itself. This theory of Kumārila which is also the Nyāya theory is called abhihitānvayavāda[1].

Lastly according to Prabhākara it is only the Veda that can be called śabda-pramāṇa, and only those sentences of it which contain injunctions (such as, perform this sacrifice in this way with these things). In all other cases the validity of words is only inferred on the ground of the trustworthy character of the speaker. But Kumārila considers the words of all trustworthy persons as śabda-pramāṇa.

The Pramāṇa of Non-perception (anupalabdhi).

In addition to the above pramāṇas Kumārila admits a fifth kind of pramāṇa, viz. *anupalabdhi* for the perception of the non-existence of a thing. Kumārila argues that the non-existence of a thing (e.g. there is no jug in this room) cannot be perceived by the senses, for there is nothing with which the senses could come into contact in order to perceive the non-existence. Some people prefer to explain this non-perception as a case of anumāna. They say that wherever there is the existence of a visible object there is the vision of it by a perceiver. When there is no vision of a visible object, there is no existence of it also. But it is easy to see that such an inference presupposes the perception of want of vision and want of existence, but how these non-perceptions are to be accounted for is exactly the point to be solved. How can the perception of want of vision or want of existence be grasped? It is for this that we have to admit a separate mode of pramāṇa namely anupalabdhi.

All things exist in places either in a positive (*sadrūpa*) or in a negative relation (*asadrūpa*), and it is only in the former case

[1] See *Prabhākaramīmāṃsā* by Dr Gaṅgānātha Jhā and S. N. Dasgupta's *Study of Patanjali*, appendix. It may be noted in this connection that Mīmāṃsā did not favour the Sphoṭa doctrine of sound which consists in the belief that apart from the momentary sounds of letters composing a word, there was a complete word form which was manifested (sphoṭa) but not created by the passing sounds of the syllables. The work of the syllable sounds is only to project this word-manifestation. See Vācaspati's *Tattvabindu*, *Ślokavārttika* and *Prakaraṇapañcikā*. For the doctrine of anvitābhidhāna see Śālikanātha's *Vākyārthamātṛkāvṛtti*.

that they come within the purview of the senses, while in the latter case the perception of the negative existence can only be had by a separate mode of the movement of the mind which we designate as a separate pramāṇa as anupalabdhi. Prabhākara holds that non-perception of a visible object in a place is only the perception of the empty place, and that therefore there is no need of admitting a separate pramāṇa as anupalabdhi. For what is meant by empty space? If it is necessary that for the perception of the non-existence of jug there should be absolutely empty space before us, then if the place be occupied by a stone we ought not to perceive the non-existence of the jug, inasmuch as the place is not absolutely empty. If empty space is defined as that which is not associated with the jug, then the category of negation is practically admitted as a separate entity. If the perception of empty space is defined as the perception of space at the moment which we associated with a want of knowledge about the jug, then also want of knowledge as a separate entity has to be accepted, which amounts to the same thing as the admission of the want or negation of the jug. Whatever attempt may be made to explain the notion of negation by any positive conception, it will at best be an attempt to shift negation from the objective field to knowledge, or in other words to substitute for the place of the external absence of a thing an associated want of knowledge about the thing (in spite of its being a visible object) and this naturally ends in failure, for negation as a separate category has to be admitted either in the field of knowledge or in the external world. Negation or abhāva as a separate category has anyhow to be admitted. It is said that at the first moment only the ground is seen without any knowledge of the jug or its negation, and then at the next moment comes the comprehension of the non-existence of the jug. But this also means that the moment of the perception of the ground is associated with the want of knowledge of the jug or its negation. But this comes to the same thing as the admission of negation as a separate category, for what other meaning can there be in the perception of "only the ground" if it is not meant that it (the perception of the ground) is associated with or qualified by the want of knowledge of the jug? For the perception of the ground cannot generate the notion of the non-existence of the jug, since even where there is a jug the ground is perceived. The qualifying phrase that "only the ground is perceived" becomes meaningless, if things whose presence is excluded are not specified as negative conditions qualifying the perception of the ground. And this would require that we had already the notion of negation in us, which appeared to us of itself in a special manner unaccountable by other means of proof. It should also be noted that non-perception of a sensible object generates the notion of negation immediately and not through other negations, and this is true not only of things of the present moment but also of the memory of past perceptions of non-existence, as when we remember that there was no jug here. Anupalabdhi is thus a separate pramāṇa by which the absence or want of a sensible object—the negation of a thing—can be comprehended.

Self, Salvation, God.

Mīmāṃsā has to accept the existence of soul, for without it who would perform the Vedic commandments, and what would be the meaning of those Vedic texts which speak of men as performing sacrifices and going to Heaven thereby? The soul is thus regarded as something entirely distinct from the body, the sense organs, and buddhi; it is eternal, omnipresent, and many, one in each body. Prabhākara thinks that it is manifested to us in all cognitions. Indeed he makes this also a proof for the existence of self as a separate entity from the body, for had it not been so, why should we have the notion of self-persistence in all our cognitions—even in those where there is no perception of the body? Kumārila however differs from Prabhākara about this analysis of the consciousness of self in our cognitions, and says that even though we may not have any notion of the parts of our body or their specific combination, yet the notion of ourselves as embodied beings always appears in all our cognitions. Moreover in our cognitions of external objects we are not always conscious of the self as the knower; so it is not correct to say that self is different from the body on the ground that the consciousness of self is present in all our cognitions, and that the body is not cognized in many of our cognitions. But the true reason for admitting that the self is different from the body is this, that movement or willing, knowledge, pleasure, pain, etc., cannot be attributed to the body, for though the body exists at death these cannot then be found. So it has to be admitted that they must belong to some other entity owing to the association with which the body appears to be endowed with movement etc. Moreover knowledge, feeling, etc. though apparent to the perceiver, are not yet perceived by others as other qualities of the body, as colour etc., are perceived by other men. It is a general law of causation that the qualities of the constituent elements (in the cause) impart themselves to the effect, but the earth atoms of which the body is made up do not contain the qualities of knowledge etc., and this also corroborates the inference of a separate entity as the vehicle of knowledge etc. The objection is sometimes raised that if the soul is omnipresent how can it be called an agent or a mover? But Mīmāṃsā does not admit that movement means atomic motion, for the principle of movement is the energy which moves the atoms, and this is possessed by the omnipresent soul. It is by the energy imparted by it to the body that the latter moves. So it is that though the soul does not move it is called an agent on account of the fact that it causes the movement of the body. The self must also be understood as being different from the senses, for even when one loses some of the senses he continues to perceive his self all the same as persisting all through.

The question now arises, how is self cognized? Prabhākara holds that the self as cognizor is never cognized apart from the cognized object, nor is the object ever cognized without the cognizor entering into the cognition as a necessary factor. Both the self and the object shine forth in the self-luminous knowledge in what we have already described as tripuṭī-pratyakṣa (perception as three-together). It is not the soul which is self-illumined but knowledge; so it is knowledge which illumines both the self and the object in one operation. But just as in the case of a man who walks, the action of walking rests upon the walker, yet he is regarded as the agent of the work and not as the object, so in the case of the operation of knowledge, though it affects the self, yet it appears as the agent and not as the object. Cognition is not soul, but the soul is manifested in cognition as its substratum, and appears in it as the cognitive element "I" which is inseparable from all cognitions. In deep sleep therefore when no object is cognized the self also is not cognized.

Kumārila however thinks that the soul which is distinct from the body is perceived by a mental perception (*mānasa-pratyakṣa*) as the substratum of the notion of "I," or in other words the self perceives itself by mental perception, and the perception of its own nature shines forth in consciousness as the "I." The objection that the self cannot itself be both subject and object to its own operation does not hold, for it applies equally to Prabhākara's theory in which knowledge reveals the self as its object and yet considers it as the subject of the operation. The analogy of linguistic usage that though the walking affects the walker yet he is the agent, cannot be regarded as an escape from this charge, for the usage of language is not philosophical analysis. Though at the time of the cognition of objects the self is cognized, yet it does not appear as the knower of the knowledge of objects, but reveals itself as an object of a separate mental perception which is distinct from the knowledge of objects. The self is no doubt known as the substratum of "I," but the knowledge of this self does not reveal itself necessarily with the cognition of objects, nor does the self show itself as the knower of all knowledge of objects, but the self is apprehended by a separate mental intuition which we represent as the "I." The self does not reveal itself as the knower but as an object of a separate intuitive process of the mind. This is indeed different from Prabhākara's analysis, who regarded the cognition of self as inseparable from the object-cognition, both being the result of the illumination of knowledge. Kumārila agrees with Prabhākara however in holding that soul is not self-illuminating (*svayamprakāśa*), for then even in deep sleep the soul should have manifested itself; but there is no such manifestation then, and the state of deep sleep appears as an unconscious state. There is also no bliss in deep sleep, for had it been so people would not have regretted that they had missed sensual enjoyments by untimely sleep. The expression that "I slept in bliss" signifies only that no misery was felt. Moreover the opposite representation of the deep sleep state is also found when a man on rising from sleep says "I slept so long without knowing anything not even my own self." The self is not atomic, since we can simultaneously feel a sensation in the head as well as in the leg. The Jaina theory that it is of the size of the body which contracts and expands according to the body it occupies is unacceptable. It is better therefore that the soul should be regarded as all-pervading as described in the Vedas. This self must also be different in different persons for otherwise their individual experiences of objects and of pleasure and pain cannot be explained[1].

[1] See *Ślokavārttika*, ātmavāda *Śāstra-dīpikā*, ātmavāda and mokṣavāda.

Kumārila considered the self to be merely the potency of knowledge (*jñānaśakti*)[1]. Cognitions of things were generated by the activity of the manas and the other senses. This self itself can only be cognized by mental perception. Or at the time of salvation there being none of the senses nor the manas the self remains in pure existence as the potency of knowledge without any actual expression or manifestation. So the state of salvation is the state in which the self remains devoid of any of its characteristic qualities such as pleasure, pain, knowledge, willing, etc., for the self itself is not knowledge nor is it bliss or ānanda as Vedānta supposes; but these are generated in it by its energy and the operation of the senses. The self being divested of all its senses at that time, remains as a mere potency of the energy of knowledge, a mere existence. This view of salvation is accepted in the main by Prabhākara also.

Salvation is brought about when a man enjoys and suffers the fruits of his good and bad actions and thereby exhausts them and stops the further generation of new effects by refraining from the performance of kāmya-karmas (sacrifices etc. performed for the attainment of certain beneficent results) and guarantees himself against the evil effects of sin by assiduously performing the nitya-karmas (such as the sandhyā prayers etc., by the performance of which there is no benefit but the non-performance of which produces sins). This state is characterized by the dissolution of the body and the non-production of any further body or rebirth.

Mīmāṃsā does not admit the existence of any God as the creator and destroyer of the universe. Though the universe is made up of parts, yet there is no reason to suppose that the universe had ever any beginning in time, or that any God created it. Every day animals and men are coming into being by the action of the parents without the operation of any God. Neither is it necessary as Nyāya supposes that dharma and adharma should have a supervisor, for these belong to the performer and

[1] It may be mentioned in this connection that unlike Nyāyā Mīmāṃsā did not consider all activity as being only of the nature of molecular vibration (*parispanda*). It admitted the existence of energy (*śakti*) as a separate category which manifested itself in actual movements. The self being considered as a śakti can move the body and yet remain unmoved itself. Manifestation of action only means the relationing of the energy with a thing. Nyāyā strongly opposes this doctrine of a non-sensible (atīndriya) energy and seeks to explain all action by actual molecular motion.

no one can have any knowledge of them. Moreover there cannot be any contact (*saṃyoga*) or inherence (*samavāya*) of dharma and adharma with God that he might supervise them; he cannot have any tools or body wherewith to fashion the world like the carpenter. Moreover he could have no motive to create the world either as a merciful or as a cruel act. For when in the beginning there were no beings towards whom should he be actuated with a feeling of mercy? Moreover he would himself require a creator to create him. So there is no God, no creator, no creation, no dissolution or pralaya. The world has ever been running the same, without any new creation or dissolution, sṛṣṭi or pralaya.

Mīmāṃsā as philosophy and Mīmāṃsā as ritualism.

From what we have said before it will be easy to see that Mīmāṃsā agrees in the main with Vaiśeṣika about the existence of the categories of things such as the five elements, the qualities, rūpa, rasa, etc. Kumārila's differences on the points of jāti, samavāya, etc. and Prabhākara's peculiarities have also been mentioned before. On some of these points it appears that Kumārila was influenced by Sāṃkhya thought rather than by Nyāya. Sāṃkhya and Vaiśeṣika are the only Hindu systems which have tried to construct a physics as a part of their metaphysics; other systems have generally followed them or have differed from them only on minor matters. The physics of Prabhākara and Kumārila have thus but little importance, as they agree in general with the Vaiśeṣika view. In fact they were justified in not laying any special stress on this part, because for the performance of sacrifices the common-sense view of Nyāya-Vaiśeṣika about the world was most suitable.

The main difference of Mīmāṃsā with Nyāya consists of the theory of knowledge. The former was required to prove that the Veda was self-valid and that it did not derive its validity from God, and also that it was not necessary to test its validity by any other means. To do this it began by trying to establish the self-validity of all knowledge. This would secure for the Veda the advantage that as soon as its orders or injunctions were communicated to us they would appear to us as valid knowledge, and there being nothing to contradict them later on there would be nothing in the world which could render the Vedic injunctions invalid. The other pramāṇas such as perception, inference, etc. were described, firstly to indicate that they could not show to us how dharma could be acquired, for dharma was not an existing thing which could be perceived by the other pramāṇas, but a thing which could only be produced by acting according to the injunctions of the Vedas. For the knowledge of dharma and adharma therefore the śabdapramāṇa of the Veda was our only source. Secondly it was necessary that we should have a knowledge of the different means of cognition, as without them it would be difficult to discuss and verify the meanings of debatable Vedic sentences. The doctrine of creation and dissolution which is recognized by all other Hindu systems could not be acknowledged by the Mīmāṃsā as it would have endangered the eternality of the Vedas. Even God had to be dispensed with on that account.

The Veda is defined as the collection of Mantras and Brāhmaṇas (also called the *vidhis* or injunctive sentences). There are three classes of injunctions (1) apūrva-vidhi, (2) niyama-vidhi, and (3) parisaṅkhyā-vidhi. Apūrva-vidhi is an order which enjoins something not otherwise known, e.g. the grains should be washed (we could not know that this part of the duty was necessary for the sacrifice except by the above injunction). Niyama-vidhi is that where when a thing could have been done in a number of ways, an order is made by the Veda which restricts us to following some definite alternative (e.g. though the chaff from the corn could be separated even by the nails, the order that "corn should be threshed" restricts us to the alternative of threshing as the only course acceptable for the sacrifice). In the niyama-vidhi that which is ordered is already known as possible but only as an alternative, and the vidhi insists upon one of these methods as the only one. In apūrva-vidhi the thing to be done would have remained undone and unknown had it not been for the vidhi. In parisaṅkhyā-vidhi all that is enjoined is already known but not necessarily as possible alternatives. A certain mantra "I take up the rein" (*imām agṛbhnāṃ raśanāṃ*) which could be used in a number of cases should not however be used at the time of holding the reins of an ass.

There are three main principles of interpreting the Vedic sentences. (1) When some sentences are such that connectively they yield a meaning but not individually, then they should be taken together connectively as a whole. (2) If the separate sentences can however yield meanings separately by themselves they should not be connected together. (3) In the case of certain sentences which are incomplete suitable words from the context of immediately preceding sentences are to be supplied.

The vidhis properly interpreted are the main source of dharma. The mantras which are generally hymns in praise of some deities or powers are to be taken as being for the specification of the deity to whom the libation is to be offered. It should be remembered that as dharma can only be acquired by following the injunctions of the Vedas they should all be interpreted as giving us injunctions. Anything therefore found in the Vedas which cannot be connected with the injunctive orders as forming part of them is to be regarded as untrustworthy or at best inexpressive. Thus it is that those sentences in the Vedas which describe existing things merely or praise some deed of injunction (called the *arthavādas*) should be interpreted as forming part of a vidhi-vākya (injunction) or be rejected altogether. Even those expressions which give reasons for the performance of certain actions are to be treated as mere arthavādas and interpreted as praising injunctions. For Vedas have value only as mandates by the performance of which dharma may be acquired.

When a sacrifice is performed according to the injunctions of the Vedas, a capacity which did not exist before and whose existence is proved by the authority of the scriptures is generated either in the action or in the agent. This capacity or positive force called *apūrva* produces in time the beneficient results of the sacrifice (e.g. leads the performer to Heaven). This apūrva is like a potency or faculty in the agent which abides in him until the desired results follow[1].

It is needless to dilate upon these, for the voluminous works of Śabara and Kumārila make an elaborate research into the nature of sacrifices, rituals, and other relevant matters in great detail, which anyhow can have but little interest for a student of philosophy.

[1] See Dr Gaṅgānātha Jhā's *Prabhākaramīmāṃsā* and Mādhava's *Nyāyamālāvistara*.

X

THE ŚAṆKARA SCHOOL OF VEDĀNTA

Comprehension of the philosophical issues more essential than the Dialectic of controversy.

Pramāṇa in Sanskrit signifies the means and the movement by which knowledge is acquired, *pramātā* means the subject or the knower who cognizes, *pramā* the result of pramāṇa—right knowledge, *prameya* the object of knowedge, and *prāmāṇya* the validity of knowledge acquired. The validity of knowledge is sometimes used in the sense of the faithfulness of knowledge to its object, and sometimes in the sense of an inner notion of validity in the mind of the subject—the knower (that his perceptions are true), which moves him to work in accordance with his perceptions to adapt himself to his environment for the attainment of pleasurable and the avoidance of painful things. The question wherein consists the prāmāṇya of knowledge has not only an epistemological and psychological bearing but a metaphysical one also. It contains on one side a theory of knowledge based on an analysis of psychological experience, and on the other indicates a metaphysical situation consistent with the theory of knowledge. All the different schools tried to justify a theory of knowledge by an appeal to the analysis and interpretation of experience which the others sometimes ignored or sometimes regarded as unimportant. The thinkers of different schools were accustomed often to meet together and defeat one another in actual debates, and the result of these debates was frequently very important in determining the prestige of any school of thought. If a Buddhist for example could defeat a great Nyāya or Mīmāṃsā thinker in a great public debate attended by many learned scholars from different parts of the country, his fame at once spread all over the country and he could probably secure a large number of followers on the spot. Extensive tours of disputation were often undertaken by great masters all over the country for the purpose of defeating the teachers of the opposite schools and of securing adherents to their own. These debates were therefore not generally conducted merely in a passionless philosophical mood with the object of arriving at the truth but in order to inflict a defeat on opponents and to establish the ascendency of some particular school of thought. It was often a sense of personal victory and of the victory of the school of thought to which the debater adhered that led him to pursue the debate. Advanced Sanskrit philosophical works give us a picture of the attitude of mind of these debaters and we find that most of these debates attempt to criticize the different schools of thinkers by exposing their inconsistencies and self-contradictions by close dialectical reasoning, anticipating the answers of the opponent, asking him to define his statements, and ultimately proving that his theory was inconsistent, led to contradictions, and was opposed to the testimony of experience. In reading an advanced work on Indian philosophy in the original, a student has to pass through an interminable series of dialectic arguments, and negative criticisms (to thwart opponents) sometimes called *vitaṇḍā*, before he can come to the root of the quarrel, the real philosophical divergence. All the resources of the arts of controversy find full play for silencing the opponent before the final philosophical answer is given. But to a modern student of philosophy, who belongs to no party and is consequently indifferent to the respective victory of either side, the most important thing is the comprehension of the different aspects from which the problem of the theory of knowledge and its associated metaphysical theory was looked at by the philosophers, and also a clear understanding of the deficiency of each view, the value of the mutual criticisms, the speculations on the experience of each school, their analysis, and their net contribution to philosophy. With Vedānta we come to an end of the present volume, and it may not be out of place here to make a brief survey of the main conflicting theories from the point of view of the theory of knowledge, in order to indicate the position of the Vedānta of the Śaṅkara school in the field of Indian philosophy so far as we have traversed it. I shall therefore now try to lay before my readers the solution of the theory of knowledge (*pramāṇavāda*) reached by some of the main schools of thought. Their relations to the solution offered by the Śaṅkara Vedānta will also be dealt with, as we shall attempt to sketch the views of the Vedānta later on in this chapter.

The philosophical situation: A Review.

Before dealing with the Vedānta system it seems advisable to review the general attitude of the schools already discussed to the main philosophical and epistemological questions which determine the position of the Vedānta as taught by Śaṅkara and his school.

The Sautrāntika Buddhist says that in all his affairs man is concerned with the fulfilment of his ends and desires (*puruṣārtha*). This however cannot be done without right knowledge (*samyagjñāna*) which rightly represents things to men. Knowledge is said to be right when we can get things just as we perceived them. So far as mere representation or illumination of objects is concerned, it is a patent fact that we all have knowledge, and therefore this does not deserve criticism or examination. Our enquiry about knowledge is thus restricted to its aspect of later verification or contradiction in experience, for we are all concerned to know how far our perceptions of things which invariably precede all our actions can be trusted as rightly indicating what we want to get in our practical experience (*arthaprāpakatva*). The perception is right (*abhrānta* non-illusory) when following its representation we can get in the external world such things as were represented by it (*saṃvādakatva*). That perception alone can be right which is generated by the object and not merely supplied by our imagination. When I say "this is the cow I had seen," what I see is the object with the brown colour, horns, feet, etc., but the fact that this is called cow, or that this is existing from a past time, is not perceived by the visual sense, as this is not generated by the visual object. For all things are momentary, and that which I see now never existed before so as to be invested with this or that permanent name. This association of name and permanence to objects perceived is called *kalpanā* or *abhilāpa*. Our perception is correct only so far as it is without the abhilāpa association (*kalpanāpoḍha*), for though this is taken as a part of our perceptual experience it is not derived from the object, and hence its association with the object is an evident error. The object as unassociated with name—the nirvikalpa—is thus what is perceived. As a result of the pratyakṣa the manovijñāna or thought and mental perception of pleasure and pain is also determined. At one moment perception reveals the object as an object of knowledge (*grāhya*), and by the fact of the rise of such a percept, at another moment it appears as a thing realizable or attainable in the external world. The special features of the object undefinable in themselves as being what they are in themselves (*svalakṣaṇa*) are what is actually perceived (*pratyakṣaviṣaya*)[1]. The *pramāṇaphala* (result of perception) is the

[1] There is a difference of opinion about the meaning of the word "svalakṣaṇa" of Dharmakīrtti between my esteemed friend Professor Stcherbatsky of Petrograd and myself. He maintains that Dharmakīrtti held that the content of the presentative element at the moment of perception was almost totally empty. Thus he writes to me, "According to your interpretation svalakṣaṇa means—the object (or idea with Vijñānavādin) *from which everything past and everything future has been eliminated*, this I do not deny at all. But I maintain that if everything past and future has been taken away, what remains? *The present* and the present is a *kṣaṇa* i.e. nothing. ... The reverse of kṣaṇa is a kṣaṇasaṃtāna or simply saṃtāna and in every saṃtāna there is a synthesis ekībhāva of moments past and future, produced by the intellect (buddhi = niścaya = kalpanā = adhyavasāya).... There is in the perception of a jug *something* (a kṣaṇa of sense knowledge) which we must distinguish from the *idea* of a jug (which is always a saṃtāna, always vikalpita), and if you take the idea away in a strict unconditional sense, no knowledge remains: kṣanasya jñānena prāpayitumaśakyatvāt. This is absolutely the Kantian teaching about *Synthesis of Apprehension*. Accordingly pratyakṣa is a *transcendental* source of knowledge, because practically speaking it gives no knowledge at all. This *pramāṇa* is *asatkalpa*. Kant says that without the elements of intuition (= sense-knowledge = pratyakṣa = kalpanāpoḍha) our cognitions would be empty and without the elements of intellect (kalpanā = buddhi = synthesis = ekībhāva) they would be blind. Empirically both are always combined. This is exactly the theory of Dharmakīrtti. He is a Vijñānavādī as I understand, because he maintains the cognizability of ideas (vijñāna) alone, but the reality is an incognizable foundation of our knowledge; he admits, it is bāhya, it is artha, it is arthakriyākṣaṇa = svalakṣaṇa; that is the reason for which he sometimes is called Sautrāntika and this school is sometimes called Sautrānta-vijñānavāda, as opposed to the Vijñānavāda of Aśvaghoṣa and Āryāsaṅga, which had no elaborate theory of cognition. If the jug as it exists in our representation were the svalakṣaṇa and paramārthasat, what would remain of Vijñānavāda? But there is the perception of the jug as opposed to the *pure idea* of a jug (śuddhā kalpanā), an element of reality, the sensational kṣaṇa, which is communicated to us by sense knowledge. Kant's 'thing in itself' is also a kṣaṇa and also an element of sense knowledge of pure sense as opposed to *pure reason*, Dharmakīrtti has also *śuddhā kalpanā* and *śuddham pratyakṣam*.... And very interesting is the opposition between pratyakṣa and anumāna, the first moves from kṣaṇa to saṃtāna and the second from saṃtāna to kṣaṇa, that is the reason that although bhrānta the anumāna is nevertheless pramāṇa because through it we indirectly also reach kṣaṇa, the arthakriyākṣaṇa. It is bhrānta directly and pramāṇa indirectly; pratyakṣa is pramāṇa directly and bhrānta (asatkalpa) indirectly...." So far as the passages to which Professor Stcherbatsky refers are concerned, I am in full agreement with him. But I think that he pushes the interpretation too far on Kantian lines. When I perceive "this is blue," the perception consists of two parts, the actual presentative element of sense-knowledge (*svalakṣaṇa*) and the affirmation (*niścaya*). So far we are in complete agreement. But Professor Stcherbatsky says that this sense-knowledge is a kṣaṇa (moment) and is nothing. I also hold that it is a kṣaṇa, but it is nothing only in the sense that it is not the same as the notion involving affirmation such as "this is blue." The affirmative process occurring at the succeeding moments is determined by the presentative

ideational concept and power that such knowledge has of showing the means which being followed the thing can be got (*yena kṛtena arthaḥ prāpito bhavati*). Pramāṇa then is the similarity of the knowledge with the object by which it is generated, by which we assure ourselves that this is our knowledge of the object as it is perceived, and are thus led to attain it by practical experience. Yet this later stage is pramāṇaphala and not pramāṇa which consists merely in the vision of the thing (devoid of other associations), and which determines the attitude of the perceiver towards the perceived object. The pramāṇa therefore only refers to the newly-acquired knowledge (*anadhigatādhigantṛ*) as this is of use to the perceiver in determining his relations with the objective world. This account of perception leaves out the real epistemological question as to how the knowledge is generated by the external world, or what it is in itself. It only looks to the correctness or faithfulness of the perception to the object and its value for us in the practical realization of our ends. The question of the relation of the external world with knowledge as determining the latter is regarded as unimportant.

element of the first moment (*pratyakṣabalotpanna* N.T., p. 20) but this presentative element divested from the product of the affirmative process of the succeeding moments is not characterless, though we cannot express its character; as soon as we try to express it, names and other ideas consisting of affirmation are associated and these did not form a part of the presentative element. Its own character is said to be its own specific nature (*svalakṣaṇa*). But what is this specific nature? Dharmakīrtti's answer on this point is that by specific nature he means those specific characteristics of the object which appear clear when the object is near and hazy when it is at a distance (*yasyārthasya sannidhānāsannidhānābhyām jñānapratibhāsabhedastat svalakṣaṇam* N., p. 1 and N. T., p. 16). Sense-knowledge thus gives us the specific characteristics of the object, and this has the same form as the object itself; it is the appearance of the "blue" in its specific character in the mind and when this is associated by the affirmative or ideational process, the result is the concept or idea "this is blue" (*nīlasarūpaṃ pratyakṣamanubhūyamānaṃ nīlabodharūpamavasthāpyate ... nīlasārūpyamasya pramāṇam nīlavikalpanarūpaṃ tvasya pramāṇaphalam*, N. T. p. 22). At the first moment there is the appearance of the blue (*nīlanirbhāsaṃ hi vijñānam*, N. T. 19) and this is direct acquaintance (*yatkiñcit arthasya sākṣātkārijñānam tatpratyakṣamucyate*, N. T. 7) and this is real (*paramārthasat*) and valid. This blue sensation is different from the idea "this is blue" (*nīlabodha*, N. T. 22) which is the result of the former (pramāṇaphala) through the association of the affirmative process (*adkyavasāya*) and is regarded as invalid for it contains elements other than what were presented to the sense, and is a *vikalpapratyaya*. In my opinion *svalakṣaṇa* therefore means pure sensation of the moment presenting the specific features of the object and with Dharmakīrtti this is the only thing which is valid in perception and vikalpapratyaya or pramānaphala is the idea or concept which follows it. But though the latter is a product of the former, yet, being the construction of succeeding moments, it cannot give us the pure stage of the first moment of sensation-presentation (*kṣaṇasya prāpayitumaśakyatvāt*, N. T. 16). N. T. = *Nyāyabinduṭīkā*, N=*Nyāyabindu* (Peterson's edition).

The Yogācāras or idealistic Buddhists take their cue from the above-mentioned Sautrāntika Buddhists, and say that since we can come into touch with knowledge and knowledge alone, what is the use of admitting an external world of objects as the data of sensation determining our knowledge? You say that sensations are copies of the external world, but why should you say that they copy, and not that they alone exist? We never come into touch with objects in themselves; these can only be grasped by us simultaneously with knowledge of them, they must therefore be the same as knowledge (*sahopalambhaniyamāt abhedo nīlataddhiyoḥ*); for it is in and through knowledge that external objects can appear to us, and without knowledge we are not in touch with the so-called external objects. So it is knowledge which is self-apparent in itself, that projects itself in such a manner as to appear as referring to other external objects. We all acknowledge that in dreams there are no external objects, but even there we have knowledge. The question why then if there are no external objects, there should be so much diversity in the forms of knowledge, is not better solved by the assumption of an external world; for in such an assumption, the external objects have to be admitted as possessing the infinitely diverse powers of diversely affecting and determining our knowledge; that being so, it may rather be said that in the beginningless series of flowing knowledge, preceding knowledge-moments by virtue of their inherent specific qualities determine the succeeding knowledge-moments. Thus knowledge alone exists; the projection of an external word is an illusion of knowledge brought about by beginningless potencies of desire (*vāsanā*) associated with it. The preceding knowledge determines the succeeding one and that another and so on. Knowledge, pleasure, pain, etc. are not qualities requiring a permanent entity as soul in which they may inhere, but are the various forms in which knowledge appears. Even the cognition, "I perceive a blue thing," is but a form of knowledge, and this is often erroneously interpreted as referring to a permanent knower. Though the cognitions are all passing and momentary, yet so long as the series continues to be the same, as in the case of one person, say Devadatta, the phenomena of memory, recognition, etc. can happen in the succeeding moments, for these are evidently illusory cognitions, so far as they refer to the permanence of the objects believed to have been perceived before, for things or knowledge-moments, whatever they may be, are destroyed the next moment after their birth. There is no permanent entity as perceiver or knower, but the knowledge-moments are at once the knowledge, the knower and the known. This thoroughgoing idealism brushes off all references to an objective field of experience, interprets the verdict of knowledge as involving a knower and the known as mere illusory appearance, and considers the flow of knowledge as a self-determining series in successive objective forms as the only truth. The Hindu schools of thought, Nyāya, Sāṃkhya, and the Mīmāṃsā, accept the duality of soul and matter, and attempt to explain the relation between the two. With the Hindu writers it was not the practical utility of knowledge that was the only important thing, but the nature of knowledge and the manner in which it came into being were also enquired after and considered important.

Pramāṇa is defined by Nyāya as the collocation of instruments by which unerring and indubitable knowledge comes into being. The collocation of instruments which brings about definite knowledge consists partly of consciousness (*bodha*) and partly of material factors (*bodhābodhasvabhāva*). Thus in perception the proper contact of the visual sense with the object (e.g. jug) first brings about a non-intelligent, non-apprehensible indeterminate consciousness (*nirvikalpa*) as the jugness (*ghaṭatva*) and this later on combining with the remaining other collocations of sensecontact etc. produces the determinate consciousness: this is a jug. The existence of this indeterminate state of consciousness as a factor in bringing about the determinate consciousness, cannot of course be perceived, but its existence can be inferred from the fact that if the perceiver were not already in possession of the qualifying factor (*viśeṣanajñāna* as jugness) he could not have comprehended the qualified object (*viśiṣṭabuddhi*) the jug (i.e. the object which possesses jugness). In inference (*anumāṇa*) knowledge of the liṅga takes part, and in upamāna the sight of similarity with other material conglomerations. In the case of the Buddhists knowledge itself was regarded as pramāṇa; even by those who admitted the existence of the objective world, right knowledge was called pramāṇa, because it was of the same form as the external objects it represented, and it was by the form of the knowledge (e.g. blue) that we could apprehend that the external object was also blue. Knowledge does not determine the external world but simply enforces our convictions about the external world. So far as knowledge leads us to form our convictions of the external world it is pramāṇa, and so far as it determines our attitude towards the external world it is pramāṇaphala. The question how knowledge is generated had little importance with them, but how with knowledge we could form convictions of the external world was the most important thing. Knowledge was called pramāṇa, because it was the means by which we could form convictions (*adhyavasāya*) about the external world. Nyāya sought to answer the question how knowledge was generated in us, but could not understand that knowledge was not a mere phenomenon like any other objective phenomenon, but thought that though as a guṇa (quality) it was external like other guṇas, yet it was associated with our self as a result of collocations like any other happening in the material world. Pramāṇa does not necessarily bring to us new knowledge (*anadhigatādhigantṛ*) as the Buddhists demanded, but whensoever there were collocations of pramāṇa, knowledge was produced, no matter whether the object was previously unknown or known. Even the knowledge of known things may be repeated if there be suitable collocations. Knowledge like any other physical effect is produced whenever the cause of it namely the pramāṇa collocation is present. Categories which are merely mental such as class (*sāmānya*), inherence (*samavāya*), etc., were considered as having as much independent existence as the atoms of the four elements. The phenomenon of the rise of knowledge in the soul was thus conceived to be as much a phenomenon as the turning of the colour of the jug by fire from black to red. The element of indeterminate consciousness was believed to be combining with the sense contact, the object, etc. to produce the determinate consciousness. There was no other subtler form of movement than the molecular. Such a movement brought about by a certain collocation of things ended in a certain result (*phala*). Jñāna (knowledge) was thus the result of certain united collocations (*sāmagrī*) and their movements (e.g. contact of manas with soul, of manas with the senses, of the senses with the object, etc.). This confusion renders it impossible to understand the real philosophical distinction between knowledge and an external event of the objective world. Nyāya thus fails to explain the cause of the origin of knowledge, and its true relations with the objective world. Pleasure, pain, willing, etc. were regarded as qualities which belonged to the soul, and the soul itself was regarded as a qualitiless entity which could not be apprehended directly but was inferred as that in which the qualities of jñāna, sukha (pleasure), etc. inhered. Qualities had independent existence as much as substances, but when any new substances were produced, the qualities rushed forward and inhered in them. It is very probable that in Nyāya the cultivation of the art of inference was originally pre-eminent and metaphysics was deduced later by an application of the inferential method which gave the introspective method but little scope for its application, so that inference came in to explain even perception (e.g. this is a jug since it has jugness) and the testimony of personal psychological experience was taken only as a supplement to corroborate the results arrived at by inference and was not used to criticize it[1].

Sāṃkhya understood the difference between knowledge and material events. But so far as knowledge consisted in being the copy of external things, it could not be absolutely different from the objects themselves; it was even then an invisible translucent sort of thing, devoid of weight and grossness such as the external objects possessed. But the fact that it copies those gross objects makes it evident that knowledge had essentially the same substances though in a subtler form as that of which the objects were made. But though the matter of knowledge, which assumed the form of the objects with which it came in touch, was probably thus a subtler combination of the same elementary substances of which matter was made up, yet there was in it another element, viz. intelligence, which at once distinguished it as utterly different from material combinations. This element of intelligence is indeed different from the substances or content of the knowledge itself, for the element of intelligence is like a stationary light, "the self," which illuminates the crowding, bustling knowledge which is incessantly changing its form in accordance with the objects with which it comes in touch. This light of intelligence is the same that finds its manifestation in consciousness as the "I," the changeless entity amidst all the fluctuations of the changeful procession of knowledge. How this element of light which is foreign to the substance of knowledge

[1] See *Nyāyamañjarī* on pramāṇa.

relates itself to knowledge, and how knowledge itself takes it up into itself and appears as conscious, is the most difficult point of the Sāmkhya epistemology and metaphysics. The substance of knowledge copies the external world, and this copy-shape of knowledge is again intelligized by the pure intelligence (*puruṣa*) when it appears as conscious. The forming of the buddhi-shape of knowledge is thus the pramāṇa (instrument and process of knowledge) and the validity or invalidity of any of these shapes is criticized by the later shapes of knowledge and not by the external objects (*svataḥ-prāmāṇya* and *svataḥ-aprāmāṇya*). The pramāṇa however can lead to a pramā or right knowledge only when it is intelligized by the puruṣa. The puruṣa comes in touch with buddhi not by the ordinary means of physical contact but by what may be called an inexplicable transcendental contact. It is the transcendental influence of puruṣa that sets in motion the original prakṛti in Sāṃkhya metaphysics, and it is the same transcendent touch (call it yogyatā according to Vācaspati or samyoga according to Bhiksu) of the transcendent entity of puruṣa that transforms the non-intelligent states of buddhi into consciousness. The Vijñānavādin Buddhist did not make any distinction between the pure consciousness and its forms (*ākāra*) and did not therefore agree that the ākāra of knowledge was due to its copying the objects. Sāṃkhya was however a realist who admitted the external world and regarded the forms as all due to copying, all stamped as such upon a translucent substance (*sattva*) which could assume the shape of the objects. But Sāṃkhya was also transcendentalist in this, that it did not think like Nyāya that the ākāra of knowledge was all that knowledge had to show; it held that there was a transcendent element which shone forth in knowledge and made it conscious. With Nyāya there was no distinction between the shaped buddhi and the intelligence, and that being so consciousness was almost like a physical event. With Sāṃkhya however so far as the content and the shape manifested in consciousness were concerned it was indeed a physical event, but so far as the pure intelligizing element of consciousness was concerned it was a wholly transcendent affair beyond the scope and province of physics. The rise of consciousness was thus at once both transcendent and physical.

The Mīmāṃsist Prabhākara agreed with Nyāya in general as regards the way in which the objective world and sense contact induced knowledge in us. But it regarded knowledge as a unique phenomenon which at once revealed itself, the knower and the known. We are not concerned with physical collocations, for whatever these may be it is knowledge which reveals things—the direct apprehension that should be called the pramāṇa. Pramāṇa in this sense is the same as pramiti or pramā, the phenomenon of apprehension. Pramāṇa may also indeed mean the collocations so far as they induce the pramā. For pramā or right knowledge is never produced, it always exists, but it manifests itself differently under different circumstances. The validity of knowledge means the conviction or the specific attitude that is generated in us with reference to the objective world. This validity is manifested with the rise of knowledge, and it does not await the verdict of any later experience in the objective field (*saṃvādin*). Knowledge as nirvikalpa (indeterminate) means the whole knowledge of the object and not merely a non-sensible hypothetical indeterminate class-notion as Nyāya holds. The savikalpa (determinate) knowledge only re-establishes the knowledge thus formed by relating it with other objects as represented by memory[1].

Prabhākara rejected the Sāṃkhya conception of a dual element in consciousness as involving a transcendent intelligence (*cit*) and a material part, the buddhi; but it regarded consciousness as an unique thing which by itself in one flash represented both the knower and the known. The validity of knowledge did not depend upon its faithfulness in reproducing or indicating (*pradarśakatva*) external objects, but upon the force that all direct apprehension (*anubhūti*) has of prompting us to action in the external world; knowledge is thus a complete and independent unit in all its self-revealing aspects. But what the knowledge was in itself apart from its self-revealing character Prabhākara did not enquire.

Kumārila declared that jñāna (knowledge) was a movement brought about by the activity of the self which resulted in producing consciousness (*jñātatā*) of objective things. Jñāna itself cannot be perceived, but can only be inferred as the movement necessary for producing the jñātatā or consciousness of things. Movement with Kumārila was not a mere atomic vibration, but was a non-sensuous transcendent operation of which vibration

[1] Sāṃkhya considered nirvikalpa as the dim knowledge of the first moment of consciousness, which, when it became clear at the next moment, was called savikalpa.

was sometimes the result. Jñāna was a movement and not the result of causal operation as Nyāya supposed. Nyāya would not also admit any movement on the part of the self, but it would hold that when the self is possessed of certain qualities, such as desire, etc., it becomes an instrument for the accomplishment of a physical movement. Kumārila accords the same self-validity to knowledge that Prabhākara gives. Later knowledge by experience is not endowed with any special quality which should decide as to the validity of the knowledge of the previous movement. For what is called saṃvādi or later testimony of experience is but later knowledge and nothing more[1]. The self is not revealed in the knowledge of external objects, but we can know it by a mental perception of self-consciousness. It is the movement of this self in presence of certain collocating circumstances leading to cognition of things that is called jñāna[2]. Here Kumārila distinguishes knowledge as movement from knowledge as objective consciousness. Knowledge as movement was beyond sense perception and could only be inferred.

The idealistic tendency of Vijñānavāda Buddhism, Sāṃkhya, and Mīmāṃsā was manifest in its attempt at establishing the unique character of knowledge as being that with which alone we are in touch. But Vijñānavāda denied the external world, and thereby did violence to the testimony of knowledge. Sāṃkhya admitted the external world but created a gulf between the content of knowledge and pure intelligence; Prabhākara ignored this difference, and was satisfied with the introspective assertion that knowledge was such a unique thing that it revealed with itself, the knower and the known; Kumārila however admitted a transcendent element of movement as being the cause of our objective consciousness, but regarded this as being separate from self. But the question remained unsolved as to why, in spite of the unique character of knowledge, knowledge could relate itself to the world of objects, how far the world of external objects or of knowledge could be regarded as absolutely true. Hitherto judgments were only relative, either referring to one's being prompted to the objective world, to the faithfulness of the representation of objects, the suitability of fulfilling our requirements, or to verification by later

[1] See *Nyāyaratnamālā*, svataḥ-prāmāṇya-nirṇaya.

[2] See *Nyāyamañjarī* on Pramāṇa, *Ślokavārttika* on Pratyakṣa, and Gāgā Bhaṭṭa's *Bhaṭṭacintāmaṇi* on Pratyakṣa.

uncontradicted experience. But no enquiry was made whether any absolute judgments about the ultimate truth of knowledge and matter could be made at all. That which appeared was regarded as the real. But the question was not asked, whether there was anything which could be regarded as absolute truth, the basis of all appearance, and the unchangeable reality. This philosophical enquiry had the most wonderful charm for the Hindu mind.

Vedānta Literature.

It is difficult to ascertain the time when the *Brahma-sūtras* were written, but since they contain a refutation of almost all the other Indian systems, even of the Śūnyavāda Buddhism (of course according to Śaṅkara's interpretation), they cannot have been written very early. I think it may not be far from the truth in supposing that they were written some time in the second century B.C. About the period A.D. 780 Gauḍapāda revived the monistic teaching of the Upaniṣads by his commentary on the Māṇḍūkya Upaniṣad in verse called *Māṇḍūkyakārikā*. His disciple Govinda was the teacher of Śaṅkara (A.D. 788—820). Śaṅkara's commentary on the *Brahma-sūtras* is the root from which sprang forth a host of commentaries and studies on Vedāntism of great originality, vigour, and philosophic insight. Thus Ānandagiri, a disciple of Śaṅkara, wrote a commentary called *Nyāyanirṇaya*, and Govindānanda wrote another commentary named *Ratnaprabhā*. Vācaspati Miśra, who flourished about A.D. 841, wrote another commentary on it called the *Bhāmatī*. Amalānanda (A.D. 1247—1260) wrote his *Kalpataru* on it, and Apyayadīkṣita (A.D. 1550) son of Raṅgarājādhvarīndra of Kāñcī wrote his *Kalpataruparimala* on the *Kalpataru*. Another disciple of Śaṅkara, Padmapāda, also called Sanandana, wrote a commentary on it known as *Pañcapādikā*. From the manner in which the book is begun one would expect that it was to be a running commentary on the whole of Śankara's bhāṣya, but it ends abruptly at the end of the fourth sūtra. Mādhava (1350), in his *Śaṅkaravijaya*, recites an interesting story about it. He says that Sureśvara received Śaṅkara's permission to write a *vārttika* on the bhāṣya. But other pupils objected to Śaṅkara that since Sureśvara was formerly a great Mīmāṃsist (Maṇḍana Miśra was called Sureśvara after his conversion to Vedāntism) he was not competent to write a good *vārttika* on the bhāṣya. Sureśvara, disappointed, wrote a treatise called *Naiṣkarmyasiddhi*. Padmapāda wrote a ṭīkā but this was burnt in his uncle's house. Śaṅkara, who had once seen it, recited it from memory and Padmapāda wrote it down. Prakāśātman (1200) wrote a commentary on Padmapāda's *Pañcapādikā* known as *Pañcapādikāvivaraṇa*. Akhaṇḍānanda wrote his *Tattvadīpana*, and the famous Nṛsiṃhāśrama Muni (1500) wrote his *Vivaraṇabhāvaprakāśikā* on it. Amalānanda and Vidyāsāgara also wrote commentaries on *Pañcapādikā*, named *Pañcapādikādarpaṇa* and *Pañcapādikāṭīkā* respectively, but the *Pañcapādikāvivaraṇa* had by far the greatest reputation. Vidyāraṇya who is generally identified by some with Mādhava (1350) wrote his famous work *Vivaraṇaprameyasaṃgraha*[1], elaborating the ideas of *Pañcapādikāvivaraṇa*; Vidyāraṇya wrote also another excellent work named *Jīvanmuktiviveka* on the Vedānta doctrine of emancipation. Sureśvara's (A.D. 800) excellent work *Naiṣkarmyasiddhi* is probably the earliest independent treatise on Śaṅkara's philosophy as expressed in his bhāṣya. It has been commented upon by Jñānotrama Miśra. Vidyāraṇya also wrote another work of great merit known as *Pañcadaśī*, which is a very popular and illuminating treatise in verse on Vedānta. Another important work written in verse on the main teachings of Śaṅkara's bhāṣya is *Saṃkṣepaśārīraka*, written by Sarvajñātma Muni (A.D. 900). This has also been commented upon by Rāmatīrtha. Śrīharṣa (A.D. 1190) wrote his *Khaṇḍanakhaṇḍakhādya*, the most celebrated work on the Vedānta dialectic. Citsukha, who probably flourished shortly after Śrīharṣa, wrote a commentary on it, and also wrote an independent work on Vedānta dialectic known as *Tattvadīpikā* which has also a commentary called *Nayanaprasādinī* written by Pratyagrūpa. Śaṅkara Miśra and Raghunātha also wrote commentaries on *Khaṇḍanakhaṇḍakhādya*. A work on Vedānta epistemology and the principal topics of Vedānta of great originality and merit known as *Vedāntaparibhāṣā* was written by Dharmarājādhvarīndra (about A.D. 1550). His son Rāmakṛṣṇādhvarin wrote his *Śikhāmaṇi* on it and Amaradāsa his *Maṇiprabhā*. The *Vedāntaparibhāṣā* with these two commentaries forms an excellent exposition of some of the fundamental principles of Vedānta. Another work of supreme importance (though probably the last great work on Vedānta) is the *Advaitasiddhi* of Madhusūdana Sarasvatī who followed Dharmarājādhvarīndra.

[1] See Narasiṃhācārya's article in the *Indian Antiquary*, 1916.

This has three commentaries known as *Gauḍabrahmānandī*, *Viṭṭhaleśopadhyāyī* and *Siddhivyākhyā*. Sadānanda Vyāsa wrote also a summary of it known as *Advaitasiddhisiddhāntasāra*. Sadānanda wrote also an excellent elementary work named *Vedāntasāra* which has also two commentaries *Subodhinī* and *Vidvanmanorañjinī*. The *Advaitabrahmasiddhi* of Sadānanda Yati though much inferior to *Advaitasiddhi* is important, as it touches on many points of Vedānta interest which are not dealt with in other Vedānta works. The *Nyāyamakaranda* of Ānandabodha Bhaṭṭārakācāryya treats of the doctrines of illusion very well, as also some other important points of Vedānta interest. *Vedāntasiddhāntamuktāvalī* of Prakāśānanda discusses many of the subtle points regarding the nature of ajñāna and its relations to cit, the doctrine of *dṛṣṭisṛṣṭivāda*, etc., with great clearness. *Siddhāntaleśa* by Apyayadīkṣita is very important as a summary of the divergent views of different writers on many points of interest. *Vedāntatattvadīpikā* and *Siddhāntatattva* are also good as well as deep in their general summary of the Vedānta system. *Bhedadhikkāra* of Nṛsiṃhāśrama Muni also is to be regarded as an important work on the Vedānta dialectic.

The above is only a list of some of the most important Vedānta works on which the present chapter has been based.

Vedānta in Gauḍapāda.

It is useless I think to attempt to bring out the meaning of the Vedānta thought as contained in the *Brahma-sūtras* without making any reference to the commentary of Śaṅkara or any other commentator. There is reason to believe that the *Brahma-sūtras* were first commented upon by some Vaiṣṇava writers who held some form of modified dualism[1]. There have been more than a half dozen Vaiṣṇava commentators of the *Brahma-sūtras* who not only differed from Śaṅkara's interpretation, but also differed largely amongst themselves in accordance with the different degrees of stress they laid on the different aspects of their dualistic creeds. Every one of them claimed that his interpretation was the only one that was faithful to the sūtras and to the Upaniṣads. Should I attempt to give an interpretation myself and claim that to be the right one, it would be only just one

[1] This point will be dealt with in the 2nd volume, when I shall deal with the systems expounded by the Vaiṣṇava commentators of the *Brahma-sūtras*.

additional view. But however that may be, I am myself inclined to believe that the dualistic interpretations of the *Brahma-sūtras* were probably more faithful to the sūtras than the interpretations of Śaṅkara.

The *Śrīmadbhagavadgītā*, which itself was a work of the Ekānti (singularistic) Vaiṣṇavas, mentions the *Brahma-sūtras* as having the same purport as its own, giving cogent reasons[1]. Professor Jacobi in discussing the date of the philosophical sūtras of the Hindus has shown that the references to Buddhism found in the *Brahma-sūtras* are not with regard to the Vijñānavāda of Vasubandhu, but with regard to the Śūnyavāda, but he regards the composition of the *Brahma-sūtras* to be later than Nāgārjuna. I agree with the late Dr S. C. Vidyābhūṣhana in holding that both the Yogācāra system and the system of Nāgārjuna evolved from the *Prajñāpāramitā*[2]. Nāgārjuna's merit consisted in the dialectical form of his arguments in support of Śūnyavāda; but so far as the essentials of Śūnyavāda are concerned I believe that the Tathatā philosophy of Aśvaghoṣa and the philosophy of the *Prajñāpāramitā* contained no less. There is no reason to suppose that the works of Nāgārjuna were better known to the Hindu writers than the *Mahāyāna sūtras*. Even in such later times as that of Vācaspati Miśra, we find him quoting a passage of the *Śālistambha sūtra* to give an account of the Buddhist doctrine of pratītyasamutpāda[3]. We could interpret any reference to Śūnyavāda as pointing to Nāgārjuna only if his special phraseology or dialectical methods were referred to in any way. On the other hand, the reference in the *Bhagavad-gītā* to the *Brahma-sūtras* clearly points out a date prior to that of Nāgārjuna; though we may be slow to believe such an early date as has been assigned to the *Bhagavad-gītā* by Telang, yet I suppose that its date could safely be placed so far back as the first half of the first century B.C. or the last part of the second century B.C. The *Brahma-sūtras* could thus be placed slightly earlier than the date of the *Bhagavad-gītā*. I do not know of any evidence that would come in conflict with this supposition. The fact that we do not know of any Hindu writer

[1] "Brahmasūtrapadaiścaiva hetumadbhirviniścitaḥ" *Bhagavad-gītā*. The proofs in support of the view that the *Bhagavad-gītā* is a Vaiṣṇava work will be discussed in the second volume of the present work in the section on *Bhagavad-gītā* and its philosophy.

[2] *Indian Antiquary*, 1915.

[3] See Vācaspati Miśra's *Bhāmatī* on Śaṅkara's bhāsya on *Brahma-sūtra*, II. ii.

who held such monistic views as Gauḍapāda or Śaṅkara, and who interpreted the *Brahma-sūtras* in accordance with those monistic ideas, when combined with the fact that the dualists had been writing commentaries on the *Brahma-sūtras*, goes to show that the *Brahma-sūtras* were originally regarded as an authoritative work of the dualists. This also explains the fact that the *Bhagavad-gītā*, the canonical work of the Ekānti Vaiṣṇavas, should refer to it. I do not know of any Hindu writer previous to Gauḍapāda who attempted to give an exposition of the monistic doctrine (apart from the Upaniṣads), either by writing a commentary as did Śaṅkara, or by writing an independent work as did Gauḍapāda. I am inclined to think therefore that as the pure monism of the Upaniṣads was not worked out in a coherent manner for the formation of a monistic system, it was dealt with by people who had sympathies with some form of dualism which was already developing in the later days of the Upaniṣads, as evidenced by the dualistic tendencies of such Upaniṣads as the Śvetāśvatara, and the like. The epic Sāṃkhya was also the result of this dualistic development.

It seems that Bādarāyaṇa, the writer of the *Brahma-sūtras*, was probably more a theist, than an absolutist like his commentator Śaṅkara. Gauḍapāda seems to be the most important man, after the Upaniṣad sages, who revived the monistic tendencies of the Upaniṣads in a bold and clear form and tried to formulate them in a systematic manner. It seems very significant that no other kārikās on the Upaniṣads were interpreted, except the *Māṇḍūkyakārikā* by Gauḍapāda, who did not himself make any reference to any other writer of the monistic school, not even Bādarāyaṇa. Śaṅkara himself makes the confession that the absolutist (*advaita*) creed was recovered from the Vedas by Gauḍapāda. Thus at the conclusion of his commentary on Gauḍapāda's kārikā, he says that "he adores by falling at the feet of that great guru (teacher) the adored of his adored, who on finding all the people sinking in the ocean made dreadful by the crocodiles of rebirth, out of kindness for all people, by churning the great ocean of the Veda by his great churning rod of wisdom recovered what lay deep in the heart of the Veda, and is hardly attainable even by the immortal gods[1]." It seems particularly significant that Śaṅkara should credit Gauḍapāda and not Bādarāyaṇa with recovering the Upaniṣad creed. Gauḍapāda was the teacher of Govinda, the teacher of Śaṅkara; but he was probably living when Śaṅkara was a student, for Śaṅkara says that he was directly influenced by his great wisdom, and also speaks of the learning, self-control and modesty of the other pupils of Gauḍapāda[2]. There is some dispute about the date of Śaṅkara, but accepting the date proposed by Bhaṇḍarkar, Paṭhak and Deussen, we may consider it to be A.D. 788[3], and suppose that in order to be able to teach Śaṅkara, Gauḍapāda must have been living till at least A.D. 800

Gauḍapāda thus flourished after all the great Buddhist teachers Aśvaghoṣa, Nāgārjuna, Asaṅga and Vasubandhu; and I believe that there is sufficient evidence in his kārikās for thinking that he was possibly himself a Buddhist, and considered that the teachings of the Upaniṣads tallied with those of Buddha. Thus at the beginning of the fourth chapter of his kārikās he says that he adores that great man (*dvipadām varam*) who by knowledge as wide as the sky realized (*sambuddha*) that all appearances (*dharma*) were like the vacuous sky (*gaganopamam*[4]). He then goes on to say that he adores him who has dictated (*deśita*) that the touch of untouch (*asparśayoga*—probably referring to Nirvāṇa) was the good that produced happiness to all beings, and that he was neither in disagreement with this doctrine nor found any contradiction in it (*avivādaḥ aviruddhaśca*). Some disputants hold that coming into being is of existents, whereas others quarrelling with them hold that being (*jāta*) is of nonexistents (*abhūtasya*); there are others who quarrel with them and say that neither the existents nor non-existents are liable to being and there is one non-coming-into-being (*advayamajātim*). He agrees with those who hold that there is no coming into being[5]. In IV. 19 of his kārikā he again says that the Buddhas have shown that there was no coming into being in any way (*sarvathā Buddhairajātiḥ paridīpitaḥ*).

[1] Śaṅkara's bhāṣya on Gauḍapāda's kārikā, Ānandāśrama edition, p. 214.

[2] Ānandāśrama edition of Śaṅkara's bhāṣya on Gauḍapāda's kārikā, p. 21.

[3] Telang wishes to put Śaṅkara's date somewhere in the 8th century, and Veṅkateśvara would have him in A.D. 805-897, as he did not believe that Śaṅkara could have lived only for 32 years. *J. R. A. S.* 1916.

[4] Compare *Laṅkāvatāra*, p. 29, *Kathaṃ ca gaganopamam*.

[5] Gauḍapāda's kārikā, IV. 2, 4.

Again, in IV. 42 he says that it was for those realists (*vastuvādi*), who since they found things and could deal with them and were afraid of non-being, that the Buddhas had spoken of origination (*jāti*). In IV. 90 he refers to *agrayāna* which we know to be a name of *Mahāyāna*. Again, in IV. 98 and 99 he says that all appearances are pure and vacuous by nature. These the Buddhas, the emancipated one (*mukta*) and the leaders know first. It was not said by the Buddha that all appearances (*dharma*) were knowledge. He then closes the kārikās with an adoration which in all probability also refers to the Buddha[1].

Gauḍapāda's work is divided into four chapters: (1) Āgama (scripture), (2) Vaitathya (unreality), (3) Advaita (unity), (4) Alātaśānti (the extinction of the burning coal). The first chapter is more in the way of explaining the Māṇḍūkya Upaniṣad by virtue of which the entire work is known as *Māṇḍūkyakārikā*. The second, third, and fourth chapters are the constructive parts of Gauḍapāda's work, not particularly connected with the Māṇḍūkya Upaniṣad.

In the first chapter Gauḍapāda begins with the three apparent manifestations of the self: (1) as the experiencer of the external world while we are awake (*viśva* or *vaiśvānara ātmā*), (2) as the experiencer in the dream state (*taijasa ātmā*), (3) as the experiencer in deep sleep (*suṣupti*), called the *prājña* when there is no determinate knowledge, but pure consciousness and pure bliss (*ānanda*). He who knows these three as one is never attached to his experiences. Gauḍapāda then enumerates some theories of creation: some think that the world has proceeded as a creation from the prāṇa (vital activity), others consider creation as an expansion (*vibhūti*) of that cause from which it has proceeded; others imagine that creation is like dream (*svapna*) and magic (*māyā*); others, that creation proceeds simply by the will of the Lord; others that it proceeds from time; others that it is for the enjoyment of the Lord (*bhogārtham*) or for his play only (*krīḍārtham*), for such is the nature (*svabhāva*) of the Lord, that he creates, but he cannot have any longing, as all his desires are in a state of fulfilment.

[1] Gauḍapāda's kārikā, IV. 100. In my translation I have not followed Śaṅkara, for he has I think tried his level best to explain away even the most obvious references to Buddha and Buddhism in Gauḍapāda's kārikā. I have, therefore, drawn my meaning directly as Gauḍapāda's kārikās seemed to indicate. I have followed the same principle in giving the short exposition of Gauḍapāda's philosophy below.

Gauḍapāda does not indicate his preference one way or the other, but describes the fourth state of the self as unseen (*adṛṣṭa*), unrelationable (*avyavahāryam*), ungraspable (*agrāhyam*), indefinable (*alakṣaṇa*), unthinkable (*acintyam*), unspeakable (*avyapadeśya*), the essence as oneness with the self (*ekātmapratyayasāra*), as the extinction of the appearance (*prapañcopaśama*), the quiescent (*śāntam*), the good (*śivam*), the one (*advaita*)[1]. The world-appearance (*prapañca*) would have ceased if it had existed, but all this duality is mere māyā (magic or illusion), the one is the ultimately real (*paramārthataḥ*). In the second chapter Gauḍapāda says that what is meant by calling the world a dream is that all existence is unreal. That which neither exists in the beginning nor in the end cannot be said to exist in the present. Being like unreal it appears as real. The appearance has a beginning and an end and is therefore false. In dreams things are imagined internally, and in the experience that we have when we are awake things are imagined as if existing outside, but both of them are but illusory creations of the self. What is perceived in the mind is perceived as existing at the moment of perception only; external objects are supposed to have two moments of existence (namely before they are perceived, and when they begin to be perceived), but this is all mere imagination. That which is unmanifested in the mind and that which appears as distinct and manifest outside are all imaginary productions in association with the sense faculties. There is first the imagination of a perceiver or soul (*jīva*) and then along with it the imaginary creations of diverse inner states and the external world. Just as in darkness the rope is imagined to be a snake, so the self is also imagined by its own illusion in diverse forms. There is neither any production nor any destruction (*na nirodho, na cotpattiḥ*), there is no one who is enchained, no one who is striving, no one who wants to be released[2]. Imagination finds itself realized in the non-existent existents and also in the sense

[1] Compare in Nāgārjuna's first kārikā the idea of *prapañcopaśamam śivam*. *Anirodhamanut pādamanucc hedamaśāśvatam anekārthamanānārthamanāgamamanirgamam yaḥ pratītyasamutpādam prapañcopaśamam śivam deśayāmāsa sambuddhastam vande vadatāmvaram*. Compare also Nāgārjuna's Chapter on *Nirvāṇaparīkṣā*, *Pūrvopalambhopaśamaḥ prapañcopaśamaḥ śivaḥ na kvacit kasyacit kaścit dharmmo buddhenadeśitaḥ*. So far as I know the Buddhists were the first to use the words *prapañcopaśaman śivam*.

[2] Compare Nāgārjuna's kārikā, "anirodhamanutpādam" in *Mādhyamikavṛtti*, *B. T. S.*, p. 3.

of unity; all imagination either as the many or the one (*advaya*) is false; it is only the oneness (*advayatā*) that is good. There is no many, nor are things different or non-different (*na nānedam ... na pṛthag nāpṛthak*)[1]. The sages who have transcended attachment, fear, and anger and have gone beyond the depths of the Vedas have perceived it as the imaginationless cessation of all appearance (*nirvikalpaḥ prapañcopaśamaḥ*), the one[2].

In the third chapter Gauḍapāda says that truth is like the void (*ākāśa*) which is falsely conceived as taking part in birth and death, coming and going and as existing in all bodies; but howsoever it be conceived, it is all the while not different from ākāśa. All things that appear as compounded are but dreams (*svapna*) and māyā (magic). Duality is a distinction imposed upon the one (*advaita*) by māyā. The truth is immortal, it cannot therefore by its own nature suffer change. It has no birth. All birth and death, all this manifold is but the result of an imposition of māyā upon it[3]. One mind appears as many in the dream, so also in the waking state one appears as many, but when the mind activity of the Togins (sages) is stopped arises this fearless state, the extinction of all sorrow, final cessation. Thinking everything to be misery (*duḥkham sarvam anusmṛtya*) one should stop all desires and enjoyments, and thinking that nothing has any birth he should not see any production at all. He should awaken the mind (*citta*) into its final dissolution (*laya*) and pacify it when distracted; he should not move it towards diverse objects when it stops. He should not taste any pleasure (*sukham*) and by wisdom remain unattached, by strong effort making it motionless and still. When he neither passes into dissolution nor into distraction; when there is no sign, no appearance that is the perfect Brahman. When there is no object of knowledge to come into being, the unproduced is then called the omniscent (*sarvajña*).

In the fourth chapter, called the Alātaśānti, Gauḍapāda further

[1] Compare *Mādhyamikakārikā*, *B. T. S.*, p. 3, *anekārtham anānārtham*, etc.

[2] Compare *Laṅkāvatārasūtra*, p. 78, *Advayāsamsāraparinirvāṇavatsarvadharmāḥ tasmāt tarhi mahāmate Śunyatānutpādādvayaniḥsvabhāvalakṣaṇe yogaḥ karaṇiyaḥ*; also 8, 46, *Yaduta svacittaviṣayavikalpadṛṣṭyānavabodhanāt vijñānānām svacittadṛśyamātrānavatāreṇa mahāmate vālapṛthagjanāḥ bhāvābhāvasvabhāvaparamārthadṛṣṭidvayavādino bhavanti*.

[3] Compare Nāgārjuna's kārikā, *B. T. S.*, p. 196, *Ākāśam śaśaśṛṅgañca bandhyāyāḥ putra eva ca asantaścābhivyajyanie tathābhāvena kalpanā*, with Gauḍapāda's kārikā, iii. 28, *Asato māyayā janma tatvato naiva jāyate bandhyāputro na tattvena māyāya vāpi jāyate*.

describes this final state[1]. All the dharmas (appearances) are without death or decay[2]. Gauḍapāda then follows a dialectical form of argument which reminds us of Nāgārjuna. Gauḍapāda continues thus: Those who regard kāraṇa (cause) as the kāryya (effect in a potential form) cannot consider the cause as truly unproduced (*aja*), for it suffers production; how can it be called eternal and yet changing? If it is said that things come into being from that which has no production, there is no example with which such a case may be illustrated. Nor can we consider that anything is born from that which has itself suffered production. How again can one come to a right conclusion about the *regressus ad infinitum* of cause and effect (*hetu* and *phala*)? Without reference to the effect there is no cause, and without reference to cause there is no effect. Nothing is born either by itself or through others; call it either being, non-being, or being-non-being, nothing suffers any birth, neither the cause nor the effect is produced out of its own nature (*svabhāvataḥ*), and thus that which has no beginning anywhere cannot be said to have a production. All experience (*prajñapti*) is dependent on reasons, for otherwise both would vanish, and there would be none of the afflictions (*saṃkleśa*) that we suffer. When we look at all things in a connected manner they seem to be dependent, but when we look at them from the point of view of reality or truth the reasons cease to be reasons. The mind (*citta*) does not come in touch with objects and thereby manifest them, for since things do not exist they are not different from their manifestations in knowledge. It is not in any particular case that the mind produces the manifestations of objects while they do not exist so that it could be said to be an error, for in present, past, and future the mind never comes in touch with objects which only appear by reason of their diverse manifestations. Therefore neither the mind nor the objects seen by it are ever produced. Those who perceive them to suffer production are really traversing the reason of vacuity (*khe*), for all production is but false imposition on the vacuity. Since the unborn is perceived as being born, the essence then is the absence of

[1] The very name Alātaśānti is absolutely Buddhistic. Compare Nāgārjuna's kārikā, *B. T. S.*, p. 206, where he quotes a verse from the *Śataka*.

[2] The use of the word dharma in the sense of appearance or entity is peculiarly Buddhistic. The Hindu sense is that given by Jaimini, "Codanālakṣaṇah arthah, dharmah." Dharma is determined by the injunctions of the Vedas.

production, for it being of the nature of absence of production it could never change its nature. Everything has a beginning and an end and is therefore false. The existence of all things is like a magical or illusory elephant (*māyāhastī*) and exists only as far as it merely appears or is related to experience. There is thus the appearance of production, movement and things, but the one knowledge (*vijñāna*) is the unborn, unmoved, the unthingness (*avastutva*), the cessation (*śāntam*). As the movement of burning charcoal is perceived as straight or curved, so it is the movement (*spandita*) of consciousness that appears as the perceiving and the perceived. All the attributes (e.g. straight or curved) are imposed upon the charcoal fire, though in reality it does not possess them; so also all the appearances are imposed upon consciousness, though in reality they do not possess them. We could never indicate any kind of causal relation between the consciousness and its appearance, which are therefore to be demonstrated as unthinkable (*acintya*). A thing (*dravya*) is the cause of a thing (*dravya*), and that which is not a thing may be the cause of that which is not a thing, but all the appearances are neither things nor those which are not things, so neither are appearances produced from the mind (*citta*), nor is the mind produced by appearances. So long as one thinks of cause and effect he has to suffer the cycle of existence (*saṃsāra*), but when that notion ceases there is no saṃsāra. All things are regarded as being produced from a relative point of view only (*saṃvṛti*), there is therefore nothing permanent (*śāśvata*). Again, no existent things are produced, hence there cannot be any destruction (*uccheda*). Appearances (*dharma*) are produced only apparently, not in reality; their coming into being is like māyā, and that māyā again does not exist. All appearances are like shoots of magic coming out of seeds of magic and are not therefore neither eternal nor destructible. As in dreams, or in magic, men are born and die, so are all appearances. That which appears as existing from an imaginary relative point of view (*kalpita saṃvṛti*) is not so in reality (*paramārtha*), for the existence depending on others, as shown in all relative appearance, is after all not a real existence. That things exist, do not exist, do exist and not exist, and neither exist nor not exist; that they are moving or steady, or none of those, are but thoughts with which fools are deluded.

It is so obvious that these doctrines are borrowed from the Mādhyamika doctrines, as found in the Nāgārjuna's kārikās and the Vijñānavāda doctrines, as found in *Laṅkāvatāra*, that it is needless to attempt to prove it. Gauḍapāda assimilated all the Buddhist Śūnyavāda and Vijñānavāda teachings, and thought that these held good of the ultimate truth preached by the Upaniṣads. It is immaterial whether he was a Hindu or a Buddhist, so long as we are sure that he had the highest respect for the Buddha and for the teachings which he believed to be his. Gauḍapāda took the smallest Upaniṣads to comment upon, probably because he wished to give his opinions unrestricted by the textual limitations of the bigger ones. His main emphasis is on the truth that he realized to be perfect. He only incidentally suggested that the great Buddhist truth of indefinable and unspeakable vijñāna or vacuity would hold good of the highest ātman of the Upaniṣads, and thus laid the foundation of a revival of the Upaniṣad studies on Buddhist lines. How far the Upaniṣads guaranteed in detail the truth of Gauḍapāda's views it was left for his disciple, the great Śaṅkara, to examine and explain.

Vedānta and Śaṅkara (A.D. 788-820).

Vedānta philosophy is the philosophy which claims to be the exposition of the philosophy taught in the Upaniṣads and summarized in the *Brahma-sūtras* of Bādarāyaṇa. The Upaniṣads form the last part of the Veda literature, and its philosophy is therefore also called sometimes the Uttara-Mīmāṃsā or the Mīmāṃsā (decision) of the later part of the Vedas as distinguished from the Mīmāṃsā of the previous part of the Vedas and the Brāhmaṇas as incorporated in the *Pūrvamīmāṃsā sūtras* of Jaimini. Though these *Brahma-sūtras* were differently interpreted by different exponents, the views expressed in the earliest commentary on them now available, written by Śaṅkarācārya, have attained wonderful celebrity, both on account of the subtle and deep ideas it contains, and also on account of the association of the illustrious personality of Śaṅkara. So great is the influence of the philosophy propounded by Śaṅkara and elaborated by his illustrious followers, that whenever we speak of the Vedānta philosophy we mean the philosophy that was propounded by Śaṅkara. If other expositions are intended the names of the exponents have to be mentioned (e.g. Rāmānuja-mata, Vallabha-mata, etc.). In this chapter we shall limit ourselves to the exposition of the Vedānta philosophy as elaborated by Śaṅkara and his followers. In Śaṅkara's work (the commentaries on the *Brahma-sūtra* and the ten Upaniṣads) many ideas have been briefly incorporated which as found in Śaṅkara do not appear to be sufficiently clear, but are more intelligible as elaborated by his followers. It is therefore better to take up the Vedānta system, not as we find it in Śaṅkara, but as elaborated by his followers, all of whom openly declare that they are true to their master's philosophy.

For the other Hindu systems of thought, the sūtras (*Jaimini sūtra*, *Nyāya sūtra*, etc.) are the only original treatises, and no foundation other than these is available. In the case of the Vedānta however the original source is the Upaniṣads, and the sūtras are but an extremely condensed summary in a systematic form. Śaṅkara did not claim to be the inventor or expounder of an original system, but interpreted the sūtras and the Upaniṣads in order to show that there existed a connected and systematic philosophy in the Upaniṣads which was also enunciated in the sūtras of Bādarāyaṇa. The Upaniṣads were a part of the Vedas and were thus regarded as infallible by the Hindus. If Śaṅkara could only show that his exposition of them was the right one, then his philosophy being founded upon the highest authority would be accepted by all Hindus. The most formidable opponents in the way of accomplishing his task were the Mīmāṃsists, who held that the Vedas did not preach any philosophy, for whatever there was in the Vedas was to be interpreted as issuing commands to us for performing this or that action. They held that if the Upaniṣads spoke of Brahman and demonstrated the nature of its pure essence, these were mere exaggerations intended to put the commandment of performing some kind of worship of Brahman into a more attractive form. Śaṅkara could not deny that the purport of the Vedas as found in the Brāhmaṇas was explicitly of a mandatory nature as declared by the Mīmāṃsā, but he sought to prove that such could not be the purport of the Upaniṣads, which spoke of the truest and the highest knowledge of the Absolute by which the wise could attain salvation. He said that in the karmakāṇḍa—the (sacrificial injunctions) Brāhmaṇas of the Vedas—the purport of the Vedas was certainly of a mandatory nature, as it was intended for ordinary people who were anxious for this or that pleasure, and were never actuated by any desire of knowing the absolute truth, but the Upaniṣads, which were intended for the wise who had controlled their senses and become disinclined to all earthly joys, demonstrated the one Absolute, Unchangeable, Brahman as the only Truth of the universe. The two parts of the Vedas were intended for two classes of persons. Śaṅkara thus did not begin by formulating a philosophy of his own by logical and psychological analysis, induction, and deduction. He tried to show by textual comparison of the different Upaniṣads, and by reference to the content of passages in the Upaniṣads, that they were concerned in demonstrating the nature of Brahman (as he understood it) as their ultimate end. He had thus to show that the uncontradicted testimony of all the Upaniṣads was in favour of the view which he held. He had to explain all doubtful and apparently conflicting texts, and also to show that none of the texts referred to the doctrines of mahat, prakṛti, etc. of the Sāṃkhya. He had also to interpret the few scattered ideas about physics, cosmology, eschatology, etc. that are found in the Upaniṣads consistently with the Brahman philosophy. In order to show that the philosophy of the Upaniṣads as he expounded it was a consistent system, he had to remove all the objections that his opponents could make regarding the Brahman philosophy, to criticize the philosophies of all other schools, to prove them to be self-contradictory, and to show that any interpretation of the Upaniṣads, other than that which he gave, was inconsistent and wrong. This he did not only in his bhāṣya on the *Brahma-sūtras* but also in his commentaries on the Upaniṣads. Logic with him had a subordinate place, as its main value for us was the aid which it lent to consistent interpretations of the purport of the Upaniṣad texts, and to persuading the mind to accept the uncontradicted testimony of the Upaniṣads as the absolute truth. His disciples followed him in all, and moreover showed in great detail that the Brahman philosophy was never contradicted either in perceptual experience or in rational thought, and that all the realistic categories which Nyāya and other systems had put forth were self-contradictory and erroneous. They also supplemented his philosophy by constructing a Vedānta epistemology, and by rethinking elaborately the relation of the māyā, the Brahman, and the world of appearance and other relevant topics. Many problems of great philosophical interest which had been left out or slightly touched by Śaṅkara were discussed fully by his followers. But it should always be remembered that philosophical reasonings and criticisms are always to be taken as but aids for convincing our intellect and strengthening our faith in the truth revealed in the Upaniṣads. The true work of logic is to adapt the mind to accept them. Logic used for upsetting the instructions of the Upaniṣads is logic gone astray. Many lives of Śaṅkārācarya were written in Sanskrit such as the *Śaṅkaradigvijaya*, *Śaṅkara-vijaya-vilāsa*, *Śaṅkara-jaya*, etc. It is regarded as almost certain that he was born between A.D. 700 and 800 in the Malabar country in the Deccan. His father Śivaguru was a Yajurvedi Brāhmin of the Taittirīya branch. Many miracles are related of Śaṅkara, and he is believed to have been the incarnation of Śiva. He turned ascetic in his eighth year and became the disciple of Govinda, a renowned sage then residing in a mountain cell on the banks of the Narbuda. He then came over to Benares and thence went to Badarikāśrama. It is said that he wrote his illustrious bhāṣya on the *Brahma-sūtra* in his twelfth year. Later on he also wrote his commentaries on ten Upaniṣads. He returned to Benares, and from this time forth he decided to travel all over India in order to defeat the adherents of other schools of thought in open debate. It is said that he first went to meet Kumārila, but Kumārila was then at the point of death, and he advised him to meet Kumārila's disciple. He defeated Maṇḍana and converted him into an ascetic follower of his own. He then travelled in various places, and defeating his opponents everywhere he established his Vedānta philosophy, which from that time forth acquired a dominant influence in moulding the religious life of India.

Śaṅkara carried on the work of his teacher Gauḍapāda and by writing commentaries on the ten Upaniṣads and the *Brahma-sūtras* tried to prove, that the absolutist creed was the one which was intended to be preached in the Upaniṣads and the *Brahma-sūtras*[1]. Throughout his commentary on the *Brahma-sūtras*, there is ample evidence that he was contending against some other rival interpretations of a dualistic tendency which held that the Upaniṣads partly favoured the Sāṃkhya cosmology of the

[1] The main works of Śaṅkara are his commentaries (bhāṣya) on the ten Upaniṣads (Īśa, Kena, Kaṭha, Praśna, Muṇḍaka, Māṇḍūkya, Aitareya, Taittirīya, Bṛhadāraṇyaka, and Chāndogya), and on the *Brahma-sūtra*..

existence of prakṛti. That these were actual textual interpretations of the *Brahma-sūtras* is proved by the fact that Śaṅkara in some places tries to show that these textual constructions were faulty[1]. In one place he says that others (referring according to Vācaspati to the Mīmāṃsā) and some of us (referring probably to those who interpreted the sūtras and the Upaniṣads from the Vedānta point of view) think that the soul is permanent. It is to refute all those who were opposed to the right doctrine of perceiving everything as the unity of the self (*ātmaikatva*) that this Śārīraka commentary of mine is being attempted[2]. Rāmānuja, in the introductory portion of his bhāṣya on the *Brahma-sūtra*, says that the views of Bodhāyana who wrote an elaborate commentary on the *Brahma-sūtra* were summarized by previous teachers, and that he was following this Bodhāyana bhāṣya in writing his commentary. In the *Vedārthasaṃgraha* of Rāmānuja mention is made of Bodhāyana, Ṭaṅka, Guhadeva, Kapardin, Bhāruci as Vedāntic authorities, and Draviḍācāryya is referred to as the "bhāṣyakāra" commentator. In Chāndogya III. X. 4, where the Upaniṣad cosmology appeared to be different from the *Viṣṇupurāṇa* cosmology, Śaṅkara refers to an explanation offered on the point by one whom he calls "ācāryya" (*atroktaḥ parihāraḥ ācāryyaiḥ*) and Ānandagiri says that "ācāryya" there refers to Draviḍācāryya. This Draviḍācāryya is known to us from Rāmānuja's statement as being a commentator of the dualistic school, and we have evidence here that he had written a commentary on the Chāndogya Upaniṣad.

A study of the extant commentaries on the *Brahma-sūtras* of Bādarāyaṇa by the adherents of different schools of thought leaves us convinced that these sūtras were regarded by all as condensations of the teachings of the Upaniṣads. The differences of opinion were with regard to the meaning of these sūtras and the Upaniṣad texts to which references were made by them in each particular case. The *Brahma-sūtra* is divided into four adhyāyas or books, and each of these is divided into four chapters or pādas. Each of these contains a number of topics of discussion (*adhikaraṇa*) which are composed of a number of sūtras, which raise the point at issue, the points that lead to doubt and uncertainty, and the considerations that should lead one to favour

[1] See note on p. 432.

[2] Śaṅkara's bhāṣya on the *Brahma-sūtras*, I. iii. 19.

a particular conclusion. As explained by Śaṅkara, most of these sūtras except the first four and the first two chapters of the second book are devoted to the textual interpretations of the Upaniṣad passages. Śaṅkara's method of explaining the absolutist Vedānta creed does not consist in proving the Vedānta to be a consistent system of metaphysics, complete in all parts, but in so interpreting the Upaniṣad texts as to show that they all agree in holding the Brahman to be the self and that alone to be the only truth. In Chapter I of Book II Śaṅkara tries to answer some of the objections that may be made from the Sāṃkhya point of view against his absolutist creed and to show that some apparent difficulties of the absolutist doctrine did not present any real difficulty. In Chapter II of Book II he tries to refute the Sāṃkhya, Yoga, Nyāya-Vaiśeṣika, the Buddhist, Jaina, Bhāgavata and Śaiva systems of thought. These two chapters and his commentaries on the first four sūtras contain the main points of his system. The rest of the work is mainly occupied in showing that the conclusion of the sūtras was always in strict agreement with the Upaniṣad doctrines. Reason with Śaṅkara never occupied the premier position; its value was considered only secondary, only so far as it helped one to the right understanding of the revealed scriptures, the Upaniṣads. The ultimate truth cannot be known by reason alone. What one debater shows to be reasonable a more expert debater shows to be false, and what he shows to be right is again proved to be false by another debater. So there is no final certainty to which we can arrive by logic and argument alone. The ultimate truth can thus only be found in the Upaniṣads; reason, discrimination and judgment are all to be used only with a view to the discovery of the real purport of the Upaniṣads. From his own position Śaṅkara was not thus bound to vindicate the position of the Vedānta as a thoroughly rational system of metaphysics. For its truth did not depend on its rationality but on the authority of the Upaniṣads. But what was true could not contradict experience. If therefore Śaṅkara's interpretation of the Upaniṣads was true, then it would not contradict experience. Śaṅkara was therefore bound to show that his interpretation was rational and did not contradict experience. If he could show that his interpretation was the only interpretation that was faithful to the Upaniṣads, and that its apparent contradictions with experience could in some way be explained, he considered that he had nothing more to do. He was not writing a philosophy in the modern sense of the term, but giving us the whole truth as taught and revealed in the Upaniṣads and not simply a system spun by a clever thinker, which may erroneously appear to be quite reasonable. Ultimate validity does not belong to reason but to the scriptures.

He started with the premise that whatever may be the reason it is a fact that all experience starts and moves in an error which identifies the self with the body, the senses, or the objects of the senses. All cognitive acts presuppose this illusory identification, for without it the pure self can never behave as a phenomenal knower or perceiver, and without such a perceiver there would be no cognitive act. Śaṅkara does not try to prove philosophically the existence of the pure self as distinct from all other things, for he is satisfied in showing that the Upaniṣads describe the pure self unattached to any kind of impurity as the ultimate truth. This with him is a matter to which no exception can be taken, for it is so revealed in the Upaniṣads. This point being granted, the next point is that our experience is always based upon an identification of the self with the body, the senses, etc. and the imposition of all phenomenal qualities of pleasure, pain, etc. upon the self; and this with Śaṅkara is a beginningless illusion. All this had been said by Gauḍapāda. Śaṅkara accepted Gauḍapāda's conclusions, but did not develop his dialectic for a positive proof of his thesis. He made use of the dialectic only for the refutation of other systems of thought. This being done he thought that he had nothing more to do than to show that his idea was in agreement with the teachings of the Upaniṣads. He showed that the Upaniṣads held that the pure self as pure being, pure intelligence and pure bliss was the ultimate truth. This being accepted the world as it appears could not be real. It must be a mere magic show of illusion or māyā. Śaṅkara never tries to prove that the world is māyā, but accepts it as indisputable. For, if the self is what is ultimately real, the necessary conclusion is that all else is mere illusion or māyā. He had thus to quarrel on one side with the Mīmāṃsā realists and on the other with the Sāṃkhya realists, both of whom accepted the validity of the scriptures, but interpreted them in their own way. The Mīmāṃsists held that everything that is said in the Vedas is to be interpreted as requiring us to perform particular kinds of action, or to desist from doing certain other kinds. This would mean that the Upaniṣads being a part of the Veda should also be interpreted as containing injunctions for the performance of certain kinds of actions. The description of Brahman in the Upaniṣads does not therefore represent a simple statement of the nature of Brahman, but it implies that the Brahman should be meditated upon as possessing the particular nature described there, i.e. Brahman should be meditated upon as being an entity which possesses a nature which is identical with our self; such a procedure would then lead to beneficial results to the man who so meditates. Śaṅkara could not agree to such a view. For his main point was that the Upaniṣads revealed the highest truth as the Brahman. No meditation or worship or action of any kind was required; but one reached absolute wisdom and emancipation when the truth dawned on him that the Brahman or self was the ultimate reality. The teachings of the other parts of the Vedas, the karmakāṇḍa (those dealing with the injunctions relating to the performance of duties and actions), were intended for inferior types of aspirants, whereas the teachings of the Upaniṣads, the jñānakāṇḍa (those which declare the nature of ultimate truth and reality), were intended only for superior aspirants who had transcended the limits of sacrificial duties and actions, and who had no desire for any earthly blessing or for any heavenly joy. Throughout his commentary on the *Bhagavadgītā* Śaṅkara tried to demonstrate that those who should follow the injunctions of the Veda and perform Vedic deeds, such as sacrifices, etc., belonged to a lower order. So long as they remained in that order they had no right to follow the higher teachings of the Upaniṣads. They were but karmins (performers of scriptural duties). When they succeeded in purging their minds of all desires which led them to the performance of the Vedic injunctions, the field of karmamārga (the path of duties), and wanted to know the truth alone, they entered the jñānamārga (the way of wisdom) and had no duties to perform. The study of Vedānta was thus reserved for advanced persons who were no longer inclined to the ordinary joys of life but wanted complete emancipation. The qualifications necessary for a man intending to study the Vedānta are (1) discerning knowledge about what is eternal and what is transitory (*nityānityavastuviveka*), (2) disinclination to the enjoyment of the pleasures of this world or of the after world (*ihāmutraphalabhogavirāga*), (3) attainment of peace, self-restraint, renunciation, patience, deep concentration and faith (*śamadamādisādhanasampat*) and desire for salvation (*mumukṣutva*). The person who had these qualifications should study the Upaniṣads, and as soon as he became convinced of the truth about the identity of the self and the Brahman he attained emancipation. When once a man realized that the self alone was the reality and all else was māyā, all injunctions ceased to have any force with him. Thus, the path of duties (*karma*) and the path of wisdom (*jñāna*) were intended for different classes of persons or adhikārins. There could be no joint performance of Vedic duties and the seeking of the highest truth as taught in the Upaniṣads (*jñāna-karma-samuccayābhāvaḥ*). As against the dualists he tried to show that the Upaniṣads never favoured any kind of dualistic interpretations. The main difference between the Vedānta as expounded by Gauḍapāda and as explained by Śaṅkara consists in this, that Śaṅkara tried as best he could to dissociate the distinctive Buddhist traits found in the exposition of the former and to formulate the philosophy as a direct interpretation of the older Upaniṣad texts. In this he achieved remarkable success. He was no doubt regarded by some as a hidden Buddhist (*pracchanna Bauddha*), but his influence on Hindu thought and religion became so great that he was regarded in later times as being almost a divine person or an incarnation. His immediate disciples, the disciples of his disciples, and those who adhered to his doctrine in the succeeding generations, tried to build a rational basis for his system in a much stronger way than Śaṅkara did. Our treatment of Śaṅkara's philosophy has been based on the interpretations of Vedānta thought, as offered by these followers of Śaṅkara. These interpretations are nowhere in conflict with Śaṅkara's doctrines, but the questions and problems which Śaṅkara did not raise have been raised and discussed by his followers, and without these one could not treat Vedānta as a complete and coherent system of metaphysics. As these will be discussed in the later sections, we may close this with a short description of some of the main features of the Vedānta thought as explained by Śaṅkara.

Brahman according to Śaṅkara is "the cause from which (proceeds) the origin or subsistence and dissolution of this world which is extended in names and forms, which includes many agents and enjoyers, which contains the fruit of works specially determined according to space, time, and cause, a world which is formed after an arrangement inconceivable even by the (imagination of the) mind[1]." The reasons that Śaṅkara adduces for the existence of Brahman may be considered to be threefold: (1) The world must have been produced as the modification of something, but in the Upaniṣads all other things have been spoken of as having been originated from something other than Brahman, so Brahman is the cause from which the world has sprung into being, but we could not think that Brahman itself originated from something else, for then we should have a *regressus ad infinitum* (*anavasthā*). (2) The world is so orderly that it could not have come forth from a non-intelligent source. The intelligent source then from which this world has come into being is Brahman. (3) This Brahman is the immediate consciousness (*sākṣi*) which shines as the self, as well as through the objects of cognition which the self knows. It is thus the essence of us all, the self, and hence it remains undenied even when one tries to deny it, for even in the denial it shows itself forth. It is the self of us all and is hence ever present to us in all our cognitions.

Brahman according to Śaṅkara is the identity of pure intelligence, pure being, and pure blessedness. Brahman is the self of us all. So long as we are in our ordinary waking life, we are identifying the self with thousands of illusory things, with all that we call "I" or mine, but when in dreamless sleep we are absolutely without any touch of these phenomenal notions the nature of our true state as pure blessedness is partially realized. The individual self as it appears is but an appearance only, while the real truth is the true self which is one for all, as pure intelligence, pure blessedness, and pure being.

All creation is illusory māyā. But accepting it as māyā, it may be conceived that God (Īśvara) created the world as a mere sport; from the true point of view there is no Īśvara who creates the world, but in the sense in which the world exists, and we all exist as separate individuals, we can affirm the existence of Īśvara, as engaged in creating and maintaining the world. In reality all creation is illusory and so the creator also is illusory. Brahman, the self, is at once the material cause (*upādāna-kāraṇa*) as well as the efficient cause (*nimitta-kāraṇa*) of the world.

[1] Śaṅkara's commentary, I. i. 2. See also Deussen's *System of the Vedānta*.

There is no difference between the cause and the effect, and the effect is but an illusory imposition on the cause—a mere illusion of name and form. We may mould clay into plates and jugs and call them by so many different names, but it cannot be admitted that they are by that fact anything more than clay; their transformations as plates and jugs are only appearances of name and form (*nāmarūpa*). This world, inasmuch as it is but an effect imposed upon the Brahman, is only phenomenally existent (*vyavahārika*) as mere objects of name and form (*nāmarūpa*), but the cause, the Brahman, is alone the true reality (*pāramārthika*)[1].

The main idea of the Vedānta philosophy.

The main idea of the advaita (non-dualistic) Vedānta philosophy as taught by the Śaṅkara school is this, that the ultimate and absolute truth is the self, which is one, though appearing as many in different individuals. The world also as apart from us the individuals has no reality and has no other truth to show than this self. All other events, mental or physical, are but passing appearances, while the only absolute and unchangeable truth underlying them all is the self. While other systems investigated the pramāṇas only to examine how far they could determine the objective truth of things or our attitude in practical life towards them, Vedānta sought to reach beneath the surface of appearances, and enquired after the final and ultimate truth underlying the microcosm and the macrocosm, the subject and the object. The famous instruction of Śvetaketu, the most important Vedānta text (*makāvākya*) says, "That art thou. O Śvetaketu." This comprehension of my self as the ultimate truth is the highest knowledge, for when this knowledge is once produced, our cognition of world-appearances will automatically cease. Unless the mind is chastened and purged of all passions and desires, the soul cannot comprehend this truth; but when this is once done, and the soul is anxious for salvation by a knowledge of the highest truth, the preceptor instructs him, "That art thou." At once he becomes the truth itself, which is at once identical with pure bliss and pure intelligence; all ordinary notions and cognitions of diversity and of the

[1] All that is important in Śaṅkara's commentary of the *Brahma-sūtras* has been excellently systematised by Deussen in his *System of the Vedānta*; it is therefore unnecessary for me to give any long account of this part. Most of what follows has been taken from the writings of his followers.

many cease; there is no duality, no notion of mine and thine; the vast illusion of this world process is extinct in him, and he shines forth as the one, the truth, the Brahman. All Hindu systems believed that when man attained salvation, he became divested of all world-consciousness, or of all consciousness of himself and his interests, and was thus reduced to his own original purity untouched by all sensations, perceptions, feelings and willing, but there the idea was this that when man had no bonds of karma and no desire and attachment with the world and had known the nature of his self as absolutely free and unattached to the world and his own psychosis, he became emancipated from the world and all his connections with the world ceased, though the world continued as ever the same with others. The external world was a reality with them; the unreality or illusion consisted in want of true knowledge about the real nature of the self, on account of which the self foolishly identified itself with world-experiences, worldly joys and world-events, and performed good and bad works accordingly. The force of accumulated karmas led him to undergo the experiences brought about by them. While reaping the fruits of past karmas he, as ignorant as ever of his own self, worked again under the delusion of a false relationship between himself and the world, and so the world process ran on. Mukti (salvation) meant the dissociation of the self from the subjective psychosis and the world. This condition of the pure state of self was regarded as an unconscious one by Nyāya-Vaiśeṣika and Mīmāṃsā, and as a state of pure intelligence by Sāṃkhya and Yoga. But with Vedānta the case is different, for it held that the world as such has no real existence at all, but is only an illusory imagination which lasts till the moment when true knowledge is acquired. As soon as we come to know that the one truth is the self, the Brahman, all our illusory perceptions representing the world as a field of experience cease. This happens not because the connections of the self with the world cease, but because the appearance of the world process does not represent the ultimate and highest truth about it. All our notions about the abiding diversified world (lasting though they may be from beginningless time) are false in the sense that they do not represent the real truth about it. We not only do not know what we ourselves really are, but do not also know what the world about us is. We take our ordinary experiences of the world as representing it correctly, and proceed on our career of daily activity. It is no doubt true that these experiences show us an established order having its own laws, but this does not represent the real truth. They are true only in a relative sense, so long as they appear to be so; for the moment the real truth about them and the self is comprehended all world-appearances become unreal, and that one truth, the Brahman, pure being, bliss, intelligence, shines forth as the absolute—the only truth in world and man. The world-appearance as experienced by us is thus often likened to the illusory perception of silver in a conch-shell; for the moment the perception appears to be true and the man runs to pick it up, as if the conch-shell were a real piece of silver; but as soon as he finds out the truth that this is only a piece of conch-shell, he turns his back on it and is no longer deluded by the appearance or again attracted towards it. The illusion of silver is inexplicable in itself, for it was true for all purposes so long as it persisted, but when true knowledge was acquired, it forthwith vanished. This world-appearance will also vanish when the true knowledge of reality dawns. When false knowledge is once found to be false it cannot return again. The Upaniṣads tell us that he who sees the many here is doomed. The one, the Brahman, alone is true; all else is but delusion of name and form. Other systems believed that even after emancipation, the world would continue as it is, that there was nothing illusory in it, but I could not have any knowledge of it because of the absence of the instruments by the processes of which knowledge was generated. The Sāṃkhya puruṣa cannot know the world when the buddhi-stuff is dissociated from it and merged in the prakṛti, the Mīmāṃsā and the Nyāya soul is also incapable of knowing the world after emancipation, as it is then dissociated from manas. But the Vedānta position is quite distinct here. We cannot know the world, for when the right knowledge dawns, the perception of this world-appearance proves itself to be false to the person who has witnessed the truth, the Brahman. An illusion cannot last when the truth is known; what is truth is known to us, but what is illusion is undemonstrable, unspeakable, and indefinite. The illusion runs on from beginningless time; we do not know how it is related to truth, the Brahman, but we know that when the truth is once known the false knowledge of this world-appearance disappears once for all. No intermediate link is necessary to effect it, no mechanical dissociation of buddhi or manas, but just as by finding out the glittering piece to be a conch-shell the illusory perception of silver is destroyed, so this illusory perception of world-appearance is also destroyed by a true knowledge of the reality, the Brahman. The Upaniṣads held that reality or truth was one, and there was "no many" anywhere, and Śaṅkara explained it by adding that the "many" was merely an illusion, and hence did not exist in reality and was bound to disappear when the truth was known. The world-appearance is māyā (illusion). This is what Śaṅkara emphasizes in expounding his constructive system of the Upaniṣad doctrine. The question is sometimes asked, how the māyā becomes associated with Brahman. But Vedānta thinks this question illegitimate, for this association did not begin in time either with reference to the cosmos or with reference to individual persons. In fact there is no real association, for the creation of illusion does not affect the unchangeable truth. Māyā or illusion is no real entity, it is only false knowledge (*avidyā*) that makes the appearance, which vanishes when the reality is grasped and found. Māyā or avidyā has an apparent existence only so long as it lasts, but the moment the truth is known it is dissolved. It is not a real entity in association with which a real world-appearance has been brought into permanent existence, for it only has existence so long as we are deluded by it (*prātītika-sattā*). Māyā therefore is a category which baffles the ordinary logical division of existence and non-existence and the principle of excluded middle. For the māyā can neither be said to be "is" nor "is not" (*tattvānyatvābhyām anirvacanīyā*). It cannot be said that such a logical category does not exist, for all our dream and illusory cognitions demonstrate it to us. They exist as they are perceived, but they do not exist since they have no other independent existence than the fact of their perception. If it has any creative function, that function is as illusive as its own nature, for the creation only lasts so long as the error lasts. Brahman, the truth, is not in any way sullied or affected by association with māyā, for there can be no association of the real with the empty, the māyā, the illusory. It is no real association but a mere appearance.

In what sense is the world-appearance false?

The world is said to be false—a mere product of māyā. The falsehood of this world-appearance has been explained as involved in the category of the indefinite which is neither *sat* "is" nor *asat* "is not." Here the opposition of the "is" and "is not" is solved by the category of time. The world-appearance is "is not," since it does not continue to manifest itself in all times, and has its manifestation up to the moment that the right knowledge dawns. It is not therefore "is not" in the sense that a "castle in the air" or a hare's horn is "is not," for these are called *tuccha*, the absolutely non-existent. The world-appearance is said to be "is" or existing, since it appears to be so for the time the state of ignorance persists in us. Since it exists for a time it is *sat* (is), but since it does not exist for all times it is *asat* (is not). This is the appearance, the falsehood of the world-appearance (*jagatprapañca*) that it is neither *sat* nor *asat* in an absolute sense. Or rather it may also be said in another way that the falsehood of the world-appearance consists in this, that though it appears to be the reality or an expression or manifestation of the reality, the being, *sat*, yet when the reality is once rightly comprehended, it will be manifest that the world never existed, does not exist, and will never exist again. This is just what we find in an illusory perception; when once the truth is found out that it is a conchshell, we say that the silver, though it appeared at the time of illusory perception to be what we saw before us as "this" (this is silver), yet it never existed before, does not now exist, and will never exist again. In the case of the illusory perception of silver, the "this" (pointing to a thing before me) appeared as silver; in the case of the world-appearance, it is the being (*sat*), the Brahman, that appears as the world; but as in the case when the "this" before us is found to be a piece of conch-shell, the silver is at once dismissed as having had no existence in the "this" before us, so when the Brahman, the being, the reality, is once directly realized, the conviction comes that the world never existed. The negation of the world-appearance however has no separate existence other than the comprehension of the identity of the real. The fact that the real is realized is the same as that the world-appearance is negated. The negation here involved refers both to the thing negated (the world-appearance) and the negation itself, and hence it cannot be contended that when the conviction of the negation of the world is also regarded as false (for if the negation is not false then it remains as an entity different from Brahman and hence the unqualified monism fails), then this reinstates the reality of the world-appearance; for negation of the world-appearance is as much false as the world-appearance itself, and hence on the realization of the truth the negative thesis, that the world-appearance does not exist, includes the negation also as a manifestation of world-appearance, and hence the only thing left is the realized identity of the truth, the being. The peculiarity of this illusion of world-appearance is this, that it appears as consistent with or inlaid in the being (*sat*) though it is not there. This of course is dissolved when right knowledge dawns. This indeed brings home to us the truth that the world-appearance is an appearance which is different from what we know as real (*sadvilakṣaṇa*); for the real is known to us as that which is proved by the pramāṇas, and which will never again be falsified by later experience or other means of proof. A thing is said to be true only so long as it is not contradicted; but since at the dawn of right knowledge this world-appearance will be found to be false and non-existing, it cannot be regarded as real[1]. Thus Brahman alone is true, and the world-appearance is false; falsehood and truth are not contrary entities such that the negation or the falsehood of falsehood will mean truth. The world-appearance is a whole and in referring to it the negation refers also to itself as a part of the world-appearance and hence not only is the positive world-appearance false, but the falsehood itself is also false; when the world-appearance is contradicted at the dawn of right knowledge, the falsehood itself is also contradicted.

Brahman differs from all other things in this that it is self-luminous (*svaprakāśa*) and has no form; it cannot therefore be the object of any other consciousness that grasps it. All other things, ideas, emotions, etc., in contrast to it are called *dṛśya* (objects of consciousness), while it is the *draṣṭā* (the pure consciousness comprehending all objects). As soon as anything is comprehended as an expression of a mental state (*vṛtti*), it is said to have a form and it becomes dṛśya, and this is the characteristic of all objects of consciousness that they cannot reveal themselves apart from being manifested as objects of consciousness through a mental state.

[1] See *Advaitasiddhi, Mithyātvanirukti.*

Brahman also, so long as it is understood as a meaning of the Upaniṣad text, is not in its true nature; it is only when it shines forth as apart from the associations of any form that it is svaprakāśa and draṣṭā. The knowledge of the pure Brahman is devoid of any form or mode. The notion of *dṛśyatva* (objectivity) carries with it also the notion of *jaḍatva* (materiality) or its nature as non-consciousness (*ajñānatva*) and non-selfness (*anātmatva*) which consists in the want of self-luminosity of objects of consciousness. The relation of consciousness (*jñāna*) to its objects cannot be regarded as real but as mere illusory impositions, for as we shall see later, it is not possible to determine the relation between knowledge and its forms. Just as the silver-appearance of the conch-shell is not its own natural appearance, so the forms in which consciousness shows itself are not its own natural essence. In the state of emancipation when supreme bliss (*ānauda*) shines forth, the ānanda is not an object or form of the illuminating consciousness, but it is the illumination itself. Whenever there is a form associated with consciousness, it is an extraneous illusory imposition on the pure consciousness. These forms are different from the essence of consciousness, not only in this that they depend on consciousness for their expression and are themselves but objects of consciousness, but also in this that they are all finite determinations (*paricchinna*), whereas consciousness, the abiding essence, is everywhere present without any limit whatsoever. The forms of the object such as cow, jug, etc. are limited in themselves in what they are, but through them all the pure being runs by virtue of which we say that the cow is, the jug is, the pot is. Apart from this pure being running through all the individual appearances, there is no other class (*jāti*) such as cowness or jugness, but it is on this pure being that different individual forms are illusorily imposed (*ghaṭādīkam sadarthekalpitam, pratyekam tadanubiddhatvena pratīyamānatvāt*). So this world-appearance which is essentially different from the Brahman, the being which forms the material cause on which it is imposed, is false (*upādānaniṣṭhātyantābhāvapratiyogitv-alakṣaṇamithyātvasiddhiḥ*—as Citsukha has it).

The nature of the world-appearance, phenomena.

The world-appearance is not however so illusory as the perception of silver in the conch-shell, for the latter type of worldly illusions is called *prātibhāsika*, as they are contradicted by other later experiences, whereas the illusion of world-appearance is never contradicted in this worldly stage and is thus called *vyavahārika* (from *vyavahāra*, practice, i.e. that on which is based all our practical movements). So long as the right knowledge of the Brahman as the only reality does not dawn, the world-appearance runs on in an orderly manner uncontradicted by the accumulated experience of all men, and as such it must be held to be true. It is only because there comes such a stage in which the world-appearance ceases to manifest itself that we have to say that from the ultimate and absolute point of view the world-appearance is false and unreal. As against this doctrine of the Vedānta it is sometimes asked how, as we see the reality (*sattva*) before us, we can deny that it has truth. To this the Vedānta answers that the notion of reality cannot be derived from the senses, nor can it be defined as that which is the content of right knowledge, for we cannot have any conception of right knowledge without a conception of reality, and no conception of reality without a conception of right knowledge. The conception of reality comprehends within it the notions of unalterability, absoluteness, and independence, which cannot be had directly from experience, as this gives only an appearance but cannot certify its truth. Judged from this point of view it will be evident that the true reality in all our experience is the one self-luminous flash of consciousness which is all through identical with itself in all its manifestations of appearance. Our present experience of the world-appearance cannot in any way guarantee that it will not be contradicted at some later stage. What really persists in all experience is the being (*sat*) and not its forms. This being that is associated with all our experience is not a universal genus nor merely the individual appearance of the moment, but it is the being, the truth which forms the substratum of all objective events and appearances (*ekenaiva sarvānugatena sarvatra satpratītiḥ*). Things are not existent because they possess the genus of being (*sat*) as Nyāya supposes, but they are so because they are themselves but appearance imposed on one identical being as the basis and ground of all experience. Being is thus said to be the basis (*adhiṣṭhāna*) on which the illusions appear. This being is not different with different things but one in all appearances. Our perceptions of the world-appearance could have been taken as a guarantee of their reality, if the reality which is supposed of them could be perceived by the senses, and if inference and śruti (scriptures) did not point the other way. Perception can of course invalidate inference, but it can do so only when its own validity has been ascertained in an undoubted and uncontested manner. But this is not the case with our perceptions of the world-appearance, for our present perceptions cannot prove that these will never be contradicted in future, and inference and śruti are also against it. The mere fact that I perceive the world-appearance cannot prove that what I perceive is true or real, if it is contradicted by inference. We all perceive the sun to be small, but our perception in this case is contradicted by inference and we have hence to admit that our perceptions are erroneous. We depend (*upajīvya*) indeed for all our transactions on perception, but such dependence cannot prove that that on which we depend is absolutely valid. Validity or reality can only be ascertained by proper examination and enquiry (*parīkṣā*), which may convince us that there is no error in it. True it is that by the universal testimony of our contemporaries and by the practical fruition and realization of our endeavours in the external world, it is proved beyond doubt that the world-appearance before us is a reality. But this sort of examination and enquiry cannot prove to us with any degree of satisfaction that the world-appearance will never be contradicted at any time or at any stage. The Vedānta also admits that our examination and enquiry prove to us that the world-appearance now exists as it appears; it only denies that it cannot continue to exist for all times, and a time will come when to the emancipated person the world-appearance will cease to exist. The experience, observation, and practical utility of the objects as perceived by us cannot prove to us that these will never be contradicted at any future time. Our perception of the world-appearance cannot therefore disprove the Vedānta inference that the world-appearance is false, and it will demonstrate itself to be so at the time when the right knowledge of Brahman as one dawns in us. The testimony of the Upaniṣads also contradicts the perception which grasps the world-appearance in its manifold aspect.

Moreover we are led to think that the world-appearance is false, for it is not possible for us to discover any true relation between the consciousness (*dṛk*) and the objects of consciousness (*dṛśya*). Consciousness must be admitted to have some kind of connection with the objects which it illumines, for had it not been so there could be any knowledge at any time irrespective of its connections with the objects. But it is not possible to imagine any kind of connection between consciousness and its objects, for it can neither be contact (*saṃyoga*) nor inherence (*samavāya*); and apart from these two kinds of connections we know of no other. We say that things are the objects of our consciousness, but what is meant by it is indeed difficult to define. It cannot be that objectivity of consciousness means that a special effect like the jñātatā of Mīmāṃsā is produced upon the object, for such an effect is not admissible or perceivable in any way; nor can objectivity also mean any practical purpose (of being useful to us) associated with the object as Prabhākara thinks, for there are many things which are the objects of our consciousness but not considered as useful (e.g. the sky). Objectivity also cannot mean that the thing is the object of the thought-movement (*jñānakāraṇa*) involved in knowledge, for this can only be with reference to objects present to the perceiver, and cannot apply to objects of past time about which one may be conscious, for if the thing is not present how can it be made an object of thought-movement? Objectivity further cannot mean that the things project their own forms on the knowledge and are hence called objects, for though this may apply in the case of perception, it cannot be true of inference, where the object of consciousness is far away and does not mould consciousness after its own form. Thus in whatever way we may try to conceive manifold things existing separately and becoming objects of consciousness we fail. We have also seen that it is difficult to conceive of any kind of relation subsisting between objects and consciousness, and hence it has to be admitted that the imposition of the world-appearance is after all nothing but illusory.

Now though all things are but illusory impositions on consciousness yet for the illumination of specific objects it is admitted even by Vedānta that this can only take place through specific sense-contact and particular mental states (*vṛtti*) or modes; but if that be so why not rather admit that this can take place even on the assumption of the absolute reality of the manifold external world without? The answer that the Vedānta gives to such a question is this, that the phenomenon of illumination has not to undergo any gradual process, for it is the work of one flash like the work of the light of a lamp in removing darkness; so it is not possible that the external reality should have to pass through any process before consciousness could arise; what happens is simply this, that the reality (*sat*) which subsists in all things as the same identical one reveals the object as soon as its veil is removed by association with the vṛtti (mental mould or state). It is like a light which directly and immediately illuminates everything with which it comes into relation. Such an illumination of objects by its underlying reality would have been continuous if there were no veils or covers, but that is not so as the reality is hidden by the veil of ajñāna (nescience). This veil is removed as soon as the light of consciousness shines through a mental mould or vṛtti, and as soon as it is removed the thing shines forth. Even before the formation of the vṛtti the illusory impositions on the reality had still been continuing objectively, but it could not be revealed as it was hidden by ajñāna which is removed by the action of the corresponding vṛtti; and as soon as the veil is removed the thing shines forth in its true light. The action of the senses, eye, etc. serves but to modify the vṛtti of the mind, and the vṛtti of the mind once formed, the corresponding ajñāna veil which was covering the corresponding specific part of the world-appearance is removed, and the illumination of the object which was already present, being divested of the veil, shows itself forth. The illusory creations were there, but they could not be manifested on account of the veil of nescience. As soon as the veil is removed by the action of the vṛtti the light of reality shows the corresponding illusory creations. So consciousness in itself is the ever-shining light of reality which is never generated but ever exists; errors of perception (e.g. silver in the conch-shell) take place not because the doṣa consisting of the defect of the eye, the glaze of the object and such other elements that contributed to the illusion, generated the knowledge, but because it generated a wrong vṛtti. It is because of the generation of the wrong vṛtti that the manifestation is illusory. In the illusion "this is silver" as when we mistake the conch-shell for the silver, it is the *cit*, consciousness or reality as underlying the object represented to us by "this" or "*idam*" that is the basis (*adhiṣṭhāna*) of the illusion of silver. The cause of error is our nescience or non-cognition (*ajñāna*) of it in the form of the conch-shell, whereas the right knowledge is the cognition of it as conch-shell. The basis is not in the content of my knowledge as manifested in my mental state (*vṛtti*), so that the illusion is not of the form that the "knowledge is silver" but of "this is silver." Objective phenomena as such have reality as their basis, whereas the expression of illumination of them as states of knowledge is made through the *cit* being manifested through the mental mould or states. Without the vṛtti there is no illuminating knowledge. Phenomenal creations are there in the world moving about as shadowy forms on the unchangeable basis of one cit or reality, but this basis, this light of reality, can only manifest these forms when the veil of nescience covering them is temporarily removed by their coming in touch with a mental mould or mind-modification (*vṛtti*). It is sometimes said that since all illumination of knowledge must be through the mental states there is no other entity of pure consciousness apart from what is manifested through the states. This Vedānta does not admit, for it holds that it is necessary that before the operation of the mental states can begin to interpret reality, reality must already be there and this reality is nothing but pure consciousness. Had there been no reality apart from the manifesting states of knowledge, the validity of knowledge would also cease; so it has to be admitted that there is the one eternal self-luminous reality untouched by the characteristics of the mental states, which are material and suffer origination and destruction. It is this self-luminous consciousness that seems to assume diverse forms in connection with diverse kinds of associations or limitations (*upādhi*). It manifests ajñāna (nescience) and hence does not by itself remove the ajñāna, except when it is reflected through any specific kind of vṛtti. There is of course no difference, no inner and outer varieties between the reality, the pure consciousness which is the essence, the basis and the ground of all phenomenal appearances of the objective world, and the consciousness that manifests itself through the mental states. There is only one identical pure consciousness or reality, which is at once the basis of the phenomena as well as their interpreter by a reflection through the mental states or vṛttis.

The phenomena or objects called the dṛśya can only be determined in their various forms and manifestations but not as to their ultimate reality; there is no existence as an entity of any relation such as saṃyoga (contact) or samavāya (inherence) between them and the pure consciousness called the dṛk; for the truth is this, that the dṛk (perceiver) and the dṛśya (perceived) have one identical reality; the forms of phenomena are but illusory creations on it.

It is sometimes objected that in the ordinary psychological illusion such as "this is silver," the knowledge of "this" as a thing is only of a general and indefinite nature, for it is perceived as a thing but its special characteristics as a conch-shell are not noticed, and thus the illusion is possible. But in Brahman or pure consciousness there are neither definite nor indefinite characteristics of any kind, and hence it cannot be the ground of any illusion as the piece of conch-shell perceived indefinitely as a mere "this" can be. The answer of Vedānta is that when the Brahman stands as the ground (*adhiṣṭhāna*) of the world-appearance its characteristic as sat or real only is manifested, whereas its special character as pure and infinite bliss is never noticed; or rather it may be said that the illusion of world-appearance is possible because the Brahman in its true and correct nature is never revealed to us in our objective consciousness; when I say "the jug is," the "isness," or "being," does not shine in its purity, but only as a characteristic of the jug-form, and this is the root of the illusion. In all our experiences only the aspect of Brahman as real shines forth in association with the manifold objects, and therefore the Brahman in its true nature being unknown the illusion is made possible. It is again objected that since the world-appearance can serve all practical purposes, it must be considered as real and not illusory. But the Vedānta points out that even by illusory perceptions practical effects are seen to take place; the illusory perception of a snake in a rope causes all the fear that a real snake could do; even in dreams we feel happy and sad, and dreams may be so bad as to affect or incapacitate the actual physical functions and organs of a man. So it is that the past impressions imbedded in us continuing from beginningless time are sufficient to account for our illusory notions, just as the impressions produced in actual waking life account for the dream creations. According to the good or bad deeds that a man has done in previous lives and according to the impressions or potencies (*saṃskāra*) of his past lives each man has a particular kind of world-experience for himself and the impressions of one cannot affect the formation of the illusory experience of the other. But the experience of the world-appearance is not wholly a subjective creation for each individual, for even before his cognition the phenomena of world-appearance were running in some unknowable state of existence (*svena adhyastasya saṃskārasya viyadādyadhyāsajanakatvopapatteḥ tatpratītyabhāvepi tadadhyāsasya pūrvam sattvāt kṛtsnasyāpi vyavahārikapadārthasya ajñātasattvābhyupagamāt*). It is again sometimes objected that illusion is produced by malobserved similarity between the ground (*adhiṣṭhāna*) and the illusory notion as silver in "this is silver," but no such similarity is found between the Brahman and the world-appearance. To this Vedānta says that similarity is not an indispensable factor in the production of an illusion (e.g. when a white conch is perceived as yellow owing to the defect of the eye through the influence of bile or *pitta*). Similarity helps the production of illusion by rousing up the potencies of past impressions or memories; but this rousing of past memories may as well be done by *adṛṣṭa*—the unseen power of our past good or bad deeds. In ordinary illusion some defect is necessary but the illusion of this world-appearance is beginningless, and hence it awaits no other doṣa (defect) than the avidyā (nescience) which constitutes the appearance. Here avidyā is the only doṣa and Brahman is the only adhiṣṭhāna or ground. Had there not been the Brahman, the self-luminous as the adhiṣṭhāna, the illusory creations could not have been manifested at all. The cause of the direct perception of illusion is the direct but indefinite perception of the adhiṣṭhāna. Hence where the adhiṣṭhāna is hidden by the veil of avidyā, the association with mental states becomes necessary for removing the veil and manifesting thereby the self-luminous adhiṣṭhāna. As soon as the adhiṣṭhāna, the ground, the reality, the blissful self-luminous Brahman is completely realized the illusions disappear. The disappearance of the phenomena means nothing more than the realization of the self-luminous Brahman.

The Definition of Ajñāna (nescience).

Ajñāna the cause of all illusions is defined as that which is beginningless, yet positive and removable by knowledge (*anādibhāvarūpatve sati jñānanivartyatvam*). Though it manifests itself in all ordinary things (veiled by it before they become objects of perception) which have a beginning in time, yet it itself has no beginning, for it is associated with the pure consciousness which is beginningless. Again though it has been described as positive (*bhāvarūpa*) it can very well constitute the essence of negation (*abhāva*) too, for the positivity (*bhāvatva*) does not mean here the opposite of abhāva (negation) but notes merely its difference from abhāva (*abhāva-vilakṣaṇatvamātram vivakṣitam*). Ajñāna is not a positive entity (*bhāva*) like any other positive entity, but it is called positive simply because it is not a mere negation (*abhāva*). It is a category which is believed neither to be positive in the ordinary sense nor negative, but a third one which is different both from position as well as from negation. It is sometimes objected that ajñāna is a mere illusory imagination of the moment caused by defect (*doṣa*) and hence it cannot be beginningless (*anādi*); but Vedānta holds that the fact that it is an imagination or rather imposition, does not necessarily mean that it is merely a temporary notion produced by the defects; for it could have been said to be a temporary product of the moment if the ground as well as the illusory creation associated with it came into being for the moment, but this is not the case here, as the cit, the ground of illusion, is ever-present and the ajñāna therefore being ever associated with it is also beginningless. The ajñāna is the indefinite which is veiling everything, and as such is different from the definite or the positive and the negative. Though it is beginningless yet it can be removed by knowledge, for to have a beginning or not to have it does not in any way determine whether the thing is subject to dissolution or not for the dissolution of a thing depends upon the presence of the thing which can cause it; and it is a fact that when knowledge comes the illusion is destroyed; it does not matter whether the cause which produced the illusion was beginningless or not. Some Vedāntists however define ajñāna as the substance constituting illusion, and say that though it is not a positive entity yet it may be regarded as forming the substance of the illusion; it is not necessary that only a positive entity should be the matter of any thing, for what is necessary for the notion of a material cause (*upādāna*) is this, that it should continue or persist as the same in all changes of effects. It is not true that only what is positive can persist in and through the effects which are produced in the time process. Illusion is unreal and it is not unnatural that the ajñāna which also is unreal should be the cause of it.

Ajñāna established by Perception and Inference.

Ajñāna defined as the indefinite which is neither positive nor negative is also directly experienced by us in such perceptions as "I do not know, or I do not know myself or anybody else," or "I do not know what you say," or more particularly "I had been sleeping so long happily and did not know anything." Such perceptions point to an object which has no definite characteristics, and which cannot properly be said to be either positive or negative. It may be objected that the perception "I do not know" is not the perception of the indefinite, the ajñāna, but merely the negation of knowledge. To this Vedānta says that had it been the perception of a negation merely, then the negation must have been associated with the specific object to which it applied. A negation must imply the thing negatived; in fact negation generally appears as a substantive with the object of negation as a qualifying character specifying the nature of the negation. But the perception "I do not know or I had no knowledge" does not involve the negation of any particular knowledge of any specific object, but the knowledge of an indefinite objectless ignorance. Such an indefinite ajñāna is positive in the sense that it is certainly not negative, but this positive indefinite is not positive in the same sense in which other definite entities are called positive, for it is merely the characterless, passive indefinite showing itself in our experience. If negation meant only a general negation, and if the perception of negation meant in each case the perception of a general negation, then even where there is a jug on the ground, one should perceive the negation of the jug on the ground, for the general negation in relation to other things is there. Thus negation of a thing cannot mean the general notion of the negation of all specific things; similarly a general negation without any specific object to which it might apply cannot manifest itself to consciousness; the notion of a general negation of knowledge is thus opposed to any and every knowledge, so that if the latter is present the former cannot be, but the perception "I do not know" can persist, even though many individual objects be known to us. Thus instead of saying that the perception of "I do not know" is the perception of a special kind of negation, it is rather better to say that it is the perception of a different category namely the indefinite, the ajñāna. It is our common experience that after experiencing the indefinite (*ajñāna*) of a specific type we launch forth in our endeavours to remove it. So it has to be admitted that the perception of the indefinite is different from the perception of mere negation. The character of our perceiving consciousness (*sākṣi*) is such that both the root ajñāna as well as its diverse forms with reference to particular objects as represented in mental states (*vṛtti-jñāna*), are comprehended by it. Of course when the vṛttijñāna about a thing as in ordinary perceptions of objects comes in, the ajñāna with regard to it is temporarily removed, for the vṛttijñāna is opposed to the ajñāna. But so far as our own perceiving consciousness (*sākṣi-caitanya*) is conceived it can comprehend both the ajñāna and the jñāna (knowledge) of things. It is thus often said that all things show themselves to the perceiving consciousness either as known or as unknown. Thus the perceiving consciousness comprehends all positives either as indefinite ajñāna or as states of knowledge or as specific kinds of ajñāna or ignorance, but it is unable to comprehend a negation, for negation (*abhāva*) is not a perception, but merely the absence of perception (*anupalabdhi*). Thus when I say I do not know this, I perceive the indefinite in consciousness with reference to that thing, and this is not the perception of a negation of the thing. An objection is sometimes raised from the Nyāya point of view that since without the knowledge of a qualification (*viśeṣana*) the qualified thing (*viśiṣṭa*) cannot be known, the indefinite about an object cannot be present in consciousness without the object being known first. To this Vedānta replies that the maxim that the qualification must be known before the qualified thing is known is groundless, for we can as well perceive the thing first and then its qualification. It is not out of place here to say that negation is not a separate entity, but is only a peculiar mode of the manifestation of the positive. Even the naiyāyikas would agree that in the expression "there is no negation of a jug here," no separate negation can be accepted, for the jug is already present before us. As there are distinctions and differences in positive entities by illusory impositions, so negations are also distinguished by similar illusory impositions and appear as the negation of jug, negation of cloth, etc.; so all distinctions between negations are unnecessary, and it may be accepted that negation like position is one which appears as many on account of illusory distinctions and impositions. Thus the content of negation being itself positive, there is no reason to object that such perceptions as "I do not know" refer to the perception of an indefinite ajñāna in consciousness. So also the perception "I do not know what you say" is not the perception of negation, for this would require that the hearer should know first what was said by the speaker, and if this is so then it is impossible to say "I do not know what you say."

So also the cognition "I was sleeping long and did not know anything" has to be admitted as referring to the perception of the indefinite during sleep. It is not true as some say that during sleep there is no perception, but what appears to the awakened man as "I did not know anything so long" is only an inference; for, it is not possible to infer from the pleasant and active state of the senses in the awakened state that the activity had ceased in the sleep state and that since he had no object of knowledge then, he could not know anything; for there is no invariable concomitance between the pleasant and active state of the senses and the absence of objects of knowledge in the immediately preceding state. During sleep there is a mental state of the form of the indefinite, and during the awakened state it is by the impression (*saṃskāra*) of the aforesaid mental state of ajñāna that one remembers that state and says that "I did not perceive anything so long." The indefinite (*ajñāna*) perceived in consciousness is more fundamental and general than the mere negation of knowledge (*jñānābhāva*) and the two are so connected that though the latter may not be felt, yet it can be inferred from the perception of the indefinite. The indefinite though not definite is thus a positive content different from negation and is perceived as such in direct and immediate consciousness both in the awakened state as well as in the sleeping state.

The presence of this ajñāna may also be inferred from the manner in which knowledge of objects is revealed in consciousness, as this always takes place in bringing a thing into consciousness which was not known or rather known as indefinite before we say "I did not know it before, but I know it now." My present knowledge of the thing thus involves the removal of an indefinite which was veiling it before and positing it in consciousness, just as the first streak of light in utter darkness manifests itself by removing the darkness[1]. Apart from such an inference its exist-

[1] See *Pañcapādikāvivaraṇa*, *Tattvadīpana*, and *Advaitasiddhi*.

ence is also indicated by the fact that the infinite bliss of Brahman does not show itself in its complete and limitless aspect. If there was no ajñāna to obstruct, it would surely have manifested itself in its fullness. Again had it not been for this ajñāna there would have been no illusion. It is the ajñāna that constitutes the substance of the illusion; for there is nothing else that can be regarded as constituting its substance; certainly Brahman could not, as it is unchangeable. This ajñāna is manifested by the perceiving consciousness (*sākṣi*) and not by the pure consciousness. The perceiving consciousness is nothing but pure intelligence which reflects itself in the states of avidyā (ignorance).

Locus and Object of Ajñāna, Ahaṃkāra, and Antaḥkaraṇa.

This ajñāna rests on the pure *cit* or intelligence. This cit or Brahman is of the nature of pure illumination, but yet it is not opposed to the ajñāna or the indefinite. The cit becomes opposed to the ajñāna and destroys it only when it is reflected through the mental states (*vṛtti*). The ajñāna thus rests on the pure cit and not on the cit as associated with such illusory impositions as go to produce the notion of ego "*aham*"or the individual soul. Vācaspati Miśra however holds that the ajñāna does not rest on the pure cit but on the jīva (individual soul). Mādhava reconciles this view of Vācaspati with the above view, and says that the ajñāna may be regarded as resting on the jīva or individual soul from this point of view that the obstruction of the pure cit is with reference to the jīva (*Cinmātrāśritam ajñānam jīvapakṣapātitvāt jīvāśritam ucyate* Vivaraṇaprameya, p. 48). The feeling "I do not know" seems however to indicate that the ajñāna is with reference to the perceiving self in association with its feeling as ego or "I"; but this is not so; such an appearance however is caused on account of the close association of ajñāna with antaḥkaraṇa (mind) both of which are in essence the same (see Vivaraṇaprameyasaṃgraha, p. 48).

The ajñāna however does not only rest on the cit, but it has the cit as its viṣaya or object too, i.e. its manifestations are with reference to the self-luminous cit. The self-luminous cit is thus the entity on which the veiling action of the ajñāna is noticed; the veiling action is manifested not by destroying the self-luminous character, nor by stopping a future course of luminous career on the part of the cit, nor by stopping its relations with the viṣaya, but by causing such an appearance that the self-luminous cit seems so to behave that we seem to think that it is not or it does not shine (*nāsti na prakāśate iti vyavahāraḥ*) or rather there is no appearance of its shining or luminosity. To say that Brahman is hidden by the ajñāna means nothing more than this, that it is such (*tadyogyatā*) that the ajñāna can so relate itself with it that it appears to be hidden as in the state of deep sleep and other states of ajñāna-consciousness in experience. Ajñāna is thus considered to have both its locus and object in the pure cit. It is opposed to the states of consciousness, for these at once dispel it. The action of this ajñāna is thus on the light of the reality which it obstructs for us, so long as the obstruction is not dissolved by the states of consciousness. This obstruction of the cit is not only with regard to its character as pure limitless consciousness but also with regard to its character as pure and infinite bliss; so it is that though we do not experience the indefinite in our pleasurable feelings, yet its presence as obstructing the pure cit is indicated by the fact that the full infinite bliss constituting the essence of Brahman is obstructed; and as a result of that there is only an incomplete manifestation of the bliss in our phenomenal experiences of pleasure. The ajñāna is one, but it seems to obstruct the pure cit in various aspects or modes, with regard to which it may be said that the ajñāna has many states as constituting the individual experiences of the indefinite with reference to the diverse individual objects of experience. These states of ajñāna are technically called tulājñāna or avasthājñāna. Any state of consciousness (vrttijñāna) removes a manifestation of the ajñāna as tulājñāna and reveals itself as the knowledge of an object.

The most important action of this ajñāna as obstructing the pure cit, and as creating an illusory phenomenon is demonstrated in the notion of the ego or ahaṃkāra. This notion of ahaṃkāra is a union of the true self, the pure consciousness and other associations, such as the body, the continued past experiences, etc.; it is the self-luminous characterless Brahman that is found obstructed in the notion of the ego as the repository of a thousand limitations, characters, and associations. This illusory creation of the notion of the ego runs on from beginningless time, each set of previous false impositions determining the succeeding set of impositions and so on. This blending of the unreal associations held up in the mind (*antaḥkaraṇa*) with the real, the false with the true, that is at the root of illusion. It is the antaḥkaraṇa taken as the self-luminous self that reflects itself in the cit as the notion. of the ego. Just as when we say that the iron ball (red hot) burns, there are two entities of the ball and the fire fused into one, so here also when I say "I perceive" there are two distinct elements of the self as consciousness and the mind or antaḥkaraṇa fused into one. The part or aspect associated with sorrow, materiality, and changefulness represents the antaḥkaraṇa, whereas that which appears as the unchangeable perceiving consciousness is the self. Thus the notion of ego contains two parts, one real and the other unreal.

We remember that this is distinctly that which Prabhākara sought to repudiate. Prabhākara did not consider the self to be self-luminous, and held that such is the threefold nature of thought (*tripuṭī*), that it at once reveals the knowledge, the object of knowledge, and the self. He further said that the analogy of the red-hot iron ball did not hold, for the iron ball and the fire are separately experienced, but the self and the antaḥkaraṇa are never separately experienced, and we can never say that these two ate really different and only have an illusory appearance of a seeming unity. Perception (*anubhava*) is like a light which illuminates both the object and the self, and like it does not require the assistance of anything else for the fulfilling of its purpose. But the Vedānta objects to this saying that according to Prabhākara's supposition it is impossible to discover any relation between the self and the knowledge. If knowledge can be regarded as revealing itself, the self may as well be held to be self-luminous; the self and the knowledge are indeed one and the same. Kumārila thinks this thought (*anubhava*) to be a movement, Nyāya and Prabḥkara as a quality of the self[1]. But if it were a movement like other movements, it could not affect itself as illumination. If it were a substance and atomic in size, it would only manifest a small portion of a thing, if all-pervasive then it would illuminate everything, if of medium size it would depend on its parts for its own

[1] According to Nyāya the *ātman* is conscious only through association with consciousness, but it is not consciousness (*cit*). Consciousness is associated with it only as a result of suitable collocations. Thus *Nyāyamañjarī* in refuting the doctrine of self-luminosity (*svaprakāśa*) says (p. 432)

sacetanaścitā yogāttadyogena vinā jaḍaḥ
nārthāvabhāsādanyaddhi caitanyaṃ nāma manmahe.

constitution and not on the self. If it is regarded as a quality of the self as the light is of the lamp, then also it has necessarily to be supposed that it was produced by the self, for from what else could it be produced? Thus it is to be admitted that the self, the ātman, is the self-luminous entity. No one doubts any of his knowledge, whether it is he who sees or anybody else. The self is thus the same as vijñāna, the pure consciousness, which is always of itself self-luminous[1].

Again, though consciousness is continuous in all stages, waking or sleeping, yet ahaṃkāra is absent during deep sleep. It is true that on waking from deep sleep one feels "I slept happily and did not know anything": yet what happens is this, that during deep sleep the antaḥkaraṇa and the ahamkāra are altogether submerged in the ajñāna, and there are only the ajñāna and the self; on waking, this ahaṃkāra as a state of antaḥkaraṇa is again generated, and then it associates the perception of the ajñāna in the sleep and originates the perception "I did not know anything." This ahaṃkāra which is a mode (*vṛtti*) of the antaḥkaraṇa is thus constituted by avidyā, and is manifested as jñānaśakti (power of knowledge) and kriyāśakti (power of work). This kriyāśakti of the ahaṃkāra is illusorily imposed upon the self, and as a result of that the self appears to be an active agent in knowing and willing. The ahaṃkāra itself is regarded, as we have already seen, as a mode or vṛtti of the antaḥkaraṇa, and as such the ahaṃkāra of a past period can now be associated; but even then the vṛtti of antaḥkaraṇa, ahaṃkāra, may be regarded as only the active side or aspect of the antaḥkaraṇa. The same antaḥkaraṇa is called manas in its capacity as doubt, buddhi in its capacity as achieving certainty of knowledge, and citta in its capacity as remembering[2]. When the pure cit shines forth in association with this antaḥkaraṇa, it is called a jīva. It is clear from the above account that the ajñāna is not a mere nothing, but is the principle of the phenomena. But it cannot stand alone, without the principle of the real to support it (*āśraya*); its own nature as the ajñāna or indefinite is perceived directly by the pure consciousness; its movements as originating the phenomena remain indefinite in themselves, the real as under-

[1] See *Nyāyamakaranda*, pp. 130-140, *Citsukha* and *Vivaraṇaprameyasaṃgraha*, pp. 53-58.

[2] See *Vedānta-paribhāṣā*, p. 88, Bombay edition.

lying these phenomenal movements can only manifest itself through these which hide it, when corresponding states arise in the antaḥkaraṇa, and the light of the real shines forth through these states. The antaḥkaraṇa of which ahaṃkāra is a moment, is itself a beginningless system of ajñāna-phenomena containing within it the associations and impressions of past phenomena as merit, demerit, instincts, etc. from a beginningless time when the jīva or individual soul began his career.

Anirvācyavāda and the Vedānta Dialectic.

We have already seen that the indefinite ajñāna could be experienced in direct perception and according to Vedānta there are only two categories. The category of the real, the self-luminous Brahman, and the category of the indefinite. The latter has for its ground the world-appearance, and is the principle by which the one unchangeable Brahman is falsely manifested in all the diversity of the manifold world. But this indefinite which is different from the category of the positive and the negative, has only a relative existence and will ultimately vanish, when the true knowledge of the Brahman dawns. Nothing however can be known about the nature of this indefinite except its character as indefinite. That all the phenomena of the world, the fixed order of events, the infinite variety of world-forms and names, all these are originated by this avidyā, ajñāna or māyā is indeed hardly comprehensible. If it is indefinite nescience, how can all these well-defined forms of world-existence come out of it? It is said to exist only relatively, and to have only a temporary existence beside the permanent infinite reality. To take such a principle and to derive from it the mind, matter, and indeed everything else except the pure self-luminous Brahman, would hardly appeal to our reason. If this system of world-order were only seeming appearance, with no other element of truth in it except pure being, then it would be indefensible in the light of reason. It has been proved that whatever notions we have about the objective world are all self-contradictory, and thus groundless and false. If they have all proceeded from the indefinite they must show this character when exposed to discerning criticism. All categories have to be shown to be so hopelessly confused and to be without any conceivable notion that though apparent before us yet they crumble into indefiniteness as soon as they are examined, and one cannot make any such assertion about them as that they are or that they are not. Such negative criticisms of our fundamental notions about the world-order were undertaken by Śrīharṣa and his commentator and follower Citsukha. It is impossible within the limits of this chapter to give a complete account of their criticisms of our various notions of reality. I shall give here only one example.

Let us take the examination of the notion of difference (*bheda*) from *Khaṇḍanakhaṇḍakhādya*. Four explanations are possible of the notion of difference: (1) the difference may be perceived as appearing in its own characteristics in our experience (*svarūpa-bheda*) as Prabhākara thinks; (2) the difference between two things is nothing but the absence of one in the other (*anyonyābhāva*), as some Naiyāyikas and Bhāṭṭas think; (3) difference means divergence of characteristics (*vaidharmya*) as the Vaiśeṣikas speak of it; (4) difference may be a separate quality in itself like the pṛthaktva quality of Nyāya. Taking the first alternative, we see that it is said that the jug and the cloth represent in themselves by their very form and existence their mutual difference from each other. But if by perceiving the cloth we perceive only its difference from the jug as the characteristic of the cloth, then the jug also must have penetrated into the form of the cloth, otherwise how could we perceive in the cloth its characteristics as the difference from the jug? i.e. if difference is a thing which can be directly perceived by the senses, then as difference would naturally mean difference from something else, it is expected that something else such as jug, etc. from which the difference is perceived must also be perceived directly in the perception of the cloth. But if the perception of difference between two things has penetrated together in the same identical perception, then the self-contradiction becomes apparent. Difference as an entity is not what we perceive in the cloth, for difference means difference from something else, and if that thing from which the difference is perceived is not perceived, then how can the difference as an entity be perceived? If it is said that the cloth itself represents its difference from the jug, and that this is indicated by the jug, then we may ask, what is the nature of the jug? If the difference from the cloth be the very nature of the jug, then the cloth itself is also involved in the nature of the jug. If it is said that the jug only indicates that it is a term from which difference is intended to be conveyed, then that also becomes impossible, for how can we imagine that there is a term which is independent of any association of its difference from other things, and is yet a term which establishes the notion of difference? If it is a term of difference, it cannot be independent of its relation to other things from which it is differentiated. If its difference from the cloth is a quality of the jug, then also the old difficulty comes in, for its difference from the cloth would involve the cloth also in itself; and if the cloth is involved in the nature of the jug as its quality, then by the same manner the jug would also be the character of the cloth, and hence not difference but identity results. Moreover, if a cloth is perceived as a character of the jug, the two will appear to be hanging one over the other, but this is never so experienced by us. Moreover, it is difficult to ascertain if qualities have any relation with things; if they have not, then absence of relation being the same everywhere everything might be the quality of everything. If there is a relation between these two, then that relation would require another relation to relate itself with that relation, and that would again require another relation and that another, and so on. Again, it may be said that when the jug, etc. are seen without reference to other things, they appear as jug, etc., but when they are viewed with reference to cloth, etc. they appear as difference. But this cannot be so, for the perception as jug is entirely different from the perception of difference. It should also be noted that the notion of difference is also different from the notions of both the jug and the cloth. It is one thing to say that there are jug and cloth, and quite another thing to say that the jug is different from the cloth. Thus a jug cannot appear as difference, though it may be viewed with reference to cloth. The notion of a jug does not require the notions of other things for its manifestation. Moreover, when I say the jug is different from the cloth, I never mean that difference is an entity which is the same as the jug or the cloth; what I mean is that the difference of the cloth from the jug has its limits in the jug, and not merely that the notion of cloth has a reference to jug. This shows that difference cannot be the characteristic nature of the thing perceived.

Again, in the second alternative where difference of two

things is defined as the absence of each thing in the other, we find that if difference in jug and cloth means that the jug is not in the cloth or that cloth is not in jug, then also the same difficulty arises; for when I say that the absence or negation of jug in the cloth is its difference from the jug, then also the residence of the absence of jug in the cloth would require that the jug also resides in the cloth, and this would reduce difference to identity. If it is said that the absence of jug in the cloth is not a separate thing, but is rather the identical cloth itself, then also their difference as mutual exclusion cannot be explained. If this mutual negation (*anyonyabhāva*) is explained as the mere absence of jugness in the cloth and of clothness in the jug, then also a difficulty arises; for there is no such quality in jugness or clothness that they may be mutually excluded; and there is no such quality in them that they can be treated as identical, and so when it is said that there is no jugness in cloth we might as well say that there is no clothness in cloth, for clothness and jugness are one and the same, and hence absence of jugness in the cloth would amount to the absence of clothness in the cloth which is self-contradictory. Taking again the third alternative we see that if difference means divergence of characteristics (*vaidharmya*), then the question arises whether the vaidharmya or divergence as existing in jug has such a divergence as can distinguish it from the divergence existing in the cloth; if the answer is in the affirmative then we require a series of endless vaidharmyas progressing *ad infinitum*. If the answer is in the negative then there being no divergence between the two divergences they become identical, and hence divergence of characteristics as such ceases to exist. If it is said that the natural forms of things are difference in themselves, for each of them excludes the other, then apart from the differences—the natural forms—the things are reduced to formlessness (*niḥsvarūpatā*). If natural forms (*svarūpa*) mean special natural forms (*svarūpa-viśeṣa*) then as the special natural forms or characteristics only represent difference, the natural forms of the things as apart from the special ones would appear to be identical. So also it may be proved that there is no such quality as pṛthaktva (separateness) which can explain differences of things, for there also the questions would arise as to whether separateness exists in different things or similar ones or whether separateness is identical with the thing in which it exists or not, and so forth.

The earliest beginnings of this method of subtle analysis and dialectic in Indian philosophy are found in the opening chapters of *Kathāvatthu*. In the great *Mahābhaṣya* on Pāṇini by Patañjali also we find some traces of it. But Nāgārjuna was the man who took it up in right earnest and systematically cultivated it in all its subtle and abstruse issues and counter-issues in order to prove that everything that appeared as a fixed order or system was non-existent, for all were unspeakable, indescribable and self-contradictory, and thus everything being discarded there was only the void (*śūnya*). Śaṅkara partially utilized this method in his refutations of Nyāya and the Buddhist systems; but Śrīharṣa again revived and developed it in a striking manner, and after having criticized the most important notions and concepts of our everyday life, which are often backed by the Nyāya system, sought to prove that nothing in the world can be defined, and that we cannot ascertain whether a thing is or is not. The refutations of all possible definitions that the Nyāya could give necessarily led to the conclusion that the things sought to be defined did not exist though they appeared to do so; the Vedāntic contention was that this is exactly as it should be, for the indefinite ajñāna produces only appearances which when exposed to reason show that no consistent notions of them can be formed, or in other words the world-appearance, the phenomena of māyā or ajñāna, are indefinable or anirvacanīya. This great work of Śrīharṣa was followed by *Tattvadīpikā* of Citsukha, in which he generally followed Śrīharṣa and sometimes supplemented him with the addition of criticisms of certain new concepts. The method of Vedānta thus followed on one side the method of Śūnyavāda in annulling all the concepts of world-appearance and on the other Vijñānavāda Buddhism in proving the self-illuminating character of knowledge and ultimately established the self as the only self-luminous ultimate reality.

The Theory of Causation.

The Vedānta philosophy looked at the constantly changing phenomena of the world-appearance and sought to discover the root whence proceeded the endless series of events and effects. The theory that effects were altogether new productions caused by the invariable unconditional and immediately preceding antecedents, as well as the theory that it was the cause which evolved and by its transformations produced the effect, are considered insufficient to explain the problem which the Vedānta had before it. Certain collocations invariably and unconditionally preceded certain effects, but this cannot explain how the previous set of phenomena could be regarded as producing the succeeding set. In fact the concept of causation and production had in it something quite undefinable and inexplicable. Our enquiry after the cause is an enquiry after a more fundamental and primary form of the truth of a thing than what appears at the present moment when we wished to know what was the cause of the jug, what we sought was a simpler form of which the effect was only a more complex form of manifestation, what is the ground, the root, out of which the effect has come forth? If apart from such an enquiry we take the pictorial representation of the causal phenomena in which some collocations being invariably present at an antecedent point of time, the effect springs forth into being, we find that we are just where we were before, and are unable to penetrate into the logic of the affair. The Nyāya definition of cause and effect may be of use to us in a general way in associating certain groups of things of a particular kind with certain other phenomena happening at a succeeding moment as being relevant pairs of which one being present the other also has a probability of being present, but can do nothing more than this. It does not answer our question as to the nature of cause. Antecedence in time is regarded in this view as an indispensable condition for the cause. But time, according to Nyāya, is one continuous entity; succession of time can only be conceived as antecedence and consequence of phenomena, and these again involve succession; thus the notions of succession of time and of the antecedence and consequence of time being mutually dependent upon each other (*anyonyāśraya*) neither of these can be conceived independently. Another important condition is invariability. But what does that mean? If it means invariable antecedence, then even an ass which is invariably present as an antecedent to the smoke rising from the washerman's house, must be regarded as the cause of the smoke[1]. If it means such an antecedence as contributes to the happening of the effect, it becomes again difficult to understand anything about its contri-

[1] Asses are used in carrying soiled linen in India. Asses are always present when water is boiled for washing in the laundry.

buting to the effect, for the only intelligible thing is the antecedence and nothing more. If invariability means the existence of that at the presence of which the effect comes into being, then also it fails, for there may be the seed but no shoot, for the mere presence of the seed will not suffice to produce the effect, the shoot. If it is said that a cause can produce an effect only when it is associated with its accessory factors, then also the question remains the same, for we have not understood what is meant by cause. Again when the same effect is often seen to be produced by a plurality of causes, the cause cannot be defined as that which happening the effect happens and failing the effect fails. It cannot also be said that in spite of the plurality of causes, each particular cause is so associated with its own particular kind of effect that from a special kind of cause we can without fail get a special kind of effect (cf. Vātsyāyana and *Nyāyamañjarī*), for out of the same clay different effects come forth namely the jug, the plate, etc. Again if cause is defined as the collocation of factors, then the question arises as to what is meant by this collocation; does it mean the factors themselves or something else above them? On the former supposition the scattered factors being always present in the universe there should always be the effect; if it means something else above the specific factors, then that something always existing, there should always be the effect. Nor can collocation (*sāmagrī*) be defined as the last movement of the causes immediately succeeding which the effect comes into being, for the relation of movement with the collocating cause is incomprehensible. Moreover if movement is defined as that which produces the effect, the very conception of causation which was required to be proved is taken for granted. The idea of necessity involved in the causal conception that a cause is that which must produce its effect is also equally undefinable, inexplicable, and logically inconceivable. Thus in whatsoever way we may seek to find out the real nature of the causal principle from the interminable series of cause-effect phenomena we fail. All the characteristics of the effects are indescribable and indefinable ajñāna of māyā, and in whatever way we may try to conceive these phenomena in themselves or in relation to one another we fail, for they are all carved out of the indefinite and are illogical and illusory, and some day will vanish for ever. The true cause is thus the pure being, the reality which is unshakable in itself, the ground upon which all appearances being imposed they appear as real. The true cause is thus the unchangeable being which persists through all experience, and the effect-phenomena are but impositions upon it of ajñāna or avidyā. It is thus the clay, the permanent, that is regarded as the cause of all clay-phenomena as jug, plates, etc. All the various modes in which the clay appears are mere appearances, unreal, indefinable, and so illusory. The one truth is the clay. So in all world-phenomena the one truth is being, the Brahman, and all the phenomena that are being imposed on it are but illusory forms and names. This is what is called the *satkāryavāda* or more properly the *satkāraṇavāda* of the Vedānta, that the cause alone is true and ever existing, and phenomena in themselves are false. There is only this much truth in them, that all are imposed on the reality or being which alone is true. This appearance of the one cause the being, as the unreal many of the phenomena is what is called the *vivarttavāda* as distinguished from the *sāṃkhyayogapariṇāmavāda*, in which the effect is regarded as the real development of the cause in its potential state. When the effect has a different kind of being from the cause it is called *vivartta* but when the effect has the same kind of being as the cause it is called *pariṇāma* (*kāraṇasvaiakṣaṇānyathābhāvaḥ pariṇāmaḥ tadvilakṣaṇo vivarttaḥ* or *vastunastatsamattāko'nyathābhāvaḥ pariṇāmaḥ tadviṣamasattākaḥ vivarttaḥ*). Vedānta has as much to object against the Nyāya as against the pariṇāma theory of causation of the Sāṃkhya; for movement, development, form, potentiality, and actuality—all these are indefinable and inconceivable in the light of reason; they cannot explain causation but only restate things and phenomena as they appear in the world. In reality however though phenomena are not identical with the cause, they can never be defined except in terms of the cause (*Tadabhedam vinaiva tadvyatirekeṇa durvacam kāryyam vivarttaḥ*).

This being the relation of cause and effect or Brahman and the world, the different followers of Śaṅkara Vedānta in explaining the cause of the world-appearance sometimes lay stress on the māyā, ajñāna or avidyā, sometimes on the Brahman, and sometimes on them both. Thus Sarvajñātmamuni, the writer of *Saṅkṣepa-śārīraka* and his followers think that the pure Brahman should be regarded as the causal substance (*upādāna*) of the world-appearance, whereas Prakāśātman Akhaṇḍānanda, and

Mādhava hold that Brahman in association with māyā, i.e. the māyā-reflected form of Brahman as Īśvara should be regarded as the cause of the world-appearance. The world-appearance is an evolution or pariṇāma of the māyā as located in Īśvara, whereas Īśvara (God) is the vivartta causal matter. Others however make a distinction between māyā as the cosmical factor of illusion and avidyā as the manifestation of the same entity in the individual or jīva. They hold that though the world-appearance may be said to be produced by the māyā yet the mind etc. associated with the individual are produced by the avidyā with the jīva or the individual as the causal matter (*upādāna*). Others hold that since it is the individual to whom both Īśvara and the world-appearance are manifested, it is better rather to think that these are all manifestations of the jīva in association with his avidyā or ajñāna. Others however hold that since in the world-appearance we find in one aspect pure being and in another materiality etc., both Brahman and māyā are to be regarded as the cause, Brahman as the permanent causal matter, upādāna and māyā as the entity evolving in pariṇāma. Vācaspati Miśra thinks that Brahman is the permanent cause of the world-appearance through māyā as associated with jīva. Māyā is thus only a sahakāri or instrument as it were, by which the one Brahman appears in the eye of the jīva as the manifold world of appearance. Prakāśānanda holds however in his *Siddhānta Muktāvalī* that Brahman itself is pure and absolutely unaffected even as illusory appearance, and is not even the causal matter of the world-appearance. Everything that we see in the phenomenal world, the whole field of world-appearance, is the product of māyā, which is both the instrumental and the upādāna (causal matter) of the world-illusion. But whatever these divergences of view may be, it is clear that they do not in any way affect the principal Vedānta text that the only unchangeable cause is the Brahman, whereas all else, the effect-phenomena, have only a temporary existence as indefinable illusion. The word māyā was used in the Ṛg-Veda in the sense of supernatural power and wonderful skill, and the idea of an inherent mystery underlying it was gradually emphasized in the Atharva Veda, and it began to be used in the sense of magic or illusion. In the Bṛhadāraṇyaka, Praśna, and Svetāśvatara Upaniṣads the word means magic. It is not out of place here to mention that in the older Upaniṣads the word māyā occurs only once in the Bṛhadāraṇyaka and once only in the Praśna. In early Pāli Buddhist writings it occurs only in the sense of deception or deceitful conduct. Buddhaghoṣa uses it in the sense of magical power. In Nāgārjuna and the *Laṅkāvatāra* it has acquired the sense of illusion. In Śaṇkara the word māyā is used in the sense of illusion, both as a principle of creation as a śakti (power) or accessory cause, and as the phenomenal creation itself, as the illusion of world-appearance.

It may also be mentioned here that Gauḍapāda the teacher of Śaṇkara's teacher Govinda worked out a system with the help of the māyā doctrine. The Upaniṣads are permeated with the spirit of an earnest enquiry after absolute truth. They do not pay any attention towards explaining the world-appearance or enquiring into its relations with absolute truth. Gauḍapāda asserts clearly and probably for the first time among Hindu thinkers, that the world does not exist in reality, that it is māyā, and not reality. When the highest truth is realized māyā is not removed, for it is not a thing, but the whole world-illusion is dissolved into its own airy nothing never to recur again. It was Gauḍapāda who compared the world-appearance with dream appearances, and held that objects seen in the waking world are unreal, because they are capable of being seen like objects seen in a dream, which are false and unreal. The ātman says Gauḍapāda is at once the cognizer and the cognized, the world subsists in the ātman through māyā. As ātman alone is real and all duality an illusion, it necessarily follows that all experience is also illusory. Śaṇkara expounded this doctrine in his elaborate commentaries on the Upaniṣads and the Brahma-sūtra, but he seems to me to have done little more than making explicit the doctrine of māyā. Some of his followers however examined and thought over the concept of māyā and brought out in bold relief its character as the indefinable thereby substantially contributing to the development of the Vedānta philosophy.

Vedānta theory of Perception and Inference[1].

Pramāṇa is the means that leads to right knowledge. If memory is intended to be excluded from the definition then

[1] Dharmarājādhvarīndra and his son Rāmakṛṣṇa worked out a complete scheme of the theory of Vedantic perception and inference. This is in complete agreement with the general Vedānta metaphysics. The early Vedantists were more interested in

pramāṇa is to be defined as the means that leads to such right knowledge as has not already been acquired. Right knowledge (*pramā*) in Vedānta is the knowledge of an object which has not been found contradicted (*abādhitārthaviṣayajñānatva*). Except when specially expressed otherwise, pramā is generally considered as being excludent of memory and applies to previously unacquired (*anadhigata*) and uncontradicted knowledge. Objections are sometimes raised that when we are looking at a thing for a few minutes, the perception of the thing in all the successive moments after the first refers to the image of the thing acquired in the previous moments. To this the reply is that the Vedānta considers that so long as a different mental state does not arise, any mental state is not to be considered as momentary but as remaining ever the same. So long as we continue to perceive one thing there is no reason to suppose that there has been a series of mental states. So there is no question as to the knowledge of the succeeding moments being referred to the knowledge of the preceding moments, for so long as any mental state has any one thing for its object it is to be considered as having remained unchanged all through the series of moments. There is of course this difference between the same percept of a previous and a later moment following in succession, that fresh elements of time are being perceived as prior and later, though the content of the mental state so far as the object is concerned remains unchanged. This time element is perceived by the senses though the content of the mental state may remain undisturbed. When I see the same book for two seconds, my mental state representing the book is not changed every second, and hence there can be no *such supposition* that I am having separate mental states in succession each of which is a repetition of the previous one, for so long as the general content of the mental state remains the same there is no reason for supposing that there has been any change in the mental state. The mental state thus remains the same so long as the content is not changed, but though it remains the same it can note the change in the time elements as extraneous

demonstrating the illusory nature of the world of appearance, and did not work out a logical theory. It may be incidentally mentioned that in the theory of inference as worked out by Dharmarājādhvarīndra he was largely indebted to the Mīmāṃsā school of thought. In recognizing arthapatti, upamāna śabda and anupalabdhi also Dharmarājādhvarīndra accepted the Mīmāṃsā view. The Vedantins, previous to Dharmarājādhvarīndra, had also tacitly followed the Mīmāṃsā in these matters.

addition. All our uncontradicted knowledge of the objects of the external world should be regarded as right knowledge until the absolute is realized.

When the antaḥkaraṇa (mind) comes in contact with the external objects through the senses and becomes transformed as it were into their forms, it is said that the antaḥkaraṇa has been transformed into a state (*vṛtti*)[1]. As soon as the antaḥkaraṇa has assumed the shape or form of the object of its knowledge, the ignorance (*ajñāna*) with reference to that object is removed, and thereupon the steady light of the pure consciousness (*cit*) shows the object which was so long hidden by ignorance. The appearance or the perception of an object is thus the self-shining of the cit through a vṛtti of a form resembling an object of knowledge. This therefore pre-sup-poses that by the action of ajñāna, pure consciousness or being is in a state of diverse kinds of modifications. In spite of the cit underlying all this diversified objective world which is but the transformation of ignorance (ajñāna), the former cannot manifest itself by itself, for the creations being of ignorance they are but sustained by modifications of ignorance. The diversified objects of the world are but transformations of the principle of ajñāna which is neither real nor unreal. It is the nature of ajñāna that it veils its own creations. Thus on each of the objects created by the ajñāna by its creating (*vikṣepa*) capacity there is a veil by its veiling (*āvaraṇa*) capacity. But when any object comes in direct touch with antaḥkaraṇa through the senses the antaḥkaraṇa becomes transformed into the form of the object, and this leads to the removal of the veil on that particular ajñāna form—the object, and as the self-shining cit is shining through the particular ajñāna state, we have what is called the perception of the thing. Though there is in reality no such distinction as the inner and the outer yet the ajñāna has created such illusory distinctions as individual souls and the external world of objects the distinctions of time, space,

[1] Vedānta does not regard manas (mind) as a sense (indriya). The same antaḥkaraṇa, according to its diverse functions, is called manas, buddhi, ahaṃkāra, and citta. In its functions as doubt it is called manas, as originating definite cognitions it is called buddhi. As presenting the notion of an ego in consciousness ahaṃkāra, and as producing memory citta. These four represent the different modifications or states (vṛtti) of the same entity (which in itself is but a special kind of modification of ajñāna as antaḥkaraṇa).

etc. and veiled these forms. Perception leads to the temporary and the partial breaking of the veil over specific ajñāna forms so that there is a temporary union of the cit as underlying the subject and the object through the broken veil. Perception on the subjective side is thus defined as the union or undifferentiation (*abheda*) of the subjective consciousness with the objective consciousness comprehending the sensible objects through the specific mental states (*tattadindriyayogyaviṣayāva-cchinnacaitanyā-bhinnatvam tattadākāraviṣayāvacchinnajñānasya tattadaṃśe pratyakṣatvam*). This union in perception means that the objective has at that moment no separate existence from the subjective consciousness of the perceiver. The consciousness manifesting through the antaḥkaraṇa is called jīvasākṣi.

Inference (*anumāna*), according to Vedānta, is made by our notion of concomitance (*vyāptijñāna*) between two things, acting through specific past impressions (*saṃskāra*). Thus when I see smoke on a hill, my previous notion of the concomitance of smoke with fire becomes roused as a subconscious impression, and I infer that there is fire on the hill. My knowledge of the hill and the smoke is by direct perception. The notion of concomitance revived in the subconscious only establishes the connection between the smoke and the fire. The notion of concomitance is generated by the perception of two things together, when no case of the failure of concomitance is known (*vyabhicārājñāna*) regarding the subject. The notion of concomitance being altogether subjective, the Vedantist does not emphasize the necessity of perceiving the concomitance in a large number of cases (*bhūyodarśanam sakṛddarśanam veti viśeṣo nādaranīyaḥ*). Vedānta is not anxious to establish any material validity for the inference, but only subjective and formal validity. A single perception of concomitance may in certain cases generate the notion of the concomitance of one thing with another when no contradictory instance is known. It is immaterial with the Vedānta whether this concomitance is experienced in one case or in hundreds of cases. The method of agreement in presence is the only form of concomitance (*anvayavyāpti*) that the Vedānta allows. So the Vedānta discards all the other kinds of inference that Nyāya supported, viz. *anvayavyatireki* (by joining agreement in presence with agreement in absence), *kevalānvayi* (by universal agreement where no test could be applied of agreement in absence) and *kevalavyatireki* (by universal agreement in absence). Vedānta advocates three premisses, viz. (1) *pratijña* (the hill is fiery); (2) *hetu* (because it has smoke) and (3) *dṛṣṭānta* (as in the kitchen) instead of the five propositions that Nyāya maintained[1]. Since one case of concomitance is regarded by Vedānta as being sufficient for making an inference it holds that seeing the one case of appearance (silver in the conch-shell) to be false, we can infer that all things (except Brahman) are false (*Brah-mabhinnam sarvam mithyā Brahmabhinnatvāt yedevam tadevam yathā śuktirūpyam*). First premiss (*pratijñā*) all else excepting Brahman is false; second premiss (*hetu*) since all is different from Brahman; third premiss (*dṛṣṭānta*) whatever is so is so as the silver in the conch[2].

Ātman, Jīva, Īśvara, Ekajīvavāda and Dṛṣṭisṛṣṭivāda.

We have many times spoken of truth or reality as self-luminous (*svayaṃprakāśa*). But what does this mean? Vedānta defines it as that which is never the object of a knowing act but is yet immediate and direct with us (*avedyatve sati aparokṣavya-vahārayogyatvam*). Self-luminosity thus means the capacity of being ever present in all our acts of consciousness without in any way being an object of consciousness. Whenever anything is described as an object of consciousness, its character as constituting its knowability is a quality, which may or may not be present in it, or may be present at one time and absent at another. This makes it dependent on some other such entity which can produce it or manifest it. Pure consciousness differs from all its objects in this that it is never dependent on anything else for its manifestation, but manifests all other objects such as the jug, the cloth, etc. If consciousness should require another consciousness to manifest it, then that might again require another, and that another, and so on *ad infinitum* (*anavasthā*). If consciousness did not manifest itself at the time of the object-manifestation, then even on seeing or knowing a thing one might doubt if he had seen or known it. It is thus to be admitted that consciousness (*anubhūti*) manifests itself and thereby maintains the appearance of

[1] Vedānta would have either pratijñā, hetu and udāharaṇa, or udāharaṇa, upanaya and nigamana, and not all the five of Nyāya, viz. pratijñā, hetu, udāharaṇa, upanaya and nigamana.

[2] Vedantic notions of the pramāṇa of upamāna, arthāpatti, śabda and anupalabdhi, being similar to the mīmāṃsā view, do not require to be treated here separately.

all our world experience. This goes directly against the jñātatā theory of Kumārila that consciousness was not immediate but was only inferable from the manifesting quality (*jñātatā*) of objects when they are known in consciousness.

Now Vedānta says that this self-luminous pure consciousness is the same as the self. For it is only self which is not the object of any knowledge and is yet immediate and ever present in consciousness. No one doubts about his own self, because it is of itself manifested along with all states of knowledge. The self itself is the revealer of all objects of knowledge, but is never itself the object of knowledge, for what appears as the perceiving of self as object of knowledge is but association comprehended under the term ahaṃkāra (ego). The real self is identical with the pure manifesting unity of all consciousness. This real self called the ātman is not the same as the jīva or individual soul, which passes through the diverse experiences of worldly life. Īśvara also must be distinguished from this highest ātman or Brahman. We have already seen that many Vedāntists draw a distinction between māyā and avidyā. Māyā is that aspect of ajñāna by which only the best attributes are projected, whereas avidyā is that aspect by which impure qualities are projected. In the former aspect the functions are more of a creative, generative (*vikṣepa*) type, whereas in the latter veiling (*āvaraṇa*) characteristics are most prominent. The relation of the cit or pure intelligence, the highest self, with māyā and avidyā (also called ajñāna) was believed respectively to explain the phenomenal Īśvara and the phenomenal jīva or individual. This relation is conceived in two ways, namely as upādhi or pratibimba, and avaccheda. The conception of pratibimba or reflection is like the reflection of the sun in the water where the image, though it has the same brilliance as the sun, yet undergoes the effect of the impurity and movements of the water. The sun remains ever the same in its purity untouched by the impurities from which the image sun suffers. The sun may be the same but it may be reflected in different kinds of water and yield different kinds of images possessing different characteristics and changes which though unreal yet phenomenally have all the appearance of reality. The other conception of the relation is that when we speak of ākāśa (space) in the jug or of ākāśa in the room. The ākāśa in reality does not suffer any modification in being within the jug or within the room. In reality it is all-pervasive and is neither limited (*avachinna*) within the jug or the room, but is yet conceived as being limited by the jug or by the room. So long as the jug remains, the ākāśa limited within it will remain as separate from the ākāśa limited within the room.

Of the Vedantists who accept the reflection analogy the followers of Nṛsiṃhāśrama think that when the pure cit is reflected in the māyā, Īśvara is phenomenally produced, and when in the avidyā the individual or jīva. Sarvajñātmā however does not distinguish between the māyā and the avidyā, and thinks that when the cit is reflected in the avidyā in its total aspect as cause, we get Īśvara, and when reflected in the antaḥkaraṇa—a product of the avidyā—we have jīva or individual soul.

Jīva or individual means the self in association with the ego and other personal experiences, i.e. phenomenal self, which feels, suffers and is affected by world-experiences. In jīva also three stages are distinguished; thus when during deep sleep the antaḥkaraṇa is submerged, the self perceives merely the ajñāna and the jīva in this state is called prājña or ānandamaya. In the dream-state the self is in association with a subtle body and is called taijasa. In the awakened state the self as associated with a subtle and gross body is called viśva. So also the self in its pure state is called Brahman, when associated with māyā it is called Īśvara, when associated with the fine subtle element of matter as controlling them, it is called hiraṇyagarbha; when with the gross elements as the ruler or controller of them it is called virāṭ puruṣa.

The jīva in itself as limited by its avidyā is often spoken of as pāramarthika (real), when manifested through the sense and the ego in the waking states as vyavahārika (phenomenal), and when in the dream states as dream-self, prātibhāṣika (illusory).

Prakāśātmā and his followers think that since ajñāna is one there cannot be two separate reflections such as jīva and Īśvara; but it is better to admit that jīva is the image of Īśvara in the ajñāna. The totality of Brahma-cit in association with māyā is Īśvara, and this when again reflected through the ajñāna gives us the jīva. The manifestation of the jīva is in the antaḥkaraṇa as states of knowledge. The jīva thus in reality is Īśvara and apart from jīva and Īśvara there is no other separate existence of

Brahma-caitanya. Jīva being the image of Īśvara is thus dependent on him, but when the limitations of jīva are removed by right knowledge, the jīva is the same Brahman it always was.

Those who prefer to conceive the relation as being of the avaccheda type hold that reflection (pratibimba) is only possible of things which have colour, and therefore jīva is cit limited (avac-chinna) by the antaḥkaraṇa (mind). Īśvara is that which is beyond it; the diversity of antaḥkaraṇas accounts for the diversity of the jīvas. It is easy however to see that these discussions are not of much fruit from the point of view of philosophy in determining or comprehending the relation of Īśvara and jīva. In the Vedānta system Īśvara has but little importance, for he is but a phenomenal being; he may be better, purer, and much more powerful than we, but yet he is as much phenomenal as any of us. The highest truth is the self, the reality, the Brahman, and both jīva and Īśvara are but illusory impositions on it. Some Vedantists hold that there is but one jīva and one body, and that all the world as well as all the jīvas in it are merely his imaginings. These dream jīvas and the dream world will continue so long as that super-jīva continues to undergo his experiences; the world-appearance and all of us imaginary individuals, run our course and salvation is as much imaginary salvation as our world-experience is an imaginary experience of the imaginary jīvas. The cosmic jīva is alone the awakened jīva and all the rest are but his imaginings. This is known as the doctrine of ekajīva (one-soul).

The opposite of this doctrine is the theory held by some Vedantists that there are many individuals and the world-appearance has no permanent illusion for all people, but each person creates for himself his own illusion, and there is no objective datum which forms the common ground for the illusory perception of all people; just as when ten persons see in the darkness a rope and having the illusion of a snake there, run away, and agree in their individual perceptions that they have all seen the same snake, though each really had his own illusion and there was no snake at all. According to this view the illusory perception of each happens for him subjectively and has no corresponding objective phenomena as its ground. This must be distinguished from the normal Vedānta view which holds that objectively phenomena are also happening, but that these are illusory only in the sense that they will not last permanently and have thus only a temporary and relative existence in comparison with the truth or reality which is ever the same constant and unchangeable entity in all our perceptions and in all world-appearance. According to the other view phenomena are not objectively existent but are only subjectively imagined; so that the jug I see had no existence before I happened to have the perception that there was the jug; as soon as the jug illusion occurred to me I said that there was the jug, but it did not exist before. As soon as I had the perception there was the illusion, and there was no other reality apart from the illusion. It is therefore called the theory of dṛṣṭisṛṣṭivāda, i.e. the theory that the subjective perception is the creating of the objects and that there are no other objective phenomena apart from subjective perceptions. In the normal Vedānta view however the objects of the world are existent as phenomena by the sense-contact with which the subjective perceptions are created. The objective phenomena in themselves are of course but modifications of ajñāna, but still these phenomena of the ajñāna are there as the common ground for the experience of all. This therefore has an objective epistemology whereas the dṛṣṭisṛṣṭivāda has no proper epistemology, for the experiences of each person are determined by his own subjective avidyā and previous impressions as modifications of the avidyā. The dṛṣṭisṛṣṭivāda theory approaches nearest to the Vijñānavāda Buddhism, only with this difference that while Buddhism does not admit of any permanent being Vedānta admits the Brahman, the permanent unchangeable reality as the only truth, whereas the illusory and momentary perceptions are but impositions on it.

The mental and physical phenomena are alike in this, that both are modifications of ajñāna. It is indeed difficult to comprehend the nature of ajñāna, though its presence in consciousness can be perceived, and though by dialectic criticism all our most well-founded notions seem to vanish away and become self-contradictory and indefinable. Vedānta explains the reason of this difficulty as due to the fact that all these indefinable forms and names can only be experienced as modes of the real, the self-luminous. Our innate error which we continue from beginningless time consists in this, that the real in its full complete light is ever hidden from us, and the glimpse that we get of it is always through manifestations of forms and names; these phenomenal forms and names are undefinable, incomprehensible, and unknowable in themselves, but under certain conditions they are manifested by the self-luminous real, and at the time they are so manifested they seem to have a positive being which is undeniable. This positive being is only the highest being, the real which appears as the being of those forms and names, A lump of clay may be moulded into a plate or a cup, but the plate-form or the cup-form has no existence or being apart from the being of the clay; it is the being of the clay that is imposed on the diverse forms which also then seem to have being in themselves. Our illusion thus consists in mutually mis-attributing the characteristics of the unreal forms—the modes of ajñāna and the real being. As this illusion is the mode of all our experience and its very essence, it is indeed difficult for us to conceive of the Brahman as apart from the modes of ajñāna. Moreover such is the nature of ajñānas that they are knowable only by a false identification of them with the self-luminous Brahman or ātman. Being as such is the highest truth, the Brahman. The ajñāna states are not non-being in the sense of nothing of pure negation (*abhāva*), but in the sense that they are not being. Being that is the self-luminous illuminates non-being, the ajñāna, and this illumination means nothing more than a false identification of being with non-being. The forms of ajñāna if they are to be known must be associated with pure consciousness, and this association means an illusion, superimposition, and mutual misattribution. But apart from pure consciousness these cannot be manifested or known, for it is pure consciousness alone that is self-luminous. Thus when we try to know the ajñāna states in themselves as apart from the ātman we fall in a dilemma, for knowledge means illusory superimposition or illusion, and when it is not knowledge they evidently cannot be known. Thus apart from its being a factor in our illusory experience no other kind of its existence is known to us. If ajñāna had been a nonentity altogether it could never come at all, if it were a positive entity then it would never cease to be; the ajñāna thus is a mysterious category midway between being and non-being and indefinable in every way; and it is on account of this that it is called *tattvānyatvābhyām anirvācya* or undefinable and undeterminable either as real or unreal. It is real in the sense that it is a necessary postulate of our phenomenal experience and unreal in its own nature, for apart from its connection with consciousness it is incomprehensible and undefinable. Its forms even while they are manifested in consciousness are self-contradictory and incomprehensible as to their real nature or mutual relation, and comprehensible only so far as they are manifested in consciousness, but apart from these no rational conception of them can be formed. Thus it is impossible to say anything about the ajñāna (for no knowledge of it is possible) save so far as manifested in consciousness and depending on this the Dṛṣṭisṛṣṭivādins asserted that our experience was inexplicably produced under the influence of avidyā and that beyond that no objective common ground could be admitted. But though this has the general assent of Vedānta and is irrefutable in itself, still for the sake of explaining our common sense view (*pratikarmavyavasathā*) we may think that we have an objective world before us as the common field of experience. We can also imagine a scheme of things and operations by which the phenomenon of our experience may be interpreted in the light of the Vedānta metaphysics.

The subject can be conceived in three forms: firstly as the ātman, the one highest reality, secondly as jīva or the ātman as limited by its psychosis, when the psychosis is not differentiated from the ātman, but ātman is regarded as identical with the psychosis thus appearing as a living and knowing being, as *jīvasākṣi* or perceiving consciousness, or the aspect in which the jīva comprehends, knows, or experiences; thirdly the antaḥkaraṇa psychosis or mind which is an inner centre or bundle of avidyā manifestations, just as the outer world objects are exterior centres of avidyā phenomena or objective entities. The antaḥkaraṇa is not only the avidyā capable of supplying all forms to our present experiences, but it also contains all the tendencies and modes of past impressions of experience in this life or in past lives. The antaḥkaraṇa is always turning the various avidyā modes of it into the jīvasākṣi (jīva in its aspect as illuminating mental states), and these are also immediately manifested, made known, and transformed into experience. These avidyā states of the antaḥkaraṇa are called its vṛttis or states. The specific peculiarity of the vṛtti-ajñānas is this that only in these forms can they be superimposed upon pure consciousness, and thus be interpreted as states of consciousness and have their indefiniteness or cover removed. The forms of ajñāna remain as indefinite and hidden or veiled only so long as they do not come into relation to these vṛttis of antaḥkaraṇa, for the ajñāna can be destroyed by the cit only in the form of a vṛtti, while in all other forms the ajñāna veils the cit from manifestation. The removal of ajñāna-vṛttis of the antaḥkaraṇa or the manifestation of vṛtti-jñāna is nothing but this, that the antaḥkaraṇa states of avidyā are the only states of ajñāna which can be superimposed upon the self-luminous ātman (*adhyāsa*, false attribution). The objective world consists of the avidyā phenomena with the self as its background. Its objectivity consists in this that avidyā in this form cannot be superimposed on the self-luminous cit but exists only as veiling the cit. These avidyā phenomena may be regarded as many and diverse, but in all these forms they serve only to veil the cit and are beyond consciousness. It is only when they come in contact with the avidyā phenomena as antaḥkaraṇa states that they coalesce with the avidyā states and render themselves objects of consciousness or have their veil of āvaraṇa removed. It is thus assumed that in ordinary perceptions of objects such as jug, etc. the antaḥkaraṇa goes out of the man's body (*śarīramadhyāt*) and coming in touch with the jug becomes transformed into the same form, and as soon as this transformation takes place the cit which is always steadily shining illuminates the jug-form or the jug. The jug phenomena in the objective world could not be manifested (though these were taking place on the background of the same self-luminous Brahman or ātman as forms of the highest truth of my subjective consciousness) because the ajñāna phenomena in these forms serve to veil their illuminator, the self-luminous. It was only by coming into contact with these phenomena that the antaḥkaraṇa could be transformed into corresponding states and that the illumination dawned which at once revealed the antaḥkaraṇa states and the objects with which these states or vṛttis had coalesced. The consciousness manifested through the vṛttis alone has the power of removing the ajñāna veiling the cit. Of course there are no actual distinctions of inner or outer, or the cit within me and the cit without me. These are only of appearance and due to avidyā. And it is only from the point of view of appearance that we suppose that knowledge of objects can only dawn when the inner cit and the outer cit unite together through the antaḥkaraṇavṛtti, which makes the external objects translucent as it were by its own translucence, removes the ajñāna which was veiling the external self-luminous cit and reveals the object phenomena by the very union of the cit as reflected through it and the cit as underlying the object phenomena. The pratyakṣa-pramā or right knowledge by perception is the cit, the pure consciousness, reflected through the vṛtti and identical with the cit as the background of the object phenomena revealed by it. From the relative point of view we may thus distinguish three consciousnesses: (1) consciousness as the background of objective phenomena, (2) consciousness as the background of the jīva or pramātā, the individual, (3) consciousness reflected in the vṛtti of the antaḥkaraṇa; when these three unite perception is effected.

Pramā or right knowledge means in Vedānta the acquirement of such new knowledge as has not been contradicted by experience (*abādhita*). There is thus no absolute definition of truth. A knowledge acquired can be said to be true only so long as it is not contradicted. Thus the world appearance though it is very true now, may be rendered false, when this is contradicted by right knowledge of Brahman as the one reality. Thus the knowledge of the world appearance is true now, but not true absolutely. The only absolute truth is the pure consciousness which is never contradicted in any experience at any time. The truth of our world-knowledge is thus to be tested by finding out whether it will be contradicted at any stage of world experience or not. That which is not contradicted by later experience is to be regarded as true, for all world knowledge as a whole will be contradicted when Brahma-knowledge is realized.

The inner experiences of pleasure and pain also are generated by a false identification of antaḥkaraṇa transformations as pleasure or pain with the self, by virtue of which are generated the perceptions, "I am happy," or "I am sorry." In continuous perception of anything for a certain time as an object or as pleasure, etc. the mental state or vṛtti is said to last in the same way all the while so long as any other new form is not taken up by the antaḥkaraṇa for the acquirement of any new knowledge. In such cases when I infer that there is fire on the hill that I see, the hill is an object of perception, for the antaḥkaraṇa vṛtti is one with it, but that there is fire in it is a matter of inference, for the antaḥkaraṇa vṛtti cannot be in touch with the fire; so in the same experience there may be two modes of mental modification, as perception in seeing the hill, and as inference in inferring the fire in the hill. In cases of acquired perception, as when on seeing sandal wood I think that it is odoriferous sandal wood, it is pure perception so far as the sandal wood is concerned, it is inference or memory so far as I assert it to be odoriferous. Vedānta does not admit the existence of the relation called *samavāya* (inherence) or *jāti* (class notion); and so does not distinguish perception as a class as distinct from the other class called inference, and holds that both perception and inference are but different modes of the transformations of the antaḥkaraṇa reflecting the cit in the corresponding vṛttis. The perception is thus nothing but the cit manifestation in the antaḥkaraṇa vṛtti transformed into the form of an object with which it is in contact. Perception in its objective aspect is the identity of the cit underlying the object with the subject, and perception in the subjective aspect is regarded as the identity of the subjective cit with the objective cit. This identity of course means that through the vṛtti the same reality subsisting in the object and the subject is realized, whereas in inference the thing to be inferred, being away from contact with antaḥkaraṇa, has apparently a different reality from that manifested in the states of consciousness. Thus perception is regarded as the mental state representing the same identical reality in the object and the subject by antaḥkaraṇa contact, and it is held that the knowledge produced by words (e.g. this is the same Devadatta) referring identically to the same thing which is seen (e.g. when I see Devadatta before me another man says this is Devadatta, and the knowledge produced by "this is Devadatta" though a verbal (*śābda*) knowledge is to be regarded as perception, for the antaḥkaraṇa vṛtti is the same) is to be regarded as perception or pratyakṣa. The content of these words (this is Devadatta) being the same as the perception, and there being no new relationing knowledge as represented in the proposition "this is Devadatta" involving the unity of two terms "this" and "Devadatta" with a copula, but only the indication of one whole as Devadatta under visual perception already experienced, the knowledge proceeding from "this is Devadatta" is regarded as an example of nirvikalpa knowledge. So on the occasion of the rise of Brahma-consciousness when the preceptor instructs "thou art Brahman" the knowledge proceeding from the sentence is not savikalpa, for though grammatically there are two ideas and a copula, yet from the point of view of intrinsic significance (*tātparya*) one identical reality only is indicated. Vedānta does not distinguish nirvikalpa and savikalpa in visual perception, but only in śābda perception as in cases referred to above. In all such cases the condition for nirvikalpa is that the notion conveyed by the sentence should be one whole or one identical reality, whereas in savikalpa perception we have a combination of different ideas as in the sentence, "the king's man is coming" (*rājapuruṣa āgacchati*). Here no identical reality is signified, but what is signified is the combination of two or three different concepts[1].

It is not out of place to mention in this connection that Vedānta admits all the six pramāṇas of Kumārila and considers like Mīmāṃsā that all knowledge is self-valid (*svataḥ-pramāṇa*). But pramā has not the same meaning in Vedānta as in Mīmāṃsā. There as we remember pramā meant the knowledge which goaded one to practical action and as such all knowledge was pramā, until practical experience showed the course of action in accordance with which it was found to be contradicted. In Vedānta however there is no reference to action, but pramā means only uncontradicted cognition. To the definition of self-validity as given by Mīmāṃsā Vedānta adds another objective qualification, that such knowledge can have svataḥ-prāmāṇya as is not vitiated by the presence of any doṣa (cause of error, such as defect of senses or the like). Vedānta of course does not think like Nyāya that positive conditions (e.g. correspondence, etc.) are necessary for the validity of knowledge, nor does it divest knowledge of all qualifications like the Mīmāṃsists, for whom all knowledge is self-valid as such. It adopts a middle course and holds that absence of doṣa is a necessary condition for the self-validity of knowledge. It is clear that this is a compromise, for whenever an external condition has to be admitted, the knowledge cannot be regarded as self-valid, but Vedānta says that as it requires only a negative condition for the absence of doṣa, the objection does not apply to it, and it holds that if it depended on the presence of any positive condition for proving the validity of knowledge like the Nyāya, then only its theory of self-validity would have been damaged. But since it wants only a negative condition, no blame can be

[1] See *Vedāntaparibhāṣā* and *Śikhāmaṇi*.

attributed to its theory of self-validity. Vedānta was bound to follow this slippery middle course, for it could not say that the pure cit reflected in consciousness could require anything else for establishing its validity, nor could it say that all phenomenal forms of knowledge were also all valid, for then the world-appearance would come to be valid; so it held that knowledge could be regarded as valid only when there was no doṣa present; thus from the absolute point of view all world-knowledge was false and had no validity, because there was the avidyā-doṣa, and in the ordinary sphere also that knowledge was valid in which there was no doṣa. Validity (prāmāṇya) with Mīmāṃsā meant the capacity that knowledge has to goad us to practical action in accordance with it, but with Vedānta it meant correctness to facts and want of contradiction. The absence of doṣa being guaranteed there is nothing which can vitiate the correctness of knowledge[1].

Vedānta Theory of Illusion.

We have already seen that the Mīmāṃsists had asserted that all knowledge was true simply because it was knowledge (*yathārthāḥ sarve vivādaspadībhūtāḥ pratyayāḥ pratyayatvāt*). Even illusions were explained by them as being non-perception of the distinction between the thing perceived (e.g. the conch-shell), and the thing remembered (e.g. silver). But Vedānta objects to this, and asks how there can be non-distinction between a thing which is clearly perceived and a thing which is remembered? If it is said that it is merely a non-perception of the non-association (i.e. non-perception of the fact that this is not connected with silver), then also it cannot be, for then it is on either side mere negation, and negation with Mīmāṃsā is nothing but the bare presence of the locus of negation (e.g. negation of jug on the ground is nothing but the bare presence of the ground), or in other words non-perception of the non-association of "silver" and "this" means barely and merely the "silver" and "this." Even admitting for argument's sake that the distinction between two things or two ideas is not perceived, yet merely from such a negative aspect no one could be tempted to move forward to action (such as stooping down to pick up a piece of illusory silver). It is positive

[1] See *Vedāntaparibhāṣā*, *Śikhāmaṇi*, *Maṇiprabhā* and Citsukha on svataḥprāmāṇya.

conviction or perception that can lead a man to actual practical movement. If again it is said that it is the general and imperfect perception of a thing (which has not been properly differentiated and comprehended) before me, which by the memory of silver appears to be like true silver before me and this generates the movement for picking it up, then this also is objectionable. For the appearance of the similarity with real silver cannot lead us to behave with the thing before me as if it were real silver. Thus I may perceive that gavaya (wild ox) is similar to cow, but despite this similarity I am not tempted to behave with the gavaya as if it were a cow. Thus in whatever way the Mīmāṃsā position may be defined it fails[1]. Vedānta thinks that the illusion is not merely subjective, but that there is actually a phenomenon of illusion as there are phenomena of actual external objects; the difference in the two cases consists in this, that the illusion is generated by the doṣa or defect of the senses etc., whereas the phenomena of external objects are not due to such specific doṣas. The process of illusory perception in Vedānta may be described thus. First by the contact of the senses vitiated by doṣas a mental state as "thisness" with reference to the thing before me is generated; then in the thing as "this" and in the mental state of the form of that "this" the cit is reflected. Then the avidyā (nescience) associated with the cit is disturbed by the presence of the doṣa, and this disturbance along with the impression of silver remembered through similarity is transformed into the appearance of silver. There is thus an objective illusory silver appearance, as well as a similar transformation of the mental state generated by its contact with the illusory silver. These two transformations, the silver state of the mind and external phenomenal illusory silver state, are manifested by the perceiving consciousness (*sākṣicaitanya*). There are thus here two phenomenal transformations, one in the avidyā states forming the illusory objective silver phenomenon, and another in the antaḥkaraṇa-vṛtti or mind state. But in spite of there being two distinct and separate phenomena, their object being the same as the "this" in perception, we have one knowledge of illusion. The special feature of this theory of illusion is that an indefinable (*anirvacanīya-khyāti*) illusory silver is created in every case where an illusory perception of silver occurs. There are three orders of reality in Vedānta, namely the

[1] See *Vivaraṇa-prameya-saṃgraha* and *Nyāyamakaranda* on akhyāti refutation.

pāramārthika or absolute, *vyavahārika* or practical ordinary experience, and *prātibhāsika*, illusory. The first one represents the absolute truth; the other two are false impressions due to doṣa. The difference between vyavahārika and prātibhāsika is that the doṣa of the vyavahārika perception is neither discovered nor removed until salvation, whereas the doṣa of the prātibhāsika reality which occurs in many extraneous forms (such as defect of the senses, sleep, etc.) is perceived in the world of our ordinary experience, and thus the prātibhāsika experience lasts for a much shorter period than the vyavahārika. But just as the vyavahārika world is regarded as phenomenal modifications of the ajñāna, as apart from our subjective experience and even before it, so the illusion (e.g. of silver in the conch-shell) is also regarded as a modification of avidyā, an undefinable creation of the object of illusion, by the agency of the doṣa. Thus in the case of the illusion of silver in the conch-shell, indefinable silver is created by the doṣa in association with the senses, which is called the creation of an indefinable (*anirvacanīya*) silver of illusion. Here the cit underlying the conch-shell remains the same but the avidyā of antaḥkaraṇa suffers modifications (*pariṇāma*) on account of doṣa, and thus gives rise to the illusory creation. The illusory silver is thus *vivartta* (appearance) from the point of view of the cit and pariṇāma from the point of view of avidyā, for the difference between vivartta and pariṇāma is, that in the former the transformations have a different reality from the cause (cit is different from the appearance imposed on it), while in the latter case the transformations have the same reality as the transforming entity (appearance of silver has the same stuff as the avidyā whose transformations it is). But now a difficulty arises that if the illusory perception of silver is due to a coalescing of the cit underlying the antaḥkaraṇa-vṛtti as modified by doṣa and the object—cit as underlying the "this" before me (in the illusion of "this is silver"), then I ought to have the experience that "I am silver" like "I am happy" and not that "this is silver"; the answer is, that as the coalescing takes place in connection with my previous notion as "this," the form of the knowledge also is "this is silver," whereas in the notion "I am happy," the notion of happiness takes place in connection with a previous vṛtti of "I." Thus though the coalescing of the two "cits" is the same in both cases, yet in one case the knowledge takes the form of "I am," and in another as "this is" according as the previous impression is "I" or "this." In dreams also the dream perceptions are the same as the illusory perception of silver in the conch-shell. There the illusory creations are generated through the defects of sleep, and these creations are imposed upon the cit. The dream experiences cannot be regarded merely as memory-products, for the perception in dream is in the form that "I see that I ride in the air on chariots, etc." and not that "I remember the chariots." In the dream state all the senses are inactive, and therefore there is no separate objective cit there, but the whole dream experience with all characteristics of space, time, objects, etc. is imposed upon the cit. The objection that since the imposition is on the pure cit the imposition ought to last even in waking stages, and that the dream experiences ought to continue even in waking life, does not hold; for in the waking stages the antaḥkaraṇa is being constantly transformed into different states on the expiry of the defects of sleep, etc., which were causing the dream cognitions. This is called *nivṛtti* (negation) as distinguished from *bādha* (cessation). The illusory creation of dream experiences may still be there on the pure cit, but these cannot be experienced any longer, for there being no doṣa of sleep the antaḥkaraṇa is active and suffering modifications in accordance with the objects presented before us. This is what is called nivṛtti, for though the illusion is there I cannot experience it, whereas bādha or cessation occurs when the illusory creation ceases, as when on finding out the real nature of the conch-shell the illusion of silver ceases, and we feel that this is not silver, this was not and will not be silver. When the conch-shell is perceived as silver, the silver is felt as a reality, but this feeling of reality was not an illusory creation, though the silver was an objective illusory creation; for the reality in the śukti (conch-shell) is transferred and felt as belonging to the illusion of silver imposed upon it. Here we see that the illusion of silver has two different kinds of illusion comprehended in it. One is the creation of an indefinable silver (*anirvacanīya-rajatotpatti*) and the other is the attribution of the reality belonging to the conch-shell to the illusory silver imposed upon it, by which we feel at the time of the illusion that it is a reality. This is no doubt the *anyathākhyāti* form of illusion as advocated by Nyāya. Vedānta admits that when two things (e.g. red flower and crystal) are both present before my senses, and I attribute the quality of one to the other by illusion (e.g. the illusion that the crystal is red), then the illusion is of the form of anyathākhyāti; but if one of the things is not present before my senses and the other is, then the illusion is not of the anyathākhyāti type, but of the anirvacanīyakhyāti type. Vedānta could not avoid the former type of illusion, for it believed that all appearance of reality in the world-appearance was really derived from the reality of Brahman, which was self-luminous in all our experiences. The world appearance is an illusory creation, but the sense of reality that it carries with it is a misattribution (*anyathākhyāti*) of the characteristic of the Brahman to it, for Brahman alone is the true and the real, which manifests itself as the reality of all our illusory world-experience, just as it is the reality of śukti that gives to the appearance of silver its reality.

Vedānta Ethics and Vedānta Emancipation.

Vedānta says that when a duly qualified man takes to the study of Vedānta and is instructed by the preceptor—"Thou art that (Brahman)," he attains the emancipating knowledge, and the world-appearance becomes for him false and illusory. The qualifications necessary for the study of Vedānta are (1) that the person having studied all the Vedas with the proper accessories, such as grammar, lexicon etc. is in full possession of the knowledge of the Vedas, (2) that either in this life or in another, he must have performed only the obligatory Vedic duties (such as daily prayer, etc. called *nitya-karma*) and occasionally obligatory duty (such as the birth ceremony at the birth of a son, called *naimittika-karma*) and must have avoided all actions for the fulfilment of selfish desires (*kāmya-karmas*, such as the performance of sacrifices for going to Heaven) and all pro-hibited actions (e.g. murder, etc. *niṣiddha-karma*) in such a way that his mind is purged of all good and bad actions (no karma is generated by the *nitya* and *naimittika-karma*, and as he has not performed the *kāmya* and prohibited karmas, he has acquired no new karma). When he has thus properly purified his mind and is in possession of the four virtues or means of fitting the mind for Vedānta instruction (called *sādhana*) he can regard himself as properly qualified for the Vedānta instruction. These virtues are (1) knowledge of what is eternal and what is transient, (2) disinclination to enjoyments of this life and of the heavenly life after death, (3) extreme distaste for all enjoyments, and anxiety for attaining the means of right knowledge, (4) control over the senses by which these are restrained from everything but that which aids the attainment of right knowledge (*dama*), (*a*) having restrained them, the attainment of such power that these senses may not again be tempted towards worldly enjoyments (*uparati*), (*b*) power of bearing extremes of heat, cold, etc., (*c*) employment of mind towards the attainment of right knowledge, (*d*) faith in the instructor and Upaniṣads; (5) strong desire to attain salvation. A man possessing the above qualities should try to understand correctly the true purport of the Upaniṣads (called *śravaṇa*), and by arguments in favour of the purport of the Upaniṣads to strengthen his conviction as stated in the Upaniṣads (called *manana*) and then by *nididhyāsana* (meditation) which includes all the Yoga processes of concentration, try to realize the truth as one. Vedānta therefore in ethics covers the ground of Yoga; but while for Yoga emancipation proceeds from understanding the difference between puruṣa and prakṛti, with Vedānta salvation comes by the dawn of right knowledge that Brahman alone is the true reality, his own self[1]. Mīmāṃsā asserts that the Vedas do not declare the knowledge of one Brahman to be the supreme goal, but holds that all persons should act in accordance with the Vedic injunctions for the attainment of good and the removal of evil. But Vedānta holds that though the purport of the earlier Vedas is as Mīmāṃsā has it, yet this is meant only for ordinary people, whereas for the elect the goal is clearly as the Upaniṣads indicate it, namely the attainment of the highest knowledge. The performance of Vedic duties is intended only for ordinary men, but yet it was believed by many (e.g. Vācaspati Miśra and his followers) that due performance of Vedic duties helped a man to acquire a great keenness for the attainment of right knowledge; others believed (e.g. Prakāśātmā and his followers) that it served to bring about suitable opportunities by securing good preceptors, etc. and to remove many obstacles from the way so that it became easier for a person to attain the desired right knowledge.

In the acquirement of ordinary knowledge the ajñānas re-

[1] See *Vedāntasāra* and *Advaitabrahmasiddhi*.

moved are only smaller states of ajñāna, whereas when the Brahma-knowledge dawns the ajñāna as a whole is removed. Brahma-knowledge at the stage of its first rise is itself also a state of knowledge, but such is its special strength that when this knowledge once dawns, even the state of knowledge which at first reflects it (and which being a state is itself ajñāna modification) is destroyed by it. The state itself being destroyed, only the pure infinite and unlimited Brahman shines forth in its own true light. Thus it is said that just as fire riding on a piece of wood would burn the whole city and after that would burn the very same wood, so in the last state of mind the Brahma-knowledge would destroy all the illusory world-appearance and at last destroy even that final state[1].

The mukti stage is one in which the pure light of Brahman as the identity of pure intelligence, being and complete bliss shines forth in its unique glory, and all the rest vanishes as illusory nothing. As all being of the world-appearance is but limited manifestations of that one being, so all pleasures also are but limited manifestations of that supreme bliss, a taste of which we all can get in deep dreamless sleep. The being of Brahman however is not an abstraction from all existent beings as the *sattā* (being as class notion) of the naiyāyika, but the concrete, the real, which in its aspect as pure consciousness and pure bliss is always identical with itself. Being (*sat*) is pure bliss and pure consciousness. What becomes of the avidyā during mukti (emancipation) is as difficult for one to answer as the question, how the avidyā came forth and stayed during the world-appearance. It is best to remember that the category of the indefinite avidyā is indefinite as regards its origin, manifestation and destruction. Vedānta however believes that even when the true knowledge has once been attained, the body may last for a while, if the individual's previously ripened karmas demand it. Thus the emancipated person may walk about and behave like an ordinary sage, but yet he is emancipated and can no longer acquire any new karma. As soon as the fruits due to his ripe karmas are enjoyed and exhausted, the sage loses his body and there will never be any other birth for him, for the dawn of perfect knowledge has burnt up for him all budding karmas of beginningless previous lives, and he is no longer subject to any

[1] *Siddhāntaleśa.*

of the illusions subjective or objective which could make any knowledge, action, or feeling possible for him. Such a man is called *jīvanmukta*, i.e. emancipated while living. For him all world-appearance has ceased. He is the one light burning alone in himself where everything else has vanished for ever from the stage[1].

Vedānta and other Indian Systems.

Vedānta is distinctly antagonistic to Nyāya, and most of its powerful dialectic criticism is generally directed against it. Śaṅkara himself had begun it by showing contradictions and inconsistencies in many of the Nyāya conceptions, such as the theory of causation, conception of the atom, the relation of sama-vāya, the conception of jāti, etc[2]. His followers carried it to still greater lengths as is fully demonstrated by the labours of Śrīharṣa, Citsukha, Madhusūdana, etc. It was opposed to Mīmāṃsā so far as this admitted the Nyāya-Vaiśeṣika categories, but agreed with it generally as regards the pramāṇas of anumāna, upamiti, arthāpatti, śabda, and anupalabdhi. It also found a great supporter in Mīmāṃsā with its doctrine of the self-validity and self-manifesting power of knowledge. But it differed from Mīmāṃsā in the field of practical duties and entered into many elaborate discussions to prove that the duties of the Vedas referred only to ordinary men, whereas men of higher order had no Vedic duties to perform but were to rise above them and attain the highest knowledge, and that a man should perform the Vedic duties only so long as he was not fit for Vedānta instruction and studies.

With Sāṃkhya and Yoga the relation of Vedānta seems to be very close. We have already seen that Vedānta had accepted all the special means of self-purification, meditation, etc., that were advocated by Yoga. The main difference between Vedānta and Sāṃkhya was this that Sāṃkhya believed that the stuff of which the world consisted was a reality side by side with the puruṣas. In later times Vedānta had compromised so far with Sāṃkhya that it also sometimes described māyā as being made up of sattva, rajas, and tamas. Vedānta also held that according to these three characteristics were formed diverse modifications

[1] See *Pañcadaśī*.

[2] See Śaṇkara's refutation of Nyāya, *Śaṇkara-bhāṣya*, II. ii.

of the māyā. Thus Īśvara is believed to possess a mind of pure sattva alone. But sattva, rajas and tamas were accepted in Vedānta in the sense of tendencies and not as reals as Sāṃkhya held it. Moreover, in spite of all modifications that māyā was believed to pass through as the stuff of the world-appearance, it was indefinable and indefinite, and in its nature different from what we understand as positive or negative. It was an unsubstantial nothing, a magic entity which had its being only so long as it appeared. Prakṛti also was indefinable or rather undemonstrable as regards its own essential nature apart from its manifestation, but even then it was believed to be a combination of positive reals. It was undefinable because so long as the reals composing it did not combine, no demonstrable qualities belonged to it with which it could be defined. Māyā however was undemonstrable, indefinite, and indefinable in all forms; it was a separate category of the indefinite. Sāṃkhya believed in the personal individuality of souls, while for Vedānta there was only one soul or self, which appeared as many by virtue of the māyā transformations. There was an adhyāsa or illusion in Sāṃkhya as well as in Vedānta; but in the former the illusion was due to a mere non-distinction between prakṛti and puruṣa or mere misattribution of characters or identities, but in Vedānta there was not only misattribution, but a false and altogether indefinable creation. Causation with Sāṃkhya meant real transformation, but with Vedānta all transformation was mere appearance. Though there were so many differences, it is however easy to see that probably at the time of the origin of the two systems during the Upaniṣad period each was built up from very similar ideas which differed only in tendencies that gradually manifested themselves into the present divergences of the two systems. Though Śaṇkara laboured hard to prove that the Sāṃkhya view could not be found in the Upaniṣads, we can hardly be convinced by his interpretations and arguments. The more he argues, the more we are led to suspect that the Sāṃkhya thought had its origin in the Upaniṣads. Śaṅkara and his followers borrowed much of their dialectic form of criticism from the Buddhists. His Brahman was very much like the śūnya of Nāgārjuna. It is difficult indeed to distinguish between pure being and pure non-being as a category. The debts of Śaṅkara to the self-luminosity of the Vijñānavāda Buddhism can hardly be overestimated. There seems to be much truth in the accusations against Śaṅkara by Vijñāna Bhikṣu and others that he was a hidden Buddhist himself. I am led to think that Śaṅkara's philosophy is largely a compound of Vijñānavāda and Śūnyavāda Buddhism with Upaniṣad notion of the permanence of self superadded.

XI

THE ŚAṄKARA SCHOOL OF VEDĀNTA (*continued*)

THE treatment of the school of Śaṅkara Vedānta in the preceding chapter may be considered fairly sufficient for all ordinary purposes. But the reputation of this school of thought stands so high, and so many people are interested in it, that it was pointed out to me that it would be desirable to go into a little more detailed study of it. An additional justification for such a suggestion is to be found in the regrettable fact that, though numerous elementary and half-informed treatises have been published both in this country and in Europe, I do not know of any systematic study of the system in any of the modern languages of Europe or Asia which has been based on a first-hand study of the works of the great thinkers of this school who followed Śaṅkara and developed his system in a remarkably recondite manner. The comparatively small compass of this chapter in a History of Indian Philosophy cannot be expected to fulfil adequately such a demand; but still it may be expected that an attempt to bring out some of these materials by some amount of detailed study will be excusable, though it may seem slightly to disturb the general plan of this work.

The World-Appearance.

The Upaniṣads, called also the Vedānta, contain passages which indicate very different lines of thought, theistic, pantheistic, of self as the only ultimate reality, creationism, etc. The works of those commentators who wrote commentaries on the Upaniṣads before Śaṅkara and tried to interpret them on the supposition that there was one uniform, systematic, dogmatic philosophy in them are now practically all lost, and all that we can know of them is contained in the meagre references that are found in Śaṅkara's commentaries or the works of other, later, commentators. As an example I may refer to Bhartṛprapañca, who tried to give a realistic interpretation of the *Bṛhad-āraṇyaka Upaniṣad* by treating the world and souls as real emanations from God or Brahman[1].

[1] Fragments of Bhartṛprapañca from the writings of Śaṅkara and his commentator Ānandajñāna and from Sureśvara's *Vārttika* have been collected by Prof. Hiriyanna, Mysore, in a short paper read at the Third Oriental Conference in Madras in 1924, published in Madras in 1925.

Śaṅkara inherited from his predecessors the opinion that the Upaniṣads teach us one consistent systematic philosophy, but, being under the influence of Gauḍapāda, differed from them on the nature of this philosophy, which he propounded so elaborately in all his commentaries on the Upaniṣads and the *Brahma-sūtras*.

The main thesis of Śaṅkara, as has already been pointed out in the preceding chapter, consists of the view that Brahman alone is the ultimate reality, while everything else is false. He was interested in proving that this philosophy was preached in the Upaniṣads; but in the Upaniṣads there are many passages which are clearly of a theistic and dualistic purport, and no amount of linguistic trickery could convincingly show that these could yield a meaning which would support Śaṅkara's thesis. Śaṅkara therefore introduces the distinction of a common-sense view (*vyāvahārika*) and a philosophic view (*pāramārthika*), and explains the Upaniṣads on the supposition that, while there are some passages in them which describe things from a purely philosophic point of view, there are many others which speak of things only from a common-sense dualistic view of a real world, real souls and a real God as creator. Śaṅkara has applied this method of interpretation not only in his commentary on the Upaniṣads, but also in his commentary on the *Brahma-sūtra*. Judging by the *sūtras* alone, it does not seem to me that the *Brahma-sūtra* supports the philosophical doctrine of Śaṅkara, and there are some *sūtras* which Śaṅkara himself interpreted in a dualistic manner. He was never afraid of indulging in realistic interpretations; for he could easily get out of the difficulty by asserting that all the realistic conceptions found in the *sūtras* or in the Upaniṣad passages were merely an estimate of things from the common-sense point of view. Though on the basis of Śaṅkara's own statements, as well as those of his later commentators and other adherents of his school, there is hardly any room for doubt regarding the meaning and force of Śaṅkara's philosophy, yet at least one Indian scholar has sought to prove that Śaṅkara's philosophy was realistic[1]. That there was some amount of realism in Śaṅkara is proved by his own confession, when he criticizes the uncompromising Buddhistic idealists (*vijñāna-vādins*) or the so-called Buddhistic nihilists (*śūnya-vādins*).

[1] *Advaita Philosophy* by K. Vidyāratna, published by the Calcutta University Press, 1924.

I have already discussed in a general way in what sense according to the Vedānta, from the point of view of the Śaṅkara school of Vedānta as interpreted by his later adherents, the world is an illusion. But in the present section I propose to discuss Śaṅkara's own statements, as well as the statements of some of his important followers, on the subject of the nature of world-illusion. This is one of the most important points of the Śaṅkara school of philosophy and needs a discussion in some detail.

But before I take it up, I am naturally reminded of the views of Buddhist idealism and the so-called Buddhistic nihilism, and it seems desirable that Śaṅkara's doctrine of illusion should be treated in connection with the doctrines of illusion in those systems of Buddhistic thought which preceded Śaṅkara. Taking the *Śūnyavāda* theory of Nāgārjuna and Candrakīrti, we see that they also introduced the distinction between limited truth and absolute truth. Thus Nāgārjuna says in his *Mādhyamika-sūtras* that the Buddhas preach their philosophy on the basis of two kinds of truth, truth as veiled by ignorance and depending on common-sense presuppositions and judgments (*saṃvṛti-satya*) and truth as unqualified and ultimate (*paramārtha-satya*)[1]. The word *saṃvṛti* literally means "closed." Candrakīrti explains *saṃvṛti* as meaning "closing on all sides" and says that it is ignorance (*ajñāna*) which is denoted by the term *saṃvṛti* here, because it covers the truth of all things[2]. In this sense the whole of the world of our experience of causes and effects, which we perceive and of which we speak, presents an appearance which is hidden by ignorance. This world is not contradicted in our world-experience; but, as each and every entity of this world is produced by other things or entities, and they again by others, and as we cannot specify the nature of each one of them without referring to others which produced them or from which they originated, and tracing those again to other causes and

[1] *dve satye samupāśritya buddhānāṃ dharma-deśanā*
loka-saṃvṛti-satyaṃ ca satyaṃ ca paramārthataḥ.
Mādhyamika-sūtra, XXIV. 8, p. 492, B.B. edition.

[2] *Ajñānaṃ hi samantāt sarva-padārtha-tattvāvacchādanāt saṃvṛtir ity ucyate. Ibid.* Candrakīrti however gives two other meanings of the word *saṃvṛti*, which do not seem to be so closely connected with the etymology. In the first of the two meanings *saṃvṛti* means interdependent origination or *pratītya-samutpāda*, and in the second it means the conventional world of common-sense, which can be expressed or indicated by speech and language and which we are supposed to know and refer to in all our experiences involving the knower and the known—*saṃvṛtiḥ saṃketo loka-vyavahāraḥ, sa ca abhidhānābhidheya-jñāna-jñeyādilak-ṣaṇaḥ.*

so on, it is not possible to assert anything as to the nature or characteristic (*svabhāva*) of anything as it is. Things are known to us only as being the result of the combination of many entities or as product complexes. Nothing is produced of itself, and so the products are never by themselves self-existent, but exist only through the coming together of different entities. That which has any nature of its own cannot owe its origination to other complexes, and so there is nothing in our world-experience which has a nature of its own. The apparent reality of the world has therefore the mysterious veil of ignorance over it, and it is this veil of ignorance which is referred to by the term *loka-saṃvṛta*. This is spoken of also as *tathya-saṃvṛti* (real ignorance), as distinguished from *mithyā-saṃvṛti* (false ignorance), properly used of the ordinary illusions and hallucinations of magic, mirage reflections, etc.[1]1 Those appearances which are due to sense-defects or other causes and are therefore contradicted in experience are called *mithyā-saṃvṛta*, because their falsehood is discovered in experience. The falsehood of the world-appearances, however, can be realized only when their real nature (*paramārtha-rūpa*) as a succession of essenceless products of causal complexes is properly understood. The world holds good and remains uncontradicted and has all the appearance of reality in all our practical experiences, and it is only when it is understood that these phenomena have no nature of their own that they are considered false. All teachings in philosophy take for granted the world-appearances, subjective and objective, and try to give a rational analysis and estimate of them; and it is only through an experience of these world-phenomena and a rational understanding of them that one realizes their truth as being a mere flow of causes and effects devoid of essence. The appearance of the world as reality is therefore true only in a limited manner during the period when the veil of ignorance is not removed from our eyes; and this is signified by designating the truth (*satya*) of the world as only *loka-saṃvṛta*. This world-appearance is however relatively true when compared with the ordinary illusions of perception (when, e.g., a piece of rope is perceived as a snake, or when one sees a mirage in a desert).

But a question arises—if the world-appearance has no essence of its own, how is it that it appears to have one, or how is it that the world-phenomena appear at all? To such a question Nāgārjuna's answer is that the appearance of the world is like the

[1] *Bodhi-caryāvatāra-pañjikā*, p. 353, Biblotheca Indica Series, 1902.

appearance of mirages or dreams, which have no reality of their own, but still present an objective appearance of reality[1]. The world is not a mere nothing, like a lotus of the sky or the hare's horn, which are simply non-existent (*avidyamāna*). Thus there is not only the ultimate truth (*paramārtha*); there is also the relative truth of the phenomenal world (*loka-saṃvṛti-satya*); there are, further, the sense-illusions, hallucinations and the like which are contradicted in ordinary experience (*aloka-saṃvṛta or mithyā-saṃvṛta*), and also that which is merely non-existent, like the hare's horn. The error (*viparyāsa*) of world-appearance is considered as being of four kinds, viz. the consideration of the momentary as eternal, the consideration of the painful as being pleasurable, the consideration of the unholy as holy, and of that which has no soul as having a soul[2]. And this error is due to ignorance (*avidyā*). Candrakīrti quotes a passage from the *Ārya-dṛḍhāśaya-paripṛcchā*, in which it is said that, just as a man may see in a dream that he is spending the night with the wife of the king, and, suddenly realizing that he is discovered, tries to fly for fear of his life (thus perceiving the presence of a woman, where there is none), so we are always falling into the error of asserting that we have perceived the manifold world-appearance where there is none[3].

Such analogies of error naturally suggest the supposition that there must be some reality which is mistaken as some other thing; but, as has already been explained, the Buddhists emphasized the fact that, in dreams, the illusory appearances were no doubt objectively known as objective presentations of which we had previously become aware—experiences through which we pass, though there is no reality on which these appearances rest or are imposed. It was here that Śaṅkara differed. Thus, in his introduction to the commentary on the *Brahma-sūtra* he says that the essence of all illusory perception is that one thing is mistaken for another, that the qualities, characteristics or attributes of one thing are taken for the qualities, characteristics or attributes of another. Illusion is defined as the false appearance in some object of something

[1] *Mādhyamika-sūtra*, XXIII. 8.

[2] *Iha catvāro viparyāsā ucyante: tadyathā pratikṣaṇa-vināśini skandha-pañcake yo nityam iti grāhaḥ sa viparyāsaḥ . . . duḥkhātmake skandha-pañcake yaḥ sukham iti viparīto grāhaḥ so 'paro viparyāsaḥ,. . . śarīram aśuci-svabhāvaṃ tatra yo śucitvena grāhaḥ sa viparyāsaḥ,. . . pañca-skandhaṃ nirātmakaṃ tasmin ya ātma-grāhaḥ anātmani ātmābhiniveśaḥ sa viparyāsaḥ.* Candrakīrti's commentary on *ibid.* XXIII. 13. Compare it with the *Yoga-sūtra*, II. 5, Ānandāśrama Series.

[3] Candrakīrti's commentary on the *Mādhyamika-sūtra*, XXIII. 13.

experienced before, resembling a memory image. It is explained by some as being the false affirmation of the characteristics of one thing in regard to another; others explain it as an error due to the nonapprehension of the difference between that which is wrongly apprehended and the misapprehended object which the former is wrongly supposed to be; others think that, when one thing is misapprehended as another, the illusion consists in the fancying of the former entity as being endowed with strange characteristics (*viparīta-dharmatva*); but in all these different ways of analysis illusion fundamentally is nothing but the false appearance of one thing with the characteristics of another. So also it may be that a conch-shell appears as silver or that one moon appears as two moons[1]. Śaṅkara then suggests that, since the universal self (*pratyag-ātman*) is felt through our feeling of "I" and since it is immediate in all experience (*aparokṣa*), it is not absolutely unrelated and unindicated (*aviṣaya*) in experience, and consequently it is quite possible that the non-self (*anātman*) and its characteristics may be illusorily imposed upon the universal self. This illusory imposition of the non-self and its characteristics on the universal self is called nescience (*avidyā*).

In his commentary on Gauḍapāda's *Kārikā*, I. 17, Śaṅkara says that, when a piece of rope falsely appears as a snake, this is merely false imposition or appearance, not existence. The illusory appearance of the snake did not really bring into existence a snake, which later on became non-existent when right knowledge supervened. It was a mere illusion, and the rope-snake had no existence at all[2]. Śaṅkara in commenting on Gauḍapāda's *Kārikā* explains with approval Gauḍapāda's view that the world of common experience is as illusory as a dream. Dreams are false; for in a dream a man may have the experience of going to distant places, and yet, when he wakes up, he finds that he has been asleep for a few seconds only, and has not moved a foot from his bed. The dream experiences are therefore false, because they are contradicted by the waking experiences. But the waking experiences, being similar to dream experiences, are equally false. For both sets of experiences involve the duality of subject and object, and are therefore fundamentally more or less the same: so that, if one of them is

[1] Śaṅkara's *Adhyāsa-bhāṣya* on the *Brahma-sūtra*, Nirṇaya-Sāgara Press, Bombay, 1904.

[2] *Rajjvāṃ sarpa iva kalpitatvāt na tu sa vidyate . . . na hi rajjvāṃ bhrānti-buddhyā kalpitaḥ sarpo vidyamānaḥ san vivekato nivṛttaḥ; tathedaṃ prapañcākhyaṃ māyā-mātram.* Gauḍapāda's *Kārikā*, I. 17, Ānandāśrama Series.

false, the other also is false. The world-experience is like other well-known instances of illusion—the mirage, for example. Since it had no existence in the beginning, and will not have any existence in the end, neither can it have existence in the intervening period of appearance. The objection that our waking experiences fulfil practical purposes and have thus associated with them the pragmatic test of truth, which is absent in the case of dream experiences, is invalid; for the pragmatic tests of the waking experiences may well be contradicted by dream experiences; a man who goes to sleep after a sumptuous feast may well dream that he has been starving for days together. Both our inner world of mind and its experiences and the outer objective world are thus false creations[1]. But Gauḍapāda and Śaṅkara differ from the Śūnyavādin Buddhists in this—that they think that even false creations must have some basis in truth. If a rope appears as a snake, the false creation of the snake has some basis in the truth of the rope: there could not be false creations and false appearances without any firm basis of truth (*āspada*) underlying them[2]. Nāgārjuna, it will be remembered, tried to prove the falsity of all appearances on the ground of their being interdependent and not having anything which could be pointed out as their own nature. The dialectic being applicable to all appearances, there was nothing left which was not relative and interdependent, nothing which was self-evident by nature and which was intelligible by itself without reference to anything else. It is this interdependence and relativity of all appearances that was called "nothingness" or *śūnyátā* by Nāgārjuna. There was nothing which could be affirmed of anything independently by itself without reference to something else; nothing therefore could be conceived as having any essence by itself. All appearances were therefore only interdependent phantom creations; and it was precisely this interdependence that proved the essencelessness of their natures. There was no basis of truth anywhere. There was nothing which had any essence. But neither Śaṅkara nor Gauḍapāda appears to have tried to show why the inner world of thoughts, ideas, emotions, volitions and the outer world of objects should be considered as being illusory appearances. Their main point seems to consist in a dogmatic statement that all

[1] Śaṅkara's commentary on Gauḍapāda's *Kārikā*, II. 1–12.

[2] *Na hi nirāspadā rajju-sarpa-mṛgatṛṣṇikādayaḥ kvacit upalabhyante. Ibid.* I. 6.

appearances or experiences are false just as dream experiences are false. The imperfect analogy of waking experiences is made into an argument, and the entire manifold of appearances is declared to be false. But it is urged at the same time that these false creations must have some basis of truth; the changing appearances must have some unchanging basis on which they are imposed—and this basis is the self (*ātman*), or Brahman, which is the only thing that is permanent, unchanging and real. This self is the being of pure intelligence, which is one identical unit, negating all differences and duality (*viśuddha-vijñapti-mātra-sattā-dvaya-rūpeṇa*)[1]. Just as the false creation of "snake" appears in the case of the "rope," so all such judgments as "I am happy," "I am unhappy," "I am ignorant," "I am born," "I am old," "I am with a body," "I perceive," etc., are all merely false predications associated with the self; they are all false, changing and illusory predications, and it is only the self which remains permanent through all such judgments. The self is entirely different from all such predications; it is self-luminous and self-manifesting, shining independently by itself.

By applying the dialectic of mutual interdependence, *pratītyasamutpāda*, Nāgārjuna tried to prove that there was nothing which could be pointed out as the essence of anything as it is; but he did not explain how the appearances which were nothing more than phantom creations came to be what they were. How did the world-appearance of essenceless interdependent phenomena show itself? Śaṅkara did not try to prove with a keen logical dialectic that the world-appearance was false: he simply took it for granted, since the Upaniṣads proclaimed Brahman as the ultimate reality. But how did the world-appearance manifest itself? Śaṅkara does not seem to go deeply into this question and simply passes it over in asserting that this world-appearance is all due to ignorance (*avidyā*); it could not be spoken of as either existing or non-existing; it was merely illusory, like the conch-shell silver. But Padmapāda, who wrote the commentary known as *Pañca-pādikā* on the first four *sūtras* of Śaṅkara's commentary on the *Brahma-sūtras,* says that the precise meaning of the term "false conception" (*mithyā-jñāna*) in Śaṅkara's introduction to his commentary on the *Brahma-sūtras* is that there is a force or power or potency (*śakti*) of nescience which constitutes materiality (*jaḍātmikā avidyā-śaktiḥ*),

[1] Gauḍapāda's *Kārikā*, II. 17.

and that it is this potency which transforms itself into the stuff (*upādāna*) of the world-appearance[1]. It is well to remember in this connection that, according to Śaṅkara's philosophy, it is not only the objective world that constitutes the world of appearance, but also the subjective world of all experiences and predicates that may be associated with the self. Thus, when one says "I," this ego-hood is analysed as involving two parts—the one, pure intelligence or pure consciousness; and the other, the concept of subjectivity, which is illuminated, expressed or manifested by the underlying pure intelligence with which it is falsely associated. The concept of subjectivity stands here as materiality, or objectivity, which is made to float up by the power of pure intelligence, thus causing the judgment "I am" or "I am a man[2]." This *avidyā-śakti*, or power of *avidyā*, subsists in the pure self and, on the one hand, arrests the revelation of its true nature as Brahman, and, on the other hand, transforms itself into the various concepts associated with the psychological self of our ordinary experience[3]. The illusion consists in the association of the psychological qualities of thinking, feeling, willing, etc. with the transcendent or universal self (*pratyak-citi*). These psychological determinations are all mutually connected with one another. Thus, to be able to enjoy pleasures, one must first act; one can only act when one has attachments, antipathies and desires, and one can have attachments and desires only when one has experienced joys and sorrows—so these psychological determinations in a beginningless cycle are always naturally associated with the transcendent self-luminous self[4].

It should be clear from the foregoing discussion that, as Padmapāda or Prakāśātman explains, *ajñāna* or nescience is some kind of indefinable stuff out of the transformations of which subjective psychological experiences and the world of objects have come into being. This *ajñāna* is not the *ajñāna* of the Buddhists, i.e. a wrong notion or misconception, and this *adhyāsa*, or illusion, is not the *viparyaya* of Nāgārjuna; for here it is a positive power or

[1] *Pañca-pādikā*, p. 4, the Vizianagram Sanskrit Series, 1891.

[2] *asmat-pratyaye yo 'nidam-aṃśaś cid-eka-rasaḥ tasmiṃs tad-bala-nirbhāsitatayā lakṣaṇato yuṣmad-arthasya manuṣyābhimānasya sambhedaivāvabhāsaḥ sa eva adhyāsaḥ. Ibid.* p. 3.

[3] *ataḥ sā pratyak-citi brahma-svarūpāvabhāsaṃ pratibadhnāti ahaṃkārādy-atad-rūpa-pratibhāsa-nimittaṃ ca bhavati. Ibid.* p. 5.

[4] Prakāśātman's *Pañca-pādikā-vivaraṇa*, p. 10, the Vizianagram Sanskrit Series, 1892.

stuff. Thus Prakāśātman argues that all effects have at their back some cause, which forms their stuff or material; the world-appearance, being also an effect, must have some stuff out of which it has evolved or was made up; and *ajñāna*, lying in the transcendent self as a separate power, is such a material cause[1]. This *avidyā*-potency in the transcendent self is positive in its nature. This positive *ajñāna* is directly perceived in such immediate perceptions as "I do not know myself or others," and can also be inferred or comprehended by implication[2]. The fact that *ajñāna* or *avidyā* is spoken of as a power inherent in the transcendent self shows that it is dependent thereon; *avidyā* is not, however, a power, but a substance or entity which has certain powers by which it transforms itself into the cosmic appearances, subjective and objective; yet it is called a power, or *śakti*, because of its dependence (*para-tantratā*) on the transcendent self, and it is in consideration of the entire dependence of *avidyā* and its transformations on the self that the self is regarded as the material cause of all effects—the cosmic appearances of the world and the mind[3]. The self thus not only holds the *ajñāna* within it as a dependent function, but in spite of its self-luminosity it can be reacted upon by the *ajñāna* with its manifold powers in such a way that it can be veiled by this *ajñāna* and made the underlying basis of all world-appearances of *ajñāna*-transformations[4].

Appaya Dīkṣita, referring in his *Siddhānta-leśa* to the view of the writer of the *Padārtha-tattva*, summarizes the matter thus: Brahman and Māyā form together the material cause (*ubhayam upādānam*), and hence it is that in the world-appearance there are two distinct characteristics, "being" (*sattā*) from Brahman and materiality (*jāḍya*) from Māyā. Brahman is the cause, as the unchanging basis of the Māyā, which is the cause as being the

[1] *sarvaṃ ca kāryam sopādānaṃ bhāva-kāryatvāt ghaṭādivad ity anumānāt . . . tasmān mithyārtha-taj-jñānātmakaṃ mithyā-bhūtam adhyāsam upādāna-kāraṇa-sāpekṣam . . . mithyā-jñānam eva adhyāsopādānam. Pañca-pādikā-vivaraṇa*, pp.11–12.

[2] *Ibid.* p. 13.

[3] *śaktir ity ātma-para-tantratayā ātmanaḥ sarva-kāryopādānasya nirvoḍhṛtvam. Ibid.* p. 13. *Ātma-kāraṇatva-nirvoḍhṛtvād ātma-para-tantratvā ca śakti-matyām api śakti-śabda upacāritaḥ.* Akhaṇḍānanda Muni's *Tattva-dīpana*, p. 65, Chowkhambā Sanskrit Book Depot, Benares, 1902.

[4] *ataḥ svaprakāśe 'pi ātmani vicitra-śakti-bhāva-rūpāvidyā-prayuktam āvaraṇaṃ durapahṇavam.* Rāmānanda Sarasvati's *Vivaraṇopanyāsa*, p. 16, Chow-khambā Sanskrit Book Depot, Benares, 1901.

stuff that actually undergoes transformation[1]. Vācaspati Miśra also conceives Brahman, jointly with its *avidyā*, to be the material cause of the world (*avidyā-sahita-brahmopādānam*)[2]. In his adoration hymn at the beginning of his *Bhāmati* he describes Brahman as being in association with its companion, the indefinable *avidyā*, the unchanging cause of the entire objective universe[3]. Sarvajñātma Muni, however, does not wish to give *māyā* the same degree of co-operation in the production of the world-appearance as Brahman, and considers the latter to be the real material cause of the world through the instrumentality of Māyā; for Brahman, being absolutely changeless, cannot by itself be considered as cause, so that, when Brahman is spoken of as cause, this can only be in a remote and modified sense (*upalakṣaṇa*), through the instrumentality of *māyā*[4]. The author of the *Siddhānta-muktāvalī* is referred to by Appaya Dīkṣita as holding that it is the *māyā* and *māyā* alone that forms the stuff of the world-appearance; and that Brahman is not in any way the material cause of the universe, but that it is only the basis of the subsistence of *māyā* and is only from that point of view spoken of as being the material cause[5].

It is clear that the above differences of view regarding the nature of the relation between *māyā* and the self or Brahman in the production of the world-appearance are mere scholastic disputes over words or modes of expression, and have but little philosophical significance. As has already been said, these questions do not seem to have arisen in Śaṅkara's mind. He did not think it worth while to explain anything definitely regarding the nature of *avidyā* and its relation with Brahman, and the part that it played in supplying the material stuff of the universe. The world was an illusion, and Brahman was the basis of truth on which these illusions appeared; for even illusions required something on which they could appear. He never faced squarely the difficulties that are naturally connected with the theory, and was not therefore concerned to explain the definite relation of *māyā* to Brahman in connection with the production of the phantom show of the universe. The natural objection against such views is that the term

[1] *Siddhānta-leśa*, p. 12, V.S. Series, 1890.

[2] *Bhāmatī* on Śaṅkara's *Bhāṣya*, I. I. 2, Nirṇaya-Sāgara Press, 1904.

[3] *Anirvācyāvidyā-dvitaya-sacivasya prabhavato vivartā yasyaite viyad-anila-tejob-avanayaḥ, ibid.* p. 1.

[4] *Saṃkṣepa-śārīraka*, I. 333, 334, Bhāū Śāstrī's edition.

[5] *Siddhānta-leśa*, p. 13, V.S. Series, 1890.

avidyā (formed by compounding the negative particle *a* and *vidyā* "knowledge") may mean either absence of knowledge (*vidyā-bhāvaḥ*) or false knowledge (*mithyā-jñānam*); and in neither of these meanings can it be supposed to behave as the material cause or substance-stuff of anything; for a false knowledge cannot be a substance out of which other things are made[1]. The answer given by Ānandabodha Bhaṭṭāraka to such an objection is that this *avidyā* is not a psychological ignorance, but a special technical category, which is beginningless and indefinable (*anādy-anirvācyāvidyāśra yaṇāt*). The acceptance of such a category is a hypothesis which one is justified in holding as valid, since it explains the facts. Effects must have some cause behind them, and a mere instrumental cause cannot explain the origination of the substratum of the effect; again, effects which are not true cannot have for their material cause (*upādāna-kāraṇa*) that which is true, nor can they have for their material cause that which is absolutely non-existent. So, since the material cause of the world can neither be true nor be anything which is absolutely non-existent, the hypothesis is naturally forced upon the Vedāntists that the material cause of this false world-appearance is an entity which is neither existent nor non-existent[2]. Ānandabodha in his *Pramāṇa-mālā* quotes approvingly from the *Brahma-tattva-samīkṣā* of Vācaspati to show that *avidyā* is called *avidyā* or nescience because it is a hypothetic category which is neither "is" nor "is not," and is therefore unintelligible; *avidyā* signifies particularly the unintelligibility of this category[3]. Ānandabodha points out that the acceptance of *avidyā* is merely the logical consequence of indicating some possible cause of the world-appearance—considering the nature of the world-appearance as it is, its cause can only be something which neither is nor is not; but what we understand by such a category, we cannot say; it is plainly unintelligible; the logical requirements of such a category merely indicate that that which is the material cause of this false world-appearance cannot be regarded either as existing or as non-existing; but this does not

[1] *avidyā hi vidyābhavo mithyā-jñānaṃ vā na cobhayaṃ kasya cit samavāyi-kāraṇam adravyatvāt.* Ānandabodha's *Nyāya-makaranda*, p. 122, Chowkhambā Sanskrit Book Depot, Benares, 1901.

[2] *Ibid.* pp. 122–124.

[3] *sad-asad-ubhayānubhayādi-prakāraiḥ anirvacanīyatvam eva hy avidyānām avidyātvam. Brahma-tattva-samīkṣā as quoted in Pramāṇa-mālā,* p. 10, Chowkhambā Sanskrit Book Depot, Benares, 1907.

make this concept either intelligible or consistent[1]. The concept of *avidyā* is thus plainly unintelligible and inconsistent.

Thought and its Object in Buddhism and in Vedānta.

The Vedānta takes a twofold view of things; the first view refers to ultimate reality and the second to appearance. This ultimate reality is pure intelligence, as identical with pure bliss and pure being. This is called ultimately real in the sense that it is regarded as changeless. By pure intelligence the Vedānta does not mean the ordinary cognitional states; for these have a subjective and an objective content which are extraneous to them. This pure intelligence is pure immediacy, identical with the fact of revelation found in all our conscious states. Our apprehensions of objects are in some sense events involving both a subjective and an objective content; but their special feature in every case is a revelatory inwardness or immediacy which is non-temporal and changeless. The fact that we see, hear, feel, touch, think, remember is equivalent to saying that there are various kinds of cognizings. But what is the nature of this cognizing? Is it an act or a fact? When I see a blue colour, there is a blue object, there is a peculiar revelation of an appearance as blue and a revelation of the "I" as perceiver. The revelation is such that it is both a revelation of a certain character as blue and of a certain thing called the blue object. When a revelation occurs in perception, it is one and it reveals both the object and its appearance in a certain character as blue. The revelation is not the product of a certain relation which happens to subsist at any time between the character-appearance and the object; for both the character-appearance as blue and the object are given in revelation. The revelation is self-evident and stands unique by itself. Whether I see, or hear, or feel, or change, the fact remains that there is some sort of an awareness which does not change. Awareness is ever present by itself and does not undergo the changes that its contents undergo. I may remember that I had seen a blue object five minutes previously; but, when I do this, what I perceive is the image of a blue object, with certain temporal and spatial relations, which arises or

[1] *Vailakṣaṇya-vāco-yuktir hi pratiyogi-nirūpaṇād yauktikatva-prakaṭanaphalā na tv evaṃ-rūpatāyāḥ sāmañjasya-sampādanāya ity avocāma. Pramāṇa-mālā*, p. 10.

becomes revealed; but the revelation itself cannot be revealed again. I may be conscious, but I cannot be conscious of consciousness. For consciousness as such, though ever present in its immediacy, cannot become an object of any other consciousness. There cannot be any such thing as the awareness of an awareness or the awareness of the awareness of an awareness, though we may multiply such phrases in language at our pleasure. When I remember that I have been to Trinity College this morning, that only means that I have an image of the way across the commons, through Church Street and Trinity Street; my movements through them are temporally pushed backward, but all this is a revelation as image at the present moment and not a revelation of a past revelation. I cannot say that this present image in any way reveals that particular image as the object of the present revelation. But the former revelation could not be held to be distinct from the present one; for distinction is always based on content and not on revelation. Revelation as such is identical and, since this is so, one revelation cannot be the object of another. It is incorrect to say that "*A* is *A*" means that one *A* becomes itself over again. It is owing to the limitations of grammatical terminology that identity is thus described. Identity thus understood is different from what we understand by identity as a relation. Identity understood as a relation presupposes some difference or otherness and thus is not self-contained. And it is because it is not self-contained that it can be called a relation. When it is said that *A* is identical with *A*, it means that on all the various occasions or contents in which *A* appeared it always signified the same thing, or that it had the same shape or that it was the same first letter of the English alphabet. Identity in this sense is a function of thought not existing by itself, but in relation to a sense of opponency or otherness. But revelation has no otherness in it; it is absolutely ubiquitous and homogeneous. But the identity of revelation of which we are speaking does not mean that the revelation signifies the same thing amidst a diversity of contents: it is simply the one essence identical in itself and devoid of any numerical or other kinds of difference. It is absolutely free from "now" and "then," "here" and "there," "such" or "not such" and "this" or "that." Consciousness of the self-shining self taken in this way cannot be regarded as the relation of an appearance to an object, but it is the fact of the revelation or the entity of the self. If we conceive of revelation in this way, it is an error to make any distinction in revelation as the revelation of the past or the revelation of the present moment. For moments are revealed as objects are revealed; they do not constitute revelation or form any part of it. This revelation is identical with the self-shining self to which everything else has to be related in order to be known.

"Is cognizing an act or a fact?" Before this can be answered the point to be made clear is what is meant by cognizing. If we ignore the aspect of revelation and speak of mental states which can be looked at from the point of view of temporal or qualitative change of character, we must speak of them as acts or events. If we look at any mental state as possessing certain characters and relations to its objects, we have to speak of these aspects. But, if we look at cognizing from the point of view of its ultimate truth and reality as revelation, we cannot call it either an act or a fact; for, as revelation, it is unique and unchangeable in itself. All relations and characters are revealed in it, it is self-evident and is at once in and beyond them all. Whether we dream or wake, whether we experience an illusion or a truth, revelation is always there. When we look at our mental states, we find that they are always changing, but this is so only with reference to the contents. Apart from this there is a continuity in our conscious life. By this continuity the Vedānta apprehends not any sort of coherence in our ideas, but the fact of the permanence of revelation. It may be asked what remains of revelation, if the mental states are taken away. This question is not admissible; for the mental states do not form part of revelation; they are rendered conscious by coming into relation with revelation. This category is the ultimate reality. It is not self or subject in the sense in which self or ego is ordinarily understood. For what is ordinarily understood as the ego or the "I" is as much a content of the perception of the moment as any other objective content. It is not impossible that any particular objective content may be revealed at any time without the corresponding "I perceive" being explicitly revealed at the same time. The notion of ego or "I" does not refer to an everlasting abiding independent self or person; for this notion is as changing as any other objective content. The "I" has no definite real content as referring to an existing entity, but is only a particular mode of mind which is often associated, as a relatively abiding content, with other changing contents of the mind. As such, it is as changeable as is any other object. "I know this" only means that there is a revelation which at one sweep reveals both the "this" and the "I." So far as the revelation appears as revealing the "this" and the "I," it is manifested in a subjective mental state having a particular conscious centre different from other similar centres. But, since revelation cannot in reality be individuated, all that we may say about "I" or "mine," "thou" or "thine," falls outside it. They are all contents, having some indefinite existence of their own and revealed by this principle of revelation under certain conditions. This principle of revelation thus has a reality in quite a different sense from that which is used to designate the existence of any other object. All other objects are dependent upon this principle of revelation for their manifestation, and their nature or essence, out of connection with it, cannot be defined or described. They are not self-evident, but are only expressed by coming into some sort of relation with this principle. We have already seen that this principle cannot be either subjective or objective. For all considerations of subject or object fall outside it and do not in any way qualify it, but are only revealed by it. There are thus two principles, the principle of revelation and all that which is revealed by it. The principle of revelation is one; for there is nothing else like it; it alone is real in the highest and truest sense. It is absolute in the sense that there is no growth, decay, evolution or change in it, and it is perfectly complete in itself. It is infinite in the sense that no finitude can form part of it, though through it all finitude is being constantly revealed. It is all-pervading in the sense that no spatial or temporal limits can be said to affect it in any way, though all these are being constantly revealed by it. It is neither in my head nor in my body nor in the space before me; but yet there is nowhere that it is not. It has sometimes been designated as the "Self" or *ātman*, but only in the sense of denoting its nature as the supreme essence and transcendent reality of all—the Brahman.

Apart from this principle of revelation, all else is constituted of a substanceless indefinable stuff called *māyā.* In some schools of Śaṅkara Vedānta it is said that all is pure and simple illusion, that things exist only when they are perceived and dissolve into nothingness as soon as we cease to perceive them; this school has been designated the *Dṛṣṭi-sṛṣṭi* school, a doctrine which has been briefly explained in the tenth chapter of the present work[1]. One of the most important texts of this school is the *Siddhānta-muktāvalī* by Prakāśānanda[2]. Prakāśānanda seems to have taken his inspiration from the *Yoga-vāsiṣṭha*, and he denied the existence of things when they are not perceived (*ajñāta-sattvānabhyupagama*). He tried to show that there were no grounds for holding that external objects existed even when they were not perceived or that external objects had a reality independent of their perceptions. Examining the capacity of perception as a proof to establish this difference between perception and its object, he argued that, since the difference between the awareness and its object was a quality of the awareness, the awareness itself was not competent to grasp this quality in the object, as it was one of the constituents of the complex quality involving a difference of the awareness and its object; to assert the contrary would be a fallacy of self-dependence (*ātmāśrayatva*). If the apprehended difference is a complex, such as "difference-between-awareness-and-its-object," and if this complex is a quality which is apprehended as existing in the object, it has to be assumed that, in order that the nature of awareness may be realized, vindicated or established, it must depend upon itself involved as a constituent in the complex "difference-between-awareness-and-its-object" directly and immediately—which comes to the same thing as saying that awareness becomes aware of itself by being aware of itself; this is impossible and is called the logical fallacy of self-

[1] *A History of Indian Philosophy*, vol. 1. pp. 477–478, by S. N. Dasgupta, published by the Cambridge University Press, 1922.

[2] Prakāśānanda refers to the arguments of Prakāśātman's (A.D. 1200) *Pañca-pādikā-vivaraṇa* and Sarvajñātma Muni's (A.D. 900) *Saṃkṣepa-śārīraka* and refers approvingly to Sureśvara, the author of the *Naiṣkarmya-siddhi*. Appaya Dīkṣita (A.D. 1620) refers to Prakāśānanda in his *Siddhānta-leśa* (pp. 13, 72). Nānā Dīkṣita, a follower of the school of Prakāśānanda and author of the *Siddhānta-dīpikā*, in a commentary on the *Siddhānta-muktāvalī*, gives a list of Vedānta teachers. In this list he mentions the names of Prakāśānubhavānanda, Nṛsiṃha and Rāghavendra Yati. Venis thinks (see *The Pandit*, 1890, pp. 487–490) that Prakāśānubhava is the same as Prakāśātman and Nṛsiṃha the same as Nṛsiṃhāśrama Muni, who is said to have converted Appaya Dīkṣita to Śaṅkara Vedānta, and thinks that Prakāśānanda lived in the last quarter of the sixteenth century, being wedged in between Nṛsiṃha and Appaya. Though it would be difficult to settle his time so precisely and definitely, yet it would not be wrong to suppose that he lived some time towards the latter half of the sixteenth centurv. Prakāśānanda's doctrine of *Dṛṣṭi-sṛṣṭi* is apparently unknown to the earlier Vedantic works and even the *Vedānta-paribhāṣā*, a work of the early sixteenth century, does not seem to be aware of him, and it appears that the earliest mention of his name can be traced only to Appaya, who lived in the sixteenth and the seventeenth centuries. Prakāśānanda may thus be believed to have lived in the latter half of the sixteenth century.

dependence[1]. If it is held that the complex quality ("difference-of-awareness-from-the-object") is directly perceived in the object through the senses, then it has to be assumed that the said complex quality existed in the object even before the production of the awareness, and this would involve the impossible supposition that the complex quality of which the awareness was a constituent was already present even before such an awareness had already come into being. If perception or direct awareness cannot be said to prove the difference between the awareness and its object, there can be no inference which may be supposed to do it. For such an inference has to take form thus—"the object is different from its own awareness, because it is associated with entirely different kinds of qualities or characteristics[2]." But how could it be known that the object has qualities of an entirely different character from its awareness, since a difference between an awareness and its object was contested and could not be proved by perception or any other means? Prakāśānanda further says that the argument by implication (*arthāpatti*), that awareness involves the acceptance of something different from the awareness of which the awareness is affirmed, because there cannot be any knowledge without a corresponding object, is invalid. In proving the invalidity of the supposition that knowledge necessarily implies an object, Prakāśānanda raises the question whether such an implication of an object as conditioning knowledge refers to the production (*utpatti*) of knowledge, its persistence (*sthiti*) or its secondary cognition. As regards the first alternative Prakāśānanda says that according to the Vedānta consciousness is ever-existent and is never a product; and, even if it is regarded as a product, the process of cognition can itself be regarded as a sufficient cause for its production. It can by no means be urged that the presence of an external object is in all cases necessary for the production of knowledge; for, though it is arguable that in perception an object is necessary, no one will suggest that an external object is to be considered necessary in the production of inferential knowledge—a fact which shows that the presence of an external object is not indispensable for the production of knowledge as such. As regards the persistence of knowledge it is said

[1] *Siddhānta-muktāvalī*, as printed in the Pandit, 1889, pp. 247–249.

[2] *vimato viṣayaḥ sva-viṣaya-jñānād bhidyate tad-viruddha-dharmāśrayatvāt. Ibid.* p. 252.

that awareness has not the object that it knows for its locus or substance (*āśraya*), in such a way that the absence of the object, as apart from the awareness, would make it impossible for the awareness to persist; and, if knowledge is supposed to be persisting in anything, that something would not be a cognized object, but the cognizer itself—as in the Nyāya view, where knowledge is regarded as an attribute of the self and the self is then regarded as the substance or locus (*āśraya*) of knowledge. Since again cognition and its object do not exist in the same space or in the same time (this is proved by the possibility of our knowing a past or a future object), there cannot be any such concomitance between the two that it would be right for any one to infer the external presence of an object because of there being a subjective cognition or awareness. So he argues that there is no proof that cognition and cognized objects are different.

In the above account of Prakāśānanda's views it is clear that he does not attempt to give any positive proof in support of his thesis that the world-appearance and all objects contained in it have no existence while they are not perceived or that the being of all objects cognized is their *percipi*. He only tries to show that it cannot be logically established that awareness of blue and blue are two different objects; or, in other words, that it cannot be proved that the cognized object is different from its cognition. It could not legitimately be held that awareness (*pratīti*) was different from its object (*pratyetavya*). The whole universe, as we perceive it, is nothing but cognition without there being any object corresponding to it. As dreams are nothing but mere awareness, without there being any real objects behind them which manifest themselves in different ways of awareness and their objects, so also is the world of awaking consciousness[1]. The world has thus no independent substratum, but is mere cognition or mere awareness (*vijñāna-mātra* or *bhāva-mātra*).

This scheme of Vedānta philosophy is surprisingly similar to the idealism of Vasubandhu (A.D. 280–360), as taught in his *Viṃśatikā* with a short commentary of his own and in his *Triṃśikā* with a commentary by Sthiramati[2]. According to this idealism

[1] *pratyetavya-pratītyoś ca bhedaḥ prāmāṇikaḥ kutaḥ*
pratīti-mātram evaitad bhāti viśvaṃ carācaram
jñāna-jñeya-prabhedena yathā svāpnaṃ pratīyate
vijñāna-mātram evaitat tathā jāgrac carācaram.
Siddhānta-muktāvalī, p. 258.

[2] *Vijñapti-mātratā-siddhi*, containing two treatises, *Viṃśatikā* and *Triṃśikā*, Paris, 1925.

(*vijñāna-vāda*) of Vasubandhu all appearances are but transformations of the principle of consciousness by its inherent movement, and none of our cognitions are produced by any external objects which to us seem to be existing outside of us and generating our ideas. Just as in dreams one experiences different objects at different places and countries without there being any objective existence of them, or as in dreams many people may come together and perform various actions, so what seems to be a real world of facts and external objects may well be explained as a mere creation of the principle of intelligence without any objective basis at all. All that we know as subjective or objective is mere ideation (*vijñapti*) and there is no substantive reality, or entity corresponding to it; but that does not mean that pure non-conceptual (*anabhilapyenātmanā*) thought, which the saints realize, is also false[1]. It is possible that the awareness of anything may become the object of a further awareness, and that of another; but in all such cases where the awarenesses are significant (*arthavatī*) there is no entity or reality represented by them; this, however, should not be interpreted as a denial of the principle of intelligence or pure knowledge as such. Vasubandhu then undertakes to show that the perceptual evidence of the existence of the objective world cannot be trusted. He says that, taking visual perception as an example, we may ask ourselves if the objects of the visual perception are one as a whole or many as atoms. They cannot be mere wholes, since wholes would imply parts; they cannot be of the nature of atoms, since such atoms are not separately perceived; they cannot be of the nature of combinations of atoms, since the existence of atoms cannot be proved[2]. For, if six atoms combine from six sides, that implies that the atoms have parts; if however six atoms combine with one another at one identical point, that would mean that the combined group would not have a size larger than that of one atom and would therefore be invisible. Again, if the objects of awareness and perception were only wholes, then succession and sequence would be inexplicable, and our perception of separate and distinct things would remain unaccountable. So they have

It seems probable that Vasubandhu flourished in A.D. 280–360 rather than in A.D. 420–500 as held by me in the first volume of the present work. See B. Bhattacharya's foreword to the *Tattva-saṃgraha*.

[1] *yo bālair dhārmāṇāṃ svabhāvo grāhya-grāhakādiḥ parikalpitaḥ tena kalpitenātmanā teṣāṃ nairātmyaṃ na tv anabhilāpyenātmanā yo buddhānāṃ viṣaya iti.* Commentary on *Viṃśatikā*, p. 6.

[2] *Nāpi te saṃhatā viṣayī-bhavanti, yasmāt paramāṇur ekaṃ dravyaṃ na sidhyati. Ibid.* p. 7.

no real objective existence, though perception leads us to believe that they have. People are dreaming of the world of objects in the sleep of the subconscious habit of false imaginative construction (*vitatha-vikalpābhyāsa-vāsanā-nidrayā*), and in their dreams they construct the objective world; it is only when they become awake with the transcendent indeterminate knowledge (*lokottara-nirvikalpa-jñāna-lābhāt prabuddho bhavati*) that they find the world-construction to be as false as the dream-construction of diverse appearances. In such a view there is no objective material world, and our cognitions are not influenced by external objects; how then are our minds influenced by good instructions and associations? and, since none of us have any real physical bodies, how can one kill another? Vasubandhu explains this by the theory that the thought-currents of one person can sometimes determine the thought-currents of another. Thus the idea of killing of a certain type may produce such a disturbance of the vital powers of another as to produce a cessation of the continuity of the thought-processes, which is called death[1]. So also the good ideas of one may influence the ideas of another for good.

In the *Triṃśikā* of Vasubandhu and its commentary by Sthiramati this idealism is more clearly explained. It is said that both the soul (or the knower) and all that it knows as subjective ideas or as external objects existing outside of us are but transformations of pure intelligence (*vijñāna-pariṇāma*). The transformation (*pariṇāma*) of pure intelligence means the production of an effect different from that of the causal moment simultaneously with the cessation of the causal moment[2]. There is neither externality nor subjectivity in pure intelligence, but these are imposed upon it (*vijñāna-svarūpe parikalpita eva ātmā dharmāś ca*). All erroneous impositions imply that there must be some entity which is mistaken for something else; there cannot be erroneous impositions on mere vacuity; so it has to be admitted that these erroneous impositions of various kinds of external characteristics, self, etc. have been made upon the transformations of pure intelligence[3]. Both Vasubandhu and Sthiramati repudiate the suggestion of those extreme idealists who

[1] *para-vijñapti-viśeṣādhipatyāt pareṣāṃ jīvitendriya-virodhinī kācit vikriyā utpadyate yayā sabhāga-santati-vicchedākhyaṃ maraṇam bhavati.* Commentary on *Viṃśatikā*, p. 10.

[2] *kāraṇa-kṣaṇa-nirodha-sama-kālaḥ kāraṇa-kṣaṇa-vilakṣaṇa-kāryasya ātmalābhaḥ pariṇāmaḥ.* Sthiramati's commentary on *Triṃśikā*, p. 16.

[3] *upacārasya ca nirādhārasyāsambhavād avaśyaṃ vijñāna-pariṇāmo vastuto' sty upagantavyo yatra ātma-dharmopacāraḥ pravartate. Ibid.* Compare Śaṅkara's commentary on Gauḍapāda's *Kārikā*, *"na hi nirāspadā mṛgatṛṣṇikādayaḥ."*

deny also the reality of pure intelligence on grounds of interdependence or relativity (*saṃvṛti*)[1]. Vasubandhu holds that pure consciousness (*vijñapti-mātratā*) is the ultimate reality. This ultimate consciousness is a permanent entity, which by its inherent power (*śakti*) undergoes threefold transformations as the inherent indeterminate inner change (*vipāka*), which again produces the two other kinds of transformations as the inner psychoses of mental operations (*manana*) and as the perception of the so-called external sensibles (*viṣaya-vijñapti*). The apprehension of all appearances or characterized entities (*dharma*) as cognized objects and that of selves as cognizers, the duality of perceivers and the perceived, are due to the threefold transformations of *vipāka*, *manana* and *viṣaya-vijñapti*. The ultimate consciousness (*vijñapti-mātra*) which suffers all these modifications is called *ālaya-vijñāna* in its modified transformations, because it is the repository of all experiences. The ultimate principle of consciousness is regarded as absolutely permanent in itself and is consequently also of the nature of pure happiness (*sukha*); for what is not eternal is painful, and this, being eternal, is happy[2]. When a saint's mind becomes fixed (*pratiṣṭhita*) in this pure consciousness (*vijñapti-mātra*), the tendency to dual thought of the subjective and the objective (*grāhya-grāhakānuśaya*) ceases and there dawns the pure indeterminate (*nir-vikalpa*) and transcendent (*lokottara*) consciousness. It is a state in which the ultimate pure consciousness returns from its transformations and rests in itself. It is divested of all afflictions (*kleśa*) or touch of vicious tendencies and is therefore called *anāsrava*. It is unthinkable and undemonstrable, because it is, on the one hand, pure self-consciousness (*pratyātma-vedya*) and omniscience (*sarvajñatā*), as it is divested of all limitations (*āvaraṇa*), and, on the other hand, it is unique in itself[3]. This pure consciousness is called the container of the seed of all (*sarva-bīja*), and, when its first indeterminate and indefinable transformations rouse the psychosis-transformations and

[1] Thus *Laṅkāvatāra*, one of the most important works on Buddhistic idealism, denies the real transformation of the pure intelligence or *ālaya-vijñāna*. See *Laṅkāvatāra*, p. 46, published by the Otani University Press, Kyoto, 1923.

[2] *dhruvo nityatvād akṣayatayā; sukho nityatvād eva yad anityaṃ tad duḥkham ayaṃ ca nitya iti asmāt sukhaḥ.* Sthiramati's commentary on *Triṃśikā*, p. 44.

[3] *Ālaya-vijñāna* in this ultimate state of pure consciousness (*vijñapti-mātratā*) is called the cause (*dhātu*) of all virtues, and, being the ultimate state in which the dharmas or characterized appearances have lost all their limitations it is called the *dharma-kāya* of the Buddha (*mahā-muniḥ bhūmi-pāramitādi-bhāva-nayā kleśa-jñeyāvaraṇa-prahāṇāt. . . sarva-dharma-vibhutva-lābhataś ca dharma-kāya ity ucyate*). *Ibid.*

also the transformations as sense-perceptions, these mutually act and react against one another, and thus the different series rise again and again and mutually determine one another. These transformations are like waves and ripples on the ocean, where each is as much the product of others as well as the generator of others[1].

In this view thought (*vijñāna*) is regarded as a real substance, and its transformations are also regarded as real; and it is these transformations that are manifested as the selves and the characterized appearances[2]. The first type of transformations, called *vipāka*, is in a way the ground of the other two transformations, which contain the indeterminate materials out of which the manifestations of the other two transformations appear. But, as has already been pointed out, these three different types of transformations again mutually determine one another. The *vipāka* transformations contain within them the seeds of the constructive instincts (*vikalpa-vāsanā*) of the selves as cognizers, the constructive instincts of colours, sounds, etc., the substantive basis (*āśraya*) of the attribution of these twofold constructive instincts, as well as the sense-faculties and the localization of space-determinations (*sthāna-vijñapti* or *bhājana-loka-sanniveśa-vijñapti*). They are also associated in another mode with sense-modifications involving the triune of the sense (*indriya*), sense-object (*viṣaya*) and cognition (and each of these triunes is again associated with a characteristic affective tone corresponding to the effective tones of the other two members of the triune in a one-to-one relation), attention (*manaskāra*), discrimination (*saṃjñā*), volition (*cetanā*) and feeling (*vedanā*)[3]. The *vipāka* transformations have no determinate or limited forms (*aparịcchinnālambanākāra*), and there are here no

[1] *tac ca varttate srotasaughavat. Ibid.* p. 21.

[2] *avaśyaṃ vijñāna-pariṇāmo vastuto'sty upagantavy oyatrātmadharmopacāraḥ-pravarttate. Ibid.* p. 16.

[3] Feeling (*vedanā*) is distinguished here as painful, pleasurable and as the basic entity which is neither painful nor pleasurable, which is feeling *per se* (*vedanā anubhava-svabhāvā sā punar viṣayasya āhlādaka-paritāpaka-tadubhaya-kara-vivikta-svarūpa-sākṣātkaraṇa-bhedāt*). This feeling *per se* must be distinguished again from the non-pleasurable-painful feeling existing along with the two other varieties, the painful and the pleasurable. Here the *vipāka* transformations are regarded as evolving the basic entity of feeling, and it is therefore undifferentiated in it as pleasure or pain and is hence called "feeling as indifference (*upekṣā*)" and undifferentiated (*avyākṛta*). The differentiation of feeling as pleasurable or as painful takes place only as a further determination of the basic entity of feeling evolved in the *vipāka* transformations of good and bad deeds (*śubhāśubha-karma-vipāka*). Good and bad (*śubhāśubha*) are to be distinguished from moral and immoral as potential and actual determinations of virtuous and vicious actions.

actualized emotional states of attachment, antipathy or the like, which are associated with the actual pleasurable or painful feelings. The *vipāka* transformations thus give us the basic concept of mind and its principal functions with all the potentialities of determinate subject-object consciousness and its processes. There are here the constructive tendencies of selves as perceivers, the objective constructive tendencies of colours, sounds, etc., the sense-faculties, etc., attention, feeling, discrimination, volition and sense-functioning. But none of these have any determinate and actualized forms. The second grade of transformations, called *manana*, represents the actual evolution of moral and immoral emotions; it is here that the mind is set in motion by the ignorant references to the mental elements as the self, and from this ignorance about the self is engendered self-love (*ātma-sneha*) and egoism (*ātma-māna*). These references are again associated with the fivefold universal categories of sense-functioning, feeling, attention, volition and discrimination. Then comes the third grade of transformations, which is associated with the fivefold universal categories together with the special manifestations of concrete sense-perceptions and the various kinds of intellectual states and moral and immoral mental states, such as desire (*chandaḥ*) for different kinds of sense-experiences, decisions (*adhimokṣa*) in conclusions firmly established by perceptions, reasoning, etc., memory, attentive reflection (*samādhi*), wisdom *(prajñā*), faith and firm will for the good *(śraddhā*), shamefulness *(hrī*) for the bad, etc. The term *ālaya-vijñāna* is given to all these three types of transformations, but there is underneath it, as the permanent passive ground, the eternal and unchangeable pure thought (*vijñapti-mātratā*).

It may be pointed out here that in this system of philosophy the eternal and unchangeable thought-substance undergoes by virtue of its inner dynamic three different orders of superficial changes, which are compared to constantly changing streams and waves. The first of these represents the basic change which later determines all subjective and objective possibilities; the second starts the process of the psychosis by the original ignorance and false attribution of self-hood to non-self elements, self-love and egoism; and in the third grade we have all the concrete mental and extra-mental facts. The fundamental categories which make the possibility of mind, mental processes and the extra-mental relations, are evolved in the first stage of transformations; and these abide through the other two stages of transformations and become more and more complex and concrete in course of their association with the categories of the other transformations. In analysing the knowledge situation Vasubandhu does not hold that our awareness of blue is only a modification of the "awareness," but he thinks that an awareness has always two relations, a relation with the subject or the knower (*grāhaka-graha*) and a relation with the object which is known (*grāhya-graha*). Blue as an object is essential for making an awareness of blue possible; for the awareness is not blue, but we have an awareness of the blue. But Vasubandhu argues that this psychological necessity is due to a projection of objectivity as a necessary function of determinate thought, and it does not at all follow that this implies that there are real external objects existing outside of it and generating the awareness as external agent. Psychological objectivity does not imply ontological objectivity. It is argued that, if the agency of objective entities in the production of sense-knowledge be admitted, there could not be any case where sense-knowledge could be admitted to be produced without the operation of the objective entities; but, since in dreams and illusions such sense-knowledge is universally regarded as being produced without the causal operation of such objective entities, no causal operation can be conceded to the objective entities for the production of sense-knowledge.

Śaṅkara, in attempting to refute the Buddhist idealism in his commentary on the *Brahma-sūtra*, II. ii. 28, seems to refer to a school of idealism which is the same as that described by Śāntarakṣita in his *Tattva-saṃgraha* (commented upon by Kamalaśīla), but largely different from that described in Vasubandhu's *Triṃśikā*. The positive arguments against the impossibility of an external world constituted by partless atoms are the same[1]. But

[1] Vācaspati, however, in his *Bhāmatī* commentary, II. ii. 28, introduces some new points. He says that spatial extension, as perceived in visual perception, cannot be due to the perception of partless atoms. Nor can it be said that the colour particles produced in uninterrupted succession generate the notion of spatial extension, though there is no spatial extension in the individual atom; for it is not possible that the groups of colour particles are not interrupted by taste, smell and the tactual particles. So it has to be admitted that the colour particles are at some distance from one another and are interrupted by other particles, and that the continuous appearance of colour in spatial distribution is a false appearance, like the appearance of continuous trees from a distance constituting a forest (*gandha-rasa-sparśa-paramāṇv-antaritā hi te rūpa-paramāṇavo na nirantarāḥ; tasmād ārāt sāntareṣu vṛkṣeṣu eka-ghana-pratyayavad eṣa sthūla-pratyayaḥ paramāṇuṣu sāntareṣu bhrānta eva*).

it is further argued on behalf of the Buddhist idealists that the awareness of a pillar, the awareness of a wall or of a jug or of a piece of cloth, implies that these individual awarenesses are mutually different in nature among themselves; and that consequently the apparent differences among objects are but differences among the ideas; and that therefore the objects are of the same nature as the particular ideas by which we are supposed to know them; and, if that be so, the hypothesis of an external world of objects becomes unnecessary. Moreover the fact that both the idea of the object and the object are taken at one and the same moment proves that both the object and the idea are identical, just as the illusory second moon perceived simultaneously with the moon is identical with it[1]. When one of them is not perceived the other also is not perceived. If they were by nature separate and different, there would be no reason why there should be such a uniform and invariable relation between them. The reason for the diversity of our ideas is to be sought not in the diversity of external objects which are ordinarily supposed to produce them, but in the beginningless diversity of the instinctive subconscious roots (*vāsanā*) which produce all our ideas in the waking state, just as they produce dreams during sleep; as dreams are admitted by all to be produced without any external objects, so are all ideas produced without any external real objects; for as ideas the dream ideas are just the same as the waking ideas. But in both cases there are the instinctive subconscious roots (*vāsanā*), without which no ideas, whether in the dream state or in the waking state, can be produced; so these, being invariably present in all cases of production of ideas, are the cause of all ideas[2].

[1] This simile is adduced by Vācaspati probably from a quotation from Diṅnāga—*sahopalambha-niyamād abhedo nīla-tad-dhiyoḥ bhedaś ca bhrānti-vijñānair dṛsyetendāv ivādvaye.*

Since both the blue and the idea of the blue are taken at the same moment, they are one and the same; for any two things which are taken simultaneously are identical. As one moon appears as two in an illusory manner, so the difference between the idea and the object is also perceived only illusorily. This argument of *sahopalambha-niyama* is absent in Vasubandhu's *Viṃśatikā* and *Triṃśikā*.

[2] Vācaspati summarizes in this connection the inference of the Sautrāntikas for the existence of an external world of objects as the causes of the corresponding ideas. The argument of the Sautrāntikas runs thus: When, the old causes remaining the same, there is a new effect, that new effect must be due to a new cause. Now, though it should be admitted that in the passing series of inner consciousness each particular moment generates the succeeding one, and that this power of productivity is called *vāsanā* (*tat-pravṛtti-vijñāna-janana-śak-tir vāsanā*), and that its tendency to effectuate itself is called its power of fruition (*paripāka*), even then it would be difficult to understand how each particular

Śaṅkara in refuting the above position says that such a view is untenable because it contradicts our experience, which always distinguishes the subject and the object from the awareness. We are directly aware of our sense-contact with external objects which we perceive, and the object of awareness and the awareness are not one and the same. Our awareness itself shows that it is different from its object. The awareness of a pillar is not the same as a pillar, but a pillar is only an object of the awareness of a pillar. Even in denying external objects, the Buddhist idealists have to say that what is knowable only within appears as if it was existing outside[1]. Śaṅkara argues thus: if externality is absolutely non-existent, how can any sense-cognition appear as external? Viṣṇumitra cannot appear as the son of a barren woman. Again, the fact that an idea has the same form as its object does not imply that there are no objects; on the other hand, if there were no objects, how could any idea have the same form as its corresponding object? Again, the maxim that any two things which are taken simultaneously are identical is false; for, if the object and its awareness are comprehended at the same moment, the very fact that one is taken along with the other shows that they cannot be identical. Moreover, we find that in all our awarenesses of blue or yellow, a jug or a wall, it is the qualifying or predicative factors of objects of knowledge that differ; awareness as such remains just the same. The objects of knowledge are like so many extraneous qualities attributed to knowledge, just as whiteness or blackness may be attributed to a cow; so whether one perceives blue or red or yellow, that signifies that the difference of perception involves a difference in objects and not in the awareness itself. So the awareness, being one, is naturally different from the objects, which are many; and, since the objects are many,

moment should have a power altogether different from other moments; for, since there is nothing else to change the character of the moments, each moment is just as much a moment as any other. So it has to be admitted that there are other things which make one moment different in its power of effectuation from any other; and these are the external objects.

[1] Śaṅkara says yad *antar-jñeya-rūpaṃ tad bahirvad avabhāsate*. This seems to be a quotation from Diṅnāga. Diṅnāga's verse, as quoted by Kamalaśīla in his commentary on the *Tattva-saṃgraha*, verses 2082–2084, runs as follows:

yad antar-jñeya-rūpaṃ tu bahirvad avabhāsate
so 'rtho vijñāna-rūpatvāt tat-pratyayatayāpi ca.

This shows that Śaṅkara had Diṅnāga in his mind when he attempted to refute the Buddhist idealists.

they are different from the one, the awareness. The awareness is one and it is different from the objects, which are many[1]. Moreover, the argument that the appearance of world objects may be explained on the analogy of dreams is also invalid; for there is a great difference between our knowledge of dreams and of worldly objects—dreams are contradicted by the waking experience, but the waking experiences are never found contradicted.

It is curious to note here the contradictions in Śaṅkara's own statements. It has been already pointed out that he himself in his commentary on Gauḍapāda's *Kārikā* built a powerful argument for the non-existence of all objects of waking experience on the analogy of the non-existence of the objects of dream experience. Śāntarakṣita (A.D. 705) and Kamalaśīla (A.D. 728) in refuting a position similar to that of the view of Śaṅkara—that consciousness is one and unchangeable and that all objects are changing, but that the change of objects does not imply any change of the consciousness itself—argue that, had this been so, then that would imply that all sensibles of different kinds of colours, sounds, etc. were known at one and the same time, since the consciousness that would reveal those objects is constant and unchangeable[2]. Kamalaśīla therefore holds that consciousness is not unchangeable and one, but that there are only the changeable ideas of the sensibles and each idea is different from the other which follows it in time. Śaṅkara's view that consciousness is only one and that it is only the objects that are many seems to be based on a separation due to an arbitrary abstraction. If the commentary on Gauḍapāda's *Kārikā* be admitted to be a work of Śaṅkara, then it may be urged that Śaṅkara's views had undergone a change when he was writing the commentary on the *Brahma-sūtra*; for in the commentary on Gauḍapāda's *Kārikā* he seems again and again to emphasize the view that the objects perceived in waking experience are as false and as non-existent as objects of dream experience. His only realism there consisted in the assertion that the world was but the result of a false illusory imposition on the real Brahman, since

[1] *dvābhyāṃ ca bheda ekasya siddho bhavati ekasmāc ca dvayoḥ; tasmād artha-jñānayor bhedaḥ.* Śaṅkara's .*Bhāṣya*, II. ii. 28, Nirṇaya-Sāgara Press. Bombay, 1904.

[2] *tad yadi nityaika-jñāna-pratibhāsātmakā amī śabdādayaḥ syus tadā vicitrās-taraṇa-pratibhāsavat sakṛd eva pratibhāseran; tat-pratibhāsātmakasya jñānasya sarvadā vasthitatvāt.* Kamalaśīla's commentary on the *Tattva-saṃgraha*, sl. 331. Gaekwad's Oriental Series, 1926.

Neither Śāntarakṣita nor Kamalaśīla seems to be familiar with Śaṅkara .

illusions such as mirage, etc. must have some underlying basis upon which they are imposed. But in the commentary on the *Brahma-sūtra* the world of objects and sensibles is seen to have an existence of some sort outside individual thought. Vācaspati in his *Bhāmatī* commentary distinguishes the position of Śaṅkara from that of Buddhist idealism by saying that the Vedānta holds that the "blue" is not an idea of the form of blue, but "the blue" is merely the inexplicable and indefinable object[1].

In discussing the views of Vasubandhu in the *Viṃśatikā* and *Triṃśikā* it has been pointed out that Vasubandhu did not try to repudiate the objectivity of the objects of awareness, but he repudiated the idea that objects of awareness existed outside of thought and produced the different kinds of awareness. His idea seems to have been that the sensibles are made up of thought-stuff and, though they are the psychological objects of awareness, they do not exist outside of thought and determine the different ideas that we have of them. But both the sensibles and their ideas are determined by some inner law of thought, which determines the nature and methods of the whole process of the growth and development of the psychosis, and which determines not only its cognitional character, but also its moral and emotional character. All the arguments of Śaṅkara in which he emphasizes the psychological duality of awareness and its object would have no force against Vasubandhu, as Vasubandhu admits it himself and holds that "blue" (*nīla*) is different from the idea of blue; the blue is an object (*ālambana*) and the idea of the blue is an awareness. According to him thought splits itself into subject and object; the idea therefore expresses itself as a subject-object awareness. The subject and the object are as much products of thought as the idea itself; the fact that he considers the blue to be thought does not mean that he denies the objectivity of the blue or that the only existence of the blue is the blue-idea. The blue is objectively present before the idea of blue as a presentation, just as there is the subject to perceive it, but this objectivity does not imply that the blue is somewhere outside thought in the space outside; for even space-locations are thought-products, and so there is no sense in attributing the sensibles of presentation to the outside world. The sensibles are objects of awareness, but they are not the excitants

[1] *na hi brahma-vādino nīlādyākārāṃ vittim abhyupagacchanti, kintu anirvacanīyaṃ nīlādīti. Bhāmatī*, II. ii. 28.

of the corresponding awareness. It does not seem that Śaṅkara says anything to refute such a view. Śaṅkara's position in the commentary on Gauḍapāda's *Kārikā* seems to have been the same sort of view as that of Diṅnāga, which he takes so much pains to refute in the *Brahma-sūtra-bhāṣya*, and as such it was opposed to the view of Nāgārjuna that there must be some essence or reality on which the illusory impositions are made. But in the *Brahma-sūtra-bhāṣya* he maintains the view that the objective world, as it appears to our consciousness, is present before it objectively and independently—only its ultimate nature is inexplicable. The difference of the objects from the awareness and their independent existence and activity have been accepted by most of the later Vedānta teachers of the Śaṅkara school; and it is well known that in sense-perception the need of the mind-contact with the object of perception through the specific sense is considered indispensable[1].

Prakāśātman (A.D. 1200) in his *Pañca-pādikā-vivaraṇa* raises this point and says that the great difference between the Mahāyānists and the Vedāntins consists in the fact that the former hold that the objects (*viṣaya*) have neither any separate existence nor any independent purpose or action to fulfil as distinguished from the momentary ideas, while the latter hold that, though the objects are in essence identical with the one pure consciousness, yet they can fulfil independent purposes or functions and have separate, abiding and uncontradicted existences[2]. Both Padmapāda and Prakāśātman argue that, since the awareness remains the same while there is a constant variation of its objects, and therefore that which remains constant (*anuvṛtta*) and that which changes (*vyāvṛtta*) cannot be considered identical, the object cannot be regarded as being only a modification of the idea[3]. It is suggested that the Buddhist idealist urges that, if the object (e.g. blue) is different from the awareness, it cannot be revealed in it, and, if the blue can be revealed in the awareness, at that moment all the other things of the world might as well be revealed; for there is no such

[1] See *Vedānta-paribhāṣā*, ch. 1, Śrīvenkateśvar Press, Bombay, 1911.

[2] *tattva-darśinas tu advitīyāt saṃvedanāt abhede 'pi viṣayasya bhedenāpi arthakriyā-sāmarthya-sattvaṃ sthāyitvaṃ cābādhitam astīti vadanti. Pañca-pādikā-vi-varaṇa*, p. 73. In addition to this work Prakāśātman also wrote two independent commentaries on *Brahma-sūtra* called *Śārīraka-mīmāṃsā-nyāya-saṃgraha* and *Laukika-nyāya-muktāvalī.*

[3] *anuvṛttasya vyāvṛttān na bhedo 'nuvṛttatvād ākāśa-ghaṭādivat. Pañca-pādikā-vivaraṇa*, p. 73.

specific relation with the blue that the blue alone should appear in consciousness at that moment. If it is urged that the blue produces the awareness of the blue, then what would be the function of the visual organ? It is better, therefore, the Buddhist suggests, to admit a natural and unique relation of identity of the idea and the object[1]. The Vedāntist objects to this and says that such a supposition cannot be true, since we perceive that the subject, object and the idea are not one and the same. To such an objection the Buddhist is supposed to reply that these three do not form a complex unity, but arise at three successive moments of time, and then by virtue of their potency or root-impression a complex of the three appears; and this complex should not therefore be interpreted as being due to a relationing of three distinct entities[2]. Thus the fact that "I perceive blue" is not to be interpreted as a conscious relationing of "I," "the blue" and the awareness, but as an ideation arising at one particular point of time, involving all the three constituents in it. Such a supposition is necessary, because all appearances are momentary, and because the relationing of the three as three independent entities would necessarily be impossible without the lapse of some time for their operation of relationing. The theory of momentariness naturally leads us to the above supposition, that what appears as relationing is nothing but one momentary flash, which has the above three as its constituent elements; so the Buddhist is supposed to admit that, psychologic-

[1] *tasmāt svābhāvikāsādharaṇābhedasambandhād eva vijñāne nīlam avabhāsate*, *Paṇca-pādikā-vivaraṇa*, p. 74.

Arguing from a similar point of view, Śāntarakṣita and Kamalaśīla urge that, if the object was not identical with the awareness, there must be some immutable law why they should appear simultaneously. This law according to the Buddhists could only be either of identity (*tādātmya*) or of causality as invariability of production (*tad-utpatti*). The first alternative is what the Buddhists here are contending for as against the Vedāntists. There cannot be the law of causality here; for there cannot be any operation of the law of causality as production between two entities which are simultaneous. *Tattva-saṃgraha* and *Pañjikā*, 2030, 2031.

[2] *tad vāsanā-sameta-samanantara-pratyaya-samutthaṃ saṅkalanātmakaṃ pratyayāntaram etan neha sambandhāgamaḥ.* Padmapāda's (A.D. 820) *Pañca-pādikā*, p. 25. This work exerted the greatest influence on the development of Vedāntic thought for about six or seven centuries, and several commentaries were written on it. Most important of these are Prakāśātman's *Pañcapādikā-vivaraṇa*, *Pañca-pādikādhyāsa-bhāṣya-vyākhyā'* *Pañca-pādikā-śāstra-darpaṇa* by Amṛtānanda, *Tattva-dīpana* by Amrtānandanātha, and also a commentary by Ānandapūrṇa Yati. Prakāśātman's commentary on it, called *Pañcapādikā-vivaraṇa*, was commented upon by Akhaṇḍānanda Muni in his *Tattva-dīpana*, by Rāmānanda Sarasvatī in his *Vivaraṇopanyāsa*, and by Nṛsiṃhāśrama in his *Pañca-pādikā-vivaraṇa-bhāva-prakāśikā*.

ally, the awareness and its object seem to be different, but such a psychological appearance can at best be considered as a mental illusion or fiction; for logically the Buddhist cannot admit that a momentary appearance could subsist long enough to have the possibility of being relationed to the self and the awareness, as in "I know the blue"; and, if the blue was not considered to be identical with awareness, there would remain no way to explain the possibility of the appearance of the blue in the awareness[1].

Padmapāda points out that the main point with the Buddhists is the doctrine of causal efficiency (*artha-kriyā-kāritva*), or the maxim that that alone exists which can prove its existence by effecting some purpose or action. They hold further that this criterion of existence can be satisfied only if all existents are momentary and if all things are momentary; the only epistemological view that can consistently be accepted is the identity of the awareness and the object. The main reason why only momentary existents can satisfy the criterion of causal efficiency is that, if the existents were not assumed to be momentary, they could not effect any purpose or action[2]. Padmapāda urges in refutation of this that, if causal efficiency means the productivity of its own awareness (*sva-viṣaya-jñāna-jananam*), then an awareness or idea has no existence; for it does not produce any other knowledge of itself (*saṃvidāṃ sva-viṣaya-jñānā-jananād asallakṣaṇatvam*), and the awareness of one cannot be known by others except by inference, which again would not be direct cognition[3]. If causal efficiency means the production of another moment, then the last moment, having no other moment to produce, would itself be non-existent; and, if the last moment is proved to be non-existent, then by turns all the other moments would be non-existent. Existence is a nature of things; and even when a thing remains silent after an operation it does not on that account cease to exist[4]. On such a basis Prakāśātman points out

[1] *nānubhavam āśritya saṃvedanād abhinnaṃ nīlaṃ brūmaḥ kintu vijñānena nīlasya pratibhāsānyathānupapattyā; kṣaṇikasya tv āgantuka-sambandhābhāve. . . pratibhāsa eva na syāt. Pañca-pādikā-vivaraṇa*, p. 74.

[2] See the first volume of this work, pp. 163–164, where the reasons in justification of the doctrine are briefly stated.

[3] Padmapāda derives the possibility of one's being aware of an awareness, which however hardly appears to be convincing. He thinks that an awareness, being of the nature of light, does not stand in need of any other light to illuminate it. *na ca saṃvit saṃvido viṣayaḥ samvid-ātmanā bhedābhāvāt pradīpasyeva pradīpāntaram. Pañca-pādikā*, p. 27.

[4] *nārtha-kriyā-kāritva-lakṣaṇaṃ sattvaṃ kintu svābhāvikam iti sakṛt kāryyaṃ kṛtvā*

that the supposed three notions of "I," "awareness" and the object are really not three distinct notions appearing as one on account of their similarity, but all the three are joined together in one identical subject-object-awareness which does not involve the three successive stages which the Buddhists suppose. This identity is proved by the fact that they are recognized (*pratyabhijñā*) to be so. We are, again, all conscious of our own identity, that we persist in all our changing states of consciousness, and that, though our ideas are continually changing with the changing objects, we remain unchanged all the same; and this shows that in knowing ourselves as pure awareness we are successively connected with the changing objects. But the question arises who is to be convinced of this identity, a notion of which can be produced only by a relationing of the previous existence (through subconscious impressions of memory) to the existence of the present moment; and this cannot be done by the Vedāntic self, which is pure self-revealing consciousness that cannot further be made an object of any other conscious state; for it is unchangeable, indestructible, and there cannot be in it a consciousness of relationing between a past state and a present state through the subconscious impressions of memory[1]. The mere persistence of the same consciousness is not the recognition of identity; for the recognition of identity would be a relation uniting the past as past with the present as present; and, since there is no one to perceive the relation of identity, the appearance of identity is false. The Vedāntic answer to such an objection is that, though the pure consciousness cannot behave as an individual, yet the same consciousness associated with mind (*antaḥkaraṇa-viśiṣṭa*) may behave as an individual who can recognize his own identity as well as that of others. The mind is associated with the subconscious impressions of a felt ego (*ahaṃvṛtti-saṃskāra-sahitam*), due to the experience of the self as associated with a past time; being responsible for the experience of the self as associated with the present time, it produces the notion of the identity of the self as persisting both in the past and in the present. A natural objection against such an explanation is that, since the Vedānta does not admit that one awareness can be the object of another awareness, the revival of a past awareness is

tuṣṇīmbhūtasyāpi sthāyinaḥ sattvaṃ na virudhyate. Pañca-pādikā-vivaraṇa, p. 80.

[1] *pūrvānubhava-saṃskāra-sahitād idānīṃtana-vastu-pramiti-kāraṇāj jātam ekasya kāla-dvaya-saṃbandha-viṣayakaṃ pratyakṣa-jñānaṃ pratyabhijñā iti cet, na tarhi ātmani sā sambhavati. . . vijñāna-svabhāvasya hy ātmanaḥ. . jñānānta-rāgamyatvāt. . . Pañca-pādikā-vivaraṇa*, p. 75.

impossible, without which recognition of identity would be impossible. The answer of the Vedāntist is that, just as an idea is remembered through its subconscious impressions, so, though recognition of identity was absent in the preceding moment, yet it could arise through the operation of the subconscious impressions at a later moment[1]. According to the Vedānta the pure consciousness is the only unchanging substance underlying; it is this consciousness associated with mind (*antaḥkaraṇa*) that behaves as the knower or the subject, and it is the same consciousness associated with the previous and later time that appears as the objective self with which the identity is felt and which is known to be identical with the knower—the mind-associated consciousness. We all have notions of self-identity and we feel it as "I am the same"; and the only way in which this can be explained is on the basis of the fact that consciousness, though one and universal, can yet be supposed to perform diverse functions by virtue of the diverse nature of its associations, by which it seems to transform itself as the knower and the thousand varieties of relations and objects which it knows. The main point which is to be noted in connection with this realization of the identity of the self is that the previous experience and its memory prove that the self existed in the past; but how are we to prove that what existed is also existing at the present moment? Knowledge of identity of the self is something different from the experience of self in the past and in the present. But the process consists in this, that the two experiences manifest the self as one identical entity which persisted through both the experiences, and this new experience makes the self known in the aforesaid relation of identity. Again, when I remember a past experience, it is the self as associated with that experience that is remembered; so it is the self as associated with the different time relations that is apprehended in an experience of the identity of self.

From all these discussions one thing that comes out clearly is that according to the Śaṅkara Vedānta, as explained by the *Vivaraṇa* school of Padmapāda and his followers, the sense-data and the objects have an existence independent of their being perceived; and there is also the mind called *antaḥkaraṇa*, which operates in its own way for the apprehension of this or that object. Are objects already there and presented to the pure consciousness through the

[1] *Pañca-pādikā-vivaraṇa*, p. 76.

mind? But what then are the objects? and the Śaṅkarite's answer is that they in themselves are unspeakable and indescribable. It is easy to notice the difference of such a view from that of the Buddhistic idealism of Diṅnāga or the *Laṅkāvatāra* on the one hand and that of Vasubandhu in his *Triṃśikā* on the other. For in the case of the former there were no objects independent of their being perceived, and in the case of the latter the objects are transformations of a thought-principle and are as such objective to the subject which apprehends them. Both the subject and the object are grounded in the higher and superior principle, the principle of thought. This grounding implies that this principle of thought and its transformations are responsible for both the subject and the object, as regards material and also as regards form. According to the Śaṅkara Vedānta, however, the stuff of world-objects, mind, the senses and all their activities, functionings and the like are but modifications of *māyā*, which is indescribable (*anirvācya*) in itself, but which is always related to pure consciousness as its underlying principle, and which in its forms as material objects hides from the view and is made self-conscious by the illuminating flash of the underlying principle of pure consciousness in its forms as intellectual states or ideas. As already described, the Śūnyavādins also admitted the objective existence of all things and appearances; but, as these did not stand the test of criticism, considered them as being essenceless (*niḥsvabhāva*). The only difference that one can make out between this doctrine of essencelessness and the doctrine of indescribableness of the Śaṅkara school is that this "indescribable" is yet regarded as an indescribable something, as some stuff which undergoes changes and which has transformed itself into all the objects of the world. The idealism of the Śaṅkara Vedānta does not believe in the *sahopalambha-niyama* of the Buddhist idealists, that to exist is to be perceived. The world is there even if it be not perceived by the individual; it has an objective existence quite independent of my ideas and sensations; but, though independent of my sensations or ideas, it is not independent of consciousness, with which it is associated and on which it is dependent. This consciousness is not ordinary psychological thought, but it is the principle that underlies all conscious thought. This pure thought is independent and self-revealing, because in all conscious thought the consciousness shines by itself; all else is manifested by this consciousness and when considered apart from it, is inconceivable and unmeaning. This independent and uncontradicted self-shiningness constitutes being (*abādhita-svayaṃ-prakāśataiva asya sattā*)[1]. All being is pure consciousness, and all appearance hangs on it as something which is expressed by a reference to it and apart from which it has no conceivable status or meaning. This is so not only epistemologically or logically, but also ontologically. The object-forms of the world are there as transformations of the indescribable stuff of *māyā*, which is not "being," but dependent on "being"; but they can only be expressed when they are reflected in mental states and presented as ideas. Analogies of world objects with dream objects or illusions can therefore be taken only as popular examples to make the conception of *māyā* popularly intelligible; and this gives the Vedāntic idealism its unique position.

Śaṅkara's Defence of Vedānta; Philosophy of Bādarāyaṇa and Bhartṛprapañca.

Śaṅkara's defensive arguments consisted in the refutation of the objections that may be made against the Vedāntic conception of the world. The first objection anticipated is that from the followers of Sāṃkhya philosophy. Thus it is urged that the effect must be largely of the same nature as the cause. Brahman, which is believed to be intelligent (*cetana*) and pure (*śuddha*), could not be the cause of a world which is unintelligent (*jaḍa* and *acetana*) and impure (*aśuddha*). And it is only because the world is so different in nature from the intelligent spirits that it can be useful to them. Two things which are identical in their nature can hardly be of any use to each other—two lamps cannot be illuminating to each other. So it is only by being different from the intelligent spirits that the world can best serve them and exist for them. Śaṅkara's answer to this objection is that it is not true that the effect should in every way be similar to the cause—there are instances of inanimate hair and nails growing from living beings, and of living insects growing out of inanimate objects like cowdung. Nor can it be denied that there is at least some similarity between Brahman and the world in this, that both have being. It cannot be urged that, because Brahman is intelligent, the world also should be intelligent; for there is no reason for such

[1] Vācaspati Miśra's *Bhāmatī*, p. 13, Nirṇaya-Sāgara edition, 1904.

an expectation. The converse of it also has not been found to be true—it has not been found that what is unintelligent has been known to have been derived from a source other than Brahman[1]. The whole point of this argument seems to lie in the fact that, since the Upaniṣads assert that Brahman is the cause of the world, the apparent incompatibility of the production of an impure and unintelligent world from the intelligent and pure Brahman has to be explained away; for such ultimate truths can be discovered not by reason, but by the testimony of the Upaniṣads. Another objection supposed to be raised by Sāṃkhya against Vedānta is that at the time of dissolution (*pralaya*), when the world of effects will dissolve back into Brahman the cause, the impurities of the worldly state might also make the causal state of Brahmahood impure. Śaṅkara refutes it by pointing out two sets of instances in which the effects do not affect the causal state when they return to it. Of these, one set of instances is to be found in those cases where articles of gold, silver, etc. are melted back into their original material states as unformed gold and silver, and are not seen to affect them with their specific peculiarities as formed articles. The other instance is to be found in the manifestation of magic by a magician. The magical creations of a magician are controlled by him and, when they vanish in this way, they cannot in any way affect the magician himself; for the magical creations have no reality. So also a dreamer is not affected by his dreams when he is awake. So the reality is one which remains altogether untouched by the changing states. The appearance of this reality as all the changing states is mere false show (*māyā-mātram*), like the appearance of a rope as a snake. Again, as a man may in deep sleep pass into a state where there is no trace of his mundane experiences and may yet, when he becomes awake, resume his normal vocation in life, so after the dissolution of the world into its causal state there may again be the same kind of creation as there was before the dissolution. So there can be no objection that the world of impure effects will affect the pure state of Brahman at the time of dissolution or that there could be no creation after dissolution.

These arguments of Śaṅkara in answer to a supposed objection

[1] *kiṃ hi yac caitanyenānanvitaṃ tad abrahma-prakṛtikaṃ dṛṣṭam iti brahma-vādinaṃ praty udāhriyeta samastasya vastujātasya brahma-prakṛtikatvābhyu-pagamāt.* Śaṅkara's *Bhāṣya*, II. i. 6.

that the world of effects, impure and unintelligent as it is, could not have been the product of pure and intelligent Brahman are not only weak but rather uncalled for. If the world of effects is mere *māyā* and magic and has no essence (*vastutva*), the best course for him was to rush straight to his own view of effects as having no substantiality or essence and not to adopt the *pariṇāma* view of real transformations of causes into effects to show that the effects could be largely dissimilar from their causes. Had he started with the reply that the effects had no real existence and that they were merely magical creations and a false show, the objection that the impure world could not come out of pure Brahman would have at once fallen to the ground; for such an objection would have validity only with those who believed in the real transformations of effects from causes, and not with a philosopher like Śaṅkara, who did not believe in the reality of effects at all. Instead of doing that he proceeded to give examples of the realistic return of golden articles into gold in order to show that the peculiar defects or other characteristics of the effect cannot affect the purity of the cause. Side by side with this he gives another instance, how magical creations may vanish without affecting the nature of the magician. This example, however, does not at all fit in with the context, and it is surprising how Śaṅkara failed to see that, if his examples of realistic transformations were to hold good, his example of the magic and the magician would be quite out of place. If the *pariṇāma* view of causation is to be adopted, the *vivarta* view is to be given up. It seems however that Śaṅkara here was obliged to take refuge in such a confusion of issues by introducing stealthily an example of the *vivarta* view of unreality of effects in the commentary on *sūtras* which could only yield a realistic interpretation. The *sūtras* here seem to be so convincingly realistic that the ultimate reply to the suggested incompatibility of the production of effects dissimilar from their causes is found in the fact that the Upaniṣads hold that this impure and unintelligent world had come out of Brahman; and that, since the Upaniṣads assert it, no objection can be raised against it on grounds of reason.

In the next section the theory of realistic transformation of causes is further supported by the *sūtra* which asserts that in spite of the identity of effects with their cause their plurality or diversity may also be explained on the analogy of many popular illustrations. Thus, though the waves are identical with the sea, yet they have an existence in their plurality and diversity as well. Here also Śaṅkara has to follow the implication of the *sūtra* in his interpretation. He, however, in concluding his commentary on this *sūtra*, says that the world is not a result of any real transformation of Brahman as effect; Brahman alone exists, but yet, when Brahman is under the conditioning phenomena of a world-creation, there is room for apparent diversity and plurality. It may be pointed out, however, that such a supplementary explanation is wholly incompatible with the general meaning of the rule, which is decidedly in favour of a realistic transformation. It is unfortunate that here also Śaṅkara does not give any reason for his supplementary remark, which is not in keeping with the general spirit of the *sūtra* and the interpretation which he himself gave of it.

In the next section the *sūtras* seem plainly to assert the identity of cause and effect, "because of the possibility of the effect, because the cause exists, because the effect exists in the cause and is due to an elaboration of the cause and also for other reasons and the testimony of the Upaniṣads." Such a meaning is quite in keeping with the general meaning of the previous sections. Śaṅkara, however, interprets the *sūtra* as meaning that it is Brahman, the cause, which alone is true. There cannot therefore be any real transformation of causes into effects. The omniscience of Brahman and His being the creator of the world have thus only a limited validity; for they depend upon the relative reality of the world. From the absolute point of view therefore there is no Īśvara who is the omniscient creator of the world[1]. Śaṅkara supports this generally on the ground of the testimony of some Upaniṣad texts (e.g. *mṛttiketyeva satyam*, etc.). He however introduces an argument in support of the *sat-kārya-vāda* theory, or the theory that the effect is already existent in the cause. This theory is indeed common both to the *pariṇāma* view of real transformation and the *vivarta* view, in two different ways. It is curious however that he should support the *sat-kārya-vāda* theory on *pariṇāma* lines, as against the generative view of *a-sat-kārya-vāda* of the Nyāya, but not on *vivarta* lines, where effects are treated as non-existent and false. Thus he

[1] *kūṭa-stha-brohmātma-vādinaḥ ekatvaikāntyāt īśitrīśitavyabhāvaḥ īśvara-kāraṇa-pratijñā-virodha iti cet*; *na*; *avidyātmaka-nāma-rūpa-bīja-vyākaraṇāpek-ṣaivāt sarvajñatvasya. Śaṅkara's Bhāṣya on Brahma-sūtra*, II. i. 14.

na tāttvikam aiśvaryyaṃ sarvajñatvaṃ ca brahmaṇaḥ kintv avidyopādhikam iti tadāśrayam pratijñā-sūtram, tattvāśrayaṃ tu tad ananyatva-sūtram. Bhāmatī on the above Bhāṣya.

says that the fact that curd is produced from milk and not from mud shows that there is some such intimate relation of curd with milk which it has not with anything else. This intimate relation consists in the special power or capacity (*śakti*) in the cause (e.g. the milk), which can produce the special effect (e.g. the curd). This power is the very essence of the cause, and the very essence of this power is the effect itself. If a power determines the nature of the effect, it must be already existent in the cause as the essence of the effect. Arguing against the Nyāya view that the cause is different from the effect, though they are mutually connected in an inseparable relation of inherence (*samavāya*), he says that, if such a *samavāya* is deemed necessary to connect the cause with the effect, then this also may require a further something to connect the *samavāya* with the cause or the effect and that another and that another *ad infinitum*. If it is urged that *samavāya*, being a relation, does not require any further relation to connect it with anything else, it may well be asked in reply how "conjunction" (*saṃyoga*), which is also regarded as a relation, should require the relation of inherence (*samavāya*) to connect it with the objects which are in conjunction (*saṃyogin*). The conception of *samavāya* connecting substances with their qualities is unnecessary; for the latter always appear identified with the former (*tādātmya-pratīti*). If the effect, say a whole, is supposed to be existing in the cause, the parts, it must exist in them all taken together or in each of the separate parts. If the whole exist only in the totality of the parts, then, since all the parts cannot be assembled together, the whole as such would be invisible. If the whole exist in the parts in parts, then one has to conceive other parts of the whole different from its constituent parts; and, if the same questions be again repeated, these parts should have other parts and these others; and thus there would be a vicious infinite. If the whole exists wholly in each of the parts at the same time, then there would be many wholes. If it exists successively in each of the parts, then the whole would at one time be existent only in one part, and so at that time the functions of the whole would be absent in the other parts. If it is said that, just as a class-concept (e.g. cow) exists wholly in each of the individuals and yet is not many, so a whole may also be wholly existent in each of the parts, it may well be replied that the experience of wholes is not like the experience of class-concepts. The class-concept of cow is realized in each and every cow; but a whole is not realized in each and every part. Again, if the effect is non-existent before its production, then, production being an action, such an action would have nothing as its agent, which is impossible—for, since the effect is non-existent before its production, it could not be the agent of its production; and, since being non-existent, it cannot be the agent of its production, such a production would be either itself non-existent or would be without any agent. If, however, production is not defined as an action, but as a relationing of an effect with its cause (*svakāraṇa-sattā-samavāya*), then also it may be objected that a relation is only possible when there are two terms which are related, and, since the effect is as yet non-existent, it cannot be related to its cause.

But, if the effect is already existent, what then is the necessity of the causal operation (*kāraka-vyāpāra*)? The answer to such a question is to be found in the view that the effect is but an elaboration of the cause into its effect. Just as a man may sit with his limbs collected together or stretched out and yet would be considered the same man, so an effect also is to be regarded as an expansion of the cause and as such identical with it. The effect is thus only a transformed state of the cause; and hence the causal operation is necessary for bringing about this transformation; but in spite of such a transformation the effect is not already existing in the cause as its potency or power.

There are seven other smaller sections. In the first of these the objection that, if the world is a direct product of the intelligent Brahman, there is no reason why such an intelligent being should create a world which is full of misery and is a prison-house to himself, is easily answered by pointing out that the transcendent creator is far above the mundane spirits that suffer misery in the prison-house of the world. Here also Śaṅkara adds as a supplementary note the remark that, since there is no real creation and the whole world is but a magical appearance, no such objection that the creator should not have created an undesirable world for its own suffering is valid. But the *sūtras* gave him no occasion for such a remark; so that indeed, as was the case with the previous sections, here also his *māyā* theory is not in keeping even with his general interpretation of the *sūtras*, and his remarks have to be appended as a note which hangs loosely and which does not appear to have any relevancy to the general meaning and purport of the *sūtras*.

In the next section an objection is raised that Brahman cannot without the help of any other accessory agents create the world; the reply to such an objection is found in the fact that Brahman has all powers in Himself and can as such create the world out of Himself without the help of anything else.

In the next section an objection is raised that, if the world is a transformation of Brahman, then, since Brahman is partless, the transformation must apply to the whole of Brahman; for a partial transformation is possible only when the substance which is undergoing the transformation has parts. A reply to such an objection is to be found in the analogy of the human self, which is in itself formless and, though transforming itself into various kinds of dream experiences, yet remains unchanged and unaffected as a whole by such transformations. Moreover, such objections may be levelled against the objectors themselves; for Sāṃkhya also admits the transformation of the formless *prakṛti*.

In another section it is urged that, since Brahman is complete in Himself, there is no reason why He should create this great world, when He has nothing to gain by it. The reply is based on the analogy of play, where one has nothing to gain and yet one is pleased to indulge in it. So Brahman also creates the world by His *līlā* or play. Śaṅkara, however, never forgets to sing his old song of the *māyā* theory, however irrelevant it may be, with regard to the purpose of the *sūtras*, which he himself could not avoid following. Thus in this section, after interpreting the *sūtra* as attributing the world-creation to God's playful activity, he remarks that it ought not to be forgotten that all the world-creation is but a fanciful appearance due to nescience and that the ultimate reality is the identity of the self and Brahman.

The above discussion seems to prove convincingly that Bādarāyaṇa's philosophy was some kind of *bhedābheda-vāda* or a theory of transcendence and immanence of God (Brahman)—even in the light of Śaṅkara's own commentary. He believed that the world was the product of a real transformation of Brahman, or rather of His powers and energies (*śakti*). God Himself was not exhausted by such a transformation and always remained as the master creator who by His play created the world and who could by His own powers create the world without any extraneous assistance. The world was thus a real transformation of God's powers, while He Himself, though remaining immanent in the world through His powers, transcended it at the same time, and remained as its controller, and punished or rewarded the created mundane souls in accordance with their bad and good deeds.

The doctrine of *bhedābheda-vāda* is certainly prior to Śaṅkara, as it is the dominant view of most of the *purāṇas*. It seems probable also that Bhartṛprapañca refers to Bodhāyana, who is referred to as *vṛttikāra* by Rāmānuja, and as *vṛttikāra* and *Upavarṣa* by Śaṅkara, and to Dramiḍācārya, referred to by Śaṅkara and Rāmānuja; all held some form of *bhedābheda* doctrine[1]. Bhartṛprapañca has been referred to by Śaṅkara in his commentary on the *Bṛhadāraṇyaka Upaniṣad*; and Ānandajñāna, in his commentary on Śaṅkara's commentary, gives a number of extracts from Bhartṛprapañca's Bhāṣya on the *Bṛhadāraṇyaka Upaniṣad*. Prof. M. Hiriyanna collected these fragments in a paper read before the Third Oriental Congress in Madras, 1924, and there he describes Bhartṛprapañca's philosophy as follows. The doctrine of Bhartṛprapañca is monism, and it is of the *bhedābheda* type. The relation between Brahman and the *jīva*, as that between Brahman and the world, is one of identity in difference. An implication of this view is that both the *jīva* and the physical world evolve out of Brahman, so that the doctrine may be described as *Brahma-pariṇāma-vāda*. On the spiritual side Brahman is transformed into the *antaryāmin* and the *jīva*; on the physical side into *avyakta*, *sūtra*, *virāj* and *devatā*, which are all cosmic; and *jāti* and *piṇḍa*, which are not

[1] Prof. S. Kuppusvāmī Śāstrī, in an article read before the Third Oriental Conference, quotes a passage from Veṅkaṭa's *Tattva-ṭīkā* on Rāmānuja's commentary on the *Brahma-sūtrās*, in which he says that Upavarṣa is a name of Bodhāyana—*vṛttikārasya Bodhāyanasyaiva hi Upavarṣa iti syān nāma—Proceedings of the Third Oriental Conference*, Madras, 1924. The commentators on Śaṅkara's *Bhāṣya* say that, when he refers to Vṛttikāra in I. i. 9, I. i. 23, I. ii. 23 and III. iii. 53, he refers to Upavarṣa by name. From the views of Upavarṣa referred to in these *sūtras* it appears that Upavarṣa believed in the theory of *jñāna-karma-samuccaya*, held also by Bhāskara (an adherent of the *bhedābheda* theory), Rāmānuja and others, but vehemently opposed by Śaṅkara, who wanted to repudiate the idea of his opponents that the performance of sacrificial and Vedic duties could be conceived as a preliminary preparation for making oneself fit for Brahma-knowledge.

References to Dramiḍācārya's commentary on the *Chāndogya Upaniṣad* are made by Ānandagiri in his commentary on Śaṅkara's commentary on the *Chāndogya Upaniṣad*. In the commentary of Sarvajñātma Muni's *Saṃkṣepa-śārīraka*, III. 217–227, by Nṛsiṃhāśrama, the Vākyakāra referred to by Sarvajñātma Muni as Ātreya has been identified with Brahmanandin or Taṅka and the bhāṣyakāra (a quotation from whose *Bhāṣya* appears in *Saṃkṣepa-śārīraka*, III. 221. "*antarguṇā bhagavatī paradevateti*," is referred to as a quotation from Dramiḍācārya in Rāmānuja's *Vedārtha-saṃgraha*, p. 138, Pandit edition) is identified with Dramiḍācārya, who wrote a commentary on Brahmanandin's *Chāndogyo-paniṣad-vārttika*.

cosmic. These are the *avasthās* or modes of Brahman, and represent the eight classes into which the variety of the universe may be divided. They are again classified into three *rāśis*, *paramātma-rāśi*, *jīva-rāśi* and *mūrttāmūrtta-rāśi*, which correspond to the triple subject-matter of Religion and Philosophy, viz. God, soul and matter. Bhartṛprapañca recognized what is known as *pramāṇa-samuccaya*, by which it follows that the testimony of common experience is quite as valid as that of the Veda. The former vouches for the reality of variety and the latter for that of unity (as taught in the Upaniṣads). Hence the ultimate truth is *dvaitādvaita. Mokṣa*, or life's end, is conceived as being achieved in two stages—the first leading to *apavarga*, where *saṃsāra* is overcome through the overcoming of *āsaṅga*; and the second leading to Brahmahood through the dispelling of *avidyā*. This means of reaching either stage is *jñāna-karma-samuccaya*, which is a corollary on the practical side to *pramāṇa-samuccaya* on the theoretical side.

It is indeed difficult to say what were the exact characteristics of Bādarāyaṇa's *bhedābheda* doctrine of Vedānta; but there is very little doubt that it was some special type of *bhedābheda* doctrine, and, as has already been repeatedly pointed out, even Śaṅkara's own commentary (if we exclude only his parenthetic remarks, which are often inconsistent with the general drift of his own commentary and the context of the *sūtras*, as well as with their purpose and meaning, so far as it can be made out from such a context) shows that it was so. If, however, it is contended that this view of real transformation is only from a relative point of view (*vyavahārika*), then there must at least be one *sūtra* where the absolute (*pāra-mārthika*) point of view is given; but no such *sūtra* has been discovered even by Śaṅkara himself. If experience always shows the causal transformation to be real, then how is one to know that in the ultimate point of view all effects are false and unreal? If, however, it is contended that there is a real transformation (*pariṇāma*) of the *māyā* stuff, whereas Brahman remains always unchanged, and if *māyā* is regarded as the power (*śakti*) of Brahman, how then can the *śakti* of Brahman as well as its transformations be regarded as unreal and false, while the possessor of the *śakti* (or the *śaktimat*, Brahman) is regarded as real and absolute? There is a great diversity of opinion on this point among the Vedāntic writers of the Śaṅkara school. Thus Appaya Dīkṣita in his *Siddhānta-leśa* refers to the author of *Padārtha-nirṇaya* as saying that

Brahman and *māyā* are both material causes of the world-appearance—Brahman the *vivarta* cause, and *māyā* the *pariṇāma* cause. Others are said to find a definition of causation intermediate between *vivarta* and *pariṇāma* by defining material cause as that which can produce effects which are not different from itself (*svābhinna-kārya janakatvam upādānatvam*). The world is identical with Brahman in as much as it has being, and it is identical with nescience in as much as it has its characteristics of materiality and change. So from two different points of view both Brahman and *māyā* are the cause of the world. Vācaspati Miśra holds that *māyā* is only an accessory cause (*sahakāri*), whereas Brahman is the real *vivarta* cause[1]. The author of the *Siddhānta-muktāvalī*, Prakāśānanda, however, thinks that it is the *māyā* energy (*māyā-śakti*) which is the material cause of the world and not Brahman. Brahman is unchangeable and is the support of *māyā*; and is thus the cause of the world in a remote sense. Sarvajñātma Muni, however, believes Brahman alone to be the *vivarta* cause, and *māyā* to be only an instrument for the purpose[2]. The difficulty that many of the *sūtras* of Bādarāyaṇa give us a *pariṇāma* view of causation was realized by Sarvajñātma Muni, who tried to explain it away by suggesting that the *pariṇāma* theory was discussed approvingly in the *sūtras* only because this theory was nearest to the *vivarta*, and by initiating people to the *pariṇāma* theory it would be easier to lead them to the *vivarta* theory, as hinted in *sūtra* II. i. 14[3]. This explanation could have some probability, if the arrangement of the *sūtras* was

[1] Vācaspati Miśra flourished in about A.D. 840. In addition to his *Bhāmatī* commentary on the *Brahma-sūtra* he wrote many other works and commentaries on other systems of philosophy. His important works are: *Tattva-bindu*, *Tattva-vaiśāradī* (yoga), *Tattva-samīkṣā Brahma-siddhi-ṭīkā*, *Nyāya-kaṇikā on Vidhi-viveka*, *Nyāya-tattvāloka*, *Nyāya-ratna-ṭīkā*, *Nyāya-vārttika-tātparya-ṭīkā*, *Brahma-tattva-saṃhitoddīpanī*, *Yukti-dīpikā* (*Sāṃkhya*), *Sāṃkhya-tattva-kaumudī*, *Vedānta-tattva-kaumudī*.

[2] He lived about A.D. 900 during the reign of King Manukulāditya and was a pupil of Deveśvara

[3] *vivarta-vādasya hi pūrva-bhūmir*
vedānta-vāde pariṇāma-vādaḥ
vyavasthite 'smin pariṇāma-vāde
svayaṃ samāyāti vivarta-vādaḥ.
Saṃkṣepa-śārīraka, II. 61.

upāyam ātiṣṭhati pūrvam uccair
upeyam āptuṃ janatā yathaiva
śrutir munīndraś ca vivarta-siddhyai
vikāra-vādaṃ vadatas tathaiva. *Ibid.* II. 62.

vikāra-vādaṃ Kapilādi-pakṣam
upetya vādena tu sūtra-kāraḥ
śrutiś ca saṃjalpati pūrvabhūmau
sthitvā vivarta-pratipādanāya. *Ibid.* II. 64.

such as to support the view that the *pariṇāma* view was introduced only to prepare the reader's mind for the *vivarta* view, which was ultimately definitely approved as the true view; but it has been shown that the content of almost all the *sūtras* of II. i. consistently support the *pariṇāma* view, and that even the *sūtra* II. i. 14 cannot be explained as holding the *vivarta* view of causation as the right one, since the other *sūtras* of the same section have been explained by Śaṅkara himself on the *pariṇāma* view; and, if the content be taken into consideration, this *sūtra* also has to be explained on the *pariṇāma* view of *bhedābheda* type.

Teachers and Pupils in Vedānta

The central emphasis of Śaṅkara's philosophy of the Upaniṣads and the *Brahma-sūtra* is on Brahman, the self-revealed identity of pure consciousness, bliss and being, which does not await the performance of any of the obligatory Vedic duties for its realization. A right realization of such Upaniṣad texts as "That art thou," instilled by the right teacher, is by itself sufficient to dispel all the false illusions of world-appearance. This, however, was directly against the Mīmāṃsā view of the obligatoriness of certain duties, and Śaṅkara and his followers had to fight hard on this point with the Mīmāṃsakas. Different Mīmāṃsā writers emphasized in different ways the necessity of the association of duties with Brahma-wisdom; and a brief reference to some of these has been made in the section on Sureśvara. Another question arose regarding the nature of the obligation of listening to the unity texts (e.g. "that art thou") of the Vedānta; and later Vedānta writers have understood it differently. Thus the author of the *Prakaṭārtha*, who probably flourished in the twelfth century, holds that it is only by virtue of the mandate of the Upaniṣads (such as "thou shouldst listen to these texts, understand the meaning and meditate") that one learns for the first time that one ought to listen to the Vedānta texts—a view which is technically called *apūrva-vidhi*. Others, however, think that people might themselves engage in reading all kinds of texts in their attempts to attain salvation and that they might go on the wrong track; and it is just to draw them on to the right path, viz. that of listening to the unity texts of the Upaniṣads, that the Upaniṣads direct men to listen to the unity texts—this view is technically called *niyama-vidhi*.

The followers of Sarvajñātma Muni, however, maintain that there can in no sense be a duty in regard to the attainment of wisdom of Brahma-knowledge, and the force of the duty lies in enjoining the holding of discussions for the clarification of one's understanding; and the meaning of the obligatory sentence "thou shouldst listen to" means that one should hold proper discussions for the clarification of his intellect. Other followers of Sureśvara, however, think that the force of the obligation lies in directing the student of Vedānta steadily to realize the truth of the Vedānta texts without any interruption; and this view is technically called *parisaṃkhyā-vidhi*. Vācaspati Miśra and his followers, however, think that no obligation of duties is implied in these commands; they are simply put in the form of commands in order to show the great importance of listening to Vedānta texts and holding discussions on them, as a means of advancement in the Vedāntic course of progress.

But the central philosophical problem of the Vedānta is the conception of Brahman—the nature of its causality, its relation with *māyā* and the phenomenal world of world-appearance, and with individual persons. Śaṅkara's own writings do not always manifest the same uniform and clear answer; and many passages in different parts of his work show tendencies which could be more or less diversely interpreted, though of course the general scheme was always more or less well-defined. Appaya Dīkṣita notes in the beginning of his *Siddhānta-leśa* that the ancients were more concerned with the fundamental problem of the identity of the self and the Brahman, and neglected to explain clearly the order of phenomenal appearance; and that therefore many divergent views have sprung up on the subject. Thus shortly after Śaṅkara's death we have four important teachers, Sureśvara and his pupil Sarvajñātma Muni, Padmapāda and Vācaspati Miśra, who represent three distinct tendencies in the monistic interpretation of the Vedānta. Sureśvara and his pupil Sarvajñātma Muni held that *māyā* was only an instrument (*dvāra*), through which the one Brahman appeared as many, and had its real nature hidden from the gaze of its individual appearances as individual persons. In this view *māyā* was hardly recognized as a substance, though it was regarded as positive; and it was held that *māyā* had, both for its object and its support, the Brahman. It is the pure Brahman that is the real cause underlying all appearances, and the *māyā* only hangs on it like a veil of illusion which makes this one thing appear as many unreal appearances. It is easy to see that this view ignores altogether the importance of giving philosophical explanations of phenomenal appearance, and is only concerned to emphasize the reality of Brahman as the only truth. Vācaspati's view gives a little more substantiality to *māyā* in the sense that he holds that *māyā* is coexistent with Brahman, as an accessory through the operation of which the creation of world-appearance is possible; *māyā* hides the Brahman as its object, but it rests on individual persons, who are again dependent on *māyā*, and *māyā* on them, in a beginningless cycle. The world-appearance is not mere subjective ideas or sensations, but it has an objective existence, though the nature of its existence is inexplicable and indescribable; and at the time of dissolution of the world (or *pralaya*) its constitutive stuff, psychical and physical, will remain hidden in *avidyā*, to be revived again at the time of the next world-appearance, otherwise called creation. But the third view, namely that of Padmapāda, gives *māyā* a little more substantiality, regarding it as the stuff which contains the double activity or power of cognitive activity and vibratory activity, one determining the psychical process and the other the physical process, and regarding Brahman in association with *māyā*, with these two powers as Iśvara, as the root cause of the world. But the roots of a very thoroughgoing subjective idealism also may be traced even in the writings of Śaṅkara himself. Thus in the *Bṛhadāraṇyaka-bhāṣya* he says that, leaving aside theories of limitation (*avaccheda*) or reflection (*pratibimba*), it may be pointed out that, as the son of Kuntī is the same as Rādheya, so it is the Brahman that appears as individual persons through beginningless *avidyā*; the individual persons so formed again delusively create the world-appearance through their own *avidyā*. It will be pointed out in a later section that Maṇḍana also elaborated the same tendency shortly after Śaṅkara in the ninth century. Thus in the same century we have four distinct lines of Vedāntic development, which began to expand through the later centuries in the writers that followed one or the other of these schools; and some additional tendencies also developed. The tenth century seems to have been very barren in the field of the Vedānta, and, excepting probably Jñānottama Miśra, who wrote a commentary on Sureśvara's *Vārttika*, no writer of great reputation is known to us to have lived in this period. In other fields of philosophical development also this century was more or less barren, and, excepting Udayana and Śrīdhara in Nyāya-Vaiśeṣika, Utpala in Astronomy and Abhinavagupta in Śaivism, probably no other persons of great reputation can be mentioned. There were, however, a few Buddhistic writers of repute in this period, such as Candragomin (junior) of Rajshahi, the author of *Nyāya-loka-siddhi*, Prajñākara Gupta of Vikramaśilā, author of *Pramāṇa-vārtikālaṅkāra* and *Sahopalambha-niścaya*, Ācārya Jetāri of Rajshahi, the author of *Hetu-tattvopadeṣa*, *Dharma-dharmi-viniścaya* and *Bālāvatāra-tarka*, Jina, the author of *Pramāṇa-vārtikālaṅkāra-ṭikā*, Ratnakīrti, the author of the *Apoha-siddhi*, *Kṣaṇa-bhaṅga-siddhi* and *Sthira-siddhi-dūṣaṇa*, and Ratna Vajra, the author of the *Yukti-prayoga*. The eleventh century also does not seem to have been very fruitful for Vedānta philosophy. The only author of great reputation seems to have been Ānandabodha Bhaṭṭārakācārya, who appears to have lived probably in the latter half of the eleventh century and the first half of the twelfth century. The *mahāvidyā* syllogisms of Kulārka Paṇḍita, however, probably began from some time in the eleventh century, and these were often referred to for refutation by Vedāntic writers till the fourteenth century, as will be pointed out in a later section. But it is certain that quite a large number of Vedāntic writers must have worked on the Vedānta before Ānandabodha, although we cannot properly trace them now. Ānandabodha says in his *Nyāya-makaranda* that his work was a compilation (*saṃgraha*) from a large number of Vedāntic monographs (*nibandha-puṣpāñjali*). Citsukha in his commentary on the *Nyāya-makaranda* points out (p. 346) that Ānandabodha was refuting a view of the author of the *Brahma-prakāśikā*. According to Govindānanda's statement in his *Ratna-prabhā*, p. 311, Amalānanda of the thirteenth century refuted a view of the author of the *Prakaṭārtha*. The author of the *Prakaṭārtha* may thus be believed to have lived either in the eleventh or in the twelfth century. It was a commentary on Śaṅkara's *Bhāṣya*, and its full name was *Śārīraka-bhāṣya-prakaṭārtha*; and Ānandajñāna (called also Janārdana) wrote his *Tattvāloka* on the lines of Vedantic interpretation of this work. Mr Tripathi says in his introduction to the *Tarka-saṃgraha* that a copy of this work is available in Tekka Maṭha; but the present writer had the good fortune of going through it from a manuscript in the Adyar Library, and a short account of its philosophical views is given below in a separate section. In the *Siddhānta*-leśa of Appaya Dīkṣita we hear of a commentary on it called *Prakaṭārtha-vivaraṇa*. But, though Ānandajñāna wrote his *Tattvāloka* on the lines of the *Prakaṭārtha*, yet the general views of Ānandajñāna were not the same as those of the author thereof; Ānandajñāna's position was very much like that of Sarvajñātma Muni, and he did not admit many *ajñānas*, nor did he admit any difference beween *māyā* and *avidyā*. But the author of the *Prakaṭārtha*, so far as can be judged from references to him in the *Siddhānta-leśa*, gave a separate place to the *antaḥkaraṇas* of individual persons and thought that, just as the jīvas could be cognizers through the reflection of pure intelligence in the *antaḥkaraṇa* states, so Īśvara is omniscient by knowing everything through *māyā* modifications. The views of the author of the *Prakaṭārtha* regarding the nature of *vidhi* have already been noted. But the way in which Ānandajñāna refers to the *Prakaṭārtha* in *Muṇḍaka*, p. 32, and *Kena*, p. 23, shows that he was either the author of the *Prakaṭārtha* or had written some commentary to it. But he could not have been the author of this work, since he refers to it as the model on which his *Tattvāloka* was written; so it seems very probable that he had written a commentary to it. But it is surprising that Ānandajñāna, who wrote commentaries on most of the important commentaries of Śaṅkara, should also trouble himself to write another commentary on the *Prakaṭārtha*, which is itself a commentary on Śaṅkara 's commentary. It may be surmised, therefore, that he had some special reasons for respecting it, and it may have been the work of some eminent teacher of his or of someone in his parental line. However it may be, it is quite unlikely that the work should have been written later than the middle of the twelfth century[1].

It is probable that Gangāpurī Bhaṭṭāraka also lived earlier than Ānandabodha, as Citsukha points out. Gaṅgāpurī must then have lived either towards the latter part of the tenth century or the first half of the eleventh century. It is not improbable that he may have been a senior contemporary of Ānandabodha. His work, *Padārtha-tattva-nirṇaya*, was commented on by Ānandajñāna. According to him both *māyā* and Brahman are to be regarded as the cause of the world. All kinds of world-phenomena exist, and being may therefore be attributed to them; and being is the same whatever may be the nature of things that exist. Brahman is thus the changeless cause in the world or the *vivarta-kāraṇa*; but all the

[1] See Tripathi's introduction to the *Tarka-saṃgraha*.

changing contents or individual existents must also be regarded as products of the transformation of some substance, and in this sense *māyā* is to be regarded as the *pariṇāmi-kāraṇa* of the world. Thus the world has Brahman as its *vivarta-kāraṇa* and *māyā* as its *pariṇāmi-kāraṇa*. The world manifests both aspects, the aspect of changeless being and that of changing materiality; so both *māyā* and Brahman form the material cause of the world in two different ways (*Brahmamāyā ca ity ubhayopādānam*; *sattva-jāḍya-rūpobhaya-dharmānugaty-upapattiś ca*). *Tarka-viveka* and *Siddhānta-viveka* are the names of two chapters of this book, giving a summary of Vaiśeṣika and Vedānta philosophy respectively. The view of Gaṅgāpurī in the *Padārtha-tattva-nirṇaya* just referred to seems to have been definitely rejected by Ānandabodha in his *Pramāṇa-mālā*, p. 16.

When Kulārka had started the *mahā-vidyā* syllogisms, and great Nyāya authors such as Jayanta and Udayana in the ninth and tenth centuries had been vigorously introducing logical methods in philosophy and were trying to define all that is knowable, the Vedāntic doctrine that all that is knowable is indefinable was probably losing its hold; and it is probable that works like Ānandabodha's *Pramāṇa-mālā* and *Nyāya-dīpāvalī* in the eleventh century or in the early part of the twelfth century were weakly attempting to hold fast to the Vedāntic position on logical grounds. It was Śrīharṣa who in the third quarter of the twelfth century for the first time attempted to refute the entire logical apparatus of the Naiyāyikas. Śrīharṣa's work was carried on in Citsukha's *Tattva-pradīpikā* in the early part of the thirteenth century, by Ānandajñāna in the latter part of the same century in his *Tarka-saṃgraha* and by Nṛsiṃhāśrama Muni in his *Bheda-dhikkāra* in the sixteenth century. On the last-named a pupil, Nārāyaṇāśrama, wrote his *Bheda-dhikkāra-satkriyā*, and this had a sub-commentary, called *Bheda-dhikkāra-satkriyojjvalā*. The beginnings of the dialectical arguments can be traced to Śaṅkara and further back to the great Buddhist writers, Nāgārjuna, Āryadeva, Candrakīrti, etc. Interest in these dialectical arguments was continuously kept up by commentaries written on these works all through the later centuries. The names of these commentators have been mentioned in the sections on Śrīharṣa, Citsukha and Ānandajñāna.

Moreover, the lines of Vedānta interpretation which started with Sureśvara, Padmapāda and Vācaspati were vigorously continued in commentaries and in independent works throughout the later centuries. Thus in the middle of the thirteenth century Vācaspati's *Bhāmatī* was commented on by Amalānanda in his *Kalpa-taru*; and this. *Kalpa-taru* was again commented on by Appaya Dīkṣita in the latter part of the sixteenth century and the first quarter of the seventeenth century, and by Lakṣmīnṛsiṃha in is *Ābhoga* towards the end of the seventeenth century or the beginning of the eighteenth[1].

Padmapāda's *Pañca-pādikā* was commented on by Prakāśātman in the thirteenth century in his *Pañca-pādikā-vivaraṇa*, by Akhaṇḍānanda in the fourteenth century in his *Tattva-dīpana*, by Vidyāraṇya in the same century in his *vivaraṇa-prameya-saṃgraha*, by Ānandapūrṇa and Nṛsiṃha in the sixteenth century and by Rāma Tīrtha in the seventeenth century[2]. The line of Sureśvara also continued in the summary of his great *Vārttika* (called *Vārt-tika-sāra*) by Vidyāraṇya and its commentaries, and also in the commentaries on the *Saṃkṣepa-śārīraka* from the sixteenth century onwards. Many independent works were also written by persons holding more or less the same kinds of views as Sarvaj-ñātma Muni[3]. The philosophy of *dṛṣṭi-sṛṣṭi-vāda* Vedānta, which was probably started by Maṇḍana, had doubtless some adherents too; but we do not meet with any notable writer on this line, except Prakāśānanda in the sixteenth century and his pupil Nānā Dīkṣita. The *Vedānta-kaumudī* is an important work which is

[1] Allāla Sūri, son of Trivikramācārya, wrote a commentary on the *Bhāmatī*, called the *Bhāmatī-tilaka.*

[2] Samyagbodhendra Saṃyamin, pupil of Gīrvāṇendra (A.D. 1450), wrote a summary of the main contents of the *Pañca-pādikā-vivaraṇa* in six chapters (*varṇaka*), and this work is called by two names, *Advaita-bhūṣaṇa* and *Vivaraṇa-prameya-saṃgraha*. There are again two other commentaries on Prakāśātman's *Pañca-pādikā-vivaraṇa*: the *Riju-vivaraṇa* by Viṣṇubhaṭṭa, son of Janārdana Sarvajña and pupil of Svāmīndrapūrṇa, and the *Ṭīkā-ratna* by Ānandapūrṇa. The *Riju-vivaraṇa* had again another commentary on it, called the *Trayyanta-bhāva-pradīpikā*, by Rāmānanda, pupil of Bhāratī Tīrtha.

There are, however, two other commentaries on the *Pañca-pādikā* called Pañca-*pādikā-vyākhyā* (by an author whose name is not definitely known) and the *Prabandha-pariśodhinī* by Ātmasvarūpa, pupil of Nṛsiṃhasvarūpa. Dharma-rāyādhvarīndra also wrote a commentary on *Pañca-pādikā*, called the *Pañca-pādikā-ṭīkā.*

[3] Apart from the two published commentaries on the *Saṃkṣepa-śārīraka*, there is another work called the *Saṃkṣepa-śārīraka-sambandhokti* by Vedānanda, pupil of Vedādhyakṣa-bhagavat-pūjyapāda, in which the author tries to show the mutual relation of the verses of it as yielding a consistent meaning. Nṛsīṃhā-śrama also wrote a commentary on the *Saṃkṣepa-śārīraka*, called the *Tattva-bodhinī.* One Sarvajñātma Bhagavat wrote a small Vedāntic work, called *Pañca prakriyā*; but it is not probable that he is the same as Sarvajñātma Muni.

referred to by Appaya Dīkṣita in his *Siddhānta-leśa*. In this work the omniscience of Brahman consists in the fact that the pure consciousness as Brahman manifests all that exists either as actually transformed or as potentially transformed, as future, or as latently transformed, as the past in the *māyā*; and it is the Parameśvara who manifests Himself as the underlying consciousness (*sākṣin*) in individual persons, manifesting the *ajñāna* transformations in them, and also their potential *ajñāna* in dreamless sleep. Many other important Vedānta views of an original character are expressed in this book. This work of Ramādvaya has been found by the present writer in the Govt. Oriental MSS. Library, Madras, and a separate section has been devoted to its philosophy. From references in it to followers of Madhva it may be assumed that the *Vedānta-kaumudī* was written probably in the fourteenth century.

From the fourteenth century, however, we have a large number of Vedānta writers in all the succeeding centuries; but with the notable exception of Prakāśānanda, Madhusūdana Sarasvatī in his *Advaita-siddhi* (in which he tried to refute the objections of Vyāsa Tīrtha against the monistic Vedānta in the sixteenth century) and probably Vidyāraṇya's *Vivaraṇa-prameya-saṃgraha* and Dharmarājādhvarindra's *Paribhāṣā*, and its *Śikhāmaṇi* commentary by Rāmakrṛṣṇa, there are few writers who can be said to reveal any great originality in Vedāntic interpretations. Most of the writers of this later period were good compilers, who revered all sorts of past Vedāntic ideas and collected them in well-arranged forms in their works. The influence of the *Pañca-pādikā-Vivaraṇa*, however, is very strong in most of these writers, and the *Vivaraṇa* school of thought probably played the most important part in Vedāntic thought throughout all this period.

These Vedāntic writers grew up in particular circles inspired by particular teachers, whose works were carried on either in their own families or among their pupils; a few examples may make this clear. Thus Jagannāthāśrama was a great teacher of south India in the latter half of the fifteenth century; he had a pupil in Nṛsiṃhāśrama, one of the most reputed teachers of Vedānta in the early half of the sixteenth century. He was generally inspired on the one hand by the *Vivaraṇa* and on the other by Śrīharṣa and Citsukha and Sarvajñātma Muni: he wrote a number of Vedānta works, such as *Advaita-dīpikā* (his pupil, Nārāyaṇāśrama, wrote a commentary called *Advaita-dīpikā-vivaraṇa* on it), *Advaita-pañca-*

ratna, *Advaita-bodha-dīpikā*, *Advaita-ratna-koṣa*, *Tattva-bodhinī*, a commentary on the *Saṃkṣepa-śārīraka*, *Tattva-viveka* (which had two commentaries, *Tattva-viveka-dīpana* of Nārāyaṇāśrama and *Tattva-vivecana* of Agnihotra, pupil of Jñānendra Sarasvatī), *Pañca-pādikā-vivaraṇa-prakāśikā*, *Bheda-dhikkāra*, *Advaita-ratna-vyākhyāna* (a commentary on Mallanārodīya's *Advaita-ratna*), and *Vedānta-tattva-viveka*. The fact that he could write commentaries both on Sarvajñātma Muni's work and also on the *Vivaraṇa*, and also write a *Bheda-dhikkāra* (a work on dialectic Vedānta on the lines of Śrīharṣa's dialectical work) shows the syncretistic tendencies of the age, in which the individual differences within the school were all accepted as different views of one Vedānta, and in which people were more interested in Vedānta as a whole and felt no hesitation in accepting all the Vedāntic ideas in their works. Nṛsiṃhāśrama had a pupil Dharmarājādhvarīndra, who wrote a *Vedānta-paribhāṣā*, a commentary called *Tarka-cūḍāmaṇi* on the *Tattva-cintāmaṇi* of Gaṅgeśa, and also on the *Nyaya-siddhānta-dīpa* of Śaśadhara Ācārya, and a commentary on the *Pañca-pādikā* of Padmapāda. His son and pupil Rāmakṛṣṇa Dīkṣita wrote a commentary on the first, called *Vedānta-śikhāmaṇi*; and Amaradāsa, the pupil of Brahmavijñāna, wrote another commentary on this *Śikhāmaṇi* of Rāmakṛṣṇa[1]. Rāmakṛṣṇa had also written a commentary on Rucidatta's *Tattva-cintāmaṇi-prakāśa*, called *Nyāya-śikhāmaṇi*, and a commentary on the *Vedānta-sāra*. Other authors, such as Kāśīnātha Śāstrin and Brahmendra Sarasvatī, had also written separate works bearing the name *Vedānta-paribhāṣā* after the *Vedānta-paribhāṣā* of Dharmarāja in the seventeenth century. Under the sphere of Nṛsiṃha's influence, but in the Śaiva and Mīmāṃsaka family of Raṅgarāja Adhvarin, was born Appaya Dīkṣita, who became one of the most reputed teachers of the sixteenth and the seventeenth centuries. His works have all been noted in the section devoted to him. He again was a teacher of Bhaṭṭojī Dīkṣita, who in addition to many works on grammar, law and ritual (*smṛti*) wrote two important works on Vedānta, called *Tattva-kaustubha* and *Vedānta-tattva-dīpana-vyākhyā*, the latter a commentary on the commentary, *Tattva-viveka-dīpana*, of Nārāyaṇāśrama (a pupil of Nṛsiṃhāśrama) on the latter's work, *Vedānta-tattva-viveka*. This Nārāyaṇāśrama had also written another commentary on

[1] Pettā Dīkṣita, son of Nārāyaṇa Dīkṣita, also wrote a commentary on the *Vedānta-paribhāṣā*, called *Vedānta-paribhāṣā-prakāśikā*.

Nṛsiṃhāśrama's *Bheda-dhikkāra*, called *Bheda-dhikkāra-satkriyā*; and later on in the eighteenth century another commentary was written on Nṛsiṃha's *Bheda-dhikkāra*, called *Advaita-candrikā*, by Narasiṃha Bhaṭṭa, pupil of Rāmabhadrāśrama and Nāgeśvara in the eighteenth century. Bhaṭṭojī Dīkṣita's son Bhānujī Dīkṣita was a commentator on the *Amara-koṣa* (*Vyākhyā-sudhā* or *Subodhinī*). Bhaṭṭojī was, however, a pupil not only of Appaya, but also of Nṛsiṃhāśrama Muni. Bhaṭṭojī's younger brother and pupil, Raṅgojī Bhaṭṭa, wrote two works, the *Advaita-cintāmaṇi* and the *Advaita-śāstra-sāroddhāra*, more or less on the same lines, containing a refutation of Vaiśeṣika categories, a determination of the nature of the self, a determination of the nature of *ajñāna* and the nature of the doctrine of reflection, proofs of the falsity of world-appearance and an exposition of the nature of Brahman and how Brahmahood is to be attained. His son Koṇḍa Bhaṭṭa was mainly a grammarian, who wrote also on Vaiśeṣika. Again Madhusūdana Sarasvatī, who was a pupil of Viśveśvara Sarasvatī (pupil of Sarvajña Viśveśa and pupil's pupil of Govinda Sarasvatī), lived in the early half of the sixteenth century and was probably under the influence of Nṛsiṃhāśrama, who is reputed to have defeated Madhusūdana Sarasvatī's teacher, Mādhava Sarasvatī. Madhusūdana had at least three pupils, Puruṣottama, who wrote on Madhusūdana's commentary the *Siddhānta-tattva-bindu* a commentary called *Siddhānta-tattva-bindu-ṭīkā*[1]; the others were Bālabhadra and Śeṣagovinda (the latter of whom wrote a commentary on Śaṅkara's *Sarva-darśana-siddhānta-saṃgraha*, called *Sarva-siddhānta-rahasya-ṭīkā*). Again Sadānanda, the author of the *Vedānta-sāra*, one of the most popular and well-read syncretistic works on Vedānta, was a contemporary of Nṛsiṃhāśrama; Nṛsiṃha Sarasvatī wrote in 1588 a commentary thereon, called *Subodhinī*. Devendra, the author of the *Svānubhūti-prakāśa*, was also a contemporary of Nṛsiṃhāśrama. It has already been pointed out that Prakāśānanda was probably a contemporary of Nṛsiṃhāśrama, though he does not seem to have been under his influence. This shows how some of the foremost Vedānta writers of the sixteenth and seventeenth centuries grew up together in a Vedāntic circle, many of whom were directly or indirectly under the influence of Nṛsiṃhāśrama and Appaya Dīkṣita.

[1] Brahmānanda wrote on the *Siddhānta-bindu* another commentary, called *Siddhānta-bindu-ṭīkā*.

Passing to another circle of writers, we see that Bhāskara Dīkṣita, who lived in the latter half of the seventeenth century, wrote a commentary, *Ratna-tūlikā*, on the *Siddhānta-siddhāñjana* of his teacher Kṛṣṇānanda. The *Siddhānta-siddhāñjana* is an excellent syncretistic work on Vedānta, which contains most of the important Vedānta doctrines regarding the difference of *dharma-vicāra* and *brahma-vicāra*, the relation of Mīmāṃsā theories of commands, and the need of Brahma-knowledge; it introduces many Mīmāṃsā subjects and treats of their relations to many relevant Vedānta topics. It also introduces elaborate discussions on the nature of knowledge and ignorance. It seems, however, to be largely free from the influence of the *Vivaraṇa*, and it does not enter into theories of perception or the nature of the *antaḥkaraṇa* and its *vṛtti*. It is thus very different from most of the works produced in the sixteenth century in the circles of Nṛsiṃha or Appaya. Kṛṣṇānanda lived probably in the middle of the seventeenth century. He had for teacher Rāmabhadrānanda; and Rāmabhadrānanda was taught by Svayaṃprakāśānanda, the author of the *Vedānta-naya-bhūṣaṇa*, a commentary on the *Brahma-sūtra* on the lines of Vācaspati Miśra's *Bhāmatī*. This Svayaṃprakāśa must be distinguished from the other Svayaṃprakāśa, probably of the same century, who was a pupil of Kaivalyānanda Yogīndra and the author of the *Rasābhi-vyañjikā*, a commentary of *Advaita-makaranda* of Lakṣmīdhara Kavi. Rāmabhadrānanda had as his teacher Rāmānanda Sarasvatī, the author of the *Vedānta-siddhānta-candrikā*, on which a commentary was written by Gaṅgādharendra Sarasvatī (A.D. 1826), pupil of Rāmacandra Sarasvatī and pupil's pupil of Sarvajña Sarasvatī, and author of the *Sāṃrājya-siddhi* with its commentary, the *Kaivalya-kalpadruma*. Prakāśānanda was a pupil of Advaitānanda, author of the *Brahma-vidyābharaṇa*, a commentary on Śaṅkara's *Śārīraka-bhāṣya*—Advaitānanda was a disciple of Rāmatīrtha, author of the *Anvaya-prakāśikā* (a commentary on the *Saṃkṣepa-śārīraka* of Sarvajñātma Muni) and a disciple of Kṛṣṇatīrtha, a contemporary of Jagannāthāśrama, the teacher of Nṛsiṃhāśrama. Rāmatīrtha's *Anvaya-prakāśikā* shows an acquaintance with Madhusūdana's *Advaita-siddhi*; and he may thus be considered to have lived in the middle of the seventeenth century. Svayaṃprakāśānanda, again, had for pupil Mahādevānanda, or Vedāntin Mahādeva, the author of the *Advaita-cintā-kaustubha* or *Tattvānusandhāna*. It seems very clear that these writers of the seventeenth and the early eighteenth centuries flourished in a different circle of Vedāntic ideas, where the views of Vācaspati, Sureśvara and Sarvajñātma Muni had greater influence than the authors of the *Vivaraṇa* school of Vedānta. Another important syncretistic Vedānta writer is Sadānanda Kāśmīraka, author of the *Advaita-brahma-siddhi*, who lived in the early part of the eighteenth century. The *Advaita-brahma-siddhi* is an excellent summary of all the most important Vedānta doctrines, written in an easy style and explaining the chief features of the Vedāntic doctrines in the different schools of Advaita teachers. Narahari's *Bodha-sāra* may be mentioned as one of the important products of the late eighteenth century[1].

The sort of relationship of teachers and students in particular circles that has been pointed out holds good of the earlier authors also, though it is difficult to trace them as well as can be done in the later years, since many of the earlier books are now missing and the footprints of older traditions are becoming more and more faint. Thus it may be pointed out that Vidyāraṇya was a contemporary of Amalānanda in the fourteenth century, as both of them

[1] A number of other important Vedānta works, written mostly during the seventeenth to nineteenth centuries, may also be mentioned. Thus Lokanātha, son of Sarvajñanārāyaṇa and grandson of Nṛsiṃhāśrama, wrote a metrical work in three chapters refuting the views of the dualists, called *Advaita-muktāsāra* with a commentary on it called *Kānti*; Brahmānanda Sarasvatī wrote the *Advaita-siddhānta-vidyotana*; Gopālānanda Sarasvatī, pupil of Yogānanda, wrote the *Akhaṇḍātma-prakāśikā*; Harihara Paramahaṃsa, pupil of Śivarāma, pupil of Viśveśvarāśrama, wrote the *Anubhava-vilāsa*, and early in the nineteenth century Sāmin, a pupil of Brahmānanda, wrote a big work in twelve chapters, called *Brahmānanda-vilāsa*. In this connection it may not be out of place to mention the names of some important works of Vedānta dialectics in refutation of other systems of philosophical views more or less on the lines of those dialectical writings which have been noticed in the present volume. Thus Ānanda-pūrṇa (A.D. 1600), who commented on Śrīharṣa's *Khaṇḍana-khaṇḍa-khādya*, wrote the *Nyāya-candrikā* in four chapters, refuting the views of the Nyāya, Mīmāṃsā and Vaiśeṣika; Ānandānubhava, pupil of Nārāyaṇa Jyotisha, who lived probably in the same century, wrote a similar work, called *Padārtha-tattva-nirṇaya*; Jñānaghana, who probably lived in the thirteenth century, wrote an elaborate dialectical work in thirty-three chapters (*prakaraṇa*), called *Tattva-śuddhi*; Śrīnivāsa Yajvan, who probably lived in the sixteenth century, wrote the *Vādāvalī* in twenty-six chapters in refutation of Viśiṣṭādvaita and Dvaita views; Bhavānīśaṅkara also wrote a similar dialectical work, called *Siddhānta-dīpikā*. As examples of semi-popular Vedānta works of a syncretistic type, such works as the *Tattva-bodha* of Vāsudevendra, the *Guṇa-traya-viveka* of Svayaṃprakāśa Yogīndra, the *fagan-mithyātva-dīpikā* of Rāmendra Yogin, the *Ānanda-dīpa* of Śivānanda Yati(which had a commentary called *Ānanda-dīpa-ṭikār* by Rāmanātha), the *Svātma-yoga-pradīpa* by Yogīśvara (which had a commentary by Amarānanda) and the *Vedānta-hṛdaya* (on the lines of the *Yoga-vāsiṣṭha* and *Gauḍapāda*) by Varada Paṇḍita may be mentioned. This latter work was probably later than Prakāśānanda's *Vedānta-siddhānta-muktāvali*, which followed the same line of thought.

were pupils of Śaṅkarānanda and Anubhavānanda respectively; these in turn were both pupils of Ānandātman. Śaṅkarānanda was the author of the *Gitā-tātparya-bodhinī* and of a number of commentaries on the various Upaniṣads, and also of a summary of the Upaniṣads, called *Upaniṣad-ratna*. Amalānanda, however, had as teacher not only Anubhavānanda, but also Sukhaprakāśa Muni, who again was a disciple of Citsukha, himself a disciple of Gauḍeśvara Ācārya (called also Jñānottama).

Vedānta Doctrine of Soul and the Buddhist Doctrine of Soullessness.

One of the most important points of Śaṅkara's criticism of Buddhism is directed against its denial of a permanent soul which could unite the different psychological constituents or could behave as the enjoyer of experiences and the controller of all thoughts and actions.

The Buddhists argue that for the production of sense-cognition, as the awareness of a colour or sound, what is required in addition to the sense-data of colours, etc. is the corresponding sense-faculties, while the existence of a soul cannot be deemed indispensable for the purpose[1]. Vasubandhu argues that what is experienced is the sense-data and the psychological elements in groups called *skandhas*. What one calls self (*ātman*) cannot be anything more than a mere apparent cognitional existence (*prajñapti-sat*) of what in reality is but a conglomeration of psychological elements. Had the apparent self been something as different from the psychological elements as colours are from sounds, it would then be regarded as an individual (*pudgala*); but, if its difference from these psychological elements be of the same nature as the difference of the constituents of milk from the appearance of milk, then the self could be admitted only to have a cognitional existence (*prajñapti-sat*)[2]. The self has, in fact, only a cognitional appearance of separateness from the psychological elements; just as, though

[1] The arguments here followed are those of Vasubandhu, as found in his *Abhidharma-kośa*, and are based on Prof. Stcherhatsky's translation of the appendix to ch. viii of that work, called the *Pudgala-viniścaya*, and Yaśomitra's commentary in manuscript from Nepal, borrowed from Viśvabhāratī, Santiniketan, Bengal.

[2] *yadi yathā rūpādiḥ śabdāder bhāvāntaram abhipreyate pudgala iti abhyu-pagato bhavati bhinna-lakṣaṇaṃ hi rūpaṃ śabdād ityādi kṣīrādivat samudāyaś cet prajñaptitaḥ. Abhidharma-kośa-vyākhyā*, Viśvabhāratī MS. p. 337.

milk appears to have a separate existence from the proper combination of its constituent elements, yet it is in reality nothing more than a definite kind of combination of its constituent elements, so the self is nothing more than a certain conglomeration of the psychological elements (*skandha*), though it may appear to have a separate and independent existence. The Vātsīputrīyas, however, think that the individual is something different from. the *skandhas* or psychological entities, as its nature is different from the nature of them. The Vātsīputrīyas deny the existence of a permanent soul, but believe in momentary individuals (*pudgala*) as category separate and distinct from the *skandhas*. Just as fire is something different from the fuel that conditioned it, so the name "individual" (*pudgala*) is given to something conditioned by the *skandhas* at a given moment in a personal life[1]. Vasubandhu, however, argues against the acceptance of such an individual and says that there is no meaning in accepting such an individual. Rain and sun have no effects on mere vacuous space, they are of use only to the skin; if the individual is, like the skin, a determiner of the value of experiences, then it must be accepted as external; if it is like vacuous space, then no purpose is fulfilled by accepting it[2]. The Vātsīputrīyas, however, thought that, just as the fuel conditioned the fire, so the personal elements conditioned the individual. By this conditioning the Vātsīputrīyas meant that the personal elements were some sort of a coexisting support[3]. What is meant by saying that the *pudgala* is conditioned by the personal elements is that, when the *skandhas* or psychological elements are present, the *pudgala* is also present there[4]. But Vasubandhu urges that a mere conditioning of this kind is not sufficient to establish the cognitional existence of an individual; for even colour is conditioned by the visual sense, light and attention in such a way that, these being present, there is the perception of light; but can anybody on that ground consider the

[1] Stcherbatsky's translation of the *Pudgala-viniścaya*, *Bulletin de l'Académie des Sciences de Russie*, p. 830.

The exact text of Vasubandhu, as translated from Tibetan in a note, runs thus: *gṛhīta-pratyutpannābhyantara-skandham upādāya pudgala-prajñaptiḥ. Ibid.* p. 953.

[2] *Vātsīputrīyāṇāṃ tīrthika-dṛṣṭiḥ prasajyate niṣprayojanatvaṃ ca*
varṣāta-pābhyāṃ kiṃ vyomnaś carmaṇy-asti tayoḥ phalam
carmopamaś cet sa nityaḥ khatulyaś ced asatphalaḥ.
MS. of Yaśomitra's commentary, p. 338.

[3] *āśraya-bhūtaḥ saha-bhūtaś ca. Ibid.*

[4] *rūpasyāpi prajñaptir vaktavyā cakṣur-ādiṣu satsu tasyopalambhāt, tāni cakṣur-ādīny upādāya rūpam prajñāpyate. Ibid.*

existence of colour to be a cognitional one? And would cognitional entities deserve to be enumerated as separate categories? Again it may be asked, if such an individual exists, how is it experienced? For, if it be experienced by any of the senses, it must be a sense-datum: for the senses can grasp only their appropriate sense-data, and the individual is no sense-datum. Therefore, just as milk is nothing but the collected sense-data of colour, taste, etc., so also the so-called individual is nothing more than the conglomerated psychological elements[1]. The Vātsīputrīyas argue that, since the psychological elements, the sense-data, etc., are the causes of our experience of the individual, the individual cannot be regarded as being identical with these causal elements which are responsible for their experience; if it were so, then even light, eye, attention, etc., which are causes of the experience of the sense-data, would have to be regarded as being identical in nature with the individual[2]. But it is not so maintained; the sense-datum of sounds and colours is always regarded as being different from the individual, and one always distinguishes an individual from a sense-datum and says "this is sound," "this is colour" and "this is individual[3]." But the individual is not felt to be as distinct from the psychological elements as colour is from sound. The principle of difference or distinctness consists in nothing but a difference of moments; a colour is different from a sound because it is experienced at a different moment, while the psychological elements and the individual are not experienced at different moments[4]. But it is argued in reply that, as the sense-data and the individual are neither different nor identical (*ratio essendi*), so their cognition also is neither different nor identical in experience (*ratio cognoscendi*)[5]. But Vasubandhu says that, if such a view is taken in this case, then it might as well be taken in all cases wherever there is any conglomeration[6]. Moreover, the separate senses are all limited to their special fields, and the mind which acts with them is also limited

[1] *yathā rūpādīny eva samastāni samuditāni kṣīram iti udakam iti vā prajñāpyate, tathā skandhāś ca samastā pudgala iti prajñāpyate, iti siddham.* MS. of Yaśomitra's commentary, p. 339 A.

[2] *yathā rūpam pudgalopalabdheḥ kāraṇaṃ bhavati sa ca tebhyo'nyo na vaktavyaḥ āloka-cakṣur-manaskārā api rūpopalabdheḥ kāraṇaṃ bhavati tad api tad-abhinna-svabhāvaḥ pudgalaḥ prāpnoti. Ibid.*

[3] *Ibid.* p. 339 B.

[4] *svalakṣaṇād api kṣaṇāntaram anyad ity udāhāryam. Ibid.*

[5] *yathā rūpa-pudgalayor anyānanyatvam avaktavyam evaṃ tadupalabdhyorapi anyānanyatvam avaktavyam. Ibid.*

[6] *yo 'yaṃ siddhāntaḥ pudgala eva vaktavyaḥ so'yam bhidyate saṃskṛtam api avaktavyam iti kṛtvā. Ibid.*

to the data supplied by them; there is, therefore, no way in which the so-called individual can be experienced. In the Ajita sermon Buddha is supposed to say: "A visual consciousness depends upon the organ of sight and a visible object. When these three (object, sense organ and consciousness) combine, a sensation is produced. It is accompanied by a feeling, a representation and a volition. Only so much is meant, when we are speaking of a human being. To these (five sets of elements) different names are given, such as a sentient being, a man, Manu's progeny, a son of Manu, a child, an individual, a life, a soul. If with respect to them the expression is used 'he sees the object with his own eyes,' it is false imputation (there being in reality nobody possessing eyes of his own). In common life such expressions with respect to them are current as 'that is the name of this venerable man, he belongs to such a caste and such a family, he eats such food, this pleases him, he has reached such an age, he has lived so many years, he has died at such an age.' These O brethren! accordingly are mere words, mere conventional designations.

'Expressions are they, (but not truth)!
Real elements have no duration:
Vitality makes them combine
In mutually dependent apparitions[1].' "

The Vātsīputrīyas however refer to the *Bhāra-hāra-sūtra*, in which Buddha is supposed to say: "O brethren, I shall explain unto you the burden (of life), and moreover I shall explain the taking up of the burden, the laying aside of it and who the carrier is...What is the burden? All the five aggregates of elements—the substrates of personal life. What is meant by the taking up of the burden? The force of craving for a continuous life, accompanied by passionate desires, the rejoicing at many an object. What is the laying aside of the burden? It is the wholesale rejection of this craving for a continuation of life, accompanied as it is by passionate desires and rejoicings at many an object, the getting rid of it in every circumstance, its extinction, its end, its suppression, an aversion to it, its restraint, its disappearance. Who is the carrier? We must answer: it is the individual, i.e. 'this venerable man having this name, of such a caste, of such a family, eating such food, finding pleasure or displeasure at such things, of such an age, who after a

[1] Stcherbatsky's translation in *Bulletin de l'Académie des Sciences de Russie*.

life of such length will pass away having reached such an age[1].'" But Vasubandhu points out that the carrier of the burden is not to be supposed to be some eternal soul or real individual. It is the momentary group of elements of the preceding moment that is designated as the burden, and the immediately succeeding one the carrier of the burden (*bhāra-hāra*)[2].

The Vātsīputrīyas again argue that activity implies an active agent, and, since knowing is an action, it also implies the knower who knows, just as the walking of Devadatta implies a Devadatta who walks. But Vasubandhu's reply to such a contention is that there is nowhere such a unity. There is no individual like Devadatta: what we call Devadatta is but a conglomeration of elements. "The light of a lamp is a common metaphorical designation for an uninterrupted production of a series of flashing flames. When this production changes its place, we say that the light has moved. Similarly consciousness is a conventional name for a chain of conscious moments. When it changes its place (i.e. appears in co-ordination with another objective element), we say that it apprehends that object. And in the same way we speak about the existence of material elements. We say matter 'is produced,' 'it exists'; but there is no difference between existence and the element which does exist. The same applies to consciousness (there is nothing that cognizes, apart from the evanescent flashing of consciousness itself)[3]."

It is easy to see that the analysis of consciousness offered by the Vedānta philosophy of the Śaṅkara school is entirely different from this. The Vedānta holds that the fact of consciousness is entirely different from everything else. So long as the assemblage of the physical or physiological conditions antecedent to the rise of any cognition, as for instance, the presence of illumination, sense-object contact, etc., is being prepared, there is no knowledge, and it is only at a particular moment that the cognition of an object arises. This cognition is in its nature so much different from each and all the elements constituting the so-called assemblage of conditions, that it cannot in any sense be regarded as the product of

[1] Stcherbatsky's translation

[2] Yaśomitra points out that there is no carrier of the burden different from the collection of the skandhas—*bhārādānavan na skandhebhyo' rthāntara-bhūtaḥ pudgala ity arthaḥ. Abhidharma-kośa-vyākhyā*, Viśvabhāratī MS.

[3] Stcherbatsky's translation in Bulletin de *l'Académie des Sciences de Russie*, pp. 938–939.

any collocation of conditions. Consciousness thus, not being a product of anything and not being further analysable into any constituents, cannot also be regarded as a momentary flashing. Uncaused and unproduced, it is eternal, infinite and unlimited. The main point in which consciousness differs from everything else is the fact of its self-revelation. There is no complexity in consciousness. It is extremely simple, and its only essence or characteristic is pure self-revelation. The so-called momentary flashing of consciousness is not due to the fact that it is momentary, that it rises into being and is then destroyed the next moment, but to the fact that the objects that are revealed by it are reflected through it from time to time. But the consciousness is always steady and unchangeable in itself. The immediacy (*aparokṣatva*) of this consciousness is proved by the fact that, though everything else is manifested by coming in touch with it, it itself is never expressed, indicated or manifested by inference or by any other process, but is always self-manifested and self-revealed. All objects become directly revealed to us as soon as they come in touch with it. Consciousness (*saṃvid*) is one. It is neither identical with its objects nor on the same plane with them as a constituent element in a collocation of them and consciousness. The objects of consciousness or all that is manifested in consciousness come in touch with consciousness and themselves appear as consciousness. This appearance is such that, when they come in touch with consciousness, they themselves flash forth as consciousness, though that operation is nothing but a false appearance of the non-conscious objects and mental states in the light of consciousness, as being identical with it. But the intrinsic difference between consciousness and its objects is that the former is universal (*pratyak*) and constant (*anuvṛtta*), while the latter are particular (*apratyak*) and alternating (*vyāvṛtta*). The awarenesses of a book, a table, etc. appear to be different not because these are different flashings of knowledge, but because of the changing association of consciousness with these objects. The objects do not come into being with the flashings of their awareness, but they have their separate existence and spheres of operation[1]. Consciousness is one and unchanging; it is only when the objects get associated with it that

[1] *tattva-darśī tu nityam advitīyaṃ vijñānaṃ viṣayāś ca tatrādhyastāḥ pṛthag-artha-kriyā-samarthās teṣāṃ cābādhitaṃ sthāyitvam astīti vadati. Vivaraṇa-prameya-saṃgraha*, p. 74, the Vizianagram Sanskrit Series, Benares, 1893.

they appear in consciousness and as identical with it in such a way that the flashing of an object in consciousness appears as the flashing of the consciousness itself. It is through an illusion that the object of consciousness and consciousness appear to be welded together into such an integrated whole, that their mutual difference escapes our notice, and that the object of consciousness, which is only like an extraneous colour applied to consciousness, does not appear different or extraneous to it, but as a specific mode of the consciousness itself. Thus what appear as but different awarenesses, as book-cognition, table-cognition, are not in reality different awarenesses, but one unchangeable consciousness successively associated with ever-changing objects which falsely appear to be integrated with it and give rise to the appearance that qualitatively different kinds of consciousness are flashing forth from moment to moment. Consciousness cannot be regarded as momentary. For, had it been so, it would have appeared different at every different moment. If it is urged that, though different consciousnesses are arising at each different moment, yet on account of extreme similarity this is not noticed; then it may be replied that, if there is difference between the two consciousnesses of two successive moments, then such difference must be grasped either by a different consciousness or by the same consciousness. In the first alternative the third awareness, which grasps the first two awarenesses and their difference, must either be identical with them, and in that case the difference between the three awarenesses would vanish; or it may be different from them, and in that case, if another awareness be required to comprehend their difference and that requires another and so on, there would be a vicious infinite. If the difference be itself said to be identical with the nature of the consciousness (*saṃvit-svarūpa-bhūto bhedaḥ*), and if there is nothing to apprehend this difference, then the non-appearance of the difference implies the non-appearance of the consciousness itself; for by hypothesis the difference has been held to be identical with the consciousness itself. The non-appearance of difference, implying the non-appearance of consciousness, would mean utter blindness. The difference between the awareness of one moment and another cannot thus either be logically proved, or realized in experience, which always testifies to the unity of awareness through all moments of its appearance. It may be held that the appearance of unity is erroneous, and that, as such, it presumes that the awarenesses are similar; for without such a similarity there could not have been the erroneous appearance of unity. But, unless the difference of the awarenesses and their similarity be previously proved, there is nothing which can even suggest that the appearance of unity is erroneous[1]. It cannot be urged that, if the existence of difference and similarity between the awarenesses of two different moments can be proved to be false, then only can the appearance of unity be proved to be true; for the appearance of unity is primary and directly proved by experience. Its evidence can be challenged only if the existence of difference between the awarenesses and their similarity be otherwise proved. The unity of awareness is a recognition of the identity of the awarenesses (*pratyabhijñā*), which is self-evident.

It has also been pointed out that the Buddhists give a different analysis of the fact of recognition. They hold that perception reveals the existence of things at the moment of perception, whereas recognition involves the supposition of their existence through a period of past time, and this cannot be apprehended by perception, which is limited to the present moment only. If it is suggested that recognition is due to present perception as associated with the impressions (*saṃskāra*) of previous experience, then such a recognition of identity would not prove the identity of the self as "I am he"—for in the self-luminous self there cannot be any impressions. The mere consciousness as the flash cannot prove any identity; for that is limited to the present moment and cannot refer to past experience and unite it with the experience of the present moment. The Buddhists on their side deny the existence of recognition as the perception of identity, and think that it is in reality not one but two concepts—"I" and "that"—and not a separate experience of the identity of the self as persisting through time. To this the Vedāntic reply is that, though there cannot be any impressions in the self as pure consciousness, yet the self as associated with the mind (*antaḥkaraṇa*) can well have impressions (*saṃskāra*), and so recognition is possible[2]. But it may be objected that the complex of the self and mind would then be playing the double role of knower and the known; for it is the mind containing the impressions and the self that together

[1] *Vivaraṇa-prameya-saṃgraha*, p. 76.

[2] *kevale cidātmani janya-jñāna-tat-saṃskārayor asambhove' py antaḥkaraṇa-viśiṣṭe tat-sambhavād ukta-pratyabhijñā kiṃ na syāt. Ibid.* p. 76.

play the part of the recognizer, and it is exactly those impressions together with the self that form the content of recognition also—and hence in this view the agent and the object have to be regarded as one. But in reply to this Vidyāraṇya Muni urges that all systems of philosophy infer the existence of soul as different from the body; and, as such an inference is made by the self, the self is thus both the agent and the object of such inferences. Vidyāraṇya says that it may further be urged that the recognizer is constituted of the self in association with the mind, whereas the recognized entity is constituted of the self as qualified by past and present time[1]. Thus the recognition of self-identity does not strictly involve the fact of the oneness of the agent and its object. If it is urged that, since recognition of identity of self involves two concepts, it also involves two moments, then the assertion that all knowledge is momentary also involves two concepts, for momentariness cannot be regarded as being identical with knowledge. The complexity of a concept does not mean that it is not one but two different concepts occurring at two different moments. If such a maxim is accepted, then the theory that all knowledge is momentary cannot be admitted as one concept, but two concepts occurring at two moments; and hence momentariness cannot be ascribed to knowledge, as is done by the Buddhists. Nor can it be supposed, in accordance with the Prabhākara view, that the existence of the permanent "this self" is admitted merely on the strength of the recognizing notion of "self-identity"; for the self which abides through the past and exists in the present cannot be said to depend on a momentary concept of recognition of self-identity. The notion of self-identity is only a momentary notion, which lasts only at the present time; and hence the real and abiding self cannot owe its reality or existence merely to a psychological notion of the moment.

Again, if it is argued that memory, such as "I had an awareness of a book," shows that the self was existing at the past time when the book was perceived, it may be replied that such memory and previous experience may prove the past existence of the self, but it cannot prove that the self that was existing in the past is identical with the self that is now experiencing. The mere existence of self at two moments of time does not prove that the self had persisted through the intervening times. Two notions of

[1] *antaḥkaraṇa-viśiṣṭatayaivātmanaḥ pratyabhijñātṛtvaṃ pūrvāpara-kāla-viśiṣṭatayā ca pratyabhijñeyatvam. Vivaraṇa-prameya-saṃgraha*, p. 77.

two different times cannot serve to explain the idea of recognition, which presupposes the notion of persistence. If it were held that the two notions produce the notion of self-persistence through the notion of recognition, then that would mean that the Buddhist admits that one can recognize himself as "I am he." It cannot be said that, since the self itself cannot be perceived, there is no possibility of the perception of the identity of the self through recognition; for, when one remembers "I had an experience," that very remembrance proves that the self was perceived. Though at the time when one remembers it the self at the time of such memory is felt as the perceiver and not as the object of that self-perception, yet at the time of the previous experience which is now being remembered the self must have been itself the object of the perception. If it is argued that it is only the past awareness that is the object of memory and this awareness, when remembered, expresses the self as its cognizer, then to this it may be replied that since at the time of remembering there is no longer the past awareness, the cognizer on whom awareness had to rest itself is also absent. It is only when an awareness reveals itself that it also reveals the cognizer on whom it rests; but, if an awareness is remembered, then the awareness which is remembered is only made an object of present awareness which is self-revealed. But the past awareness which is supposed to be remembered is past and lost and, as such, it neither requires a cognizer on which it has to rest nor actually reveals such a cognizer. It is only the self-revealed cognition that also immediately reveals the cognizer with its own revelation. But, when a cognition is mediated through memory, its cognizer is not manifested with its remembrance[1]. So the self which experienced an awareness in the past can be referred to only through the mediation of memory. So, when the Prabhākaras hold that the existence of the self is realized through such a complex notion as "I am he," it has to be admitted that it is only through the process of recognition (*pratyabhijñā*) that the persistence of the self is established. The main point that Vidyāraṇya Muni urges in his *Vivaraṇa-prameya-saṃgraha* is that the fact of recognition or the experience of self-identity cannot be explained by any assumption of two separate concepts, such as the memory of a past cognition or cognizer and the present awareness.

[1] *svayaṃprakāśamānaṃ hi saṃvedanam āśrayaṃ sādhayati na tu smṛti-viṣayatayā para-prakāśyam. Vivaraṇa-prameya-saṃgraha*, p. 78.

We all feel that our selves are persisting through time and that I who experienced pleasure yesterday and I who am experiencing new pleasures today are identical; and the only theory by which this notion of self-persistence or self-identity can be explained is by supposing that the self exists and persists through time. The Buddhist attempts at explaining this notion of self-identity by the supposition of the operation of two separate concepts are wholly inadequate, as has already been shown. The perception of self-identity can therefore be explained only on the basis of a permanently existing self.

Again, the existence of self is not to be argued merely through the inference that cognition, will and feeling presuppose some entity to which they belong and that it is this entity that is called self; for, if that were the case, then no one would be able to distinguish his own self from that of others. For, if the self is only an entity which has to be presupposed as the possessor of cognition, will, etc., then how does one recognize one's own cognition of things as differing from that of others? What is it that distinguishes my experience from that of others? My self must be immediately perceived by me in order that I may relate any experience to myself. So the self must be admitted as being self-manifested in all experience; without admitting the self to be self-luminous in all experience the difference between an experience as being my own and as belonging to others could not be explained. It may be objected by some that the self is not self-luminous by itself, but only because, in self-consciousness, the self is an object of the cognizing operation (*saṃvit-karma*). But this is hardly valid; for the self is not only cognized as an object of self-consciousness, but also in itself in all cognitional operations. The self cannot be also regarded as being manifested by ideas or percepts. It is not true that the cognition of the self occurs after the cognition of the book or at any different time from it. For it is true that the cognition of the self and that of the book take place at the same point of time; for the same awareness cannot comprehend two different kinds of objects at the same time. If this was done at different points of time, then that would not explain our experience—"I have known this". For such a notion implies a relation between the knower and the known; and, if the knower and the known were grasped in knowledge at two different points of time, there is nothing which could unite them together in the same act of knowledge. It is also wrong to maintain that the self is manifested only as the upholder of ideas; for the self is manifested in the knowing operation itself. So, since the self cannot be regarded as being either the upholder or cognizer of ideas or their object, there is but one way in which it can be considered as self-manifesting or self-revealing (*sva-prakāśa*). The immediacy of the self is thus its self-revealing and self-manifesting nature. The existence of self is thus proved by the self-luminous nature of the self. The self is the cognizer of the objects only in the sense that under certain conditions of the operation of the mind there is the mind-object contact through a particular sense, and, as the result thereof, these objects appear in consciousness by a strange illusion; so also ideas of the mind, concepts, volitions and emotions appear in consciousness and themselves appear as conscious states, as if consciousness was their natural and normal character, though in reality they are only illusorily imposed upon the consciousness—the self-luminous self.

Ānandabodha Bhaṭṭārakācārya, from whom Vidyāraṇya often borrows his arguments, says that the self-luminosity of the self has to be admitted, because it cannot be determined as being manifested by anything else. The self cannot be regarded as being perceived by a mental perception (*mānasa pratyakṣa*); for that would involve the supposition that the self is the object of its own operation; for cognition is at any rate a function of the self. The functions of cognition belonging to the self cannot affect the self itself[1]. The Vedānta has also to fight against the Prabhākara view which regards cognition as manifesting the object and the self along with itself, as against its own view that it is the self which is identical with knowledge and which is self-manifesting. Ānandabodha thus objects to the Prabhākara view, that it is the object-cognition which expresses both the self and the not-self, and holds that the self cannot be regarded as an object of awareness. Ānandabodha points out that it may be enunciated as a universal proposition that what is manifested by cognition must necessarily be an object of cognition, and that therefore, if the self is not an object of cognition, it is not manifested by cognition[2]. Therefore the self or the cognizer is not manifested by cognition; for, like

[1] *tathā sati svādhāra-vijñāna-vṛtti-vyāpyatvād ātmanaḥ karmatve svātmani vṛtti-virodhād iti brūmaḥ. Nyāya-makaranda*, p. 131.

[2] *Ibid.* pp. 134–135.

cognition, it is self-manifested and immediate without being an object of cognition[1].

The self-luminosity of cognition is argued by Ānandabodha. He says that, if it is held that cognition does not manifest itself, though it manifests its objects, it may be replied that, if it were so, then at the time when an object is cognized the cognizer would have doubted if he had any cognition at the time or not. If anyone is asked whether he has seen a certain person or not, he is sure about his own knowledge that he has seen him and never doubts it. It is therefore certain that, when an object is revealed by any cognition, the cognition is itself revealed as well. If it is argued that such a cognition is revealed by some other cognition, then it might require some other cognition and that another and so on *ad infinitum*; and thus there is a vicious infinite. Nor can it be held that there is some other mental cognition (occurring either simultaneously with the awareness of the object or at a later moment) by which the awareness of the awareness of the object is further cognized. For from the same mind-contact there cannot be two different awareneses of the type discussed. If at a later moment, then, there is mind-activity, cessation of one mind-contact, and again another mind-activity and the rise of another mind-contact, that would imply many intervening moments, and thus the cognition which is supposed to cognize an awareness of an object would take place at a much later moment, when the awareness which it has to reveal is already passed. It has therefore to be admitted that cognition is itself self-luminous and that, while manifesting other objects, it manifests itself also. The objection raised is that the self or the cognition cannot affect itself by its own functioning (*vṛtti*); the reply is that cognition is like light and has no intervening operation by which it affects itself or its objects. Just as light removes darkness, helps the operation of the eye and illuminates the object and manifests itself all in one moment without any intervening operation of any other light, so cognition also in one flash manifests itself and its objects, and there is no functioning of it by which it has to affect itself. This cognition cannot be described as being mere momentary flashes, on the ground that, when there is the blue awareness, there is not the yellow awareness; for apart from the blue awareness, the

[1] *saṃveditā na saṃvid-adhīna-prakāśaḥ saṃvit-karmatām antareṇa aparokṣatvāt saṃvedanavat. Nyāya-makaranda*, p. 135. This argument is borrowed verbatim by Vidyāraṇya in his *Vivaraṇa-prameya-saṃgraha*, p. 85.

yellow awareness or the white awareness there is also the natural basic awareness or consciousness, which cannot be denied. It would be wrong to say that there are only the particular awarenesses which appear and vanish from moment to moment; for, had there been only a series of particular awarenesses, then there would be nothing by which their differences could be realized. Each awareness in the series would be of a particular and definite character, and, as it passed away, would give place to another, and that again to another, so that there would be no way of distinguishing one awareness from another; for according to the theory under discussion there is no consciousness except the passing awarenesses, and thus there would be no way by which their differences could be noticed; for, even though the object of awareness, such as blue and yellow, differed amongst themselves, that would fail to explain how the difference of a blue awareness and a yellow awareness could be apprehended. So the best would be to admit the self to be of the nature of pure consciousness.

It will appear from the above discussion that the Vedānta had to refute three opponents in establishing its doctrine that the self is of the nature of pure consciousness and that it is permanent and not momentary. The first opponent was the Buddhist, who believed neither in the existence of the self nor in the nature of any pure permanent consciousness. The Buddhist objection that there was no permanent self could be well warded off by the Vedānta by appealing to the verdict of our notion of self-identity—which could not be explained on the Buddhist method by the supposition of two separate notions of a past "that self" and the present "I am." Nor can consciousness be regarded as being nothing more than a series of passing ideas or particular awarenesses; for on such a theory it would be impossible to explain how we can react upon our mental states and note their differences. Consciousness has thus to be admitted as permanent. Against the second opponent, the Naiyāyika, the Vedānta urges that the self is not the inferred object to which awarenesses, volitions or feelings belong, but is directly and immediately intuited. For, had it not been so, how could one distinguish his own experiences as his own and as different from those of others? The internalness of my own experiences shows that they are directly intuited as my own, and not merely supposed as belonging to some self who was the possessor of his experiences. For inference cannot reveal the internalness of any cognition or feeling. Against the third opponent, the Mīmāṃsaka, the Vedānta urges that the self-revealing character belongs to the self which is identical with thought—as against the Mīmāṃsa view, that thought as a self-revealing entity revealed the self and the objects as different from it. The identity of the self and thought and the self-revealing character of it are also urged; and it is shown by a variety of dialectical reasoning that such a supposition is the only reasonable alternative that is left to us.

This self as pure consciousness is absolutely impersonal, unlimited and infinite. In order to make it possible that this one self should appear as many individuals and as God, it is supposed that it manifests itself differently through the veil of *māyā.* Thus, according to the *Siddhānta-leśa*, it is said in the *Prakaṭārthavivaraṇa* that, when this pure consciousness is reflected through the beginningless, indescribable *māyā*, it is called Īśvara or God. But, when it is reflected through the limited parts of *māyā* containing powers of veiling and of diverse creation (called *avidyā*), there are the manifestations of individual souls or *jīvas*. It is again said in the *Tattva-viveka* of Nṛsiṃhāśrama that, when this pure consciousness is reflected through the pure *sattva* qualities, as dominating over other impure parts of *prakṛti*, there is the manifestation of God. Whereas, when the pure consciousness is reflected through the impure parts of *rajas* and *tamas*, as dominating over the *sattva* part of *prakṛti* (called also *avidyā*), there are the manifestations of the individual selves or *jīvas*. The same *prakṛti* in its two aspects, as predominating in *sattva* and as predominating in *rajas* and *tamas*, goes by the name of *māyā* and *avidyā* and forms the conditioning factors (*upādhi*) of the pure consciousness, which on account of the different characters of the conditioning factors of *māyā* and *avidyā* appear as the omniscient God and the ignorant individual souls. Sarvajñātma Muni thinks that, when the pure consciousness is reflected through *avidyā*, it is called Īśvara, and, when it is reflected through mind (*antaḥkaraṇa*), it is called *jīva.*

These various methods of accounting for the origin of individual selves and God have but little philosophical significance. But they go to show that the principal interest of the Vedānta lies in establishing the supreme reality of a transcendental principle of pure consciousness, which, though always untouched and unattached in its own nature, is yet the underlying principle which can explain all the facts of the enlivening and enlightening of all our conscious experiences. All that is limited, be it an individual self or an individual object of awareness, is in some sense or other an illusory imposition of the modification of a non-conscious principle on the principle of consciousness. The Vedānta is both unwilling and incapable of explaining the nature of the world-process in all its details, in which philosophy and science are equally interested. Its only interest is to prove that the world-process presupposes the existence of a principle of pure consciousness which is absolutely and ultimately real, as it is immediate and intuitive. Reality means what is not determined by anything else; and in this sense pure consciousness is the only reality—and all else is indescribable—neither real nor unreal; and the Vedānta is not interested to discover what may be its nature.

Vedāntic Cosmology.

From what has been said above it is evident that *māyā* (also called *avidyā* or *ajñāna*) is in itself an indefinable mysterious stuff, which has not merely a psychological existence, but also an ontological existence as well. It is this *ajñāna* which on the one hand forms on the subjective plane the mind and the senses (the self alone being Brahman and ultimately real), and on the other hand, on the objective plane, the whole of the objective universe. This *ajñāna* has two powers, the power of veiling or covering (*āvaraṇa*) and the power of creation (*vikṣepa*). The power of veiling, though small, like a little cloud veiling the sun with a diameter of millions of miles, may, in spite of its limited nature, cover up the infinite, unchangeable self by veiling its self-luminosity as cognizer. The veiling of the self means veiling the shining unchangeable self-perception of the self, as infinite, eternal and limitless, pure consciousness, which as an effect of such veiling appears as limited, bound to sense-cognitions and sense-enjoyments and functioning as individual selves[1]. It is through this covering power of *ajñāna* that the self appears as an agent and an enjoyer of pleasures and pains and subject to ignorant fears of rebirth, like the illusory perception of a piece of rope in darkness as a snake. Just as through the creative power of ignorance a piece of

[1] ***vastuto' jñānasyātmāchādakatvābhāve'pi pramātṛ-buddhimātrāchādakatvena ajñānasyātmāchādakatvam upacārād ucyate. Subodhinī on Vedānta-sāra***, p. 13, Nirnaya-Sāgara Press, Bombay, 1916.

rope, the real nature of which is hidden from view, appears as a snake, so does ignorance by its creative power create on the hidden self the manifold world-appearance. As the *ajñāna* is supposed to veil by its veiling power (*āvaraṇa-śakti*) only the self-cognizing and self-revealing aspect of the self, the other aspect of the self as pure being is left open as the basis on which the entire world-appearance is created by the creative power thereof. The pure consciousness, veiled as it is by *ajñāna* with its two powers, can be regarded as an important causal agent (*nimitta*), when its nature as pure consciousness forming the basis of the creation of the world-appearance is emphasized; it can be regarded as the material cause, when the emphasis is put on its covering part, the ajñāna. It is like a spider, which, so far as it weaves its web, can be regarded as a causal agent, and, so far as it supplies from its own body the materials of the web, can be regarded as the material cause of the web, when its body aspect is emphasized. The creative powers (*vikṣepa-śakti*) of *ajñāna* are characterized as being threefold, after the manner of Sāṃkhya *prakṛti*, as *sattva*, *rajas* and *tamas*. With the pure consciousness as the basis and with the associated creative power of *ajñāna* predominating in *tamas*, space (*ākāśa*) is first produced; from *ākāśa* comes air, from air fire, from fire water, from water earth. It is these elements in their fine and uncompounded state that in the Sāṃkhya and the Purāṇas are called *tan-mātras*. It is out of these that the grosser materials are evolved as also the subtle bodies[1]. The subtle bodies are made up of seventeen parts,

[1] As to how the subtle elements are combined for the production of grosser elements there are two different theories, viz. the *trivṛt-karaṇa* and the *pañcī-karaṇa*. The *trivṛt-karaṇa* means that fire, water and earth (as subtle elements) are each divided into two halves, thus producing two equal parts of each; then the three half parts of the three subtle elements are again each divided into two halves, thus producing two quarter parts of each. Then the original first half of each element is combined with the two quarters of other two elements. Thus each element has half of itself with two quarter parts of other two elements. Vācaspati and Amalānanda prefer *trivṛt-karaṇa* to *pañcī-karaṇa*; for they think that there is no point in admitting that air and *ākāśa* have also parts of other elements integrated in them, and the Vedic texts speak of *trivṛt-karaṇa* and not of *pañcī-karaṇa*. The *pañcī-karaṇa* theory holds that the five subtle elements are divided firstly into two halves, and then one of the two halves of these five elements is divided again into four parts, and then the first half of each subtle element is combined with the one-fourth of each half of all the other elements excepting the element of which there is the full half as a constituent. Thus each element is made up of one-half of itself, and the other half of it is constituted of the one-fourth of each of the other elements (i.e. one-eighth of each of the other four elements), and thus each element has at least some part of other elements integrated into it. This view is supported by the *Vedānta-paribhāṣā* and its *Śikhāmaṇi* commentary, p. 363.

excluding the subtle elements, and are called *sūkṣma-śarīra* or *liṅga-śarīra.* This subtle body is composed of the five cognitive senses, the five conative senses, the five *vāyus* or biomotor activities, *buddhi* (intellect) and *manas,* together with the five subtle elements in tanmātric forms. The five cognitive senses, the auditory, tactile, visual, gustatory and olfactory senses, are derived from the *sattva* parts of the five elements, *ākāśa*, *vāyu*, *agni*, *ap* and *pṛthivi* respectively. *Buddhi*, or intellect, means the mental state of determination or affrimation (*niścayātmikā antaḥkaraṇa-vṛtti*). *Manas* means the two mental functions of *vikalpa* and *saṅkalpa* or of *saṅkalpa* alone resulting in doubt[1]. The function of mind (*citta*) and the function of egoism (*ahaṃkāra*) are included in *buddhi* and *manas*[2]. They are all produced from the *sattva* parts of the five elements and are therefore elemental. Though they are elemental, yet, since they are produced from the compounded *sattva* parts of all the elements, they have the revealing function displayed in their cognitive operations. *Buddhi* with the cognitive senses is called the sheath of knowledge (*vijñānamaya-koṣa*). Manas with the cognitive senses is called the sheath of *manas* (*manomaya-koṣa*). It is the self as associated with the *vijñānamaya-koṣa* that feels itself as the agent, enjoyer, happy or unhappy, the individual self (*jīva*) that passes through worldly experience and rebirth. The conative senses are produced from the *rajas* parts of the five elements. The five *vāyus* or biomotor activities are called *Prāṇa* or the breathing activity, *Udāna* or the upward activity and *Samāna* or the digestive activity. There are some who add another five *vāyus* such as the Nāga, the vomiting *Apāna troyānes* activity, Kūrma, the reflex activity of opening the eyelids, Kṛkala, the activity of coughing, Devadatta, the activity of yawning, and Dhanañjaya, the nourishing activity. These *prāṇas*

[1] The *Vedānta-sāra* speaks of *saṅkalpa* and *vikalpa,* and this is explained by the *Subodhinī* as meaning doubt. See *Vedānta-sāra* and *Subodhinī*, p. 17. The *Vedānta-paribhāṣā* and its (commentators speak of *saṅkalpa* as being the only function of *manas,* but it means "doubt." See pp. 88–89 and 358.

[2] *smaraṇākāra-vṛttimad antaḥkaraṇaṃ cittam* (*Vedānta-paribhāṣā-Maṇi-prabhā*, p. 89). *anayor eva cittāhṃkārayor antarbhāvaḥ* (*Vedānta-sāra*, p. 17). But the *Vedānta-paribhāṣā* says that *manas*, *buddhi*, *ahaṃkāra* and *citta*, all four, constitute the inner organ (*antaḥkaraṇa*). See *Vedānta-paribhāṣā*, p. 88. The *Vedānta-sāra* however does not count four functions *buddhi*, *manas*, *citta*, *ahaṃkāra*; *citta* and *ahaṃkāra* are regarded as the same as *buddhi* and *manas*. Thus according to the *Vedānta-sāra* there are only two categories. But since the *Vedānta-paribhāṣā* only mentions *buddhi* and *manas* as constituents of the subtle body, one need not think that there is ultimately any difference between it and the *Vedānta-sāra*.

together with the cognitive senses form the active sheath of *prāṇa* (*prāṇamaya-koṣa*). Of these three sheaths, the *vijñānamaya*, *manomaya* and *prāṇamaya*, the *vijñānamaya* sheath plays the part of the active agent (*kartṛ-rūpaḥ*); the *manomaya* is the source of all desires and volition, and is therefore regarded as having an instrumental function; the *prāṇamaya* sheath represents the motor functions. These three sheaths make up together the subtle body or the *sūkṣma-śarīra*. Hiraṇyagarbha (also called *Sūtrātmā* or *prāṇa*) is the god who presides over the combined subtle bodies of all living beings. Individually each subtle body is supposed to belong to every being. These three sheaths, involving as they do all the subconscious impressions from which our conscious experience is derived, are therefore called a dream (*jāgrad-vāsanāmayatvāt svapna*).

The process of the formation of the gross elements from the subtle parts of the elements is technically called *pañcīkaraṇa*. It consists in a compounding of the elements in which one half of each rudimentary element is mixed with the eighth part of each other rudimentary element. It is through such a process of compounding that each element possesses some of the properties of the other elements. The entire universe consists of seven upper worlds (*Bhuḥ*, *Bhuvaḥ*, *Svar*, *Mahar*, *Janaḥ*, *Tapaḥ* and *Satyam*), seven lower worlds (*Atala*, *Vitala*, *Sutala*, *Rasātala*, *Talātala*, *Mahātala* and *Pātāla*) and all the gross bodies of all living beings. There is a cosmic deity who presides over the combined physical bodies of all beings, and this deity is called Virāṭ. There is also the person, the individual who presides over each one of the bodies, and, in this aspect, the individual is called Viśva.

The *ajñāna* as constituting *antaḥkaraṇa* or mind, involving the operative functions of *buddhi* and *manas*, is always associated with the self; it is by the difference of these *antaḥkaraṇas* that one self appears as many individual selves, and it is through the states of these *antaḥkaraṇas* that the veil over the self and the objects are removed, and as a result of this there is the cognition of objects. The *antaḥkaraṇa* is situated within the body, which it thoroughly pervades. It is made up of the *sattva* parts of the five rudimentary elements, and, being extremely transparent, comes into touch with the sense objects through the specific senses and assumes their forms. It being a material stuff, there is one part inside the body, another part in touch with the sense-objects, and a third part between the two and connected with them both as one whole.

The interior part of the *antaḥkaraṇa* is the ego or the agent. The intervening part has the action of knowledge, called also *vṛtti-jñāna.* The third part, which at the time of cognition is transformed into the form of the sense-objects, has the function of making them manifested in knowledge as its objects. The *antaḥkaraṇa* of three parts being transparent, pure consciousness can well be manifested in it. Though pure consciousness is one, yet it manifests the three different parts of the *antaḥkaraṇa* in three different ways, as the cognizer (*pramātṛ*), cognitive operation (*pramāṇa*) and the cognition, or the percept (*pramiti*). In each of the three cases the reality is the part of the pure consciousness, as it expresses itself through the three different modifications of the *antaḥkaraṇa*. The sense-objects in themselves are but the veiled pure consciousness, *brahman*, as forming their substance. The difference between the individual consciousness (*jīva-caitanya*) and the *brahman*-consciousness (*brahma-caitanya*) is that the former represents pure consciousness, as conditioned by or as reflected through the *antaḥkaraṇa*, while the latter is the unentangled infinite consciousness, on the basis of which all the cosmic creations of *māyā* are made. The covering of *avidyā*, for the breaking of which the operation of the *antaḥkaraṇa* is deemed necessary, is of two kinds, viz. subjective ignorance and objective ignorance. When I say that I do not know a book, that implies subjective ignorance as signified by "I do not know," and objective ignorance as referring to the book. The removal of the first is a precondition of all kinds of knowledge, perceptual or inferential, while the second is removed only in perceptual knowledge. It is diverse in kind according to the form and content of the sense-objects; and each perceptual cognition removes only one specific ignorance, through which the particular cognition arises[1].

Śaṅkara and his School.

It is difficult to say exactly how many books were written by Śaṅkara himself. There is little doubt that quite a number of books attributed to Śaṅkara were not written by him. I give here a list of those books that seem to me to be his genuine works, though it is extremely difficult to be absolutely certain.

[1] See Madhusūdana Sarasvatī's *Siddhānta-bindu*, pp. 132–150; and Brahmānanda Sarasvatī's *Nyāya-ratnāvalī*, pp. 132–150, Śrīvidyā Press, Kumbakonam, 1893.

I have chosen only those works which have been commented on by other writers, since this shows that these have the strength of tradition behind them to support their authenticity. The most important works of Śaṅkara are his commentaries on the ten Upaniṣads, *Īśā*, *Kena*, *Kaṭha*, *Praśna*, *Muṇḍaka*, *Māṇḍūkya*, *Aitareya*, *Taittirīya*, *Chāndogya* and *Bṛhad-āraṇyaka* and the *Śārīraka-mīmāṃsā-bhāṣya*. The main reasons why a number of works which probably were not written by him were attributed to him seem to be twofold; first, because there was another writer of the same name, i.e. Śaṅkarācārya, and second, the tendency of Indian writers to increase the dignity of later works by attributing them to great writers of the past. The attribution of all the Purāṇas to Vyāsa illustrates this very clearly. Śaṅkara's *Īśopaniṣad-bhāṣya* has one commentary by Ānandajñāna and another, *Dīpikā*, by the other Śaṅkara Ācārya. His *Kenopaiṣad-bhāṣya* has two commentaries, *Kenopaniṣad-bhāṣya-vivaraṇa* and a commentary by Ānandajñāna. The *Kāṭhakopaniṣad-bhāṣya* has two commentaries, by Ānandajñāna and by Bālagopāla Yogīndra. The *Praśnopanṣad-bhāṣya* has two commentaries, by Ānandajāna and Nārāyaṇendra Sarasvatī. The *Muṇḍakopaniṣad-bhāṣya* has two commentaries, by Ānandajñāna and Abhinavanārāyaṇendra Sarasvatī. The *Māṇḍūkyopaniṣad-bhāṣya* has two commentaries, by Ānandajñāna and Mathurānātha Śukla, and a summary, called *Māṇḍūkyopaniṣad-bhāṣyārtha-saṃgraha*, by Rāghavānanda. The *Aitareyopaniṣad-bhāṣya* has six commentaries, by Ānandajñāna, Abhinavanārāyaṇa, Nṛsimha Ācārya, Bālakṛṣṇadāsa, Jñānāmṛta Yati, and Viśveśvara Tīrtha. The *Taittirīyopaniṣad-bhāṣya* seems to have only one commentary on it, by Ānandajñāna. The *Chāndogyopaniṣad* has two commentaries, called *Bhāṣya-ṭippana*, and a commentary by Ānandajñāna. The *Bṛhad-āraṇyakopaniṣad-bhāṣya* has a commentary by Ānandajñāna and a big independent work on it by Sureśvara, called *Bṛhad-āraṇyakopaniṣad-bhāṣya-vārttika*, or simply *Vārttika*, which has also a number of commentaries; these have been noticed in the section on Sureśvara. His *Aparokṣānubhava* has four commentaries, by Śaṅkara Ācārya, by Bālagopāla, by Caṇḍeśvara Varman (*Anubhava-dīpikā*), and by Vidyāraṇya. His commentary on Gauḍapāda's *Māṇḍūkya-kārikā*, called *Gauḍapādīya-bhāṣya* or *Āgama-śāstra-vivaraṇa*, has two commentaries, one by Śuddhānanda and one by Ānandajñāna. His *Ātma-jñānopadeśa* has two commentaries, by Ānandajñāna and by Pūrṇānanda Tīrtha; the *Eka-śloka* has a commentary called *Tattva-dīpana*, by Svayaṃprakāśa Yati; no commentary however is attributed to the *Viveka-cūdāmaṇi*, which seems to be genuinely attributed to Śaṅkara; the *Ātma-bodha* has at least five commentaries, by Advayānanda, Bhāsurānanda, Bodhendra (*Bhāva-prakāśika*), Madhusūdana Sarasvatī and RāmānandaTīrtha; The *Ātmānātma-viveka* has at least four commentaries, by Padmapāda, Pūrṇānanda Tīrtha, Sāyaṇa and Svayaṃprakāśa Yati. The *Ātmopadeśa-vidhi* is said to have a commentary by Ānandajñāna; the *Ānanda-laharī* has about twenty-four commentaries, by Appaya Dīkṣita, Kavirāja, Kṛṣṇa Ācārya (*Mañju-bhāṣinī*), Keśava-bhaṭṭa, Kaivalyāśrama (*Saubhāgya-vardhinī*), Gaṅgāharī (*Tattvadīpikā*), Gaṅgādhara, Gopīrāma, Gopīkānta Sārvabhauma (*Ānandalaharī-tarī*), Jagadīśa?, Jagannātha Pañcānana, Narasiṃha, Brahmānanda (*Bhāvārtha-dīpikā*), Malla Bhaṭṭa, Mahādeva Vidyāvagīśa, Mahādeva Vaidya, Rāmacandra, Rāmabhadra, Ramānanda Tīrtha, Lakṣmīdhara Deśika and Viśvambhara and Śrīkaṇṭha Bhaṭṭa and another called *Vidvan-manoramā*. The *Upadeśa-sāhasrī* has at least four commentaries, by Ānandajñāna, by Rāmā Tīrtha (*Padayojanikā*), *Bodha-vidhi* by a pupil of Vidyādhāman, and by Śaṅkarācārya. His *Cid-ānanda-stava-rāja* called also *Cid-ānanda-daśaślokī* or simply *Daśa-ślokī*, has also a number of commentaries and sub-commentaries, such as the *Siddhānta-tattva-bindu* by Madhusūdana Sarasvatī; Madhusūdana's commentary was commented on by a number of persons, such as Nārāyaṇa Yati (*Laghu-ṭikā*), Puruṣottama Sarasvatī (*Siddhānta-bindu-sandīpana*), Pūrṇānanda Sarasvatī (*Tattva-viveka*), Gauḍa Brahmānanda Sarasvatī (*Siddhānta-bindu-nyāya-ratnāvalī*), by Saccidānanda and Śivalāla Śarman. Gauḍa Brahmānanda's commentary, *Siddhānta-bindu-nyāyaratnāvalī*, was further commented on by Kṛṣṇakānta (*Siddhāntanyāya-ratna-pradīpikā*). Śaṅkara's *Dṛg-dṛśya-prakaraṇa* was commented on by Rāmacandra Tīrtha; his *Pañcīkaraṇa-prakriyā* has again a number of commentaries—that by Sureśvara is *Pañcīkaraṇa-vārttika*, and this has a further commentary, called *Pañcīkaraṇa-vārttikābharaṇa*, by Abhinavanārāyaṇendra Sarasvatī, pupil of Jñānendra Sarasvatī. Other commentaries on the *Pañcīkaraṇā prakriyā* are *Pañcīkaraṇa-bhāva-prakāśikā*, *Pañcīkaraṇa-ṭīkā-tattva-candrikā*, *Pañcīkaraṇa-tātparya-candrikā* and *Pañcīkaraṇa-vivaraṇa* by Ānandajñāna, *Pañcīkaraṇa-vivaraṇa* by Svayaṃprakāśa Yati and by Prajñānānanda, and a sub-commentary called *Tattva-candrikā*. Śaṅkara also commented on the *Bhagavadgītā*;

this commentary has been examined in the chapter on the *Bhagavad-gitā* in the present volume. His *Laghu-vākya-vṛtti* has a commentary called *Puṣpāñjali*, and another, called *Laghuvākya-vṛtti-prakāśikā*, by Rāmānanda Sarasvatī; his *Vākya-vṛtti* has a commentary by Ānandajñāna, and another commentary, called *Vākya-vṛtti-prakāśikā*, by Viśveśvara Paṇḍita. He starts his *Vākya-vṛtti* in the same manner as Īśvarakṛṣṇa starts his *Sāṃkhya-kārikā*, namely by stating that, suffering from the threefold sorrows of life, the pupil approaches a good teacher for instruction regarding the ways in which he may be liberated from them. Sureśvara in his *Naiṣkarmya-siddhi* also starts in the same manner and thus gives a practical turn to the study of philosophy, a procedure which one does not find in his *Brahma-sūtra-bhāṣya.* The answer, of course, is the same as that given in so many other places, that one is liberated only by the proper realization of the Upaniṣad texts that declare the unity of the self with Brahman. He then goes on to show that all external things and all that is called mind or mental or psychical is extraneous to self, which is of the nature of pure consciousness; he also declares here that the effects of one's deeds are disposed by God (Īśvara), the superior illusory form of Brahman, and not by the mysterious power of *apūrva* admitted by the Mīmāṃsists. He concludes this short work of fifty-three verses by insisting on the fact that, though the unity texts (*advaita-śruti*) of the Upaniṣads, such as "that (Brahman) art thou," may have a verbal construction that implies some kind of duality, yet their main force is in the direct and immediate apperception of the pure self without any intellectual process as implied by relations of identity. The *Vākya-vṛtti* is thus conceived differently from the *Aparokṣānubhūti*, where yoga processes of posture and breath-regulations are described, as being helpful for the realization of the true nature of self. This may, of course, give rise to some doubts regarding the true authorship of the *Aparokṣānubhūti*, though it may be explained as being due to the different stages of the development of Śaṅkara's own mind; divergences of attitude are also noticeable in his thoroughgoing idealism in his commentary on Gauḍapāda's *Kārikā*, where the waking life is regarded as being exactly the same as dream life, and external objects are deemed to have no existence whatsoever, being absolutely like dream-perceptions—as contrasted with his *Śārīraka-mīmāṃsā-bhāṣya*, where external objects are considered to have an indescribable existence, very different from dream-creations. The *Upadeśa-sāhasrī*, which in its nineteen chapters contains only six hundred and seventy-five stanzas, is more in a line with the *Vākya-vṛtti*, and, though the well-known Vedānta topics are all slightly touched upon, greater emphasis is laid on the proper realization of the Vedāntic unity texts, such as "that art thou," as means to the attainment of Brahmahood. There are also a number of short poems and hymns attributed to Śaṅkarācarya, such as the *Advaitānubhūti*, *Ātma-bodha*, *Tattvopadeśa*, *Prauḍhānubhūti*, etc., some of which are undoubtedly his, while there are many others which may not be so; but in the absence of further evidence it is difficult to come to any decisive conclusion[1]. These hymns do not contain any additional philosophical materials, but are intended to stir up a religious favour and emotion in favour of the monistic faith. In some cases, however, the commentators have found an excuse for extracting from them Vedāntic doctrines which cannot be said to follow directly from them. As an illustration of this, it may be pointed out that out of the ten ślokas of Śaṅkara Madhusūdana made a big commentary, and Brahmānanda Sarasvatī wrote another big commentary on that of Madhūsudana and elaborated many of the complex doctrines of the Vedānta which have but little direct bearing upon the verses themselves. But Śaṅkara's most important work is the *Brahma-sūtra-bhāṣya*, which was commented on by Vācaspati Miśra in the ninth century. Ānandajñāna in the thirteenth, and Govindānanda in the fourteenth century. Commentaries on Vācaspati's commentary will be noticed in the section on Vācaspati Miśra. Subrahmaṇya wrote a verse summary of Śaṅkara's commentary which he calls *Bhāṣyārtha-nyāya-mālā*; and Bhāratī Tīrtha wrote also the *Vaiyāsika-nyāya-mālā*, in which he tried to deal with the general arguments of the *Brahma-sūtra* on the lines of Śaṅkara's commentary. Many other persons, such as Vaidyanātha Dīkṣita, Devarāma Bhaṭṭa, etc., also wrote topical summaries of the main lines of the general arguments of the *Brahma-sūtra* on the lines of Śaṅkara's commentary, called *Nyāya-mālā* or *Adhikaraṇa-mālā*. But many other persons were inspired by Śaṅkara's commentary (or by the commentaries of Vācaspati Miśra and other great writers of the Śaṅkara school) and under the name of independent commentaries on the *Brahma-sūtra* merely repeated what was contained in these. Thus

[1] The *Ātma-bodha* was commented upon by Padmapāda in his commentary *Ātma-bodha-vyākhyāna*, called also *Vedānta-sāra*.

Amalānanda wrote his *Śāstra-darpaṇa* imitating the main lines of Vācaspati's commentary on Saṅkara's commentary; and Svayaṃprakāśa also wrote his *Vedānta-naya-bhūṣaṇa*, in which for the most part he summarized the views of Vācaspati's *Bhāmatī* commentary. Hari Dīkṣita wrote his *Brahma-sūtra-vṛtti*, Śaṅkarānanda his *Brahma-sūtra-dipīkā* and Brahmānanda his *Vedānta-sūtra-muktā-valī* as independent interpretations of the *Brahma-sūtra*, but these were all written mainly on the lines of Śaṅkara's own commentary, supplementing it with additional Vedāntic ideas that had been developed after Śaṅkara by the philosophers of his school of thought or explaining Śaṅkara's *Bhāṣya*[1].

Maṇḍana, Sureśvara and Viśvarūpa

General tradition has always identified Maṇḍana with Sureśvara and Viśvarūpa; and Col. G. A. Jacob in his introduction to the second edition of the *Naiṣkarmya-siddhi* seems willing to believe this tradition. The tradition probably started from Vidyāraṇya's *Śaṅkara-dig-vijaya*, where Maṇḍana is spoken of as being named not only Umbeka, but also Viśvarūpa (VIII. 63). He further says in X. 4 of the same work that, when Maṇḍana became a follower of Śaṅkara, he received from him the name Sureśvara. But the *Śaṅkara-dig-vijaya* is a mythical biography, and it is certainly very risky to believe any of its statements, unless corroborated by other reliable evidences. There is little doubt that Sureśvara was

[1] Some of these commentaries are: *Brahma-sūtra-bhāṣyārtha-saṃgraha* by Brahmānanda Yati, pupil of Viśveśvarānanda, *Brahma-sūtrārtha-dīpikā* by Veṅkaṭa, son of Gaurī and Śiva, *Brahma-sūtra-vṛtti* (called also *Mitākṣarā*) by Annam Bhaṭṭa, and *Brahma-sūtra-bhāṣya-vyākhyā* (called also *Vidyā-śrī*) by Jñānottama Bhaṭṭāraka, pupil of Jñānaghana. The peculiarity of this last work is that it is the only commentary on the *eka-jīva-vāda* line that the present writer could trace. In addition to these some more commentaries may be mentioned, such as *Brahma-sūtra-vṛtti* by Dharma Bhaṭṭa, pupil of Rāmacandrārya and pupil's pupil of Mukundāśrama, *Sūtra-bhāṣya-vyākhyāna* (called also *Brahma-vidyā-bharaṇa*) by Advaitānanda, pupil of Rāmānanda and pupil's pupil of Brahmānanda, *Brahma-sūtra-bhāṣya-vyākhyā* (called also *Nyāya-rakṣā-maṇi*) by Appaya Dīkṣita, *Brahma-tattva-prakāśikā* (which is different from an earlier treatise called *Brahma-prakāśikā*) by Sadāśivendra Sarasvatī, *Brahma-sūtro-panyāsā* by Rāmeśvara Bhāratī, by a pupil of Rāmānanda, *Sārīraka-mīmāṃsā-sūtra-siddhānta-kaumudī* by Subrahmaṇya Agnicin Makhīndra, *Vedānta-kaustu-bha* by Sītārāma; none of which seem to be earlier than the sixteenth century. But Ananyānubhava, the teacher of Prakāśātman (A.D. 1200), seems to have written another commentary, called *Sārīraka-nyāya-maṇimālā*. Prakāśātman himself also wrote a metrical summary of the main contents of Śaṅkara's *Bhāṣya* called *Sārīraka-mīmāṃsā-nyāya-saṃgraha*, and Kṛṣṇānubhūti, in much later times, wrote a similar metrical summary, called *Sārīraka-mīmāṃsā-saṃgraha*.

the author of a *Vārttika*, or commentary in verse, on Śaṅkara's *Bṛhadāraṇyaka* Upaniṣad (which was also summarized by Vidyrāṇya in a work called *Vārttika-sāra*, which latter was further commented on by Maheśvara Tīrtha in his commentary, called the *Laghu-saṃgraha*). The *Vārttika* of Sureśvara was commented on by at least two commentators, Ānandagiri in his *Śāstra-prakāśikā* and Ānandapūrṇa in his *Nyāya-kalpa-latikā*. In a commentary on the *Parāśara-smṛti* published in the Bib. Ind. series (p. 51) a quotation from this *Vārttika* is attributed to Viśvarūpa; but this commentary is a late work, and in all probability it relied on Vidyāraṇya's testimony that Viśvarūpa and Sureśvara were identically the same person. Vidyāraṇya also, in his *Vivaraṇa-prameya-saṃgraha*, p. 92, quotes a passage from Sureśvara's *Vārttika* (IV. 8), attributing it to Viśvarūpa. But in another passage of the *Vivaraṇaprameya-saṃgraha* (p. 224) he refers to a Vedānta doctrine, attributing it to the author of the *Brahma-siddhi*. But the work has not yet been published, and its manuscripts are very scarce: the present writer had the good fortune to obtain one. A fairly detailed examination of the philosophy of this work will be given in a separate section. The *Brahma-siddhi* is an important work, and it was commented on by Vācaspati in his *Tattva-samīkṣā*, by Ānandapūrṇa in his *Brahma-siddhi-vyākhyā-ratna*, by Śaṅkhapāṇi in his *Brahma-siddhi-ṭīkā*, and by Citsukha in his *Abhiprāya-prakāśikā*. But only the latter two works are available in manuscripts. Many important works however refer to the *Brahma-siddhi* and its views generally as coming from the author of *Brahma-siddhi* (*Brahma-siddhi-kāra*). But in none of these references, so far as it is known to the present writer, has the author of *Brahma-siddhi* been referred to as Sureśvara. The *Brahma-siddhi* was written in verse and prose, since two quotations from it in Citsukha's *Tattva-pradīpikā* (p. 381, Nirṇaya-Sāgara Press) and *Nyāya-kaṇikā* (p. 80) are in verse, while there are other references, such as *Tattva-pradīpikā* (p. 140) and elsewhere, which are in prose. There is, however, little doubt that the *Brahma-siddhi* was written by Maṇḍana or Maṇḍana Miśra; for both Śrīdhara in his *Nyāya-kandalī* (p. 218) and Citsukha in his *Tattva-pradīpikā* (p. 140) refer to Maṇḍana as the author of the *Brahma-siddhi*. Of these the evidence of Śrīdhara, who belonged to the middle of the tenth century, ought to be considered very reliable, as he lived within a hundred years of the death of Maṇḍana; whoever Maṇḍana may have been, since he lived after Śaṅkara (A.D. 820), he could not have flourished very much earlier than the middle of the ninth century. It is, therefore, definitely known that the *Naiṣkarmya-siddhi* and the *Vārttika* were written by Sureśvara, and the *Brahma-siddhi* by Maṇḍana. The question regarding the identity of these two persons may be settled, if the views or opinions of the *Brahma-siddhi* can be compared or contrasted with the views of the *Naiṣkarmya-siddhi* or the *Vārttika*. From the few quotations that can be traced in the writings of the various writers who refer to it is possible to come to some fairly decisive conclusions[1].

Of all passages the most important is that quoted from the *Brahma-siddhi* in the *Vivaraṇa-prameya-saṃgrana* (p. 224). It is said there that according to the author of the *Brahma-siddhi* it is the individual persons (*jīvāḥ*, in the plural) who by their own individual ignorance (*svāvidyayā*) create for themselves on the changeless Brahman the false world-appearance. Neither in itself, nor with the *māyā*, or as reflection in *māyā*, is Brahman the cause of the world (*Brahma na jagat-kāraṇam*). The appearances then are but creations of individual ignorance, and individual false experiences of the world have therefore no objective basis. The agreement of individual experiences is due to similarity of illusions in different persons who are suffering under the delusive effects of the same kinds of ignorance; this may thus be compared with the delusive experience of two moons by a number of persons. Not all persons experience the same world; their delusive experiences are similar, but the objective basis of their experience is not the same (*saṃvādas tu bahu-puruṣāvagata-dvitīya-candravat sādṛśyād upapadyate*). If this account is correct, as may well be supposed, then Maṇḍana Miśra may be regarded as the originator of the Vedāntic doctrine of *dṛṣti-sṛṣṭi-vāda*, which was in later times so forcefully formulated by Prakāśānanda. Again, in Prakāśātman's *Pañca-pādikā-vivaraṇa* (p. 32), it is held that according to the author of the *Brahma-siddhi* both *māyā* and *avidyā* are nothing but false experiences (*avidyā māyā mithyā-pratyaya iti*). About the function

[1] A copy of the manuscript of the *Brahma-siddhi* and its commentary was consulted by me in the Adyar and the Govt. Sanskrit MSS. Libraries after the above section had been written, and a thorough examination of its contents, I am happy to say, corroborates the above surmises. The *Brahma-siddhi* is expected to be shortly published by Prof. Kuppusvāmi Śāstrī, and I consulted the tarka-pāda of it in proof by the kind courtesy of Prof. Śāstrī in Madras in December 1928. A separate section has been devoted to the philosophy of Maṇḍana's *Brahma-siddhi*.

of knowledge as removing doubts he is said to hold the view (as reported in the *Nyāya-kandalī*, p. 218) that doubt regarding the validity of what is known is removed by knowledge itself. In the *Nyāya-kaṇikā* (p. 80) it is said that Maṇḍana held that reality manifests itself in unlimited conceptions of unity or universality, whereas differences appear only as a result of limited experience. Again, in the *Laghu-candrikā* (p. 112, Kumbakonam edition) Maṇḍana is introduced in the course of a discussion regarding the nature of the dispersion of ignorance and its relation to Brahma-knowledge or Brahmahood. According to Śaṅkara, as interpreted by many of his followers, including Sureśvara, the dissolution of ignorance (*avidyā-nivṛtti*) is not a negation, since negation as a separate category has no existence. So dissolution of ignorance means only Brahman. But according to Maṇḍana there is no harm in admitting the existence of such a negation as the cessation of ignorance; for the monism of Brahman means that there is only one positive entity. It has no reference to negations, i.e. the negation of duality only means the negation of all positive entities other than Brahman (*bhāvādvaita*). The existence of such a negation as the cessation of ignorance does not hurt the monistic creed. Again, Sarvajñātma Muni in his *Saṃkṣepa-śārīraka* (II. 174) says that ignorance (*avidyā*) is supported (*āśraya*) in pure consciousness (*cin-mātrāśrita-viṣayam ajñānam*), and that, even where from the context of Śaṅkara's *Bhāṣya* it may appear as if he was speaking of the individual person (*jīva*) as being the support of *ajñāna*, it has to be interpreted in this sense. Objections of Maṇḍana, therefore, to such a view, viz. that ignorance rests with the individuals, are not to be given any consideration; for Maṇḍana's views lead to quite different conclusions (*parihṛtya Maṇḍana-vācaḥ tad dhy anyathā prasthitam*)[1]. The commentator of the *Saṃkṣepa-śārīraka*, Rāmatīrtha Svāmin, also, in commenting on the passage referred to, contrasts the above view of Maṇḍana with that of Sureśvara, who according to him is referred to by an adjective *bahu-śruta* in the *Saṃkṣepa-śārīraka* text, and who is reported to have been in agreement with the views of Sarvajñātma Muni, as against the views of Maṇḍana. Now many of these views which have been attributed to Maṇḍana are not shared by Sureśvara, as will appear from what will be said below concerning him. It does not therefore appear that Maṇḍana Miśra and Sureśvara were the same

[1] Mr Hiriyanna, in *J.R.A.S.* 1923, mentions this point as well as the point concerning *avidyā-nivṛtti* in Maṇḍana's view as admission of negation.

person. But, if Vidyāraṇya, who knows so much about the views of Maṇḍana, had identified them in the *Śaṅkara-dig-vijaya*, that might lead one to pause. Now Mr Hiriyanna seems to have removed this difficulty for us by his short note in *J.R.A.S.* 1924, where he points out that Vidyāraṇya in his *Vārttika-sāra* refers to the author of the *Brahma-siddhi* as a different authority from the author of the *Vārttika*, viz. Sureśvara. Now, if Vidyāraṇya, the author of the *Vārttika-sāra*, knew that Maṇḍana, the author of the *Brahma-siddhi*, was not the same person as Sureśvara, he could not have identified them in his *Śaṅkara-dig-vijaya*. This naturally leads one to suspect that the Vidyāraṇya who was the author of the *Vivaraṇa-prameya-saṃgraha* and the *Vārttika-sāra* was not the same Vidyāraṇya as the author of *Śaṅkara-dig-vijaya*. Another consideration also leads one to think that Vidyāraṇya (the author of the *Vivaraṇa-prameya-saṃgraha*) could not have written the *Śaṅkara-dig-vijaya*. Ānandātman had two disciples, Anubhavānanda and Śaṅkarānanda. Anubhavānanda had as his disciple Amalānanda, and Śaṅkarānanda had Vidyāraṇya as his disciple. So Amalānanda may be taken as a contemporary of Vidyāraṇya. Now Amalānanda had another teacher in Sukhaprakāśa, who had Citsukha as his teacher. Thus Citsukha may be taken to be a contemporary of the grand teacher (*parama-guru*), Ānandātman, of Vidyāraṇya. If this was the case, he could not have written in his *Śaṇkara-dig-vijaya* (XIII. 5) that Citsukha, who lived several centuries after Padmapāda, was a disciple of Padmapāda. It may therefore be safely asserted that the author of the *Śaṅkara-dig-vijaya* was not the author of the *Vivaraṇa-prameya-saṃgraha*. Now, if this is so, our reliance on the author of the *Vivaraṇa-prameya-saṃgraha* cannot be considered to be risky and unsafe. But on p. 92 of the *Vivaraṇa-prameya-saṃgraha* a passage from the *Vārttika* of Sureśvara (IV. 8) is attributed to Viśvarūpa Ācārya. It may therefore be concluded that Maṇḍana, the author of the *Brahma-siddhi*, was not the same person as Sureśvara, unless we suppose that Maṇḍana was not only a Mīmāṃsā writer, but also a Vedānta writer of great repute and that his conversion by Śaṅkara meant only that he changed some of his Vedāntic views and accepted those of Śaṅkara, and it was at this stage that he was called Sureśvara. On this theory his *Brahma-siddhi* was probably written before his conversion to Śaṅkara's views. It seems likely that this theory may be correct, and that the author of the *Vidhi-viveka* was also the author of the

Brahma-siddhi; for the passage of the *Brahma-siddhi* quoted by Vācaspati in his *Nyāya-kaṇikā* is quoted in a manner which suggests that in all probability the author of the *Vidhi-viveka* was also the author of the *Brahma-siddhi*. It may also be concluded that in all probability Viśvarūpa was the same person as Sureśvara, though on this subject no references of value are known to the present writer other than by the author of the *Vivaraṇa-prameya-saṃgraha*.

Maṇḍana (A.D. 800)

Maṇḍana Miśra's *Brahma-siddhi* with the commentary of Śaṅkhapāṇi is available in manuscript, and Mahāmahopādhyāya Kuppusvāmi Śāstrī of Madras is expected soon to bring out a critical edition of this important work. Through the courtesy of Mahāmahopādhyāya Kuppusvāmi Śāstrī the present writer had an opportunity of going through the proofs of the *Brahma-siddhi* and through the courtesy of Mr C. Kunhan Raja, the Honorary Director of the Adyar Library, he was able also to utilize the manuscript of Śaṅkhapāṇi's commentary[1]. The *Brahma-siddhi* is in four chapters, *Brahma-kāṇḍa*, *Tarka-kāṇḍa*, *Niyoga-kāṇḍa*, and *Siddhi-kāṇḍa*, in the form of verses (*kārikā*) and long annotations (*vṛtti*). That Maṇḍana must have been a contemporary of Śaṅkara is evident from the fact that, though he quotes some writers who flourished before Śaṅkara, such as Śabara, Kumārila or Vyāsa, the author of the *Yoga-sūtra-bhāṣya*, and makes profuse references to the Upaniṣad texts, he never refers to any writer who flourished after Śaṅkara[2]. Vācaspati also wrote a commentary, called *Tattvasamīkṣā*, on Maṇḍana's *Brahma-siddhi*; but unfortunately this text, so far as is known to the present writer, has not yet been

[1] Citsukha, the pupil of Jñānottama, also wrote a commentary on it, called *Abhiprāya-prakāśikā*, almost the whole of which, except some portions at the beginning, is available in the Government Oriental Manuscript Library, R. No. 3853. Ānandapūrṇa also wrote a commentary on the *Brahma-siddhi*, called *Bhāva-śuddhi*.

[2] Maṇḍana's other works are *Bhāvanā-viveka*, *Vidhi-viveka*, *Vibhrama-viveka* and *Sphoṭa-siddhi*. Of these the *Vidhi-viveka* was commented upon by Vācaspati Miśra in his *Nyāya-kaṇikā*, and the *Sphoṭa-siddhi* was commented upon by the son of Bhavadāsa, who had also written a commentary, called *Tattva-vibhāvanā*, on Vācaspati Miśra's *Tattva-bindu*. The commentary on the *Sphoṭa-siddhi* is called *Gopālika*. Maṇḍana's *Vibhrama-viveka* is a small work devoted to the discussion of the four theories of illusion (*khyāti*), *ātma-khyāti*, *asat-khyāti*, *anyathā-khyāti* and *akhyāti*. Up till now only his *Bhāvanā-viveka* and *Vidhi-viveka* have been published.

discovered. In the *Brahma-kāṇḍa* chapter Maṇḍana discusses the nature of Brahman; in the *Tarka-kāṇḍa* he tries to prove that we cannot perceive "difference" through perception and that therefore one should not think of interpreting the Upaniṣad texts on dualistic lines on the ground that perception reveals difference. In the third chapter, the *Niyoga-kāṇḍa*, he tries to refute the Mīmāṃsā view that the Upaniṣad texts are to be interpreted in accordance with the Mīmāṃsā principle of interpretation, that all Vedic texts command us to engage in some kind of action or to restrain ourselves from certain other kinds of action. This is by far the longest chapter of the book. The fourth chapter, the *Siddhi-kāṇḍa*, is the shortest: Maṇḍana says here that the Upaniṣad texts show that the manifold world of appearance does not exist at all and that its apparent existence is due to the *avidyā* of *jīva*.

In the *Brahma-kāṇḍa* the most important Vedāntic concepts are explained by Maṇḍana according to his own view. He first introduces the problem of the subject (*draṣṭṛ*) and the object (*dṛśya*) and says that it is only by abolishing the apparent duality of subject and object that the fact of experience can be explained. For, if there was any real duality of subject and object, that duality could not be bridged over and no relation between the two could be established; if, on the other hand, there is only the subject, then all things that are perceived can best be explained as being illusory creations imposed on self, the only reality[1]. Proceeding further with the same argument, he says that attempts have been made to bring about this subject-object relation through the theory of the operation of an intermediary mind (*antaḥkaraṇa*); but whatever may be the nature of this intermediary, the pure unchangeable intelligence, the self or the subject, could not change with its varying changes in accordance with its connection with different objects; if it is held that the self does not undergo any transformation or change, but there is only the appearance of a transformation through its reflection in the *antaḥkaraṇa*, then it is plainly admitted that objects are not in reality perceived and that there is only an appearance of perception. If objects are not perceived in reality, it is wrong to think that they have a separate

[1] *ekatva evāyaṃ draṣṭṛ-dṛśya-bhāvo'vakalpate, draṣṭur eva cid-ātmanaḥ tathā tathā vipariṇāmād vivartanād vā; nānātve tu vivikta-svabhāvayor asaṁsṛṣṭaparaspara-svarūpayor asambaddhayoḥ kīdṛśo draṣṭṛ-dṛśya-bhāvaḥ.* Kuppusvāmi Śāstrī's edition of *Brahma-siddhi*, p. 7 (In the press.)

and independent existence from the self[1]. Just as the very same man sees his own image in the mirror to be different from him and to exist outside of him as an object, so the same self appears as all the diverse objects outside of it. It is difficult to conceive how one could admit the existence of external objects outside the pure intelligence (*cit*); for in that case it would be impossible to relate the two[2].

According to Maṇḍana *avidyā* is called *māyā*, or false appearance, because it is neither a characteristic (*sva-bhāva*) of Brahman nor different from it, neither existent nor non-existent. If it was the characteristic of anything, then, whether one with that or different from it, it would be real and could not therefore be called *avidyā*; if it was absolutely non-existent, it would be like the lotus of the sky and would have no practical bearing in experience (*na vyavahāra-bījam*) such as *avidyā* has; it has thus to be admitted that *avidyā* is indescribable or unspeakable (*anirvacanīyā*)[3].

According to Maṇḍana *avidyā* belongs to the individual souls (*jīva*). He admits that there is an inconsistency in such a view; but he thinks that, *avidyā* being itself an inconsistent category, there is no wonder that its relation with *jīva* should also be incon-

[1] *ekāntaḥkaraṇa-saṃkrāntāv asty eva sambandha iti cet, na, citeḥ śuddhatvād apariṇāmād aprati-saṃkramāc ca; dṛśya buddhiḥ citi-sannidheś chāyaya vivartata iti ced atha keyaṃ tac chāyatā? a-tad-ātmanaḥ tad-avabhāsaḥ; na tarhi paramārthato dṛśyaṃ dṛśyate, paramārthataś ca dṛśyamānaṃ draṣṭṛ-vyatiriktam asti iti dur-bhaṇam. Ibid.* Śaṅkhapāṇi in commenting on this discards the view that objects pass through the sense-channels and become superimposed on the *antaḥkaaṇa* or *durbhaṇam* and thereby become related to the pure intelligence of the self and objectified: *na tu sphaṭikopame cetasi indriya-praṇālī-saṃkrāntānām arthānāṃ tatraiva saṃkrāntena ātma-caitanyena sambaddhānāṃ tad-dṛśyatvaṃ ghaṭiṣyate.* Adyar MS. p. 75.

It may not be out of place to point out in this connection that the theory of Padmapāda, Prakāsātman, as developed later on by Dharmarājādhvarīndra, which held that the mind (*antaḥkaraṇa*) becomes superimposed on external objects in perception, was in all probability borrowed from the Sāṃkhya doctrine of *cic-chāyāpatti* in perception, which was somehow forced into Śaṅkara's loose epistemological doctrines and worked out as a systematic epistemological theory. The fact that Maṇḍana discards this epistemological doctrine shows, on the one hand, that he did not admit it to be a right interpretation of Śaṅkara and may, on the other hand, be regarded as a criticism of the contemporary interpretation of Padmapāda. But probably the reply of that school would be that, though they admitted extra-individual reality of objects, they did not admit the reality of objects outside of pure intelligence (*cit*).

[2] *tathā hi darpaṇa-tala-stham ātmānaṃ vibhaktam ivātmanaḥ pratyeti*; *cites tu vibhaktam asaṃsṛṣṭaṃ tayā cetyata iti dur-avagamyam. Ibid.*

[3] *Ibid.* p. 9. It may not be out of place here to point out that Ānandabodha's argument in his *Nyāya-makaranda* regarding the unspeakable nature of *avidyā*, which has been treated in a later section of this chapter, is based on this argument of Maṇḍana.

sistent and unexplainable. The inconsistency of the relationship of *avidyā* with the *jīvas* arises as follows: the *jīvas* are essentially identical with Brahman, and the diversity of *jīvas* is due to imagination (*kalpanā*); but this imagination cannot be of Brahman, since Brahman is devoid of all imagination (*tasyā vidyātmanaḥ kalpnā-śūnyatvāt*); it cannot be the imagination of the *jīvas*, since the *jīvas* themselves are regarded as being the product of imagination[1]. Two solutions may be proposed regarding this difficulty, firstly, that the word *māyā* implies what is inconsistent; had it been a consistent and explainable concept, it would be reality and not *māyā*[2]. Secondly, it may be said that from *avidyā* come the *jīvas* and from the *jīvas* comes the *avidyā*, and that this cycle is beginningless and therefore there is no ultimate beginning either of the *jīvas* or of the *avidyā*[3]. This view is held by those who think that *avidyā* is not the material cause of the world: these are technically called *avidyopādāna-bheda-vādins*. It is through this *avidyā* that the *jīvas* suffer the cycle of births and rebirths, and this *avidyā* is natural to the *jīvas*, since the *jīvas* themselves are the products of *avidyā*[4]. And it is through listening to the Vedāntic texts, right thinking, meditation, etc. that true knowledge dawns and the *avidyā* is destroyed ; it was through this *avidyā* that the *jīvas* were separated from Brahman; with its destruction they attain Brahmahood[5].

In defining the nature of Brahman as pure bliss Śaṅkhapāṇi the commentator raises some very interesting discussions. He starts by criticizing the negative definition of happiness as cessation of pain or as a positive mental state qualified by such a negative condition[6]. He says that there are indeed negative pleasures which are enjoyed as negation of pain (e.g. a plunge into cold water is an escape from the painful heat); but he holds that there are cases where pleasures and pains are experienced simultaneously

[1] *itaretarāśraya prasaṅgāt kalpanādhīno hi*
jīva vibhāgaḥ, jīvāśrayā kalpanā. *Ibid.* p. 10.

[2] *anupapadyamānārthaiva hi māyā; upapadyamānārthatve yathārtha-bhāvān na māyā syāt. Ibid.*

[3] *anāditvān netaretarāśrayatva-doṣah. Ibid.*

[4] *na hi jīveṣu nisarga-jā vidyāsti, avidyaiva hi naisargikī, āgantukyā vidyāyāh pravilayaḥ. Ibid.* pp. 11–12.

[5] *avidyayaiva tu brahmaṇo jīvo vibhaktaḥ, tan-nivṛttau brahma-svarūpam eva bhavati, yathā ghaṭādi-bhede tad-ākāśam pariśuddham paramākaśam eva bhavati. Ibid.*

[6] *duḥkha nivṛttir vā tad-viśiṣṭātmopatabdhir vā sukham astu, sarvathā sukhaṃnāma na dharmāntaram asti.* Adyar MS. of the Śaṅkhapāṇi commentary, p. 18.

and not as negation of each other. A man may feel painful heat in the upper part of his body and yet feel the lower part of his body delightfully cool and thus experience pleasure and pain simultaneously (*sukha-duḥkhe yugapaj janyete*). Again, according to the scriptures there is unmixed pain in Hell, and this shows that pain need not necessarily be relative. Again, there are many cases (e.g. in the smelling of a delightful colour of camphor) where it cannot be denied that we have an experience of positive pleasure[1]. Śaṅkhapāṇi then refutes the theory of pain as unsatisfied desire and happiness as satisfaction or annulment of desires (*viṣayaprāptiṃ vinā kāma eva duḥkham ataḥ tan-nivṛttir eva sukham bhaviṣyati*) by holding that positive experiences of happiness are possible even when one has not desired them[2]. An objection to this is that experience of pleasures satisfies the natural, but temporarily inactive, desires in a subconscious or potential condition[3]. Again, certain experiences produce more pleasures in some than in others, and this is obviously due to the fact that one had more latent desires to be fulfilled than the other. In reply to these objections Śaṅkhapāṇi points out that, even if a thing is much desired, yet, if it is secured after much trouble, it does not satisfy one so much as a pleasure which comes easily. If pleasure is defined as removal of desires, then one should feel happy before the pleasurable experience or after the pleasurable experience, when all traces of the desires are wiped out, but not at the time of enjoying the pleasurable experience; for the desires are not wholly extinct at that time. Even at the time of enjoying the satisfaction of most earnest desires one may feel pain. So it is to be admitted that pleasure is not a relative concept which owes its origin to the sublation of desires, but that it is a positive concept which has its existence even before the desires are sublated[4]. If negation of desires be defined as happiness, then even disinclination to food through bilious attacks is to be called happiness[5]. So it is to be admitted that positive pleasures are in the first instance experienced and then are desired. The theory that pains and pleasures are relative and that without pain there can be no experience of pleasure and that there can be no experience of pain without an

[1] *Ibid.* pp. 20, 21.
[2] *Ibid.* p. 22.
[3] *sahajo hi rāgaḥ sarva-puṃsām asti sa tu viṣaya-viśeṣeṇa āvir-bhavati. Ibid* .p. 23.
[4] *ataḥ kāma-nivṛtteḥ prāg-bhāvi sukha-vastu-bhūtam eṣṭavyam . Ibid.* p. 27.
[5] *Ibid.* p. 25.

experience of pleasure is false and consequently the Vedāntic view is that the state of emancipation as Brahmahood may well be described as an experience of positive pure bliss[1].

Śaṅkara in his commentary on the *Brahma-sūtra* and in his commentaries on some of the Upaniṣads and the *Māṇḍūkya-kārikā* had employed some elements of dialectical criticism, the principles of which had long been introduced in well-developed forms by the Buddhists. The names of the three great dialecticians, Śrīharṣa, Ānandajñāna and Citsukha, of the Śaṅkara school, are well known, and proper notice has been taken of them in this chapter. But among the disciples of Śaṅkara the man who really started the dialectical forms of argument, who was second to none in his dialectical powers and who influenced all other dialecticians of the Śaṅkara school, Ānandabodha, Śrīharṣa, Ānandajñāna, Citsukha, Nṛsiṃhāśrama and others, was Maṇḍana. Maṇḍana's great dialectical achievement is found in his refutation of the perception of difference (*bheda*) in the *Tarka-kāṇḍa* chapter of his *Brahma-siddhi*.

The argument arose as follows: the category of difference (*bheda*) is revealed in perception, and, if this is so, the reality of difference cannot be denied, and therefore the Upaniṣad texts should not be interpreted in such a way as to annul the reality of "difference." Against such a view-point Maṇḍana undertakes to prove that "difference," whether as a quality or characteristic of things or as an independent entity, is never experienced by perception (*pratyakṣa*)[2]. He starts by saying that perception yields three possible alternatives, viz. (1) that it manifests a positive object, (2) that it presents differences from other objects, (3) that it both manifests a positive object and distinguishes it from other objects[3]. In the third alternative there may again be three other alternatives, viz. (i) simultaneous presentation of the positive object and its distinction from others, (ii) first the presentation of the positive object and then the presentation of the difference, (iii) first the presentation of the difference and then the presentation of the positive object[4]. If by perception differences

[1] *yadi duḥkhā-bhāvaḥ sukhaṃ syāt tataḥ syād evam bhāvāntare tu sukhe duḥhābhāve ca tathā syād eva. Ibid.* p. 161.

[2] This discussion runs from page 44 of the *Brahma-siddhi* (in the press) to the end of the second chapter.

[3] *tatra pratyakṣe trayaḥ kalpāḥ, vastu-svarūpa-siddhih vastv-antarasya vyavacchedaḥ ubhayaṃ vā. Brahma-siddhi*, II.

[4] *ubhayasminn api traividhyam, yaugapadyam, vyavaccheda-pūrvako vidhiḥ, vidhi-pūrvako vyavacchedaḥ. Ibid.*

from other objects are experienced, or if it manifests both the object and its differences, then it has to be admitted that "difference" is presented in perception; but, if it can be proved that only positive objects are presented in perception, unassociated with any presentation of difference, then it has to be admitted that the notion of difference is not conveyed to us by perception, and in that case the verdict of the Upaniṣads that reality is one and that no diversity can be real is not contradicted by perceptual experience. Now follows the argument.

Perception does not reveal merely the difference, nor does it first reveal the difference and then the positive object, nor both of them simultaneously; for the positive object must first be revealed, before any difference can be manifested. Difference must concern itself in a relation between two positive objects, e.g. the cow is different from the horse, or there is no jug here. The negation involved in the notion of difference can have no bearing without that which is negated or that of which it is negated, and both these are positive in their notion. The negation of a chimerical entity (e.g. the lotus of the sky) is to be interpreted as negation of a false relation of its constituents, which are positive in themselves (e.g. both the lotus and the sky are existents, the incompatibility is due to their relationing, and it is such a relation between these two positive entities that is denied), or as denying the objective existence of such entities, which can be imagined only as a mental idea[1]. If the category of difference distinguishes two objects from one another, the objects between which the difference is manifested must first be known. Again, it cannot be held that perception, after revealing the positive object, reveals also its difference from other objects; for perception is one unique process of cognition, and there are no two moments in it such that it should first reveal the object with which there is present sense-contact and then reveal other objects which are not at that moment in contact with sense, as also the difference between the two[2]. In the case of the discovery of one's own illusion, such as "this is not silver, but conch-shell," only the latter knowledge is perceptual, and this knowledge refers to and negates after the previous knowledge of the object as silver has been negated. It was

[1] *kutaścin nimittād buddhau labdha-rūpāṇām bahir niṣedhaḥ kriyate.*
Brahma-siddhi, II.

[2] *kramaḥ saṃgacchate yuktyā naika-vijñāna-karmaṇoḥ*
na sannihita-jaṃ tac ca tadanyāmarśi jāyate. Ibid. II. *Kārikā* 3.

only when the presented object was perceived as "this before" that it was denied as being the silver for which it was taken, and when it was thus negated there was the perception of the conch-shell. There is no negative concept without there first being a positive concept; but it does not therefore follow that a positive concept cannot be preceded by a negative concept[1]. This is therefore not a case where there are two moments in one unique perception, but there are here different cognitive experiences[2].

Again, there is a view (Buddhist) that it is by the power or potency of the indeterminate cognition of an object that both the positive determinate cognition and its difference from others are produced. Though the positive and the negative are two cognitions, yet, since they are both derived from the indeterminate cognition, it can well be said that by one positive experience we may also have its difference from others also manifested (*eka-vidhir eva anya-vyavacchedaḥ*)[3]. Against such a view Maṇḍana urges that one positive experience cannot also reveal its differences from all other kinds of possible and impossible objects. A colour perceived at a particular time and particular place may negate another colour at that particular place and time, but it cannot negate the presence of taste properties at that particular place and time; but, if the very perception of a colour should negate everything else which is not that colour, then these taste properties would also be negated, and, since this is not possible, it has to be admitted that perception of a positive entity does not necessarily involve as a result of that very process the negation of all other entities.

There is again a view that things are by their very nature different from one another (*prakṛtyaiva bhinnā bhāvāḥ*), and thus, when by perception an object is experienced, its difference from other objects is also grasped by that very act. In reply to this objection Maṇḍana says that things cannot be of the nature of differences; firstly, in that case all objects would be of the nature of difference, and hence there would be no difference among them; secondly, as

[1] *pūrva-vijñāna-vihite rajatādau "idam" iti ca sannihitārtha-sāmānye niṣedho vidhi-pūrva eva, śuktikā-siddhis tu virodhi-niṣedha-pūrva ucyate; vidhi-pūrvatā ca niyamena niṣedhasyocyate, na vidher niṣedha-pūrvakatā niṣidhyate. Brahmasiddhi*, II. *Kārikā* 3.

[2] *na ca tatra eka-jñānasya kramavad-vyāpāratā ubhaya-rūpasya utpatteḥ. Ibid.*

[3] *nīlasya nirvikalpaka-darśanasya yat sāmarthyaṃ niyataika-kāraṇatvaṃ tena anādi-vāsanā-vaśāt pratibhāsitaṃ janitam idaṃ nedam iti vikalpo bhāvābhāva-vyavahāram pravartayati...satyaṃ jñāna-dvayam idaṃ savikalpakaṃ tu nirvikalpakaṃ tayor mūla-bhūtaṃ tat pratyakṣaṃ tatra ca eka-vidhir eva anyavyavaccheda iti brūma iti.* Śaṅkhapāṇi's commentary, *ibid.*

"difference" has no form, the objects themselves would be formless; thirdly, difference being essentially of the nature of negation, the objects themselves would be of the nature of negation; fourthly, since difference involves duality or plurality in its concept, no object could be regarded as one; a thing cannot be regarded as both one and many[1]. In reply to this the objector says that a thing is of the nature of difference only in relation to others (*parāpekṣaṃvastuno bheda-svabhāvaḥ nātmāpekṣam*), but not in relation to itself. In reply to this objection Maṇḍana says that things which have been produced by their own causes cannot stand in need of a relation to other entities for their existence; all relationing is mental and as such depends on persons who conceive the things, and so relationing cannot be a constituent of objective things[2]. If relationing with other things constituted their essence, then each thing would depend on others—they would depend on one another for their existence (*itaretarāśraya-prasaṅgāt*). In reply to this it may be urged that differences are different, corresponding to each and every oppositional term, and that each object has a different specific nature in accordance with the different other objects with which it may be in a relation of opposition; but, if this is so, then objects are not produced solely by their own causes; for, if differences are regarded as their constituent essences, these essences should vary in accordance with every object with which a thing may be opposed. In reply to this it is urged by the objector that, though an object is produced by its own causes, yet its nature as differences appears in relation to other objects with which it is held in opposition. Maṇḍana rejoins that on such a view it would be difficult to understand the meaning and function of this oppositional relation (*apekṣā*); for it does not produce the object, which is produced by its own causes, and it has no causal efficiency and it is also not experienced, except as associated with the other objects (*nānāpekṣa-pratiyogināṃ bhedaḥ pratīyate*). Difference also cannot be regarded as being of the essence of oppositional relation; it is only when there is an oppositional relation between objects already experienced that difference manifests

[1] *na bhedo vastuno rūpaṃ tad-abhāva-prasaṅgataḥ*
arūpeṇa ca bhinnatvaṃ vastuno nāvakalpate.

Brahma-siddhi, II. 5.

[2] *nāpekṣā nāma kaścid vastu-dharmo yena vastuni vyavasthāpyeran, na khalu sva-hetu-prāpitodayeṣu sva-bhāva-vyavasthiteṣu vastuṣu sva-bhāva-sthitaye vastv-antarāpekṣā yujyate. Ibid.* II. 6, *vṛtti.*

itself. Relations are internal and are experienced in the minds of those who perceive and conceive[1]. But it is further objected to this that concepts like father and son are both relational and obviously externally constitutive. To this Maṇḍana's reply is that these two concepts are not based on relation, but on the notion of production; that which produces is the father and that which is produced is the son. Similarly also the notions of long and short depend upon the one occupying greater or less space at the time of measurement and not on relations as constituting their essence.

In reply to this the objector says that, if relations are not regarded as ultimate, and if they are derived from different kinds of actions, then on the same ground the existence of differences may also be admitted. If there were no different kinds of things, it would not be possible to explain different kinds of actions. But Maṇḍana's reply is that the so-called differences may be but differences in name; the burning activity of the same fire is described sometimes as burning and sometimes as cooking. In the Vedānta view it is held that all the so-called varied kinds of actions appear in one object, the Brahman, and so the objection that varied kinds of actions necessarily imply the existence of difference in the agents which produce them is not valid. Again, the difficulty in the case of the Buddhist is in its own way none the less; for according to him all appearances are momentary, and, if this be so, how does he explain the similarities of effects that we notice ? It can be according to them only on the basis of an illusory notion of the sameness of causes; so, if the Buddhist can explain our experience of similarity on the false appearance of sameness of causes, the Vedāntist may also in his turn explain all appearances of diversity through illusory notions of difference, and there is thus no necessity of admitting the reality of differences in order to explain our notions of difference in experience[2] . Others again argue that the world must be a world of diversity, as the various objects of our experience serve our various purposes, and it is impossible that one and the same thing should serve different purposes. But this objection is not valid, because even the self-same thing can serve diverse purposes; the same fire can burn, illuminate and cook. There is no objection to there being a number of limited (*avacchinna*) qualities

[1] *pauruṣeyīm apekṣām na vastv anuvartate, ato na vastu-svabhāvaḥ. Ibid.*

[2] *atha nir-anvaya-vināśānām api kalpanā-viṣayād abhedāt kāryasya tulyatā hanta tarhi bhedād eva kalpanā-viṣayāt kāryābheda-siddher mūḍhā kāraṇa-bheda-kalpanā. Ibid.*

or characters in the self-same thing. It is sometimes urged that things are different from one another because of their divergent powers (e.g. milk is different from sesamum because curd is produced from milk and not from sesamum); but divergence of powers is like divergence of qualities, and, just as the same fire may have two different kinds of powers or qualities, namely, that of burning and cooking, so the same entity may at different moments both possess and not possess a power, and this does not in the least imply a divergence or difference of entity. It is a great mystery that the one self-same thing should have such a special efficiency (*sāmarthyātiśaya*) that it can be the basis of innumerable divergent appearances. As one entity is supposed to possess many divergent powers, so one self-same entity may on the same principle be regarded as the cause of divergent appearances.

Again, it is held by some that "difference" consists in the negation of one entity in another. Such negations, it may be replied, cannot be indefinite in their nature; for then negations of all things in all places would make them empty. If, however, specific negations are implied with reference to determinate entities, then, since the character of these entities, as different from one another, depends on these implied negations, and since these implied negations can operate only when there are these different entities, they depend mutually upon one another (*itaretarāśraya*) and cannot therefore hold their own. Again, it cannot be said that the notion of "difference" arises out of the operation of perceptual processes like determinate perception (occurring as the culmination of the perceptual process); for there is no proof whatsoever that "difference," as apart from mutual negation, can be definitely experienced. Again, if unity of all things as "existents" (*sat*) was not realized in experience, it would be difficult to explain how one could recognize the sameness of things. This sameness or unity of things is by far the most fundamental of experiences, and it is first manifested as indeterminate experience, which later on transforms itself into various notions of difference[1]. In this connection Maṇḍana also takes great pains in refuting the view that things are twofold in their nature, both unity and difference, and also

[1] *pratyekam anubiddhatvād abhedena mṛṣā mataḥ*
bhedo yathā taraṅgāṇām bhedād bhedaḥ kalāvataḥ.
Brahma-siddhi, 11. *Kārikā* 31.

the Jaina view that unity and difference are both true in their own respective ways. But it is not necessary to enter into these details. The main point in his refutation of the category of difference consists in this, that he shows that it is inconceivable and dialectically monstrous to suppose that the category of difference can be experienced through perception and that it is philosophically more convenient to suppose that there is but one thing which through ignorance yields the various notions of difference than to suppose that there are in reality the infinite agreements of unity and difference just as they are experienced in perception[1].

In the third chapter of the *Brahma-siddhi*, called the *Niyoga-kāṇḍa*, Maṇḍana refutes the Mīmāṃsā view that the Vedāntic texts are to be interpreted in accordance with the Mīmāṃsā canon of interpretation, viz. that Vedic texts imply either a command or a prohibition. But, as this discussion is not of much philosophical importance, it is not desirable to enter into it. In the fourth chapter, called the *Siddhi-kāṇḍa*, Maṇḍana reiterates the view that the chief import of the Upaniṣad texts consists in showing that the manifold world of appearance does not exist and that its manifestation is due to the ignorance (*avidyā*) of the individual souls (*jīva*). The sort of ultimate reality that is described in the Upaniṣad texts is entirely different from all that we see around us, and it is as propounding this great truth, which cannot be known by ordinary experience, that the Upaniṣads are regarded as the only source from which knowledge of Brahman can be obtained.

Sureśvara (A.D. 800)

Sureśvara's chief works are the *Naiṣkarmya-siddhi* and *Bṛhad-āraṇyakopaniṣad-bhāṣya-vārttika*. The *Naiṣkarmya-siddhi* has at least five commentaries, such as the *Bhāva-tattva-prakāśikā* by Citsukha, which is based on Jñānottama's *Candrikā*. This *Candrikā* is thus the earliest commentary on the *Naiṣkarmya-siddhi*. It is difficult to determine Jñānottama's date. In the concluding verses of this commentary the two names Satyabodha and Jñānottama occur; and Mr Hiriyanna points out in his introduction to the *Naiṣkarmya-siddhi* that these two names also occur in the Sarvajña-pīṭha of Conjeeveram, to which he claims to have belonged as teacher and pupil,

[1] *ekasyaivāstu mahimā yan nāneva prakāśate*
lāghavān na tu bhinnānām yac cakāśaty abhinnavat.
Brahma-siddhi, 11. *Kārikā* 32.

and according to the list of teachers of that Maṭha Jñānottama was the fourth from Śaṅkara. This would place Jñānottama at a very early date; if, however, the concluding verses are not his, but inserted by someone else, then of course they give no clue to his date except the fact that he must have lived before Citsukha, since Citsukha's commentary was based on Jñānottama's commentary *Candrikā*. Another commentary is the *Vidyā-surabhi* of Jñānāmṛta, the pupil of Uttamāmṛta; another is the *Naiṣkarmya-siddhi-vivaraṇa* of Akhilātman, pupil of Daśarathapriya; and there is also another commentary, called *Sārārtha*, by Rāmadatta, which is of comparatively recent date.

Sureśvara's *Naiṣkarmya-siddhi* is divided into four chapters. The first chapter deals with discussions regarding the relation of Vedic duties to the attainment of Vedāntic wisdom. *Avidyā* is here defined as the non-perception in one's experience of the ultimate oneness of the self: through this rebirths take place, and it is the destruction of this ignorance which is emancipation (*tan-nāśo muktir ātṃanaḥ*). The Mīmāṃsists think that, if one ceases to perform actions due to desire (*kāmya-karma*) and prohibited actions, then the actions which have already accumulated will naturally exhaust themselves in time by yielding fruits, and so, since the obligatory duties do not produce any new *karma*, and since no other new *karmas* accumulate, the person will naturally be emancipated from *karma*. There is, however, in the Vedas no injunction in favour of the attainment of right knowledge. So one should attain emancipation through the performance of the Vedic duties alone. As against this Mīmāṃsā view Sureśvara maintains that emancipation has nothing to do with the performance of actions. Performance of Vedic duties may have an indirect and remote bearing, in the way of purifying one's mind, but it has certainly no direct bearing on the attainment of salvation. Sureśvara states a view attributed to Brahmadatta in the *Vidyā-ṣurabhi* commentary, that ignorance is not removed merely by the knowledge of the identity of oneself with Brahman, as propounded in Vedānta texts, but through long and continuous meditation on the same. So the right apprehension of the Upaniṣadic passages on the identity of the Brahman and the individual does not immediately produce salvation; one has to continue to meditate for a long time on such ideas of identity; and all the time one has to perform all one's obligatory duties, since, if one ceased to perform them, this would be a transgression of one's duties and would naturally produce sins, and hence one would not be able to obtain emancipation. So knowledge must be combined with the performance of duties (*jñāna-karma-samuccaya*), which is vehemently opposed by Śaṅkara. Another view which occurs also in the *Vārttika*, and is there referred to by the commentator Ānandajñāna as being that of Maṇḍana, is that, as the knowledge derived from the Vedāntic texts is verbal and conceptual, it cannot of itself lead to Brahma-knowledge, but, when these texts are continually repeated, they produce a knowledge of Brahman as a mysterious effect by just the same kind of process as gives rise to the mysterious effects of sacrificial or other Vedic duties. The *Vārttika* refers to various schools among the adherents of the joint operation of knowledge and of duties (*jñāna-karma-samuccaya*), some regarding *jñāna* as being the more important, others regarding karma as more important, and still others regarding them both as being equally important, thus giving rise to three different schools of *jñāna-karma-samuccaya*. Sureśvara tries to refute all these views by saying that true knowledge and emancipation are one and the same thing, and that it does not in the least require the performance of any kind of Vedic duties. Sureśvara also refutes the doctrine of the joint necessity of *karma* and *jñāna* on the view of those modified dualists, like Bhartṛprapañca, who thought that reality was a unity in differences, so that the doctrine of differences was as true as that of unity, and that, therefore, duties have to be performed even in the emancipated state, because, the differences being also real, the necessity of duties cannot be ignored at any stage of progress, even in the emancipated state, though true knowledge is also necessary for the realization of truth as unity. Sureśvara's refutation of this view is based upon two considerations, viz. that the conception of reality as being both unity and difference is self-contradictory, and that, when the oneness is realized through true knowledge and the sense of otherness and differences is removed, it is not possible that any duties can be performed at that stage; for the performance of duties implies experience of duality and difference[1].

The second chapter of the *Naiṣkarmya-siddhi* is devoted to the exposition of the nature of self-realization, as won through the proper interpretation of the unity texts of the Upaniṣads by a

[1] See also Prof. Hiriyanna's introduction to his edition of the *Naiṣkarmya-siddhi*.

proper teacher. The experience of the ego and all its associated experiences of attachment, antipathy, etc., vanish with the dawn of true self-knowledge of unity. The notion of ego is a changeful and extraneous element, and hence outside the element of pure consciousness. All manifestations of duality are due to the distracting effects of the *antaḥkaraṇa*. When true knowledge dawns, the self together with all that is objectivity in knowledge vanishes. All the illusory appearances are due to the imposition of *ajñāna* on the pure self, which, however, cannot thereby disturb the unperturbed unity of this pure self. It is the *antaḥkaraṇa*, or the intellect, that suffers all modifications in the cognitive operations; the underlying pure consciousness remains undisturbed all the same. Yet this non-self which appears as mind, intellect, and its objects is not a substantive entity like the *prakṛti* of the Sāṃkhya; for its appearance is due merely to ignorance and delusion. This world-appearance is only a product of nescience (*ajñāna*) or false and indescribable illusion on the self, and is no real product of any real substance as the Sāṃkhya holds. Thus it is that the whole of the world-appearance vanishes like the illusory silver in the conch-shell as soon as truth is realized.

In the third chapter Sureśvara discusses the nature of *ajñāna*, its relation with the self, and the manner of its dissolution. There are two entities, the self and the non-self; now the non-self, being itself a product of *ajñāna* (nescience or ignorance), cannot be regarded as its support or object; so the *ajñāna* has for its support and object the pure self or Brahman; the ignorance of the self is also in regard to itself, since there is no other object regarding which ignorance is possible—the entire field of objective appearance being regarded as the product of ignorance itself. It is the ignorance of the real nature of the self that transforms itself into all that is subjective and objective, the intellect and its objects. It is thus clear that according to Sureśvara, unlike Vācaspati Miśra and Maṇḍana, the *avidyā* is based not upon individual persons (*jīva*), but upon the pure intelligence itself. It is this ignorance which, being connected and based upon the pure self, produces the appearances of individual persons and their subjective and objective experiences. This *ajñāna*, as mere ignorance, is experienced in deep dreamless sleep, when all its modifications and appearances shrink within it and it is experienced in itself as pure ignorance, which again in the waking state manifests itself in the whole series of experiences. It is easy to see that this view of the relation of *ajñāna* to pure intelligence is different from the idealism preached by Maṇḍana, as noticed in the previous section. An objection is raised that, if the ego were as much an extraneous product of *ajñāna* as the so-called external objects, then the ego should have appeared not as a subject, but as an object like other external or internal objects (e.g. pleasure, pain, etc.). To this Sureśvara replies that, when the *antaḥkaraṇa* or mind is transformed into the form of the external objects, then, in order to give subjectivity to it, the category of the ego (*ahaṃkāra*) is produced to associate objective experiences with particular subjective centres, and then through the reflection of the pure intelligence by way of this category of the ego the objective experience, as associated with this category of the ego, appears as subjective experience. The category of the ego, being immediately and intimately related to the pure intelligence, itself appears as the knower, and the objectivity of the ego is not apparent, just as in burning wood the fire and that which it burns cannot be separated. It is only when the pure intelligence is reflected through the *ajñāna* product of the category of the ego that the notion of subjectivity applies to it, and all that is associated with it is experienced as the "this," the object, though in reality the ego is itself as much an object as the objects themselves. All this false experience, however, is destroyed in the realization of Brahman, when Vedāntic texts of unity are realized. In the third chapter of the *Naiṣkarmya-siddhi* the central ideas of the other three chapters are recapitulated. In the *Vārttika* Sureśvara discusses the very same problems in a much more elaborate manner, but it is not useful for our present purposes to enter into these details.

Padmapāda (A.D. 820)

Padmapāda is universally reputed to be a direct disciple of Śaṅkarācārya, and, since the manner of his own salutation to Śaṅkarācārya confirms this tradition, and since no facts are known that can contradict such a view, it may safely be assumed that he was a younger contemporary of Śaṅkarācārya. There are many traditional stories about him and his relations with Śaṅkarācārya; but, since their truth cannot be attested by reliable evidence, it is not possible to pronounce any judgment on them. Only two works are attributed to him, viz. the *Pañca-pādikā*, which is a commentary on

Śaṅkara's commentary on the first four *sūtras* of the *Brahma-sūtra* and Śaṅkara's introduction to his commentary known as the *adhyāsa* and the *sambhāvanā-bhāṣya*, and the *Ātma-bodha-vyākhyāna*, called also *Vedānta-sāra*. This *Pañca-pādikā* is one of the most important of the Vedānta works known to us. It was commented on by Prakāśātman (A.D. 1200) in his *Pañca-pādikā-vivaraṇa*[1]. The *Pañca-pādikā-vivaraṇa* was further commented on by Akhaṇḍānanda (A.D. 1350), a pupil of Ānandagiri, in his *Tattva-dīpana*. Ānanda-pūrṇa (A.D. 1600), who wrote his *Vidyā-sāgarī* commentary on Śrīharṣa's *Khaṇḍana-khaṇḍa-khādya* and also a commentary on the *Mahā-vidyā-viḍambana*, wrote a commentary on the *Pañca-pādikā*[2]. Nṛsiṃhāśrama also wrote a commentary on the *Pañca-pādikā-vivaraṇa*, called the *Pañca-pādikā-vivaraṇa-prakāśikā*, and Śrīkṛṣṇa also wrote one on the *Pañca-pādikā-vivaraṇa*. Aufrecht refers to another commentary by Amalānanda as *Pañca-pādikā-śāstra-darpaṇa*; but this is undoubtedly a mistake for his *Śāstra-darpaṇa*, which is noticed below. Amalānanda was a follower of the Vācaspati line and not of the line of Padmapāda and Prakāśātman. Rāmānanda Sarasvatī, a pupil of Govindānanda, the author of the *Ratna-prabhā* commentary on the *Śāṅkara-bhāṣya*, wrote his *Vivaraṇopanyāsa* (a summary of the main theses of the *Vivaraṇa*) as a commentary on Śaṅkara's *Bhāṣya*; but this was strictly on the lines of the *Pañco-pādikā-vivaraṇa*, though it was not a direct commentary thereon. Vidyāraṇya also wrote a separate monograph, called *Vivaraṇa-prameya-saṃgraha*, in which he interpreted the Vedāntic doctrines on the lines of the *Pañca-pādikā-vivaraṇa*. Of all these the *Vivaraṇopanyāsa* of Rāmānanda Sarasvatī was probably the last important work on the *Vivaraṇa* line; for Rāmānanda's teacher Govindānanda, the pupil of Gopāla Sarasvatī and the pupil's pupil of Śivarāma, refers in his *Ratna-prabhā* commentary to Jagannāthāśrama's commentary on the *Śāṅkara-bhāṣya*, called the *Bhāṣya-dīpikā*, and also to Ānandagiri's commentary as "*vṛddhāh,*" p. 5 (Nirṇaya-Sāgara Press, 1904). Jagannātha was the teacher of Nṛsiṃhāśrama; Govindānanda must therefore have lived towards the end of the sixteenth century. Rāmānanda may

[1] Prakāśātman also wrote a metrical summary of Śaṇkara's *Bhāṣya* and a work called *Śabda-nirṇaya*, in which he tried to prove the claims of scriptural testimony as valid cognition.

[2] As Mr Telang points out in his introduction to the *Mahā-vidyā-viḍambana*, it seems that Ānandapūrṇa lived after Śaṅkara Miśra (A.D. 1529), as is seen from his criticism of his reading of a passage of the *Khaṇḍana-khaṇḍa-khādya*, p. 586 (Chowkhambā).

therefore be placed in the early part of the seventeenth century. Govindānanda himself also in his *Ratna-prabhā* commentary followed the *Vivaraṇa* line of interpretation, and he refers to Prakāśātman with great respect as *Prakāśātma-śrī-caraṇaiḥ* (*Ratna-prabhā*, p. 3).

Padmapāda's method of treatment, as interpreted by Prakāśātman, has been taken in the first and the second volumes of the present work as the guide to the exposition of the Vedānta. It is not therefore necessary that much should be said in separate sections regarding the Vedāntic doctrines of these two great teachers. But still a few words on Padmapāda's philosophy may with advantage be read separately. Padmapāda says that *māyā*, *avyākṛta*, *prakṛti*, *agrahaṇa*, *avyakta*, *tamaḥ*, *kāraṇa*, *laya*, *śakti*, *mahāsupti*, *nidrā*, *kṣara* and *ākāśa* are the terms which are used in older literature as synonymous with *avidyā*. It is this entity that obstructs the pure and independently self-revealing nature of Brahman, and thus, standing as the painted canvas (*citra-bhitti*) of ignorance (*avidyā*), deeds (*karma*) and past impressions of knowledge (*pūrva-prajñā-saṃskāra*) produce the individual persons (*jīvatvāpādikā*). Undergoing its peculiar transformations with God as its support, it manifests itself as the two powers of knowledge and activity (*vijñāna-kriyā-śakti-dvayāśraya*) and functions as the doer of all actions and the enjoyer of all experiences (*kartṛtva-bhoktṛtvaikā-dhāraḥ*). In association with the pure unchangeable light of Brahman it is the complex of these transformations which appears as the immediate ego (*ahaṃkāra*). It is through the association with this ego that the pure self is falsely regarded as the enjoyer of experiences. This transformation is called *antaḥkaraṇa*, *manas*, *buddhi* and the ego or the ego-feeler (*ahaṃ-pratyayin*) on the side of its cognitive activity, while on the vibratory side of its activity (*spanda-śaktyā*), it is called *prāṇa* or biomotor functions. The association of the ego with the pure *ātman*, like the association of the redness of a *japā* flower with a crystal, is a complex (*granthi*) which manifests the dual characteristics of activity of the *avidyā* stuff and the consciousness of the pure self (*saṃbhinnobhaya-rūpatvāt*).

On the question as to whether *avidyā* has for both support (*āśraya*) and object (*viṣaya*) Brahman Padmapāda's own attitude does not seem to be very clear. He only says that *avidyā* manifests itself in the individual person (*jīva*) by obstructing the real nature of the Brahman as pure self-luminosity and that the

Brahman by its limitation (*avaccheda*) through beginningless *avidyā* is the cause of the appearance of infinite individual persons. But Prakāśātman introduces a long discussion, trying to prove that Brahman is both the support and the object of *avidyā* as against the view of Vācaspati Miśra that *avidyā* has the Brahman as its object and the *jīva* as its support (*āśraya*). This is thus one of the fundamental points of difference between the *Vivaraṇa* line of interpretation and the interpretation of the Vācaspati line. In this Prakāśātman agrees with the view of Sureśvara and his pupil Sarvajñātman, though, as will be noticed, Sarvajñātman draws some nice distinctions which are not noticed by Sureśvara.

Padmapāda draws a distinction between two meanings of falsehood (*mithyā*), viz. falsehood as simple negation (*apahnava-vacana*) and falsehood as the unspeakable and indescribable (*anirvacanī-yatā-vacana*). It is probably he who of all the interpreters first described *ajñāna* or *avidyā* as being of a material nature (*jaḍātmikā*) and of the nature of a power (*jaḍātmikā avidyā-śakti*), and interpreted Śaṅkara's phrase "*mithyā-jñāna-nimittaḥ*" as meaning that it is this material power of *ajñāna* that is the constitutive or the material cause of the world-appearance. Prakāśātman, however, elaborates the conception further in his attempts to give proofs in support of the view that *avidyā* is something positive (*bhāva-rūpa*). These proofs have been repeatedly given by many other later writers, and have already been dealt with in the first volume of the present work. Padmapāda is also probably the first to attempt an explanation of the process of Vedāntic perception which was later on elaborated by Prakāśātman and later writers, and his views were all collected and systematized in the exposition of the *Vedānta-paribhāṣā* of Dharmarāja Adhvarīndra in the sixteenth century. Describing this process, Padmapāda says that, as a result of the cognitive activity of the ego, the objects with which that is concerned become connected with it, and, as a result of that, certain changes are produced in it, and it is these changes that constitute the subject-object relation of knowledge (*jñātur jñeya-sambandhaḥ*). The *antaḥkaraṇa*, or psychical frame of mind, can lead to the limited expression of the pure consciousness only so far as it is associated with its object. The perceptual experience of immediacy (*aparokṣa*) of objects means nothing more than the expression of the pure consciousness through the changing states of the *antaḥkaraṇa*. The ego thus becomes a perceiver (*pramātṛ*) through its connection with the underlying consciousness. Prakāśātman, however, elaborates it by supposing that the *antaḥkaraṇa* goes out to the objective spatial positions, and assumes the spatial form of the objects perceived. Hence what Paḍmapāda conceived merely as the change of the *antaḥkaraṇa* states through the varying relation of the *antaḥkaraṇa* with its objects, is interpreted in the definite meaning of this relation as being nothing more than spatial superposition of the *antaḥkaraṇa* on its objects. In inference, however, there is no immediate knowledge, as this is mediated through relations with the reason (*liṅga*). Knowledge however would mean both mediate and immediate knowledge; for it is defined as being the manifestation of the object (*artha-prakāśa*).

On the subject of the causality of Brahman Padmapāda says that that on which the world-appearance is manifested, the Brahman, is the cause of the world. On this point Prakāśātman offers three alternative views, viz. (1) that, like two twisted threads in a rope, *māyā* and Brahman are together the joint cause of the world, (2) that that which has *māyā* as its power is the cause, and (3) that the Brahman which has *māyā* supported on it is the cause of the world, but in all these the ultimate causality rests with Brahman, since *māyā* is dependent thereon. Brahman is *sarva-jña* (omniscient) in the sense that it manifests all that is associated with it, and it is the Brahman that through its *māyā* appears as the world of experience. The doctrines of *avaccheda-vāda* and *pratibimba-vāda* explained in the first volume of the present work are also at least as old as Padmapāda's *Pañca-pādikā*, and both Padmapāda and Prakāśātman seem to support the reflection theory (*pratibimba-vāda*), the theory that the *jīva* is but a reflected image of Brahman[1]

Vācaspati Miśra (A.D. 840)

Vācaspati Miśra, the celebrated author of a commentary called *Bhāmatī* on Śaṅkara's commentary, is the author of a *Tattva-samīkṣā*, a commentary on Maṇḍana's *Brahma-siddhi*; he also commented on the *Sāṃkhya-kārikā*, *Vidhi-viveka*, *Nyāya-vārttika*, and he was

[1] See volume I, pp. 475, 476. These two doctrines were probably present in germinal forms as early as the ninth century. But gradually more and more attention seems to have been paid to them. Appaya Dīkṣita gives a fairly good summary of these two doctrines in the *Parimala*, pp. 335–343, Śri Vāṇi Vilāsa Press, Srirangam, without committing either himself or Vācaspati to any one of these views.

the author of a number of other works. In his *Nyāya-sūcīni-bandha* he gives his date as 898 (*vasv-aṅka-vasu-vatsare*), which in all probability has to be understood as of the Vikrama-saṃvat, and consequently he can safely be placed in A.D. 842. In his commentary called *Bhāmatī* he offers salutation to Mārtaṇḍa-tilaka-svāmin, which has been understood to refer to his teacher. But Amalānanda in commenting thereon rightly points out that this word is a compound of the two names Mārtaṇḍa and Tilakasvāmin, belonging to gods adored with a view to the fruition of one's actions. Tilakasvāmin is referred to in *Yājñavalkya*, 1. 294 as a god, and the *Mitākṣarā* explains it as being the name of the god Kārttikeya or Skanda. Udayana, however, in his *Nyāya-vārttika-tātparya-pariśuddhi* (p. 9), a commentary on Vācaspati's *Tātparya-ṭīkā*, refers to one Trilocana as being the teacher of Vācaspati, and Vardhamāna in his commentary on it, called *Nyāya-nibandha-prakāśa*, confirms this: Vācaspati himself also refers to Trilocanaguru, whom he followed in interpreting the word *vyavasāya* (*Nyāya-sūtra*, I. i. 4) as determinate knowledge (*savikalpa*)[1]. It is however interesting to note that in the *Nyāya-kaṇikā* (verse 3) he refers to the author of the *Nyāya-mañjarī* (in all probability Jayanta) as his teacher (*vidyā-taru*)[2]. Vācaspati says at the end of his *Bhāmatī* commentary that he wrote that work when the great king Nṛga was reigning. This king, so far as the present writer is aware, has not yet been historically traced. *Bhāmatī* was Vācaspati's last great work; for in the colophon at the end of the *Bhāmatī* he says that he had already written his *Nyāya-kaṇikā*, *Tattva-samīkṣā*, *Tattva-bindu* and other works on Nyāya, Sāṃkhya and Yoga.

Vācaspati's Vedāntic works are *Bhāmatī* and *Tattva-samīkṣā* (on *Brahma-siddhi*). The last work has not yet been published. Aufrecht, referring to his work, *Tattva-bindu*, says that it is a Vedānta work. This is however a mistake, as the work deals with the *sphoṭa* doctrines of sound, and has nothing to do with Vedānta. In the absence of Vācaspati's *Tattva-samīkṣā*, which has not been published, and manuscripts of which have become extremely scarce, it is difficult to give an entirely satisfactory account of the special features of Vācaspati's view of Vedānta. But his *Bhāmatī*

[1] *trilocana-gurūnnīta-mārgānugamanonmukhaiḥ*
yathāmānaṃ yathā-vastu vyākhyātam idam īdṛśam.
Nyāya-vārttika-tātparya-ṭīkā, p. 87. Benares, 1898.

[2] *ajñāna-timira-śamanīṃ nyāya-mañjarīṃ rucirām*
prasavitre prabhavitre vidyā-tarave namo gurave.
Nyāya-kaṇikā, introductory verse.

commentary is a great work, and it is possible to collect from it some of the main features of his views. As to the method of Vācaspati's commentary, he always tries to explain the text as faithfully as he can, keeping himself in the background and directing his great knowledge of the subject to the elucidation of the problems which directly arise from the texts and to explaining the allusions and contexts of thoughts, objections and ideas of other schools of thought referred to in the text. The *Bhāmatī* commentary on Śaṅkara's *Bhāṣya* is a very important one, and it had a number of important sub-commentaries. The most important and earliest of these is the *Vedānta-kalpa-taru* of Amalānanda (A.D. 1247–1260), on which Appaya Dīkṣita (about A.D. 1600) wrote another commentary called *Vedānta-kalpa taru-parimala*[1]. The *Vedānta-kalpa-taru* was also commented on by Lakṣmīnṛsiṃha, author of the *Tarka-dīpikā*, son of Koṇḍabhaṭṭa and grandson of Raṅgojī Bhaṭṭa, towards the end of the seventeenth century, and this commentary is called *Ābhoga*. The *Ābhoga* commentary is largely inspired by the *Vedānta-kalpa-taru-parimala*, though in many cases it differs from and criticizes it. In addition to these there are also other commentaries on the *Bhāmatī*, such as the *Bhāmatī-tilaka*, the *Bhāmatī-vilāsa*, the *Bhāmatī-vyākhyā* by Śrīraṅganātha and another commentary on the *Vedānta-kalpa-taru*, by Vaidyanātha Payaguṇḍa, called the *Vedānta-kalpa-taru-mañjarī*.

Vācaspati defines truth and reality as immediate self-revelation (*sva-prakāśatā*) which is never contradicted (*abādhita*). Only the pure self can be said to be in this sense ultimately real. He thus definitely rejects the definition of reality as the participation of the class-concept of being, as the Naiyāyikas hold, or capacity of doing work (*artha-kriyā-kāritva*), as the Buddhists hold. He admits two kinds of *ajñāna*, as psychological and as forming the material cause of the mind and the inner psychical nature of man or as the material world outside. Thus he says in his commentary on the *Śaṅkara-*

[1] Amalānanda also wrote another work, called *Śāstra-darpaṇa*, in which, taking the different topics (*adhikaraṇas*) of the *Brahma-sūtras*, he tried to give a plain and simple general explanation of the whole topic without entering into much discussion on the interpretations of the different sūtras on the topic. These general lectures on the *adhikaraṇas* of the *Brahma-sūtras* did not, however, reveal any originality of views on the part of Amalānanda, but were based on Vācaspati's interpretation, and were but reflections of his views, as Amalānanda himself admits in the second verse of the *Śāstra-darpaṇa* (*Vācaspati-mati-vimbitam ādarśam prārabhe vimalam*)—Śri Vāṇi Vilāsa Press, 1913, Srirangam, Madras.

bhāṣya, I. iii. 30, that at the time of the great dissolution (*mahā-pralaya*) all products of *avidyā*, such as the psychical frame (*antaḥkaraṇa*), cease to have any functions of their own, but are not on account of that destroyed; they are at that time merged in the indescribable *avidyā*, their root cause, and abide there as potential capacities (*sūkṣmeṇa śakti-rūpeṇa*) together with the wrong impressions and psychological tendencies of illusion. When the state of *mahā-pralaya* is at an end, moved by the will of God, they come out like the limbs of a tortoise or like the rejuvenation during rains of the bodies of frogs which have remained inert and lifeless all the year round, and then, being associated with their proper tendencies and impressions, they assume their particular names and forms as of old before the *mahā-pralaya*. Though all creation takes place through God's will, yet God's will is also determined by the conditions of *karma* and the impressions produced by it. This statement proves that he believed in *avidyā* an objective entity of an indescribable nature (*anirvācyā avidyā*), into which all world-products disappear during the *mahā-pralaya* and out of which they reappear in the end and become associated with psychological ignorance and wrong impressions which had also disappeared into it at the time of the *mahā-pralaya*. *Avidyā* thus described resembles very much the *prakṛti* of Yoga, into which all the world-products disappear during a *mahā-pralaya* together with the fivefold *avidyā* and their impressions, which at the time of creation become associated with their own proper *buddhis*. In the very adoration hymn of the *Bhāmatī* Vācaspati speaks of *avidyā* being twofold (*avidyā-dvitaya*), and says that all appearances originate from Brahman in association with or with the accessory cause (*sahakāri-kāraṇa*) of the two *avidyās* (*avidyā-dvitaya-sacivasya*). In explaining this passage Amalānanda points out that this refers to two *avidyās*, one as a beginningless positive entity and the other as the preceding series of beginningless false impressions (*anyā pūrvāpūrva-bhrama-saṃskāraḥ*). There is thus one aspect of *avidyā* which forms the material stuff of the appearances; but the appearances could not have been appearances if they were not illusorily identified with the immediate and pure self-revelation (*sva-prakāśā cit*). Each individual person (*jīva*) confuses and misapprehends his psychical frame and mental experiences as intelligent in themselves, and it is by such an illusory confusion that these psychical states attain any meaning as appearances; for otherwise these appearances could not have been expressed at all. But how does the person come in, since the concept of a person itself presupposes the very confusion which it is supposed to make? To this Vācaspati's reply is that the appearance of the personality is due to a previous false confusion, and that to another previous false confusion (cf. Maṇḍana). So each false confusion has for its cause a previous false confusion, and that another false confusion and so on in a beginning–less series. It is only through such a beginningless series of confusions that all the later states of confusion are to be explained. Thus on the one hand the *avidyā* operates in the individual person, the *jīva*, as its locus or support (*āśraya*), and on the other hand it has the Brahman or pure self-revealing intelligence as its object (*viṣaya*), which it obscures and through which it makes its false appearances to be expressed, thereby giving them a false semblance of reality, whereby all the world-appearances seem to be manifestations of reality[1]. It is easy to see how this view differs from the view of the *Saṃkṣepa-śārīraka* of Sarvajñātma Muni; for in the opinion of the latter, the Brahman is both the support (*āśraya*) and the object (*viṣaya*) of *ajñāna*, which means that the illusion does not belong to the individual person, but is of a transcendental character. It is not the individual person as such (*jīva*), but the pure intelligence that shines through each individual person (*pratyak-cit*), that is both obscured and diversified into a manifold of appearances in a transcendental manner. In Vācaspati's view, however, the illusion is a psychological one for which the individual person is responsible, and it is caused through a beginningless chain of illusions or confusions, where each succeeding illusory experience is explained by a previous illusory mode of experience, and that by another and so on. The content of the illusory experiences is also derived from the indescribable *avidyā*, which is made to appear as real by their association with Brahman, the ultimately real and self-revealing Being. The illusory appearances, as they are, cannot be described as being existent or non-existent; for, though they seem to have their individual existences, they are always negated by other existences, and none of them have that kind of reality which can be said to defy all negation and contradiction; and it is only such uncontradicted self-revelation that can be said to be

[1] It is in the latter view that Vācaspati differs from Maṇḍana, on whose *Brahma-siddhi* he wrote his *Tattva-samīkṣā*.

ultimately real. The unreality of world-appearances consists in the fact that they are negated and contradicted; and yet they are not absolutely non-existent like a hare's horn, since, had they been so, they could not have been experienced at all. So in spite of the fact that the appearances are made out of *avidyā*, they have so far as any modified existence can be ascribed to them, the Brahman as their underlying ground, and it is for this reason that Brahman is to be regarded as the ultimate cause of the world. As soon as this Brahman is realized, the appearances vanish; for the root of all appearances is their illusory confusion with reality, the Brahman. In the *Bhāmatī* commentary on Śaṅkara's commentary, II. ii. 28, Vācaspati points out that according to the Śaṅkara Vedānta the objects of knowledge are themselves indescribable in their nature (*anirvacanīyaṃ nīlādi*) and not mere mental ideas (*na hi brahma-vādino nīlādy-ākārāṃ vittim abhyupagacchanti kintu anirvacanīyaṃnīlādi*). The external objects therefore are already existent outside of the perceiver, only their nature and stuff are indescribable and irrational (*anirvācya*). Our perceptions therefore refer always to such objects as their excitants or producers, and they are not of the nature of pure sensations or ideas generated from within, without the aid of such external objects.

Sarvajñātma Muni (A.D. 900).

Sarvajñātma Muni was a disciple of Sureśvarācārya, the direct disciple of Śaṅkara, to whom at the beginning of his work *Saṃkṣepa-śārīraka* he offers salutation by the name Deveśvara, the word being a synonym of the word *sura* in Sureśvara. The identification of Deveśvara with Sureśvara is made by Rāma Tīrtha, the commentator on the *Saṃkṣepa-śārīraka*, and this identification does not come into conflict with anything else that is known about Sarvajñātma Muni either from the text of his work or from other references to him in general. It is said that his other name was Nityabodhācārya. The exact date of neither Sureśvara nor Sarvajñātma can be definitely determined. Mr Pandit in his introduction to the *Gauḍavaho* expresses the view that, since Bhavabhūti was a pupil of Kumārila, Kumārila must have lived in the middle of the seventh century, and, since Śaṅkara was a contemporary of Kumārila (on the testimony of the *Śaṅkara-dig-vijaya*), he must have lived either in the seventh century or in the first half of the eighth century. In the first volume of the present work Śaṅkara was placed between A.D. 780–820. The arguments of Mr Pandit do not raise any new point for consideration. His theory that Bhavabhūti was a pupil of Kumārila is based on the evidence of two manuscripts, where, at the end of an act of the *Mālatī-Mādhava*, it is said that the work was written by a pupil of Kumārila. This evidence, as I have noticed elsewhere, is very slender. The tradition that Śaṅkara was a contemporary of Kumārila, based as it is only on the testimony of the *Śaṅkara-dig-vijaya*, cannot be seriously believed. All that can be said is that Kumārila probably lived not long before Śaṅkara, if one can infer this from the fact that Śaṅkara does not make any reference to Kumārila. Hence there seems to be no reason why the traditionally accepted view that Śaṅkara was born in Saṃvat 844, or A.D. 788, or Kali age 3889, should be given up[1]. Taking the approximate date of Śaṅkara's death to be about A.D. 820 and taking into consideration that Sureśvara, the teacher of Sarvajñātman, occupied his high pontifical position for a long time, the supposition that Sarvajñātman lived in A.D. 900 may not be very far wrong. Moreover, this does not come into conflict with the fact that Vācaspati, who probably wrote his earlier work the *Nyāya-sūcī-nibandha* in A.D. 842, also wrote his commentary on Maṇḍana's *Brahma-siddhi* when Sureśvara was occupying the pontifical position.

Sarvajñātma Muni was thus probably a younger contemporary of Vācaspati Miśra. In his *Saṃkṣepa-śārīraka* he tries to describe the fundamental problems of the Vedānta philosophy, as explained by Śaṅkara. This work, which is probably the only work of his that is known to us, is divided into four chapters, written in verses of different metres. It contains in the first chapter 563 verses, in the second 248, in the third 365 and in the fourth 63. In the first chapter of the work he maintains that pure Brahman is the ultimate cause of everything through the instrumentality (*dvāra*) of *ajñāna*. The *ajñāna*, which rests on (*āśraya*) the pure self and operates on it as its object (*viṣaya*), covers its real nature (*ācchādya*) and creates delusory appearances (*vikṣipati*), thereby producing the threefold appearances of God (*Īśvara*), soul (*jīva*) and the world. This *ajñāna* has no independent existence, and its effects are seen only through the pure self (*cid-ātman*) as its ground and object, and its creations are all false. The pure self is directly perceived in the state of dreamless sleep as being of the nature

[1] See *Ārya-vidyā-sudhā-kara*, pp. 226, 227.

of pure bliss and happiness without the slightest touch of sorrow; and pure bliss can only be defined as that which is the ultimate end and not under any circumstances a means to anything else; such is also the pure self, which cannot be regarded as being a means to anything else; moreover, there is the fact that everyone always desires his self as the ultimate object of attainment which he loves above anything else. Such an infinite love and such an ultimate end cannot be this limited self, which is referred to as the agent of our ordinary actions and the sufferer in the daily concerns of life. The intuitive perception of the seers of the Upaniṣads also confirms the truth of the self as pure bliss and the infinite. The illusory impositions on the other hand are limited appearances of the subject and the object which merely contribute to the possibility of false attribution and cannot therefore be real (*na vāstavaṃ tat*). When the Brahman is associated with *ajñāna* there are two false entities, viz. the *ajñāna* and the Brahman as associated with the *ajñāna*; but this does not imply that the pure Brahman, which underlies all these false associations, is itself also false, since this might lead to the criticism that, everything being false, there is no reality at all, as some of the Buddhists contend. A distinction is drawn here between *ādhāra* and *adhiṣṭhāna*. The pure Brahman that underlies all appearances is the true *adhiṣṭhāna* (ground), while the Brahman as modified by the false *ajñāna* is a false *ādhāra* or a false object to which the false appearances directly refer. All illusory appearances are similarly experienced. Thus in the experience "I perceive this piece of silver" (in the case of the false appearance of a piece of conch-shell as silver) the silvery character or the false appearance of the silver is associated with the "this" element before the perceiver, and the "this" element in its turn, as the false object, becomes associated with the false silver as the "this silver." But, though the objectivity of the false silver as the "this" before the perceiver is false, the "this" of the true object of the conch-shell is not false. It is the above kind of double imposition of the false appearance on the object and of the false object on the false appearance that is known as *parasparādhyāsa*. It is only the false object that appears in the illusory appearance and the real object lies untouched. The inner psychical frame (*antaḥkaraṇa*) to a certain extent on account of its translucent character resembles pure Brahman, and on account of this similarity it is often mistaken for the pure self and the pure self is mistaken for the *antaḥkaraṇa*. It may be contended that there could be no *antaḥkaraṇa* without the illusory imposition, and so it could not itself explain the nature of illusion. The reply given to such an objection is that the illusory imposition and its consequences are beginningless and there is no point of time to which one could assign its beginning. Hence, though the present illusion may be said to have taken its start with the *antaḥkaraṇa*, the *antaḥkaraṇa* is itself the product of a previous imposition, and that of a previous *antaḥkaraṇa*, and so on without a beginning. Just as in the illusion of the silver in the conch-shell, though there is the piece of conch-shell actually existing, yet it is not separately seen, and all that is seen to exist is the unreal silver, so the real Brahman exists as the ground, though the world during the time of its appearance is felt to be the only existing thing and the Brahman is not felt to be existent separately from it. Yet this *ajñāna* has no real existence and exists only for the ignorant. It can only be removed when the true knowledge of Brahman dawns, and it is only through the testimony of the Upaniṣads that this knowledge can dawn; for there is no other means of insight into the nature of Brahman. Truth again is defined not as that which is amenable to proof, but as that which can be independently and directly felt. The *ajñāna*, again, is defined as being positive in its nature (*bhāva-rūpam*) and, though it rests on the pure Brahman, yet, like butter in contact with fire, it also at its touch under certain circumstances melts away. The positive character of *ajñāna* is felt in the world in its materiality and in ourselves as our ignorance. The real ground cause, however, according to the testimony of the Upaniṣads, is the pure Brahman, and the *ajñāna* is only the instrument or the means by which it can become the cause of all appearances; but, *ajñāna* not being itself in any way the material cause of the world, Sarvajñātman strongly holds that Brahman in association and jointly with *ajñāna* cannot be regarded as the material cause of the world. The *ajñāna* is only a secondary means, without which the transformation of appearances is indeed not possible, but which has no share in the ultimate cause that underlies them. He definitely denies that Brahman could be proved by any inference to the effect that that which is the cause of the production, existence and dissolution of the world is Brahman, since the nature of Brahman can be understood only by the testimony of the scriptures. He indulges in long discussions in order to show how the Upaniṣads can lead to a direct and immediate apprehension of reality as Brahman.

The second chapter of the book is devoted mainly to the further elucidation of these doctrines. In that chapter Sarvajñātma Muni tries to show the difference of the Vedānta view from the Buddhist, which difference lies mainly in the fact that, in spite of the doctrine of illusion, the Vedānta admits the ultimate reality to be Brahman, which is not admitted by the Buddhists. He also shows how the experiences of waking life may be compared with those of dreams. He then tries to show that neither perception nor other means of proof can prove the reality of the world-appearance and criticizes the philosophic views of the Sāṃkhya, Nyāya and other systems. He further clarifies his doctrine of the relation of Brahman to *ajñāna* and points out that the association of *ajñāna* is not with the one pure Brahman, nor with individual souls, but with the pure light of Brahman, which shines as the basis and ground of individual souls (*pratyaktva*); for it is only in connection with this that the *ajñāna* appears and is perceived. When with the dawn of right knowledge pure Brahman as one is realized, the *ajñāna* is not felt. It is only in the light of Brahman as underlying the individual souls that the *ajñāna* is perceived, as when one says, "I do not know what you say"; so it is neither the individual soul nor the pure one which is Brahman, but the pure light as it reveals itself through each and every individual soul[1]. The true light of Brahman is always there, and emancipation means nothing more than the destruction of the *ajñāna*. In the third chapter Sarvajñātman describes the ways (*sādhana*) by which one should try to destroy this *ajñāna* and prepare oneself for this result and for the final Brahma knowledge. In the last chapter he describes the nature of emancipation and the attainment of Brahmahood.

The *Saṃkṣepa-śārīraka* was commented upon by a number of distinguished writers, none of whom seem to be very old. Thus Nṛsiṃhāśrama wrote a commentary called *Tattva-bodhinī*, Puruṣottama Dīkṣita wrote another called *Subodhinī*, Rāghavānanda another called *Vidyāmṛta-varṣiṇī*, Viśvadeva another called *Siddhānta-dīpa*, on which Rāma Tīrtha, pupil of Kṛṣṇa Tīrtha,

[1] *nājñānam advayasamāśrayam iṣṭam evaṃ*
nādvaita-vastu-viṣayaṃ niśitekṣaṇānām
nānanda-nitya-viṣayāśrayam iṣṭam etat
pratyaktva-mātra-viṣayāśrayatānubhūteḥ
Saṃkṣepa-śārīraka, II. 211.

based his commentary *Anvayārtha-prakāśikā*. Madhusūdana Sarasvatī also wrote another commentary, called *Saṃkṣepa-śārīraka-sāra-saṃgraha.*

Ānandabodha Yati

Ānandabodha is a great name in the school of Śaṅkara Vedānta. He lived probably in the eleventh or the twelfth century[1] He refers to Vācaspati's *Tattva-samīkṣā* and criticizes, but without mentioning his name, Sarvajñātman's view of the interpretation of the nature of self as pure bliss. He wrote at least three works on Śaṅkara Vedānta, viz. *Nyāya-makaranda*, *Nyāya-dīpāvalī* and *Pramāṇa-mālā*. Of these the *Nyāya-makaranda* was commented upon by Citsukha and his pupil Sukhaprakāśa in works called *Nyāya-makaranda-ṭīkā* and *Nyāya-makaranda-vivecanī*. Sukha-prakāśa also wrote a commentary on the *Nyāya-dīpāvatī*, called *Nyāya-dīpāvalī-tātparya-ṭīkā*. Anubhūtisvarūpa Ācārya (late thirteenth century), the teacher of Ānandajñāna, also wrote commentaries on all the three works of Ānandabodha. Ānandabodha does not pretend to have made any original contribution and says that he collected his materials from other works which existed in his time[2]. He starts his *Nyāya-makaranda* with the thesis that the apparent difference of different selves is false, since not only do the Upaniṣads hold this doctrine, but it is also intelligible on grounds of reason that the apparent multiplicity of selves can be explained on an imaginary supposition of diversity (*kālpanika-puruṣa-bheda*), even though in reality there is but one soul. Arguing on the fact that even the illusory supposition of an imaginary diversity may explain all appearances of diversity, Ānandabodha tries to refute the argument of the *Sāṃkhya-kārikā* that the diversity of souls is proved by the fact that with the birth and death of some there is not birth or death of others. Having refuted the plurality of subjects in his own way, he turns to the refutation of plurality of objects. He holds that difference (*bheda*) cannot be perceived by sense-perception, since difference cannot be perceived without perceiving both the object and all else from which it differs. It cannot be said that first the object is perceived and then the difference; for perception will naturally

[1] Mr Tripathi in his introduction to Ānandajñāna's *Tarka-saṃgraha* gives Ānandabodha's date as A.D. 1200.

[2] *Nānā-nibandha-kusuma-prabhavāvadāta-*
nyāyāpadeśa-makaranda-kadamba eṣa.
Nyāya-makaranda, p. 359.

cease with awareness of its object, and there is no way in which it can operate for the comprehension of difference; neither can it be held that the comprehension of difference can in any way be regarded as simultaneous with the perception of the sensibles. Nor is it possible that, when two sensibles are perceived at two different points of time, there could be any way in which their difference could be perceived; for the two sensibles cannot be perceived at one and the same time. It cannot, again, be said that the perception of any sensible, say blue, involves with it the perception of all that is not blue, the yellow, the white, the red, etc.; for in that case the perception of any sensible would involve the perception of all other objects of the world. The negation of the difference of an entity does not mean anything more than the actual position of it. It is not, however, right to hold that all positive entities are of the nature of differences; for this is directly against all experience. If differences are perceived as positive entities, then to comprehend their differences further differences would be required, and there would thus be a vicious infinite. Moreover, differences, being negative in their nature, cannot be regarded as capable of being perceived as positive sensibles. Whether difference is taken as a subject or a predicate in the form "the difference of the jug from the pillar," or "the jug is different from the pillar," in either case there is comprehension of an earlier and more primitive difference between the two objects, on the basis of which the category of difference is realized.

Ānandabodha then discusses the different theories of error held by the Nyāya, Mīmāṃsā, Buddhism, etc. and supports the *anirvacanīya* theory of error[1]. In this connection he records his view as to why nescience (*avidyā*) has to be admitted as the cause of world-appearance. He points out that the variety and multiplicity of world-appearance cannot be explained without the assumption of a cause which forms its substance. Since this world-appearance is unreal, it cannot come out of a substance that is real, nor can it come out of something absolutely non-existent and unreal, since such a thing evidently could not be the cause of anything; hence, since the cause of world-appearance cannot be either real or unreal, it must have for its cause something which is neither real nor unreal, and the neither-real-nor-unreal entity is *avidyā*[2].

[1] See the first volume of the present work, ch. X, p. 485.
[2] *Nyāya-makaranda*, pp. 122, 123.

He next proceeds to prove the doctrine that the self is of the nature of pure consciousness (*ātmanaḥ samvid-rūpatva*). This he does, firstly, by stating the view that awareness in revealing itself reveals also immediately its objects, and secondly, by arguing that even though objects of awareness may be varying, there is still the unvarying consciousness which continues the same even when there is no object. If there were only the series of awarenesses arising and ceasing and if there were constant and persistent awarenesses abiding all the time, how could one note the difference between one awareness and another, between blue and yellow? Referring to *avidyā*, he justifies the view of its being supported on Brahman, because *avidyā*, being indefinable in its nature, i.e. being neither negative nor positive, there can be no objection to its being regarded as supported on Brahman. Moreover, Brahman can only be regarded as omniscient in its association with *avidyā*, since all relations are of the nature of *avidyā* and there cannot be any omniscience without a knowledge of the relations. In his *Nyāya-dīpavalī* he tries by inference to prove the falsity of the world-appearance on the analogy of the falsity of the illusory silver. His method of treatment is more or less the same as the treatment in the *Advaita-siddhi* of Madhusūdana Sarasvatī at a much later period. There is practically nothing new in his *Pramāṇa-mālā*. It is a small work of about twenty-five pages, and one can recognize here the arguments of the *Nyāya-makaranda* in a somewhat different form and with a different emphasis. Most of Ānandabodha's arguments were borrowed by the later writers of the Vedānta school. Vyāsatīrtha of the Madhva school of Vedānta collected most of the standard Vedānta arguments from Ānandabodha and Prakāśātman for refutation in his *Nyāyāmṛta*, and these were again refuted by Madhusūdana's great work, the *Advaita-siddhi*, and these refuted in their turn in Rāma Tīrtha's *Nyāyāmṛta-taraṅgiṇī*. The history of this controversy will be dealt with in the third volume of the present work.

Mahā-vidyā and the Development of Logical Formalism.

The Buddhists had taken to the use of the dialectic method of logical discussions even from the time of Nāgārjuna. But this was by no means limited to the Buddhists. The Naiyāyikas had also adopted these methods, as is well illustrated by the writings of Vātsyāyana, Udyotakara, Vācaspati, Udayana and others. Śaṅkara himself had utilized this method in the refutation of Buddhistic, Jaina, Vaiśeṣika and other systems of Indian philosophy. But, though these writers largely adopted the dialectic methods of Nāgārjuna's arguments, there seems to be little attempt on their part to develop the purely formal side of Nāgārjuna's logical arguments, viz. the attempt to formulate definitions with the strictest formal rigour and to offer criticisms with that overemphasis of formalism and scholasticism which attained their culmination in the writings of later Nyāya writers such as Raghunātha Śiromaṇi, Jagadīśa Bhaṭṭācārya, Mathurānātha Bhaṭṭācārya and Gadādhara Bhaṭṭācārya. It is generally believed that such methods of overstrained logical formalism were first started by Gaṅgeśa Upādhyāya of Mithilā early in the thirteenth century. But the truth seems to be that this method of logical formalism was steadily growing among certain writers from as early as the tenth and eleventh centuries. One notable instance of it is the formulation of the *mahā-vidyā* modes of syllogism by Kulārka Paṇḍita in the eleventh century. There is practically no reference to this *mahā-vidyā* syllogism earlier than Śrīharṣa (A.D. 1187)[1]. References to this syllogism are found in the writings of Citsukha Ācārya (A.D. 1220), Amalānanda, called also Vyāsāśrama (A.D. 1247), Ānandajñāna (A.D. 1260), Veṅkaṭa (A.D. 1369), Śeṣa Śārṅgadhara (A.D. 1450) and others[2]. The *mahā-vidyā* syllogisms were started probably some time in the eleventh century, and they continued to be referred to or refuted by writers till the fifteenth century, though it is curious to notice that they were not mentioned by Gaṅgeśa or any of his followers, such as Raghunātha, Jagadīśa and others, in their discussions on the nature of *kevalānvayi* types of inference.

[1] *gandhe gandhāntara-prasañjikā na ca yuktir asti; tadastitve vā kā no hāniḥ; tasyā apy asmābhiḥ khaṇḍanīyatvāt.* Śrīharṣa's *Khaṇḍana-khaṇḍa-khādya*, p. 1181, Chowkhambā edition.

[2] *athavā ayam ghaṭaḥ etadghaṭānyatve sati vedyatvānadhikaraṇānya-padār-hatvāt paṭavad ity-ādimahāvidyā-prayogair api vedyatva-siddhir apy ūhanīyā.*—Citsukha Ācārya's *Tattva-pradīpikā*, p. 13, also p. 304. The commentator Pratyag-rūpa-bhagavān mentions Kulārka Paṇḍita by name. *evaṃ sarvā mahavidyās tac-chāyā vānye prayogāḥ khaṇḍanīyā iti.*—Amalānanda's *Vedānta-kalpa-taru*, p. 304 (Benares, 1895). *sarvāsv eva mahāvidyāsu*, etc.—Ānandajñāna's *Tarka-saṃrgaha*, p. 22. Also Veṅkaṭa's *Nyāya-pariśuddhi*, pp. 125, 126, 273–276, etc., and *Tattva-muktā-kalāpa* with *Sarvārtha-siddhi*, pp. 478, 485, 486–491. Mr M. R. Telang has collected all the above references to *mahā-vidyā* in his introduction to the *Mahā-vidyā-viḍambana*, Gaekwad's Oriental Series, Baroda, 1920.

In all probability *mahā-vidyā* syllogisms were first started by Kulārka Paṇḍita in his *Daśa-śloki-mahā-vidyā-sūtra* containing sixteen different types of definitions for sixteen different types of *mahā-vidyā* syllogisms. Assuming that Kulārka Paṇḍita, the founder of *mahā-vidyā* syllogisms, flourished in the eleventh century, it may well be suggested that many other writers had written on this subject before Vādīndra refuted them in the first quarter of the thirteenth century. Not only does Vādīndra refer to the arguments of previous writers in support of *mahā-vidyā* and in refutation of it in his *Mahā-vidyā-viḍambana*, but Bhuvanasundara Sūri also in his commentary on the *Mahā-vidyā-viḍambana* refers to other critics of *mahā-vidyā*. Recently two different commentaries have been discovered on *mahā-vidyā*, by Puruṣottamavana and Pūrṇaprajña. Veṅkaṭa in his *Nyāya-pariśuddhi* refers to the *Mahā-vidyā*, the *Māna-manohara* and the *Pramāṇa-mañjarī*, and Śrīnivāsa in his commentary *Nyāya-sāra* on the *Nyāya-pari-śuddhi* describes them as works which deal with roundabout syllogisms (*vakrānumāna*)[1]. This shows that for four or five centuries *mahā-vidyā* syllogisms were in certain quarters supported and refuted from the eleventh century to the sixteenth century.

It is well known that the great Mīmāṃsā writers, such as Kumārila Bhaṭṭa and his followers, believed in the doctrine of the eternity of sounds, while the followers of the Nyāya and Vaiśeṣika, called also Yaugācāryas, regarded sound as non-eternal (*anitya*). *Mahā-vidyā* modes were special modes of syllogism, invented probably by Kulārka Paṇḍita for refuting the Mīmāṃsā arguments of the eternity of sounds and proving the non-eternity of sounds. If these modes of syllogism could be regarded as valid, they would also have other kinds of application for the proving or disproving of other theories and doctrines. The special feature of the *mahā-vidyā* syllogisms consisted in their attempt to prove a thesis by the *kevalānvayi* method. Ordinarily concomitance (*vyāpti*) consists in the existence of the reason (*hetu*) in association with the probandum and its non-existence in all places where the probandum is absent (*sādhyābhāvavad-avṛttitvam*). But the *kevalānvayi* form of inference which is admitted by the Naiyāyikas applies to those cases where the probandum is so universal that there is no case where it is absent, and consequently it cannot have a reason (*hetu*) whose concomitance with it can be determined by

[1] See M. R. Telang's introduction to the *Mahā-vidyā-viḍambana.*

its non-existence in all cases where the probandum is absent and its existence in all cases where the probandum is present. Thus in the proposition, "This is describable or nameable (*idam abhi-dheyam*) because it is knowable (*prameyatvāt*)," both the probandum and the reason are so universal that there is no case where their concomitance can be tested by negative instances. *Mahā-vidyā* syllogisms were forms of *kevalānvayi* inference of this type, and there were sixteen different varieties of it which had this advantage associated with them, that, they being *kevalānvayi* forms of syllogism, it was not easy to criticize them by pointing out defects or lapses of concomitance of the reason and the probandum, as no negative instances are available in their case. In order to make it possible that a *kevalānvayi* form of syllogism should be applicable for affirming the non-eternity of sound, Kulārka tried to formulate propositions in sixteen different ways so that on *kevalānvayi* lines such an affirmation might be made about a subject that by virtue of it the non-eternity of sound should follow necessarily as the only consequence, other possible alternatives being ruled out. It is this indirect approach of inference that has been by the critics of *mahā-vidyā* styled roundabout syllogism. Thus *mahā-vidyā* has been defined as that method of syllogism by which a specific probandum which it is desired to prove by the joint method of agreement and difference (3, *anvaya-vyatireki-sādhya-viśeṣaṃ vādy-abhimatam sādhayati*) is proved by the necessary implication of the existence of a particular probandum in a particular subject (2, *pakṣe vyāpaka-pratītya-paryavasāna-balāt*), affirmed by the existence of hetu in the subject on *kevalānvayi* lines (1, *kevalān-vayini vyāpake pravartamāno hetuḥ*). In other words, a reason which exists in a probandum inseparably abiding in a subject (*pakṣa)* without failure (proposition 1) proves (*sādhayati*), by virtue of the fact, that such an unfailing existence of that probandum in that subject in that way is only possible under one supposition (proposition 2), namely, the affirmation of another probandum in another subject (e.g. the affirmation of the probandum "non-eternity" to the subject "sound"), which is generally sought to be proved by the direct method of agreement and difference (proposition 3). This may be understood by following a typical *mahā-vidyā* syllogism. Thus it is said that by reason of knowability (*meya-tva*) as such the self, dissociated from the relations of all eternal and non-eternal qualities of all other objects excepting sound, is related to a non-eternal entity (*ātmā śabdetarānitya-nitya-yavṛttitvānadhikaraṇānitya-vṛtti-dharmavān meyatvād ghaṭavat*). Now by the qualifying adjunct of "self" the self is dissociated from all qualities that it shares with all other eternal and non-eternal objects excepting sound, and the consequence is that it is left only with some kind of non-eternal quality in relation with sound, as this was left out of consideration in the qualifying adjunct, which did not take sound within its purview. Since many relations are also on the Nyāya view treated as qualities, such a non-eternal relation of the self to sound may be their mutual difference or their mutual negation (*anyonyābhāva*). Now, if the self, which is incontestably admitted to be eternal, has such a non-eternal quality or relation to sound, then this can only be under one supposition, viz. that sound is non-eternal. But, since all other non-eternal relations that the self may have to other non-eternal objects, and all other eternal relations that it may have to other eternal objects, and all other such relations that it may have to all eternal and non-eternal objects jointly, except sound, have already been taken out of consideration by the qualifying phrase, the inseparable and unfailing non-eternal quality that the self may have, in the absence of any negative instances, is in relation to sound; but, if it has a non-eternal quality in relation to sound, then this can be so only under one supposition, viz. that sound is itself non-eternal; for the self is incontestably known as eternal. This indirect and roundabout method of syllogism is known as *mahā-vidyā*. It is needless to multiply examples to illustrate all the sixteen types of propositions of *mahā-vidyā* syllogism, as they are all formed on the same principle with slight variations.

Vādīndra in his *Mahā-vidyā-viḍambana* refuted these types of syllogism as false, and it is not known that any one else tried to revive them by refuting Vādīndra's criticisms. Vādīndra styles himself in the colophon at the end of the first chapter of his *Mahā-vidyā-viḍambana* "*Hara-kiṅkara-nyāyācārya-parama-paṇḍita-bhaṭṭa-vādīndra*," and in the concluding verse of his work refers to Yogīśvara as his preceptor. The above epithets of *Hara-kiṅkara*, *nyāyācārya*, etc. do not show however what his real name was. Mr Telang points out in his introduction to the *Mahā-vidyā-viḍambana* that his pupil Bhaṭṭa Rāghava in his commentary on Bhāsa-rvajña's *Nyāya-sāra*, called *Nyāya-sāra-vicāra*, refers to him by the name Mahādeva. Vādīndra's real name, then, was Mahādeva, and the rest of the epithets were his titles. Bhaṭṭa Rāghava says that the name of Vādīndra's father was Sāraṅga. Bhaṭṭa Rāghava gives his own date in the Śakaera. The sentence however is liable to two different constructions, giving us two different dates, viz. A.D. 1252 and 1352. But, judging from the fact that Vādīndra was a religious counsellor of King Śrīsiṃha (also called Śiṅghana), who reigned in Devagiri A.D. 1210–1247, and that in all probability he lived before Veṅkaṭa (A.D. 1267–1369), who refers to his *Mahā-vidyā-viḍambana*, Mr Telang suggests that we should take A.D. 1252 to be the date of Bhaṭṭa Rāghava; and, since he was a pupil of Vādīndra, one may deduct about 27 years from his date and fix Vādīndra's date as A.D. 1225. Mr Telang points out that such a date would agree with the view that he was a religious counsellor of King Śrīsiṃha. Vādīndra refers to Udayana (A.D. 984) and Śivāditya Miśra (A.D. 975–1025). Mr Telang also refers to two other works of Vādīndra, viz. *Rasa-sāra* and *Kaṇāda-sūtra-nibandha*, and argues from allusions contained in Vādīndra's *Mahā-vidyā-viḍambana* that he must have written other works in refutation of *mahā-vidyā*. Vādīndra's *Mahā-vidyā-viḍambana* consists of three chapters. In the first chapter he gives an exposition of the *mahā-vidyā* syllogisms; the second and third chapters are devoted to the refutation of these syllogisms. Vādīndra's Mahā-vidyā-viḍambana has two commentaries, one called *Mahā-vidyā-viḍambana-vyākhyāna*, by Ānandapūrṇa (A. D. 1600), and the other, called *Vyākhyāna-dīpikā*, by Bhuvanasundara Sūri (A.D. 1400). In addition to these Bhuvanasundara Sūri also wrote a small work called the *Laghu-mahā-vidyā-viḍambana* and a commentary, *Mahā-vidyā-vivaraṇa-ṭippana*, on a *Mahā-vidyā-daśaślokī-vivaraṇa* by an unknown author.

The main points of Vādīndra's criticisms may briefly be stated as follows: He says that it is not possible that there should be a proper reason (*hetu*) which has no negative instances (*kevalānvayi-hetor eva nirvaktum aśakyatvāt*). It is difficult to prove that any particular quality should exist everywhere and that there should not be any instance or case where it does not occur. In the third chapter he shows that not only is it not possible to have *kevalānvayi hetus*, but that even in arguments on the basis of such *kevalānvayi hetu* there would be great scope for fallacies of self-contradiction (*sva-vyāghāta*) and fallacies of illicit distribution of the middle term (*anaikāntikatva*) and the like. He also shows how all these fallacies apply to all the *mahā-vidyā* syllogisms invented by Kulārka Paṇḍita.

It is needless for our present purposes to enter into any elaborate logical discussion of Vādindra; for the present digression on *mahā-vidyā* syllogisms is introduced here only to show that scholastic logicisms were not first introduced by Śrīharṣa, but had already come into fashion a few centuries before him, though Śrīharṣa was undoubtedly the most prominent of those who sought to apply these scholastic methods in philosophy.

It will thus be seen that the fashion of emphasizing the employment of logical formalism as a method in philosophy was inherited by the Naiyāyikas and Vedāntists alike from Buddhists like Nāgārjuna, Āryadeva and others in the third and the fourth centuries and their later successors in the fifth, sixth and seventh centuries. But during the eighth, ninth and tenth centuries one notices a steady development on this side in the works of prominent Nyāya writers such as Vātsyāyana, Udyotakara, Vācaspati Miśra and Udayana and Vedāntic authors such as the great master Śaṅkarācārya, Vācaspati Miśra and Ānandabodha Yati. But the school of abstract and dry formalism may be said to have properly begun with Kulārka Paṇḍita, or the authors of the *Māna-manohara* and *Pramāṇa-mañjarī* in the latter part of the eleventh century, and to have been carried on in the works of a number of other writers, until we come to Gaṅgeśa of the early thirteenth century, who enlivened it with the subtleties of his acute mind by the introduction of the new concepts of *avacchedakatā*, which may be regarded as a new turning point after *vyāpti*. This work was further carried on extremely elaborately by his later successors, the great writers of this new school of logic (*navya-nyāya*), Raghunātha Śiromaṇi, Jagadīśa Bhaṭṭācārya, Gadādhara Bhaṭṭācārya and others. On the Vedānta side this formalism was carried on by Śrīharṣa (A.D. 1187), Citsukha of about A.D. 1220 (of whom Vādīndra was a contemporary), Ānandajñāna or Ānandagiri of about A.D. 1260 and through a number of minor writers until we come to Nṛsiṃhāśrama and Madhusūdana Sarasvatī of the seventeenth century. It may be surmised that formal criticisms of Śrīharṣa were probably largely responsible for a new awakening in the Naiyāyikas, who began to direct their entire attention to a perfecting of their definitions and discussions on strict lines of formal accuracy and preciseness to the utter neglect of the collection of new data, new experiences or the investigation of new problems or new lines of enquiry, which is so essential for the development of true philosophy. But, when once they started perfecting the purely logical appliances and began to employ them successfully in debates, it became essential for all Vedāntists also to master the ways of this new formalism for the defence of their old views, with utter neglect of new creations in philosophy. Thus in the growth of the history of the dialectic of logical formalism in the Vedānta system of thought it is found that during the eighth, ninth, tenth and eleventh centuries the element of formalism was at its lowest and the controversies of the Vedānta with the Buddhists, Mīmāṃsists and Naiyāyikas were based largely on the analysis of experience from the Vedāntic standpoint and its general approach to philosophy. But in the twelfth and the thirteenth centuries the controversy was largely with the Nyāya and Vaiśeṣika and dominated by considerations of logical formalism above everything else. Criticisms became for the most part nothing more than criticisms of Nyāya and Vaiśeṣika definitions. Parallel to this a new force was gradually growing during these centuries in the writings of Rāmānuja and his followers, and in the succeeding centuries the followers of Madhva, the great Vaiṣṇava writer, began to criticize the Vedāntists (of the Śaṅkara school) very strongly. It is found therefore that from the thirteenth or fourteenth century the Vedāntic attack was largely directed against the followers of Rāmānuja and Madhva. A history of this controversy will be given in the third and fourth volumes of the present work. But the method of logical formalism had attained such an importance by this time that, though the Vaiṣṇavas brought in many new considerations and points of view in philosophy, the method of logical formalism never lost its high place in dialectic discussions.

Vedānta Dialectic of Śrīharṣa (A.D. 1150)

Śrīharṣa flourished probably during the middle of the twelfth century A.D. Udayana, the great Nyāya writer, lived towards the end of the tenth century, as is evident from the colophon of his *Lakṣaṇāvalī*[1]. Śrīharṣa often refutes the definitions of Udayana, and therefore must have flourished after him. Again, the great logician Gaṅgeśa of Mithilā refers to Śrīharṣa and refutes his

[1] *tarkāmbarāṅka*(906)*pramiteṣv atīteṣu śakāntataḥ*
varṣesūdayanaś cakre subodhāṃ lakṣaṇāvalīm.
Lakṣaṇāvalī, p. 72, Surendralāl Gosvāmin's edition, Benares, 1900.

views, and, since Gaṅgeśa lived in A.D. 1200, Śrīharṣa must have lived before that date. Accordingly Śrīharṣa was after Udayana and before Gaṅgeśa, i. e. between the tenth and twelfth centuries A.D. At the end of his book he refers to himself as honoured by the King of Kanauj (*Kānyakubjeśvara*). It is probable that this king may be Jayacandra of Kanauj, who was dethroned about A.D. 1195[1]. In his poetical work *Naiṣadha-carita* he mentions at the end of the several chapters many works of his, such as *Arṇava varṇana*, *Gauḍorvīśa-kula-praśasti*, *Nava-sāhasāṅka-carita*, *Vijaya-praśasti*, *Śiva-śakti-siddhi*, *Sthairya-vicāraṇa*, *Chandaḥ-praśasti*, and also *Īśvarābhisandhi* and *Pañcanalīya kāvya*[2]. The fact that he wrote a work eulogizing the race of the kings of Gauḍa leads one to suspect that he may have been one of the five Brahmans invited by Ādiśūra of Bengal from Kanauj in the early part of the eleventh century, in which case Śrīharṣa would have to be placed at that time, and cannot be associated with Jayacandra, who was dethroned in A.D. 1195. Śrīharṣa's most important philosophical contribution was the *Khaṇḍana-khaṇḍa-khādya* (lit. "the sweets of refutation"), in which he attempts to refute all definitions of the Nyāya system intended to justify the reality of the categories of experience and tries to show that the world and all world-experiences are purely phenomenal and have no reality behind them. The only reality is the self-luminous Brahman of pure consciousness[3]. His polemic is against the Nyāya, which holds that

[1] Ānandapūrṇa in his commentary on the *Khaṇḍana-khaṇḍa-khādya*, called *Khaṇḍana-phakkikā*, explains Kānyakubjeśvara as Kāśīrāja, i. e. King of Kāśī or Benares.

[2] None of these however are available.

[3] Śrīharṣa at the end of this work speaks of having purposely made it extremely knotty here and there, so that no one could understand its difficulties easily except when explained by the teacher. Thus he says:

grantha-granthir iha kvacit kvacid api nyāsi prayatnān mayā
prājñammanya-manā haṭhena paṭhitīmāsmin khalaḥ khelatu,
śraddhārāddha-guruḥ ślathīkṛta-dṛḍha-granthiḥ samāsādayat
tv etat-tarkarasormmi-majjana sukheṣv āsañjanaṃ sajjanaḥ.

Khaṇḍana-khaṇḍa-khādya, p. 1341. Chowkhambā Sanskrit Book Depot, Benares, 1914.

Several commentaries have been written on this celebrated work by various people, e. g. *Khaṇḍana-maṇḍana*, by Paramānanda, *Khaṇḍana-maṇḍana* by Bhavanātha, *Dīdhiti* by Raghunātha Śiromaṇi, *Prakāśa* by Vardhamāna, *Vidyā-bharaṇī* by Vidyābharana, *Vidyā-sāgarī* by Vidyāsāgara, *Khaṇḍana-ṭīkā* by Padmanābha Paṇḍita, *Ānanda-vardhana* by Śaṅkara Miśra, *Śrī-darpaṇa* by Śubhaṅkara, *Khaṇḍana-mahā-tarka* by Caritrasiṃha, *Khaṇḍana-khaṇḍana* by Pragalbha Miśra, *Śiṣya-hitaiṣiṇī* by Padmanābha, *Khaṇḍana-kuṭhāra* by Goku-lanātha Upādhyāya. At least one refutation of it was attempted by the Naiyā-yikas, as is evidenced by the work of a later Vācaspati (A.D. 1350) from Bengal, called *Khaṇḍanoddhāra*.

whatever is known has a well-defined real existence, and Śrīharṣa's main point is to prove that all that is known is indefinable and unreal, being only of a phenomenal nature and having only a relative existence based on practical modes of acceptance, customs and conventions. But, though his chief polemic is against the Nyāya, yet, since his criticisms are almost wholly of a destructive nature like those of Nāgārjuna, they could be used, with modifications, no less effectively against any other system. Those who criticize with the object of establishing positive definitions would object only to certain definitions or views of other schools; but both Śrīharṣa and the nihilists are interested in the refutation of all definitions as such, and therefore his dialectic would be valid against all views and definitions of other systems[1].

He starts with the proposition that none of our awarenesses ever stand in need of being further known or are capable of being the objects of any further act of knowledge. The difference of the Vedānta from the idealistic Buddhists consists in this, that the latter hold that everything is unreal and indefinable, not even excepting cognitions (*vijñāna*); while the Vedānta makes an exception of cognitions and holds that all the world, excepting knowledge or awareness, is indefinable either as existent or non-existent (*sad-asadbhyāṃ vilakṣaṇam*) and is unreal[2]. This indefinableness is in the nature of all things in the world and all experiences (*meya-svabhāvānugāminyām anirvacanīyatā*), and no amount of ingenuity or scholarship can succeed in defining the nature of that which has no definable nature or existence. Śrīharṣa undertakes to show that all definitions of things or categories put forward by the Nyāya writers are absolutely hollow and faulty even according to the canons of logical discussions and definitions accepted by the Naiyāyika; and, if no definition can stand or be supported, it necessarily follows that there can be no definitions, or, in other words, that no definitions of the phenomenal world are possible and that the world of phenomena and all our so-called experiences

[1] Śrīharṣa himself admits the similarity of his criticisms to those of Nāgārjuna and says: "*tathā hi yadi darśaneṣu śūnya-vādānirvacanīya-pakṣayor āśrayaṇaṃ tada tāvad amūṣāṃ nir-bādhaiva sārva-pathīnatā*," etc. *Khaṇḍana-khaṇḍa-khādya*, pp. 229–230, Chowkhambā Sanskrit Book Depot, Benares, 1914.

[2] By the idealistic Buddhists Śrīharṣa here means the idealism of the *Laṅkāvatāra*, from which he quotes the following verse:

buddhyā vivicyamānānāṃ svabhāvo nāvadhāryate
ato nirabhilapyās te nissvabhāvāś ca deśitāḥ.

Laṅkāvatāra-sūtra, p. 287, Otani University Press, 1923.

of it are indefinable. So the Vedāntist can say that the unreality of the world is proved. It is useless for any one to attempt to find out what is true by resorting to arguments; for the arguments can be proved to be false even by the canons on which they are based. If anyone, however, says that the arguments of Śrīharṣa are open to the same objection and are not true, then that would only establish his own contention. For Śrīharṣa does not believe in the reality of his arguments and enters into them without any assumption of their reality or unreality. It can be contended that it is not possible to argue without first admitting the reality of the arguments. But such reality cannot be established without first employing the *pramāṇas* or valid means of proof; and the employment of the *pramāṇas* would require further arguments, and these further employment of the *pramāṇas* and so on until we have vicious infinite regress. If, however, the very arguments employed in accordance with the canons of the opponents to destroy their definitions be regarded as false, this would mean that the opponents reject their own canons, so that the Vedāntic arguments in refuting their position would be effective. The Vedānta is here interested only in destroying the definitions and positions of the opponents; and so, unless the opponents are successful in defending their own positions against the attacks of the Vedānta, the Vedānta point of view is not refuted. So the manifold world of our experience is indefinable, and the one Brahman is absolutely and ultimately real.

Regarding the proof that may be demanded of the ultimate oneness Śrīharṣa says that the very demand proves that the idea of ultimate oneness already exists, since, if the idea were not realized, no one could think of asking for a proof of it. Now, if it is admitted that the idea of absolute oneness is realized (*pratīta*), then the question arises whether such realization is right knowledge (*pramā*) or error (*apramā*). If it is a right idea, then, whatever may have produced it, this right idea is to be regarded as valid proof. If such an idea is false, one cannot legitimately ask the Vedāntist to adduce any proofs to demonstrate what is false. It may be urged that, though the Naiyāyika considers it false, it is regarded by the Vedāntist as true and hence the Vedāntist may be called upon to prove that the way in which or the means of proof through which he came to have his idea was true. This, however, the Vedāntist would readily deny; for, even though the idea of the absolute oneness may be right, yet the way in which one happened to come by this idea may be wrong. There may be a fire on a hill; but yet, if one infers the existence of such a fire from fog appearing as smoke, then such an inference is false, even though the idea of the fire may itself be right. Leaving aside the discussion of the propriety of such demands on the part of the opponents, the Vedāntist says that the Upaniṣadic texts demonstrate the truth of the ultimate oneness of reality.

The ultimate oneness of all things, taught in the Upaniṣad texts, cannot be said to be negatived by our perceptual experience of "many." For our perception deals with individual things of the moment and therefore cannot apply to all things of the past, present, and future and establish the fact of their all being different from one another. Perception applies to the experience of the immediate present and is therefore not competent to contradict the universal proposition of the oneness of all things, as taught by the Upaniṣads. Again, as Śrīharṣa says, in our perception of the things of experience we do not realize the differences of the perceptual objects from ourselves, but the differences among the objects themselves. The self-revelation of knowledge also fails to show its difference from all objects of the world. The difference, again, of the perceived objects from all other things is not revealed in the nature of the perceived objects themselves as *svarūpa-bheda*, or difference as being of the nature of the objects which are differenced—if that were the case, then the false and erroneous perception of silver would also at once manifest its difference from the object (the conch-shell) on which the false silver is imposed. In this way Śrīharṣa tried to prove that the purport of non-duality, as asserted in the Vedic texts, is not contradicted by any other, stronger, proof. Most of these arguments, being of a verbal nature, may better here be dropped. The main stress seems to rest on the idea that the immediate differences between the things perceived do not in the least suggest or imply that they, in their essence or in their totality, could not ultimately, as a result of our progressive and better knowledge of things, be considered as one identical reality (as is asserted in the Upaniṣads). If perception cannot prove anything, inferences by themselves cannot stand alone or contradict the non-duality taught in the Upaniṣads. In our world of phenomenal experience our minds are always impressed with the concept of difference; but Śrīharṣa says that the mere existence of an idea does not prove its reality. Words can give rise to ideas relating even to absolutely non-existing things.

Again, the concept of "difference" can hardly be defined. If it lies involved within the essential nature of all things that differ, then difference would be identical with the nature of the things that differ. If difference were different from the things that differ, then it would be necessary to find out some way of establishing a relation between "difference" and the things that differ, and this might require another connection, and that another, and so we should have a vicious endless series. He says that "difference" may be looked upon from a number of possible points of view. Firstly, "difference" is supposed to be of the nature of things. But a "difference" which is of the nature of the things which differ must involve them all in one; for there cannot be any difference without referring to the things from which there is difference. If by "book" we mean its difference from table, then the table has to enter into the nature of the book, and that would mean the identity of the table and the book. There is no meaning in speaking of "difference" as being the thing, when such differences can only be determined by a reference to other things. If "difference" be the nature of a thing, such a nature cannot be in need of being determined by other things. One thing, say a book, is realized as being different from a table—the nature of the difference may here be described as being "the quality of being distinguished from a table"; but "the quality of being distinguished" would have no meaning or *locus standi*, unless "the table" were also taken with it. If anyone says that a book is identical with "the quality of being distinguished from," then this will invariably include "the table" also within the essence of the book, as "the table" is a constituent of the complex quality "to be distinguished from," which necessarily means "to be distinguished from a table." So on this view also "the table" and all other things which could be distinguished from the book are involved in the very essence of all things—a conclusion which contradicts the very concept of difference. It may also be pointed out that the concept of difference is entirely extraneous to the concept of things as they are understood or perceived. The notion of "difference" is itself different from the notion of the book and the table, whether jointly or separately. The joint notion of the book and the table is different from the notion that "the book differs from the table". For understanding the nature of a book it is not necessary that one should understand previously its difference from a table. Moreover, even though the notion of difference may in some sense be said to lead to our apprehension of individual things, the apprehension of such individual things docs not carry with it the idea that it is on account of such difference that the individual things are perceived. It is through similarity or resemblance between two things—say between a wild cow (*gavaya*) and the domestic cow (*go*)—that a man can recognize an animal as a wild cow; but yet, when he so considers an animal as a wild cow, he does not invariably because of such a resemblance to a cow think the animal to be a wild cow. The mental decision regarding an animal as a cow or a wild cow takes place immediately without any direct participation of the cause which produced it. So, even though the notion of difference may be admitted to be responsible for our apprehension of the different individual things, an apprehension of an individual thing does not involve as a constituent any notion of difference. It is therefore wrong to think that things are of the nature of difference.

In another view, wherein difference is interpreted as "mental negation" or "otherness" (*anyonyābhāva*), this "otherness" (say of the book from the table) is explained as being the negation of the identity of one with the other. When one says that the book is other than the table, what is meant is that identity of the book with the table is denied. Śrīharṣa here raises the objection that, if the identity of the book with the table was absolutely chimerical, like the hare's horn, such a denial of identity would be absolutely meaningless. It cannot, again, be suggested that this mental negation, or negation as otherness, means the denial of one class-concept in respect of another, (e.g. that of book on the table); for there is in these class-concepts no such special characteristic (*dharma*) by virtue of which one could be denied of the other or they could be distinguished from each other, since the Naiyāyika, against whom Śrīharṣa's arguments are directed, does not admit that class-concepts possess any distinguishing qualities. In the absence of such distinguishing qualities they may be regarded as identical: but in that case the denial of one class-concept (say of the table) would involve the denial of the class-concept of the thing itself (e.g. the book), since the class-concepts of the book and the table, not having any distinguishing qualities, are identical; and, further, through mental denial both the book and the table would be devoid of the class-concepts of book and table, and so there would be no way of distinguishing one thing from another, book from table. It is easy to see therefore that there is no way of making a special case regarding negation as otherness (*anyonyābhāva*). Again, if difference is regarded as the possession of opposite characters (*vaidharmya*), then also it may be asked whether the opposite characters have further opposite characters to distinguish them from one another, and these again others, and so there is a vicious infinite; if these are supposed to stop anywhere, then the final characters at that stage, not having any further opposite characters to distinguish them, would be identical, and hence all opposite characters in the backward series would be meaningless and all things would be identical. If on the contrary it is admitted at the very first stage that opposite or differing characters have no differing characters to distinguish them from one another, then the characters will be identical. Again, it may be asked whether these distinguishing characters are themselves different from the objects which possess them or not. If they are different, one may again ask concerning the opposing characters which lead to this difference and then again about other opposing characters of these, and so on. If these infinite differences were to hold good, they could not arrive in less than infinite time, whereas the object is finite and limited in time. If, again, they came all at once, there would be such a disorderly medley of these infinite differences that there would be no way of determining their respective substrates and their orderly successive dependence on one another. And, since in the series the earlier terms of difference can only be established by the establishment of the later terms of difference, the forward movement in search of the later terms of difference, in support of the earlier terms of difference, makes these earlier terms of difference unnecessary[1].

It cannot, therefore, be said that our perception of differences has any such intrinsic validity that it can contradict the ultimate unity taught in the Upaniṣad texts. Śrīharṣa does not deny that we perceive seeming differences in all things, but he denies their

[1] *prathama-bhedāsvīkāra-prayojanasya bheda-vyavahārāder dvitīya-bhedād eva siddheḥ prathama-bhedo vyarthaḥ syād eva, dvitīya-bhedādi-prayojanasya tṛtīya-bhedādinaiva siddheḥ so pi vyarthaḥ syāt. Vidyā-sāgarī on Khaṇḍana-khaṇḍa-khādya*, p. 206. Chowkhambā Sanskrit Book Depot, Benares, 1914.

ultimate validity, since he considers them to be due to *avidyā* or nescience alone[1].

The chief method of Śrīharṣa's dialectic depends upon the assumption that the reality of the things that one defines depends upon the unimpeachable character of the definitions; but all definitions are faulty, as they involve the fallacy of argument in a circle (*cakraka*), and hence there is no way in which the real nature of things can be demonstrated or defined. Our world of experience consists of knower, known and knowledge; if a knower is defined as the possessor of knowledge, knowledge can only be understood by a reference to the knower; the known, again, can be understood only by a reference to knowledge and the knower, and so there is a circle of relativity which defies all attempts at giving an independent definition of any of these things. It is mainly this relativity that in specific forms baffles all attempts at definition of all categories.

Application of the Dialectic to the Different Categories and Concepts

Śrīharṣa first takes for his criticism the definitions of right cognition. Assuming the definition of right cognition to be the direct apprehension of the real nature of things, he first urges that such a definition is faulty, since, if one accidentally guesses rightly certain things hidden under a cover and not perceived, or makes a right inference from faulty data or by fallacious methods, though the awareness may be right, it cannot be called right cognition[2]. It is urged that cognition, in order to be valid, must be produced through unerring instruments; here, however, is a case of chance guesses which may sometimes be right without being produced by unerring instruments of senses. Nor can correspondence of the cognition with its object (*yathārthānubhavaḥ pramā*) be regarded as a proper definition of right cognition. Such correspondence can be defined as meaning either that which represents the reality of the object itself or similarity to the object. The real nature of

[1] *na vayaṃ bhedasya sarvathaivāsattvam abhyutpagacchāmaḥ, kiṃ nāma na pāramār thikaṃ sattvaṃ; avidyā-vidyamānatvaṃ tu tadīyam iṣyata eva. Khaṇ-ḍana-khaṇḍa-khādya*, p. 214.

[2] E.g. when a man rightly guesses the number of shells closed in another man's hand, or when one makes a false inference of fire on a hill from a fog looking like smoke from a distance and there is fire on the hill by chance—his judgment may be right though his inference may be false.

an object is indeterminable, and so correspondence of awareness with the object may rather be defined as similarity of the former to the latter. If this similarity means that the awareness must have such a character as is possessed by the object (*jñāna-viṣayīkṛtena rūpeṇa sādṛśyam*), then this is clearly impossible; for qualities that belong to the object cannot belong to the awareness—there may be an awareness of two white hard marbles, but the awareness is neither two, nor white, nor hard[1]. It may be urged that the correspondence consists in this, that the whiteness etc. belong to the object as qualities possessed by it, whereas they belong to awareness as being qualities which it reveals[2]. But that would not hold good in the case of illusory perception of silver in a conch-shell; the awareness of "before me" in the perception of "before me the silver" has to be admitted as being a right cognition. If this is admitted to be a right cognition, then it was meaningless to define right cognition as true correspondence; it might as well have been defined as mere cognition, since all cognition would have some object to which it referred and so far as that only was concerned all cognitions would be valid. If, however, entire correspondence of thought and object be urged, then partial correspondence like the above can hardly be considered satisfactory. But, if entire correspondence is considered indispensable, then the correctness of the partial correspondence has to be ignored, whereas it is admitted by the Naiyāyika that, so far as reference to an object is concerned, all cognitions are valid; only the nature of cognition may be disputed as to right or wrong, when we are considering the correspondence of the nature of the object and the nature characterized by the awareness of the object. If entire correspondence with the object is not assured, then cognition of an object with imperfect or partial correspondence, due to obstructive circumstances, has also to be rejected as false. Again, since the correspondence always refers to the character, form or appearance of the thing, all our affirmations regarding the objects to which the characters are supposed to belong would be false.

Referring to Udayana's definition of right cognition as *samyak paricchitti*, or proper discernment, Śrīharṣa says that the word

[1] *dvau ghaṭau śuklav ityatra rūpa-saṃkhyādi-samavāyitvaṃ na jñānasya guṇatvād ataḥ prakāśamāna-rūpeṇa artha-sādṛśyaṃ jñānasya nāsti—asti ca tasya jñānasya tatra ghaṭayoḥ pramātvam. Vidyā-sāgarī on Khaṇḍana*, p. 398.

[2] *arthasya hi yathā samavāyād rūpaṃ viśeṣaṇībhavati tathā viṣayabhāvāj jñānasyāpi tad-viśeṣaṇam bhavaty eva. Khaṇḍana*, p. 399.

"*samyak*" (proper) is meaningless; for, if *samyak* means "entire," then the definition is useless, since it is impossible to see all the visible and invisible constituent parts of a thing, and no one but an omniscient being could perceive a thing with all its characters, properties or qualities. If right discernment means the discernment of an object with its special distinguishing features, this again is unintelligible; for even in wrong cognition, say of conch-shell as silver, the perceiver seems to perceive the distinguishing marks of silver in the conch-shell. The whole point lies in the difficulty of judging whether the distinguishing marks observed are real or not, and there is no way of determining this. If, again, the distinguishing features be described as being those characteristics without the perception of which there can be no certain knowledge and the perception of which ensures right cognition, then it may well be pointed out that it is impossible to discover any feature of any cognition of which one can be positively certain that it is not wrong. A dreamer confuses all sorts of characters and appearances and conceives them all to be right. It may be urged that in the case of right perception the object is perceived with its special distinguishing features, as in the case of the true perception of silver, whereas in the case of the false perception of silver in the conch-shell no such distinguishing features are observed. But even in this case it would be difficult to define the essential nature of the distinguishing features; for, if any kind of distinguishing feature would do, then in the case of the false perception of silver in the conch-shell the distinguishing feature of being before the eyes is also possessed by the conch-shell. If all the particular distinguishing features are insisted on, then there will be endless distinguishing features, and it would be impossible to make any definition which would include them all. The certitude of a cognition which contradicts a previous wrong cognition would often be liable to the same objection as the wrong cognition itself, since the nature of the special distinguishing features which would establish its validity cannot be established by any definition of right knowledge.

Arguing against the definition of right cognition as "apprehension which is not incorrect or not defective" (*avyabhicārī anubhavaḥ*), Śrīharṣa says that "not incorrect" or "not defective" cannot mean that the cognition must exist only at the time when the object exists; for then inferential cognition, which often refers to past and future things, would be false. Neither can it mean that the cognition coexists in space with its objects; nor can it mean that the right cognition is similar to its object in all respects, since cognition is so different in nature from the object that it is not possible that there should be any case in which it would be similar there to in all respects. And, if the view that an awareness and its object are one and the same be accepted, then this would apply even to those cases where one object is wrongly perceived as another; and hence the word "*avyabhicārī*" is not sufficient to distinguish right knowledge from wrong cognition.

Arguing against the Buddhist definition of right cognition as "an apprehension which is not incompatible (*avisaṃvādi*) with the object known," Śrīharṣa tries to refute the definition in all the possible senses of incompatibility of cognition with object which determines wrong knowledge. If the definition is supposed to restrict right cognition to cognition which is cognized by another cognition as being in agreement with its object, then a wrong cognition, repeated successively through a number of moments and found to be in agreement with its object through all the successive moments until it is contradicted, would also have to be admitted as right, because in this case the previous cognition is certified by the cognition of the succeeding moments. If, again, right cognition is defined as a cognition the incompatibility of which with its object is not realized by any other cognition, then also there are difficulties in the way. For even a wrong cognition may for some time be not contradicted by any other cognition. Moreover, the vision of the conch-shell by the normal eye as white may be contradicted by the later vision by the jaundiced eye as yellow. If it is urged that the contradiction must be by a faultless later cognition, then it may be pointed out that, if there had been any way of defining faultless cognition, the definition of right cognition would have been very easy. On the other hand, unless right cognition is properly defined, there is no meaning in speaking of faulty or wrong cognition. If right cognition is defined as a cognition which has causal efficiency, that in fact is not a proper definition; for even the wrong cognition of a snake might cause fear and even death. If it is urged that the causal efficiency must be exercised by the object in the same form in which it is perceived, then it is very difficult to ascertain this; and there may be a false cognition of causal efficiency also; hence it would be very difficult to ascertain the nature of right cognition on the basis of causal efficiency. Śrīharṣa points out again that in a similar way Dharmakīrti's definition of right cognition as enabling one to attain the object (*artha-prāpakatva*) is also unintelligible, since it is difficult to determine which object can be actually attained and which not, and the notion that the thing may be attained as it is perceived may be present even in the case of the wrong perception of silver in the conch-shell. If right cognition is defined as cognition which is not contradicted, then it may be asked whether the absence of contradiction is at the time of perception only, in which case even the wrong perception of silver in the conch-shell would be a right cognition, since it is uncontradicted at least at the time when the illusion is produced. If it is urged that a right cognition is that which is not contradicted at any time, then we are not in a position to assert the rightness of any cognition; for it is impossible to be certain that any particular cognition will never at any time be contradicted.

After showing that it is impossible to define right cognition (*pramā*) Śrīharṣa tries to show that it is impossible to define the idea of instruments (*karaṇa*) or their operative action (*vyāpāra*) as involved in the idea of instruments of cognition (*pramāṇa)*. Śrīharṣa attempts to show that instrumentality as an agent cannot be separately conceived as having an independent existence, since it is difficult to determine its separate existence. It would be a long tale to go into all the details of this discussion as set forth by Śrīharṣa, and for our present purposes it is enough to know that Śrīharṣa refuted the concept of "instrumentality" as a separate agent, both as popularly conceived or as conceived in Sanskrit grammar. He also discusses a number of alternative meanings which could be attributed to the concept of "*karaṇa*"or instrument, and shows that none of these meanings can be satisfactorily justified[1].

In refuting the definition of perception he introduces a long discussion showing the uselessness of defining perception as an instrument of right knowledge. Perception is defined in the Nyāya as cognition which arises through the contact of a particular sense with its object; but it is impossible to know whether any cognition has originated from sense-contact, since the fact of the production

[1] Among many other definitions Śrīharṣa also refutes the definition of *karaṇa* as given by Udyotakara—"*yadvān eva karoti tat karaṇam.*" *Khaṇḍana*, p. 506.

of knowledge from sense-contact cannot itself be directly perceived or known by any other means. Since in perception the senses are in contact on the one hand with the self and on the other hand with the external objects, Śrīharṣa urges by a series of arguments that, unless the specific object with which the sense is in contact is mentioned in each case, it would be difficult to formulate a definition of perception in such a way that it would imply only the revelation of the external object and not the self, which is as much in contact with the sense as is the object. Again, the specification of the object in the case of each perception would make it particular, and this would defeat the purposes of definition, which can only apply to universal concepts. Arguing against a possible definition of perception as immediateness, Śrīharṣa supposes that, if perception reveals some specific quality of the object as its permanent attribute, then, in order that this quality may be cognized, there ought to be another attribute, and this would presuppose another attribute, and so there would be an infinite regress; and, if at any stage of the infinite regress it is supposed that no further attribute is necessary, then this involves the omission of the preceding determining attributes, until the possibility of the perception is also negatived. If this immediateness be explained as a cognition produced by the instrumentality of the sense-organs, this again is unintelligible; for the instrumentality of sense-organs is incomprehensible. Śrīharṣa takes a number of alternative definitions of perceptions and tries to refute them all more or less in the same way, mostly by pointing out verbal faults in the formulation of the definitions.

Citsukha Ācārya, a commentator on Śrīharṣa's *Khaṇḍana-khaṇḍa-khādya*, offers a refutation of the definition of perception in a much more condensed form. He points out that the definition of perception by Akṣapāda as an uncontradicted cognition arising out of sense-contact with the object is unintelligible. How can we know that a cognition would not be contradicted? It cannot be known from a knowledge of the faultlessness of the collocating circumstances, since the faultlessness can be known only if there is no contradiction, and hence faultlessness cannot be known previously and independently, and the collocating circumstances would contain many elements which are unperceivable. It is also impossible to say whether any experience will for ever remain uncontradicted. Nor can it again be urged that right cognition is that which can produce an effort on the part of the perceiver (*pravṛtti-sāmarthya*); for even an illusory knowledge can produce an effort on the part of the perceiver who is deceived by it. Mere achievement of the result is no test for the rightness of the cognition; for a man may see the lustre of a gem and think it to be a gem and really get the gem, yet it cannot be doubted that his apprehension of the ray of the gem as the gem was erroneous[1]. In the case of the perception of stars and planets there is no chance of any actual attainment of those objects, and yet there is no reason to deny the validity of the cognitions.

Passing over the more or less verbal arguments of Śrīharṣa in refutation of the definitions of inference (*anumāna*) as *liṅga-parāmarśa* or the realization of the presence in the minor term (*pakṣa*, e.g. the mountain) of a reason or probans (*liṅga*, e.g. smoke) which is always concomitant with the major term (*sādhya*, e.g. fire), or as invariable concomitance of the probans with the probandum or the major term (*sādhya*, e.g. fire), and its other slightly modified varieties, I pass on to his criticism of the nature of concomitance (*vyāpti*), which is at the root of the notion of inference. It is urged that the universal relationship of invariable concomitance required in *vyāpti* cannot be established unless the invariable concomitance of all the individuals involved in a class be known, which is impossible. The Naiyāyika holds that the mind by a sort of mental contact with class-concepts or universals, called *sāmānya-pratyāsatti*, may affirm of all individuals of a class without actually experiencing all the individuals. It is in this way that, perceiving the invariable concomitance of smoke and fire in a large number of cases, one understands the invariable concomitance of smoke with fire by experiencing a sort of mental contact with the class-concept "smoke" when perceiving smoke on a distant hill. Śrīharṣa argues in refutation of such an interpretation that, if all individual smoke may be known in such a way by a mental contact with class-concepts, then by a mental contact with the class-concept "knowable" we might know all individual knowables and thus be omniscient as well. A thing is knowable only as an individual with its specific qualities as such, and therefore to know a thing as a knowable would involve the knowledge of all such specific qualities; for the

[1] *dṛśyate hi maṇi-prabhāyāṃ maṇi-buddhyā pravartamānasya maṇi-prāpteḥ pravṛtti-sāmarthyaṃ na cāvyabhicāritvam. Tattva-pradīpikā*, p. 218. Nirṇaya-Sāgara Press, Bombay, 1915.

class-concept "knowable" would involve all individuals which have a specific knowable character. It may be urged that knowability is one single character, and that things may be otherwise completely different and may yet be one so far as knowability is concerned, and hence the things may remain wholly unknown in their diversity of characters and may yet be known so far as they are merely knowable. To this Śrīharṣa answers that the class-concept "knowable" would involve all knowables and so even the diversity of characters would be involved within the meaning of the term "knowable".

Again, assuming for the sake of argument that it is possible to have a mental contact with class-concepts through individuals, how can the invariable concomitance itself be observed? If our senses could by themselves observe such relations of concomitance, then there would be no possibility of mistakes in the observation of such concomitance. But such mistakes are committed and corrected by later experience, and there is no way in which one can account for the mistake in the sense-judgment. Again, if this invariable concomitance be defined as *avinābhāva*, which means that when one is absent the other is also absent, such a definition is faulty; for it may apply to those cases where there is no real invariable concomitance. Thus there is no real concomitance between "earth" and "possibility of being cut"; yet in *ākāśa* there is absence of earth and also the absence of "possibility of being cut". If it is urged that concomitance cannot be determined by a single instance of the absence of one tallying with the absence of the other, it must be proved that universally in all instances of the absence of the one, e.g. the fire, there is also the absence of the other, e.g. the smoke. But it is as difficult to ascertain such universal absence as it is to ascertain universal concomitance. Again, if this concomitance be defined as the impossibility of the presence of the middle term, the reason or the probans, where the major term or the probandum is also absent, then also it may be said that it is not possible to determine such an impossibility either by sense-knowledge or by any other means.

Now *tarka* or eliminatory consideration in judging of possibilities cannot be considered as establishing invariable concomitance; for all arguments are based on invariable concomitance, and such an assumption would lead to a vicious mutual interdependence. The great logician Udayana objects to this and says that, if invariable concomitance between smoke and fire be denied, then there are strong arguments (*tarka*) against such a denial (*bādhakas tarkaḥ*), namely, that, if smoke is not regarded as concomitant with fire, then smoke would either exist without any cause or not exist at all, which is impossible. But Śrīharṣa says that there is room for an alternative proposition which Udayana misses, namely, that smoke is due to some cause other than fire. It may be that there are smokes which are not caused by fire. How can one be sure that all smokes are caused by fire? There may be differences in these two classes of fire which remain unnoticed by us, and so there is always room for the supposition that any particular smoke may not be caused by fire, and such doubts would make inference impossible. Udayana had however contended that, if you entertain the doubt, with regard to a future case, that it is possible that there may be a case in which the concomitance may be found wrong, then the possibility of such a doubt (*śaṅkā*) must be supported by inference, and the admission of this would involve the admission of inference. If such an exaggerated doubt be considered illegitimate, there is no obstruction in the way of inference. Doubts can be entertained only so long as such entertainment of doubts is compatible with practical life. Doubts which make our daily life impossible are illegitimate. Every day one finds that food appeases hunger, and, if in spite of that one begins to doubt whether on any particular day when he is hungry he should take food or not, then life would be impossible[1]. Śrīharṣa, however, replies to this contention by twisting the words of Udayana's own *kārikā*, in which he says that, so long as there is doubt, inference is invalid; if there is no doubt, this can only be when the invalidity of the inference has been made manifest, and until such invalidity is found there will always be doubts. Hence the argument of possibilities (*tarka*) can never remove doubts[2].

Śrīharṣa also objects to the definition of "invariable concomitance" as a natural relation (*svābhāvikaḥ sambandhaḥ*). He rejects the term "natural relation" and says that invariable concomitance

[1] *śaṅkā ced anumāsty eva*
na cec chaṅkā tatastarām
vyāghātāvadhir āśaṅkā
tarkaḥ śaṅkāvadhir mataḥ.

Kusumāñjali, III, 7. Chowkhambā Sanskrit Book Depot, Benares, 1912.

[2] *vyāghāto yadi śaṅkāsti*
na cec chaṅkā tatastarām
vyāghātāvadhir āśaṅkā
tarkaḥ śaṅkāvadhiḥ kutaḥ

Khaṇḍana-khaṇḍa-khādya, p. 693.

would not be justifiable in any of its possible meanings, such as (i) depending on the nature of the related (*sambandhi-svabhāva-śrita*), (ii) produced by the nature of the related (*sambandhi-svabhāva-janya*), (iii) not different from the nature constituting the relatedness, since, as these would be too wide and would apply even to those things which are not invariable concomitants, e.g. all that is earthen can be scratched with an iron needle. Though in some cases earthen objects may be scratched with an iron needle, not all earthen objects can be so scratched. He further refutes the definition of invariable concomitance as a relation not depending upon conditional circumstances (*upādhi*). Without entering into the details of Śrīharṣa's argument it may be pointed out that it rests very largely on his contention that conditionality of relations cannot be determined without knowledge of the nature of invariable concomitance and also that invariable concomitance cannot be determined without a previous determination of the conditionality of relations.

Śrīharṣa's brief refutation of analogy, implication and testimony, as also his refutation of the definitions of the different fallacies of inference, are not of much importance from a philosophical point of view, and need not be detailed here.

Turning now to Śrīharṣa's refutation of the Nyāya categories, we note that he begins with the refutation of "being" or positivity (*bhāvatva*). He says that being cannot be defined as being existent in itself, since non-being is also existent in itself; we can with as much right speak of being as existing as of non-being as existing; both non-being and being may stand as grammatical nominatives of the verb "exists". Again, each existing thing being unique in itself, there is no common quality, such as "existence" or "being," which is possessed by them all. Again, "being" is as much a negation of "non-being" as "non-being" of "being"; hence "being" cannot be defined as that which is not a negation of anything. Negation is a mere form of speech, and both being and non-being may be expressed in a negative form.

Turning to the category of non-being (*abhāva*), Śrīharṣa says that it cannot be defined as negation of anything; for being may as well be interpreted as a negation of non-being as non-being of being (*bhāvābhāvayor dvayor api paraspara-pratikṣepātmakatvāt*). Nor again can non-being be defined as that which opposes being; for not all non-being is opposed to all being (e.g. in "there is no jug on the ground" the absence of jug does not oppose the ground in respect of which the jug is denied); if non-being opposes some existent things, then that does not differentiate negation; for there are many existent things which are opposed to one another (e.g. the horse and the bull).

In refuting the Nyāya definition of substance (*dravya*) as that which is the support of qualities, Śrīharṣa says that even qualities appear to have numeral and other qualities (e.g. we speak of two or three colours, of a colour being deep or light, mixed or primary—and colour is regarded as quality). If it is urged that this is a mistake, then the appearance of the so-called substances as being endowed with qualities may also be regarded as equally erroneous. Again, what is meant by defining substance as the support (*āśraya*) of qualities? Since qualities may subsist in the class-concept of quality (*guṇatva*), the class-concept of quality ought to be regarded as substance according to the definition. It may be urged that a substance is that in which the qualities inhere. But what would be the meaning here of the particle "in"? How would one distinguish the false appearance, to a jaundiced eye, of yellowness in a white conch-shell and the real appearance of whiteness in the conch-shell? Unless the falsity of the appearance of yellow in the conch-shell is realized, there can be no difference between the one case and the other. Again, substance cannot be defined as the inhering or the material cause (*samavāyi-kāraṇa*), since it is not possible to know which is the inhering cause and which is not; for number is counted as a quality, and colour also is counted as a quality, and yet one specifies colours by numbers, as one, two, or many colours.

Furthermore, the Nyāya definition of quality as that which has a genus and is devoid of qualities is unintelligible; for the definition involves the concept of quality, which is sought to be defined. Moreover, as pointed out above, even qualities, such as colours, have numeral qualities; for we speak of one, two or many colours. It is only by holding to this appearance of qualities endowed with numeral qualities that the definition of quality can be made to stand, and it is again on the strength of the definition of quality that such appearances are to be rejected as false. If colours are known as qualities in consideration of other reasons, then these, being endowed with numeral qualities, could not for that very reason be called qualities; for qualities belong according to definition only to substances. Even the numerals themselves are endowed with the quality of separateness. So there would not be a single instance that the Naiyāyika could point to as an example of quality.

Speaking of relations, Śrīharṣa points out that, if relation is to be conceived as something subsisting in a thing, then its meaning is unintelligible. The meaning of relation as "in" or "herein" is not at all clear; for the notion of something being a container (*ādhāra*) is dependent on the notion of the concept of "in" or "herein," and that concept again depends on the notion of a container, and there is no other notion which can explain either of the concepts independently. The container cannot be supposed to be an inhering cause; for in that case such examples as "there is a grape in this vessel" or "the absence of horns in a hare" would be unexplainable. He then takes a number of possible meanings which can be given to the notion of a container; but these, not being philosophically important, are omitted here. He also deals with the impossibility of defining the nature of the subject-object relation (*viṣaya-viṣayi-bhāva*) of knowledge.

In refuting the definition of cause Śrīharṣa says that cause cannot be defined as immediate antecedence; for immediate antecedence can be ascribed only to the causal operation, which is always an intervening factor between the cause and the effect. If, on the theory that what (e.g. the causal operation) belongs to a thing (e.g. the cause) cannot be considered as a factor which stands between it (cause) and that which follows it (effect), the causal operation be not regarded as a separate and independent factor, then even the cause of the cause would have to be regarded as one with the cause and therefore cause. But, if it is urged that, since the cause of the cause is not an operation, it cannot be regarded as being one with the cause, one may well ask the opponent to define the meaning of operation. If the opponent should define it as that factor without which the cause cannot produce the effect, then the accessory circumstances and common and abiding conditions, such as the natural laws, space, and so forth, without which an effect cannot be produced, are also to be regarded as operation, which is impossible. Further, "operation" cannot be qualified as being itself produced by the cause; for it is the meaning of the concept of cause that has still to be explained and defined. If, again, cause is defined as the antecedence of that which is other than the not-cause, then this again would be faulty; for one cannot understand the "not-cause" of the definition without understanding what is the nature of cause, and vice-versa. Moreover, space, being a permanent substance, is always present as a not-cause of anything, and is yet regarded as the cause of sound. If, again, cause is defined as that which is present when the effect is present and absent when the effect is absent, this would not explain the causality of space, which is never known to be absent. If, again, cause is defined as invariable antecedence, then permanent substances such as space are to be regarded as the sole causes of effects. If, however, invariable antecedence be understood to mean unconditional antecedence, then two coexistent entities such as the taste and the colour of an earthen pot which is being burnt must mutually be the cause of the colour and the taste of the burnt earthen pot; for neither does the colour condition taste, nor does the taste condition colour. Moreover, if mere invariable antecedents be regarded as cause, then the invariably preceding symptoms of a disease are to be regarded as the cause of the disease on account of their invariable antecedence. Again, causality cannot be regarded as a specific character or quality belonging to certain things, which quality can be directly perceived by us as existing in things. Thus we may perceive the stick of the potter's wheel to be the cause of the particular jugs produced by it, but it is not possible to perceive causality as a general quality of a stick or of any other thing. If causality existed only with reference to things in general, then it would be impossible to conceive of the production of individual things, and it would not be possible for anyone to know which particular cause would produce a particular effect. On the other hand, it is not possible to perceive by the senses that an individual thing is the cause of a number of individual effects; for until these individual effects are actually produced it is not possible to perceive them, since perception involves sense-contact as its necessary condition. It is not necessary for our present purposes to enter into all the different possible concepts of cause which Śrīharṣa seeks to refute: the above examination is expected to give a fairly comprehensive idea of the methods of Śrīharṣa's refutation of the category of cause.

Nor is it possible within the limited range of the present work to give a full account of all the different alternative defences of the various categories accepted in Nyāya philosophy, or of all the various ways in which Śrīharṣa sought to refute them in his

Khaṇḍana-khaṇḍa-khādya. I have therefore attempted to give here only some specimens of the more important parts of his dialectical argument. The chief defect of Śrīharṣa's criticisms is that they often tend to grow into verbal sophisms, and lay greater stress on the faults of expression of the opponent's definitions and do not do him the justice of liberally dealing with his general ideas. It is easy to see how these refutations of the verbal definitions of the Nyāya roused the defensive spirit of the Naiyāyikas into re-stating their definitions with proper qualificatory phrases and adjuncts, by which they avoided the loopholes left in their former definitions for the attack of Śrīharṣa and other critics. In one sense, therefore, the criticisms of Śrīharṣa and some of his followers had done a great disservice to the development of later Nyāya thought; for, unlike the older Nyāya thinkers, later Nyāya writers, like Gaṅgeśa, Raghunātha and others, were mainly occupied in inventing suitable qualificatory adjuncts and phrases by which they could define their categories in such a way that the undesirable applications and issues of their definitions, as pointed out by the criticisms of their opponents, could be avoided. If these criticisms had mainly been directed towards the defects of Nyāya thought, later writers would not have been forced to take the course of developing verbal expressions at the expense of philosophical profundity and acuteness. Śrīharṣa may therefore be said to be the first great writer who is responsible indirectly for the growth of verbalism in later Nyāya thought.

Another defect of Śrīharṣa's criticisms is that he mainly limits himself to criticizing the definitions of Nyāya categories and does not deal so fully with the general ideas involved in such categories of thought. It ought, however, in all fairness to Śrīharṣa to be said that, though he took the Nyāya definitions as the main objective of his criticisms, yet in dealing with the various alternative variations and points of view of such definitions he often gives an exhaustive treatment of the problems involved in the discussion. But in many cases his omissions become very glaring. Thus, for example, in his treatment of relations he only tries to refute the definitions of relation as container and contained, as inherence, and as subject-object relation of cognitions, and leaves out many other varieties of relation which might well have been dealt with. Another characteristic feature of his refutation is, as has already been pointed out, that he has only a destructive point of view and is not prepared to undertake the responsibility of defining any position from his own point of view. He delights in showing that none of the world-appearances can be defined in any way, and that thus, being indescribable, they are all false. But incapacity to define or describe anything in some particular way cannot mean that the thing is false. Śrīharṣa did not and could not show that the ways of definition which he attempted to refute were the only ways of defining the different categories. They could probably be defined in other and better ways, and even those definitions which he refuted could be bettered and improved by using suitable qualificatory phrases. He did not attempt to show that the concepts involved in the categories were fraught with such contradictions that, in whatever way one might try to define, one could not escape from those inner contradictions, which were inherent in the very nature of the concepts themselves. Instead of that he turned his attention to the actual formal definitions which had been put forward by the Nyāya and sometimes by Prabhākara and tried to show that these definitions were faulty. To show that particular definitions are wrong is not to show that the things defined are wrong. It is, no doubt, true that the refutation of certain definitions involves the refutation of the concepts involved in those definitions; but the refutation of the particular way of presentation of the concept does not mean that the concept itself is impossible. In order to show the latter, a particular concept has to be analysed on the basis of its own occurrences, and the inconsistencies involved in such an analysis have to be shown.

Citsukha's Interpretations of the Concepts of Śaṅkara Vedānta.

Citsukha (about A.D. 1220), a commentator on Śrīharṣa, had all Śrīharṣa's powers of acute dialectical thought, but he not only furnishes, like Śrīharṣa, a concise refutation of the Nyāya categories, but also, in his *Tattva-pradīpikā*, commented on by Pratyagbhagavān (A.D. 1400) in his *Nayana-prasādinī*[1], gives us a very acute

[1] Citsukha, a pupil of Gauḍeśvara Ācārya, called also Jñānottama, wrote a commentary on Ānandabodha Bhaṭṭārakācārya's *Nyāya-makaranda* and also on Śrīharṣa's *Khaṇḍana-khaṇḍa-khādya* and an independent work called *Tattva-pradīpikā* or *Cit-sukhī*, on which the study of the present section is based. In this work he quotes Udayana, Udyotakara, Kumārila, Padmapāda, Vallabha (*Līlāvatī*), Śālikanātha, Sureśvara, Śivāditya, Kulārka Paṇḍita and Śridhara (*Nyāya-kandatī*). In addition to these he also wrote a commentary on the *Brahma-sūtra-bhāṣya* of Śaṅkara, called *Bhāṣya-bhāva-prakāśikā*, *Vivaraṇa-tātparya-dīpikā*, a commentary on the *Pramāṇa-mālā* of Ānandabodha, a commentary on Maṇḍana's *Brahma-siddhi*, called *Abhiprāya-prakāśikā*, and an index to the *adhikaraṇas*

analysis and interpretation of some of the most important concepts of Śaṅkara Vedānta. He is not only a protector of the *Advaita* doctrine of the Vedānta, but also an interpreter of the Vedāntic concepts[1]. The work is written in four chapters. In the first chapter Citsukha deals with the interpretation of the Vedānta concepts of self-revelation (*sva-prakāśa*), the nature of self as consciousness (*ātmanaḥ saṃvid-rūpatva*), the nature of ignorance as darkness, the nature of falsity (*mithyātva*), the nature of nescience (*avidyā*), the nature of the truth of all ideas (*sarva-pratyayānām yathā-thatvam*), the nature of illusions, etc. In the second chapter he refutes the Nyāya categories of difference, separateness, quality, action, class-concepts, specific particulars (*viśeṣa*), the relation of inherence (*samavāya*), perception, doubt, illusion, memory, inference, invariable concomitance (*vyāpti*), induction (*vyāpti-graha*), existence of the reason in the minor term (*pakṣa-dharmatā*), reason (*hetu*), analogy (*upamāna*), implication, being, non-being, duality, measure, causality, time, space, etc. In the third chapter, the smallest of the book, he deals with the possibility of the realization of Brahman and the nature of release through knowledge. In the fourth chapter, which is much smaller than the first two, he deals with the nature of the ultimate state of emancipation.

Citsukha starts with a formal definition of the most fundamental concept of the Vedānta, namely the concept of self-revelation or self-illumination (*sva-prakāśa*). Both Padmapāda and Prakāśātman in the *Pañca-pādikā* and *Pañca-pādikā-vivaraṇa* had distinguished the self from the ego as self-revelation or self-illumi-

of the *Brahma-sūtra*, called *Adhikaraṇa-mañjarī*. His teacher Jñānottama wrote two works on Vedānta, called *Nyāya-sudhā* and *Jñāna-siddhi*; but he seems to have been a different person from the Jñānottama who wrote a commentary on Sureśvara's *Naiṣkarmya-siddhi*; for the latter was a householder (as he styles himself with a householder's title, *miśra*), and an inhabitant of the village of Mangala in the Cola country, while the former was an ascetic and a preceptor of the King of Gauḍa, as Citsukha describes him in his colophon to his *Tattva-pradīpikā*. He is also said to have written the *Brahma-stuti*, *Viṣṇu-purāṇa-ṭīkā*, *Ṣaḍ-darśana-saṃgraha-vṛtti*, *Adhikaraṇa-saṅgati* (a work explaining the inter-relation of the topics of the *Brahma-sūtra*) and a commentary on the *Naiṣkarmya siddhi*, called the *Naiṣkarmya-siddhi-ṭīkā* or the *Bhāva-tattva-prakāśikā*. His pupil Sukhaprakāśa wrote a work on the topics of the *Brahma-sūtra*, called *Adhikaraṇa-ratna-mālā*.

[1] Thus Paṇḍita Harinātha Śarmā in his Sanskrit introduction to the *Tattva-pradīpikā* or *Cit-sukhī* speaks of this work as *advaita-siddhānta-rakṣako'py advaita-siddhānta-prakāśako vyutpādakaś ca*.

nation (*svayam-prakāśa*). Thus Prakāśātman says that consciousness (*saṃvid*) is self-revealing and that its self-revelation is not due to any other self-revealing cause[1]. It is on account of this natural self-revelation of consciousness that its objects also appear as self-revealing[2]. Padmapāda also says the same thing, when he states that the self is of the nature of pure self-revealing consciousness; when this consciousness appears in connection with other objects and manifests them, it is called experience (*anubhava*), and, when it is by itself, it is called the self or *ātman*[3]. But Citsukha was probably the first to give a formal definition of the nature of this self-revelation.

Citsukha defines it as that which is entitled to be called immediate (*aparokṣa-vyavahāra-yogya*), though it is not an object of any cognition or any cognizing activity (*avedyatve'pi*)[4]. It may be objected that desires, feelings, etc. also are not objects of any cognition and yet are entitled to be regarded as immediate, and hence the definition might as well apply to them; for the object of cognition has a separate objective existence, and by a mind-object contact the mind is transformed into the form of the object, and thereby the one consciousness, which was apparently split up into two forms as the object-consciousness which appeared as material objects and the subject-consciousness which appeared as the cognizer, is again restored to its unity by the super-imposition of the subjective form on the objective form, and the object-form is revealed in consciousness as a jug or a book. But in the case of our experience of our will or our feelings these have no existence separate from our own mind and hence are not cognized in the same way as external objects are cognized. According to Vedānta epistemology these subjective experiences of will, emotions, etc. are different mental constituents, forms or states, which, being directly and illusorily imposed upon the self-revealing consciousness, become experienced. These subjective states are therefore not cognized in the same way as external objects. But, since the

[1] *saṃvedanaṃ tu svayam-prakāśa eva na prakāśāntara-hetuḥ. Pañca-pādikā-vivaraṇa*, p. 52.

[2] *tasmād anubhavaḥ sajātīya-prakāśāntara-nirapekṣaḥ prakāśamāna eva viṣaye prakāśādi-vyavahāra-nimittaṃ bhavitum arhati avyavadhānena viṣaye prakāśā-di-vyavahāra-nimittatvāt. Ibid.*

[3] *tasmāt cit-svabhāva evātmā tena tena prameya-bhedenaupadhīyamāno'nubha-vābhidhānīyakaṃ labhate avivakṣitopādhir ātmādi-śabdaiḥ. Pañca-pādikā*, p. 10.

[4] *avedyatve saty aparokṣa-vyavahāra-yogyatvaṃ svayam-prakāśa-lakṣaṇam. Cit-sukhī*, p. 9.

experience of these states is possible only through a process of illusory imposition, they are not entitled to be called immediate[1]. So, though they appear as immediate, they have no proper *yogyatā*, or, in other words, they are not entitled to be called immediate. But in the true sense even external objects are but illusory impositions on the self-revealing consciousness, and hence they also cannot be said to be entitled to be called immediate. There is therefore no meaning in trying to distinguish the self-revealing consciousness as one which is not an object of cognition ; for on the Vedānta theory there is nothing which is entitled to be called immediate, and hence the phrase *avedyatve* (not being an object of cognition) is unnecessary as a special distinguishing feature of the self-revealing consciousness; the epithet "immediate" is therefore also unnecessary. To such an objection Citsukha's reply is that the experience of external objects is only in the last stage of world-dissolution and Brahmahood found non-immediate and illusory, and, since in all our ordinary stages of experience the experience of world-objects is immediate, the epithet *avedyatva* successfully distinguishes self-revealing consciousness from all cognitions of external objects which are entitled to be called immediate and are to be excluded from the range of self-revealing consciousness only by being objects of cognition. In the field of ordinary experience the perceived world-objects are found to be entitled to be called immediate no less than the self-revealing consciousness, and it is only because they are objects of cognition that they can be distinguished from the self-revealing. consciousness.

The main argument in favour of the admission of the category of independent self-revealing consciousness is that, unless an independent self-revealing consciousness is admitted, there would be a vicious series in the process preceding the rise of any cognition; for, if the pure experience of self-revealing consciousness has to be further subjected to another process before it can be understood, then that also might require another process, and that another, and so there would be an unending series. Moreover, that the pure experience is self-revealing is proved by the very fact of the experience itself; for no one doubts his own experience or stands in need of any further corroboration or confirmation as to whether he experienced or not. It may be objected

[1] *avedyatve 'pi nāparokṣa-vyavahāra-yogyatā teṣām, adhyastatayaiva teṣāṃ siddheḥ. Cit-sukhī*, p. 10. Nirṇaya-Sāgara Press, Bombay, 1915.

that it is well known that we may be aware of our awareness of anything (*anu-vyavasāya*), and in such a case the self-revealing consciousness may become further cognized. Citsukha's reply to this is that, when one perceives a jug, there is the mental activity, then a cessation of that activity, then a further starting of new activity and then the knowledge that I know the jug, or rather I know that I know the jug—and hence such a cognition cannot be said to be directly and immediately cognizing the first awareness, which could not have stayed through so many moments[1]. Again, since neither the senses nor the external objects can of themselves produce the self-revelation of knowledge, if knowledge were not admitted as self-revealing, the whole world would be blind and there would be no self-revelation. When one knows that he knows a book or a jug, it is the cognized object that is known and not the awareness that is cognized; there can be no awareness of awareness, but only of the cognized object[2]. If the previous awareness could be made the object of subsequent awareness, then this would amount to an admission of the possibility of the self being known by the self (*svasyāpi svena vedyatvāpātāt*)—a theory which would accord not with the Vedānta idealism, but with the Buddhistic. It is true, no doubt, that the pure self-revealing consciousness shows itself only on the occasion of a mental state; but its difference from other cognitive states lies in the fact that it has no form or object, and hence, though it may be focussed by a mental state, yet it stands on a different footing from the objects illuminated by it.

The next point that Citsukha urges is that the self is of the nature of pure self-revealing consciousness (*ātmanaḥ saṃvid-rūpatva*). This is, of course, no new contribution by Citsukha, since this view had been maintained in the Upaniṣads and repeated by Śaṅkara, Padmapāda, Prakāśātman and others. Citsukha says that, like knowledge, the self also is immediately revealed or experienced without itself being the object of any cognizing activity or cognition, and therefore the self is also of the nature of knowledge. No one doubts about his own self; for the self always stands directly and

[1] *ghaṭa-jñānodaya-samaye manasi kriyā tato vibhāgas tataḥ pūrva-saṃyoga-vināśas tata uttara-saṃyogotpattis tato jñānāntaram iti aneka-kṣaṇa-vilambena utpa-dyamānasya jñānasya aparokṣatayā pūrva-jñāna-grāhakatvānupapatteḥ. Cit-sukhī*, p. 17.

[2] *vidito ghaṭa ity atra anuvyavasāyena ghaṭasyaiva viditatvam avasīyate na tu vitteḥ. Ibid.* p. 18.

immediately self-revealed. Self and knowledge being identical, there is no relation between the two save that of identity (*jñānātmanoḥ sambandhasyaiva abhāvāt*).

Citsukha defines falsity (*mithyātva*) as the non-existence of a thing in that which is considered to be its cause[1]. He shows this by pointing out that a whole, if it is to exist anywhere, must exist in the parts of which it is made, and, if it does not exist even there, it does not exist anywhere and is false. It is, however, evident that a whole cannot exist in the parts, since, being a whole, it cannot be in the parts[2]. Another argument adduced by Citsukha for the falsity of the world-appearance is that it is impossible that there should be any relation between the self-revealing consciousness, the knower (*dṛk*), and the objects which are cognized (*dṛśya*). Knowledge cannot be said to arise through sense-contact; for in the illusory perception of silver there is the false perception of silver without any actual sense-contact with silver. A reference to subject-object relation (*viṣaya-viṣayi-bhāva*) cannot explain it, since the idea of subject-object relation is itself obscure and unexplainable. Arguing as to the impossibility of properly explaining the subject-object relation (*viṣaya-viṣayi-bhāva*) in knowledge, Citsukha says that it cannot be held that the subject-object relation means that knowledge produces some change in the object (*viṣaya*) and that the knower produces such a change. For what may be the nature of such a change? If it be described as *jñātatā*, or the character of being known, how can such a character be by my knowledge at the present moment generated as a positive quality in an object which has now ceased to exist? If such a quality can be produced even in past objects, then there would be no fixed law according to which such qualities should be produced. Nor can such a relationship be explained on a pragmatic basis by a reference to actual physical practical action with reference to objects that we know or the internal volitions or emotions associated with our knowledge of things. For in picking up a piece of silver that we see in front of us we may quite unknowingly be drawing with it the dross contained in the silver, and hence the fact of the physical

[1] *sarveṣām api bhāvānām āśrayatvena saṃmate*
pratiyogitvam atyantābhāvaṃ prati mṛṣātmatā. Cit-sukhī, p. 39.
Some of these definitions of falsity are collected in Madhusūdana's *Advaita-siddhi*, a work composed much later than the *Cit-sukhī*.

[2] *aṃśinaḥ svāṃśa-gātyantābhāvasya pratiyoginaḥ aṃśitvād itarāṃśīva. . . vimataḥ paṭaḥ etat-tantu-niṣṭhātyantābhāva-pratiyogī avayavitvāt paṭāntaravat. Cit-sukhī*, pp. 40, 41.

drawing of the dross cannot on that ground alone make it an object of my knowledge, and hence the subject-object relation of knowledge cannot be defined as a mere physical action following cognition. The internal mental states of volition and the emotions associated with knowledge belong to the knower and have nothing to do with the object of knowledge. If, however, it is urged that objectivity consists in the fact that whatever is known appears in consciousness, the question arises, what does this appearing in consciousness mean? It cannot mean that consciousness is the container and the object is contained in it; for, consciousness being internal and the object external, the object cannot be contained in it. It cannot be a mere undefined relatedness; for in that case the object may as well be considered subject and the subject, object. If objectivity be defined as that which can induce knowledge, then even the senses, the light and other accessories which help the rise of knowledge may as well be regarded as objects. Object cannot be defined as that to which knowledge owes its particular form; for, knowledge being identical with its form, all that helps the rise of knowledge, the senses, light, etc., may as well be regarded as objects. So, in whatever way one may try to conceive the nature of the subject-object relation, he will be disappointed.

Citsukha follows the traditional view of nescience (*ajñāna*) as a positive entity without beginning which disappears with the rise of true knowledge[1]. Nescience is different from the conception of positivity as well as of negativity, yet it is called only positive because of the fact that it is not negative[2]. Ignorance or nescience is described as a positive state and not a mere negation of knowledge; and so it is said that the rise of right knowledge of any object in a person destroys the positive entity of ignorance with reference to that object and that this ignorance is something different from what one would understand by negation of right knowledge[3]. Citsukha says that the positive character of ignorance becomes apparent when we say that "We do not know whether what you say is true." Here there is the right knowledge of the fact that

[1] *anādi-bhāva-rūpaṃ yad-vijñānena vilīyate tad ajñānam iti prājñā-lakṣaṇam saṃpracakṣate anāditve sati bhāva-rūpaṃ vijñāna-nirāsyam ajñānam iti lakṣaṇaṃ iha vivakṣitam. Cit-sukhī*, p. 57.

[2] *bhāvābhāva-vilakṣaṇasya ajñānasya abhāva-vilakṣaṇatva-mātreṇa bhāvatvo-pacārāt. Ibid.*

[3] *vigītaṃ Deva-datta-niṣṭha-pramāṇa-jñānaṃ Devadatta-niṣṭha-pramābhāvā-tiriktānādernivarttakaṃ pramāṇatvād Yajñadattādigata-pramāṇa-jñānavad ity anumā-nam. Ibid.* p. 58.

what is said is known, but it is not known whether what is said is valid[1]. Here also there is a positive knowledge of ignorance of fact, which is not the same as mere absence of knowledge. Such an ignorance, however, is not experienced through sense-contact or sense-processes, but directly by the self-revealing consciousness—the *sākṣin.* Just before the rise of right knowledge about an object there is ignorance (*ajñāna*), and the object, as qualified by such an ignorance, is experienced as being unknown. All things are the objects of the inner unmoved intuitive consciousness either as known or as unknown[2]. Our reference to deep dreamless sleep as a state in which we did not know anything (*na kiṃcid-avediṣam*) is also referred to as a positive experience of ignorance in the dreamless state.

One of the chief tenets of Vedānta epistemology lies in the supposition that a presentation of the false is a fact of experience. The opposite view is that of Prabhākara, that the false is never presented in experience and that falsehood consists in the wrong construction imposed upon experience by the mind, which fails to note the actual want of association between two things which are falsely associated as one. According to this theory all illusion consists of a false association or a false relationing of two things which are not presented in experience as related. This false association is not due to an active operation of the mind, but to a failure to note that no such association was actually presented in experience (*asaṃsargāgraha*). According to Prabhākara, the great Mīmāṃsā authority, the false is never presented in experience, nor is the false experience due to an arbitrary positive activity of wrong construction of the mind, but merely to a failure to note certain distinctions presented in experience. On account of such a failure things which are distinct are not observed as distinct, and hence things which are distinct and different are falsely associated as one, and the conch-shell is thus regarded as silver. But here there is no false presentation in experience. Whatever is known is true; falsehood is due to omissions of knowledge and failure in noting differences.

Citsukha objects to this view and urges that such an explanation

[1] *tvadukte 'rthe pramāṇa-jñānaṃ mama nāsti ity asya viśiṣṭa-viṣaya-jñānasya pramātvāt. Cit-sukhī*, p. 59.

[2] *asman-mate ajñānasya sākṣi-siddhatayā pramāṇābodhyatvāt, pramāṇa-jñāno-dayāt prāk-kāle ajñānaṃ tad-viśeṣito 'rthaḥ sākṣi-siddhaḥ ajñāta ity anuvāda gocaraḥ. . .sarvaṃ vastu jñātatayā ajñātatayā vā sākṣi-caitanyasya viṣayaḥ. Ibid.* p. 60.

can never explain all cases of false apprehension. Take the proposition, "There are false apprehensions and false presentations"; if this proposition is admitted to be correct, then Prabhākara's contention is false; if it is admitted to be false, then here is a false proposition, the falsehood of which is not due to a failure to note differences. If the falsity of all propositions be said to be due to a failure to note differences, then it would be hard to find out any true proposition or true experience. On the analogy of our false experience of the everchanging flame of a lamp as the same identical one all cases of true recognition might no less be regarded as false, and therefore all inferences would be doubtful. All cases of real and true association could be explained as being due to a failure to note differences. There could be no case in which one could assure himself that he was dealing with a real association and not a failure to apprehend the absence of association (*asaṃsargāgraha*). Citsukha therefore contends that it is too much to expect that all cases of false knowledge can be explained as being due to a mere non-apprehension of difference, since it is quite reasonable to suppose that false knowledge is produced by defective senses which oppose the rise of true knowledge and positively induce false appearance[1]. Thus in the case of the illusory perception of conch-shell as silver it is the conch-shell that appears as a piece of silver. But what is the nature of the presentation that forms the object (*ālambana*) of false perception? It cannot be regarded as absolutely non-existent (*asat*), since that which is absolutely non-existent cannot be the object of even a false perception, and moreover it cannot through such a perception (e.g. the tendency of a man to pick up the piece of silver, which is but a false perception of a piece of conch-shell) induce a practical movement on the part of the perceiver. Neither can it be regarded as existent; for the later experience contradicts the previous false perception, and one says that there is no silver at the present time and there was no silver in the past—it was only the conch-shell that appeared as silver. Therefore the false presentation, though it serves all the purposes of a perceptual object, cannot be described either as existent or as non-existent, and it is precisely this character that constitutes the indefinable nature (*anirvacanīyatā*) of all illusions[2].

[1] *tathā doṣāṇām api yathārtha-jñāna-pratibandhakatvam ayathārtha-jñāna-janakatvaṃ ca kiṃ na syāt. Cit-sukhī*, p. 66.

[2] *pratyekaṃ sad asattvābhyāṃ vicāra-padavīṃ na yad gāhate tad anirvācyam āhur vedānta-vedinaḥ. Ibid.* p. 79.

It is unnecessary to deal with the other doctrines of Vedānta which Citsukha describes, since there is nothing new in them and they have already been described in chapter X of volume I of this work. It is therefore desirable to pass on to his dialectic criticism of the Nyāya categories. It will suffice, however, to give only a few of these criticisms, as they mostly refer to the refutation of such kinds of categories as are discussed in Śrīharṣa's great work *Khaṇḍana-khaṇḍa-khādya*, and it would be tedious to follow the refutation of the same kinds of categories by two different writers, though the arguments of Citsukha are in many cases new and different from those given by Śrīharṣa. Citsukha's general approach to such refutations is also slightly different from that of Śrīharṣa. For, unlike Śrīharṣa, Citsukha dealt with the principal propositions of the Vedānta, and his refutations of the Nyāya categories were not intended so much to show that they were inexplicable or indefinable as to show that they were false appearances, and that the pure self-revealing Brahman was the only reality and truth.

Thus, in refuting time (*kāla*), Citsukha says that time cannot be perceived either by the visual sense or by the tactual sense, nor can it be apprehended by the mind (*manas*), as the mind only operates in association with the external senses. Moreover, since there are no perceptual data, it cannot be inferred. The notions of before and after, succession and simultaneity, quickness and duration, cannot by themselves indicate the nature of time as it is in itself. It may be urged that, since the solar vibrations can only be associated with human bodies and worldly things, making them appear as young or old only through some other agency such as days, months, etc., such an agency, which brings about the connection of solar vibrations with worldly things, is called time[1]. To this Citsukha replies that, since the self itself can be regarded as the cause of the manifestation of time in events and things in accordance with the varying conditions of their appearance, it is unnecessary to suppose the existence of a new category called time. Again, it cannot be said that the notions of before and after have time as their material cause; for the validity of these notions is challenged by the Vedāntist. They may be regarded as the im-

[1] *taraṇi-parispanda-viśeṣāṇāṃ yuva-sthavira-śarīrādi-piṇḍeṣu māsādi-vicitra-buddhi-janana-dvāreṇa tad-upahiteṣu paratvāparatvādi-buddhi-janakatvaṃ na ca tair asaṃbaddhānāṃ tatra buddhi-janakatvaṃ, na ca sākṣāt sambandho ravi-parispandānāṃ piṇḍair asti ataḥ tat-saṃbandhakatayā kaścid aṣṭadravya-vilakṣaṇo dravya-viśeṣaḥ svīkartavyaḥ, tasya ca kāla iti saṃjñā.* (This is Vallabha's view of time.) *Nayana-prasādinī* commentary on *Cit-sukhī*, p. 321, by Pratyak-svarupa-bhagavat. Nirṇaya-Sāgara Press, Bombay, 1915.

pressions produced by a greater or lesser quantity of solar vibrations. There is therefore no necessity to admit time as a separate category, since its apprehension can be explained on the basis of our known data of experience. From considerations of some data relative space (*dik*) has to be discarded; for relative space cannot be perceived by the senses or inferred for want of data of experience. Both time and relative space originate from a sense of relativity (*apekṣā-buddhi*), and, given that sense of relativity, the mind can in association with our experience of bodily movements form the notion of relative space. It is therefore unnecessary to admit the existence of relative space as a separate category.

In refuting the atomic theory of the Vaiśeṣikas Citsukha says that there is no ground for admitting the Vaiśeṣika atoms. If these atoms are to be admitted on the ground that all things are to be conceived as being divisible into smaller and smaller parts, then the same may apply to the atoms as well. If it is urged that one must stop somewhere, that the atoms are therefore regarded as the last state, and are uniform in size and not further divisible, then the specks of dust that are seen in the windows when the sun is shining (called *trasareṇus*) may equally be regarded as the last stage of divisible size. If it is contended that, since these are visible, they have parts and cannot therefore be considered as indivisible, it may be said in reply that, since the Nyāya writers admit that the atoms can be perceived by the yogins, visibility of the *trasareṇus* could not be put forward as a reason why they could not be regarded as indivisible. Moreover, if the atoms were partless, how could they be admitted to combine to produce the grosser material forms? Again, it is not indispensable that atoms should combine to form bigger particles or make grosser appearances possible; for, like threads in a sheet, many particles may make gross appearances possible even without combining. Citsukha then repeats Śaṅkara's refutation of the concept of wholes and parts, saying that, if the wholes are different from the parts, then they must be in the parts or they would not be there; if they are not in the parts, it would be difficult to maintain that the wholes were made of parts; if they are in the parts, they must be either wholly or partly in them; if they are wholly in the parts, then there would be many such wholes, or in each part the whole would be found; and, if they are partly in the parts, then the same difficulty of wholes and parts would appear.

Again, the concept of contact (*saṃyoga*) is also inexplicable. It cannot be defined as the coming together of any two things which are not in contact (*aprāptayoḥ prāptiḥ saṃyogaḥ*); for, until one knows the meaning of the concept of contact, one cannot understand the meaning of the phrase "not in contact." If it is defined as the coming together of two things which are unrelated, then contact (*saṃyoga*) would include even the relation of inherence, such as that which exists between a piece of cloth and the threads. If it is defined as a relation which is produced in time and is transitory (*anityaḥ sambandhaḥ janyatva-viśeṣito vā*), then cases of beginningless contact would not be included, and even the possession of an article by purchase would have to be included as contact, since this relation of possession is also produced in time. It cannot be objected that "possession" is not a relation, since a relation to be such must be between two things; for, if the objection were valid, the relation between substance and quality would not be a relation, since quality and substance exist together, and there are no two separate things which can be related. If the objector means that the relation must be between two terms, then there are two terms here also, namely, the article possessed and the possessor. Moreover, if contact is defined as relation which does not connect two things in their entirety (*avyāpya-vṛttitva-viśeṣito*), then again it would be wrong, since in the case of partless entities the relation of contact cannot connect the parts, as they have no parts. Citsukha refutes the concept of separation (*vibhāga*) on the same lines and passes over to the refutation of number, as two, three and the like.

Citsukha urges that there is no necessity of admitting the existence of two, three, etc. as separate numbers, since what we perceive is but the one thing, and then by a sense of oscillation and mutual reference (*apekṣā-buddhi*) we associate them together and form the notions of two, three, etc. These numbers therefore do not exist separately and independently, but are imaginatively produced by mental oscillation and association from the experience of single objects. There is therefore no necessity of thinking that the numbers, two, three, etc., are actually produced. We simply deal with the notions of two, three, etc. on the strength of our powers of mental association[1].

[1] *āropita-dvitva-tritvādi-viśeṣitaikatva-samuccayālambanā buddhir dvitvādi-janiketi cet; na; tathābhūtāyā eva buddher dvitvādi-vyavahāra-janakatvopapattau dvitvādy-utpādakatva-kalpanā-vaiyarthyāt. Nayana-prasādinī*, p. 300.

Citsukha then refutes the notion of class-concept (*jāti*) on the ground that it cannot be proved either by perception or by inference. The question is what exactly is meant by class-concept. If it is said that, when in perceiving one individual animal we have the notion of a cow, and in perceiving other individual animals also we have the same notion of cow, there is *jāti*, then it may be replied that this does not necessarily imply the admission of a separate class-concept of cow; for, just as one individual had certain peculiarities which entitled it to be called a cow, so the other individuals had their peculiarities which entitled them to be called cows. We see reflections of the moon in different places and call each of them the moon. What constitutes the essentials of the concept of cow? It is difficult to formulate one universal characteristic of cows; if one such characteristic could be found, then there would be no necessity of admitting the class-concept of cow. For it would then be an individual characteristic, and one would recognize it as a cow everywhere, and there would be no necessity of admitting a separate class-concept. If one admits a class-concept, one has to point out some trait or quality as that which indicates the class-concept. Then again one could not get at this trait or quality independently of the class-concept or at the class-concept independently of it, and this mutual dependence would make the definition of either of them impossible. Even if one admits the class-concept, one has to show what constitutes the essentials of it in each case, and, if such essentials have to be found in each case, then those essentials would be a sufficient justification for knowing a cow as cow and a horse as horse: what then is the good of admitting a class-concept? Again, even if a class-concept be admitted, it is difficult to see how it can be conceived to be related to the individuals. It cannot be a relation of contact, identity, inherence or any other kind of relation existing anywhere. If all class-concepts existed everywhere, there would be a medley of all class-concepts together, and all things would be everywhere. Again, if it is held that the class-concept of cow exists only in the existing cows, then how does it jump to a new cow when it is born? Nor has the class-concept any parts, so as to be partly here and partly there. If each class-concept of cow were wholly existent in each of the individual cows, then there would be a number of class-concepts; and, if each class-concept of cow were spread out over all the individual cows, then, unless all the individual cows were brought together, one could not have the notion of any class-concept.

Speaking of the refutation of cause (*kāraṇa*), Citsukha says that cause cannot be defined as mere antecedence (*pūrva-kāla-bhāvitva*); for then the ass which is always found in the house of a washerman and on the back of which the washerman carries his clothes might be regarded as a thing antecedent to the smoky fire kindled in the washerman's house and thus as a cause of fire. If this antecedence be further qualified as that which is present in all cases of the presence of the effect and absent in all cases of the absence of the effect, then also the washerman's ass may be considered to satisfy the conditions of such an antecedence with reference to the fire in the washerman's house (when the washerman is away from the house with his ass, the fire in the washerman's house is also absent, and it is again kindled when he returns to his house with his ass). If "unconditionality" (*ananyathā-siddha*) is further added as a qualifying condition of antecedence, even then the ass and the common abiding elements such as space, ether and the like may be regarded as causes of the fire. If it be argued that the ass is present only because of the presence of other conditioning factors, the same may be said of seeds, earth, water, etc., which are all however regarded as being causes for the production of the shoots of plants. If objection be raised against the possibility of ether (*ākāśa*) being regarded as the cause of smoke on the ground of its being a common, abiding and all-pervasive element, then the same argument ought to stand as an objection against the soul (which is an all-pervasive entity) being regarded on the Nyāya view as the cause of the production of pleasure and pain. The cause cannot be defined as that which being there the effect follows; for then a seed cannot be regarded as the cause of the shoot of the plant, since the shoots cannot be produced from seeds without the help of other co-operating factors, such as earth, water, light, air, etc. Cause, again, cannot be defined as that which being present in the midst of the co-operating factors or even accessories (*sahakāri*), the effect follows; for an irrelevant thing, like an ass, may be present among a number of co-operating circumstances, but this would not justify anybody calling an irrelevant thing a cause. Moreover, such a definition would not apply to those cases where by the joint operation of many co-operating entities the effect is produced. Furthermore, unless the cause can be properly defined, there is no way of defining the co-operating conditions. Nor can a cause be defined as that which being there the effect follows, and which not being there there is no effect (*sati bhāvo 'saty abhāva eva*); for such a maxim is invalidated by the plurality of causes (fire may be produced by rubbing two pieces of wood, by striking hard against a flint, or by a lens). It may be urged that there are differences in each kind of fire produced by the different agencies: to which it may be replied that, even if there were any such difference, it is impossible to know it by observation. Even when differences are noticeable, such differences do not necessarily imply that the different effects belong to different classes; for the differences might well be due to various attendant circumstances. Again, a cause cannot be defined as a collocation of things, since such a collocation may well be one of irrelevant things. A cause cannot be defined as a collocation of different causes, since it has not so far been possible to define what is meant by "cause." The phrase "collocation of causes" will therefore be meaningless. Moreover, it may be asked whether a collocation of causes (*sāmagrī*) be something different from the causes, or identical with them. If the former alternative be accepted, then effects would follow from individual causes as well, and the supposition of a collocation of causes as producing the effects would be uncalled-for. If the latter alternative be accepted, then, since the individuals are the causes of the collocation, the individuals being there, there is always the collocation and so always the effect, which is absurd. Again, what does this collocation of causes mean? It cannot mean occurrence in the same time or place; for, there being no sameness of time and place for time and place respectively, they themselves would be without any cause. Again, it cannot be said that, if the existence of cause be not admitted, then things, being causeless, would be non-existent; for the Nyāya holds that there are eternal substances such as atoms, souls, etc., which have no cause.

Since cause cannot be defined, neither can effect (*kārya*) be satisfactorily defined, as the conception of effect always depends upon the notion of cause.

In refuting the conception of substance (*dravya*) Citsukha says that a substance can be defined only as being that in which the qualities inhere. But, since even qualities are seen to have qualities and a substance is believed by the Naiyāyikas to be without any quality at the moment of its origination, such a definition cannot properly distinguish or define a substance. If a substance be defined in a roundabout way as that in which there is no presence of the absolute negation of possessing qualities (*guṇavattvātyantābhāvānadhikaraṇatā*), then also it may be objected that such a definition would make us regard even negation (*abhāva*) as a quality, since the absence of the negation of qualities, being itself a negation, cannot exist in a negation[1]. It may again be asked whether the absence of the negation of qualities refers to the negation of a number of qualities or the negation of all qualities; in either case it is wrong. For in the first case a substance, which contains only some qualities and does not possess others, would not be called a substance, and in the latter case it would be difficult to find anything that cannot be called a substance; for where is the substance which lacks all qualities? The fact also remains that even such a roundabout definition cannot distinguish a substance from a quality; for even qualities have the numerical qualities and the qualities of separateness[2]. If it is argued that, if qualities are admitted to have further qualities, there will be a vicious infinite, it may be said in reply that the charge of vicious infinite cannot be made, since the qualities of number and separateness cannot be said to have any further qualities. Substances, again, have nothing in common by virtue of which they could be regarded as coming under the class-concept of substances[3]. Gold and mud and trees are all regarded as substances, but there is nothing common in them by virtue of which one can think that gold is the same as mud or tree; therefore it cannot be admitted that in the substances one finds any characteristic which remains the same in them all[4].

Referring to qualities (*guṇa*), Citsukha deals with the definition of *guṇa* in the *Vaiśeṣika-bhāṣya* of Praśastapāda. There Praśastapāda defines *guṇa* as that which inheres in a substance, is associated with the class-concept of substance, is itself without any quality

[1] *tatraiva atyantābhave 'tivyāpteḥ*; *sopi hi guṇavattvātyantābhāvas tasyādhi-karaṇam svasya svasminnavṛtteḥ. Cit-sukhī*, p. 176.

[2] *asminnapi vakra-lakṣaṇe guṇādṣu api saṃkhyā-pṛthaktva-guṇayoḥ pratīteḥ kathaṃ nātivyāptiḥ. Ibid.* p. 177.

[3] *jātim abhyupagacchatā tajjāti-vyañjakaṃ kiṃcid-avaśyam abhyupeyam na ca tannirupaṇam suśakam. Ibid.* p. 178.

[4] *dravyaṃ dravyam iti anugata-pratyayaḥ pramāṇaṁ iti cenna suvarṇam-upalabhya mṛttikām-upalabhyamānasya laukikasya tad evedaṃ dravyam iti pratyayā-bhāvāt parīkṣakāṇāṃ cānugata-pratyaye vipratipatteḥ. Ibid.* p. 179.

and which has no motion (*niṣkriya*)[1]. But the definition of a quality cannot involve the phrase "without a quality"; for quality is still to be defined. Again, unless the *guṇa* is properly defined, its difference from motion is not known, and so the phrase "which has no motion" is meaningless. The class-concept of quality, again, can be determined only when the general character of qualities is known and the nature of class-concepts also is determined. Hence, from whatever point of view one may look at the question, it is impossible to define qualities.

It is needless now to multiply examples of such refutation by Citsukha. It will appear from what has been adduced that Citsukha enters into detail concerning most concepts of particular categories and tries to show their intrinsic impossibility. In some cases, however, he was not equal to the task and remained content with criticizing the definitions given by the Naiyāyikas. But it may be well to point out here that, though Śrīharṣa and Citsukha carried out an elaborate scheme of a critique of the different categories in order to show that the definitions of these categories, as given by the Nyāya, are impossible, yet neither of them can be regarded as the originator of the application of the dialectic method in the Vedānta. Śaṅkara himself had started it in his refutation of the Nyāya and other systems in his commentary on the *Vedānta-sūtras* II. 11.

The Dialectic of Nāgārjuna and the Vedānta Dialectic.

The dialectic of Śrīharṣa was a protest against the realistic definitions of the Nyāya-Vaiśeṣika, which supposed that all that was knowable was also definable. It aimed at refuting these definitions in order to prove that the natures of all things are indefinable, as their existence and nature are all involved in *māyā*. The only reality is Brahman. That it is easy to pick holes in all definitions was taught long ago by Nāgārjuna, and in that sense (except for a tendency to find faults of a purely verbal nature in Nyāya definitions) Śrīharṣa's method was a continuation of Nāgārjuna's, and an application of it to the actual definitions of the Nyāya-Vaiśeṣika. But the most important part of Nāgārjuna's method was deliberately ignored by Śrīharṣa and his followers, who made no attempt to refute Nāgārjuna's conclusions. Nāgārjuna's main thesis is that all things are relative and hence indefinable in

[1] *rūpādīnāṃ guṇānāṃ sarveṣāṃ guṇatvābhisambandho dravyāśritatvaṃ nirguṇatvaṃ niṣkriyatvam. Praśastapāda-bhāṣya*, p. 94, The Vizianagram Sanskrit Series, Benares, 1895.

themselves, and so there is no way of discovering their essences; and, since their essences are not only indefinable and indescribable, but incomprehensible as well, they cannot be said to possess any essences of their own. Nāgārjuna was followed by Āryadeva, a Ceylonese by birth, who wrote a separate work on the same subject in 400 verses. For about two centuries after this the doctrines of Nāgārjuna lay dormant, as is evidenced by the fact that Buddha-ghoṣa of the fourth century A.D. does not refer to them. During the Gupta empire, in the fifth century A.D., Asaṅga and Vasubandhu flourished. In the sixth century A.D the relativist philosophy of Nāgārjuna again flourished in the hands of Buddhapālita, of Valabhī in Surat, and of Bhavya, or Bhāvaviveka, of Orissa. The school of Bhavya was called Mādhyamika-Sautrāntika on account of his supplementing Nāgārjuna's arguments with special arguments of his own. At this time the Yogācāra school of Mahāyāna monism developed in the north, and the aim of this school was to show that for the true knowledge of the one consciousness (*vijñāna*) all logical arguments were futile. All logical arguments showed only their own inconsistency[1]. It seems very probable that Śrīharṣa was inspired by these Yogācāra authors, and their relativist allies from Nāgārjuna to Bhavya, and Candrakīrti, the master commentator on Nāgārjuna's *Mādhyamika-kārikā*. Buddha-pālita sought to prove that the apprehension and realization of the idealistic monism cannot be made by any logical argument, since all logic is futile and inconsistent, while Bhāvaviveka sought to establish his idealistic monism by logical arguments. Candrakīrti finally supported Buddhapālita's scheme as against the scheme of Bhāvaviveka and tried to prove the futility of all logical arguments. It was this Mādhyamika scheme of Candrakīrti that finally was utilized in Tibet and Mongolia for the realization of idealistic monism.

In taking up his refutation of the various categories of being Nāgārjuna begins with the examination of causation. Causation in the non-Buddhistic systems of philosophy is regarded as being production from the inner changes of some permanent or abiding stuff or through the conglomeration (*sāmagrī*) of several factors or through some factors operating upon an unchangeable and abiding stuff. But Nāgārjuna denies not only that anything is ever produced, but also that it is ever produced in any one of the above ways. Buddhapālita holds that things cannot arise

[1] *The Conception of Buddhist Nirvāṇa*, pp. 66–67. Published by the Academy of Sciences of the U.S.S.R. Leningrad, 1927.

of themselves, since, if they are already existing, there is no meaning in their being produced; if things that are existing are regarded as capable of being produced again, then things would eternally continue to be produced. Bhāvaviveka, criticizing Buddhapālita, says that the refutation of Buddhapālita should have been supplemented with reasons and examples and that his refutation would imply the undesirable thesis that, if things are not produced of themselves, they must be produced by other factors. But Candrakīrti objects to this criticism of Bhāvaviveka and says that the burden of proof in establishing the identity of cause and effect lies with the opponents, the Sāṃkhyists, who hold that view. There is no meaning in the production of what already exists, and, if that which is existent has to be produced again, and that again, there will be an infinite regress. It is unnecessary to give any new argument to refute the Sāṃkhya *sat-kārya-vāda* view; it is enough to point out the inconsistency of the Sāṃkhya view. Thus Āryadeva says that the Mādhyamika view has no thesis of its own which it seeks to establish, since it does not believe in the reality or unreality of anything or in the combination of reality and unreality[1]. This was exactly the point of view that was taken by Śrīharṣa. Śrīharṣa says that the Vedāntists have no view of their own regarding the things of the world and the various categories involved in them. Therefore there was no way in which the Vedānta view could be attacked. The Vedānta, however, is free to find fault with other views, and, when once this is done and the inconsistencies of other positions are pointed out, its business is finished; for it has no view of its own to establish. Nāgārjuna writes in his *Vigraha-vyāvartanī* thus:

> When I have these (of my own to prove),
> I can commit mistakes just for the sake (of proving);
> But I have none. I cannot be accused (of being inconsistent).
> If I did (really) cognize some (separate) things,
> I could then make an affirmation or a denial
> Upon the basis of these things perceived or (inferred).
> But these (separate) things do not exist for me.
> Therefore I cannot be assailed on such a basis[2].

[1] *sad asat sad-asac ceti yasya pakṣo na vidyate*
upālambhaś cireṇāpi tasya vaktuṃ na śakyate. *Mādhyamika-vṛtti*, p. 16.

[2] *anyat pratītya yadi nāma paro* 'bhaviṣyat
jāyeta tarhi bahulaḥ śikhino 'ndhakāraḥ
sarvasya janma ca bhavet khalu sarvataś ca
tulyam paratvam akhile 'janake 'pi yasmāt. *Ibid*. p. 36.

Candrakīrti thus emphasizes the fact that it is not possible for the Mādhyamikas to offer new arguments or new examples in criticizing any view, since they have no view of their own to support. They cannot even prove their own affirmations, and, if their affirmations contain any thesis, they quarrel with it also themselves. So the Mādhyamika scheme of criticism consists only in finding fault with all theses, whatever they may be, and in replying to the counter-charges so far as inconsistencies can be found in the opponents' theses and methods, but not in adducing any new arguments or any new counter-theses, since the Mādhyamikas have no theses of their own. In an argument one can only follow the principles that one admits; no one can be defeated by arguments carried on on the basis of principles admitted only by his opponents.

Things are not produced by any conglomeration of foreign factors or causes; for, were it so, there would be no law of such production and anything might come from any other thing, e.g. darkness from light[1]. And, if a thing cannot be produced out of itself or out of others, it cannot be produced by a combination of them both. Again, the world could not have sprung into being without any cause (*ahetutaḥ*).

The Buddhist logicians try to controvert this view by pointing out that, whatever a view may be, it must be established by proper proof. So, in order to prove the thesis that all existents are unproduced, the Mādhyamikas must give some proofs, and this would involve a further specification of the nature of such proofs and a specification of the number of valid proofs admitted by them. But, if the thesis that "all existents are unproved" is a mere assertion without any proof to support it, then any number of counter-assertions may be made for which no proof need be shown; and, if proofs are not required in one case, they cannot be required in the other. So one could with equal validity assert that all existents are real and are produced from causes. The Mādhyamika answer to such an objection, as formulated by Candrakīrti, is that the Mādhyamika has no thesis of his own and so the question whether his thesis is supported by valid proof or not is as meaningless as the question regarding the smallness or the greatness of a mule's horn. Since there is no thesis, the Mādhyamika has nothing to

[1] *Mādhyamika-vṛtti*, p. 36. See also Stcherbatsky's *The Conception of Buddhist Nirvāṇa*, to which the author is indebted for the translation and some of the materials of the last two paragraphs.

say regarding the nature of valid proofs (*pramāṇa*) or their number. But it may well be asked why, if the Mādhyamika has no thesis of his own, should he hold the proposition that all existents are unproduced (*sarve bhāvā anutpannāḥ*)? To this the Mādhyamika replies that such propositions appear as definite views only to ordinary people, not to the wise. The proper attitude for the wise is always to remain silent. They impart instruction only from a popular point of view to those who want to listen to them. Their arguments are not their own or those which they believe to be right, but only such as would appeal to their hearers.

It is not out of place here to mention that the Mādhyamika school wishes to keep the phenomenal and the real or the transcendental views wide apart. In the phenomenal view things are admitted to be as they are perceived, and their relations are also conceived as real. It is interesting to refer to the discussion of Candrakīrti with Diṅnāga regarding the nature of sense-perceptions. While Diṅnāga urges that a thing is what it is in itself (*sva-lakṣaṇa*), Candrakīrti holds that, since relations are also perceived to be true, things are relational as well. Phenomenally substances exist as well as their qualities. The "thing in itself" of Diṅnāga was as much a relative concept as the relational things that are popularly perceived as true; that being so, it is meaningless to define perception as being only the thing in itself. Candrakīrti thus does not think that any good can be done by criticizing the realistic logic of the Naiyāyikas, since, so far as popular perceptions or conceptions go, the Nyāya logic is quite competent to deal with them and give an account of them. There is a phenomenal reality and order which is true for the man in the street and on which all our linguistic and other usages are based. Diṅnāga, in defining perception, restricts it to the unique thing in itself (*sva-lakṣaṇa*) and thinks that all associations of quality and relations are extraneous to perceptions and should be included under imagination or inference. This however does violence to our ordinary experience and yet serves no better purpose; for the definition of perception as given by Diṅnāga is not from the trānscendental point of view. If that is so, why not accept the realistic conceptions of the Nyāya school, which fit in with the popular experience? This reminds us of the attitude of the Vedāntists, who on the one hand accepted the view-point of popular experience and regarded all things as having a real objective existence, and on the other hand considered them as false and unreal from the transcendental point of view of ultimate reality. The attitude of the Vedāntists on this point seems to have been directly inspired by that of the Mādhyamikas. The attempts of Śrīharṣa to refute the realistic definitions of the Nyāya were intended to show that the definitions of the Nyāya could not be regarded as absolute and true, as the Naiyāyikas used to think. But, while the Mādhyamikas, who had no view-points of their own to support, could leave the field of experience absolutely undisturbed and allow the realistic definitions of the Nyāya to explain the popular experience in any way they liked, the Vedānta had a thesis of its own, namely, that the self-luminous Brahman was the only reality and that it was through it that everything else was manifested. The Vedānta therefore could not agree with Nyāya interpretations of experience and their definitions. But, as the Vedānta was unable to give the manifold world-appearance a footing in reality, it regarded it as somehow existing by itself and invented a theory of perception by which it could be considered as being manifested by coming in touch with Brahman and being illusorily imposed on it.

Continuing the discussion on the nature of causation, Nāgārjuna and Candrakīrti hold that collocations of causal conditions which are different from the effect cannot produce the effect, as is held by the Hīnayāna Buddhists; for, since the effect is not perceived in those causal conditions, it cannot be produced out of them, and, if it is already existent in them, its production becomes useless. Production of anything out of some foreign or extraneous causes implies that it is related to them, and this relation must mean that it was in some way existent in them. The main principle which Nāgārjuna employs in refuting the idea of causation or production in various ways is that, if a thing exists, it cannot be produced, and, if it does not exist, it cannot be produced at all. That which has no essence in itself cannot be caused by anything else, and, having no essence in itself, it cannot be the cause of anything else[1].

Nāgārjuna similarly examines the concepts of going and coming and says that the action of going is not to be found in the space traversed, nor is it to be found in that which is not traversed; and apart from the space traversed and not traversed there cannot be any action of going. If it is urged that going is neither in the space

[1] *Mādhyamika-vṛtti*, p. 90, 1. 6.

traversed nor in the space untraversed, but in the person who continues to go, since going is in him in whom there is the effort of going, then this again cannot be right. For, if the action of going is to be associated with the person who goes, it cannot be associated with the space traversed. One action cannot be connected with both; and, unless some space is gone over, there cannot be a goer. If going is in the goer alone, then even without going one could be called a goer, which is impossible. If both the goer and the space traversed have to be associated with going, then there must be two actions and not one; and, if there are two actions, that implies that there are also two agents. It may be urged that the movement of going is associated with the goer and that therefore going belongs to the goer; but, if there is no going without the goer and if there is no goer without going, how can going be associated with the goer at all? Again, in the proposition "the goer goes" (*gantā gacchati*) there is only one action of going, and that is satisfied by the verb "goes"; what separate "going" is there by virtue of association with which a "goer" can be so called? and, since there are no two actions of going, there cannot be a goer. Again, the movement of going cannot even be begun; for, when there is the motion of going, there is no beginning and when there is no motion of going, there cannot be any beginning. Again, it cannot be urged that "going" must exist, since its opposite, "remaining at rest " (*sthiti*), exists; for who is at rest? The goer cannot be at rest, since no one can be a goer unless he goes; he who is not a goer, being already at rest, cannot be the agent of another action of being at rest. If the goer and going be regarded as identical, then there would be neither verb nor agent. So there is no reality in going."Going" stands here for any kind of passage or becoming, and the refutation of "going" implies the refutation of all kinds of passage (*niṣkarṣaṇa*) as well. If seeds passed into the state of shoots (*aṅkura*), then they would be seeds and not shoots; the shoots neither are seeds nor are different from them; yet, the seeds being there, there are the shoots. A pea is from another pea, yet no pea becomes another pea. A pea is neither in another pea nor different from it. It is as one may see in a mirror the beautiful face of a woman and feel attracted by it and run after her, though the face never passed into the mirror and there was no human face in the reflected image. Just as the essenceless reflected image of a woman's face may rouse attachment in fools, so are world-appearances the causes of our delusion and attachment.

It is needless to multiply examples and describe elaborately Nāgārjuna's method of applying his dialectic to the refutation of the various Buddhistic and other categories. But from what has been said it may be possible to compare or contrast Nāgārjuna's dialectic with that of Śrīharṣa. Neither Nāgārjuna nor Śrīharṣa is interested to give any rational explanation of the world-process, nor are they interested to give a scientific reconstruction of our world-experience. They are agreed in discarding the validity of world-experience as such. But, while Nāgārjuna had no thesis of his own to uphold, Śrīharṣa sought to establish the validity and ultimate reality of Brahman. But, it does not appear that he ever properly tried to apply his own dialectic to his thesis and attempted to show that the definition of Brahman could stand the test of the criticism of his own dialectic. Both Nāgārjuna and Śrīharṣa were, however, agreed in the view that there was no theory of the reconstruction of world-appearance which could be supported as valid. But, while Śrīharṣa attacked only the definitions of the Nyāya, Nāgārjuna mainly attacked the accepted Buddhistic categories and also some other relevant categories which were directly connected with them. But the entire efforts of Śrīharṣa were directed to showing that the definitions of the Nyāya were faulty and that there was no way in which the Nyāya could define its categories properly. From the fact that the Nyāya could not define its categories he rushed to the conclusion that they were intrinsically indefinable and that therefore the world-appearance which was measured and scanned in terms of those categories was also false. Nāgārjuna's methods differ considerably from those of Śrīharṣa in this, that the concepts which he criticized were shown by him to have been intrinsically based and constructed on notions which had no essential nature of their own, but were understood only in relation to others. No concept revealed any intrinsic nature of its own, and one could understand a concept only through another, and that again through the former or through another, and so on. The entire world-appearance would thus be based on relative conceptions and be false. Nāgārjuna's criticisms are, however, largely of an a *priori* nature, and do not treat the concepts in a concrete manner and are not based on the testimony of our psychological experience. The oppositions shown are therefore very often of an abstract nature and occasionally degenerate into verbalism. But as a rule they are based on the fundamentally relative nature of our experience. They are never half so elaborate as the criticisms of Śrīharṣa; but at the same time they are fundamentally more convincing and more direct than the elaborate roundabout logical subtleties of Śrīharṣa's dialectic. It cannot be denied that, based on the dialectical methods of Nāgārjuna, Buddhapālita and Candrakīrti, Śrīharṣa's criticisms, following an altogether different plan of approach, show wonderful powers of logical subtlety and finesse, though the total effect can hardly be regarded as an advance from the strictly philosophical point of view, while the frequent verbalism of many of his criticisms is a discredit to his whole venture.

Dialectical criticisms of Śāntarakṣita and Kamalaśīla (A.D. 760) as forerunners of Vedānta Dialectics.

(a) Criticisms of the Sāṃkhya Pariṇāma Doctrine.

In tracing the history of the dialectical ways of thinking in the Vedānta it has been pointed out in the previous sections that the influence of Nāgārjuna and Candrakīrti on Śaṅkara and some of his followers, such as Śrīharṣa, Citsukha and others, was very great. It has also been pointed out that not only Nāgārjuna and Candrakīrti, but many other Buddhist writers, had taken to critical and dialectical ways of discussion. The criticism of the different schools of Indian thought, as contained in Śāntarakṣita's *Tattva-saṃgraha* with Kamalaśīla's commentary *Pañjikā*, is a remarkable instance of this. Śāntarakṣita lived in the first half of the eighth century A.D., and Kamalaśīla was probably his junior contemporary. They refuted the views of Kambalāśvatara, a follower of the Lokāyata school, the Buddhist Vasumitra (A.D. 100), Dharmatrāta (A.D. 100), Ghoṣaka (A.D. 150), Buddhadeva (A.D. 200), the Naiyāyika Vātṣyāyana (A.D. 300), the Mīmāṃsist Śabarasvāmin (A.D. 300), the Sāṃkhyist Vindhyasvāmin (A.D. 300), the Buddhist Saṅghabhadra (A.D. 350), Vasubandhu (A.D. 350), the Sāṃkhyist Iśvarakṛṣṇa (A.D. 390), the Buddhist Diṅnāga (A.D. 400), the Jaina Ācāryasūri (A.D. 478), the Sāṃkhyist Māṭhara Ācārya (A.D. 500), the Naiyāyika Udyotakara (A.D. 600), the rhetorician Bhāmaha (A.D. 640), the Buddhist Dharmakīrti (A.D. 650), the grammarian-philosopher Bhartṛhari (A.D. 650), the Mīmāṃsist Kumārila Bhaṭṭa (A.D. 680), the Jaina Śubhagupta (A.D. 700), the Buddhist Yugasena (A.D. 700), the Naiyāyika Āviddhakarṇa (A.D. 700), Śaṅkarasvāmin (A.D. 700), Praśastamati (A.D. 700), Bhāvivikta (A.D. 700), the Jaina Pātrasvāmin (A.D. 700), Āhrika (A.D. 700), Sumati (A.D. 700), and the Mīmāṃsist Uveyaka (A.D. 700)[1]. It is not possible here, of course, to enter into a complete analysis of all the criticisms of the different philosophers by Śāntarakṣita and Kamalaśīla; yet some of the important points of these criticisms may be noted in order to show the nature and importance of this work, which also reveals the nature of the critical thinking that prevailed among the Buddhists before Śaṅkara and by which Śaṅkara and his followers, like Śrīharṣa, Citsukha or Ānandajñāna, were in all probability greatly influenced.

In criticizing the Sāṃkhya views they say that, if the effects, the evolutes, be identical with the cause, the *pradhāna*, why should they be produced from the *pradhāna*? If they are identical, then the evolutes themselves might be regarded as cause or the *pradhāna* as effect. The ordinary way of determining causality is invariable antecedence, and that is avowedly not available here. The idea of *pariṇāma*, which means identity in diversity, the causal scheme of the Sāṃkhya, is also inadmissible; for, if it is urged that any entity changes into diverse forms, it may be asked whether the nature of the causal entity also changes or does not change. If it does not change, then the causal and the effect states should abide together in the later product, which is impossible; if it changes, then there is nothing that remains as a permanent cause; for this would only mean that a previous state is arrested and a new state is produced. If it is urged that causal transformation means the assumption of new qualities, it may be asked whether such qualities are different from the causal substance or not; if they are, then the occurrence of new qualities cannot entitle one to hold the view that the causal substance is undergoing transformations (*pariṇāma*). If the changing qualities and the causal substance are identical, then the first part, of the argument would reappear. Again, the very arguments that are given in favour of the *sat-kārya-vāda* (existence of the effect in the cause) could be turned against it. Thus, if curds, etc. already exist

[1] These dates are collected from Dr B.Bhattacharya's foreword to the *Tattvasaṃgraha*. The present author, though he thinks that many of these dates are generally approximately correct, yet, since he cannot spare the room for proper discussions, does not take responsibility for them.

in the nature of the milk, then what is the meaning of their being produced from it? If there is no idea of production, there is no idea of causality. If it is urged that the effects are potentially existent in the cause, and causal operations only actualize them, then it is admitted that the effects are actually non-existent in the cause, and we have to admit in the cause some specific characteristic, brought about by the causal operation, on account of the absence of which the effects remained in the potential state in the cause, and that the causal operations which actualize the effects produce some specific determinations in the cause, in consequence of which the effect, which was non-existent before, is actualized; this would mean that what was non-existent could be produced, which would be against the *sat-kārya-vāda* theory. In the light of the above criticisms, since according to the *sat-kārya-vāda* theory causal productions are impossible, the arguments of Sāṃkhya in favour of *sat-kārya-vāda*, that only particular kinds of effects are produced from particular kinds of causes, are also inadmissible.

Again, according to Sāṃkhya, nothing ought to be capable of being definitely asserted, since according to the *sat-kārya-vāda* theory doubts and errors are always existent as a modification of either *buddhi*, *manas* or *caitanya*. Again, the application of all Sāṃkhya arguments might be regarded as futile, since all arguments are intended to arrive at decisive conclusions; but decisive conclusions, being effects, are already existent. If, however, it is contended that decisive conclusions were not existent before, but were produced by the application of arguments, then there is production of what was non-existent, and thus the *sat-kārya-vāda* theory fails. If it is urged that, though the decisive conclusion (*niścaya*) is already existent before the application of the argumentative premises, yet it may be regarded as being manifested by the application of those premises, the Sāṃkhyist may be asked to define what he means by such manifestation (*abhivyakti*). This manifestation may mean either some new characteristic or some knowledge or the withdrawal of some obscuration to the comprehension. In the first alternative, it may again be asked whether this new character (*svabhāvātiśaya*) that is generated by the application of the premises is different from the decisive conclusion itself or identical with it. If it is identical, there is no meaning in its introduction; if it is different, no relation is admissible between these two, since any attempt to introduce a relation between two unrelated entities would launch us into a vicious infinite (*anavasthā*). It cannot mean the rise of the knowledge about that particular object for the manifestation of which the premises are applied; for, according to the *sat-kārya-vāda* theory, that knowledge is already there. Again, it cannot mean the removal of the obscuration of knowledge; for, if there is obscuration, that also must be ever-existent. As a matter of fact, the whole of the teachings of Sāṃkhya philosophy directed to the rise of true knowledge ought to be false, for true knowledge is ever-existent, and therefore there ought to be no bondage, and therefore all persons should always remain emancipated. Again, if there is any false knowledge, it could not be destroyed, and therefore there could be no emancipation.

Śāntarakṣita and Kamalaśīla then urge that, though the above refutation of the *sat-kārya-vāda* ought naturally to prove the *a-sat-kārya-vāda* (the production of that which did not exist before) doctrine, yet a few words may be said in reply to the Sāṃkhya refutation of *a-sat-kārya-vāda*. Thus the argument that that which is non-existent has no form (*nairūpya*) and therefore cannot be produced is false ; for the operation of production represents itself the character of the thing that is being produced. As the Satkāryavādins think that out of the same three *guṇas* different kinds of effects may be produced according to causal collocations, so here also, according to the law of different kinds of causal forces (*karaṇa-śakti-pratniyamāt*), different kinds of non-existing effects come into being. It is meaningless to hold that the limitation of causal forces is to be found in the pre-existence of effects; for, in reality, it is on account of the varying capacities of the causal forces that the various effects of the causes are produced. The production of various effects is thus solely due to the diverse nature of the causal forces that produce them. The law of causal forces is thus ultimately fundamental. The name *a-sat-kārya-vāda*, however, is a misnomer; for certainly there is no such non-existent entity which comes into being[1]. Production in reality means nothing more than the characteristic of the moment only, divested from all associations of a previous and a succeeding point of time[2]. The meaning of *a-sat-kārya-*

[1] *na hy asan-nāma kiñcid asti yad utpattim āviśet, kintu kālpaniko 'yaṃ vyava-hāro yad asad utpadyata iti yāvat. Tattva-saṃgraha-pañjikā*, p. 33.

[2] *vastūnāṃ pūrvāpara-koṭi-śūnya-kṣaṇa-mātrāvasthāyī svabhāva eva utpādaḥity ucyate. Ibid.*

vāda is that an entity called the effect is seen immediately after a particular causal operation; and it certainly did not exist before this second moment, since, if it did exist at the first moment of the causal operation, it would have been perceived ; it is therefore said that the effect did not exist before; but this should not be interpreted to mean that the Buddhists believed in the non-existing existence of the effect, which suddenly came into being after the causal operation.

Refuting the other Sāṃkhya doctrines, Śāntarakṣita and Kamalaśīla point out that, if an effect (e.g. curd) is said to exist in the cause (e.g. milk), it cannot do so in the actual form of the effect, since then milk would have tasted as curd. If it is said to exist in the form of a special capacity or potency (*śakti*), then the existence of the effect in the cause is naturally denied ; for it is the potency of the effect that exists in the cause and not the effect itself. Again, the Sāṃkhyists believe that all sensible things are of the nature of pleasure and pain; this, however, is obviously impossible, since only conscious states can be regarded as pleasurable or painful. There is no sense at all in describing material things as of the nature of pleasure or pain. Again, if objective material things were themselves pleasurable or painful, then the fact that the same objects may appear pleasurable to some and painful to others would be unexplainable. If, however, it is held that even pleasurable objects may appear painful to someone, on account of his particular state of mind or bad destiny, then the objects themselves cannot be pleasurable or painful. Again, if objects are regarded as being made up of three *guṇas*, there is no reason for admitting one eternal *prakṛti* as the source of them all. If causes are similar to effects, then from the fact that the world of objects is many and limited and non-eternal one ought to suppose that the cause of the objects also should be many, limited and noneternal. It is sometimes held that, as all earthen things are produced from one earth, so all objects are produced from one *prakṛti*; but this also is a fallacious argument, since all earthen things are produced not out of one lump of earth, but from different lumps. Thus, though it may be inferred that the world of effects must have its causes, this cannot lead us to infer that there is one such cause as the *prakṛti* of the Sāṃkhyists.

(b) Criticism of Iśvara.

One of the chief arguments of the Naiyāyika theists in favour of the existence of God is based on the fact that the specific forms and shapes of the different objects in the world cannot be explained except on the supposition of an intelligent organizer or shaper. To this Śāntarakṣita and Kamalaśīla reply that we perceive only the different kinds of visual and tactile sensibles and that there are no further shaped wholes or so-called objects, which men fancy themselves to be perceiving. It is meaningless to think that the visual sensibles and tactile sensibles go together to form one whole object. When people say that it is the same coloured object, seen in the day, that we touched in the night when we did not see it, they are wrong; for colour sensibles or sense-data are entirely different kinds of entities from tactile sense-data, and it is meaningless to say that it is the same object or whole which has both the colour and tactile characteristics. If two colour sensibles, say yellow and blue, are different, then still more different are the colour sensibles and the tactile ones. What exist therefore are not wholes having colour and tactile characters, but only discrete elements of colour and tactile sense-data; the combining of them into wholes is due only to false imagination. There are no objects which can be perceived by the two senses; there is no proof that it is one identical object that is perceived by the eye as well as touched. There exist therefore only loose and discrete sense-data. There being thus no shaped wholes, the supposition of the existence of God as shaper and organizer is inadmissible. The mere fact that there are the effects cannot lead to the inference that there is one intelligent creator and organizer, since a causal inference cannot be made from mere similarity of any description; there must be a law of unconditional and invariable connection (*pratibandha*). The argument that, since jugs, etc. are made by an intelligent potter, so trees, etc. must also have been made by an intelligent creator, is faulty; for trees, etc., are so different in nature from jugs, etc., that it is wrong to make any assertion from the former to the latter. The general Buddhist arguments against the existence of any eternal entity will also apply against the existence of any eternal God. The argument that, since a state of arrest breaks up into a state of motion or production in all natural phenomena, there must be an intelligent creator, is wrong;

for there is no state of arrest in nature; all things in the world are momentary. Again, if things are happening in succession, at intervals, through the operation of a causal agent, then God also must be operating at intervals and, by the arguments of the opponents themselves, He must have another being to guide His operations, and that another, and that another, and there would thus be a vicious infinite. If God had been the creator, then everything would have sprung into being all at once. He ought not to depend on accessory assistance; for, He being the creator of all such accessory circumstances, they could not render Him any assistance in His creation. Again, if it is urged that the above argument does not hold, because God only creates when He wishes, then it may be replied that, since God's will is regarded as eternal and one, the old objection of simultaneous production holds good. Moreover, since God is eternal and since His will depends only on Him and Him alone, His will cannot be transitory. Now, if He and His will be always present, and yet at the moment of the production of any particular phenomenon all other phenomena are not produced, then those phenomena cannot be regarded as being caused by God or by His will. Again, even if for argument's sake it may be granted that all natural objects, such as trees, hills, etc., presuppose intelligent creators, there is no argument for supposing that one intelligent creator is the cause of all diverse natural objects and phenomena. Therefore there is no argument in favour of the existence of one omniscient creator.

The arguments urged in refutation of *prakṛti* and Iśvara would also apply against the Pātañjala-Sāṃkhya, which admits the joint causality of Iśvara and *prakṛti*; for here also, *prakṛti* and Iśvara being eternal causes, one would expect to have simultaneous production of all effects. If it is urged that the three *guṇas* behave as accessory causes with reference to God's operation, then also it may be asked whether at the time of productive activity (*sarga*) the activity of dissolution or of maintenance (*sthiti*) may also be expected to be operated, or whether at the time of dissolution, there might be productive operation as well. If it is urged that, though all kinds of forces are existent in *prakṛti*, yet it is only those that become operative that take effect, it may be objected that some other kind of cause has to be admitted for making some powers of *prakṛti* operative, while others are inoperative, and this would introduce a third factor; thus the joint causality of *puruṣa* and *prakṛti* is also easily refuted. Again, the view that God produces the world through kindness is also false; for, had it been so, the world would not have been so full of misery. Again, there being before creation no beings, God could not feel kindness to nonexistent beings. He would not have destroyed the world had He been so kind; if He created and destroyed the world in accordance with the good or bad deeds, then He would not be independent. Had He been independent, He would not have allowed Himself to be influenced by the consequences of bad deeds in producing misery in the world. If He created the world out of mere playful instincts, then these playful instincts would be superior to Him. If He derived much enjoyment from His productive and destructive play, then, if He were able, He would have created and destroyed the world simultaneously. If He is not capable of creating and destroying the world simultaneously, then there is no reason to suppose that He would be able to do it at intervals. If it is urged that the world was produced naturally by His own existence, then there would be simultaneous production. If it is objected that, just as spiders, though they naturally go on producing webs, yet do not produce them all at once, so God also may be producing the world gradually and not all at once, it may then be pointed out that the analogy of spider's webs is false, since the spider does not naturally produce webs, but only through greed for eating insects, and its activities are determined by such motives. God, however, is One who can have only one uniform motive. If it is urged that creation flows from God unconsciously, as it were, it may readily be objected that a being who creates such a great universe without any intelligent purpose would indeed be very unintelligent.

(c) Refutation of the Soul Theory.

The Nyāya view of the soul, that our thoughts must have a knower and that our desires and feelings must have some entity in which they may inhere and that this entity is soul and that it is the existence of this one soul that explains the fact of the unity of all our conscious states as the experience of one individual, is objected to by Śāntarakṣita and Kamalaśīla. They hold that no thought or knowledge requires any further knower for its illumination; if it had been so, there would be a vicious infinite. Again, desires, feelings, etc., are not like material objects, which would require a receptacle in which they might be placed. The so-called unity of consciousness is due to a false unifying imagination of the momentary ones as one. It is also well known that different entities may be regarded as combined on account of their fulfilling the same kinds of functions. It is knowledge in its aspect of ego that is often described as the self, though there is no objective entity corresponding to it. It is sometimes argued that the existence of the soul is proved by the fact that a man is living only so long as his vital currents are connected with the soul, and that he dies when they are disconnected from it; but this is false, since, unless the existence of soul be proved, the supposition of its connection with vital currents as determining life is untenable. Some, however, say that the self is directly perceived in experience; if it had not been, there would not have been such diversity of opinion about its existence. The sense of ego cannot be said to refer to the self; for the sense of ego is not eternal, as it is supposed to be. On the other hand, it refers sometimes to our body (as when I say, "I am white"), sometimes to the senses (as when I say, "I am deaf"), and sometimes to intellectual states. It cannot be said that its reference to body or to senses is only indirect; for no other permanent and direct realization of its nature is found in experience. Feelings, desires, etc., also often arise in succession and cannot therefore be regarded as inhering in a permanent self. The conclusion is that, as all material objects are soulless, so also are human beings. The supposed eternal soul is so different from the body that it cannot be conceived how one can help the other or even be related to it. Thus there is hardly any argument in favour of the soul theory of the Nyāya and Vaiśeṣika.

(d) Refutation of the Mīmāṃsā Theory of the Self.

Kumārila believed that, though the nature of the self as pure consciousness was eternal and unchangeable, yet it passed through various changing phases of other feeling and volitional states. That the self was of the nature of pure consciousness was proved by the fact that it perceives itself to be knower in the past and in the present. So the existence of the self is proved by the fact of self-consciousness. To this Śāntarakṣita and Kamalaśīla reply that, if the self is regarded as one eternal consciousness, then knowledge or the knowing faculty (*buddhi*) ought also to be regarded as similarly one and eternal; but seemingly Kumārila does not consider *buddhi* to be such. If the knowing faculty be regarded as eternal and one, how are the varying states of cognition, such as colour-cognition, taste-cognition, etc., to be explained? If it is urged that, though the knowing faculty is one, yet (just as a fire, though it has always a capacity of burning, yet burns only when combustible substances are put in it) it only passes through various kinds of perception according as various kinds of objects are presented to it; or, just as a mirror, though it has always the power of reflecting, yet only reflects when the objects are presented to it, so the selves are eternally conscious and yet operate only in connection with their specific bodies and grasp the various kinds of sense-data, and all cognitions are forged from them(selves). If the change of cognitions is due to the changing operations of the senses and the sense-objects, then such a cognizing faculty cannot be regarded as eternal and one. If the knowing faculty is to be regarded as eternal owing to an experience of continuity of consciousness, then how can one explain the variety of cognitions? If it is urged that the variety of cognitions is due to the assumption by the cognizing faculty of various forms of objects, then how can one explain the experience of the variety of cognitions in hallucinations, when there are no objects? Moreover the Mīmāṃsist does not think that the cognizing faculty assumes the forms of the objects cognized, but believes that cognition reveals the objects in the objective world and the cognizing faculty has itself no forms (*nirākārā buddhiḥ*). The fact that there may be cognitions without a corresponding real objective presentation proves that our cognitions are subjective and self-revealed and that they do not reveal objective entities. If it is urged that the knowing faculty has always the power of revealing all things, then sound-cognition would be the same as colour-cognition. The analogy of fire is also false, since there is not one fire that is constant; the analogy of the reflecting mirror is also false, since there is really no reflection in the mirror itself; one can see a reflection in a mirror at a particular angle, the mirror therefore is only an apparatus for producing an illusory cognition. Again, the *buddhi* cannot be compared to a mirror as an apparatus for producing illusory images; for then some other *buddhi* would be necessary for perceiving illusory images. Again, if the self is regarded as one and eternal, then it cannot pass through the varying feeling and volitional states. If these states are not entirely different from the self, then their changes would imply the change of the self; and again, if they are entirely different from the self, how should their change affect the self? Again, if these states all belong to the self and it is urged that it is when the pleasurable state is submerged in the nature of the common self, that the painful state may arise, it may be pointed out in objection that, if the pleasurable states could be submerged in the nature of the self in identity with itself, then they would be identical with the nature of the self. It is also wrong to suppose that the sense of self-consciousness refers to a really existing entity corresponding to it. It has in reality no specific object to refer to as the self. It may therefore be safely asserted that the existence of the self is not proved by the evidence of self-consciousness.

(e) Refutation of the Sāṃkhya View of the Self.

Against the Sāṃkhya view of the self it is pointed out that the Sāṃkhya regards the self as pure consciousness, one and eternal, and that, as such, it ought not to beable to enjoy diverse kinds of experiences. If it is held that enjoyment, etc., all belong to *buddhi* and the *puruṣa* only enjoys the reflections in the *buddhi*, it may well be objected that if the reflections in the *buddhi* are identical with *puruṣa*, then with their change the *puruṣa* also undergoes a change; and if they are different, the *puruṣa* cannot be considered to be their enjoyer. Again, if the *prakṛti* concentrates all its activities for the enjoyment of the *puruṣa*, how can it be regarded as unconscious? Again, if all actions and deeds belong to *buddhi*, and if *buddhi* be different from *puruṣa*. why should the *puruṣa* suffer for what is done by the *buddhi*? If, again, the nature of *puruṣa* cannot be affected by the varying states of pleasure and pain, then it cannot be regarded as an enjoyer; and, if it could be affected, it would itself be changeable.

(f) The Refutation of the Upaniṣad View of the Self.

The Upaniṣadic thinkers hold that it is one eternal consciousness that illusorily appears as all objects, and that there is in reality no perceiver and perceived, but only one eternal consciousness. Against this view it is urged by Śāntarakṣita and Kamalaśīla that, apart from the individual cognitions of colour, taste, etc., no eternal, unchangeable consciousness is experienced. If one eternal consciousness is the one reality, then there cannot be a distinction of false knowledge and right knowledge, bondage and emancipation. There being only one reality, there is no right knowledge which need be attained.

(g) Refutation of the Theory of the Persistence of Existing Entities.

Śāntarakṣita and Kamalaśīla point out that the Naiyāyikas divide existing entities into two classes, as produced (*kṛtaka*) and unproduced (*a-kṛtaka*), and they hold that those which are produced are destructible. The Vātsīputrīyas also similarly divide existing entities into momentary (e.g. ideas, sound, flame, etc.) and non-momentary (e.g. earth, sky, etc.). On this point Śāntarakṣita and Kamalaśīla urge that whatever is produced is momentary, since the destructibility of momentary things does not depend on any cause excepting the fact that they are produced; for, had the destructibility of such entities depended on conditions or causes other than the fact of their being produced, then the premise that whatever is produced is necessarily destructible would be false. The Naiyāyika view, therefore, that produced entities depend for their destruction on other conditions, is false. If produced entities do not depend for their destruction on any other condition or cause than the fact of their being produced, then they must be destroyed the moment they are produced, or in other words they are momentary. Moreover, destruction, being negation, is not a positive entity and is absolutely contentless, and only positive entities depend on other conditions or causes for their production. Destruction, being negation, is not produced by any conditions or causes like a positive entity. Destruction therefore is not generated by any separate causal apparatus, but the very causes that lead to the production of an entity lead also to its destruction the next moment. Destructibility being a necessary characteristic of productibility, destruction cannot need the interference of any causes. It has also been stated above that destruction is pure negation and has therefore no characteristics which have to be generated by any positive set of causes or conditions.[1]

[1] The word *kṣaṇika*, which is translated as "momentary," is, according to Śāntarakṣita, a technical term. The character in an entity of dying immediately after production, is technically called *kṣaṇa*, and whatever has this quality is called *kṣaṇika* (*utpādānāntara-vināśi-svabhāvo vastunaḥ kṣaṇa ucyate, sa yasyāsti sa kṣaṇika iti. Tattva-saṃgraha*, p. 142); *kṣaṇa* therefore does not mean time moment. It means the character of dying immediately after being produced. The objection of Udyotakara that what only stays for a moment of time (*kṣaṇa*) cannot be called *kṣaṇika*, because at the expiry of the moment nothing remains which can be characterized as momentary, is therefore inadmissible. There is, however, no entity separate from the momentary character, and the use of the term *kṣaṇika*, which grammatically distinguishes the possessor of the momentary character from the momentary character itself, is due only to verbal license.

Kumalaśīla and Śāntarakṣita urge that existence (*sattva*) can be affirmed only of those entities which are capable of serving a purpose (*artha-kriyā-samarthā*). They urge that entities can only serve a purpose, if they are momentary. Entities that persist cannot serve any purpose and therefore cannot have any existence. In order to prove their thesis they enter into the following argument. If any purpose is to be served, then that can be either in succession or simultaneously, and no middle alternative is possible. If an existing entity persists in time, then all its effects ought to come about simultaneously; for, the complete cause being there, the effects must also be there, and there is no reason why the effects should happen in succession; but it is well known in experience that effects happen only in succession and not simultaneously. If, however, it is objected that even a persisting entity can perform actions in succession owing to its association with successive accessories (*kramiṇaḥ sahakāriṇaḥ*), then one may well enquire as to the nature of the assistance given by the successive accssories to the persisting entity in the production of the effect; is it by producing a special modification (*atiśayādhāna*) of the persisting cause or by independent working in consonance with the productive action of the persisting entity? In the first alternative, the special modification may be either identical with or different from the nature of the persisting entity, and both these alternatives are impossible; for, if it is identical, then, since the effect follows in consequence of the special modification of the accessories, it is the element of this special modification that is to be regarded as the cause of the effect, and not the persisting entity. If it is again urged that the effect is due to the association of the special modification with the persisting entity, then it would be impossible to define the nature of such association; for an association may be either of identity or of productivity (*tādātmya* and *tad-utpatti*), and neither of them is possible in the present case, since the special modification is recognized as being different from the persisting entity and is acknowledged by assumption to be produced by the accessories. Again, such association cannot be regarded as being of the nature of *samavāya*; for this special modification, being of the nature of an additional assistance (*upakāra*), cannot be regarded as being of the nature of inseparable inherence (*samavāya*). If this special modification be regarded as being neither of the nature of an additional assistance (*upakāra*) nor of the nature of an essence identical with the persisting entity, and if it is still regarded as being associated with the persisting entity in a relation of *samavāya*, then anything in the world could be regarded as being in the *samavāya* relation with anything else. In the other alternative, in which it is maintained that the persisting entity awaits only the independent working of the accessories, it may well be asked whether the causal nature of the persisting entity is the same together with the totality of the accessories as it is without them? In the former case, the accessories would also be persistent. In the latter case, the persisting entity can no longer be regarded as persisting.

Regarding the objection of Bhadanta Yogasena, that the same difficulties would arise in the assumption of entities as momentary, Śāntarakṣita and Kamalaśīla reply that in their view the accessories behave in two ways, firstly, as independent co-operation (*ekārtha-kriyā-kāritā*) and, secondly, as mutual help (*parasparopakāritā*). Thus in the first moment the different accessory-units are only independently co-operant, since, in one moment, their mutual actions cannot help one another; but in the second moment, the effects may be regarded as being of a joint nature, and therefore mutually determining one another, in the production of the effect of the third moment. In this view, though each entity operates independently, yet none of their operations are irrelevant. They are ali being produced and determined by the respective causes and conditions in a beginningless series.

The objection against the momentariness of all things on the ground that things are perceived and recognized to be the same, and as persisting, is not a valid one. For the fact of persistence cannot be perceived by the senses and must be regarded as due to false imagination. All recognition is due to the operation of memory, which is almost universally recognized as invalid for purposes of right knowledge. On this point it may be argued that in recognition, if the entity now perceived be the same as the entity perceived at a previous time, then how can a cognition in the past comprehend an entity of the present time? If they are held to be different, then it is acknowledged that the entities perceived as the same in recognition are not really the same. The objector's argument that, since things pass by the same name, they must be persistent is invalid; for it is well known that even in ordinary perception, where a flame is known to be destroyed every moment, and produced anew, it is still said in common verbal usage to be the same flame. Thus all existing things must be regarded as momentary.

(h) Refutation of Criticisms of the Non-permanency of Entities.

It is objected by the Naiyāyikas and others that, if things are momentary, then the theory of karma would fail; for how can it be understood that the deeds be performed by one, and the fruits reaped by another? How, again, can it be understood that a momentary cause which does not abide till the rise of the effect should produce the same? Again, if objects are momentary, how can they be perceived by the eye? The phenomena of recognition would also be inexplicable, as there would be no permanent perceiver who would identify the present and the past as being one. How, again, would the phenomenon of bondage and of emancipation apply to a non-permanent being? In reply to this Śāntarakṣita and Kamalaśīla say that, just as a seed by means of its invariable power produces the shoots, without being superintended by any conscious agent, so the inner states of a man may generate other states, without being superintended by any permanent conscious agent; the formula (*dharma-saṃketa*) for all production is, "this happening, that happens"; "this being produced, that is produced." It is through ignorance that a man cannot discern that all subsequent states are determined by the natural forces of the preceding ones and thinks of himself as performing this or that action or as striving for emancipation. The true nature of things cannot be determined by the illusory experience of ignorant people. It is sometimes objected that the parts of a seed attain a due constitution by assimilating nutritive elements at the second stage, and then again at the third stage attain a new constitution by further accretion of new nutritive elements, and that therefore it cannot be held that the parts of the seed are entirely destroyed at the second stage. To this the reply of Śāntarakṣita is that in the second moment the effect is produced in dependence on the undestroyed causal efficiency of the first causal moment; so that the effect is produced by the causal efficiency of the first moment, when the cause is not destroyed. The cause however perishes in the second moment; for, once the cause has produced the effect, it cannot be producing it again and again; if it did, there would be a vicious infinite. It must therefore be admitted that the causal efficiency of the cause ceases immediately after production[1]. The view that the effect is produced simultaneously with the cause (*saha-bhūtaṃ kāryam*) is unreasonable, since the cause cannot produce the effect before it is itself produced; again, it cannot produce after it is itself produced ; for then the effect also has to be acknowledged to be of the same nature as the cause; but at the same moment it can have no scope for its efficiency. Thus the cause and effect cannot be produced simultaneously. There is no necessity also for admitting a causal operation (*vyāpāra*), as separate and distinct from the cause. Invariable antecedence is the only qualification of cause[2]. If a causal operation has to be admitted for connecting the cause with the effect, then that would require another operation, and that another, and there would be a vicious infinite. If the causal operation is admitted to be able to generate the effect independently by itself, so can the cause be also admitted to be able to produce the effect. The objection that, if antecedence be admitted to be alone the determinant of causality, then the fact, that a thing is smelled after it is seen may also lead one to infer that colour is the cause of smell, is invalid, for the Buddhists have no objection to regarding colour as an accessory cause of smell. It must also be remembered that the Buddhists do not regard mere antecedence as the definition of cause, but invariable and necessary antecedence[3]. Again, no difficulty need be experienced in perception, if the objects are admitted to be momentary; for ideas may be considered to have forms akin to the objects, or to be formless, but revealing the objects. In either case the ideas are produced by their causes, and the momentariness or permanence of objects has nothing to do with their determination[4]. There are in reality no agent and no enjoyer, but only the series of passing mental phenomena. Causality consists in the determination of the succeeding states by the previous ones. The objection of Udyotakara, that, if the mind is momentary, it cannot be modified (*vāsanā*) by deeds (*karma*), is invalid; for, in the Buddhist view, this modification

[1] The Vaibhāṣikas are spoken of by Śāntarakṣita as holding the view that the effect is produced at the third moment. In this view the effect is produced by the destroyed cause.

[2] *idam eva hi kāryasya kāraṇāpekṣā yat tad-anantara-bhāvitvam. Tattva-saṃgraha*, p. 177.

[3] *na hi vayam ānantarya-mātraṃ kārya-kāraṇa-bhāvādhigati-nibandhanaṃ . . . yasyaivānantaraṃ yad bhavati tat tasya kāraṇam iṣyate. Ibid.* p. 180.

[4] Sāntarakṣita and Kamalaśīla are Buddhists who style themselves *nirākāra-vijñāna-vādin.*

(*vāsanā*) means nothing more than the production of a new mental state of a modified nature. There is again no permanent perceiver who remembers and recognizes; it is only when in a particular series of conscious states, on account of the strength of a particular perception, such particularly modified mental states are generated as may be said to contain seeds of memory, that memory is possible. The Buddhists also do not consider that there is one person who suffers bondage and is liberated; they think that bondage means nothing more than the production of painful states due to ignorance (*avidyā*) and other mental causes, and that liberation also means nothing more than purity of the mental states due to cessation of ignorance through right knowledge.

(i) Refutation of the Nyāya Vaiśeṣika Categories.

Śāntarakṣita and Kamalaśīla attempt to refute the categories of substance (*dravya*) with its subdivisions, quality (*guṇa*), action (*karma*), generality, or class concepts (*sāmānya*), specific peculiarities (*viśeṣa*), relation of inherence (*samavāya*), and the connotation and denotation of words (*śabdārtha*). This refutation may briefly be set out here.

Speaking against the eternity of atoms, they hold that, since no special excellence can be produced in eternal entities, no conditions or collocations of any kind can produce any change in the nature of the atoms; thus, the atoms being always the same in nature, all objects should be produced from them either at once, or not at all. The mere fact that no cause of atoms is known is no ground for thinking that they are causeless. Again, substance, as different from characters and qualities, is never perceived. The refutation of wholes (*avayavī*), which has already been effected, also goes against the acceptance of substantive wholes, and so the four substances earth, water, air and fire, which are ordinarily regarded as substantive—wholes made up of atoms—also stand refuted. Again, it is not easy to prove the existence of separate and independent time and space entities; for spatial and temporal determinations may well be explained as mental modifications due, like other facts of experience, to their specific causes. The Buddhists of course accept the existence of *manas* as an instrument separate from the sense-organs, but they do not admit its existence as an eternal and single entity.

The refutation of substances implies the refutation of *guṇas*, which are supposed to be dependent on substances. If the substances do not exist, there can also be no relation of inherence, in which relation the *guṇas* are supposed to exist in substances. There is, again, no meaning in acknowledging colours, etc., as different from the atoms in which they are supposed to exist. The perception of numbers also ought to be regarded as due to mental modifications associated with particular cognitions. There is no reason for holding that numbers should stand as separate qualities. In a similar manner Śāntarakṣita and Kamalaśīla proceed with the refutation of the other Nyāya qualities.

Proceeding with the refutation of action (*karma*), they hold that, if all things are admitted to be momentary, then action cannot be attributed to them; for action, involving as it does successive separation of parts and association of contact-points, implies many moments for its execution. If things are admitted to be persistent or eternal, then also movement cannot be explained. If things are admitted to be always moving, then they will be in motion while they are perceived to be at rest, which is impossible. If things are at rest by nature, there cannot be any vibratory movement in them. The main principle involved in the refutation of *guṇas* and *karmas* consists in the fact that the *guṇas* and *karmas* are regarded by the Buddhists as being identical with the particular sense-data cognized. It is wrong, in their view, to analyse the sense-data as substances having qualities and motion as different categories inhering in them. Whatever may be the substance, that is also the quality which is supposed to be inhering in it, as also the motion which it is supposed to execute.

Regarding the refutation of class-concepts the main drift of Buddhist argument is that, though the perception of class-natures may be supposed to be due to some cause, yet it is wrong to assume the existence of eternal class-nature existing constantly in all the changing and diverse individual members of a class. For, howsoever we may try to explain it, it is difficult to see how one thing can remain constantly the same, though all the individual members in which it is supposed to exist are constantly changing. If class-natures are said to inhere owing to specific qualities, e.g. cooking in the cook, then also it may be objected that, since the operation of cooking is different in each case, there is no one character "cooking" by virtue of which the class-nature of cook is admissible. Moreover, a cook is called a cook even when he is not cooking. Considerations like these should lead any thinking person to deny the existence of eternal class-natures.

Regarding the refutation of specific qualities (*viśeṣa*) it is held that, if *yogins* can perceive the ultimate specific qualities as different from one another, they might equally perceive the atoms to be different from one another; if the atoms cannot be perceived as different except through some other properties, then the same may be required of the specific properties themselves.

Regarding the refutation of *samavāya*, or relation of inherence, the Buddhist objects mainly to the admission of a permanent *samavāya* relation, though all the individuals in which this relation may be supposed to exist should be changing or perishing. It is a false supposition that the relation of inherence, such as that of the cloth in the thread, is ever felt to be, as if the one (e.g. the cloth) was existing in the other (threads), as the Naiyāyikas suppose.

Dialectic of Śaṅkara and Ānandajñāna.

It is well known that Śaṅkarācārya in his commentary on the *Brahma-sūtra*, II. ii 11–17, criticizes the atomic theory of the Vaiśeṣikas. His first thesis is that the production of an effect different in nature from the cause, as in the case of the production of the impure world from pure Brahman, can be justified on the analogy of even the critics of the Vedānta, the Vaiśeṣikas. The Vaiśeṣikas hold that in the production of the *dvy-aṇuka* (containing two atoms) from the *paramāṇu* (single atom) and of the *catur-aṇuka* (containing four atoms) from the *dvy-aṇuka*, all other qualities of the *paramāṇu* and the *dvy-aṇuka* are transferred to the *dvy-aṇuka* and *catur-aṇuka* respectively, excepting the specific measures of *pārimāṇḍalya* (specific atomic measure) and *aṇu-hrasva* (specific measure of the dyads), which are peculiar to *paramāṇu* and *dvy-aṇuka* respectively. Thus, though all other qualities of *paramāṇus* pass over to *dvy-aṇukas* produced by their combination, yet the specific *pārimāṇḍalya* measure of the *paramāṇus* does not pass to the *dvy-aṇukas*, which are of the *aṇu-hrasva parimāṇa*. So also, though all the qualities of *dvy-aṇukas* would pass on to the *catur-aṇuk*as made out of their combination, yet their own specific *aṇu-hrasva parimāṇa* would not pass on to the *catur-aṇukas*, which are possessed of their own measure, viz. the *mahat parimāṇa*, uncaused by the *parimāṇa* of the *dvy-aṇukas*. This shows that the

Vaiśeṣikas believe that the *pārimāṇḍalya* measure (*parimāṇa*) of the *paramāṇus* may produce an altogether different measure in their product, the *dvy-aṇukas*, and so the *aṇu-hrasva* measure of the *dvy-aṇukas* may produce an altogether different measure in their product, the *catur-aṇukas*, viz. the *mahat parimāṇa*. On this analogy it may be contended that the Vaiśeṣikas have nothing to object to in the production of an altogether different effect (viz. the impure world) from an altogether different cause, the pure Brahman. If it is urged that the measure of the *paramāṇu* cannot pass on to the *dvy-aṇuka* only because its passage is rendered impossible by the taking possession of it by an opposite quality (the *aṇu-hrasva parimāṇa*), then a similar reply may be given in the case of the difference between the world and Brahman. Moreover, since, according to the Vaiśeṣika theory, all products remain for a moment without qualities, there is no reason why, when the *dvy-aṇuka* was produced, the *pārimāṇḍalya* measure should not pass on to it. At that moment, since the *pārimāṇḍalya* measure did not pass on to it as did the other qualities, it follows, not that the passing of the *pārimāṇḍalya* measure is opposed by the other *parimāṇa*, but that it naturally did not pass on to it. Again, it cannot be objected that the analogy of dissimilarity of qualities (*guṇa*) cannot be cited in support of the dissimilarity of substances.

Śaṅkara's second thesis is that the Vaiśeṣika view that atoms combine is wrong, because, since the atoms are partless, and since combination implies contact and contact implies parts which come in contact, there cannot be any combination of atoms. Moreover, since before creation there is no one who can make an effort, and since the contact of atoms cannot be effected without effort, and since the selves, being unconscious at that time, cannot themselves make any effort, it is impossible to account for the activity without which the contact of the atoms would also be impossible. So the atoms cannot combine, for want of the effort needed for such a contact. Śaṅkara's third point is that the relation of *samavāya* upheld by the Vaiśeṣikas cannot be admitted; for, if to unite two different objects the relation of *samavāya* is needed, then *samavāya*, being itself different from them, would require another *samavāya* to connect itself with them, and that another, and that another, and so on *ad infinitum*. If the relation of contact requires a further relation of *samavāya* to connect it with the objects in contact, there is no reason why *samavāya* should not require some other relation in its turn. Again, if the atoms are regarded as always operative and combining, then there can be no dissolution (*pralaya*), and, if they are always disintegrating, then creation would be impossible. Again, since the atoms possess the qualities of colour, etc., they must be the product of some simpler causes, just as other objects having qualities are made up of simpler entities. Moreover, it is not right to suppose that, since we have the idea of non-eternality, this must imply eternality and that therefore the atoms must be eternal; for, even though it implies the existence of eternality, it does not imply that the atoms should be eternal, since there is such an eternal thing as Brahman. Again, the fact that the cause of the destruction of the atoms is not known does not imply that they are eternal; for mere ignorance of the ways of destruction does not imply etemality. Again, the Vaiśeṣikas are wrong in speaking of six different categories and yet hold that all the five other categories depend on substance for their existence or manifestation. A substance and its quality do not appear to be as different as two substances. A substance appears black or white, and this implies that the qualities are at bottom identical with the substance (*dravyātmakatā guṇasya*). It cannot, moreover, be urged that the dependence of other categories on substance consists in their inseparableness (*ayuta-siddhatva*) from it. This inseparableness cannot be inseparableness of space ; for, when threads constitute as their product a piece of cloth, then the threads and the cloth cannot be regarded as having the same space, yet, being cause and effect, they are to be regarded as *ayuta-siddha*, or inseparable; and yet the whiteness of the cloth is not regarded as abiding in the threads. If inseparableness means inseparableness of time, then the two horns of a bull, which exist at the same time, should also be regarded as inseparable; and, if inseparableness means inseparableness of character or sameness of character, then quality cannot be regarded as being different from substance. Again, since the cause exists prior to the effect, it cannot be regarded as inseparable from the cause, and yet it is asserted by the Vaiśeṣikas that their relation is one of *samavāya*, since they are inseparable in their nature.

Śaṅkara, however, seldom indulges in logical dialectic like the above, and there are only a few rare instances in which he attacks his opponents from a purely logical point of view. But even here he does not so much criticize the definitions of the Vaiśeṣikas as point out the general logical and metaphysical confusions that result from some of the important Vaiśeṣika theories. It is easy to note the difference of a criticism like this from the criticism of Śrīharṣa in his *Khaṇḍana-khaṇḍa-khādya*, where he uses all the power of his dialectical subtleties to demolish the cherished principles of pure logic as formulated by the Nyāya logicians. It is not a criticism of certain doctrines in support of others, but it is a criticism which aims at destroying the possibility of logical or perceptual knowledge as a whole. It does not touch any specific metaphysical views, but it denies the power of perception and inference to give us right knowledge, and it supposes that it achieves its purpose by proving that the Nyāya modes of definition of perception and inference are faulty and self-contradictory. Citsukha's attempts are more positive; for he criticizes not only the Nyāya categories of logic, but also the categories of Vaiśeṣika metaphysics, and makes some positive and important statements, too, about the Vedānta doctrine itself. Ānandajñāna's *Tarka-saṃgraha* is another important work of negative criticism of the Vaiśeṣika categories and in that sense a continuation on a more elaborate scale of Citsukha's criticisms of the Vaiśeṣika categories. The importance of the Vaiśeṣika was gradually increasing, as it was gradually more and more adopted by Vaiṣṇava realistic writers, such as Madhva and his followers, and it was supposed that a refutation of the Vaiśeṣika would also imply a refutation of the dualistic writers who draw their chief support from Vaiśeṣika physics and metaphysics.

Ānandajñāna, also called Ānandagiri, was probably a native of Gujarat and lived in the middle of the thirteenth century. Mr Tripathi points out in his introduction to Ānandajñāna's *Tarka-saṃgraha* that Ānandajñāna was a spiritual head of the Dvārakā monastery of Śaṇkara, of which Sureśvarācārya was the first teacher. He was a pupil of two teachers, Anubhūtisvrūpācārya and Śuddhānanda. Anubhūtisvarūpācārya wrote five works, viz. (1) a grammatical work called *Sārasvata-prakriyā*, (2) a commentary on Śaṅkara's commentary on Gauḍapāda's *Māṇḍūkya-kārikā*, (3) a commentary on Ānandabodha Yati's *Nyāya-makaranda*, called *Nyāya-makaranda-saṃgraha*, (4) a commentary, called *Candrikā*, on Ānandabodha's *Nyāya-dīpāvalī*, and (5) another commentary, called *Nibandha*, on Ānandabodha's *Pramāṇa-mālā*. Nothing is known about his other teacher, Śuddhānanda, who is different from the other Śuddhānanda, the teacher of Svayamprakāśa of the seventeenth century, author of the *Advaita-makaranda-ṭīkā*. One of the most distinguished of Ānandagiri's pupils was Akhaṇḍānanda, author of the *Tattva-dīpana*, a commentary on Prakāśātman's *Pañca-pādikā-vivaraṇa*, as he refers to him as *śrīmad-ānanda-śailāhva-pañcāsyaṃ satataṃ bhaje* in the fourth verse of his *Tattva-dīpana*. Ānandagiri wrote a large number of works, which are mostly commentaries. Of these his *Iśāvāsya-bhāṣya-ṭippaṇa*, *Kenopaniṣad-bhāṣya-ṭippaṇa*, *Vākya-vivaraṇa-vyākhyā*, *Kaṭhopaniṣad-bhāṣya-ṭīkā*, *Muṇḍaka-bhāṣya-vyākhyāna*, *Māṇḍūkya-Gauḍapādīya-bhāṣya-vyākhyā*, *Taittirīya-bhāṣya-ṭippaṇa*, *Chāndogya-bhāṣya-ṭīkā*, *Tait-tirīya-bhāṣya-vārttika-ṭīkā*, *Śāstra-prakāśikā*, *Bṛhad-āraṇyaka-bhāṣya-vārttika-ṭikā*, *Bṛhad-āraṇyaka-bhāṣya-tīkā*, *Śārīraka-bhāṣya-ṭīkā* (called also *Nyāya-nirṇaya*), *Gītā-bhāṣya-vivecana*, *Pañcikaraṇa-vivaraṇa*, with a commentary called *Tattva-candrikā* by Rāma Tīrtha, a pupil of Jagannāthāśrama (latter part of the fifteenth century), and *Tarka-saṃgraha* have already been printed. But some of his other works, such as *Upadeśa-sāhasrī-vivṛti*, *Vākya-vṛtti-ṭīkā*, *Ātma-jñānopadeśa-ṭīkā*, *Svarūpa-nirṇaya-ṭīkā*, *Tripurī-prakaraṇa-ṭīkā*, *Padārtha-tattva-nirṇaya-vivaraṇa* and *Tattvāloka*, still remain to be printed. It will thus be seen that almost all his works are but commentaries on Śaṅkara's commentaries and other works. The *Tarka-saṃgraha* and *Tattvāloka* (attributed to "Janārdana," which was probably the name of Ānandagiri when he was a householder) seem to be his only two independent works[1]. Of these the manuscript of the second work, in which he refutes the doctrines of many other philosophers, including Bhāskara's *pariṇāma* doctrines, has, unfortunately, not been available to the present writer. The *Tarka-saṃgraha* is devoted almost wholly to a detailed refutation of the Vaiśeṣika philosophy. The book is divided into three chapters. In the first chapter, dealing with the criticism of substances (*dravya*), he starts with a refutation of the concepts of duality, reality (*tattva*), existence (*sattva*), non-existence, positivity (*bhāva*) and negativity (*abhāva*). Ānandojñāna then passes on to a refutation of the definition of substance and its division into nine kinds (according to the Vaiśeṣika philosophy). He then criticizes the first substance, earth, and its diverse forms, as atoms (*paramāṇu*) and molecules

[1] See Mr Tripathi's introduction to his edition of the *Tarka-saṃgraha*, Baroda, 1917.

(*dvyaṇuka*), and its grosser forms and their modified states, as bodies, senses and sense-objects, and continues to criticize the other substances such as water, fire, air, and the theory of creation and dissolution, *ākāśa*, time, space, self (*ātman*) and *manas*. In the second chapter he goes on to the criticism of qualities (*guṇa*), such as colour (*rūpa*), taste (*rasa*), smell (*gandha*), touch (*sparśa*), the effects of heat on the transformations of objects through molecular or atomic changes (*pīlu-pāka* and *piṭhara-pāka*), number (*saṅkhyā*), measure (*parimāṇa*), separateness (*pṛthaktva*), contact (*saṃyoga*), separation (*vibhāga*), the nature of knowledge, illusion and dreams, the nature of right knowledge and its means (*pramāṇa* and *pramā*), perception (*pratyakṣa*), inference (*anumāna*), concomitance (*vyāpti*), reason (*hetu*), fallacies (*hetv ābhāsa*), examples (*dṛṣṭānta*), discussions, disputations and wranglings, testimony of the scriptures (*āgama*), analogy (*upamāna*), memory, pleasure, pain, will, antipathy (*dveṣa*), effort (*prayatna*), heaviness, liquidity (*dravatva*), virtue, vice, etc. In the third chapter he refutes the notion of action, class-concept or universality (*jāti*), the relation of inherence (*samavāya*) and different kinds of negation. The thesis designed to be proved in all these refutations is the same as that of Śrīharṣa or Citsukha, viz. that in whatsoever manner the Vaiśeṣikas have attempted to divide, classify or define the world of appearances they have failed.

The conclusion at which he arrives after this long series of criticisms and refutations reminds us of Ānandabodha's conclusions in his *Nyāya-makaranda*, on which a commentary was written by his teacher Anubhūtisvarūpa Ācārya, to which reference has already been made when Ānandabodha's views were under discussion. Thus Ānandajñāna says that an illusory imposition cannot be regarded as existent (*sat*); for, since it is non-existent in the substratum (*adhiṣṭhāna*) of its appearance, it cannot be existent anywhere else. Neither can it be regarded as absolutely non-existent (*atyantāsat*); for, had it been so, it would not have appeared as immediately perceived (*aparokṣa-pratīti-virodhāt*); nor can it be regarded as existent and non-existent in the same object. The only alternative left is that the illusory imposition is indescribable in its nature[1]. This indescribability (*anirvācyatva*) means that, in whichever way one may try to describe it, it is found that none of those ways

[1] *pāriśeṣyād anirvācyam āropyam upagamyatāṃ sattvādīnāṃ prakārāṇāṃ prāg-ukta-nyāya-bādhanāt. Tarka-saṃgraha*, p. 135.

can be affirmed of it or, in other words, that it is indescribable in each and every one of those ways[1]. Now, since all appearances must have something for their cause and since that which is not a real thing cannot have a real thing as its material cause (*na ca avastuno vastu upādānam upapadyate*), and, since they are all indescribable in their nature, their cause must also be of that nature, the nescience of the substratum[2].

He then asserts that this nescience (*ajñāna*), which is the material out of which all appearances take their form, is associated with Brahman; for Brahman could not be regarded as omniscient or the knower of all (*sarva-jña*) without its association with *ajñāna*, which is the material stuff of the *all* (the knower, the means of knowledge, the objects and their relations)[3]. Everything else that appears except the one reality, the self, the Brahman, is the product of this *ajñāna*. This one *ajñāna* then can explain the infinite kinds of appearances, and there is not the slightest necessity of admitting a number of *ajñānas* in order to explain the diversity or the plurality of appearances. The many selves are thus but appearances produced by this one *ajñāna* in association with Brahman[4]. It is the one *ajñāna* that is responsible for appearances of the dream state as well as of the waking state. It is the one *ajñāna* which produces all kinds of diversity by its diversity of functions or modes of operation. If there is only one reality, which through one *ajñāna* appears in all diverse forms of appearances, how is the phenomenon of self-consciousness or self-recognition to be explained? To this difficulty Ānandajñāna's reply is that both the perceiving and the perceived self are but false appearances in the *antaḥkaraṇa* (an *ajñāna* product), and that it does not in any way infect the one true self with any kind of activity. Thus there is the one Brahman and there is one beginningless, indescribable *ajñāna* in connection with it, which is the cause of all the infinitely diverse appearances through which the former appears impure and suffers

[1] *yena yena prakāreṇa paro nirvaktum icchati*
tena tenātmanā 'yogas tad-anirvācyatā matā. Tarka-saṃgraha, p. 136.

[2] *tasmād rūpyādi-kāryasyānirvācyatvāt tad-upādānam api adhiṣṭhānājñānam upādeyam. Ibid* p. 137.

[3] *pramāṇataḥ sarvajñatve 'pi pramātṛtvasya pramāṇa-prameya-sambandhasya cājñāna-sambandham antareṇāsiddheḥ tasmin ajñānavattvam avaśyam āsrayita-vyam anyathā sarvajñatvāyogāt. Ibid*. pp. 137, 138.

[4] *ekas tāvad ātmā dvayor api āvayoḥ sampratipanno 'sti, tasya svādjñānād eva avivāda-siddhād ekasmād atiriktaṃ sarvam pratibhāti;...samastasyaiva bheda-bhānasyāpārarmārthikasyaikajñāna-sāmarthyād eva sambhavān nājñāna-bhede hetur asti. Ibid*. pp. 138, 139.

bondage, as it were, and again appears liberated, as it were, through the realization of the Vedāntic truth of the real nature of the self[1]. In fact there is neither bondage nor emancipation.

In view of the above it may be suggested that Ānandajñāna is following the same line of interpretation of the relation of *ajñāna* to Brahman which was upheld by Vācaspati and Ānandabodha. Ānandajñāna's position as an interpreter of Śaṅkara's philosophy is evident from the number of able commentaries which he wrote on the commentaries of Saṅkara and also from the references made to him by later writers. Mr Tripathi collects the names of some of these writers, as Prajñānānanda, Śeṣa Śārṅgadhara, Vādivāgīśvara, Vādīndra, Rāmānanda Sarasvatī, Sadānanda Kāśmīraka (A.D. 1547), Kṛṣṇānanda (A.D. 1650), Maheśvara Tīrtha (A.D. 1650) and others.

Philosophy of the Prakaṭārtha-vivaraṇa (A.D. 1200).

The *Prakaṭārtha-vivaraṇa* (as the writer himself calls it in the colophon of the work—*prārabhyate vivaraṇaṃ prakaṭārtham etat*) is an important commentary still in manuscript on Śaṅkara's commentary on the *Brahma-sūtra*, which the present writer had an opportunity of going through from a copy in the Adyar Library, Madras, through the kind courtesy of the Librarian, Mr T. R. Chintamani, who is intending to bring out an edition. The author, however, does not anywhere in the work reveal his own name and the references which can be found in other works are all to its name as *Prakaṭar* or to the author of the *Prakaṭārtha* (*prakaṭārtha-kāra*), and not to the author's personal name[2]. This work has been referred to by Ānandajñāna, of the thirteenth century (*Muṇḍaka*, p. 32; *Kena*, p. 23; Ānandāśrama editions A.D. 1918 and 1917), and it may well be supposed that the

[1] *Advitīyam ātma-tattvam, tatra ca anādy anirvācyam ekam ajñānam ananta-bheda-pratibhāna-nidānam, tataś cānekārtha-kaluṣitam ātma-tattvam baddham ivānubhūya-mānam, vedānta-vākyottha-tattva-sākṣātkāra-parākṛta-sakāryājñānaṃ muktam iva bhāti; paramārthato na bandho na muktir iti sakaryājñāna-nivṛtty-upalakṣitam paripūrṇam ātma-tattvam eva parama-puruṣārtha-rūpaṃ sidhyati. Tarka-saṃgraha*, p. 141.

[2] The colophon of the work runs as follows :

jñātvāpi yasya bahu-kālam acintanena
vyākhyātum akṣamatayā paritāpi cetaḥ
tasyopatāpa-haraṇāya mayeha bhāṣye
prārabhyate vivaraṇam prakaṭārtham etat.

MS. No. I, 38. 27, Govt. MSS. Library, Madras.

author of the work lived in the latter half of the twelfth century. He certainly preceded Rāmādvaya, the author of the *Vedānta-kaumudī*, who not only refers to the *Prakaṭārtha*, but has been largely influenced in many of his conceptions by the argument of this work[1]. The author of the latter holds that the indefinable *māyā* in association with pure consciousness (*cin-mātra-sambandhinī*) is the mother of all existence (*bhūta-prakṛti*). Through the reflection of pure consciousness in *māyā* is produced Iśvara (God), and by a transformation of Him there arises the creator Brahmā, and it is by the reflection of the pure consciousness in the infinite parts of this Brahmā that there arise the infinite number of individual souls through the veiling and creating functions of the *māyā*. *Māyā* or *ajñāna* is not negation, but a positive material cause, just as the earth is of the jug (*ajñānaṃ nābhāva upādānatvān mṛdvat*). But, being of the nature of veiling (*āvaraṇatvāt*) and being destructible through right knowledge (*prakāśa-heyatvāt*), it cannot be known as it is: still it may well be regarded as the positive cause of all illusions[2]. The well-known Vedāntic term *svaprakāśa* is defined in the *Prakaṭārtha* as illumination without the cognition of its own idea (*sva-saṃvin-nairapekṣeṇa sphuraṇam*). The self is to be regarded as self-revealing; for without such a supposition the revelation of the self would be inexplicable[3]. The author of the *Prakaṭārtha* then criticizes the Kumārila view of cognition as being a subjective act, inferable from the fact of a particular awareness, as also the Nyāyā-Vaiśeṣika and Prabhākara views of knowledge as an illumination of the object inhering in the subject (*ātma-samavāyī viṣaya-prakāśo jñānam*), and the Bhāskara view of knowledge as merely a particular kind of activity of the self; and he ultimately holds the view that the mind or *manas* is a substance with a preponderance of *sattva*, which has an illuminating nature, and that it is this *manas* which, being helped by the moral destiny (*adṛṣṭādi-sahakṛtam*), arrives at the place where the objects stand like a long ray of light and comes in contact with it, and then as a result thereof pure consciousness is reflected upon the object, and this leads to its cognition. Perceptual cognition, thus

[1] *Vedānta-kaumudī*, MS. transcript copy, p. 99.

[2] *āvaraṇatvāt prakāśa-heyatvād vā tamovat-svarūpeṇa pramāṇa-yogyatve 'py abhāva-vyāvṛtti-bhrama-kāraṇatvādi-dharma-viśiṣṭasya prāmāṇikatvaṃ na viru-dhyate.* MS. p. 12.

[3] *ātmā sva-prakāśas tato 'nyathā'nupapadyamānatve sati prakāśamānatvān na ya evaṃ na sa evaṃ yathā kumbhaḥ. Prakaṭārtha* MS.

defined, would be a mental transformation which can excite the revelation of an object (*manaḥ-pariṇāmaḥ samvid-vyañjako jñānam*)[1]. In the case of inference, however, the transformation of *manas* takes place without any actual touch with the objects; and there is therefore no direct excitation revealing the object; for the *manas* there, being in direct touch with the reason or the *linga*, is prevented from being in contact with the object that is inferred. There is here not an operation by which the knowledge of the object can be directly revealed, but only such a transformation of the *manas* that a rise of the idea about the object may not be obstructed[2]. The author of the *Prakaṭārtha* accepted the distinction between *māyā* and *ajñāna* as conditioning *Iśvara* and *jīva.*

Vimuktātman (A.D. 1200).

Vimuktātman, a disciple of Avyayātman Bhagavat Pūjyapāda, wrote his *Īṣṭa-siddhi* probably not later than the early years of the thirteenth century. He is quoted and referred to by Madhusūdana in his *Advaita-siddhi* and by Rāmādvaya in his *Vedānta-kaumudī* of the fourteenth century. It was commented upon by Jñānottama, the teacher of Citsukha, and this commentary is called *Īṣṭa-siddhi-vyākhyā* or *Iṣṭa-siddhi-vivaraṇa.* For reasons stated elsewhere Jñānottama could not have flourished later than the latter half of the thirteenth century. Vimuktātman wrote also another work, called *Pramāṇa-vṛtti-nirṇaya*, to which he refers in his *Īṣṭa-siddhi* (MS. p. 72). The work has not yet been published, and the manuscript from the Adyar Library, which is a transcript copy of a manuscript of the Nāḍuvil Maṭham, Cochin State, and which has been available to the present writer, is very fragmentary in many parts; so much so, that it is often extremely difficult to follow properly the meaning of the discussions. The work is divided into eight chapters, and is devoted in a very large part to discussions relating to the analysis of illusions in the Vedānta school and in the other schools of philosophy. This work is to be regarded as one of the four traditional *Siddhis*, such as

[1] MS. p. 54.

[2] *upalabdha-sambandhārthā kāreṇa pariṇatam mano 'nāvabhāsa-vyāvṛtti-mātraphalam, na tu saṃvid-vyañjakam lingādi-samvid-vyavadhāna-pratibandhāt.* MS. p. 54.

It is easy to see how Dharmarājādhvarīndra elaborated his Vedāntic theory of perception and inference with these and other data worked out by his predecessors.

the *Brahma-siddhi* by Maṇḍana, the *Naiṣkarmya-siddhi* by Sureśvara, the *Īṣṭa-siddhi* by Vimuktātman and the *Advaita-siddhi* by Madhusūdana. Hitherto only the *Naiṣkarmya-siddhi* and the *Advaita-siddhi* have been published. The *Brahma-siddhi* is expected to be published soon in Madras; but as yet the present writer is not aware of any venture regarding this important work.

The work begins with the interpretation of a salutation made by the author, in which he offers his adoration to that birthless, incognizable, infinite intuitive consciousness of the nature of selfjoy which is the canvas on which the illusory world-appearance has been painted. Thus he starts the discussion regarding the nature of the ultimate reality as pure intuitive consciousness (*anubhūti*). Nothing can be beginningless and eternal, except pure consciousness. The atoms are often regarded as beginningless ; but, since they have colours and other sense-properties, they are like other objects of nature, and they have parts also, as without them no combination of atoms would be possible. Only that can be indivisible which is partless and beginningless, and it is only the intuitive consciousness that can be said to be so. The difference between consciousness and other objects is this, that, while the latter can be described as the "this" or the object, the former is clearly not such. But, though this difference is generally accepted, dialectical reasoning shows that the two are not intrinsically different. There cannot logically be any difference between the perceiving principle (*dṛk*) and the perceived (*dṛśya*); for the former is unperceived (*adṛśyatvāt*). No difference can be realized between a perceived and an unperceived entity; for all difference relates two cognized entities. But it may be argued that, though the perceiver may not be cognized, yet he is self-luminous, and therefore the notion of difference ought to be manifested. A reply to this objection involves a consideration regarding the nature of difference. If difference were of the nature of the entities that differed, then difference should not be dependent on a reference to another (*na svarūpa-dṛṣṭih prati-yogy-apekṣā*). The difference has thus to be regarded as a characteristic (*dharma*) different from the nature of the differing entities and cognized by a distinct knowing process like colours, tastes, etc.[1] But this view also is not correct, since it is

[1] *tasmāt kathañcit bhinno jñānāntara-gamyo rūpa-rasādivad bhedo 'bhyupeyaḥ.* Adyar *Īṣṭa-siddhi* MS. p. 5.

difficult to admit "difference" as an entity different from the differing entities; for such a difference would involve another difference by which it is known, and that another and that another, we should have an infinite regress; and the same objection applies to the admission of mutual negation as a separate entity. This being so, it is difficult to imagine how "difference" or mutual negation between the perceiver and the perceived can be cognized; for it is impossible that there should be any other cognition by which this "difference," or mutual negation which has the perceiver as one of its alternating poles, could be perceived[1]. Moreover, the self-luminous perceiving power is always present, and it is impossible that it could be negated—a condition without which neither difference nor negation could be possible. Moreover, if it is admitted that such a difference is cognized, then that very fact proves that it is not a characteristic of the perceiving self. If this difference is admitted to be self-luminous, then it would not await a reference to another, which is a condition for all notions of difference or mutual negation. Therefore, "difference" or "mutual negation" cannot be established, either as the essence of the perceiving self or as its characteristics; and as there is no other way in which this difference can be conceived, it is clear that there is no difference between the perceiving self and its characteristics.

Again, negation is defined as the non-perception of a perceivable thing; but the perceiving self is of the very nature of perception, and its non-perception would be impossible. Admitting for the sake of argument that the perceiving self could be negated, how could there be any knowledge of such a negation? for without the self there could be no perception, as it is itself of the nature of perception. So the notion of the negation of the perceiving self cannot be anything but illusion. Thus the perceiving self and the perceived (*dṛk* and *dṛśya*) cannot be differentiated from each other. The difficulty, however, arises that, if the perceiving self and the perceived were identical, then the infinite limitations and differences that are characteristic of the perceived would also be characteristic of the perceiver; and there are the further objections to such a supposition that it is against all ordinary usage and experience. It

[1] *evaṃ ca sati na dṛg-dṛśyayor bhedo draṣṭum śakyaḥ*
nāpy anyonyābhāvaḥ na hi dṛśaḥ svayaṃ dṛṣṭeḥ
prati-yogy-apekṣa-dṛṣṭy-antara-dṛśyaṃ rūpāntaraṃ svaṃ
samasti svayaṃ dṛṣṭitva-hānāt. MS. p. 6.

may be argued that the two are identical, since they are both experienced simultaneously (*sahopalambha-niyamāt*); but the reply is that, as two are experienced and not one, they cannot be regarded as identical, for in the very experience of the two their difference is also manifested[1]. In spite of such obvious contradiction of experience one could not venture to affirm the identity of the perceiver and the perceived[2]. The maxim of identity of the perceiver and the perceived because of simultaneous perception cannot be regarded as true; for, firstly, the perceiver is never a cognized object, and the perceived is never self-luminous, secondly, the perceiver is always self-revealing, but not so the perceived, and, thirdly, though the "perceived" cannot be revealed without the perceiver, the latter is always self-revealed. There is thus plainly no simultaneity of the perceiver and the perceived. When a perceived object *A* is illuminated in consciousness, the other objects *B*, *C*, *D*, etc. are not illuminated, and, when the perceived object *B* is illuminated, *A* is not illuminated, but the consciousness (*samvid*) is always self-illuminated; so no consciousness can be regarded as being always qualified by a particular objective content; for, had it been so, that particular content would always have stood self-revealed[3]. Moreover, each particular cognition (e.g. awareness of blue) is momentary and self-revealed and, as such, cannot be the object of any other cognition; and, if any particular awareness could be the object of any other awareness, then it would not be awareness, but a mere object, like a jug or a book. There is thus an intrinsic difference between awareness and the object, and so the perceiver, as pure awareness, cannot be identified with its object[4]. It has already been pointed out that the perceiver and the perceived cannot be regarded as different, and now it is shown that they cannot be regarded as identical. There is another alternative, viz. that they may be both identical and different (which is the *bhedābheda* view of Bhāskara and Rāmānuja and others), and Vimuktātman tries to show that

[1] *abhede saha-bhānāyogād dvayor hi saha-bhānam na ekasyaiva na hi dṛśaiva dṛk saha bhātīti bhavatāpy ucyate, nāpi dṛśyenaiva dṛśyaṃ saha bhātīti kintu dṛg-dṛśyayoḥ saha bhānam ucyate atas tayor bhedo bhāty eva.* MS. p. 25.

[2] *tasmāt sarva-vyavahāra-lopa-prasaṅgān na bhedo dṛg-dṛśyaoḥ. Ibid.*

[3] *kiṃ vidyud-viśeṣitatā nāma saṃvidaḥ svarūpam uta saṃvedyasya, yadi samvidaḥ sāpi bhāty eva saṃvid-bhānāt saṃvedya-svarūpaṃ cet tadā bhānān na saṃvido bhānam. Ibid.* p. 27.

[4] *asaṃvedyaiva saṃvit samvedyaṃ cāsaṃvid eva, ataḥ saṃvedyasya ghaṭasukhādeḥ saṃvidaś cābheda-gandho 'pi na pramāṇavān. Ibid.* p. 31.

this alternative is also impossible and that the perceiver and the perceived cannot be regarded as being both identical and different. The upholder of the *bhedābheda* view is supposed to say that, though the perceiver and the perceived cannot, as such, be regarded as identical, yet they may be regarded as one in their nature as Brahman. But in reply to this it may be urged that, if they are both one and identical with Brahman, there would be no difference between them. If it is argued that their identity with Brahman is in another form, then also the question arises whether their forms as perceiver and perceived are identical with the form in which they are identical with Brahman; and no one is aware of any form of the perceiver and the perceived other than their forms as such, and therefore it cannot be admitted that in spite of their difference they have any form in which they are one and identical. If again it is objected that it is quite possible that an identical entity should have two different forms, then also the question arises whether these forms are one, different or both identical with that entity and different. In the first alternative the forms would not be different; in the second they would not be one with the entity. Moreover, if any part of the entity be identical with any particular form, it cannot also be identical with other forms; for then these different forms would not be different from one another; and, if again the forms are identical with the entity, how can one distinguish the entity (*rūpin*) from the forms (*rūpa*)? In the third alternative the question arises whether the entity is identical with one particular form of it and different from other forms, or whether it is both identical with the same form and different. In the first case each form would have two forms, and these again other two forms in which they are identical and different, and these other two forms, and so on, and we should have infinite regress: and the same kind of infinite regress would appear in the relation between the entity and its forms. For these and similar reasons it is impossible to hold that the perceiver and the perceived are different as such and yet one and identical as Brahman.

If the manifold world is neither different nor identical nor both different and identical with the perceiver, what then is its status? The perceiver is indeed the same as pure perception and pure bliss, and, if it is neither identical nor different nor both identical with the manifold world and different, the manifold world must necessarily be unsubstantial (*avastu*); for, if it had any substantiality, it might have been related in one of the above three ways of relation. But, if it is unsubstantial, then none of the above objections would apply. But it may again be objected that, if the world were unsubstantial, then both our common experience and our practical dealing with this world would be contradicted. To this Vimuktātman's reply is that, since the world is admitted to be made up of *māyā* (*māyā-nirmitatvābhyupagamāt*), and since the effects of *māyā* canot be regarded either as substantial or as unsubstantial, none of the above objections would be applicable to this view. Since the manifold world is not a substance, its admission cannot disturb the monistic view, and, since it is not unsubstantial, the facts of experience may also be justified[1]. As an instance of such an appearance which is neither *vastu* (substance) nor *avastu*, one may refer to dream-appearances, which are not regarded as unreal because of their nature as neither substance nor not-substance, but because they are contradicted in experience. Just as a canvas is neither the material of the picture painted on it nor a constituent of the picture, and just as the picture canot be regarded as being a modification of the canvas in the same way as a jug is a modification of clay, or as a change of quality, like the redness in ripe mangoes, and just as the canvas was there before the painting, and just as it would remain even if the painting were washed away, whereas the painting would not be there without the canvas, so the pure consciousness also is related to this world-appearance, which is but a painting of *māyā* on it[2].

Māyā is unspeakable and indescribable (*anirvacanīyā*), not as different from both being and non-being, but as involving the characters of both being and non-being. It is thus regarded as a power of ignorance (*avidyā-śakti*) which is the material cause of all objects of perception otherwise called matter (*sarva-jaḍopādāna-bhūtā*). But, just as fire springing from bamboos may burn up the same bamboos even to their very roots, so Brahma-knowledge, which is itself a product of ignorance and its processes, destroys the self-same ignorance from which it was produced and its processes and at last

[1] *prapañcasya vastutvābhāvān nādvaita-hāniḥ avastutvābhāvāc ca pratyakṣādy-aprāmāṇyam apy-ukta-doṣābhāvāt.* MS. p. 64.

[2] *yatha citrasya bhittiḥ sākṣāt nopādānam nāpi sahajaṃ citraṃ tasyāh nāpyavasthāntaraṃ mṛda iva ghaṭādiḥ nāpi guṇāntarāgamaḥ āmrasyeva raktatādiḥ na cāsyāh janmādiś citrāt prāg ūrdhaṃ ca bhāvāt, yady api bhittiṃ vinā na citraṃ na bhāti tathāpi na sā citraṃ vinā bhāti ity evam-ādy-anubhūtir bhitti-jagac-citrayor yojyam. Ibid.* p. 73.

itself subsides and leaves the Brahman to shine in its own radiance[1]. The functions of the *pramāṇas*, which are all mere processes of ignorance, *ajñāna* or *avidyā*, consist only in the removal of obstructions veiling the illumination of the self-luminous consciousness, just as the digging of a well means the removal of all earth that was obstructing the omnipresent *ākāśa* or space; the *pramāṇas* have thus no function of manifesting the self-luminous consciousness, and only remove the veiling *ajñāna*[2]. So Brahma-knowledge also means the removal of the last remnants of *ajñāna*, after which Brahma-knowledge as conceptual knowledge, being the last vestige of *ajñāna*, also ceases of itself. This cessation of *ajñāna* is as unspeakable as *ajñāna* itself. Unlike Maṇḍana, Vimuktātman does not consider *avidyā* to be merely subjective, but regards it as being both subjective and objective, involving within it not only all phenomena, but all their mutual relations and also the relation with which it is supposed to be related to the pure consciousness, which is in reality beyond all relations. Vimuktātman devotes a large part of his work to the criticism of the different kinds of theories of illusion (*khyāti*), and more particularly to the criticism of *anyathākhyāti*. These contain many new and important points; but, as the essential features of these theories of illusion and their criticisms have already been dealt with in the tenth chapter of the first volume, it is not desirable to enter into these fresh criticisms of Vimuktātman, which do not involve any new point of view in Vedāntic interpretation. He also deals with some of the principal Vedāntic topics of discussion, such as the nature of bondage, emancipation, and the reconciliation of the pluralistic experience of practical life with the monistic doctrine of the Vedānta; but, as there are not here any strikingly new modes of approach, these may be left out in the present work.

Rāmādvaya (A.D. 1300).

Rāmādvaya, a pupil of Advayāśrama, wrote an important work, called *Vedānta-kaumudī*, in four chapters, in which he discussed in a polemical way many Vedāntic problems while dealing with the subject matter of Śaṅkara's commentary on the first four topics of the *Brahma-sūtra*. The work has not yet been published; but at least one manuscript of it is available in the Government

[1] MS. p. 137.
[2] *Ibid.* p. 143.

Oriental Manuscript Library, Madras: this through the kindness of the Curator the present author had the opportunity of utilizing. Rāmādvaya also wrote a commentary on his *Vedānta-kaumudī*, called *Vedānta-kaumudī-vyākhyāna*, a manuscript of the first chapter of which has been available to the present writer in the library of the Calcutta Asiatic Society. These are probably the only manuscripts of this work known till now. The date of the writing of the copy of the *Vedānta-kaumudī-vyākhyāna* is given by the copyist Śeṣanṛsiṃha as A.D. 1512. It is therefore certain that the work cannot have been written later than the fifteenth century. Rāmādvaya in the course of his discussions refers to many noted authors on Nyāya and Vedānta, none of whom are later than the thirteenth century. Vimuktātman, author of the *Iṣṭa-siddhi*, has been placed by the present author in the early half of the thirteenth century; but Rāmādvaya always refers to him approvingly, as if his views were largely guided by his; he also in his *Vedānta-kaumudī-vyākhyāna* (MS. p. 14) refers to Janārdana, which is Ānandajñāna's name as a householder; but Janārdana lived in the middle of the thirteenth century; it seems therefore probable that Rāmādvaya lived in the first half of the fourteenth century.

In the enunciation of the Vedāntic theory of perception and inference Rāmādvaya seems to have been very much under the influence of the views of the author of the *Prakaṭārtha*; for, though he does not refer to his name in this connection, he repeats his very phrases with a slight elaboration[1]. Just as the cloudless sky covers itself with clouds and assumes various forms, so the pure consciousness veils itself with the indefinable *avidyā* and appears in diverse limited forms. It is this consciousness that forms the real ground of all that is known. Just as a spark of fire cannot manifest itself as fire if there are no fuels as its condition, so the pure consciousness, which is the underlying reality of all objects, cannot illuminate them if there are not the proper conditions to help it in its work[2]. Such a conditioning factor is found in

[1] See *Vedānta-kaumudī*, MS. transcript copy, pp. 36 and 47.

[2] Rāmādvaya refers here to the *daharādhikaraṇa* of Śaṅkara's commentary on the *Brahma-sūtra*, presumably to I. 3, 19, where Śaṅkara refers to the supposed distinction between the individual soul (*jīva*) and Brahman. Here Śaṅkara says that his commentary is directed towards the regulation of those views, both outside and inside the circle of Upaniṣadic interpreters, which regard individual souls as real (*apare tu vādinaḥ*

manas, which is of the stuff of pure *sattva*: on the occasion of sense-object contact this manas, being propelled by the moral destiny (*adṛṣṭādi-kṣubdhaṃ*), transforms itself into the form of a long ray reaching to the object itself[1]. The pure consciousness, as conditioned or limited by the *antaḥkaraṇa* (*antaḥkaraṇāvacchinnaṃcaitanyaṃ*), does by such a process remove its veil of *avidyā*, (though in its limited condition as individual soul this *avidyā* formed its own body), and the object also being in contact with it is manifested by the same process. The two manifestations of the subject and the object, having taken place in the same process (*vṛtti*) there, are joined together in the same cognition as "this object is known by me" (*vṛtter ubhayasaṃlagnatvāc ca tad-abhivyakta-caitanya-syāpi tathātvena mayedam viditam iti saṃśleṣa-pratyayaḥ*); and, as its other effect, the consciousness limited by the *antaḥkaraṇa*, transformed into the form of the process (*vṛtti*) of right knowledge (*pramā*), appears as the cognizer (*vṛtti-lakṣaṇa-pramāśrayāntaḥ-karaṇāvacchinnas tat-pramātetyapi vyapadiśyate*)[2]. The object also attains a new status in being manifested and is thus known as the object (*karma-kārakābhivyaktaṃ. ca tat prakāśātmanā phalavyapadeśa-bhāk*). In reality it is the underlying consciousness that manifests the *vṛtti* transformation of the *antaḥkaraṇa*; but, as it is illusorily identified with the *antaḥkaraṇa* (*antaḥkaraṇa-caitanyayor aikyādhyāsāt*), like fire and iron in the heated iron, it is also identified with the *vṛtti* transformation of the *antaḥkaraṇa*, and, as the *vṛtti* becomes superimposed on the object, by manifesting the *vṛtti* it also manifests the object, and thus apart from the subjective illumination as awareness, there is also the objective fact of an illumination of the object (*evaṃ vṛtti-vyañjakam api taptā-yaḥ-piṇḍa-nyāyena tad-ekatām ivāptaṃ vṛttivad-viṣaya-prākaṭyāt-manā sampadyate*)[3]. The moments in the cognitive process in perception according to Rāmādvaya may thus be described. The

pāramārthikam eva jaivaṃ rūpam iti manyante asmadīyāś ca kecit). Such a view militates against the correct understanding of the self as the only reality which through *avidyā* manifests itself as individual souls and with its removal reveals itself in its real nature in right knowledge as *parameśvara*, just as an illusory snake shows itself as a piece of rope. *Parameśvara*, the eternal unchangeable and upholding consciousness, is the one reality which, like a magician, appears as many through *avidyā*. There is no consciousness other than this (*eka eva parameśvaraḥ kūṭastha-nityo vijñāna-dhātur avidyayā-māyayā māyāvivad anekadhā vibhāvyate nānyo vijñāna-dhātur asti*).

[1] This passage seems to be borrowed directly from the *Prakaṭārtha*, as may be inferred from their verbal agreement. But it may well be that both the *Vedāntakaumudī* and the *Prakaṭārtha* borrowed it from the *Pañca-pādikā-vivaraṇa*.

[2] *Vedānta-kaumudī*, MS. transcript copy, p. 36.

[3] *Ibid.* p. 37.

sense-object contact offers an occasion for the moral destiny (*adṛṣṭa*) to stir up the *antaḥkaraṇa*, and, as a result thereof, the *antaḥkaraṇa* or mind is transformed into a particular state called *vṛtti*. The pure consciousness underlying the *antaḥkaraṇa* was lying dormant and veiled, as it were, and, as soon as there is a transformation of the *antaḥkaraṇa* into a *vṛtti*, the consciousness brightens up and overcomes for the moment the veil that was covering it. The *vṛtti* thus no longer veils the underlying consciousness, but serves as a transparent transmitter of the light of consciousness to the object on which the *vṛtti* is superimposed, and, as a result thereof, the object has an objective manifestation, separate from the brightening up of consciousness at the first moment of the *vṛtti* transformation. Now, since the *vṛtti* joins up the subjective brightening up of consciousness and the objective illumination of the object, these two are joined up (*saṃśleṣa-pratyaya*) and this results in the cognition "this object is known by me"; and out of this cognition it is possible to differentiate the knower as the underlying consciousness, as limited by the *antaḥkaraṇa* as transformed into the *vṛtti*, and the known as that which has been objectively illuminated. In the *Vedānta-paribhāṣā* we hear of three consciousnesses (*caitanya*), the *pramātṛ-caitanya* (the consciousness conditioned by the *antahkaraṇa*), the *pramāṇa-caitanya* (the same consciousness conditioned by the *vṛtti* of the *antaḥkaraṇa*), and the *viṣaya-caitanya* (the same consciousness conditioned by the object). According to this perception (*pratyakṣa*) can be characterized either from the point of view of cognition (*jñāna-gata-pratyakṣatva*) or from the point of view of the object, both being regarded as two distinct phases, cognitional and objective, of the same perceptual revelation. From the point of view of cognition it is defined as the non-distinction (*abheda*) of the *pramāṇa-caitanya* from the *viṣaya-caitanya* through spatial superimposition of the *vṛtti* on the object. Perception from the point of view of the object (*viṣaya-gata-pratyakṣatva*) is defined as the non-distinction of the object from the *pramātṛ-caitanya* or the perceiver, which is consciousness conditioned by the *antaḥkaraṇa*. This latter view, viz. the definition of perception from the point of view of the object as the non-distinction of the object from the consciousness as limited by *antaḥkaraṇa* (*ghaṭāder antaḥkaraṇāvacchinna-caitanyābhedaḥ*), is open to the serious objection that really the non-distinction of the object (or the consciousness conditioned by the *antaḥkaraṇa—antaḥkaraṇāvacchinna-caitanya*) but with the cognition (*pramāṇa-caitanya or vṛtti-caitanya*); for the cognition or the *vṛtti* intervenes between the object and the perceiver, and the object is in immediate contact with the *vṛtti* and not with the perceiver (*antaḥkaraṇāvacchinna-caitanya*). That this is so is also admitted by Dharmarāja Adhvarīndra, son of Rāmakṛṣṇa Adhvarin, in his *Śikhā-maṇi* commentary on the *Vedānta-paribhāṣā* [1]. But he tries to justify Dharmarāja Adhvarīndra by pointing out that he was forced to define *viṣaya-gata-pratyakṣatva* as non-distinction of the object from the subject, since this view was taken in Prakāśātman's *Vivaraṇa* and also in other traditional works on Vedānta[2]. This however seems to be an error. For the passage of the *Vivaraṇa* to which reference is made here expounds an entirely different view[3]. It says there that the perceptibility of the object consists in its directly and immediately qualifying the cognitional state or sense-knowledge (*saṃvid*)[4]. That other traditional Vedāntic interpreters entirely disagreed with the view of Dharmarāja Adhvarīndra is also evident from the account of the analysis of the perceptual process given by Rāmādvaya. Rāmādvaya says, as has just been pointed out, that it is the illuminated cognitive process, or the *vṛtti*, that has the subject and the object at its two poles and thus unites the subject and the object in the complex subject-predicate form "this is known by me." The object is thus illuminated by the *vṛtti*, and it is not directly with the subject, but with the *vṛtti*, that the object is united. Dharmarāja Adhvarīndra himself raises an objection against his interpretation, that it might be urged, if in perception there was non-distinction of the object from the subject, then in perceiving an object, e.g. a book, one should feel "I am the book," and not "I perceive the book" in reply to such an objection he says that in the perceptual process

[1] *yad vā yogyatve sati viṣaya-caitanyābhinna-pramāṇa-caitanya-viṣayatvaṃ ghaṭāder viṣayasya pratyakṣatvaṃ tathāpi viṣayasyāparokṣatvaṃ samvidabhedāt iti vivaraṇe tatra tatra ca sāṃpradāyikaiḥ pramātrabhedasyaiva viṣayapratyakṣa-lakṣaṇatvenābhidhānād evaṃ uktam. Śikhā-maṇi* on *Vedānta-paribhāṣā*, p. 75, Bombay, 1911, Venkatesvara Press.

[2] *Ibid.*

[3] *Tasmād avyavadhānena saṃvid-upādhitayāparokṣatā viṣayasya. Pañcapādikā-vivaraṇa*, p. 50, Benares, 1892.

[4] It should be noted here that *saṃvid* means cognitional idea or sense-knowledge and not the perceiver (*antaḥkaraṇāvacchinna-caitanya*), as the author of the *Śikhāmaṇi* says. Thus Akhaṇḍānanda in his *Tattva-dīpana* commentary explains the word *saṃvid* as *saṃvic-chabdena indriyārtha-samprayoga-ja-jñānasya vivakṣitatvāt. Tattva-dīpana*, p. 194, Benares, 1902.

there is only a non-distinction between the consciousness underlying the object and the consciousness underlying the perceiver, and this non-distinction, being non-relational, does not imply the assertion of a relation of identity resulting in the notion "I am the book"[1]. This is undoubtedly so, but it is hardly an answer to the objection that has been raised. It is true that the object and the subject are both but impositions of *avidyā* on one distinctionless pure consciousness; but that fact can hardly be taken as an explanation of the various modes of experiences of the complex world of subject-object experience. The difference of the Vedāntic view of perception, as expounded in the *Pañca-pādikā-vivaraṇa*, from the Buddhist idealism (*vijñāna-vāda*) consists in this, that, while the Buddhists did not accord any independent status to objects as outside the ideas or percepts, the Vedānta accepted the independent manifestation of the objects in perception in the external world[2]. There is thus a distinction between visional percept and the object; but there is also a direct and immediate connection between them, and it is this immediate relationship of the object to its awareness that constitutes the perceptivity of the object (*avyavadhānena samvid-upādhitā aparokṣatā viṣayasya—Vivaraṇa*, p. 50). The object is revealed in perception only as an object of awareness, whereas the awareness and the subject reveal themselves directly and immediately and not as an object of any further intuition or inference (*prameyaṃ karmatvena aparokṣam pramātṛ-pramitī punar aparokṣe eva kevalaṃ na karmatayā*)[3].

The views of the *Vedānta-kaumudī*, however, cannot be regarded as original in any sense, since they are only a reflection of the exposition of the subject in Padmapāda's *Pañca-pādikā* and Prakāśātman's *Pañca-pādikā-vivaraṇa*. The development of the whole theory of perception may be attributed to the *Pañca-pādikā-vivaraṇa*, since all the essential points of the perceptual theory can be traced in that work. Thus it holds that all the world objects are veiled by *avidyā*; that, as the *antaḥkaraṇa* is transformed into states by superimposition on objects, it is illuminated by the underlying consciousness; and that through the spatial contact with the objects the veil of the objects is removed by these *antaḥkaraṇa* transformations; there are thus two illuminations, namely

[1] *Vedānta-paribhāṣā*, pp. 76, 77.

[2] *na ca vijñānābhedād eva āparokṣyam avabhāsate bahiṣṭvasyāpi rajatāder āparokṣyāt. Pañca-pādikā-vivaraṇa*, p. 50.

[3] *Pañca-pādikā*, p. 17, Benares, 1891.

of the *antaḥkaraṇa* transformations (called *vṛtti* in the *Vedānta-kaumudī*, and *Vedānta-paribhāṣā* and pure consciousness); to the question that, if there were unity of the consciousness underlying the object and the consciousness underlying the *antaḥkaraṇa* (i.e. the subject) and the consciousness underlying the *antaḥkaraṇa* modification (or *vṛtti*), there would be nothing to explain the duality in perception (e.g. "I perceive the book," and not "I am the book," and it is only the latter form that could be expected from the unity of the three consciousnesses), Prakāśātman's reply is that, since the unity of the object-consciousness with the *antaḥkaraṇa*-consciousness (subject) is effected through the modification or the *vṛtti* of the *antaḥkaraṇa* and, since the *antaḥkaraṇa* is one with its *vṛtti*, the *vṛtti* operation is rightly attributed to the *antaḥkaraṇa* as its agent, and this is illuminated by the consciousness underlying the *antaḥkaraṇa* resulting in the perception of the knower as distinguished from the illumination of object to which the operation of the *vṛtti* is directed in spatial superimposition—the difference between the subject and the object in perception is thus due to the difference in the mode or the condition of the *vṛtti* with reference to the subject and the object[1].This is exactly the interpretation of the *Vedānta-kaumudī*, and it has been pointed out above that the explanations of the *Vedānta-paribhāṣā* are largely different therefrom and are in all probability inexact. As this unity is effected between individual subjects (consciousness limited by specific *antaḥkaraṇas*) and individual objects (consciousness limited by specific *avidyā* materials constituting the objects) through the *vṛtti*, it can result only in revelation of a particular subject and a particular object and not in the revelation of all subjects and all objects[2]. This has been elaborated into the view that there is an infinite number of *ajñāna*-veils, and that each cognitive illumination removes only one *ajñāna* corresponding to the illumination of one object[3]. But this also is not an original contribution of Rāmādvaya, since it was also propounded by his predecessor Ānandajñāna in his *Tarka-*

[1] See *Pañca-pādikā-vivaraṇa*, p. 70, and *Tattva-dīpana*, pp. 256-259, Benares, 1902.

[2] *etat pramātṛ-caitanyābhinnatayaiva abhivyaktaṃ tad viṣaya-caitanyaṃ na pramātr-antara-caitanyābhedena abhivyaktam ato na sarveṣām avabhāsyatvam. Pañca-pādikā-vivaraṇa*, p. 71.

[3] *yāvanti jñānāni tāvanti sva-tantrāṇi para-tantrāṇi vā ajñānāni tato na doṣaḥ. Vedānta-kaumudī*, MS. copy, p. 43.

saṃgraha and by others[1]. The upshot of the whole discussion is that on the occasion of a cognitive operation of the mind both the mind and the cognitive operation become enlivened and illuminated by the indwelling pure consciousness as subject-consciousness and awareness, and through contact with this cognitive operation the object also becomes revealed not as a mere content of awareness, but as an objective fact shining forth in the external world. Cognition of objects is thus not a mere quality of the self as knower, as the Nyāya holds, nor is there any immediate contact of the self with the object (the contact being only through the cognitive operation); the cognition is also not to be regarded as unperceived movement, modification or transforation of the self which may be inferred from the fact of the enlightenment of the object (*jñātatā*), as Kumārila held, nor is the illumination of the object to be regarded mere form of awareness without there being a corresponding as a objective entity (*viṣayābhivyaktir nāma vijñāne tad-ākārollekha-mātraṃ na bahir-aṅga-rūpasya vijñānābhivyāptiḥ*), as is held by the Buddhist subjective idealists. The cognitive operation before its contact with the object is a mere undifferentiated awareness, having only an objective reference and devoid of all specifications of sense characters, which later on assumes the sense characteristics in accordance with the object with which it comes in contact. It must be noted, however, that the cognitive operation is not an abstract idea, but an active transformation of a real *sattva* stuff, the mind (*antaḥkaraṇa*)[2]. Since in the continuous perception of the same object we have only a rapid succession of cognitive acts, each

[1] The theory is that there is an infinite number of the *ajñāna*-veils; as soon as there is the *vṛtti*-object contact, the veil is removed and the object is illuminated; the next moment there is again an *ajñāna*-veil covering the object, and again there is the *vṛtti*-object contact, and again illumination of the object, and thus there is very quick succession of veils and their removals, as the perception of the object continues in time. On account of the rapidity of this succession it is not possible to notice it (*vṛtti-vijñānasya sāvayavatvāc ca hrāsa-daśāyāṃ dīpa-jvālāyā iva tamo 'ntaraṃ mohāntaram āvaritum viṣayaṃ pravartate tato' pi kramamāṇaṃ kṣaṇāntare sāmagry-anusāreṇa vijñānāntaraṃ viṣay āvaraṇa-bhaṅgenaiva sva-kāryaṃ karoti, tathā sarvāṇy api atiśaighryāt tu jñāna-bhedavad āvaraṇāntaraṃ na lakṣyate. Vedānta-kaumudī*, MS. copy, p. 46). This view of the *Vedānta-kaumudī* is different from the view of the *Vedānta-paribhāṣā*, which holds that in the case of continuous perception of the same object there are not different successive awarenesses, but there is *one* unchanged continuous *vṛtti* and not different *vṛttis* removing different *ajñānas* (*kiñ ca siddhānte dhārā-vāhika-buddhi-sthale na jñānā-bhedaḥ kintu yāvād ghaṭa-sphuraṇam tāvad ghaṭākārāntaḥkaraṇa-vrttir ekaiva na tu nānā vṛtteḥ sva-virodhi-vṛtty-utpattiparyaṇtaṃ sthāyitvābhyupagamāt. Vedānta-paribhāṣā*, pp. 26, 27, Bombay, 1911).

[2] *ataḥ sāvayava-sattvātmakam antaḥkaraṇam eva anudbhūta-rūpa-sparśam adṛśyam aspṛśyaṃ ca viṣayākāreṇa pariṇamate, Vedānta-kaumudi*, MS. copy, p. 42.

dispelling an intellectual darkness enfolding the object before its illumination, there is no separate perception of time as an entity standing apart from the objects; perception of time is but the perception of the succession of cognitive acts, and what is regarded as the present time is that in which the successive time-moments have been fused together into one concrete duration: it is this concrete duration, which is in reality but a fusion of momentary cognitive acts and awarenesses, that is designated as the present time[1]. According to Rāmādvaya the definition of perception would not therefore include the present time as a separate element over and above the object as a separate datum of perception; for his view denies time as an objective entity and regards it only as a mode of cognitive process.

Rāmādvaya's definition of right knowledge is also different from that of Dharmarāja Adhvarīndra. Rāmādvaya defines right knowledge (*pramā*) as experience which does not wrongly represent its object (*yathārthānubhavaḥ pramā*), and he defines the instrument of right knowledge as that which leads to it[2]. Verbally this definition is entirely different from that of Dharmarāja Adhvarīndra, with whom the two conditions of *pramā* or right knowledge are that it should not be acquaintance with what was already known (*anadhigata*) and that it should be uncontradicted[3]. The latter condition, however, seems to point only to a verbal difference from Rāmādvaya's definition; but it may really mean very much more than a verbal difference. For, though want of contradiction (Dharmarāja Adhvarīndra's condition) and want of wrong representation (Rāmādvaya's condition) may mean the same thing, yet in the former case the definition of truth becomes more subjective than in the latter case; for want of wrong representation refers to an objective correspondence and objective certainty. An awareness may wrongly represent an object, but yet may not be found contradicted in the personal history of one or even many observers. Such a definition of truth becomes very relative, since its limits are not fixed by correspondence with its object. Considering the fact

[1] *na kālaḥ pratyakṣa-gocaraḥ...stambhādir eva prāg-abhāva-nivṛtti-pradhvaṃsānutpatti-rūpo vartamānaḥ tad-avacchinaḥ kālo' pi vartamānaḥ sa ca tathāvidho' neka-jñāna-sādhāraṇa eva, na caitāvatā jñāna-yaugapadyāpattiḥ ṣūksmakālāpekṣayā kramasambhavāt, na ca sūkṣma-kālopādhīnām apratītiḥ kārya-krameṇaiva unnīyamānatvāt. Vedānta-kaumudī*, MS. copy, pp. 20–22.

[2] *Ibid.* p.16.

[3] *tatra smṛti-vyāvṛttam pramātvam anadhigatābādhitārtha-viṣaya-jñānatvam. Vedānta-paribhāṣā*, p. 20.

that the Vedānta speaks of a real spatial superimposition of the modification of the *antaḥkaraṇa* (which is its cognitive operation) on the object, a Vedānta definition of truth might well be expected to be realistic and not subjectivistic or relativistic. The idealism of the Vedānta rests content in the view that, however realistic these cognitive relations to objects may be, they are impositions and appearances which have as their ultimate ground one changeless consciousness. The definition of *pramā* by Rāmādvaya as an awareness which does not give a wrong representation (*yathārthā-nubhava*) of objects could not be found faulty because of the fact that according to the Vedānta all dual experience of the world was false; for, though it was ultimately so, for all practical purposes it had a real existence, and Rāmādvaya refers to the *Iṣṭa-siddhi* to justify his view on this point.

As to the other point, viz. that a *pramā* must always be that which acquaints us with what is unknown before (*anadhigata*), Rāmādvaya definitely repudiates such a suggestion[1]. He says that it often happens that we perceive things that we perceived before, and this makes recognition possible, and, if we deny that these are cases of right knowledge, we shall have to exclude much that is universally acknowledged as right knowledge. Also it cannot be conceived how in the case of the continuous perception of an object there can be new qualities accruing to the object, so as to justify the validity of the consciousness as right knowledge at every moment; nor can it be said that the sense-organs after producing the right knowledge of an object (which lasts for some time and is not momentary) may cease to operate until a new awareness is produced. There is therefore no justification for introducing *anadhigatatva* as a condition of perception. Turning to the difference between perception and inference, Rāmādvaya says that in inference the inferred object does not form a datum and there is no direct and immediate contact of the *antaḥkaraṇa* with the inferred object (e.g. fire). In inference the *antaḥkaraṇa* is in touch only with the reason or the *liṅga* (e.g. smoke), and through this there arises (*liṅgādibala-labdhākārollekha-mātreṇa*) an idea in the mind (e.g. regarding the existence of fire) which is called inference[2].

[1] *ajñāta-jñāpanaṃ pramāṇam iti tad asāram. Vedānta-kaumudī*, MS. copy, p. 18.

2 *Ibid*. p. 47. One of the earliest explanations of the Vedāntic view of inference occurs in the *Prakaṭārtha-vivaraṇa*, to which the *Vedānta-kaumudī* is in all probability indebted.

On the subject of the self-validity of knowledge (*svataḥ-prāmāṇya*) Rāmādvaya does not, like Dharmarājādhvarīndra, include the absence of defects (*doṣābhāva*) in the definition of *svataḥ-prāmāṇya.* It may well be remembered that Dharmarāja Adhvarīndra defines validity (*prāmāṇya*) of knowledge as an awareness that characterizes an object as it is (*tadvati tat-prakārakajñānatvam*), while self-validity (*svataḥ-prāmāṇya*) is defined as the acceptance by the underlying *sākṣi* consciousness of this validity in accordance with the exact modes of the awareness (of which the validity is affirmed), and in accordance with the exact objective conditions of the awareness, in absence of any defects[1]. Rāmādvaya, however, closely follows Kumārila's view of the self-validity of knowledge and defines it as that which, being produced by the actual data of that cognition, does not contain any element which is derived from other sources[2]. Later knowledge of the presence of any defects or distorting elements may invalidate any cognition; but, so long as such defects are not known, each cognition is valid of itself for reasons similar to those held by Kumārila and already discussed[3]. In this connection Rāmādvaya points out that our cognitions are entirely internal phenomena and are not in touch with objects, and that, though the objects are revealed outside, yet it is through our own internal conditions, merit and demerit, that they may be perceived by us[4].

Vidyāraṇya (A.D. 1350)

In addition to the *Sarva-darśana-saṃgraha* Mādhava wrote two works on the Śaṅkara Vedānta system, viz. *Vivaraṇa-prameyasaṃgraha* and *Pañcadaśī*; and also *Jīvan-mukti-viveka.* Of these the former is an independent study of Prakāśātman's *Pañca-pādikāvivaraṇa*, in which Mādhava elaborates the latter's arguments in his own way. His other work, *Pañcadaśī*, is a popular compendium in verse. Both these works attained great celebrity on account of

[1] *doṣābāve sati yāvat-svāśraya-grāhaka-sāmagrī-grāhyatvam; svāśrayo vṛtti-jñānam, tad-grāhakaṃ sākṣi-jñānam tenāpi vṛtti-jñāne gṛhyamāṇe tad-gataprāmāṇyam api gṛhyate. Vedānta-paribhāṣā*, pp. 336, 337.

[2] *vijñāna-sāmagrī-janyatve sati yat tad-anya-janyatvaṃ tad-abhāvasyaiva svatastvokty-angīkārāt. Vedānta-kaumudī*, MS. copy, p. 52.

jñaptāvapi jñāna-jñāpaka-sāmagrī-mātra-jñāpyatvaṃ svatastvam. Ibid. p. 61.

[3] *A History of Indian Philosophy*, vol. 1, Cambridge, 1922, pp. 372–375.

[4] *prākaṭyena yuktasyāpi tasya na sarvair viditatvaṃ sva-prakāśam api prākaṭyaṃ kasyacid evādṛṣṭa-yogāt sphurati na guṇatve jñānasya kathañcid artha-yogaḥ samastīti. Vedānta-kaumudī*, MS. copy, pp. 67, 68.

their clear and forcible style and diction. Vidyāraṇya is reputed to be the same as Mādhava, brother of Sāyaṇa, the great Vedic commentator. He was a pupil of Śaṅkarānanda, who had written some works of minor importance on the Upaniṣads[1].

Vidyāraṇya in his *Pañcadaśī* repeats the *Vivaraṇa* view of the Vedānta, that, whether in our awakened state or in our dreams or in our dreamless condition, there is no moment when there is no consciousness; for even in dreamless sleep there must be some consciousness, as is evident from the later remembrance of the experience of the dreamless state. The light of consciousness is thus itself ever present without any change or flickering of any kind. It should therefore be regarded as ultimately real. It is self-luminous and neither rises nor sets[2]. This self is pure bliss, because nothing is so much loved by us as our own selves. If the nature of self had been unobscured, we could not have found any enjoyment in sense-objects. It is only because the self is largely obscured to us that we do not rest content with self-realization and crave for other pleasures from sense-objects. *Māyā* is the cause of this obscuration, and it is described as that power by which can be produced the manifold world-appearance. This power (*śakti*), cannot be regarded either as absolutely real or as unreal. It is, however, associated only with a part of Brahman and not with the whole of it, and it is only in association with a part of Brahman that it transforms itself into the various elements and their modifications. All objects of the world are thus but a complex of Brahman and *māyā*. The existence or being of all things is the Brahman, and all that appears identified with being is the *māyā* part. *Māyā* as the power of Brahman regulates all relation and order of the universe. In association with the intelligence of Brahman this behaves as an intelligent power which is responsible for the orderliness of all qualities of things, their inter-relations and interactions[3]. He compares the world-appearance to a painting, where the white canvas stands for the pure Brahman, the white paste for the inner controller (*antaryāmin*), the dark colour for the dispenser of the crude elements (*sūtrātman*) and the coloration for

[1] Bhāratītīrtha and his teacher Vidyātīrtha also were teachers of Vidyāraṇya. Vidyāraṇya thus seems to have had three teachers, Bhāratī Tirtha, Vidyā Tirtha and Śaṅkarānanda.

[2] *nodeti nāstamety ekā saṃvid eṣā svayam-prabhā. Pañcadaśī*, I. 7, Basumati edition, Calcutta, 1907.

[3] *śaktir asty aiśvarī kācit sarva-vastu-niyāmikā.* 38....*cic-chāyāveśataḥ śaktiś cetaneva vibhāti sā.* 40. *Ibid.* III.

the dispenser of the concrete elemental world (*virāṭ*), and all the figures that are manifested thereon are the living beings and other objects of the world. It is Brahman that, being reflected through the *māyā*, assumes the diverse forms and characters. The false appearance of individual selves is due to the false identification of subjectivity—a product of *māyā*—with the underlying pure consciousness—Brahman. Vidyāraṇya then goes on to describe the usual topics of the Vedānta, which have already been dealt with. The chief and important feature of Vidyāraṇya's *Pañcadaśī* is the continual repetition of the well-established Vedāntic principles in a clear, popular and attractive way, which is very helpful to those who wish to initiate their minds into the Vedāntic ways of self-realization[1]. His *Vivaraṇa-prameya-saṃgraha* is a more scholarly work; but, as it is of the nature of an elaboration of the ideas contained in *Pañca-pādikā-vivaraṇa*, which has generally been followed as the main guide in the account of Vedānta given in this and the preceding chapter, and there being but few ideas which can be considered as an original contribution of Vidyāraṇya to the development of Vedāntic thought, no separate account of its contents need be given here[2]. The *Jīvan-mukti-viveka*, the substance of which has already been utilized in section 17 of chapter X, volume 1 of the present work, is an ethical treatise, covering more or less the same ground as the *Naiṣkarmya-siddhi* of Sureśvara.

Nṛsiṃhāśrama Muni (A.D. 1500).

Nṛsiṃhāśrama Muni (A.D. 1500) was a pupil of Gīrvāṇendra Sarasvatī and Jagannāthāśrama and teacher of Nārāyaṇāśrama, who wrote a commentary on his *Bheda-dhikkāra*. He wrote many works, such as *Advaita-dīpikā*, *Advaita-pañca-ratna*, *Advaita-bodha-dipikā*, *Advaita-vāda*, *Bheda-dhikkāra*, *Vācārambhaṇa*, *Vedānta-tattva-viveka*, and commentaries on the *Saṃkṣepa-śārīraka* and *Pañca-*

[1] There are four commentaries on the *Pañcadaśī:—Tattva-bodhinī*, *Vṛtti-prabhākara* by Niścaladāsa Svāmin, *Tātparya-bodhinī* by Rāmakṛṣṇa and another commentary by Sadānanda. It is traditionally believed that the *Pañcadaśī* was written jointly by Vidyāraṇya and Bhāratī Tīrtha. Niścaladāsa Svāmin points out in his *Vṛtti-prabhākara* that Vidyāraṇya was author of the first ten chapters of the *Pañcadaśī* and Bhāratī Tīrtha of the other five. Rāmakṛṣṇa, however, in the beginning of his commentary on the seventh chapter, attributes that chapter to Bhāratī Tīrtha, and this fits in with the other tradition that the first six chapters were written by Vidyāraṇya and the other nine by Bhāratītīrtha.

[2] He also wrote another work on the *Vivaraṇa*, called *Vivaraṇopanyāsa*, which is referred to by Appaya Dīkṣita in his *Siddhānta-leśa*, p. 68—*Vivaraṇopanyāse Bhāratītīrtha-vacanam*.

pādikā-vivaraṇa, called *Tattva-bodhinī* and *Pañca-pādikā-vivaraṇa-prakāśikā*. Nṛsiṃhāśrama was very well reputed among his contemporaries, but it does not seem that he introduced any new ideas into the Vedānta. He is more interested in emphasizing the fact of the identity of Brahman with the self and the illusory character of the world-appearance than in investigating the nature and constitution of *māyā* and the way in which it can be regarded as the material stuff of world-appearance. He defines the falsehood of world-appearance as its non-existence in the locus in which it appears (*pratipannopādhāv abhāva-pratiyogitva*)[1]. When a piece of conch-shell appears to be silver, the silver appears to be existent and real (*sat*), but silver cannot be the same as being or existence (*na tāvad rajata-svarūpaṃ sat*). So also, when we take the world-appearance as existent, the world-appearance cannot be identical with being or existence; its apparent identification with these is thus necessarily false[2]. So also the appearance of subjectivity or egoistic characters in the self-luminous self is false, because the two are entirely different and cannot be identified. Nṛsiṃhāśrama, however, cannot show by logical arguments or by a reference to experience that subjectivity or egoism (*ahaṃkāra*, which he also calls *antaḥkaraṇa* or mind) is different from self, and he relies on the texts of the Upaniṣads to prove this point, which is of fundamental importance for the Vedānta thesis. In explaining the nature of the perceptual process he gives us the same sort of account as is given by his pupil Dharmarāja Adhvarīndra in his *Vedānta-paribhāṣā*, as described in the tenth chapter in the first volume of this work[3]. He considers the self to be bliss itself (*sukha-rūpa*) and does not admit that there is any difference between the self and bliss (*sa cātmā sukhān na bhidyate*)[4]. His definition of *ajñāna* is the same as that of Citsukha, viz. that it is a beginningless constitutive cause, which is removable by true knowledge[5]. There is thus practically

[1] *Vedānta-tattva-viveka*, p. 12. *The Pandit*, vol. XXV, May 1903. This work has two important commentaries, viz. *Tattva-viveka-dīpana*, and one called *Tattva-viveka-dīpana-vyākhyā* by Bhaṭṭojī.

[2] *Vedānta-tattva-viveka*, p. 15.

[3] *yadā antaḥkaraṇa-vṛttyā ghaṭāvacchinnaṃ caitanyam upadhīyate tadā antaḥkaraṇāvacchinna-ghaṭāvacchinna-caitanyayor vastuta ekatve'py upādhibhedād bhinnayor abhedopādhi-sambandhena aikyād bhavaty abheda ity antaḥkara-ṇāvacchinna-caitanyasya viṣayābhinna-tad-adhiṣṭhāna-caitanyasyābheda-siddhyartham vṛtter nirgamanaṃ vācyam. Ibid.* p. 22.

[4] *Ibid.* p. 29.

[5] *anādy upādānatve sati jñāna-nivartyam ajñānam, nikhila-prapañcopādānabrahma-*

no new line of argument in his presentation of the Vedānta. On the side of dialectical arguments, in his attempts to refute "difference" (*bheda*) in his *Bheda-dhikkāra* he was anticipated by his great predecessors Śrīharṣa and Citsukha.

Appaya Dīkṣita[1] (A.D. 1550).

Appaya Dīkṣita lived probably in the middle of the sixteenth century, as he refers to Nṛsiṃhāśrama Muni, who lived early in that century. He was a great scholar, well-read in many branches of Sanskrit learning, and wrote a large number of works on many subjects. His grandfather was Ācārya Dīkṣita, who is said to have been famous for his scholarship from the Himalayas to the south point of India: the name of his father was Raṅgarāja Makhīndra (or simply Rāja Makhīndra). There is, however, nothing very noteworthy in his Vedāntic doctrines. For, in spite of his scholarship, he was only a good compiler and not an original thinker, and on many occasions where he had opportunities of giving original views he contents himself with the views of others. It is sometimes said that he had two different religious views at two different periods of his life, Śaiva and the Vedānta. But of this one cannot be certain; for he was such an all-round scholar that the fact that he wrote a Śaiva commentary and a Vedāntic commentary need not lead to the supposition that he changed his faith. In the beginning of his commentary *Śivārka-maṇi-dīpikā* on Śrīkaṇṭha's Śaiva commentary to the *Brahma-sūtra* he says that, though the right interpretation of the *Brahma-sūtra* is the monistic interpretation, as attempted by Sankara and others, yet the desire for attaining this right wisdom of oneness (*advaita-vāsanā*) arises only through the grace of Śiva, and it is for this reason that Vyāsa in his *Brahma-sūtra* tried to establish the superiority of the qualified Brahman Śiva as interpreted by Śrīkaṇṭhācārya. This shows that even while writing his commentary on Śrīkaṇṭha's *Saiva-bhāṣya* he had not lost respect for the monistic interpretations of Śaṅkara, and he was somehow able to reconcile in his mind the Śaiva doctrine of qualified Brahman (*saguṇa-brahma*) as Śiva with the Śaṅkara doctrine of unqualified pure Brahman. It is possible,

gocaram eva ajñānam. Ibid. p. 43.

[1] He was also called Appayya Dīkṣita and Avadhāni Yajvā, and he studied Logic (*tarka*) with Yajñeśvara Makhīndra. See colophon to Appaya Dīkṣita's commentary on the *Nyāya-siddhānta-mañjarī* of Jānakīnātha, called *Nyāyasiddhānta-mañjarī-vyākhyāna* (MS.).

however, that his sympathies with the monistic Vedānta, which at the beginning were only lukewarm, deepened with age. He says in his *Śivārka-maṇi-dīpikā* that he lived in the reign of King Cinnabomma (whose land-grant inscriptions date from Sadāśiva, mahārāja of Vijayanagara, A.D. 1566 to 1575; *vide* Hultzsch, *S.I. Inscriptions*, vol. I), under whose orders he wrote the *Śivārka-maṇi-dīpikā* commentary on Śrīkaṇṭha's commentary. His grandson Nīlakaṇṭha Dīkṣita says in his *Śiva-līlārṇava* that Appaya Dīkṣita lived to the good old age of seventy-two. In the *Oriental Historical Manuscripts* catalogued by Taylor, vol.II, it is related that at the request of the Pāṇḍya king Tirumalai Nayaka he came to the Pāṇḍya country in A.D. 1626 to settle certain disputes between the Śaivas and the Vaiṣṇavas. Kālahasti-śaraṇa-Śivānanda Yogīndra, in his commentary on the *Ātmārpaṇa-stava*, gives the date of Appaya Dīkṣita's birth as Kali age 4654, or A.D. 1554, as pointed out by Māhāmahopādhyāya Kuppusvami Sastri in his Sanskrit introduction to the *Śiva-līlārṇava*. Since he lived seventy-two years, he must have died some time in 1626, the very year when he came to the Pāṇḍya country. He had for his pupil Bhaṭṭojī-Dīkṣita, as is indicated by his own statement in the *Tantrasiddhānta-dīpikā* by the latter author. Bhaṭṭojī Dīkṣita must therefore have been a junior contemporary of Appaya Dīkṣita, as is also evidenced by his other statement in his *Tattva-kaustubha* that he wrote this work at the request of King Keladī-Veṅkaṭendra, who reigned from 1604 to 1626 (*vide* Hultzsch's second volume of *Reports on Sanskrit Manuscripts*)[1].

It is said that Appaya Dīkṣita wrote about four hundred works. Some of them may be mentioned here: *Advaita-nirṇaya*, *Catur-mata-sāra-saṃgraha* (containing in the first chapter, called *Nyāya-muktāvalī*, a brief summary of the doctrines of Madhva, in the second chapter, called *Naya-mayūkha-mālikā*, the doctrines of Rāmānuja, in the third chapter the decisive conclusions from the point of view of Śrikaṇṭha's commentary called *Naya-maṇi-mālā* and in the fourth chapter, called *Naya-mañjarī*, decisive conclusions in accordance with the views of Saṅkarācārya); *Tattva-muktāvalī*, a work on Vedānta; *Vyākaraṇa-vāda-nakṣatra-mālā*, a work on grammar; *Pūrvottara-mīmāṃsā-vāda-nakṣatra-mālā* (containing various separate topics of discussion in Mīmāṃsā and

[1] See Mahāmahopādhyāya Kuppusvami Sastri's introduction to the *Śiva-līlārṇava*, Srirangam, 1911.

Vedānta); *Nyāya-rakṣā-maṇi*, a commentary on the *Brahma-sūtra* following the monistic lines of Śaṅkara; *Vedānta-kalpa-taru-parimala*, a commentary on Amalānanda's *Vedānta-kalpa-taru*, a commentary on Vācaspati's *Bhāmatī* commentary; *Siddhānta-leśa-saṃgraha*, a collection of the views of different philosophers of the monistic school of Śaṅkara on some of the most important points of the Vedānta, without any attempt at harmonizing them or showing his own preference by reasoned arguments, and comprising a number of commentaries by Acyutakṛṣṇānanda Tīrtha (*Kṛṣṇālaṃkāra*), Gaṅgādharendra Sarasvatī (*Siddhānta-bindu-śīkara*), Rāmacandra Yajvan (*Gūḍhārtha-prakāśa*), Viśvanātha Tīrtha, Dharmaya Dīkṣita and others; *Śivārka-maṇi-dīpikā*, a commentary on Śrīkaṇṭha's *Śaiva-bhāṣya* on the *Brahma-sūtra*; *Śiva-karṇāmṛta*; *Śiva-tattva-viveka*; *Śiva-purāṇa-tāmasatva-khaṇḍana*; *Śivādvaita-nirṇaya*; *Śivānanda-laharī-candrikā*, a commentary on *Śaṅkara's Śivānanda-laharī*; *Śivārcana-candrikā*; *Śivotkarṣa-candrikā*; *Śivotkarṣa-mañjarī*; *Śaiva-kalpa-druma*; *Siddhānta-ratnā-kara*; *Madhva-mukha-bhaṅga*, an attempt to show that Madhva's interpretation of the *Brahma-sūtra* is not in accordance with the meaning of the texts of the Upaniṣads; *Rāmānuja-mata-khaṇḍana*; *Rāmāyaṇa-tātparya-nirṇaya*; *Rāmāyaṇa-tātparya-saṃgraha*; *Rāmāyaṇa-bhārata-sāra-saṃgraha*; *Rāmāyaṇa-sāra*; *Rāmāyaṇa-sārasaṃgraha*; *Rāmāyaṇa-sāra-stava*; *Mīmāṃsādhikaraṇa-mālā Upakrama-parākrama*, a short Mīmāṃsa work; *Dharma-mīmāṃsā-paribhāṣā*; *Nāma-saṃgraha-mālikā*; *Vidhi-rasāyana*; *Vidhi-rasāyanopajīvanī*; *Vṛtti-vārttika*, a short work on the threefold meanings of words; *Kuvalayānanda*, a work on rhetoric on which no less than ten commentaries have been written; *Citra-mīmāṃsā*, a work on rhetoric; *Jayollāsa-nidhi*, a commentary on the *Bhāgavata-purāṇa*; *Yādavābhyudaya-ṭīkā*, a commentary on Veṅkaṭa's *Yādavā-bhyudaya*; a commentary on the *Prabodha-candrodaya nāṭaka*, etc.

Prakāśānanda (A.D. 1550–1600).

It has been pointed out that the Vedānta doctrine of monism as preached by Śaṅkara could not shake off its apparent duality in association with *māyā*, which in the hands of the later followers of Śaṅkara gradually thickened into a positive stuff through the evolution or transformation of which all the phenomena of world-appearance could be explained. The Vedāntists held that this *māyā*, though it adhered to Brahman and spread its magical creations thereon, was unspeakable, indescribable, indefinable, changeable and unthinkable and was thus entirely different from the self-revealing, unchangeable Brahman. The charge of dualism against such a system of philosophy could be dodged by the teachers of Vedānta only byholding that, since Brahman was the ultimate reality, *māyā* was unreal and illusory, and hence the charge of duality would be false. But when one considers that *māyā* is regarded as positive and as the stuff of the transformations of world-appearance, it is hardly intelligible how it can be kept out of consideration as having no kind of existence at all. The positive character of *māyā* as being the stuff of all world-appearance has to be given up, if the strictly, monistic doctrine is to be consistently kept. Almost all the followers of Śaṅkara had, however, been interpreting their master's views in such a way that the positive existence of an objective world with its infinite varieties as the ground of perceptual presentation was never denied. The whole course of the development of Vedānta doctrine in the hands of these Vedānta teachers began to crystallize compactly in the view that, since the variety and multiplicity of world-appearance cannot be explained by the pure changeless Brahman, an indefinable stuff, the *māyā*, has necessarily to be admitted as the ground of this world. Prakāśānanda was probably the first who tried to explain Vedānta from a purely sensationalistic view-point of idealism and denied the objective existence of any stuff. The existence of objects is nothing more than their perception (*dṛṣṭi*). The central doctrine of Prakāśānanda has already been briefly described in chapter X, section 15, of volume I of the present work, and his analysis of the nature of perceptual cognition has already been referred to in a preceding section of the present chapter.

Speaking on the subject of the causality of Brahman, he says that the attribution of causality to Brahman cannot be regarded as strictly correct; for ordinarily causality implies the dual relation of cause and effect; since there is nothing else but Brahman, it cannot, under the circumstances, be called a cause. Nescience (*avidyā*), again, cannot be called a cause of the world; for causality is based upon the false notion of duality, which is itself the outcome of nescience. The theory of cause and effect thus lies outside the scope of the Vedānta (*kārya-kāraṇa-vādasya vedānta-bahirbhūtatvāt*). When in reply to the question, "what is the cause of the world?" it is said that nescience (*ajñāna*—literally, want of knowledge) is the cause, the respondent simply wants to obviate the awkward silence. The nature of this nescience cannot, however, be proved by any of the *pramāṇas*; for it is like darkness and the *pramāṇas* or the valid ways of cognition are like light, and it is impossible to perceive darkness by light. Nescience is that which cannot be known except through something else, by its relation to something else, and it is inexplicable in itself, yet beginningless and positive. It will be futile for any one to try to understand it as it is in itself. Nescience is proved by one's own consciousness: so it is useless to ask how nescience is proved. Yet it is destroyed when the identity of the self with the immediately presented Brahman is realized. The destruction of nescience cannot mean its cessation together with its products, as Prakāśātman holds in the *Vivaraṇa*; for such a definition would not apply, whether taken simply or jointly. Prakāśānanda, therefore, defines it as the conviction, following the realization of the underlying ground, that the appearance which was illusorily imposed on it did not exist. This view is different from the *anyathā-khyāti* view, that the surmised appearance was elsewhere and not on the ground on which it was imposed; for here, when the underlying ground is immediately intuited, the false appearance absolutely vanishes, and it is felt that it was not there, it is not anywhere, and it will not be anywhere; and it is this conviction that is technically called *bādha.* The indefinability of nescience is its negation on the ground on which it appears (*pratipannopādhau niṣedha-pratiyogitvam*). This negation of all else excepting Brahman has thus two forms; in one form it is negation and in another form this negation, being included within "all else except Brahman," is itself an illusory imposition, and this latter form thus is itself contradicted and negated by its former form. Thus it would be wrong to argue that, since this negation remains after the realization of Brahman, it would not itself be negated, and hence it would be a dual principle existing side by side with Brahman[1]

True knowledge is opposed to false knowledge in such a way

[1] *Brahmaṇy adhyasyamānaṃ sarvaṃ kālatraye nāstītiniścayasya asti rūpadvayam ekam bādhātmakam aparam adhyasyamānatvaṃ; tatra adhyas amānatvena rūpeṇa sva-viṣayatvam; bādhatvena viṣayitvam iti nātmāśraya ity arthaḥ tathā ca nādvaita-kṣatiḥ.* Compare also *Bhāmatī* on *Adhyāsa-bhāṣya.* Nānā. Dīkṣita seems to have borrowed his whole argument from the Bhāmatī. See his commentary on the *Siddhānta-muktāvalī. The Pandit*, 1890, p. 108.

This idea, however, is not by any means a new contribution of Prakāśānanda. Thus Citsukha writes the same thing in his *Tattva-dīpikā* (also called *Pratyak-tattva-pradīpikā*), that, when the former dawns, the latter is dispelled altogether. An objection is sometimes raised that, if this be so, then the person who has realized Brahma knowledge will cease to have a bodily existence; for bodily existence is based on illusion and all illusion must vanish when true knowledge dawns. And, if this is so, there will be no competent Vedānta teacher. To this Prakāśānanda replies that, even though the Vedānta teacher may be himself an illusory production, he may all the same lead any one to the true path, just as the Vedas, which are themselves but illusory products, may lead any one to the right path[1].

On the subject of the nature of the self as pure bliss (*ānanda*) he differs from Sarvajñātma Muni's view that what is meant by the statement that the self is of the nature of pure bliss is that there is entire absence of all sorrows or negation of bliss in the self. Bliss, according to Sarvajñātma Muni, thus means the absence of the negation of bliss (*an-ānanda-vyavṛtti-mātram ānandatvam*)[2]. He differs also from the view of Prakāśātman that ānanda, or bliss, means the substance which appears as blissful, since it is the object that we really desire. Prakāśātman holds that it is the self on which the character of blissfulness is imposed. The self is called blissful, because it is the ground of the appearance of blissfulness. What people consider of value and desire is not the blissfulness, but that which is blissful. Prakāśānanda holds that this view is not correct, since the self appears not only as blissful, but also as painful, and it would therefore be as right to call the self blissful as to call it painful. Moreover, not the object of blissfulness, which in itself is dissociated from blissfulness, is called blissful, but that which is endowed with bliss is called blissful (*viśiṣṭasyaiva ānandapadārthatvāt*)[3]. If blissfulness is not a natural character of the self, it cannot be called blissful because it happens to be the ground on which blissfulness is illusorily imposed. So Prakāśānanda holds that the self is naturally of a blissful character.

Prakāśānanda raises the question regarding the beholder of the

p. 39, as follows: "*sarveṣām api bhāvānām āsrayatvena sammate pratiyogitvam atyantābhāvam prati mṛṣātmatā*," which is the same as *pratipannopādhau niṣedha-pratiyogitvam*. Compare also *Vedānta-paribhāṣā*, pp. 219 and 220, *mithyātvaṃ ca svāśrayatvenābhimata-yāvanniṣṭhātyantābhāva-pratiyogitvam*. In later times Madhusūdana freely used this definition in his *Advaita-siddhi*.

[1] *kalpito 'pyupadeṣṭā syād yathā-śāstraṃ samādiśet*
na cāvinigamo doṣo 'vidyāvattvena nirṇayāt. *The Pandit*, 1890, p. 160.

[2] *Saṃkṣepa-śārīraka*, I. I. 174.

[3] *Siddhānta-muktāvalī. The Pandit*, 1890, p. 215.

experienced duality and says that it is Brahman who has this experience of duality; but, though Brahman alone exists, yet there is no actual modification or transformation (*pariṇāma*) of Brahman into all its experiences, since such a view would be open to the objections brought against the alternative assumptions of the whole of Brahman or a part of it, and both of them would land us in impossible consequences. The *vivarta* view holds that the effect has no reality apart from the underlying ground or substance. So *vivarta* really means oneness with the substance, and it virtually denies all else that may appear to be growing out of this one substance. The false perception of world-appearance thus consists in the appearance of all kinds of characters in Brahman, which is absolutely characterless (*niṣprakārikāyāḥ saprakārakatvena bhāvaḥ*). Since the self and its cognition are identical and since there is nothing else but this self, there is no meaning in saying that the Vedānta admits the *vivarta* view of causation; for, strictly speaking, there is no causation at all (*vivartasya bāla-vyutpatti-prayojana-tayā*)[1]. If anything existed apart from self, then the Vedāntic monism would be disturbed. If one looks at *māyā* in accordance with the texts of the Vedas, *māyā* will appear to be an absolutely fictitious non-entity (*tuccha*), like the hare's horn; if an attempt is made to interpret it logically, it is indefinable (*anirvacanīya*), though common people would always think of it as being real (*vāstavī*)[2]. Prakāśānanda thus preaches the extreme view of the Vedānta, that there is no kind of objectivity that can be attributed to the world, that *māyā* is absolutely non-existent, that our ideas have no objective substratum to which they correspond, that the self is the one and only ultimate reality, and that there is no causation or creation of the world. In this view he has often to fight with Sarvajñātma Muni, Prakāśātman, and with others who developed a more realistic conception of *māyā* transformation; but it was he who, developing probably on the lines of Maṇḍana, tried for the first time to give a consistent presentation of the Vedānta from the most thorough-going idealistic point of view. In the colophon of his work he says that the essence of the Vedānta as

[1] *bālān prati vivarto 'yaṃ brahmaṇaḥ sakalaṃ jagat*
avivarttitam ānandam āsthitāḥ kṛtinaḥ sadā.
The Pandit, 1890, p. 326.

[2] *tucchānirvacanīyā ca vāstavī cety asau tridhā*
jñeyā māyā tribhir bodhaiḥ śrauta-yauktika-laukikaiḥ.
Ibid. p. 420.

preached by him is unknown to his contemporaries and that it was he who first thoroughly expounded this doctrine of philosophy[1]. Prakāśānanda wrote many other works in addition to his *Siddhānta-muktāvalī*, such as *Tārā-bhakti-taraṅgiṇī*, *Manoramā tantra-rāja-ṭīkā*, *Mahā-lakṣmī-paddhati* and *Śrī-vidyā-paddhati*, and this shows that, though a thoroughgoing Vedāntist, he was religiously attached to tantra forms of worship. Nānā Dīkṣita wrote a commentary on the *Muktāvalī*, called *Siddhānta-pradīpikā*, at a time when different countries of India had become pervaded by the disciples and disciples of the disciples of Prakāśānanda[2].

Madhusūdana Sarasvatī (A.D. 1500).[3]

Madhusūdana Sarasvatī, who was a pupil of Viśveśvara Sarasvatī and teacher of Puruṣottama Sarasvatī, in all probability flourished in the first half of the sixteenth century. His chief works are *Vedānta-kalpa-latikā*, *Advaita-siddhi*, *Advaita-mañjarī*, *Advaita-ratna-rakṣaṇa*, *Ātma-bodha-ṭīkā*, *Ānanda-mandākinī*, *Kṛṣṇa-kutūhalanāṭaka*, *Prasthāna-bheda*, *Bhakti-sāmānya-nirūpaṇa*, *Bhagavad-gītā-gūḍhārtha-dīpikā*, *Bhagavad-bhakti-rasāyana*, *Bhāgavata-purāṇa-prathama-śloka-vyākhyā*, *Veda-stuti-ṭīkā*, *Śāṇḍilya-sūtra-ṭīkā*, *Śāstra-siddhānta-leśa-ṭīkā*, *Saṃkṣepa-śārīrakasāra-saṃgraha*, *Siddhānta-tattva-bindu*, *Hari-līlā-vyākhyā*. His most important work, however, is his *Advaita-siddhi*, in which he tries to refute the objections raised in Vyāsātīrtha's *Nyāyāmṛta*[4]

[1] *vedānta-sāra-sarvasvam ajñeyam adhunātanaiḥ*
aśeṣeṇa mayoktaṃ tat puruṣottama-yatnataḥ.
The Pandit, 1890, p. 428.

[2] *yacchiṣya-śiṣya-sandoha-vyāptā bhārata-bhūmayaḥ*
vande tam yatibhir vandyaṃ Prakāśānandam īśvaram.
Ibid. p. 488.

[3] Rāmājñā Pāṇḍeya in his edition of Madhusūdana's *Vedānta-kalpa-latikā* suggests that he was a Bengali by birth. His pupil Puruṣottama Sarasvatī in his commentary on the *Siddhānta-bindu-ṭīkā* refers to Balabhadra Bhaṭṭācārya as a favourite pupil of his, and Pāṇḍeya argues that, since Bhaṭṭācārya is a Bengali surname and since his favourite pupil was a Bengali, he also must have been a Bengali. It is also pointed out that in a family genealogy (*Kula-pañjikā*) of Kotalipara of Faridpur, Bengal, Madhusūdana's father is said to have been Pramodapurandara Ācārya, who had four sons—Śrīnātha Cūḍāmaṇi, Yādavānanda Nyāyācārya, Kamalajanayana and Vāgīśa Gosvāmin. Some of the important details of Madhusūdana's philosophical dialectics will be taken up in the treatment of the philosophy of Madhva and his followers in the third volume of the present work in connection with Madhusūdana's discussions with Vyāsatīrtha.

[4] The *Advaita-siddhi* has three commentaries, *Advaita-siddhy-upanyāsa*, *Bṛhat-ṭīkā*, and *Laghu-candrikā*, by Brahmānanda Sarasvatī.

against the monistic Vedānta of Śaṅkara and his followers. Materials from this book have already been utilized in sections 6, 7, 8, 9 and 10 of the tenth chapter of the present work. More will be utilized in the third volume in connection with the controversy between Vyāsatīrtha and Madhusūdana, which is the subject-matter of *Advaita-siddhi.* Madhusūdana's *Siddhānta-bindu* does not contain anything of importance, excepting that he gives a connected account of the perceptual process, already dealt with in the tenth chapter and also in the section "Vedāntic Cosmology" of the present volume. His *Advaita-ratna-rakṣaṇa* deals with such subjects as the validity of the Upaniṣads: the Upaniṣads do not admit duality; perception does not prove the reality of duality; the duality involved in mutual negation is false; indeterminate knowledge does not admit duality; duality cannot be proved by any valid means of proof, and so forth. There is practically nothing new in the work, as it only repeats some of the important arguments of the bigger work *Advaita-siddhi* and tries to refute the view of dualists like the followers of Madhva, with whom Madhusūdana was in constant controversy. It is unnecessary, therefore, for our present purposes to enter into any of the details of this work. It is, however, interesting to note that, though he was such a confirmed monist in his philosophy, he was a theist in his religion and followed the path of *bhakti*, or devotion, as is evidenced by his numerous works promulgating the *bhakti* creed. These works, however, have nothing to do with the philosophy of the Vedānta, with which we are concerned in the present chapter. Madhusūdana's *Vedānta-kalpa-latikā* was written earlier than his *Advaita-siddhi* and his commentary on the *Mahimnaḥ stotra*[1]. Rāmājñā Pāṇḍeya points out in his introduction to the *Vedānta-kalpa-latikā* that the *Advaita-siddhi* contains a reference to his *Gītā-nibandhana*; the *Gītā-nibandhana* and the *Śrīmad-bhāgavata-ṭīkā* contain references to his *Bhakti-rasāyana*, and the *Bhakti-rasāyana* refers to the *Vedānta-kalpa-latikā*; and this shows that the *Vedānta-kalpa-latikā* was written prior to all these works. The *Advaita-ratna-rakṣaṇa* refers to the *Advaita-siddhi* and may therefore be regarded as a much later work. There is nothing particularly new in the *Vedānta-kalpa-latikā* that deserves special mention as a contribution to Vedāntic thought. The special feature of the work consists in the frequent

[1] He refers to the *Vedānta-kalpa-latikā* and *Siddhānta-bindu* in his *Advaita-siddhi*, p. 537 (Nirṇaya-Sāgara edition). See also *Mahimnaḥ-stotra-ṭīkā*, p. 5.

brief summaries of doctrines of other systems of Indian philosophy and contrasts them with important Vedānta views. The first problem discussed is the nature of emancipation (*mokṣa*) and the ways of realizing it: Madhusūdana attempts to prove that it is only the Vedāntic concept of salvation that can appeal to men, all other views being unsatisfactory and invalid. But it does not seem that he does proper justice to other views. Thus, for example, in refuting the Sāṃkhya view of salvation he says that, since the Sāṃkhya thinks that what is existent cannot be destroyed, sorrow, being an existent entity, cannot be destroyed, so there cannot be any emancipation from sorrow. This is an evident misrepresentation of the Sāṃkhya; for with the Sāṃkhya the destruction of sorrow in emancipation means that the *buddhi*, a product of *prakṛti* which is the source of all sorrow, ceases in emancipation to have any contact with *puruṣa*, and hence, even though sorrow may not be destroyed, there is no inconsistency in having emancipation from sorrow. It is unnecessary for our present purposes, however, to multiply examples of misrepresentation by Madhusūdana of the views of other systems of thought in regard to the same problem. In the course of the discussions he describes negation (*abhāva*) also as being made up of the stuff of nescience, which, like other things, makes its appearance in connection with pure consciousness. He next introduces a discussion of the nature of self-knowledge, and then, since Brahma knowledge can be attained only through the Upaniṣadic propositions of identity, he passes over to the discussion of import of propositions and the doctrines of *abhihitān-vaya-vāda*, *anvitābhidhāna-vāda* and the like. He then treats of the destruction of nescience. He concludes the work with a discussion of the substantial nature of the senses. Thus the mind-organ is said to be made up of five elements, whereas other senses are regarded as being constituted of one element only. *Manas* is said to pervade the whole of the body and not to be atomic, as the Naiyāyikas hold. Finally, Madhusūdana returns again to the problem of emancipation, and holds that it is the self freed from nescience that should be regarded as the real nature of emancipation.

XII

THE PHILOSOPHY OF THE *YOGA-VĀSIṢṬHA*

THE philosophical elements in the various Purāṇas will be taken in a later volume. The *Yoga-vāsiṣṭha-Rāmāyaṇa* may be included among the *purāṇas*, but it is devoid of the general characteristics of the *purāṇās* and is throughout occupied with discussions of Vedāntic problems of a radically monistic type, resembling the Vedāntic doctrines as interpreted by Śaṅkara. This extensive philosophical poem, which contains twenty-three thousand seven hundred and thirty-four verses (ignoring possible differences in different manuscripts or editions) and is thus very much larger than the *Śrīmad-bhagavad-gītā*, is a unique work. The philosophical view with which it is concerned, and which it is never tired of reiterating, is so much like the view of Śaṅkara and of Vijñānavāda Buddhism, that its claim to treatment immediately after Śaṅkara seems to me to be particularly strong. Moreover, the various interpretations of the *Vedānta-sūtra* which will follow are so much opposed to Śaṅkara's views as to make it hard to find a suitable place for a treatment like that of the *Yoga-vāsiṣṭha* unless it is taken up immediately after the chapter dealing with Śaṅkara.

The work begins with a story. A certain Brahmin went to the hermitage of the sage Agastya and asked him whether knowledge or work was the direct cause of salvation (*mokṣa-sādhana*). Agastya replied that, as a bird flies with its two wings, so a man can attain the highest (*paramaṃ padaṃ*) only through knowledge and work. To illustrate this idea he narrates a story in which Kāruṇya, the son of Agniveśya, having returned from the teacher's house after the completion of his studies, remained silent and did no work. When he was asked for the reason of this attitude of his, he said that he was perplexed over the question as to whether the action of a man in accordance with scriptural injunction was or was not more fitted for the attainment of his highest good than following a course of self-abnegation and desirelessness (*tyāga-mātra*). On hearing this question of Kāruṇya' Agniveśya told him that he could answer his question only by narrating a story, after hearing which he might decide as he chose. A heavenly damsel (*apsarāḥ*), Suruci by name, sitting on one of the peaks of the Himālayas, once saw a messenger of Indra flying through the sky. She asked him where he was going. In reply he said that a certain king, Ariṣṭanemi by name, having given his kingdom to his son and having become free from all passions, was performing a course of asceticism (*tapas*), and that he had had to go to him on duty and was returning from him. The damsel wanted to know in detail what happened there between the messenger and the king. The messenger replied that he was asked by Indra to take a well-decorated chariot and bring the king in it to heaven, but while doing so he was asked by the king to describe the advantages and defects of heaven, on hearing which he would make up his mind whether he would like to go there or not. In heaven, he was answered, people enjoyed superior, medium and inferior pleasures according as their merits were superior, medium or inferior: when they had exhausted their merits by enjoyment, they were reborn again on earth, and during their stay there they were subject to mutual jealousy on account of the inequality of their enjoyments. On hearing this the king had refused to go to heaven, and, when this was reported to Indra, he was very much surprised and he asked the messenger to carry the king to Vālmīki's hermitage and make Vālmīki acquainted with the king's refusal to enjoy the fruits of heaven and request him to give him proper instructions for the attainment of right knowledge, leading to emancipation (*mokṣa*). When this was done, the king asked Vālmīki how he might attain *mokṣa*, and Vālmīki in reply wished to narrate the dialogue of Vaśiṣṭha and Rāma (*Vaśiṣṭha-rāma-saṃvāda*) on the subject.

Vālmīki said that, when he had finished the story of Rāma—the work properly known as *Rāmāyaṇa*—and taught it to Bharadvāja, Bharadvāja recited it once to Brahmā (the god), and he, being pleased, wished to confer a boon on him. Bharadvāja in reply said that he would like to receive such instructions as would enable people to escape from sorrow. Brahmā told him to apply to Vālmīki and went himself to him (Vālmīki), accompanied by Bharadvāja, and asked him not to cease working until he finished describing the entire character of Rāma, by listening to which people will be saved from the dangers of the world. When Brahmā disappeared from the hermitage after giving this instruction, Bharadvāja also asked Vālmīki to describe how Rāma and his wife, brother and followers behaved in this sorrowful and dangerous world and lived in sorrowless tranquillity.

In answer to the above question Vālmīki replied that Rāma, after finishing his studies, went out on his travels to see the various places of pilgrimage and hermitages. On his return, however, he looked very sad every day and would not tell anyone the cause of his sorrow. King Daśaratha, Rāma's father, became very much concerned about Rāma's sadness and asked Vaśiṣṭha if he knew what might be the cause of it. At this time the sage Viśvāmitra also visited the city of Ayodhyā to invite Rāma to kill the demons. Rāma's dejected mental state at this time created much anxiety, and Viśvāmitra asked him the cause of his dejection.

Rāma said in reply that a new enquiry had come into his mind and had made him averse to all enjoyments. There is no happiness in this world, people are born to die and they die to be born again. Everything is impermanent (*asthira*) in this world. All existent things are unconnected (*bhāvāḥ . . . parasparam asaṅginaḥ*). They are collected and associated together only by our mental imagination (*manaḥ-kalpanayā*). The world of enjoyment is created by the mind (*manaḥ*), and this mind itself appears to be non-existent. Everything is like a mirage.

Vaśiṣṭha then explained the nature of the world-appearance, and it is this answer which forms the content of the book. When Vālmīki narrated this dialogue of Vaśiṣṭha and Rāma, king Ariṣṭanemi found himself enlightened, and the damsel was also pleased and dismissed the heavenly messenger. Kāruṇya, on hearing all this from his father Agniveśya, felt as if he realized the ultimate truth and thought that, since he realized the philosophical truth, and since work and passivity mean the same, it was his clear duty to follow the customary duties of life. When Agastya finished narrating the story, the Brahmin Sutīkṣṇa felt himself enlightened.

There is at least one point which may be considered as a very clear indication of later date, much later than would be implied by the claim that the work was written by the author of the *Rāmāyaṇa*. It contains a *śloka* which may be noted as almost identical with a verse of Kālidāsa's *Kumāra-saṃbhava*[1]. It may, in my opinion, be almost unhesitatingly assumed that the author borrowed it from Kālidāsa, and it is true, as is generally supposed, that Kālidāsa

[1] *Yoga-vāsiṣṭha*, III. 16. 50:

atha tām atimātra-vihvalāṃ
sakṛpākāśabhavā sarasvatī
śapharīṃ hrada-śoṣa-vihvalāṃ
prathamā vṛṣṭir ivānvakampata.

lived in the fifth century A.D. The author of the *Yoga-vāsiṣṭha*, whoever he may have been, flourished at least some time after Kālidāsa. It may also be assumed that the interval between Kālidāsa's time and that of the author of the *Yoga-vāsiṣṭha* had been long enough to establish Kālidāsa's reputation as a poet. There is another fact which deserves consideration in this connection. In spite of the fact that the views of the *Yoga-vāsiṣṭha* and Śaṅkara's interpretation of Vedānta have important points of agreement neither of them refers to the other. Again, the views of the *Yoga-vāsiṣṭha* so much resemble those of the idealistic school of Buddhists, that the whole work seems to be a Brahmanic modification of idealistic Buddhism. One other important instance can be given of such a tendency to assimilate Buddhistic idealism and modify it on Brahmanic lines, viz. the writings of Gauḍapāda and Śaṅkara. I am therefore inclined to think that the author of the *Yoga-vāsiṣṭha* was probably a contemporary of Gauḍapāda or Śaṅkara, about A.D. 800 or a century anterior to them.

The work contains six books, or *prakaraṇas*, namely, *Vairāgya*, *Mumukṣu-vyavahāra*, *Utpatti*, *Sthiti*, *Upaśama and Nirvāṇa. It is known also by the names of Ārṣa-Rāmāyaṇa*, *Jñāna-vāsiṣṭha*, *Mahā-Rāmāyaṇa*, *Vāsiṣṭha-Rāmāyaṇa* or *Vāsiṣṭha*. Several commentaries have been written on it. Of these commentaries I am particularly indebted to the *Tātparya-prakāśa* of Ānandabodhendra.

The *Yoga-vāsiṣṭha* is throughout a philosophical work, in the form of popular lectures, and the same idea is often repeated again and again in various kinds of expressions and poetical imagery. But the writer seems to have been endowed with extraordinary poetical gifts. Almost every verse is full of the finest poetical imagery; the choice of words is exceedingly pleasing to the ear, and they often produce the effect of interesting us more by their poetical value than by the extremely idealistic thought which they are intended to convey.

The *Yoga-vāsiṣṭha* had a number of commentaries, and it was also summarized in verse by some writers whose works also had commentaries written upon them. Thus Advayāraṇya, son of Narahari, wrote a commentary on it, called *Vāsiṣṭha-Rāmāyaṇa-candrikā*. Ānandabodhendra Sarasvatī, pupil of Gaṅgādharendra Sarasvatī of the nineteenth century, wrote the *Tātparya-prakāśa*. Gaṅgādharendra also is said to have written a commentary of the same name. Rāmadeva and Sadānanda also wrote two commentaries on the work, and in addition to these there is another commentary, called *Yoga-vasiṣṭha-tātparya-saṃgraha*, and another commentary, the *Pada-candrikā*, was written by Mādhava Sarasvatī. The names of some of its summaries are *Bṛhad-yoga-vasiṣṭha*, *Laghu-jñāna-vasiṣṭha*, *Yoga-vāsiṣṭha-ślokāḥ* and *Yoga-vāsiṣṭha-saṃkṣepa* by Gauḍa Abhinanda of the ninth century, *Yoga-vāsiṣṭha-sāra* or *Jñāna-sāra*, *Yoga-vāsiṣṭha-sāra-saṃgraha* and *Vāsiṣṭha-sāra* or *Vāsiṣṭha-sāra-gūḍhārthā* by Ramānanda Tirthā, pupil of Advaitānanda. The *Yoga-vāsiṣṭha-saṃkṣepa* of Gauḍa Abhinanda had a commentary by Ātmasukha, called *Candrikā*, and another called *Saṃsārataraṇī*, by Mummaḍideva. The *Yoga-vāsiṣṭha-sāra* also had two commentaries by Pūrṇānanda and Mahīdhara. Mr Sivaprasad Bhattacarya in an article on the *Yoga-vāsiṣṭha-Rāmāyaṇa* in the *Proceedings of the Madras Oriental Conference* of 1924 says that the *Mokṣopāya-sāra*, which is another name for the *Yoga-vāsiṣṭha-sāra*, was written by an Abhinanda who is not to be confused with Gauḍa Abhinanda. But he misses the fact that Gauḍa Abhinanda had also written another summary of it, called *Yoga-vāsiṣṭha-saṃkṣepa*. Incidentally this also refutes his view that the *Yoga-vāsiṣṭha* is to be placed between the tenth and the twelfth centuries. For, if a summary of it was written by Gauḍa Abhinanda of the ninth century, the *Yoga-vāsiṣṭha* must have been written at least in the eighth century. The date of the *Yoga-vāsiṣṭha* may thus be regarded as being the seventh or the eighth century.

The Ultimate Entity.

The third book of the *Yoga-vāsiṣṭha* deals with origination (*utpatti*). All bondage (*bandha*) is due to the existence of the perceptible universe (*dṛśya*), and it is the main thesis of this work that it does not exist. At the time of each dissolution the entire universe of appearance is destroyed, like dreams in deep sleep (*suṣupti*). What is left is deep and static (*stimita-gambhīra*), neither light nor darkness, indescribable and unmanifested (*anākhyam anabhivyaktam*), but a somehow existent entity. This entity manifests itself as another (*svayam anya ivollasan*); and through this dynamic aspect it appears as the ever-active mind (*manas*)—like moving ripples from the motionless ocean. But in reality whatever appears as the diversified universe is altogether non-existent; for, if it was existent, it could not cease under any circumstances[1]. It does not exist at all. The ultimate indefinite and indescribable entity, which is pure extinction (*nirvāṇa-mātra*), or pure intelligence (*paro bodhaḥ*), remains always in itself and does not really suffer any transformations or modifications. Out of the first movement of this entity arises ego (*svatā*), which, in spite of its appearance, is in reality nothing but the ultimate entity. Gradually, by a series of movements (*spanda*) like waves in the air, there springs forth the entire world-appearance. The ultimate entity is a mere entity of pure conceiving or imagining (*saṃkalpa-puruṣa*)[2]. The Muni held that what appears before us is due to the imagination of *manas*, like dreamland or fairyland (*yathā saṃkalpa-nagaraṃ yathā gandharva-pattanam*). There is nothing in essence except that ultimate entity, and whatever else appears does not exist at all—it is all mere mental creations, proceeding out of the substanceless, essenceless mental creations of the ultimate entity. It is only by the realization that this world-appearance has no possibility of existence that the false notion of ourselves as knowers ceases, and, though the false appearance may continue as such, there is emancipation (*mokṣa*).

This *manas*, however, by whose mental creations everything springs forth in appearance, has no proper form, it is merely a name, mere nothingness[3]. It does not exist outside or subjectively inside us; it is like the vacuity surrounding us everywhere. That anything has come out of it is merely like the production of a mirage stream. All characteristics of forms and existence are like momentary imaginations. Whatever appears and seems to have existence is nothing but *manas*, though this *manas* itself is merely a hypothetical starting-point, having no actual reality. For the *manas* is not different from the dreams of appearance and cannot be separated from them, just as one cannot separate liquidity from water or movement from air. *Manas* is thus nothing but the hypothetical entity from which all the dreams of appearance proceed, though these dreams and *manas* are merely the same and

[1] *Yoga-vāsiṣṭha*, iii. 3.

[2] *sarveṣāṃ bhūta-jātānāṃ saṃsāra-vyavahāriṇām*
prathamo' sau pratispandaś citta-dehaḥ svatodayaḥ
asmāt pūrvāt pratispandād ananyaitat-svarūpiṇī
iyaṃ pravisṛtā sṛṣṭiḥ spanda-sṛṣṭir ivānilāt.
III. 3. 14, 15.

[3] *rāmāsya manaso rūpaṃ na kiṃcid api dṛśyate*
nāma-mātrād ṛte vyomno yathā śūnya-jaḍākṛteḥ.
III. 4. 38.

it is impossible to distinguish between them[1]. *Avidyā, saṃsṛti, citta, manas, bandha, mala, tamas* are thus but synonyms for the same concept[2]. It is the perceiver that appears as the perceived, and it is but the perceptions that appear as the perceiver and the perceived. The state of emancipation is the cessation of this world-appearance. There is in reality no perceiver, perceived or perceptions, no vacuity (*śūnya*), no matter, no spirit or consciousness, but pure cessation or pure negation, and this is what we mean by Brahman[3]. Its nature is that of pure cessation (*śānta*), and it is this that the Sāṃkhyists call *puruṣa*, the Vedāntins call "Brahman," the idealistic Buddhists call "pure idea" (*vijñāna-mātra*) and the nihilists "pure essencelessness" (*śūnya*)[4]. It is of the nature of pure annihilation and cessation, pervading the inner and the outer world[5]. It is described as that essencelessness (*śūnya*) which does not appear to be so, and in which lies the ground and being of the essenceless world-appearance (*yasmin śūnyaṃ jagat sthitam*), and which, in spite of all creations, is essenceless[6]. The illusory world-appearance has to be considered as absolutely non-existent, like the water of the mirage or the son of a barren woman. The ultimate entity is thus neither existent nor non-existent and is both statical and dynamical (*spandāspandātmaka*)[7] ; it is indescribable and unnameable (*kimapy-avyapadeśātmā*) and neither being nor non-being nor being-non-being, neither statical being nor becoming (*na bhāvo bhavanaṃ na ca*). The similarity of the philosophy of the *Yoga-vāsiṣṭha* to the idealistic philosophy of the *Laṅkāvatāra-sūtra* is so definite and deep that the subject does not require any elaborate discussion and the readers are referred to the philosophy of the *Laṅkāvatāra* in the first volume of the present work. On Vedānta lines it is very similar to Prakāśānanda's interpretation of the Vedānta in later times, called *dṛṣṭi-sṛṣṭi-vāda,* which can probably be traced at least as far back as Gauḍapāda or Maṇḍana. Prakāśātman refers to the *Yoga-vāsiṣṭha* as one of his main authorities.

[1] *pūrṇe pūrṇaṃ prasarati śānte śāntaṃ vyavasthitam*
vyomany evoditaṃ vyoma brahmaṇi brahma tiṣṭhati
na dṛśiyam asti sad-rūpaṃ na draṣṭā na ca darśanaṃ
na śūnyaṃ na jaḍaṃ no cic chāntam evedam ātatam.

III. 4. 69, 70.

[2] III. 4. 46.

[3] III. 5. 6–7.

[4] *nāśa-rūpo vināśātmā.* III. 5. 16.

[5] III. 7. 22.

[6] III. 9. 59.

[7] III. 9. 49.

Origination.

The world as such never existed in the past, nor exists now, nor will exist hereafter; so it has no production or destruction in any real sense[1]. But yet there is the appearance, and its genesis has somehow to be accounted for. The ultimate entity is, of course, of the nature of pure cessation (*śānta*), as described above. The order of moments leading to the manifestation of the world-appearance can be described in this way: At first there is something like a self-reflecting thought in the ultimate entity, producing some indescribable objectivity which gives rise to an egohood. Thus, on a further movement, which is akin to thought, is produced a state which can be described as a self-thinking entity, which is clear pure intelligence, in which everything may be reflected. It is only this entity that can be called conscious intelligence (*cit*). As the thought-activity becomes more and more concrete (*ghana-saṃvedana*), other conditions of soul (*jīva*) arise out of it. At this stage it forgets, as it were, its subject-objectless ultimate state, and desires to flow out of itself as a pure essence of creative movement (*bhāvanā-mātra-sāra*). The first objectivity is *ākāśa*, manifested as pure vacuity. At this moment arise the ego (*ahaṃtā*) and time (*kāla*). This creation is, however, in no sense real, and is nothing but the seeming appearances of the self-conscious movement (*sva-saṃvedana-mātrakam*) of the ultimate being. All the network of being is non-existent, and has only an appearance of existing. Thought(*saṃvit*), which at this moment is like the *ākāśa* and the ego and which is the seed (*bīja*) of all the conceivings of thought (*bhāvanā*), formulates by its movement air[2]. Again,

[1] *bandhyā-putra-vyoma-bane yathā na staḥ kadācana*
jagad-ādy akhilaṃ dṛśyaṃ tathā nāsti kadācana
na cotpannaṃ na ca dhvaṃsi yat kilādau na vidyate
utpattiḥ kīdṛśī tasya nāśa-śabdasya kā kathā. III. 11.4, 5

[2] *manaḥ sampadyate lolaṃ kalanā-kalanonmukham;*
kalayantī manaḥ śaktir ādau bhāvayati kṣaṇāt.
ākāśa-bhāvanāmacchāṃ śabda-bīja-rasonmukhīm;
tatas tāṃ ghanatāṃ jātaṃ ghana-spanda-kramān manaḥ.
IV. 44. 16, 17.

A comparison of numerous passages like these shows that each mental creation is the result of a creative thought-movement called *bhāvanā,* and each successive movement in the chain of a succession of developing creative movements is said to be *ghana*, or concrete. *Ghana* has been paraphrased in the *Tātparya-prakāśa* as accretion (*upacaya*). *Bhāvāna* is the same as *spanda*; as the result of each thought-movement, there was thought-accretion (*ghana*), and corresponding to each *ghana* there was a semi-statical creation, and following each *ghana* there was a *spanda* (*ghana-spanda-kramāt*).

following the ākāśa moment and from it as a more concrete state (*ghanībhūya*), comes forth the sound-potential (*kha-tan-mātra*). This sound-potential is the root of the production of all the Vedas, with their words, sentences and valid means of proof. Gradually the conceivings of the other *tan-mātras* of *sparśa*, *tejas*, *rasa* and *gandha* follow, and from them the entire objective world, which has no other reality than the fact that they are conceptions of the self-conscious thought[1]. The stages then are, that in the state of equilibrium (*sama*) of the ultimate indescribable entity called the Brahman, which, though pure consciousness in essence, is in an unmanifested state, there first arises an objectivity (*cetyatva*) through its self-directed self-consciousness of the objectivity inherent in it (*sataś cetyāṃśa-cetanāt*); next arises the soul, where there is objective consciousness only through the touch or connection of objectivity (*cetya-saṃyoga-cetanāt*) instead of the self-directed consciousness of objectivity inherent in itself. Then comes the illusory notion of subjectivity, through which the soul thinks that it is only the conscious subject and as such is different from the object (*cetyaika-paratā-vaśāt*). This moment naturally leads to the state of the subjective ego, which conceives actively (*buddhitvākalanaṃ*), and it is this conceiving activity which leads to the objective conceptions of the different *tan-mātras* and the world-appearance. These are all, however, ideal creations, and as such have no reality apart from their being as mere appearance. Since their nature is purely conceptual (*vikalpa*), they cannot be real at any time. All that appears as existent does so only as a result of the conceptual activity of thought. Through its desire, "I shall see," there comes the appearance of the two hollows of the eye, and similarly in the case of touch, smell, hearing and taste. There is no single soul, far less an infinite number of them. It is by the all-powerful conceptual activity of Brahman that there arises the appearance of so many centres of subjective thought, as the souls (*jīvas*). In reality, however, the *jīvas* have no other existence than the conceptualizing activity which produces their appearance. There is no materiality or form: these are nothing but the self-flashings of thought (*citta-camatkāra*).

Manas, according to this theory, is nothing but that function of pure consciousness through which it posits out of itself an object of itself. Here the pure conscious part may be called the spiritual

[1] III. 12.

part and its objectivity aspect the material part[1]. In its objectivity also the *cit* perceives nothing but itself, though it appears to perceive something other than itself (*svam evānyatayā dṛstvā*), and this objectivity takes its first start with the rise of egohood (*ahaṃtā*).

But to the most important question, namely, how the original equilibrium is disturbed and how the present development of the conceptual creation has come about, the answer given in the *Yoga-vāsiṣṭha* is that it is by pure accident (*kākatālīya-yogena*) that such a course of events took place. It is indeed disappointing that such a wonderful creation of world-appearance should have ultimately to depend on accident for its origin[2]. It is considered irrelevant to enquire into the possibility of some other cause of the ultimate cause, the Brahman[3].

Karma, Manas and the Categories.

Karma in this view is nothing but the activity of the *manas*. The active states of *manas* are again determined by their preceding moments and may in their turn be considered as determining the succeeding moments. When any particular state determines any succeeding state, it may be considered as an agent, or *kartā*; but, as this state is determined by the activity of the previous state, otherwise called the *karma*, it may be said that the *karma* generates the *kartā*, the *kartā* by its activity again produces *karma*, so that *karma* and *kartā* are mutually determinative. As in the case of the seed coming from the tree and the tree coming from the seed, the cycle proceeds on from *kartā* to *karma* and from *karma* to *kartā*, and no ultimate priority can be affirmed of any one of them[4]. But, if this is so, then the responsibility of *karma* ceases; the root desire (*vāsanā*) through which a man is born also makes him suffer or enjoy in accordance with it; but, if *kartā* and *karma* spring forth together, then a particular birth ought not to be determined by the *karma* of previous birth, and this would mean

[1] *cito yac cetya-kalanaṃ tan-manastvam udāhṛtam*
cid-bhāgo'trājaḍo bhāgo jāḍyam atra hi cetyatā. III. 91. 37.

[2] III. 96. 15, IV. 54. 7.

[3] *Brahmaṇah kāraṇaṃ kiṃ syād iti vaktuṃ na yujyate*
svabhāvo nirviśeṣatvāt paro vaktuṃ na yujyate. IV. 18. 22.

[4] *yathā karma ca kartā ca paryāyeṇeha saṃgatau*
karmaṇā kriyate kartā kartrā karma praṇīyate
bījāṅkurādivan-nyāyo loka-vedokta eva saḥ. III. 95. 19, 20.

that man's enjoyment and sorrow did not depend on his *karma*. In answer to such a question, raised by Rāmacandra, Vaśiṣṭha says that *karma* is due not to *ātman*, but to *manas*. It is the mental movement which constitutes *karma*. When first the category of *manas* rises into being from Brahman, *karma* also begins from that moment, and, as a result thereof, the soul and the body associated with it are supposed to be manifested. *Karma* and *manas* are in one sense the same. In this world the movement generated by action (*kriyā-spanda*) is called *karma*, and, as it is by the movement of *manas* that all effects take place, and the bodies with all their associated sufferings or enjoyments are produced, so even the body, which is associated with physical, external *karma*, is in reality nothing but the *manas* and its activity. *Manas* is essentially of the nature of *karma*, or activity, and the cessation of activity means the destruction of *manas* (*karma-nāśe mano-nāśaḥ*)[1]. As heat cannot be separated from fire or blackness from collyrium, so movement and activity cannot be separated from *manas*. If one ceases, the other also necessarily ceases. *Manas* means that activity which subsists between being and non-being and induces being through non-being: it is essentially dynamic in its nature and passes by the name of *manas*. It is by the activity of *manas* that the subject-objectless pure consciousness assumes the form of a self-conscious ego. *Manas* thus consists of this constantly positing activity (*ekānta-kalanaḥ*). The seed of *karma* is to be sought in the activity of *manas* (*karma-bījaṃ manaḥ-spanda*), and the actions (*kriyā*) which follow are indeed very diverse. It is the synthetic function (*tad-anusandhatte*) of *manas* that is called the functioning of the conative senses, by which all actions are performed, and it is for this reason that *karma* is nothing but *manas*. *Manas*, *buddhi*, *ahaṃkāra*, *citta*, *karma*, *kalpanā*, *saṃsṛti*, *vāsanā*, *vidyā*, *prayatna*, *smṛti*, *indriya*, *prakṛti*, *māyā* and *kriyā* are different only in name, and they create confusion by these varied names; in reality, however, they signify the same concept, namely, the active functioning of *manas* or *citta*. These different names are current only because they lay stress on the different aspects of the same active functioning. They do not mean different entities, but only different moments, stages or aspects. Thus the first moment of self-conscious activity leading in different directions is called *manas*. When, after such oscillating movement, there is

[1] III. 95.

the position of either of the alternatives, as "the thus," it is called *buddhi*. When by the false notions of associations of body and soul there is the feeling of a concrete individual as "I," it is called *ahaṃkāra*. When there is reflective thought associated with the memory of the past and the anticipations of the future, it is called *citta*. When the activity is taken in its actual form as motion or action towards any point, it is called *karma*. When, leaving its self-contained state, it desires anything, we have *kalpanā*. When the *citta* turns itself to anything previously seen or unseen, as being previously experienced, we have what is called memory (*smṛti*). When certain impressions are produced in a very subtle, subdued form, dominating all other inclinations, as if certain attractions or repulsions to certain things were really experienced, we have the root inclinations (*vāsanā*). In the realization that there is such a thing as self-knowledge, and that there is also such a thing as the false and illusory world-appearance, we have what is called right knowledge (*vidyā*). When the true knowledge is forgotten and the impressions of the false world-appearance gain ground, we have what are called the impure states (*mala*). The functions of the five kinds of cognition please us and are called the senses (*indriya*). As all world-appearance has its origin and ground in the highest self, it is called the origin (*prakṛti*). As the true state can neither be called existent nor non-existent, and as it gives rise to all kinds of appearance, it is called illusion (*māyā*)[1]. Thus it is the same appearance which goes by the various names of *jīva*, *manas*, *citta* and *buddhi*[2].

One of the peculiarities of this work is that it is not a philosophical treatise of the ordinary type, but its main purpose lies in the attempt to create a firm conviction on the part of its readers, by repeating the same idea in various ways by means of stories and elaborate descriptions often abounding in the richest poetical imagery of undeniably high aesthetic value, hardly inferior to that of the greatest Sanskrit poet, Kālidāsa.

[1] III. 96.17–31.

[2] *Jīva ity ucyate lohe mana ity apt kathyate*
cittam ity ucyate saiva buddhir ity ucyate tathā.
III. 96.34.

The World-Appearance.

The *Yoga-vāsiṣṭha* is never tired of repeating that this world is like a hare's horn, a forest in the sky, or a lotus in the sky. The state of Brahman is higher than the state of *manas*. It is by becoming *manas* that Brahman transforms itself into thought-activity and thus produces the seeming changeful appearances. But Brahman in itself cannot have anything else (*brahma-tattve 'nyatā nāsti*). But, though there is this change into *manas*, and through it the production of the world-appearance, yet such a change is not real, but illusory; for during all the time when this change makes its appearance and seems to stay, Brahman remains shut up within itself, changeless and unchangeable. All objective appearance is thus nothing but identically the same as the Brahman, and all that appears has simply no existence. The seer never transforms himself into objectivity, but remains simply identical with himself in all appearances of objectivity. But the question arises, how, if the world-appearance is nothing but the illusory creative conception of *manas*, can the order of the world-appearance be explained? The natural answer to such a question in this system is that the seeming correspondence and agreement depend upon the similarity of the imaginary products in certain spheres, and also upon accident. It is by accident that certain dream series correspond with certain other dream series[1]. But in reality they are all empty dream constructions of one *manas*. It is by the dream desires that physical objects gradually come to be considered as persistent objects existing outside of us. But, though during the continuance of the dreams they appear to be real, they are all the while nothing but mere dream conceptions. The self-alienation by which the pure consciousness constructs the dream conception is such that, though it always remains identical with itself, yet it seems to posit itself as its other, and as diversified by space, time, action and substance (*deśa-kāla-kriyā-dravyaiḥ*).

The difference between the ordinary waking state and the dream state consists in this, that the former is considered by us as associated with permanent convictions (*sthira-pratyaya*), whereas the latter is generally thought to have no permanent basis. Any experience which persists, whether it be dream or not,

[1] *melanam api svakīya-parakīya-svapnānāṃ daivāt kvacit saṃvādavat svāntaḥ-kalpanātmakam eva. Yoga-vāsiṣṭha-tātparya-prakāśa*, IV. 18. 46.

comes to be regarded as permanent, whereas, if even our waking conceptions come to be regarded as changeful, they lose their validity as representing permanent objects, and our faith in them becomes shaken. If the dream experiences persisted in time and the waking experiences were momentary, then the waking state would be considered as a dream and the dream experiences would be considered as ordinary experiences in the dream state. It is only with the coming of the waking state that there is a break of the dream experiences, and it is then that the latter are contradicted and therefore regarded as false. But so long as the dream experiences lasted in the dream state, we did not consider them to be false; for during that time those dream experiences appeared somehow to be permanent and therefore real. There is thus no difference between dream states and waking states except this, that the latter are relatively persistent, continuous and permanent (*sthira*), while the former are changeful and impermanent (*asthira*)[1].

There is within us a principle of pure consciousness, which is also the vital principle (*jīva-dhātu*), vitality (*vīrya*), and body heat (*tejas*). In the active condition, when the body is associated with manas, action and speech, the vital principle moves through the body, and on account of this all sorts of knowledge arise, and the illusion of world-appearance inherent in it is manifested as coming from outside through the various sense apertures. This being of a steady and fixed character is called the waking state (*jāgrat*). The *suṣupta*, or deep sleep state, is that in which the body is not disturbed by the movement of the *manas*, action or speech. The vital principle remains still in itself, in a potential state without any external manifestation, as the oil remains in the sesamum (*taila-saṃvid yathā tile*)[2]. When the vital principle (*jīva-dhātu*) is very much disturbed, we have experiences of the dream state.

Whenever the *manas* strongly identifies itself with any of its concepts, it appears to itself as that concept, just as an iron ball in fire becomes itself like fire. It is the *manas* that is both the perceiver (*puruṣa*) and the perceived universe (*vīśva-rūpatā*)[3].

[1] *jāgrat-svapna-daśā-bhedo na sthirāsthirate vinā*
samaḥ sadaiva sarvatra samasto 'nubhavo 'nayoḥ
svapno 'pi svapna-samaye sthairyājjāgrattvam ṛcchati
asthairyāt jāgrad evāste svapnas tādṛśa-bodhataḥ.

IV. 19. 11, 12.

[2] IV. 19. 23.
[3] IV. 20. 4.

The followers of the Sāṃkhya consider *manas* to be pure consciousness; they have also explained their doctrines in other details, and they think that emancipation cannot be attained by any way other than that which the Sāṃkhya suggests. The followers of the Vedānta also consider that emancipation is attained if one understands that all this world is Brahman and if there is self-control and cessation of desires together with this knowledge, and that this is the only way of salvation. The Vijñānavādins (Idealistic Buddhists) think that, provided there is complete self-control and cessation of all sense desires, one may attain emancipation, if he understands that the world-appearance is nothing but his own illusion. Thus each system of thought thinks too much of its own false methods of salvation (*svair eva niyama-bhramaiḥ*), springing from the traditional wrong notions. But the truth underlying all these conceptions is that *manas* is the root of all creations. There is nothing intrinsically pleasurable or painful, sweet or bitter, cold or hot, and such appearances arise only through the habitual creations of the mind. When one believes and thinks with strong faith in any particular manner, he begins to perceive things in that particular manner during that particular time[1].

Nature of Agency (Kartṛtva) and the Illusion of World-Creation.

Whenever we ascribe agency (*kartṛtva*) to any person in respect of deeds producing pleasure or pain, or deeds requiring strenuous exercise of will-power, as those of the Yoga discipline, we do it wrongly; for agency consists in the grasp of will and resolution, and so it is an internal determination of the mind, of the nature of dominant and instinctive desires and inclinations (*vāsanābh-idhānaḥ*)[2]. The inner movement of feeling in the person towards the enjoyment of experiences takes place in accordance with these fixed desires or inclinations leading him to specific forms of enjoyment. All enjoyment is thus a natural consequence of our nature and character as active agents. Since all active agency (*kartṛtva*) consists in the

[1] *na jñeneha padārtheṣu rūpam ekam udīryate*
dṛḍha-bhāvanayā ceto yad yathā bhāvayaty alam
tat tat-phalaṃ tad-ākāraṃ tāvat-kālaṃ prapaśyati.
na tad asti na yat satyaṃ na tad asti na yan mṛṣā.
IV. 21. 56, 57.

[2] *yohyantara-sthāyāḥ manovṛtter niścayaḥ upādeyatā-pratyayo vāsanābhidhā-natatkartṛtva-śabdenocyate.* IV. 38. 2.

inner effort of will, the enjoyment following such an inner exercise of will is nothing but the feeling modifications of the mind following the lead of the active exercise of the will. All action or active agency is thus associated with root inclinations (*vāsanā*), and is thus possible only for those who do not know the truth and have their minds full of the root inclinations. But those who have no *vāsanā* cannot be said to have the nature of active agents or of enjoying anything. Their minds are no doubt always active and they are active all the time; but, as they have no *vāsanā*, they are not attached to fruit, and there is the movement without any attachment. Whatever is done by *manas* is done, and what is not done by it is not done; so it is the *manas* that is the active agent, and not the body; the world has appeared from the mind (*citta or manas*), is of the essence of *manas*, and is upheld in *manas*. Everything is but a mental creation and has no other existence.

Ultimately, everything comes from Brahman; for that is the source of all powers, and therefore all powers (*śaktayaḥ*) are seen in Brahman–existence, non-existence, unity, duality and multiplicity all proceed from Brahman. The *citta*, or mind, has evolved out of pure consciousness (*cit*) or Brahman, as has already been mentioned, and it is through the latter that all power of action (*karma*), root desires (*vāsanā*), and all mental modifications appear. But, if everything has proceeded from Brahman, how is it that the world-appearance happens to be so different from its source, the Brahman? When anything comes out of any other thing, it is naturally expected to be similar thereto in substance. If, therefore, the world-appearance has sprung forth from Brahman, it ought to be similar in nature thereto; but Brahman is sorrowless, while the world-appearance is full of sorrow; how is this to be explained? To such a question the answer is, that to a person who has a perfect realization of the nature of the world-appearance, as being a mere conceptual creation from the Brahman and having no existence at all, there is no sorrow in this world-appearance nor any such quality which is different from Brahman. Only in the eyes of a person who has not the complete realization does this difference between the world-appearance and Brahman seem to be so great, and the mere notion of the identity of Brahman and the universe, without its complete realization, may lead to all sorts of mischief. On this account instruction in the identity of the Brahman and the world-appearance should never be given to anyone whose mind has not been properly purified by the essential virtues of self-control and disinclination to worldly pleasures[1]. As in magic (*indrajāla*), non-existent things are produced and existent things are destroyed, a jug becomes a cloth, and a cloth becomes a jug, and all sorts of wonderful sights are shown, though none of these appearances have the slightest essence of their own; so is the entire world-appearance produced out of the imagination of the mind. There is no active agent (*kartṛ*) and no one enjoyer (*bhoktṛ*) of the pleasures and sorrows of the world, and there is no destruction whatsoever[2].

Though the ultimate state is the indescribable Brahman or *cit*, yet it is from *manas* that all creation and destruction from cycle to cycle take their start. At the beginning of each so-called creation the creative movement of *manas* energy is roused. At the very first the outflow of this *manas* energy in the direction of a conceptual creation means an accumulation of energy in *manas*, called *ghana*, which is a sort of statical aspect of the dynamical energy (*spanda*). At the next stage there is a combination of this statical state of energy with the next outflow of energy, and the result is the stabilized accretion of energy of the second order; this is again followed by another outflow of energy, and that leads to the formation of the stabilized energy of the third order, and so on. The course of thought-creation is thus through the interaction of the actualized energy of thought with the active forms of the energy of thought, which join together, at each successive outflow from the supreme fund of potential energy. Thus it is said that the first creative movement of *manas* manifests itself as the *ākāśa* creation, and that, as a result of this creative outflow of energy, there is an accretion of energy in *manas*; at this moment there is another outflow (*spanda*) or movement on the part of *manas*, as modified by the accretion of energy of the previous state, and this outflow of *manas* thus modified is the creation of air. The outflow of this second order, again, modifies *manas* by its accretion, and there is a third outflow of energy of the *manas* as modified by the previous accretion, and so on. This process of the modification of energy by the outflow of the *manas* modified at each stage by the accretion of the outflow of energy at each of the preceding states is called

[1] *ādau śama dama-prāyair guṇaiḥ śiṣyaṃ viśodhayet*
paścāt sarvam idaṃ brahma śuddhas tvam iti bodhayet.
IV. 39. 23.

[2] *nātra kaścit kartā na bhoktā na vināśam eti.* IV. 39. 41.

ghana-spanda-krama[1]. The creation of all the so-called *tan-mātras* (subtle states) of *ākāśa*, *vāyu*, *tejas*, ap and *kṣiti* takes place in this order, and afterwards that of the *ahaṃkāra* and *buddhi*, and thus of the subtle body (*pury-aṣṭaka*); thereafter the cosmic body of Brahman is formed and developed in accordance with the root desire (*vāsanā*) inherent in *manas*. Thus here we have first the *ākāśa tan-mātra*, then the *vāyu tan-mātra* from the *ākāśa tan-mātra* plus the outflow of energy, then, from the *ākāśa tan-mātra* plus the *vāyu tan-mātra* plus the outflow of energy of the third order, *tejas tan-mātra*, and so on. Then, after the *tan-mātra*, the *ahaṃkāra* and the *buddhi*, we have the subtle body of eight constituents (*five tan-mātras*, *ahaṃkāra*, *buddhi* and the root *manas*), called the *pury-aṣṭaka* of Brahmā. From this develops the body of Brahmā, and from the creative imagination of Brahmā we have the grosser materials and all the rest of the world-appearance. But all this is pure mental creation, and hence unreal, and so also are all the scriptures, gods and goddesses and all else that passes as real.

The Stage of the Saint (Jīvan-mukta).

Emancipation (*mukti*) in this system can be attained in the lifetime of a person or after his death; in the former case it is called *sa-deha-muktatā*, or *jīvan-muktatā*. The *jīvan-mukta* state is that in which the saint has ceased to have any desires (*apagataiṣaṇaḥ*), as if he were in a state of deep sleep (*suṣuptavat*). He is self-contained and thinks as if nothing existed. He has always an inward eye, even though he may be perceiving all things with his external eye and using his limbs in all directions. He does not wait for the future, nor remain in the present, nor remember the past. Though sleeping, he is awake and, though awake, he is asleep. He may be doing all kinds of actions externally, though he remains altogether unaffected by them internally. He internally renounces all actions, and does not desire anything for himself. He is full of bliss and happiness, and therefore appears to ordinary eyes to be an ordinary happy man; but in reality, though he may be doing all kinds of things, he has not the delusion of being himself an active agent (*tyakta-kartṛtva-vibhramaḥ*). He has no antipathy, grief, emotions, or outbursts of pleasure. He is quite neutral to all who

[1] IV. 44. 13–30.

do him ill or well; he shows sympathetic interest in each person in his own way; he plays with a child, is serious with an old man, an enjoyable companion to a young man, sympathetic with the sorrows of a suffering man. He is wise and pleasant and loving to all with whom he comes in contact. He is not interested in his own virtuous deeds, enjoyments, sins, in bondage or emancipation. He has a true philosophic knowledge of the essence and nature of all phenomena, and, being firm in his convictions, he remains neutral to all kinds of happenings, good, bad, or indifferent. But from the descriptions it appears that this indifference on the part of a saint does not make him an exclusive and unnatural man; for, though unaffected in every way within himself, he can take part in the enjoyment of others, he can play like a child and can sympathize with the sorrows of sufferers[1].

Jīvan-mukti, or emancipation while living, is considered by Śaṅkara also as a possible state, though he does not seem to have used the term in his works. Thus, on the basis of *Chāndogya*, VI. 14. 2, he says that knowledge destroys only those actions which have not already begun to yield their fruits; those actions which have already begun to yield fruits cannot be destroyed by true knowledge, and so it is not possible for anyone to escape from their effects, good or bad; and it has to be admitted that even after the dawning of true knowledge the body remains until the effects of the actions which have already begun to yield fruits are exhausted by enjoyment or suffering. In explaining such a condition Śaṅkara gives two analogies: (1) as a potter's wheel goes on revolving when the vessel that it was forming is completed, so the body, which was necessary till the attainment of true knowledge, may continue to exist for some time even after the rise of knowledge; (2) as, when a man through some eye-disease sees two moons instead of one, he continues to do so even when he is convinced that there are not two moons but one, so, even when the saint is firmly convinced of the unreality of the world-appearance, he may still continue to have the illusion of world-appearance, though internally he may remain unaffected by it[2] Of the Upaniṣads only the later *Muktika Upaniṣad*, which seems to have drawn its inspiration from the *Yoga-vāsiṣṭha*, mentions the word *jīvan-mukta*, meaning those saints who live till their fruit-yielding

[1] V. 77.

[2] Śaṅkara's *Śārīraka-bhāṣya* or the *Brahma-sūtra*, IV. i. 15, 19.

actions (*prārabdha-karma*) are exhausted[1]. But, though the word is not mentioned, the idea seems to be pretty old.

The conception of *sthita-prajña* in the *Śrīmad-bhagavad-gītā* reminds us of the state of a *jīvan-mukta* saint. A *sthita-prajña* (man of steady wisdom) has no desires, but is contented in himself, has no attachment, fear or anger, is not perturbed by sorrow nor longs for pleasure, and is absolutely devoid of all likes and dislikes. Like a tortoise within its shell, he draws himself away from the sense-objects[2]. This conception of the *Śrīmad-bhagavad-gītā* is referred to in the *Yoga-vāsiṣṭha*, which gives a summary of it in its own way[3]. But it seems as if the conception of the saint in the *Yoga-vāsiṣṭha* has this advantage over the other, that here the saint, though absolutely unaffected by all pleasures and sufferings, by virtue and vice, is yet not absolutely cut off from us; for, though he has no interest in his own good, he can show enjoyment in the enjoyment of others and sympathy with the sufferings of others; he can be as gay as a child when with children, and as serious as any philosopher when with philosophers or old men. The *Śrīmad-bhagavad-gītā*, though it does not deny such qualities to a saint, yet does not mention them either, and seems to lay stress on the aspect of the passivity and neutral character of the saint; whereas the *Yoga-vāsiṣṭha*, as we have already said, lays equal stress on both these special features of a saint. He is absolutely unattached to anything, but is not cut off from society and can seemingly take part in everything without losing his mental balance in any way. The *Gītā*, of course, always recommends even the unattached saint to join in all kinds of good actions; but what one misses there is the taking of a full and proper interest in life along with all others, though the saint is internally absolutely unaffected by all that he may do.

The saint in the *Yoga-vāsiṣṭha* not only performs his own actions in an unattached manner, but to all appearance mixes with the sorrows and joys of others.

The question whether a saint is above the tyranny of the effects of his own deeds was also raised in Buddhist quarters. Thus we find in the *Kathā-vatthu* that a discussion is raised as to whether a saint can be killed before his proper time of death, and it is said that no one can attain *nirvāṇa* without enjoying the

[1] *Muktika Upaniṣad*, I. 42, also II. 33, 35, 76.
[2] *Śrīmad-bhagavad-gītā*, II. 55–58.
[3] *Yoga-vāsiṣṭha*, VI. 52–58.

fruits of accumulated intentional deeds[1]. A story is told in the *Dhammapada* commentary (the date of which, according to E. W. Burlingame, is about A.D. 450), how the great saint Moggallāna was torn in pieces by thieves, and his bones were pounded until they were as small as grains of rice; such a miserable death of such a great saint naturally raised doubts among his disciples, and these were explained by Buddha, who said that this was due to the crime of parricide, which Moggallāna had committed in some previous birth; even though he had attained sainthood (*arhattva*) in that life, he could not escape suffering the effect of his misdeeds, which were on the point of bearing fruit[2]. This would naturally imply the view that sainthood does not necessarily mean destruction of the body, but that even after the attainment of sainthood the body may continue to exist for the suffering of the effects of such actions as are on the point of bearing fruit.

The different Indian systems are, however, not all agreed regarding the possibility of the *jīvan-mukta* state. Thus, according to the Nyāya, *apavarga*, or emancipation, occurs only when the soul is absolutely dissociated from all the nine kinds of qualities (will, antipathy, pleasure, pain, knowledge, effort, virtue, vice and rooted instincts). Unless such a dissociation actually occurs, there cannot be emancipation; and it is easy to see that this cannot happen except after death, and so emancipation during the period while the body remains is not possible[3]. The point is noticed by Vātsyāyana in a discussion on *Nyāya-sūtra*, IV. 2. 42-45, where he raises the question of the possibility of knowledge of external objects through the senses and denies it by declaring that in emancipation (*apavarga*) the soul is dissociated from the body and all the senses, and hence there is no possibility of knowledge; and that with the extinction of all knowledge there is also ultimate and absolute destruction of pain[4]. The Vaiśeṣika holds the same view on the subject. Thus Śrīharṣa says that, when through right knowledge (*paramārtha-darśana*) all merit ceases, then the

[1] *Kathā-vatthu*, XVII. 2.

[2] Buddhist Legends by E. W. Burlingame, vol. 2. p. 304. The same legend is repeated in the introduction to *Jātaka* 522.

[3] *tad evam navānām ātma-guṇānāṃ nirmūlocchedo 'pavargaḥ*
tad evedam uktaṃ bhavati tad-atyanta-viyogo 'pavargaḥ.
Nyāya-mañjarī, p. 508.

yasmāt sarva-duḥkha-bījaṃ sarva-duḥkhāyatanaṃ cāpavarge
vichidyate tasmāt sarveṇa duḥkhena vimuktiḥ
apavargo no nirbījaṃ nirāyatanaṃ ca duḥkham utpadyate.
Vātsyāyana on Nyāya-sūtra, IV. 2. 43.

soul, being devoid of the seeds of merit and demerit, which produce the body and the senses, etc., and the present body having been destroyed by the exhaustive enjoyment of the fruits of merit and demerit, and there being no further production of any new body by reason of the destruction of all the seeds of *karma*, there is absolute cessation of the production of body, like the extinction of fire by the burning up of all the fuel; and such an eternal non-production of body is called *mokṣa* (emancipation)[1].

Prabhākara seems to hold a similar view. Thus Śālikanātha, in explaining the Prabhākara view in his *Prakaraṇa-pañcikā*, says that emancipation means the absolute and ultimate destruction of the body, due to the total exhaustion of merit and demerit[2]. The difficulty is raised that it is not possible to exhaust by enjoyment or suffering the fruits of all the *karmas* accumulated since beginningless time; he who, being averse to worldly sorrows and all pleasures which are mixed with traces of sorrow, works for emancipation, desists from committing the actions prohibited by Vedic injunctions, which produce sins, exhausts by enjoyment and suffering the good and bad fruits of previous actions, attains true knowledge, and is equipped with the moral qualities of passionless tranquillity, self-restraint and absolute sex-control, exhausts in the end all the potencies of his *karmas* (*niḥśeṣa-karmāśaya*) and attains emancipation[3]. This view, however, no doubt has reference to a very advanced state in this life, when no further *karma* is accumulating; but it does not call this state *mokṣa* during life; for *mokṣa*, according to this view, is absolute and ultimate non-production of body.

The *Sāṃkhya-kārikā*, however, holds that, when true knowledge is attained (*samyagjñānādhigama*), and when in consequence none of the *karmas* of undetermined fruition (*aniyata-vipāka*), accumulated through beginningless time, are able to ripen for bearing fruit, the body may still continue to remain simply by the inertia, as it were, of the old *avidyā*; just as even after the potter has ceased to operate the potter's wheel may continue to move as a

[1] *yathā dagdhendhanasyānalasyopaśamaḥ punar anutpāda evaṃ punaḥ śarīr-ānutpādo mokṣaḥ. Nyāya-kandalī*, p. 283.

Praśastapāda also writes: *tadā nirodhāt nirbījasyātmanaḥ śarīrādi-nivṛttiḥ punaḥ śarīrādy-anutpattau dagdhendhanānalavad upaśamo mokṣa iti. Praśastapādabhāṣya*, p. 282.

[2] *ātyantikas tu dehocchedo niḥśeṣa-dharmādharma-parikṣaya-nibandhano mokṣa iti. Prakaraṇa-pañcikā*, p. 156 .

[3] *Ibid*. p. 157.

result of the momentum which it has acquired (*cakra-bhramivad dhṛta-śarīraḥ*)[1].

The word *jīvan-mukta* is not used either in the *Kārikā* or in the *Tattva-kaumudī* or in the *Tattva-vibhākara*. The *Sāṃkhya-sūtra*, however, uses the term and justifies it on the same grounds as does Vācaspati[2]. The *Sāṃkhya-sūtra*, more particularly the *Pravacana-bhāṣya*, raises the threefold conception of *manda-viveka* (feeble discrimination), *madhya-viveka* (middle discrimination), and *viveka-niṣpatti* (finished discrimination)[3]. The stage of *manda-viveka* is that in which the enquirer has not attained the desired discrimination of the difference between *prakṛti* and *puruṣa*, but is endeavouring to attain it ; the *madhya-viveka* stage is the state of the *jīvan-mukta*. But this is an *asamprajñāta* state, i.e. a state in which there is still subject-object knowledge and a full conscious discrimination. The last stage, *viveka-niṣpatti*, is an *asamprajñāta* state in which there is no subject-object knowledge, and therefore there cannot in this stage be any reflection of pleasure or sorrow (due to the fructifying *karma—prārabdha-karma*) on the *puruṣa*.

The Yoga also agrees with the general conclusion of the Sāṃkhya on the subject. A man who nears the state of emancipation ceases to have doubts about the nature of the self, and begins to re-live the nature of his own self and to discriminate himself as being entirely different from his psychosis (*sattva*); but, as a result of the persistence of some decayed roots of old impressions and instincts, there may, in the intervals of the flow of true discriminative knowledge, emerge other ordinary cognitive states, such as "I am," "mine," "I know," "I do not know"; yet, inasmuch as the roots of the old impressions have already been burnt, these occasional ordinary cognitive states cannot produce further new impressions. The general impressions of cognition (*jñāna-saṃskāra*), however, remain until the final destruction of *citta*. The point here is that, the roots in the world of subconscious impressions being destroyed, and the occasional appearance of ordinary cognitive states being but remnants produced by some of the old impressions, the roots of which have already

[1] *Sāṃkhya-kārikā*, 67, 68. The *Tattva-kaumudī* here essays to base its remarks on *Chāndogya*, VI. 14. 2, as Śaṅkara did in his *bhāṣya* on the *Brahma-sūtra*. The *Tattva-vibhākara* of Vaṃśīdhara Miśra, in commenting on Vācaspati's *Tattva-kaumudī*, quotes *Muṇḍaka Upaniṣad*, II. 2. 8, and also *Śrīmad-bhagavad-gītā*, IV. 37, for its support. Compare *Yoga-vāsiṣṭha: ghanā na vāsanā yasya punarjanana-varjitā*.

[2] *Sāṃkhya-sūtra*, III. 77–83.

[3] *Ibid*. III. 77, 78.

been burnt, these occasional ordinary cognitive states are like passing shadows which have no basis anywhere; they cannot, therefore, produce any further impressions and thus cannot be a cause of bondage to the saint. With the advance of this state the sage ceases to have inclinations even towards his processes of concentration, and there is only discriminative knowledge; this state of *samādhi* is called *dharma-megha*. At this stage all the roots of ignorance and other afflictions become absolutely destroyed, and in such a state the sage, though living (*jīvann eva*), becomes emancipated (*vimukta*). The next stage is, of course, the state of absolute emancipation (*kaivalya*), when the citta returns back to *prakṛti*, never to find the *puruṣa* again[1].

Among later writers Vidyāraṇya wrote on this subject a treatise which he called *Jīvan-mukti-viveka*[2]. It is divided into five chapters. In the first he deals with the authorities who support *jīvan-mukti*; in the second, with the nature of the destruction of instinctive root inclinations (*vāsanā*); in the third, with the destruction of *manas* (*mano-nāśa*); in the fourth, with the final object for which *jīvan-mukti* is sought; and in the fifth, with the nature and characteristics of those saints who have attained *jīvan-mukti* by wisdom and right knowledge (*vidvat-saṃnyāsa*), and have virtually renounced the world, though living. The work is more a textual compilation from various sources than an acute philosophical work examining the subject on its own merits. The writer seems to have derived his main inspiration from the *Yoga-vāsiṣṭha*, though he refers to relevant passages in several other works, such as *Bṛhadāraṇyaka Upaniṣad*, *Maitreyī-brāhmaṇa*, *Kahola-brāhmaṇa*, *Śārīra-brāhmaṇa*, *Jābāla-brāhmaṇa*, *Kaṭha-vallī*, *Gītā*, *Bhāgavata*, *Bṛhaspati-smṛti*, *Sūta-saṃhitā*, *Gauḍa-pāda-kārikā*, *Śaṅkara-bhāṣya*, *Brahma-sūtra*, *Pañca-pādikā*, *Viṣṇu-purāṇa*, *Taittirīya-brāhmaṇa*, *Yoga-sūtra*, *Naiṣkarmya-siddhi*, *Kauṣītaki*, *Pañcadaśī*, *Antaryāmibrāhmaṇa*, *Vyāsa-bhāṣya*, *Brahma-upaniṣad*, the works of Yama, Parāśara, Bodhāyana, Medhātithi, Viśvarūpa Ācārya, etc.

Disinclination to passions and desires (*virakti)* is, according to him, of two kinds, intense (*tīvra*) and very intense (*tīvratara*).

[1] *Yoga-sūtra* and *Vyāsa-bhāṣya*, IV. 29–32.

[2] This Vidyāraṇya seems to be later than the Vidyāraṇya who wrote the *Pañcadaśī*, as quotations from the chapter *Brahmānanda* of the *Pañcadaśī* are found in it (chap. II, pp. 195, 196, Chowkhamba edition). So my identification of the Vidyāraṇya of the *Pañcadaśī* with the writer of *Jīvan-mukti-viveka* in the first volume (p. 419) of the present work seems to be erroneous.

Intense *virakti* is that in which the person does not desire anything in this life, whereas very intense *virakti* is that in which the person ceases to have any desires for all future lives[1]. Vidyāraṇya takes great pains to prove, by reference to various scriptural texts, that there are these two distinct classes of renunciation (*sannyāsin*), though one might develop into the other[2]. As regards the nature of *jīvan-mukti*, Vidyāraṇya follows the view of the *Yoga-vāsiṣṭha*, though he supports it by other scriptural quotations. On the subject of bodiless emancipation (*videha-mukti*) also he refers to passages from the *Yoga-vāsiṣṭha*. *Jīvan-mukti* is the direct result of the cessation of all instinctive root desires (*vāsanā-kṣaya*), the dawning of right knowledge (*tattva-jñāna*), and the destruction of *manas* (*mano-nāśa*). Vidyāraṇya, however, holds that on account of steady right knowledge even the seeming appearance of passions and attachment cannot do any harm to a *jīvan-mukta*, just as the bite of a snake whose fangs have been drawn cannot do him any harm. Thus he gives the example of Yājñavalkya, who killed Śākalya by cursing and yet did not suffer on that account, because he was already a *jīvan-mukta*, firm in his knowledge of the unreality of the world. So his anger was not real anger, rooted in instinctive passions, but a mere appearance (*ābhāsa*) of it[3].

Energy of Free-will (Pauruṣa).

One of the special features of the *Yoga-vāsiṣṭha* is the special emphasis that it lays upon free-will and its immense possibilities, and its power of overruling the limitations and bondage of past *karmas*. *Pauruṣa* is defined in the *Yoga-vāsiṣṭha* as mental and physical exertions made in properly advised ways (*sādhūpadiṣṭa*

[1] If the ascetic has ordinary desires he is called *haṃsa*; if he desires emancipation, he is called *parama-haṃsa*. The course of their conduct is described in the *Parāśara-smṛti*, *Jīvan-mukti-viveka*, I. II. When a man renounces the world for the attainment of right knowledge, it is called *vividiṣā-saṃnyāsa* (renunciation for thirst of knowledge), as distinguished from *vidvat-saṃnyāsa* (renunciation of the wise) in the case of those who have already attained right knowledge. The latter kind of *saṃnyāsa* is with reference to those who are *jīvan-mukta*.

[2] It is pointed out by Vidyāraṇya that the *Āruṇikopaniṣad* describes the conduct and character of *vividiṣā-saṃnyāsa*, in which one is asked to have a staff, one loin-cloth and to repeat the Āraṇyakas and the Upaniṣads only, and the *Parama-haṃsopaniṣat* describes the conduct and character of *vidvat-saṃnyāsa*, in which no such repetition of the Upaniṣads is held necessary, since such a person is fixed and steady in his Brahma knowledge. This makes the difference between the final stages of the two kinds of renunciation (*Jīvan-mukti-viveka*, I. 20–24).

[3] *Jīvan-mukti-viveka*, pp. 183-186.

mārgeṇa), since only such actions can succeed[1]. If a person desires anything and works accordingly in the proper way, he is certain to attain it, if he does not turn back in midway[2]. Pauruṣa is of two kinds, of the past life (*prāktana*) and of this life (*aihika*), and the past *pauruṣa* can be overcome by the present *pauruṣa*[3]. The karma of past life and the *karma* of this life are thus always in conflict with each other, and one or the other gains ground according to their respective strength. Not only so, but the endeavours of any individual may be in conflict with the opposing endeavours of other persons, and of these two also that which is stronger wins[4]. By strong and firm resolution and effort of will the endeavours of this life can conquer the effect of past deeds. The idea that one is being led in a particular way by the influence of past *karmas* has to be shaken off from the mind; for the efforts of the past life are certainly not stronger than the visible efforts of the moment.

All efforts have indeed to be made in accordance with the direction of the scriptures *(śāstra)*. There is, of course, always a limit beyond which human endeavours are not possible, and therefore it is necessary that proper economy of endeavours should be observed by following the directions of the scriptures, by cultivating the company of good friends, and by adhering to right conduct, since mere random endeavours or endeavours on a wrong line cannot be expected to produce good results[5]. If one exerts his will and directs his efforts in the proper way, he is bound to be successful. There is nothing like destiny *(daiva)*, standing as a separate force: it has a continuity with the power of other actions performed in this life, so that it is possible by superior exertions to destroy the power of the actions of previous lives, which would have led to many evil results. Whenever a great effort is made or a great energy is exerted, there is victory. The whole question, whether the *daiva* of the past life or the *pauruṣa* of this life will win, depends upon the relative strength of the two, and any part of the *daiva* which becomes weaker than the efforts of the present life

[1] *sādhūpadiṣṭa-mārgeṇa yan mano-'ṅga-viceṣṭitam*
tat pauruṣaṃ tat saphalam anyad unmatta-ceṣṭitam.

Yoga-vāsiṣṭha, II. 4. 11.

[2] *yo yam arthaṃ prārthayate tad-arthaṃ cehate kramāt*
avaśyaṃ sa tam āpnoti na ced ardhān nivartate.

Ibid. II. 4. 12.

[3] Ibid. II. 4. 17.

[4] Ibid. II. 5. 5, 7.

[5] *sa ca sac-chāstra-sat-saṅga-sad-ācārair nijaṃ phalaṃ*
dadātīti svabhāvo 'yam anyathā nārtha-siddhaye.

Ibid. II. 5. 25.

in a contrary direction is naturally annulled. It is only he who thinks that destiny must lead him on, and consequently does not strive properly to overcome the evil destiny, that becomes like an animal at the mercy of destiny or God, which may take him to heaven or to hell. The object of all endeavours and efforts in this life is to destroy the power of the so-called destiny, or *daiva*, and to exert oneself to his utmost to attain the supreme end of life.

The *Yoga-vāsiṣṭha* not only holds that *pauruṣa* can conquer and annul *daiva*, but it even goes to the extreme of denying *daiva* and calling it a mere fiction, that, properly speaking, does not exist at all. Thus it is said that endeavours and efforts manifest themselves as the movement of thought (*saṃvit-spanda*), the movement of manas (*manaḥ-spanda*), and the movement of the senses (*aindriya*). Thought movement is followed by movement of the psychosis or *ceias*; the body moves accordingly, and there is also a corresponding enjoyment or suffering. If this view is true, then *daiva* is never seen anywhere. Properly speaking, there is no *daiva*, and wherever any achievement is possible, it is always by continual strenuous effort of will, standing on its own account, or exercised in accordance with the *śāstra* or with the directions of a teacher[1]. It is for all of us to exert ourselves for good and to withdraw our minds from evil. By all the *pramāṇas* at our disposal it is found that nothing but the firm exercise of will and effort achieves its end, and that nothing is effected by pure *daiva*; it is only by the effort of eating that there is the satisfaction of hunger, it is only by the effort of the vocal organs that speech is effected, and it is only by the effort of the legs and corresponding muscles that one can walk. So everything is effected by personal efforts, when directed with the aid of the *śāstra* and proper advisers or teachers. What passes as *daiva* is a mere fiction; no one has ever experienced it, and it cannot be used by any of the senses; and the nature of efforts being essentially vibratory (*spanda*), one can never expect such movement from the formless, insensible, so-called *daiva*, which is only imagined and can never be proved. Visible efforts are all tangible and open to immediate perception; and, even if it is admitted that *daiva* exists, how can this supposed formless (*amūrta*) entity come in contact with it? It is only fools who conceive the

[1] *śāstrato gurutaś caiva svataś ceti tri-siddhayaḥ*
sarvatra puruṣārthasya na daivasya kadācana.

Yoga-vāsiṣṭha, II. 7. II.

existence of *daiva*, and depend on it, and are ruined, whereas those who are heroes, who are learned and wise, always attain their highest by their free-will and endeavour[1].

Rāma points out to Vaśiṣṭha in II. 9 that *daiva* is fairly well accepted amongst all people, and asks how, if it did not exist, did it come to be accepted, and what does it mean after all? In answer to this Vaśiṣṭha says that, when any endeavour (*pauruṣa*) comes to fruition or is baffled, and a good or a bad result is gained, people speak of it as being *daiva*. There is no *daiva*, it is mere vacuity, and it can neither help nor obstruct anyone in any way. At the time of taking any step people have a particular idea, a particular resolution; there may be success or failure as the result of operation in a particular way, and the whole thing is referred to by ordinary people as being due to *daiva*, which is a mere name, a mere consolatory word. The instinctive root inclinations (*vāsanā*) of a prior state become transformed into *karma*. A man works in accordance with his *vāsanā* and by *vāsanā* gets what he wants. *Vāsanā* and *karma* are, therefore, more or less like the potential and actual states of the same entity. *Daiva* is but another name for the *karmas* performed with strong desire for fruit, *karma* thus being the same as *vāsanā*, and *vāsanā* being the same as *manas*, and *manas* being the same as the agent or the person (*puruṣa*); so *daiva* does not exist as an entity separate from the *puruṣa*, and they are all merely synonyms for the same indescribable entity (*durniścaya*). Whatever the *manas* strives to do is done by itself, which is the same as being done by *daiva*. There are always in *manas* two distinct groups of *vāsanās*, operating towards the good and towards the evil, and it is our clear duty to rouse the former against the latter, so that the latter may be overcome and dominated by the former. But, since man is by essence a free source of active energy, it is meaningless to say that he could be determined by anything but himself; if it is held that any other entity could determine him, the question arises, what other thing would determine that entity, and what else that entity, and there would thus be an endless vicious regression[2]. Man is thus a free source

[1] *mūḍhaiḥ prakalpitaṃ daivaṃ tat-parās te kṣayaṃ gatāḥ*
prājñās tu pauruṣārthena padam uttamatāṃ gatāḥ.

Yoga-vāsiṣṭha, II. 8. 16.

[2] *anyas tvāṃ cetayati cet taṃ cetayati ko 'paraḥ*
ka imaṃ cetayet tasmād anavasthā na vāstavī.

Ibid. II. 9. 29.

of activity, and that which appears to be limiting his activity is but one side of him, which he can overcome by rousing up his virtuous side. This view of *puruṣa-kāra* and *karma* seems to be rather unique in Indian literature.

Prāṇa and its Control.

The mind (*citta*), which naturally transforms itself into its states (*vṛtti*), does so for two reasons, which are said to be like its two seeds. One of these is the vibration (*parispanda)* of *prāṇa*, and the other, strong and deep-rooted desires and inclinations which construct *(dṛḍha-bhāvanā)*[1]. When the *prāṇa* vibrates and is on the point of passing through the nerves *(nāḍī-saṃsparśanodyata)*, then there appears the mind full of its thought processes *(saṃveda-namaya)*. But when the *prāṇa* lies dormant in the hollow of the veins (*śirā-saraṇi-koṭare*), then there is no manifestation of mind, and its processes and the cognitive functions do not operate[2]. It is the vibration of the *prāṇa* (*prāṇa-spanda*) that manifests itself through the *citta* and causes the world-appearance out of nothing. The cessation of the vibration of *prāṇa* means cessation of all cognitive functions. As a result of the vibration of *prāṇa*, the cognitive function is set in motion like a top (*vīṭā*). As a top spins round in the yard when struck, so, roused by the vibration of *prāṇa*, knowledge is manifested; and in order to stop the course of knowledge, it is necessary that the cause of knowledge should be first attacked. When the *citta* remains awake to the inner sense, while shut to all extraneous cognitive activities, we have the highest state. For the cessation of *citta* the yogins control *prāṇa* through *prāṇāyāma* (breath-regulation) and meditation (*dhyāna*), in accordance with proper instructions[3].

Again, there is a very intimate relation between *vāsanā* and *prāṇa-spanda*, such that *vāsanā* is created and stimulated into activity, *prāṇa-spanda*, and *prāṇa-spanda* is set in motion through *vāsanā*. When by strong ideation and without any proper deliberation of the past and the present, things are conceived to be one's own—the body, the senses, the ego and the like—we have what is

[1] *Yoga-vāsiṣṭha*, V. 91. 14.

[2] I have translated *śirā* as veins, though I am not properly authorized to do it. For the difference between veins and arteries does not seem to have been known.

[3] *Yoga-vāsiṣṭha*, V. 91. 20–27.

called *vāsanā*. Those who have not the proper wisdom always believe in the representations of the ideations of *vāsanā* without any hesitation and consider them to be true; and, since both the *vāsanā* and the *prāṇa-spanda* are the ground and cause of the manifestations of *citta*, the cessation of one promptly leads to the cessation of the other. The two are connected with each other in the relation of seed and shoot (*bījāṅkuravat*); from *prāṇa-spanda* there is *vāsanā*, and from *vāsanā* there is *prāṇa-spanda*. The object of knowledge is inherent in the knowledge itself, and so with the cessation of knowledge the object of knowledge also ceases[1].

As a description of *prāṇa* we find in the *Yoga-vāsiṣṭha* that it is said to be vibratory activity (*spanda-śakti*) situated in the upper part of the body, while *apāna* is the vibratory activity in the lower part of the body. There is a natural *prāṇāyāma* going on in the body in waking states as well as in sleep. The mental outgoing tendency of the *prāṇas* from the cavity of the heart is called *recaka*, and the drawing in of the *prāṇas* (*dvādaśāṅguli*) by the *apāna* activity is called *pūraka*. The interval between the cessation of one effort of *apāna* and the rise of the effort of *prāṇa* is the stage of *kumbhaka*. Bhuśuṇḍa, the venerable old crow who was enjoying an exceptionally long life, is supposed to instruct Vaśiṣṭha in VI. 24 on the subject of *prāṇa*. He compares the body to a house with the ego (*ahaṃkāra)* as the householder. It is supposed to be supported by pillars of three kinds[2], provided with nine doors (seven apertures in the head and two below), tightly fitted with the tendons (*snāyu*) as fastening materials and cemented with blood, flesh and fat. On the two sides of it there are the two *nāḍīs*, *iḍā and piṅgalā*, lying passive and unmanifested (*nimīlite*). There is also a machine (*yantra*) of bone and flesh *(asthi-māṃsa-maya*) in the shape of three double lotuses *(padma-yugma-traya*) having pipes attached to them running both upwards and downwards and with their petals closing upon one another *(anyonya-milat-komala-saddala*). When it is slowly

[1] *samūlaṃ naśyataḥ kṣipraṃ mūla-cchedād iva drumaḥ.*
saṃvidaṃ viddhi saṃvedyaṃ bījaṃ dhīratayā vinā
na saṃbhavati saṃvedyaṃ taila-hīnas tilo yathā
na bahir nāntare kiṃcit saṃvedyaṃ vidyate pṛthak.

Yoga-vāsiṣṭha, V. 91. 66 and 67.

[2] *tri-prakāra-mahā-sthūṇam*, VI. 24. 14. The commentator explains the three kinds of pillars as referring to the three primal entities of Indian medicine—*vāyu* (air), *pitta* (bile) and *kapha* (phlegm)—*vāta-pitta-kapha-lakṣaṇa-tri-prakārā mahāntaḥ sthūṇā viṣṭambha-kāṣṭhāni yasya*. I am myself inclined to take the three kinds of pillars as referring to the bony structure of three parts of the body—the skull, the trunk, and the legs.

filled with air, the petals move, and by the movement of the petals the air increases. Thus increased, the air, passing upwards and downwards through different places, is differently named as *prāṇa*, *apāna*, *samāna*, etc. It is in the threefold machinery of the lotus of the heart (*hṛt-padma-yantra-tritaye*) that all the *prāṇa* forces operate and spread forth upwards and downwards like the rays from the moon's disc. They go out, return, repulse and draw and circulate. Located in the heart, the air is called *prāṇa*: it is through its power that there is the movement of the eyes, the operation of the tactual sense, breathing through the nose, digesting of food and the power of speech[1]. The *prāṇa* current of air stands for exhalation (*recaka*) and the *apāna* for inhalation (*pūraka*), and the moment of respite between the two operations is called *kumbhaka*; consequently, if the *prāṇa* and *apāna* can be made to cease there is an unbroken continuity of *kumbhaka*. But all the functions of the *prāṇa*, as well as the upholding of the body, are ultimately due to the movement of *citta*[2] Though in its movement in the body the *prāṇa* is associated with air currents, still it is in reality nothing but the vibratory activity proceeding out of the thought-activity, and these two act and react upon each other, so that, if the vibratory activity of the body be made to cease, the thought-activity will automatically cease, and vice-versa. Thus through *spanda-nirodha* we have *prāṇa-nirodha* and through *prāṇa-nirodha* we have *spanda-nirodha*. In the *Yoga-vāsiṣṭha*, III. 13. 31, *vāyu* is said to be nothing but a vibratory entity (*spandate yat sa tad vāyuḥ*).

In V. 78 it is said that *citta* and movement are in reality one and the same, and are therefore altogether inseparable, like the snow and its whiteness, and consequently with the destruction of one the other is also destroyed. There are two ways of destroying the *citta*, one by Yoga, consisting of the cessation of mental states, and the other by right knowledge. As water enters through the crevices of the earth, so air (*vāta*) moves in the body through the *nāḍīs* and is called *prāṇa*. It is this *prāṇa* air which, on account of its diverse functions and works, is differently named as *apāna*, etc.

[1] *Yoga-vāsiṣṭha*, VI. 24. It is curious to note in this connection that in the whole literature of the Āyur-veda there is probably no passage where there is such a clear description of the respiratory process. *Pupphusa*, or lungs are mentioned only by name in *Suśruta-saṃhitā*, but none of their functions and modes of operation are at all mentioned. It is probable that the discovery of the respiratory functions of the lungs was made by a school of thought different from that of the medical school.

[2] *Ibid.* VI. 25. 61–74.

But it is identical with *citta*. From the movement of *prāṇa* there is the movement of *citta*, and from that there is knowledge (*samvid*). As regards the control of the movement of *prāṇa*, the *Yoga-vāsiṣṭha* advises several alternatives. Thus it holds that through concentrating one's mind on one subject, or through fixed habits of long inhalation associated with meditation, or through exhaustive exhalation, or the practice of not taking breath and maintaining *kumbhaka*, or through stopping the inner respiratory passage by attaching the tip of the tongue to the uvula[1], or, again, through concentration of the mind or thoughts on the point between the two brows, there dawns all of a sudden the right knowledge and the consequent cessation of *prāṇa* activities[2].

Professor Macdonell, writing on *prāṇa* in the *Vedic Index*, vol. II, says, "*prāṇa*, properly denoting ' breath,' is a term of wide and vague significance in Vedic literature." In the narrow sense *prāṇa* denotes one of the vital airs, of which five are usually enumerated, viz. *prāṇa*, *apāna*, *vyāna*, *udāna* and *samāna*. The exact sense of each of these breaths, when all are mentioned, cannot be determined. The word *prāṇa* has sometimes merely the general sense of breath, even when opposed to *apāna*. But its proper sense is beyond question "breathing forth," "expiration." But, though in a few cases the word may have been used for "breath" in its remote sense, the general meaning of the word in the Upaniṣads is not air current, but some sort of biomotor force, energy or vitality often causing these air currents[3]. It would be tedious to refer to the large number of relevant Upaniṣad texts and to try to ascertain after suitable discussion their exact significance in each

[1] *tālu-mūla-gatāṃ yatnāj jihvayākramya ghanṭikām*
ūrdhva-randhra-gate prāṇe prāṇa-spando nirudhyate.

Yoga-vāsiṣṭha, V. 78. 25.

[2] It is important to notice in this connection that most of the forms of *prāṇa-yāma* as herein described, except the *haṭha-yoga* process of arresting the inner air passage by the tongue, otherwise known as *khecarī-mūdrā*, are the same as described in the *sūtras* of Patañjali and the *bhāṣya* of Vyāsa; and this fact has also been pointed out by the commentator Ānandabodhendra Bhikṣu in his commentary on the above.

[3] Difference between *prāṇa* and *vāyu*, *Aitareya*, II. 4; the *nāsikya prāṇa*, I. 4. Relation of *prāṇa* to other functions, *Kauṣītaki*, II. 5; *prāṇa* as life, II. 8; *prāṇa* connected with *vāyu*, II. 12; *prāṇa* as the most important function of life, II. 14; *prāṇa* as consciousness, III. 2. Distinction of *nāsikya* and *mukhya prāṇa*, *Chāndogya*, II. 1–9; the function of the five *vāyus*, III. 3-5; *prāṇa* as the result of food, 1. 8. 4; of water, VI. 5. 2, VI. 6. 5, VI. 7. 6; *prāṇa* connected with *ātman*, as everything else connected with *prāṇa*, like spokes of a wheel, *Bṛhadāraṇyaka*, II. 5. 15; *prāṇa* as strength, *ibid.* v. 14. 4; *prāṇa* as force running through the *suṣumṇā* nerve, *Maitrī*, VI. 21; etc.

case. The best way to proceed therefore is to refer to the earliest traditional meaning of the word, as accepted by the highest Hindu authorities. I refer to the *Vedānta-sūtra* of Bādarāyaṇa, which may be supposed to be the earliest research into the doctrines discussed in the Upaniṣads. Thus the *Vedānta-sūtra*, II. 4. 9 (*na vāyu-kriye pṛthag upadeśāt*), speaking of what may be the nature of *prāṇa*, says that it is neither air current (*vāyu*) nor action (*kriyā*), since *prāṇa* has been considered as different from air and action (in the Upaniṣads). Śaṅkara, commenting on this, says that from such passages as *yaḥ prāṇaḥ sa eṣa vāyuḥ pañca 'vidhaḥ prāṇo pāno vyāna udānaḥ samānaḥ* (what is *prāṇa* is *vāyu* and it is fivefold, *prāṇa, apāna, vyāna, udāna, samāna*), it may be supposed that *vāyu* (air) is *prāṇa*, but it is not so, since in *Chāndogya*, III. 18. 4, it is stated that they are different. Again, it is not the action of the senses, as the Sāṃkhya supposes; for it is regarded as different from the senses in *Muṇḍaka*, II. 1.3. The passage which identifies *vāyu* with *prāṇa* is intended to prove that it is the nature of *vāyu* that has transformed itself into the entity known as *prāṇa* (just as the human body itself may be regarded as a modification or transformation of *kṣiti*, earth). It is not *vāyu*, but, as Vācaspati says, *"vāyu-bheda,"* which Amalānanda explains in his *Vedānta-kalpa-taru* as *vāyoḥ pariṇāma-rūpa-kārya-viśeṣaḥ*, i.e. it is a particular evolutionary product of the category of *vāyu*. Śaṅkara's own statement is equally explicit on the point. He says, *vāyur evāyam adhyātmam āpannaḥ pañca-vyūho viśeṣātmanāvatiṣṭhamānaḥ prāṇo nāma bhaṇyate na tattvāntaraṃ nāpi vāyu-mātram,*" i.e. it is *vāyu* which, having transformed itself into the body, differentiates itself into a group of five that is called *vāyu*; *prāṇa* is not altogether a different category, nor simply air. In explaining the nature of *prāṇa* in II. 4. 10–12, Śaṅkara says that *prāṇa* is not as independent as *jīva* (soul), but performs everything on its behalf, like a prime minister (*rāja-mantrivaj jīvasya sarvārtha-karaṇatvena upakaraṇa-bhūto na svatantraḥ*). *Prāṇa* is not an instrument like the senses, which operate only in relation to particular objects; for, as is said in *Chāndogya*, V. 1. 6, 7, *Bṛhad-āraṇyaka*, IV. 3. 12 and *Bṛhad-āraṇyaka*, 1. 3. 19, when all the senses leave the body the *prāṇa* continues to operate. It is that by the functioning of which the existence of the soul in the body, or life (*jīva-sthiti*), and the passage of the *jīva* out of the body, or death (*jīvotkrānti*), are possible. The five *vāyus* are the five functionings of this vital principle, just as the fivefold mental states of right knowledge, illusion, imagination (*vikalpa*), sleep and memory are the different states of the mind. Vācaspati, in commenting on *Vedānta-sūtra*, II. 4. 11, says that it is the cause which upholds the body and the senses (*dehendriya-vidhāraṇa-kāraṇaṃ prāṇaḥ*), though it must be remembered that it has still other functions over and above the upholding of the body and the senses (*na kevalaṃ śarīrendriya-dhāraṇam asya kāryam*, Vācaspati, *ibid.*). *In Vedānta-sūtra*, II. 4. 13, it is described as being atomic (*aṇu*), which is explained by Śaṅkara as "subtle" (*sūkṣma*), on account of its pervading the whole body by its fivefold functionings. Vācaspati in explaining it says that it is called "atomic" only in a derivative figurative sense (*upacaryate*) and only on account of its inaccessible or indefinable character (*duradhigamatā*), though pervading the whole body. Govindānanda, in commenting upon *Vedānta-sūtra*, II. 4. 9, says that *prāṇa* is a vibratory activity which upholds the process of life and it has no other direct operation than that (*parispanda-rupa-prāṇanānukūlatvād avāntara-vyāpārābhāvāt*). This seems to be something like biomotor or life force. With reference to the relation of *prāṇa* to the motor organs or faculties of speech, etc., Śaṅkara says that their vibratory activity is derived from *prāṇa* (*vāg-ādiṣu parispanda-lābhasya prāṇāyattatvam*, II. 4. 19). There are some passages in the *Vedānta-sūtra* which may lead us to think that the five *vāyus* may mean air currents, but that it is not so is evident from the fact that the substance of the *prāṇa* is not air (*etat prāṇādi-pañcakam ākāśādi-gata-rajo-'ṃśebhyo militebhya utpadyate*), and the *rajas* element is said to be produced from the five *bhūtas*, and the *prāṇas* are called *kriyātmaka*, or consisting of activity. Rama Tīrtha, commenting on the above passage of the *Vedāntasāra*, says that it is an evolutionary product of the essence of *vāyu* and the other *bhūtas*, but it is not in any sense the external air which performs certain physiological functions in the body (*tathā mukhya-prāṇo'pi vāyor bāhyasya sūtrātmakasya vikāro na śārīramadhye nabhovad vṛtti-lābha-mātreṇa avasthito bāhya-vāyur eva*)[1]. Having proved that in Vedānta *prāṇa* or any of the five *vāyus* means biomotor force and not air current, I propose now to turn to the Sāṃkhya-Yoga.

The Sāṃkhya-Yoga differs from the Vedānta in rejecting the view that the *prāṇa* is in any sense an evolutionary product of the

[1] *Vidvan-mano-rañjanī*, p. 105, Jacob's edition, Bombay, 1916.

nature of *vāyu*. Thus Vijñānabhikṣu in his *Vijñānāmṛta-bhāṣya* on *Vedānta-sūtra*, II. 4. 10, says that *prāṇa* is called *vāyu* because it is self-active like the latter (*svataḥ kriyāvattvena ubhayoḥ prāṇa-vāyvoḥ sājātyāt*). Again, in II. 4. 9, he says that *prāṇa* is neither air nor the upward or downward air current (*mukhya-prāṇo na vāyuḥ nāpi śārīrasya ūrdhv-ādho-vgamana-lakṣaṇā vāyu-kriyā*).

What is *prāṇa*, then, according to Sāṃkhya-Yoga? It is *mahat-tattva*, which is evolved from *prakṛti*, which is called *buddhi* with reference to its intellective power and *prāṇa* with reference to its power as activity. The so-called five *vāyus* are the different functionings of the *mahat-tattva* (*sāmānya-kārya-sādhāraṇaṃ yat kāraṇaṃ mahat-tattvaṃ tasyaiva vṛtti-bhedāḥ prāṇāpānādayaḥ*; *see Vijñānāmṛta-bhāṣya*, II. 4. 11). Again, referring to *Sāṃkhya-kārikā*, 29, we find that the five *vāyus* are spoken of as the common functioning of *buddhi*, *ahaṃkāra* and *manas*, and Vācaspati says that the five *vāyus* are their life. This means that the three, *buddhi*, *ahaṃkāra* and *manas*, are each energizing, in their own way, and it is the joint operation of these energies that is called the fivefold *prāṇa* which upholds the body. Thus in this view also *prāṇa* is biomotor force and no air current. The special feature of this view is that this biomotor force is in essence a mental energy consisting of the specific functionings of *buddhi*, *ahaṃkāra* and *manas*[1]. It is due to the evolutionary activity of *antaḥkaraṇa*. In support of this view the *Sāṃkhya-pravacana-bhāṣya*, II. 31, *Vyāsa-bhāṣya*, III. 39, Vācaspati's *Tattva-vaiśāradī*, Bhikṣu's *Yogavarttika*, and Nāgeśa's *Chāyā-vyākhyā* thereon may be referred to. It is true, no doubt, that sometimes inspiration and expiration of external air are also called *prāṇa*; but that is because in inspiration and expiration the function of *prāṇa* is active or it vibrates. It is thus the entity which moves and not mere motion that is called *prāṇa*[2]. Rāmānuja agrees with Śaṅkara in holding that *prāṇa* is not air (*vāyu*), but a transformation of the nature of air. But it should be noted that this modification of air is such a modification as can only be known by Yoga methods[3].

The Vaiśeṣika, however, holds that it is the external air which

[1] Gauḍapāda's *bhāṣya* on the *Śaṃkhya-kārikā*, 29 compares the action of *prāṇa* to the movement of birds enclosed in a cage which moves the cage: compare Śaṅkara's reference to *Vedānta-sūtra*, II. 4. 9.

[2] *Rāmānuja-bhāṣya* on *Vedānta-sūtra*, II. 4. 8.

[3] See the *Tattva-muktā-kalāpa*, 53-55, and also *Rāmānuja-bhāṣya* and *Śrutaprakāśikā*, II. 4. 1–15.

according to its place in the body performs various physiological functions[1]. The medical authorities also support the view that *vāyu* is a sort of driving and upholding power. Thus the *Bhāva-prakāśa* describes *vāyu* as follows: It takes quickly the *doṣas*, *dhātus* and the *malas* from one place to another, is subtle, composed of *rajo-guṇa*; is dry, cold, light and moving. By its movement it produces all energy, regulates inspiration and expiration and generates all movement and action, and by upholding the keenness of the senses and the *dhātus* holds together the heat, senses and the mind[2]. Vāhaṭa in his *Aṣṭāṅga-saṃgraha* also regards *vāyu* as the one cause of all body movements, and there is nothing to suggest that he meant air currents[3]. The long description of Caraka (I. 12), as will be noticed in the next chapter, seems to suggest that he considered the *vāyu* as the constructive and destructive force of the universe, and as fulfilling the same kinds of functions inside the body as well. It is not only a physical force regulating the physiological functions of the body, but is also the mover and controller of the mind in all its operations, as knowing, feeling and willing. Suśruta holds that it is in itself *avyakta* (unmanifested or unknowable), and that only its actions as operating in the body are manifested (*avyakto vyakta-karmā ca*).

In the *Yoga-vāsiṣṭha*, as we have already seen above, *prāṇa* or *vāyu* is defined as that entity which vibrates (*spandate yat sa tad vāyuḥ*, III. 13) and it has no other reality than vibration. *Prāṇa* itself is, again, nothing but the movement of the intellect as *ahaṃkāra*[4].

Prāṇa is essentially of the nature of vibration (*spanda*), and mind is but a form of *prāṇa* energy, and so by the control of the mind the five *vāyus* are controlled[5]. The Śaiva authorities also agree with the view that *prāṇa* is identical with cognitive activity, which passes through the *nāḍīs* (nerves) and maintains all the body movement and the movement of the senses. Thus Kṣemarāja says that it is the cognitive force which passes in the form. of *prāṇa* through the *nāḍīs*, and he refers to Bhaṭṭa Kallaṭa as also holding the same view, and *prāṇa* is definitely spoken of by him as force (*kuṭila-vāhinī prāṇa-śaktiḥ*)[6]. Śivopādhyaya in his *Vivṛti* on the

[1] *Nyāya-kandalī* of Śrīdhara, p. 48.
[2] *Bhāva-prakāśa*, Sen's edition, Calcutta, p. 47.
[3] Vāhaṭa's *Aṣṭāṅga-saṃgraha* and the commentary by Indu, Trichur, 1914, pp. 138, 212.
[4] *Yoga-vāsiṣṭha*, III. 14.
[5] *Ibid.* V. 13, 78.
[6] *Śiva-sūtra-vimarśinī*, III. 43, 44.

Vijñāna-bhairava also describes *prāṇa* as force (*śakti*), and the *Vijñāna-bhairava* itself does the same[1]. Bhaṭṭa Ānanda in his *Vijñāna-kaumudī* describes *prāṇa* as a functioning of the mind (*citta-vṛtti*).

Stages of Progress.

It has been already said that the study of philosophy and association with saintly characters are the principal means with which a beginner has to set out on his toil for the attainment of salvation. In the first stage (*prathamā bhūmikā*) the enquirer has to increase his wisdom by study and association with saintly persons. The second stage is the stage of critical thinking (*vicāraṇā*); the third is that of the mental practice of dissociation from all passions, etc. (*asaṅga-bhāvanā*); the fourth stage (*vilāpanī*) is that in which through a right understanding of the nature of truth the world-appearance shows itself to be false; the fifth stage is that in which the saint is in a state of pure knowledge and bliss (*śuddha-saṃvit-mayā-nanda-rūpa*). This stage is that of the *jīvan-mukta*, in which the saint may be said to be half-asleep and half-awake (*ardha-supta-prabuddha*). The sixth stage is that in which the saint is in a state of pure bliss; it is a state which is more like that of deep dreamless sleep (*suṣupta-sadṛśa-sthiti*). The seventh stage is the last transcendental state (*turyātīta*), which cannot be experienced by any saint while he is living. Of these the first three stages are called the waking state (*jāgrat*), the fourth stage is called the dream state (*svapna*), the fifth stage is called the dreamless (*suṣupta*) state, the sixth stage is an unconscious state called the *turya*, and the seventh stage is called the *turyātīta*[3].

Desire (*icchā*) is at the root of all our troubles. It is like a mad elephant rushing through our system and trying to destroy it. The senses are like its young, and the instinctive root inclinations (*vāsanā*) are like its flow of ichor. It can only be conquered by the close application of patience (*dhairya*). Desire means the imaginations of the mind, such as "let this happen to me," and this is also called *saṅkalpa*. The proper way to stop this sort of imagining is to cease by sheer force of will from hoping or desiring in this manner, and for this one has to forget his memory; for

[1] *Vijñāna-bhairava* and *Vivṛti*, verse 67.

[2] See the *Nyāya-kandalī* of Śrīdhara, p. 48, and also *Dinakarī* and *Rāmarūdrī* on the *Siddhānta-muktāvalī* on *Bhāṣā-parichcheda*, p. 44.

[3] *Yoga-vāsiṣṭha*, VI. 120.

so long as memory continues such hopes and desires cannot be stopped. The last stage, when all movement has ceased (*aspanda*) and all thoughts and imaginations have ceased, is a state of unconsciousness (*avedanam*)[1]. *Yoga* is also defined as the ultimate state of unconsciousness (*avedana*), the eternal state when everything else has ceased[2]. In this state *citta* is destroyed, and one is reduced to the ultimate entity of consciousness; and thus, being free of all relations and differentiations of subject and object, one has no knowledge in this state, though it is characterized as *bodhātmaka* (identical with consciousness). This last state is indeed absolutely indescribable (*avyapadeśya*), though it is variously described as the state of Brahman, Śiva, or the realization of the distinction of *prakṛti* and *puruṣa*[3]. The *Yoga-vāsiṣṭha*, however, describes this state not as being essentially one of bliss, but as a state of unconsciousness unthinkable and indescribable. It is only the fifth state that manifests itself as being of the nature of *ānanda*; the sixth state is one of unconsciousness, which, it seems, can somehow be grasped; but the seventh is absolutely transcendental and indescribable.

The division of the progressive process into seven stages naturally reminds one of the seven stages of *prajñā* (wisdom) in Patañjali's *Yoga-sūtra* and *Vyāsa-bhāṣya*. The seven stages of *prajñā* are there divided into two parts, the first containing four and the second three. Of these the four are psychological and the three are ontological, showing the stages of the disintegration of *citta* before its final destruction or *citta-vimukti*[4]. Here also the first four stages, ending with *vilāpanī*, are psychological, whereas the last three stages represent the advance of the evolution of *citta* towards its final disruption. But, apart from this, it does not seem that there is any one to one correspondence of the *prajñā* states of the *Yoga-vāsiṣṭha* with those of Patañjali. The *Yoga-vāsiṣṭha* occasionally mentions the name *Yoga* as denoting the highest state and defines it as the ultimate state of unconsciousness (*avedanaṃvidur yogam*) or as the cessation of the poisonous effects of desire[5]. In the first half of the sixth book, chapter 125, the ultimate state is described as the state of universal negation (*sarvāpahnava*). Existence of *citta* is pain, and its destruction bliss; the destruction

[1] *Yoga-vāsiṣṭha*, VI. 126.

[2] *Ibid.* VI. 126. 99.

[3] *Ibid.* VI. 126. 71–72.

[4] See my *A History of Indian Philosophy*, vol. 1, Cambridge, 1922, p. 273.

[5] *Icchā-viṣa-vikārasya viyogaṃ yoga-nāmakam. Yoga-vāsiṣṭha*, VI. 37. 1; also *ibid.* VI. 126. 99.

of *citta* by cessation of knowledge—a state of neither pain nor pleasure nor any intermediate state—a state as feelingless as that of the stone (*pāṣāṇavat-samam*), is the ultimate state aimed at[1].

Karma, according to the *Yoga-vāsiṣṭha*, is nothing but thought-activity manifesting itself as subject-object knowledge. Abandonment of *karma* therefore means nothing short of abandonment of thought-activity or the process of knowledge[2]. Cessation of *karma* thus means the annihilation of knowledge. The stirring of *karma* or activity of thought is without any cause; but it is due to this activity that the ego and all other objects of thought come into being; the goal of all our endeavours should be the destruction of all knowledge, the unconscious, stone-like knowledgeless state[3].

As there are seven progressive stages, so there are also seven kinds of beings according to the weakness or strength of their *vāsanās*. There are *svapna-jāgara*, *saṅkalpa-jāgara*, *kevala-jāgrat-sthita*, *cirāj-jāgrat-sthita*, *ghana-jāgrat-sthita*, *jāgrat-svapna* and *kṣīṇa-jāgaraka*. *Svapna-jāgara* (dream-awake) persons are those who in some past state of existence realized in dream experience all our present states of being and worked as dream persons (*svapna-nara*). The commentator in trying to explain this says that it is not impossible; for everything is present everywhere in the spirit, so it is possible that we, as dream persons of their dream experience, should be present in their minds in their *vāsanā* forms (*tad-antaḥ-karaṇe vāsanātmanā sthitāḥ*)[4]. As both past and present have no existence except in thought, time is in thought reversible, so that our existence at a time future to theirs does not necessarily prevent their having an experience of us in dreams. For the limitations of time and space do not hold for thought, and as elements in thought everything exists everywhere (*sarvaṃ sarvatra vidyate*)[5]. By dreams these persons may experience changes of life and even attain to final emancipation. The second class, the *saṅkalpa-jāgaras*, are those who without sleeping can by mere imagination continue to conceive all sorts of activities and existences, and may ultimately attain emancipation. The third class, the *kevala-jāgaras*, are those who are born in this life for the first time. When such beings pass

[1] This *turīyātīta* stage should not be confused with the sixth stage of *suṣupti*, which is often described as a stage of pure bliss.

[2] *sarveṣāṃ karmaṇāṃ evaṃ vedanaṃ bījam uttamam*
svarūpaṃ cetayitvāntas tataḥ spandaḥ pravartate. *Yoga-vāsiṣṭha*, VI. II. 2. 26.

[3] *Ibid.* III. 15. 16.

[4] *Ibid.* VI. 2. 50. 9. *Tātparya-prakāśa*.

[5] *Ibid.*

through more than one life, they are called *cira-jāgaras.* Such beings, on account of their sins, may be born as trees, etc., in which case they are called *ghana-jāgaras.* Those of such beings suffering rebirth who by study and good association attain right knowledge are called *jāgrat-svapna-sthita*; and finally, those that have reached the *turya* state of deliverance are called *kṣīṇa-jāgaraka.*

Bondage (*bandha*), according to the *Yoga-vāsiṣṭha*, remains so long as our knowledge has an object associated with it, and deliverance (*mokṣa*) is realized when knowledge is absolutely and ultimately dissociated from all objects and remains in its transcendent purity, having neither an object nor a subject[1]

Methods of Right Conduct.

The *Yoga-vāsiṣṭha* does not enjoin severe asceticism or the ordinary kinds of religious gifts, ablutions or the like for the realization of our highest ends, which can only be achieved by the control of attachment (*rāga*), antipathy (*dveṣa*), ignorance (*tamaḥ*), anger (*krodha*), pride (*mada*), and jealousy (*mātsarya*), followed by the right apprehension of the nature of reality[2]. So long as the mind is not chastened by the clearing out of all evil passions, the performance of religious observances leads only to pride and vanity and does not produce any good. The essential duty of an enquirer consists in energetic exertion for the achievement of the highest end, for which he must read the right sort of scriptures (*sac-chāstra*) and associate with good men[3]. He should somehow continue his living and abandon even the slightest desire of enjoyment (*bhogagandham parityajet*), and should continue critical thinking (*vicāra*). On the question whether knowledge or work, *jñāna* or *karma*, is to be accepted for the achievement of the highest end, the *Yoga-vāsiṣṭha* does not, like Śaṅkara, think that the two cannot jointly be taken up, but on the contrary emphatically says that, just as

[1] *jñānasya jñeyatāpattir bandha ity abhidhīyate*
tasyaiva jñeyatā-śāntir mokṣa ity abhidhīyate.

Yoga-vāsiṣṭha, VI. II. 190. 1.

[2] *sva-pauruṣa-prayatnena vivekena vikāśinā*
sa devo jñāyate rāma na tapaḥ-snāna-karmabhiḥ.

Ibid. III. 6. 9.

[3] Good men are defined in the *Yoga-vāsiṣṭha* as follows:
deśe yaṃ sujana-prāyā lokāḥ sādhuṃ pracakṣate
sa viśiṣṭaḥ sa sādhuḥ syāt taṃ prayainena saṃśrayet.

Ibid. III. 6. 20.

a bird flies with its two wings, so an enquirer can reach his goal through the joint operation of knowledge and work[1].

The main object of the enquirer being the destruction of *citta*, all his endeavours should be directed towards the uprooting of instinctive root inclinations (*vāsanā*), which are the very substance and root of the *citta*. The realization of the truth (*tattva-jñāna*), the destruction of the *vāsanās* and the destruction of the *citta* all mean the same identical state and are interdependent on one another, so that none of them can be attained without the other. So, abandoning the desire for enjoyment, one has to try for these three together; and for this one has to control one's desires on one hand and practise breath-control (*prāṇa-nirodhena*) on the other; and these two would thus jointly co-operate steadily towards the final goal. Such an advancement is naturally slow, but this progress, provided it is steady, is to be preferred to any violent efforts to hasten (*haṭha*) the result[2]. Great stress is also laid on the necessity of self-criticism as a means of loosening the bonds of desire and the false illusions of world-appearance and realizing the dissociation from attachment (*asaṅga*)[3].

Yoga-vāsiṣṭha, Śaṅkara Vedānta and Buddhist Vijñānavāda.

To a superficial reader the idealism of the *Yoga-vāsiṣṭha* may appear to be identical with the Vedānta as interpreted by Śaṅkara; and in some of the later Vedānta works of the Śaṅkara school, such as the *Jīvan-mukti-viveka*, etc., so large a number of questions dealt with in the *Yoga-vāsiṣṭha* occur that one does not readily imagine that there may be any difference between this idealism and that of Śaṅkara. This point therefore needs some discussion.

The main features of Śaṅkara's idealism consist in the doctrine that the self-manifested subject-objectless intelligence forms the ultimate and unchangeable substance of both the mind (*antaḥkaraṇa*) and the external world. Whatever there is of change and mutation is outside of this Intelligence, which is also the Reality. But, nevertheless, changes are found associated with this reality or Brahman, such as the external forms of objects and the diverse mental states. These are mutable and have therefore a different kind of indescribable existence from Brahman; but still they are

[1] *Yoga-vāsiṣṭha*, I. I. 7, 8.
[2] *Ibid.* V. 92.
[3] *Ibid.* V. 93.

somehow essentially of a positive nature[1]. Śaṅkara's idealism does not allow him to deny the existence of external objects as apart from perceiving minds, and he does not adhere to the doctrine of *esse est percipi.* Thus he severely criticizes the views of the Buddhist idealists, who refuse to believe in the existence of external objects as apart from the thoughts which seem to represent them. Some of these arguments are of great philosophical interest and remind one of similar arguments put forth by a contemporary British Neo-realist in refutation of Idealism.

The Buddhists there are made to argue as follows: When two entities are invariably perceived simultaneously they are identical; now knowledge and its objects are perceived simultaneously; therefore the objects are identical with their percepts. Our ideas have nothing in the external world to which they correspond, and their existence during dreams, when the sense-organs are universally agreed to be inoperative, shows that for the appearance of ideas the operation of the sense-organs, indispensable for establishing connection with the so-called external world, is unnecessary. If it is asked how, if there are no external objects, can the diversity of percepts be explained, the answer is that such diversity may be due to the force of *vāsanās* or the special capacity of the particular moment associated with the cognition[2]. If the so-called external objects are said to possess different special capacities which would account for the diversity of percepts, the successive moments of the mental order may also be considered as possessing special distinctive capacities which would account for the diversity of percepts generated by those cognition moments. In dreams it is these diverse cognition moments which produce diversity of percepts.

Śaṅkara, in relating the above argument of the Buddhist idealist, says that external objects are directly perceived in all our perceptions, and how then can they be denied? In answer to this, if it is held that there is no object for the percepts excepting the sensations, or that the existence of anything consists in its being perceived, that can be refuted by pointing to the fact that the independent existence of the objects of perception, as apart from their being perceived, can be known from the perception itself, since the

[1] See the account of Śaṅkara Vedānta in my *A History of Indian Philosophy*, vol. 1, Cambridge, 1922, chapter X.

[2] *Kasyacid eva jñāna-kṣaṇasya sa tādṛśaḥ sāmarthyātiśayo vāsanā-pariṇāmaḥ. Bhāmatī*, II. II. 28.

perceiving of an object is not the object itself; it is always felt that the perception of the blue is different from the blue which is perceived; the blue stands forth as the object of perception and the two can never be identical. This is universally felt and acknowledged, and the Buddhist idealist, even while trying to refute it, admits it in a way, since he says that what is inner perception appears as if it exists outside of us, externally. If externality as such never existed, how could there be an appearance of it in consciousness ? When all experiences testify to this difference between knowledge and its object, the inner mental world of thoughts and ideas and the external world of objects, how can such a difference be denied? You may see a jug or remember it: the mental operation in these two cases varies, but the object remains the same[1].

The above argument of Śaṅkara against Buddhist idealism conclusively proves that he admitted the independent existence of objects, which did not owe their existence to anybody's knowing them. External objects had an existence different from and independent of the existence of the diversity of our ideas or percepts.

But the idealism of the *Yoga-vāsiṣṭha* is more like the doctrine of the Buddhist idealists than the idealism of Śaṅkara. For according to the *Yoga-vāsiṣṭha* it is only ideas that have some sort of existence. Apart from ideas or percepts there is no physical or external world having a separate or independent existence. *Esse est percipi* is the doctrine of the *Yoga-vāsiṣṭha*, while Śaṅkara most emphatically refutes such a doctrine. A later exposition of Vedānta by Prakāśānanda, known as *Vedānta-siddhānta-muktāvalī*, seems to derive its inspiration from the *Yoga-vāsiṣṭha* in its exposition of Vedānta on lines similar to the idealism of the *Yoga-vāsiṣṭha*, by denying the existence of objects not perceived (*ajñāta-sattvānabhyupagama*)[2]. Prakāśānanda disputes the ordinarily accepted view that cognition of objects arises out of the contact of senses with objects; for objects for him exist only so long as they are perceived, i.e. there is no independent external existence of objects apart from their perception. All objects have only perceptual existence (*prātītikasattva*). Both Prakāśānanda and the *Yoga-vāsiṣṭha* deny the existence of objects when they are not perceived, while Śaṅkara not only admits their existence, but also holds that they exist in the same form in which they are known; and this amounts virtually to the admission that our knowing an object does not add

---

[1] Śaṅkara's *bhāṣya* on the *Brahma-sūtra*, II. 2. 28.
[2] *Siddhānta-muktāvalī*. See *The Pandit*, new series, vol. XI, pp. 129–139.

anything to it or modify it to any extent, except that it becomes known to us through knowledge. Things are what they are, even though they may not be perceived. This is in a way realism. The idealism of Śaṅkara's Vedānta consists in this, that he held that the Brahman is the immanent self within us, which transcends all changeful experience and is also ultimate reality underlying all objects perceived outside of us in the external world. Whatever forms and characters there are in our experience, internal as well as external, have an indescribable and indefinite nature which passes by the name of *māyā*[1]. Śaṅkara Vedānta takes it for granted that that alone is real which is unchangeable; what is changeful, though it is positive, is therefore unreal. The world is only unreal in that special sense; *māyā* belongs to a category different from affirmation and negation, namely the category of the indefinite.

The relation of the real, the Brahman, to this *māyā* in Śaṅkara Vedānta is therefore as indefinite as the *māyā*; the real is the unchangeable, but how the changeful forms and characters become associated with it or what is their origin or what is their essence, Śaṅkara is not in a position to tell us. The *Yoga-vāsiṣṭha* however holds that formless and characterless entity is the ultimate truth; it is said to be the Brahman, *cit*, or void (*śūnya*); but, whatever it may be, it is this characterless entity which is the ultimate truth. This ultimate entity is associated with an energy of movement, by virtue of which it can reveal all the diverse forms of appearances. The relation between the appearances and the reality is not external, indefinite and indescribable, as it is to Śaṅkara, but the appearances, which are but the unreal and illusory manifestations of the reality, are produced by the operation of this inner activity of the characterless spirit, which is in itself nothing but a subject-objectless pure consciousness. But this inner and immanent movement does not seem to have any dialectic of its own, and no definite formula of the method of its operation for its productions can be given; the imaginary shapes of ideas and objects, which have nothing but a mere perceptual existence, are due not to a definite order, but to accident or chance (*kākatālīya*). Such a conception is indeed very barren, and it is here that the system of the *Yoga-vāsiṣṭha* is particularly defective. Another important defect of the system is that it does not either criticize knowledge or admit its validity, and the characterless entity which forms its absolute is never revealed in experience.

[1] See my *A History of Indian Philosophy*, vol. 1, ch. X.

With Śaṅkara the case is different; for he holds that this absolute Brahman is also the self which is present in every experience and is immediate and self-revealed. But the absolute of the *Yoga-vāsiṣṭha* is characterless and beyond experience. The state of final emancipation, the seventh stage, is not a stage of bliss, like the Brahmahood of the Vedānta, but a state of characterlessness and vacuity almost. In several places in the work it is said that this ultimate state is differently described by various systems as Brahman, distinction of *prakṛti* and *puruṣa*, pure *vijñāna* and void (*śūnya*), while in truth it is nothing but a characterless entity. Its state of *mukti* (emancipation) is therefore described, as we have already seen above, as *pāṣāṇavat* or like a stone, which strongly reminds us of the Vaiśeṣika view of *mukti*. On the practical side it lays great stress on *pauruṣa*, or exertion of free-will and energy, it emphatically denies *daiva* as having the power of weakening *pauruṣa* or even exerting a superior dominating force, and it gives us a new view of *karma* as meaning only thought-activity. As against Śaṅkara, it holds that knowledge (*jñāna*) and *karma* may be combined together, and that they are not for two different classes of people, but are both indispensable for each and every right-minded enquirer. The principal practical means for the achievement of the highest end of the *Yoga-vāsiṣṭha* are the study of philosophical scripture, association with good men and self-criticism. It denounces external religious observances without the right spiritual exertions as being worse than useless. Its doctrine of *esse est percipi* and that no experiences have any objective validity outside of themselves, that there are no external objects to which they correspond and that all are but forms of knowledge, reminds us very strongly of what this system owes to Vijñānavāda Buddhism. But, while an important Vijñānavāda work like the *Laṅkāvatāra-sūtra* tries to explain through its various categories the origin of the various appearances in knowledge, no such attempt is made in the *Yoga-vāsiṣṭha*, where it is left to chance. It is curious that in the Sanskrit account of Vijñānavāda by Hindu writers, such as Vācaspati and others, these important contributions of the system are never referred to either for the descriptive interpretation of the system or for its refutation. While there are thus unmistakable influences of Vijñānavāda and Gauḍapāda on the *Yoga-vāsiṣṭha*, it seems to have developed in close association with the Śaiva, as its doctrine of *spanda*, or immanent activity, so clearly shows. This point will, however, be more fully discussed in my treatment of Śaiva philosophy.

APPENDIX TO VOLUME I

THE *LOKĀYATA, NĀSTIKA* AND *CĀRVAKA*

THE materialistic philosophy known as the *Lokāyata,* the *Cārvāka* or the *Bārhaspatya* is probably a very old school of thought. In the *Śvetāśvatara Upaniṣad* a number of heretical views are referred to and among these we find the doctrine which regarded matter or the elements (*bhūtāni*) as the ultimate principle. The name *Lokāyata* is also fairly old. It is found in Kauṭilya's *Artha-śāstra,* where it is counted with Śaṃkhya and Yoga as a logical science (*ānvīkṣikī*)[1]. Rhys Davids has collected a number of Pāli passages in which the word *Lokāyata* occurs and these have been utilized in the discussion below[2]. Buddhaghoso speaks of *Lokāyata* as a *vitaṇḍā-vāda-sattham*[3]. *Vitaṇḍā* means tricky disputation and it is defined in the *Nyāya-sūtra,* I. 2. 3, as that kind of tricky logical discussion (*jalpa)* which is intended only to criticize the opponent's thesis without establishing any other counter-thesis (*sā pratipakṣa-sthāpanā-hīnā vitaṇḍā*), and it is thus to be distinguished from *vāda* which means a logical discussion undertaken in all fairness for upholding a particular thesis. *Vitaṇḍā,* however, has no thesis to uphold, but is a kind of *jalpa* or tricky argument which seeks to impose a defeat on the opponent by wilfully giving a wrong interpretation of his words and arguments (*chala*), by adopting false and puzzling analogies (*jāti*), and thus to silence or drive him to self-contradiction and undesirable conclusions (*nigraha-sthāna*) by creating an atmosphere of confusion. But *vitaṇḍā* cannot then be a *vāda*, for *vāda* is a logical discussion for the ascertainment of truth, and thus the word *vitaṇḍā-vāda* would be self-contradictory. Jayanta, however, points out that the Buddhists did not make any distinction

[1] Kauṭilya, *Artha-śāstra,* I. I.

[2] *Dialogues of the Buddha,* vol. I, p. 166. In recent times two Italian scholars, Dr Piszzagalli and Prof. Tucci, have written two works called *Nāstika, Cārvāka Lokāyatika* and *Linee di una storia del Materialismo Indiano* respectively in which they attempt to discover the meaning of the terms *nāstika, cārvāka* and *lokāyata* and also the doctrines of the sects. Most of the Pāli passages which they consider are those already collected by Rhys Davids.

[3] *Abhidhāna-ppadīpikā,* V. 112, repeats Buddhaghoso's words "*vitaṇḍā-sattham viññeyaṃ yaṃ taṃ lokāyatam.*"

between a pure logical argument and a tricky disputation and used the same word *vāda* to denote both these forms of argument[1]. This explains why *Lokāyata,* though consisting merely of *vitaṇḍā,* could also be designated as *vāda* in Buddhist literature. A few examples of this *vitaṇḍā* are given by Buddhaghoso in the same commentary in explaining the term "*loka-khāyikā*" (lit. "popular story," but "popular philosophy" according to P. T. S. Pali Dictionary)—the crows are white because their bones are white the geese are red because their blood is red[2]. Such arguments are there designated as being *vitaṇḍā-sallāpa-kathā,* where *sallāpa* and *kathā* together mean conversational talk, *sallāpa* being derived from *sam* and *lap.* According to the definitions of the *Nyāya-sūtra,* 2. 18, these would not be regarded as instances of *vitaṇḍā* but of *jāti,* i. e. inference from false analogies where there is no proper concomitance, and not *vitaṇḍā* as just explained. Rhys Davids quotes another passage from the *Sadda-nīti* of the *Aggavaṃsa* (early twelfth century) which, in his translation, runs as follows: "*Loka* means 'the common world' (*bāla-loka*). *Lokāyata* means '*āyatanti, ussāhanti vāyamanti vādassadenāti*'; that is, they exert themselves about it, strive about it, through the pleasure they take in discussion. Or perhaps it means 'the world does not make any effort (*yatati*) by it,' that it does not depend on it, move on by it (*na yatati na īhati vā*). For living beings (*sattā*) do not stir up their hearts (*cittaṃ na uppādenti*) by reason of that book (*taṃ hi gandhaṃ nissāya*)[3]." Now the *Lokāyata* is the book of the unbelievers (*titthia-satthaṃ yaṃ loke vitaṇḍā-sattham uccati*), full of such useless disputations as the following: "All is impure; all is not impure; the crow is white, the crane is black; and for this reason or for that"—the book which is known in the world as the *vitaṇḍā-sattha,* of which the Bodhisattva, the incomparable leader, Vidhura the Pundit, said: "Follow not the *Lokāyata,* that works not for the

[1] *ity udāhṛtam idaṃ kathā-trayaṃ yat paraspara-vivikta-lakṣaṇam*
sthūlam apy anavalokya kathyate vāda eka iti śākya-śiṣyakaiḥ.
Nyāya-mañjarī, p. 596.

[2] *Sumaṅgala-vilāsinī,* I. 90, 91.

[3] This translation is inexact. There is no reference to any book in the Pāli passage; in the previous sentence there was a word *vādassādana* which was translated. as "through the pleasure they take in discussion, " whereas the literal translation would be "by the taste (*assāda*) of the disputation," and here it means "pursuing that smell" people do not turn their minds to virtuous deeds.

progress in merit[1]." Thus, from the above and from many other passages from the Pāli texts it is certain that the *Lokāyata* means a kind of tricky disputation, sophistry or casuistry practised by the non-Buddhists which not only did not lead to any useful results but did not increase true wisdom and led us away from the path of Heaven and of release. The common people were fond of such tricky discourses and there was a systematic science (*śāstra* or *sattha*) dealing with this subject, despised by the Buddhists and called the *vitaṇḍā-sattha*[2]. *Lokāyata* is counted as a science along with other sciences in *Dīghanikāya,* III. I. 3, and also in *Aṅguttara*, I. 163, and in the *Divyāvadāna* it is regarded as a special branch of study which had a bhāṣya and a *pravacana* (commentaries and annotations on it)[3].

There seems to be a good deal of uncertainty regarding the meaning of the word *Lokāyata.* It consists of two words, *loka* and *āyata* or *ayata; āyata* may be derived as *ā* + *yaṃ* + *kta* or from *ā*+*yat* (to make effort) + *a* either in the accusative sense or in the sense of the verb itself, and *ayata* is formed with the negative particle *a* and *yat* (to make effort). On the passage in the *Agga-vaṃsa* which has already been referred to, it is derived firstly as *a* + *yatanti* (makes great effort) and the synonyms given are *ussāhanti vāyamanti,* and secondly as *a* + *yatanti*, i.e. by which people cease to make efforts (*tena loko na yatati na īhati vā lokā-yatam*). But Prof. Tucci quotes a passage from Buddhaghoso's *Sārattha-pakāsinī* where the word *āyata* is taken in the sense of

[1] See *Dialogues of the Buddha,* I. 168. The translation is inexact. The phrase "All is impure; all is not impure" seems to be absent in the Pāli text. The last passage quoted from *Vidhura-paṇḍita-jātaka* (Fausboll, VI, p. 286) which is one of the most ancient of the *jātakas* runs as follows: "*na seve lokāyatikaṃ na' etam paññāya vaddhanaṃ.*" The unknown commentator describes the *lokāyatika* as "*lokayātikan ti anattha-nissitam sagga-maggānāṃ adāyakaṃ aniyyānikam vitaṇḍa-sallāpam lokāyatika-vādaṃ seveyya.*" The *Lokāyata* leads to mischievous things and cannot lead to the path of Heaven or that of release and is only a tricky disputation which does not increase true wisdom.

[2] Rhys Davids seems to make a mistake in supposing that the word *Vidaddha* in *Vidaddhavādi* is only the same word as *vitaṇḍā* wrongly spelt (*Dialogues of the Buddha,* i. 167) in the *Aṭthasālinī,* pp. 3, 90, 92, 241. The word *vidaddha* is not *vitaṇḍā* but *vidagdha* which is entirely different from *vitaṇḍā*.

[3] *lokāyataṃ bhāṣya-pravacanam, Divyāvadāna*, p. 630; also *chandasi vā vyākaraṇe vā lokāyate vā pramāṇa-mīmāṃsāyāṃ vā na cai-ṣāṃ ūhā-pohaḥ pra-jñāyate Ibid.* p. 633.

It is true, however, that *lokāyata* is not always used in the sense of a technical logical science, but sometimes in its etymological sense (i. e. what is prevalent among the people, *lokeṣu āyato lokā-yataḥ*) as in *Divyāvadāna,* p. 619, where we find the phrase "*lokāyata-yajña-mantreṣu niṣṇātaḥ.*"

āyatara (basis), and *lokāyata* according to this interpretation means "the basis of the foolish and profane world[1]." The other meaning of *lokāyata* would be *lokeṣu āyata,* i. e. that which is prevalent among the common people, and this meaning has been accepted by Cowell in his translation of *Sarva-darśana-saṃgraha* and here the derivation would be from *a+ yam + kta* (spreading over)[2]. The *Amara-koṣa* only mentions the word and says that it is to be in the neuter gender as *lokāyatam.* It seems that there are two *lokāyata* words. One as adjective meaning "prevalent in the world or among the common people" and another as a technical word meaning "the science of disputation, sophistry and casuistry" (*vitaṇḍā-vāda-sattaṃ*); but there seems to be no evidence that the word was used to mean "nature-lore," as suggested by Rhys Davids and Franke, or "polity or political science" as suggested by other scholars. The *Śukra-nīti* gives a long enumeration of the science and arts that were studied and in this it counts the *nāstika-śāstra* as that which is very strong in logical arguments and regards all things as proceeding out of their own nature and considers that there are no Vedas and no god[3]. Medhātithi, in commenting upon *Manu,* VII. 43, also refers to the *tarka-vidyā* of the Cārvākas, and all the older references that have been discussed show that there was a technical science of logic and sophistry called the *Lokāyata.* Fortunately we have still further conclusive evidence that the *Lokāyata-śāstra* with its commentary existed as early as the time of Kātyāyana, i. e. about B.C. 300. There is a *Vārtika* rule associated with VII. 3. 45 "*varṇaka-tāntave upasaṃkhyānam,*" that the word *varṇaka* becomes *varṇakā* in the feminine to mean a blanket or a wrapper (*prāvaraṇa*), and Patañjali (about B.C. 150), in interpreting this *vārtika sutra,* says that the object of restricting the formation of the word *varṇaka* only to the sense of a cotton or woollen wrapper is that in other senses the feminine form would

[1] *Linee di una storia del Materialismo Indiano*, p. 17. *Sārattha-pakāsinī* (Bangkok), II. 96.

[2] Rhys Davids describes *lokāyata* as a branch of Brahmanic learning, probably Nature-lore, wise sayings, riddles, rhymes and theories, handed down by tradition, as to the cosmogony, the elements, the stars, the weather, scraps of astronomy, of elementary physics, even of anatomy, and knowledge of the nature of precious stones, and of birds and beasts and plants (*Dialogues of the Buddha,* I. 171). Franke translates it as "logische beweisende Naturerklärung," *Digha,* I9.

[3] *yuktir valīyasī yatra sarvaṃ svābhavikaṃ mataṃ-kasyā'pi ṇe'śvaraḥ kartā na vedo nāstikaṃ hi tat. Śukra-nīti-sāra,* IV. 3. 55.

be *varṇikā* or *varttikā* (e. g. meaning a commentary) as in the case of the *Bhāguri* commentary on the *Lokāyata—varṇikā bhāguri-lokāyatasya, vartikā bhāguri lokāyatasya*[1]. Thus it seems to be quite certain that there was a book called the *Lokāyata* on which there was at least one commentary earlier than B.C. 150 or even earlier than B.C. 300, the probable date of Kātyāyana, the author of the *vārttika-sātra.* Probably this was the old logical work on disputation and sophistry, for no earlier text is known to us in which the *Lokāyata* is associated with materialistic doctrines as may be found in later literature, where *Cārvāka* and *Lokāyata* are identified[2]. Several *sūtras* are found quoted in the commentaries of Kamalaśīla, Jayanta, Prabhācandra, Guṇaratna, etc. from the seventh to the fourteenth century and these are attributed by some to *Cārvāka* by others to *Lokāyata* and by Guṇaratna (fourteenth century) to Bṛhaspati[3]. Kamalaśīla speaks of two different commentaries on these *sūtras* on two slightly divergent lines which correspond to the division of *dhūrta* Cārvāka and *suśikṣita* Cārvāka in the *Nyāya-mañjarī.* Thus it seems fairly certain that there was at least one commentary on the *Lokāyata* which was probably anterior to Patañjali and Kātyāyana; and by the seventh century the *lokāyata* or the *Cārvāka-sūtras* had at least two commentaries representing two divergent schools of interpretation. In addition to this there was a work in verse attributed to Bṛhaspati, quotations from which have been utilized for the exposition of the Cārvāka system in the *Sarva-darśana-saṃgraha.* It is difficult, however, to say how and when this older science of sophistical logic or of the art of disputation became associated with materialistic theories and revolutionary doctrines of morality, and came to be hated by Buddhism, Jainism and Hinduism alike. Formerly it was hated only by the Buddhists, whereas the Brahmins are said to have learnt this science as one of the various auxiliary branches of study[4].

It is well known that the cultivation of the art of disputation is very old in India. The earliest systematic treatise of this is to be found in the *Caraka-saṃhitā* (first century A.D.) which is only a

[1] Patañjali's *Mahā-bhāṣya* on *Pāṇini,* VII. 3 45, and Kaiyaṭa's commentary on it.

[2] *tan-nāmāni cārvāka-lokāyate-ty-ādīni.* Guṇaratna's commentary on *Sad-darśana-samuccaya,* p. 300. *Lokāyata* according to Guṇaratna means those who behave like the common undiscerning people—*lokā nirvicārāḥ sāmānyā lokās tadvād ācaranti sma iti lokāyatā lokāyatikā ity api.*

[3] *Ibid.* p. 307, *Tattva-saṃgraha,* p. 520.

[4] *Aṅguttara,* I. 163.

revision of an earlier text (*Agniveśa-saṃhitā*), which suggests the existence of such a discussion in the first or the second century B. C. if not earlier. The treatment of this art of disputation and sophistry in the *Nyāya-sūtras* is well known. Both in the Āyur-veda and in the Nyāya people made it a point to learn the sophistical modes of disputation to protect themselves from the attacks of their opponents. In the *Kathā-vatthu* also we find the practical use of this art of disputation. We hear it also spoken of as *hetu-vāda* and copious reference to it can be found in the *Mahābhārata*[1]. In the *Aśva-medha-parvan* of the *Mahābhārata* we hear of *hetu-vādins* (sophists or logicians) who were trying to defeat one another in logical disputes[2]. Perhaps the word *vākovākya* in the *Chāndogya Upaniṣad,* VII. I. 2, VII. 2. I, VII. 7 I, also meant some art of disputation. Thus it seems almost certain that the practice of the art of disputation is very old. One other point suggested in this connection is that it is possible that the doctrine of the orthodox Hindu philosophy, that the ultimate truth can be ascertained only by an appeal to the scriptural texts, since no finality can be reached by arguments or inferences, because what may be proved by one logician may be controverted by another logician and that disproved by yet another logician, can be traced to the negative influence of the sophists or logicians who succeeded in proving theses which were disproved by others, whose findings were further contradicted by more expert logicians[3]. There were people who tried to refute by arguments the Vedic doctrines of the immortality of souls, the existence of a future world either as rebirth or as the *pitṛ-yāna* or the *deva-yāna,* the efficacy of the Vedic sacrifices and the like, and these logicians or sophists (*haituka*) who reviled the Vedas were called *nāstikas*. Thus, Manu says that the Brahmin who through a greater confidence in the science of logic (*hetu-śāstra*) disregards the authority of the Vedas and the *smṛti* are but *nāstikas* who should be driven out by good

[1] *Mahābhārata,* III. I 3034, v. 1983; XIII. 789, etc.

[2] *Ibid.* xiv. 85. 27.

[3] Compare *Brahma-sūtra* "*tarkā-pratiṣṭhānād apy anyathā-numānam iti ced evam api avimokṣa-prasaṅgaḥ.* II. I. II.

Śaṅkara also says: *yasmān nirāgamāḥ puruṣo-prekṣā-mātra-nibandhanāḥ tarkāḥ a pratiṣṭhitā bhavanti utprekṣāyāḥ nirankuśatvāt kair apy utprekṣitāḥ santaḥ tato'nyair ābhāsyante iti na pratiṣṭhitatvaṃ tarkānaṃ śakyam aśrayitum.*

Vācaspati, commenting on the commentary of Śaṅkara, quotes from *Vākya-padīya: yatnenā' numito'py arthaḥ kuśalair anumāṭrbhiḥ abhiyuktatarair anyair anyathai'vo'papādyate.*

men[1]. The *Bhāgavata-purāṇa* again says that one should neither follow the Vedic cult, nor be a heretic (*pāṣaṇḍī*, by which the Buddhists and Jains were meant), nor a logician (*haituka*) and take the cause of one or the other party in dry logical disputations[2]. Again, in *Manu*, IV. 30, it is said that one should not even speak with the heretics (*pāṣaṇḍino*), transgressors of caste disciplines (*vikarmasthān*), hypocrites (*vaiḍāla-vratika*), double-dealers and sophists (*haituka*)[3]. These *haitukas*, sophists or logicians thus indulged in all kinds of free discussions and controverted the Vedic doctrines. They could not be the Naiyāyikas or the Mīmāṃsists who were also sometimes called *haituka* and *tarkī* because they employed their logical reasonings in accordance with the Vedic doctrines[4]. Thus we reach another stage in our discussion in which we discover that the *haitukas* used sophistical reasonings not only in their discussions, but also for repudiating the Vedic, and probably also the Buddhistic doctrines, for which they were hated both by the Vedic people and the Buddhists; and thus the sophistical or logical science of disputation and criticism of Vedic or Buddhistic doctrines grew among the Brahmanic people and was cultivated by the Brahmins. This is testified by *Manu*, II. II, where Brahmins are said to take this *hetu-śāstra*, and this also agrees with *Aṅguttara*, I. 163, and other Buddhistic texts.

But who were these *nāstikas* and were they identical with the *haitukas*? The word is irregularly formed according to Paṇini's rule, IV. 460 (*asti-nāsti-diṣtaṃ matiḥ*)-Patañjali, in his commentary, explains the word *āstika* as meaning one who thinks "it exists" and *nāstika* as one who thinks "it does not exist." Jayāditya, in his *Kāśikā* commentary on the above *sūtra*, explains *āstika* as one who believes in the existence of the other world (*para-loka*), *nāstika* as one who does not believe in its existence, and *diṣṭika* as one who believes only what can be logically demonstrated[5]. But we have the

[1] *yo'vamanyeta te mūle hetu-śāstrā-śrayād dvijaḥ | sa sādhubhir vahiṣ-kāryo nāstiko veda-nindakaḥ. Manu*, II. II.

[2] *veda-vāda-rato na syān na pāṣand Ina haitukaḥ | śuṣka-vāda-vivāde na kañ cit pakṣaṃ samāśrayet. Bhāgavata*, XI. 18. 30.

[3] Medhātithi here describes the *haitukas* as *nāstikas*, or those who do not believe in the future world (*para-loka*) or in the sacrificial creed. Thus he says, *haitukā nāstikā nāsti paraloko, nāsti dattam, nāsti hutam ity evaṃ sthita-prajñāḥ.*

[4] *Manu*, XII. III.

[5] *paralokaḥ asti'ti yasya matir asti sa āstikaḥ, tadviparito nāstikaḥ; pramā-ṇā-nupātinī yasya matiḥ sa diṣṭikaḥ. Kāśikā* on Paṇini, IV. 4. 60. Jayāditya lived in the first half of the

definition of *nāstika* in Manu's own words as one who controverts the Vedic doctrines (*veda-nindaka*[1]). Thus the word *nāstika* means, firstly, those who do not believe in the existence of the other world or life after death, and, secondly, those who repudiate the Vedic doctrines. These two views, however, seem to be related to each other, for a refusal to believe in the Vedic doctrines is equivalent to the denial of an after-life for the soul and also of the efficacy of the sacrifice. The *nāstika* view that there is no other life after the present one and that all consciousness ceases with death seems to be fairly well established in the Upaniṣadic period; and this view the Upaniṣads sought to refute. Thus, in the *Kaṭha Upaniṣad* Naciketa says that there are grave doubts among the people whether one does or does not exist after death, and he was extremely anxious to have a final and conclusive answer from Yama, the lord of death[2]. Further on Yama says that those who are blinded with greed think only of this life and do not believe in the other life and thus continually fall victims to death[3]. Again, in the *Bṛhad-āraṇyaka Upaniṣad* (II. 4. 12, IV. 5. 13) a view is referred to by Yājñavalkya that consciousness arises from the elements of matter and vanishes along with them and that there is no consciousness after death[4]. Jayanta says in his *Nyāya-mañjarī* that the *Lokāyata* system was based on views expressed in passages like the above which represent only the opponent's (*pūrva-pakṣa*) view[5]. Jayanta further states in the same passage that no duties are prescribed in the *lokāyata*; it is only a work of tricky disputation (*vaitaṇḍika-kathai'vā'sau*) and not an *āgama*[6].

References to the *nāstikas* are found also in the Buddhist literature

seventh century.

[1] *Manu,* II. II. *Medhātithi in explaining* nāstikā'-krāntam (Manu, VIII. 22) identifies *nāstikas* with *lokāyatas* who do not believe in the other world. Thus he says, *yathā nāstikaiḥ para-lokā-pavādibhir lokāyatikā-dyṇir ākrāntam.* But in *Manu,* IV. 163, *nāstikya* is explained by him as meaning the view that the Vedic doctrines are false: *veda-pramāṇakānām arthānāṃ mithyātvā-dhyavasāysya nāstikya-śabdena pratipādanam.*

[2] *ye'yam prete vicikitsā manuṣye astī'ty eke nā'yam asti'ti cai'ke, etad-vidyām anuśiṣṭas tvayā'haṃ varāṇāṃ eṣa varas tṛtīyah. Kaṭha,* I. 20.

[3] *na sāmparāyaḥ pratibhāti bālaṃ pramādy-antaṃ vitta-mohena mūḍham; ayaṃ loko nāsti para iti mānī punah punar vaśam āpadyate me. Ibid.* II. 6.

[4] *vijñāna-ghana eva etebhyaḥ bhūtebhyo samutthāya tāny evā'nuvinaśyati, na pretya samjñā'sti ity are bravīmi. Bṛhad-āraṇyaka,* II. 4. 12.

[5] *tad evaṃ pūrva-pakṣa-vacana-mūlatvāt lokāyata-śāstram api na svatantram. Nyāya-mañjarī,* p. 271, V. S. Series, 1895.

[6] *nahi lokāyate kiñ cit kartavyam upadiśyate vaitaṇḍika-kathai'va'san* na *punaḥ kaś cid āgamaḥ. Ibid.* p. 270.

The P. T. S. Pāli Dictionary explains the meaning of the word *natthika* as one who professes the motto of "*natthi*," a sceptic, nihilist, and *natthika-diṭṭhi* as scepticism or nihilistic view. It may, however, seem desirable here to give brief accounts of some of the heretics referred to in Buddhistic literature who could in some sense or other be regarded as sceptics or nihilists. Let us first take up the case of Pūraṇa Kassapa described in *Dīgha Nikāya,* II. 16, 17. Buddhaghoso, in commenting on the *Dīgha Nikāya,* II. 2, in his *Sumaṅgala-vilāsinī,* says that, in a family which had ninety-nine servants, Kassapa was the hundredth servant and he having thus completed (*pūraṇa*) the hundredth number was called by his master *pāraṇa* (the completer), and Kassapa was his family name. He fled away from the family and on the way thieves robbed him of his cloth and he somehow covered himself with grass and entered a village. But the villagers finding him naked thought him to be a great ascetic and began to treat him with respect. From that time he became an ascetic and five hundred people turned ascetics and followed him. King Ajātaśatru once went to this Purāṇa Kassapa and asked him what was the visible reward that could be had in this life by becoming a recluse, and Pūraṇa Kassapa replied as follows: "To him who acts, O king, or causes another to act, to him who mutilates or causes another to mutilate, to him who punishes or causes another to punish, to him who causes grief or torment, to him who trembles or causes others to tremble, to him who kills a living creature, who takes what is not given, who breaks into houses, who commits dacoity, or robbery, or highway robbery, or adultery, or who speaks lies, to him thus acting there is no guilt. If with a discus with an edge sharp as a razor he should make all the living creatures on the earth one heap, one mass of flesh, there would be no guilt thence resulting, no increase of guilt would ensue. Were he to go along the south bank of the Ganges giving alms and ordering gifts to be given, offering sacrifices or causing them to be offered, there would be no merit thence resulting, no increase of merit. In generosity, in self-mastery, in control of the senses, in speaking truth, there is neither merit, nor increase of merit. Thus, Lord, did Pūraṇa Kassapa, when asked what was the immediate advantage in the life of a recluse, expound his theory of non-action (*akiriyam*)[1]."

[1] *Dialogues of the Buddha,* I. 69–70.

This theory definitely repudiates the doctrine of *karma* and holds that there is neither virtue nor vice and thus no action can lead to any fruit[1]. This is what is here called the doctrine of *akiriya* and it is in a way an answer to the question what may be the visible reward in this life of being a recluse. Since there is neither virtue nor vice, no action can produce any meritorious or evil effect—this is one kind of *nātthikavāda.* But it is wrong to confuse this *akiriya*[2] doctrine with the doctrine of inactivity (*akāraka-vāda*) attributed to Sāṃkhya by Śīlaṅka in his commentary on *Sūtra-kṛtāñga-sūtra,* I. I. 13. That *akāraka* doctrine refers to the Sāṃkhya view that the souls do not participate in any kind of good or bad deeds[3].

Let us now turn to another nihilistic teacher, viz. Ajita Keśakambalī His doctrines are briefly described in *Dīgha,* II. 22–24, where Ajita says: "There is no such thing as alms or sacrifice or offering. There is neither fruit nor result of good or evil deeds. There is no such thing as this world or the next (*n'atthi ayaṃ loko na paro loko*). There is neither father nor mother, nor beings springing into life without them. There are in the world no recluses or Brahmins who have reached the highest point, who walk perfectly and who, having understood and realized, by themselves alone, both this world and the next, make their wisdom known to others. A human being is built up of the four elements; when he dies the earth in him returns and relapses to the earth, the fluid to the water, the heat to the fire, his wind to the air, and his faculties pass into space. The four bearers, with the bier as the fifth, take the dead body away; till they reach the burning ground men utter eulogies, but there his bones are bleached and his offerings end in ashes. It is a doctrine of fools, this talk of gifts. It is an empty lie, mere idle talk, when men say there is profit therein. Fools and wise alike, on the dissolution of the body, are cut off, annihilated and after death they are not."[4] Ajita Keśakambalī was so called because he used to wear a garment made of human hair which was hot in summer and cold in winter and was thus a source of suffering[4]. It is easy to see that Ajita Keśakambalī's views were very similar to

[1] Buddhaghoso, in commenting on it says, *sabbathāpi pāpapunnānam kiriyam eva paṭikkhipati. Sumaṅgala-vilāsinī,* I. 160.

[2] This has been interpreted by Dr Barua as representing the doctrine of Pūraṇa Kassapa, which is evidently a blunder. *Prebuddhistic Indian Philosophy,* Calcutta, 1921, p. 279.

[3] *bāle ca paṇḍite kāyassa bhedā ucchijjanti vinassanti, na honti param maraṇd ti. Dīgha,* II. 23. *Dialogues of the Buddha,* pp. 73–74.

[4] *Sumaṅgala-vilāsinī,* I. 144.

the views of the Cārvākas as known to us from the fragments preserved as quotations and from accounts of them given by other people. Thus, Ajita did not believe in the other world, in virtue or vice, and denied that *karmas* produced any fruits. He, however, believed in the view that the body was made up of four elements, that there was no soul separate from the body, that with the destruction of the body everything of this life was finished, and that there was no good in the Vedic sacrifices.

Let us now turn to the doctrine of Makkhali Gosāla or Mankhaliputta Gosāla or Makkhali Gosāla who was a contemporary of the Buddha and Mahāvīra. Buddhaghoso says that he was born in a cow-shed (*go-sāla*). As he grew up he was employed as a servant; while going in the mud to bring oil he was cautioned by his master to take care not to let his feet slip (*mākhali*) in the mud; but in spite of the caution he slipped and ran away from his master, who, following him in a rage, pulled the ends of his *dhoti,* which was left in his hands, and Makkhali ran away naked. Thus left naked he afterwards became an ascetic like Pūrana Kassapa[1]. According to the *Bhagavatī-sūtra,* XV. I, however, he was the son of Makkhali who was a *mankha* (a mendicant who makes his living by showing pictures from house to house) and his mother's name was Bhaddā. He was born in a cow-shed and himself adopted the profession of a *mankha* in his youth. At his thirtieth year he met Mahāvīra and after two years he became his disciple and lived with him for six years practising penances. Then they fell out, and Makkhali Gosāla, after practising penances for two years, obtained his Jina-hood while Mahāvīra became a Jina two years after the attainment of Jina-hood by Gosāla. After this Gosāla continued to be a Jina for sixteen years and Mahāvīra met him at the end of that period in Sāvatthi where there was a quarrel between the two and Gosāla died through fever by the curse of Mahāvīra Hoernlé shows in his edition of the text and translation of *Uvāsagadasāo,* pp. 110–111, that Mahāvīra died in 450–451 B.C. at the age of 56. Makkhali was the founder of the *Ājīvaka* sect. *Ājīvakas* are mentioned in the rock-hewn cave (which was given to them) on Barabar hills near Gaya, in the seventh Pillar Edict of Asoka in 236 B.C. and in the rock-hewn caves on Nāgārjuni hill in 227 B.C. in the reign of Asoka's successor Dāsaratha. They are also mentioned in the

1 *Sumangala-vilāsinī,* I. 143, 144.

Bṛhaj-jātaka (XV. I) of Varāha Mihira in the middle of the sixth century A.D. Silāṅka (ninth century) also refers to them in his commentary on the *Sūtra-kṛtāṅga-sūtra* (I. I. 3. 12 and I. 3. 3. II), in which the *Ājīvakas* are mentioned along with *Trai-rāśikas* as being followers of Makkhali Gosāla[1]. Halāyudha also mentions the *ājīvas* as being the same as the Jains in general; but does not distinguish the *nirgranthas* from the *Digambaras* or identify the latter with the *Ājīvakas* as Hoernlé says in his article on the *Ājīvakas*[2]. Hoernle further points out in the same article that in the thirteenth-century inscriptions on the walls of the Perumāl Temple at Poygai near Virinchipuram reference is made to the taxes imposed on the *Ājīvakas* by the Chola king Rājarajā in the years A.D. 1238, 1239, 1243 and 1259. Thus it is clear that the *Ājīvaka* School of Makkhali which was started by Makkhali in the fifth century B.C. continued to exist and spread not only in North India but also in South India, and other schools also have developed out of it such as the *Trai-rāsikas.* Pāṇini's grammar has a rule (IV. I. 54), *maskara-maskariṇau veṇuparivrājakayoḥ,* which signifies that *maskara* means a bamboo and *maskarin* a travelling ascetic. Patañjali, however, in commenting on it, says that *maskarins* were those who advised the non-performance of actions and held that cessation (*śānti*) was much better (*māskṛta karmaṇi śāntir vah śreyasī ityāha ato maskarī parivrā-jakaḥ*). The word, therefore, does not necessarily mean *ekadaṇḍins* or those who bore one bamboo staff. The identification of Makkhali with *maskarins* is therefore doubtful[4]. It is also very doubtful whether the *Ājīvakas* can be regarded as the same as *Digambara* Jains, as Hoernlé supposes, for neither Varāha nor Bhoṭṭolpala identifies the *Ājīvakas* with the Jains, and Śīlāṅka treats them as different and not as identical[2]. Halāyudha also does not speak of the *Digambaras*

[1] The *Trai-rāśikas* are those who think that the self by good deeds. becomes pure and free from *karma* and thus attains *mokṣa,* but seeing the success of its favourite doctrines it becomes joyous and seeing them neglected it becomes angry, and then being born again attains purity and freedom from *karma* by the performance of good deeds and is again born through joy and antipathy as before. Their canonical work is one containing twenty-one *sūtras.* In commenting on I. 3. 3. II Śīlaṅka mentions also the *Digambaras* along with the *Ājīvakas,* but it does not seem that he identifies them in the way Hoernlé states in his scholarly article on the *Ājīvakas* in the *Encyclopaedia of Religion and Ethics.* The exact phrase of Śīlāṅka is *ājīvakā-dīnāṃ para-tīrthikānāṃ digamvarāṇāṃ ca asad-ācaraṇair upaneyā.*

[2] Hoernlé, in his article on the *Ājīvakas* in the *Encyclopaedia of Religion and Ethics,* says: "From this fact that Gosāla is called Makkhaliputta or Mankhali (*Maskarin*), i.e. the

as *Ājīvakas*[1] It is, therefore, very doubtful whether the *Ājīvakas* could be identified with the *Digambara* Jains unless by a confusion in later times, probably on account of the fact that both the *Digambaras* and the *Ājīvakas* went about naked[2].

The fundamental tenet of Gośala appears in more or less the same form in *Uvāsagadasāo,* I. 97, 115, II. III, 132, *Saṃyutta Nikāya,* III. 210, *Añguttara Nikāya,* I. 286 and the *Dīgha Nikāya,* II 20. In the last-mentioned work Gosāla is reported to say to king Ajāta śatru: "There is no cause for the sufferings of beings; they therefore all suffer without any cause; there is no cause for the purity (*viśuddhi*) of beings; they all become pure without any cause; there is no efficiency in one's own deeds or in the deeds of others (*n'atthi atta-kāre na'tthi parakāre*) or in one's free efforts (*puriṣakāre*); there is no power, no energy, no human strength or heroic endeavours (*parākkama*)[3]. All vertebrates (*sabbe sattā*), all animals with one or more senses (*sabbe pāṇā),* all lives emanating from eggs or ovaries (*sabbe bhūtā*), all vegetable lives, are without any power or efficiency. They become transformed in various forms by their inherent destiny, by their manifestation in various life-forms, and by their different natures (*niyati-saṅgati-bhava-pariṇati*), and it is in accordance with their six kinds of life-states that they suffer pains and enjoy pleasures." Again, in the *Sūtra-kṛtāṅga sūtra,* II. 6. 7, Gosāla is reported to say that there is no sin for ascetics in having intercourse with women[4]. These doctrines of Gosāla

man of the bamboo staff, it is clear that originally he belonged to the class of *eka-daṇḍins* (or *daṇḍin*) ascetics; and, though he afterwards joined Mahāvīra and adopted his system, he held some distinguishing tenets of his own, and also retained his old distinguishing mark, the bamboo staff." This is all very doubtful, for firstly *mankha* and *maskarin* cannot be identified; secondly, *mankha* means a beggar who carried pictures in his hands—*mankhaś citra-phalaka-vyagra-karo bhikṣuka-viśesaḥ* (Abhayadeva Sūri's comment on the *Bhagavatī-sūtra,* p. 662. Nirnaya Sagara ed.). Gosāla's father was a *mankha* and his name was Mankhali from which Gosāla was called Makkhaliputta. Both Jacobi (*Jaina Sūtras,* II. 267 footnote) and Hoernlé *(Ājīvaka, Encyclopaedia of Religion and Ethics,* p. 266) are here wrong, for the passage referred to is Śīlāṅka's commentary on *Sūtra-kṛtāṅga-sūtra,* III. 3. II *(ājīvakā-dinām para-tīrthikānāṃ digamvarārāṇm ca),* and the "*ca*" in the passage which is to be translated as "and" and not as "or" distinguishes the *Ājīvakas* from the *Digamvaras.*

[1] *nagnā to dig-vāsāḥ kṣapaṇaḥ śramaṇaś ca jīvako jainaḥ, ājivo mala-dhārī nirgranthaḥ kathyate ṣaḍbhiḥ.* II. 190.

[2] *Divyāvadāna,* p. 427, refers to an episode where a Buddha image was dishonoured by a *nirgrantha* and in consequence of that 8000 *Ājīvakas* were killed in the city of Puṇḍravardhana. Dr Barua also refers to this passage in his small work, *The Ājīvakas.*

[3] As Buddhaghoso says, these are all merely specifications of *puriṣa-kāra* (*sarvaiva puriṣa-kāra-viv'ecanam eva*). *Sumaṅgala-vilāsinī,* II. 20.

[4] There is another passage in the *Sūtra-kṛtāṅga-sūtra,* III. 4. 9 (*evamege u asattha*

interest us only so far as they may be considered similar to the other *nāstika* teachings. But unlike other *nāstikas*, Gosāla believed not only in rebirths but also introduced a special doctrine of reanimation[1]. Several other doctrines which are not of philosophical, ethical or eschatological interest but which refer only to *Ājīvakas* dogmatics are related both in the *Dīgha Nikāya*, II. 20, and in the *Bhagavatī-sūtra*, XV, and have been elaborately dealt with by Hoernlé in his article on the *Ājīvakas* and his translation of the *Uvāsagadasāo.* The two important points that we need take note of here are that the *Ājīvakas* who were an important sect did not believe in the efficiency of our will or our *karma* and regarded sex-indulgence as unobjectionable to recluses. Other heretics are also alluded to in the *Sūtra-kṛtāṅga sūtra*, I. III. 4. 9–14, where they also are alluded to as having similar tendencies[2]. Thus it is said: "Some unworthy heretics, slaves of women, ignorant men who are averse to the Law of the Jainas, speak thus: 'As the squeezing of a blister or boil causes relief for some time, so it is with (the enjoyment of) charming women. How could there be any sin in it? As a ram

paṇṇavanti anāriyā; itthivāsam gayā bālā jinasāsana-parāmmuha), where it is said that some wrongdoers and others who belong to the Jaina circle have turned their faces from the laws imposed upon them by Jina and are slaves of women. Hoernlé says (*Ājīvakas, Encyclopaedia of Religion and Ethics,* p. 261) that this passage refers to the followers of Gosāla. But there is no evidence that it is so, if at least we believe in Śīlāṅka's commentary. Śīlāṅka's explains "*ege*" or "*eke*" as *bauddha-viśessā nīla-paṭādayaḥ nātha-vādika-maṇḍala-praviṣṭā vā śaiva-viśesāḥ* and *pasattha* as *sad-anuṣṭhānāt pārśve tiṣṭhanti iti parivaśthāḥ sva-yūthyā vā pārśvasthā-vasanna-kuśa-lā-dayaḥ strī-pariṣaha-parājitāḥ*. Thus, according to him, it refers to some Buddhists wearing blue garments, the *nātha-vādins*, the *Śaivas*, or some Jains with bad characters, or bad people in general.

[1] Gosāla thought that it was possible that one person's soul could reanimate other dead bodies. Thus, when he was challenged by Mahāvīra, who forbade his disciples to hold any intercourse with him, he is reported to have said that the Makkhaliputta Gosāla who was the disciple of Mahāvīra was long dead and born in the abode of the gods while he was in reality Udāyī-kuṇḍiyāyaṇīya, who in the seventh and the last change of body through reanimation had entered Gosāla's body. According to Gosāla, a soul must finish eighty-four thousand *mahā-kalpas* during which it must be born seven times in the abode of the gods and seven times as men, undergoing seven reanimations, exhausting all kinds of *karmas.* See *Bhagavati-sūtra,* XV. 673, Nirṇaya Sagaraed. See also Hoernlé's two Appendices to his translation of *Uvāsagadasāo* and the article on *Ājīvika, Encyclopaedia of Religion and Ethics*, p. 262. A *mahā-kalpa* is equal to 300,000 *saras* and one *sara* is the time required to exhaust the sands of the seven Ganges (each Ganges being 500 *yojanas* or 2250 miles in length, 2¼ miles in breadth, and 50 *dhanus* or 100 yards in depth), at the rate of putting 100 years for the removal of one grain of sand. See *ibid.;* also Rockhill's Appendix I to his Life of *the Buddha.*

[2] According to Śīlāṅka they were a sect of Buddhists wearing blue garments, Śaivas, the Nāthas, and some degraded Jains also.

drinks the quiet water, so it is with (the enjoyment of) charming women. How can there be any sin in it?' So say some unworthy heretics who entertain false doctrines and who long for pleasures as the ewe for her kid. Those who do not think of the future but only enjoy the present will repent of it afterwards when their life or their youth is gone[1]."

Again, some heretics (identified by Śīlāṅka with the *Lokāyata*) are reported in the *Sūtra-krtāṅga-sūtra*, II. I. 9-10, as instructing others as follows: Upwards from the sole of the feet up to the bottom of the tips of hair and in all transverse directions the soul is up to the skin; so long as there is the body there is the soul and there is no soul apart from this body, so the soul is identical with the body; when the body is dead there is no soul. When the body is burnt no soul is seen and all that is seen is but the white bones. When one draws a sword from a scabbard, one can say that the former lies within the latter, but one cannot say similarly of the soul that it exists in the body; there is in reality no way of distinguishing the soul from the body such that one may say that the former exists in the latter. One can draw the pith from a grass stalk, or bones from flesh or butter from curd, oil from sesamum and so forth, but it is not possible to find any such relation between the soul and the body. There is no separate soul which suffers pains and enjoys pleasures and migrates to the other world after the death of the body, for even if the body is cut into pieces no soul can be perceived, just as no soul can be perceived in a jug even when it is broken to pieces, whereas in the case of a sword it is found to be different from the scabbard within which it is put. The *Lokāyatas* thus think that there is no fault in killing living beings, since striking a living body with a weapon is like striking the ground. These *Lokāyatas,* therefore, cannot make any distinction between good and bad deeds as they do not know of any principle on which such a distinction can be made, and there is thus no morality according to them. Some slight distinction is made between the ordinary nihilists and the haughty nihilists (*pragalbha nāstika*) who say that if the soul was different from the body then it would have some specific kind of colour, taste or the like, but no such separate entity is discoverable, and therefore it cannot be believed that there is a separate soul. The *Sūtra-kṛtāṅga-sūtra,* II. 1.9 (p. 277), speaks

[1] See Jacobi's translation of *Sūtra-kṛtāṅga-sūtra*. *Jaina Sūtras*, II. 270.

of these *Pragalbha Nāstikas* as renouncing (*niṣkramya*) the world and instructing other people to accept their doctrines. But Śīlāṅka says that the *Lokāyata* system has no form of initiation and thus there cannot be any ascetics of that school; it is the ascetics of other schools such as the Buddhists who sometimes in their ascetic stage read the *Lokāyata,* became converted to *lokāyata* views, and preached them to others[1].

After the treatment of the views of the *lokāyata nāstikas* the *Sūtra-kṛtāṅga-sūtra* treats of the Sāṃkhyas. In this connection Śīlāṅka says that there is but little difference between the *lokāyata* and the Sāṃkhya, for though the Sāṃkhyas admit souls, these are absolutely incapable of doing any work, and all the work is done by *prakṛti* which is potentially the same as the gross elements. The body and the so-called mind is therefore nothing but the combination of the gross elements, and the admission of separate *puruṣas* is only nominal. Since such a soul cannot do anything and is of no use (*akiṃcitkara*), the *Lokāyatas* flatly deny them. Śīlāṅka further says that the Sāṃkhyists, like the *Lokāyatikas,* do not find anything wrong in injuring animal lives, for after all the living entities are but all material products, the so-called soul being absolutely incapable of taking interest or part in all kinds of activities[2]. Neither the *nāstikas* nor the Sāṃkhyists can, therefore, think of the distinction between good and bad deeds or between Heaven and Hell, and they therefore give themselves up to all kinds of enjoyments. Speaking of the *lokāyata nāstikas,* the *Sūtra-kṛtāṅga-sūtras* say as follows: "Thus some shameless men becoming monks propagate a law of their own. And others believe it, put their faith in it, adopt it (saying): 'Well you speak the truth, O Brahmaṇa (or) O Śramaṇa, we shall present you with food, drink, spices and sweetmeats, with a robe, a bowl, or a broom.' Some have been induced to honour them, some have made (their proselytes) to honour them. Before (entering an order) they were determined to become Śramaṇas,

[1] *yady api lokāyatikānāṃ nāsti dīkṣādikaṃ tathā'pi apareṇa śākyā-dinā pravrajyā-vidhānena pravrajyā paścāt lokāyatikam adhīyānasya tathāvidha-pariṇateḥ tad evā' bhirucitam.* Śīlāṅka's commentary on the *Sūtra-kṛtāṅga-sūtra,* p. 280 a (Nirṇaya Sagaraed).

In pp. 280–281 Śīlaṅka points out that the *Bhāgavatas* and other ascetics at the time of their renouncement of the world take the vow of all kinds of self-restraint, but as soon as they become converted to the *lokāyata* views they begin to live an unrestrained life. They then wear blue garments (*nīla-paṭa*).

[2] *Ibid.* pp. 281, 283.

houseless, poor monks, who would have neither sons nor cattle, to eat only what should be given them by others, and to commit no sins. After having entered their Order they do not cease (from sins), they themselves commit sins and they assent to another's committing sins. Then they are given to pleasures, amusements and sensual lust; they are greedy, fettered, passionate, covetous, the slaves of love and hate[1]."

But we find references to the *lokāyata* doctrines not only in the *Sūtra-kṛtāṅga-sūtra* but also in the *Bṛhad-āraṇyaka,* the *Kaṭha* as described above and in the *Chāndogya Upaniṣad,* VIII.7, 8, where Virocana, the representative of the demons who came to Prajāpati for instruction regarding the nature of self, went away satisfied with the view that the self was identical with the body. Prajāpati asked both Indra and Virocana to stand before a cup of water and they saw their reflections, and Prajāpati told them that it was that well dressed and well adorned body that was the self and both Indra and Virocana were satisfied; but Indra was later on dissatisfied and returned for further instructions, whereas Virocana did not again come back. The *Chāndogya Upaniṣad* relates this as an old story and says that it is for this reason that those, who at the present time believe only in worldly pleasures and who have no faith (in the efficiency of deeds or in the doctrine of the immortality of the soul) and who do not perform sacrifices, are called demons (*asura*); and it is therefore their custom to adorn the dead body with fine clothes, good ornaments and provide food for it with which they probably thought that the dead would conquer the other world.

This passage of the *Chāndogya* seems to be of special importance. It shows that there was a race different from the Aryans, designated here as *asuras,* who dressed their dead bodies with fine clothes, adorned them with ornaments, provided them with food, so that when there was a resurrection of these dead bodies they might with that food, clothes and ornaments prosper in the other world and it is these people who believed that the body was the only self. The later *Lokāyatas* or *Cārvākas* also believed that this body was the self, but the difference between them and these *dehātmavādins* referred to in the *Chāndogya* is that they admitted "another world" where the bodies rose from the dead and prospered in the fine clothes, ornaments and food that were given to

[1] See Jacobi, *Jaina Sūtras,* II 341-342.

the dead body. This custom is said to be an *asura* custom. It seems possible, therefore, that probably the *lokāyata* doctrines had their beginnings in the preceding Sumerian civilization in the then prevailing customs of adorning the dead and the doctrine of bodily survival after death. This later on became so far changed that it was argued that since the self and the body were identical and since the body was burnt after death, there could not be any survival after death and hence there could not be another world after death. Already in the *Kaṭha* and the *Bṛhad-āraṇyaka* we had proof of the existence of people who did not believe in the existence of any consciousness after death and thought that everything ended with death; and in the *Chāndogya* we find that Virocana believed in the doctrine that the body was the *ātman* and this doctrine is traced here to the custom of adorning the dead body among the *asuras*.

The tenets and doctrines of these *asuras* are described in the *Gīta,* XVI. 7-18, as follows: The *asuras* cannot distinguish between right and wrong conduct; they do not have any purity, truthfulness and proper behaviour. They do not think that the world is based on any truth and reality; they do not believe in God and consider all beings to have come out from the desires of the sexes and from nothing more than from mutual sex-relations. These foolish people with such views do harm to the world, engage themselves in ferocious deeds and destroy their own selves (as they have no faith in the other world or in the means thereto)[1]. Full of insatiable desire, egoism, vanity and pride, they take the wrong course through ignorance and live an impure life. They think that existence ends finally at death and that there is nothing beyond this world and its enjoyments, and they therefore give themselves up to earthly enjoyments. Bound with innumerable desires, anger, attachment, etc., they busy themselves in collecting materials of earthly enjoyments through wrong means. They always think of their riches, which they earn daily, and which they accumulate, with which they fulfil their desires in the present or wish to fulfil in the future; of the enemies whom they have destroyed, or whom they wish to destroy; of their powers, their success, their joys, their strength, and so forth.

A doctrine similar to that of the *Lokāyatikas* is preached by Jābali in *Rāmāyaṇa,* II.108, where he says that it is a pity that there

[1] Śrīdhara says that these refer to the *Lokāyatikas. Gītā,* XVI. 9.

Should be some people who prefer virtue in the other world to eathly goods of this world; the perfermance of the different sacrifices for the satisfaction of the dead is but waste of food, for being dead no one can eat. If food eaten by people here should be of use to other bodies, then it is better to perform *śrāddhas* for people who make a sojourn to distant countries than to arrange for their meals. 'Though intelligent men wrote books praising the merit of gifts, sacrifices, initiation and asceticism, in reality there is nothing more than what is directly perceived by the senses.

In the *Viṣṇu Purāṇa* (1, 6. 29–31) certain people are alluded to who did not believe in the efficacy of the performance of sacrifices and spoke against the Vedas and the sacrifices; and in the *Mahābhārata,* XII. 186, it has been urged by Bharadvāja that life-functions can be explained by purely physical and physiological reasons and that the assumption of a soul is quite unnecessary. In the *Mahāhhārata* references are made also to *haitukas* who did not believe in the other world; they were people with strong old convictions (*dṛḍha-pūrve*) who could hardly change their views; they were learned in the Vedas (*vahuśruta*), were well read in older *śāstras,* made gifts, performed sacrifices, hated falsehood, were great orators in assemblies, and went among the people explaining their views. This passage reveals a curious fact that even in the Vedic circles there were people who performed sacrifices, made gifts and were well read in the Vedas and in older literature, who despised falsehood, were great logicians and speakers and yet did not believe in anything except what exists in this world (*nai'tad astī-vāidinaḥ*). We know from the Buddhistic sources that the Brahmins were well versed in the *lokāyata* learning; we know also that in the Upaniṣadic circles the views of those who did not believe in life after death are referred to and reproached, and the *Chāndogya* refers to people among whom the doctrine that the self and the body were identical was current as a corollary underlying their custom of adorning the dead. In the *Rāmāyaṇa* we find that Jāvāli taught the doctrine that there was no life after death and that the ritualistic offerings for the satisfaction of the dead were unnecessary. In the *Gītā* we find also the holders of such views referred to, and they are there reported as performing sacrifices only in name, as they did not adhere to the proper ritualistic course[1]. But in the

[1] *yajante nāma-jajñais te dambhenā' vidhi-pūrvakam. Gītā,* XVI. 17.

Mahābharata certain people are referred to who were well read in the Vedas and other older literature and yet did not believe in the other world and in the immortality of the soul. This shows that this heterodox view (that there was no life after death) was gradually spreading amongst certain sections of the Vedic people, and that though some of them were worthless people who utilized the doctrine only to indulge in sense-gratifications and to live in a lower plane of life, there were others who performed the Vedic practices, were well read in Vedic and other literature and yet did not believe in the doctrine of immortality or in a world beyond the present. Thus, even in those early times, on the one hand there were in the Vedic circle many moral and learned people who believed in these heretical views, whereas there were also immoral and bad people who lived a vicious life and held such heretical views either tacitly or openly[1].

We thus know that the *lokāyata* views were very old, probably as early as the Vedas, or still earlier, being current among the Sumerian people of pre-Aryan times. We know further that a commentary on the *Lokāyata-śāstra* by Bhāgurī was very well known in B.C. 200 or 300, but it is exceedingly difficult to say anything regarding the author of the *Lokāyata-śāstra.* It is attributed to Brhaspati or to Cārvāka[2]. But it is difficult to say who this Bṛhaspati may have been. One *Bṛhaspati-sūtra*, a work on polity, has been edited with translation by Dr F. W. Thomas and published from Lahore. In this work the *lokāyatas* have been mentioned in II 5, 8, 12, 16, 29, and III. 15. Here they are very severely abused as thieves who regard religion as a mere means of advantage and who are destined to go to Hell. It is therefore absolutely certain

[1] The *Maitrāyaṇa Upaniṣad*, VII. 8, 9, says that there are many others who by adopting useless arguments, illustrations, false analogies and illusory demonstrations wish to oppose the Vedic ways of conduct; they do not believe in the self and are like thieves who would never go to Heaven and with whom no one should associate. One sometimes forgets that the doctrine of these people is nothing new but is only a different kind of Vedic science (*veda-vidyā'ntaran tu tat*). Bṛhaspati became Śukra and taught the *Asuras* this doctrine so that they might be inclined to despise the Vedic duties and consider bad to be good and good to be bad.

[2] The *Maitrāyaṇīya* attributes these doctrines to Bṛhaspati and Śukra; the *Prabodha-candro-daya* of Kṛṣṇa Miśra says that these were first formulated by Bṛhaspati and then handed over to Cārvāka who spread them among people through his pupils.

See also Mr D. Śāstrī's *Cārvāka-ṣaṣti*, pp. 11–13, where he refers to a number of authorities who attribute this to Bṛhaspti.

that the Bṛhaspati who was the author of these *sūtras* on polity could not have been the author of the *lokāyata* science. Nor could it have been the legal writer Bṛhaspati. In Kauṭilya's *Artha-śāstra* a Bṛhaspati is referred to as a writer on polity, but this must be a different one from the *Bārhaspatya-sūtra* published by Dr Thomas[1]. The Bṛhaspati of Kauṭilya's *Artha-śāstra* is reported there as admitting agriculture, trade and commerce (*vārtā*), law and statecraft (*daṇḍa-nīti*), as the only sciences; in the next passage of the same chapter (*Vidyā-samuddeśa*) *daṇḍa-nīti* is regarded as the one subject of study by Uśanas. In the *Prabodha-candro-daya* Kṛṣṇa Miśra makes Cārvāka hold the view that law and statecraft are the only sciences and that the science of *vārtā* (i.e. agriculture, commerce, trade, dairy, poultry, etc.) falls within them. According to this report the Cārvākas took only *daṇḍa-nīti* and *vārtā* into account, and thus their views agreed with those of Bṛhaspati and Uśanas, and more particularly with those of the latter. But we cannot from this assume that either Bṛhaspati or Uśanas mentioned by Kauṭilya could be regarded as the author of the original *lokāyata*. Bṛhaspati, the author of the *Lokāyata-śāstra,* is thus a mythical figure, and we have practically no information regarding the originator of the *lokāyata* system. It is probable that the original *lokāyata* work was written in the form of *sūtras* which had at least two commentaries, the earliest of which was probably as early as B.C. 300 or 400. There was at least one metrical version of the main contents of this system from which extracts are found quoted in Mādhava's *Sarva-darśana-saṃgraha* and in other places.

It is difficult to say whether Cārvāka was the name of a real person or not. The earliest mention of the name is probably to be found in the *Mahābhārata,* XII. 38 and 39, where Cārvāka is described as a Rākṣasa in the garb of an ascetic Brahmin with three staffs (*tridaṇḍī*), but nothing is said there about the doctrine that he professed. In most of the early texts the *lokāyata* doctrines are either mentioned as the *lokāyata* view or attributed to Bṛhaspati. Thus, in the *Padma Purāṇa* in the *Sṛṣt-khaṇḍa,* XII. 318-340, some of the *lokāyata* doctrines are described as being the instructions of Bṛhaspati. Kamalaśīla, of the eighth century, refers to the Cārvākas as being the adherents of the *lokāyata* doctrine; the *Prabodha-candro-daya* speaks of Cārvāka as being the greatteacher who

[1] Kautilya's *Artha-śāstra*, pp. 6, 29, 63, 177, 192, Mysore ed. 1924.

propagated through a succession of pupils and pupils of pupils the *Lokāyata-śāstra* written by Vācaspati and handed over to him. Mādhava, in his *Sarva-darśana-saṃgraha,* describes him as one who follows the views of Bṛhaspati and the chief of the nihilists (*bṛhaspati-matā-nusāriṇā nāstika-śiromaṇinā*). Guṇaratna, however, in his commentary on the *Ṣaḍ-darśana-samuccaya,* speaks of the Cārvākas as being a nihilistic sect who only eat but do not regard the existence of virtue and vice and do not trust anything else but what can be directly perceived. They drank wines and ate meat and were given to unrestricted sex-indulgence. Each year they gathered together on a particular day and had unrestricted intercourse with women. They behaved like common people and for this reason they were called *lokāyata* and because they held views originally framed by Bṛhaspati they were also called *Bārhaspatya.* Thus it is difficult to say whether the word Cārvāka was the name of a real personage or a mere allusive term applied to the adherents of the *lokāyata* view.

Both Haribhadra and Mādhava have counted the Lokāyata or Cārvāka philosophy as a *darśana* or system of philosophy. It had a new logic, a destructive criticism of most of the cherished views of other systems of Indian philosophy, a materialistic philosophy, and it denied morality, moral responsibility and religion of every kind.

Let us, therefore, first take up the Cārvāka logic. The Cārvākas admitted the validity only of perception. There is nothing else but what can be perceived by the five senses. No inference can be regarded as a valid means of knowledge, for inference is possible only when the universal concomitance of the reason (*hetus*) with the probandum is known, and such a reason is known to be existing in the object of the minor term (*vyāpti-pakṣa-dharmatā-śāli hi lingaṃ gamakam*). Such a concomitance is possible when it is known not only to be unconditional but when there is no doubt in the mind that it could be conditional. Such a concomitance must first be known before an inference is possible; but how can it be known? Not by perception, for concomitance is not an objective entity with which the senses can come in contact. Moreover, the concomitance of one entity with another means that the entities are associated with each other in the past, present and future (*sarvo-pasaṃhārayatrī vyāptiḥ*), and the sense-organs can have no scope with regard to future associations or even with regard to all past time. If it is urged that the concomitance is between the class-character (*sāmānya-gocaram*) of the probandum (e.g. fire) and the class-character of the reason (e.g. smoke), then it is not necessary that the concomitance of the reason with the probandum should have actually to be perceived at all times by the sense-organs. But if the concomitance is between the class-character of smoke and fire, why should any individual fire be associated with every case of smoke? If the concomitance cannot be perceived by the sense-organs, it cannot be perceived by the mind either, for the mind cannot associate itself with the external objects except through the sense-organs. The concomitance cannot be known through inference, for all inference presupposes it. Thus, there being no way of perceiving concomitance, inference becomes impossible. Again, a concomitance which can lead to a valid inference must be devoid of all conditions; but the absence of such conditions in the past or in the future cannot be perceived at the time of making the inference. Moreover, a condition (*upādhi*) is defined as that which, having an unfailing concomitance with the probandum, has not the same concomitance with the reason (*sādhanā-vyāpakatve sati sādhya-sama-vyaptih*)[1].

Again it is said that an inference is possible only when the reason (e.g. smoke) is perceived to be associated with the object denoted by the minor term (*pakṣa*, e.g. hill), but in reality there is no association of the smoke with the hill nor can it be a character of it, for it is a quality of fire. There is no universal agreement between smoke and hill so that one can say that wherever there is a hill there is smoke. Nor can it be said that wherever there is smoke there is both the hill and the fire. When the smoke is first seen it is not perceived as the quality of fire associated with a hill; therefore it is not enough to say that the reason (e.g. smoke) belongs to the minor term (*pakṣa,* e.g. hill) as its character (*pakṣa-dharma*), but that the reason belongs to the minor term associated with the probandum. The assertion that in an inference the reason must be known as a quality of the minor term (*pakṣa*) has therefore to be interpreted as being a quality of a part of the minor term as associated with the probandum.

A valid inference can be made when the two following con-

[1] *Sarva-darśana-saṃgraha*, I.

ditions are satisfied: (1) An invariable and unconditional concomitance is known between the reason and the probandum such that in every case when the reason is present the probandum must also be present in all places and in all times, without the association of any determining condition. (2) That a reason having such a concomitance with the probandum must be known to exist in the minor term (*pakṣa*) in which the probandum is asserted. Now the Cārvāka contention is that none of these conditions can be fulfilled and that therefore valid inference is impossible. Firstly, concomitance is ascertained through an experience of a very large number of cases (*bhūyo-darśana*) of agreement between the reason (*hetu*) and the probandum (*sādhya*). But according to the difference of circumstances, time and place, things differ in their power or capacity and thus since the nature and qualities of things are not constant it is not possible that any two entities should be found to agree with each other under all circumstances in all times and in all places[1]. Again, an experience of a large number of cases cannot eliminate the possibility of a future failure of agreement. It is not possible to witness all cases of fire and smoke and thus root out all chances of a failure of their agreement, and if that were possible there would be no need of any inference[2]. The Cārvākas do not admit "universals," and therefore they do not admit that the concomitance is not between smoke and fire but between smoke-ness (*dhūmatva*) and fire-ness (*vahnitva*)[3]. Again, it is impossible to assure oneself that there are no conditions (*upādhi*) which would vitiate the concomitance between the *hetu* and the *sādhya*, for though they may not now be perceivable they may still exist imperceivably[4]. Without a knowledge of agreement in absence (i.e. in a case where there is no fire there is no smoke), there cannot be any assurance of concomitance. It is impossible to exhaust in

[1] *deśa-kāla-daśā-bheda-vicitrā-tmasu vastuṣu*
avinā-bhāva-niyamo na śakyo vastum āha ca. *Nyāya-mañjarī*, p. 119.

[2] *na pratyakṣī-kṛtā yāvad dhūmā-gni-vyaktayo' khilāḥ*
tāvat syād api dhūmo' sau yo' nagner iti śaṅkyate
ye tu pratyakṣato viśvaṃ paśyanti hi bhavādṛsaḥ
kiṃ divya-cakṣuṣām eṣām anumāna-prayojanam *Ibid.*

[3] *sāmānya-dvārako' py asti nā' vinābhāva-niścayaḥ*
vāstavaṃ hi na sāmānyaṃ nāma kāiñcana vidyate. *Ibid.*

[4] Compare *Khaṇḍana-khaṇḍa-khādya*, p. 693:
vyāghāto yadi śaṅkā' sti na cer chaṅkā tatastarām
vyāghātā-vadhir āśaṅkā tarkaḥ śaṅkā-vadhiḥ kutaḥ.

experience all cases of absence of fire as being also the cases of the absence of smoke. Thus since without such a joint method of agreement in presence and absence the universal invariable concomitance cannot be determined, and since it is not possible to assure oneself of the universal agreement in presence or in absence, the concomitance itself cannot be determined[1].

Purandara, however, a follower of Cārvāka (probably of the seventh century), admits the usefulness of inference in determining the nature of all worldly things where perceptual experience is available; but inference cannot be employed for establishing any dogma regarding the transcendental world, or life after death or the laws of *Karma* which cannot be available to ordinary perceptual experience[2]. The main reason for upholding such a distinction between the validity of inference in our practical life of ordinary experience, and in ascertaining transcending truths beyond experience, lies in this, that an inductive generalization is made by observing a large number of cases of agreement in presence together with agreement in absence, and no cases of agreement in presence can be observed in the transcendent sphere; for even if such spheres existed they could not be perceived by the senses. Thus, since in the supposed supra-sensuous transcendent world no case of a *hetu* agreeing with the presence of its *sādhya* can be observed, no inductive generalization or law of concomitance can be made relating to this sphere[3]. In reply to this contention Vādideva says that such a change may be valid against the Mīmāṃsists who depend upon the joint method of agreement and difference for making any inductive generalization, but this cannot

[1] *niyamaś cā'numānā-ṅgaṃ gṛhītaḥ pratipadyate*
grahaṇaṃ cā'sya nā'nyatra nāstitā-niścayaṃ vinā
darśanā-darśanābhyaṃ hi niyama-grahaṇaṃ yadi
tad apy asad anagnau hi dhūmasye'ṣṭam adarśanam
anagniś ca kiyān sarvaṃ jagaj-jvalana-varjitam
tatra dhūmasya nāstitvaṃ nai'va paśyanty ayoginaḥ.

Nyāya-mañjarī, p. 120

[2] He is mentioned in Kamalaśīla's *Pañjikā*, p. 431, *Purandaras tv āha loka-prasiddham anumānaṃ cārvākair apī'ṣyate eva, yat tu kaiś cit laukikaṃ mārgam atikramya anumānam ucyate tan niṣidhyate.* Vādideva Sūri also quotes a *sūtra* of Purandara in his commentary *Syādvāda-ratnākāra* on his *Pramāṇa-naya-tattva-lokā-laṅkāra,* II. 131: *pramāṇasya gauṇatvād anumānād artha-niścaya-durlabhāt*

[3] *avyabhicārā-vagamo hi laukika-hetūnām*
Anumeyā'vagame nimittaṃ sā nāsti tantra-siddheṣu
iti na tebhyaḥ parokṣā-rthā'vagamo nyāyyo'ta idam
uktam anumānād artha-niścayo durlabhaḥ.

apply against the Jaina view of inference which is based on the principle of necessary implication (*anyathā-nupapattāv eva tat-svarū-patvena svīkārāt*).

Other objections also made against the possibility of a valid inference are as follows: (1) impressions made by inferential knowledge are dim and not so vivid (*aspaṣṭatvāt*) as those produced by perception; (2) inference has to depend on other things for the determination of its object (*svārtha-niścaye parā-pekṣatvāt*); (3) inference has to depend on perception (*pratyakṣa-pūrvakatvāt*); (4) inferential cognitions are not directly produced by the objects (*arthād anupajāyamānatvāt*); (5) inference is not concrete (*avastu-viṣayatvāt*); (6) it is often found contradicted (*bādhyamānatvāt*); (7) there is no proof which may establish the law that every case of the presence of the *hetu* should also be a case of the presence of the *sādhya* (*sādhya-sādhanayoḥ pratibandha-sādhaka-pramāṇā-bhāvād vā*)[1]. None of these can be regarded as a reason why inference should be regarded as invalid from the Jaina point of view. For in reply to the first objection it may be pointed out that vividness has never been accepted as a definition of *pramāṇa,* and therefore its absence cannot take away the validity of an inference; illusory perceptions of two moons are vivid, but are not on that account regarded as valid. Again, an inference does not always depend on perception, and even if it did, it utilized its materials only for its own use and nothing more. Perception also is produced from certain materials, but is not on that account regarded as invalid. The inference is also produced from objects and is as concrete as perception since like it it involves universals and particulars. Again, false inferences are indeed contradicted, but that is no charge against right inferences. The invariable relationship between a *hetu* and a *sādhya* can be established through mental reasoning (*tarka*)[2].

Jayanta points out in this connection that a law of universal agreement of the *sādhya* with the *hetu* has to be admitted. For an inference cannot be due to any mere instinctive flash of intelligence (*pratibhā*). If a knowledge of invariable and unconditional agreement was not regarded as indispensable for an inference, and if it was due to a mere instinctive flash, then the people of the Cocoanut

[1] Vādideva Sūri's *Syādvāda-ratnākāra*, pp. 131, I32. Nirṇaya Sagara Press, 1914.
[2] *Ibid.*

island who do not know how to make fire would have been able to infer fire from smoke. Some say that the invariable association of the *hetu* with the *sādhya* is perceived by mental perception (*mānasa-pratyakṣa*). They hold that in perceiving the association of smoke with fire and the absence of the former when the latter is absent, the mind understands the invariable association of smoke with fire. It is not necessary in order to come to such a generalization that one should perceive the agreement of smoke and fire in all the infinite number of cases in which they exist together, for the agreement observed in the mind is not between smoke and fire but between smoke-ness and fire-ness (*jvalanatvā-di-sāmānya-puraḥsaratayā vyāpti-grahaṇāt*). The objection against this view would be the denial of class-concepts as held by the Cārvākas, Buddhists, and others. There are others, again, who say that even if universals are admitted, it is impossible that there should be universals of all cases of absence of fire as associated with the absence of smoke, and under the circumstances unless all positive and negative instances could be perceived the inductive generalization would be impossible. They, therefore, hold that there is some kind of mystic intuition like that of a yogin (*yogi-pratyakṣa-kalpaṃ*) by which the invariable relation (*pratibandha*) is realized. Others hold that an experience of a large number of positive instances unaccompanied by any experience of any case of failure produces the notion of concomitance. But the Nyāya insists on the necessity of an experience of a large number of instances of agreement in presence and absence for arriving at any inductive generalization of concomitance[1]. The Cārvākas, of course, say to this that in determining the unconditional invariable agreement of every case of a *hetu* with its *sādhya* the absence of visible conditions may be realized by perception; but the possibility of the existence of invisible conditions cannot be eliminated even by the widest experience of agreement in presence, and thus there would always be the fear that the invariable concomitance of the *hetu* with *the sādhya* may be conditional, and thus all inference has the value of more or less probability but not of certainty, and it is only through perceptual corroboration that the inferences come to be regarded as valid[2]. The reply of Nyāya to this is that the assertion that in-

[1] *Nyāya-mañjarī*, p. 122.

[2] *athā-numānaṃ na pramāṇaṃ yogyo-pādhīnāṃ yogyā-nupalabdhyā' bhāva-niś-caye' py' ayogyo-pādhi-śaṅkayā vyabhicāra-saṃśayāt śataśaḥ sahacaritayor api vyabhicāro-*

ference is not valid is itself an inference based on the similarity of inferential processes with other invalid mental processes. But this does not properly refute the Cārvāka position that inductive generalizations are only probable, and that therefore (as Purandara says) they acquire some amount of validity by being corroborated by experience and that they have no force in spheres where they cannot be corroborated by perceptual experience.

Since the Cārvākas do not attribute any more validity to inference than probability, other forms of *pramāṇas,* such as the testimony of trusty persons or the scriptures, analogy or implication, also were not regarded as valid. According to Udayana's statement, the Cārvākas denied the existence of anything that was not perceived, and Udayana points out that if this doctrine is consistently applied and people begin to disbelieve all that they do not perceive at any particular time, then all our practical life will be seriously disturbed and upset[1]. The school of *dhūrta Cārvākas,* in their *Sūtra* work, not only denied the validity of inference but criticized the Nyāya categories as enunciated in the *Nyāya-sūtra,* I. I. I, and tried to establish the view that no such enumeration of categories was possible[2]. It is no doubt true that the Cārvākas admitted perception as the only valid *pramāṇa,* but since illusions occurred in perception also, ultimately all *pramāṇas* were regarded as indeterminable by them.

The Cārvākas had to contend on the one hand with those who admitted a permanent soul, such as the Jains, the Naiyāyikas, the Sāṃkhya-yoga and the Mīmāṃsā, and on the other hand with the idealistic Buddhists who believed in a permanent series of conscious states; for the Cārvākas denied all kinds of existence after death. Thus they say that since there is no permanent entity that abides after death, there is no existence after death. As the body, understanding and sense-functions, are continually changing, there cannot be any existence after death, and hence no separate soul can be admitted. According to some, Cārvākas consciousness is pro-

palabdheś ca loke dhūmā-di-darśanā-ntaraṃ vahnyā'di-vyavahāraś ca sambhāvana-mātrāt saṃvādena ca prāmāṇyā-bhimānād. Tattva-cintāmaṇi Annumiti. For a similar view see Russel, "On the notion of Cause" in his *Mysticism and Logic.*

[1] Udayana's *Nyāya-kusumānjali,* III. 5, 6.

[2] *cārvāka-dhūrtas tu athā'tas tattvaṃ vyākhyāsyāma iti pratijñāya pramāṇa-prameya-saṃkhyā-lakṣaṇa-niyamā-sakya-karaṇīyatvam eva tattvaṃ vyākhyā-tavān; pramāṇa-saṃkhyā-myam-āśakya-karaṇiyatva-siddhaye ca pramiti-bhedān pratyakṣā-di-pramāṇān upajanyān īdṛśān upādarśayat. Nyāya-mañjarī,* p. 64.

duced (*utpadyate*) from the four elements, and according to others it is manifested (*abhivyajyate*) from them like fermenting intoxication (*surā*) or acids. It is on account of diverse kinds of arrangements and rearrangements of the atoms of air, water, fire and earth that consciousness is either produced or manifested and the bodies and senses are formed or produced. There is nothing else but these atomic arrangements, and there is also no further separate category[1].

The school of *Suśikṣita Cārvākas* holds that, so long as the body remains, there is an entity which remains as the constant perceiver and enjoyer of all experiences. But no such thing exists after the destruction of the body. If there was anything like a permanent self that migrated from one body to another, then it would have remembered the incidents of the past life just as a man remembers the experiences of his childhood or youth[2]. Arguing against the Buddhist view that the series of conscious states in any life cannot be due to the last conscious state before death in a previous life, or that no state of consciousness in any life can be the cause of the series of conscious states in another future life, the Cārvākas say that no consciousness that belongs to a different body and a different series can be regarded as the cause of a different series of conscious states belonging to a different body. Like cognitions belonging to a different series, no cognition can be caused by the ultimate state of consciousness of a past body[3]. Again, since the last mental state of a saint cannot produce other mental states in a separate birth, it is wrong to suppose that the last mental state of a dying man should be able to produce any series of mental states in a new birth. For this reason the Cārvāka teacher Kambalāśvatara says that consciousness is produced from the body through the operation of the vital functions of *prāṇa, apāna* and other bio-motor faculties. It is also wrong to suppose that there is any dormant consciousness in the early stages of the foetal life, for consciousness means the cognition of objects, and there cannot be any consciousness in the foetal state when no sense-organs are properly developed; so also there is no consciousness in a state of swoon, and

[1] *tat-samudāye viṣaye-ndriya-saṃjñā. Cārvāka-sūtra* quoted in. Kamalaśīla's *Pañjikā*, p. 520.

[2] *Nyāya-mañjarī*, p. 467.

[3] *yadi jñānam na tad vivakṣitā-tīta-deha-varti-caram ajñāna-janyam. jñānatvāt yathānya-santāna-varti-jñānam. Kamalaśīla's Pañjikā*, p. 521.

it is wrong to suppose that even in these stages consciousness exists as a potential power, for power presupposes something in which it exists and there is no other support for consciousness excepting the body, and, therefore, when the body is destroyed, all consciousness ceases with it. It cannot also be admitted that at death consciousness is transferred to another intermediary body, for no such body is ever perceived and cannot therefore be accepted. There cannot also be the same series of consciousness in two different bodies; thus the mental states of an elephant cannot be in the body of a horse.

The Buddhist reply to this objection of the Cārvākas is that if by discarding after-life the Cārvākas wish to repudiate the existence of any permanent entity that is born and reborn, then that is no objection to the Buddhists, for they also do not admit any such permanent soul. The Buddhist view is that there is a beginningless and endless series of states of conscious states which, taken as a period of seventy, eighty or a hundred years, is called the present, past or future life. It is wrong on the part of the Cārvākas to deny the character of this series as beginningless and endless; for if it is so admitted, then a state of consciousness at birth has to be regarded as the first and that would mean that it had no cause and it would thus be eternal, for since it existed without any cause there is no reason why it should ever cease to exist. It could not also have been produced by some eternal consciousness or god, for no such eternal entities are admitted; it cannot be admitted as being eternal by itself; it cannot be produced by eternal atoms of earth, water, etc., for it may be shown that no eternal entities can produce anything. Thus, the last alternative is that it must have been produced by the previous states of consciousness. Even if the atoms are regarded as momentary it would be difficult to prove that consciousness was produced by them. The principle which determines causation is, firstly, that something is the cause which, being present, that which was worthy of being seen but was not seen before becomes seen[1]. Secondly, when two instances are such that though all the other conditions are present in them both, yet with the introduction of one element there happens a new phenomenon in the one which does not happen in the other, then that element is the cause of that

[1] *yeṣām upalambhe sati upalabdhi-lakṣaṇa-prāptaṃ pūrvam anupalabdhaṃ sad upalabhyate ity evam āśrayaṇīyam.* Kamalaśīla, *Pañjikā*, p. 525.

phenomenon[1]. The two instances, which differ from each other only in this that there is the effect in the one and not in the other, agree with each other in all other respects excepting that that in which there is the effect has also a new clement which is not present in the other, and it is only in such a case that that element may be regarded as the cause of that effect. Otherwise, if the cause is defined as that which being absent the effect is also absent, then there is the alternative possibility of the presence of another element which was also absent, and it might be that it was on account of the absence of this element that the effect was absent. Thus, the two instances where an effect occurs and where it does not occur must be such that they are absolutely the same in every respect, except the fact that there is one element in the case where there is the effect which was absent in the other instance. The causal relation between body and mind cannot be established by such a rigorous application of the joint method of agreement and difference. It is not possible to employ the method of agreement to determine the nature of relation between one's own body and mind, for it is not possible to observe the body in the early foetal stage before the rise of mind, for without mind there cannot be any observation. In other bodies also the mind cannot be directly observed and so it is not possible to say that the body is prior to mind. The method of difference also cannot be employed, for no one can perceive whether with the cessation of the body his mind also ceases or not; and since the minds of other people cannot be directly perceived, such a negative observation cannot be made with reference to other people, and no assertion can therefore be made as to whether with the cessation of other people's bodies their minds also ceased or not. No inference can be drawn from the immobility of the body at death that it must be due to the destruction of mind, for it may still exist and yet remain inoperative in moving the body. Moreover, the fact that a particular body is not moved by it, is due to the fact that the desires and false notions which were operative with reference to that body were then absent.

Again, there are other reasons why the body cannot be regarded as the cause of mind: for if the body as a whole was the cause of

[1] *satṣu tad-anyeṣu samartheṣu ta-dhetuṣu yasyai'kasyā' bhāve na bhavatī'ty evam āśrayaṇiyam anyathā hi kevalaṃ tad-abhāve na bhavatī'ty upadarśane sandigdham atra tasya sāmarthyaṃ syāt anyasyā'pi tat-samarthasyā' bhāvāt*. Kamalaśīla, *Pañjikā*, p. 526.

mind, then slight deformities of the body would have changed the character of the mind, or minds associated with big bodies like those of elephants would be greater than those of men. If with the change of one there is no change in the other, the two cannot be said to be related as cause and effect. Nor can it be said that the body with the complete set of senses is the cause of mind, for in that case with the loss of any sense the nature and character of the mind would also be changed. But we know that this is not so, and when by paralysis all the motor organs are rendered inoperative, the mind may still continue to work with unabated vigour[1]. Again, though the body may remain the same, yet the mental temperament, character or tone might considerably change, or sudden emotions might easily unhinge the mind though the body might remain the same. Even if instances are found which prove that the conditions of the body affect the conditions of the mind, yet that is no reason why the mind or soul should cease to exist with the destruction of the body. If on account of co-existence (*saha-sthiti-niyama*) of body and mind they may be said to be connected with each other in bonds of causation, then since body is as much co-existent with mind as mind with body, the mind may as well be said to be the cause of body. Co-existence does not prove causation, for co-existence of two things may be due to a third cause. Heated copper melts, so through heat the foetal elements may be supposed to produce on the one hand the body and on the other hand to manifest mind or consciousness. So the co-existence of body and mind does not necessarily mean that the former is the material cause of the latter.

It is said that though the later mental states are perceived to be produced by the previous ones, yet the first manifested consciousness has a beginning and it is produced by the body, and thus the theory of the Buddhists that the series of conscious states is without beginning is false. But if the mental states are in the first instance produced by the body, then these could not in later cases be produced in other ways through the visual or other sense organs. If it is urged that the body is the cause of the first origin of knowledge, but not of the later mental states, then the later mental states ought to be able to raise themselves without being in any way dependent

[1] *prasuptikā-di-rogā-dinā kārye-ndriyā-dīnām upaghāte'pi mano-dhīr avi-kṛtaikā-vikalāṃ sva-sattām anubhavati.* Kamalaśīla, *Pañjikā,* p. 527.

on the body. If it is held that a mental state can produce a series of other mental states only with the help of the body, then each of them would produce an infinite series of such mental states, but such an infinite number of infinite series is never experienced. It cannot also be said that the body generates consciousness only at the first stage and that in all later stages the body remains only as an accessory cause, for that which once behaves as a generating cause cannot behave as an accessory cause. Thus, even if the physical elements be admitted to be impermanent, they cannot be regarded as the cause. If the mental states be regarded as having a beginning, it may be asked whether by mental states the sense-knowledge or the mental ideas are meant. It cannot be the former, for during sleep, swoon or inattentive conditions there is no sense-knowledge, even though the sense-organs are present, and it has therefore to be admitted that attention is the necessary pre-condition of knowledge, and the sense-organs or the sense-faculties cannot be regarded as the sole cause of sense-knowledge. The mind cannot also be regarded as the sole cause, for unless the sense-data or the sense-objects are perceived by the senses, the mind cannot work on them. If the mind could by itself know objects, then there would have been no blind or deaf people. Admitting for argument's sake that mind produces the cognitions, it may be asked whether this cognition is *savikalpa* or *nirvikalpa*; but there cannot be any *savikalpa* unless the association of names and objects (*saṅketa*) is previously learnt. It cannot be also *nirvikalpa* knowledge, for *nirvikalpa* represents the objects as they are in their unique character, which cannot be grasped by the mind alone without the help of the sense-organs. If it is held that even the sense-data are produced by the mind, then that would be the admission of extreme idealism and the giving up of the Cārvāka position. Thus, the conscious states are to be regarded as beginning-less and without any origin. Their specific characters are determined by experiences of past lives, and it is as a reminiscence of these experiences that the instincts of sucking or fear show themselves even with the newly-born baby[1]. It has therefore to be admitted that the conscious states are produced neither by the body nor by the mind, but that they are beginningless and are generated by the previous

[1] *tasmāt pūrvā-bhyāsa-kṛta evā'yaṃ bālānām iṣṭā-niṣṭo-pādāna-parityāga-lakṣaṇo vyavahāra iti siddhā buddher anāditā.* Kamalaśīla, *Pañjikā*, p. 532.

states, and these by other previous states, and so on. The parental consciousness cannot be regarded as being the cause of the consciousness of the offspring, for the latter are not similar in nature, and there are many beings which are not of parental origin. It has, therefore, to be admitted that the conscious states of this life must be produced by the states of another life previous to it. Thus, the existence of a past life is proved. And since the mental states of this life are determined by the mental states of other lives, the mental states of this life also are bound to determine other mental states, and this establishes the existence of future lives; provided, however, that these mental states are associated with the emotions of attachment, anger, antipathy, etc. For the mental states can produce other mental states only when they are affected by the emotions of attachment, anger, etc., and these are inherited by the new-born baby from the mental states of his previous life which determined the series of experiences of his present life. Though the past experiences are transferred to the present life, yet owing to a severe shock due to the intervention of the foetal period these experiences do not at once show themselves in infancy, but reveal themselves gradually with age. One does not always remember what one experienced before; thus, in dreams and deliriums, though the elements of the past experience are present, yet they are reconstructed in a distorted form and do not present themselves in the form of memory. So the past experiences cannot ordinarily be remembered by the infant, though there are some gifted beings who can remember their past lives. It is wrong to suppose that the mind is supported by the body or inheres in it, for the mind is formless. Again, if the mind inhered in the body and was of the same stuff as the body, then the mental states should be as perceptible by the visual organ as the body itself. The mental states can be perceived only by the mind in which they occur, but the body can be perceived both by that mind as well as by others; therefore, these two are of entirely different character and are hence entirely different. The body is continually changing, and it is the unitary series of conscious states that produces the impression of the identity of the body. For though the individual consciousnesses are being destroyed every moment, yet the series remains one in its continuity in the past lives, the present life and the future. When the series is different, as in that of a cow and a horse or between two different persons, the states of the one series cannot affect those in the other. One conscious state is thus admitted to be determining another conscious state, and that another, and so on, within the series. Thus it has to be admitted that consciousness exists, even in the unconscious state; for had it not been so, then there would be a lapse of consciousness at that time and this would mean the breaking up of the series. States of consciousness are independent of the sense-organs and the sense-objects, as they are determined by the previous states; in dreams, when the sense-organs are not operating and when there is no sense-object contact, the conscious states continue to be produced; and in the case of the knowledge of past or future events, or the knowledge of chimerical things like the hare's horn, the independence of conscious states is clearly demonstrated. Thus it is proved that consciousness is neither produced by the body nor is in any way determined or conditioned by it, and it is determined only by its past states and itself determines the future states. Thus also the existence of the past and the future lives is proved.

The arguments of the Jains and of the Naiyāyikas against the Cārvākas are somewhat of a different nature from those of the idealistic Buddhists just described, as the former admitted permanent souls which the latter denied. Thus Vidyānandi, in his *Tattvārtha-śloka-vārtika,* says that the chief reason why the soul cannot be regarded as a product of matter is the fact of undisputed, unintermittent and universal self-consciousness unlimited by time or space. Such perceptions as "this is blue" or "I am white" depend upon external objects or the sense-organs, and cannot therefore be regarded as typical cases of self-consciousness. But such perceptions as "I am happy" which directly refer to the self-perception of the ego do not depend on the operation of any external instruments such as the sense-organs or the like. If this self-consciousness were not admitted to be established by itself, no other doctrine, not even the Cārvāka doctrine which seeks to demolish all attested convictions, could be asserted, for all assertions are made by virtue of this self-consciousness. If any consciousness required another consciousness to have itself attested, then that would involve a vicious infinite and the first consciousness would have to be admitted as unconscious. Thus, since the self manifests itself in self-consciousness (*sva-samvedana*), and since the body is perceived through the operation of the senses like all other physical things, the former is entirely different from the latter and cannot be produced by the latter, and because it is eternal it cannot also be manifested by the latter. Again, since consciousness exists even without the senses, and since it may not exist even when there is the body and the senses (as in a dead body), the consciousness cannot be regarded as depending on the body. Thus, the self is directly known as different from the body by the testimony of self-consciousness. The other arguments of Vidyānandi are directed against the idealistic Buddhists who do not believe in a permanent self but believe in the beginningless series of conscious states, and this discussion had better be omitted here[1].

Jayanta argues in the *Nyāya-mañjarī* that the body is continually changing from infancy to old age, and therefore the experiences of one body cannot belong to the new body that has been formed through growth or decay, and therefore the identity of the ego and recognition which form the essential constitutive elements of knowledge cannot belong to the body[2]. It is true no doubt that good diet and medicine which are helpful to the body are also helpful to the proper functioning of the intellect. It is also true that curds and vegetable products and damp places soon begin to germinate into insects. But this is no proof that matter is the cause of consciousness. The selves are all-pervading, and when there is appropriate modifications of physical elements they manifest themselves through them according to the conditions of their own *karmas*. Again, consciousness cannot also be admitted to belong to the senses, for apart from the diverse sense-cognitions there is the apperception of the ego or the self which co-ordinates these diverse sense-cognitions. Thus I feel that whatever I perceive by the eyes I touch by the hand, which shows distinctly that apart from the sense-cognitions there is the individual perceiver or the ego who co-ordinates these sensations, and without such a co-ordinator the unity of the different sensations could not be attained. The Suśikṣita Cārvākas, however, hold that there is one perceiver so long as the body exists, but that this perceiver (*pramātṛ-tattva*) does not transmigrate, but is destroyed with the destruction of the body; the soul is thus not immortal, and there is no after-world after the destruction of this body[3]. To this Jayanta's reply is that if

[1] *Tattvārtha-śloka-vārtika*, pp. 26-52.
[2] *Nyāya-mañjarī*, pp. 439–441.
[3] *Ibid.* pp. 467, 468.

a self is admitted to exist during the lifetime of this body, then since this self is different from the body, and since it is partless and non-physical by nature, there cannot be anything which can destroy it. No one has ever perceived the self to be burnt or torn to pieces by birds or animals as a dead body can be. Thus, since it has never been found to be destroyed, and since it is not possible to infer any cause which can destroy it, it is to be regarded as immortal. Since the self is eternal, and since it has a present and past association with a body, it is not difficult to prove that it will have also a future association with a body. Thus, self does not reside either in any part of the body or throughout the body, but is all-pervading and behaves as the possessor of that body with which it becomes associated through the bonds of *karma*. *Para-loka* or after-life is defined by Jayanta as rebirth or the association of the soul with other bodies after death. The proofs that are adduced in favour of such rebirths are, firstly, from the instinctive behaviour of infants in sucking the mother's breast or from their unaccountable joys and miseries which are supposed to be due to the memory of their past experiences in another birth; and, secondly, from the inequalities of powers, intelligence, temper, character and habits, inequalities in the reaping of fruits from the same kind of efforts. These can be explained only on the supposition of the effects of *karma* performed in other births[1].

Śaṅkara, in interpreting the *Brahma-sūtra,* III. 3. 53, 54, tries to refute the *lokayatika* doctrine of soullessness. The main points in the *lokayatika* argument here described are that since consciousness exists only when there is a body, and does not exist when there is no body, this consciousness must be a product of the body. Life-movements, consciousness, memory and other intellectual functions also belong to the body, since they are experienced only in the body and not outside of it[2]. To this Śaṅkara's reply is that life-movements, memory, etc., do not sometimes exist even when the body exists (at death), therefore they cannot be the products of the body. The qualities of the body, such as colour, form, etc., can be

[1] *Nyāya-mañjarī,* pp. 470–473.

[2] *yad dhi yasmin sati bhavaty asati ca na bhavati tat tad-dharmatvena adhyavasīyate yathā'gni-dharmāv auṣṇya-prakāśau; prāṇa-ceṣṭā-caitaṇya-smṛtyā-dayaś cā'tma-dharmatvenā'bhimatā ātma-vā-dināṃ te' py antar eva deha upala-bhyamānā bahiś cā'nupalabhyamanā asiddhe deha-vyat irikte dharmiṇi deha-dharmā eva bhavitum arhanti; tasmād avyatireko dehād ātmāna iti. Śaṅkara-bhāṣya* on *Brahma-sūtra,* III. 3. 53.

perceived by everyone, but there are some who cannot perceive consciousness, memory, etc. Again, though these are perceived so long as the living body exists, yet there is no proof that it does not exist when this body is destroyed. Further, if consciousness is a product of the body, it could not grasp the body; no fire can burn itself and no dancer can mount his own shoulders. Consciousness is always one and unchangeable and is therefore to be regarded as the immortal self. Though ordinarily the self is found to manifest itself in association with a body, that only shows that the body is its instrument, but it does not prove that the self is the product of the body, as is contended by the Cārvākas. The Cārvākas criticized the entire social, moral and religious programme of orthodox Hindus. Thus Śrīharṣa, in representing their views in his *Naiṣadh-acarita,* says as follows: "The scriptural view that the performance of sacrifices produces wonderful results is directly contradicted by experience, and is as false as the Purāṇic story of the floating of stones. It is only those who are devoid of wisdom and capacity for work who earn a livelihood by the Vedic sacrifices, or the carrying of three sticks (*tridaṇḍa*), or the besmearing of the forehead with ashes. There is no certainty of the purity of castes, for, considering the irrepressible sex-emotions of men and women, it is impossible to say that any particular lineage has been kept pure throughout its history in the many families on its maternal and paternal sides. Men are not particular in keeping themselves pure, and the reason why they are so keen to keep the women in the harem is nothing but jealousy; it is unjustifiable to think that unbridled sex-indulgence brings any sin or that sins bring suffering and virtues happiness in another birth; for who knows what will happen in the other birth when in this life we often see that sinful men prosper and virtuous people suffer?" The Vedic and the *smṛti* texts are continually coming into conflict with one another, and are reconciled only by the trickery of the commentators; if that is so, why not accept a view in which one may act as one pleases? It is held that the sense of ego is associated with the body, but when this body is burnt, what remains there of virtue or vice, and even if there is anything that will be experienced by another ego and in another body and as such that cannot hurt me. It is ridiculous to suppose that any one should remember anything after death, or that after death the fruits of *karma* will be reaped, or that by feeding Brahmins after death the so-called departed soul will have any satisfaction. The image-worship, or the worship of stones with flowers, or of bathing in the Ganges as a religious practice is absolutely ridiculous. The practice of performing *śrāddha* ceremonies for the satisfaction of the departed is useless, for if the offering of food could satisfy the dead then the hunger of travellers could also be removed by their relations offering them food at home. In reality with death and destruction of the body everything ends, for nothing returns when the body is reduced to ashes. Since there is no soul, no rebirth, no god and no after-life, and since all the scriptures are but the instructions of priests interested in cheating the people, and the Purāṇas are but false mythical accounts and fanciful stories, the one ideal of our conduct is nothing but sense-pleasures. Sins and virtues have no meaning, they are only the words with which people are scared to behave in a particular manner advantageous to the priests. In the field of metaphysics the Cārvākas are materialists and believe in nothing beyond the purely sensible elements of the atoms of earth, water, air and fire and their combinations; in the field of logic they believe in nothing but what can be directly perceived; they deny *karma,* fruits of *karma,* rebirth or souls. The only thing that the Cārvākas cared for was the momentary sense-pleasures, unrestrained enjoyment of sensual joys. They did not believe in sacrificing present joys to obtain happiness in the future, they did not aim at increasing the total happiness and wellbeing of the whole life as we find in the ethical scheme of Caraka; with them a pigeon today was better than a peacock tomorrow, better to have a sure copper coin today than a doubtful gold coin in the future[1]. Thus, immediate sense-pleasures were all that they wanted and any display of prudence, restraint, or other considerations which might lead to the sacrifice of present pleasures was regarded by them as foolish and unwise. It does not seem that there was any element of pessimism in their doctrine. Their whole ethical position followed from their general metaphysical and logical doctrine that sense-objects or sense-pleasures were all that existed, that there was no supra-sensible or transcendent reality, and thus there was no gradation or qualitative difference between the pleasures and no reason why any restraint should be put upon our normal tendency to indulge in sense-pleasures.

[1] *varam adya kapotaḥ śvo mayūrāt*
varam saṃśayikān niṣkād asaṃśayikaḥ
kārṣāpaṇa iti lokāyatikāh.

Kāma-sūtra, 1. 2. 29, 30.

INDEX

Abhidhammas, 82–83, 166
Abhidhammatthasaṅgaha, 90, 92, 94
Abhidharmakośa, 92, 114–15, 117, 119–21, 128
Abhidharma Kośabhāṣya, 120
Abhidharmakośa kārikā, 114
Abhidharmakośaśāstra, 114
Abhidharmakośa vyākhyā, 120
Abhihitānvayavāda, 396–97
Abhilāpa association (*kalpanāpoḍha*), 408
Ābhoga, 546, 602
Absence of knowledge (*vidyā-bhāvaḥ*), 506
Absolute cessation (*mokṣe nivṛttirniḥśeṣā*), 216
Absolute momentariness, doctrine of, 209
Absolute monism, school of, 70
Ācārya, Śaṅkara, 572
Adharma, 197–98, 316
Adhikaraṇa-mālā, 575
Advaita-bodha-dipikā, 710
Advaita-brahma-siddhi, 420, 490, 551
Advaita-cintā-kaustubha, 550
Advaita-dīpikā, 547, 710
Advaita-makaranda, 550, 687
Advaita-nirṇaya, 713
Advaitānubhūti, 575
Advaita-pañca-ratna, 710
Advaita-ratna-rakṣaṇa, 720
Advaita-siddhi, 67, 419–20, 444, 456, 547, 550, 612, 646, 692–93, 717, 719–20 *ddhisiddhāntasāra*, 420
Advaita-vāda, 710
Advayāraṇya, 725
Adyar Library, 543, 581, 690, 692
Agastya, 722, 724
Agni (fire), 37
Ahaṃkāra, 213–14, 216, 225–26, 248–51, 253, 262, 276, 301, 458, 460–61, 472, 475, 569, 711, 732–33, 739, 756–57
Ahaṃkāra, 248–51, 457
Ahiṃsā, 199–200, 236, 270
Ahirbudhnya Saṃhitā, 219–21
Āhrika, 666
Airy organ (organ of touch), 377
Aitareya, 28, 30, 36, 39, 57, 432, 572, 753
Ajātaśatru, 33–34
Ajita Kesakambali, 80
Ajñāna-consciousness, 458
Ajñāna modification, 491
Ākāśa, 197–98, 253, 288, 292, 326
Ākāśāstikāya, 195, 198
Ākāśic organ (organ of sound), 377
Akhaṇḍānanda, 419, 504, 525, 597, 687, 702
Akhyāti theory of Mīmāṃsā, 386
Akṣapāda, 63, 71, 279, 306, 309, 632
Ālayavijñāna, 86, 131–34, 136–37, 146, 167
Alberuni, 233–35, 237
Amalānanda, 86, 114, 418–19, 543, 546, 551–52, 568, 576, 580, 597, 601–3, 613, 714, 754
Ānandabodha, 420, 506, 543–45, 563–64, 583, 586, 610–12, 618, 641, 686, 688, 690
Ānandagiri, 418, 433, 537, 577, 597, 618, 687, *See also* Ānandajñāna
Ānandajñāna, 537, 543–45, 572–75, 586, 594, 610, 613, 618, 666, 686, 688–90, 699, 704
Ānandamaya ātman, 46
Ānandapūrṇa, 546, 551, 577, 581, 597, 617, 620
Anirvacanīya theory of error, 611
Annamaya, 46, 60
Annamaya koṣa, 60
Antaḥkaraṇa, 299, 457–61, 472–73, 476–77, 480–83, 486–88, 527–28, 544, 550, 559–60, 566, 569–71, 582–83, 595–96, 598–600, 603, 607–8, 689, 700–5, 707, 711, 756
Antaḥkaraṇa transformations, 482, 704
Antarāya karma, 191, 194
Antarvyāptisamarthana, 156, 346
Anthropomorphism, 18
Anvaya-prakāśikā, 550
Anyathākhyāti theory of illusion, 385
Aparigraha (abandoning attachment for all things), 199
Aparokṣānubhava, 572
Aparokṣānubhūti, 574

Āpastamba, 276
Appanāsamādhi, 102–3
Aqueous organ (organ of taste), 377
Āraṇyakas, 12, 14, 27–29, 33, 35–36, 746
Aristotle, 279
Arthakriyākāritva, doctrine of, 155, 161, 163, 187, 209
Arthaśāstra, 227
Āruṇi, 33–34
Āryadeva, 122, 128–29, 166, 545, 618, 658–59
Aśaraṇabhāvanā (meditation of helplessness), 202
Asceticism, 36, 39, 54, 58, 81, 201–2, 226–27, 723, 761
Āstika, 67–68, 72
Āstika-mata or orthodox schools, 68
Astronomy, 32
Aśvaghoṣa, 120, 128–29, 135–36, 138, 161, 166, 280, 409, 423
doctrine of, 147
Tathatā philosophy of, 129–38
Aśvapati Kaikeya, 33–34
Atharva-Veda, 12–13, 24, 31, 469
Atheism, 203–6, *See also* Jaina philosophy
Ātma-bodha, 573, 575, 597, 719
Ātma-bodha-vyākhyāna, 597
Ātma-jñānopadeśa, 572, 687
Ātman doctrine, 27, 45–48
Ātman Upaniṣad, 31
Atomic contact (*ārambhaka-saṃyoga*), 328
Atomic theory of the Vaiśeṣikas, 651
Ātreyasaṃthitā, 213
Ātreyatantra, 213
Attainment of the goal (*sādhana*), 77
Attainment of wisdom (*Brahma*-knowledge), 541
Atthakathā, 83
Atthasālinī, 82–83, 85, 89, 97–99, 108
Authoritative old Sāṃkhya view, 218
Avaccheda-vāda, doctrines of, 600
Avataṃsaka, 128
Āyuṣka karma, 191

Bādarāyaṇa, 70, 223, 279, 422–23, 429–30, 433, 530, 536, 538–39, 754
philosophy of, 530–40
Badarikāśrama, 432
Bālabhadra, 549
Bālāki Gārgya, 33–34
Bhagavad-gītā, 8, 64, 227, 421–22, 436, 574
Bhāmaha, 665
Bhāmatī, 114, 143, 418, 421, 505, 519, 523, 530, 533, 539, 546, 550, 576, 600–3, 605, 714, 716, 763
Bhāra-hāra-sūtra, 555
Bhartṛhari, 231, 665
Bhartṛprapañca, 495, 530, 537–38, 594
philosophy of, 530–40
Bhāṣāpariccheda, 280–81, 307, 339
Bhāskara, 537, 550, 687, 691, 695
Bhāṣya-ṭippana, 572
Bhāṣyavāttika, 63
Bhaṭṭa Ānanda, 758
Bhaṭṭācārya, Gadādhara, 308, 613, 618
Bhaṭṭācārya, Jagadīśa, 308, 613, 618
Bhaṭṭācarya, Jānakīnātha, 308
Bhattacarya, Sivaprasad, 726
Bhaṭṭa, Devarāma, 575
Bhaṭṭa, Kumārila, 67, 69, 129, 145, 167, 209, 284, 355, 359, 369–72, 378–80, 382, 384, 386–89, 391–92, 395–97, 399–403, 405, 416–17, 432, 459, 475, 581, 605–6, 614, 641, 665, 673, 691, 705, 708
Bhaṭṭa, Malla, 573
Bhaṭṭa-mata, 69
Bhaṭṭa Rāghava, 616–17
Bhaṭṭārakācarya, Ānandabodha, 543, 563, 641
Bhaṭṭāraka, Gangāpurī, 544
Bhaṭṭa, Śrīkaṇṭha, 573
Bhāvāgaṇeśa, 212, 243
Bhāvasaṃvaras, 195
Bhāvivikta, 666
Bhedābheda doctrine of Vedānta, 537–38
Bhedābheda-vāda, 536–37
Bheda-dhikkāra, 420, 545, 548–49, 710, 712
Bheda-dhikkāra-satkriyā, 545, 549
Bhīmācārya, M. M., 2
Bhojavṛtti, 212
Bibliotheca Indica, 165, 168, 337, 346
Birth/death, cycle of, 130
Birth/rebirths, cycle of, 215
Birth ceremony at the birth of a son, *See* Naimittika-karma

Bodhāyana bhāṣya, 433
Bodhibhāvanā, 202
Brahmacaryya (celibacy), 199–200, 226, 236
Brahmadatta, 593
Brahmahood, 55, 538, 549, 575, 579, 584, 586, 609, 644, 766
causal state of, 531
Brahmajāla sutta, 236
Brahma-kāṇḍa, 581–82
Brāhmaṇas, 12–14, 24–31, 33, 35, 208, 369, 404, 429–30
and the Early Upaniṣads, 31–37
Brahmaṇaspati, 23, 32, 43
Brahman-consciousness (*brahma-caitanya*), 571
Brahman
material representation of, 43
unknowability of, 44–45
Brahman Padmapāda, 598, 600
Brahma-prakāśikā, 543
Brahma Samaj, 40
Brahma-siddhi, 539, 577–78, 580–82, 586–87, 589, 591–92, 600–1, 604, 606, 641, 692–93
Brahma-sūtra, 8, 45, 64, 70, 85–86, 70, 91, 121, 143, 279, 418, 420–22, 429–33, 439, 470, 496, 499–500, 502, 519, 522–24, 533, 539–40, 550, 574–76, 586, 597, 602, 641–42, 683, 690, 698–99, 712, 714, 740, 744–45, 764
Brahma-sūtra-bhāṣya, 524, 574–76, 641
Brahmavihāra, 103
Brahmin Sutīkṣṇa, 724
Bṛhad-āraṇyaka-bhāṣya-ṭīkā, 687
Bṛhadāraṇyaka Upaniṣad, 14, 28, 31, 35, 39, 50, 87, 226, 263, 432, 469–70, 537, 542, 745, 753
Bṛhad-āraṇyakopaniṣad-bhāṣya, 572
Bṛhad-yoga-vasiṣṭha, 726
Buddhadeva, 115–16, 665
Buddhaghoṣa, 82–83, 88–89, 94, 96, 99, 105, 161, 470
Buddhahood, 84, 136–37
Buddhi, 232, 259–62, 265, 569
Buddhism, 9, 74–75, 78, 83–84, 88–90, 95, 99, 107–11, 113, 122, 129, 138, 161, 165–67, 169, 175, 208–10, 212, 219, 237–38, 312–13, 322, 421, 424, 478, 494, 507, 552, 611, 722
Brahmanic modification, 725
criticism of, 274–75
nāstika schools of, 208
non-Sautrāntika school of, 168
non-Vaibhāṣika school of, 168
Buddhist Dharmakīrti, 665
Buddhist Diṅnāga, 63, 665
Buddhist doctrine of soullessness, 552–67
Buddhistic idealism of Diṅnāga, 529
Buddhistic nihilists (*śūnya-vādins*), 496–97
Buddhist idealism, 497, 519, 523, 703, 764
Buddhist Paṇḍitāśoka, 318
Buddhist philosophy, 3, 7, 78, 84, 115, 145, 164
Avijjā and Āsava, 99–100
Buddhaghoṣa, 89
Buddha's Life, 81–82
definition of being or existence (sattva), 160
Buddhist Literature, 82–84
Abhidhammas, 83
Nikāyas, 83
Sthaviravāda or Theravāda, 83
Thera Vāda, 83
doctrine of causal connection, 84–93
abhiññānena, 98
abhisandahana, 98
anubhava, 97
āyatana, 85
bhava, 85
Bhavacakra (wheel of existence), 86
Buddhaghoṣa, 96
cetanā, 97
consciousness (*viññāna*), 85
decay and death (*jarāmaraṇa*), 86
ekacittasmiṃ, 97
paccabhiññā, 98
paṭiccasamuppāda, 84
sabbasaṅgahikavasena, 98
Saṃyutta Nikāya, 84
saññā, 97
sense-contact (*phassa*), 85
taṇhā, 85
upādāna, 85
vedanā, 97
doctrine of causal efficiency, 163–64
doctrine of momentariness, 158–64
evolution of Buddhist Thought, 166–68
kamma, 106–9

khandhas, 93–98
mahāyānism, 125–29
nihilism, 138–45
ontological issues, 164–66
pāli buddhism, 83
sautrāntika theory of inference, 155–58
sautrāntika theory of perception, 151–54
school of vijñānavāda buddhism, 145–51
sīla and samādhi, 100–6
state of philosophy, 78–81
tathatā philosophy of aśvaghoṣa, 129–38
upaniṣads, 109–11
Buddhist Saṅghabhadra, 665
Buddhist Vasumitra, 665
Buddhist Vijñānavāda, 762–66
Buddhist Yugasena, 666
Buddhitattva, 249–50
Burlingame, E.W., 742

Calcutta Asiatic Society, 699
Candrakānta Tarkālaṃkāra, 279
Candrakīrti, 85–88, 109, 125, 128–29, 138, 140, 155, 166, 497, 499, 545, 658–62, 665
Candrikā, 212, 592–93, 686, 726
Caraka-saṃhitā, 302
Cārvākas, schools of (Dhūrtta and Suśikṣita), 78
Cārvāka sūtras, 87
Cattle-keeping, 15
Catuḥśataka, 129
Catuḥsūtrī, 70
Caturmata-sāra-saṃgraha, 713
Causal connection, doctrine of, 84–93
Causal efficiency, doctrine of, 168, 526
Causal forces (*karaṇa-śakti-pratniyamāt*), 668
Causation
principle of, 254–25
Sāṃkhya theories of, 258
Cause-effect relation, 141, 352–53
Chāndogya-bhāṣya-ṭīkā, 687
Chāndogya Upaniṣad, 28, 30, 36, 39, 53, 93, 110, 133, 173–74, 226, 263, 432–33, 537, 572, 687, 740, 744, 753–54
Chāyā-vyākhyā, 756
Chintamani, T. R., 690
Citsukha, 238, 419, 445, 460, 462, 465, 485, 492, 543–45, 547, 552, 577, 580–81, 586, 592–93, 610, 613, 618, 632, 641–57, 665–66, 686, 688, 692, 711–12, 716
Citsukha Ācārya, 613, 632
class-concept of quality, 657
class-concept of substances, 656
conception of substance (*dravya*), 655
dialectical thought, 641
ignorance or nescience, 647
notion of class-concept (*jāti*), 653
qualities (guṇa), 656–57
refutation of cause (*kāraṇa*), 654
subject-object relation, 646
traditional view of nescience, 647
Citta, 91, 265, 268–70
characteristic of, 269
characteristics of, 261–64
kind of, 268
stage of, 268
state of, 268
Cittaviśuddhiprakaraṇa, 129
Class-concept (*jāti*), 168, 203, 534, 602, 625–26, 633–34, 637, 642, 653–57, 682
"knowable", 634
refutation of, 682
Cognition (*saṃvedana*), 115, 118, 154, 182, 189, 191, 207, 214, 225, 250, 268, 273, 277, 280–81, 285, 289–91, 296, 304, 331–33, 336, 339, 342–43, 356–58, 376–79, 383–84, 386–87, 390–91, 395, 400–1, 404, 409, 411, 417, 438–39, 449, 452, 456, 484, 512–13, 517, 526, 554, 556, 558, 561–64, 566, 570–71, 587–88, 597, 627–33, 643–45, 647, 674, 678, 691, 694–95, 700–2, 705, 708, 716, 718, 733–44, 763–64
Cognitive process, 261–64
Colour-cognition, 674
Conservation of Energy, 254–55
Construction of mind (*buddhi-nirmāṇa*), 256
Correctness of knowledge, 375, 485
Cosmic golden egg, 25
Cosmography (Jaina philosophy), 199
Cosmology, Jaina, 202
Creative powers (*vikṣepa-śakti*), 568
Dārā Shiko, 39

Darśanāvaraṇīya, 190, 193–94
Daśa-śloki-mahā-vidyā-sūtra, 614

Dasgupta, S. N., 238, 397, 511
Davids, Rhys, 92, 96, 99, 108, 112, 120, 158
Deśika, Lakṣmīdhara, 573
Destructibility, 676
Devadatta, 117–18, 176, 290, 391–93, 411, 483, 556, 569, 647
Devakṣema, 120
Devayāna, doctrine of, 58
Dhammapada, 83, 742
Dhammas, 84, 89, 104, 166
Dhammasaṅgaṇi, 82–83, 94–95, 99
Dhāraṇāśāstra, 229
Dharma, 94, 197–98, 316, 427, 543, 546, 576, 714
Dharmakīrtti, 151, 153, 155, 309, 340, 351, 362, 409–10
Dharmarājādhvarīndra, 67, 419, 471, 548, 583, 692, 708
Dharma-saṃgraha, 94
Dharmaskandha, 120
Dharmatrāta, 115, 120, 665
Dharmmakīrtti, 168
Dharmmottara, 152, 155, 168
Dhātukāya, 120
Dialectical Vedānta, 1
Dīgha Nikāya, 83, 106
Dīkṣita, Ācārya, 712
Dīkṣita, Appaya, 504–5, 511, 538, 541, 543, 546–49, 573, 576, 600, 710, 712–14
Dīkṣita, Bhaṭṭojī, 549
Dīkṣita, Nānā, 546, 719
Dīkṣita, Nīlakaṇṭha, 713
Dīkṣita, Rāmabhadra, 230
Dīkṣita, Vaidyanātha, 575
Dīpavaṃsa, 83, 112, 119
Direct perception (*pratyakṣa*), 344
Doctine(s)
absolute momentariness, 209
arthakriyākāritva, 155, 161, 163, 187, 209
Aśvaghoṣa, 147
Ātman, 25–26
avaccheda-vāda, 600
Bhedābheda doctrine of Vedānta, 527–38
Buddhist doctrine of Soullessness, 552–67
causal connection, 84–93
causal efficiency, 168, 526
Devayāna, 58
ekajīva (one-soul), 477
illusion, 303, 337, 497, 609
inference, 280
Madhva, 713
māyā, 50
Mīmāṃsā doctrines, 281
momentariness, 158–64, 168, 212, 274, 310
mukti, 74–75
nayas, 176–79
negation, 360
nihilistic Buddhists, 301
Nyaya-Vaiśeṣika, 310–13
arataḥ-prāmāṇya, 372–75
paṭiccasamuppāda, 166
perception, 379–82
philosophical doctrine of Śaṅkara, 496
philosophical doctrines of European philosophy, 9
pīlupāka, 327
piṭharapāka, 327
pralaya and sṛṣṭi, 323
pratibimba-vāda, 600
relative pluralism, 175–76
Sautrāntika doctrine of Buddhism, 155
self-validity of knowledge, 372
soul, 75, 362–63
syādvāda, 179–81
tathāgatagarbha, 147
Tathatā doctrine, 166–67
transmigration, 25–27, 53–57
Vedānta doctrine of Soul, 522–67
Vijñāna vādins, 332
viparyyaya, 220
vyāpti, 303
Yoga Doctrine of Soul, 238–41
Draviḍācāryya, 433
Dravya, 175, 191, 197–98, 231–32, 285–87, 294, 304, 306, 312–13, 317–20, 334, 340, 380, 428, 637, 650, 655, 681, 687
aparatva, 316
gandha (odour), 313
paratva, 316
parimiti (measure), 314–16
pṛthaktva (mutual difference), 316
rasa (taste), 313
rūpa (colour), 313
śabda (sound), 314
saṃkhyā (number), 314

saṃyoga (connection), 316
sparśa (touch), 314
vibhāga (separation), 316
Dravya karma, 191
Dravya-leśyā, 191
Dṛṣṭi-sṛṣṭi school, 510
Dṛṣṭi-sṛṣṭi-vāda, philosophy of, 546
Dṛṣṭi-sṛṣṭi-vāda theory, 478
Dvārakā monastery, 686, *See also* Ānandajñāna

Early School of Sāṃkhya, 213–22
Earthly organ (organ of smell), 377
Eating and drinking (*āhāre paṭikkūlasaññā*), 102
Ego (*ahaṃkāra*), 111, 133–34, 214, 225, 250, 284, 457–59, 472, 475–76, 503, 509, 527, 571, 595–96, 598–99, 642, 673, 727, 729–30, 750–51, 760
ego-consciousness, 134
ego-feeler (*ahaṃ-pratyayin*), 598
ego-hood, parts, 503
egoism, function of (*ahaṃkāra*), 569
immediate ego (*ahaṃkāra*), 598
self-conscious ego, 732
Ekajīva (one-soul), doctrine of, 477
Eka-śloka, 572
Emancipation (*mukti*) , 58–61, 203, 489
Energy of free-will (*Pauruṣa*), 746–50
Eschatology (Doctrine of Ātman), 25–26
Essencelessness (*śūnya*), 728
European philosophy, 6, 9, 62

False knowledge (*mithyā-jñānam*), 183, 293, 365, 502, 506
Feelings, 242–43, 673

Garbha Upaniṣad, 31
Gauḍa Abhinanda, 726
Gauḍabrahmānandī, 420
Gauḍapāda, 212, 223, 243, 418, 420, 422–27, 429, 432, 435, 437, 470, 496, 500–2, 515, 522, 524, 551, 574, 686, 725, 728, 756, 766
Gauḍapādīya-bhāṣya, 572
Gauḍeśvara Ācārya, 552, 641
Gautama, 59, 63, 65, 71, 81, 186, 279, 289, 306
Ghana-spanda-krama, 739
Ghoṣaka, 120, 665
Gītā-bhāṣya-vivecana, 687
Gitā-tātparya-bodhinī, 552
Goldstücker, 227, 279
Gotra karma, 191, 194
Govardhana, 329–30
Govindānanda, 85–86, 89–91, 418, 543, 575, 597–98, 755
Greek philosophy, 42
Guṇaratna, 2–3, 7, 78–79, 114–15, 119, 162–63, 170, 175–76, 186, 194, 203, 206, 213, 217–18, 220, 222–23
Guṇas, 243–45, 286
meanings, 243
modifications of, 273
nature of, 223–24, 273
state of the mutual equilibrium, 245
tamo-guṇas, 244
as things of secondary importance, 244
transformations of, 267
types, 243
ultimate entities, 244
Guṇasthānas, 192
Gupta, Prajñākara, 543

Haribhadra, 2, 7, 68, 222
Hastabālaprakaraṇavṛtti, 129
Heaven, attainment of, 350
Hemacandra, 171–72, 180, 199, 203, 237
Henotheism, 17–19, 27
Hetuvādins (Sarvāstivādins), 112
Hīnayāna Buddhists, 662
Hindu Chemistry, 251, 254, 321–22, 327, *See also* Ray, P.C.
Hindu Law, 11, 69
Hiraṇyagarbha, 19, 23, 32, 52, 476, 570
Hiriyanna, 495, 537, 579–80, 592, 594
History of Philosophy, 3
Holy student life (*brahmacarya*), 283
Horse sacrifice (*aśvamedha*), 14

Idealistic school of Buddhists, 725
Identity, knowledge of, 528
Illusion
doctrine of, 303, 337, 497, 609
example of, 385
psychology of, 384–87
Image-worship, 11
Individual consciousness (*jīva-caitanya*), 571
Indriya, 193, 232, 472, 517, 583, 732–33
Inner concomitance (*antarvyāpti*), 157

Instrumentality, concept of, 631
Intelligence
principle of, 240–41, 514
super-translucent transcendent principle of, 241
Inter-atomic space (*ghanapratarabhedena*), 196
Invariable concomitance, definition of, 635
Īśā Upaniṣad, 28, 31, 39, 50, 572
Īśopaniṣadbhāṣya, 572
Iṣṭa-siddhi, 692–93, 699, 707
Īśvara, 68, 203, 218–20, 222–23, 234, 248, 255, 258–59, 267, 270–71, 282, 284, 300, 304, 307, 311, 322–27, 355, 363–66, 438, 469, 474–77, 493, 533, 544, 566, 574, 606, 670–72
Īśvarakṛṣṇa, 218–20, 222, 574
Īśvarānumāna, 326, 365

Jacob, G. A., 576
Jacobi, 277–79
Jaigīṣavya, 229
Jaimini, 69, 281–82, 369–70, 427, 429–30
Jaina Ācāryasūri, 665
Jaina Philosophy, 7, 169–207
adharma, 197–98
ākāśa, 197–98
āsrava, 192–95
canonical literature of, 171–72
characteristics of the Jains, 172–73
cosmography, 199
dharma, 197–98
doctrine of nayas, 176–79
doctrine of relative pluralism, 175–76
doctrine of syādvāda, 179–81
fundamental ideas of Jaina ontology, 173–75
jaina atheism, 203–6
jaina yoga, 199–203
jīvas, 188–90
kāla and samaya, 198
karma, 190–95
knowledge as revelation, 186–88
literature of, 171–72
Mahāvīra's Life, 173
mokṣa (emancipation), 207
nirjarā, 192–95
non-perceptual knowledge, 185–86
origin of Jainism, 169–70
pudgala, 195–97
sects of Jainism, 170–71
Digambaras, 170
Śvetāmbaras, 170
theory of perception, 183–85
value of knowledge, 181–83
Jaina Śubhagupta, 666
Jaina thought, 7
Jāti, apprehension of, 381
Jayanta, 67, 79, 160, 212, 307, 321, 326, 330, 337, 355, 362, 545, 601
Jhā, Gaṅgānātha, 370, 372, 378, 384, 397, 405
Jhānasamādhi, acquirement of, 102
Jīvan-mukta, 492, 708, 710, 739–42, 744–46, 758, 762
Jīvan-mukti-viveka, 419, 708, 710, 745–46, 762
Jīvas, 188–90
Jivāstikāya, 189
Jñāna-karma-samuccaya, 537–38, 594
Jñānaprasthāna Śāstra, 120
Jñānaśakti (power of knowledge), 460
Jñānāvaraṇīya, 190, 193–94
Journal of the Bengal Asiatic Society, 278

Kāla and Samaya, 198
Kalāpa Vyākaraṇa, 282
Kālidāsa, 277, 724–25, 733
Kalpataru, 418
Kalpataruparimala, 418
Kāma, 57, 88, 144, 585
Kamalaśīla, 519, 521–22, 525, 665–66, 668–70, 672–73, 675–76, 678–82
Kāmāsavas, 100
Kamma, 106–9
Kaṇāda-sūtra-nibandha, 617
Kāpila Sāṃkhya, 68
Kāpya Pataṃchala, 230
Karaṇa, concept of, 631
Kārikā, 67, 122, 125, 128, 212, 218, 220, 222, 224, 238, 242, 273, 281, 342, 422–24, 429, 500–2, 515, 522, 524, 574, 587–88, 591–92, 744
Karma doctrine, complexities of, 57
Karmamārga (path of duties), 436
Kār-maśarīra, 73
Karma theory, 71–74, 190–92
adṛṣṭa (the unseen), 72
apūrva (new), 72

aśuklā-kṛṣṇa, 73
conception of ṛta, 72
mukta, 73
śukla-kṛṣṇa, 73
vāsanā, 73
Kāśmīraka, 690
Kaṭha, 28, 31, 39, 45, 50, 59–60, 109, 211, 226, 432, 572, 745
Kathāvatthu, 83, 108, 112–13, 119–20, 157–58, 465, 741–42
Kaṭhopaniṣad-bhāṣya-ṭīkā, 687
Kātyāyana, 230, 279
Kātyāyanīputtra, 120
Kauṭilya, 227, 277–79
Kavi, Lakṣmīdhara, 550
Kavirāja, 573
Kāyika-vijñapti karma, 124
Kena, 28, 30, 37, 39, 432, 544, 572, 690
Kenopaniṣad-bhāṣya-vivaraṇa, 572
Khaṇḍana-khaṇḍakhādya, 318, 419, 462, 551, 597, 613, 620–21, 626, 632, 635, 640, 650, 686
Khandha Yamaka, 94
Khecarī-mūdrā, 753
Kingship, 15
Kiraṇāvalībhāskara, 306
Kitāb Pātanjal, 233
Knowledge
Bhāskara view of, 691
characteristic of, 242, 376
false knowledge (*mithyā-jñānam*), 183, 293, 365, 502, 506
nature of, 382–84
non-perceptual, 185–86
origin of, 330–32, 414
production principles of, 376
revelation, 240
rise of, 188, 374–76, 413, 416, 647, 740
self-illuminating character of, 465
self-knowledge, 59
self-revelation of, 623, 645
self-validity of, 284, 303, 372–74, 389, 396, 417, 484–85, 492, 708
sense-contact as a condition, 376
of sense-objects (indriyārtha), 288
sheath of knowledge (*vijñānamaya-koṣa*), 569
subject-object relation of, 599, 647
thought-movement (jñānakāraṇa) involved in, 448
transcendent indeterminate, 515
validity or truth of, 373
Kriyāśakti (power of work), 460
Kṛṣṇa Ācārya, 573
Kṛṣṇānanda, 550, 690
Kumalaśīla, 677
Kumārajīva, 122, 128, 166
Kumārasambhava, 277, 724
Kumārila, six pramāṇas of, 484
Kusumāñjali, 326

Laghu-candrikā, 579, 719
Laghu-jñānavasiṣṭha, 726
Laghu-vākya-vṛtti, 574
Lakṣmīnṛsiṃha, 546, 602
Laṅkāvatāra, 84, 125–26, 128, 130, 138, 147, 149–50, 280, 423, 429, 470, 516, 529, 621, 728, 766
Laṅkāvatāra sūtra, 280
Law of Karma, 21–22, 26
Linguistic trickery, 496
Logical formalism, 612–19
Lokabhāvanā, 202
Loka-saṃvṛta, 498
Lokāyata school, 665

Macdonell, A. A., 12–13, 18–19, 22–23, 25–26, 753
Madhusūdana, Śaṅkara, 575
Madhva, doctrines of, 713
Madhyamaka (*Śūnya* system), 141
Mādhyamika doctrine, 127, 138, 429
Mādhyamika kārikā, 138, 658
Mādhyamikas, 113, 660, 662
Mādhyamika-sūtras, 497
Magical force, 36–37
Magic (*indrajāla*), 738
Mahābhārata, 79, 216–20, 224, 279
Mahābhāṣya, 219, 230–33, 235, 465
Mahādeva Vaidya, 573
Mahādeva Vidyāvagīśa, 573
Mahānārayaṇa, 31
Mahāsatipaṭṭhāna sutta, 107
Mahat, 248–51
Mahā Vibhāṣā, 120
Mahāvibhāṣāśāstra, 120–21
Mahā-vidyā syllogism, 543, 545, 613–17, 618
Mahā-vidyā-viḍambana, 597, 613–14, 616–17
Mahāvīra, 79, 169–71, 173
Mahāyāna, 125–28, 166, 279, 421, 424

Mahāyānasamparigraha śāstra, 128
Mahāyāna, schools of, 128
Mahāyāna scriptures, 166
Mahāyāna sūtra, 125–26, 128, 279, 421
Mahāyānasūtrālaṃkāra, 125, 128, 146–47, 151
Mahāyānism, 125–29
Maheśvara Tīrtha, 577, 690
Mahimnaḥ stotra, 720
Maitrāyaṇa Upaniṣad, 236
Maitrāyaṇī school, 31
Maitrāyaṇī Upaniṣad, 236
Maitreyī, 28, 35, 61, 745
Majjhima Nikāya, 83, 90, 93, 100, 106, 111
Mālatī-Mādhava, 606
Malliṣena, 171
Māna-manohara, 614, 618
Manas, 25–26, 43, 124, 133–34, 146, 184, 189, 213–15, 225, 228, 261–62, 289, 291–93, 295, 298–300, 303, 311, 316, 323, 343, 365, 377–78, 402, 413, 441–42, 460, 472, 569–70, 598, 650, 667, 681, 691–92, 700, 726–28, 731–39, 745–46, 748–49, 756
Māṇḍūkya, 28, 31, 39, 418, 424, 432, 572, 586, 686–87
Māṇḍūkya-Gauḍapādīya-bhāṣya-vyākhyā, 687
Māṇḍūkyakārikā, 418, 422, 424, 572, 586, 686
Māṇḍūkyopaniṣad-bhāṣya, 572
Māṇikya Nandī, 309
Manomaya, 46, 60, 569–70
Material cause, 53, 254–55, 286, 320, 322–23, 376–77, 380, 438, 445, 453, 504–6, 539, 545, 568, 584, 599, 602, 608, 637, 650, 689, 691, 697
Maṭha Jñānottama, 593
Māṭharabhāṣya, 213
Maudgalyāyana, 120
Māyā
doctrine of, 50
instrumentality of, 505
modifications of, 529
transformations, 493
Mechanical, physical and chemical theories of the Ancient Hindus, 213
Meditation, 14, 29, 35, 37, 44, 73, 82–83, 102–5, 115, 127, 144, 150, 161, 173, 195, 201–2, 227, 233–36, 266, 270, 272, 317, 436, 490, 492, 584, 593, 750, 753
Metaphysical theories, 8
Milinda Pañha, 83, 89, 107
Mīmāṃsā philosophy
Arthāpatti, 391–94
doctrines, 281
indeterminate and determinate perception, 378–79
inference, 387–90
Mīmāṃsā literature, 369–72
nature of knowledge, 382–84
ontological problems, 379–82
Parataḥ-prāmāṇya doctrine of Nyāya, 372–75
as philosophy, 403–5
pramāṇa of non-perception, 397–99
psychology of illusion, 384–87
as ritualism, 403–5
śabda pramāṇa, 394–97
school of, 280–85, 346
self, salvation, god, 399–403
sense organs in perception, 375–78
sūtras of, 69
svataḥ-prāmāṇya doctrine, 372–75
upamāna, 391–94
Mīmāṃsā sūtras, 280–82, 369–70, 372, 394
Mīmāṃsā theories of commands, 550
Mīmāṃsā theory of the self, 673–75
Mīmāṃsā view of the obligatoriness, 540
Mind-associated consciousness, 528
Miśra, Keśava, 307
Miśra, Maṇḍana, 371, 418, 432, 542, 546, 576–92, 594–96, 600, 604, 606, 641, 692, 698, 718, 728
Miśra, Padmanābha, 63, 306
Miśra, Pārthasārathi, 371
Miśra, Śālikanātha, 370, 397, 641, 743
Miśra, Śaṅkara, 63, 284, 288, 291, 306–7, 314, 419, 597, 620
Miśra, Śivāditya, 617
Miśra, Vācaspati, 63, 86, 161, 212, 218–19, 221–26, 229, 233, 260–62, 269, 271, 277–78, 307, 330, 337–38, 340–41, 351–52, 355, 371, 397, 415, 418, 421, 433, 457, 469, 490, 505–6, 519–20, 523, 530, 539, 541–42, 545–46, 550–51, 568, 575–77, 581, 595, 597, 599–6, 610, 613, 618, 620, 690, 714,

744, 754–56, 766
Mithyā-saṃvṛta, 498–99
Moggallāna, 108, 263, 742
Mokṣa (salvation), 170, 173, 190, 192, 207, 215–17, 305, 538, 743
Molasses (*madaśakti*), 79
Momentariness, doctrine of, 158–64, 168, 212, 274, 310
Monotheism, 17–19
Monotheistic tendency, 19–20, 27
Moral endeavours, 216
Mukti, Doctrine of, 74–75
Muktika Upaniṣad, 263, 740–41
Mukti stage, 491
Mukti, state of (liberation), 248
Müller, Max, 10, 13, 18, 38–40, 45
Muṇḍaka, 28, 39, 49, 432, 544, 572, 687, 690, 744, 754
Muṇḍaka-bhāṣyavyākhyāna, 687
Muṇḍakopaniṣad-bhāṣya, 572
Mutual interdependence, dialectic of, 502
Mutual negation (*anyonyabhāva*), 464, 616

Naciketas, 59
Nāgārjuna, 109, 124–26, 128–29, 138, 144, 155, 166, 215, 233, 235, 279, 421, 423, 425–27, 429, 465, 470, 493, 497–98, 501–3, 524, 545, 612–13, 618, 621, 657–65
Naimittika-karma, 489
Naiṣadha-carita, 620
Naiṣkarmyasiddhi, 418–19, 511, 574, 576, 578, 592–94, 642, 692–93, 710, 745
Naiyāyika Āviddhakarṇa, 666
Naiyāyika Uddyotakara, 665
Naiyāyika Vātṣyāyana, 665
Nāma karma, 191, 194
Nārāyaṇāśrama, 545, 547–48, 710
Nāstika, 67, 208
Natural Philosophy of the Ancient Hindus, 213
Nature of Agency (*Kartṛtva*), 736–39
Nature of death (*maraṇānussati*), 102
Nayanaprasādinī, 419, 641, 650, 652
Nayas, Doctrine of, 176–79
Negation
doctrine of, 360
existence of, 357–58
kinds of, 149, 359–60, 688
of knowledge (*jñānābhāva*), 456
non-existence (abhāva), 357
Nemicandra, 171, 193–94
Neti neti, 44–45, 61, 65, 110
Nigodas, 190
Nihilism, 138–45
Nihilistic Buddhists, doctrine of, 301
Nihilistic conceptions, 80
Nihilists (*śūnyavādins*), 140, 302, 496, 621, 728
Nirīśvara Sāṃkhya, 259
Nirvāṇa, 28, 75, 100, 108, 128, 133, 135–36, 142, 169, 190, 215, 423, 658, 660, 725
Nirvikalpa pratyakṣa (indeterminate perception), 261
Niyama-vidhi, 404, 540
Niyoga-kāṇḍa, 581–82, 592
Non-enlightenment, 135
Non-intelligent transformations, 260
Non-perception, kinds of, 358
Non-phenomenal consciousness, 299
Nṛsiṃhāśrama Muni, 419–20, 476, 511, 525, 537, 545, 547–51, 566, 586, 597, 609, 618, 710–12
Nyāyabindu, 151–52, 154–55, 168, 181, 309, 358, 410
Nyāyabinduṭikā, 152, 154–55, 156, 359, 410
Nyāyabodhinī, 330
Nyāya-dīpāvalī, 545, 610, 686
Nyāya doctrine of inference, 280
Nyāya-kandalī, 306, 310–12, 314, 316–17, 324, 326, 328, 337–38, 351, 355, 359, 577, 579, 743, 757–58
Nyāya-kaṇikā, 539, 577, 579, 581, 601
Nyāyakośa, 2
Nyāya Literature, 305–10
Nyāya-makaranda, 506, 543, 563–64, 583, 610, 612, 641, 686, 688
Nyāyamālā, 575
Nyāyamañjarī, 67, 79, 160–63, 212, 276, 307, 311, 322, 326–27, 330, 332–33, 336–37, 340, 345, 347, 353, 355, 358–59, 362–63, 365–66, 373, 380, 414, 417, 459, 467
Nyāyā Mīmāṃsā, 402
Nyāyāmṛta, 612, 719
Nyāyamuktāvalī, 713
Nyāya-nibandha-prakāśa, 63, 601

Nyāyanirṇaya, 307, 418
Nyāyānusāra, 120
Nyāya philosophy, new school of, 308
Nyāya, Pleasures and pains (sukha and duḥkha) are held by, 342
Nyāyaratnākara, 370, 378, 388–90
Nyāya-sāra, 616
Nyāya schools, 177
of philosophy, 159
of thought, 157
Nyāyasūci, 278
Nyāya-sūcīni-bandha, 601
Nyāya sūtras, 71, 229, 276–80, 294–307, 327, 342, 360, 362, 430
Nyāyasūtravivaraṇa, 307
Nyāya-tātparyamaṇḍana, 63, 307
Nyāya-tātparyaṭīkā, 63
Nyāya theory, 397
Nyāya-Vaiśeṣika
caraka, nyāya sūtras and vaiśeṣika sūtras, 301–5
categories, 312
contrasting it with Sāṃkhya or Buddhism, 312
criticism of Buddhism and Sāṃkhya, 274–76
doctrines, 281, 284
dravya, 313–19
existence of Īśvara, 325–26
guṇa, 313–19
inference, 343–54
Īśvara and salvation, 363–66
kāla in, 311
karma, 313–19
negation in, 355–60
nyāya sūtras philosophy, 276–80, 294–301
nyāya-vaiśeṣika physics, 326–30
old school of Mīmāṃsā, 280–85
origin of knowledge, 330–32
perception, 333–43
physics, 326–30
pluralistic system, 312
pralaya and *sṛṣṭi*, 323–25
pramāṇas of nyāya, 332–33
refutation of categories, 681–83
sāmānya, 313–19
samavāya, 313–19
seeker of Salvation, 360–62
theory of causation, 319–23
upamāna and śabda, 354–55
vaiśeṣika and nyāya literature, 305–10
vaiśeṣika sūtras, 276–80, 285–94
viśeṣa, 313–19

Object-consciousness, 643, 704
Optimistic Faith, 75
Oriental Historical Manuscripts, 713
Oriental Manuscript Library, 581, 699
Outer concomitance (*bahirvyāpti*), 157

Pada-candrikā, 726
Padārtha-nirṇaya, 538
Padmapāda, 546, 596–600
Pāli, 1, 3, 31, 82–83, 84, 87, 92, 108, 110–11, 114, 139, 161, 263, 470
Pāli Scriptures, 82, 139
Pali Text Society Journal, 109
Pañcadaśī, 419, 492, 708–10, 745
Pañcāgnividyā, 37
Pañcakāraṇī, method of, 352
Pañca-pādikā, 418–19, 502–4, 511, 524–28, 546–48, 596–97, 600, 642–43, 687, 700, 702–4, 710–11, 745
Pañcaśikha, 216–19, 221
Pañcīkaraṇa, 570
Pañcikaraṇavivaraṇa, 687
Paṇḍita, Kulārka, 543, 613–14, 617–18, 641
Pañjikā, 525, 665
Paramāṇu, 121, 251–54, 683–84, 687
Paramātman, 214
Parameśvara, 547, 700
Parārthānumāna, 155–56, 186, 350, 353
Parasparādhyāsa, 607
Parataḥ-prāmāṇya doctrine of Nyāya, 372–75
Pariṇāma theory of causation, 53
Pariṇāmavāda, 258
Parmenides (Plato), 42
Pātanjal, 233, 237
Pātañjala mahābhāṣya, 231
Pātañjala Sāṃkhya, 68, 221, 671
Pātañjala school of *Sāṃkhya*, 221, 229
Pātañjala tantra, 231, 235
Pātañjala Yoga sūtras, 68
Patañjali, 68, 203, 212, 219, 222, 227–36, 238, 268, 279, 317, 365, 465, 753, 759
Patañjalicarita, 230
Paṭiccasamuppāda, doctrine of, 166
Pātrasvāmin, 666

Perception
of class (*jāti*), 379
of class-natures, 682
of concomitance, 473
conditions of, 334
definition of, 294, 297, 303, 333, 342, 631–32, 661, 686, 701, 706
determinate perception, 378–79
doctrine of, 379–82
gradual development of, 341
illusory perception, 152, 154, 375, 384–86, 440–43, 451, 477, 486–88, 499, 567, 628, 646, 649
indeterminate, 334, 378–79
kinds of, 378
mental perception (*mānasa pratyakṣa*), 563, 400
of mirage, 373
nature of, 168, 358, 694
negation, 358–59
of non-existence, 356
Nyāya view of, 382
Nyāya-Vaiśeṣika theory of, 335
pramāṇa of non-perception, 397–99
Śabda pramāṇa, 394–97
Sautrāntika Theory of, 151–54
savikalpa, 341
sense organs in, 375–78
as sound-knowledge (*śabda-pramāṇa*), 334
stages, 378
Perceptual cognition, 338, 571, 715
Perceptual illusion, 337
Performance of duties, 317, 436, 594
Pettā Dīkṣita, 548
Phenomenal consciousness, 299
Philosophic literature, growth of, 65–67
Philosophic thought, history of, 31
Pīlupāka, doctrine of, 327
Piṭharapāka, doctrine of, 327
Pitṛyāna theory, 56
Pleasurable character, sense of, 336
Polytheism, 17–19
Positive Sciences of the Ancient Hindus, 213, 246, 251–52, 322, 326, 329
Poussin, De la Vallée, 108
Prabhākara, 415
Prabhākaramīmāṃsā, 372, 378, 383–84, 397, 405
Prajāpati, 19–20, 25–26, 32, 36, 43, 46–47, 55
Prajñānānanda, 573, 690
Prajñāpāramitā, 125, 128, 421
Prajñaptiśāstra, 120
Prakaraṇapāda, 120
Prakaraṇapañcikā, 370, 378–79, 386, 390, 392, 397, 743
Prakāśa, 326
Prakāśānanda, 420, 469, 511–13, 539, 546–47, 549–51, 578, 714–19, 728, 764
Prakāśātman, 419, 468, 503–4, 511, 524–26, 546, 576, 578, 597–600, 612, 642–43, 645, 687, 702–4, 708, 716–18, 728
Prakaṭārtha, 540, 543–44, 690–92, 699–700, 707
Prakaṭārtha-vivaraṇa, 544, 566, 690–92, 707
Prakṛti and its Evolution, 245–47
Prakṛti equilibrium, disturbance of, 247–48
Pralaya (periodical cosmic dissolution), 214, 223, 247–49, 261, 323–25, 403, 531, 542, 603, 685, *See also* Sṛṣṭi
Pramāṇa, 154, 181, 268, 277, 294, 296–97, 304, 330–32, 343, 354–56, 365, 389–91, 394, 397–99, 406, 409–10, 412–16, 471, 474, 484, 538, 571, 631, 647–48, 661, 688–89, 691, 701–2
Pramāṇa-mālā, 506–7, 545, 610, 612, 641, 686
Pramāṇa-mañjarī, 614, 618
Pramāṇasamuccaya, 120, 153, 155, 167, 307, 309, 538
Prāna, 36, 750–58
Prāṇamaya ātman, 46
Prāṇa-maya koṣa, 60
Prāṇāyāma, 227, 236, 272, 750–51, *See also* Yoga
Praśastamati, 666
Praśastapāda, 67, 305–6, 312, 314, 316–17, 328, 332, 337, 348–51, 355, 359, 362, 656–57, 743
Praśastapāda bhāsya, 67
Praśna, 28, 31, 39, 51, 432, 469–70, 572
Pratibimba-vāda, doctrine of, 600
Pratyagbhagavān, 641
Prauḍhānubhūti, 575
Pravacanabhāṣya, 212, 245, 259
Pravicayabuddhi, 148
Progress, stages of, 758–61

Pudgala, 195–97, 552–53
Pure cessation (*śānta*), 728–29
Pūrṇa, 120
Puruṣa, 20–21, 43, 52, 213, 216, 238–39, 259–61
Pūrva Mīmāṃsā, 68
Pūrvamīmāṃsā sūtras, 429
Puṣpāñjali, 574

Quality, Nyāya definition of, 637

Rāghavānanda, 572, 609
Raghunātha, 326, 365
Raghunātha Śiromaṇi, 308, 613, 618, 620
Raja, C. Kunhan, 581
Rājamṛgāṅka, 231
Rājavārttika, 212, 219
Rāma, 546, 605, 609, 612, 687, 723–24, 749
Rāmabhadra, 230, 573
Rāmacandra, 550, 573, 714, 732
Rāmādvaya, 691–92, 698–708
definition of *pramā*, 707
definition of right knowledge, 706
Rāmājñā Pāṇḍeya, 719–20
Ramānanda Tīrtha, 573, 726
Rāmānuja, 50, 70–71, 168, 429, 433, 537, 619, 695, 713–14, 756
Rama Tīrtha, 755
Rāmatīrtha, 419, 550, 579
Rāmāyaṇa, 714, 723–24, 725
Raṅgarāja Adhvarin, 548
Rasābhi-vyañjikā, 550
Rasa-sāra, 617
Ratnākaraśānti, 156, 346
Ratnakīrtti, 68, 158–61, 163–64, 168
Ratna-prabhā, 89–90, 306, 418, 543, 597–98
Ratnatraya, 128
Ratna-tūlikā, 550
Ray, P. C., 321–22, 327
Relative pluralism, doctrine of, 175–76
Religio-philosophical quest, 35
Revelation, principle of, 510
Revival of Upaniṣad studies in modern times, 39–40
Ṛg-Veda, 12, 14–16, 23–26, 32, 45, 226, 469
advancement of thought, 26
its civilization, 14–16
conception of the supreme man (Puruṣa), 21
cosmogony of, 23–25
Puruṣasūkta of, 32
Uktha (verse) of, 36
Viśvakarman, 32
Right Conduct, methods of, 761–62
Ritualism, 21, 403–5
Roy, Ram Mohan, 40

Śabara, 69, 369–72, 387, 405, 581
Śabarasvāmin, 665
Śabda pramāṇa, 355, 394–95, 397
Sacrifice, 21–22, 35, 37, 316
Sacrificial duties, 26, 30, 44, 436
nature of, 26
Sacrificial fees (*dakṣiṇā*), 36
Sacrificial gifts, 36
Sacrificial Karma, 80
Sadānanda Kāśmīraka, 551, 690
Sadānanda Vyāsa, 420
Ṣaḍdarśana, 68
Ṣaḍdarśanasamuccaya, 2, 114, 170, 175–76, 186, 206, 222
Saddharmapuṇḍarīka, 125, 128
Saint, stage of the (*Jīvan-mukta*), 739–46
Śaivism, 543
Salvation, 29, 38, 76–77, 115–27, 138, 199, 214, 220, 233–35, 237, 244, 258, 278, 283, 285, 294–95, 300–1, 305, 316–17, 360–62, 363–66, 394, 402, 430, 437, 439–40, 477, 487, 490, 540, 593, 721–22, 736, 758
Samādhi, 82, 100–3, 119, 136, 166, 236, 271–72, 518, 745
Sāmānya, 281, 317–19
Samavāya, 171, 319, 322
Samavāya, refutation of, 683
Sāma-Veda, 12
Samaveta-samavāya, 335
Samayapradīpa, 120
Saṃhitās, 12–13, 72
Saṃkalpa, 225, 261, 727
Sāṃkhya, 7, 9, 51, 53, 67–68, 71, 75, 78, 80, 95, 116, 165, 167–68, 178, 188, 196, 211–13, 216–29, 232, 235–36, 238–45, 247–48, 251–54, 256–66, 268–69, 273, 275–78, 281, 286, 299, 302, 310–12, 317, 320–21, 325, 330–33, 363, 367–69, 378, 380, 382, 385,

394, 403, 412, 414–17, 422, 431–32, 434–35, 440–41, 468, 492–93, 530–31, 536, 539, 568, 574, 583, 595, 600–1, 609–10, 659, 665–69, 675, 721, 736, 743–44, 754–56
and the Yoga Doctrine of Soul, 238–41
and Yoga Literature, 212–13
Atheism, 258–59
conception of power, 321
cosmology, 221, 310
criticism of, 274–76
distinction of buddhi (cognition) and cit, 299
doctrine, 80, 116, 216–17, 219, 221–24, 257, 330, 583, 669
conception of the guṇas, 224
features of, 216
Pariṇāma Doctrine, 665–69
Early School of, 213–22
metaphysics on the Yoga, 228
philosophy, 211, 213, 238, 243, 265, 530, 668
school, 51, 53, 68, 217, 222
theories of causation, 258
refutation of the of the self, 675
Sāṃkhya kārikā, 67, 212, 218, 221–66, 574, 600, 610, 743–44
Sāṃkhyapravacanabhāṣya, 223
Sāṃkhya puruṣa, 241, 441
Sāṃkhyasāra, 212
Sāṃkhya sūtra, 212, 222–26, 744
Sāṃkhya-Yoga, 196, 212–13, 222, 254, 260, 273, 286, 299, 317, 330, 378, 380, 394, 755–56
Sāṃkhyist Iśvarakṛṣṇa, 665
Sāṃkhyist Māṭhara Ācārya, 665
Sāṃkhyist Vindhyasvāmin, 665
Saṃkṣepa-śārīraka, 419, 505, 511, 537, 539, 546, 548, 550, 579, 604–6, 609–10, 710, 717
Sammitīyaśāstra, 119
Saṃskāras, 86, 91, 127, 139, 143, 263–64, 266, 272
Samyagbodhendra Saṃyamin, 546
yuktābhidharmaśāstra, 120
Saṃyutta Nikāya, 83–84, 86, 94–96, 98, 110–11
Saṅgītiparyyāya, 120
Śaṅkarācārya, 369, 429, 572–73, 575, 596, 618, 683
Śaṅkara, dialectic of, 683–90
Śaṅkaradigvijaya, 432
Śaṇkara-dig-vijaya, 580
Śaṅkara-jaya, 432
Śaṅkara, philosophical doctrine of, 496
Śaṅkara school, 406–7, 439, 495, 497, 524, 529, 538, 575, 586, 619, 762
Ahaṃkāra, 457–61
Ajñāna, 457–61
Ānandabodha Yati, 610–12
Ānandajñāna's dialectic, 683–90
Antaḥkaraṇa, 457–61
Appaya Dīkṣita, 712–14
Ātman, 474–85
Bādarāyaṇa's philosophy, 530–40
Bhartṛprapañca's philosophy, 530–40
Buddhism and in Vedānta, 507–40
Buddhist Doctrine of Soullessness, 552–67
Citsukha's Interpretations, 641–57
dialectic application, 627–41
dialectic of controversy, 406–07
Dṛṣṭisṛṣṭivāda, 474–85
Ekajīvavāda, 474–85
forerunners of Vedānta Dialectics, 665–83
Īśvara, 474–85
Jīva, 474–85
logical formalism development of, 612–19
Madhusūdana Sarasvatī, 719–21
Mahā-vidyā, 612–19
Maṇḍana, 581–92
Nāgārjuna's dialectic, 657–65
nature of the world-appearance, 445–52
Nṛsiṃhāśrama Muni, 710–12
Padmapāda, 596–600
perception and inference, 454–61
philosophical situation, 408–18
Prakāśānanda, 714–19
Prakaṭārtha-vivaraṇa's philosophy, 690–92
Rāmādvaya, 698–708
Śaṅkara and his School, 571–76
Śaṅkara Vedānta, 641–57
Śaṅkara's Defence of Vedānta, 530–40
Śaṅkara's dialectic, 683–90
Sarvajñātma Muni, 605–10
Sureśvara, 592–96
Teachers and Pupils in Vedānta, 540–52
Theory of Causation, 465–70
Vācaspati Miśra, 600–5

Vedānta and other Indian Systems, 492–94
Vedānta and Śaṅkara, 429–39
Vedānta Dialectic of Śrīharṣa, 619–27
Vedānta dialectic, 461–65
Vedānta Dialectic, 657–65
Vedānta Doctrine of Soul, 522–67
Vedānta in Gauḍapāda, 420–29
Vedānta Literature, 418–20
Vedānta theory of Illusion, 485–89
Vedānta theory of Perception and Inference, 470–74
Vedāntic cosmology, 567–71
Vidyāraṇya, 708–10
Vimuktātman, 692–98
world-appearance, 443–45, 495–507
Śaṅkarasvāmin, 666
Śaṅkara Vedānta, 407, 495, 510–11, 528–29, 605, 610, 641–57, 708, 762–66
Śaṅkaravijaya, 418
Śaṅkara-vijayavilāsa, 432
Sānka (*Sāṃkhya*), 233
Śaṅkhapāṇi, 577, 581, 583–85, 588
Sanmātra-viṣayam pratyakṣaṃ, 382
Śāntabhadra, 168
Śāntarakṣita, 519, 522, 525, 665–66, 668–70, 672–73, 675–82
Saptadaśabhūmi sūtra, 128
Sarasvatī, Abhinavanārāyaṇendra, 572–73
Sarasvatī, Brahmānanda, 551, 571, 573, 575, 719
Sarasvatī, Brahmendra, 548
Sarasvatī, Gaṅgādharendra, 550, 714, 725
Sarasvatī, Govinda, 549
Sarasvatī, Mādhava, 549, 726
Sarasvatī, Madhusūdana, 67, 419, 492, 547, 549–50, 571, 573, 610, 612, 618, 646, 692–93, 717, 719–21
Sarasvatī, Pūrṇānanda, 573
Sarasvatī, Rāmānanda, 525, 550, 574, 597, 690
Sarasvatī, Viśveśvara, 549, 719
Śāriputtra, 120
Śārīraka-bhāṣya-ṭīkā (*Nyāya-nirṇaya*), 687
Śārīraka-mīmāṃsā-bhāṣya, 572, 574
Sarva-darśana-saṃgraha, 2, 68, 79, 114, 235, 305, 322, 708
Sarvajñātma Muni, 419, 505, 537, 539, 541, 544, 546, 548, 550–51, 566, 579, 604–10, 717–18
Sarvajña Viśveśa, 549
Ṣaṣṭitantra, 219–21
Ṣaṣṭitantroddhāra, 220
Śāstra-darpaṇa, 576, 597, 602
Śāstra-prakāśikā, 577, 687
Śāstrī, Haraprasāda, 278, 303, 371
Sastri, Māhāmahopādhyāya Kuppusvami, 713
Śāstrin, Kāśīnātha, 548
Śāstrī, S. Kuppusvāmī, 537
Śatapatha Brāhmaṇa, 20, 24–25, 31, 226, 230
Satipaṭṭhāna sutta, 227
Satkāryavāda, 257–58, 468
Satkāryavāda, Causation as, 257–58
Sat-kārya-vāda theory, 533, 667–68
Sattva preponderance, 249–50, 260
Satyasiddhi school, 124
Sautrānta-vijñānavāda, 409
Sautrāntika Buddhist, 165, 302, 408, 411
Sautrāntika doctrine of Buddhism, 155
Sautrāntikas, 112–15, 120, 161, 167–68, 188, 520
Sautrāntika Theory of Perception, 151–54
Savikalpa perception, 341
School of logic (*navya-nyāya*), 618
School of Vijñānavāda Buddhism, 145–51
Schopenhauer, 39–40
Scriptural duties, 317, 436
Seal, B. N., 213, 246, 251–53, 321–22, 326–29
Self-identity, notion of, 560, 562, 565
Self-purification, 492
Self-revelation or self-illumination, 642
Self-validity of knowledge, doctrine of, 372
Sense-cognition, 298, 336, 521, 552, 567
Sense-contact, cause of, 340
Separate jāti, conception of a, 381
Separation-consciousnes, 134
Śeṣagovinda, 549
Śeṣanṛsiṃha, 699
Śeṣa Śārṅgadhara, 613, 690
Seśvara Sāṃkhya, 259
Sex-desires, 57
Shāh Jahān, 39

Siddhānta-bindu, 549, 571, 573, 714, 719–20
Siddhānta-dīpa, 609
Siddhānta-leśa, 420, 504–5, 511, 538, 541, 543–44, 547, 566, 710, 714
Siddhānta-muktāvalī, 339, 469, 505, 511–13, 716–17, 758
Siddhānta-pradīpikā, 719
Siddhāntatattva, 420
Siddhasena Divākara, 171, 309
Siddhi-kāṇḍa, 581–82, 592
Siddhivyākhyā, 420
S.I. Inscriptions, 713
Śikhā-maṇi, 318, 419, 484–85, 547–48, 568, 702
Śiva-līlārṇava, 713
Śivārka-maṇi-dīpikā, 712–14
Six Buddhist Nyāya Tracts, 168, 297, 318, 346, 371, 380
Skambha, 24
Ślokavārttika, 67, 218, 370, 378, 380, 382, 386, 390, 397, 401, 417
Sorrow and its dissolution, 264–68
cessation of the rebirth-process, 265
Vedic sacrifices, 264
Soul Theory, refutation of the, 672–73
Sound-potential (*kha-tan-mātra*), 730
Śraddhā, 58, 199, 271, 317, 518
Śrāvakas (theravādin monks), 137
Śrīdhara, 306, 313, 316–17, 338, 359, 379, 543, 577, 758
Śrīharṣa, 318, 419, 462, 465, 492, 545, 547–48, 551, 586, 597, 613, 618–41, 650, 657–59, 662, 664–66, 686, 688, 712, 742
Śrīkṛṣṇa, 597
Śrīmālāsiṃhanāda, 128
Sṛṣṭi, 323–25
Stcherbatsky or Keith, 351
Subject-consciousness, 643, 705
Subject-object-awareness, 527
Subodhinī, 371, 420, 549, 567, 569, 609
Substance, Nyāya definition of, 637
Suhṛllekha, 144
Sumati, 666
Śūnyavāda Buddhism, 418, 494
Śūnyavāda doctrine, 166–67 *Śūnyavāda* theory, 497
Śūnyavādin Buddhists, 501
Sureśvara, 67, 418–19, 495, 511, 540–42, 545–46, 551, 572–74, 576–81, 592–96, 599, 605–6, 641–42, 692, 710
Sūri, Allāla, 546
Sūri, Bhuvanasundara, 614, 617
Sūri, Deva, 172
Sūtrasthāna, 280
Suvarṇaprabhāsa sūtra, 301
Svalakṣaṇam, 154, 410
Svataḥ-prāmāṇya doctrine of Mīmāṃsā, 372–75
Svayaṃprakāśa Yati, 573
Śvetāśvatara, 28, 31, 39, 49–50, 52, 78, 227, 281–82, 422, 469
Syādvāda, doctrine of, 179
Syllogism, 156, 186, 280, 293, 613–16
kevalānvayi form of, 615
mahā-vidyā syllogism, 543, 545, 613–17, 618
types of, 616
of thought, 4–5, 7–8, 65, 67, 309, 394, 430, 434–35, 721

Tadasya brahmacaryam, 227
Taittirīya, 23, 26, 28, 30–31, 39, 51, 432, 572, 687, 745
Taittirīyabhāṣya-ṭippaṇa, 687
Taittirīya-Brāhmaṇa, 23
Taittirīyopaniṣad-bhāṣya, 572
Tāmasika ahaṃkāra, 249
Tamas preponderance, 249–50
Tanmātras, 251–54
colour-potential, 252
smell-potential, 252
sound-potential, 252
sound-potential, 253
taste-potential, 252
touch-potential, 252
Tapas (asceticism), 226
Tarka-kāṇḍa, 581–82, 586
Tarkarahasyadīpikā, 79, 114–15, 162–63, 203, 217–18, 221
Tarkasaṃgraha, 322, 330, 543–45, 610, 686–90
Taste-cognition, 674
Tathāgatagarbha, doctrine of, 147
Tathatā doctrine, 166–67
Tathya-saṃvṛti (real ignorance), 498
Tātparya-prakāśa, 725, 729, 760
Tātparyaṭīkā, 229, 269, 307, 330, 338, 341, 352
Tātparyaṭīkāpariśuddhi, 307

Tattva-bindu, 539, 601
Tattva-bodhinī, 546, 548, 609, 710–11
Tattva-dīpana, 504, 525, 546, 573, 597, 687, 702, 704
Tattvadīpikā, 419, 465, 573
Tattvakaumudī, 212, 218, 243, 257, 262, 264
Tattvāloka, 543–44, 687
Tattva-pradīpikā, 238, 545, 577, 613, 633, 641–42
Tattvārthādhigamasūtra, 171, 175–76, 184
Tattvasamāsa, 212
Tattva-saṃgraha, 514, 519, 521–22, 525, 665, 668, 676, 680
Tattva-samīkṣā, 581, 600–1, 604, 610
Tattvavaiśāradī, 212, 239, 245, 254, 256–57, 260, 264, 266–67
Tattva-viveka, 548, 566, 711
Tattvopadeśa, 575
Testimony (*śabda-pramāṇa*), 354
Theories
illusion, 384–85, 581, 698
akhyāti theory of Mīmāṃsā, 386
anirvacanīya theory of error, 611
anyathākhyāti theory of illusion, 385
atomic theory of Vaiśeṣikas, 651, 683
dṛṣṭisṛṣṭivāda theory, 478
nyāya, 397
Causation, 52, 257, 319–23, 465–70
dṛṣṭisṛṣṭivāda, 478
karma and rebirth, 71
knowledge, 374, 403, 406–7
perception, 183–85
pariṇāma theory of causation, 53
pitṛyāna theory, 56
sat-kārya-vāda theory, 533, 667–68
sautrāntika theory of inference, 155–58
Sautrāntika theory of perception, 151–54
vedānta theory of illusion, 485–89
Theravāda Buddhism, 150
Schools of, 112–24
Thilly, Frank, 3
Tilak, Bāl Gaṅgādhar, 10
Tiryaksāmānya, 196
Transmigration, 26, 34, 53–54, 58, 192
doctrine of, 25–27, 53–57
Triṃśikā, 513, 515–16, 519–20, 523, 529
Udayana, 63, 306–7, 312, 326, 329, 365, 543, 545, 601, 613, 617–20, 628, 634–35, 641
Udyotakara, 63, 228, 269, 298, 305, 307, 309, 327–28, 330, 337, 342, 351, 353, 355 , 613, 618, 631, 641, 676, 680
Ultimate entity, 726–28
Ultimate oneness, 623
Ultimate substances, 242–43
Universal self (*pratyag-ātman*), 500
Universal self (*pratyak-citi*), 503
Upacāra samādhi, 102–3
Upadeśa-sāhasrī, 575, 687
Upamāna and Śabda, 354–55
Upaniṣad
absolutism of, 31
Ātman Upaniṣad, 31
Brahman place in, 48–50
Bṛhadāraṇyaka Upaniṣad, 14, 28, 31, 35, 39, 50, 87, 226, 263, 432, 469–70, 537, 542, 745, 753
Buddhism, 109–11
Chāndogya Upaniṣad, 28, 30, 36, 39, 53, 93, 110, 133, 173–74, 226, 263, 432–33, 537, 572, 687, 740, 744, 753–54
composition and growth of, 38–39
conception of Brahman, 50, 436
disparateness of the teachings, 31
doctrines, 31, 42, 52, 434
ātman doctrine, 27, 45–48
constructive system, 442
formation of the, 31
Garbha Upaniṣad, 31
interpretations, 41–42
Kauṣītaki Upaniṣad, 30, 50
Maitrāyaṇa Upaniṣad, 236
Muktika Upaniṣad, 263, 740–41
names of the Upaniṣads, 30–31
philosophy of, 8, 30, 41, 431, 540
Svetāśvatara Upaniṣads, 469
teachings, 38
Vedic literature, 28–30
adherents of the Vedānta (*Upaniṣads*), 9
exponent of the Upaniṣads, 30
path of knowledge (*jñāna-mārga*), 29
path of works (*karma-mārga*), 29
vedic commandment, 29
vedic teaching, 29
view of the self, 675
Upaskāra, 282–86, 288, 290–93, 306, 314

Upavarṣa, 370, 537
Ūrdhvasāmānya, 197
Uttānapada, 23
Uttarādhyayanasūtra, 169, 236
Uttara Mīmāṃsā, 7, 70, 429
Uveyaka, 666

Vācārambhaṇa, 710
Vācaspatimiśra, 143, 307
Vācikāvijñapti karma, 124
Vādīndra, 614, 616–18, 690
Vādīndra, 690
Vādivāgīśvara, 690
Vaibhāṣika, 113–17, 120, 122
Vaikārika ahaṃkāra, 249
Vaināśikas (nihilists), 257
Vaipulyasūtras, 125
Vaiśeṣika-bhāśya, 656
Vaiśeṣika schools, 177
Vaiśeṣika sūtra, 68, 71, 279–82, 284–94, 291, 301, 303–6, 311–12, 327, 332, 355, 359
Vaiśeṣika sūtras, 276–80, 327
Vaiṣṇava philosophy, 8, 221
Vaiṣṇava schools of thought, 77
Vājasaneyi schools, 31
Vākya-vivaraṇavyākhyā, 687
Vākya-vṛtti, 574–75, 687
Vālmīki, 723–24
Vanamālī Vedāntatīrtha, 281, 305
Varddha-mānendu, 63
Vārttika, 63, 67, 188, 230, 307, 309, 327, 353, 495, 542, 546, 572, 577–78, 580, 594, 596
Vārttika-tātparyaṭīkā, 63
Vaśiṣṭha, 723–24, 732, 749, 751
Vāsiṣṭha-Rāmāyaṇa, 725
Vasubandhu, 114, 117, 120, 124, 128, 167, 218, 233, 421, 423, 513–16, 519–20, 523, 529, 552–54, 556, 658, 665
Vasumitra, 112, 115–16, 120
Vātsīputrīyas, 553–56, 676
Vātsyāyana, 63, 120, 167, 186, 228–29, 269, 277–78, 280, 294–98, 301, 304, 306–7, 309, 327, 351, 467, 613, 618, 742
Vātsyāyana bhāṣya, 63, 278, 296–97, 306, 309
Vāyus (bio-motor force), 262
Vāyu (wind), 37

Vedānta philosophy, 20, 30, 70, 371, 429–30, 432, 439, 465, 470, 545, 556, 606
absolutist, 434
ātman, 241
doctrine, 41–42, 419, 550–51, 577, 686, 714–15
Bhedābheda, 537–38
of monism, 714
of soul, 522–67
instruction, 489
exponent of, 50, 52
principal interest of, 566
scheme of, 513
school of, 556, 612
sūtras of the, 62
theory
of Illusion, 485–89
of Inference, 470–74
of perception, 470–74
way of looking at things, 177
Vedārthasaṃgraha, 433
Vedārthasaṃgraha, 433
Vedāntic Cosmology, 567, 720
Vedāntic doctrines, 551, 575, 597–98, 712, 722
Vedāntic monism, 718
Vedāntin Mahādeva, 550
Vedāntist objects, 525
Vedas, 1, 6, 10–14, 20, 22, 24–26, 29–30, 33, 40–41, 67, 69–70, 79, 186, 208–11, 234, 277–78, 284–85, 291, 294, 297, 304, 326, 332–33, 355, 394, 401, 404–5, 422, 426–27, 429–31, 435–36, 489–90, 492, 593, 717–18, 730
antiquity of, 10
classification of the Vedic literature, 11–12
place in the Hindu mind, 10–11
Saṃhitās, 12–13
Vedic duties, performance of, 29, 437, 490, 593
Vedic Gods, 16–17
plurality of, 17
Vedic hymns, 6, 18, 31
devotion of, 22
Vedic Index, 753
Vedic Mythology, 18–19, 22–23, 25–26
Vedic rites, 11, 265
Vedic ritualism, 14

Vedic sacrifices and rituals, 11
Veṅkaṭa, 222, 537, 576, 613–14, 617, 714
Verbal cognition, 293
Vidhi-viveka, 539, 580–81, 600
Vidvan-manoramā, 573
Vidvanmanorañjinī, 420
Vidyābhūṣaṇa, S. C., 172, 279, 309, 421
Vidyāmṛta-varṣiṇī, 609
Vidyāraṇya, 419, 546–47, 551, 560–61, 563–64, 572, 576–77, 580, 597, 708–10, 745–46
Vigraha-vyāvartanī, 659
Vijñāna Bhikṣu, 212, 220–26, 229, 256, 260, 262, 494, 756
Vijñānakaumudī, 758
Vijñānakāya, 120
Vijñānamātrasiddhi, 128
Vijñānamaya, 46, 60, 569–70
Vijñānāmṛta Bhāṣya, 220, 223
Vijñānaskandha, 124
Vijñānavāda, 85, 127–28, 138, 145, 151, 166–67, 302, 409, 417, 421, 429, 465, 478, 493–94, 766
Vijñānavāda Buddhism, 145, 465, 478, 493, 766
idealistic tendency of, 417
Vijñānavāda Buddhists, 302
Vijñānavāda doctrine, 166–67, 429
Vijñānavāda, 145
Vijñānavāda school, 128, 151
Vijñānavādin Buddhist, 415
Vijñāna vādins, 332, 736
Vikrama-saṃvat, 601
Vimalakīrtti, 128
Viṃśatikā, 513–15, 520, 523
Vimuktātman, 692–99
Vinītadeva, 152, 163, 168
Viparyyaya, doctrine of, 220
Viṣṇu, 39, 642, 745
Viṣṇumitra, 521
Viṣṇupurāṇa cosmology, 433
Visual perception, 182, 219, 298, 336, 340, 356, 483–84, 514, 519
Viśuddhādvaita-vāda school, 70
Visuddhimagga, 83, 88, 99, 101–6, 111, 161
Viśvakarma, 19–20, 32, 52
Viśvakarman, 32, 43
Viśvambhara, 573
Viśvāmitra, 724
Viśvanātha, 281, 307, 339, 714
Viśvanāthavṛtti, 307
Viśvarūpa, 576–81, 745
Viśveśvara Paṇḍita, 574
Vital principle (*jīva-dhātu*), 735
Viṭṭhaleśopadhyāyī, 420
Vivaraṇa-prameya-saṃgraha, 419, 457, 460, 486, 546–47, 557, 560–61, 564, 577, 580, 710
Vivaraṇa school
of Padmapāda, 528
of thought, 547
of Vedānta, 551
Vivarttavāda, 258, 468
Viveka-cūḍāmaṇi, 573
Vṛtti transformation, 700–1
Vyākhyāna-dīpikā, 617
Vyāpti, doctrine of, 303
Vyāsabhāṣya, 225, 228–29, 231–33, 235–37, 239, 254, 256–57, 263, 266, 269, 273, 380, 613, 745, 756, 759
Vyavahāra-naya standpoint, 178

Welt als Wille und Vorstellung, 40
Woods, J. H., 231
World-Appearance, 495, 734–36
World-creation, illusion of, 736–37
World-Soul, 52

Yājñavalkya, 28, 34–35, 44, 54, 601, 746
Yajur-Veda, 12
Yaśomitra, 114, 120, 167, 552–54, 556
Yati, Ānandabodha, 610–12, 618, 686
Yoga, 7, 9, 28, 39, 68, 74–75, 77–78, 80, 93, 199, 201, 208, 211–13, 217, 219–23, 226–38, 248, 251, 255, 258–59, 261–66, 268–73, 277–78, 286, 292–93, 301, 303, 317, 325, 385, 434, 440, 490, 492, 499, 511, 551, 581, 601, 603, 722, 724–28, 731, 734, 736, 740–41, 744–53, 756–62, 764–66
Patañjali, 226–38
Avidyā of, 261
Haṭhayoga, 229
Karmas in are divided into four classes, 266
kinds of yoga, 229
Laya Yoga, 229
Mantra Yoga, 229
meditation, 270–73
Yoga doctrine, 226, 235–36

Yoga doctrine, of Soul, 238–41
Purificatory Practices (*Parikarma*), 270–71
Rājayoga, 229
strength of, 230
validity of, 228
Yogācārabhūmi śāstra, 128
Yogācāra school of Mahāyāna monism, 658
Yoga Psychology, 270
Yoga sūtra, 212, 219, 227, 230, 232–38, 263, 266, 268
idea of metempsychosis, 234
idea of soul, 234
siddhis (miraculous powers), 234
stages of meditation, 234
tarka, 236
Yoga Theism, 258–59
Yoga Upaniṣads, 228
Yogavārttika, 212, 223, 239, 243, 245, 254, 256–57, 259–64
Yoga-vāsiṣṭha, 511, 551, 722, 724–28, 734, 740–41, 744–53, 757–62, 764–66
absolute of, 766
Buddhist Vijñānavāda, 762–66
energy of free-will (*Pauruṣa*), 746–50
idealism of, 762, 764
Illusion of World Creation, 736–39
Karma, Manas and the Categories, 731–34
methods of right conduct, 761–62
nature of agency (*Kartṛtva*), 736–39
origination, 729–31
philosophy of the, 728
Prāṇa and its control, 750–58
Śaṅkara Vedānta, 762–66
stage of the saint (*Jīvan-mukta*), 739–46
stages of progress, 758–61
world-appearance, 734–36
ultimate entity, 726–28
Yoga-vāsiṣṭha-Rāmāyaṇa, 722, 726
Yoga-vāsiṣṭha-saṃkṣepa, 726
Yoga-vāsiṣṭha-ślokā, 726
Yoga-vasiṣṭha-tātparya-saṃgraha, 726

Zend-Avesta, 39
Zeus, 18